1998 Tax Legislation

IRS Restructuring and Reform

Law, Explanation and Analysis

CCH INCORPORATED
Chicago

This publication is designed to provide accurate and authoritative information in regard to the subject matter covered. It is sold with the understanding that the publisher is not engaged in rendering legal, accounting, or other professional service. If legal advice or other expert assistance is required, the services of a competent professional person should be sought.

ISBN 0-8080-0281-3

©1998, **CCH** INCORPORATED

4025 W. Peterson Ave.
Chicago, IL 60646-6085
1-800-248-3248
http://www.cch.com

A Great Day for Taxpayers and Practitioners Alike:

Sorting Out the IRS Restructuring and Reform Bill

On June 25, 1998, the House passed the Internal Revenue Service Restructuring and Reform Bill of 1998 (H.R. 2676) by an overwhelming 402-8 majority. It is expected to be passed by the Senate after its Fourth of July recess and signed into law by the President shortly thereafter. Looking at recent articles in the popular press, one could cynically dismiss this legislation as merely addressing an IRS internal reorganization, an orchestrated beltway rally against an unpopular agency and an easy political target. One would not be more wrong as the new law is multi-faceted combining several discrete legislative packages into one bill. Many of the specific changes themselves are surprisingly complex in subtle ways affecting a broad range of taxpayers in a variety of significant ways.

Most notably, the bill makes a number of changes in what had been fundamental tenets of tax law procedure. Shifting the burden of proof, extending attorney-client privilege to accountants and enrolled agents, facilitating more liberal compromise procedures, and introducing interest, penalty and innocent spouse relief all dramatically change the rules of taxpayer/IRS engagement. Thus, practitioners need not only review and understand the new rules laid out in this electronic publication—but more basically, they must reconsider their tactics for dealing with the IRS personally developed through repeated interaction with various agents over time. The battlefield has changed.

Many of the provisions in the new law are designed to address the myriad problems inherent in the Taxpayer Relief Act of 1997 (P.L. 105-34). Some of these "technical corrections" significantly affect planning assumptions associated with the omnipresent Roth IRA. Still others affect netting capital losses, education tax breaks and various estate tax changes.

Other areas of the new law clearly bestow additional benefits on taxpayers such as the new shorter holding period for long-term capital gain rates, and liberalized rules for converting IRAs to Roth IRAs. As to the latter, the taxpayer benefit is really the by-product of the need to raise revenue to pay for some of the more expensive components of the reform legislation. Other revenue raisers such as the reversal of the Tax Court's decision in *Schmidt Baking Co.* are certainly not as taxpayer friendly.

Above and beyond these other provisions, change in the IRS organization, the purported focus of this bill, is perhaps the most dramatic aspect of the new law. The IRS is literally being turned inside out with a shift from its current geographically based structure to a structure that will be set up to serve particular groups of taxpayers with similar needs—individuals, small businesses, large businesses and tax-exempts. Given the magnitude of this shift, and the IRS's need to concurrently address pressing year 2000 issues at the heart of its technology infrastructure, the IRS is likely to be an organization in transition for some time.

The timing of this new law is also not without significance. This bill literally comes on the heels of the demise of the line item veto. The Supreme Court struck down the Line Item Veto Act as unconstitutional in *Clinton v. City of New York* on June 25, 1998; the very same day IRS Restructuring and Reform Act passed the House. As this has direct bearing on procedural aspects of this bill and last year's tax legislation, CCH has included a special discussion of the affect of the overturning of the Line Item Veto Act on recent tax legislation. This discussion appears at ¶ 30,025.

In this work, CCH editors, together with a number of leading tax professionals, are providing CCH customers with a single integrated reference tool that covers the Internal Revenue Service Restructuring and Reform Bill of 1998 (HR 2676), as well as the tax provisions of the Surface Transportation Revenue Act of 1998 (P.L. 105-178) that was signed into law by the President on June 9, 1998. The Conference report for HR 2676 is available in a separate publication, IRS Restructuring and Reform Bill of 1998 (HR 2676), dated June 24, 1998. This print edition of *1998 Legislation: Law, Explanation and Analysis* is being sent to subscribers together with a complimentary copy of *CCH's 1998 Tax Legislation: Highlights of the IRS Restructuring and Reform Act* and legislation study guide/quizzer. Taken together CCH has put together this complete package to orient professionals to the new law.

Mark Hevrdejs

Executive Editor

June 1998

OUTSIDE CONTRIBUTORS

Paul M. Bodner
Great Neck, New York

David R. Brennan
Faegre & Benson LLP
Minneapolis, Minnesota

Jim Carlisle
PricewaterhouseCoopers LLP
Washington, D.C.

Denis J. Conlon
Ernst & Young, LLP
Chicago, Illinois

C. VanLeer Davis III
Dechert Price & Rhoads
Philadelphia, Pennsylvania

J. Earl Epstein
Epstein, Shapiro & Epstein
Philadelphia, Pennsylvania

Donna Steele Flynn
Ernst & Young, LLP
Washington, D.C.

Wallace L. Head
Sanford C. Bernstein & Co., Inc.
Chicago, Illinois

Lawrence M. Hill
Brown & Wood LLP
New York, New York

Prof. David Hudson
Holland Law Center
University of Florida
Gainesville, Florida

Sidney Kess
New York, New York

S. Timothy Kochis
Kochis Fitz
San Francisco, California

Prof. Karen V. Kole
University of Tulsa School of Law
Tulsa, Oklahoma

Charles R. Levun
Levun Goodman & Cohen
Northbrook, Illinois

Robert McKenzie
McKenzie & McKenzie PC
Chicago, Illinois

William H. Mears, Jr.
Brown Brothers, Harriman Trust Company
New York, New York

Keith Nakamoto
PricewaterhouseCoopers LLP
Chicago, Illinois

Robert Nath
Odin, Feldman & Pittleman, PC
Fairfax, Virginia

Martin Nissenbaum
Ernst & Young, LLP
New York, New York

Shirley Peterson
President, Hood College
Frederick, Maryland

Sanford J. Schlesinger
Kaye, Scholer, Fierman, Hays & Handler, LLP
New York, New York

Arthur D. Sederbaum
Patterson, Belknap, Webb & Tyler LLP
New York, New York

Steven M. Surdell
Baker & McKenzie
Chicago, Illinois

CCH EDITORIAL STAFF

Pamela K. Carron, J.D., LL.M.

Karen Heslop, J.D.
Project Coordinators

Washington News Division

John Carpenter
Sheila Cherry
Paula Cruickshank
Gwen Jenkins
Rosalyn Johns

Craig Lebamoff, J.D.
Ann Marie Maloney, M.P.P.
Joyce Mutcherson-Ridley
Kevin Thomas

Analysis

Mark A. Luscombe, J.D., LL.M., C.P.A.

George G. Jones, J.D., LL.M.

John J. Mueller, J.D., LL.M.

Explanations

Ray G. Suelzer, Jr., J.D., LL.M.

Karin Huyck, J.D.
Coordinating Editors

Maureen C. Bornstein, J.D.
Anne E. Bowker, J.D.
Carina E. Callahan, J.D.
Mildred Carter, J.D.
Maurice M. Cashin, J.D.
Tom Cody, J.D., LL.M., M.B.A.
Kurt Diefenbach, J.D.
David F. Dotson, J.D.
Adrienne G. Gershon, J.D.
Bruno L. Graziano, J.D., M.S.A.
Kay Harris, J.D.
Marilynn Helt, J.D.
Nicholas J. Kaster, J.D.
Robert K. Kauffman, J.D., LL.M.
Thomas H. Kabaker, J.D.
Frank Kmiec, J.D.

Laura M. Lowe, J.D.
Michael A. Luster, J.D., LL.M.
Peter J. Melcher, J.D., LL.M., M.B.A.
Jean T. Nakamoto, J.D.
Jerome Nestor, J.D., C.P.A., M.B.A.
Karen A. Notaro, J.D., LL.M.
Marie T. O'Donnell, J.D., LL.M.
Carol D. Olbinsky, J.D.
Lawrence A. Perlman, J.D., LL.M., C.P.A.
Elizabeth Shepard Putnam, J.D.
Neil A. Ringquist, J.D., C.P.A.
Richard Ryndak, J.D.
Tracey A. Salinski, J.D., LL.M.
Carla Scarsella, J.D., C.P.A.
Carolyn M. Schiess, J.D.
Glenn Sulzer, J.D.

Internal Revenue Code

Karen J. Elsner, C.P.A.

Kathleen M. Higgins
Coordinating Editors

Ernest Deak
Lisa Moore
Kathleen Rogers
Warren L. Rosenbloom

Lisa A. Weder
Lynn Wilson
Christine C. Wyllie

Committee Reports

Mary E. Hamlin, J.D.
Coordinating Editor

Kris Bond
Sheri Miller, J.D.

Ellen Mitchell

Effective Dates

Jennifer A. Thalman, J.D.
Coordinating Editor

Katherine Baransky, J.D.   Kenneth L. Swanson, J.D., LL.M.
Julie S. Genz, J.D.

Production

Doris M. Heaney

Mary Ellen Guth
Production Coordinators

Elizabeth Albers   Nick Kursell
David Amyotte   Faina Lerin
Diana Bernhard   Marc Ludena
LB Brumage   Helen Miller
Odette Calderon   Catherine Olsen
Jane Easterly   Al Parzygnat
Chris Freeman   William Pegler
Katherine Grela   Thomas Potaczek
Kathy Hough   James C. Walschlager

Editorial Assistants

Kenneth R. Kuehl

Paula Weglarz
Coordinators

Diane L. McComb   Sandy Silverman
Tracy Deak   Whitney K. Ward

Electronic Release Development

Douglas L. Bretschneider

David Schuster
Coordinators

Kathleen M. Kowalski   James Waddick
Diane Lockwood, M.B.A.

Administrative Support

Gina Carbone   Eileen Slivka
Sue Gorman   Monika Stefan

How to Use

¶ 1

This edition of CCH 1998 TAX LEGISLATION: LAW, EXPLANATION AND ANALYSIS provides you with CCH explanations and analysis of both the IRS Restructuring and Reform Act (as passed by the House of Representatives on June 24, 1998) and the Surface Transportation Revenue Act of 1998 (P.L. 105-178), which was signed into law on June 9, 1998. In conjunction with CCH editors, practitioners and academics have infused the explanations in this text with practical guidance and planning strategies, and warn of latent pitfalls in the provisions contained in these new legislative packages. The details of the plan to reform the Internal Revenue Service are also thoroughly articulated and analyzed. Included in this text are the provisions of the Internal Revenue Code as amended, added or repealed by the new laws, and the relevant controlling Committee Reports.

Here is a guide to the numerous features provided in this text:

HIGHLIGHTS

A segment entitled "Highlights" precedes the CCH explanations, and provides references to the explanations to give you a quick overview of the major provisions in this legislative package. The Highlights are topically arranged by subject and provide a means of entry into the explanations. Subscribers to electronic versions of this product (on-line and CD-Rom) are able to link directly from a Highlights summary of interest to the related detailed explanation of the provision. *See ¶ 5.*

CCH EXPLANATIONS

CCH-prepared explanations of the IRS Restructuring and Reform Act of 1998 and the Surface Transportation Revenue Act of 1998 (ISTEA) are arranged according to subject matter for ease of use. The material is also flagged as either a technical correction, an IRS reform or an ISTEA provision. The first chapter of the explanation material is focussed on identifying taxpayers and industries significantly impacted by the new laws. In subsequent chapters, each explanation includes a discussion of background or prior law that helps to put into perspective the corrections and changes introduced by the IRS Restructuring and Reform Act or ISTEA.

Incorporated throughout the explanations is expert commentary provided by practitioners and academics. This commentary highlights planning opportunities and strategies engendered by the new laws and identifies how to avoid pitfalls and hazards in the legislative language.

Each explanation ends with the applicable effective date of the provision discussed. The effective date is preceded by a ★ symbol for easy reference.

The explanation paragraphs are followed by boldface amendment captions which: (1) identify the Act section of the applicable Act and the Code Section, added, amended, or repealed; and (2) provide cross references to the law and to the reproduced controlling Committee Reports. *The CCH explanations begin at ¶ 201.*

INDEX. Because the topical or subject matter approach to new legislation is usually the easiest to navigate, you may also access the material in the CCH Explanations through the extensive index. The index is located at the end of the book. *See page 809.* The index is also available on the electronic publication of this text on CCH Access On-Line and on CCH CD-Rom products.

AMENDED CODE PROVISIONS

CCH has reflected the changes to the Internal Revenue Code initiated by the IRS Restructuring and Reform Act of 1998 and ISTEA in the Law Added, Amended or Repealed provisions. Deleted Code material or the text of the Code provision prior to amendment appears in the Amendment Notes following each reconstructed Code provision. *Any changed or added portion is set out in italics.*

The applicable date for each Amendment Note is set out in boldface type. Preceding each set of amendment notes, CCH provides references to: (1) the corresponding controlling Committee Reports; and (2) the CCH explanation of that amended, added, or repealed Code provision. Electronic product subscribers can link to the related explanation or committee report material using these references. *The text of the Code begins at ¶5001.*

NON-CODE PROVISIONS

The sections of the IRS Restructuring and Reform Act of 1998 and ISTEA that do *not* amend the Internal Revenue Code appear in full text in Act section order following the Law Added, Amended or Repealed section of the text. Included is the text of Act sections that amend prior tax acts, such as the Taxpayer Relief Act of 1997 (P.L. 105-34), Small Business Job Protection Act of 1996 (P.L. 104-188), and the Technical and Miscellaneous Revenue Act of 1988 (P.L. 100-647). *The text of these provisions appears in Act section order beginning at ¶8001.*

COMMITTEE REPORTS

The Controlling Committee Reports officially explain the intent of Congress regarding the provisions in the IRS Restructuring and Reform Act and ISTEA. At the end of the Committee Report text, CCH provides a caption line that includes references to the corresponding Explanation and Code provisions. Electronic product subscribers can link from these references to the corresponding material. *These Controlling Committee Reports—House, Senate, and Conference Committee Reports—appear in Act section order beginning at ¶10,001.*

EFFECTIVE DATES

A table listing the major effective dates provides you with a reference bridge between Code sections and Act sections and indicates the retroactive or prospective nature of the laws explained. *This effective date table appears at ¶20,001.*

SPECIAL FINDING DEVICES

A table cross-referencing Code sections to the CCH explanations is included *(see ¶25,001).* Other tables include Code sections added, amended, or repealed *(see ¶25,005),* provisions of other acts that were amended *(see ¶25,010),* Act sections not amending Internal Revenue Code sections *(see ¶25,015),* and Act sections amending Code sections *(see ¶25,020),* so that you can immediately determine whether a provision in which you are interested is affected.

Each explanation chapter is preceded by a chapter table of contents listing the chapter contents. A detailed table of contents for the entire LAW, EXPLANATION AND ANALYSIS text is also included for easy identification of subject matter.

¶1

SPECIAL TABLES

Provisions that were initially included in the House or Senate versions of the IRS Restructuring and Reform Act of 1998 but were dropped in conference agreement are included *(see ¶ 30,001).*

Also, because the Line Item Veto Act (P.L. 104-130) was declared unconstitutional on the very day that the House of Representatives passed the IRS Restructuring and Reform Act, CCH editors have included a discussion of the impact of this development on recent bills at *¶ 30,025*. None of the provisions in ISTEA were subject to the Line Item Veto.

Finally, a listing of those provisions that were stricken or repealed as deadwood from the Internal Revenue Code appear at *¶ 30,050*.

CLIENT LETTERS

Client letters explaining the ramifications of the tax law changes are included. These memoranda are intended to be used by practitioners as the foundation for drafting letters to inform their clients of the recent law changes and their impact on a client's tax, financial, or estate plan. Sample client letters on financial and retirement planning, tax planning for individuals, small business tax breaks, and a Taxpayer Relief Act of 1997 follow-up are provided. Subscribers to CCH's CD-Rom and Access On-line products can copy the letter text over into their word-processing application for easy text manipulation and customization. *The client letters begin at ¶ 50,001.*

Table of Contents

Detailed Table of Contents

CHAPTER 1. TAXPAYERS AFFECTED

TECHNICAL CORRECTIONS AND REVENUE RAISERS
CHAPTER 2. INDIVIDUALS

CHAPTER 3. INDIVIDUAL RETIREMENT ACCOUNTS AND QUALIFIED PLANS

CHAPTER 4. ESTATE AND GIFT TAX

CHAPTER 5. BUSINESS AND INVESTMENT

CHAPTER 7. EXCISE TAXES

IRS RESTRUCTURING AND REFORM PROVISIONS

CHAPTER 8. IRS STRUCTURE AND FUNCTIONS

CHAPTER 9. IMPROVEMENTS IN PERSONNEL FLEXIBILITIES

CHAPTER 10. ELECTRONIC FILING INITIATIVES

CHAPTER 11. TAXPAYER RIGHTS—EXAMINATION ACTIVITIES

CHAPTER 12. TAXPAYER RIGHTS—COLLECTION ACTIVITIES

CHAPTER 13. TAXPAYER RIGHTS—JUDICIAL PROCEEDINGS

CHAPTER 14. TAXPAYER RIGHTS—INTEREST, PENALTIES, AND REFUNDS

Highlights

¶ 5

INDIVIDUALS

Earned Income Credit (EIC). Individuals otherwise eligible for the EIC, who fail to provide their taxpayer identification numbers (TINs) or the TINs of their spouses, are not allowed the EIC for the year for which the credit is claimed. A qualifying child is not taken into account in computing an eligible individual's EIC unless that child's name, age, and TIN are included on the return for the year for which the credit is claimed. Also, eligible individuals with qualifying children will not be allowed EICs if they fail to identify those children by name, age, and TIN on their returns .... ¶ 216

Education Individual Retirement Accounts (IRAs). Any balance remaining in an education IRA is deemed distributed within 30 days after the beneficiary reaches age 30, or within 30 days of the death of a beneficiary under age 30. The earnings portion of the distribution is includible in the beneficiary's gross income .... ¶ 236

Student Loan Interest. Individuals are allowed to deduct interest paid on qualified education loans beginning in 1998. However, the debt must be incurred solely for purposes of paying qualified higher education expenses, and the deduction is limited to interest paid during the first 60 months in which such payments are required... ¶ 242

Sale of Principal Residence. The $250,000 exclusion ($500,000 for certain joint filers) of gain on the sale or exchange of a principal residence is prorated for taxpayers who do not meet the two-year ownership and use requirements in the case of sales or exchanges attributable to a change in place of employment, health, or unforeseen circumstances. Where joint filers fail to qualify for the $500,000 exclusion, the limit on the amount of excludable gain is computed separately for each spouse .... ¶ 246, ¶ 248

Exclusion for Transportation Fringe Benefits. Employers may offer employees the option of electing cash compensation in lieu of any qualified transportation benefit or combination of benefits after 1997 without jeopardizing the exclusion available to the employees for noncash transportation fringe benefits. No amount will be includible in income merely because the employee is offered the choice of cash and one or more qualified transportation benefits. To the extent that the employee elects to receive cash, the funds will constitute taxable income. Further, for tax years beginning in 1999, the base amount for the maximum exclusion for qualified parking benefits will increase from $155 to $175. Also, the base amount for the maximum exclusion for employer-provided qualified transportation benefits such as van pooling and transit passes will increase from $60 to $65 for tax years beginning in 1999, and will further increase from $65 to $100 for tax years beginning in 2002................... ¶ 253

IRS Levies. Use of a "continuous levy," which attaches both to property held on the date of levy and to property or payments acquired after the date of levy, is at the IRS's discretion and must be specifically approved by the IRS before the levy takes effect... ¶ 266

INDIVIDUAL RETIREMENT ACCOUNTS AND QUALIFIED PLANS

Roth IRAs. The rules dealing with conversions of regular IRAs into Roth IRAs have been modified in order to prevent taxpayers from receiving premature distributions from Roth Conversion IRAs while reaping the benefits of the four-year income spread. A 10% early withdrawal tax is imposed on premature, unqualified withdrawals, and ordering rules are provided for determining which amounts are withdrawn for tax purposes when a Roth IRA contains both conversion and contributory amounts, or conversion amounts from different years. Also, the four-year income spread has been made elective, and taxpayers can elect to recognize all income in the conversion year . . . . ¶ 301

Erroneous Conversions. Taxpayers who erroneously convert their regular IRAs into Roth IRAs have until the due date of their returns, including extensions, in which to "undo" the transactions by completing trustee-to-trustee transfers of the converted amounts from Roth IRAs to regular IRAs . . . . ¶ 311

Death of Account Holder. If a taxpayer who converted a regular IRA to a Roth IRA dies during the four-year spread period, any amount remaining to be included in income as a result of the conversion will be includible on the decedent's final return. However, a surviving spouse who is the beneficiary of a Roth Conversion IRA can elect to continue to defer income over the remainder of the spread period . . . . ¶ 315

Computation of Adjusted Gross Income (AGI). For purposes of determining eligibility to convert a regular IRA to a Roth IRA after 2004, minimum required IRA distributions made to taxpayers over age 70½ will be excluded from AGI and will not count toward the $100,000 maximum AGI level . . . . ¶ 323

Contribution Limit. The maximum amount that individuals may contribute to their various IRAs is limited to $2,000 per year. Simplified employee pensions (SEPs) and SIMPLE IRAs cannot be designated as Roth IRAs. Also, contributions to SEPs and SIMPLE IRAs cannot be taken into account for purposes of the $2,000 contribution limit and will not affect the amount that can be contributed to a Roth IRA . . . . ¶ 331

ESTATE AND GIFT TAX

Family-Owned Businesses. The qualified family-owned business interest (QFOBI) exclusion which, in combination with the applicable exclusion amount, shields a maximum of $1.3 million from the estate tax has been converted into a deduction. The deduction is not available for gift tax or generation-skipping transfer tax purposes . . . . ¶ 401, ¶ 406

BUSINESS AND INVESTMENT

Capital Gains and Losses. Law changes made by the Taxpayer Relief Act of 1997 (1997 TRA) regarding the taxation of long-term capital gains have been rewritten and restructured to fill in gaps in coverage. Amendments to Code Sec. 1(h), which consist largely of "technical corrections," are designed to present the provision in a more logical and coherent style . . . . ¶ 501-¶ 524

Long-Term Capital Gains. The 18-month holding period for long-term capital assets eligible for the lower capital gain rates set by the 1997 TRA has been eliminated. Instead, property held for more than one year will qualify for the favorable rates effective for tax years ending after 1997 . . . . ¶ 502

Maximum Capital Gains Rate. The formula for determining an individual's tax on long-term capital gains has been revamped and simplified . . . . ¶ 518

Rollover of Gain. The election to roll over gain realized from the sale of qualified small business stock held for more than six months can now be made by "a taxpayer other than a corporation." Thus, the election, which was previously available only to individuals, can be made by certain partnerships and S corporations . . . . ¶ 531

¶ 5

Deferred Compensation. Employers can deduct accrued vacation or severance pay in a particular year only if those amounts are actually received by their employees on or before 2½ months after the close of the tax year. "Actual receipt" is not intended to include the furnishing of a letter of credit, promissory note, other evidence of indebtedness, or a promise to provide services or property in the future. Also, amounts transferred as loans, refundable deposits, or contingent payments, and funds set aside in a trust for employees are not considered to be actually received. This provision legislatively overrules the Tax Court's decision in *Schmidt Baking Co., Inc.* (107 TC 271, Dec. 51,650) . . . . ¶591

Employer-Provided Meals. Where more than half of the employees receiving employer-provided meals on work premises are furnished those meals for the convenience of the employer, all meals furnished to employees at the employer's place of business are treated as provided for the convenience of the employer. In these circumstances, the value of the meals is excludable from employees' incomes and is fully deductible by the employer . . . . ¶593

CORPORATIONS AND SPECIAL ENTITIES

Stapled Real Estate Investment Trusts (REITs). The Tax Reform Act of 1984 curtailed the tax benefits of the stapled REIT structure, under which a REIT was stapled to an active business corporation in order to eliminate the corporate tax on active business income from the real estate. However, grandfather relief from the elimination of stapled REITS was provided to a group of stapled entities that included a REIT on June 30, 1983. The benefits enjoyed by grandfathered stapled REITs have generally been eliminated for real property interests acquired after March 26, 1998. Additional rules apply to mortgages acquired after that date and to acquisitions of real property interests through entities after that date. Also, relief has been provided for transactions that were in progress on March 26, 1998 . . . . ¶655

Contributions of Computer Technology. The "augmented charitable deduction" allowed for certain gifts of computer technology and equipment by C corporations for elementary or secondary school purposes applies to contributions made after 1997 and before 2001 . . . . ¶696

EXCISE TAXES

Rail Fuels Excise Tax. 1.25 cents per gallon of the excise tax on diesel fuel and gasoline used in trains, which was imposed through September 30, 1999, has been repealed effective November 1, 1998 . . . . ¶727

Fuel Tax Refunds. The refund procedures for all taxable motor fuels have been combined, effective October 1, 1998. Once taxpayers have paid a single $750 minimum amount of motor fuel excise taxes for fuel used for a nontaxable purpose, they can file refund claims using the simplified procedures. Tax on specified fuels can be aggregated to arrive at the $750 amount, which is determined on a year-to-year basis, rather than on a quarterly basis . . . . ¶729

Highway-Related Taxes and Trust Fund. Highway Trust Fund excise taxes that were scheduled to expire in 1999 have been extended for a six-year period. The taxes include those imposed on heavy trucks and trailers; highway motor vehicles; heavy tires; special motor fuels; certain buses; certain alcohol fuels; and gasoline, diesel fuel, and kerosene . . . . ¶750

IRS STRUCTURE AND FUNCTIONS

Reorganization of IRS. Geographic regional divisions within the IRS will be replaced by units serving groups of taxpayers with similar needs. These groups are broken down into individuals, small businesses, large sector corporations, and exempt organizations. The reorganization will not affect existing tax laws, taxpayer rights, or pending lawsuits. Meeting taxpayers' needs and providing public service will be key elements of a revised IRS mission statement . . . . ¶801, ¶806

IRS Commissioner. The duties of the Commissioner have been specifically prescribed, the Commissioner will be appointed to serve a five-year term in office, and candidates must have a "demonstrated ability in management." The Chief Counsel will report directly to the Commissioner and will have an expanded role in policy matters . . . . ¶811, ¶816

National Taxpayer Advocate. The renamed *National* Taxpayer Advocate will be appointed by the Treasury Secretary and will report directly to the Commissioner. Local advocates, who report directly to the National Advocate, operate independently of other IRS offices . . . . ¶821

Oversight of the IRS. A nine-member IRS Oversight Board will oversee the administration, management, conduct, direction, and supervision of the IRS. Among other duties, the board is to ensure that taxpayers are properly treated by IRS employees, to review and approve IRS strategic plans, and to recommend placement and removal of high-level officials, including the Commissioner and the National Taxpayer Advocate . . . . ¶826

Treasury IG for Tax Administration. The Office of the IRS Chief Inspector is being replaced by a new, independent Office of the Treasury Inspector General for Tax Administration, which is charged with oversight and inspection of the IRS. . . . . ¶831

Low-Income Taxpayer Clinics. Matching grants will be awarded to fund taxpayer clinics targeted at low-income and non-English-speaking clients, training and technical assistance providing support to such clinics, and volunteer taxpayer assistance programs. . . . . ¶851

Disclosures by "Whistle Blowers." To facilitate the reporting of IRS employee misconduct and taxpayer abuse, persons with authorized access to taxpayer return information may disclose that information when reporting such abuse to Congressional committees charged with IRS oversight . . . . ¶863

Tax Protestors. The IRS is barred from designating taxpayers as illegal tax protestors and must remove such designation from its Individual Master File . . . . ¶891

IMPROVEMENTS IN PERSONNEL FLEXIBILITIES

Performance Management and Staffing. The IRS has been given one year in which to establish a new performance-management system that allows for the evaluation of each employee's performance and sets a minimum level at which the employees are expected to perform. The IRS has been provided with a broader range of options to motivate its employees and refocus the agency toward improved taxpayer assistance. . . . . ¶941-¶966

Employee Misconduct. Specific acts of misconduct that will result in an IRS employee's termination have been enumerated. The Commissioner has discretion to take a personnel action other than mandatory termination . . . . ¶976

Employee Evaluations. The IRS is barred from using records of tax enforcement results to evaluate its employees' performance or to impose or suggest production quotas or goals with respect to the employees . . . . ¶981

¶5

ELECTRONIC FILING INITIATIVES

Promotion of Electronic Filing. Within 180 days of enactment, the IRS must establish a strategic plan to increase taxpayer use of electronic filing. A new electronic commerce advisory group is to report on the IRS's progress in meeting its goal of 80% electronic filing by 2007 .... ¶ 1001

Information Returns. As an incentive to encourage the use of electronic filing for information returns reporting such items as dividends, partnership distributions, and interest, the filing due date has been extended from February 28 to March 31 .... ¶ 1005

Paperless Filing. Pending the development of procedures that will allow the IRS to accept electronic signatures in connection with electronically filed returns, it is authorized either to waive the signature requirement or to provide for alternative signature methods .... ¶ 1009

TAXPAYER RIGHTS—EXAMINATION ACTIVITIES

Extension of Rights to Civil Damages. Taxpayers may recover up to $100,000 in civil damages if an IRS officer or employee negligently disregards the Tax Code or regulations. Damages are also recoverable for willful violations by IRS personnel of certain Bankruptcy Code provisions and regulations pertaining to automatic stays and discharges. Nontaxpayers may also sue for civil damages in connection with unauthorized collection actions...................... ¶ 1101

Taxpayer Assistance Orders (TAOs). The National Taxpayer Advocate can issue a TAO based on the determination that a taxpayer will suffer a significant hardship due to the manner in which the tax laws are being administered. Such a hardship includes an immediate threat of adverse action; a delay of more than 30 days in resolving taxpayer account problems; potential liability for significant costs if relief is not granted; and the possibility of irreparable injury to, or a long-term adverse impact on, the taxpayer...................... ¶ 1106

Financial Status Audits. The IRS's use of financial status audit techniques, which scrutinize a taxpayer's lifestyle to determine the existence of unreported income, is limited to situations where a routine examination has established a reasonable likelihood of unreported income.................. ¶ 1111

Expanded Explanation of Taxpayer Rights. The IRS has been directed to revise Publication 1, *Your Rights as a Taxpayer*, in order to better explain both a taxpayer's rights during administrative interviews and the criteria and procedures used in selecting taxpayers for audit .... ¶ 1121, ¶ 1126

Executive Branch Audit Influence. Executive Branch requests for taxpayer audits are prohibited. Parties barred from making audit requests include the President and Vice President and their staffs, as well as cabinet-level personnel other than the Attorney General .... ¶ 1131

Prohibition on Requesting Waiver of Right to Sue. Government officers and employees are generally prohibited from requesting taxpayers to waive their right to sue with respect to any action taken in connection with the tax laws .... ¶ 1133

Privileged Communications. Communications between taxpayers and "federally authorized tax practitioners," who include nonattorneys licensed to practice before the IRS, in connection with any noncriminal proceedings that are before the IRS or that are brought by or against the government in federal court, are accorded the same protections as communications with attorneys. This privilege does not extend to written communications regarding corporate tax shelters.. ¶ 1141

¶ 5

Third-Party Contacts. The IRS can serve summonses on third-party recordkeepers either in person or by certified or registered mail. Also, it is generally required to notify taxpayers prior to contacting third parties regarding examination or collection activities . . . . ¶ 1151, ¶ 1156

IRS Use of Pseudonyms. As a prerequisite for using pseudonyms, IRS employees must provide adequate justification for the use and obtain the approval of their supervisors . . . . ¶ 1176

TAXPAYER RIGHTS—COLLECTION ACTIVITIES

Approval of Liens and Levies. Written approval of the IRS Chief Counsel or his delegate must be obtained as a prerequisite for jeopardy and termination assessments or jeopardy levies. Also, "where appropriate," revenue officers must obtain a supervisor's approval before issuing a notice of lien or levy against a taxpayer's property or before seizing property . . . . ¶ 1201, 1206

Increased Levy Exemption Amounts. The levy exemption amount for a taxpayer's personal effects has been increased from $2,500 to $6,250, and the levy exemption for books, equipment, and tools used in a taxpayer's trade, business or profession has been increased from $1,250 to $3,125. These amounts will be adjusted for inflation . . . . ¶ 1210

Lien Exemption Amounts. The dollar amounts of certain "superpriority interests" that are exempt from federal tax liens have been increased. For casual sales for amounts under $1,000 with respect to household goods, personal effects, or other tangible property, a lien is invalid against a purchaser who lacks knowledge of the lien. Mechanic's liens of $5,000 or less that are related to repairs or improvements to a taxpayer's personal residence have priority over a tax lien on the residence. The exemption amounts will be adjusted for inflation . . . . ¶ 1214

Collection Barred During Refund Proceedings. The IRS cannot collect any unpaid "divisible tax" (amounts paid periodically, such as employment taxes) by levy or court proceeding while a refund suit for the paid portion of the tax is pending. The prohibition does not apply if the taxpayer executes a written waiver or if collection of the tax is in jeopardy . . . . ¶ 1222

Levies on Retirement Plans and IRAs. The 10% tax on premature withdrawals from employer-sponsored retirement plans or IRAs will not apply to distributions after 1999 that result from an IRS levy against the plan or IRA . . ¶ 1226

Release of Erroneous Liens. A third-party owner of property against which a tax lien has been filed may, as a matter of right, obtain a certificate of discharge with respect to such lien upon the posting of security satisfactory to the IRS. Such relief is not available to delinquent taxpayers . . . . ¶ 1230

Seizure of Residence or Business. The IRS cannot seize the personal residence of the taxpayer or any other person in order to satisfy a liability of $5,000 or less. Further, unless collection of the tax is in jeopardy, written approval by the IRS District Director or Assistant Director is required prior to the seizure of a taxpayer's principal residence or of the real or personal property used in the taxpayer's trade or business. . . . . ¶ 1234

Accounting for Sales. The recordkeeping requirements applicable to IRS sales of real property have been extended to sales of all types of property. The IRS must furnish those records, excluding the identity of the purchaser, to the taxpayer along with an accounting of the amount of the sale proceeds applied to the tax liability and the remaining balance due . . . . ¶ 1242

Due Process in Collection Activities. The IRS has five business days after the filing of a lien in which to provide notice to the taxpayer. Also, notice of the right to a hearing must be provided at least 30 days before levying on a person's property or right to property. The notice must indicate the amount owed and explain the taxpayer's right to a hearing, the availability of administrative appeals and their procedures, and how to obtain a release of lien. In addition, the notice must outline the proposed action and identify the taxpayer's rights with respect to each action, including any available alternatives to the levy ... ¶ 1254

Fair Debt Collection Practices Act (FDCPA). The IRS is required to adhere to certain requirements of the FDCPA, including limiting communications with taxpayers to convenient times; refraining from communications with taxpayers who are known to be represented by counsel; restricting communications with taxpayers at their place of employment; and curtailing actions that constitute harassment, oppression, or abuse .... ¶ 1262

Explanation of Appeal and Collection Process. The IRS must include an explanation of its entire examination and collection process with the first deficiency letter that it sends to a taxpayer .... ¶ 1266

Offers in Compromise. While an offer in compromise or an installment agreement offer is pending, and for 30 days thereafter or until resolution of any appeal, the IRS cannot levy against the taxpayer's property in satisfaction of the liability covered by the offer. The IRS is to develop guidelines for determining whether an offer in compromise is adequate and procedures for independent administrative review of its rejection of an offer prior to communicating that rejection to the taxpayer. Taxpayers must be notified of their right to appeal any rejection to the IRS Office of Appeals .... ¶ 1270

Installment Agreements. Generally, the IRS must enter into an installment agreement with an individual who requests such an arrangement if the tax debt does not exceed $10,000 and the taxpayer has not, during the preceding five-year period, failed to file, failed to pay income tax, or entered into any other installment payment agreements. Taxpayers who make payments under installment agreements are to be furnished with annual statements indicating the status of their tax debts. The penalty for failure to pay taxes has been reduced for any month in which an installment agreement is in effect .... ¶ 1274-¶ 1282

Extension of Statute of Limitations. The IRS has to notify taxpayers of their right to refuse to extend the limitations period for tax assessments each time that an extension request is made .... ¶ 1286

Innocent Spouse. The requirements for obtaining innocent spouse relief from joint and several tax liability have been relaxed in a number of ways. Relief is now available with respect to all tax understatements attributable to erroneous items of the other spouse; the understatement no longer has to be substantial. Further, it is sufficient that the income items in question be merely "erroneous," not "grossly erroneous." Also, relief can be obtained on an apportioned basis; taxpayers have two years in which to elect innocent spouse relief following a tax assessment; certain legally separated couples can elect separate tax liability even if they filed jointly; the Tax Court has been granted jurisdiction to review denials of innocent spouse relief and separate liability elections; and the IRS is authorized to provide expanded equitable relief .... ¶ 1290

TAXPAYER RIGHTS—JUDICIAL PROCEEDINGS

Refund Jurisdiction. In circumstances where decedents' estates have elected to pay estate tax relating to certain closely held businesses on an installment basis, federal district courts and the U.S. Court of Federal Claims have jurisdiction to determine the correct amount of estate tax liability or the estate's entitlement to a refund prior to final payment .... ¶ 1301

Small Case Calendar. The dollar cap for small tax case treatment of actions filed in the Tax Court cases has increased from $10,000 to $50,000 .... ¶ 1316

30 IRS Restructuring and Reform Act of 1998

Refund of Improperly Collected Amounts. Proper courts, including the Tax Court, have jurisdiction to order a refund of any amount wrongfully collected during the pendency of a Tax Court petition .... ¶ 1321

Tax Court Deadlines. All deficiency notices mailed after 1998 must indicate the last date on which a taxpayer can file a timely petition with the Tax Court. The IRS is bound by the filing deadline specified in the notice .... ¶ 1326

Burden of Proof in Court Proceedings. The burden of proof on a factual issue that is relevant in determining a taxpayer's income tax liability is shifted to the government if the taxpayer presents credible evidence on the issue and satisfies substantiation and recordkeeping requirements, cooperates with the IRS, and, for taxpayers other than individuals, satisfies the net worth limitations. In circumstances where statistical information from unrelated taxpayers is used to reconstruct an individual's income, the IRS has the burden of proof as to that item. The burden of proof is also on the IRS with respect to penalties assessed against individuals .... ¶ 1331

Awards of Fees and Costs. The hourly rate cap on attorneys' fee awards has been increased to $125 per hour and will be indexed for inflation; increased awards may be granted based on the complexity of the issues presented. Fees may be awarded to *pro bono* individuals representing prevailing parties. The circumstances in which the government's position will be deemed "substantially justified" and the taxpayer will be treated as the prevailing party have been enumerated .... ¶ 1336

TAXPAYER RIGHTS—INTEREST, PENALTIES, AND REFUNDS

Accrual of Interest and Penalties. The accrual of interest and penalties on individuals' income tax delinquencies will be suspended if the IRS fails to issue a notice specifically stating the liability and the basis for such liability within 18 months (one year for tax years beginning after 2003) following the later of the original due date of the return or the date on which a timely return is filed. The suspension will end 21 days after the date when notice is provided by the IRS . ¶ 1401

Interest Rates. The interest rate for tax overpayments and underpayments has essentially been equalized for any period of mutual debt between a taxpayer and the IRS. To the extent that underpayment and overpayment interest runs simultaneously on equal amounts, no interest will be imposed .... ¶ 1406

Elimination of Interest Rate Differential. The interest rate paid by the IRS with respect to noncorporate taxpayers' overpayments has been increased. The interest rate applicable to such taxpayers' underpayments and overpayments is now the same .... ¶ 1411

Imposition of Penalties. A notice of penalty sent by an IRS employee to a taxpayer after December 31, 2000, must state the name of the penalty, the statutory provision authorizing imposition of the penalty, and the computation resulting in the penalty. With the exception of certain additions to tax, including those imposed for failure to file or pay and for underpayment of estimated tax, supervisory approval is a prerequisite before penalties can be assessed .... ¶ 1436

Refund Offset Program. For tax refunds payable after 1999, the IRS's refund offset program will include past-due, legally enforceable state income tax debts that have been reduced to judgment .... ¶ 1446

Disallowance of Refunds. Taxpayers whose refund claims are being disallowed must be provided with an explanation of the IRS's reasons for the disallowance .... ¶ 1451

Limitations Period for Financially Disabled Taxpayers. The statute of limitations on refund claims may be tolled during any period in which "financially disabled" taxpayers with determinable medical or physical impairments are unable to manage their financial affairs due to such impairments. The limitations period will not be tolled if a third party is authorized to act on behalf of a taxpayer in financial matters .... ¶ 1461

¶ 5

Chapter 1
Taxpayers Affected

IRS RESTRUCTURING AND REFORM ACT OF 1998

Overview

¶ 101

Although labeled the IRS Restructuring and Reform Act of 1998, it is the provisions unrelated to IRS restructuring that will have the most significant impact on the majority of taxpayers. These provisions include a last minute change shortening the capital gain holding period from 18 to 12 months and a variety of provisions labeled technical corrections, many of which will have a significant impact on tax planning. The technical correction provisions primarily relate to the Taxpayer Relief Act of 1997 (P.L. 105-34). The Taxpayer Relief Act of 1997 was one of the most significant pieces of tax legislation in over a decade in terms of its impact on tax planning for the average taxpayer. However, it also added a great deal of complexity to tax provisions that individual and small business taxpayers must deal with regularly. There were also a number of last minute compromises with the administration that resulted in statutory language that was put together quickly and without time for the usual amount of review and analysis. As a result, the technical corrections to those provisions have taken on a greater significance than has often been the case with past technical correction legislation.

In many cases with prior tax laws, technical corrections have not emerged until several years after the underlying legislation has passed. In contrast, many of the technical corrections to the Taxpayer Relief Act of 1997 have such a significant impact on tax planning and tax return preparation that there was a particular sense of urgency to promptly enact these technical corrections. In the capital gains area, the IRS found it necessary to seek assurance from Congress of its intent to pass technical correction legislation before proceeding with the revised Schedule D that was utilized for preparation of 1997 returns. The return of the capital gain holding period to 12 months should help to simplify Schedule D on future returns.

Most of the major provisions of the Taxpayer Relief Act of 1997 are modified by the technical corrections contained in this legislation. There are changes to the child tax credit, the education incentives, the IRA provisions, the capital gain provisions, the estate and gift tax provisions, and the alternative minimum tax provisions, as well as to many of the miscellaneous provisions and revenue raisers. These technical corrections do not make any attempt to solve the complexities inherent in many of the provisions of the Taxpayer Relief Act of 1997. They do, however, clarify the scope of many of those provisions and significantly impact the planning opportunities associated with those provisions.

In addition to technical corrections, the focus of the IRS Restructuring and Reform Act of 1998 is on changes to the organization of the IRS and a set of enhanced taxpayer protections and rights. Also included are a number of revenue offsets to help pay for those reforms that are anticipated to result in a loss of tax dollars to the government. While the changes to the organizational structure may have a long-term benefit to taxpayers in terms of a more efficient and responsive agency, the specific changes will be largely of interest to those tax practitioners that deal with the IRS on a regular basis. Many of the new taxpayer protections and rights, however, will be of great interest to taxpayers. Of particular interest, and with a significant revenue cost, will be the expansion of the protections for an innocent spouse when filing a joint tax return. Reduced penalties and interest under prescribed circumstances will also be of importance to a broad spectrum of taxpayers. Many of the other provisions, relating to shifting the burden of proof, protections during audits and collection activities, and disclosures to taxpayers, will improve the position of the taxpayer in dealing with the IRS, but the specifics will be of interest primarily to the taxpayer's representative.

Collectively, these changes are the most extensive restructuring of the IRS and the laws under which it operates in at least 40 years. They will create many planning opportunities for tax practitioners and their clients in determining how best to handle tax issues and resolve disputes with the IRS.

IMPACT ON TAXPAYERS

Individuals

¶ 105

The Taxpayer Relief Act of 1997 had its primary impact on individual taxpayers. It is no surprise, therefore, that a large number of the technical corrections to that '97 Act also impact individuals. Key areas that will affect planning involve Roth IRAs; capital gains, including sales of principal residences; and estate and gift planning. Significant provisions in this law affecting individuals include the reduction in the capital gains holding period to 12 months, expanded relief for innocent spouses, greater availability of conversions to Roth IRAs to higher income taxpayers, and a new privilege of confidentiality in discussing tax matters with an accountant or enrolled agent.

Provisions affecting individuals include the following:

Capital Gains:

Individual Retirement Accounts:

Estate and Gift:

Families

¶ 111

The Taxpayer Relief Act of 1997 also had a primary focus on families. Important clarifications are made in this legislation to the child tax credit, education provisions, and the adoption tax credit.

Small Business

¶ 115

Clarification of the workings of the family-owned business exclusion, new with the 1997 Tax Act, is the most significant change affecting small business.

Business Generally

¶ 121

Business has a mixed bag of provisions in this legislation, some restrictive but several helpful.

Corporations

¶ 125

Some provisions affecting corporations were removed in the final negotiations, such as foreign tax credit carryover and carryback changes and provisions with respect to foreign hybrid entities (¶ 633). Those that remain are significant clarifications of law.

Exempt Organizations

¶ 131

Provisions with respect to exempt organizations are primarily clarification of prior law.

Partnerships

¶ 135

Many of the partnership provisions in this legislation are detailed and narrowly focused, with allocation of basis clarifications and the stapled-REIT provision being perhaps the most significant.

Investors

¶ 141

Investors will be particularly cheered by the shortening of the capital gains holding period.

Specialized Industries

¶ 145

The following industries have provisions in the legislation particularly focused on them.

Transportation and Fuels (including provisions from the Surface Transportation Revenue Act of 1998):

Beverages:

Financial Institutions and Markets:

IRS Procedures and Practices

¶ 151

Changes affecting dealings with the IRS are extensive and pervasive. They are subcategorized by topic for ease of locating matters of particular interest.

¶ 151

IRS Structure

¶ 155

These provisions reflect the most significant changes in IRS structure in over 40 years.

TECHNICAL CORRECTIONS AND REVENUE RAISERS

Chapter 2

Individuals

CREDITS

Child Credit Stacking Rules

¶ 201

Background

For 1998, taxpayers may claim a $400 child tax credit for each qualifying child under the age of 17 (Code Sec. 24, as added by the Taxpayer Relief Act of 1997 (P.L. 105-34)). The child credit is generally a nonrefundable credit, but a portion may be treated as a refundable credit by taxpayers who claim the additional credit for families with three or more qualifying children (Code Sec. 24(d)) or the supplemental child credit that is part of the earned income credit (EIC) (Code Sec. 32(m)[(n)], as added by P.L. 105-34).

The maximum additional credit for families with three or more children ("additional credit") is limited to the greater of:

(1) the excess of the taxpayer's regular tax liability (net of applicable credits other than the EIC) over the taxpayer's tentative minimum tax liability (as defined at Code Sec. 55 and determined without regard to the alternative minimum tax (AMT) foreign tax credit), or

(2) the excess of (a) the taxpayer's regular income tax liability (net of applicable credits other than the EIC) plus the employee share of FICA liability (and one-half of any SECA tax liability), over (b) the EIC.

If the amount determined in (2), above, exceeds the amount determined in (1), above, the excess is treated as a refundable credit.

Under Code Sec. 26, nonrefundable personal credits may not be used to reduce tax liability below a taxpayer's tentative minimum tax. Special "stacking" rules determine the order in which credits are used to reduce a taxpayer's tax liability— first, nonrefundable personal credits, then other credits, business credits, and the investment tax credit (Senate Committee Report to the IRS Restructuring and Reform Act of 1998). Within the group of nonrefundable personal credits, those that cannot be carried forward are used to reduce the tax liability for the current year before those that can be carried forward.

Technical Corrections Impact

Families with three or more children.—A technical correction clarifies the application of the Code Sec. 26(a) income tax liability limitation to the refundable portion of the child credit for families with three or more children. The additional credit for families with three or more children ("additional credit") is treated in the same way as other refundable credits. After all the other credits are applied according to the stacking rules to reduce the taxpayer's tax liability for the year, then the refundable credits are applied. The refundable credits first reduce the taxpayer's tax liability for the year, and any remaining credit in excess of the tax liability for the year is payable to the taxpayer (Senate Committee Report to the IRS Restructuring and Reform Act of 1998).

Specifically, for families with three or more children, the additional credit is equal to the lesser of:

(1) the child credit that would be allowed if computed without regard to the refundable additional credit and the Code Sec. 26(a) tax liability limitation, or

(2) the amount that the total nonrefundable personal credits (including the child credit but without regard to the refundable additional credit) would increase if the Code Sec. 26(a) tax liability limitation were increased by the excess of (a) the taxpayer's social security taxes for the tax year, over (b) the earned income credit determined without regard to the supplemental child credit for the tax year (Code Sec. 32(n)).

The amount of the additional credit reduces the amount of the nonrefundable child credit otherwise allowable without regard to the Code Sec. 26(a) tax liability limitation (Code Sec. 24(d)(1), as amended by the 1998 Act).

For taxpayers subject to the AMT, the additional credit is reduced by the excess of (1) the taxpayer's AMT under Code Sec. 55 for the tax year, over (2) the amount of the reduction of the EIC under Code Sec. 32(h) with respect to the taxpayer for the tax year (Code Sec. 24(d)(2), as amended by the 1998 Act).

PRACTICAL ANALYSIS. Professor Karen V. Kole of the University of Tulsa School of Law observes that, as she noted in previous commentary to the Taxpayer Relief Act of 1997, the child tax credit is yet another provision ostensibly designed to benefit lower and middle class taxpayers but is so difficult to understand (not only by laypersons but also by practitioners) that very few

¶ 201

deserving taxpayers will benefit from the provision. For example, definitions are used in this section such as "modified gross income" (meaning adjusted gross income increased by certain foreign income under Code Secs. 911, 932 and 933) that the section and qualification are made exceedingly complex.

The new law does not change this complexity. However, it does clarify the child tax credit in some respects. The Act clarifies the application of the income tax liability limitation on the child tax credit by treating the refundable portion of it in the same way as the other refundable credits. Specifically, after all the other credits are applied according to the stacking rules of the income tax limitation, then the refundable credits are applied first to reduce the taxpayer's tax liability for the year and then to provide a credit in excess of income tax liability for the year. Also, with respect to the supplemental child credit, the portion of the child tax credit that is a supplemental child credit under the earned income credit and the offsetting reduction of the child tax credit does not affect the total tax credits allowed to the taxpayer or any other credit available to the taxpayer. The Act also clarifies the amount of the child tax credit that is treated as a supplemental child credit.

While some clarification has been added to the child tax provisions of the Internal Revenue Code, a large amount of complexity has not been eliminated. This complexity will still cause those taxpayers who potentially are to benefit from the child tax credit to seek the help of costly tax advisors, thus eating into the benefit of those the credit is designed to help.

★ *Effective date.* The provision is effective for tax years beginning after December 31, 1997 (Act Sec. 6024 of the IRS Restructuring and Reform Act of 1998; Act Sec. 101(e) of the Taxpayer Relief Act of 1997 (P.L. 105-34)).

Act Sec. 6003(a)(1), amending Code Sec. 24(d)(1) and (2), striking Code Sec. 24(d)(3) and (4), and redesignating Code Sec. 24(d)(5) as (3); Act Sec. 6003(a)(2), amending Code Sec. 24(d)(3), as redesignated by Act Sec. 6003(a)(1). Law at ¶ 5020. Committee Report at ¶ 10,815.

Coordination of Child and Supplemental Credit

¶ 206

Background ———————————————————————————

For 1998, taxpayers may claim a $400 child tax credit for each qualifying child under the age of 17 (Code Sec. 24). The child credit is a nonrefundable credit, but a portion may be treated as the supplemental child credit—a refundable credit that is part of the earned income credit (EIC) (Code Sec. 32(m)[(n)], as added by the Taxpayer Relief Act of 1997 (P.L. 105-34)). The amount of any supplemental child credit claimed as part of the EIC reduces the amount of the otherwise allowable child credit.

The supplemental child credit is equal to:

(1) the lesser of (a) $400 (for 1998) times the number of qualifying children or (b) the Code Sec. 26(a) limit (the taxpayer's regular tax liability (net of all credits except the EIC) over the taxpayer's tentative minimum tax (as defined at Code Sec. 55 and determined without regard to the alternative minimum tax foreign tax credit)), over

(2) the taxpayer's regular income tax liability (net of all applicable credits other than the EIC), plus the employee share of FICA liability (and one-half of any SECA liability), and minus the EIC (Code Sec. 32(m)[(n)](2), as added by P.L. 105-34).

Technical Corrections Impact

Supplemental child credit computation.—A technical correction clarifies that the amount of the supplemental child credit is equal to the lesser of:

(1) the amount by which the taxpayer's total nonrefundable personal credits (as limited by Code Sec. 26(a)) are increased by reason of the child credit, or

(2) the excess of (a) the taxpayer's total tax credits (including the EIC, but not the supplemental child credit or credits for excess social security tax withheld, tax withheld on nonresident aliens and foreign corporations, or excise taxes on gasoline and certain fuels used in farming and other qualified purposes), over (b) the sum of the taxpayer's regular income taxes and social security taxes (Code Sec. 32(n)(1), as amended by the IRS Restructuring and Reform Act of 1998).

Example. In 1998, James Lee has a regular tax liability of $700 and no tentative minimum tax liability, pays social security taxes of $900, and is entitled to an earned income credit of $1,500. If Lee has two qualifying children, he could claim a nonrefundable child credit of $700 (as limited by Code Sec. 26(a)). However, Lee is entitled to a refundable supplemental child credit of $600. This is equal to the lesser of (1) $700 or (2) the excess of his total tax credits of $2,200 over the sum of his regular tax liability of $700 and his social security taxes of $900 ($2,200 − ($900 + $700) = $600). Lee's otherwise allowable child credit of $700 is reduced by the supplemental child credit of $600 to $100.

Treatment of a portion of the child credit as a supplemental child credit with the corresponding reduction of the otherwise allowable child credit does not affect the total amount of tax credits available to the taxpayer or any other tax credit available to the taxpayer (Code Sec. 32(n)(2), as amended by the 1998 Act). A technical correction also clarifies that the phaseout of the EIC and other EIC rules do not apply to the computation of the supplemental child credit.

Planning Note. Although the total amount of the child credit is the same whether or not part of it is treated as the supplemental credit, it is advantageous for lower-income taxpayers to claim the supplemental credit as part of the refundable EIC rather than as a nonrefundable child credit. Nonrefundable credits are subtracted from the total tax for the year and may only reduce it to zero—any excess is not refunded. In contrast, refundable credits are treated as tax payments and added to withheld federal income taxes and any estimated tax payments—if this is more than the total tax, the excess is refunded.

★ *Effective date.* The provision is effective for tax years beginning after December 31, 1997 (Act Sec. 6024 of the IRS Restructuring and Reform Act of 1998; Act Sec. 101(e) of the Taxpayer Relief Act of 1997 (P.L. 105-34)).

Act Sec. 6003(b), amending Code Sec. 32(m). Law at ¶ 5040. Committee Report at ¶ 10,820.

¶ 206

Earned Income Credit Phaseout

¶ 211

Background _____

An eligible low-income worker may claim a refundable earned income credit (EIC) which is equal to the worker's earned income (up to a limited amount) multiplied by a credit percentage (Code Sec. 32). The available credit may be reduced for workers at certain earned income or modified adjusted gross income (AGI) levels according to phaseout percentages. Different credit and phaseout percentages are used depending on the number of the taxpayer's qualifying children (Code Sec. 32(b)).

In determining the phaseout, an individual's modified AGI is adjusted gross income determined without regard to:

(1) net capital losses to the extent that they do not exceed $3,000 (the annual limit on the deduction of net capital losses provided in Code Sec. 1211(b)(1));

(2) net losses from trusts and estates;

(3) net losses relating to nonbusiness rents and royalties;

(4) for tax years beginning after 1997, 75 percent of net losses from trades or businesses, computed separately for sole proprietorships engaged in farming, sole proprietorships not engaged in farming, and other trades or businesses;

(5) for tax years beginning after 1997, tax-exempt interest;

(6) for tax years beginning after 1997, nontaxable distributions from pensions, annuities, and individual retirement accounts (IRAs), unless the distributions are rolled over into similar vehicles (Code Sec. 32(c)(5), as amended by the Taxpayer Relief Act of 1997 (P.L. 105-34)).

For purposes of item (4), above, trades or businesses that consist of the performance of services by the individual as an employee are excluded.

_____

Technical Corrections Impact

Modified adjusted gross income defined.—A technical correction clarifies that in computing a worker's modified AGI for purposes of the earned income credit phaseout, the following nontaxable items are added back to AGI for tax years beginning after 1997:

(1) tax-exempt interest; and

(2) nontaxable distributions from pensions, annuities, and individual retirement accounts (IRAs), unless the distributions were not included in income due to a trustee-to-trustee transfer of funds or a rollover distribution (Code Sec. 32(c)(5)(B)(iv) and Code Sec. 32(c)(5)(C), as amended by the IRS Restructuring and Reform Act of 1998).

Only the following items are losses that are disregarded in computing modified AGI:

(1) net capital losses to the extent that they do not exceed the $3,000 limit under Code Sec. 1211(b)(1);

(2) net losses from trusts and estates;

(3) net losses relating to nonbusiness rents and royalties; and

(4) for tax years beginning after 1997, 75 percent of net losses from trades or businesses, computed separately for sole proprietorships engaged in

farming, sole proprietorships not engaged in farming, and other trades or businesses.

Item (4), above, excludes trades or businesses that consist of the performance of services by the individual as an employee.

Comment. Prior to the technical correction, tax-exempt interest and the specified nontaxable distributions were disregarded in computing modified AGI. Since such amounts are not included in income or AGI, they were not included in modified AGI under prior law. These amounts are now specifically added back to AGI in computing modified AGI.

>***Example.*** Jill Moore is eligible for the EIC and has one qualifying child, earned income of $14,000, and $500 of tax-exempt interest on municipal bonds for 1998. For 1998, the maximum EIC for one qualifying child is $2,271, subject to the phaseout (Rev. Proc. 97-57, I.R.B. 1997-52, 20). Moore's phaseout amount is $358 (15.98% $\times$ (modified AGI of $14,500 − $12,260)). Thus, her EIC for 1998 is $1,913 ($2,271 maximum EIC − $358 phaseout amount). (Note: The amount of the credit is normally determined by using the EIC tables released by the IRS each year, rather than by using the above formula.)

★ *Effective date.* The provision is effective for tax years beginning after December 31, 1997 (Act Sec. 6024 of the IRS Restructuring and Reform Act of 1998; Act Sec. 1085(e)(2) of the Taxpayer Relief Act of 1997 (P.L. 105-34)).

Act Sec. 6010(p)(1), amending Code Sec. 32(c)(5); Act Sec. 6010(p)(2), amending Code Sec. 32(c)(2)(B)(v); and Act Sec. 6010(p)(3), amending Act Sec. 1085(a)(3) of the Taxpayer Relief Act of 1997 (P.L. 105-34). Law at ¶ 5040 and ¶ 8255. Committee Report at ¶ 11,215.

Earned Income Credit Qualification Rules

¶ 216

Background

Among other eligibility requirements for claiming the earned income credit (EIC), individuals must provide their taxpayer identification number (TIN) (social security number) on their returns and, if married, the TIN of their spouse (Code Sec. 32(c)(1)(F), as added by the Personal Responsibility and Work Opportunity Reconciliation Act of 1996 (P.L. 104-193)). Similarly, among other requirements, individuals who are claiming the EIC with respect to a child or children must indicate their child's name, age, and TIN on their returns in order for the child to be considered a qualifying child. This identification requirement covers children born during the year for which the return is filed (Code Sec. 32(c)(3)(D)(i)). The omission of the correct TIN is treated as a mathematical or clerical error and any additional tax resulting from the disallowance of the credit may be summarily assessed (Code Sec. 6213(g)(2)(F)).

Technical Corrections Impact

Taxpayer identification number (TIN).—A technical correction clarifies that no EIC is allowed to an eligible individual who fails to provide his or her TIN or the TIN of his or her spouse (if married) on the tax return for the year for which the credit is claimed (Code Sec. 32(c)(1)(F), as amended by the IRS Restructuring and Reform Act of 1998). Similarly, a qualifying child is not taken into account in computing the EIC of an eligible individual unless the child's name, age, and TIN are included on the taxpayer's return for the year for which the credit is claimed (Code Sec. 32(c)(3)(D), as amended by the 1998 Act). Moreover, no EIC is allowed to an eligible individual who has one or more qualifying children if none of the qualifying children are properly identified by name, age, and TIN on the tax return for the year for which the credit is claimed (Code Sec. 32(c)(1)(G), as added by the 1998 Act).

Comment. The changes are intended to treat the identification requirements as prerequisites for claiming the EIC, rather than as part of the definitions of eligible individuals and qualifying children.

★ *Effective date.* The provision on supplying TINs of the taxpayer and the taxpayer's spouse is effective with respect to returns the due date for which, without regard to extensions, is after September 21, 1996 (Act Sec. 6021(c)(1) of the IRS Restructuring and Reform Act of 1998; Act Sec. 451(d) of the Personal Responsibility and Work Opportunity Reconciliation Act of 1996 (P.L. 104-193)). The provision on supplying TINs of qualifying children is effective for tax years beginning after December 31, 1990 (Act Sec. 6021(c)(2) of the IRS Restructuring and Reform Act of 1998; Act Sec. 11111(f) of the Omnibus Budget Reconciliation Act of 1990 (P.L. 101-508)).

Act Sec. 6021(a), amending Code Sec. 32(c)(1)(F); Act Sec. 6021(b)(1), amending Code Sec. 32(c)(3)(D); Act Sec. 6021(b)(2), adding Code Sec. 32(c)(1)(G); and Act Sec. 6021(b)(3), amending Code Sec. 32(c)(3)(A). Law at ¶ 5040. Committee Report at ¶ 11,375.

Adoption Credit Carryovers

¶ 221

*Background*_____

Individuals may claim a nonrefundable adoption credit for up to $5,000 of qualified adoption expenses for each eligible child. For an eligible child with special needs, up to $6,000 of qualified adoption expenses qualifies for the credit (Code Sec. 23, as added by the Small Business Job Protection Act of 1996 (P.L. 104-188)). The amount of the adoption credit is phased out ratably for taxpayers with adjusted gross income (AGI) between $75,000 and $115,000.

Code Sec. 26 generally limits the amount of nonrefundable credits that can be claimed to the excess of the taxpayer's regular tax liability over the taxpayer's tentative minimum tax liability. If the amount of the allowable adoption credit exceeds the Code Sec. 26 limit, any unused portion of the adoption credit may be carried forward for up to five years, with credits used on a first-in, first-out basis. Any credit that remains unused after five years is lost (Code Sec. 23(c), as added by P.L. 104-188).

Technical Corrections Impact

Effect of carryovers on credit phaseout.—A technical correction clarifies that the phaseout of the adoption credit based on the taxpayer's AGI is applied without regard to any carryovers of the credit (Code Sec. 23(b)(2)(A), as amended by the IRS Restructuring and Reform Act of 1998). Thus, the phaseout is applied only once in the year that the credit is generated and is not reapplied in future years to further reduce any credit carryovers.

Example. Robert and Susan Brady pay $5,000 of qualified expenses to adopt a child and the adoption is finalized in the same year. Their AGI for the year is $85,000. The Bradys also have an adoption credit carryover of $1,000 from the previous year. Since the Bradys' AGI of $85,000 exceeds the $75,000 floor of the credit phaseout range, they must reduce their otherwise allowable credit for the current year of $5,000 by $1,250 (($10,000 ÷ $40,000) × $5,000), but do not have to reduce their $1,000 credit carryover from the prior year.

★ *Effective date.* The provision is effective for tax years beginning after December 31, 1996 (Act Sec. 6018(h) of the IRS Restructuring and Reform Act of 1998; Act Sec. 1807(e) of the Small Business Job Protection Act of 1996 (P.L. 104-188)).

Act Sec. 6018(f)(1), amending Code Sec. 23(b)(2)(A); Act Sec. 6018(f)(2), amending Act Sec. 1807(c)(3) of the Small Business Job Protection Act of 1996 (P.L. 104-188). Law at ¶ 5010 and ¶ 8280. Committee Report at ¶ 11,345.

Credit for Prior-Year Minimum Tax Liability

¶ 224

Background

Refundable credits claimed by a taxpayer under Code Secs. 31 through 35 are treated as an overpayment of tax to the extent such credits exceed a taxpayer's income tax liability after reduction by the nonrefundable personal credits (Code Secs. 21 through 26), "other tax credits" (Code Secs. 27 through 30A) and the business-related credits (Code Secs. 38 through 45C) (Code Sec. 6401(a)).

Technical Corrections Impact

Credit for prior year minimum tax liability taken into account in determining overpayment.—The Act clarifies that for purposes of determining the amount of an overpayment attributable to refundable credits, a taxpayer's income tax liability is also reduced by any credit claimed under Code Sec. 53 for a prior year minimum tax liability (Code Sec. 6401(b)(1), as amended by the IRS Restructuring and Reform Act of 1998).

★ *Effective date.* The provision is generally effective for tax years beginning after 1986 (Act Sec. 6022(b) of the IRS Restructuring and Reform Act of 1998; Act Sec. 701(f) of the Tax Reform Act of 1986).

Act Sec. 6022(a), amending Code Sec. 6401(b)(1). Act Sec. 6022(b). Law at ¶ 6340.

EDUCATION INCENTIVES

Education Tax Credit Reporting Requirements

¶ 226

Background

Individuals may claim a nonrefundable Hope scholarship credit or lifetime learning credit if they pay qualified tuition and related expenses to eligible postsecondary educational institutions and certain vocational institutions (Code Sec. 25A, as added by the Taxpayer Relief Act of 1997 (P.L. 105-34)). The qualified tuition must be paid for the taxpayer, the taxpayer's spouse or the taxpayer's dependents.

Information returns have to be filed with the IRS by any eligible educational institution that receives qualified tuition and related expenses and any person which, in the course of a trade or business, reimburses or refunds such expenses (Code Sec. 6050S, as added by P.L. 105-34). Information returns must also be filed by any person engaged in a trade or business that receives from any individual interest aggregating $600 or more for any calendar year on one or more education loans. These institutions and persons must also provide payee statements to students and persons claiming them as dependents on or before January 31 of the year following the calendar year for which the information return is made.

Technical Corrections Impact

Filing of information returns.—Although eligible educational institutions that receive or reimburse qualified tuition and related expenses must file information returns, a technical correction clarifies that a person that is not an eligible educational institution is only required to file information returns if the person is in the trade or business of making reimbursements or refunds of qualified tuition and expenses to individuals *under an insurance arrangement* (Code Sec. 6050S(a)(1) and (2), as amended by the IRS Restructuring and Reform Act of 1998).

Caution. The technical correction does not affect the current information return filing requirement for persons who receive, in the course of their trade or business, interest from any individual that totals $600 or more for any calendar year on one or more qualified education loans (Code Sec. 6050S(a)(3)). For 1998, Form 1098-E (Student Loan Interest Statement) may be used for this purpose.

Comment. Educational institutions that are required to file information returns for 1998 concerning qualified tuition and expenses should use Form 1098-T (Tuition Payments Statement). A copy of Form 1098-T or other substitute may be used as the required payee statement that is provided to students or persons claiming them as dependents. According to the 1998 Instructions for Form 1099, 1098, 5498, and W2-G, persons other than eligible educational institutions are not required to file Form 1098-T for 1998.

Currently, a properly completed Form 1098-T must include:

(1) the name, address, and TIN of the eligible institution,

(2) the name, address, and TIN of the individual with respect to whom payments of qualified tuition and related expenses were paid during 1998,

(3) an indication as to whether the individual named in item (2), above, was enrolled for at least half the full-time academic workload during any academic period commencing in 1998, and

(4) an indication as to whether the individual named in (2), above, was enrolled exclusively in a program or programs leading to a graduate-level degree, graduate-level certificate, or other recognized graduate-level educational credential (Notice 97-73, I.R.B. 1997-51, 16).

In addition to the above identifying information, the information return must report the aggregate amount:

(1) received on behalf of an individual for qualified tuition and related expenses for the year;

(2) refunded or reimbursed to such individual for the year; and

(3) received during the year from such individual as interest (Code Sec. 6050S(b)(2)(C)).

Until final regulations are adopted, no penalties will be imposed under Code Sec. 6721 for failure to provide correct information returns or under Code Sec. 6722 for failure to furnish correct statements to the individuals with respect to whom information reporting is required. Even after final regulations are adopted, no penalties will be imposed under Code Sec. 6721 or Code Sec. 6722 for 1998 if the institution made a good-faith effort to file information returns and to otherwise comply with Notice 98-73.

★ *Effective date.* This provision is effective for expenses paid after December 31, 1997, in tax years ending after such date, for education furnished in academic periods beginning after such date (Act Sec. 6024 of the IRS Restructuring and Reform Act of 1998; Act Sec. 201(f)(1) of the Taxpayer Relief Act of 1997 (P.L. 105-34)).

IRS Restructuring and Reform Impact

Reporting grant money.—Educational institutions that receive payments for qualified tuition and related expenses on behalf of any individual must now also report any grant money received by that same individual and processed by the reporting institution for the calendar year (Code Sec. 6050S(b)(2)(C)(ii), as amended by the IRS Restructuring and Reform Act of 1998). The 1998 Act also clarifies that the institution needs to report refunds or reimbursements paid to such individual only to the extent that the reporting institution was the payor of the refund or reimbursement (Code Sec. 6050S(b)(2)(C)(iii), as amended by the 1998 Act).

According to the Conference Committee Report to the 1998 Act, educational institutions must separately report for each student:

(1) the aggregate amount of qualified tuition and related expenses (not including expenses relating to sports, games, hobbies or nonacademic fees);

(2) any grant amount (regardless of whether it is excludable from income) received by the student to pay the costs of attendance and processed through the institution during the year; and

(3) total reimbursements or refunds paid by the institution to the student during the calendar year.

Minimizing the reporting burden. The Conference Committee Report to the 1998 Act expresses congressional intent to minimize the reporting burden imposed on educational institutions, while maintaining the ability of the IRS to monitor compliance with the Hope scholarship and lifetime learning credits. In furtherance of this aim, the 1998 Act clarifies that the term "qualified tuition and related expenses" (Code Sec. 25A(f)(1)) does not require the adjustments for scholarships required by Code Sec. 25A(g). Thus, the reporting institution need not reduce the qualified tuition and related expenses amount reported under Code Sec. 6050S(a) by: (1) employer-paid educational expenses, (2) scholarships and fellowships received tax free, (3) amounts deducted by the student as business expenses, (4) the amount of educational expenses excludable from gross income of either the student or the taxpayer claiming the credit, or (4) any payments for an individual's educational expenses or attributable to the individual's enrollment at an institution that are excludable from gross income under any U.S. law (Code Sec. 6050S(e), as amended by the 1998 Act).

Noting that the Treasury Department is drafting guidance for education tax credit reporting, the Conferees urged the Treasury to further minimize reporting burdens by:

(1) conforming the definition of "qualified tuition and related expenses" with that provided under section 472(l) of the Higher Education Act,

(2) providing an effective date for the regulatory guidance that will give the educational institutions sufficient time to implement additional required reporting,

(3) providing that no further reporting be required beyond that required by Notice 97-73 until final regulatory guidance is issued,

(4) providing further clarification regarding the reasonable cause exception under Code Sec. 6724(a), as it relates to education information reporting, and

(5) considering exempting institutions from the reporting requirements with respect to certain categories of students (such as nondegree students enrolled in a noncredit course) provided compliance is not undermined.

¶ 226

Finally, the Conference Committee Report encourages IRS computer modernization efforts to incorporate the ability to match a dependent's TIN with the return filed by the person claiming the individual as a dependent.

★ *Effective date.* This provision applies to returns required to be filed with respect to tax years beginning after December 31, 1998 (Act Sec. 3712(c) of the IRS Restructuring and Reform Act of 1998).

Act Sec. 6004(a)(2), amending Code Sec. 6050S(a); Act Sec. 6004(a)(3), amending Act Sec. 201(c)(2) of the Taxpayer Relief Act of 1997 (P.L. 105-34); Act Sec. 3712(a), amending Code Sec. 6050S(b)(2)(C); Act Sec. 3712(b)(1), amending Code Sec. 6050S(d)(2); Act Sec. 3712(b)(2), amending Code Sec. 6050S(e); Act Sec. 3712(c). Law at ¶ 6080 and ¶ 8239. Committee Report at ¶ 10,690 and ¶ 10,835.

Qualified State Tuition Programs

¶ 228

Background

Under a qualified state tuition program, a person may either:

(1) make cash purchases of tuition credits or certificates that entitle a designated beneficiary to a waiver of or payment of qualified higher education expenses; or

(2) make cash contributions to an account established for meeting the qualified higher education expenses of the designated beneficiary (Code Sec. 529).

These programs are generally exempt from tax except for the tax on unrelated business income under Code Sec. 511. Distributions from the program are taxed under the annuity rules of Code Sec. 72(b). Thus, amounts distributed or educational benefits provided to a beneficiary in excess of contributions made on behalf of the beneficiary are included in the beneficiary's income unless excludable under another Code section. Amounts distributed to a contributor or other distributee in excess of contributions made on behalf of the beneficiary are included in the contributor's or distributee's income (Code Sec. 529(c)(3)).

A change in beneficiaries is not treated as a distribution subject to tax under the annuity rules as long as the new beneficiary is a member of the family of the previously designated beneficiary (Code Sec. 529(c)(3)(C)(ii)). Similar treatment applies to a distribution to a beneficiary that is rolled over within 60 days to the credit of a family member of the previously designated beneficiary under a qualified state tuition program (Code Sec. 529(c)(3)(C)(i)). A member of the family is defined as the beneficiary's son or daughter or other descendant; stepson or stepdaughter; brother, sister, stepbrother or stepsister; father or mother or other ancestor; stepfather or stepmother; niece or nephew; aunt or uncle; son-in-law, daughter-in-law, father-in-law, mother-in-law, brother-in-law, or sister-in-law (Code Sec. 152(a)(1)-(8)); or the spouse of any of those individuals (Code Sec. 529(e)(2), prior to amendment by the IRS Restructuring and Reform Act of 1998).

Technical Corrections Impact

Distributions.—A technical correction clarifies that distributions from a qualified state tuition program are taxed to the beneficiary under the Code Sec. 72 annuity rules unless excludable from income under another Code section (Code Sec. 529(c)(3)(A), as amended by the IRS Restructuring and Reform Act of 1998). Thus, distributions are treated as consisting of principal or contributions which are generally not taxed and earnings which may be subject to tax (Code Sec. 72(e)(2)(B); Code Sec. 72(e)(9), as added by the 1998 Act). The portion of a

·distribution that is treated as paid from contributions is determined by multiplying the distribution by the ratio that the total amount of contributions bears to the balance of the account at the time the distribution is made (Code Sec. 72(e)(8); Code Sec. 72(e)(9), as added by the 1998 Act).

> **Example.** Julie Anderson is the beneficiary of a qualified state tuition program who receives a $2,000 distribution from the program to pay her qualified higher education expenses. On the distribution date, the total account balance is $20,000, of which $15,000 represents contributions of principal and $5,000 represents earnings. The portion of the $2,000 distribution that is treated as a nontaxable return of contributions is $1,500 ($2,000 × ($15,000 ÷ $20,000)).

Although distributions from a qualified state tuition program are generally taxable under the annuity rules, exceptions are provided for a change in beneficiary to a family member of the previously designated beneficiary and for rollovers from one program to another to the credit of the family member of the previously designated beneficiary. A technical correction expands the definition of a family member to include the spouse of the designated beneficiary (Code Sec. 529(e)(2), as amended by the 1998 Act).

Thus, a member of the family, with respect to any designated beneficiary, includes:

> (1) the spouse of the beneficiary;

> (2) the son or daughter or other descendant; stepson or stepdaughter; brother, sister, stepbrother or stepsister; father or mother or other ancestor; stepfather or stepmother; niece or nephew; aunt or uncle; son-in-law, daughter-in-law, father-in-law, mother-in-law, brother-in-law, or sister-in-law (Code Sec. 152(a)(1)-(8)); and

> (3) a spouse of any of the individuals listed in (2), above (Code Sec. 529(e)(2), as amended by the 1998 Act).

★ *Effective date.* This provision is effective on January 1, 1998 (Act Sec. 6024 of the IRS Restructuring and Reform Act of 1998; Act Sec. 211(f)(1) of the Taxpayer Relief Act of 1997 (P.L. 105-34)).

Act Sec. 6004(c)(2), amending Code Sec. 529(c)(3)(A); Act Sec. 6004(c)(3), amending Code Sec. 529(e)(2); and Act Sec. 6004(d)(3)(B), adding Code Sec. 72(e)(9). Law at ¶ 5150 and ¶ 5410. Committee Report at ¶ 10,850.

U.S. Savings Bond Interest Exclusion

¶ 231

Background ⎯⎯⎯⎯⎯⎯⎯⎯⎯⎯⎯⎯⎯⎯⎯⎯⎯⎯⎯⎯⎯⎯⎯⎯⎯⎯⎯⎯⎯

Interest on U.S. savings bonds that are redeemed and used to pay for higher education costs of an individual, the individual's spouse, or the individual's dependents is excludable from income (Code Sec. 135). The exclusion is also available if the redemption proceeds are contributed to a qualified state tuition program or an education individual retirement account ("education IRA") on behalf of the individual, the individual's spouse, or the individual's dependents, rather than being used to pay the expenses directly (Code Sec. 135(c)(2)(C)).

The excludable amount is reduced on a pro rata basis where the redemption proceeds exceed the amount of qualified higher education expenses and is subject to a phaseout for individuals at higher levels of modified adjusted gross income (AGI) (Code Sec. 135(b)). In addition, the amount of qualified higher education expenses that is taken into account in applying the interest exclusion must be reduced by the amount of expenses that are taken into account in computing the Hope scholarship credit or the lifetime learning credit (Code Secs. 25A and 135(d)(2)).

Qualified higher education expenses are the costs of attending an eligible educational institution. An eligible educational institution is one defined in section 1201(a) or subparagraph (C) or (D) of section 481(a)(1) of the Higher Education Act of 1965 (20 U.S.C. §§ 1141(a) and 1088(a)), as in effect on October 21, 1988 (Code Sec. 135(c)(3)(A)). The term generally includes accredited universities, colleges, junior colleges, and other institutions that provide postsecondary education. Also included are collegiate and associate degree schools of nursing. A vocational school is also treated as an eligible educational institution if it is an "area vocational education school" defined in subparagraph (C) or (D) of section 521(3) of the Carl D. Perkins Vocational Education Act (20 U.S.C. § 2471(3)(C) and (D)) that is in any "state" as defined in section 521(27) of that Act (20 U.S.C. § 2471(27)), as those sections are in effect on October 21, 1988 (Code Sec. 135(c)(3)(B)).

Technical Corrections Impact

Redemption proceeds used for education.—The qualified higher education expenses that are taken into account in determining the excludable amount of interest on redeemed U.S. savings bonds are the costs of attending an eligible educational institution. A technical correction conforms the definition of the term "eligible educational institution" in Code Sec. 135 with the definition used for purposes of Code Secs. 529 and 530 with respect to qualified state tuition programs and education IRAs (Code Sec. 135(c)(3), as amended by the IRS Restructuring and Reform Act of 1998).

Thus, for purposes of the exclusion for U.S. savings bond interest, an eligible educational institution is defined under Code Sec. 529(e)(5) as an institution which is described in section 481 of the Higher Education Act of 1965 (20 U.S.C. § 1088) and is eligible to participate in Department of Education student aid programs under title IV of that Act. The term generally includes accredited postsecondary educational institutions offering credit toward a bachelor's degree, an associate's degree, a graduate or professional degree, or another recognized postsecondary credential. Certain proprietary institutions and postsecondary vocational institutions also qualify.

Coordination with other education benefits. A technical correction provides that the qualified higher education expenses that are taken into account in determining the excludable amount of interest on redeemed U.S. savings bonds must be reduced by the amount of expenses that are taken into account in determining the exclusion for distributions from an education IRA (Code Sec. 135(d)(2), as amended by the 1998 Act). This reduction is in addition to the current reduction for expenses taken into account in determining the allowable Hope scholarship credit or the lifetime learning credit.

★ *Effective date.* This provision applies to tax years beginning after December 31, 1997 (Act Sec. 6024 of the IRS Restructuring and Reform Act of 1998; Act Sec. 213(f) of the Taxpayer Relief Act of 1997 (P.L. 105-34)).

Act Sec. 6004(c)(1), amending Code Sec. 135(c)(3); Act Sec. 6004(d)(4), amending Code Sec. 135(d)(2); and Act Sec. 6004(d)(9), amending Code Sec. 135(c)(2)(C). Law at ¶ 5190. Committee Report at ¶ 10,845.

Education Individual Retirement Accounts

¶ 236

Background

Education individual retirement accounts ("education IRAs") are trusts or custodial accounts used to accumulate funds for payment of a designated beneficiary's qualified higher education expenses (Code Sec. 530, as added by the Taxpayer Relief Act of 1997 (P.L. 105-34)). Up to $500 of annual contributions per beneficiary may be made to an education IRA, subject to a phaseout that starts for joint filers with modified adjusted gross income (AGI) of $150,000 and for other filers with modified AGI of $95,000.

Distributions from education IRAs are deemed paid from contributions, which are always tax free, and from earnings, which may be excludable if they are used to pay the beneficiary's qualified education expenses (Code Sec. 530(d)). The portion of a distribution that is treated as paid from contributions is determined by multiplying the distribution by the ratio that the aggregate amount of contributions bears to the total balance of the education IRA at the time the distribution is made.

If the beneficiary's education expenses are at least as much as the aggregate distributions from the education IRA, then no part of the distribution is includible in income (Code Sec. 530(d)(2)(A)). However, if the aggregate distributions exceed the education expenses, the expenses are deemed to be paid from a pro rata share of both principal and interest. Thus, the portion of the earnings that may be excluded from income is based on the ratio that the education expenses bear to the total amount of the distribution (Code Sec. 530(d)(2)(B)). The remainder is included in the income of the recipient of the distribution.

A taxpayer who claims tax-favored treatment for education IRA distributions may not also claim the HOPE scholarship credit or the lifetime learning credit in the same year (Code Sec. 25A(e)(2)). A six-percent excise tax may be imposed on excess contributions to an education IRA (Code Sec. 4973(e)) and an additional 10-percent tax imposed on distributions includible in income (Code Sec. 530(d)(4)). However, amounts held in an education IRA may be distributed and rolled over into an education IRA for a member of the beneficiary's family or into another education IRA for the benefit of the same beneficiary without penalty (Code Sec. 530(d)(5)).

Technical Corrections Impact

Distributions, contributions and coordinating rules.—A technical correction clarifies that an education individual retirement account (" education IRA") must be established for the purpose of paying the qualified higher education expenses of *an individual* who is a designated beneficiary of the education IRA (Code Sec. 530(b)(1), as amended by the IRS Restructuring and Reform Act of 1998). Thus, the designated beneficiary must be a life-in-being (Senate Finance Committee Report to the 1998 Act).

Termination of education IRAs. In order to reflect congressional intent, as set forth in the Conference Committee Report to the Taxpayer Relief Act of 1997 (P.L. 105-34), a technical correction provides that the balance remaining in an education IRA must be distributed within 30 days after a beneficiary reaches age 30. This is in addition to the rule requiring distribution of the account balance within 30 days after the death of a beneficiary under age 30 (Code Sec. 530(b)(1)(E), as amended by the 1998 Act). Where such a distribution is required, the balance at the close of the 30-day period is deemed to be distributed at that time (Code Sec. 530(d)(8), as added by the 1998 Act), and the earnings portion of the distribution is includible in the beneficiary's gross income (Code Sec. 530(d)(1), as amended by the 1998 Act).

Planning Note. Before a beneficiary reaches age 30, the balance of an education IRA may be transferred or rolled over to another education IRA for a member of the former beneficiary's family in order to further defer or possibly avoid payment of tax on the earnings in the account.

Rollovers and beneficiary changes. Amounts held in an education IRA may be distributed and rolled over into an education IRA for a member of the beneficiary's family or into another education IRA for the benefit of the same beneficiary without having to be included in the income of the distributee (Code Sec. 530(d)(5), prior to amendment by the 1998 Act). Also, a change in beneficiaries will not be treated as a distribution that is includible in income if the new beneficiary is a member of the former beneficiary's family (Code Sec. 530(d)(6), prior to amendment by the 1998 Act). A technical correction clarifies that the new beneficiaries following a rollover of a distribution to another education IRA or a change in beneficiary must be under age 30 as of the date of such distribution or change (Code Sec. 530(d)(5) and (6), as amended by the 1998 Act).

Transfers upon death and divorce. In general, the transfer of an interest in an education IRA to a spouse or former spouse under a divorce or separation agreement is not treated as a taxable transfer (Code Sec. 530(d)(7), prior to amendment by the 1998 Act; Code Sec. 220(f)(7)). In addition, a surviving spouse who obtains an interest in an education IRA as a designated beneficiary upon the death of the original beneficiary steps into the shoes of the original beneficiary and is treated as the account holder (Code Sec. 530(d)(7), prior to amendment by the 1998 Act; Code Sec. 220(f)(8)). A technical correction provides that the rule for survivors who acquire the original beneficiary's interest in an education IRA upon the beneficiary's death applies to the beneficiary's family members as well as to the beneficiary's spouse (Code Sec. 530(d)(7), as amended by the 1998 Act).

Account earnings v. investment. A technical correction clarifies that distributions from an education IRA are taxed under the Code Sec. 72 annuity rules (Code Sec. 530(d)(1), as amended by the 1998 Act). Thus, distributions are treated as consisting of principal or contributions which are generally not taxed and earnings which may be subject to tax depending on the amount of qualified education expenses (Code Sec. 72(e)(2)(B); Code Sec. 72(e)(9), as added by the 1998 Act). The portion of a distribution that is treated as paid from contributions is determined by multiplying the distribution by the ratio that the total amount of contributions bears to the balance of the account at the time the distribution is made (Code Sec. 72(e)(8); Code Sec. 72(e)(9), as added by the 1998 Act).

Example (1). Alicia Bryant receives a $1,000 distribution from an education IRA. On the distribution date, the total account balance is $10,000, of which $6,000 represents contributions and $4,000 represents earnings. The portion of the $1,000 distribution that is treated as a nontaxable return of contributions is $600 ($1,000 × ($6,000 ÷ $10,000)). If Bryant's qualified higher education expenses are at least $1,000, then the $400 portion of the distribution that represents earnings may also be excluded from income.

Example (2). Assume the same facts as in *Example (1),* above, except that Bryant's qualified higher education expenses are only $750. Of the $400 portion of the distribution that represents earnings, Bryant may only exclude $300 from income ($400 × ($750 ÷ $1,000)). Bryant must include the remaining $100 in income.

No double benefit. Under Code Sec. 25A(e)(2), a taxpayer's election to apply the Hope scholarship or lifetime learning credits with respect to an individual's qualified tuition and related expenses is not effective if any portion of any distribution from an education IRA is excluded from income under Code Sec.

530(d)(2). A technical correction further provides that *no* deduction or credit is allowed to a taxpayer for any qualified higher education expenses that are taken into account in determining the amount of an education IRA distribution that is excludable from income under Code Sec. 530(d)(2) (Code Sec. 530(d)(2)(D), as added by the 1998 Act).

Comment. One example of a deduction or credit for education expenses that would be denied if the taxpayer also took the expenses into account for purposes of the exclusion for education IRA distributions is the Code Sec. 162 business expense deduction. This deduction would apply to the cost of education that maintains or improves a necessary skill for the taxpayer's trade or business or that meets requirements of the taxpayer's employer, law, or regulations that are a condition of continued employment.

Ten-percent tax on nonqualifying distributions. Although an additional 10-percent tax is generally imposed on excess distributions from an education IRA that are includible in income, a technical correction provides an exception for amounts that are includible in income because a taxpayer elected to waive the exclusion for distributions used to pay for qualified higher education expenses (Code Sec. 530(d)(4)(B)(iv), as added by the 1998 Act). Thus, the 10-percent additional tax will not apply to a distribution from an education IRA that is includible in the beneficiary's income because the taxpayer elected to claim a Hope scholarship credit or lifetime learning credit with respect to the beneficiary (Senate Committee Report to the 1998 Act).

The 10-percent additional tax also does not apply to certain distributions of excess contributions. The distribution must be made by the due date (including extensions) for filing the beneficiary's tax return for the tax year in which the contribution was made and be accompanied by the amount of income attributable to the excess contribution (Code Sec. 530(d)(4)(C), as amended by the 1998 Act). If the beneficiary does not have to file a return, then the distribution must be made by the 15th day of the fourth month of the tax year following the tax year in which the contribution was made.

Comment. Where excess contributions have been made to an education IRA but are subsequently distributed, this rule limits the tax impact to the six-percent tax on the excess contributions rather than both the six-percent tax and the 10-percent tax on the distribution or return of the contribution.

Six-percent excise tax on excess contributions. A technical correction expands the definition of the term "excess contributions" for purposes of the six-percent excise tax on excess contributions to an education IRA. The first item treated as an excess contribution is any excess over the $500 maximum annual contribution amount per beneficiary. The correction clarifies that if the contributor's allowable contribution for the year is reduced based on the modified AGI phaseout (Code Sec. 530(c)), then the amount treated as an excess contribution is the sum of the allowable reduced contributions if less than the excess over $500 (Code Sec. 4973(e)(1)(A), as amended by the 1998 Act).

In addition, as under current law, any contributions to a qualified state tuition program (Code Sec. 529) for the benefit of the same beneficiary covered by the education IRA are treated as excess contributions to the education IRA (Code Sec. 4973(e)(1)(B), as amended by the 1998 Act).

Finally, the technical correction applies the excise tax in each year in which an excess contribution remains in an education IRA and not just the year in which the excess contribution is originally made (Code Sec. 4973(e)(1)(C), as amended by the 1998 Act).

¶ 236

PRACTICAL ANALYSIS. Professor David Hudson of the Graduate Tax Program at the University of Florida College of Law in Gainesville, Florida, comments that particularly in light of the new rules, those who open up Education IRAs in a family situation in which there are other siblings should, as a matter of course, designate another child as the beneficiary in case of death. In spite of the new law's more liberal treatment, however, Professor Hudson cautions parents to weigh the risk of an unqualified education IRA withdrawal in which earnings are taxed as ordinary income against the benefits of outright gifts to the child which are then invested in capital assets that, in turn, will be taxed at a capital gains rate as low as eight percent upon liquidation for whatever reason.

★ *Effective date.* This provision applies to tax years beginning after December 31, 1997 (Act Sec. 6024 of the IRS Restructuring and Reform Act of 1998; Act Sec. 213(f) of the Taxpayer Relief Act of 1997 (P.L. 105-34)).

Act Sec. 6004(d)(1), amending Code Sec. 530(b)(1); Act Sec. 6004(d)(2), amending Code Sec. 530(b)(1)(E) and (d)(7) and adding Code Sec. 530(d)(8); Act Sec. 6004(d)(3), amending Code Sec. 530(d)(1) and adding Code Sec. 72(e)(9); Act Sec. 6004(d)(5), adding Code Sec. 530(d)(2)(D); Act Sec. 6004(d)(6), amending Code Sec. 530(d)(4)(B); Act Sec. 6004(d)(7), amending Code Sec. 530(d)(4)(C); Act Sec. 6004(d)(8), amending Code Sec. 530(d)(5) and (6); Act Sec. 6004(d)(10), amending Code Sec. 4973(e)(1), striking Code Sec. 4973(e)(2)(B) and redesignating Code Sec. 4973(e)(2)(C) as (B). Law at ¶ 5150, ¶ 5420 and ¶ 5940. Committee Report at ¶ 10,845.

Cancellation of Student Loans

¶ 241

Background

Persons whose student loans were forgiven or discharged because they worked for a certain period of time in a designated profession for any of a broad class of employers generally do not have to include the discharged amount in income (Code Sec. 108(f)). The types of student loans that are covered by this exclusion include loans made by the United States, a state, certain other governmental entities, or a tax-exempt corporation controlling a state, county or municipal hospital whose employees are public employees.

In addition, a student loan includes loans by educational organizations that (1) received the loaned funds from one of the above entities or (2) made the loans under a program in which students work in occupations or areas with unmet needs. Loans by a tax-exempt organization to refinance such loans are also treated as student loans for this purpose (Code Sec. 108(f)(2)(D), as amended by the Taxpayer Relief Act of 1997 (P.L. 105-34)). In these situations, the work must be performed under the direction of a governmental entity or a tax-exempt Code Sec. 501(c)(3) organization and the student may not be employed by the lender (Code Sec. 108(f)(3), as added by P.L. 105-34).

Technical Corrections Impact

Refinancing loans.—A technical correction clarifies that the exclusion from gross income for forgiven or discharged student loans applies to loans made by certain tax-exempt organizations to refinance *any* existing student loan and not just loans made by educational organizations (Code Sec. 108(f)(2)(D), as amended by the IRS Restructuring and Reform Act of 1998). The correction further clarifies that refinancing loans made by both educational organizations and certain tax-exempt organizations must be made under a program of the refinancing organization that requires the student to fulfill a public service requirement by working in occupations or areas with unmet needs under the direction of a governmental entity or a tax-exempt Code Sec. 501(c)(3) organization.

★ *Effective date.* The provision is effective with respect to discharges of indebtedness after August 5, 1997 (Act Sec. 6024 of the IRS Restructuring and Reform Act of 1998; Act Sec. 225(b) of the Taxpayer Relief Act of 1997 (P.L. 105-34)).

Act Sec. 6004(f)(1), amending Code Sec. 108(f)(2); Act Sec. 6004(f)(2), amending Code Sec. 108(f)(3). Law at ¶ 5160. Committee Report at ¶ 10,860.

Deduction for Student Loan Interest

¶ 242

Background ————————————————————————————————

Beginning in 1998, individuals may deduct interest paid during the tax year on any qualified education loan (Code Sec. 221(a), as added by the Taxpayer Relief Act of 1997 (P.L. 105-34)). A qualified education loan is any debt incurred to pay the qualified higher education expenses of the taxpayer, the taxpayer's spouse, or an individual who was the taxpayer's dependent at the time that the debt was incurred (Code Sec. 221(e), as added by P.L. 105-34). A qualified education loan also encompasses debt used to refinance the qualified education loan but not debt owed to a related party (Code Sec. 221(c)(1), as added by P.L. 105-34).

The maximum deductible amount of interest is $1,000 in 1998, $1,500 in 1999, $2,000 in 2000, and $2,500 in 2001 and thereafter. The amount of interest on a qualified education loan that may be deducted is phased out beginning at modified adjusted gross incomes (AGI) over $40,000 ($60,000 for joint filers), as adjusted for inflation after 2002 (Code Sec. 221(b) and (g), as added by P.L. 105-34). No deduction is allowed if the interest is deductible under another section of the Code, such as deductible interest on a home equity loan.

The deduction for interest on a qualified education loan is allowed only with respect to interest paid on the loan during the first 60 months in which interest payments are required. The 60 months do not have to be consecutive. The original loan and all refinancings of the loan are treated as one loan for this purpose (Code Sec. 221(d), as added by P.L. 105-34). The deduction applies to a qualified education loan taken out at any time but only with respect to interest payments due after December 31, 1997, and the portion of the 60-month period after December 31, 1997.

Technical Corrections Impact

Qualified education loan.—A technical correction clarifies that, in order for interest to be deductible on a qualified education loan, the debt must be incurred by the taxpayer solely to pay qualified higher education expenses (Code Sec. 221(e)(1), as amended by the IRS Restructuring and Reform Act of 1998).

Caution. Revolving lines of credit generally would not constitute qualified education loans unless the borrower agreed to use the line of credit to pay only qualifying education expenses (Conference Committee Report to the 1998 Act).

Sixty-month period. Only interest paid on a qualified education loan during the first 60 months in which interest payments are required may be deductible. If interest payments were first required before January 1, 1998, the months in which those payments were required count against the 60-month time limit for that loan (Notice 97-60, 1997-46, 8).

¶ 242

The original loan and all refinancings of the loan are treated as one loan for this purpose. In the case of multiple loans that are refinanced by or serviced as a single loan (consolidated and collapsed loans) and loans that were made before August 5, 1997, the IRS has been authorized to issue regulations on the proper calculation of the 60-month period (Code Sec. 221(d), as amended by the 1998 Act). Such regulations would follow the guidance in Notice 98-7 (I.R.B. 1998-3, 54) on the establishment of the 60-month period with respect to such loans for reporting purposes (Conference Committee Report to the 1998 Act).

Comment. Under Notice 98-7, the 60-month period ("covered period") for consolidated and collapsed loans begins on (1) the most recent date on which any of the loans subject to consolidation or collapse went into repayment status, if the payee knows or has reason to know that date, or (2) January 1, 1998, if the payee does not know or have reason to know that date.

PRACTICAL ANALYSIS. Professor David Hudson of the Graduate Tax Program at the University of Florida College of Law in Gainesville, Florida, cautions that even though under state law a parent's obligation to support may include college tuition in certain circumstances, the tax law is clear that the parent must be primarily obligated under the loan agreement itself to be entitled to the deduction. As a practical matter, however, the student usually is the family member who does better taking out the student loan not only because many student loans carry a subsidized rate of interest but also because the adjusted gross income limitations on claiming the deduction foreclose many parents from taking a deduction in any event. Parents who want to claim a deduction for interest payments should plan to take out a home equity loan, which generally will allow them a full below-the-line interest deduction.

★ *Effective date.* This provision is effective for interest payments due and paid after December 31, 1997, on any qualified education loan and the portion of the 60-month period after December 31, 1997 (Act Sec. 6024 of the IRS Restructuring and Reform Act of 1998; Act Sec. 202(e) of the Taxpayer Relief Act of 1997 (P.L. 105-34)).

Act Sec. 6004(b)(1), amending Code Sec. 221(e)(1); Act Sec. 6004(b)(2), amending Code Sec. 221(d). Law at ¶ 5250. Committee Report at ¶ 10,840.

Qualified Zone Academy Bond Credit

¶ 244

Background

Banks, insurance companies, and certain corporate lenders that hold qualified zone academy bonds are entitled to a nonrefundable credit (Code Sec. 1397E(a) and (d)(6), as added by the Taxpayer Relief Act of 1997 (P.L. 105-34)). Qualified zone academy bonds are bonds issued by a state or local government where a substantial portion of the funds raised are used to renovate, provide equipment to, develop course materials for, or train teachers and others at certain public schools that are located in empowerment zones or enterprise communities or that have a certain percentage of students from low-income families. A percentage of the bond proceeds must also be matched by private entities (Code Sec. 1397E(d), as added by P.L. 105-34; Conference Committee Report to P.L. 105-34).

The credit is allowed to taxpayers holding a qualified zone academy bond on the credit allowance date, which is the anniversary of the issuance of the bond (Code Sec. 1397E(f)(1), as added by P.L. 105-34). The amount of the credit is equal

Background

to a credit rate set monthly by the IRS multiplied by the face amount of the bond (Code Sec. 1397E(b), as added by P.L. 105-34; Temporary Reg. § 1.1397E-1T(b)). The credit is includible in income as if it were an interest payment on the bond and may be claimed against regular income tax and alternative minimum tax (AMT) liability (Code Sec. 1397E(g), as added by P.L. 105-34; Temporary Reg. § 1.1397E-1T(a)).

Technical Corrections Impact

Treatment for estimated tax and overpayment purposes.—The credit for holders of qualified zone academy bonds is includible in income as if it were an interest payment on the bond and may be claimed against regular income tax and alternative minimum tax (AMT) liability (Code Sec. 1397E(g), as added by the Taxpayer Relief Act of 1997 (P.L. 105-34); Temporary Reg. § 1.1397E-1T(a)). A technical correction clarifies that, for purposes of subtitle F of the Internal Revenue Code (Code Secs. 6001-7873), the qualified zone academy bond credit is treated as a credit allowable under part IV of subchapter A of chapter 1 of the Code. Thus, the credit may be claimed for corporate estimated tax purposes under Code Sec. 6655(g)(1)(B) and is taken into account when determining whether a taxpayer has made an overpayment of tax under Code Sec. 6401(b)(1) (Code Sec. 1397E(h), as added by the IRS Restructuring and Reform Act of 1998; Senate Finance Committee Report to the 1998 Act).

★ *Effective date.* This provision is effective for obligations issued after December 31, 1997 (Act Sec. 6024 of the IRS Restructuring and Reform Act of 1998; Act Sec. 226(c) of the Taxpayer Relief Act of 1997 (P.L. 105-34)).

Act Sec. 6004(g)(1), amending Act Sec. 226(a) of the Taxpayer Relief Act of 1997 (P.L. 105-34); Act Sec. 6004(g)(2), amending Code Sec. 1397E(d)(4)(B); Act Sec. 6004(g)(3), adding Code Sec. 1397E(h); Act Sec. 6004(g)(4), amending Code Sec. 1397E(g); Act Sec. 6004(g)(5), amending Code Sec. 42(j)(4)(D); Act Sec. 6004(g)(6), amending Code Sec. 49(b)(4); Act Sec. 6004(g)(7), amending Code Sec. 50(a)(5)(C)). Law at ¶ 5070, ¶ 5090, ¶ 5100, ¶ 5680, ¶ 5690, and ¶ 8239. Committee Report at ¶ 10,865.

PRINCIPAL RESIDENCE

Exclusion of Gain

¶ 246

Background

An individual may elect to exclude up to $250,000 of gain on the sale or exchange of a principal residence (Code Sec. 121, as amended by the Taxpayer Relief Act of 1997 (P.L. 105-34)). The individual must own and occupy the residence for at least two of the five years before the sale or exchange. Although the exclusion may be applied to only one sale or exchange every two years, sales occurring before May 7, 1997, are not taken into consideration (Code Sec. 121(b)(3), as amended by P.L. 105-34).

The amount of excludable gain is increased to $500,000 for married individuals filing jointly if (1) either spouse meets the two-year ownership test, (2) both spouses meet the two-year use test, and (3) neither spouse is rendered ineligible for the exclusion because he or she sold or exchanged a residence within the last two years (Code Sec. 121(b), as amended by P.L. 105-34).

Even if a taxpayer does not meet the two-year ownership and use requirements, a pro rata amount of the *realized gain* is excludable where the sale or

Background

exchange is due to a change in place of employment, health, or unforeseen circumstances (Code Sec. 121(c), as amended by P.L. 105-34).

Technical Corrections Impact

Proration of exclusion.—A technical correction provides that the $250,000 or $500,000 *exclusion,* not the realized gain, is prorated for a taxpayer who does not meet the two-year ownership and use requirements in the case of a sale or exchange due to a change in place of employment, health, or unforeseen circumstances (Code Sec. 121(c)(1), as amended by the IRS Restructuring and Reform Act of 1998).

The prorated amount is equal to the $250,000 or $500,000 exclusion (whichever applies) multiplied by the ratio of:

(1) the shorter of (a) the aggregate periods that the property was owned and used as a principal residence during the five-year period ending on the date of the sale or exchange or (b) the period after the date of the most recent prior sale or exchange to which the exclusion applied, over

(2) two years.

Example. On September 1, 1997, Al and Lisa Jackson purchased a townhouse in Boston for $450,000. Lisa receives an offer of employment in Atlanta, and, on July 1, 1998, the Jacksons sell their townhouse for $480,000 and purchase a home in an Atlanta suburb for $350,000. The Jacksons realize $30,000 of gain on their townhouse. Since they owned and resided in the townhouse for 10 months, they may exclude up to $208,333 of gain from income ($500,000 exclusion × 10 months ÷ 24 months = $208,333). Since their actual gain is only $30,000, the entire amount of gain is excludable. Before the technical correction was made, the Jacksons could only exclude $12,500 ($30,000 realized gain × 10 months ÷ 24 months = $12,500).

Comment. 1997 Form 2119 (Sale of Your Home) was drafted by the IRS on the assumption that this technical correction would be enacted into law. Thus, a taxpayer who was affected by this provision in 1997 and filed Form 2119 should not need to file an amended return.

PRACTICAL ANALYSIS. Sidney Kess, New York, CCH contributing editor, author and lecturer, observes that the technical correction to the home sale rules for sales that do not satisfy the two-year minimum ownership and use requirements because of job relocation, illness or other unforeseeable events will insulate virtually all such sales from any reportable gains. The new partial exclusion is the ratio of the time that ownership and use bears to two years. Someone who moves because of a job change after owning and using a home for a year, for example, is entitled to one-half of the regular exclusion ($250,000 or $500,000 depending on marital status). It is highly unlikely that a home will appreciate *more than* this partial exclusion within this shortened period.

★ *Effective date.* This provision is generally effective for sales and exchanges after May 6, 1997 (Act Sec. 6024 of the IRS Restructuring and Reform Act of 1998; Act Sec. 312(d)[(e)] of the Taxpayer Relief Act of 1997 (P.L. 105-34)).

Act Sec. 6005(e)(2), amending Code Sec. 121(c)(1). Law at ¶ 5180. Committee Report at ¶ 10,925.

Joint Returns

¶ 248

Background ————————————————————————————

An individual may elect to exclude up to $250,000 of gain on the sale or exchange of a principal residence (Code Sec. 121, as amended by the Taxpayer Relief Act of 1997 (P.L. 105-34)). The individual must own and occupy the residence for at least two of the five years before the sale or exchange. Although the exclusion may be applied to only one sale or exchange every two years, sales occurring before May 7, 1997, are not taken into consideration (Code Sec. 121(b)(3), as amended by P.L. 105-34).

The amount of excludable gain is increased to $500,000 for married individuals filing jointly if (1) either spouse meets the two-year ownership test, (2) both spouses meet the two-year use test, and (3) neither spouse is rendered ineligible for the exclusion because he or she sold or exchanged a residence within the last two years (Code Sec. 121(b), as amended by P.L. 105-34).

———————————————————————————————————————

Technical Corrections Impact

Dollar limitation.—For married individuals filing jointly who fail to qualify for the $500,000 exclusion for gain on a residence because they do not satisfy the two-year ownership test, two-year use test, and the prohibition on any other sale or exchange of a residence within the last two years, a technical correction clarifies that the limit on the amount of excludable gain is computed separately for each spouse. Thus, the maximum exclusion for the couple is equal to the sum of the exclusions to which the spouses would otherwise be entitled if they had not been married (Code Sec. 121(b)(2), as amended by the IRS Restructuring and Reform Act of 1998). Each spouse is treated as owning the property during the period that either spouse owned the property.

Example (1). Susan and Craig Hart married in April 1998 and will file a joint return. Before they married, each owned a condominium that each used separately as a principal residence for over two years. The condominiums were finally sold at a gain in June 1998. The $500,000 exclusion for married taxpayers filing jointly does not apply because Susan and Craig did not use the same condominium as their joint principal residence for the required two-year period. Susan and Craig, however, are each entitled to exclude up to $250,000 of gain on the sale of each of their separate condominiums, that is, the exclusion that each would have been entitled to had they not married.

Example (2). Assume the same facts as in *Example (1),* above, except that Susan lived in her parents' home prior to marriage instead of in her own condominium. In this case, the $500,000 exclusion is not available with respect to Craig's condominium because the joint use test is not satisfied. However, since Craig would have been entitled to a $250,000 exclusion if he had not been married, Craig and Susan may exclude up to $250,000 of the gain from the sale of his condominium on their joint return.

Comment. The IRS anticipated this clarification and stated in IRS Pub. 17, "Your Federal Income Tax" (for 1997 returns), that gain can be excluded by spouses who file a joint return if either spouse meets the ownership and use tests. According to the IRS's examples, the maximum amount of gain that can be excluded is: (1) $250,000 where only one spouse meets the use test, and (2) $250,000 by each spouse where each spouse sells a home for which the ownership and use tests are met by that spouse.

★ *Effective date.* This provision is generally effective for sales and exchanges after May 6, 1997 (Act Sec. 6024 of the IRS Restructuring and Reform Act of 1998; Act Sec. 312(d)[(e)] of the Taxpayer Relief Act of 1997 (P.L. 105-34)).

Act Sec. 6005(e)(1), amending Code Sec. 121(b)(2). Law at ¶ 5180. Committee Report at ¶ 10,920.

Effective Date

¶ 251

Background

An individual may elect to exclude up to $250,000 ($500,000 for joint filers) of gain on the sale or exchange of a principal residence after May 6, 1997 (Code Sec. 121, as amended by the Taxpayer Relief Act of 1997 (P.L. 105-34)). However, a taxpayer could elect to apply prior law to any sale or exchange (1) before August 5, 1997, (2) after August 5, 1997, pursuant to a binding contract in effect on that date, or (3) where a replacement residence was acquired on or before August 5, 1997, or pursuant to a binding contract in effect on that date, and the former Code Sec. 1034 rollover-of-gain provision would apply (Act Sec. 312(d)[(e)] of P.L. 105-34, prior to amendment by the IRS Restructuring and Reform Act of 1998).

Under the rules in effect prior to enactment of the 1997 Act, individuals who were age 55 or older on the date of the sale of their principal residence could elect a once-in-a-lifetime exclusion of up to $125,000 of gain ($62,500, if married filing separately) (Code Sec. 121, prior to amendment by P.L. 105-34). In addition, under the prior rollover-of-gain rule, taxpayers could postpone recognition of gain on the sale of their home if they purchased or built a home that was at least equal in cost to the sales price of the old home and the replacement occurred during the period that generally began two years before and ended two years after the date of sale of the old home (Code Sec. 1034, prior to repeal by P.L. 105-34).

Technical Corrections Impact

Sales or exchanges on enactment date.—A technical correction provides that a taxpayer may elect to apply prior law to a sale or exchange occurring *on August 5, 1997,* as well as to sales and exchanges occurring before August 5, 1997 (Act Sec. 312(d)[(e)](2) of P.L. 105-34, as amended by the IRS Restructuring and Reform Act of 1998). Thus, taxpayers who sold or exchanged a home on or before August 5, 1997, could choose to use the $125,000 once-in-a-lifetime exclusion for taxpayers age 55 or over or the rollover-of-gain rule for homes that are replaced within the replacement period.

Comment. 1997 Form 2119 (Sale of Your Home) was drafted by the IRS on the assumption that this technical correction would be enacted into law. Thus, the IRS allowed a taxpayer to elect to use the prior law rules if the residence was sold before August 6, 1997 (1997 Instructions for Form 2119).

Election. To elect to use the prior law rules that applied to sales before May 7, 1997, taxpayers should have completed Part II and/or Part III of 1997 Form 2119 (Sale of Your Home). Part I of the form is completed by all filers, whether they apply the present or prior law rules.

PRACTICAL ANALYSIS. Sidney Kess, New York, CCH contributing editor, author and lecturer, notes that another technical correction allows individuals who sold their homes *on or before* August 5, 1997 (the date of enactment of the Taxpayer Relief Act of 1997), to elect to use the old home sale rules. Prior language limited this option to those who sold *before* this date. Thus,

individuals who sold their homes on August 5, 1997, and used the new exclusion should review their situation and consider whether the old rules would have been preferable. These individuals should consider filing amended returns to elect the old rules if they result in lower tax.

★ *Effective date.* This provision is effective as if originally included in Act Sec. 312(d)[(e)](2) of the Taxpayer Relief Act of 1997 (P.L. 105-34), which, as so amended, provides that, at the election of the taxpayer, the provisions in Act Sec. 312 of P.L. 105-34 will not apply to any sale or exchange on or before August 5, 1997 (Act Sec. 6024 of the IRS Restructuring and Reform Act of 1998).

Act Sec. 6005(e)(3), amending Act Sec. 312(d)[(e)](2) of the Taxpayer Relief Act of 1997 (P.L. 105-34). Law at ¶ 8240. Committee Report at ¶ 10,930.

TRANSPORTATION FRINGE BENEFITS AND TRAVEL EXPENSES

Exclusion for Transportation Fringe Benefits

¶ 253

Background

The value of qualified transportation fringe benefits provided to an employee is excluded from gross income and wages for income and employment tax purposes. Qualified transportation fringe benefits include: (1) transportation in a commuter highway vehicle if the transportation is in connection with travel between the employee's residence and place of employment (e.g., van pooling); (2) a transit pass; or (3) qualified parking (Code Sec. 132(f)(1)).

The maximum amount of qualified parking that is excludable from an employee's gross income in 1998 is $175 per month, as indexed for inflation. Other qualified transportation fringes are excludable from gross income to the extent that the aggregate value of benefits does not exceed $65 per month in 1998, as indexed for inflation (Rev. Proc. 97-57, I.R.B. 1997-52, 20). These inflation-indexed amounts were derived from base amounts of $155 per month for qualified parking and $60 per month for other transportation benefits (van pooling and transit passes) (Code Sec. 132(f)(2) and (6), prior to amendment by the Surface Transportation Revenue Act of 1998 (ISTEA) (P.L. 105-178)).

For tax years beginning after 1997, employers may offer employees a choice between cash and qualified parking without causing the employees to lose the exclusion for qualified parking benefits (Code Sec. 132(f)(4), prior to amendment by P.L. 105-178).

ISTEA Impact

Exclusion amounts increased.—In tax years beginning in 1999 and thereafter, the base amount for the maximum exclusion for qualified parking benefits has been increased from $155 to $175 (Code Sec. 132(f)(2)(B), as amended by the Surface Transportation Revenue Act of 1998 (ISTEA) (P.L. 105-178)). In tax years beginning in 1999 and thereafter, the base amount for the maximum exclusion for other qualified transportation benefits, such as van pooling and transit passes, has been increased from $60 to $65 (Code Sec. 132(f)(2)(A), as amended by P.L. 105-178).

For tax years beginning in 2000 and thereafter, these base amounts for the exclusion are indexed for inflation under Code Sec. 1(f)(3) for the calendar year in which the tax year begins. The base year for computing the inflation adjustment applicable to this period is calendar year 1998, and any increase is rounded down to the next lowest multiple of $5 (Code Sec. 132(f)(6)(A) and (B), as amended by P.L. 105-178). The exclusion limits are not adjusted for inflation in a tax year beginning in 1999 (Senate Finance Committee Report to P.L. 105-178).

For tax years beginning in 2002 and thereafter, the base amount for the exclusion limit for qualified transportation benefits other than parking, such as van pooling and transit passes, is increased from $65 to $100 (Code Sec. 132(f)(2)(A), as amended by P.L. 105-178, effective for tax years beginning after 2001). The base amount for the exclusion limit for qualified parking benefits remains at $175.

For tax years beginning in 2003 and thereafter, the $100 base amount for qualified transportation benefits other than parking is indexed for inflation under Code Sec. 1(f)(3), but the base year for computing the inflation adjustment is calendar year 2001 and any increase is rounded down to the next lowest multiple of $5 (Code Sec. 132(f)(6)(A), as amended by P.L. 105-178, effective for tax years beginning after 2001).

Comment. The maximum exclusion amount for qualified transportation benefits other than parking may be larger than Congress anticipated for the year 2002. The base amounts for that year are $100 and $175, and it appears that Congress did not intend for the $100 amount to be indexed for inflation until 2003 by using a base year of 2001. However, as currently drafted, the base amounts for 2002 would still be subject to the indexing procedure for tax years beginning after 1999, which relies on a base year of 1998. This would likely result in a large inflation adjustment to the $100 base amount only for 2002.

The base amounts and base years for inflation indexing for tax years beginning in 1999-2003 are as follows.

Tax Year Beginning In	Base Amounts	Base Year for Indexing
1999, 2000, 2001	$175 for parking	1998
	$ 65 for other transportation benefits	1998
2002	$175 for parking	1998
	$100 for other transportation benefits	1998
2003	$175 for parking	1998
	$100 for other transportation benefits	2001

Cash option. For tax years beginning after 1997, employers who provide *any* qualified transportation fringe benefits for their employees may offer employees a choice between cash and one or more qualified transportation benefits without causing the employees to lose the exclusion from income for noncash transportation fringe benefits (Code Sec. 132(f)(4), as amended by P.L. 105-178). The amount of cash offered is includible in the employee's income only to the extent that the employee *chooses* the cash option (Senate Finance Committee Report to P.L. 105-178). Previously, employers could only offer employees a choice between cash and qualified parking without causing the employees to lose the exclusion (Code Sec. 132(f)(4), prior to amendment by P.L. 105-178).

Comment. In addition to the cash option, no amount is included in an employee's income or wages merely because the employee is offered a choice among qualified transportation benefits (Conference Committee Report to P.L. 105-178).

★ *Effective date.* The provision on increasing the base amounts for the exclusion for transportation benefits to $65 and $175 is effective for tax years beginning after December 31, 1998 (Act Sec. 9010(b)(3) of the Surface Transportation Revenue Act of 1998 (P.L. 105-178)). The provision on increasing the base amount for the exclusion for transportation benefits other than parking to $100 is effective for tax years beginning after December 31, 2001 (Act Sec. 9010(c)(3) of P.L. 105-178). The provision on choosing to take cash instead of a transportation benefit is effective for tax years beginning after December 31, 1997 (Act Sec. 9010(a)(2) of P.L. 105-178).

Act Sec. 9010(a)(1), amending Code Sec. 132(f)(4); Act Sec. 9010(b)(1), amending Code Sec. 132(f)(6); Act Sec. 9010(b)(2), amending Code Sec. 132(f)(2); Act Sec. 9010(c)(1), amending Code Sec. 132(f)(2)(A); Act Sec. 9010(c)(2), amending Code Sec. 132(f)(6)(A); Act Sec. 9010(a)(2), (b)(3), and (c)(3). Law at ¶ 5185. Committee Report at ¶ 15,135. Act section references are to the Surface Transportation Revenue Act of 1998 (P.L. 105-178).

Federal Employees on Temporary Duty Status

¶ 256

Background ─────────────────────────────────────

Unreimbursed ordinary and necessary travel expenses, including meals and lodging expenses, that are incurred while temporarily away from home in pursuit of a trade or business are deductible (Code Sec. 162(a)(2)). However, in order for a taxpayer's time away from home to be considered temporary, it must be one year or less in length. If the taxpayer's assignment in the second location is expected to exceed one year in length, it is considered indefinite, rather than temporary, and travel expenses with respect to that location are not deductible.

The one-year rule does not apply to a federal employee who is traveling on temporary duty status to investigate or to provide support services for the investigation of a federal crime. The travel must be certified by the Attorney General (Code Sec. 162(a), as amended by the Taxpayer Relief Act of 1997 (P.L. 105-34)). Thus, such an employee's travel expenses are deductible even if the employee's time away from home exceeds one year in length.

──

Technical Corrections Impact

Participation in criminal prosecutions.—A technical correction expands the exception to the one-year rule on deductibility of travel expenses of federal employees. Travel expenses of federal employees who are traveling on temporary duty status in order to *prosecute* or to provide support services for the *prosecution* of a federal crime, as well as to investigate or to support the investigation of a federal crime, are deductible even if they are away from home for more than one year (Code Sec. 162(a), as amended by the IRS Restructuring and Reform Act of 1998). Proper certification of the travel by the Attorney General, or his or her designee, is still required.

Example. Steve Adams works for the U.S. Department of Justice and maintains his permanent home in Chicago. He is placed on temporary duty status and assigned to assist in the investigation and prosecution of a major money laundering case in the Miami area. Adams rents an apartment in Miami in May 1998 and begins gathering evidence and taking depositions related to the case. He is expected to continue working on the case through the trial which will begin in June 1999. Assuming the travel has been properly certified by the Attorney General, Adams' unreimbursed travel expenses, including meals and lodging expenses, are deductible even though he is expected to be away from home for more than one year.

Comment. Although federal employees and other taxpayers on temporary job assignments cannot deduct meals and lodging expenses incurred in their tax home when they return on days off, meals and lodging expenses incurred while traveling from the temporary place of work to the hometown and back to work are deductible up to the amount that it would have cost for meals and lodging at the temporary place of work (IRS Pub. 17, "Your Federal Income Tax" (for 1997 returns)).

★ *Effective date.* The provision is effective for amounts paid or incurred with respect to tax years ending after August 5, 1997 (Act Sec. 6024 of the IRS Restructuring and Reform Act of 1998; Act Sec. 1204(b) of the Taxpayer Relief Act of 1997 (P.L. 105-34)).

Act Sec. 6012(a), amending Code Sec. 162(a). Law at ¶ 5205. Committee Report at ¶ 11,255.

POLICE AND FIRE DEPARTMENT EMPLOYEES

Disability Payments

¶ 261

Background

Certain amounts received by full-time police or fire department employees or their survivors in 1989, 1990 or 1991 due to heart disease or hypertension of the employee are excludable from gross income under Code Sec. 104(a)(1) as compensation for personal injuries or sickness under a worker's compensation act. The amount had to be payable under a state law, as amended on May 19, 1992, that irrebuttably presumed that heart disease and hypertension are work-related illnesses. This treatment only applied to employees separating from service before July 1, 1992 (Act Sec. 1529 of the Taxpayer Relief Act of 1997 (P.L. 105-34)).

Technical Corrections Impact

Work-related illnesses.—The technical correction expands the scope of the exclusion for amounts received by full-time police or fire department employees or their survivors in 1989, 1990 or 1991 due to heart disease or hypertension of the employee. The exclusion applies to amounts payable under a state law, as amended on May 19, 1992, that irrebuttably presumed that heart disease and hypertension are work-related illnesses, but only for employees *hired* before July 1, 1992 (Act Sec. 1529(b)(1)(B)(i) of P.L. 105-34, as amended by the IRS Restructuring and Reform Act of 1998). In addition, the exclusion also applies to amounts received by employees referred to in that state law that are payable under any other statute, ordinance, labor agreement, or similar provision as a disability pension payment or in the nature of a disability pension payment attributable to employment as a police officer or fireman (Act Sec. 1529(b)(1)(B)(ii) of P.L. 105-34, as amended by the 1998 Act).

Planning Note. Claims for refund or credit for overpayments resulting from the provision can be filed by August 5, 1998, regardless of any statute of limitation that might otherwise apply (Act Sec. 1529(c) of P.L. 105-34).

★ *Effective date.* The provision is effective August 5, 1997 (Act Sec. 6024 of the IRS Restructuring and Reform Act of 1998; Act Sec. 1529 of the Taxpayer Relief Act of 1997 (P.L. 105-34)).

Act Sec. 6015(c), amending Act Sec. 1529(a) and (b)(1)(B) of the Taxpayer Relief Act of 1997 (P.L. 105-34). Law at ¶ 8270. Committee Report at ¶ 11,315.

IRS LEVIES

Continuous Levies

¶ 266

Background

The IRS has the authority to issue a "continuous levy" on "specified payments" in order to collect unpaid taxes (Code Sec. 6331(h), as added by the

Background _____

Taxpayer Relief Act of 1997 (P.L. 105-34)). A continuous levy is a special levy that attaches to both property and rights to property held on the date of the levy and certain payments due to or received by the taxpayer after the date of the levy.

Specified payments are defined as (1) any federal payments other than payments for which eligibility is based on the income or assets, or both, of a payee; (2) certain amounts that would otherwise be exempt from levy, such as unemployment benefits described in Code Sec. 6334(a)(4), workers' compensation benefits described in Code Sec. 6334(a)(7), wages described in Code Sec. 6334(a)(9), and public assistance payments described in Code Sec. 6334(a)(11); and (3) certain railroad annuity, pension, or unemployment benefits. The continuous levy applies to up to 15 percent of any specified payment, including amounts otherwise exempt from levy under Code Sec. 6334 (item (2), above).

_____

Technical Corrections Impact

Approval of continuous levy required.—A technical correction clarifies that the use of a continuous levy is at the IRS's discretion and must be specifically approved by the IRS before the levy takes effect (Code Sec. 6331(h), as amended by the IRS Restructuring and Reform Act of 1998). Thus, if the IRS issues a levy on a taxpayer's property and such property is a specified payment, the levy is not considered a continuous levy that attaches to future payments unless it is specifically designated as such.

Example. The IRS issues a levy which attaches to Jane Brown's social security benefits. These benefits are not paid on the basis of her income or assets and, thus, constitute a specified payment. Unless the levy is approved as a continuous levy, it does not attach to any social security benefits that are received by Brown after the date of the levy. The levy only applies to benefits held by Brown on the date of the levy.

★ *Effective date.* The provision applies to levies issued after August 5, 1997 (Act Sec. 6024 of the IRS Restructuring and Reform Act of 1998; Act Sec. 1024(b) of the Taxpayer Relief Act of 1997 (P.L. 105-34)).

Act Sec. 6010(f), amending Code Sec. 6331(h)(1). Law at ¶ 6280. Committee Report at ¶ 11,170.

Chapter 3
Individual Retirement Accounts and Qualified Plans

ROTH IRAs

Early Withdrawals of Converted Amounts

¶ 301

Background _____

A taxpayer with adjusted gross income (AGI) of less than $100,000 may convert a regular IRA into a Roth IRA at any time. (Code Sec. 408A(c)(3)(B), as added by the Taxpayer Relief Act of 1997 (P.L. 105-34)). The amount converted is generally includible in income in the year of the conversion. However, if the conversion occurs in 1998, the amount converted is includible in income ratably over the four-year period beginning with the year in which the conversion occurs. Under prior law, this four-year income spread was mandatory, not elective (Code Sec. 408A(d)(3)(A)(iii), prior to amendment by the IRS Restructuring and Reform Act of 1998). The 10 percent tax on early withdrawals does not apply to conversions of regular IRAs into Roth IRAs. (Code Sec. 408A(d)(3)(A)(ii), as added by the Taxpayer Relief Act of 1997 (P.L. 105-34)). Under prior law, taxpayers under age 59½ could escape the 10 percent early withdrawal tax by rolling over funds from a regular IRA to a Roth IRA and then immediately thereafter taking a distribution from the Roth IRA.

Technical Corrections Impact

Early Withdrawals of Amounts Converted From Regular IRAs to Roth IRAs.—The IRS Restructuring and Reform Act of 1998 modifies the rules relating to conversions of regular IRAs into Roth IRAs in order to prevent taxpayers from receiving premature distributions from a Roth Conversion IRA while retaining the benefits of the four-year income spread.

Acceleration of income inclusion. Where amounts are converted in 1998, and are thus subject to the four-year income spread, income inclusion is accelerated for any amounts withdrawn before 2001, the fourth year of the spread. Under this rule, a taxpayer that withdraws converted amounts prior to the last year of the four-year spread will be required to include in income the amount otherwise includible under the four-year rule, plus the lesser of (1) the taxable amount of the withdrawal, or (2) the remaining taxable amount of the conversion (i.e., the taxable amount of the conversion not included in income under the four-year rule in the current or a prior taxable year). In subsequent years (assuming no further withdrawals), the amount includible in income will be the lesser of (1) the amount otherwise required under the four-year rule (determined without regard to the withdrawal) or (2) the remaining taxable amount of the conversion (Code Sec. 408A(d)(3)(E)(i), as added by the 1998 Act).

The 1998 Act provides "ordering rules" to determine which amounts are withdrawn for tax purposes where a Roth IRA contains both conversion and contributory amounts, or conversion amounts from different years. See ¶ 305.

Example (1). John Adams, age 50, has a nondeductible IRA with a value of $100,000, consisting of $75,000 in contributions and $25,000 in earnings. He has no other IRAs. Adams converts the nondeductible IRA into a Roth IRA in 1998 and elects the four-year spread. As a result of the conversion, $25,000 is includible in income ratably over four years (i.e., $6,250 in each of the years 1998, 1999, 2000, and 2001). The 10% early withdrawal tax does not apply to the conversion. At the beginning of 1999, the value of the account is $110,000 and Adams withdraws $10,000. The withdrawal is treated as attributable entirely to amounts that were includible in income due to the conversion. Thus, in 1999, $16,250 is included in income (the $6,250 includible in the year of withdrawal under the four-year rule, plus $10,000 ($10,000 is less than the remaining taxable amount of $12,500 ($25,000 minus $12,500)). In 2000, $2,500 (the remaining taxable amount of the conversion ($12,500 minus $10,000)) is included in income under the four-year rule. No amount is included in income in 2001 due to the conversion.

Specific rules are provided under the 1998 Act where a Roth IRA account holder dies during the four year spread period. See ¶ 315.

Election. The 1998 Act makes the four-year income spread elective. There are some taxpayers who would not find it advantageous to spread out income over four years. Such taxpayers may now elect to recognize all the income in the year of conversion. According to the Senate Finance Committee Report, the election is to be made in the time and manner prescribed by the Secretary of the Treasury. If the account holder fails to make an election, the four-year spread will be deemed to be elected. An election, or deemed election, with respect to the four-year spread cannot be changed after the due date for the return for the first year of the income inclusion (including extensions) (Code Sec. 408A(d)(3)(A)(iii), as amended by the 1998 Act).

Application of early withdrawal tax to converted amounts. The 1998 Act modifies the rules relating to conversions to prevent taxpayers from receiving premature distributions (i.e., within five years) while retaining the benefit of the nonpayment of the early withdrawal tax. If converted amounts are withdrawn within the five-year period beginning with the year of the conversion, then, only to the extent attributable to amounts that were includible in income due to the conversion, the amount withdrawn will be subject to the 10 percent early withdrawal tax. (Code Sec. 408A(d)(3)(F), as added by the 1998 Act).

Example (2). Assume the facts in *Example (1)*. The $10,000 withdrawal made by Adams in 1999 would be subject to the 10% early withdrawal tax (unless one of the exceptions under Code Sec. 72(t) applies) because Adams is under age 59½.

PRACTICAL ANALYSIS. William H. Mears, Jr., of Brown Brothers, Harriman Trust Co., New York, NY, observes that much of the technical corrections relates to adding clarity and has little substantive effect. However, there are several provisions which are of special interest.

Mears notes that some commentators have pointed out that it may be possible under current law to deposit funds into a Roth IRA and then withdraw them before the due date of the taxpayer's tax return. The earnings would then be tax-free. The Act makes it clear that the payment by the IRA is not a qualified distribution and therefore the withdrawn deposit, along with its earnings, is subject to tax. The deposited amount, of course, would otherwise have not been taxable.

Significantly, the Act now allows, in the case of conversions of IRAs into Roth IRAs, the taxpayer to elect to have the amount converted entirely includible in income in the year of conversion (or rollover) rather than ratably over four years (last year's enacted four-year averaging provision). For any number of reasons, the taxpayer may not want to defer three-fourths of the income from conversion over the next three years. A higher tax rate may be forecast, either from personal circumstances or from a view of future tax rates increases emanating from Washington. On the other hand, a taxpayer may want to have a certain amount taxable in 1998 and be able to control the amount includible in future years by deferring other IRA conversions until future years.

★ *Effective date.* These provisions are effective for tax years beginning after December 31, 1997 (Act Sec. 6024 of the IRS Restructuring and Reform Act of 1998; Act Sec. 302(f) of the Taxpayer Relief Act of 1997 (P.L. 105-34)).

Act Sec. 6005(b)(4)(A), amending Code Sec. 408A(d)(3)(A)(iii). Act Sec. 6005(b)(4)(B), adding Code Sec. 408A(d)(3)(E) and 408A(d)(3)(F). Act Sec. 6005(b)(6)(B). Law at ¶ 5370. Committee Report at ¶ 10,890.

Determination of Five-Year Holding Period

¶ 305

Background

In general, distributions of earnings from a Roth IRA are "qualified distributions" and, hence, excludable from income, if the individual has held a Roth IRA for at least five years and certain other requirements are satisfied. The five-year holding period begins with the first tax year for which a contribution was made. However, under prior law, the five-year holding period with respect to conversion Roth IRAs began with the tax year of the conversion (Code Sec. 408A(d)(2)(B), prior to amendment by the IRS Restructuring and Reform Act of 1998).

Technical Corrections Impact

Applying the Five-Year Holding Period for Roth IRAs.—The IRS Restructuring and Reform Act of 1998 eliminates the special rule under which a separate five-year holding period applied for purposes of determining whether a distribution of amounts attributable to a conversion is a qualified distribution.

Thus, the five-year holding rule for Roth IRAs will begin with the year for which a contribution is first made to a Roth IRA. A subsequent conversion will not start the running of a new five-year period (Code Sec. 408A(d)(2)(B), as amended by the 1998 Act).

Return of excess contributions. Distributions of excess contributions and earnings allocable to the contributions are not considered qualified distributions (Code Sec. 408A(d)(2)(C), as added by the 1998 Act).

Planning Note. With only one five-year holding period, taxpayers contemplating a conversion in the future should make a Roth IRA contribution (even if only a token one) by April 15, 1999, and designate it for the 1998 tax year. This will start the five-year clock running on January 1, 1998.

Ordering rules. Ordering rules will apply to determine what amounts are withdrawn in the event a Roth IRA contains both conversion amounts (possibly from different years) and other contributions (Code Sec. 408A(d)(4), as amended by the 1998 Act). Under these rules, regular Roth IRA contributions will be deemed to be withdrawn first, then converted amounts (starting with the amounts first converted). Withdrawals of converted amounts will be treated as coming first from converted amounts that were includible in income. Earnings will continue to be treated as withdrawn after contributions.

Comment. Prior IRS guidance (see IRS Announcement 97-122, I.R.B. 1997-50, 63) advising sponsors to keep conversion Roth IRAs separate from contributory Roth IRAs may need to be reconsidered in light of this change. Having only one five-year holding period appears to remove the necessity of keeping separate IRAs for contributions and conversions. However, in light of the new ordering rules, if one Roth IRA is used for both contributory and conversion contributions, taxpayers under age 59 1/2 will need to keep track of which amounts are attributable to contributions and which amounts are attributable to conversions, in the event a withdrawal is taken within the five-year period.

Multiple Roth IRAs treated as one Roth IRA. For purposes of these rules, all Roth IRAs, whether or not maintained in separate accounts, will be considered a single Roth IRA (Code Sec. 408A(d)(4), as amended by the 1998 Act).

★ *Effective date.* These provisions are effective for tax years beginning after December 31, 1997 (Act Sec. 6024 of the IRS Restructuring and Reform Act of 1998; Act Sec. 302(f) of the Taxpayer Relief Act of 1997 (P.L. 105-34)).

Act Sec. 6005(b)(3)(A), amending Code Sec. 408A(d)(2)(B). Act Sec. 6005(b)(3)(B), adding Code Sec. 408A(d)(2)(C). Act Sec. 6005(b)(5)(A), amending Code Sec. 408A(d)(4). Law at ¶ 5370.

Corrections of Erroneous Conversions

¶ 311

Background

A taxpayer with adjusted gross income (AGI) above $100,000 is not eligible to convert a regular IRA into a Roth IRA (Code Sec. 408A(c)(3)(B), as added by the Taxpayer Relief Act of 1997 (P.L. 105-34)). Prior law did not provide a mechanism by which a taxpayer could correct or "undo" an erroneous conversion. Such a circumstance could arise if a taxpayer makes a conversion early in a tax year and then discovers by the end of the year that his AGI has exceeded the $100,000 limit, rendering him ineligible to make the conversion.

Technical Corrections Impact

Corrections of Erroneous Conversions of Regular IRAs to Roth IRAs.—In order to assist individuals who erroneously convert regular IRAs into Roth IRAs, or who otherwise wish to change the nature of an IRA contribution, the IRS Restructuring and Reform Act of 1998 provides that (except as provided by the Treasury Secretary) contributions to an IRA and earnings on those contributions may be transferred in a trustee-to-trustee transfer from any IRA to another IRA by the due date for the taxpayer's return for the year of the contribution (including extensions). Any such transferred contributions will be treated as if contributed to the transferee IRA (and not to the transferor IRA) (Code Sec. 408A(d)(6)(A) and Code Sec. 408A(d)(7), as added by the 1998 Act).

> **Example.** Judith Jones converts a regular IRA into a Roth IRA early in 1998, when she anticipates her AGI for the year will be $85,000. Later in the year, she receives a $25,000 bonus from her employer. She can "undo" the transaction by completing a trustee-to-trustee transfer of the converted amounts (including the earnings on those amounts) from the Roth IRA to a regular IRA by April 15, 1999 (the due date of her return).

Comment. According to the Senate Finance Committee Report, trustee-to-trustee transfers include transfers between IRA trustees as well as IRA custodians, apply to transfers from and to IRA accounts and annuities, and apply to transfers between IRA accounts and annuities with the same trustee or custodian.

Any transfer of contributions must be accompanied by any net income allocable to the contributions. Also, such transfers are permitted only if no deduction was allowed with respect to the contribution to the transferor plan (Code Sec. 408A(d)(6)(B), as added by the 1998 Act).

★ *Effective date.* These provisions are effective for tax years beginning after December 31, 1997 (Act Sec. 6024 of the IRS Restructuring and Reform Act of 1998; Act Sec. 302(f) of the Taxpayer Relief Act of 1997 (P.L. 105-34)).

Act Sec. 6005(b)(6)(A) and Act Sec. 6005(b)(7), adding Code Sec. 408A(d)(6) and 408A(d)(7). Law at ¶ 5370.

Effect of Account Holder's Death During Four-Year Spread Period

¶ 315

Background

If a taxpayer makes a conversion from a regular IRA to a Roth IRA, the amount converted is generally included in income in the year of the conversion. However, if the conversion occurs in 1998, the amount converted may be includible in income ratably over the four-year period beginning with the year in which the conversion occurs (Code Sec. 408A(d)(3)(A)(iii), as added by the Taxpayer Relief Act of 1997 (P.L. 105-34)). Prior law did not contain a specific rule addressing what happens if an individual dies during the four-year spread period for 1998 conversions.

Technical Corrections Impact

Effect of Account Holder's Death During Four-Year Averaging Period.—Under the IRS Restructuring and Reform Act of 1998, any amounts remaining to be included in income as a result of a 1998 conversion will be includible in income on the final return of the deceased taxpayer (Code Sec. 408A(d)(3)(E)(ii)(I), as added by the 1998 Act).

Election by surviving spouse to continue deferral. If the surviving spouse is the sole beneficiary of the Roth IRA, the spouse may elect to continue the deferral by including the remaining amounts in his or her income over the remainder of the four-year period. However, such an election may not be made or changed after the due date for the spouse's tax year which includes the date of death (Code Sec. 408A(d)(3)(E)(ii)(II), as added by the 1998 Act).

Example. In 1998, Judith Jones rolls over $40,000 from her regular IRA to a Roth IRA. She elects the four-year income spread. The amount of $10,000 is included in her gross income for 1998. If she dies in 1999, and is unmarried, the remaining amount ($30,000) is included on her final tax return. If she is married, her spouse may make an election by April 15, 2000, to continue the deferral. If so, he will include in his gross income $10,000 in each of the years 1999, 2000, and 2001.

★ *Effective date.* This provision is effective for tax years beginning after December 31, 1997 (Act Sec. 6024 of the IRS Restructuring and Reform Act of 1998; Act Sec. 302(f) of the Taxpayer Relief Act of 1997 (P.L. 105-34)).

Act Sec. 6005(b)(4)(B), adding Code Sec. 408A(d)(3)(E)(ii). Law at ¶ 5370. Committee Report at ¶ 10,890.

Determination of AGI Limit for Conversions

¶ 321

Background

A taxpayer with adjusted gross income (AGI) of less than $100,000 may convert a regular IRA into a Roth IRA. (Code Sec. 408A(c)(3)(B), as added by the Taxpayer Relief Act of 1997 (P.L. 105-34)). Amounts includible in income as a result of the conversion are not taken into account in determining whether the $100,000 AGI threshold is exceeded (Code Sec. 408A(c)(3)(C), as added by the Taxpayer Relief Act of 1997 (P.L. 105-34)). Under prior law, the deduction for a contribution to a regular IRA was taken into account in determining AGI for the tax year.

Technical Corrections Impact

Calculation of AGI Limit for Conversions.—Under the IRS Restructuring and Reform Act of 1998, AGI, for purposes of applying the $100,000 threshold, is determined in the same manner as under Code Sec. 219(g)(3) for regular IRAs. Under Code Sec. 219(g)(3), AGI includes taxable social security and railroad retirement benefits (Code Sec. 86), and the application of the passive activity loss rules of Code Sec. 469. However, the exclusions for interest on U.S. savings bonds used to pay higher education expenses (Code Sec. 135), for employer-provided adoption assistance programs (Code Sec. 137), and for foreign earned income (Code Sec. 911) are not taken into account in determining AGI. In addition, the deduction for a contribution to a regular IRA is not taken into account (Code Sec. 408A(c)(3)(C)(i), as amended by the 1998 Act).

The 1998 Act makes it clear that the applicable AGI is the AGI for the year of the distribution to which the conversion relates (Code Sec. 408A(c)(3)(B), as amended by the IRS Restructuring and Reform Act of 1998).

Comment. The conference agreement clarifies that, for purposes of determining the $100,000 AGI threshold, the conversion amount is not taken into account. Thus, the conference report states, for this purpose, AGI and all AGI-based phaseouts are to be determined without taking into account the conversion amount. However, for purposes of computing taxable income, the conversion amount (to the extent otherwise includible in AGI) is to be taken into account in computing the AGI-based phaseout amounts.

★ *Effective date.* This provision is effective for tax years beginning after December 31, 1997 (Act Sec. 6024 of the IRS Restructuring and Reform Act of 1998; Act Sec. 302(f) of the Taxpayer Relief Act of 1997 (P.L. 105-34)).

Act Sec. 6005(b)(2)(B), amending Code Sec. 408A(c)(3)(B); Act Sec. 6005(b)(2)(C), amending Code Sec. 408A(c)(3)(C)(i). Law at ¶ 5370. Committee Report at ¶ 10,890.

AGI Limit and Minimum Required Distributions

¶ 323

Background ———————————————————————————

A taxpayer with adjusted gross income (AGI) of $100,000 or less may convert a regular IRA into a Roth IRA (Code Sec. 408A(c)(3)(B), as added by the Taxpayer Relief Act of 1997 (P.L. 105-34)). Generally, uniform minimum required distribution rules apply to tax-qualified plans and regular IRAs. These rules require that participants must begin taking minimum distributions no later than the "required beginning date." For qualified plans, the required beginning date is April 1 of the calendar year following the later of (1) the calendar year in which the employee attains age 70½ or (2) the calendar year in which the employee retires. For IRA distributions, the required beginning date is April 1 of the calendar year following the calendar year in which the holder attains age 70½. Prior law did not exclude minimum required distributions from AGI for purposes of calculating the $100,000 threshold.

IRS Restructuring and Reform Impact

Minimum Required Distributions Excluded From AGI for Purposes of Making Roth IRA Conversions.—For tax years beginning in 2005, the IRS Restructuring and Reform Act of 1998 modifies the definition of AGI to exclude minimum required distributions from AGI solely for the purposes of determining eligibility to convert a regular IRA to a Roth IRA (Code Sec. 408A(c)(3)(C)(i), as amended by the 1998 Act). As under present law, the required minimum distribution would not be eligible for conversion to a Roth IRA and would be included in gross income.

Comment. This change will allow more taxpayers over age 70½ (in 2005) to qualify for Roth IRA conversions, since the amount of their required distributions will not count toward the $100,000 threshold. Taxpayers over age 70½ today will have to wait several more years to take advantage of this change.

PRACTICAL ANALYSIS. William H. Mears, Jr., of Brown Brothers, Harriman Trust Co., New York, NY, comments that for purposes of computing adjusted gross income to determine if the taxpayer is qualified to convert an IRA, the Act amendment provides that mandatory IRA distributions need not be considered. This will in many cases allow a taxpayer who is otherwise ineligible to convert an IRA into a Roth IRA to do so. However, this provision is not effective until 2005, meaning that this opportunity is more than six years away.

Accordingly, advisors should be watchful and not allow clients to reach age 70 1/2, the age when distribution must begin, without considering conversion. This change in the statute should not be used as a reason for delaying consideration. The change is only helpful to those who are receiving distributions today and who presumably will also be receiving distributions in 2005. Existing law does not permit required minimum distributions to be converted to Roth IRAs.

★ *Effective date.* This provision is effective for tax years beginning after December 31, 2004 (Act Sec. 7004(b) of the IRS Restructuring and Reform Act of 1998).

Act Sec. 7004(a), amending Code Sec. 408A(c)(3)(C)(i). Act Sec. 7004(b). Law at ¶ 5370. Committee Report at ¶ 11,545.

Clarification of Phaseout Range

¶ 325

Background

The $2,000 Roth IRA maximum contribution limit is phased out for individual taxpayers with adjusted gross income (AGI) between $95,000 and $110,000 and for married taxpayers filing a joint return with AGI between $150,000 and $160,000 (Code Sec. 408A(c)(3)(A) and Code Sec. 408A(c)(3)(C), as added by the Taxpayer Relief Act of 1997 (P.L. 105-34)). The phaseout range for married individuals filing separately was intended to be $0 to $10,000, but this intent was not reflected in the prior law (Joint Committee on Taxation, *General Explanation of Tax Legislation Enacted in 1997*, (JCS-23-97), December 17, 1997, p. 46).

Technical Corrections Impact

Clarification of Phaseout Range for Married Taxpayers Filing Separately.—The IRS Restructuring and Reform Act of 1998 clarifies that the phaseout range for the Roth IRA maximum contribution limit for a married individual filing a separate return is $0 to $10,000 of AGI (Code Sec. 408A(c)(3)(A)(ii), as amended by the 1998 Act).

★ *Effective date.* This provision is effective for tax years beginning after December 31, 1997 (Act Sec. 6024 of the IRS Restructuring and Reform Act of 1998; Act Sec. 302(f) of the Taxpayer Relief Act of 1997 (P.L. 105-34)).

Act Sec. 6005(b)(2)(A), amending Code Sec. 408A(c)(3)(A)(ii). Law at ¶ 5370.

Clarification of Contribution Limit

¶ 331

Background

An individual may make contributions up to the lesser of $2,000 or 100 percent of compensation to a Roth IRA if the individual's AGI does not exceed certain limits (Code Sec. 408A(c)(2) and 408A(c)(3)(A), as added by the Taxpayer Relief Act of 1997 (P.L. 105-34)). The Conference Committee Report to the Taxpayer Relief Act of 1997 stated that contributions to all of an individual's IRAs for a tax year may not exceed $2,000.

Technical Corrections Impact

Clarification of Roth IRA Contribution Limit.—The IRS Restructuring and Reform Act of 1998 makes clear that the maximum amount of contributions an individual may make to all of his or her IRAs is limited to a cumulative total of $2,000 per year (Code Sec. 408A(c)(3)(A), as amended by the 1998 Act).

Example. Jordan Cox is a single taxpayer with AGI of $102,500. He participates in his company's 401(k) plan and therefore is ineligible to make a deductible IRA contribution. Because of his income level, he is eligible to make only a $1,000 Roth IRA contribution. Jordan is therefore permitted to make an additional $1,000 contribution to a regular nondeductible IRA.

SEPs and SIMPLE IRAs. Under the 1998 Act, a simplified employee pension (SEP) or a SIMPLE IRA may not be designated as a Roth IRA and contributions to an SEP or SIMPLE IRA cannot be taken into account for purposes of the $2,000 contribution limit (Code Sec. 408A(f), as added by the 1998 Act). Thus, contributions to an SEP or SIMPLE IRA will not affect the amount that an individual can contribute to a Roth IRA.

★ *Effective date.* This provision is effective for tax years beginning after December 31, 1997 (Act Sec. 6024 of the IRS Restructuring and Reform Act of 1998; Act Sec. 302(f) of the Taxpayer Relief Act of 1997 (P.L. 105-34)).

Act Sec. 6005(b)(1), amending Code Sec. 408A(c)(3)(A). Act Sec. 6005(b)(8)(B), amending Code Sec. 4973(b). Act Sec. 6005(b)(9), adding Code Sec. 408A(f). Law at ¶ 5370 and 5940. Committee Report at ¶ 10,880.

INDIVIDUAL RETIREMENT ARRANGEMENTS
Deductible IRA Contribution Limits
¶ 356

Background———————————————————————————

The generally applicable $2,000 limit on deductible IRA contributions is phased out over graduated levels of adjusted gross income for married individuals (filing jointly) who are active participants in an employer-sponsored retirement plan. For 1998, the phase-out range for joint filers is $50,000—$60,000 of AGI (Code Sec. 219(g)(3)(B), as amended by the Taxpayer Relief Act of 1997 (P.L. 105-34)).

Under pre-1998 law, an individual was treated as an active participant in an employer-sponsored plan if his or her spouse was an active participant. However, beginning in the 1998 tax year, an individual is not considered to be an active participant in an employer-sponsored retirement plan merely because the individual's spouse is an active participant (Code Sec. 219(g)(1), as amended by the Taxpayer Relief Act of 1997 (P.L. 105-34)). The $2,000 maximum deductible IRA contribution for an individual who is not an active participant, but whose spouse is, is phased out for taxpayers with AGI between $150,000—$160,000 (Code Sec. 219(g)(7), as amended by the Taxpayer Relief Act of 1997 (P.L. 105-34)

Technical Corrections Impact

Deductible IRA contribution limits for active participants in employer-sponsored retirement plans.—The IRS Restructuring and Reform Act of 1998 makes clear that the phased out dollar limitation for deductible IRA contributions applies whether a married individual or the individual's spouse is an active participant in an employer-sponsored retirement plan (Code Sec. 219(g)(1), as amended by the 1998 Act). However, the 1998 Act further states that, if the phase-out rule applies to an individual merely because his or her spouse is an active participant in an employer-sponsored plan, the $2,000 maximum deductible IRA contribution for the individual, but not for the active participant spouse, will be phased out at AGI between $150,000 and $160,000 (jointly computed) (Code Sec. 219(g)(7), as amended by the 1998 Act). Thus, individuals who are married to active participants, but who are not active participants themselves, are not subject to the maximum deductible IRA contribution phase-out range of $50,000—$60,000 of AGI that is applicable to married active participants in 1998.

Example (1). Barney is covered by a 401(k) plan sponsored by his employer. His wife, Betty, is not employed. The couple files a joint income tax return for 1998, reporting adjusted gross income of $120,000. Betty may make a deductible IRA contribution to an IRA for the year because she is not an active participant in an employer-sponsored retirement plan and the combined AGI of the couple is below $150,000. Barney, however, may not make a deductible IRA contribution because the combined AGI of the couple is outside the threshold range for active participants who are married and filing jointly ($50,000—$60,000 in 1998).

Example (2). Assume the same facts as in Example (1), except that the couple's AGI was $200,000 for 1998. Neither Barney nor Betty would be able to make a deductible IRA contribution.

Example (3). Betty is employed, earns $38,000 a year, and is covered by her employer's 401(k) plan. Betty and Barney file a joint return for 1998, reporting combined AGI of $75,000. Because Betty is an active participant in an employer-sponsored plan and the couple's AGI exceeds the applicable $50,000—$60,000 phase-out range, she is not able to make a deductible IRA contribution.

★ *Effective date.* The provisions are effective for tax years beginning after December 31, 1997 (Act Sec. 6024 of the IRS Restructuring and Reform Act of 1998; Act Sec. 301(c) of the Taxpayer Relief Act of 1997 (P.L. 105-34)).

Act Sec. 6005(a), amending Code Sec. 219(g)(1) and (7). Law at ¶ 5240. Committee Report at ¶ 10,875.

Eligible Rollover Distributions

¶ 361

Background

Generally, distributions received by an IRA owner before he or she attains age 59½ are subject to a ten-percent penalty tax. However, in addition to other exceptions enumerated in Code Sec. 72(t), the ten-percent early withdrawal tax, effective for distributions occurring after 1997, does not apply to IRA distributions used to pay stipulated qualified higher education expenses or expenses (up to $10,000) incurred by qualified first-time home buyers (Code Secs. 72(t)(2)(E) and (F), as added by the Taxpayer Relief Act of 1997 (P.L. 105-34)).

The exceptions from the penalty tax for early distributions from an IRA to pay for higher education expenses and first-time home buyer expenses do not apply to distributions, including hardship distributions, from employer-sponsored retirement plans. However, certain "eligible rollover distributions," including hardship distributions from a 401(k) or 403(b) plan, may be rolled over to an IRA. Accordingly, under prior law, participants in 401(k) or 403(b) plans could effectively avoid the ten-percent early withdrawal tax by rolling over hardship distributions to an IRA and withdrawing the funds from the IRA pursuant to the authorized exemptions under Code Sec. 72(t). In addition, by rolling over the distributions, the participants could avoid the 20-percent withholding rule that generally applies to eligible rollover distributions that are not rolled over directly to an IRA or another retirement plan.

Technical Corrections Impact

Hardship 401(k) or 403(b) distributions are not eligible rollover distributions.—The IRS Restructuring and Reform Act of 1998, effective for distributions occurring after 1998, provides that hardship distributions from a 401(k) or 403(b) plan are not eligible rollover distributions and, thus, may not be rolled over to any IRA (Code Secs. 402(c)(4) and 403(b)(8)(B), as amended by the 1998 Act) However, because the hardship distributions are not eligible rollover distributions, they will not be subject to the 20-percent withholding that is generally applicable to eligible rollover distributions that are not transferred directly to another retirement plan or an IRA.

Planning Note. A hardship distribution from a 401(k) plan may not be made unless it is necessary to meet an "immediate and heavy financial need" of the plan participant. Deemed hardship events include the purchase of the participant's principal residence (but not mortgage payments) and the payment of tuition, related fees, and room and board for the next 12 months of post-secondary education for the employee, the employee's spouse, children, or dependents. However, hardship distributions from a 401(k) plan to a participant who has not attained age 59½ remain subject to the ten-percent early distribution penalty unless an exception under Code Sec. 72(t) applies. Although 401(k) participants may no longer shield a distribution from tax by taking advantage of the exception provided for IRA owners who incur qualified higher education or first-time home buyer expenses, the distribution may be exempt from tax under Code Sec. 72(t) if, among other stipulated exceptions, it is: (1) made to a beneficiary on or after the employee's death; (2) attributable to the employee's disability; (3) part of series of substantially equal periodic payments made not less frequently than annually over the life of the employee or the joint lives of the employee and a designated beneficiary; (4) made to an employee who retires after reaching age 55; or (5) less than medical expense deductions.

Planning Note. In addition, 401(k) plan participants looking to purchase a home should, prior to electing a hardship distribution, investigate whether the plan authorizes loans. Loans from 401(k) plans must be repaid to the plan, but are not subject to the early withdrawal tax.

★ *Effective date.* The provision is effective for distributions occurring after December 31, 1998 (Act Sec. 6005(c)(2)(C) of the IRS Restructuring and Reform Act of 1998).

Act Sec. 6005(c)(2), adding Code Sec. 402(c)(4)(C) and amending Code Sec. 403(b)(8)(B). Law at ¶ 5330 and 5340. Committee Report at ¶ 10,895.

SIMPLE IRAs

Mergers or Acquisitions

¶ 366

Background —————————————————————————————————

An employer may maintain a SIMPLE IRA if it employed no more than 100 employees who received at least $5,000 in compensation for the preceding calendar year and if it does not currently maintain another qualified plan. However, employers who have maintained a SIMPLE plan for at least one year, but who fail to be eligible in subsequent years because they employ more than 100 eligible employees may continue to maintain the plan for the two calendar years following the last year in which the employer satisfied the 100-employee rule (Code Sec. 408(p)(2)(C)(i)(II), as added by the Small Business Job Protection Act of 1996 (P.L. 104-188)). If the employer employs more than 100 employees because of an acquisition, disposition, or similar transaction, the grace period will not apply unless rules similar to the coverage requirements of Code Sec. 410(b)(6)(C)(i) are met.

A SIMPLE IRA that is maintained by an employer for one or more years will also not immediately cease to be a qualified salary reduction arrangement if the employer, because of an acquisition, disposition, or similar transaction with another employer, maintains a qualified plan in the same year that the SIMPLE plan

Background

is maintained (Code Sec. 408(p)(2)(D)(iii), as amended by the Taxpayer Relief Act of 1997 (P.L. 105-34)). However, the authorized grace period allows the SIMPLE IRA to be treated as a qualified salary reduction arrangement only from the date of the transaction to the last day of the *first* plan year beginning after the date of the transaction.

Technical Corrections Impact

Maintaining a SIMPLE IRA following a merger or acquisition.—The IRS Restructuring and Reform Act of 1998 imposes a uniform grace period during which a SIMPLE IRA may be maintained following an acquisition, disposition, or similar transaction that affects an employer's capacity to meet the 100-employee limit, the exclusive plan requirement, or the coverage rules for participation. Specifically, the 1998 Act provides that, if an employer fails to meet the 100-employee limit, the exclusive plan requirement, or the participation rules because of an acquisition, disposition, or similar transaction, the SIMPLE IRA may be maintained as a qualified salary reduction arrangement during a "transition period" that begins on the date of the transaction and ends on the last day of the second calendar year following the calendar year in which the transaction occurs (Code Sec. 408(p)(10), as added by the 1998 Act).

In order for the grace period to apply, the employer must satisfy rules similar to the coverage requirements of Code Sec. 410(b)(6)(C)(i)(II), which generally provide that coverage under the plan not be significantly changed during the transition period. In addition, the SIMPLE IRA may not be maintained during the transition period unless it would have met the requirements applicable to qualified salary reduction arrangements after the transaction, if the employer maintaining the arrangement had remained a separate employer.

Caution. An employer may not use a merger or acquisition to shield an arrangement that could not have been maintained as a qualified salary reduction arrangement before the transaction.

Comment. Under prior law, the grace period applicable to an employer that failed to meet the exclusive plan requirement or the 100-employee restriction following a merger or acquisition was available only to employers that had maintained the SIMPLE IRA for one or more years. However, the express conditions of Code Sec. 408(p)(10) do not include the requirement that the employer have maintained the SIMPLE IRA for one or more years. In addition, the statutory provisions that contain the requirement that a SIMPLE plan have been maintained for one or more years in order for the grace period to apply no longer apply to mergers and acquisitions (Code Secs. 408(p)(2)(C)(i)(II) and 408(p)(2)(D)(iii), as amended by the 1998 Act). Thus, presumably, an employer that has maintained a SIMPLE IRA for a period of less than one year, may avail itself of the exception in the event of a merger or acquisition, as long as the stipulated statutory conditions are otherwise met.

Example. Company A employs 60 employees and maintains a SIMPLE IRA. Company B employs 80 employees and sponsors a qualified defined benefit pension plan. Following A's purchase of B on June 1, 1998, A may continue to maintain the SIMPLE IRA as a qualified salary reduction arrangement during the period from June 1, 1998 to December 31, 2000. The coverage under the SIMPLE IRA may not be significantly changed and only individuals who would have been employees of Company A had the transaction not occurred may be eligible to participate

¶ 366

★ *Effective date.* The provision is effective for tax years beginning after December 31, 1996 (Act Sec. 6024 of the IRS Restructuring and Reform Act of 1998; Act Sec. 1601(j) of the Taxpayer Relief Act of 1997 (P.L. 105-34); Act Sec. 1421(a) of the Small Business Job Protection Act (P.L. 104-188)).

Act Sec. 6016(a)(1)(B), adding Code Sec. 408(p)(10); Act Sec. 6016(a)(1)(C), amending Code Secs. 408(p)(2)(C)(i)(II) and 408(p)(2)(D)(iii). Law at ¶ 5360. Committee Report at ¶ 11,325.

Exclusive Plan Requirement

¶ 368

Background _____

An employer make not make contributions under a SIMPLE IRA for a calendar year if the employer, or a predecessor employer, maintains a qualified plan pursuant to which any of its employees receives an allocation of contributions (in the case of defined contribution plan) or has an increase in accrued benefits (in the case of a defined benefit plan) for a plan year beginning or ending in that calendar year. However, an employer may adopt a SIMPLE IRA for noncollectively bargained employees even if it also maintains a qualified plan for collectively bargained employees (Code Sec. 408(p)(2)(D)(i), as amended by the Taxpayer Relief Act of 1997 (P.L. 105-34)). Thus, the fact that an employer maintains a qualified plan in which only collectively bargained employees may participate will not prevent it from establishing a SIMPLE IRA in which only noncollectively bargained employees may participate.

Technical Corrections Impact

Plans for noncollectively bargained employees.—The IRS Restructuring and Reform Act of 1998 confirms that the exception to the single plan rule applies if the SIMPLE plan is maintained for employees who are not covered by a collective bargaining agreement. Prior law had provided that, if an employer maintained a qualified plan in which only employees who were not covered by a collective bargaining agreement between employers and airline pilots under the Railway Labor Act were allowed to participate, the employer could not sponsor a SIMPLE plan for which such employees were eligible. Under the 1998 Act, an employer who sponsors a qualified plan for collectively bargained employees may maintain a SIMPLE IRA for noncollectively bargained employees, including employees who are not covered by a collective bargaining agreement between employers and airline pilots under the Railway Labor Act (Code Sec. 408(p)(2)(D)(i), as amended by the 1998 Act).

★ *Effective date.* The provision is effective for tax years beginning after December 31, 1996 (Act Sec. 6024 of the IRS Restructuring and Reform Act of 1998; Act Sec. 1601 (j) of the Taxpayer Relief Act of 1997 (P.L. 105-34); Act Sec. 1421(a) of the Small Business Job Protection Act (P.L. 104-188)).

Act Sec. 6016(a)(1)(A), amending Code Sec. 408(p)(2)(D)(i). Law at ¶ 5360. Committee Report at ¶ 11,325.

Return of Excess Contributions

¶ 369

Background _____

Excess IRA contributions that are returned before the due date of the IRA holder's tax return for the year are not included in the taxpayer's income and are not subject either to the six-percent excise tax imposed on excess contributions or to the 10-percent penalty tax assessed on premature distributions. However, in order

Background

for a taxpayer to take advantage of these rules, no deduction may have been allowable or allowed under Code Sec. 219 for the excess contribution. The maximum deductible contribution to an IRA for 1998 is $2,000 per person.

For purposes of the return of excess contribution rules, Code Sec. 408(d)(7)(B) stipulates that contributions to a simplified employee pension plan that may be excluded from an employee's income are treated as amounts allowed or allowable as a deduction under Code Sec. 219, even though they exceed the $2,000 limit applicable to deductible IRA contributions. Under prior law, however, a comparable provision did not apply to SIMPLE IRA contributions.

Technical Corrections Impact

The IRS Restructuring and Reform Act of 1998 extends Code Sec. 408(d)(7)(B) to SIMPLE IRAs. Accordingly, in applying the rules governing the distribution of excess contributions and in determining whether the six-percent excise tax under Code Sec. 4973 applies, amounts contributed under a SIMPLE IRA that fall within the applicable limits ($6,000 per year) and, thus, may be excluded from an employee's income are treated as allowed or allowable as a deduction under Code Sec. 219, even though they exceed the $2,000 maximum deductible IRA contribution (Code Sec. 408(d)(7)(B), as amended by 1998 Act). Thus, a SIMPLE IRA contribution that may be excluded from an employee's income may not be included in a corrective distribution. However, a SIMPLE IRA contribution that exceeds the applicable limit and is not excludable from an employee's income may be included in a corrective distribution.

★ *Effective date.* The provision is effective for tax years beginning after December 31, 1996 (Act Sec. 6018(h) of the IRS Restructuring and Reform Act of 1998; Act Sec. 1421 of the Small Business Job Protection Act (P.L. 104-188)).

Act Sec. 6018(b), amending Code Sec. 408(d)(7). Law at ¶ 5360.

403(b) PLANS

Indian Tribal Governments

¶ 371

Background

Amounts from a Code Sec. 403(b) tax-sheltered annuity may not generally be rolled over to a 401(k) plan. However, amounts received under a 403(b) tax-sheltered annuity contract purchased before 1995 by an Indian tribal government may be rolled over to a 401(k) plan maintained by the Indian tribal government (Small Business Job Protection Act of 1996 (P.L. 104-188), Sec. 1450(b)(2)). The rollover may be made whether or not the annuity contract is terminated (Taxpayer Relief Act of 1997 (P.L. 105-34), Sec. 1601(d)(4)(A)).

Technical Corrections Impact

Rollover of 403(b)(7) custodial accounts to 401(k) plans.—The IRS Restructuring and Reform Act of 1998 clarifies that the existing grandfather exemption also allows an employee participating in a 403(b)(7) custodial account of an Indian tribal government to roll over amounts from the account to a 401(k) plan maintained by the Indian tribal government (Taxpayer Relief Act of 1997 (P.L. 105-34), Sec. 1601(d)(4)(A), as amended by the 1998 Act).

¶ 371

Comment. Generally, amounts may be paid or made available from a custodial account only upon the occurrence of death, disability, attainment of age 59½, separation from service, or financial hardship.

Planning Note. With the exception of the grandfather rule for TSAs maintained by Indian tribal governments, TSA assets may only be transferred to another TSA or to an IRA. Thus, assets in 403(b) contracts purchased by employers, including Indian tribal governments after 1995, may not be rolled over to a 401(k) plan.

★ *Effective date.* The provision is effective as of August 20, 1996 (the effective date of Act Sec. 1450(b), Small Business Job Protection Act (P.L. 104-188)); (Act Sec. 6024, IRS Restructuring and Reform Act of 1998; Act Sec. 1601(d)(4) of the Taxpayer Relief Act of 1997 (P.L. 105-34)).

Act Sec. 6016(a)(2), amending Act Sec. 1601(d)(4)(A) of the Taxpayer Relief Act of 1997 (P.L. 105-34). Law at ¶ 8275. Committee Report at ¶ 11,330.

Chapter 4
Estate and Gift Tax

QUALIFIED FAMILY-OWNED BUSINESS DEDUCTION

Conversion of Exclusion to Deduction

¶ 401

Background

A provision for excluding the value of qualified family-owned business interests (QFOBIs) from the value of the gross estate was created for estates of decedents dying after December 31, 1997 (Code Sec. 2033A, prior to redesignation as Code Sec. 2057 by the IRS Restructuring and Reform Act of 1998). The maximum QFOBI exclusion in combination with the applicable exclusion amount shields a maximum of $1,300,000 from the estate tax. It is unclear whether the provision, as originally written, provides an exclusion of property or an exclusion of value from the estate. If the provision excludes property, the estate tax value of any remaining QFOBIs includible in the gross estate would be unaffected by the exclusion and the excluded QFOBI would not qualify for the marital deduction. On the other hand, if the provision provides an exclusion of value only, it could be argued that the estate tax value of a QFOBI included in the gross estate is reduced by its pro-rata share of the QFOBI exclusion. Therefore, it is not apparent how Code Sec. 2033A interacts with Code Sec. 1014 (basis of property acquired from a decedent), Code Sec. 2032A (special use valuation), Code Sec. 2056 (marital deduction), Code Sec. 2612 (GST taxable terminations, taxable distributions and direct skips), and Code Sec. 6166 (installment payments).

Technical Corrections Impact

QFOBI deduction clarified.—The qualified family-owned business exclusion is converted into a deduction and Code Sec. 2033A is redesignated as Code Sec. 2057 (Act Sec. 6007(b)(1)(A) of the IRS Restructuring and Reform Act of 1998). The ownership and material-participation requirements that must be met in order to be eligible for the qualified family-owned business deduction remain the same as they had been for the Code Sec. 2033A exclusion (Code Sec. 2057(b)(1) and Code Sec. 2057(b)(2), as redesignated by the 1998 Act). Code Sec. 2057 also clarifies that the deduction applies only for estate tax purposes. The deduction is not available for gift tax or generation-skipping transfer tax purposes (Code Sec. 2057(a)(1), as redesignated and amended by the 1998 Act).

Election. The general election and related recapture agreement requirements that pertained to the prior Code Sec. 2033A exclusion remain unchanged for the Code Sec. 2057 deduction (Code Sec. 2057(b)(1)(B) and Code Sec. 2057(h), as redesignated by the 1998 Act).

PRACTICAL ANALYSIS. Arthur D. Sederbaum, of Patterson, Belknap, Webb & Tyler LLP, New York, NY, comments that the qualified family-owned business provisions, enacted as Code Sec. 2033A by the 1997 Act, were criticized on several grounds. First, since the family-owned business provisions were providing an exclusion from estate taxes, it was unclear how the new provisions interacted with other Code sections. Would the excluded business interest qualify for date-of-death basis under Code Sec. 1014 as property acquired from a decedent? Would the interest qualify for the marital deduction under Code Sec. 2056 as passing to the decedent's spouse? Would the interest affect the percentage requirements for the inclusion of a closely-held business in the decedent's gross estate so that the estate qualified for the fifteen-year extension of time to pay estate tax provisions under Code Sec. 6166? These questions are answered in the 1998 Act by converting the qualified family-owned business exclusion into a deduction and redesignating Code Sec. 2033A as Code Sec. 2057. By classifying the family-owned business interest as a deduction, the decedent's estate is benefited, since the value of the closely-held business is being subtracted from the gross estate at the highest marginal estate tax rate.

A second criticism arose from the interaction of the family-owned business exclusion with the increase in the unified credit from an exemption equivalent of $600,000 in 1997 to $1,000,000 in 2006. The 1997 Act provided that the exclusion was only applicable to the extent that the amount covered by the exclusion plus the amount effectively exempted by the unified credit would not exceed $1,300,000. Therefore, as the unified credit amount increased from 1998 through 2006 and the family-owned business exclusion was likewise decreasing, the total estate tax impact on estates that qualified for the family-owned business exclusion was actually increasing. This was due to the fact that the corresponding increase in the unified credit created a benefit at the decedent's lowest estate tax bracket, while the decrease of the amount eligible for the family-owned business exclusion meant that less of a value was being eliminated from the decedent's highest estate tax bracket.

The 1998 Act rectifies this situation by giving the executor an election opportunity. If the executor so elects, the estate would be entitled to a maximum qualified family-owned business deduction of $675,000 and an "applicable exclusion amount" (the term introduced by the 1998 Act signifying the exemption equivalent) of $625,000, for total of $1.3 million, regardless of the year of the decedent's death. If a decedent's estate includes qualified family-owned business interests with a value of at least $675,000, the qualified family-owned business deduction thereby becomes more attractive, since it is removing a maximum amount from the decedent's highest estate tax bracket that could be as high as 55 percent. Thus, in 2006, this election will result in an effective estate tax savings of $62,500. The savings result from the election of $675,000 to qualify for the family-owned business deduction beginning in 2006 instead of $300,000, and this increase of $375,000 could be deducted at the highest estate tax bracket of 55 percent for a savings of $206,250. The savings is offset by the fact that the applicable exclusion amount is reduced from $1 million to $625,000, causing a corresponding increase in estate taxes of $143,750. The difference is the $62,500 saved. The total savings for decedents dying between 1997 and 2006 is less, since under the 1997 legislation more of the family-owned business exclusion was available in those earlier years.

If a recapture event occurs with respect to any qualified family-owned business interest, the total amount of estate taxes potentially subject to recapture is calculated as the difference between the actual amount of estate tax liability for the estate, and the amount of estate taxes that would have been owed had the qualified family-owned business election not been made.

Although the 1998 changes address several of the major criticisms of the original legislation, the tax advisor must still weigh the perceived benefits of the qualified family-owned business deduction against many of the complicated rules for eligibility and recapture which still exist.

★ *Effective date.* The qualified family-owned business deduction is effective for the estates of decedents dying after December 31, 1997 (Act Sec. 6024 of the IRS Restructuring and Reform Act of 1998; Act Sec. 502(c) of the Taxpayer Relief Act of 1997 (P.L. 105-34)).

Act Sec. 6007(b)(1)(A), redesignating Code Sec. 2033A as Code Sec. 2057; Act Sec. 6007(b)(1)(B), amending redesignated Code Sec. 2057(a); Act Sec. 6007(b)(1)(C), amending redesignated Code Sec. 2057(b)(2)(A); and Act Sec. 6007(b)(1)(D), amending redesignated Code Sec. 2057(c). Law at ¶ 5770. Committee Report at ¶ 10,975.

Coordination With Unified Credit

¶ 406

Background

The unified credit against federal estate and gift taxes is scheduled to increase in the years 1998 through 2006 (Code Sec. 2010(c), as added by the Taxpayer Relief Act of 1997 (P.L. 105-34)). The amount of the unified credit in effect for any particular year is referred to as the "applicable credit amount." In turn, the applicable credit amount protects a certain amount of property (referred to as the "applicable exclusion amount") from estate or gift taxes. The applicable exclusion amount will increase from $625,000 in 1998 to $1 million in 2006.

In addition to the applicable exclusion amount, the 1997 Act provided an exclusion from a decedent's gross estate for certain qualified family-owned business interests (QFOBIs) (Code Sec. 2033A, prior to redesignation as Code Sec. 2057 by the IRS Restructuring and Reform Act of 1998). The maximum QFOBI exclusion provided under the 1997 Act is equal to the excess of $1,300,000 over the applicable exclusion amount in effect for the year of the decedent's death. Thus, when combined with the applicable exclusion amount, up to $1.3 million of the value of qualified family-owned business interests (QFOBIs) can be passed free of the estate tax. However, the 1997 Act also provided that the maximum exclusion amount for QFOBIs decreases proportionately as the applicable exclusion amount increases from $625,000 in 1998 to $1,000,000 in 2006. This results in the possibility that an estate electing the exclusion for QFOBIs could pay a greater amount of estate tax if the decedent died in 2006 versus what would have been paid on the same size estate in 1998. This anomaly occurs because the applicable exclusion amount is directly related to the applicable credit amount, the impact of which is felt at the lowest estate tax rates. On the other hand, the QFOBI exclusion reduces the taxable estate at the decedent's highest marginal estate tax rates.

Technical Corrections Impact

Adjustments to applicable exclusion amount.—In valuing the taxable estate, an estate may elect to deduct up to $675,000 of qualified family-owned business interests (QFOBIs) from the gross estate. If the maximum $675,000 QFOBI deduction is taken, the applicable exclusion amount under Code Sec. 2010 is limited to $625,000, regardless of the date of death. In order to coordinate the deduction with the unified credit, if the QFOBI deduction is less than $675,000, the $625,000 applicable exclusion amount is increased by the excess of $675,000 over the amount of the QFOBI deduction allowed. However, the applicable exclusion amount may not be increased above the amount that would apply to the estate if no QFOBI deduction had been elected (Code Sec. 2057(a), as redesignated and amended by the IRS Restructuring and Reform Act of 1998). Therefore, a maximum of $1.3 million in family-owned business assets may be shielded from the estate tax by the QFOBI deduction in combination with the applicable exclusion amount.

Comment. Since the applicable credit amount (unified credit) is the amount of the tentative estate tax on the applicable exclusion amount, the unified credit for an estate that takes a QFOBI deduction will have to be calculated separately in order to determine the estate tax liability. The unified credit will vary from estate to estate, depending on the amount of the QFOBI deduction. Accordingly, the applicable credit amount for an estate claiming the QFOBI deduction will not be obtainable from the Code or from tax reference material.

Example (1). Pam Rich dies in 1999 when the Code Sec. 2010 applicable exclusion amount is $650,000. Rich's estate includes $1,400,000 of QFOBIs and her estate elects to take the maximum $675,000 deduction. Rich's estate is entitled to a Code Sec. 2057 deduction of $675,000 and an applicable exclusion amount of $625,000, thereby shielding a maximum of $1.3 million QFOB assets from the estate tax.

Example (2). Adam Brook dies in 2002 when the Code Sec. 2010 applicable exclusion amount is $700,000. Brook's $1,400,000 estate includes $600,000 of QFOBIs and his estate qualifies for and elects to take a $600,000 deduction. Brook's estate will be entitled to a Code Sec. 2057 deduction of $600,000 and an applicable exclusion amount of $700,000 ($625,000 + ($675,000 − $600,000)). Again, the estate is able to shield a maximum of $1.3 million of estate assets from the estate tax.

Example (3). Ruth Roth dies in 2000 when the Code Sec. 2010 applicable exclusion amount is $675,000. Roth's $1,300,000 estate includes $500,000 of QFOBIs and her estate qualifies for and elects a $500,000 deduction. Roth's estate will be entitled to a Code Sec. 2057 deduction of $500,000 and an applicable exclusion amount of $675,000. The applicable exclusion amount under Code Sec. 2010 cannot exceed the amount which would apply to the

¶ 406

estate without regard to Code Sec. 2057. Only $1.175 million of estate assets will be shielded from the estate tax because of the limited QFOBI deduction.

Additional estate tax.—The 1998 Act also clarifies the amount of additional estate tax imposed if a recapture event occurs with respect to a QFOBI by removing a cross-reference to Code Sec. 2032A and adding a descriptive formula. The total amount of tax potentially subject to recapture is the difference between the actual amount of estate tax liability for the estate and the amount of estate tax that would have been owed had the qualified family-owned business deduction not been taken (Code Sec. 2057(f)(2), as redesignated and amended by the 1998 Act).

> **Example (4).** Nate Worth's estate includes $800,000 of QFOBIs and the estate elected to take a $675,000 QFOBI deduction. The estate tax liability paid was $578,750. The estate tax would have been $916,500 if the QFOBI deduction had not been taken. Slim Worth, the decedent's son, inherited the entire estate and disposed of $100,000 of the QFOBI property three years after his father's death. The additional tax of $42,219 plus interest is calculated as follows. The "adjusted tax difference with respect to the estate" is $337,750 ($916,500 − $578,750). Because the recapture event occurred within the third year of Slim's material participation, the additional tax is 100 percent of the "adjusted tax difference attributable to the qualified family-owned business interest" disposed of plus interest. That is, 100 percent of the amount ($42,219) that bears the same ratio to the "adjusted tax difference with respect to the estate" ($337,750) as the value of such QFOBI interest disposed of ($100,000) bears to the value of all of the QFOBI interests ($800,000) or ($337,750 × ($100,000 ÷ $800,000) = $42,219 additional tax (plus interest)).

PRACTICAL ANALYSIS. Sanford J. Schlesinger, chair of Kaye, Scholer, Fierman, Hays & Handler, LLP's Wills and Estates Dept., New York, New York, observes that the provision converts the qualified family-owned business exclusion into a deduction and redesignates Code Sec. 2033A as Code Sec. 2057. Under the 1997 legislation, during the period of the increasing unified credit, the amount which could be excluded as a qualified family-owned business interest was automatically reduced to the extent that the applicable exclusion amount increased in phases between 1998 and 2006. Since the applicable exclusion amount by definition saves taxes at the lowest rates, and the qualified family-owned business exclusion in effect saved taxes at the highest otherwise applicable rates, an increase in the applicable exclusion amount did not "compensate" for a corresponding reduction in the same amount of the qualified business exclusion.

To address this inequity between taxpayers otherwise in the same circumstances who die in different years during the phase-in of the applicable exclusion amount, the new legislation fixes the applicable exclusion amount at $625,000 (the amount generally applicable in 1998) regardless of the year of death, increased by the excess of the maximum potential qualified family-owned business deduction over the amount of the deduction actually taken (provided that such increased amount is limited to the otherwise applicable exclusion amount for the year in question, i.e., $650,000 in 1999, $675,000 in 2000 and $1,000,000 in 2006).

The maximum potential qualified family-owned business deduction is set at $675,000. This correction effectively treats taxpayers who die in any year in the same manner with respect to the family-owned business deduction regardless of changes from year to year in the applicable exclusion amount. However, the qualified family-owned business deduction, like the exclusion which it replaces, continues to be of a potentially greater benefit to larger taxable estates because such deduction will effectively shield assets of the estate where the otherwise applicable estate tax rates would be higher.

Schlesinger notes that although the potential qualified family-owned business deduction is an amount up to $675,000, an election should be made to take such deduction only to the extent that such assets cannot otherwise be covered by the applicable exclusion amount. For example, if an estate consisted solely of assets which could be qualified for the family-owned business deduction having a total value of $675,000 in 1998 when the applicable exclusion amount is $625,000, it is only desirable to take a qualified family-owned business deduction of $50,000. Although a deduction of up to $675,000 would be permissible, the qualified family-owned business deduction restricts the use of the assets for a ten year period and exposes the assets to taxation in the event that such restrictions are violated. Conversely, assets which are shielded from tax by reason of the applicable exclusion amount are not subject to restrictions or subsequent tax recapture.

On the other hand, it should always be tax efficient to elect assets for the qualified family-owned business deduction if such assets cannot otherwise be shielded from tax by the applicable exclusion amount. For example, if an estate has $3,675,000 of assets in the year 2006 and $675,000 could be made to qualify for the family-owned business deduction, it is tax efficient to elect the full $675,000. This will save the estate 55% of $675,000, or $371,250, because the deduction is applied to assets otherwise subject to the highest estate tax rate, i.e. 55%. However, this election will cause the applicable exclusion amount to be limited to $625,000, rather than $1,000,000 as will be available in 2006 if the election is not taken. Thus, the "tax cost" of the election resulting from the reduction in the applicable exclusion amount is $143,750 (the additional tax resulting from the loss of a credit applicable to $675,000 of assets subject to tax at progressive rates ranging from 37% to 39%). Thus, the net savings of electing the full amount of the qualified family-owned business deduction in this example would be $227,500 (the gross tax savings of $371,250 less the associated tax cost of $143,750).

Schlesinger notes, however, that a reduction in the federal taxable estate by reason of a qualified family-owned business deduction will also reduce the maximum amount of federal credit for state death tax paid. If the state in question is not a "sop tax" state, the impact of this should be considered, especially if the state does not conform to the federal definition of the taxable estate.

★ *Effective date.* The coordination of the unified credit with the qualified family-owned business deduction and the additional estate tax formula are effective for the estates of decedents dying after December 31, 1997 (Act Sec. 6024 of the IRS Restructuring and Reform Act of 1998; Act Sec. 502(c) of the Taxpayer Relief Act of 1997 (P.L. 105-34)).

Act Sec. 6007(b)(1)(B), amending redesignated Code Sec. 2057(a). Act Sec. 6007(b)(4), amending redesignated Code Sec. 2057(f)(2). Law at ¶ 5770. Committee Report at ¶ 10,980.

Businesses Eligible
¶ 411

Background

In general, under Code Sec. 2033A(b), prior to redesignation as Code Sec. 2057(b) by the IRS Restructuring and Reform Act of 1998, more than 50 percent of a decedent's adjusted gross estate must consist of qualified family-owned business interests (QFOBIs) in order to exclude a portion of the value of such interests from the gross estate. To qualify, the sum of (1) the adjusted value of the QFOBIs includible in the decedent's gross estate, plus (2) the adjusted value of gifts of such interests to the decedent's family members that are not includible in the gross estate, must exceed 50 percent of the decedent's adjusted gross estate.

Technical Corrections Impact

Definition of includible gifts clarified.—In addition to changing the qualified family-owned business exclusion to a deduction (see ¶ 401), the IRS Restructuring and Reform Act of 1998 clarifies the formula used to determine gifts of QFOBIs that are includible in the definition of the decedent's "adjusted gross estate" for purposes of determining whether the estate meets the 50-percent requirement by removing redundant language (Code Sec. 2057(b)(3), as redesignated and amended by the 1998 Act). Prior to the amendment, includible gifts were defined as *the excess of* the sum of (1) the amount of QFOBI gifts to members of the decedent's family taken into account as adjusted taxable gifts, plus (2) the amount of QFOBI gifts to members of the decedent's family otherwise excluded under the annual gift exclusion, *over the amount of such gifts otherwise included in the gross estate.* As amended, the includible gifts are defined as the sum of (1) and (2) above.

★ *Effective date.* This provision is effective for the estates of decedents dying after December 31, 1997 (Act Sec. 6024 of the IRS Restructuring and Reform Act of 1998; Act Sec. 502(c) of the Taxpayer Relief Act of 1997 (P.L. 105-34)).

Act Sec. 6007(b)(2), amending redesignated Code Sec. 2057(b)(3). Law at ¶ 5770. Committee Report at ¶ 10,985.

Transfers in Trust
¶ 416

Background

The qualified family-owned business provision applies only to qualified family-owned business interests (QFOBIs) acquired by, or passing to, a qualified heir from the decedent (Code Sec. 2033A(b)(2), prior to redesignation as Code Sec. 2057(b)(2) by the IRS Restructuring and Reform Act of 1998). Members of the decedent's family and individuals employed by a trade or business for at least 10 years prior to the date of the decedent's death are considered qualified heirs (Code Sec. 2033A(i)(1), prior to redesignation as Code Sec. 2057(i)(1) by the 1998 Act). It is unclear from the statutory language, as originally enacted by the Taxpayer Relief Act of 1997 (P.L. 105-34), whether QFOBIs passing to a qualified heir in a trust satisfy the "passing to" requirement.

Technical Corrections Impact

Qualified heir clarified.—The IRS Restructuring and Reform Act of 1998 clarifies that, if all the beneficiaries of a trust are qualified heirs, property passing to the trust may be treated as having passed to a qualified heir (Code Sec. 2057(i)(3)(L), as added by the 1998 Act). The 1998 Act accomplishes this by adding a cross reference to Code Sec. 2032A(g) (concerning the application of the special use valuation provisions to interests in partnerships, corporations, and trusts).

Comment. The Senate Committee Report indicates that the IRS may designate other circumstances under which trust beneficiaries are qualified heirs.

★ *Effective date.* This provision is effective for the estates of decedents dying after December 31, 1997 (Act Sec. 6024 of the IRS Restructuring and Reform Act of 1998; Act Sec. 502(c) of the Taxpayer Relief Act of 1997 (P.L. 105-34)).

Act Sec. 6007(b)(7), amending redesignated Code Sec. 2057(i)(3). Law at ¶ 5770. Committee Report at ¶ 11,015.

Trade or Business Requirement

¶ 421

Background

There is a trade or business requirement and a material-participation requirement that must be met in order to qualify for relief from estate tax under the family-owned business provision (Code Sec. 2033A(e) and Code Sec. 2033A(f), prior to redesignation as Code Sec. 2057(e) and Code Sec. 2057(f) by the IRS Restructuring and Reform Act of 1998). A qualified family-owned business interest (QFOBI) is defined as an interest in a trade or business that meets certain requirements. A certain percentage of the trade or business must be owned by the decedent and members of his or her family. In addition, the decedent or members of the decedent's family must have materially participated in the trade or business for five of the eight years preceding the decedent's death. Further, a qualified heir or member of the decedent's family must materially participate in the trade or business for at least five years of any eight-year period within 10 years following the decedent's death. However, the statutory language, as originally enacted in the Taxpayer Relief Act of 1997 (P.L. 105-34), does not make it clear whether the decedent must have personally materially participated in the trade or business or whether participation in the trade or business by the decedent's family members can be attributed to the decedent for purposes of satisfying the trade or business requirement. The same lack of clarity also exists with respect to a qualified heir during the 10-year recapture period.

Technical Corrections Impact

Trade and business requirement clarified.—Statutory language has been added to clarify that a decedent is treated as engaged in a trade or business if any member of his or her family is engaged in the trade or business (Code Sec. 2057(e)(1), as redesignated and amended by the IRS Restructuring and Reform Act of 1998). In addition, with respect to the recapture tax, a qualified heir will not be treated as disposing of an interest in a trade or business by reason of ceasing to be engaged in a trade or business if any member of the qualified heir's family continues in the trade or business (Code Sec. 2057(f)(3), as redesignated and amended by the 1998 Act).

Example (1). Sue Farmer dies owning a farm that she had cash-leased to her son Joe for the last eight years of her life. Joe has materially participated in the farming operation for the entire eight years. The Code Sec. 2057 pre-death material-participation requirement and the trade or business require-ment have been satisfied with respect to the decedent's interest in the farm by reason of her son's satisfaction of these requirements.

Example (2). Jane and Joe Farmer, brother and sister, each inherit a one-half interest in the farm in *Example (1)* from their mother. Jane cash-leases her QFOBI to Joe who is engaged in the trade or business of farming and he continues to operate the farm for the 10 years following their mother's death. Both Jane and Joe have satisfied the trade or business requirement and Jane will not be treated as having disposed of her QFOBI for purposes of the recapture tax.

★ *Effective date.* These provisions are effective for the estates of decedents dying after December 31, 1997 (Act Sec. 6024 of the IRS Restructuring and Reform Act of 1998; Act Sec. 502(c) of the Taxpayer Relief Act of 1997 (P.L. 105-34)).

Act Sec. 6007(b)(5), amending redesignated Code Sec. 2057(e)(1) and adding Code Sec. 2057(f)(3). Law at ¶ 5770. Committee Report at ¶ 10,995.

Additional Modifications to Qualified Family-Owned Business Rules

¶ 426

Background

Certain types of business interests are not eligible for estate tax relief as qualified family-owned business interests (QFOBIs). For example, the definition of a QFOBI excludes any interest in a trade or business if more than 35 percent of the adjusted ordinary gross income of the trade or business for the tax year which includes the decedent's death would qualify as personal holding company rental type income (Code Sec. 2033A(e)(2)(C), prior to redesignation as Code Sec. 2057(e)(2)(C) by the IRS Restructuring and Reform Act of 1998). Also excluded from the definition of a QFOBI is that portion of an interest in a trade or business attributable to any other assets which produce, or are held for the production of, personal holding company rental type income (Code Sec. 2033A(e)(2)(D), prior to redesignation as Code Sec. 2057(e)(2)(D) by the 1998 Act). These exceptions do not apply to banks or domestic savings and loan associations.

In addition, the QFOBI provisions incorporate by cross-reference many provi-sions from the Code Sec. 2032A special use valuation rules and the Code Sec. 543(a) personal holding company rules. However, no cross-references were provided by the Taxpayer Relief Act of 1997 (P.L. 105-34) to the Code Sec. 2032A(h) provision on involuntary conversions (as defined in Code Sec. 1033) nor to the Code Sec. 2032A(i) provision on like-kind exchanges (see Code Sec. 1031), as they relate to exceptions to imposition of the recapture tax.

Technical Corrections Impact

Rental type income clarified.—The technical corrections clarify that, in determining whether assets produce personal holding company rental type income, Code Sec. 543(a) is applied without regard to Code Sec. 543(a)(2)(B) (Code Sec. 2057(e)(2)(C) and Code Sec. 2057(e)(2)(D), as redesignated and amended by the IRS Restructuring and Reform Act of 1998). Therefore, rental income is not personal holding company income as defined in Code Sec. 543(a)(2) if the adjusted income for rent constitutes 50 percent or more of the adjusted ordinary income. The additional Code Sec. 543(a)(2)(B) rental exception requirement, that dividends for the tax year equal or exceed the amount, if any, by which personal holding company income for the taxable year exceeds 10 percent of the ordinary gross income, does not apply for purposes of Code Sec. 2057.

The effect of a cash lease by a decedent to a family member has also been clarified. An interest in property will not be disqualified, in whole or in part, as an interest in a qualified family-owned business where the decedent leases the interest on a net cash basis to a family member who uses the leased property in an active business. The decedent's interest in the property will qualify for the family-owned business deduction (Code Sec. 2057(e)(2), as redesignated and amended by the 1998 Act). In addition, the rental income derived by the decedent from such a net cash lease is not treated as personal holding company income for purposes of Code Sec. 2057.

Noncitizen spouses.—The provision regarding the security requirements for noncitizen spouses has been modified by deleting an inappropriate cross reference relating to the acceleration of payments under Code Sec. 6166(g)(1) (Code Sec. 2057(g), as redesignated and amended by the 1998 Act).

Recapture rules clarified.—Rules similar to the special use valuation rules in Code Sec. 2032A(h) and Code Sec. 2032A(i), regarding involuntary conversions and like-kind exchanges, respectively, are made applicable to Code Sec. 2057 family-owned business interests (Code Sec. 2057(i)(3)(M), as redesignated and added by the 1998 Act). These rules generally provide exceptions to the imposition of the recapture tax if there is an involuntary conversion or like-kind exchange of QFOBI property.

★ *Effective date.* These provisions are effective for the estates of decedents dying after December 31, 1997 (Act Sec. 6024 of the IRS Restructuring and Reform Act of 1998; Act Sec. 502(c) of the Taxpayer Relief Act of 1997 (P.L. 105-34)).

Act Sec. 6007(b)(3), Act Sec. 6007(b)(6), and Act Sec. 6007(b)(7), amending redesignated **Code Sec. 2057(e)(2), Code Sec. 2057(g)(1), and Code Sec. 2057(i)(3). Law at ¶ 5770. Committee Report at ¶ 10,990.**

GENERATION-SKIPPING TRANSFER TAX

Indexing of Generation-Skipping Transfer Tax Exemption

¶ 431

Background———————————————————————

The generation-skipping transfer (GST) tax is applied to three basic types of transfers (direct skips, taxable terminations, and taxable distributions). The amount of the GST tax is the taxable amount multiplied by the "applicable rate" (Code Sec. 2602). The applicable rate is the maximum federal estate tax rate in effect on the date of the transfer multiplied by the "inclusion ratio" (Code Sec. 2641). The inclusion ratio is the proportion of the taxable amount not offset by the $1 million GST exemption, calculated as the excess of "1" over the "applicable fraction." The numerator of the applicable fraction is the amount of the GST exemption allocated to the trust or outright transfer. The denominator is the value of the property transferred outright or in trust, reduced by (1) any federal estate tax and state death tax actually recovered from the property and (2) any charitable deduction allowed with respect to such property (Code Sec. 2642). Generally, under Code Sec. 2632, an allocation of the GST exemption with respect to an individual may be made at any time on or before the due date, including extensions, for filing that individual's estate tax return.

The Taxpayer Relief Act of 1997 (P.L. 105-34) provided that the $1 million GST tax exemption would be indexed for inflation for decedents dying and gifts made after December 31, 1998 (Act Sec. 501(d) of the 1997 Act). The 1997 Act also did not specifically indicate whether the inflation adjustment was applicable to all types of GST transfers (direct skips, taxable terminations, and taxable

Background
distributions), nor did it indicate the effect of the adjustment on the allocation of any additional GST exemption to an existing trust.

Technical Corrections Impact

Indexing of GST exemption clarified.—The IRS Restructuring and Reform Act of 1998 clarifies that indexing of the GST exemption is applicable to direct skips, taxable terminations, and taxable distributions made after 1998 (Code Sec. 2631(c), as amended by the 1998 Act).

Comment. According to the Senate Committee Report, for purposes of allocating the GST exemption to an existing trust, transferors are permitted to make a late allocation of any additional GST exemption resulting from the inflation adjustment pursuant to the current rules provided in Code Sec 2632 and Code Sec. 2642.

> **Example.** Al Carlyle transferred $2 million to a GST trust in 1995 and allocated his entire $1 million GST exemption to the trust, resulting in an inclusion ratio applicable to the trust of .50. Assume that by the year 2003 the inflation-adjusted amount of the GST exemption is $1,200,000 and the value of the trust assets has risen to $4 million. If Carlyle is still alive in 2003, he is allowed to make a late allocation of the additional $200,000 GST exemption that resulted from the inflation adjustment. Accordingly, the inclusion ratio applicable to the trust would then be $1 - (($2,000,000 + $200,000) \div $4,000,000) = .45$.

PRACTICAL ANALYSIS. Sanford J. Schlesinger, chair of Kaye, Scholer, Fierman, Hays & Handler, LLP's Wills and Estates Dept., New York, New York, emphasizes that the effect of the change is to allow taxpayers to utilize an increase in the exemption resulting from the indexing during life. Under prior law, the indexing applied only in the year of a decedent's death as the Code specifically referred to decedents dying after December 31, 1997, whereas the clarification applies to all generation-skipping transfers (direct skips, taxable terminations and taxable distributions) made after 1998.

★ *Effective date.* This provision is effective for generation-skipping transfers made after December 31, 1998 (Code Sec. 2631(c), as amended by Act Sec. 6007(a)(1) of the IRS Restructuring and Reform Act of 1998; Act Sec. 501(f) of the Taxpayer Relief Act of 1997 (P.L. 105-34), as amended by Act Sec. 6007(a)(2) of the 1998 Act).

Act Sec. 6007(a)(1), amending Code Sec. 2631(c). Act Sec. 6007(a)(2), amending Act Sec. 501(f) of P.L. 105-34. Law at ¶ 5790. Committee Report at ¶ 10,970.

Generation-Skipping Treatment of Revocable Trusts Limited

¶ 433

Background
The Taxpayer Relief Act of 1997 (P.L. 105-34) provided an election to treat a qualified revocable trust as part of a decedent's estate for federal income tax purposes (Code Sec. 646, prior to redesignation as Code Sec. 645 by the IRS Restructuring and Reform Act of 1998). The election is effective for two years from the date of the decedent's death, if no federal estate tax return is required to be

Background _____

filed, or six months after the final determination of estate tax liability, in a case in which a federal estate tax return is required. The election is irrevocable and must be made by *both* the trustee of the revocable trust and the executor of the decedent's estate, if any, by the due date for filing the estate's income tax return for its first tax year (including extensions). In order to be a qualified revocable trust, the trust must be one that was treated as owned by the decedent as a result of a power held by him or her. A trust treated as owned by the decedent solely because of a power held by a nonadverse party would not qualify. In addition to the aforementioned changes, in order to provide comparable treatment under the generation-skipping transfer (GST) tax, the 1997 Act also modified the definition of a trust for GST tax purposes.

Technical Corrections Impact

GST purposes limited.—A clarification limits the election to treat a revocable trust as part of a decedent's estate for GST purposes. Accordingly, the election is limited to the parameters of Code Sec. 2654(b), which allows portions of a trust attributable to transfers from different transferors or substantially separate and independent shares of different beneficiaries in a trust to be treated as separate trusts (Code Sec. 2652(b)(1) and Code Sec. 2654(b), as amended by the IRS Restructuring and Reform Act of 1998).

★ *Effective date.* This provision is effective for the estates of decedents dying after August 5, 1997 (Act Sec. 6024 of the IRS Restructuring and Reform Act of 1998; Act Sec. 1305(d) of the Taxpayer Relief Act of 1997 (P.L. 105-34)).

Act Sec. 6013(a), redesignating Code Sec. 646 as Code Sec. 645, and amending Code Sec. 2652(b)(1), and Code Sec. 2654(b). Law at ¶ 5450, ¶ 5800, and ¶ 5810. Committee Report at ¶ 11,275.

INSTALLMENT PAYMENTS

Interest Rate on Installment Payments of Estate Tax

¶ 436

Background _____

If various ownership and other tests are met, Code Sec. 6166 provides for the installment payment of federal estate taxes attributable to certain closely held business assets owned by a decedent at death. Generally, the installment payment election is available only if the entity owned by the decedent was actively engaged in a trade or business at the time of the decedent's death. However, an exception applies to certain holding company stock and non-readily-tradable business interests.

The Taxpayer Relief Act of 1997 (P.L. 105-34) lowered the interest rates applicable to deferred estate taxes and changed the computation for determining the portion of the estate taxes eligible for these rates. Under the 1997 Act, a special two-percent interest rate is applied to that portion of the deferred estate tax attributable to the first $1 million in *taxable* value of the decedent's closely held business (referred to as the "two-percent portion"). The interest rate applicable to that portion of the deferred estate tax attributable to the value of the closely held business in excess of the two-percent portion is 45 percent of the rate applicable to underpayments of tax. The 1997 Act also provided that the interest on deferred payments of estate tax is not deductible for income or estate tax purposes.

Technical Corrections Impact

Application of two-percent rate clarified.—A clarification of the application of the special two-percent interest rate on deferred payments of estate tax has been made. Specifically, the special two-percent interest rate is not available with respect to deferred estate tax payments on certain holding company stock and other non-readily-tradable business assets. In such cases, the applicable interest rate is 45 percent of the rate applicable to underpayments of tax. No deduction is allowed with respect to such interest payments for income or estate tax purposes (Code Sec. 6166(b)(7)(A)(iii) and Code Sec. 6166(b)(8)(A)(iii), as amended by the IRS Restructuring and Reform Act of 1998).

Comment. Prior to the Taxpayer Relief Act of 1997, the then-applicable four-percent rate on deferred payments of estate tax did not apply to such taxes payable on holding company stock or non-readily-tradable business assets. Because the 1997 Act provided for two special interest rates under Code Sec. 6601(j) instead of only one special rate, it was not sufficient to simply substitute the words "two-percent rate" for "four-percent rate" in Code Sec. 6166 in order to preserve this exception. The 1998 Act clarifies that while an estate is denied the "two-percent rate," it is eligible for the other special interest rate on the taxes payable on holding company stock or non-readily-tradable business assets.

★ *Effective date.* This provision is effective for the estates of decedents dying after December 31, 1997 (Act Sec. 6024 of the IRS Restructuring and Reform Act of 1988; Act Sec. 503(d) of the Taxpayer Relief Act of 1997 (P.L. 105-34)).

Act Sec. 6007(c), amending Code Sec. 6166(b)(7)(A)(iii) and Code Sec. 6166(b)(8)(A)(iii). Law at ¶ 6160. Committee Report at ¶ 11,020.

Tax Court Jurisdiction Over Installment Payment Eligibility

¶ 441

Background

A decedent's estate that is denied relief under Code Sec. 6166, pertaining to the installment payment of estate tax on closely held business assets, is entitled to seek a declaratory judgment before the U.S. Tax Court as to the estate's eligibility for installment payments. This provision (Code Sec. 7479, as added by the Taxpayer Relief Act of 1997 (P.L. 105-34)) applies to both the initial and continued eligibility for installment payment treatment.

Technical Corrections Impact

Tax Court jurisdiction clarified.—The Tax Court's jurisdiction to determine an estate's eligibility for the installment payment of estate taxes extends to the issue of which businesses that are includible in the decedent's gross estate are eligible for the deferral of tax (Code Sec. 7479(a), as amended by the IRS Restructuring and Reform Act of 1998).

Comment. Estates that seek installment-payment treatment are ordinarily at a financial disadvantage as a result of lack of liquidity. Accordingly, the Taxpayer Relief Act of 1997 provision granting judicial review of an adverse determination on the issue of eligibility for installment payment of estate taxes, without first having to pay the full amount of estate taxes due, was beneficial for estates with qualified, closely held business interests. The amendment by the IRS Restructuring and Reform Act of 1998 serves to broaden the scope of this provision.

★ *Effective date.* This provision is effective for estates of decedents dying after August 5, 1997 (Act Sec. 6024 of the IRS Restructuring and Reform Act of 1998; Act Sec. 505(c) of the Taxpayer Relief Act of 1997 (P.L. 105-34)).

Act Sec. 6007(d), amending Code Sec. 7479(a). Law at ¶ 6710. Committee Report at ¶ 11,025.

OTHER ESTATE AND GIFT TAX PROVISIONS

Revaluation of Gifts

¶ 446

Background ————————————————————————

Gifts made during life, in excess of the annual gift tax exclusion and not otherwise protected by the applicable marital or charitable deduction, are subject to gift tax. A person's lifetime taxable gifts are also a component in the computation of the federal estate tax. Prior to the Taxpayer Relief Act of 1997 (P.L. 105-34), it was possible for the IRS to successfully argue that a decedent's lifetime taxable gifts be revalued in computing adjusted taxable gifts for estate tax purposes, even though the gift tax statute of limitations had expired and the gift had been adequately disclosed. This discrepancy created administrative and record-keeping problems for estate administrators and fiduciaries.

The 1997 Act provided that, in computing adjusted taxable gifts for estate tax purposes, the IRS may not revalue gifts made during life if the gift tax statute of limitations has expired (Code Sec. 2001(f), as added by the Taxpayer Relief Act of 1997). However, in order for this provision to apply, the gift in question must have been adequately disclosed. Accordingly, the gift tax statute of limitations will not run with respect to a gift that is not adequately disclosed, even if a gift tax return was filed for other transfers in the same year.

Technical Corrections Impact

Final determination of gift tax value clarified.—In determining the amount of prior taxable gifts for estate tax purposes, the value of such gifts is the value as finally determined, even if no gift tax was paid or assessed on that gift. For purposes of this provision, the final determination of a gift's value could be the value (1) reported on a gift tax return (if not challenged by the IRS prior to expiration of the statute of limitations), (2) determined by the IRS (if not challenged by the taxpayer in court), (3) determined by a court, or (4) agreed upon by the taxpayer and the IRS in a settlement (Code Sec. 2001(f), as amended by the IRS Restructuring and Reform Act of 1998).

Comment. The Taxpayer Relief Act of 1997 provision was welcomed because it added a degree of certainty that, if properly disclosed, gifts could not be revalued for estate tax purposes after the gift tax statute of limitations had run, thus shielding the donor's estate from additional estate tax on these gifts. The amendment by the 1998 Act should make it easier for taxpayers to assure the finality of a gift tax valuation.

PRACTICAL ANALYSIS. Sanford J. Schlesinger, chair of Kaye, Scholer, Fierman, Hays & Handler, LLP's Wills and Estates Dept., New York, New York, comments that the legislation, which is effective with respect to gifts made after August 5, 1997, clarifies that in determining the amount of taxable gifts made in preceding calendar periods, the value of prior gifts is the value of such gifts as finally determined, even if no gift tax was assessed or paid on that gift. Final determinations include: (1) the value reported on the gift tax return if not challenged by the IRS prior to the expiration of the statute of limitations, (2) the value determined by the IRS, if not challenged in court by the taxpayer, (3) the value determined by the courts, or (4) the value agreed to by the IRS and the taxpayer in a settlement agreement.

The correction gives instances where certainty exists. It continues to be essential that the value of gifts be reported on timely filed gift tax returns. If the value of the gift is challenged by the IRS, it would be important to either enter into a written settlement agreement at the audit level or perhaps at the appellate conferee level where settlements are often reached. In addition, practitioners should be aware that the IRS has announced that special attention would be given to gift tax returns showing a discount claimed as well as to gift tax transfers related to family limited partnerships. It has been suggested that practitioners submit copies of family limited partnership agreements with gift and estate tax returns to facilitate adequate disclosure.

★ *Effective date.* This provision is effective with respect to gifts made after August 5, 1997 (Act Sec. 6024 of the IRS Restructuring and Reform Act of 1998; Act Sec. 506(e)(1) of the Taxpayer Relief Act of 1997 (P.L. 105-34), as amended by the 1998 Act).

Act Sec. 6007(e), amending Code Sec. 2001(f), Code Sec. 2504(c), Code Sec. 6501(c)(9), and Act Sec. 506(e)(1) of P.L. 105-34. Law at ¶ 5740, ¶ 5780, and ¶ 6400. Committee Report at ¶ 11,030.

Conservation Easements

¶ 451

Background

A contribution of a qualified real property interest to a charity or other qualified organization exclusively for a conservation purpose is eligible for an estate tax or gift tax charitable deduction under Code Sec. 2055(f) or Code Sec. 2522(d). A similar deduction is provided under Code Sec. 170(h) for income tax purposes.

In addition to these deductions, the Taxpayer Relief Act of 1997 (P.L. 105-34) added a provision that allows an executor to elect to exclude from a decedent's estate up to 40 percent (the "applicable percentage") of the value of land subject to a qualified conservation easement (Code Sec. 2031(c), as amended by the Taxpayer Relief Act of 1997). The exclusion is to be reduced by the amount of any charitable deduction allowed under Code Sec. 2055(f) with respect to the land. In addition, the amount of the exclusion is limited to the lesser of the "applicable percentage" or the "exclusion limitation." The exclusion limitation is $100,000 in 1998, $200,000 in 1999, $300,000 in 2000, $400,000 in 2001, and $500,000 in 2002 and thereafter.

The exclusion election is to be made on the decedent's estate tax return and, once made, is irrevocable. A post-mortem conservation easement may be granted by the executor of a decedent's estate or the trustee of the trust holding title to the land so long as it is granted prior to the date of the election. The 1997 Act provision was silent as to the income tax ramifications of a post-mortem conservation easement.

Technical Corrections Impact

Timing of exclusion election clarified.—The election to exclude from a decedent's estate a certain percentage of the value of land subject to a qualified conservation easement must be made on or before the due date (including extensions) for filing the decedent's estate tax return (Code Sec. 2031(c)(6), as amended by the IRS Restructuring and Reform Act of 1998).

Deduction for post-mortem conservation easement limited to estate tax.—An estate tax deduction is allowed for a qualified conservation easement contribution made after the decedent's death. However, no income tax deduction is allowed to the decedent's estate or to the decedent's qualified heirs with respect to such a post-mortem conservation easement (Code Sec. 2031(c)(9), as amended by the 1998 Act).

Even without an income tax deduction, the combination of a Code Sec. 2055(f) estate tax deduction and the exclusion allowed under Code Sec. 2031(c) can yield important tax savings to a decedent's estate.

Example. Assume Al Barker dies in 1999 owning unencumbered real property valued at $500,000. Barker's executor grants a conservation easement valued at 30% of the total land value and the estate takes a Code Sec. 2055(f) charitable deduction. The executor also makes a timely election to take an exclusion from Barker's gross estate with respect to the qualified conservation easement. The computation of the benefits is as follows:

Total Value of Land: $500,000

Estate Tax Deduction: $150,000 (.3 × $500,000)

Balance After Deduction: $350,000 ($500,000 − $150,000)

Estate Tax Exclusion: $140,000 (.4 × $350,000 < $200,000)

Amount Subject to Estate Tax: $210,000 ($350,000 − $140,000)

★ *Effective date.* These provisions are effective with respect to estates of decedents dying after December 31, 1997 (Act Sec. 6024 of the IRS Restructuring and Reform Act of 1998; Act Sec. 508(e)(1) of the Taxpayer Relief Act of 1997 (P.L. 105-34)).

Act Sec. 6007(g), amending Code Sec. 2031(c). Law at ¶ 5750. Committee Report at ¶ 11,035.

INCOME TAXATION OF TRUSTS

Pre-Need Funeral Trusts

¶ 456

Background

A funeral trust is an arrangement whereby an individual purchases funeral services or merchandise from a funeral home prior to death. The payment amount is held in trust and paid to the seller upon the individual's death. The only allowable beneficiaries of such a trust are the individuals to whom such property or services are to be provided at their death (Code Sec. 685, as added by the Taxpayer Relief Act of 1997 (P.L. 105-34)). Prior to the 1997 Act, such trusts were generally treated as grantor trusts and any income earned by the trust was taxed to the purchaser/grantor.

If the trustee of a pre-need qualified funeral trust elects special tax treatment under Code Sec. 685, the funeral trust is not treated as a grantor trust for income tax purposes and the tax on the annual earnings of the trust is payable by the trustee. Because one person or entity is often the trustee of numerous funeral

Background _____

trusts, the IRS is granted regulatory authority to prescribe rules to simplify the reporting of all trusts having a single trustee.

_____

Technical Corrections Impact

Funeral trust income.—A technical correction clarifies that a pre-need qualified funeral trust will continue to qualify for the Code Sec. 685 special rules during the 60-day period beginning on the date of the grantor's death, even though the death of the grantor causes the trust to no longer qualify as a grantor trust (Code Sec. 685(b), as amended by the IRS Restructuring and Reform Act of 1998).

Comment. The IRS's regulatory authority to prescribe rules relating to simplified reporting for all trusts having a single trustee is also extended to cover trusts that are terminated (such as by the beneficiary's death) during the tax year (Code Sec. 685(f), as amended by the 1998 Act).

★ *Effective date.* These provisions are effective for tax years ending after August 5, 1997 (Act Sec. 6024 of the IRS Restructuring and Reform Act of 1998; Act Sec. 1309(c) of the Taxpayer Relief Act of 1997 (P.L. 105-34)).

Act Sec. 6013(b), amending Code Sec. 685(b) and Code Sec. 685(f). Law at ¶ 5490. Committee Report at ¶ 11,280.

Chapter 5
Business and Investment

CAPITAL GAINS
Clarification of Provisions
¶ 501

Background

For a decade, investors pressed Congress for a reduction in the income tax rates imposed on long-term capital gains. Finally, in 1997, Congress passed legislation that brought about a reduction in the capital gains tax rate (Code Sec. 1(h), as amended by the Taxpayer Relief Act of 1997 (P.L. 105-34)). However, because of the 11th hour horse trading that went on during the legislative process, the new capital gains law presented a bewildering array of complicated formulas, obscure terms and significant gaps in coverage. The confusion over the new law was so great that within a few weeks of its enactment, the IRS was obliged to write to Congress asking it to provide more details concerning various aspects of the capital gains rules. The congressional leadership responded by letter to the IRS and provided the requested information. On the basis of this letter, the IRS issued a

Notice (Notice 97-59, I.R.B. 1997-45, 7) that addressed many of the issues that were left unresolved by the 1997 legislation.

Planning Note. The most significant change made by the IRS Restructuring and Reform Act of 1998 to the tax treatment of capital gains is that the 18-month holding period has been eliminated for tax years ending after December 31, 1997 (Code Sec. 1(h)(5), as amended by the IRS Restructuring and Reform Act of 1998). This change is discussed in detail at ¶ 502. It is important to note that all the other capital gains changes fall under the category of "technical corrections." The aim of these technical corrections is to clarify and/or provide rules for capital gains changes that were part of the 1997 legislation. Thus, most of the material in the following paragraphs discusses these technical corrections. As you read the following material, however, please keep in mind that after December 31, 1997, the 18-month holding period no longer applies.

Technical Corrections Impact

Code provisions reorganized, clarified and expanded.—The technical correction has rewritten and restructured the 1997 legislation dealing with the taxation of long-term capital gains (Code Sec. 1(h), as amended by the IRS Restructuring and Reform Act of 1998). The obvious goal of the technical correction is to present this Code provision in a more logical and coherent style. In addition, the amended Code Sec. 1(h) fills in the gaps in coverage that were evident in the 1997 legislation and that were addressed by IRS Notice 97-59.

Planning Note. It is very important to note that, with a few exceptions, the technical correction to Code Sec. 1(h) *does not* substantially change the basic capital gains rules that were in place after the 1997 Act. The technical correction merely clarifies and simplifies how the rules are to be applied. Thus, it would be a very unusual circumstance in which an individual who had filed a 1997 tax return would be forced to file an amended tax return in order to comply with the provisions of the technical correction. The IRS did an excellent job of incorporating the anticipated technical correction into its 1997 tax forms and instructions.

★ *Effective date.* This provision applies to tax years ending after May 6, 1997 (Act Sec. 6024 of the IRS Restructuring and Reform Act of 1998; Act Sec. 311(d)(1) of the Taxpayer Relief Act of 1997 (P.L. 105-34)).

Act Sec. 6005(d)(1), amending Code Sec. 1(h). Law at ¶ 5001. Committee Report at ¶ 10,915.

Elimination of 18-Month Holding Period

¶ 502

The 1997 legislation that brought about the welcome reduction in the tax rates imposed on long-term capital gains also provided that the lowest rates would only apply to capital assets that had been held more than 18 months. This was a marked increase from the traditional rule that held that long-term rates applied if the property had been held more than 12 months. The change in the holding period was effective for sales and exchanges after July 28, 1997 (Code Sec. 1(h), as amended by the Taxpayer Relief Act of 1997 (P.L. 105-34)).

At first blush, the increase in the holding period seemed innocuous from a tax compliance standpoint, and while it changed the playing field for investors, Congress explained that the change was a necessary trade-off for the lower capital gains rates. However, when the IRS began to design the 1997 Schedule D, it

Background ——————————————————————————————

became obvious that Congress had created a nightmare of complexity when one went to apply the new capital gains rules. Even though the IRS successfully incorporated the new rules into its 1997 Schedule D, most individuals found the required computations to be beyond their understanding. Even tax professionals spent a good many hours plumbing the mysteries that had been incorporated into the 1997 Schedule D.

IRS Restructuring and Reform Impact

18-month holding period eliminated.—The new legislation eliminates the 18-month holding period and provides that the 10-percent, 20-percent and/or 25-percent long-term rates apply to most capital assets held more than 12 months (Code Sec. 1(h)(5), as amended by the IRS Restructuring and Reform Act of 1998). The reduction in the holding period is generally effective for tax years ending after December 31, 1997.

Planning Note. The availability of the long-term capital gains rates for investments held more than 12 months will certainly accelerate the desire for individuals to develop tax planning strategies that produce capital gains instead of ordinary income. Remember that individuals in the highest marginal tax rates will face a tax rate of 39.6 percent on ordinary income, yet ordinarily pay a maximum rate of only 20 percent on long-term capital gains.

In order to reflect the elimination of the 18-month holding period, the 1998 legislation made the following changes in the Code:

(1) 28-percent gain. Prior to the 1998 Act, a maximum capital gains rate of 28 percent applied to (1) gains from capital assets held for more than one year, but not more than 18 months, (2) collectibles gain (see ¶ 512), and (3) Code Sec. 1202 gain (e.g., gain from small business stock) (see ¶ 531). The new legislation, which is effective for tax years ending after December 31, 1997, retains the 28-percent maximum rate for collectibles and Code Sec. 1202 gain, but provides that most capital assets (e.g., shares of stock) that are held more than 12 months, but not more than 18 months, are no longer subject to the 28-percent capital gains rate (Code Sec. 1(h)(5)(A) and (B), as amended by the 1998 Act).

Comment. Although some capital assets (e.g., collectibles) are still subject to the maximum capital gains rate of 28-percent, like other types of capital assets, they need only be held for more than 12 months.

Under the new rules, 28-percent gain property is the excess, if any, of (a) the total of collectibles gain and Sec. 1202 gain over (b) the total of collectibles loss, net short-term capital loss, and the amount of long-term capital loss carried over to the current tax year (Code Sec. 1(h)(5), as amended by the 1998 Act). The special rules of prior Code Sec. 1(h)(5)(B) that generally imposed a more than 18-month holding period on options, short sale gains, and some other types of investment assets (see ¶ 505) have been eliminated (Code Sec. 1(h)(5), as amended by the 1998 Act).

Planning Note. The elimination of the 18-month holding period is generally effective after December 31, 1997. This change may have an effect on an individual's estimated tax payments for 1998. For example, if an individual sold stock for a gain on January 3, 1998 and the stock had been held more than 12 months, but not more than 18 months, the individual may have based the April 15, 1998 estimated tax payment on the assumption that the gain would be taxed at 28 percent. Because of the retroactive elimination of the 18-month holding period, the gain would probably be subject to a maximum capital gains rate of 20 percent. Individuals may find that they overpaid their estimated tax for the first half of

1998. If so, decreasing the remaining estimated tax payments for 1998 should be considered.

PRACTICAL ANALYSIS. Tim Kochis, of Kochis Fitz, San Francisco, Cal., comments that the return to the former one-year holding period to qualify for long-term capital gain treatment should be very good news for the Treasury. Tax collections will at least accelerate (and, based on historical experience, will probably increase) as taxable transactions accelerate and probably increase as well.

Kochis also observes that it's great news for investors as the benefits of these low rates are now easier to achieve. For investors, this shorter holding period further enhances the already preferential treatment of capital appreciation returns and further diminishes the relative appeal of dividends, interest or rents since the lower capital gains rates can now be achieved much sooner, and consequently, at less risk. The shorter holding period also further erodes somewhat the relative merits of tax deferred vehicles such as traditional IRAs and 401(k) plans since their returns are ultimately taxed as ordinary income when investments outside of these types of plans can now more readily qualify for the favorable long-term capital gains rates. Still, in most cases, the balance tips heavily in favor of maximizing investment in tax-deferred plans when an income tax deduction or exclusion is available for the contribution. When there is not, however, such as with variable annuities, the disadvantage is now more pronounced since investments outside such arrangements can now qualify for favorable treatment at less risk and often much less cost.

Since this provision is retroactive to the beginning of 1998, many taxpayers may be able to recalculate the impacts of the quarterly estimated tax payments already made in April and June, relating to prior transactions this year. This could reduce what otherwise might need to be paid in future estimated tax payments.

Under a special rule, 28-percent gain also includes long-term capital gain that was taken into account for the portion of the tax year before May 7, 1997, or from property held more than 18 months and taken into account for the portion of the tax year after July 28, 1997 and before January 1, 1998 (Code Sec. 1(h)(13)(A)(i), as amended by the 1998 Act). Similarly, in determining the amount of 28-percent loss, the amount taken into account generally consists of long-term capital loss for the portion of the tax year before May 7, 1997, or from property held not more than 18 months that is taken into account for the portion of the tax year after July 28, 1997, and before January 1, 1998 (Code Sec. 1(h)(13)(A)(ii), as amended by the 1998 Act). The rules that pertained to certain types of investment vehicles (e.g., short sales) before the latest amendment to Code Sec. (1)(h) (i.e., Code Sec. 1(h)(5)(B), as amended by the technical correction portion of the 1998 Act) (see ¶ 505) remain in effect for amounts taken into account before January 1, 1998 (Code Sec. 1(h)(13)(A)(iii), as amended by the 1998 Act).

(2) Collectibles gain or loss. The new legislation provides that a collectible that is a capital asset need only be held for more than 12 months in order for the gain or loss to be classified as a "collectible gain or loss" (see ¶ 512) (Code Sec. 1(h)(6), as amended by the 1998 Act.)

(3) Unrecaptured Section 1250 gain. A new formula is provided for determining the amount of unrecaptured Section 1250 gain (Code Sec. 1(h)(7)(A)(i) and (ii),

as amended by the 1998 Act). This new formula is effective for tax years ending after December 31, 1997. See ¶ 510 for a complete discussion of what constitutes unrecaptured Section 1250 gain. Under the new formula, the amount of such gain is the excess, if any, of (a) the amount of long-term capital gain that is not otherwise treated as ordinary income, that would be treated as ordinary income if Section 1250(b)(1) included all depreciation and the applicable percentage under Section 1250(a) were 100 percent, over (b) the excess, if any, of 28-percent loss over 28-percent gain (Code Sec. 1(h)(7)(A)(i) and (ii), as amended by the 1998 Act). A special rule applies when calculating the amount of unrecaptured Section 1250 gain. Under this rule, the amount determined under the new formula does not include gain that is taken into account for the portion of the tax year before May 7, 1997, or from property not held more than 18 months that is taken into account for the portion of the tax year after July 28, 1997, and before January 1, 1998 (Code Sec. (1)(h)(13)(B), as amended by the 1998 Act).

(4) Inherited property and transfer of patents. A technical correction made by the 1998 Act (see ¶ 503) provides that, in most situations, inherited property and certain transferred patents will be eligible for the lowest applicable capital gains rate because the property will be treated as though it were held more than *18* months. However, since the new legislation also eliminated the 18-month rule, it was necessary for Congress to amend the Code to provide that inherited property and certain transferred patents will be eligible for the lowest applicable capital gains rates because they will be treated as if held more than *12* months (Code Sec. 1223(11) and (12) and Code Sec. 1235(a), as amended by the 1998 Act.)

PRACTICAL ANALYSIS. Martin Nissenbaum, National Director of Personal Income Tax Planning at Ernst & Young LLP, New York, NY, observes that the retroactive change in the holding period requirement for long-term capital gain eligibility back to more than a year will be a welcome relief for many taxpayers and for the designers of the Schedule D. The three-tier holding period regime (12 months or less, more than 12 months, and more than 18 months) which was in effect for 1997 resulted in an inordinate level of complexity with millions of returns completed incorrectly.

Especially relieved will be shareholders in mutual funds and the fund companies themselves. Under prior law, mutual funds were required to bifurcate capital gains between those realized after 12 months and those realized after 18 months. The 1997 Form 1099-DIV was not changed to accommodate this bifurcated reporting which resulted in different funds having completely different methods of reporting. Although the 1998 Form 1099-DIV was scheduled to reflect proper reporting, large numbers of taxpayer errors were still expected.

Other areas of the tax law also suffered from the three-tier holding period rules. For example, confusion reigned as to the proper holding period requirements with respect to appreciated property contributed to charity and the sale of property held by a decedent. Although the IRS and the technical corrections provisions of the Act clarify the application of these rules, having a clear distinction between short-term and long-term capital gains will make planning much simpler.

Holders of incentive stock options (ISOs) will find planning less complex since the holding period for long-term capital gains will again be the same as that necessary to avoid a disqualifying disposition of stock received on the exercise of an ISO. On the other hand, the reenactment of the 12-month holding period still does not solve two problems which afflict ISO holders:

(1) The payment of alternative minimum tax (AMT) at a rate of 28 percent even though the gain on sale of stock received on the exercise of an ISO would only be taxed at a maximum rate of 20 percent if held for more than 12 months.

(2) Capital gains on the sale of ISO stock are included in AMT income which may reduce the AMT exemption amount. This could result in an effective tax rate imposed on long-term capital gains of more than 20 percent.

The law still leaves behind a rate structure that is more complex than the one in effect prior to the Taxpayer Relief Act of 1997. A rate of 25 percent will continue to apply to gain on the sale of real estate attributable to depreciation. The gain on the sale of collectibles held for more than a year will still be subject to a maximum rate of 28 percent. But, in general, most taxpayers will be able to breathe a sigh of relief.

Planning Note. More changes to come? The elimination of the 18-month holding period came about during the last few hours of the negotiations by the Conference Committee and took most observers by surprise. Already, a proposal has been made in Congress to further reduce the tax rates that apply to long-term capital gains. At this point, passage of the proposal appears unlikely. However, the restoration of the 12-month holding period shows that Congress always has the power to do the unexpected.

Caution. As part of the 1998 legislation, Congress also made a number of technical corrections to the capital gains provisions that were enacted into law in 1997. The discussion in the following paragraphs focuses on these technical corrections. Reference is made to the "18-month holding period." The 18-month holding period was generally effective for sales after July 28, 1997. However, as discussed above, in most situations, it was eliminated for tax years ending after December 31, 1997.

Caution. According to the Conference Committee Report, the elimination of the 18-month holding period is effective for "amounts properly taken into account on or after January 1, 1998." However, Act Sec. 5001(b)(1) specifies that the new rules generally apply to tax years ending after December 31, 1997. We have opted to use the effective date specified by the Act.

PRACTICAL ANALYSIS. Wally Head, Managing Director, Chicago office of Sanford C. Bernstein & Co., Inc., observes that the elimination of the mid-term capital gains treatment will affect investment planning and management decisions by individual investors.

Head notes that lowering the tax rate for gains on marketable securities held more than one year but not more than 18 months improves the after-tax risk premium of these securities, eliminates a tax-related reason to delay their sale, makes it easier to analyze the tax cost of selling them, and makes it easier to report these gains for compliance purposes. Accordingly, this change modestly improves the relative attractiveness of equities versus bonds, modestly reduces the attractiveness of deferral strategies, and makes it even more important for investors to understand how their investment managers reflect tax costs when deciding whether to sell an appreciated security in a taxable account.

More specifically, the change should produce:

A slight increase in allocations to equities by investors who base their decision on risk/return analyses;

A slight decrease in allocations to equities by investors who invest in equities only to the extent necessary to achieve particular goals;

A slight decrease in contributions to deferral strategies that will be allocated to equities; and

An increase in the use of tax-sensitive investment managers who use sophisticated methodologies to enhance after-tax returns.

These impacts are not expected to meaningfully affect the securities markets, but they reinforce the needs most individual investors have for quality assistance with asset allocation and tax-sensitive investment management decisions.

★ *Effective date.* The provisions generally apply to tax years ending after December 31, 1997 (Act Sec. 5001(b)(1) of the IRS Restructuring and Reform Act of 1998). However, the provisions dealing with inherited property and patents took effect on January 1, 1998 (Act Sec. 5001(b)(2) of the IRS Restructuring and Reform Act of 1998).

Act Sec. 5001(a), amending Code Secs. 1(h)(5), 1(h)(6), 1(h)(7)(A), 1(h)(13)(A) and (B), 1223(11) and (12), and 1235(a). Law at ¶ 5001, ¶ 5600, and ¶ 5605. Committee Report at ¶ 10,785.

Holding Period for Certain Assets

¶ 503

Background

The Taxpayer Relief Act of 1997 (P.L. 105-34) did *not* change the traditional rule that, in order for an individual to realize a long-term capital gain, the individual must hold a capital asset for more than 12 months (Code Sec. 1222). What the 1997 legislation did impose was the requirement that an individual must generally hold a capital asset for more than 18 months in order to obtain the lowest possible capital gains rate (Code Sec. 1(h)(4), as amended by the Taxpayer Relief Act of 1997 (P.L. 105-34)). However, during the 1997 legislative rush, Congress left unclear how the change in the holding period would affect certain capital assets (e.g., inherited property).

Caution. Remember that the technical correction that is discussed below no longer applies to tax years ending after December 31, 1997. This is due to the fact that the IRS Restructuring and Reform Act of 1998 reduced the holding period for long-term capital assets to "more than 12 months." See ¶ 502 for the discussion on the reduction in the holding period.

Technical Corrections Impact

Clarification of holding period.—The technical correction changed the presumed holding period from "more than 12 months" to "more than 18 months." This was done to ensure that certain individuals can easily obtain the benefits of the lowest capital gains tax rates without being forced to hold the property for an additional six months. The types of property that are impacted by this technical correction are discussed in the following material.

Inherited property. Inherited property may be sold within 18 months after it was acquired by the heir and, in most situations, the heir will still be treated as if the holding period of the property was *more* than 18 months (Code Sec. 1223(11) and Code Sec. 1223(12), as amended by the IRS Restructuring Act of 1998).

Comment. The Taxpayer Relief Act of 1997 did not change the rule that inherited property is generally treated as having been held by the heir for more than 12 months. Therefore, if the technical correction had not lengthened the presumed holding period to "more than 18 months," the heir would have had to hold the property for an additional six months in order to benefit from the lowest possible long-term capital gains tax rate.

Example. On December 1, 1997, Max Brand inherited 100 shares of stock. The fair market value of the shares at the time of death was $1,000. On December 10, 1997, Brand sells the shares for $1,200. His $200 recognized gain is eligible to be taxed at a maximum capital gains rate of 20%. This is because Brand is considered to have held the stock for more than 18 months even though his actual period of ownership was only 10 days.

The same presumed 18-month holding period applies to "special use property" distributed to a qualified heir (Code Sec. 1223(12), as amended by the 1998 Act).

Transfer of patents. Unless the transfer is made by gift, inheritance, or devise, when an inventor or certain investors transfer a patent before it is reduced to practice, it will be treated as if the inventor or investor held the patent for more than 18 months regardless of the actual holding period (Code Sec. 1235(a), as amended by the 1998 Act).

★ *Effective date.* This provision applies to tax years ending after May 6, 1997 (Act Sec. 6024 of the IRS Restructuring and Reform Act of 1998; Act Sec. 311(d)(1) of the Taxpayer Relief Act of 1997 (P.L. 105-34)).

Act Sec. 6005(d)(4), amending Code Secs. 1223(11) and (12) and 1235(a). Law at ¶ 5600 and ¶ 5605. Committee Report at ¶ 10,915.

28-Percent Rate Gain

¶ 505

Background

The phrase "mid-term gain" was a tax term coined by the 1997 tax legislation (Code Sec. 1(h)(8), as added by the Taxpayer Relief Act of 1997 (P.L. 105-34)). In a nutshell, the phrase refers to a capital gain that was classified as long-term because it arose from an asset that was held more than 12 months, but that did not qualify for the lowest capital gain rate because the asset was not held more than 18 months. In short, the term helped to define what long-term capital gain would be taxed at a 28-percent rate.

From its inception, the term "mid-term gain" was a source of confusion because it gave the impression that there were now three types of capital gains, namely "short-term," "mid-term," and "long-term." This impression was erroneous because the 1997 legislation did not touch the traditional principle that all capital gains could be divided into either "short-term" or "long-term," depending on the length of time that an asset was held by the individual.

Comment. This change made by the technical correction portion of the IRS Restructuring and Reform Act of 1998 was rendered somewhat moot by the fact that the same legislation also eliminated the 18-month holding period requirement. For tax years ending after December 31, 1997, most capital assets will qualify for the lowest capital gains rate provided they are held more than 12 months. The elimination of the 18-month holding period is discussed at ¶ 502. Therefore, while the following material is relevant to the determination of 28-percent rate gain, it must be kept in mind that the 18-month holding period was generally eliminated as of December 31, 1997.

Technical Corrections Impact

28-percent rate gain.—The technical correction eliminates the phrase "mid-term gain" from the Code and provides a clearer, more comprehensive process by which one may determine what portion, if any, of an individual's long-term capital gain is subject to the maximum rate of 28 percent (Code Sec. 1(h)(5), as amended by the IRS Restructuring and Reform Act of 1998).

An individual's "28-percent rate gain" is the:

(1) total amount of long-term capital gain from property held for more than 12 months, but not more than 18 months; collectibles gain (see ¶ 512); and Code Section 1202 gain (i.e., recognized gain from certain small business stock), reduced by

(2) the total amount of long-term capital loss from property held for more than 12 months, but not more than 18 months; collectibles loss; net short-term capital loss; and the amount of long-term capital loss carried over from an earlier tax year (Code Sec. 1(h)(5)(A), as amended by the 1998 Act).

Planning Note. This new provision makes clear that any long-term capital loss carryforward is used to reduce the individual's 28-percent, long-term gain. It does not matter if the carryforward long-term loss arose from property held more or less than 18 months, as long as it is classified as a long-term loss. The application of this rule is illustrated in the following example.

Example. During 1997, Jack Aubrey recognized a $20,000 gain from a sale of stock sold on November 1 that had been held more than 18 months. He also had a $30,000 loss from the sale of stock sold on December 1 that he had held more than 18 months. He had no other capital transactions in 1997 (or unrecaptured Section 1250 gain). He may claim a $3,000 capital loss on his 1997 tax return. The remaining long-term loss is carried forward and may be used to reduce any 28% gain that Aubrey realizes in 1998 or future years.

Comment. The importance of this technical correction is that it provides taxpayers with detailed directions on how their 28-percent gain, if any, is to be computed. The 1997 legislation did not provide the necessary details.

Special rules for determining if 28-percent rate applies.—The technical correction also contains special rules that are applied when determining if the 28-percent rate applies to the following financial transactions: (1) short sales (Code Sec. 1(h)(5)(B)(i), as amended by the 1998 Act); (2) long-term losses that result from the closing of a short sale (Code Sec. 1(h)(5)(B)(ii), as amended by the 1998 Act); (3) options (Code Sec. 1(h)(5)(B)(iii), as amended by the 1998 Act); and (4) Section 1256 contracts marked to market (e.g., regulated future contracts) (Code Sec. 1(h)(5)(B)(iv), as amended by the 1998 Act). These four special rules are discussed in the following material.

(1) Short-term gains from short sales. The technical correction provides that when determining if the 28-percent rate applies to short sale gains and holding periods, the rules that are used when determining short-term gains and holding periods (Code Sec. 1233(b)) are to be applied in a modified form. This modification provides that when the substantially identical property has been held more than 12 months, but not more than 18 months, any gain on the closing of the short sale will be deemed to be gain from property held not more than 18 months (i.e., 28-percent gain) (Code Sec. 1(h)(5)(B)(i)(I), as amended by the 1998 Act). In addition, the substantially identical property is to be treated as held for 12 months on the day

before the *earlier* of the date of the closing of the short sale or the date the property is disposed of (Code Sec. 1(h)(5)(B)(i)(II), as amended by the 1998 Act).

Comment. A short sale occurs when an individual agrees to sell property that the individual does not own (or owns, but does not want to sell). The property sold is property the seller believes is overvalued. A short sale is made in two steps: (1) *Selling short.* The individual borrows property and delivers it to the buyer. (2) *Closing the sale.* At a later date, the individual either buys substantially identical property and delivers it to the lender, or the individual makes delivery of the property that was held at the time of the short sale. If the value of the property sold short does drop in value, the seller will realize a profit on the transaction.

(2) Long-term losses from short sales. Under the technical correction, when determining the tax consequences of a long-term loss from a short sale, the general rules (Code Sec. 1233(d)) will be applied in the following modified form (Code Sec. 1(h)(5)(B)(ii), as amended by the 1998 Act). When, on the date of the short sale, the substantially identical property had been held more than 18 months, any loss on the closing of the short sale is to be treated as a loss from the sale or exchange of a capital asset held more than 18 months (i.e., a 20-percent gain or loss).

(3) Options. The technical correction states that when determining the tax treatment of options, a rule similar to that which pertains to covered call options (Code Sec. 1092(f)) is to be applied when the stock has been held more than 18 months (Code Sec. 1(h)(5)(B)(iii), as amended by the 1998 Act). Thus, according to the Senate Finance Committee Report, any loss with respect to the option is to be treated as a loss from the sale or exchange of a capital asset held more than 18 months (i.e., a loss in the 20-percent group), provided that at the time the loss is realized, gain on the sale or exchange of the stock would be treated as gain from a capital asset held more than 18 months.

Comment. The Senate Finance Committee Reports state that any loss treated as a long-term capital loss by reason of the application of Code Sec. 1233(d) or Code Sec. 1092(f) (i.e., Items (2) or (3), above) is to be taken into account in computing an individual's 28-percent rate gain when the property causing the loss to be treated as a long-term capital loss was held *not more* than 18 months on the applicable date.

(4) Section 1256 contracts. The term "Section 1256 contract" refers to regulated futures contracts, foreign currency contracts, nonequity options, and dealer equity options (Code Sec. 1256(b)). A Section 1256 contract is treated as if it was sold at its fair market value at the end of the taxpayer's tax year (i.e., "mark to market"), even though the taxpayer continues to hold the contract (Code Sec. 1256(a)(1)). Any gain or loss that the taxpayer is forced to recognize as a result of the "mark to market" rule is treated as 40-percent short-term and 60-percent long-term. The technical correction clarifies that the long-term portion of the gain or loss will be treated as if it arose from property held more than 18 months (i.e., gain or loss will be in the 20-percent group) (Code Sec. 1(h)(5)(B)(iv), as amended by the 1998 Act).

★ *Effective date.* These provisions apply to tax years ending after May 6, 1997 (Act Sec. 6024 of the IRS Restructuring and Reform Act of 1998; Act Sec. 311(d)(1) of the Taxpayer Relief Act of 1997 (P.L. 105-34)).

Act Sec. 6005(d)(1), amending Code Sec. 1(h)(5)(A) and (B). Law at ¶ 5001. Committee Report at ¶ 10,915.

Special Rules for 1997

¶ 506

Background _____

The 1997 law that impacted the taxation of long-term capital gains was unusual in its complexity. A great deal of this complexity arose from the fact that an individual's capital gain would be taxed differently depending upon when the

Background _____

sale of the capital asset took place. For example, sales before May 7, 1997 would be taxed under the traditional rules that imposed a maximum tax rate of 28 percent on the gain if the asset had been held more than 12 months. Property sold after May 6, 1997, and before July 29, 1997, was generally taxed at a maximum rate of 20 percent if held more than 12 months. For property sold after July 28, 1997, the maximum tax depended on how long the property was held. Thus, a maximum tax of 28 percent usually applied if the property was held more than 12 months, but no more than 18 months. Property held more than 18 months was generally subject to a maximum tax of 20 percent. Under the 1997 amendment to the Code, these rules were not clear (Code Sec. 1(h)(1), as amended by the Taxpayer Relief Act of 1997 (P.L. 105-34)).

Technical Corrections Impact

1997 rules clarified.—A technical correction has clarified the rules that apply to the tax treatment of capital gains recognized during 1997 (Code Sec. 1(h)(13), as added by the IRS Restructuring and Reform Act of 1998). For example, the Code now makes clear that a 28-percent rate (see ¶ 505) applies to a long-term capital gain taken into account before May 7, 1997 (Code Sec. 1(h)(13)(A)(i), as added by the 1998 Act). In addition, the technical correction makes it easy to determine that a "28-percent gain" (see ¶ 505) does *not* include a gain from property held more than 12 months, but not more than 18 months, and sold after May 6, 1997, and before July 29, 1997 (Code Sec. 1(h)(13)(A)(iii), as added by the 1998 Act). In short, because of the technical correction, an individual can cut through the Gordian knot that was created by the original 1997 legislation and determine how the capital gains rules are to be applied to transactions that occurred during the 1997 tax year.

Comment. It must be emphasized that this technical correction did *not* change how long-term capital gains are taxed for 1997, but merely clarified how the rules are to be applied.

Comment. The same 1998 legislation that made the technical corrections to the 1997 legislation also eliminated the 18-month holding period for tax years ending after December 31, 1997. This significant change in the taxation of long-term capital gains is discussed at ¶ 502.

★ *Effective date.* This provision applies to tax years ending after May 6, 1997 (Act Sec. 6024 of the IRS Restructuring and Reform Act of 1998; Act Sec. 311(d)(1) of the Taxpayer Relief Act of 1997 (P.L. 105-34)).

Act Sec. 6005(d)(1), adding Code Sec. 1(h)(13). Law at ¶ 5001. Committee Report at ¶ 10,915.

Adjusted Net Capital Gain

¶ 508

Background _____

In order to compute an individual's capital gains tax, one must determine the amount of an individual's "adjusted net capital gain." This amount, as defined by the 1997 legislation (Code Sec. 1(h)(4), as amended by the Taxpayer Relief Act of 1997), was difficult to compute and the required formula contained obscure terms that added to the confusion.

Technical Corrections Impact

Determination process simplified.—The process of determining an individual's "adjusted net capital gain" has been greatly simplified by the technical correction (Code Sec. 1(h)(4), as amended by the IRS Restructuring and Reform Act of 1998). The revised definition provides that an individual's adjusted capital gain is net capital gain reduced (but not below zero) by:

(1) the total amount of unrecaptured Section 1250 gain (see ¶510), and

(2) the 28-percent rate gain (see ¶505).

Planning Note. Even after the technical correction, the rule remains in effect that in determining an individual's "adjusted net capital gain," net capital gain must also be reduced by any amount taken into account as investment income under Code Sec. 163(d)(4)(B)(iii) (Code Sec. 1(h)(3), as amended by the IRS Restructuring and Reform Act of 1998).

The process of determining an individual's adjusted net capital gain is illustrated in the following example.

Example. At the end of 1997, Steve Matrin determined that he had a total net capital gain of $50,000. Of the $50,000 in gain, $10,000 was classified as unrecaptured Section 1250 gain (see ¶510), and $15,000 was classified as 28% rate gain (see ¶505). As a result of the computations required by the technical correction, Matrin's "adjusted net capital gain" for 1997 is $25,000.

Planning Note. Remember that a capital asset sold after July 28, 1997, must have been held more than 18 months in order for it to be included in "adjusted net capital gain." However, the 18-month holding period was eliminated for tax years ending after December 31, 1997. See ¶502 for the impact of the termination of the 18-month rule.

★ *Effective date.* This provision applies to tax years ending after May 6, 1997 (Act Sec. 6024 of the IRS Restructuring and Reform Act of 1998; Act Sec. 311(d)(1) of the Taxpayer Relief Act of 1997 (P.L. 105-34)).

Act Sec. 6005(d)(1), amending Code Sec. 1(h)(4). Law at ¶5001. Committee Report at ¶10,915.

Unrecaptured Section 1250 Gain

¶510

Background————————

The capital gains changes brought about in 1997 provided a maximum 25-percent rate for any long-term gain attributable to certain prior depreciation that had been claimed on real property. The legislation referred to such depreciation as "unrecaptured section 1250 gain" (Code Sec. 1(h)(6), as amended by the Taxpayer Relief Act of 1997 (P.L. 105-34)). After enactment of the legislation, questions arose concerning how the term was defined and the process by which the exact amount of such gain was to be determined.

—————————————

Caution. In addition to the technical correction discussed in the following material, the 1998 legislation eliminated the 18-month holding period. This elimination is effective for tax years ending after December 31, 1997. See ¶502 for a discussion of the elimination of the 18-month holding period. While the technical correction discussed below is still of importance, it must be remembered that reference to the 18-month holding period does not generally pertain after December 31, 1997.

¶510

Technical Corrections Impact

Definition revised and clarified.—A technical correction makes clear that a taxpayer's "adjusted net capital gain" does not include "unrecaptured section 1250 gain" (see ¶ 508) (Code Sec. 1(h)(4), as amended by the IRS Restructuring and Reform Act of 1998). The technical correction further clarifies that the maximum rate on such gain is 25 percent (Code Sec. 1(h)(1)(D), as amended by the 1998 Act). Finally, the technical correction changed and clarified the process by which a taxpayer's "unrecaptured section 1250 gain" is determined (Code Sec. 1(h)(7)(A), as amended by the 1998 Act).

Under the revised definition, unrecaptured Section 1250 gain is the *excess* of:

(1) the amount of long-term capital gain (not otherwise treated as ordinary income) that would be treated as ordinary income if (a) Code Sec. 1250(b)(1) included all depreciation and the applicable percentage that applied under Code Sec. 1250(a) were 100 percent, and (b) only gain from property held for more than 18 months were taken into account, over

(2) the excess of 28-percent rate loss over 28-percent rate gain (see ¶ 505).

Note that the 18-month time period mentioned in the above formula is changed to "more than 12 months" for property sold after May 6, 1997, and before July 29, 1997 (Code Sec. 1(h)(13)(B)(ii), as amended by the 1998 Act).

Planning Note. The upshot of this revised computational format is that any net 28-percent rate loss acts first to offset unrecaptured Section 1250 gain, and the excess of such loss, if any, is then applied to offset capital gains that are taxed at the maximum 20-percent rate.

Comment. Even under the new capital gains rules, Code Sec. 1250 will continue to treat some prior claimed depreciation (i.e., usually the amount claimed in excess of the amount allowable under the straight-line method) as ordinary income. This fact is illustrated in the following example.

Example (1). On December 7, 1997, William Drake sold a building for $1,000,000. The building had originally cost $500,000 and, over the years, Drake had claimed $400,000 in depreciation. Of the $400,000 in depreciation, $100,000 was in excess of that allowed under the straight line method. Under the capital gains rules (Code Sec. 1(h)(7)(A), as amended by the 1998 Act), $300,000 of the depreciation would be classified as unrecaptured Section 1250 gain. This is because if Section 1250 had applied to all depreciation (and not only additional depreciation), $300,000 of Drake's long-term capital gain would have been treated as ordinary income.

Planning Note. Under MACRS, all depreciation on real property must be computed using the straight-line method. As a result, any gain on the sale of MACRS real property that is due to claimed depreciation will be classified as "unrecaptured Section 1250 gain." Of course, the property will have to be held more than 18 months for this rule to apply.

Example (2). On December 30, 1997, Nat Spar sold a building for $100,000. He had owned the property for more than 18 months. Spar had purchased the building for $50,000 and under MACRS had claimed $20,000 in straight-line depreciation. His basis in the building at the time of sale was $30,000. As a result, his long-term capital gain was $70,000. However, in determining Spar's "adjusted net capital gain" (see ¶ 508), he must subtract his $20,000 of unrecaptured Section 1250 gain. The $20,000 will be taxed at a maximum rate of 25% and his remaining $50,000 in adjusted net capital gain will be taxed as a maximum rate of 20%.

Limitation for Section 1231 property. The technical correction provides that the amount of unrecaptured Section 1250 gain from certain sales, exchanges and conversions (Code Sec. 1231(a)(3)(A)) for any tax year will not exceed the net Section 1231 gain (Code Sec. 1231(c)(3)) for that tax year (Code Sec. 1(h)(7)(B), as amended by the 1998 Act).

★ *Effective date.* This provision applies to tax years ending after May 6, 1997 (Act Sec. 6024 of the IRS Restructuring and Reform Act of 1998; Act Sec. 311(d)(1) of the Taxpayer Relief Act of 1997 (P.L. 105-34)).

Act Sec. 6005(d)(1), amending Code Sec. 1(h)(7)(A) and (B). Law at ¶ 5001. Committee Report at ¶ 10,915.

Collectibles

¶ 512

Background

Under the 1997 law, gain from collectibles (e.g., rugs, stamps and coins) were excluded from the definition of "adjusted net capital gain" (Code Sec. 1(h)(4) and (5), as amended by the Taxpayer Relief Act of 1997 (P.L. 105-34)).

Planning Note. In addition to the technical correction discussed below, the IRS Restructuring and Reform Act of 1998 eliminated the 18-month holding period rule. The elimination is effective for tax years ending after December 31, 1997. See ¶ 502 for a discussion of the impact of dropping the 18-month holding requirement. Of course, collectible gain from property held more than 12 months is still subject to a maximum rate of 28 percent (Code Sec. 1(h)(5), as amended by the IRS Restructuring and Reform Act of 1998).

Technical Corrections Impact

Collectibles gain and loss.—The technical correction defines "collectible gain" and "collectible loss" as gain or loss from collectibles (Code Sec. 408(m)) that is taken into consideration in computing gross income or taxable income and arises from a capital asset held for more than 18 months (Code Sec. 1(h)(6)(A), as amended by the IRS Restructuring and Reform Act of 1998). A "more-than-12-month rule" applies for collectibles sold after May 6, 1997, and before July 29, 1997 (Code Sec. 1(h)(13)(B)(ii), as amended by the 1998 Act).

Planning Note. The technical correction provides that, in determining the amount of an individual's 28-percent rate gain (see ¶ 505), the individual may offset long-term collectible gain with long-term collectible loss (Code Sec. 1(h)(5)(A), as amended by the 1998 Act). The correction does not change the rule that long-term collectible gain is taxed at a maximum rate of 28 percent.

Collectibles gain passed through from partnerships. Any long-term collectible gain passed through to an individual by a partnership, S corporation or trust is subject to a maximum tax rate of 28 percent (Code Sec. 1(h)(6)(B), as amended by the 1998 Act).

★ *Effective date.* The provision applies to tax years ending after May 6, 1997 (Act Sec. 6024 of the IRS Restructuring and Reform Act of 1998; Act Sec. 311(d)(1) of the Taxpayer Relief Act of 1997 (P.L. 105-34)).

Act Sec. 6005(d)(1), amending Code Sec. 1(h)(6). Law at ¶ 5001. Committee Report at ¶ 10,915.

Pass-Through Entities

¶515

Background

The 1997 capital gains legislation ensured that the rules governing short-term and long-term gains as well as effective dates could not be bypassed just because the taxpayer received the gain from a pass-through entity (e.g., a mutual fund) (Code Sec. 1(h)(10), as amended by the Taxpayer Relief Act of 1997 (P.L. 105-34)). The legislation included the following as pass-through entities: a regulated investment company, a real estate investment trust, an S corporation, a partnership, an estate or trust, and a common trust fund (Code Sec. 1(h)(10)(C), as amended by the 1997 Act).

Technical Corrections Impact

Expanded list of pass-through entities.—The list of pass-through entities has now been expanded by a technical correction to include certain foreign investment companies engaged in the trading of securities or commodities (Code Sec. 1246(b)) and certain passive foreign investment companies (i.e., those termed "qualified electing funds") (Code Sec. 1295(a)) (Code Sec. 1(h)(12)(G) and Code Sec. 1(h)(12)(H), as amended by the IRS Restructuring and Reform Act of 1998).

Authority to issue regulations. The IRS is given authority to issue regulations pertaining to the application of Code Sec. 1(h) to sales and exchanges and reporting requirements of pass-through entities (Code Sec. 1(h)(11), as amended by the 1998 Act).

★ *Effective date.* The provision applies to tax years ending after May 6, 1997 (Act Sec. 6024 of the IRS Restructuring and Reform Act of 1998; Act Sec. 311(d)(1) of the Taxpayer Relief Act of 1997 (P.L. 105-34)).

Act Sec. 6005(d)(1), amending Code Sec. 1(h)(11) and (12). Law at ¶5001. Committee Report at ¶10,915.

Maximum Capital Gains Rate

¶518

Background

One of the greatest criticisms leveled against the 1997 capital gains legislation was that the formula used to determine the correct tax was nearly incomprehensible (Code Sec. 1(h)(1), as amended by the Taxpayer Relief Act of 1997 (P.L. 105-34)). Although the IRS did a masterful job of developing and incorporating the required formula into its 1997 forms (e.g., Schedule D), many individuals found the law inexplicable and, as a result, had to rely blindly on the IRS forms in order to compute their capital gains tax.

Technical Corrections Impact

Tax computation formula simplified.—The formula used to determine an individual's tax on long-term capital gains has been revamped and simplified (Code Sec. 1(h)(1), as amended by the IRS Restructuring and Reform Act of 1998). While this revised formula will result in the same tax as that determined under the 1997 legislation, it is presented in a more understandable and coherent manner than its predecessor.

Comment. Because the law used to determine an individual's correct capital gains tax is so complicated, any relevant formula can only be simplified to a limited extent. The revised formula is no panacea, and determining the correct tax is still a daunting task. Congress is aware of the nightmare that it created in the 1997 legislation and, as part of the IRS Restructuring and Reform Act of 1998, it eliminated the 18-month holding period for tax years beginning after December 31, 1997 (see ¶ 502). Proposals have also been made to further reduce the maximum capital gains.

Revised formula. Under the revised formula, an individual's tax on net long-term capital gains cannot exceed the sum of:

(1) a tax computed as if there were no special tax rates for long-term capital gains on the *greater* of (a) taxable income reduced by net capital gain, or (b) the *lesser* of (i) the amount of taxable income taxed at a rate below 28 percent, or (ii) taxable income reduced by adjusted net capital gain (see ¶ 508 for definition of adjusted net capital gain) (Code Sec. 1(h)(1)(A), as amended by the 1998 Act);

(2) 10 percent of the individual's adjusted capital gain (or if less, taxable income) that does not exceed the *excess,* if any, of (a) the amount of taxable income that would (without regard to the capital gains rules) be taxed at a rate below 28 percent, over (b) taxable income reduced by adjusted net capital gain (Code Sec. 1(h)(1)(B), as amended by the 1998 Act);

(3) 20 percent of the taxpayer's adjusted net capital gain (or, if less, taxable income) in excess of the amount of tax determined under Step (2), above (Code Sec. 1(h)(1)(C), as amended by the 1998 Act);

(4) 25 percent of the excess, if any, of the unrecaptured Section 1250 gain (see ¶ 510) (or, if less, net capital gain), over the *excess,* if any, of: (a) the sum of the amount of tax computed under Step (1), above, *plus* net capital gain, over (b) taxable income (Code Sec. 1(h)(1)(D), as amended by the 1998 Act), plus

(5) 28 percent of the amount of taxable income in *excess* of the sum of the amounts on which the individual's tax is determined under Steps (1), (2), (3), and (4), above (Code Sec. 1(h)(1)(E), as amended by the 1998 Act).

The computations required by the above formula are illustrated in the following examples. For purposes of the examples, assume that, according to the tax rate schedule that applies to the individual, the first $40,000 of taxable income is taxed at 15 percent, the next $40,000 of taxable income is taxed at 28 percent, and that any taxable income above $80,000 is taxed at 31 percent.

Example (1). Assume an individual has taxable income of $100,000, including an adjusted net capital gain of $70,000. The individual's $30,000 of regular income will be taxed at 15%. $10,000 of the adjusted capital gain will be taxed at 10% (i.e., the amount of taxable income that would have been taxed at 15% if the lower capital gains rates did not exist). The remaining $60,000 of adjusted net capital gain will be taxed at 20% (i.e., the amount of taxable income that would have been taxed at 28% or 31% if the lower capital gains tax rates did not exist).

Example (2). Assume an individual has taxable income of $150,000, with a net capital gain of $50,000. The net capital gain includes an unrecaptured Section 1250 gain of $10,000, and a 28% rate gain of $10,000. This results in an adjusted net capital gain of $30,000. $100,000 of the individual's taxable income will be taxed at regular income tax rates (i.e., $40,000 at 15%, $40,000 at 28%, and $20,000 at 31%). The unrecaptured Section 1250 gain of $10,000 will be taxed at 25%, the $10,000 of 28% gain will be taxed at 28%, and the remaining $30,000 of adjusted capital gain will be taxed at 20%.

★ *Effective date.* The provision applies to tax years ending after May 6, 1997 (Act Sec. 6024 of the IRS Restructuring and Reform Act of 1998; Act Sec. 311(d)(1) of the Taxpayer Relief Act of 1997 (P.L. 105-34)).

Act Sec. 6005(d)(1), amending Code Sec. 1(h)(1). Law at ¶ 5001. Committee Report at ¶ 10,915.

Netting of Gains and Losses

¶ 521

Background _____

The 1997 changes to the capital gains rules created three separate tax rate groups: a 28-percent group, a 25-percent group, and a 20-percent group (the 20-percent group becomes a 10-percent group if the taxpayer is in the 15-percent tax bracket) (Code Sec. 1(h)(1), as amended by The Taxpayer Relief Act of 1997 (P.L. 105-34)). After enactment of the 1997 legislation, it became clear that the Code did not spell out the exact procedures that were to be used in netting the gains and losses from the various tax rate groups. Late in 1997, the IRS issued a Notice (Notice 97-59, I.R.B. 1997-45, 7) that provided the details on how the netting was to be carried out. The Notice was based on the information that the IRS had received from the Congressional leadership (Letter of September 29, 1997, from Representatives Bill Archer and Charles Rangel and Senators Daniel P. Moynihan and William Roth).

Caution. The same legislation that added the technical corrections discussed below eliminated the 18-month holding period that was required to have the lowest applicable long-term rates apply. The elimination of the 18-month rule (generally effective for tax years ending after December 31, 1997) is discussed at ¶ 502. Therefore, in reading the following material, remember that after December 31, 1997, the 28-percent group no longer includes capital assets held more than 12 months but not more than 18 months (Code Sec. 1(h)(5), as amended by the 1998 Act).

Technical Corrections Impact

Netting procedures.—A technical correction provides the necessary information that individuals need in order to follow the correct netting procedures and to accurately determine the net amount of their capital gains or losses (Code Sec. 1(h)(1), as amended by the IRS Restructuring and Reform Act of 1998).

Comment. The netting procedures embodied in the Code follow the netting procedures set forth in IRS Notice 97-59, so there are no surprises.

The basic netting procedure provides that within each tax rate group (e.g., 20-percent group), gains and losses are netted in order to arrive at a net gain or loss for the group (Notice 97-59). After this basic process has been completed, the following netting and ordering rules must be applied:

(1) *Short-term capital gains and losses.* A technical correction provides that, as under the traditional rules, short-term capital losses (including short-term loss carryovers from a prior year) are applied first to reduce short-term capital gains, if any, that would otherwise be taxable at ordinary income tax rates. A net short-term loss is used first to reduce any net long-term capital gain from the 28-percent group (Code Sec. 1(h)(5)(A)(III), as amended by the 1998 Act). Any remaining short-term loss is then used to reduce gain from the 25-percent group and then the 20-percent group (Code Sec. 1(h)(1), as amended by the 1998 Act, and Notice 97-59).

(2) *Long-term capital gains and losses.* A net loss from the 28-percent group (including long-term capital loss carryovers) is used first to reduce gain

from the 25-percent group, then to reduce net gain from the 20-percent group. A net loss from the 20-percent group is used first to reduce net gain from the 28-percent group, and then to reduce gain from the 25-percent group (Notice 97-59).

Any resulting net capital gain that is attributable to a particular rate group is taxed at that group's marginal tax rate (Notice 97-59).

Example. At the end of 1997, Ralph Helm had a short-term capital loss of $35,000. He also had long-term capital gains in the following amounts and tax rate groups: $28,000 (25% group-unrecaptured Section 1250 gain), $5,000 (28% group-collectibles gain), and $10,000 (20% group). Helm would first apply $5,000 of his short-term loss against his 28% collectibles gain. Next he would apply $28,000 of his short-term loss against the 25% unrecaptured Section 1250 gain. His remaining $2,000 of short-term loss would then be applied against his $10,000 gain in the 20% group. The result of this netting and ordering procedure is that he has $8,000 of long-term gain subject to a 20% capital gains tax.

★ *Effective date.* This provision applies to tax years ending after May 6, 1997 (Act Sec. 6024 of the IRS Restructuring and Reform Act of 1998; Act Sec. 311(d)(1) of the Taxpayer Relief Act of 1997 (P.L. 105-34)).

Act Sec. 6005(d)(1), amending Code Sec. 1(h)(1). Law at ¶ 5001. Committee Report at ¶ 10,915.

Impact on Alternative Minimum Tax

¶ 523

Background

Prior to the 1997 capital gains legislation, no special alternative minimum tax (AMT) treatment was provided for capital gains because the maximum tax rate on capital gains (i.e., 28 percent) was equal to the maximum AMT rate (also 28 percent). However, the 1997 legislation specifically provided that the new lower capital gains rates (e.g., 20 percent) would apply when computing an individual's AMT liability (Code Sec. 55(b)(3), as amended by the Taxpayer Relief Act of 1997 (P.L. 105-34)).

Technical Corrections Impact

Maximum AMT rate.—A technical correction reordered the formula for computing the AMT on capital gains (Code Sec. 55(b)(3), as amended by the IRS Restructuring and Reform Act of 1998).

Comment. Although the technical correction reordered the formula that must be used to determine the impact of capital gains on an individual's AMT, it did *not* change the principle that the lower capital gains rates are to be used when computing the individual's AMT.

Under the reordered formula, an individual's tentative minimum tax may not exceed the total of:

(1) the tentative minimum tax computed without regard to Code Sec. 55(b)(3) on the individual's "taxable excess" (i.e., alternative minimum taxable income in excess of the applicable exemption amount) reduced by the *lesser* of (a) net capital gain or (b) the total of adjusted net capital gain (see ¶ 508) and unrecaptured Section 1250 gain (see ¶ 510) (Code Sec. 55(b)(3)(A), as amended by the 1998 Act);

(2) 10 percent of so much of the adjusted net capital gain (or, if less, taxable excess) that does not exceed the amount on which tax is computed

under Code Sec. 1(h)(1)(B) (i.e., the 10-percent rate) (Code Sec. 55(b)(3)(B), as amended by the 1998 Act);

(3) 20 percent of the adjusted net capital gain (or, if less, taxable excess) in excess of the amount on which tax is determined under step (2), above (Code Sec. 55(b)(3)(C), as amended by the 1998 Act); and

(4) 25 percent of the amount of taxable income in excess of the total of the amounts determined under steps (1), (2), and (3), above (Code Sec. 55(b)(3)(D), as amended by the 1998 Act).

Comment: The 1998 Act changed the rate ordering from (1) 25%, (2) 10%, (3) 20% to (1) 10%, (2) 20%, (3) 25%.

Caution. Even though net capital gains are still subject to the lower capital gains tax rates when computing an individual's AMT, it must be remembered that such gains are fully included in an individual's alternative minimum taxable income. Thus, in some situations, a substantial amount of capital gains may make an individual liable for AMT. In addition, large amounts of capital gains may increase an individual's gross income to the point where itemized deductions and personal exemptions are subject to being phased out.

Tax years beginning after December 31, 2000. The technical correction makes clear that the lower capital gains rates of 8 percent or 18 percent that will apply after December 31, 2000, to certain property held for more than 5 years (see ¶ 524) will be used when applying the above formula (i.e., steps (2) and (3)) (Code Sec. 55(b)(3), last paragraph, as amended by the 1998 Act).

Small business stock sold after December 31, 2000. When small business stock has a holding period that begins after December 31, 2000, an amount equal to 28 percent of the gain excluded from income under Code Sec. 1202 will be treated as an item of tax preference for AMT purposes (instead of the 42 percent that was excluded under previous law) (Code Sec. 57(a)(7), as amended by the 1998 Act).

★ *Effective date.* This provision applies to tax years ending after May 6, 1997 (Act Sec. 6024 of the IRS Restructuring and Reform Act of 1998; Act Sec. 311(d)(1) of the Taxpayer Relief Act of 1997 (P.L. 105-34)).

Act Sec. 6005(d)(2), amending Code Sec. 55(b)(3). Law at ¶ 5110. Committee Report at ¶ 10,915.

Reduced Rates After 2000

¶ 524

Background

In general, the lower capital gains rates of 20 percent and 10 percent will continue to apply after December 31, 2000, provided that the regular long-term holding period has been satisfied (i.e., more than 12 months). (See ¶ 502 for a discussion concerning the elimination of the 18-month holding period for tax years ending after December 31, 1997.) However, a lower capital gains rate of 18 percent (8 percent for individuals in a 15-percent tax bracket) will apply if the individual held the asset more than five years (Code Sec. 1(h)(2), as amended by the Taxpayer Relief Act of 1997 (P.L. 105-34)). As a general rule, an individual in a marginal tax bracket higher than 15 percent must acquire the capital asset after December 31, 2000 in order to have the lower capital gains tax apply to an asset held more than five years (Code Sec. 1(h)(2)(B)(ii), as amended by P.L. 105-34). However, these individuals may make a special election to treat certain assets (e.g., readily tradable stock) acquired before January 1, 2001, as sold on January 1, 2001 (or the next business day) and pay the appropriate amount of tax. The asset will then be treated as if it was acquired after December 31, 2000 (Act Sec. 311(e) of P.L. 105-34).

Technical Corrections Impact

Cross references changed.—The technical correction did not change, alter or modify the rules concerning the lower rates that may apply to certain capital assets acquired after December 31, 2000. Its only change to the relevant Code Section (Code Sec. 1(h)(2), as amended by the IRS Restructuring and Reform Act of 1998) was to alter some cross references. These changes in the cross references were made necessary by the reordering of the rate structure under Code Sec. 1(h)(1) (Code Sec. 1(h)(2), as amended by the 1998 Act).

Election. The technical correction did *not* make any change with regard to the 1997 Act provision that provides for the special election concerning the five-year holding period (Act Sec. 311(e) of P.L. 105-34).

★ *Effective date.* This provision applies to tax years ending after May 6, 1997 (Act Sec. 6024 of the IRS Restructuring and Reform Act of 1998; Act Sec. 311(d)(1) of the Taxpayer Relief Act of 1997 (P.L. 105-34)).

Act Sec. 6005(d)(1), amending Code Sec. 1(h)(2). Law at ¶ 5001. Committee Report at ¶ 10,915.

SMALL BUSINESS STOCK

Rollover of Gain by Partnerships and S Corporations

¶ 531

Background

An individual may elect to roll over gain realized from the sale of qualified small business stock (as defined in Code Sec. 1202(c)) if the stock is held by the individual for more than six months. The gain may be rolled over into other small business stock, provided that such stock is purchased by the individual during the 60-day period that begins on the date of the sale of the original small business stock (Code Sec. 1045, as added by the Taxpayer Relief Act of 1997 (P.L. 105-34)). Although certain partnerships and S corporations may purchase qualified small business stock, the rollover provision mentions individuals only.

Technical Corrections Impact

Application of rollover provisions to partnerships and S corporations.—A technical correction changes the word "individual" in Code Sec. 1045(a) to "taxpayer other than a corporation," making it clear that the rollover provisions apply to certain partnerships and S corporations (Code Sec. 1045(a), as amended by the IRS Restructuring and Reform Act of 1998).

Rules to apply to rollovers.—The 1998 Act also clarifies that rules similar to the rules of Code Secs. 1202(f) through 1202(k) (pertaining to the 50-percent exclusion for gain from certain small business stock) are to apply to rollover of gain from qualified small business stock to another qualified small business stock (Code Sec. 1045(b)(5), as added by the IRS Restructuring and Reform Act of 1998).

Comment. Making the rollover provisions apply to certain partnerships and S corporations without limiting the types of partners or shareholders the entities may have is an important change from the Senate Bill. The Senate bill had limited the types of partners or shareholder that a partnership or S corporation could have in order for the benefits of Code Sec. 1045 to apply to a noncorporate partner or shareholder.

¶ 531

Comment. The Conference Committee Report points out that one effect of applying rules similar to those in Code Secs. 1202(f) through 1202(k) to rollovers is that the benefit of a tax-free rollover with respect to the sale of small business stock by a partnership will flow through to a partner that is not a corporation if the partner held its partnership interest at all times the partnership held the small business stock. A similar rule applies to S corporations.

PRACTICAL ANALYSIS. George Jones, Esq., of CCH INCOR-PORATED, New York, NY, observes that this technical correction brings reality to Code Sec. 1045 by validating the one practical way in which a relatively large number of individuals will be able to take advantage of the rollover—through venture capital partnerships. In the high-risk business of investing in small, emerging growth companies, the Act now lowers that risk by permitting individuals both the tax-advantage of the rollover and the investment-advantage gained through pooling their resources with more sophisticated institutional investors in funds run by skilled, professional managers.

However, this latter advantage came very close to not happening, since both the House and Senate bills had used language that would have extended the rollover benefits to investment partnerships in which only individuals were members. A lobbying blitz by existing venture capital partnership funds convinced the conferees that there is no tax policy reason to exclude partnerships with corporate members, as long as the rollover benefits are confined only to those partners who are not corporations. Since the inception of venture capital partnership funds in 1986, it has been very rare to find a fund without a mix of partners who are institutional investors (such as pension funds and university endowments) and individuals. The final language of the Act reflects that reality.

★ *Effective date.* The provision applies to sales after August 5, 1997 (Act. Sec. 6024 of the IRS Restructuring and Reform Act of 1998; Act Sec. 313(c) of the Taxpayer Relief Act of 1997 (P.L. 105-34)).

Act Sec. 6005(f), amending Code Sec. 1045(a) and Code Sec. 1045(b). Law at ¶ 5580. Committee Report at ¶ 10,935.

APPRECIATED FINANCIAL POSITIONS

Exception for Debt Instruments

¶ 536

Background

When a taxpayer enters into a constructive sale of an appreciated financial position, gain (but not loss) is recognized as if the position were sold, assigned, or otherwise terminated at its fair market value on the date of the constructive sale and then immediately repurchased (Code Sec. 1259, as added by the Taxpayer Relief Act of 1997 (P.L. 105-34)).

The term "appreciated financial position" generally means any position with respect to any stock, debt instrument, or partnership interest in which there would be gain if such position were sold, assigned, or otherwise terminated at its fair market value (Code Sec. 1259(b)(1), as added by P.L. 105-34). However, there are two exceptions (Code Sec. 1259(b)(2), as added by P.L. 105-34). One exception applies to any position that is marked to market. A second exception applies to any position with respect to a debt instrument if the following three conditions are satisfied:

> (1) the debt unconditionally entitles the holder to receive a specified principal amount;

> (2) the interest payments (or other similar amounts) with respect to the debt meet the requirements of Code Sec. 860G(a)(1)(B)(i); that is, they are payable based on a fixed rate or, to the extent provided for in regulations, at a variable rate; and

> (3) the debt is not convertible, either directly or indirectly, into stock of the issuer or any related person.

Technical Corrections Impact

Exceptions clarified.—A technical correction makes two changes in the exception relating to debt instruments. First, the correction makes it clear that the three requirements listed above refer to a position in a debt instrument rather than to the debt instrument itself. In addition, it clarifies that the exception applies either to a position that satisfies the three requirements or to a hedge of a position that meets the three requirements (Code Sec. 1259(b)(2), as amended by the IRS Restructuring and Reform Act of 1998).

Comment. The Senate Finance Committee Report states that a hedge for this purpose includes any position that reduces the taxpayer's risk of interest-rate or price-rate changes or currency fluctuations with respect to another position.

PRACTICAL ANALYSIS. Steven M. Surdell of Baker & McKenzie, Chicago, Illinois, observes that in order for a constructive sale to occur under Code Sec. 1259, a taxpayer must have eliminated sufficient amounts of the risk of loss and opportunity for gain in respect of an "appreciated financial position." Code Sec. 1259(b) broadly defines the term to include any position with respect to any stock, debt instrument, or partnership interest if such position has appreciated in value.

Code Sec. 1259(b)(2) contains what is commonly referred to as the "straight debt" exception to the appreciated financial position definition. In order to qualify for the exception, Code Sec. 1259(b)(2)(A)(i)-(iii) provides that a debt instrument must: (1) unconditionally entitle the holder to a specified principal payment, (2) bear adequate interest, and (3) not be convertible into the stock of the issuer or any related party (collectively, the "straight debt characteristics"). Once a debt instrument qualifies for the straight debt exception, it will not be deemed an "appreciated financial position" even if it has appreciated in value due to, for example, a general decline in market interest rates.

As originally enacted, Code Sec. 1259(b)(2)(A) provided that the straight debt exception applied to any *position with respect to debt* so long as the debt itself contained the straight debt characteristics. Code Sec. 1259 does not define the term "position," but most practitioners assume that the term should be interpreted in the same or similar manner as it is interpreted under the straddle rules of Code Sec. 1092. Under these rules, two or more positions may be a part of a straddle (with all the attendant complications which that characterization causes) if they economically offset each other. It has generally been understood that a straddle may occur even if the offsetting positions do not perfectly inversely correlate (i.e., do not perfectly offset each other as an economic matter).

Given this background, Code Sec. 1259(b)(2)(A) could have been interpreted to provide that a position in respect to debt could have qualified for the straight debt exception even if the position itself did not contain all of the straight debt characteristics—so long as the debt that the position hedged met those characteristics. For example, if a party took a derivative position which economically hedged an appreciated straight debt instrument, but the position also entitled the holder to economically convert into the debt issuer's stock, an argument existed that the position itself qualified for the straight debt exception notwithstanding the fact that it did not meet all of the straight debt characteristics. The Act clarifies that in order for the position to qualify for the straight debt exception the position itself, and not merely the underlying debt, must contain the straight debt characteristics or, alternatively, be a "hedge" of a position that contains the straight debt characteristics. For those purposes, a "hedge" is defined as a position that reduces the taxpayer's risk of interest rate, price or currency fluctuations with respect to another position.

★ *Effective date.* These changes are generally effective for constructive sales after June 8, 1997 (Act Sec. 6024 of the IRS Restructuring and Reform Act of 1998; Act Sec. 1001(a) of the Taxpayer Relief Act of 1997 (P.L. 105-34)).

Act Sec. 6010(a)(1), amending Code Sec. 1259(b)(2). Law at ¶ 5620. Committee Report at ¶ 11,125.

Definition of Forward Contract

¶ 541

Background ───────────────────────────────────

A constructive sale of the position generally results when a taxpayer holding an appreciated financial position enters into a forward contract to deliver the same or substantially identical property (Code Sec. 1259(c)(1)(C), as added by the Taxpayer Relief Act of 1997 (P.L. 105-34)). For this purpose, a forward contract is defined as a contract to deliver a substantially fixed amount of property for a substantially fixed price (Code Sec. 1259(d)(1), as added by the 1997 Act).

Technical Corrections Impact

Definition of forward contract clarified.—A technical correction makes it clear that the definition of a forward contract includes a contract that provides for cash settlement with respect to a substantially fixed amount of property at a substantially fixed price (Code Sec. 1259(d)(1), as amended by the IRS Restructuring and Reform Act of 1998).

Comment. In some cases, it is inconvenient or impossible to actually deliver the underlying asset. When a contract is settled for cash, it is marked to market at the end of the last trading day and all positions are declared closed. The cash changing hands is the difference between the contract price and the closing spot (market) price on that date.

Example. In June, Farmer Fred agrees to sell 100 bushels of grain for $4 per bushel on October 15. Baker Bob agrees to buy the grain for $4 per bushel on October 15. When October 15 arrives, the market price of the grain is $4.25 per bushel. Instead of selling the grain to Baker Bob for $4.00 per bushel, Farmer Fred could pay him $0.25 per bushel ($25) instead. If Baker Bob then buys the grain elsewhere for $4.25 per bushel, his net price is $4.00 per bushel ($4.25—$0.25). Farmer Fred then sells his grain on the market for $4.25 per bushel and receives a net price of $4.00 per bushel ($4.25 selling price—$0.25 paid to Baker Bob).

★ *Effective date.* This provision is generally effective for constructive sales entered into after June 8, 1997 (Act Sec. 6024 of the IRS Restructuring and Reform Act of 1998; Act Sec. 1001(a) of the Taxpayer Relief Act of 1997 (P.L. 105-34)).

Act Sec. 6010(a)(2), amending Code Sec. 1259(d)(1). Law at ¶ 5620. Committee Report at ¶ 11,130.

Special Effective Date Rule

¶ 546

Background

For decedents dying after June 8, 1997, the constructive sales rules for appreciated financial positions (Code Sec. 1259) include a special effective date provision if four conditions are satisfied (Act Sec. 1001(d)(3) of the Taxpayer Relief Act of 1997 (P.L. 105-34)). These conditions are:

(1) a constructive sale of an appreciated financial position must have occurred before June 8, 1997;

(2) the transaction must remain open for at least two years;

(3) the transaction must remain open at any time during the three years prior to the decedent's death; and

(4) the transaction is not closed within the 30-day period beginning on the August 5, 1997, date of enactment of the Taxpayer Relief Act of 1997 (P.L. 105-34).

If these requirements are satisfied, both the appreciated financial position and the transaction resulting in the constructive sale are generally treated as rights to receive income in respect of a decedent (IRD) under Code Sec. 691. Gain with respect to a position in a constructive sales transaction that accrues after the transaction is closed, however, is not treated as an IRD item (Act Sec. 1001(d)(3) of the 1997 Act).

Technical Corrections Impact

Clarification of special effective date.—The language "within the 30-day period beginning on the date of enactment of the Act" is clarified to read "before the close of the 30th day after enactment of the Act" (Act Sec. 1001(d)(3)(C) of the Taxpayer Relief Act of 1997, as amended by the IRS Restructuring and Reform Act of 1998).

Comment. The effective date of the Taxpayer Relief Act of 1997 was August 5, 1997. Thus, the rule applies to transactions not closed before the end of September 4, 1997.

★ *Effective date.* This provision is effective for decedents dying after June 8, 1997 (Act Sec. 6024 of the IRS Restructuring and Reform Act of 1998; Act Sec. 1001(d)(3) of the Taxpayer Relief Act of 1997 (P.L. 105-34)).

Act Sec. 6010(a)(4), amending Act Sec. 1001(d)(3)(C) of the Taxpayer Relief Act of 1997 (P.L. 105-34). Law at ¶ 8255. Committee Report at ¶ 11,140.

ACCOUNTING METHODS

Mark-to Market Election for Traders in Securities or Commodities

¶ 551

Background

Securities and commodities traders may elect to have the mark-to-market accounting rules apply to them (Code Sec. 475(f)(1), as added by the Taxpayer Relief Act of 1997 (P.L. 105-34)). If they make the election, any gain or loss recognized is treated as ordinary gain or loss (Code Sec. 475(d)(3)(A)(i), as added by P.L. 105-34).

The Self-Employment Contributions Act of 1954 (SECA) imposes a tax on net earnings from self-employment (NESE) (Code Sec. 1402). Gain or loss on the sale or exchange of a capital asset is excluded from NESE (Code Sec. 1402(a)(3)(A)).

For federal income tax purposes, a publicly traded partnership is generally treated as a corporation (Code Sec. 7704). Such treatment does not apply, however, if 90 percent or more of the partnership's gross income consists of passive-type income. Passive-type income includes gain from the sale or disposition of a capital asset (Code Sec. 7704(c)).

Technical Corrections Impact

Tax treatment of gain or loss clarified.—A technical correction makes it clear that gain or loss of a commodities or securities trader that is treated as ordinary gain or loss because of the election made by the trader to use the mark-to-market accounting rules is treated as gain or loss from a capital asset, and not as ordinary income. Such treatment applies for purposes of determining NESE or for determining whether the passive-type income exception to the publicly-traded partnership rules applies (Code Sec. 475(f)(1), as amended by the IRS Restructuring and Reform Act of 1998). Thus, it is not subject to the self-employment tax and is treated as passive income for purposes of determining the amount of a publicly traded partnership's passive income.

Comment. The Senate Finance Committee Report states that gain or loss that is treated as ordinary solely by reason of election of the mark-to-market rules will *not* be treated as other than gain or loss from a capital asset for purposes of any other Code provisions specified in IRS regulations.

★ *Effective date.* The provision applies to tax years of electing securities and commodities traders ending after August 5, 1997 (Act Sec. 6024 of the IRS Restructuring and Reform Act of 1998; Act Sec. 1001(d)(4)(A) of the Taxpayer Relief Act of 1997 (P.L. 105-34)).

Act Sec. 6010(a)(3), amending Code Sec. 475(f)(1)(D). Law at ¶ 5380. Committee Report at ¶ 11,135.

Manufacturer-to-Dealer Installment Sale Election

¶ 553

Background

In general, the installment sales method may not be used by dealers in personal property. Prior to enactment of the Taxpayer Relief Act of 1997 (P.L. 105-34), a special rule (Act Sec. 811(c)(2) of the Tax Reform Act of 1986 (P.L.

Background ————————————————————————

99-514)) allowed manufacturers of tangible personal property to use the installment method to report the income from sales of property to dealers if certain requirements were met. The 1997 Act repealed this special rule effective for tax years beginning more than one year after the August 5, 1997 date of enactment and treated affected manufacturers as making a change of accounting method. Any adjustments required by this change of accounting method, however, were required to be taken into account ratably over a four-year period beginning with the first tax year *beginning after the date of enactment,* even if such tax year did not begin more than one year after the date of enactment (Act Sec. 1088 of the Taxpayer Relief Act of 1997 (P.L. 105-34)).

Technical Corrections Impact

Change in beginning of four-year period.—A technical correction changes the period for making the required adjustments to the four-year period beginning with the first tax year beginning *more than one year* after date of enactment of the 1997 Act (i.e., August 5, 1997) (Act Sec. 6010(q) of the IRS Restructuring and Reform Act of 1998, amending Act Sec. 1088(b)(2)(C) of the Taxpayer Relief Act of 1997 (P.L. 105-34)).

★ *Effective date.* This provision applies to tax years beginning more than one year after August 5, 1997 (Act Sec. 6024 of the IRS Restructuring and Reform Act of 1998; Act Sec. 1088(b) of the Taxpayer Relief Act of 1997 (P.L. 105-34)).

Act Sec. 6010(q) amending Act Sec. 1088(b)(2)(C) of the Taxpayer Relief Act of 1997 (P.L. 105-34). Law at ¶ 8255.

Mark-to-Market Treatment Denied to Customer Receivables

¶ 554

Background ————————————————————————

Dealers in securities must value securities included in year-end inventory at fair market value. Securities dealers are also required to recognize gain or loss based on the fair market value of noninventory securities at the end of the year. The gain or loss is generally ordinary, rather than capital (Code Sec. 475(d)(3)(A)(i)).

A dealer in securities is a person who regularly purchases securities from or sells securities to customers in the ordinary course of a trade or business. A securities dealer is also defined as one who regularly offers to enter into, assume, offset, assign or otherwise terminate positions in certain types of securities with customers in the ordinary course of business. The definition of a security includes a note, bond, debenture, or other evidence of indebtedness (Code Sec. 475(c)(1)).

A taxpayer is ordinarily exempt from dealer treatment if the taxpayer is considered a dealer only by virtue of its purchases and sales of debt instruments that are customer paper with respect to the taxpayer or another member of its consolidated group.

A debt instrument is considered customer paper with respect to a person if:

(1) the person's principal activity is selling nonfinancial goods or services;

(2) the debt instrument was issued by the purchaser of the goods or services at the time of the purchase for the purpose of financing the purchase; and

Background

(3) at all times since the debt instrument was issued, it has been held either by the person selling the goods or services or by a corporation that is a member of the same consolidated group.

Taxpayers holding customer paper, however, may elect out of the dealer status exception (Reg. § 1.475(c)-1(b)(3)). In other words, a taxpayer holding customer paper may elect to be treated as a dealer. This "customer paper election" out of dealer status allows a taxpayer whose principal activity is selling nonfinancial goods or providing nonfinancial services to use the mark-to-market accounting method to obtain a loss deduction for their receivables.

IRS Restructuring and Reform Impact

Customer paper exemption limited.—The mark-to-market accounting rules were not intended to be used by dealers in nonfinancial goods and services to obtain a loss deduction that otherwise would not be available. Consequently, the new law amends the definition of a security to exclude any "nonfinancial customer paper" (Code Sec. 474(c)(4)(A), as added by the IRS Restructuring and Reform Act of 1998).

For this purpose, "nonfinancial customer paper" means any receivable in the form of a note, bond, debenture, or other evidence of indebtedness that is produced from the sale of nonfinancial goods or services by a person whose principal activity is selling or providing nonfinancial goods and services. The receivable must have been held by the seller of nonfinancial goods and services at all times since it was issued (Code Sec. 475(c)(4)(B), as added by the 1998 Act).

Comment. Nonfinancial customer paper held by related persons as defined under Code Sec. 267(b) or Code Sec. 707(b) is treated as held by the seller.

Example (1). Pulp Bros., a paper manufacturer, sells paper products on credit to the federal government. These accounts receivable do not bear interest. Under a mark-to-market method, this pool of receivables would be valued below its face value, which would result in a deductible loss. However, because Pulp Bros.'s primary activity is manufacturing and selling goods (paper products), it is not permitted to claim the customer paper exception to the definition of a securities dealer, or use the mark-to-market accounting rules to value the accounts receivable and deduct a loss.

Independent contractors. The Conference Agreement clarifies that nonfinancial customer paper received by a taxpayer in exchange for services performed by independent contractors is ineligible for mark-to-market treatment just as it would if the services had been performed by the taxpayer's employees. The Conference Agreement intends that, under the authority granted by Code Sec. 475(g)(1), the Treasury Department will issue regulations proscribing abuse of the new mark-to-market ineligibility provisions, including through independent contractor arrangements.

Example (2). Bob's Floors is in the business of refinishing hardwood floors. Potential customers contact Bob's Floors to obtain estimates and to arrange for the refinishing work to be done. However, Bob's Floors hires independent contractors to do the actual floor refinishing work. Payment plans (receivables) held by Bob's Floors through which customers finance the floor refinishing work are not eligible for mark-to-market treatment, even though the work is done by independent contractors, because Bob's Floors' primary business is to provide nonfinancial services.

Regulations. The Treasury Department is directed to prescribe regulations aimed at preventing security dealers (or related persons) from using these new mark-to-market ineligibility provisions to avoid the mark-to-market rules under Code Sec. 475 (Code Sec. 475(g)(3), as added by the 1998 Act). Thus, the Conference Agreement contemplates that a taxpayer will not be treated as a securities dealer based on sales to unrelated persons of receivables subject to these new provisions unless the regulatory exception for receivables held for sale to a customer applies. The Conference Agreement intends that mark-to-market or lower-of-cost-or-market will not be considered accounting methods that clearly reflect income when applied to trade receivables that are excepted from the statutory mark-to-market rules under the new provisions.

★ *Effective date.* The provision applies to tax years ending after the date of enactment (Act Sec. 7003(c)(1) of the IRS Restructuring and Reform Act of 1998). In the case of any taxpayer required by these amendments to change its method of accounting for its first tax year ending after date of enactment, (1) such change will be treated as initiated by the taxpayer; (2) such change will be treated as made with the consent of the Secretary of the Treasury; and (3) the net amount of the adjustments required to be taken into account by the taxpayer under Code Sec. 481 will be taken into account ratably over the four-tax-year periods beginning with the first tax year (Act Sec. 7003(c)(2) of the 1998 Act).

Comment. If the taxpayer terminates its existence or stops engaging in the trade or business that generated the receivable (except as a result of a tax-free transfer), any remaining balance of the Code Sec. 481 adjustment is taken into account in the year of cessation or termination.

Act Sec. 7003(a), adding Code Sec. 475(c)(4); Act Sec. 7003(b), adding Code Sec. 475(g)(3); Act Sec. 7003(c). Law at ¶ 5380. Committee Report at ¶ 11,535.

COMPANY-OWNED LIFE INSURANCE

Master Contracts

¶ 556

Background

The Taxpayer Relief Act of 1997 (P.L. 105-34) provided limitations on the deductibility of interest and premiums with respect to life insurance, endowment, and annuity contracts. One of these limitations is a pro rata interest disallowance provision (Code Sec. 264(f), as added by P.L. 105-34). An exception is made, however, for any policy or contract owned by an entity engaged in a trade or business if (1) the policy or contract covers only one individual and (2) that individual is either a 20-percent owner of the entity or is an officer, director, or employee of the trade or business (Code Sec. 264(f)). This provision says nothing about the treatment of such an individual under a master contract, however. Finally, to the extent of additional covered lives under a contract issued after the effective date (i.e., June 8, 1997), a contract is treated as a new contract (Act Sec. 1084(d) of P.L. 105-34).

Technical Corrections Impact

Coverage of individual by master contract.—A technical correction provides that if coverage of each insured individual under a master contract is treated as a separate contract for purposes of Code Sec. 817(h) (Treatment of Certain Nondiversified Contracts), Code Sec. 7702 (Life Insurance Contract Defined), and Code Sec. 7702A (Modified Endowment Contract Defined), coverage of each such insured will be treated as a separate contract for purposes of the Code Sec. 264(f) exception. For purposes of this rule, a master contract does not include any group life insurance contract, as defined in Code Sec. 848(e)(2) (Code Sec. 264(f)(3)(A), as amended by the IRS Restructuring and Reform Act of 1998).

The technical correction also clarifies that the treatment of additional covered lives under the effective date of the 1997 Act provision applies only with respect to coverage provided under a master contract, provided that coverage for each insured individual is treated as a separate contract and that the master contract is not a group life insurance contract (Act Sec. 1084(d) of the Taxpayer Relief Act of 1997 (P.L. 105-34), as amended by the 1998 Act).

Comment. The Senate Finance Committee Report states that no inference is intended that coverage provided under a master contract, for each such individual, is not treated as a separate contract for each of these individuals for other purposes under present law.

★ *Effective date.* This provision is effective for contracts issued after June 8, 1997, in tax years ending after that date (Act Sec. 6024 of the IRS Restructuring and Reform Act of 1998; Act. Sec. 1084(d) of the Taxpayer Relief Act of 1997 (P.L. 105-34)).

Act Sec. 6010(o)(3) amending Code Sec. 264(f)(4) and Act Sec. 1084(d) of the Taxpayer Relief Act of 1997 (P.L. 105-34). Law at ¶ 5260. Committee Report at ¶ 11,205.

Reporting Requirements

¶ 561

Background

The limitations on the deductibility of interest and premiums with respect to certain company-owned life insurance (Code Sec. 264, as amended by the Taxpayer Relief Act of 1997 (P.L. 105-34)) do not apply to a policy or contract held by a natural person. If a trade or business is directly or indirectly the beneficiary under the policy or contract, however, the policy is treated as held by the trade or business rather than by the natural person. The 1997 Act included a provision stating that the IRS would require such reporting as was necessary to carry out the rule when the trade or business was the beneficiary under a contract held by a natural person. Further, the 1997 Act stated that any report required under the provision would be treated as a Code Sec. 6724(d)(1) information return (Code Sec. 264(f)(5)(A)(iv), as added by P.L. 105-34).

Technical Corrections Impact

Reporting requirements.—A technical correction clarifies that the required reporting to the IRS is a Code Sec. 6724(d)(1) information return and that any other required reporting is a Code Sec. 6724(d)(2) payee statement (Code Sec. 6724(d), as amended by the IRS Restructuring and Reform Act of 1998).

Caution. The Senate Finance Committee Report notes that this means that the $50-per-report penalty imposed by Code Secs. 6722 and 6723 for failure to file or provide such information return or payee statement applies.

Comment. Although not included in the 1998 Act, the Senate Finance Committee Report clarifies that the IRS may require reporting of any relevant information either by regulations or by any other appropriate guidance (including, but not limited to, publication of a form).

★ *Effective date.* This provision is effective for contracts issued after June 8, 1997, in tax years ending after that date (Act Sec. 6024 of the IRS Restructuring and Reform Act of 1998; Act Sec. 1084(d) of the Taxpayer Relief Act of 1997 (P.L. 105-34)).

Act Sec. 6010(o)(4)(B) and (C), adding Code Sec. 6724(d)(1)(B)(xvii) and 6724(d)(2)(AA). Law at ¶ 6520. Committee Report at ¶ 11,210.

ALTERNATIVE MINIMUM TAX

Small Corporation Exemption

¶ 566

Background _____

The corporate alternative minimum tax (AMT) was repealed for small corporations for tax years beginning after 1997 (Code Sec. 55(e), as added by the Taxpayer Relief Act of 1997 (P.L. 105-34)). A corporation initially qualifies as a small corporation if it had gross receipts of $5 million or less for the three tax years that ended with its first tax year beginning after 1996. Once a corporation is recognized as a small corporation, it will continue to be exempt from the AMT as long as its average gross receipts for the prior three-tax-year period do not exceed $7.5 million. Average annual gross receipts are generally determined using the rules described in Code Sec. 448(c) for determining whether a taxpayer is exempt from the limitation on the use of the cash method of accounting because its average annual gross receipts are $5 million or less.

Technical Corrections Impact

Gross receipts tests clarified.—A technical correction clarifies how the gross receipts tests are applied. To qualify as a small business corporation, a corporation's average gross receipts for all three-tax-year periods ending before the year for which the exemption is claimed must not exceed $7.5 million. In making this computation, only tax years *beginning* after December 31, 1993, and *ending* before the tax year for which exemption from AMT is claimed are considered. However, this $7.5 million amount is reduced to $5 million for the corporation's first three-tax-year period (or portion thereof) that begins after 1993 and ends before the year in which the exemption is claimed (Code Sec. 55(e)(1)(A) and (B), as amended by the IRS Restructuring and Reform Act of 1998).

If a corporation's first tax year after beginning after 1997 is the first year of the corporation's existence, the corporation is generally treated as an exempt small corporation regardless of its gross receipts for the year (Code Sec. 55(e)(1)(C), as amended by the 1998 Act). This rule does not apply if the corporation loses its status as a small corporation because it is aggregated with one or more corporations under Code Sec. 448(c)(2) or is treated as a predecessor corporation under Code Sec. 448(c)(3)(D) (Code Sec. 55(e)(1)(D), as amended by the 1998 Act).

Example (1). ABC Corp. is a calendar-year corporation that was in existence on January 1, 1994. To qualify as a small corporation in 1998, ABC's average gross receipts for the three-tax-year period from 1994 through 1996 must be $5 million or less and its average gross receipts for the period from 1995 through 1997 must be $7.5 million or less. If ABC qualifies for 1998, it will also qualify for 1999 if its average gross receipts for the three-tax-year period 1996 through 1998 is $7.5 million or less. If ABC does not qualify for 1998, it cannot qualify for 1999 or for any subsequent year.

Example (2). XYZ Corp., a calendar-year corporation, is first incorporated in 1999. Assume that it is neither aggregated with a related, existing corporation under Code Sec. 448(c)(2) nor treated as having a predecessor corporation under Code Sec. 448(c)(3)(D). XYZ will qualify as a small corporation for 1999 regardless of its gross receipts for the year. To qualify as a small corporation in 2000, however, its gross receipts for 1999 must be $5 million or less. If XYZ qualifies for 2000, it will also qualify for 2001 if its average gross receipts for the two-tax-year period 1999 through 2000 are $7.5 million or less. If XYZ does not qualify for 2000, it cannot qualify for 2001 or any subsequent year. If XYZ qualifies for 2001, it will qualify for 2002 if its average gross receipts for the three-tax-year period 1999 through 2001 are $7.5 million or less.

Comment. In Example (2), above, the 1999 gross receipts (i.e., the first year of incorporation) must be annualized under Code Sec. 448(c)(3)(B), if the 1999 tax year is less than 12 months.

★ ***Effective date.*** This provision is effective for tax years beginning after December 31, 1997 (Act Sec. 6024 of the IRS Restructuring and Reform Act of 1998; Act Sec. 401(b) of the Taxpayer Relief Act of 1997 (P.L. 105-34)).

Act Sec. 6006(a), amending Code Sec. 55(e)(1). Law at ¶ 5110. Committee Report at ¶ 10,945.

Depreciation

¶ 571

Background

For regular tax purposes, the 200-percent declining balance method may be used to calculate depreciation deductions on certain short-lived tangible property (e.g., cars and office furniture). Depending on the type of property involved, the recovery period is three, five, seven, or 10 years. For alternative minimum tax (AMT) purposes, depreciation on such property placed in service after 1986, but before 1999, is computed using the 150-percent declining balance method and the longer class lives of the Code Sec. 168(g) alternative depreciation system (ADS). An election may be made to use the 150-percent declining balance method and ADS recovery period for regular tax purposes in order to conform regular tax and AMT depreciation (Code Sec. 168(b)(2); Code Sec. 168(c)(2), prior to amendment by the IRS Restructuring and Reform Act of 1998).

For property placed in service after 1998, the Taxpayer Relief Act of 1997 (P.L. 105-34) conformed the regular tax and AMT recovery periods by providing that the regular tax recovery periods also apply for AMT purposes (Code Sec. 56(a)(1)(A)(i), as amended by P.L. 105-34). The 1997 Act, however, failed to provide taxpayers who depreciated property using the 200-percent declining balance method for regular tax purposes with an election to use the 150-percent declining balance AMT recovery method *over the regular tax recovery period* in order to eliminate the need to make an AMT depreciation adjustment.

Technical Corrections Impact

Election clarified.—A technical correction allows taxpayers to elect, for regular tax purposes, to compute depreciation on tangible personal property that is qualified for the 200-percent declining balance method by using the 150-percent declining balance method over the recovery periods applicable for regular tax purposes (Code Sec. 168(c), as amended by the IRS Restructuring and Reform Act of 1998).

Caution. This method is available only for tangible personal property that would otherwise qualify for the 200-percent declining balance method (Code Sec. 168(b)(2)).

Election. The technical correction creates a new depreciation election that conforms regular tax and AMT depreciation. The election is irrevocable and applies to all property in the same class placed in service during the tax year for which the election is made (Code Sec. 168(b)(3) and Code Sec. 168(b)(5)).

★ *Effective date.* The amendment to the effective date related to Act Sec. 402 of the Taxpayer Relief Act of 1997 is effective August 5, 1997. However, the provision applies to property placed in service after December 31, 1998. (Act Sec. 6024 of the IRS Restructuring and Reform Act of 1998; Act Sec. 402 of the Taxpayer Relief Act of 1997 (P.L. 105-34)).

Act Sec. 6006(b), amending Code Sec. 168(c). Law at ¶ 5210. Committee Report at ¶ 10,950.

DISTRICT OF COLUMBIA TAX INCENTIVES

Eligible Census Tracts

¶ 574

Background ——————————————————————————

Certain economically depressed census tracts within the District of Columbia are designated as the D.C. Enterprise Zone (Code Sec. 1400, as added by the Taxpayer Relief Act of 1997 (P.L. 105-34)). Businesses and individual residents within the zone are eligible for special tax incentives. These incentives include a 20-percent wage credit, an additional $20,000 of expensing under Code Sec. 179 for qualified zone property placed in service by a "Qualified D.C. Zone Business," special tax-exempt financing for certain zone facilities, and a zero-percent capital gains rate on the sale of certain qualified D.C. zone assets. For purposes of the wage credit, expensing, and tax-exempt financing incentives, the D.C. Enterprise Zone consists of all census tracts that are presently part of the D.C. enterprise community (an area designated by the Secretary of Housing and Urban Development as eligible for special tax incentives) and census tracts within the District of Columbia where the poverty rate is at least 20 percent (Code Sec. 1400), as added by P.L. 105-34). For purposes of the zero-percent capital gains rate, the D.C. enterprise zone is defined to include all census tracts where the poverty rate is not less than 10 percent (Code Sec. 1400B).

——————————————————————————

Technical Corrections Impact

Census tract based on 1990 census data.—A technical correction makes it clear that the determination of whether a census tract satisfies the 20-percent poverty test applicable to the wage credit, expensing, and tax-exempt financing incentives (Code Sec. 1400(b)(2)(B), as amended by the IRS Restructuring and Reform Act of 1998), or whether a census tract satisfies the 10-percent poverty test applicable to the zero-percent capital gains rate (Code Sec. 1400B(d)(2), as amended by the IRS Restructuring and Reform Act of 1998) is to be based on 1990 decennial census data).

Comment. The Senate Finance Committee Report points out that the purpose of the technical correction is to make it clear that data from the 2000 census will not result in the expansion or reconfiguration of the D.C. Enterprise Zone.

★ *Effective date.* The provision is effective August 5, 1997 (Act Sec. 6024 of the IRS Restructuring and Reform Act of 1998; Act Sec. 701(d) of the Taxpayer Relief Act of 1997 (P.L. 105-34)).

Act Sec. 6008(a) and (c)(4), amending Code Sec. 1400(b)(2)(B) and Code Sec. 1400B(d)(2). Law at ¶ 5700 and ¶ 5720. Committee Report at ¶ 11,045 and ¶ 11,055.

Homebuyer Credit

¶ 577

Background _____

A tax credit of up to $5,000 of the amount of the purchase price is available for first-time homebuyers of a principal residence in the District of Columbia. The credit is phased out for individual taxpayers with adjusted gross income (AGI) between $70,000 and $90,000 and for joint filers with AGI between $110,000 and $130,000. The credit is available for a residence purchased after August 4, 1997, and before January 1, 2001 (Code Sec. 1400C, as added by the Taxpayer Relief Act of 1997 (P.L. 105-34)).

Technical Corrections Impact

Definitions clarified.—A technical correction makes it clear that the term "first-time homebuyer" means any individual (and, if married, the individual's spouse) who did not have a present ownership interest in a principal residence in the District of Columbia during the one-year period ending on the date of the purchase of the principal residence to which the credit applies (Code Sec. 1400C(c)(1), as amended by the IRS Restructuring and Reform Act of 1998).

The definition of "purchase price" is also clarified. The term means the adjusted basis of the principal residence on the date the residence is purchased (Code Sec. 1400C(e)(3), as amended by the 1998 Act).

A newly constructed residence is treated as purchased by the taxpayer on the date the taxpayer first occupied the residence (Code Sec. 1400C(e)(2)(B), as amended by the 1998 Act).

The technical correction also clarifies that the first-time homebuyer credit is a nonrefundable personal credit and that it is claimed after the adoption expense credit (Code Sec. 23(c), as amended by the IRS Restructuring and Reform Act of 1998) and the credit for interest on certain home mortgages (Code Sec. 25(e)(1)(C), as amended by the 1998 Act).

The technical correction further provides that the phaseout of the credit for taxpayers above the specified adjusted gross income levels applies only in the year the credit is generated. The phaseout does not apply in subsequent years to which the credit may be carried (Code Sec. 1400C(b)(1), as amended by the 1998 Act).

Finally, the technical correction makes it clear that the credit applies only to property purchased after August 4, 1997, and before January 1, 2001 (Code Sec. 1400C(i), as amended by the 1998 Act).

Comment. The Senate Finance Committee Report states that the effective date technical correction means that it is the date on which the taxpayer acquires title to the residence and not the date the purchase contract was entered into that determines whether the time requirement is satisfied.

★ *Effective date.* The provision is effective as of August 5, 1997 (Act Sec. 6024 of the IRS Restructuring and Reform Act of 1998; Act Sec. 701(a) of the Taxpayer Relief Act of 1997 (P.L. 105-34)).

Act Sec. 6008(d), amending Code Secs. 23(c), 25(e), and 1400C. Law at ¶ 5010, ¶ 5030, and ¶ 5730. Committee Report at ¶ 11,060.

Qualified D.C. Zone Business

¶ 580

Background _____

For purposes of the zero-percent capital gains rate, a D.C. Zone business is defined as any entity that is an enterprise zone business as defined in Code Sec. 1397B (Code Sec. 1400B(c), as added by the Taxpayer Relief Act of 1997 (P.L.

Background――――――――――――――――――――――――――――――――

105-34)). The definition of "D.C. Zone Business" (as added by P.L. 105-34), could be construed to mean that the term applies only to corporations and partnerships.

If a business satisfies certain requirements applicable to a qualified D.C. Zone business for a three-year testing period following the end of a start-up period, qualification requirements are subsequently reduced (Code Sec. 1394(b)(3), as amended by the Taxpayer Relief Act of 1997), but at least 35 percent of the employees of the business must still be residents of an empowerment zone or enterprise community.

――

Technical Corrections Impact

Proprietorships included in definition.—The definition of a D.C. Zone business is modified to make it clear that a proprietorship, as well as a corporation or partnership, can constitute a D.C. Zone business for purposes of the zero-percent capital gains rate (Code Sec. 1400B(c), as amended by the IRS Restructuring and Reform Act of 1998).

Residency requirement. The technical correction clarifies that qualified D.C. Zone businesses that take advantage of special tax-exempt financing incentives are not subject to the 35-percent residency rule after the close of the testing period (Code Sec. 1400A(a), as amended by the IRS Restructuring and Reform Act of 1998).

★ *Effective date.* The provision is effective August 5, 1997 (Act Sec. 6024 of the IRS Restructuring and Reform Act of 1998; Act Sec. 701(d) of the Taxpayer Relief Act of 1997 (P.L. 105-34)).

Act Sec. 6008(b), amending Code Sec. 1400A(a); Act Sec. 6008(c)(3), amending Code Sec. 1400B(c). Law at ¶ 5710 and ¶ 5720. Committee Report at ¶ 11,050 and ¶ 11,055.

Zero-Percent Capital Gains Rate

¶ 583

Background――――――――――――――――――――――――――――――――

Certain qualified D.C. Zone assets held for more than five years are subject to a zero-percent capital gains rate. For purposes of this rate, the D.C. Enterprise Zone is defined to include all census tracts in the District of Columbia where the poverty rate is at least 10 percent. Only qualified capital gains that are attributable to the 10-year period beginning on January 1, 1998, and ending on December 31, 2007, are eligible for the zero-percent rate.

The term "qualified D.C. Zone assets" generally means stock or partnership interests held in, or tangible property held by, a D.C. Zone business. In general, such assets must be acquired after 1997 and before 2003. Under a special rule, however, qualified D.C. Zone assets may include property that was a qualified D.C. Zone asset in the hands of a prior owner. This special rule applies if, at the time of the acquisition, and during substantially all of the subsequent purchaser's holding period, either (1) substantially all of the use of the property is in a qualified D.C. Zone business or (2) the property is an ownership interest in a qualified D.C. Zone business (Code Sec. 1400B, as added by the Taxpayer Relief Act of 1997 (P.L. 105-34)).

Technical Corrections Impact

Subsequent purchasers.—A technical correction makes it clear that to qualify under the special rule, there is no requirement that D.C. Zone business property be acquired by a subsequent purchaser prior to January 1, 2003 (Code Sec. 1400B(b)(6), as amended by the IRS Restructuring and Reform Act of 1998).

Effect of termination of D.C. enterprise zone designation. The technical correction also clarifies that termination of the D.C. Enterprise Zone designation at the end of 2002 will not, by itself, result in property failing to be treated as a qualified D.C. Zone asset for purposes of the zero-percent capital gains rate, assuming the property would otherwise continue to qualify (Code Sec. 1400B(b)(5), as added by the 1998 Act).

★ *Effective date.* This provision is effective as of August 5, 1997 (Act Sec. 6024 of the IRS Restructuring and Reform Act of 1998; Act Sec. 701(d) of the Taxpayer Relief Act of 1997 (P.L. 105-34)).

Act Secs. 6008(c)(1) and (2), amending Code Sec. 1400B(b). Law at ¶ 5720. Committee Report at ¶ 11,055.

EMPLOYMENT TAXES

Employer Social Security Credit

¶ 586

Background

A business tax credit is available to food and beverage establishments for a portion of the employer social security taxes paid on employee cash tips (Code Sec. 45B, as added by the Revenue Reconciliation Act of 1993 (P.L. 103-66)). This credit is classified as one of the general business credits (Code Sec. 38(b)(11), as added by the 1993 Act). Usually, unused general business credits can only be carried forward for a period of 20 years (15 years for credits that arose in tax years beginning before January 1, 1998) (Code Sec. 39(a), as amended by the Taxpayer Relief Act of 1997 (P.L. 105-34)). Thus, if the employer did not use the carryforward social security credit within the applicable time period (15 or 20 years), it was lost.

Technical Corrections Impact

Deduction for unused credit.—A technical correction adds the employer social security credit to the list of qualified business credits that may be deducted after the normal carryforward time period has expired (i.e., 15 or 20 years) (Code Sec. 196(c)(8), as added by the IRS Restructuring and Reform Act of 1998). The deduction for the unused credit is taken in the year after the expiration of the normal carryforward time period.

Example. In 1994, an employer had an unused employer social security tax credit of $5,000. After the end of the normal carryforward period (15 years because the credit arose in a tax year beginning before January 1, 1998), the employer has an unused credit of $1,000. In the first tax year after the expiration of the carryforward period, the employer may claim a deduction for the amount of the unused credit.

Comment. Among the other types of credits that may be deducted after the expiration of the normal carryforward period are the work opportunity credit, the empowerment zone credit, and the Indian employment credit (Code Sec. 196(c)).

¶ 586

★ *Effective date.* This provision is effective for taxes paid after December 31, 1993 (Act Sec. 6020(b) of the IRS Restructuring and Reform Act of 1998; Act Sec. 13443(a) of the Revenue Reconciliation Act of 1993 (P.L. 103-66)).

Act Sec. 6020(a), adding Code Sec. 196(c)(8); Act Sec. 6020(b). Law at ¶ 5230. Committee Report at ¶ 11,365.

Montana Demonstration Project

¶ 589

Background

Under a test project on the feasibility and desirability of expanding combined federal and state employment tax reporting, the 1997 law authorized a demonstration project between the IRS and the state of Montana (Act Sec. 976 of the Taxpayer Relief Act of 1997 (P.L. 105-34)). The project is limited to a five-year period and to disclosure of the name, taxpayer identification number, and signature of the taxpayer, which is information that is common to the Montana and federal portions of the combined form. The 1997 Act also amended the Code to permit the IRS to disclose certain information with regard to this demonstration project (Code Sec. 6103(d)(5), as added by the 1997 Act). Implementation of the project was, nevertheless, hindered by the fact that the IRS interpreted the Code Sec. 6103 penalties for disclosure of information to apply to information common to federal and state forms.

Technical Corrections Impact

Exemption from penalties for disclosure of information.—A technical correction makes clear that the usual restrictions on the unauthorized disclosure of information (Code Sec. 7213) and/or the unauthorized inspection of returns or return information (Code Sec. 7213A) do not apply to information disclosed as part of the Montana Demonstration Project (Code Sec. 6103(d)(5), as amended by the IRS Restructuring and Reform Act of 1998).

Comment. Without this additional language, IRS officials who disclosed taxpayer information to the state of Montana as part of the demonstration project might have been subject to prosecution for committing a felony and/or monetary penalties.

★ *Effective date.* This provision is effective as of August 5, 1997 (Act Sec. 6024 of the IRS Restructuring and Reform Act of 1998; Act Sec. 976(b)(1) of the Taxpayer Relief Act of 1997 (P.L. 105-34)).

Act Sec. 6009(d), amending Code Sec. 6103(d)(5). Law at ¶ 6110. Committee Report at ¶ 11,110.

DEDUCTIONS

Deduction for Deferred Compensation

¶ 591

Background

Vacation pay is deductible by an employer for the tax year during which it is earned and not treated as deferred compensation, provided that it is paid to employees on or before 2½ months after the end of the tax year (Temporary Reg. § 1.404(b)-1T, A-2). In *Schmidt Baking Co., Inc.* (107 TC 271, Dec. 51,650), the Tax Court considered when compensation is "paid" to an employee. It held that an employer that obtained an irrevocable letter of credit for its accrued liabilities for vacation pay and severance pay within 2½ months after the end of the tax year could deduct those liabilities for the tax year. The basis of the Tax Court's decision

Background _____

was the fact that the irrevocable letter of credit caused vacation and severance pay to be included in the taxable income of the employees. In *Schmidt Baking Co., Inc.*, the employees were considered to have been paid the vacation and severance pay on the date the letter of credit went into effect (within 2½ months of the end of the tax year), even though the employees did not actually receive the vacation and severance pay within 2½ months of the end of the tax year. Therefore, the Schmidt Baking Company was able to use a letter of credit to obtain a tax deduction for accrued vacation and severance pay liabilities for one tax year even though the actual receipt of that pay by employees was more than 2½ months after the end of that year.

IRS Restructuring and Reform Impact

Actual receipt required.—An employer may deduct accrued vacation or severance pay in a particular year only if the vacation or severance pay is actually *received* by the employee on or before 2½ months after the end of the tax year (Code Sec. 404(a)(11), as added by the IRS Restructuring and Reform Act of 1998). The deduction may not be based solely on the funding or vesting of vacation or severance pay, even if that funding or vesting results in the inclusion of the vacation or severance pay in the taxable income of the employee on or before 2½ months after the end of the tax year.

The actual receipt requirement clarifies what constitutes deferred compensation. For purposes of determining whether an item is deferred compensation, the compensation is not considered to be paid or received until it is actually received by the employee. This provision is intended to overturn the result in *Schmidt Baking Co., Inc.*

Comment. The change in definition of deferred compensation to require actual receipt affects not only constructive receipt within the 2½-month period after the end of the tax year, but also constructive receipt during the tax year. Even if the employee is required to include vacation or severance pay in income in the current year based on constructive receipt principles, the employer is not entitled to a deduction in the current year unless the actual receipt occurs on or before 2½ months after the end of the tax year.

"Actually received" not defined. The term "actually received" is not defined. The Conference Committee Report describes actual receipt in terms of what it is not. Actual receipt is not intended to include letters of credit, promissory notes or other evidences of indebtedness, whether or not the evidence is guaranteed by any other instrument or by any third party. Actual receipt also does not include a promise to provide services or property in the future, whether or not evidenced by a written agreement. In addition, actual receipt does not include an amount transferred as a loan, refundable deposit, contingent payment, or amount set aside in a trust.

Example. Acme Metal Company has accrued vacation pay liability of $60,000 at the end of 1998. On February 28, 1999, Acme issues to each employee a secured promissory note equal to the accrued vacation pay earned by that employee. No employees actually receive their vacation pay by March 15, 1999. Even assuming that the notes constitute constructive receipt of the vacation pay by the employees and result in the inclusion of the vacation pay on their 1999 tax returns, the employees have not actually received their vacation pay. Therefore, Acme is not entitled to a deduction of the accrued vacation pay in 1998. Acme would not have been entitled to a deduction in 1998 even if the promissory notes had been issued on December 28, 1998, unless actual receipt occurred on or before March 15, 1999.

¶ 591

Comment. Introducing the term "actually received" into the Code without providing a clear definition is likely to result in future issues as to the scope of its meaning. The term "constructive receipt" has been extensively analyzed, and the Conference Committee Report focuses on forms of constructive receipt that do not constitute actual receipt. Potential issues include:

(1) Is there actual receipt by an employee if compensation is paid in any form other than cash or a cash equivalent?

(2) Can payment be made to a person other than the employee and still constitute actual receipt by the employee? For example, would payment to a creditor under a garnishment order qualify?

Planning Note. The Conference Committee Report invites the Secretary of the Treasury to rethink whether the IRS should be using limited resources to challenge arrangements such as those carried out in *Schmidt Baking Co., Inc.,* for years prior to the effective date of this provision. Taxpayers involved in such disputes with the IRS may find this invitation to the IRS helpful in the disposition of such cases.

Change of accounting method. Any change in a taxpayer's method of accounting required by this provision is treated as initiated by the taxpayer with the consent of the IRS, and, therefore, a request to the IRS to change accounting methods is not required. Any adjustment required under Code Sec. 481 as a result of the change will be taken into account over a three-year period beginning with the first year for which this provision is effective (Act Sec. 7001(b) of the 1998 Act).

★ *Effective date.* The provision is effective for tax years ending after the date of enactment (Act Sec. 7001(b) of the IRS Restructuring and Reform Act of 1998).

Act Sec. 7001(a), adding Code Sec. 404(a)(11); Act Sec. 7001(b). Law at ¶ 5350. Committee Report at ¶ 11,515.

Depreciation Limitations for Electric Cars

¶ 592

Background

Since 1984, limitations under the so-called "luxury car" rules have been placed on the annual depreciation that may be claimed on business vehicles, such as cars and light trucks (Code Sec. 280F). Portions of the cost not recovered during the regular five-year MACRS depreciation period may be recovered, subject to similar limitations. (In actuality, the regular depreciation period is six years due to the depreciation convention that must be used.) In 1997, these annual depreciation limits were tripled for vehicles which are propelled primarily by electricity (Code Sec. 280F(a)(1)(C), as added by the Taxpayer Relief Act of 1997 (P.L. 105-34)). This increase in the amount of annual depreciation that may be claimed applies to electric vehicles placed in service after August 5, 1997, and before January 1, 2005.

Technical Corrections Impact

Depreciation limit after third year.—A technical correction clarifies that the maximum depreciation amounts that may be claimed for electric cars in the years following the regular depreciation period are tripled (Code Sec. 280F(a)(1)(C), as amended by the IRS Restructuring and Reform Act of 1998).

Comment. In the absence of this technical correction, it could have been argued that the increased depreciation limits applied only to the regular depreciation period. That is, after the sixth tax year of use, an electric car no longer could use triple the depreciation limit imposed on other types of luxury cars.

¶ 592

Comment. Due to the rounding of the figures used when calculating the depreciation limits imposed on electric cars, the limits may not be exactly triple the depreciation limits imposed on luxury cars. This fact is illustrated in the Example below.

Example. According to the IRS (Rev. Proc. 98-30, I.R.B. 1998-17, 6), for nonelectric cars first placed in service in 1998, the maximum annual depreciation that may be claimed after the third year of business use is $1,775. However, for electric cars, the maximum annual depreciation after the first three years of business use, and for all succeeding years, is $5,425. (Without the necessary rounding of figures, the limit on electric cars would have been $5,325 after the first three years of business use.)

★ *Effective date.* This provision applies to property placed in service after August 5, 1997, and before January 1, 2005 (Act Sec. 6024 of the IRS Restructuring and Reform Act of 1998; Act Sec. 971(a) of the Taxpayer Relief Act of 1997 (P.L. 105-34)).

Act Sec. 6009(c), amending Code Sec. 280F(a)(1)(C)(ii). Law at ¶ 5270. Committee Report at ¶ 11,105.

Meals Provided for Convenience of Employer

¶ 593

Background

As a general rule, only 50 percent of business meals and entertainment expenses are allowed as an income tax deduction (Code Sec. 274(n)). There are several exceptions, however. Under one of these exceptions, meals that are deductible as a *de minimis* fringe benefit (Code Sec. 132) are fully deductible by the employer. Courts have held that if substantially all of the meals provided by an employer are for the employer's convenience, pursuant to Code Sec. 119, the cost of such meals is fully deductible because the employer is treated as operating a *de minimis* eating facility within the meaning of Code Sec. 132(e)(2) (e.g., *Boyd Gaming Corp.*, 106 TC 343; CCH Dec. 51,348).

IRS Restructuring and Reform Impact

Easing of exclusion.—The Act provides a more generous rule for deducting the cost of meals provided to employees on an employer's business premises. If, without regard to the new provision, more than one-half of the employees to whom such meals are provided are furnished the meals for the convenience of the employer, all such meals are treated as furnished for the convenience of the employer (Code Sec. 119(b)(4), as added by the IRS Restructuring and Reform Act of 1998).

Comment. If the test is satisfied, the value of all such meals would be excludable from the employee's income and fully deductible to the employer.

Planning Note. The Conference Report states that no inference is intended as to whether such meals are fully deductible under present law. This statement appears to be inconsistent with the effective date provision, which seems to give taxpayers the opportunity to file an amended return to claim additional meal deductions for previous tax years.

Example. Xenon Company serves meals to 100 employees on its business premises and 60 of the employees are furnished the meals for the company's convenience. All the meals provided are treated as furnished for the convenience of Xenon Company.

★ *Effective date.* This provision is effective for tax years beginning before, on, or after the date of enactment of the Act (Act Sec. 5002(b) of the IRS Reform and Restructuring Act of 1998).

PRACTICAL ANALYSIS. Mark Luscombe, Principal Analyst for the Federal and State Tax Group at CCH INCORPORATED, notes that Example (9) in Reg. § 1.119-1(f) provides that all of a hospital's 230 employees may exclude from their gross income meals provided in the hospital cafeteria even though only 210 employees received meals under terms that met the "convenience of the employer" test. This example created a "substantially all" safe harbor under which a showing that at least 90 percent of the furnished meals were for the convenience of the employer meant that all employees could exclude the employer provided meals. This new provision in the law effectively expands the safe harbor by reducing the threshold from 90 percent to 50 percent. However, it should be noted that the IRS now will have clearer authority to deny exclusions where employers fall just short of the 50 percent test. As demonstrated in *Boyd Gaming Corp.*, TC Memo 1997-445, Dec. 52,280(M), meeting even a reduced 50 percent test will remain a challenge for many employers that provide employee meals on the premises.

Act Sec. 5002, adding Code Sec. 119(b)(4). Law at ¶ 5170. Committee Report at ¶ 10,790.

Chapter 6
Corporations and Special Entities

DISTRIBUTIONS OF CONTROLLED CORPORATION STOCK
Gain Recognition on Distributions of Controlled Corporation Stock
¶601

Background

The Taxpayer Relief Act of 1997 (P.L. 105-34) requires a distributing corporation to recognize corporate-level gain on the distribution of stock of a controlled corporation in certain Code Sec. 355 spin-offs. Gain must be recognized if, pursuant to a plan or series of related transactions, one or more persons *acquire* a 50-percent or greater interest in either the distributing or controlled corporation (Code Sec. 355(e), as added by P.L. 105-34). A 50-percent or greater interest is defined as 50 percent or more of the voting power or value of the stock (Code Sec. 355(d)(4)).

These provisions, although commonly referred to as the *Morris Trust* (CA-4, 66-2 USTC ¶9718, 367 F2d 794) repeal, only limit the ability to use a *Morris Trust* type spin-off to distribute appreciated assets tax-free.

Background

Certain transactions are excepted from the definition of acquisition for this purpose. An exception exists if the same shareholders own either directly or indirectly more than 50 percent of the stock (by vote and value) in both the distributing and controlling corporations, both before and after the acquisition and distribution (Code Sec. 355(e)(3)(A)(iv)).

This exception is not applicable if the stock held before the acquisition was acquired pursuant to a plan, or series of related transactions, to acquire a 50-percent or greater interest in the distributing or controlled corporation.

In the case of an acquisition of either a distributing or a controlled corporation, the amount of gain recognized is the amount the distributing corporation would have recognized had stock of the controlled corporation been sold for fair market value on the date of distribution. No adjustment to the basis of the stock or assets of either corporation is allowed by reason of the recognition of the gain (Code Sec. 355(e)(1), as added by P.L. 105-34).

Regulatory authority, intragroup spin-offs. The 1997 Act provides that, in the case of any distribution of stock of one member of an affiliated group of corporations to another member under Code Sec. 355 (an intragroup spin-off), the IRS has regulatory authority to provide adjustments to the basis of any stock in a corporation that is a member of group to reflect appropriately the proper treatment of the distribution (Code Sec. 358(g), as added by P.L. 105-34). The Joint Committee Report for P.L. 105-34 states that the same approach used under the Code Sec. 358 regulations may be used in connection with regulations issued under Code Sec. 355(f).

Control. For purposes of determining whether certain divisive transactions qualify as "D" reorganizations, the 1997 Act provided special control requirements. Under those provisions, if the transaction otherwise qualified under Code Sec. 354(b)(1)(A) and Code Sec. 354(b)(1)(B) (nonrecognition of gain or loss if substantially all the assets are transferred and the stock, securities and properties received by the transferor are distributed under a plan of reorganization), then the control test of Code Sec. 304(c) was applicable. The control test of Code Sec. 304(c) is generally satisfied if at least 50 percent of the total combined voting power and 50 percent of the value of all classes of stock are owned by shareholders receiving stock in a distributed corporation. In a transaction that otherwise meets the requirements of Code Sec. 355, shareholders receiving stock in a distributed corporation would be treated as controlling the distributed corporation immediately after the distribution if they hold stock representing greater than 50 percent of the total combined voting power and 50 percent of the value of all classes of stock of the distributed corporation (Code Sec. 368(a)(2)(H)).

Technical Corrections Impact

Acquisition of a 50-percent or greater interest.—In determining whether there has been an acquisition of a 50-percent or greater interest in a corporation, the IRS Restructuring and Reform Act of 1998 clarifies that the acquisitions described in Code Sec. 355(e)(3)(A) are disregarded (Code Sec. 355(e)(3)(A), as amended by the 1998 Act). However, acquisitions are not disregarded that are part of a plan or series of related transactions that could result in an acquisition of a 50-percent or greater interest.

Additionally, the 1998 Act clarifies the rules under Code Sec. 355(e)(3)(A)(iv) regarding the extent to which a stock acquisition is disregarded. The acquisition of stock in the distributing corporation or any controlled corporation is disregarded only to the extent that the percentage of stock owned directly or indirectly in the corporation by any stockholder immediately before the acquisition does not decrease (Code Sec. 355(e)(3)(A)(iv), as amended by the 1998 Act). Therefore, if a stockholder's interest in a corporation decreases from 50 percent to 30 percent, only 30 percent is disregarded in determining whether a 50-percent or greater interest in the corporation has been acquired.

Caution. It is possible that the identity of shareholders before and after an acquisition could remain the same and yet the distributing corporation would have to recognize corporate level gain.

Example (1). Bergo Thomas owns 10 percent of the vote and value of the stock of Distributing, which owns all of TarCo. There are nine other equal shareholders of Distributing. Thomas also owns 100 percent of the vote and value of the stock of an unrelated corporation, AcqCo. Distributing distributes TarCo to all the shareholders of Distributing. Thereafter, pursuant to a plan, Distributing (fair market value of $1 million) merges with AcqCo (fair market value of $10 million). After the merger, Thomas, owns 91 percent of the stock of the merged corporation and each of the other former Distributing shareholders owns one percent of the stock of the merged corporation. In determining whether a 50-percent or greater interest in Distributing has been acquired, the interest of each of the continuing shareholders is disregarded only to the extent there has been no decrease in such shareholder's direct or indirect ownership. Thus, the 10% interest of Thomas, and the one percent interest of each of the nine other former shareholder of Distributing, is not counted. The remaining 81 percent ownership of the merged corporation, representing a decrease of nine percent in the interests of each of the nine former shareholders other than Thomas, is counted in determining the extent of an acquisition. Therefore, a 50-percent or greater interest in Distributing has been acquired.

Control in certain divisive transactions. The 1998 Act clarifies the "control immediately after" requirement of Code Sec. 351(a) or Code Sec. 368(a)(1)(D) in the case of certain divisive transactions in which a corporation contributes assets to a controlled corporation and then distributes the stock of the controlled corporation. Provided such a transaction meets the Code Sec. 355 requirements, then, solely for purposes of determining the tax treatment of the transfers of property to the controlled corporation by the distributing corporation, the fact that the shareholders of the distributing corporation dispose of part or all of the distributed stock is *not* to be taken into account for purposes of the "control immediately after" requirement. If "boot" is received in the exchange under Code Sec. 356, then the above rule applies only to the extent of the additional consideration that relates to Code Sec. 355. For purposes of determining the tax treatment of transfers of property to the controlled corporation by parties other than the distributing corporation, the disposition of part or all of the distributed stock continues to be taken into account in determining whether the "control immediately after" requirement is satisfied (Code Sec. 351(c), as amended by the 1998 Act).

Comment. Prior to P.L. 105-34, the treatment of Code Sec. 355 spin-offs involving contributions of assets to a controlled corporation before a spin-off could differ depending on whether the distributing or controlled corporation was acquired subsequent to the spin-off. The 1997 Act modified the "control immediately after" requirement of Code Sec. 351(c) and Code Sec. 368(a)(2)(H) to make the tax treatment less dependent on which of the corporations was acquired subsequent to the Code Sec. 355 spin-off (see Senate Committee Report on the IRS Restructuring and Reform Act of 1998).

Example (2). Distributing Corp. transfers an appreciated business unit, Division X, to a newly formed subsidiary, Receive Corp., in exchange for 100 percent of Receive stock. Distributing distributes its Receive stock to Distributing shareholders. As part of a plan, Receive merges into an unrelated

¶ 601

acquiring corporation AcqCo, and the Receive shareholders receive 25 percent of the vote or value of AcqCo stock. Assuming the requirements of Code Sec. 355 are satisfied with respect to the distribution, the "control immediately after" requirement will be satisfied solely for purposes of determining the tax treatment of the transfers of property by Distributing to Receive. Accordingly, the Division X assets transferred to Receive and held by AcqCo after the merger will have a carryover basis from Distributing. However, Code Sec. 355(e) will require Distributing to recognize gain as if the Receive stock had been sold at fair market value.

Example (3). Assume the same facts as in *Example (2)*, above, except unrelated persons transfer appreciated assets to Receive in exchange for the remaining 15 percent of Receive stock. In the initial exchange, Distributing obtains 85 percent of Receive stock, and after the merger of Receive into AcqCo, Distributing obtains 25 percent of the vote and value of AcqCo stock. With respect to Distributing, the same results as in *Example (2)* occur. However, the unrelated persons who transferred assets to Receive for 15 percent of stock will recognize gain on the appreciation in their transferred assets if the "control immediately after" requirement is not satisfied after taking into account any post-spin-off dispositions that would have been taken into account under prior law.

Example (4). Assume the same facts as in *Example (3)*, above, except that the Distributing shareholders obtain 52 percent of the vote and value of AcqCo stock in the merger. Assuming the requirements of Code Sec. 355 are met with respect to the distribution, then the "control immediately after" requirement is satisfied solely for purposes of determining the tax treatment of the transfers by Distributing to Receive. The Division X assets in Receive, and in AcqCo after the merger, will have a carryover basis from Distributing. Since the Distributing shareholders retain more than 50 percent of the stock of AcqCo, Code Sec. 355(e) does not apply. The unrelated persons who transferred property for the 15 percent of Receive stock recognize gain on the appreciation in their assets transferred to Receive if the control-immediately-after requirement is not satisfied after taking into account any post-spin-off dispositions.

Regulatory authority, intragroup spin-offs. The 1998 Act clarifies that the IRS regulatory authority under Code Sec. 358(g) applies to distributions after April 16, 1997, without regard to whether a distribution involves a plan, or series of related transactions, which involves an acquisition (Act Sec. 6010(c)(1) of the 1998 Act). This provision is concerned with the IRS regulatory authority under Code Sec. 358(g) as applied to intragroup spin-off transactions that are not part of a plan or series of related transactions that involve an acquisition of a 50-percent or greater interest under new Code Sec. 355(f) (Senate Committee Report to the 1998 Act).

It is expected that any regulations will be applied prospectively, except in cases to prevent abuse (Senate Committee Report to the 1998 Act).

Comment. Further guidance to potential regulations is provided in the Conference Committee Report to the Taxpayer Relief Act of 1997 (P.L. 105-34), which notes the Committee's concerns with the current consolidated return regulations regarding basis adjustments resulting from a distribution. One concern is that excess loss accounts may not be recaptured when there is an internal spin-off followed by the subsidiary leaving the group. The Report states that the IRS may consider providing rules that require a carryover basis within the group for the stock of the distributed corporation, including a carryover of an excess loss account. Also suggested is that the change in the value and basis of the distributing corporation's assets should be reflected in basis reduction to the stock of the distributing corporation.

★ *Effective date.* The changes made by the 1998 Act regarding gain recognition are generally effective for distributions after April 16, 1997 which are pursuant to a plan (or series of related transactions) which involve an acquisition occurring after that date (unless certain transition provisions apply) (Act Sec. 6010(c)(1) of the IRS Restructuring and Reform Act of 1998, amending Act Sec. 1012(d)(1) of the Taxpayer Relief Act of 1997 (P.L. 105-34)). The changes made by the 1998 Act regarding regulatory authority for intragroup spin-offs apply to distributions after April 16, 1997 (Act Sec. 6010(c)(1) of the IRS Restructuring and Reform Act of 1998, amending Act Sec. 1012(d)(1) of P.L. 105-34). Finally, changes made by the 1998 Act regarding control in certain divisive transactions generally apply to transfers after August 5, 1997 (Act Sec. 6024 of the IRS Restructuring and Reform Act of 1998; Act Sec. 1012(d)(2) of the Taxpayer Relief Act of 1997 (P.L. 105-34)).

Act Sec. 6010(c)(1), amending Act Sec. 1012(d)(1) of the Taxpayer Relief Act of 1997 (P.L. 105-34); Act Sec. 6010(c)(2), amending Code Sec. 355(e)(3)(A); Act Sec. 6010(c)(3)(A), amending Code Sec. 351(c); Act Sec. 6010(c)(3)(B), amending Code Sec. 368(a)(2)(H)(ii). Law at ¶ 5290, ¶ 5310, ¶ 5320, and ¶ 8255. Committee Report at ¶ 11,150.

NONQUALIFIED PREFERRED STOCK

Preferred Stock Treated as Boot

¶ 616

Background

In a Code Sec. 351 transfer to a controlled corporation, gain is generally recognized only if "other property" (i.e., property other than stock) is received. The term "other property" is often referred to as "boot." The Taxpayer Relief Act of 1997 (P.L. 105-34) provides that "nonqualified preferred stock" must be treated as boot for purposes of Code Sec. 351. Thus, when a taxpayer exchanges property for nonqualified preferred stock in a transaction that qualifies under Code Sec. 351, gain, but not loss, would be recognized.

Although nonqualified preferred stock may be treated as boot under these rules, nonqualified stock is considered stock for purposes of *qualifying* for nonrecognition treatment under Code Sec. 351(a), unless and until regulations provide otherwise. To qualify for nonrecognition treatment under Code Sec. 351, property must be transferred to a corporation solely in exchange for stock by one or more persons who are in control of the corporation, as defined by Code Sec. 368(c). Thus, if a transferor transfers appreciated property to a corporation in exchange for both common stock and nonqualified preferred stock, the transferor will only recognize gain to the extent of the fair market value of the nonqualified preferred stock received in the transaction. The Code Sec. 351 nonrecognition rules are applicable to the property transferred to the corporation for stock other than nonqualified preferred stock.

Nonqualified preferred stock means preferred stock if:

(1) the holder has the right to require the issuer or a related person (within the meaning of Code Sec. 267(b) or Code Sec. 707(b)) to redeem or purchase the stock,

(2) the issuer or a related person is required to redeem or purchase the stock,

(3) the issuer or a related person has the right to redeem or purchase the stock and, as of the issue date, it is more likely than not that such right will be exercised, or

(4) the dividend rate on the stock varies in whole or in part (directly or indirectly) with reference to interest rates, commodity prices, or other similar indices (Code Sec. 351(g)(2), as added by P.L. 105-34)).

Technical Corrections Impact

Treatment of transferor, loss property.—The IRS Restructuring and Reform Act of 1998 clarifies that Code Sec. 351(b) applies to a transferor who transfers property in a Code Sec. 351 exchange and receives nonqualified preferred stock *in addition* to stock that is not treated as "other property." If the transferor receives only nonqualified preferred stock, the general nonrecognition treatment under Code Sec. 351(a) will not apply to the transferor (Code Sec. 351(g)(1)(B), as amended by the 1998 Act). Thus, if a transferor received only nonqualified preferred stock, but the transaction in the aggregate otherwise qualified as a Code Sec. 351 exchange, the transferor would recognize loss under Code Sec. 1001 and the basis of the nonqualified preferred stock and of the property in the hands of the transferee corporation would reflect the transaction in the same manner as if that particular transferor had received solely "other property" of any other type (Senate Committee Report on the 1998 Act).

Nonqualified preferred stock continues to be treated as stock received by a transferor for purposes of qualification of a transaction under Code Sec. 351(a), unless and until regulations provide otherwise (Senate Committee Report on the 1998 Act).

Caution. Other Code provisions may still disallow or defer recognition of a loss. For example, losses in transactions between corporations and controlling shareholders can be disallowed under Code Sec. 267.

Example. Honus Wagner and Pie Traynor each own 50 percent of Pyrate Corporation. In a contribution otherwise qualifying under Code Sec. 351, Wagner contributes property with a basis of $100,000 to Pyrate for preferred stock and Traynor contributes property for common stock. The preferred stock is considered nonqualified preferred stock and is valued at $80,000. Wagner recognizes a loss of $20,000 ($80,000, value of other property received, less $100,000, basis). Since the nonqualified preferred stock is treated as stock for purposes of qualifying for nonrecognition under Code Sec. 351(a) and Code Sec. 368(c), the contribution qualifies as a Code Sec. 351 contribution. Therefore, Traynor does not recognize gain or loss for his contribution.

★ *Effective date.* The provision generally applies to transactions after June 8, 1997 (Act Sec. 6024 of the IRS Restructuring and Reform Act of 1998; Act Sec. 1014(f) of the Taxpayer Relief Act of 1997 (P.L. 105-34)).

Act Sec. 6010(e)(1), amending Code Sec. 351(g)(1). Law at ¶ 5290. Committee Report at ¶ 11,160.

Family-Owned Corporation Assessment Period

¶ 621

Certain rights to acquire stock and securities can be received tax-free under Code Sec. 354. Nonqualified preferred stock (see ¶ 616) received in exchange for

Background ————————————————————————

stock (or a right to acquire stock) other than nonqualified preferred stock is not treated as a stock or security for this purpose. This rule, which results in the taxation of the nonqualified preferred stock as "other property," does not apply to exchanges of stock in certain recapitalizations of family-owned corporations. For this purpose, a family-owned corporation is defined as any corporation if at least 50 percent of the total combined voting power of all classes of stock entitled to vote and at least 50 percent of all other classes of stock of the corporation are owned by members of the same family. The stock-ownership requirements must be met for five years preceding the recapitalization and for three years following the recapitalization (Code Sec. 447(d)(2)(C)(i)).

The IRS may be hampered in timely assessing tax against a family-owned corporation that fails to meet the ownership requirement for the full three-year period following the recapitalization because there is no requirement that the corporation notify the IRS of the failure and the statute of limitations for assessing the tax generally expires three years after the filing of the return on which the exchange was reported.

Technical Corrections Impact

Extended assessment period for family-owned corporation.—The statutory period for the assessment of any deficiency attributable to a corporation failing to be a family-owned corporation does not expire before the expiration of three years after the date the IRS is notified by the corporation of the failure. Limitations on assessments of tax under other provisions, such as Code Sec. 6501(a), will not apply (Code Sec. 354(a)(2)(C)(ii)(III), as added by the IRS Restructuring and Reform Act of 1998).

The IRS may prescribe notification requirements for the corporation to inform the IRS of its failure to continue to qualify as a family-owned corporation (Code Sec. 354(a)(2)(C)(ii)(III), as added by the 1998 Act).

Comment. Although the IRS generally has three years from the time the return is filed to make assessments of tax under Code Sec. 6501(a), there are numerous exceptions similar to the one added by the 1998 Act. For example, the assessment period against certain taxpayers required to file information returns regarding foreign transfers can expire no sooner than three years after the IRS receives the information returns (Code Sec. 6501(c)(8)).

★ *Effective date.* The provision generally applies to transactions after June 8, 1997 (Act Sec. 6024 of the IRS Restructuring and Reform Act of 1998; Act Sec. 1014(f) of the Taxpayer Relief Act of 1997 (P.L. 105-34)).

Act Sec. 6010(e)(2), adding Code Sec. 354(a)(2)(C)(ii)(III). Law at ¶ 5300. Committee Report at ¶ 11,165.

EXTRAORDINARY DIVIDENDS
Extraordinary Dividends Within Consolidated Groups
¶ 626

Background ————————————————————————

The consolidated return regulations provide basis-adjustment rules with respect to dividends paid within a consolidated group of corporations (see Reg. § 1.1502-32). These rules provide that a dividend paid from one member of a group to its parent reduces the parent's basis in the stock of the payor. If the reduction exceeds the parent's basis, an excess loss account is created or increased. Excess loss accounts generally are not restored to income until the occurrence of certain specified events. Thus, for example, if the parent is considered to have disposed of the subsidiary to which the excess loss account relates, then the parent recognizes income to the extent of the excess loss account (see Reg. § 1.1502-19(c)).

A corporate shareholder that receives an "extraordinary dividend" must reduce the basis of the stock with respect to which the dividend was received by the nontaxed portion of the dividend unless the stock was held for more than two years before the dividend announcement date (Code 1059(a)). An extraordinary dividend is generally a dividend that equals or exceeds five percent of the taxpayer's adjusted basis in preferred stock and 10 percent of the taxpayer's adjusted basis in all other stock. Dividends resulting from non-pro rata redemptions or partial liquidations are also considered extraordinary dividends.

The Taxpayer Relief Act of 1997 (P.L. 105-34) amended Code Sec. 1059(a)(2) to require immediate gain recognition for certain extraordinary dividends. When making the basis reduction, the nontaxed portion of the dividend cannot reduce basis below zero. Gain must be recognized in the tax year in which the extraordinary dividend is received to the extent that the nontaxed portion exceeds basis.

The legislative history of Code Sec. 1059 addresses the interplay between the consolidated return regulations and the extraordinary dividend provisions where the corporate shareholder and payor are members of an affiliated group filing consolidated returns. The legislative history indicates that, except as provided in regulations, the extraordinary dividend provisions do not apply where the result would be a double reduction in basis in the case of distributions between members of an affiliated group filing consolidated returns (i.e., where the dividend is excluded or eliminated under the consolidated return regulations). Further, the extraordinary dividend provisions should not apply if the result would be the double inclusion of earnings and profits (i.e., from the dividend and from the disposition of stock with a reduced basis) (Conference Committee Report on the Tax Reform Act of 1986 (P.L. 99-514)).

The IRS may prescribe regulations to carry out the purposes and to prevent avoidance of the extraordinary dividend provisions, including regulations that relate to pass-through entities.

Technical Corrections Impact

Extraordinary dividends within consolidated groups.—The IRS is provided with regulatory authority to coordinate the basis-adjustment rules of Code Sec. 1059 with the consolidated return regulations (Code Sec. 1059(g)(1), as amended by the IRS Restructuring and Reform Act of 1998). The Conference Committee Report to the 1998 Act clarifies that, except as provided in regulations to be issued, Code Sec. 1059 will not cause current gain recognition to the extent that the consolidated return regulations require the creation or increase of an excess loss account with respect to a distribution. Thus, current Reg. § 1.1509(e)-1(a) does not result in gain recognition with respect to distributions within a consolidated group to the extent such distribution results in the creation or increase of an excess loss account under the consolidated return regulations.

Comment. Regulations may be issued under the consolidated return rules, rather than Code Sec. 1059. For example, Reg. § 1.701-2(f), Example (2), is an example of a regulation issued under Code Sec. 1059(g) that applies the extraordinary-dividend provision where a corporation is a partner in a partnership,

★ *Effective date.* The provision generally is effective for distributions after May 3, 1995 (Act Sec. 6024 of the IRS Restructuring and Reform Act of 1998; Act Sec. 1011(d) of the Taxpayer Relief Act of 1997 (P.L. 105-34)).

Act Sec. 6010(b), amending Code Sec. 1059(g)(1). Law at ¶ 5590. Committee Report at ¶ 11,145.

INTERNATIONAL TRANSACTIONS

Redemptions

¶ 631

Background

In a Code Sec. 304 transaction, the purchase by one corporation of stock in a related corporation is generally recharacterized as a redemption. The extent to which a Code Sec. 304 redemption is treated as a dividend distribution (under Code Sec. 301) is determined by reference to the earnings and profits of the acquiring and issuing corporations.

A deemed dividend distribution from a foreign corporation may carry with it foreign tax credits. Under Rev. Rul. 92-86, 1992-2 CB 199, and Rev. Rul. 91-5, 1991-1 CB 114, a domestic transferor in a Code Sec. 304 transaction may compute a deemed-paid credit under Code Sec. 902 on the dividends from both a foreign acquiring and a foreign issuing corporation. In the case of a foreign acquiring corporation, the Taxpayer Relief Act of 1997 (P.L. 105-34) placed limitations on the amount of the acquiring corporation's earnings and profits that could be taken into account in applying Code Sec. 304 (Code Sec. 304(b)(5), as added by P.L. 105-34). The provision was intended to prevent the inappropriate claim of foreign tax credits from a Code Sec. 304 transaction.

Technical Corrections Impact

Regulations covering foreign acquisitions.—The IRS is authorized to issue regulations that would prevent the multiple inclusion of an item in income in a Code Sec. 304 transaction where the issuing or acquiring corporation is a foreign corporation. These regulations would also provide for appropriate adjustments to basis. Specifically, the regulations could modify the Code Sec. 959 previously-taxed-income rules and the Code Sec. 961 adjustment-to-basis rules that apply to controlled foreign corporations (CFCs) (Code Sec. 304(b)(6), as added by the IRS Restructuring and Reform Act of 1998).

According to the Senate Committee Report to the 1998 Act, it is expected that the regulations would provide an exclusion from income for distributions of earnings and profits of an acquiring and issuing corporation that have already been taxed under the CFC rules of subpart F. It is further expected that the regulations will provide for appropriate adjustments to the basis of (1) the stock of the corporation treated as receiving the distribution, or (2) the stock of the corporation that had the prior inclusion with respect to the previously taxed income. The Senate Committee Report also states that no inference is intended with respect to the treatment of previously taxed income under the current rules.

In connection with this authorization to issue regulations, a cross reference to Code Sec. 1248(d) for purposes of determining earnings and profits is eliminated (Act Sec. 6010(d)(2) of the 1998 Act, striking Code Sec. 304(b)(5)(B)). Code Sec. 1248(d) provides rules for determining exclusions from earnings and profits in connection with the deemed-dividend rules that apply upon the sale of CFC stock.

Caution. The amendments made by the Taxpayer Relief Act of 1997 (P.L. 105-34) were not intended to change the foreign tax credit results reached in Rev.

Rul. 92-86, 1992-2 CB 199, and Rev. Rul. 91-5, 1991-1 CB 114. The Senate Committee Report to the 1998 Act notes that Rev. Rul. 92-86 and Rev. Rul. 91-5 involve transactions in which both the domestic transferor and the foreign acquiror are wholly owned by a domestic parent.

PRACTICAL ANALYSIS. Paul Bodner, Esq., Great Neck, NY, observes that because Code Sec. 304 creates a tax fiction whereby a person receives a dividend from a corporation that it does not own directly or indirectly, there was a question whether a foreign tax credit could accompany the dividend. Rev. Rul. 92-86, 1992-2 CB 199 and Rev. Rul. 91-5, 1991-1 CB 114 resolved the issue by holding that the US shareholder is deemed to own the stock of the paying corporation so that the deemed paid foreign tax credit would accompany the deemed dividend. These rulings involved transactions in which the domestic transferor and the foreign acquiring corporations are wholly owned by a domestic corporation. Practitioners sought a similar ruling for fact patterns not covered by these rulings, in order to avoid multiple inclusion of an item of income and to have appropriate correlative adjustments, such as treatment of taxed earnings and profits as previously taxed income rather than as a mere capital contribution. Although the IRS was receptive, there was a question as to whether it had authority to issue the ruling. This provision provides legislative support.

★ *Effective date.* The provision generally applies to distributions and acquisitions after June 8, 1997 (Act Sec. 6024 of the IRS Restructuring and Reform Act of 1998; Act Sec. 1013(d) of the Taxpayer Relief Act of 1997 (P.L. 105-34)).

Act Sec. 6010(d)(1), striking Code Sec. 304(b)(5)(B) and redesignating Code Sec. 304(b)(5)(C) as Code Sec. 304(b)(5)(B); Act Sec. 6010(d)(2), adding Code Sec. 304(b)(6). Law at ¶ 5280. Committee Report at ¶ 11,155.

IRS Notices on Foreign Tax Provisions

¶ 633

Background

On December 23, 1997, the IRS issued Notice 98-5 (I.R.B. 1998-3, 49), addressing abusive tax-motivated transactions involving foreign tax credits. The Notice discusses transactions designed to acquire or generate foreign tax credits that can be used to shelter low-taxed foreign source income. The transactions yield little economic benefit compared to the U.S. tax benefit from the foreign tax credits acquired or generated.

The Notice covers two classes of transactions identified by the IRS as creating the potential for abuse with respect to foreign tax credits. The two classes of transactions are those that involve:

(1) the acquisition of an asset that generates an income stream subject to foreign withholding tax, or

(2) the effective duplication of tax benefits through the use of certain structures designed to exploit inconsistencies between U.S. and foreign law.

In one specific example contained in the Notice, a taxpayer can effectively purchase foreign tax credits when it purchases a copyright for $75 that yields one $100 royalty payment from which $30 in foreign tax is withheld. Although the taxpayer incurs an economic loss of $5, he acquires a $30 foreign tax liability.

Four other examples of the these transactions are contained in the Notice.

Background

The IRS concludes in the Notice that these transactions are contrary to the U.S. tax policy behind the foreign tax credit, which seeks to preserve neutrality between U.S. and foreign investments. The Notice states that regulations will be issued to disallow the foreign tax credits generated in these abusive arrangements. The regulations will generally be effective for taxes paid or accrued on or after December 23, 1997. The Notice further states that the IRS is considering additional guidance to ensure that foreign tax credits are allowed in a manner consistent with the Code and the intent of Congress.

On January 16, 1998, the IRS issued Notice 98-11 (I.R.B. 1998-6, 18), addressing hybrid branch arrangements designed to circumvent the purposes of subpart F (Code Secs. 951-964). Hybrid arrangements are designed to take advantage of the differences between U.S. and foreign law. The Notice provides examples of hybrid arrangements identified by the Treasury and the IRS as being inconsistent with the policies and rules of subpart F. These hybrid arrangements involve structures that are identified as controlled foreign corporations (CFCs) under U.S. tax law, but that are considered separate entities in the country in which the CFC is incorporated. The IRS concludes in the Notice that the use of hybrid arrangements to reduce foreign tax and avoid subpart F income is contrary to U.S. international tax policy and that these arrangements will be the subject of forthcoming regulations.

On March 23, 1998, temporary and proposed regulations were issued under Notice 98-11. The temporary regulations address the treatment under subpart F of certain branches of a CFC, or partnership in which a CFC is a partner, that are treated as separate entities for foreign tax purposes (T.D. 8767). The temporary regulations provide that hybrid branch payments made between a CFC and its hybrid branch or between hybrid branches may give rise to currently taxable subpart F income if certain conditions are met. In certain instances, the recharacterization rules will apply to a CFC's proportionate share of a hybrid branch payment made between a partnership in which the CFC is a partner and a hybrid branch of the partnership or between the hybrid branches of the partnership. The proposed regulations cover the treatment of a CFC partner's distributive share of partnership income (REG-104537-97).

The regulations generally apply to amounts paid or accrued pursuant to a hybrid branch arrangement entered into or substantially modified on or after January 16, 1998. In the case of hybrid arrangements involving partnerships, the regulations generally apply to amounts paid or accrued pursuant to an arrangement that is entered into or substantially modified on or after March 23, 1998.

IRS Restructuring and Reform Impact

Foreign tax notices.— The IRS Restructuring and Reform Act of 1998 does not contain the Senate amendment concerning regulations issued under Notice 98-11 (I.R.B. 1998-6, 18). The 1998 Act also does not contain in the Senate amendment concerning Notice 95-5 (I.R.B. 1998-3, 49) and Notice 98-11.

Regulation moratorium. Under the Senate amendment, a moratorium was proposed for any final or temporary regulations with respect to Notice 98-11, dealing with hybrid branch arrangements, including hybrid branch arrangements involving partnerships. The moratorium period was to begin on January 16, 1998 and end six months after the date of enactment (Sec. 3713(a)(1) of H.R. 2676, as approved by the Senate on 5/7/98). The Senate Committee stated that the moratorium would allow Congress to consider issues associated with the impact of the regulations on U.S. businesses operating abroad. The Senate Committee also stated that delay in the implementation of the regulations was not intended to affect the effective date of the regulations and that no inference was intended regarding the authority of the IRS and Treasury to issue the Notice or regulations.

Sense of the Senate. Under the Senate amendment, it was the sense of the Senate that (1) Notice 98-11, dealing with hybrid arrangements and the regulations issued with respect to the Notice be withdrawn, and (2) Congress, and not the IRS or Treasury, should determine the policy issues that pertain to hybrid transactions under subpart F (Act Sec. 3713(a)(2) of H.R. 2676, as approved by the Senate on 5/7/98).

It was also the sense of the Senate that the Treasury should limit regulations issued under Notice 98-5, dealing with foreign tax credits to the specific transactions contained in the Notice. The regulations should (1) not affect transactions undertaken in the ordinary course of business, (2) not have an effective date earlier than the effective date of the proposed regulations, and (3) be issued under the normal procedures that provide an opportunity for comment. Nothing in the sense of Senate was intended to limit the Secretary's ability to limit abusive transactions (Sec. 3713(b) of H.R. 2676, as approved by the Senate on 5/7/98).

Conference Committee Report. In Notice 98-35 (I.R.B. 1998-26, 1), the IRS withdrew Notice 98-11 and announced its intention to withdraw the regulations issued under Notice 98-11. In the Notice, the IRS also announced its intention to issue proposed regulations covering hybrid transactions that would not be finalized before January 1, 2000.

The Conference Committee Report states that it expects Congress to consider the international tax policy issues relating to the treatment of hybrid transactions under the subpart F provisions and to take any necessary legislative action. The Conference Committee Report further states that both Congress and the Treasury Department should take into account the impact of legislation or administrative guidance in the area on affected taxpayers and industries. No inference is intended regarding the authority of the IRS and Treasury to issue the Notice 98-11 or the regulations (or any similar notice or regulations).

With respect to Notice 98-5, the Conference Committee expresses its belief that any regulations under the Notice be issued under normal regulatory procedures that allow for public comment. The Conference Committee advises the IRS and Treasury to limit issuing administrative notices that describe principles to be reflected in future regulations.

Action is deferred on temporary and proposed regulations issued on March 2, 1998 (T.D. 8764) covering the special sourcing rule under the foreign sales corporation provisions, based on the Conference Committee's good faith reliance on the Treasury Department's commitment to withdraw the regulations.

PRACTICAL ANALYSIS. Paul Bodner, Esq., Great Neck, NY, notes that Notice 98-11 and the regulations issued with it did more to unite the Republicans and Democrats on the Hill than any action in the recent past. Messrs. Archer and Rangel may disagree on many things, but Congressional prerogative is not one of them. The unified action, in both houses by both parties, caused Treasury to withdraw Notice 98-11 and the regulations. However, in Notice 98-35, Treasury reissued proposed regulations (without accompanying temporary regulations) essentially reinstating its position. Although the new regulations will not be finalized until January 1, 2000, they only provide very limited relief to transactions entered into after June 19, 1998. Meanwhile, the fight will continue as Congress considers the policy issues raised by the Notice. The congressional position regarding the Notice 98-11 regulations should be contrasted with its position on the Notice

98-5 regulations (regarding the treatment of certain types of transactions under the foreign tax credit provisions). In the latter case, Congress said that the regulations should be issued after the opportunity for public comment.

The Conference Report contains the usual language that no inference is intended regarding the authority of Treasury or the IRS to issue the Notice or regulations. The Conference Report, however, goes on to state that "the conferees are concerned about the potential disruptive effect of the issuance of an administrative notice that describes general principles to be reflected in regulations that will be issued in the future ... that ... will be effective as of the date of the issuance of the notice..."

The new regulations accompanying Notice 98-5 have a similar disruptive effect. Taxpayers will have time to plan around the regulations, while continuing their lobbying efforts to convince Congress to take more definitive action to prevent the regulations from ever being finalized. A hint of the status of this fight may be gleaned from Treasury's agreement to simultaneously withdraw the proposed new sourcing rules under the foreign sales corporation provisions and to reinstate the rule contained in the prior temporary regulations. Chairman Archer has publicly stated that he is against any additional U.S. tax on foreign source income.

Committee Reports at ¶ 11,580 and ¶ 11,585.

PASSIVE FOREIGN INVESTMENT COMPANIES

Attribution Rules

¶ 636

Background

Attribution rules under Code Sec. 1298 apply for purposes of determining whether a U.S. person is an indirect shareholder of a passive foreign investment company (PFIC). Under the attribution rules, the stock in a PFIC held by a corporation is attributed to a U.S. person only if the person directly or indirectly owns 50 percent or more of the stock in the corporation (Code Sec. 1298(a)(2)(A)). Ownership is attributed to the shareholder based on the shareholder's proportionate interest in the value of the stock. The stock in a PFIC held by a foreign corporation that is also a PFIC is attributed to a U.S. person, regardless of the 50 percent limitation (Code Sec. 1298(a)(2)(B)).

The Taxpayer Relief Act of 1997 (P.L. 105-34) eliminated overlap between the controlled foreign corporation (CFC) rules of subpart F and the PFIC provisions by adding Code Sec. 1297(e). Under Code Sec. 1297(e), a 10 percent shareholder who is subject to current inclusion of subpart F income with respect to a CFC that is also a PFIC generally is not subject to the PFIC rules with respect to the same stock. Thus, a corporation is not treated as a PFIC during the qualified portion of the shareholder's holding period, which is the period after the effective date of P.L. 105-34 and during which the shareholder is a U.S. shareholder and the corporation is a CFC.

Technical Corrections Impact

Attribution rules for non-PFIC shareholders.—The IRS Restructuring and Reform Act of 1998 clarifies that the attribution rules that determine whether a U.S. person indirectly owns stock in a PFIC apply regardless of the provision that treats a corporation as a non-PFIC with respect to a shareholder under Code Sec. 1297(e) (Code Sec. 1298(a)(2)(B), as amended by the 1998 Act). As a result, stock owned directly or indirectly by a foreign corporation that is not treated as a PFIC under Code 1297(e) is attributed to the shareholder regardless of the shareholder's percentage of ownership interest in the corporation.

> **Example.** FIX, Inc., a U.S. domestic corporation, owns 20% of the stock in a PFIC that in turn wholly owns stock in a second-tier PFIC. Code Sec. 1297(e) applies to the stock held by FIX in the first-tier PFIC so that the stock is not treated as PFIC stock. To determine the indirect ownership of FIX in the second-tier PFIC under the PFIC attribution rules, the first-tier PFIC is still considered a PFIC so that any stock ownership FIX has in the PFIC will trigger the attribution rules.

★ *Effective date.* The provision applies to tax years of U.S. persons beginning after December 31, 1997, and tax years of foreign corporations ending with or within such tax years of U.S. persons (Act Sec. 6024 of the IRS Restructuring and Reform Act of 1998; Act Sec. 1124 of the Taxpayer Relief Act of 1997 (P.L. 105-34)).

Act Sec. 6011(b)(2), amending Code Sec. 1298(a)(2)(B). Law at ¶ 5660. Committee Report at ¶ 11,230.

Option Holders

¶ 641

Background _____

The Taxpayer Relief Act of 1997 (P.L. 105-34) eliminated the overlap between the subpart F rules for controlled foreign corporations (CFCs) and the passive foreign investment company (PFIC) provisions by adding Code Sec. 1297(e). Under Code Sec. 1297(e), a shareholder that is subject to current inclusion rules under the subpart F with respect to stock of a PFIC that is a CFC is generally not subject to the PFIC provisions with respect to the same stock. If an option is held on the stock, Code Sec. 1297(e) will not apply because an option cannot be taken into account in determining a subpart F inclusion under the CFC rules.

For purposes of determining whether the *CFC stock ownership requirements* are met, both stock held directly and indirectly through a foreign entity and stock held constructively are taken into account. An option on stock of a corporation is generally considered in determining stock ownership under the constructive ownership rules (Code Sec. 318(a)(4) and Code Sec. 958).

In contrast, when determining a U.S. shareholder's pro rata share of the CFC's income and earnings subject to *a current inclusion under the subpart F rules,* only stock held directly or indirectly through a foreign entity is taken into account (Code Sec. 951(b) and Code Sec. 958). Since an option held on CFC stock is not considered held directly or indirectly through a foreign entity, the current inclusion rules of subpart F will not apply with respect to the stock. Thus, Code Sec. 1297(e) cannot be applied where the option is also held on PFIC stock. Code Sec. 1298(a)(4) provides that, to the extent set forth by regulations, a person that holds an option to acquire PFIC stock is treated as a shareholder of PFIC stock. Proposed Reg. § 1.1291-1(d) provides that a person will be treated as subject to Code Sec. 1291 rules for taxing the distribution or disposition of PFIC stock upon the disposition of an option on such stock. Further, the holding period of PFIC stock acquired upon exercise of the option includes the period the option was held.

Technical Corrections Impact

Option holders treated as non-PFIC shareholders.—The elimination of the overlap between the CFC and PFIC provisions under Code Sec. 1297(e) by the Taxpayer Relief Act of 1997 (P.L. 105-34) applies only to the extent that a shareholder is subject to the current inclusion rules under subpart F with respect to stock in the corporation. Option holders with respect to stock of a corporation that is both a PFIC and a CFC will be able to apply Code Sec. 1297(e), even though the shareholder is not subject to the current inclusion rules of subpart F with respect to the stock.

Under a technical correction, the option holder is allowed to look to the owner of the stock that is the subject of the option in order to establish that the current inclusion requirement is met and that the PFIC rules will not apply. Specifically, the option holder must establish that (1) the stock is owned by a U.S. shareholder either directly or indirectly through a foreign entity within the meaning of Code Sec. 958(a), and (2) the shareholder is not a tax-exempt person and is subject to the current inclusion rules of subpart F with respect to the stock (Code Sec. 1297(e)(4), as added by the IRS Restructuring and Reform Act of 1998).

Comment. With respect to publicly traded options, it is not clear how it could be established that the stock owner is a U.S. person.

PRACTICAL ANALYSIS. Paul Bodner, Esq., Great Neck, NY, comments that this change to the Taxpayer Relief Act of 1997 effectively eliminates a planning opportunity (i.e. loophole) by maintaining an economic interest in the foreign corporation as an option holder that is not subject to direct taxation on the PFIC's income.

★ *Effective date.* The provision applies to tax years of U.S. persons beginning after December 31, 1997, and to tax years of foreign corporations ending with or within such tax years of U.S. persons (Act Sec. 6024 of the IRS Restructuring and Reform Act of 1998; Act Sec. 1124 of the Taxpayer Relief Act of 1997 (P.L. 105-34)).

Act Sec. 6011(b)(1), adding Code Sec. 1297(e)(4). Law at ¶ 5650. Committee Report at ¶ 11,225.

Mark-to-Market Rules for RICs

¶ 646

Background ———————————————————————————————

A regulated investment company (RIC) is allowed to make a mark-to-market election under Proposed Reg. § 1.1291-8 with respect to passive foreign investment company (PFIC) stock that it owns as a direct or indirect stockholder. Under the proposed regulation, the RIC would recognize gain on a share-by-share basis at the end of the RIC's tax year. No loss could be recognized as a result of making the election.

Subsequent to the proposed regulations, the Taxpayer Relief Act of 1997 (P.L. 105-34) enacted Code Sec. 1296, which allows a shareholder of a PFIC to make a mark-to-market election with respect to marketable stock. Under the mark-to-market rules of Code Sec. 1296, the shareholder's income inclusion for each year is the excess of the fair market value of the PFIC stock at the close of the tax year over the shareholder's adjusted basis in the stock. In contrast to the proposed regulation, a shareholder is allowed a deduction under Code Sec. 1296 for the excess

Background

of the shareholder's adjusted basis of the PFIC stock over its fair market value at the close of the tax year, to the extent of net mark-to-market gain for previous years.

Technical Corrections Impact

Shareholder deduction.—The IRS Restructuring and Reform Act of 1998 clarifies that the shareholder deduction is allowed under the statutory mark-to-market rule with respect to a regulated investment company (RIC) that elects to use the rule for its PFIC stock. The deduction for the excess of the stock's adjusted basis over its fair market value is allowed, in the case of a RIC, to the extent of prior mark-to-market inclusions under Code Sec. 1296 (Code Sec. 1296(d), as amended by the 1998 Act). The Senate Committee Report states that deductions are also allowed for prior mark-to-market inclusions under Proposed Reg. § 1.1291-8.

★ *Effective date.* The provision applies to tax years of U.S. persons beginning after December 31, 1997, and tax years of foreign corporations ending with or within such tax years of U.S. persons (Act Sec. 6024 of the IRS Restructuring and Reform Act of 1998; Act Sec. 1124 of the Taxpayer Relief Act of 1997 (P.L. 105-34)).

Act Sec. 6011(c)(3), amending Code Sec. 1296(d). Law at ¶ 5640. Committee Report at ¶ 11,240.

Mark-to-Market Election

¶ 651

Background

The Taxpayer Relief Act of 1997 (P.L. 105-34) added Code Sec. 1296, which allows a U.S. shareholder in a passive foreign investment company (PFIC) to make a mark-to-market election with respect to marketable PFIC stock. If a taxpayer makes the election after the beginning of the taxpayer's holding period with respect to the stock, a special coordination rule applies under Code Sec. 1296(j). Under the coordination rule, the tax and interest charge rules that apply to nonqualified funds under Code Sec. 1291 are not avoided on amounts attributable to periods before the election.

The Taxpayer Relief Act did not address the application of either the Code Sec. 1291 rules or the coordination rule where PFIC stock is marked to market under provisions other than Code Sec. 1296. For example, mark-to-market accounting may be required by securities dealers or elected by securities and commodities traders (Code Sec. 475(e) and (f)). Other provisions, such as Code Sec. 1092(b)(1) and Temp. Reg. § 1.1092(b)-4T that relate to mixed straddle accounts, similarly allow stock to be marked to market.

Technical Corrections Impact

Coordination with other mark-to-market provisions.—The tax and interest charge rules under Code Sec. 1291 will not apply to PFIC stock that is marked to market under Code Sec. 475 or any other provision. Rules similar to the special coordination rules of Code Sec. 1296(j) will apply (Code Sec. 1291(d)(1), as amended by the IRS Restructuring and Reform Act of 1998).

Comment. The Senate Committee Report provides that no inference is intended as to the treatment of PFIC stock that was marked to market before the effective date of Code Sec. 1291 (i.e., prior to tax years of U.S. persons beginning after 1997, and tax years of foreign corporations ending with or within such tax years of U.S. persons).

PRACTICAL ANALYSIS. Paul Bodner, Esq., Great Neck, NY, notes that this provision serves merely to coordinate two mark-to-market regimes, making it unnecessary to elect to mark-to-market under both provisions.

★ *Effective date.* The provision is effective for tax years of U.S. persons beginning after December 31, 1997, and tax years of foreign corporations ending with or within such tax years of U.S. persons (Act Sec. 6024 of the IRS Restructuring and Reform Act of 1998; Act Sec. 1124 of the Taxpayer Relief Act of 1997 (P.L. 105-34)).

Act Sec. 6011(c)(2), amending Code Sec. 1291(d)(1). Law at ¶ 5630. Committee Report at ¶ 11,235.

REAL ESTATE INVESTMENT TRUSTS

Stapled REITs

¶ 655

Background ———————————————————————

A real estate investment trust (REIT) is an entity that receives most of its income from passive real estate related investments. Tax is generally not paid at the REIT level for income that is distributed to shareholders. REITs were created in 1960 to give small investors access to the commercial real estate market, then controlled by large commercial investors.

To qualify as a REIT, an entity must satisfy certain tests, including source-of-income tests. Under the source-of-income tests, at least 95 percent of a REIT's income must come from passive sources and at least 75 percent of its income must come from real estate (Code Sec. 856(c)(2) and Code Sec. 865(c)(3)). These source-of-income tests generally prevent REITs from operating properties that required significant management services (e.g., hotels and casinos).

Prior to the Tax Reform Act of 1984 (P.L. 98-369), a stapled REIT structure could be used to integrate both the ownership and operation of real estate without running afoul of the REIT rules. In a stapled REIT structure, the stock of a REIT is stapled or paired with the stock of an active business corporation so that the shareholders cannot trade the stock separately. This results in identical ownership in both entities and allows the shareholders to eliminate the corporate level tax on the portion of an active business corporation's income from ownership of real estate. In a stapled REIT structure, the REIT may hold all of the real estate assets used in the corporation's business and then lease those assets to the corporation. The rent payments are deducted by the corporation and are taxed to the REIT shareholders. This eliminates the corporate tax on the corporation's income used to pay the rent as if the corporation were a REIT.

The 1984 Act eliminated the tax benefits of the stapled REIT structure by providing that stapled entities are generally treated as one entity in determining whether any stapled entity is a REIT under Code Sec. 269B. However, because the IRS had sanctioned stapled REIT groups in private letter rulings, Congress believed that it should not change the tax treatment for the few REIT groups already in existence. Accordingly, grandfather relief from the single-entity analysis was provided for any REIT that was part of a group of stapled entities if:

Background

> (1) all members of the group were stapled entities as of June 30, 1983, and

> (2) as of June 30, 1983, the group included at least one REIT (Act Sec. 136(c)(3) of P.L. 98-369).

IRS Restructuring and Reform Impact

Stapled REITs, property acquisition prohibited.—The benefits of a stapled real estate investment trust (REIT) structure enjoyed by stapled REIT groups grandfathered under the Tax Reform Act of 1984 are generally eliminated for real property interests acquired after March 26, 1998. To prevent REITs from gaining the benefit of the stapled REIT structure through mortgages and interests in entities, additional rules also apply to mortgages acquired after March 26, 1998, and to acquisitions of real property interests through entities after that date. In general, relief is provided for transactions that were in progress on March 26, 1998.

Comment. Since 1984, many of the grandfathered stapled groups have been acquired by new owners, some have entered into new lines of business, and most have used the stapled structure to engage in large-scale asset acquisition. The IRS Restructuring and Reform Act of 1998 provision addresses the concern that these grandfathered REITs may have an unfair competitive advantage with respect to these asset acquisitions over companies that cannot use a stapled structure. The 1998 Act provision also accounts for the perception that revoking stapled group benefits for real estate already acquired by grandfathered REITs would be unfair.

General rule. Real property interests acquired by a member of a stapled REIT group after March 26, 1998 ("nonqualified real property interests") are subject to rules similar to those of Code Sec. 269B. Under Code Sec. 269B, all stapled entities are treated as a single entity for purposes of determining REIT status. Grandfather relief from the Code Sec. 269B rules, which was provided for existing stapled REITs under the 1984 Act, is frozen and will not apply to nonqualified real property interests. As a result, all of the activities and gross income of any member of the stapled REIT group with respect to the nonqualified real property interest will be attributable to the REIT under the single-entity analysis (Act Sec. 7002(a) and Act Sec. 7002(b)(1) of the 1998 Act). This may cause the REIT to lose its REIT status because it can not meet the 95 percent and 75 percent source-of-income tests (Code Sec. 865(c)(2) and (3)). Liability for the special tax on excess gross income for REITs with net income from prohibited transactions may also result from the single-entity analysis (Code Sec. 857(b)(5)).

The *stapled REIT group* includes the exempt REIT, a stapled entity or a 10-percent subsidiary entity in the exempt REIT or stapled entity (Act Sec. 7002(e)(3) of the 1998 Act). An *exempt REIT* is a REIT that qualifies for grandfather relief from the rules of Code Sec. 269B under Act Sec. 136(c) of the 1984 Act (Act Sec. 7002(e)(2) of the 1998 Act). A *stapled entity* is defined in Code Sec. 269B (Act Sec. 7002(e)(5) of the 1998 Act). See Stapled groups include 10-percent subsidiaries, below.

Example (1). REX REIT is stapled to XER, Inc., a property management company, so that REX and XER have the same shareholders. The stapled entity is grandfathered by the 1984 Act. REX begins to negotiate the purchase of a hotel on April 5, 1998, buys the property three months later, and immediately leases it to XER. The gross income from operating the hotel is subject to the single-entity analysis. REX and XER are treated as a single entity so that the lease payments to XER are ignored. The gross income from operating the property would be attributable to REX with the possibility that

REX might lose its REIT status for failure to meet the REIT source-of-income tests.

1998 Act grandfather rules. Real property interests acquired by a member of a stapled REIT group may not be treated as nonqualified real property interests under special grandfather rules in the 1998 Act. For the grandfather rules to apply, the stapled REIT must be stapled as of March 26, 1998 and at all times thereafter. Further, the REIT must qualify as a REIT on March 26, 1998 and at all times thereafter (Act Sec. 7002(b)(5) of the 1998 Act).

Grandfathered real property interests include real property interests acquired by a member of a REIT group on or before March 26, 1998 (Act Sec. 7002(b)(6) of the 1998 Act). A grandfathered real property interest also includes a real property interest acquired after March 26, 1998 pursuant to a contract that was binding on and at all times after that date. For this purpose, a written agreement includes a put option, buy-sell agreement and an agreement relating to a third party default (Act Sec. 7002(b)(2)(A) of the 1998 Act). The Conference Committee Report states that the exception is intended to apply only to substantive economic arrangements that are outside of the control of the stapled REIT group. The binding contract exception also applies to real property interests acquired after March 26, 1998 if the acquisition is described on or before that date in a public announcement or in a filing with the Securities and Exchange Commission (Act Sec. 7002(b)(2)(B) of the 1998 Act).

Stapled REIT groups include 10-percent subsidiaries. In addition to a REIT and the entities stapled to the REIT, a stapled REIT group also includes entities that are 10-percent subsidiaries of the exempt REIT or any stapled entity. A 10-percent subsidiary entity is any entity in which the exempt REIT or the stapled entity directly or indirectly holds at least a 10-percent interest (Act Sec. 7002(e)(4)(A) of the 1998 Act).

In the case of a corporate subsidiary owned by a stapled entity (not a REIT), the stapled entity must owns 10 percent of the corporation's stock by either vote or value (Act Sec. 7002(e)(4)(B) and Act Sec. 7002(e)(4)(C)(i) of the 1998 Act). For this purpose, changes in proportionate ownership that are attributable to fluctuations in the fair market value of the different classes of stock are not taken into account, unless otherwise provided in IRS guidance (Act Sec. 7002(c)(4)(C) of the 1998 Act).

The ownership test with respect to a partnership is met if either the REIT or the stapled entity own a 10-percent or greater interest in the partnership's capital or profits. The ownership test with respect to an entity such as a trust is met if the REIT or other stapled entity owns directly or indirectly at least 10 percent of the beneficial interests in the entity (Act Sec. 7002(e)(4)(C)(ii) of the 1998 Act).

Indirect ownership rules. If an exempt REIT or stapled entity owns, directly or indirectly, a 10-percent-or-greater interest in a subsidiary or partnership (10-percent subsidiary) that owns a real property interest, the REIT or stapled entity is considered to own a proportionate part of the 10-percent subsidiary's real property interest (Act Sec. 7002(c)(1) of the 1998 Act). Therefore, if a 10-percent subsidiary acquires nonqualified real property, the exempt REIT or stapled entity is considered to have acquired a nonqualified real property interest in the same percentage as its ownership interest in the 10-percent subsidiary. Likewise, the same proportion of the subsidiary's income from the nonqualified property will be attributed to the exempt REIT or stapled entity.

Example (2). XER, Inc., an entity stapled to REX REIT has a contract to manage a nonqualified real property interest held by SubREX, a partnership in which XER owns an 85% interest. For purposes of applying the REIT source-of-income tests, 85% of SubREX's activities and gross income from the property are attributable to REX. As a result, 85% of the stapled group's income from the contract is ignored under the single-entity analysis. The remaining 15% of the management fee is not treated as gross income to REX because it is not from an interest deemed held by REX or the stapled group.

A real property interest held or acquired by a 10-percent subsidiary will be treated as a qualified real property interest if it would be a qualified real property interest if held directly by the REIT or stapled entity. For the exception to apply, the entity must be a 10-percent subsidiary entity of the exempt REIT or stapled entity on March 26, 1998 and at all times thereafter (Act Sec. 7002(c)(2)(B) of the 1998 Act).

> **Example (3).** REX REIT contributes grandfathered property to Sub-REX, a partnership in which REX owns a 40% percent interest on March 26, 1998. The interest would continue to be grandfathered if held directly by the REIT, and, therefore, is grandfathered in the hands of SubREX.

If the exempt REIT or stapled entity *increases* its ownership interest in the subsidiary after March 26, 1998, the additional portion of each interest in real property treated as held by the exempt REIT or stapled entity will be treated as a nonqualified real property interest (Act Sec. 7002(c)(3) of the 1998 Act).

An exception to the indirect ownership rules exists for interests acquired by an exempt REIT or a member of a stapled REIT group after March 26, 1998 pursuant to a binding written contract that was binding on or after that date. An exception also exists for interests acquired after March 26, 1998 if the acquisition is described on or before that date in a public announcement or in a filing with the Securities and Exchange Commission (Act Sec. 7002(c)(4)(B) of the 1998 Act).

Special rules for 60-percent partnerships (UPREITs). In general, if, after March 26, 1998, an exempt REIT or stapled entity increases its ownership interest in a subsidiary entity with qualified real property interests, the REIT's or stapled entity's share of the qualified interest does not experience a corresponding increase. The additional portion of the real property interest is treated as a nonqualified real property interest (Act Sec. 7002(c)(3) of the 1998 Act). A special rule applies in the case of Umbrella Partnership Real Estate Investment Trusts (UPREITs), described in Reg. § 1.701-2(d), Example (4). In the transaction described in Reg. § 1.701-2(d), a partnership can properly be used to avoid the gain recognition that would occur if encumbered property were contributed to a corporation that elects to be treated as a REIT. Under the regulation, partnerships with substantial real estate holdings can combine business with a REIT by contributing the property to a limited partnership formed with the REIT. The partnerships then terminate, with the partners obtaining future rights to obtain stock in the REIT. The transaction does not result in gain because the new partnership is not considered an investment company under Code Sec. 351(e). By using the partnership form and gradually exchanging encumbered property for stock in the REIT, the parties are able to use the nonrecognition rules of Code Sec. 721.

The special rule that applies in the case of UPREITs treats 100 percent of the real property interests, mortgages, activities and gross income of the UPREITs as interests, activities and gross income of the exempt REIT or stapled entity that owns the partnership interest. The rule will apply if, on March 26, 1998:

> (1) the exempt REIT or stapled entity owns directly or indirectly at least 60 percent of the capital or property interest in a partnership, and

> (2) 90 percent or more of the capital and 90 percent or more of the profit interests in the partnership (other than those held by the exempt REIT or stapled entity) are, or will be, redeemable or exchangeable for consideration that is determined by reference to the value of the stock in the exempt REIT and/or the stapled entity (Act Sec. 7002(c)(5)(A) of the 1998 Act).

In applying the requirements, above, only the largest partnership owned by an exempt REIT or stapled entity on January 1, 1999 (determined by aggregate asset bases) will be treated as meeting the requirements (Act Sec. 7002(c)(5)(B) of the 1998 Act). Additionally, in applying the requirements above, a partnership formed after March 26, 1998 may be treated as being held by an exempt REIT or stapled entity on March 26, 1998. The partnership must be formed to mirror the stapling of an exempt REIT and a stapled entity in connection with an acquisition agreed to or announced on or before March 26, 1998 (Act Sec. 7002(c)(5)(C) of the 1998 Act).

Leases and improvements. A qualified real property interest will not generally become a nonqualified property interest as a result of repairs to, or improvements of, an improvement owned or leased by a REIT or stapled entity. Similarly, any improvement to land owned or leased by a REIT or stapled group member will not convert the interest to a nonqualified real property interest (Act Sec. 7002(b)(3)(A) of the 1998 Act). If a REIT leases a grandfathered interest, the interest remains grandfathered. The renewal of such a lease likewise will not affect the status of the interest. However, status is unaffected only if the rent involved does not exceed an arm's-length rate. Therefore, a REIT may lease or renew a lease of grandfathered real property to a stapled entity at an arm's-length rent without losing the property's grandfathered status (Act Sec. 7002(b)(3)(B) of the 1998 Act; Senate Committee Report). The Conference Committee Report states that the renewal of a lease from a third party to a member of a stapled REIT group will not terminate qualified real property status, whether or not the renewal is pursuant to the terms of the original lease. The Conference Committee cautions that a significant time period between the tenancies would cause the renewal not to qualify.

Despite the general rule, certain improvements may cause the real property to lose its status as a qualified real property interest. The Senate Committee Report states that an expansion beyond the boundaries of the land of a grandfathered interest that occurs after March 26, 1998 may change the status of the interest to the extent of the expansion. Further, an improvement of a qualified real property interest that is placed in service after December 31, 1999 is treated as a separate nonqualified real property interest if:

(1) the improvement changes the use of the property, and

(2) the cost is greater than (a) 200 percent of the undepreciated cost of the pre-improved property or (b) in the case of substitute basis property, the fair market value of the property on the date it was acquired by the REIT or stapled entity (Act Sec. 7002(b)(3)(C)(i) of the 1998 Act).

The Senate Committee Report provides an example of when improvements can change the status of a qualified real property interest. Undeveloped raw land acquired on or before March 26, 1998 is a qualified real property interest. The status of the land would change if a member of the REIT group constructs a building after December 31, 1999 on the undeveloped land.

A binding-contract exception exists for improvements significant enough to cause property to lose its exempt status as a qualified real property interest. Improvements placed in service before January 1, 2004, pursuant to a binding contract in effect on December 31, 1999 and at all times thereafter, are grandfathered from nonqualified real property status (Act Sec. 7002(b)(3)(C)(ii) of the 1998 Act).

Transfers between members of a stapled REIT group. A nonqualified real property interest will not include any interest in real property acquired as a result of a direct or indirect contribution, distribution or other transfer between members of the stapled REIT group. The exception applies to the extent that the aggregate interest of all stapled entities in the real property interest, after applying the indirect ownership rules, does not increase as a result of the transfer (Act Sec.

7002(b)(4) of the 1998 Act). The Conference Committee Report states that the exception applies to all types of transfers, whether or not taxable.

Example (4). REX REIT, an exempt REIT is stapled to XER, Inc. REX sells a portion of a grandfathered property interest to XER, Inc. The real property interest remains grandfathered because the total interests of REX and XER, Inc. remain at 100 percent both before and after the transfer.

Example (5). REX REIT, an exempt REIT is stapled to XER, Inc. REX contributes grandfathered property to a 10-percent subsidiary partnership, SubREX. The real property interest remains grandfathered because the 100 percent interests of REX and XER, Inc. in the property before the contribution are not increased.

Example (6). REX REIT, an exempt REIT, that is stapled to XER, Inc., owns a 50-percent interest in a partnership, SubREX, that distributes a grandfathered real property interest to the REX in complete liquidation of its interest. The 50-percent interest in the real property that REX was deemed to own continues to be grandfathered. The remaining 50-percent interest will become a non-grandfathered interest because it represents an increase in the direct and indirect interests of REX and XER, Inc.

Mortgage rules. Apart from the rules for real property interests described above, special rules apply in the case of certain mortgages acquired after March 26, 1998 (Act Sec. 7002(d) of the 1998 Act). The mortgage rules apply where a member of a stapled REIT group holds an obligation secured by an interest in real property and one of the members of the stapled group engages in certain activities with respect to that property (i.e., the rules apply where a member holds a nonqualified obligation) (Act Sec. 7002(d)(2) of the 1998 Act). These activities are those that would result in impermissible tenant service income under Code Sec. 856(d)(7). In general, impermissible tenant service income includes income from services rendered by the REIT to its tenants, unless the services are performed by an independent contractor.

Under the mortgage rules, interest income allocated to the nonqualified obligation and income from services performed by a member of the stapled group are considered impermissible tenant income of the REIT (Act Sec. 7002(d)(1) of the 1998 Act). As a result, the income will not be considered when determining if at least 95 percent of the REIT's gross income is derived from certain passive sources under Code Sec. 856(c)(2) or whether at least 75 percent of its income is from real estate sources under Code Sec. 856(c)(3). If the REIT or stapled entity owns a 10-percent-or-greater interest in a subsidiary or partnership, a proportionate part of the entity's nonqualified obligations, interest and gross income is attributable to the REIT or stapled entity (Act Sec. 7002(d)(1) of the 1998 Act).

Example (7). REX REIT makes a mortgage loan on a casino owned and operated by a member of the stapled REIT group, XER, Inc., under a management contract. Both the management fees earned by XER and the interest earned by REX are impermissible tenant services income to REX.

An exception to the mortgage rule applies to obligations with interest that does not exceed an arm's-length rate and which would be treated as interest under the REIT rules (Act Sec. 7002(d)(3) of the of the 1998 Act). Another exception applies for existing mortgages. This exception applies to mortgages held by a member of the stapled REIT group on March 26, 1998 and at all times thereafter. The mortgage must be secured by an interest in real property on March 26, 1998 and all times thereafter. However, the exception ceases to apply if the interest rate is changed so that it does not meet an arm's-length standard, unless the change is pursuant to the agreement in effect on March 26, 1998. Similarly, the exception will continue to apply if the mortgage is refinanced provided the principal amount is not increased by the refinancing and the new interest rate meets the arm's-length standard (Act Sec. 7002(d)(4) of the 1998 Act).

The Senate Committee Report states that if a REIT or a stapled entity acquires a 10-percent-or-greater interest in a partnership or corporation after March 26, 1998, no mortgage held by the partnership or subsidiary on March 26, 1998 would qualify for the existing-mortgage exception. Similarly, if the REIT or stapled entity acquires a greater interest in a subsidiary in which it was a 10-percent shareholder on March 26, 1998, the REIT's (or entity's) additional proportion of each of the subsidiary's mortgages does not qualify for the existing-mortgage exception (Act Sec. 7002(d)(6) of the 1998 Act).

> **Example (8).** REX REIT acquires a 40% interest in SubREX partnership on April 1, 1998. No mortgage held by SubREX on the acquisition date would qualify for the existing-mortgage exception because it would not be not attributable to REX on March 26, 1998.

Priority rules. The mortgage rules will not apply to any part of a real property interest owned or deemed owned by a REIT or stapled entity under the rules that apply to real property interests under the general nonqualified real property interest rule of Act Sec. 7002(a), described above (Act Sec. 7002(d)(7) of the 1998 Act). For example, if a REIT makes a mortgage loan on a property owned by a stapled entity, the mortgage rules would not apply. If the property is a nonqualified real property interest, the interest on the mortgage would be ignored under the single-entity analysis and the stapled entity's gross income from the property would be attributable to the REIT.

Rules applied on partial-year basis. The Conference Committee Report clarifies that the single-entity analysis will be applied on a partial-year basis where a stapled REIT group ceases to be stapled or there are changes in an exempt REIT's or stapled entity's ownership in a 10-percent owned subsidiary during the year.

Guidance. The IRS is authorized to issue guidance on the rules that apply to stapled REITs discussed above. Guidance may be issued to help carry out the rules, to prevent avoidance of the rules or to prevent the double counting of income (Act Sec. 7002(f) of the 1998 Act).

PRACTICAL ANALYSIS. Keith Nakamoto, tax partner at the Chicago office of PricewaterhouseCoopers LLP, notes that in the 1970's and the early 1980's, a few real estate investment trusts (REITs) formed "paired" relationships with other companies. The purpose of these relationships was to enable the REIT to actively manage its properties (through the other companies), while still meeting the REIT qualification rules, which generally did not allow the REIT to operate businesses.

In the typical "paired" structure, a REIT and an "operating" company have their stock "paired" such that they trade as a single unit. The REIT owns real estate which it leases to an operating company. The operating company is usually organized as a C corporation and unlike the REIT, the operating company is unrestricted in the business that it may operate.

In 1984, Congress passed legislation which effectively prevented the formation of new paired share REITs. After the effective date of the 1984 legislation, any newly formed paired share REIT must include the "paired" company in applying the REIT qualification tests. Existing paired share REITs were grandfathered and today five continue to exist.

Nakamoto observes that the current provision grandfathers the existing activities of these five paired share REITs. Any new activities will be subject to the inclusion rules of the 1984 legislation, that is, the REIT tests will be applied on a combined basis for these new activities. The reason for removing the grandfather status for all new activities in these five REITs is that Congress believes these entities have an unfair competitive advantage in relation to other companies that cannot benefit from this structure.

PRACTICAL ANALYSIS. C. VanLeer Davis of Dechert, Price & Rhoads, Philadelphia, PA, observes that, in response to claims of unfair competition from others in the REIT industry, the Act restricts future activities of "paired share" REITs. These REITs issue shares "paired" with shares of a C corporation, in that the two shares always trade as a unit. 1984 legislation effectively outlawed paired share REITs but permanently grandfathered existing paired share REITs. Although only five public paired share REITs remain in existence, two have recently received considerable notoriety as the result of aggressive acquisition programs.

The perceived vice of the paired share REIT is that it can arrange its affairs so as to own or finance (through the REIT) and operate (through the C corporation) active businesses, such as nursing homes and hotels. Most hotel REITs, for example, own hotel properties that are leased to an operator. This avoids the REIT's having impermissible income as the hotel's receipts are not "rents from real property" under the REIT rules, but the rent received by the REIT from the paired lessee is permissible income. A paired REIT could set the terms of the lease to maximize the REIT's income, which is not subject to corporate tax, and minimize the taxable income of the paired C corporation. Since the shares of the two entities are paired, shareholders profit from this arrangement by receiving a larger portion of their return undiminished by corporate tax. A hotel REIT which is not paired must, however, negotiate with an unaffiliated operator with no interest in maximizing the REIT's income.

Act Sec. 7002 essentially prevents expansion of the use of pairing by existing grandfathered paired share REITs. In the case of new acquisitions or new financings in which the paired entities are involved, their operations are integrated. For example, if a paired REIT buys a hotel, the activities of the REIT and the C corporation are aggregated, and if the C corporation operates the hotel, the REIT is treated as operating the hotel and therefore any income it receives is impermissible REIT income. In the case of mortgages held by the REIT where the mortgagor is the paired entity, the interest income is good income to the REIT only if the interest rate does not exceed an "arm's length" rate. Existing arrangements of paired share REITs are unaffected but become subject to the new rules if renegotiated or renewed at other than an "arm's length" price. The new provision also ensures that entities related to the paired REIT, such as corporations 10 percent or more owned by a paired entity, are included in the aggregation, to the extent of the paired group's interest.

The net effect of Act Sec. 7002 is to put paired REITs on a par with other REITs for future acquisitions, thus prohibiting entities paired with REITs from actively managing businesses occupying the REIT's real estate or owning operating entities on which the REIT holds an above-market interest rate mortgage. The new rule does not affect so-called "paper-clipped" REITs that issue operating company shares intended, but not required, to remain commonly owned with the REIT. These REITs remain outside the stapled REIT provisions.

★ *Effective date.* The provision applies to tax years ending after March 26, 1998 (Act Sec. 7002(g) of the IRS Restructuring and Reform Act of 1998).

Act Sec. 7002 of the IRS Restructuring and Reform Act of 1998. Law at ¶ 8285. Committee Report at ¶ 11,525.

Distribution Rules

¶ 661

Background

To qualify as a real estate investment trust (REIT), an entity must elect REIT status and meet other tests. An entity that elects REIT status for the first time cannot have earnings and profits that were accumulated in non-REIT years. Accordingly, a newly electing REIT must distribute earnings and profits accumulated in non-REIT years to its shareholders in its first tax year.

The Taxpayer Relief Act of 1997 (P.L. 105-34) changed the ordering rules for purposes of earnings and profits distributions. Distributions of accumulated earnings and profits by the entity are generally treated as being made from the entity's earliest, rather than most recently, accumulated earnings and profits. In making the required distribution, the earliest accumulated earnings and profits, do not consider earnings and profits of an entity that qualified as a REIT for *all* tax years beginning after February 28, 1986 (Code Sec. 857(a)(2)(A) and Code Sec. 857(d)(3)(A), prior to amendment by the IRS Restructuring and Reform Act of 1998).

Technical Corrections Impact

Distributions of non-REIT earnings and profits.—The ordering rule that applies when a REIT is required to distribute earnings and profits accumulated in non-REIT years is modified. Specifically, the term "earliest accumulated earnings and profits" now refers to the earliest earnings and profits accumulated *in any tax year* in which the entity did *not* qualify as a REIT (Code Sec. 857(d)(3)(A), as amended by the IRS Restructuring and Reform Act of 1998).

Example. RITECo has $400 of accumulated earnings and profits from 1996, a tax year in which it qualified as a REIT. In December 1997, a C corporation, ABC Corp., with $300 of accumulated earnings and profits from 1997, merged into RITECo. RITECo must distribute the non-REIT earnings and profits inherited from ABC in order to maintain its REIT status. A distribution by RITECo of $300 is deemed to first come from 1997, the earliest year with non-REIT earnings and profits. Therefore, the $300 distribution eliminates the non-REIT earnings and profits inherited from ABC.

Comment. The 1998 Act distribution rule facilitates the purging of non-REIT earnings and profits from existing REITs, as well as from newly electing REITs. Act Sec. 1262 of the Taxpayer Relief Act of 1997 (P.L. 105-34) amended Code Sec. 856(i)(2) to allow existing REITs to acquire wholly owned subsidiaries. Similar to a newly electing REIT, an existing REIT must distribute the pre-REIT earnings and profits of the subsidiary before the end of the REIT's tax year.

Caution. This provision does not change the requirement that a REIT must distribute at least 95 percent of its REIT earnings every year (Code Sec. 857(a)(1)).

PRACTICAL ANALYSIS. Keith Nakamoto, tax partner at the Chicago office of PricewaterhouseCoopers LLP, comments that the Taxpayer Relief Act of 1997 (TRA '97) eliminated a potential tax trap for a newly electing real estate investment trust (REIT). Under the REIT qualification rules, a newly electing REIT must distribute all earnings and profits from non-REIT years by the end of its first REIT tax year. Prior to TRA '97, a newly electing REIT might find it impossible to distribute all non-REIT earnings and profits because the normal ordering rules required the current year's earnings and profits to be distributed before distributing prior years' earnings and profits. TRA '97 eliminated this potential tax trap when it reversed the ordering rules and deemed all non-REIT earnings and profits to be distributed first.

The current provision clarifies that this reversal of the ordering rules applies to non-REIT earnings and profits from merged companies as well as to the REIT's own earnings and profits. With the increased merger activity among the REITs, this clarification is an important provision for the industry.

★ *Effective date.* The provision is effective for tax years beginning after August 5, 1997 (Act Sec. 6024 of the IRS Restructuring and Reform Act of 1998; Act Sec. 1263 of the Taxpayer Relief Act of 1997 (P.L. 105-34)).

Act Sec. 6012(g), amending Code Sec. 857(d)(3)(A). Law at ¶ 5530. Committee Report at ¶ 11,270.

FOREIGN TAX CREDIT

Regulated Investment Companies (RICs)

¶ 666

Background———————————————————————————————

The Taxpayer Relief Act of 1997 (P.L. 105-34) imposed a stock holding period requirement for claiming foreign tax credits with respect to dividends received from a corporation or a regulated investment company (RIC). To claim foreign tax credits, the shareholder must hold the stock for a minimum holding period of 16 days for common stock and 46 days for certain preferred stock.

The holding period requirements also apply in the case of taxes deemed paid by a RIC shareholder under the Code Sec. 853 RIC flow-through rules, which allow a RIC shareholder to either deduct or claim a credit for foreign taxes paid by the RIC. If the holding period is not met, the foreign tax credit for foreign withholding taxes is disallowed. RICs are required to notify their shareholders of the amount of foreign taxes that would be disallowed for failure to meet the holding period requirements.

Technical Corrections Impact

Holding period requirements.—A RIC may not elect to flow through to its shareholders foreign tax credits for foreign taxes paid by the RIC if its failure to meet the holding period requirements under Code Sec. 901(k) would disallow the credit for those taxes (Code Sec. 853(e), as added by the IRS Restructuring and

Reform Act of 1998). Although the foreign taxes may not be claimed as a credit by the RIC or the shareholder, they may be deducted at the RIC level.

Comment. The provision in Code Sec. 901(k)(2) denies the foreign tax credit in the case of a Code Sec. 853 election with respect to stock that does not meet the holding requirements of Code Sec. 901(k)(1). Since, under the Taxpayer Relief Act of 1997 (P.L. 105-34), the election was not precluded with respect to the stock, the RIC shareholder could deduct the foreign taxes. By eliminating the Code Sec. 853 election with respect to the stock that does not meet the holding period requirements, only the RIC can deduct the taxes.

Election. The Code Sec. 853 election is precluded with respect to stock where the holding period requirements of Code Sec. 901(k) are not met.

Notice requirement. The provision under the P.L. 105-34 that requires a RIC to notify its shareholders of the foreign taxes that are disallowed as a credit for failure to meet the holding period requirements is eliminated (Code Sec. 853(c), as amended by the 1998 Act).

Comment. Since these foreign taxes can no longer be passed through to the shareholder, they would not be included in the foreign tax amount in the shareholder notice in any event.

★ *Effective date.* The provision applies to dividends paid or accrued more than 30 days after August 5, 1997 (Act Sec. 6024 of the IRS Restructuring and Reform Act of 1998; Act Sec. 1053(c) of the Taxpayer Relief Act of 1997 (P.L. 105-34)).

PRACTICAL ANALYSIS. Paul Bodner, Esq., Great Neck, NY, observes that this technical correction ensures that Code Sec. 901(k) prevents taxpayers from selling foreign tax credits even if the dividend flows through a RIC. The big fight, however, is the regulation under Notice 98-5. Negotiations between the IRS and the securities industry are seeking to prevent some of the more abusive transactions while permitting normal business to continue. In addition, it is anticipated that there will be a lengthy comment period before any regulations are finalized. The Conference Report indicates that Congress is amenable to some regulatory action.

Act Sec. 6010(k)(1), redesignating Code Sec. 853(e) as Code Sec. 853(f) and adding new Code Sec. 853(e); Act Sec. 6010(k)(2), amending Code Sec. 853(c). Law at ¶ 5520. Committee Report at ¶ 11,195.

Securities Dealers

¶ 668

Background

The Taxpayer Relief Act of 1997 (P.L. 105-34) imposed a stock holding period requirement for claiming foreign tax credits with respect to dividends received from a corporation or regulated investment company (RIC). An exception exists for stock that is held in the active conduct of a securities business in a foreign country. Both the Senate and House Committee Reports for P.L. 105-34 indicate that additionally, for the exception to apply, the stock must be held by a *securities dealer* engaged in the active conduct of a securities business in a foreign country.

Technical Corrections Impact

Exception from holding period requirements.—The IRS Restructuring and Reform Act of 1998 clarifies that the exception from the stock holding period requirement for claiming foreign tax credits applies to stock that is held by a *securities dealer* engaged in the active conduct of a securities business in a foreign country (Code Sec. 901(k)(4)(A), as amended by the IRS Restructuring and Reform Act of 1998). This correction was needed to reflect congressional intent, as set forth in the House and Senate Committee Reports to the Taxpayer Relief Act of 1997 (P.L. 105-34), that the exception apply only to securities dealers.

★ *Effective date.* The provision applies to dividends paid or accrued more than 30 days after August 5, 1997 (Act Sec. 6024 of the IRS Restructuring and Reform Act of 1998; Act Sec. 1053(c) of the Taxpayer Relief Act of 1997 (P.L. 105-34)).

Act Sec. 6010(k)(3), amending Code Sec. 901(k)(4)(A). Law at ¶ 5550. Committee Report at ¶ 11,195.

PARTNERSHIPS

Electing Large Partnerships

¶ 671

Background ——————————————————————

The Taxpayer Relief Act of 1997 (P.L. 105-34) enacted numerous rules applicable to certain large partnerships with more than 100 partners. For example, simplified flowthrough, recordkeeping and audit provisions were made applicable to large nonservice partnerships and their partners that elected to be treated under the tax regime delineated within Code Sec. 771 through Code Sec. 777 (which address "electing large partnerships") (Code Sec. 775(a)).

Furthermore, to improve the ability of partners in large partnerships with more than 100 partners to file their own income tax returns on time, the 1997 Act required such large partnerships to send the partners their Schedules K-1 on or before the first March 15 following the close of the large partnership's tax year, a month sooner than that required of other partnerships (Code Sec. 6031(b)).

The 1997 Act also added a new rule providing that large partnerships with more than 100 partners must file their annual information returns (Form 1065) and their copies of their partners' Schedules K-1 on magnetic media (Code Sec. 6011(e)(2)).

Finally, the 1997 Act modified the treatment of partnership items of individual retirement arrangements (Code Sec. 6012(b)(6)).

The Conference Committee Report to the 1997 Act provided that these provisions were applicable to partnership tax years *beginning after* December 31, 1997. However, the statutory language contained in the 1997 Act inconsistently provided that the simplified audit procedure, Schedule K-1 reporting date, magnetic media and individual retirement arrangement rules applied to partnership tax years *ending on or after* December 31, 1997 (Act Sec. 1226 of the 1997 Act).

In a subsequent Notice, the IRS acknowledged this legislative drafting error regarding the effective date, and assured partnerships with more than 100 partners (large partnerships) that the IRS would not require magnetic media filing of large partnership information returns for tax years beginning before January 1, 1998 (Notice 97-77, I.R.B. 1997-52, 18).

However, a technical correction was necessary to provide that all of the affected provisions would apply to partnership tax years beginning after December 31, 1997, and would be effective as if enacted in the 1997 Act.

Technical Corrections Impact

Revised effective date for certain 1997 Act large partnership provisions.—The IRS Restructuring and Reform Act of 1998 provides that the provisions in the 1997 Act relating to large partnerships, the due date for reporting certain Schedules K-1, partnership returns required on magnetic media, and the treatment of partnership items of individual retirement arrangements are actually effective for partnership tax years beginning after December 31, 1997 (Act Sec. 6012(e) of the IRS Restructuring and Reform Act of 1998, amending Act Sec. 1226 of the Taxpayer Relief Act of 1997 (P.L. 105-34)).

★ *Effective date.* These provisions are effective for partnership tax years beginning after December 31, 1997.

Act Sec. 6012(e), amending Act Sec. 1226 of the Taxpayer Relief Act of 1997 (P.L. 105-34). Law at ¶ 8265. Committee Report at ¶ 11,265.

Publicly Traded Partnerships

¶ 676

Background

The Taxpayer Relief Act of 1997 (P.L. 105-34) provided that certain publicly traded partnerships that could date their continued existence back to December 17, 1987, could elect to be subject to a 3.5-percent annual tax on their "gross income" from the active conduct of a trade or business (Code Sec. 7704(g)(3), as added by P.L. 105-34). If this election was made, then the generally applicable rule treating such a publicly traded partnership as a corporation in its first tax year beginning after 1997 for income tax purposes would not apply (Code Sec. 7704(g)(1) and Code Sec. 7704(g)(3)(A)). The 1997 Act called a publicly traded partnership that could elect to be subject to this special tax an "electing 1987 partnership."

However, when Code Sec. 7704(g)(3) was enacted, the provision did not specifically make inapplicable the general rule contained in Code Sec. 701 that a partnership is not subject to the income tax. Code Sec. 701 provides that partnership tax items of income, loss, credit and deduction flow through the entity and are reflected on the returns of the partners, who are liable for any resultant tax in their separate or individual capacities.

Furthermore, the 1997 Act did not specifically make the corporate estimated tax payment requirements applicable to this 3.5-percent tax.

Technical Corrections Impact

Payment of tax by electing 1987 partnerships.—A technical correction clarifies that the 3.5-percent tax applicable to electing 1987 partnerships is in fact payable by the partnership, at the entity level, and not by the partners. The general provision of Code Sec. 701 that a partnership is not subject to the income tax does not apply to this special 3.5-percent tax (Code Sec. 7704(g)(3)(C), as amended by the IRS Restructuring and Reform Act of 1998). This special tax is voluntarily paid by electing 1987 partnerships in order to retain their partnership treatment under the Code.

Comment. This 3.5-percent tax is intended to approximate the corporate tax that these publicly traded partnerships would pay if they were treated as corporations for federal income tax purposes.

Furthermore, the 1998 Act provides that the corporate estimated tax payment rules of Code Sec. 6655 are applicable to the 3.5-percent tax payable by an electing 1987 partnership in the same manner as if the partnership were a corporation and the tax were imposed under Code Sec. 11 (relating to corporate tax rates). For this purpose, all Code Sec. 11 references to "taxable income" are to be applied as if they were references to the "gross income" of the electing 1987 partnership for the tax year from the active conduct of trades and businesses by the partnership (Code Sec. 7704(g)(3)(C), as amended by the 1998 Act).

★ *Effective date.* The provision clarifying that the partnership is responsible for the payment of the 3.5-percent tax is effective for tax years beginning after December 31, 1997 (Act Sec. 6024 of the IRS Restructuring and Reform Act of 1998; Act Sec. 964 of the Taxpayer Relief Act of 1997 (P.L. 105-34)). The provision making applicable the corporate estimated tax payment rules is effective for tax years beginning after the date of enactment (Act Sec. 6009(b)(2) of the IRS Restructuring and Reform Act of 1998).

Act Sec. 6009(b), amending Code Sec. 7704(g)(3)(C). Law at ¶ 6840. Committee Report at ¶ 11,100.

Basis of Distributed Properties

¶ 681

Background ⎯⎯⎯⎯⎯⎯⎯⎯⎯⎯⎯⎯⎯⎯⎯⎯⎯⎯⎯⎯⎯⎯⎯⎯⎯⎯⎯⎯⎯⎯⎯

When multiple properties are distributed by a partnership to a partner in a liquidating distribution, or when there is a limitation on the carryover basis from the partnership to the partner in a non-liquidating distribution, a portion of the partner's basis in the partner's partnership interest must be allocated to each of the distributed assets that the partner receives. Code Sec. 732, as amended by the Taxpayer Relief Act of 1997 (P.L. 105-34), provides the requisite mechanism for allocating this basis.

Prior to the 1997 Act, certain partners possessed a·basis-shifting opportunity that could be used to artificially increase the partner's bases in some of the distributed assets, giving rise to inflated depreciation deductions and to larger losses. Accordingly, the 1997 Act amended Code Sec.· 732(c) to eliminate basis allocations based upon the partnership's proportionate bases in the distributed assets. Instead, the amended statute adopted a "fair market value" standard. Under this new standard, the *unrealized* appreciation or depreciation of the partnership's distributed assets is taken into account when a partner determines the partner's substituted basis in the distributed partnership property.

Under Code Sec. 732(c), as amended by P.L. 105-34, a distributee partner's substituted basis is first allocated to any unrealized receivables and inventory items in an amount equal to the partnership's adjusted bases in these properties (Code Sec. 732(c)(1)(A)). To the extent that any basis attributable to the partner's partnership interest is not fully allocated to any distributed unrealized receivables and inventory under the above rules, basis is then allocated to any other distributed properties. The remaining basis is first allocated to the extent of each distributed property's adjusted basis to the partnership. Any remaining basis adjustment, if an increase, is allocated among those properties with unrealized appreciation in proportion to their respective amounts of unrealized appreciation (to the extent of each property's appreciation), and then in proportion to their respective fair market values. If the remaining basis adjustment is a decrease, the decrease is allocated among those properties with unrealized depreciation in proportion to their respective amounts of unrealized depreciation (to the extent of each property's depreciation), and then in proportion to their respective adjusted bases (taking into account the adjustments already made).

Background

For purposes of these basis allocation rules, the term "unrealized receivables" is defined by reference to Code Sec. 751(c) (Code Sec. 732(c)(1)(A)(i)). Code Sec. 751(c) provides that unrealized receivables include certain accrued but unreported income attributable to goods and services delivered or rendered, or to be delivered or rendered. In addition, the last two sentences of Code Sec. 751(c) provide that, for purposes of Code Sec. 731 (extent of recognition of gain or loss on distribution), Code Sec. 741 (recognition and character of gain or loss on sale or exchange) and Code Sec. 751 (tax treatment of unrealized receivables and inventory items), unrealized receivables also include property the sale of which will generate ordinary income (for example, depreciation recapture under Code Sec. 1245 or Code Sec. 1250). However, the amount of the unrealized receivables is limited to the amount that would be treated as ordinary income upon the sale of that property at fair market value.

For tax practitioners attempting to apply the new Code Sec. 732(c) allocation rules, the applicability of these last two definitional sentences of Code Sec. 751(c), relating to those items of property that give rise to ordinary income, and their computational impact, was unclear.

Technical Corrections Impact

Basis allocations and "unrealized receivables".—A statutory amendment now clarifies that, for purposes of the allocation rules of Code Sec. 732(c), "unrealized receivables" possesses the meaning given by Code Sec. 751(c), *including* the last two sentences of Code Sec. 751(c), which relate to those items of property that give rise to ordinary income. Thus, when applying the new allocation rules, the more expansive definition of unrealized receivables applies so that property generating ordinary income is taken into account (Code Sec. 751(c), as amended by the IRS Restructuring and Reform Act of 1998). Accordingly, in applying the Code Sec. 732(c) allocation rules to property listed in the last two sentences of Code Sec. 751(c), such as property giving rise to potential depreciation recapture, the amount of unrealized appreciation in any such property does not include any amount that would be treated as ordinary income if the property were sold at fair market value. Rather, this amount must be treated as a *separate asset* for purposes of the basis allocation rules.

Example. The Wadsworth Partnership has three partners: Sabina, Sean and Brian. The partnership has six assets. Three of these are capital assets, each with an adjusted basis equal to its fair market value, which is $20,000. The remaining three assets are depreciable equipment, each with an adjusted basis of $5,000 and a fair market value of $30,000. Each of the three pieces of equipment would have $25,000 of depreciation recapture if sold by the partnership for its $30,000 value. Sabina has a basis in her partnership interest of $60,000. If one of the capital assets and one of the pieces of equipment are distributed to Sabina in liquidation of her partnership interest, Sabina would be treated as receiving not two but rather *three* assets: (1) depreciation recapture (an unrealized receivable) with a basis to the partnership of zero and a value of $25,000; (2) a piece of equipment with a basis to the partnership of $5,000 and a value of $5,000 (its $30,000 value having been reduced by the $25,000 of depreciation recapture); and (3) a capital asset with a basis to the partnership of $20,000 and a value of $20,000.

Under the Code Sec. 732 basis allocation rules, as clarified by the technical correction, Sabina's $60,000 basis in her partnership interest is allocated among the three assets as follows. First, basis is allocated to the depreciation recapture, an unrealized receivable, in an amount equal to the partnership's adjusted basis in it, which is zero (Code Sec. 732(c)(1)(A)(i)). Then, basis is allocated to the extent of each of the other distributed properties' adjusted bases to the partnership, that is, $5,000 to the equipment (not including the depreciation recapture), and $20,000 to the capital asset. Sabina's remaining $35,000 of basis is then allocated among those properties, if any, with unrealized appreciation in proportion to their respective amounts of unrealized appreciation (to the extent of each property's appreciation). In this example, neither of the distributed properties to which basis may be allocated has any unrealized appreciation. Accordingly, basis is allocated in proportion to the properties' respective fair market values (which are $5,000 for the equipment and $20,000 for the capital asset). Thus, of the remaining $35,000, $7,000 (that is, one-fifth ($5,000 ÷ $25,000) of $35,000) is allocated to the equipment, making its total basis in Sabina's hands $12,000; the remaining $28,000 is allocated to the capital asset, making its total basis in Sabina's hands $48,000.

PRACTICAL ANALYSIS. Chuck Levun, of Levun, Goodman & Cohen, Northbrook, Ill., comments that the amendment to Code Sec. 751(c) is intended to clarify that depreciation recapture is treated as a separate zero basis unrealized receivable for purposes of allocating a partner's outside basis to the partnership assets distributed to him under the rules of Code Sec. 732(c). This rule has the effect of preserving the ordinary income element in recapture-type assets (e.g., equipment) at the expense of having an uneconomic basis allocation to the other assets distributed to the distributee partner.

★ *Effective date.* The provision applies to distributions after August 5, 1997 (Act Sec. 6024 of the IRS Restructuring and Reform Act of 1998; Act Sec. 1061(b) of the Taxpayer Relief Act of 1997 (P.L. 105-34)).

Act Sec. 6010(m), amending Code Sec. 751(c). Law at ¶ 5500. Committee Report at ¶ 11,200.

Magnetic Media Returns for Partnerships

¶ 682

Background ———————————————————————————

Under a generally uniform "magnetic media" filing requirement, any person who files more than 250 information returns in a calendar year must use magnetic media (i.e., magnetic tape, diskette, cassette, mini-disk, and other authorized formats (see Reg. § 301.6011-2(a)(1)). The Taxpayer Relief Act of 1997 (P.L. 105-34) amended this general rule to provide that those partnerships with more than 100 partners must also file their information returns using magnetic media (Code Sec. 6011(e)(2)).

For partnership tax years beginning after December 31, 1997, a partnership with more than 100 partners must provide the partnership's tax return (Form 1065), as well as copies of the schedule sent to each partner (Schedule K-1), to the IRS on magnetic media. Congress instituted this change to the magnetic media filing requirements to conform the reporting provisions for such large partnerships to the generally applicable information-reporting rules. Congress also wished to facilitate the integration of such partnership information into the already existing data systems. Partnerships with 100 or fewer partners have the option, but not the obligation, to utilize magnetic media.

Prior to amendment by the IRS Restructuring and Reform Act of 1998, Code Sec. 6724(c) provided a broader exception to the statutory penalty imposed in the

Background

case of certain failures to meet the magnetic media filing requirements. Under the penalty imposed by Code Sec. 6721, the filing of a paper form when magnetic media was required resulted in a $50 penalty for each violative form filed on paper, up to a maximum annual penalty of $250,000 for one filer. However, pursuant to Code Sec. 6724(c), the Code Sec. 6721(a)(1) penalty for the failure to file information returns on magnetic media was imposed only on the number of information returns that exceeded 250 in a calendar year. No penalty was applicable to the first 250 information returns that were not filed using magnetic media. Former Code Sec. 6724(c), however, did not take into account the aforementioned amendment of Code Sec. 6011(e)(2) requiring magnetic media filing by partnerships with more than 100 partners. Without a change to Code Sec. 6724(c), partnerships with more than 100 partners which were required to file their information returns using magnetic media were not subject to any non-filing penalty so long as the number of their information returns in any given year did not exceed 250.

Technical Corrections Impact

Magnetic media filing requirement and applicable penalty conformed.—The IRS Restructuring and Reform Act of 1998 clarifies that the penalty under Code Sec. 6724(c) for the failure to comply with the requirement of filing returns on magnetic media applies not only, in the usual case, to each failure to so file an information return in excess of 250, but also, in the case of a partnership with more than 100 partners, to each failure to so file an information return in excess of 100 (Code Sec. 6724(c), as amended by the IRS Restructuring and Reform Act of 1998).

Comment. The new amendment basically conforms the Code Sec. 6724(c) penalty with the filing requirement mandated by Code Sec. 6011(e)(2), as amended by the Taxpayer Relief Act of 1997 (P.L. 105-34).

★ *Effective date.* This provision is effective for partnership tax years beginning after December 31, 1997.

Act Sec. 6012(d), amending Code Sec. 6724(c). Law at ¶ 6520. Committee Report at ¶ 11,260.

Information Reporting for Foreign Partnerships

¶ 683

Background

The Taxpayer Relief Act of 1997 (P.L. 105-34) extended annual information reporting requirements applicable to U.S. persons that control foreign corporations to U.S. partners that control foreign partnerships (Code Sec. 6038(a)(1), as amended by the Taxpayer Relief Act of 1997 (P.L. 105-34)). The information must be furnished at the time and in the manner prescribed in *regulations* (Code Sec. 6038(a)(2)). No information is required with respect to a business entity's annual accounting period unless the information is required under *regulations* in effect on the first day of the annual accounting period (Code Sec. 6038(a)(3)).

Technical Corrections Impact

Guidance need not be issued in regulations.—The IRS Restructuring and Reform Act of 1998 clarifies that the IRS does not need to issue the information-reporting guidance in a regulation (Code Sec. 6038(a)(2) and (3), as amended by the 1998 Act). The definition of "annual accounting period" is clarified to apply to noncorporate business entities as well as corporate business entities.

Comment. IRS Form 5471 is used by U.S. persons who control foreign corporations to comply with the Code Sec. 6038 reporting requirements. Corporate information reporting requirements are prescribed in Reg. § 1.6038-2.

★ *Effective date.* The provision is effective for annual accounting periods beginning after August 5, 1997 (Act Sec. 6024 of the IRS Restructuring and Reform Act of 1998; Act Sec. 1142(f) of the IRS Taxpayer Relief Act of 1997 (P.L. 105-34)).

Act Sec. 6011(f)(1), amending Code Sec. 6038(a)(2); Act Sec. 6011(f)(2), amending Code Sec. 6038(a)(3); Act Sec. 6011(f)(3), amending Code Sec. 6038(e)(4). Law at ¶ 6050. Committee Report at ¶ 11,245.

TAX-EXEMPT ORGANIZATIONS

Subsidiaries of Tax-Exempt Organizations

¶ 686

Background————————————————————————

The Taxpayer Relief Act of 1997 (P.L. 105-34) modified the control requirement for purposes of determining whether interest, rents, royalties and annuities constitute unrelated business income (UBI) of a tax-exempt organization. Prior to the amendment, income was UBI if it was derived from a taxable or tax-exempt subsidiary that was 80-percent controlled by the parent tax-exempt organization. Indirect ownership rules did not apply, and, thus, income from a second-tier subsidiary did not constitute UBI to the tax-exempt parent.

Under the modified requirements, control was defined as ownership by vote or value of more than 50 percent of the corporate stock (or 50 percent of the profits, capital or beneficial interests, in the case of a partnership or other entity). Additionally, the constructive ownership rules under Code Sec. 318 were made applicable in determining control. Payments made by a controlled entity and *received* by a tax-exempt organization are subject to unrelated business income tax (UBIT) to the extent that the payments reduce the net unrelated income (or increase any net unrelated loss).

Technical Corrections Impact

UBI clarifications.—Three clarifications are made to the rules under Code Sec. 512(b)(13) for determining whether interest, rents, royalties and annuities constitute UBI of a tax-exempt organization. Under the new rules, Code Sec. 512(b)(13) applies to payments made by a controlled entity and *accrued* by a tax-exempt organization. Thus, payments made by a controlled entity and *received* or *accrued* by a tax-exempt organization are subject to unrelated business income tax (UBIT) to the extent that the payments reduce the net unrelated income (or increase any net unrelated loss) (Code Sec. 512(b)(13)(A), as amended by the IRS Restructuring and Reform Act of 1998).

Additionally, a cross-reference to a nonexistent Code section is eliminated in the definition of net unrelated income (Code Sec. 512(b)(13)(B)(i)(I), as amended by the 1998 Act).

Finally, the binding contract exception to the August 5, 1997 effective date is corrected so that the binding contract exception applies to amounts received or accrued rather than to payments made, as originally provided for in the 1997 Act. Accordingly, the binding contract exception applies to amounts received or accrued during the first two tax years beginning on or after August 5, 1997, if the amounts are received or accrued pursuant to a binding written contract in effect on June 8, 1997. The contract must be in effect at all times after June 8, 1997 and before the amounts are received or accrued. Amounts that would be received or accrued on or after the two-year period, but that are accelerated by the exercise of an option to accelerate payment, are not subject to the binding contract exception (Act Sec. 1041(b)(2) of the Taxpayer Relief Act of 1997 (P.L. 105-34), as amended by the 1998 Act).

★ *Effective date.* The provisions are generally effective for tax years beginning after August 5, 1997 (Act Sec. 6024 of the IRS Restructuring and Reform Act of 1998; Act Sec. 1041(b) of the Taxpayer Relief Act of 1997 (P.L. 105-34)).

Act Sec. 6010(j)(1), amending Code Sec. 512(b)(13)(A); Act Sec. 6010(j)(2), amending Code Sec. 512(b)(13)(B)(i)(I); and Act Sec. 6010((j)(3), amending Act Sec. 1041(b)(2) of the Taxpayer Relief Act of 1997 (P.L. 105-34). Law at ¶ 5400 and ¶ 8255. Committee Report at ¶ 11,190.

Apostolic Organization Disclosure Requirements

¶ 691

Background _____

Tax-exempt organizations, including a religious or apostolic organization exempt from tax under Code Sec. 501(d), are subject to public disclosure requirements with respect to their annual returns under Code Sec. 6104(b) and Code Sec. 6104(e). Under Code Sec. 6104(e)(1), a tax-exempt organization, other than a private foundation, must allow inspection at the organization's principal office of its three most recent annual information returns. The Taxpayer Bill of Rights 2 (P.L. 104-168) added to the disclosure requirements by providing that, upon request, copies of annual returns must be made available by these tax-exempt organizations. Information concerning contributors to the organizations, however, is not required to be disclosed.

An exempt religious or apostolic organization is an organization that engages in communal activities, such as farming, for the benefit of its members. The exemption under Code Sec. 501(d) is designed to provide limited tax relief by eliminating tax on the organization and shifting the tax to the organization's members. Accordingly, a religious or apostolic organization exempt from income tax under Code Sec. 501(d) must file Form 1065, U.S. Partnership Return of Income, to report its taxable income. The organization's taxable income is then reported as dividend income on Form 1065, Schedule K. Each member's pro rata share of the dividend income is reported on Schedule K-1. The Schedule K-1 must identify each member of the association.

Technical Corrections Impact

Disclosure protection for member information.—The protection from the public disclosure requirements of Code Sec. 6104(b) and Code Sec. 6104(e) that applies to contributors to tax-exempt organizations is extended to members of exempt religious or apostolic organizations described in Code Sec. 501(d). A religious or apostolic organization exempt from tax under Code Sec. 501(d) is not required to make available for public inspection copies of Schedules K-1 that show the pro rata share of the organization's taxable income that is allocated to its members as a dividend (Code Sec. 6104(b), as amended by the IRS Restructuring and Reform Act of 1998, and Code Sec. 6104(e)(1)(C), as amended by the 1998 Act). Similarly, a religious or apostolic organization is not required to provide copies of the Schedules K-1 upon request (Code Sec. 6104(e)(1)(C), as amended by the 1998 Act).

Comment. A religious or apostolic organization should consider the effective date of the provision protecting member information from disclosure when filing its

Form 1065. The provision is effective on the date of enactment of the IRS Restructuring and Reform Act of 1998; it does not relate back to the Taxpayer Bill of Rights 2 (P.L. 104-168).

★ *Effective date.* The provision is effective on the date of enactment of the IRS Restructuring and Reform Act of 1998 (Act Sec. 6019(d) of the 1998 Act).

Act Sec. 6019(a), amending Code Sec. 6104(b); Act Sec. 6019(b), amending Code Sec. 6104(e)(1)(C). Law at ¶ 6120. Committee Report at ¶ 11,355.

NATIONAL RAILROAD PASSENGER CORPORATION

Net Operating Losses

¶ 694

Background ————————————————————————————————

To help increase the intercity passenger rail service within the United States, the Taxpayer Relief Act of 1997 (P.L. 105-34) enacted certain elective procedures to help the National Railroad Passenger Corporation (Amtrak) with its capital needs. Amtrak is the principal passenger rail service provider in the United States. In general, the elective procedures allow Amtrak to consider the tax attributes of its predecessors in the use of its net operating losses, provided certain conditions are met. Use of the elective procedures by Amtrak is conditioned on (1) the payment of one percent of any resulting refund to non-Amtrak states to offset certain qualified expenses of the state, and (2) the use of the balance of any resulting refund for certain qualified expenses of Amtrak.

Qualified expenses in the case of a non-Amtrak state are expenses incurred to acquire capital improvements, upgrade maintenance facilities or maintain equipment in connection with an intercity passenger rail service or intercity bus service. Qualified expenses also include expenses incurred to purchase intercity rail service from Amtrak and the payment of interest and principal on obligations incurred for any qualified purpose. If a non-Amtrak state provides its own rail service on August 5, 1997, only the expenses incurred in connection with the intercity passenger rail services are qualified.

Technical Corrections Impact

Non-Amtrak states.—The definition of a non-Amtrak state has been changed to provide that a non-Amtrak state is a state that was not receiving intercity passenger rail service from Amtrak on August 5, 1997 (Act Sec. 977(e)(2) of the Taxpayer Relief Act of 1997 (P.L. 105-34), as amended by the IRS Restructuring and Reform Act of 1998). Under the prior definition, non-Amtrak state status applied to a state without Amtrak service on August 5, 1997, but terminated when the state received the required payment from Amtrak of a portion of any refund resulting from the special use of net operating losses. Terminating non-Amtrak state status upon receipt of the Amtrak payment was inconsistent with the requirement that a non-Amtrak state use the Amtrak payment to finance qualified expenses, including the purchase of intercity passenger rail services from Amtrak.

Comment. The elective procedures enacted by P.L. 105-34 became effective on August 5, 1997, the date of enactment. However, no refund could be received before the date of enactment of federal legislation authorizing Amtrak reform. The Amtrak Reform and Accountability Act of 1997 (P.L. 105-134) was signed into law on December 2, 1997. Act Sec. 301(b) of that legislation provides that it is the applicable reform legislation for purposes of the effective date of the elective procedures.

¶ 694

★ *Effective date.* The provision is generally effective on August 5, 1997 (Act Sec. 6024 of the IRS Restructuring and Reform Act of 1998; Act Sec. 977 of the Taxpayer Relief Act of 1997 (P.L. 105-34)).

ISTEA Impact

Non-Amtrak states, qualified expenses.—The Surface Transportation Revenue Act of 1998 (P.L. 105-178) (ISTEA) expands the definition of qualified expenses in the case of a non-Amtrak state. Qualified expenses also include expenses incurred for:

(1) capital expenditures related to state-owned rail services within the state;

(2) the funding of eligible projects under 49 U.S.C. §§ 5309-5311 (relating to mass transportation) or 23 U.S.C. §§ 103, 130, 133, 144, 149 or 152 (relating to federal-aid highways);

(3) the upgrade and maintenance of intercity primary and rural air service facilities;

(4) the purchase of intercity air service between primary and rural airports and regional hubs; and

(5) the provision of either passenger ferryboat service or harbor improvements within the state.

Qualified expenses also include interest and principal payments on obligations incurred for these additional qualified purposes.

★ *Effective date.* The provision is generally effective on August 5, 1997 (Act Sec. 9007(b) of the Surface Transportation Revenue Act of 1998 (P.L. 105-178); Act Sec. 977 of the Taxpayer Relief Act of 1997 (P.L. 105-34)).

Act Sec. 6009(e) of the IRS Restructuring and Reform Act of 1998, amending Act Sec. 977(e)(2) of the Taxpayer Relief Act of 1997 (P.L. 105-34); Act Sec. 9007(a) of the Surface Transportation Revenue Act of 1998 (P.L. 105-178), amending Act Sec. 977(e)(1)(B) of the Taxpayer Relief Act of 1997 (P.L. 105-34); Act Sec. 9007(b) of the IRS Restructuring and Reform Act of 1998. Law at ¶ 8250 and ¶ 8392. Committee Report at ¶ 11,115 and ¶ 15,105.

CHARITABLE CONTRIBUTIONS

Donations of Computer Technology and Equipment

¶ 696

Background

The Taxpayer Relief Act of 1997 (P.L. 105-34) expanded the list of contributions that qualify for the "augmented charitable deduction" to include certain gifts to schools of computer technology and equipment. Qualification for the augmented charitable deduction permits the grantor a greater deduction in situations, such as the contribution of inventory or other ordinary income property, in which the deduction is normally limited to the basis of the donated property. These rules are only applicable to gifts by C corporations (Code Sec. 170(e)(6), as added by P.L. 105-34).

An eligible donee for these purposes is:

(1) an educational organization that normally maintains a regular faculty and curriculum and has a regularly enrolled body of pupils in attendance at the place where its educational activities are regularly conducted; and

(2) a Code Sec. 501(c)(3) entity that is organized primarily for purposes of supporting elementary and secondary education.

A private foundation may be treated as an eligible donee if, within 30 days after receipt of the contribution, the foundation contributes the property to an eligible donee and notifies the donor of the contribution. As the result of a drafting error, it is unclear whether an eligible donee includes educational organizations as well as tax-exempt charitable entities.

The donated property must substantially be used within the United States for educational purposes in any of grades K-12 and fit productively into the education plans of the school.

The legislative history of this provision states that the special tax treatment for contributions of computer and other equipment was to be effective for contributions made during a three-year period in tax years beginning after December 31, 1997, and before January 1, 2001 (Conference Committee Report to P.L. 105-34). However, as a result of a drafting error, the statutory provision does not apply to contributions made during taxable years beginning after December 31, 1999 (Senate Committee Report to the IRS Restructuring and Reform Act of 1998).

Technical Corrections Impact

Rules on charitable contribution of computers by C corporations clarified.—The IRS Restructuring and Reform Act of 1998 corrects the termination date of the provision permitting an increased charitable contribution for gifts of computer technology and equipment by C corporations. The increased charitable contribution deduction applies to contributions made during tax years beginning after December 31, 1997, and before January 1, 2001 (Code Sec. 170(e)(6)(F), as amended by the 1998 Act).

Additionally, the 1998 Act clarifies that the requirements regarding use of the donated property apply regardless of whether the donee is an educational organization or a tax-exempt charitable entity (Code Sec. 170(e)(6)(B)(ii)-(vii), as amended by the 1998 Act). Similarly, the rule regarding subsequent contributions by private foundations is clarified to permit contributions to either educational organizations or tax-exempt charitable entities described in Code Sec. 170(e)(6)(B)(i) (Code Sec. 170(e)(6)(C)(ii)(I), as amended by the 1998 Act).

★ *Effective date.* This provision is effective for tax years beginning after December 31, 1997 (Act Sec. 6024 of the IRS Restructuring and Reform Act of 1998; Act Sec. 224(b) of the Taxpayer Relief Act of 1997 (P.L. 105-34)).

Act Sec. 6004(e)(1), amending Code Sec. 170(e)(6)(B)(vi) and (vii); Act Sec. 6004(e)(2), amending Code Sec. 170(e)(6)(B)(iv); Act Sec. 6004(e)(3), amending Code Sec. 170(e)(6)(C)(ii)(I); Act Sec. 6004(e)(4), amending Code Sec. 170(e)(6)(F). Law at ¶ 5220. Committee Report at ¶ 10,855.

Chapter 7
Excise Taxes

AVIATION FUEL

Aviation Excise Tax Refunds

¶701

Background

The Taxpayer Relief Act of 1997 (P.L. 105-34) extended the 15-cents-per-gallon rate portion of the aviation gasoline tax for 10 years, through September 30, 2007, and expanded deposits to the Airport and Airway Trust Fund to include revenues from the 4.3-cents-per-gallon rate originally imposed in 1993 for deficit reduction on such gasoline. The combined 19.4-cents-per-gallon tax (which includes the 0.1-cents-per-gallon Leaking Underground Storage Tank (LUST) Trust Fund tax) does not apply to fuel used in flight segments outside the United States (Code Sec. 4221) or to flight segments from the United States to foreign countries (Code Sec. 4261(b), as amended by P.L. 105-34).

Technical Corrections Impact

Aviation excise tax refunds clarified.—The IRS Restructuring and Reform Act of 1998 clarifies that the gasoline tax refund provisions apply to aviation gasoline used in flight segments outside the United States and to flight segments from the United States to foreign countries (Code Sec. 6421(c), as amended by the 1998 Act).

★ *Effective date.* The provision is effective on October 1, 1997 (Act Sec. 6024 of the IRS Restructuring and Reform Act of 1998; Act Sec. 1031(e)(1) of the Taxpayer Relief Act of 1997 (P.L. 105-34)).

Act Sec. 6010(g)(3)(A)-(B), amending Code Sec. 6421(c). Law at ¶6380. Committee Report at ¶11,175.

Aviation Fuel Taxes Previously Refunded or Credited

¶716

Background

If a producer uses aviation fuel before tax has been paid on it, that use is considered a taxable sale, unless the producer employed the fuel in a nontaxable use (Code Sec. 4091(a)(2)). Aviation fuel is exempt from tax if sold for any uses that are exempt under Code Sec. 4041, except by reason of prior taxation (Code Sec. 4092(a) and Code Sec. 6427(l)(2)(B)). These include uses in farming, as supplies for vessels or aircraft, exclusively by a state or its political subdivision, for export, and exclusively by a nonprofit school and qualifying aircraft museums. If tax is paid for fuel and the fuel is not used for taxable purposes, a refund or credit may be obtained (Code Sec. 6427(a)).

Technical Corrections Impact

Aviation fuel taxes may apply to tax previously refunded or credited.— The 1998 Act clarifies that the aviation fuel excise tax is imposed upon the taxable use of aviation fuel for which the aviation tax has been previously credited or refunded (Code Sec. 4091(a)(2), as amended by the IRS Restructuring and Reform Act of 1998).

★ *Effective date.* The provision applies to fuel acquired by the producer after September 30, 1997 (Act Sec. 6024 of the IRS Restructuring and Reform Act of 1998; Act Sec. 1436(c) of the Taxpayer Relief Act of 1997 (P.L. 105-34)).

Act Sec. 6014(d), amending Code Sec. 4091(a)(2). Law at ¶5870.

Credit for Exempt Use

¶721

Background

A refund or credit can be claimed for gasoline taxes (Code Sec. 4081) or for any diesel fuel, kerosene, special motor fuels, or noncommercial aviation fuel taxes (Code Sec. 4041) paid by the ultimate purchaser on fuel used in a helicopter for certain exempt purposes described in Code Sec. 4041(l) (Code Sec. 6427(d)). Similarly, under Code Sec. 4041(l), the purchase of such fuels is nontaxable if it was to be used for one of those exempt purposes. For purposes of these rules, "certain exempt purposes" is a purpose meeting the requirements of Code Sec. 4261(f) (concerning specific mining and agricultural uses) or Code Sec. 4261(g) (concerning air ambulances providing certain emergency medical transportation) (Code Sec. 4041(l)).

The Taxpayer Relief Act of 1997 (P.L. 105-34) added the phrase "fixed-wing aircraft" to Code Sec. 4041(l), effective August 27, 1996, so that the purchase of fuel for certain exempt purposes for use in either a helicopter or a "fixed-wing aircraft" was not taxable. However, a corresponding change was not made to Code Sec. 6427(d). Therefore, although the initial sale of fuel for certain exempt uses by a fixed-wing aircraft was nontaxable, a refund or credit was not technically available if the tax had been paid.

Technical Corrections Impact

Fuels tax refund or credit extended to fixed-wing aircraft.—The technical correction adds the phrase "or a fixed-wing aircraft" after the word "helicopter" in Code Sec. 6427(d), so a refund or credit can be claimed for fuel taxes paid by the ultimate purchaser on fuel used in a helicopter or fixed-wing aircraft for certain exempt purposes. This exemption is limited to fixed-wing aircraft equipped for and exclusively dedicated to acute care emergency medical services as described in Code Sec. 4261(g).

Caution. The exempt use under Code Sec. 4261(f) for certain mining and agricultural uses is still restricted to helicopters.

Comment. Note this change is effective retroactive to August 27, 1996, as if included in the Small Business Job Protection Act of 1996 (P.L. 104-188). Thus, affected taxpayers may be able to file amended returns and claim refunds or credits for fuel taxes paid.

★ *Effective date.* The provision is effective August 27, 1996 (Act Sec. 6024 of the IRS Restructuring and Reform Act of 1998; Act Sec. 1601(j)(1) of the Taxpayer Relief Act of 1997 (P.L. 105-34); Act Sec. 1609(i) of the Small Business Job Protection Act of 1996 (P.L. 104-188)).

Act Sec. 6016(b), amending Code Sec. 6427(d). Law at ¶ 6390.

OTHER FUEL TAXES

Effective Date Delay for Terminals Offering Dyed Fuel

¶ 723

Background

The Taxpayer Relief Act of 1997 (P.L. 105-34) provided that registration as a terminal facility eligible to handle nontax-paid diesel fuel and kerosene is conditioned upon the facility offering its customers dyed fuel for nontaxable sales of diesel fuel and kerosene (Code Sec. 4101(e), as added by the 1997 Act). This provision was to take effect on July 1, 1998 (Act Sec. 1032(f) of the 1997 Act).

ISTEA Impact

Delay in effective date for approved diesel fuel and kerosene terminals.—The Surface Transportation Revenue Act of 1998 (ISTEA) (P.L. 105-178) delayed two years, from July 1, 1998, to July 1, 2000, the effective date of the requirement that terminals offer dyed diesel fuel and dyed kerosene for removal for nontaxable use (Act Sec. 1032(f)(2) of the Taxpayer Relief Act of 1997, as amended by ISTEA).

★ *Effective date.* No specific effective date was provided by the Act. The provision is, therefore, considered effective on June 9, 1998, the date of enactment of ISTEA.

Act Sec. 9008 of the Surface Transportation Revenue Act of 1998 (P.L. 105-178), amending Act Sec. 1032(f) of the Taxpayer Relief Act of 1997 (P.L. 105-34). Law at ¶ 8395. Committee Report at ¶ 15,115.

Dyed Fuel Requirement

¶ 724

Background

The Taxpayer Relief Act of 1997 (P.L. 105-34) provided that registration of fuel terminals that handle nontax-paid diesel fuel and kerosene is conditioned on the terminal operator offering both undyed fuel, which is taxable, and dyed fuel, which is nontaxable (Code Sec. 4101(e), as added by P.L. 105-34).

Technical Corrections Impact

Dyed fuel requirement clarified.—The IRS Restructuring and Reform Act of 1998 clarifies that terminals eligible to handle nontax-paid diesel fuel are required to offer dyed diesel fuel and terminals eligible to handle nontax-paid kerosene are required to offer such fuel in a dyed form (Code Sec. 4101(e)(1), as amended by the IRS Restructuring and Reform Act of 1998). Kerosene includes diesel fuel #1 and kerosene-type aviation fuel (Senate Committee Report to the 1998 Act).

Comment. Thus, a terminal is not required to offer kerosene for sale as a condition of receiving diesel fuel on a nontax-paid basis. Conversely, a terminal that sells only kerosene is not required to offer diesel fuel as a condition of receiving nontax-paid kerosene.

★ *Effective date.* This provision is effective on July 1, 2000 (Act Sec. 6024 of the IRS Restructuring and Reform Act of 1998; Act Sec. 1032(f)(2) of the Taxpayer Relief Act of 1997 (P.L. 105-34), as amended by Act Sec. 9008 of the Surface Transportation Revenue Act of 1998 (P.L. 105-178)).

Act Sec. 6010(h)(5), amending Code Sec. 4101(e)(1). Law at ¶ 5890. Committee Report at ¶ 11,180.

Kerosene Taxed as Diesel Fuel

¶ 725

Background

The Taxpayer Relief Act of 1997 (P.L. 105-34) extended the diesel fuel excise tax rules to kerosene. Thus, the diesel fuel tax rate of 24.3 cents per gallon of fuel used as a transportation motor fuel is applicable to kerosene.

Kerosene is taxed when removed from a registered terminal unless it is indelibly dyed and destined for a nontaxable use. Registration as a terminal facility eligible to handle nontax-paid diesel fuel and kerosene is conditional on the facility offering its customers dyeing for nontaxable sales of diesel fuel and kerosene.

Aviation-grade kerosene removed from the terminal by a registered producer of aviation fuel is not subject to the dyeing requirement if the person receiving the kerosene is registered under Code Sec. 4101 with respect to the tax imposed by Code Sec. 4091 (Code Sec. 4082(d)(1), as added by P.L. 105-34).

Technical Corrections Impact

Exceptions to dyeing requirement for kerosene amended.—Under the IRS Restructuring and Reform Act of 1998, the dyeing requirement does not apply to aviation-grade kerosene (as determined by IRS regulations) which the IRS determines is destined for use as a fuel in an aircraft. (Code Sec. 4082(d)(1), as amended by the 1998 Act).

★ *Effective date.* This provision is effective on July 1, 1998 (Act Sec. 6024 of the IRS Restructuring and Reform Act of 1998; Act Sec. 1032(f)(1) of the Taxpayer Relief Act of 1997 (P.L. 105-34), as amended by Act Sec. 9008 of the Surface Transportation Revenue Act of 1998 (P.L. 105-178)).

Act Sec. 6010(h)(3), amending Code Sec. 4082(d)(1). Law at ¶ 5860. Committee Report at ¶ 11,178.

Wholesale Distributors of Kerosene

¶ 726

Background

The diesel fuel excise tax rules that were extended to kerosene by the Taxpayer Relief Act of 1997 (P.L. 105-34) specifically address the sale of kerosene to wholesale distributors. While kerosene is ordinarily subject to tax when removed from a registered terminal, the tax does not apply to kerosene which is indelibly dyed in accordance with regulations which the Secretary prescribes (Code Sec. 4082(a)(2), as amended by P.L. 105-34). However, to the extent provided in regulations, this exemption from the diesel fuel excise tax does not apply to a removal, entry, or sale of kerosene to certain wholesale distributors of kerosene. These wholesale distributors must satisfy registration requirements and sell kerosene exclusively to ultimate vendors of kerosene (Code Sec. 4082(d)(3), as added by P.L. 105-34).

Technical Corrections Impact

Exceptions to dyeing requirement for kerosene amended.—Under the IRS Restructuring and Reform Act of 1998, the exemption from the kerosene tax does not apply to kerosene *received* by a wholesale distributor of kerosene who satisfies registration requirements and sells kerosene exclusively to retailers eligible for refunds with respect to undyed kerosene sold by them for a nontaxable use (Code Sec. 4082(d)(3), as amended by the 1998 Act).

★ *Effective date.* This provision is effective on July 1, 1998 (Act Sec. 6024 of the IRS Restructuring and Reform Act of 1998; Act Sec. 1032(f)(1) of the Taxpayer Relief Act of 1997 (P.L. 105-34), as amended by Act Sec. 9008 of the Surface Transportation Revenue Act of 1998 (P.L. 105-178)).

Act Sec. 6010(h)(4), amending Code Sec. 4082(d)(3). Law at ¶ 5860. Committee Report at ¶ 11,178.

Reduction of Rail Fuel Tax

¶ 727

Background

Fuel used in trains, whether diesel or gasoline, is subject to a 5.65 cents per gallon excise tax. Of the total 5.65 cents per gallon tax, 5.55 cents per gallon is a general fund tax, with 4.3 cents per gallon of that amount being permanently imposed, and 1.25 cents per gallon imposed through September 30, 1999. The remaining 0.1 cents per gallon is dedicated to the Leaking Underground Storage Tank Trust Fund (Code Sec. 4081(a)(2)(B)) through March 31, 2005 (Code Sec. 4041(a)(1)(C)).

ISTEA Impact

Rail fuel tax reduced.—The Surface Transportation Revenue Act of 1998 (P.L. 105-178) reduces the 5.65 cents per gallon tax imposed on diesel and gasoline fuel used in trains by 1.25 cents per gallon as of November 1, 1998. Noting that 5.55 cents per gallon of the tax is applied to the general fund, the Senate Committee Report to the 1998 Act states that it is inappropriate for railroads to pay a fuel tax for deficit reduction when most other transportation modes pay taxes only to support trust fund programs that benefit those industries (Code Sec. 4041(a)(1)(C)(ii), as amended by P.L. 105-178).

★ *Effective date.* No specific effective date is provided by the Surface Transportation Act of 1998. The provision is, therefore, considered effective on June 9, 1998, the date of enactment.

Act Sec. 9006(a)(1), amending Code Sec. 4041(a)(1)(C)(ii)(II); Act Sec. 9006(a)(2), amending Code Sec. 4041(a)(1)(C)(ii)(III); Act Sec. 9006(b)(1)(A), amending Code Sec. 6421(f)(3)(B)(ii); Act Sec. 9006(b)(1)(B), amending Code Sec. 6421(f)(3)(B)(iii); Act Sec. 9006(b)(2)(A), amending Code Sec. 6427(l)(3)(B)(ii); Act Sec. 9006(b)(2)(B), amending Code Sec. 6427(l)(3)(B)(iii). Law at ¶5840. Committee Report at ¶15,095. Act section references are to the Surface Transportation Revenue Act of 1998 (P.L. 105-178).

REFUND PROCEDURES

Simplification of Fuel Tax Refunds

¶729

Background ————————————————————————

Generally, a purchaser or user who has paid the excise tax on diesel or special motor fuel (or kerosene on or after July 1, 1998) and has used the fuel for a nontaxable purpose or resold the fuel during the tax year is entitled to a refund payment rather than a tax credit only if the purchaser or user is a governmental entity or a tax-exempt organization (Code Sec. 6427(k)).

Prior to October 1, 1998, however, other eligible purchasers or users of diesel or special motor fuel may file a claim for a refund payment rather than obtaining a tax credit if they have paid at least $1,000 in diesel or special motor fuel excise taxes with respect to fuel used during any of the first three quarters of a tax year. The claim for a quarterly refund must be filed on or before the last day of the first quarter following the quarter for which the claim is filed. Other claims must be filed by the due date for filing a credit or refund of overpayment of income tax for the tax year (Code Sec. 6427(i)(2)(A)). Similar rules apply to refunds and credits of gasoline tax under Code Sec. 6421(d)(2). A special $750 threshold and rules apply to certain tax-exempt aviation fuel (Code Sec. 6427(i)(4)).

ISTEA Impact

Simplified fuel tax refund procedures.—The Surface Transportation Revenue Act of 1998 (ISTEA) (P.L. 105-178) combined the refund procedures for all taxable motor fuels, effective October 1, 1998. Once a taxpayer has paid $750 or more of motor fuel excise taxes for fuel used for a nontaxable purpose, a refund claim may be filed under the simplified procedures. Unlike prior law, tax on the following fuels may be aggregated to arrive at the $750 amount:

(1) special fuels such as benzol, benzene, napththa, liquefied petroleum gas, casing head, natural gas, compressed natural gas and noncommercial aviation fuel that are used for a purpose other than the one for which they were sold or that are resold;

(2) fuel other than gasoline used in intercity, local, or school buses;

(3) gasoline or other fuel used by aircraft museums or in certain helicopters;

(4) gasoline blendstocks or additives not used in producing gasoline;

(5) diesel fuel, kerosene, and aviation fuel used for a nontaxable purpose;

(6) gasohol used in noncommercial aviation; and

(7) gasoline used for certain nonhighway purposes, used by local transit systems, or sold for certain exempt purposes.

In addition, the $750 minimum amount is determined on a year-to-year basis, rather than on a quarterly basis. Under the new rules, taxpayers may request a fourth-quarter refund, rather than claiming the fourth-quarter amount as a tax credit. The claim must be filed on or before the last day of the first quarter following the quarter or period for which the claim is filed (Code Sec. 6421(d)(2) and Code Sec. 6427(i)(2)(A), as amended by ISTEA (P.L. 105-178).

★ *Effective date.* The new refund procedures are effective on October 1, 1998 (Act Sec. 9009(c) of the Surface Transportation Revenue Act of 1998 (P.L. 105-178)).

Act Sec. 9009(a), amending Code Sec. 6427(i)(2)(A); Act Sec. 9009(b)(1), striking Code Sec. 6427(i)(4) and redesignating Code Sec. 6427(i)(5) as Code Sec. 6427(i)(4); Act Sec. 9009(b)(2), amending Code Sec. 6427(k)(2); Act Sec. 9009(b)(3), amending Code Sec. 6421(d)(2). Law at ¶ 6380 and ¶ 6390. Committee Report at ¶ 15,125. Act section references are to the Surface Transportation Revenue Act of 1998 (P.L. 105-178).

Filing Claims for Refund of Fuel Tax

¶ 730

Background

Consumers that use previously taxed highway motor fuels for a nontaxable purpose may file claims for refunds with the IRS. The Surface Transportation Revenue Act of 1998 (P.L. 105-178) simplified the refund procedure for fuels used for a nontaxable purpose. Under the simplified procedures, claims may be filed once a $750 threshold is reached for gasoline, diesel fuel, and kerosene combined, and multiple calendar quarters may be aggregated in determining whether this threshold has been met. P.L. 105-178, however, neglected to modify the time period for filing a claim to allow for aggregation of multiple calendar quarters. No claim filed for a refund is allowed unless filed on or before the last day of the first quarter following the quarter for which the claim is filed.

Technical Corrections Impact

Clarification of claim filing period.—Under the IRS Restructuring and Reform Act of 1998, a refund claim for previously taxed highway motor fuels used for a nontaxable purpose must be filed during the first quarter following the last quarter included in the claim (Code Sec. 6427(i)(2)(B), as amended by the IRS Restructuring and Reform Act of 1998).

★ *Effective date.* This provision is effective on October 1, 1998 (Act Sec. 6017(b) of the IRS Restructuring and Reform Act of 1998; Act Sec. 9009(c) of the Surface Transportation Revenue Act of 1998 (P.L. 105-178)).

Act Sec. 6017(a), amending Code Sec. 6427(i)(2)(B); Act Sec. 6017(b). Law at ¶ 6390. Committee Report at ¶ 11,335.

ALCOHOL TAXES

Apple Cider

¶ 731

Background

Prior to enactment of the Taxpayer Relief Act of 1997 (P.L. 105-34), hard cider was taxed as a wine for excise tax purposes. The 1997 Act generally reduced

Background

the excise tax rate on hard cider to 22.6 cents per gallon for taxpayers producing more than 250,000 gallons per year (Code Sec. 5041(b)(6), as amended by P.L. 105-34). A five-cents-per-gallon credit is provided on the first 100,000 gallons of production of qualifying small producers of less than 250,000 gallons annually. The credit is phased out for production between the 100,000 to 250,000 gallon range. The reduced rates were provided due to the belief that cider is in more direct competition with beer than with wine.

Hard cider was defined by the 1997 Act as a wine fermented solely from apples or apple concentrate and water, containing no other fruit product and containing at least one-half of one percent and less than seven percent alcohol by volume (Code Sec. 5041(b)(6)). Once fermented, eligible hard cider may not be altered by the addition of other fruit juices, flavor, or other ingredients that alter the flavor that results from the fermentation process.

The 1997 Act intended that the reduced rates would only apply to hard cider which meets the preceding requirements and is also a *still* wine.

Technical Corrections Impact

Reduced excise tax on cider clarified.—The 1998 Act clarifies that the 22.6-cents-per-gallon tax rate applies only to apple cider that contains one-half to seven percent of alcohol, meets the additional requirements of Code Sec. 5041(b)(6) described above, and is also a *still* wine (Code Sec. 5041(b)(6), as amended by the IRS Restructuring and Reform Act of 1998).

Comment. The primary effect of this change appears to impose a requirement, applicable to still wines, that qualifying cider may not contain more than 0.392 grams of carbon dioxide per hundred milliliters (Code Sec. 5041(a)).

★ *Effective date.* This provision is effective on October 1, 1997 (Act Sec. 6024 of the IRS Restructuring and Reform Act of 1998; Act Sec. 908(c) of the Taxpayer Relief Act of 1997 (P.L. 105-34)).

Act Sec. 6009(a), amending Code Sec. 5041(b)(6). Law at ¶ 5960. Committee Report at ¶ 11,095.

Collection of Taxes on Wines

¶ 732

Background

All wines (including imitation, substandard, or artificial wine, and compounds sold as wine) having not more than 24 percent alcohol by volume, in bond in, produced in, or imported into the United States are taxed with reference to the time of removal for consumption or sale (Code Sec. 5041(a)). The tax rates for still wines, champagne and other sparkling wine, artificially carbonated wines, and hard cider derived primarily from apples or apple concentrate and water, range from $1.07 to $3.40 per gallon (Code Sec. 5041(b)). In the case of foreign wines, this tax is paid by the importer of the wine (Code Sec. 5043(a)(2)).

Technical Corrections Impact

Tax liability for foreign wine.—The IRS Restructuring and Reform Act of 1998 provides that the tax paid by an importer is on foreign wines that are not transferred to a bonded wine cellar free of tax under Code Sec. 5364 (Code Sec. 5043(a)(2), as amended by the 1998 Act). Code Sec. 5364 applies to wine imported in bulk.

★ *Effective date.* This provision is effective on April 1, 1998 (Act Sec. 6024 of the IRS Restructuring and Reform Act of 1998; Act Sec. 1422(c) of the Taxpayer Relief Act of 1997 (P.L. 105-34)).

Act Sec. 6014(b)(1), amending Code Sec. 5043(a)(2). Law at ¶ 5970. Committee Report at ¶ 11,285.

Refund of Tax on Wine

¶ 733

Background

The Taxpayer Relief Act of 1997 (P.L. 105-34) expanded the refund and credit provisions to include domestic wine returned to bond regardless of whether the wine was merchantable (Code Sec. 5044(a), as amended by the 1997 Act). The refund and credit provisions of Code Sec. 5044 only applied to wine produced in the United States.

Technical Corrections Impact

Time for filing refund claim.—The IRS Restructuring and Reform Act of 1998 strikes the requirement that refunds or credits of, or relief from liability for, the tax on wine applies only to wine produced in the United States and replaces it with the requirement that the wine be removed from a bonded wine cellar (Code Sec. 5044(a), as amended by the 1998 Act).

★ *Effective date.* This provision is effective on April 1, 1998 (Act Sec. 6024 of the IRS Restructuring and Reform Act of 1998; Act Sec. 1416(c) of the Taxpayer Relief Act of 1997 (P.L. 105-34)).

Act Sec. 6014(b)(2), amending Code Sec. 5044(a). Law at ¶ 5980. Committee Report at ¶ 11,290.

Bulk Importation of Natural Wine

¶ 741

Background

Wine that is imported in bulk may be withdrawn from customs custody and transferred to a bonded wine cellar without payment of tax on the wine. Wine is normally subject to an excise tax ranging from $1.07 per gallon to $3.40 per gallon, depending on its alcohol content. The winery that receives the wine is liable for the tax imposed on the wine withdrawn from customs custody, and the wine importer is relieved of the tax liability (Code Sec. 5364, as added by the Taxpayer Relief Act of 1997 (P.L. 105-34)). U.S. law follows the laws of the country of origin in classifying imported wine.

Technical Corrections Impact

Bulk importation of wine provisions apply to "natural wine."—The IRS Restructuring and Reform Act of 1998 clarifies that the provisions permitting wine that is imported in bulk to be withdrawn from customs custody and transferred to a bonded wine cellar without payment of tax applies only to alcohol that would qualify as a natural wine if produced in the United States (Code Sec. 5364, as amended by the 1998 Act). U.S. law defines wine generally as alcohol that is derived from fruit or fruit residues ("natural wine"). Natural wine may not be fortified with grain or other nonfruit-derived alcohol if produced in the United States. Certain other countries allow wine that is marketed as a natural wine to be fortified with alcohol from other sources (Senate Committee Report to the IRS Restructuring and Reform Act of 1998).

★ *Effective date.* This provision takes effect on April 1, 1998 (Act Sec. 6024 of the IRS Restructuring and Reform Act of 1998; Act Sec. 1422(c) of the Taxpayer Relief Act of 1997 (P.L. 105-34)).

Act Sec. 6014(b)(3), amending Code Sec. 5364. Law at ¶ 6010. Committee Report at ¶ 11,295.

Determination, Collection and Refund of Tax on Beer

¶ 743

Background _____

The tax imposed on beer produced in the United States is determined at the time it is removed for consumption or sale and paid for by the brewer (Code Sec. 5054(a)(1)). A brewer may obtain a refund or credit for beer previously taxed if the beer is returned to the brewery, lost, stolen, destroyed under the supervision required by regulations, or destroyed by fire, casualty, or act of God before the transfer of title to the beer occurred (Code Sec. 5056(a) and (b)).

Beer tax.—The IRS Restructuring and Reform Act of 1998 expands the categories of beer that fall under Code Sec. 5054. Thus, in addition to "beer produced in the United States," beer imported into the United States and transferred to a brewery free of tax under Code Sec. 5418 will be taxed at the time it is removed for consumption or sale (Code Sec. 5054(a)(1) and (2), as amended by the 1998 Act). The tax is paid by the brewer.

In addition, the Code provisions relating to the refund or credit of, or relief from liability for, the beer tax have been modified to include beer imported into the United States and transferred to a brewery tax-free (Code Sec. 5056, as amended by the 1998 Act).

★ *Effective date.* This provision is effective on April 1, 1998 (Act Sec. 6024 of the IRS Restructuring and Reform Act of 1998; Act Sec. 1421(c) of the Taxpayer Relief Act of 1997 (P.L. 105-34)).

Act Sec. 6014(a)(1), amending Code Sec. 5054(a)(1); Act Sec. 6014(a)(2), amending Code Sec. 5054(a)(2); Act Sec. 6014(a)(3), amending Code Sec. 5056. Law at ¶ 5990 and ¶ 6000. Committee Report at ¶ 11,285 and ¶ 11,290.

COMMUNICATIONS TAX

Prepaid Telephone Cards

¶ 746

Background _____

A three-percent excise tax is currently imposed on amounts paid for local and long-distance telephone service and teletypewriter exchange service (Code Sec. 4251(b)). The tax is collected by the provider of the service from the consumer (Code Sec. 4251(a)). The Taxpayer Relief Act of 1997 (P.L. 105-34) clarified that this excise tax applies to amounts paid by third parties to communication service providers for pre-paid telephone cards. The tax applies without regard to whether telephone service ultimately is provided pursuant to the transferred rights.

As a result, prepaid telephone cards offered by service stations, convenience stores, and other companies not in the business of telecommunications are subject to the tax. A prepaid telephone card is any card or other arrangement that entitles

Background

a holder to obtain communications services and pay for the services in advance (Code Sec. 4251(d), as added by P.L. 105-34).

Technical Corrections Impact

Treatment of prepaid telephone cards clarified.—The 1998 Act clarifies that payment to a telecommunications carrier from a third party such as a joint venture credit card company is treated as payment made by the holder of the credit card to obtain communication services. The tax is treated as paid in a manner similar to that applied to prepaid telephone cards (Code Sec. 4251(d)(3), as amended by the IRS Restructuring and Reform Act of 1998). The tax applies to payments if the rights to telephone service for which payments are made can be used in whole or in part for telephone service that, if purchased directly, would be subject to the three-percent excise tax on telephone service (Conference Committee to the IRS Restructuring and Reform Act of 1998).

★ *Effective date.* This provision applies to amounts paid in calendar months beginning more than 60 days after August 5, 1997 (Act Sec. 6024 of the IRS Restructuring and Reform Act of 1998; Act Sec. 1034(b) of the Taxpayer Relief Act of 1997 (P.L. 105-34)).

Act Sec. 6010(i), amending Code Sec. 4251(d)(3). Law at ¶ 5920. Committee Report at ¶ 11,185.

HIGHWAY AND OTHER TRUST FUND TAXES

Extension of Taxes and Trust Fund

¶ 750

Background

Highway Trust Fund taxes are imposed on gasoline, diesel fuel, kerosene, special motor fuels, heavy truck and tire sales, and on the use of heavy trucks. In general, these taxes are scheduled to expire after September 30, 1999. Receipts from the highway excise taxes are dedicated to the Highway Trust Fund for taxes imposed through September 30, 1999 and received in the Treasury before July 1, 2000. Expenditures from the Highway Trust Fund are authorized through September 30, 1998 for purposes provided in authorizing legislation.

The Highway Trust Fund is divided into two Accounts: a Highway Account and a Mass Transit Account. The Highway Account receives revenues from all non-fuel highway-related excise taxes plus revenues from all but 2.85 cents per gallon of the highway motor fuels excise taxes. The Mass Transit Account receives the 2.85 cents per gallon not transferred to the Highway Account.

ISTEA Impact

Extension of highway excise taxes and Highway Trust Fund provisions.—The Surface Transportation Revenue Act of 1998 (ISTEA) (P.L. 105-178) generally provides for a six-year extension of the Highway Trust Fund excise taxes scheduled to expire in 1999. Conforming amendments are made to floor stock taxes and tax exemptions. The Highway Trust Fund is also extended (Act Sec. 9002 of ISTEA (P.L. 105-178)).

Tax on heavy trucks and trailers. The scheduled October 1, 1999, termination date of the 12-percent excise tax on heavy trucks and trailers is delayed until October 1, 2005 (Code Sec. 4051(c), as amended by ISTEA (P.L. 105-178)).

The provision denying taxpayers the privilege of paying the highway motor vehicle tax on trucks and trailers for taxes incurred during July, August, and September of 1999 is made applicable to taxes incurred in July, August, and September of 2005 (Code Sec. 6156(e)(2), as amended by ISTEA (P.L. 105-178)).

Highway motor vehicle use tax. The expiration of the excise tax on highway motor vehicles with a taxable gross weight of at least 55,000 pounds is delayed from uses on or after October 1, 1999, to uses on or after October 1, 2005 (Code Sec. 4481(e) and Code Sec. 4482(c)(4) and (d), as amended by ISTEA (P.L. 105-178)).

Tax on heavy tires. The scheduled October 1, 1999, termination date of the excise tax on tires is delayed until October 1, 2005 (Code Sec. 4071(d), as amended by ISTEA (P.L. 105-178)).

Special motor fuels. The reduction of the tax rates applicable to special motor fuels used in motor vehicles and motorboats is delayed from sales and uses after September 30, 1999, to sales and uses after September 30, 2005 (Code Sec. 4041(a)(2)(B), as amended by ISTEA (P.L. 105-178)).

Diesel fuel used in certain buses. The reduction of the 7.3 cents per gallon tax on diesel fuel used in public and school buses to 4.3 cents per gallon is delayed to cover sales after September 30, 2005. Previously, the reduction related to sales after September 30, 1999 (Code Sec. 4041(a)(1)(C)(iii)(I), as amended by ISTEA (P.L. 105-178)).

Alcohol fuel. The reduction in the rate of tax imposed on partially exempt methanol fuel (9.15 cents per gallon to 2.15 cents per gallon) or ethanol (11.3 cents per gallon to 4.3 cents per gallon) sold or used after September 30, 1999, is delayed to sales and uses after September 30, 2005 (Code Sec. 4041(m)(1)(A), as amended by ISTEA (P.L. 105-178)).

Gasoline, diesel, and kerosene. Code Sec. 4081 imposes a tax on gasoline, diesel fuel, and kerosene removed from terminals and refineries, imported into the United States, or sold to certain unregistered persons. The scheduled reduction of the 18.3 cents per gallon tax on gasoline other than aviation fuel to 4.3 cents per gallon after September 30, 1999, is delayed until after September 30, 2005. The scheduled reduction of the 24.3 cents per gallon tax on diesel fuel or kerosene to 4.3 cents per gallon after September 30, 1999, is delayed until after September 30, 2005 (Code Sec. 4081(d)(1), as amended by ISTEA (P.L. 105-178)).

Floor stocks refunds. Floor stock refunds provided for the tire tax imposed by Code Sec. 4071 and the fuels tax imposed by Code Sec. 4081 on certain removals, entries, and sales to unregistered persons will be determined with reference to tax-paid articles held by a dealer on October 1, 2005, rather than October 1, 1999 (Code Sec. 6412(a), as amended by ISTEA (P.L. 105-178)).

Extension of exemptions for extended taxes. The expiration of the exemption from the tire tax (Code Sec. 4071) and the tax on heavy trucks and trailers sold at retail (Code Sec. 4051) for sales to state and local governments and tax-exempt organizations is delayed from October 1, 1999, to October 1, 2005 (Code Sec. 4221(a), as amended by ISTEA (P.L. 105-178)).

The expiration of the exemption from the tax on highway motor vehicles with a gross weight of at least 55,000 pounds (Code Sec. 4481) used by state and local governments and certain transit buses is delayed from October 1, 1999, to October 1, 2005 (Code Sec. 4483(g), as amended by ISTEA (P.L. 105-178)).

Extension of Highway Trust Fund deposits and withdrawals. The transfer of excise taxes to the Highway Trust Fund is extended to include taxes received in the Treasury before October 1, 2005, rather than taxes received in the Treasury before October 1, 1999 (Code Sec. 9503(b), as amended by ISTEA (P.L. 105-178)). The authorization of transfers from the Highway Trust Fund to the general fund of the Treasury for excise tax repayments and credits is extended to amounts paid before

July 1, 2006. Previously, it covered amounts paid before July 1, 2000 (Code Sec. 9503(c)(2) and (3), as amended by ISTEA (P.L. 105-178)). Authorization for the transfers of motorboat fuel taxes and small engine fuel taxes from the Highway Trust Fund to the Aquatic Resources Trust Fund (Code Sec. 9504) is extended from amounts received before October 1, 1998, to amounts received before October 1, 2005 (Code Sec. 9503(c)(4) and (5), as amended by ISTEA (P.L. 105-178)).

Extension and expansion of expenditures from Highway Trust Fund and Mass Transit Account. ISTEA extends authority for transferring amounts from the Highway Trust Fund to pay for federal-aid highway programs from expenditures incurred before October 1, 1998, to expenditures incurred before October 1, 2003. The list of federal-aid highway programs for which expenditures may be transferred is expanded to include the Transportation Equity Act for the 21st Century (Code Sec. 9503(c)(1), as amended by ISTEA (P.L. 105-178)).

ISTEA also extends the authority to makes expenditures from the Mass Transit Account of the Highway Trust Fund to expenditures before October 1, 2003. Previously, the authority related to expenditures before October 1, 1998. The Mass Transit Account may be used to pay for expenditures made in accordance with the Transportation Equity Act for the 21st Century (Code Sec. 9503(e)(3), as amended by ISTEA (P.L. 105-178)).

Clarification of taxes transferred to Mass Transit Account. The Act provides that fuel taxes imposed by Code Secs. 4041 and 4081 will generally be deposited into the Mass Transit Account at the rate of 2.86 cents per gallon. The transfer rates are 1.43 cents per gallon for partially exempt methanol or ethanol fuel, none of the alcohol in which consists of ethanol; 1.86 cents per gallon rate for liquefied natural gas; 2.13 cents per gallon for liquefied petroleum gas; and 9.71 cents per MCF for compressed natural gas (Code Sec. 9503(e)(2), as amended by ISTEA (P.L. 105-178)).

★ *Effective date.* No specific effective date is provided by the Surface Transportation Revenue Act of 1998 (P.L. 105-178). The provision is, therefore, considered effective on June 9, 1998, the date of enactment. However, the provision clarifying the amount of taxes transferred to the Mass Transit Account applies to taxes received in the Treasury after September 30, 1997 (Act Sec. 9002(e)(2) of the Surface Transportation Revenue Act of 1998 (P.L. 105-178); Act Sec. 901(f) of the Taxpayer Relief Act of 1997 (P.L. 105-34)).

Act Sec. 9002(a)(1), amending Code Sec. 4041(a)(1)(C)(iii)(I), Code Sec. 4041(a)(2)(B), Code Sec. 4041(m)(1)(A), Code Sec. 4051(c), Code Sec. 4071(d), Code Sec. 4081(d)(1), Code Sec. 4481(e), Code Sec. 4482(c)(4) and Code Sec. 4482(d); Act Sec. 9002(a)(2), amending Code Sec. 6412(a)(1) and Code Sec. 6156(e)(2); Act Sec. 9002(b), amending Code Sec. 4221(a) and Code Sec. 4483(g); Act Sec. 9002(c)(1), amending Code Sec. 9503(b), Code Sec. 9503(c)(2) and Code Sec. 9503(c)(3); Act Sec. 9002(c)(2)(A), amending Code Sec. 9503(c)(4)(A)(i) and Code Sec. 9503(c)(5)(A); Act Sec. 9002(c)(2)(B), amending 16 U.S.C. 4601-11(b); Act Sec. 9002(c)(3), amending Code Sec. 9503(c)(3); Act Sec. 9002(d), amending Code Sec. 9503(c)(1) and Code Sec. 9503(e)(3); Act Sec. 9002(e), amending Code Sec. 9503(e)(2); Act Sec. 9003(f), amending Code Sec. 9503(b)(1) and Code Sec. 9503(c)(2)(A). Law at ¶5845, ¶5857, and ¶6940. Committee Report at ¶15,015 and ¶15,025. Act section references are to the Surface Transportation Revenue Act of 1998 (P.L. 105-178).

Modifications to Highway Trust Fund

¶751

Background —————————————————————————————

Two anti-deficit provisions limit Highway Trust Fund spending. Under the first anti-deficit provision, unfunded Highway Account authorizations are limited at the end of any fiscal year to amounts not exceeding the unobligated balance plus revenues projected to be collected for that account during the following two fiscal years. The second anti-deficit provision limits unfunded Mass Transit Account authorizations to excise tax revenues projected to be collected for that account during the next fiscal year. Violation of either provision results in a proportionate reduction in spending for programs funded by the relevant Trust Fund Account, similar to a general Budget Act sequester.

The Taxpayer Relief Act of 1997 (P.L. 105-34) transferred revenues from additional 4.3-cents-per-gallon highway fuel taxes to the Highway Trust Fund, effective on October 1, 1997. The 1997 Act provided that those revenues could not be used to increase direct spending under 1991 authorizing legislation.

ISTEA Impact

Determination of Highway and Mass Transit Trust Fund balances.— The Surface Transportation Revenue Act of 1998 (ISTEA) (P.L. 105-178) provides that for purposes of determining the balances of the Highway Trust Fund and the Mass Transit Account after September 30, 1998, the October 1, 1998 opening balance of the Highway Trust Fund (other than the Mass Transit Account) will be treated as $8 billion. The Secretary of Treasury will cancel obligations held by the Highway Trust Fund to reflect the resulting reduction in the Fund balance. Furthermore, the Fund will not receive credit for interest accruing after September 30, 1998, on obligations that it holds (Code Sec. 9503(f), as added by ISTEA (P.L. 105-178)).

Repeal of limitation on expenditures. ISTEA retroactively repeals the limitation on Highway Trust Fund expenditures contained in Code Sec. 9503(c)(7) that was added by the Taxpayer Relief Act of 1997 (P.L. 105-34) (Act Sec. 9004(b) of ISTEA (P.L. 105-178)).

Limitation on expenditure authority. ISTEA provides that expenditures from the Highway Trust Fund may occur only as provided in the Internal Revenue Code. Specifically, no amount may be appropriated to the Highway Trust Fund on or after any expenditure from the Highway Trust Fund that is not permitted by Code Sec. 9503. The determination of whether an expenditure is permitted by Code Sec. 9503 is made without regard to (1) any provision of law that is not contained in the Internal Revenue Code or in a Revenue Act and (2) whether such provision of law is a subsequently enacted provision or directly or indirectly seeks to waive the application of this rule.

Under an exception, however, this provision does not preclude disbursements to liquidate contracts or other obligations that are validly entered into before the October 1, 2003, expiration date of the Highway Trust Fund expenditure authority (Code Sec. 9503(b)(6), as added by ISTEA (P.L. 105-178)).

Comment. The controlling House Committee Report to ISTEA provides that expenditures for contracts entered into after the expiration date of the Trust Fund expenditure authority are not permitted, notwithstanding subsequently enacted authorization or appropriations legislation. If any such subsequent legislation authorizes such expenditures, or such expenditures occur by administrative action in contravention of this restriction on expenditure authority, excise tax revenues otherwise to be deposited in the Highway Trust Fund are to be retained in the General Fund beginning on the date of such unauthorized action.

¶751

Mass Transit Account rules on adjustments of apportionments. ISTEA conforms the one-year deficit rule in the Mass Transit Account to the two-year rule in the Highway Account (Code Sec. 9503(e)(4), as amended by ISTEA (P.L. 105-178)).

★ *Effective date.* The provision relating to the determination of the balances of the Highway Trust Fund and the Mass Transit Account balances takes effect on October 1, 1998 (Act Sec. 9004(a)(2) of the Surface Transportation Revenue Act of 1998 (P.L. 105-178)). The provision repealing the Code Sec. 9503(c)(7) limitation on expenditures added by the Taxpayer Relief Act of 1997 (P.L. 105-34) is effective for taxes received in the Treasury after September 30, 1997 (Act Sec. 9004(b)(2) of the Surface Transportation Revenue Act of 1998 (P.L. 105-178); Act Sec. 901(f) of the Taxpayer Relief Act of 1997 (P.L. 105-34)). No effective date is provided for the remaining provisions. These provisions are, therefore, considered effective on June 9, 1998, the date of enactment of ISTEA (P.L. 105-178).

Act Sec. 9004(a), adding Code Sec. 9503(f); Act Sec. 9004(b), repealing Code Sec. 9503(c)(7); Act Sec. 9004(c), adding Code Sec. 9503(b)(6); Act Sec. 9004(d), amending Code Sec. 9503(e)(4). Law at ¶ 6940. Committee Report at ¶ 15,055. Act section references are to the Surface Transportation Revenue Act of 1998 (P.L. 105-178).

Aquatic Resources Trust Fund

¶ 752

Background

The Aquatic Resources Trust Fund combines funding for sport fish restoration and boating safety programs. The Fund consists of two separate accounts, the Sport Fish Restoration Account and the Boat Safety Account.

The Sport Fish Restoration Account is funded by motorboat gasoline taxes, by an excise tax on sport fishing equipment, and by a special tax on gasoline used in off-highway small engines, as well as by import duties imposed on fishing equipment and certain yachts and pleasure craft. Money in the Sport Fish Restoration Account may be expended, subject to appropriation, for restoring and managing species of fish that have value in connection with sport and recreation in U.S. waters, and for education programs to increase public understanding of water resources and aquatic life forms.

The Boat Safety Account is funded solely by motorboat fuel taxes (Code Sec. 9503(c)(4)(A)). The amount transferred to the Fund is subject to a limit of $70 million during any fiscal year, and no amount is transferred if the resulting balance in the Boat Safety Account would exceed $45 million. The Boat Safety Account pays for state boating safety programs and expenses of the Coast Guard.

Of the tax revenues generated from motorboat and small-engine fuels, 11.5 cents per gallon was transferred to the Aquatic Resources Trust Fund. Those receipts were deposited in the Wetlands subaccount of the Aquatic Fund for sole use in wetlands conservation efforts (Code Sec. 9504(b)(2)).

Expenditures from the Boat Safety Account must be specifically appropriated. Expenditures from the Account were authorized through September 30, 1998, as provided by appropriation acts (Act Sec. 9(b) of the Surface Transportation Extension Act of 1997, P.L. 105-130, amending Code Sec. 9504(c)). The Sport Fish Restoration Account has operated under a permanent appropriations act, approved in 1950 (Code Sec. 9504(b)(2)(A)).

ISTEA Impact

Extensions, funding increase for Aquatic Resources Trust Fund.— Authority for transfers of motorboat fuel tax funds to the Boat Safety Account and for transfers of small-engine gasoline tax funds to the wetlands subaccount is extended through September 30, 2003 (Act Sec. 9005(b) of the Surface Transportation Revenue Act of 1998 (Title IX of the Transportation Equity Act for the 21st Century) (ISTEA) (P.L. 105-178). Expenditure authority of the Boat Safety Account is also extended through September 30, 2003.

Additional revenue transfers. Additional motorboat fuels taxes and small-engine gasoline tax revenues will be transferred to the Aquatic Fund. The portion of the total motorboat fuels revenues that is transferred to the Aquatic fund will be gradually increased from 11.5 cents per gallon to 13.5 cents per gallon with respect to taxes imposed in fiscal year 2004. The portion of motorboat fuels taxes transferred to the general Highway Trust Fund will correspondingly decrease. The funding increase for the Aquatic Fund will be implemented gradually according to the following revenue transfer schedule:

> (1) 11.5 cents per gallon with respect to taxes imposed before October 1, 2001;

> (2) 13 cents per gallon with respect to taxes imposed after September 30, 2001, and before October 1, 2003; and

> (3) 13.5 cents per gallon with respect to taxes imposed after September 30, 2003 (Act Sec. 9005(a)(1) of ISTEA (P.L. 105-178)).

Limits on transfers to Boat Safety Account. In determining whether transfers to the Boat Safety Account have exceeded the total Account limit of $45 million under Code Sec. 9503(c)(4)(A)(ii)(II), the Treasury Secretary is not to take into account any amount that was appropriated from the Boat Safety Account in any preceding fiscal year but not distributed (Act Sec. 9005(a)(2) of ISTEA (P.L. 105-178)).

Expenditure purposes amended. The expenditure purposes of the Aquatic Resources Trust Fund have been amended to conform to the purposes in the authorizing provisions of ISTEA as of the date of enactment of the TEA 21 Restoration Act (Title IX of the IRS Restructuring and Reform Act) (Act Sec. 9005(b) and (c) of ISTEA (P.L. 105-178); Act Sec. 9015(b) of the IRS Restructuring and Reform Act of 1998). An additional provision expands the expenditure purposes for expenditures from the Sport Fish Restoration Account to expenditures to carry out the purposes of Act Sec. 7404(d) of ISTEA (P.L. 105-178), as in effect on its date of enactment (June 9, 1998) (Act Sec. 9005(b)(3) of ISTEA (P.L. 105-178)).

ISTEA clarifies that expenditures from the Aquatic Resources Trust Fund may be made only to the extent permitted by Code Sec. 9504. Unauthorized expenditures from any Account in the Aquatic Fund will result in an end to new appropriations to be paid into the Fund (Code Sec. 9504(d), as added by Act Sec. 9005(d) of ISTEA (P.L. 105-178)). Permitted expenditures may not be determined by reference to any provision of law outside of Title 26, whether or not the provision is enacted subsequent to ISTEA or seeks to waive the application of Code Sec. 9504(d) (as added by Act Sec. 9005(d) of ISTEA (P.L. 105-178)).

★ *Effective date.* The provisions are effective on June 9, 1998 (Act Sec. 9005(e) of the Surface Transportation Revenue Act of 1998 (P.L. 105-178)).

Act Sec. 9005(a)(1), amending Code Sec. 9503(b)(4)(D); Act Sec. 9005(a)(2), amending Code Sec. 9503(c)(4)(A)(ii); Act Sec. 9005(b), amending Code Sec. 9504(b)(2); Act Sec. 9005(c), amending Code Sec. 9504(c); Act Sec. 9005(d), redesignating Code Sec. 9504(d) as Code Sec. 9504(e) and adding new Code Sec. 9504(d); Act Sec. 9005(e). Law at ¶ 6940. Committee

Report at ¶ 15,075. Act section references are to the Surface Transportation Revenue Act of 1998 (P.L. 105-178).

Repeal of National Recreational Trails Trust Fund

¶753

Background ————————————————————————

The National Recreational Trails Trust Fund (Code Sec. 9511) was established by the Intermodal Surface Transportation Efficiency Act of 1991 (P.L. 101-240). As originally enacted, all monies appropriated to this Trails Fund were to be used to finance the acquisition, maintenance, restoration and growth of the recreational trail systems in the United States. The original legislation also provided that a portion of the revenues generated by the 11.5 cents per gallon of motor fuels taxes on fuel used in nonhighway recreational vehicles could be transferred from the Highway Trust Fund to the Trails Fund to finance these projects. However, no appropriations from the Highway Trust Fund to the Trails Fund were ever made. While no transfer appropriations were ever authorized, Congress extended the Trails Fund for one year (to October 1, 1998) under the Surface Transportation Extension Act of 1997 (P.L. 105-130).

ISTEA Impact

Repeal of Trails Fund.—The Act repeals the National Recreational Trails Trust Fund as well as the transfer of nonhighway recreational fuels taxes to the Trails Fund. However, the Conference Committee Report authorizes Highway Trust Fund expenditures (Code Sec. 4081) for similar purposes to those of the Trails Fund (Code Sec. 9511, repealed by ISTEA (P.L. 105-178)).

★ *Effective date.* No specific effective date is provided by the Act. The provision is, therefore, considered effective on June 9, 1998, the date of enactment.

Act Sec. 9011(a), repealing Code Sec. 9511; Act Sec. 9011(b)(1), striking Code Sec. 9503(c)(6); Act Sec. 9011(b)(2), amending Code Sec. 9503(b)(4)(D); Act Sec. 9011(b)(3). Law at ¶ 6955. Committee Report at ¶ 15,145. Act section references are to the Surface Transportation Revenue Act of 1998 (P.L. 105-178).

ALCOHOL FUELS CREDIT

Tax Benefits for Alcohol Fuels

¶760

Background ————————————————————————

In order to encourage the production of gasohol, a nonrefundable income tax credit is available for alcohol and alcohol-blended fuels. This credit for ethanol and methanol derived from renewable sources (e.g., biomass) was scheduled to expire after December 31, 2000 (Code Sec. 40(e)(1)). The alcohol fuels credit is equal to 54 cents per gallon for ethanol and 60 cents per gallon for methanol.

In addition, the 54 cents per gallon ethanol and 60 cents per gallon renewable source methanol tax credits may be claimed through reduced excise taxes paid on gasoline, special motor fuel and aviation fuel, rather than as an income tax credit.

Special motor fuels that contain at least 85 percent methanol, ethanol, or other alcohol produced from a substance other than petroleum or natural gas are considered qualified methanol or ethanol. Prior to January 1, 2001, the rate of tax on qualified ethanol is 12.95 cents per gallon.

Background———————————————————————————————

Qualified gasoline mixtures with alcohol (gasohol) are taxed at lower rates to encourage fossil fuel conservation. The rates depend upon the type of alcohol used and its volume in the mixture. The rates generally favor blends with higher alcohol content. The lower rates also apply to alcohol mixtures used in producing other alcohol mixtures. The rates for gasoline mixtures vary depending on whether the mixture is 10 percent, 7.7 percent or 5.7 percent gasohol and whether the mixture is used to produce gasohol.

A reduced rate of tax also applies to diesel fuel or kerosene that is combined with alcohol, so long as at least 10 percent of the finished mixture is alcohol. The rate of tax is 19 cents per gallon for diesel fuel or kerosene mixed with alcohol. These special rates for gasoline, diesel fuel or kerosene mixed with alcohol were scheduled to terminate after September 30, 2000 (Code Sec. 4081(c)(8)).

Aviation fuel mixtures with alcohol are also taxed at lower rates to encourage fossil fuel conservation. Prior to January 1, 2001, if aviation fuel is used to make a mixture with at least 10 percent alcohol, the rate of tax on the sale of the mixture is reduced to 8.5 cents per gallon (Code Sec. 4091(c)(1)). These rates apply only if the aviation fuel has not already been taxed as fuel intended for a mixture before the actual blending was done. Aviation fuel sold for use in producing a mixture with alcohol is taxed at 9.44 cents per gallon (if the fuel is to be used in a mixture containing ethanol) (Code Sec. 4091(c)(2)).

ISTEA Impact

Extension and modification of tax benefits for alcohol fuels.—The Surface Transportation Revenue Act of 1998 (ISTEA) (P.L. 105-178) extended the ethanol and renewable source methanol tax provision through September 30, 2007, for the excise tax reduction, and December 31, 2007, for the income tax credit, respectively. The income tax credit will not apply, however, for any period before January 1, 2008, during which the Highway Trust Fund financing rate under Code Sec. 4081(a)(2)(A) is 4.3 cents per gallon (Code Sec. 40(e)(1), as amended by ISTEA (P.L. 105-178)).

ISTEA, although extending the ethanol credit, also reduced its rate beginning in the year 2001. For 190 or greater proof ethanol, the income tax credit is 53 cents per gallon in calendar years 2001 and 2002, 52 cents per gallon in calendar years 2003 and 2004, and 51 cents per gallon in calendar years 2005 through 2007. For ethanol at least 150 proof and less than 190 proof, the income tax credit is 39.26 cents per gallon in calendar years 2001 and 2002, 38.52 cents per gallon in calendar years 2003 and 2004, and 37.78 cents per gallon in calendar years 2005 through 2007 (Code Sec. 40(h), as amended by ISTEA (P.L. 105-178)).

Comment. Although the income tax credit and related excise tax rate reductions do not take effect until January 1, 2001, the expiration of the credit is not scheduled to terminate until December 31, 2000. Thus, there will be no disruption in the application of the credit or rate reductions.

Special motor fuel. ISTEA extended the tax benefit accorded to special motor fuels that contain at least 85 percent methanol, ethanol, or other alcohol produced from a substance other than petroleum or natural gas from October 1, 2001, through September 30, 2007 (Code Sec. 4041(b)(2)(C), as amended and redesignated as Code Sec. 4041(b)(2)(D) by ISTEA (P.L. 105-178)). Between January 1, 2001, and December 31, 2002, the rate of tax on qualified ethanol is 13.05 cents per gallon. Between January 1, 2003, and December 31, 2004, the rate of tax on qualified ethanol is 13.15 cents per gallon. Between January 1, 2005, and September 31, 2007, the rate of tax on qualified ethanol is 13.25 cents per gallon

(Code Sec. 4041(b)(2), as amended by P.L. 105-178). Although ISTEA extended the tax benefit for special fuels containing methanol, the rate of 12.35 cents per gallon remains constant (Code Sec. 4041(b)(2)(A)).

The Surface Transportation Revenue Act of 1998 (ISTEA) (P.L. 105-178) also extended the reduced rate of tax for sales or uses of diesel fuel, special motor fuel or nongasoline aviation fuel mixtures containing at least 10 percent alcohol for sales and uses before October 1, 2007 (Code Sec. 4041(k)(3), as amended by ISTEA (P.L. 105-178)).

Gasoline mixtures. ISTEA extended the beneficial tax rates for ethanol mixed with gasoline (gasohol) through September 31, 2007 (Code Sec. 4081(c)(8), as amended by ISTEA (P.L. 105-178)). ISTEA, however, reduced the beneficial tax rates for mixtures containing ethanol beginning in year 2001 (Code Sec. 4081(c)(4)(A), as amended by ISTEA (P.L. 105-178)).

For calendar years 2001 and 2002 the following rates apply for mixtures containing ethanol:

	Mixture with any alcohol	Mixture used in producing gasohol
10% gasohol	13.100 cents/gallon	14.556 cents/gallon
7.7% gasohol	14.319 cents/gallon	15.514 cents/gallon
5.7% gasohol	15.379 cents/gallon	16.309 cents/gallon

For calendar years 2003 and 2004 the following rates apply:

	Mixture with any alcohol	Mixture used in producing gasohol
10% gasohol	13.200 cents/gallon	14.667 cents/gallon
7.7% gasohol	14.396 cents/gallon	15.597 cents/gallon
5.7% gasohol	15.436 cents/gallon	16.369 cents/gallon

For the period January 1, 2005, through September 30, 2007, the following rates apply:

	Mixture with any alcohol	Mixture used in producing gasohol
10% gasohol	13.300 cents/gallon	14.778 cents/gallon
7.7% gasohol	14.473 cents/gallon	15.680 cents/gallon
5.7% gasohol	15.493 cents/gallon	16.429 cents/gallon

The tax rates for mixtures with nonethanol alcohol, although not modified by ISTEA, were also extended until September 30, 2007.

Diesel fuel or kerosene mixed with alcohol. A reduced rate of tax also applies to diesel fuel or kerosene that is combined with alcohol so long as at least 10 percent of the finished mixture is alcohol. ISTEA extended the tax benefit accorded to ethanol until October 1, 2007. For the period January 1, 2001, through December 31, 2002, the rate of tax on alcohol mixtures containing ethanol is 19.1 cents per gallon. For the period January 1, 2003, through December 31, 2004, the rate of tax on alcohol mixtures containing ethanol is 19.2 cents per gallon. For the period January 1, 2005, through September 30, 2007, the rate of tax on alcohol mixtures containing ethanol is 19.3. cents per gallon (Code Sec. 4081(c)(5)).

Aviation fuel mixtures. ISTEA extended the tax benefit accorded to ethanol mixed with aviation fuel through September 30, 2007 (Code Sec. 4091(c)(5), as amended by ISTEA (P.L. 105-178)). ISTEA, however, reduced the benefit over the course of seven years. As a result, a qualified mixture of aviation fuel and at least 10 percent alcohol is taxed at the following rates (Code Sec. 4091(c)(1), as amended by ISTEA (P.L. 105-178)):

Period	Rate of Tax
1/1/01—12/31/02	8.6 cents/gallon
1/1/03—12/31/04	8.7 cents/gallon
1/1/05—9/30/07	8.8 cents/gallon

★ *Effective date.* No specific effective date was provided by ISTEA for the extension of the ethanol benefit. That provision is, therefore, considered effective on June 9, 1998, the date of enactment of ISTEA. The modifications to the income tax credit and related excise tax rates are effective on January 1, 2001 (Act Sec. 9003(b)(3) of the Surface Transportation Revenue Act of 1998 (P.L. 105-178).

Act Sec. 9003(a)(1), amending Code Sec. 4041(b)(2)(C), Code Sec. 4041(k)(3), Code Sec. 4081(c)(8) and Code Sec. 4091(c)(5); Act Sec. 9003(a)(2), amending Code Sec. 6427(f)(4); Act Sec. 9003(a)(3), amending Code Sec. 40(e)(1); Act Sec. 9003(a)(4) amending Headings 9901.00.50 and 9901.00.52 of the Harmonized Tariff Schedule of the United States (19 U.S.C. § 3007); Act Sec. 9003(b)(1), amending Code Sec. 40(h); and Act Sec. 9003(b)(2), amending Code Sec. 4041(b)(2), Code Sec. 4081(c)(4)(A), Code Sec. 4081(c)(5) and Code Sec. 4091(c)(1). Law at ¶ 5065 and ¶ 5857. Committee Report at ¶ 15,035. Act section references are to the Surface Transportation Revenue Act of 1998 (P.L. 105-178).

IRS RESTRUCTURING AND REFORM PROVISIONS

Chapter 8

IRS Structure and Functions

ORGANIZATION AND STRUCTURE

Reorganization of IRS

¶ 801

Background

The IRS is the Treasury Department unit that has responsibility for determining, assessing and collecting taxes and enforcing internal revenue laws. The IRS consists of a National Office in Washington, D.C. and a field organization. The field offices are divided geographically into four regions, each headed by a Regional Commissioner. In addition to the Regional Commissioner, each of these regions has a regional counsel and a regional director of appeals. There are also 33 district offices, 10 service centers, and two computing centers.

The IRS is organized by functions, each of which is conducted separately in each of the geographic districts. Functions of the IRS include customer service,

¶ 801

Background

forms processing, examination, collection, and criminal investigation. Functions related to International and Employee Plans and Exempt Organizations are structured in separate offices.

IRS Restructuring and Reform Impact

Reorganization of IRS.—The Commissioner of the IRS is directed to reorganize the IRS in a way that eliminates or substantially modifies the current structure. Instead of geographic regional divisions, the IRS is to be organized into units serving groups of taxpayers with similar needs (Act Sec. 1001(a)(3) of the IRS Restructuring and Reform Act of 1998). The reorganization must also ensure the independence of the appeals function within the IRS. Expressly forbidden is any *ex parte* communication between appeals officers and other IRS employees that compromises the independence of the appeals officers (Act Sec. 1001(a)(4) of the 1998 Act). This provision, according to the Senate Committee Report, was enacted to provide for an independent appeals function.

According to the Senate Committee Report, the geographic structure of the IRS contributed to its perceived failure to properly serve taxpayers. The Report identifies four groups of taxpayers with similar needs (individuals, small businesses, large sector corporations and tax exempts) and intends that the restructuring will provide units within the IRS that concentrate on these groups. If a taxpayer changes his residence, the current system would transfer functions related to the taxpayer to the new district wherein the taxpayer resides; under the reorganized system, the taxpayer's change in residence would not prompt a change in responsibility for the taxpayer. The IRS would also benefit in being able to assign responsibilities to persons with expertise in specific areas. The current system makes an IRS official responsible for handling every type of problem that arises in a district office or in a service center. Accountability and continuity would be achieved by a move away from the division to districts and service centers.

Comment. The restructuring provisions reflect a shift to a customer service-oriented organization similar to changes that major corporations have put into place. The directive to reorganize based on the needs of taxpayers reflects a change of emphasis from revenue collection to providing service to taxpayers.

Savings provisions smooth transition and ensure preservation of taxpayer rights and remedies. Savings provisions ensure that the reorganization will not change any existing tax laws or taxpayer rights or affect the legality of ongoing IRS actions. Rights or remedies currently available to taxpayers, including trial by jury, the right to recover taxes alleged to be illegally or erroneously assessed or collected, or any penalty unlawfully collected or any other wrongful collection activity are not affected by the reorganization. If a statute, rule or regulation under which a taxpayer attempts to recover any such tax refers to the collector of internal revenue, the principal officer for the internal revenue district or the Secretary, the statute, rule or regulation is deemed to refer to the officer whose acts or acts gave rise to the taxpayer's claim. Venue does not change as a result of the reorganization (Act Sec. 1001(b)(1) of the 1998 Act).

The reorganization does not affect the integrity of legal documents in effect before the reorganization. Thus, all orders, determinations, rules, regulations, permits, agreements, grants, contracts, certificates, licenses, registrations, and privileges that were effective prior to the reorganization will be effective according to their terms until modified, terminated, set aside or revoked in accordance with law by the President, the Treasury Secretary, the Commissioner or other authorized official, a court of competent jurisdiction or by operation of law, even though

¶ 801

the reorganization may have eliminated or changed the officers responsible for the document (Act Sec. 1001(b)(2) of the 1998 Act).

The transfer or reassignment of functions within the IRS as a result of the reorganization will not interfere with any proceedings, including notices of proposed rulemaking, or any application for any license, permit, certificate or financial assistance pending before the Treasury Department. Orders will be issued, appeals from such orders may be filed, and payments pursuant to such orders will be made as if the reorganization had not occurred, and the orders are operative until modified, terminated, superseded or revoked by authorized officials, a court of competent jurisdiction or by operation of law. The reorganization provisions will not prohibit the discontinuance or modification of any such proceeding under the same terms and conditions and to the same extent that the proceeding could have been discontinued or modified if the reorganization provisions had not been enacted. (Act Sec. 1001(b)(3) of the 1998 Act).

Lawsuits filed prior to the reorganization will continue as if the IRS has not been reorganized. Appeals taken and judgments rendered have the same effect as if there were no reorganization. If an action is filed by or against the Treasury Department or the IRS, or is filed by or against individuals in their capacity as an officer of the Treasury Department, such actions are not abated merely because of the reorganization (Act Sec. 1001(b)(4) of the 1998 Act; Act Sec. 1001(b)(5) of the 1998 Act).

Administrative actions relating to the promulgation of regulations will continue as if the reorganization had not occurred, even though the person handling the function may be affected by the reorganization (Act Sec. 1001(b)(6) of the 1998 Act).

PRACTICAL ANALYSIS. Donna Steele Flynn of Ernst & Young, LLP, Washington, DC (former Staff Director, Subcommittee on Oversight, House Ways and Means Committee), observes that the Act's directive to the IRS Commissioner to restructure the IRS "by eliminating or substantially modifying the present-law three-tier geographic structure and replacing it with an organizational structure that features operating units serving particular groups of taxpayers with similar needs" reinforces the plan announced on January 28, 1998, by IRS Commissioner Charles Rossotti to reorganize the Service around the needs of taxpayers.

Under the plan outlined by Commissioner Rossotti, the IRS would be reorganized into four major business units, each charged with end-to-end responsibility for serving particular groups of taxpayers with similar needs. One unit would serve the approximately 100 million individual taxpayers who have only wage and investment income. A second unit would serve small business taxpayers, including sole proprietors and small business corporations. The third unit would serve middle market and large corporate taxpayers, and the final unit would serve the tax-exempt sector, including employee plans, exempt organizations, and state and local governments. These business units are intended to replace the IRS's four regional offices and much of the national office, leaving the remaining national office structure to focus on oversight and broad policy concerns rather than on operations.

The legislation also requires that the reorganized IRS must ensure "an independent appeals function within the IRS" which is to "prohibit ex parte communications between appeals officers and other IRS employees to the extent that such communications appear to compromise the independence of appeals officers." What isn't clear from the legislation is whether the conferees intend that each operating unit should have its own independent appeals function or whether an independent appeals office is to be set up as a separate unit. Presumably, this decision is left to the Commissioner's discretion.

While there are a number of remaining questions about the new organizational structure, two major issues to be resolved are: (1) where in the organizational structure will estate and gift, excise tax, and foreign taxpayer functions be placed; and (2) what will happen to the 33 District Offices and 10 Service Centers?

★ *Effective date.* The provision is effective on the date of enactment (Act Sec. 1001(c) of the IRS Restructuring and Reform Act of 1998).

Act Sec. 1001. Law at ¶ 8005. Committee Report at ¶ 10,115.

Mission Statement

¶ 806

Background ————————————————————————————————————

The current mission statement of the IRS emphasizes tax collection. Even though it directs the IRS to serve the public by improving the quality of products and services and to maintain integrity and fairness in performing tax collection services, the focus is on enforcement rather than taxpayer service.

In its entirety, the mission statement reads: "The purpose of the Internal Revenue Service is to collect the proper amount of tax revenue at the least cost; serve the public by continually improving the quality of our products and services; and perform in a manner warranting the highest degree of public confidence in our integrity, efficiency, and fairness."

IRS Restructuring and Reform Impact

IRS to revise mission statement.—The IRS is to review and restate its mission to place a greater emphasis on serving the public and meeting taxpayers' needs (Act Sec. 1002 of the IRS Restructuring and Reform Act of 1998). According to the Senate Committee Report, taxpayers have been frustrated with the IRS's lack of appropriate attention to taxpayer needs. Taxpayers have a right to receive the same level of service from the IRS that they receive from the private sector.

★ *Effective date.* No specific effective date is provided by the Act. The provision is, therefore, considered effective on the date of enactment .

Act Sec. 1002. Law at ¶ 8010. Committee Report at ¶ 10,120.

IRS Commissioner

¶ 811

Background ————————————————————————————————————

Federal tax laws are administered and enforced under the supervision of the Secretary of the Treasury. The Treasury Secretary delegates the responsibility for administering the tax laws to the IRS Commissioner. The IRS Commissioner is the official immediately in charge of the IRS. The duties and powers of the IRS Commissioner were not specifically listed in the Code. Prior to the 1998 Act, the Code described the Commissioner's duties as "those that may be prescribed by the Treasury Secretary." Tax policy decisions are outside the scope of the Commis-

Background _____

sioner's responsibilities. Authority over tax policy is delegated to the Assistant Treasury Secretary for Tax Policy.

The Commissioner is a Presidential appointee (with the advice and consent of the Senate). The Commissioner may be removed at will by the President.

The IRS Commissioner was not appointed to a specific term of office. The IRS Restructuring Commission found that the average tenure of an IRS Commissioner was under three years (A Vision for a New IRS: Report of the National Commission on Restructuring the Internal Revenue Service, June 25, 1997). In their view, this high turnover worked against the goal of fostering continuity and focus in the IRS management team. A longer term of service would also help insulate the Commissioner from political influences. Both Treasury Secretary Robert Rubin and Deputy Secretary Lawrence Summers have spoken in favor of a five-year, fixed term of office for the Commissioner as a way of establishing continuity at the IRS.

Specific qualifications for the position of IRS Commissioner were not described in the Code. Most IRS Commissioners have been lawyers with professional tax backgrounds. The current IRS Commissioner, Charles Rossotti, has a strong background in business management and information technology, but is not a tax lawyer.

IRS Restructuring and Reform Impact

Five-year term, enumerated duties for IRS Commissioner.—Any IRS Commissioner appointed is required to have, among other qualifications, a "demonstrated ability in management" (Code Sec. 7803(a)(1)(A), as amended by the IRS Restructuring and Reform Act of 1998). The Commissioner remains an appointee of the President, with advice and consent of the Senate, and may be removed at any time by the President.

Five-year term. The IRS Commissioner will now be appointed to serve a five-year term (Code Sec. 7803(a)(1)(A), as amended by the 1998 Act). A Commissioner may be reappointed to more than one five-year term. Should an individual be appointed to fill a vacancy occurring before the expiration of the Commissioner's term, the appointee would finish the term. The five-year term of the Commissioner in office on the date of enactment (Commissioner Rossotti) is considered to have begun on the date of his appointment (Act Sec. 1102(f)(4)(A) of the 1998 Act). Commissioner Rossotti was sworn in on November 13, 1997; thus, his term in office is scheduled to last until November 13, 2002.

PRACTICAL ANALYSIS. Shirley Peterson, President, Hood College, Frederick, Maryland, and former Commissioner of the Internal Revenue Service, observes that one of the principal organizational deficiencies of the Internal Revenue Service has been the absence of a fixed term for the Commissioner. The Commissioner, who is appointed by the President and confirmed by the Senate, has, in the past, changed with almost every presidential election. Historically, the average tenure of the Commissioner is three years.

The constant turnover at the top of the organization has made it difficult to ensure that needed reforms are implemented and sustained; and, too often, it has resulted in a lack of accountability.

A five-year term should produce much needed continuity for the organization and should provide additional assurances that the IRS is free of political interference.

¶ 811

The addition of the five-year term will be a crucial element of IRS reform. It will increase the likelihood that other reforms included in this legislation will be implemented to make the Internal Revenue Service more effective and efficient in administering the laws while, at the same time, being fair and responsive to taxpayers.

Duties of the Commissioner. The duties of the IRS Commissioner are specifically listed, rather than left to the complete discretion of the Treasury Secretary. The listed duties, all of which are subject to delegation by the Treasury Secretary, are:

> (1) to administer, manage, direct and supervise the execution and application of the tax laws and tax treaty provisions; and

> (2) to recommend candidates for Chief Counsel to the President when a vacancy occurs and recommend the removal of Chief Counsel.

If the Treasury Secretary decides *not* to delegate any of these powers, all six of the Congressional committees with jurisdiction over the IRS must first be notified (the House Committees on Ways and Means, Government Reform and Oversight, and Appropriations, and the Senate Committees on Finance, Governmental Affairs, and Appropriations). The decision will not be effective until 30 days after the appropriate House and Senate Committees are notified (Code Sec. 7803(a)(2), as amended by the 1998 Act).

Comment. The Report of the National Commission on Restructuring the IRS provides some insight on Congress's expansion of the Commissioner's duties and the enactment of a five-year term for the Commissioner (A Vision for a New IRS: Report of the National Commission on Restructuring the Internal Revenue Service, June 25, 1997). The IRS Commissioner has not had the power to recruit personnel to hold significant management positions. Thus, while the average term of the IRS Commissioner has declined over the past 20 years, most of the senior executives at the IRS have served more than 15 years. The Report suggests that the lack of continuity of leadership, coupled with the insular nature of the high-level executives, has made it extremely difficult for the IRS to implement new management perspectives. The 1998 Act gives the Commissioner some control over the appointment and removal of high-level executives (see ¶ 817 for discussion of these provisions). This, plus the requirement that the Commissioner serve a five-year term, empowers the IRS Commissioner to make significant directional and operational changes within the IRS.

Consulting with Oversight Board. The IRS Commissioner is required to consult with the Oversight Board on issues relating to operational functions of the IRS, such as plans for modernization, managed competition, or training and education. These issues are within the Oversight Board's responsibilities under Code Sec. 7802(d)(2). The Commissioner is also required to consult with the Oversight Board on the selection, evaluation, and compensation of senior IRS executives (within the Oversight Board's management responsibilities under Code Sec. 7802(d)(3), as amended by the 1998 Act). Staffing issues that involve the Commissioner's own office do not require his involvement (Code Sec. 7803(a)(3), as amended by the 1998 Act).

★ *Effective date.* The provision is effective on the date of enactment (Act Sec. 1102(f)(1) of the IRS Restructuring and Reform Act of 1998). The five-year term of the Commissioner in office on the date of enactment shall begin as of the date of appointment (Act Sec. 1102(f)(4) of the IRS Restructuring and Reform Act of 1998).

Act Sec. 1102(a), amending Code Sec. 7803(a); Act Sec. 1102(f)(1); Act Sec. 1102(f)(4). Law at ¶ 6860. Committee Report at ¶ 10,140.

¶ 811

IRS Chief Counsel

¶816

Background ————————————————————————————

The Chief Counsel is the IRS's chief law officer, whose duties are prescribed by the Treasury Secretary. The Chief Counsel is appointed by the President with the advice and consent of the Senate as an Assistant General Counsel of the Treasury. Prior to the Act, the Chief Counsel reported to the Treasury General Counsel.

IRS Restructuring and Reform Impact

Chief Counsel's duties.—The Chief Counsel's powers are delegated by the Treasury Secretary. These powers are to include the duty to be the legal advisor to the Commissioner and to IRS officers and employees; to furnish legal opinions for the preparation and review of rulings and technical advice memoranda; to prepare, review and assist in preparing proposed legislation, treaties, regulations and executive orders relating to laws affecting the IRS; to represent the Commissioner before the Tax Court; and to determine which civil actions under the Code should be litigated and to recommend to the Justice Department the commencement of such actions (Code Sec. 7803(b)(2), as amended by the IRS Restructuring and Reform Act of 1998).

If the Treasury Secretary decides *not* to delegate the powers specified above, such decision is not effective until 30 days after the Treasury Secretary notifies the appropriate House and Senate Committees of this action (Code Sec. 7803(b)(2), as amended by the 1998 Act). The committees which must be notified are the House Committees on Ways and Means, Government Reform and Oversight, and Appropriations, and the Senate Committees on Finance, Governmental Affairs, and Appropriations.

Chief Counsel generally to report to Commissioner. The Chief Counsel is appointed by the President with the advice and consent of the Senate (Code Sec. 7803(b)(1), as amended by the 1998 Act). The IRS Commissioner is responsible for recommending candidates for Chief Counsel to the President when a vacancy occurs (Code Sec. 7803(a)(2)(B), as amended by the 1998 Act).The Chief Counsel will report directly to the IRS Commissioner *except* in the following circumstances:

(1) with respect to legal advice or interpretation of tax law not relating solely to tax policy and with respect to tax litigation, the Chief Counsel is to report to both the Commissioner *and* the General Counsel for the Treasury Department; and

(2) with respect to legal advice or interpretation of tax law relating solely to tax policy, the Chief Counsel is to report to the General Counsel only (Code Sec. 7803(b)(3), as amended by the 1998 Act).

If there is any disagreement between the Commissioner and the General Counsel with any matter that is jointly referred to them, the matter is to be submitted to the Treasury Secretary or Deputy Secretary for resolution (Code Sec. 7803(b)(3), as amended by the 1998 Act).

According to the Conference Committee Report, it is intended that the dual reporting to the Commissioner and the General Counsel include reporting with respect to legal advice or interpretations of the tax law set forth in regulations, revenue rulings and revenue procedures, technical advice and other similar memoranda, private letter rulings, and published guidance not described in the actual law. The Chief Counsel is to report directly to the Commissioner on matters relating to day-to-day operations of the IRS, such as management of the IRS and procurement.

Comment. The Senate version of this amendment would have had the Chief Counsel report directly to the IRS Commissioner on all matters. The finalized version, providing that the Chief Counsel report to the Treasury Secretary on matters of tax policy, preserves the traditional separation of the IRS Commissioner from influencing tax policy.

All personnel in the Office of Chief Counsel are to report to the Chief Counsel (Code Sec. 7803(b)(4), as amended by the 1998 Act).

★ *Effective date.* This provision is effective on the date of enactment (Act Sec. 1102(f)(1) of the IRS Restructuring and Reform Act of 1998). However, Code Sec. 7803(b)(3), providing rules for persons to whom the Chief Counsel reports, is effective 90 days from the date of enactment (Act Sec. 1102(f)(2) of the 1998 Act).

Act Sec. 1102(a), amending Code Sec. 7803(b); Act Sec. 1102(f)(1); Act Sec. 1102(f)(2). Law at ¶ 6860. Committee Report at ¶ 10,145.

IRS Personnel

¶ 817

Background —————————————————————————————

The Treasury Secretary is authorized to employ such persons as the Secretary deems appropriate for the administration and enforcement of the internal revenue laws and to assign posts of duty. The Treasury Secretary is also responsible for issuing notices and demands to delinquent IRS officers and employees who have failed to turn over monies collected in connection with internal revenue laws.

IRS Restructuring and Reform Impact

Commissioner's appointment duties expanded.—Unless otherwise specified by the Treasury Secretary, the Commissioner is authorized to employ such persons as the Commissioner deems proper for the administration and enforcement of the tax laws, and is responsible for issuing all necessary directions, instructions, orders and rules applicable to such persons (Code Sec. 7804(a), as amended by the IRS Restructuring and Reform Act of 1998).

The Commissioner also has the power to designate posts of duty and to detail personnel from field service to duty in the District of Columbia (Code Sec. 7804(b), as amended by the 1998 Act).

Delinquent Treasury Department employees who fail to account for and pay over any money collected are subject to notice and demand for payment to be issued by the Treasury Secretary (Code Sec. 7804(c), as amended by the 1998 Act). Upon failure to pay, the amount owing can be assessed as taxes against the delinquent employee. This provision remains unchanged under the 1998 Act.

Comment. These provisions were formerly contained in Code Sec. 7803. Except for changing the source of authorization to the Commissioner, rather than the Secretary, to appoint personnel and assign posts of duty, the former rules remain intact under new Code Sec. 7804. Former Code Sec. 7804, dealing with savings clauses on reorganizations under reorganization plans of 1950 and 1952, is replaced by this provision. The savings clauses for the old reorganization plans are now moot due to the reorganization provisions under the 1998 Act (see ¶ 801, discussing Act Sec. 1001).

¶ 817

★ *Effective date.* The provision is effective on the date of enactment (Act Sec. 1104(c) of the IRS Restructuring and Reform Act of 1998).

Act Sec. 1104(a), amending Code Sec. 7804; Act Sec. 1104(b)(1), amending Code Sec. 6344(b); Act Sec. 1104(c). Law at ¶ 6870. Committee Report at ¶ 10,165.

National Taxpayer Advocate

¶ 821

Background ———————————————————————————————

For nearly 20 years, the IRS has provided some form of assistance to taxpayers who have problems with the agency. The IRS established the Taxpayer Ombudsman Office in 1979. The Office of the Taxpayer Advocate was created by Congress in 1996, and the Taxpayer Ombudsman was replaced by the Taxpayer Advocate. The Taxpayer Advocate, who was appointed by the IRS Commissioner and who received higher compensation than the Ombudsman, was expected to independently represent the taxpayers' interests in disputes with the IRS. The Taxpayer Advocate submits an annual report to the House Ways and Means Committee and the Senate Finance Committee. The information included in the report is specified by statute.

During the Restructuring Commission's investigation of the IRS, questions arose about the perceived independence of the Taxpayer Advocate. As an appointee of the Commissioner whose office was within the IRS, the position was likely to attract career IRS employees with an interest in continuing their IRS career after their term as Taxpayer Advocate. Also, local taxpayer advocates were subject to review by District and Service Center Directors, which detracted from their independence. Detracting further from the objectivity of local operations, the Taxpayer Advocate delegated the authority to issue taxpayer assistance orders to the local and regional problem resolution officers, who worked directly for the IRS.

IRS Restructuring and Reform Impact

Enhanced responsibilities of the National Taxpayer Advocate.—The Taxpayer Advocate is renamed the National Taxpayer Advocate (Code Sec. 7803(c)(1)(B), as amended by the IRS Restructuring and Reform Act of 1998). The National Taxpayer Advocate is to be appointed by the Treasury Secretary, after consulting with the Commissioner and the Oversight Board. The advocate does not need to be selected from candidates chosen by the IRS Oversight Board, as was suggested in the Senate amendment. Provisions in Title 5 of the U.S. Code, dealing with appointments in the Competitive Service or the Senior Executive Service, do not apply in the selection of the National Taxpayer Advocate.

The National Taxpayer Advocate is entitled to compensation at the same rate as the highest rate of basic pay established for the Senior Executive Service under 5 USC § 5382 (ES-6) or, if the Treasury Secretary determines, at a rate fixed under 5 USC § 9503 (as added by the 1998 Act; see ¶ 926 for a discussion of the Treasury Secretary's streamlined pay authority). The National Taxpayer Advocate will report directly to the IRS Commissioner (Code Sec. 7803(c)(1)(B), as amended by the 1998 Act).

Comment. Six grades of pay are listed as basic pay rates for the Senior Executive Service in 5 USC § 5382. As of January 1, 1998, the highest rate of pay (ES-6) is $118,400 (Ex. Ord. No. 13071, Dec. 29, 1997, 62 F.R. 68521, 68526).

An individual appointed to the office of National Taxpayer Advocate must have a background in customer service as well as a background in tax law and experience in representing individual taxpayers (Code Sec. 7803(c)(1)(B)(iii), as amended by the 1998 Act). He or she may not have been an officer or employee of the IRS during the two-year period ending with the appointment. The individual appointed must also agree that he or she will not accept any employment with the IRS for at least five years after leaving the position of National Taxpayer Advocate. Service as an officer or employee of the Office of the Taxpayer Advocate is not to be taken into account for purposes of the two-year and five-year requirements (Code Sec. 7803(c)(1)(B)(iv), as amended by the 1998 Act).

General responsibilities. The functions of the National Taxpayer Advocate Office are to:

(1) assist taxpayers in resolving problems with the IRS;

(2) identify areas in which taxpayers have problems in dealing with the IRS;

(3) propose changes to IRS administrative practices that would mitigate the problems identified in item (2) above (to the extent possible); and

(4) identify possible law changes which might mitigate the problems identified (Code Sec. 7803(c)(2)(A), as amended by the 1998 Act).

The National Taxpayer Advocate is responsible for issuing Taxpayer Assistance Orders, the use of which has been expanded by the 1998 Act (under Code Sec. 7811(a); see ¶1106); for supervising local taxpayer offices; and for preparing detailed semiannual reports for use by Congress.

Operation of local offices. The National Taxpayer Advocate is to monitor the coverage and geographical allocation of local offices of taxpayer advocates. Guidelines for IRS officers and employees outlining the criteria for referral of taxpayer inquiries to local advocate offices will be developed by the National Advocate. He or she must see to it that local telephone numbers for each office are published and available. Working with the Commissioner, the National Taxpayer Advocate is to develop career paths for local taxpayer advocates choosing to make a career in the office of the Taxpayer Advocate (Code Sec. 7803(c)(2)(C), as amended by the 1998 Act).

Personnel. The National Taxpayer Advocate is responsible for appointing local taxpayer advocates, making sure that each state has at least one taxpayer advocate. The local advocates and their employees are subject to evaluation (including dismissal) by the National Taxpayer Advocate. (Code Sec. 7803(c)(2)(D)(i), as amended by the 1998 Act).

Each local taxpayer advocate reports directly to the National Taxpayer Advocate or delegate thereof. Appropriate supervisory personnel may be consulted by the National Taxpayer Advocate in evaluating or taking an action with respect to persons employed in local taxpayer advocate offices (Code Sec. 7803(c)(2)(D)(ii), as amended by the 1998 Act). When an advocate meets initially with any taxpayer, the advocate must inform the taxpayer that it operates independently of any other IRS offices and that it reports directly to Congress through the National Taxpayer Advocate. The local taxpayer advocate has the discretion not to inform the IRS of any contact with that taxpayer or of any information provided to the local office by the taxpayer (Code Sec. 7803(c)(4)(A), as amended by the 1998 Act).

Each local office must maintain means of communication that are independent of the IRS. Each office must have a separate phone, fax machine, and separate post office address, as well as other independent electronic communication access (Code Sec. 7803(c)(4)(B), as amended by the 1998 Act).

Comment. The Conference Report states that it intends that a local taxpayer advocate be available to taxpayers in each state. Also, even though the local taxpayer advocate may report to a delegate of the National Taxpayer Advocate, the committee intends that the reporting remain in the Taxpayer Advocate organization. It is not intended that the local advocates report to a District Director or other IRS official. The authorization to report to a delegate is to provide reporting flexibility sufficient to take into account any reorganizations that the IRS may undertake.

Deficiency notices to include notice of right to contact. Deficiency notices are required to inform the taxpayer of the taxpayer's right to contact a local office of the Taxpayer Advocate as well as the location and phone number of the appropriate office (Code Sec. 6212(a), as amended by Act Sec. 1102(b) of the 1998 Act).

Semiannual reports to Congress. The National Taxpayer Advocate must annually provide two reports to the House Ways and Means Committee and the Senate Finance Committee. The reports must be submitted directly to the committees without any prior comment from the IRS Commissioner, the Treasury Secretary or any other Treasury officer, or the Office of Management and Budget (Code Sec. 7803(c)(2)(B)(iii), as amended by the 1998 Act).

The first report, to be submitted by June 30 of each year, must report on the objectives of the Office of the National Taxpayer Advocate for the fiscal year beginning in that calendar year (Code Sec. 7803(c)(2)(B)(i), as amended by the 1998 Act). This report should contain a full and substantive analysis in addition to statistical information.

The second annual report, required to be submitted by December 31 of each year, reports on the activities of the Office of the National Taxpayer Advocate, and must contain specific information about developing problem areas and initiatives for solving them. Eleven specific topics are listed in the Code for inclusion in the activities report. In general, the report must identify initiatives and problems and specify what actions have been taken on them. The report must also identify areas of the tax law that impose significant compliance burdens on either the taxpayer or the IRS and propose remedies for these situations and identify the ten most litigated issues (Code Sec. 7803(c)(2)(B)(ii), as amended by the 1998 Act).

Specifically, the activities report must:

(1) identify any initiatives the National Advocate's office has taken on improving taxpayer service and IRS responsiveness;

(2) contain recommendations received from individuals with authority to issue Taxpayer Assistance Orders;

(3) contain a summary of at least 20 of the most serious problems faced by taxpayers;

(4) contain an inventory of the problems or initiatives identified in the topics (1) through (3) for which action has been taken and the result of the action;

(5) contain an inventory of the problems or initiatives identified for which action remains to be completed, and the period during which such action has remained incomplete;

(6) contain an inventory of the problems or initiatives for which no action has been taken, including the period during which the item has been in the inventory, as well as the identity of any IRS official who is responsible for the inaction;

(7) identify any Taxpayer Assistance Order that was not honored by the IRS in a timely manner;

(8) contain recommendations for appropriate administrative and legislative action to resolve problems encountered by taxpayers;

(9) identify areas of the tax law that impose significant compliance burdens on taxpayers or the IRS, including specific recommendations for solving these problems;

(10) identify the ten most litigated issues including recommendations for mitigating the disputes; and

(11) include any other information deemed advisable by the National Advocate (Code Sec. 7803(c)(2)(B)(ii), as amended by the 1998 Act).

In preparing the activities report, if any information is required to be submitted by the Treasury Inspector General for Tax Administration, the Taxpayer Advocate does not have to provide the information to Congress (Code Sec. 7803(c)(2)(B)(iv)).

Comment. Items (1) through (8) in the Taxpayer Advocate's activity report are carryovers from prior law. The 1998 Act added the requirements to identify areas of the law imposing significant compliance burdens and the ten most litigated issues.

IRS Commissioner required to respond. The IRS Commissioner must establish procedures for a formal response to the recommendations submitted by the National Taxpayer Advocate. The procedure should provide for a response within three months after the recommendations are submitted to the Commissioner (Code Sec. 7803(c)(3), as amended by the 1998 Act).

★ *Effective date.* The provisions are generally effective on the date of enactment (Act Sec. 1102(f)(1) of the IRS Restructuring and Reform Act of 1998). However, in appointing the first National Taxpayer Advocate after the date of enactment, the Treasury Secretary shall not appoint any individual who was an officer or employee of the IRS at any time during the two-year period ending on the date of appointment. The Treasury Secretary need not consult with the Oversight Board if the Board has not been appointed (Act Sec. 1102(f)(3) of the 1998 Act).

PRACTICAL ANALYSIS. Robert G. Nath of Odin, Feldman & Pittleman, P.C., Fairfax, Virginia, observes that the authority of the National Taxpayer Advocate is expanded greatly under the bill. The most important expansions are: (1) the requirement to advertise and publicize the local Offices of Taxpayer Advocate; (2) the fact that local Taxpayer Advocates now are independent of any other IRS office and constitute their own separate career path; and (3) the vastly increased Taxpayer Assistance Order authority. Clearly, these three features are mutually reinforcing.

The local Taxpayer Advocate will no longer be a well-kept secret; the telephone number is required to be published on statutory notices of deficiency, as well as in the more traditional media such as telephone directories. That alone may result in a large influx of new cases. Second, the fact that the advocate is much more independent, including advocacy as a career path, may mean that the normally semi-reluctant revenue officers who currently staff the Office of Taxpayer Advocate may wield their authority more broadly. Third, and most important, the definition of "significant hardship" essentially overturns the Anti-Injunction Act, 26 U.S.C. § 7421(a). In particular, a Taxpayer Assistance Order may be issued if there is: (1) an immediate "threat" of adverse action, (2) a delay of more than thirty days in resolving a taxpayer problem, (3) the incurring by the taxpayer of significant costs (including attorneys' or accountants' fees) if relief is not granted, or (4)

irreparable injury or long-term adverse impact on the taxpayer if relief is not granted.

Each of these, on paper, is very significant in broadening the grounds on which a Taxpayer Assistance Order can be issued. If applied as intended, hundreds or thousands of new TAOs will be authorized. Moreover, under the conference agreement, additional authority to define "significant hardship" is granted based on considerations of equity, a broad term that allows the Office of Taxpayer Advocate even wider discretion to intervene.

Nath concludes that these provisions, if applied as intended, will mean a tremendous benefit to many taxpayers, but will not permit scofflaws or repeat offenders to take advantage of the system.

Act Sec. 1102(a), amending Code Sec. 7803(c); Act Sec. 1102(b), amending Code Sec. 6212(a); Act Sec. 1102(d), amending Code Sec. 6323(j)(1)(D), Code Sec. 6343(d)(2)(D), Code Sec. 7811(b)(2)(D), Code Sec. 7811(c), Code Sec. 7811(d)(1), Code Sec. 7811(d)(2), Code Sec. 7811(e) and Code Sec. 7811(f). Law at ¶ 6180, ¶ 6250, ¶ 6320, ¶ 6800, ¶ 6860 and ¶ 6890. Committee Report at ¶ 10,150.

IRS Oversight Board

¶ 826

Background

The Treasury Department is ultimately responsible for the actions of its agency, the IRS. However, the Treasury has generally viewed the IRS as an independent agency. The IRS Commissioner sets forth policies and strategies for the IRS and, accordingly, exercises an oversight role. No one from the private sector exercises oversight control over the IRS (although groups drawing from the private sector have been formed to give feedback on various IRS functions).

The Congressional committees with IRS oversight responsibilities generally have not focused on long-term planning or budget issues. Instead, the committees have tended to focus on specific problems that arise, such as browsing or system modernization. The Joint Committee on Taxation focuses mainly on legislation and on investigating the effects of the federal tax system.

The National Committee on Restructuring the IRS, noting that the average term of the officials with oversight responsibilities (i.e., the Treasury Secretary and the IRS Commissioner) is under three years, concluded that there must be some focus and direction for the agency, and that management skills and private sector expertise is needed if the IRS is to maintain public confidence and appropriately carry out its functions (A Vision for a New IRS: Report of the National Commission on Restructuring the Internal Revenue Service, June 25, 1997).

IRS Restructuring and Reform Impact

IRS Oversight Board: Creation and responsibility.—Congress has created a nine-member IRS Oversight Board as part of its attempt to rebuild public faith in the tax system. The Board is responsible for overseeing the IRS in its administration, management, conduct, direction and supervision of the execution and application of the internal revenue laws or related statutes and tax treaties (Code Sec. 7802(c)(1)(A), as amended by the IRS Restructuring and Reform Act of 1998). Specifically, the Board will ensure that the IRS is organized and operated to carry out its mission (Code Sec. 7802(c)(1)(B), as amended by the 1998 Act). In carrying out its duties, the Board is to exercise "appropriate confidentiality" (Code Sec. 7802(c)(1)(C) as amended by the 1998 Act).

Comment. The Oversight Board has actual authority to control actions taken within the IRS. In this sense, the provision does more than add to an already long list of groups that have been formed to advise the IRS on policy and management matters. The advisory groups already in existence include the Commissioner's Advisory Group, the IRS Management Board, the Modernization Management Board, the IRS Executive Committee (comprised of senior IRS executives), and the Executive Planning Board (comprised of lower-level IRS managers).

Board membership. The nine board members will consist of six private-life individuals who are not otherwise Federal officers or employees, plus the Treasury Secretary (or Deputy Treasury Secretary), the IRS Commissioner, and an individual who is a full-time Federal Employee or a representative of employees (the "employee representative") (Code Sec. 7802(b), as amended by the 1998 Act). The private-life members and the employee representative must be appointed by the President with the advice and consent of the Senate.

The selection of Board members is to be made without taking into account political affiliations. However, each candidate must have professional experience and expertise in one or more of the following areas: (1) management of large service corporations; (2) customer service; (3) federal tax laws, including tax administration and compliance; (4) information technology; (5) organization development; (6) the needs and concerns of taxpayers; and (7) the needs and concerns of small business. The private-life members appointed to the Board should, in the aggregate, cover all the mentioned areas of expertise (Code Sec. 7802(b)(2) as amended by the 1998 Act).

Terms. The private-life Board members will be appointed for five-year terms, except that the first group of members appointed to serve on the board will be staggered. Two members from the first group of appointees will have two-year terms, two members will have four-year terms and two members will serve five-year terms. The private-life members and the employee representative are limited to two five-year terms on the Board. If there is a vacancy on the Board, it is to be filled in the same manner as the original appointment. Any member filling a vacancy will serve out the term (Code Sec. 7802(b)(2) as amended by the 1998 Act).

Role of the Board. One role of the Board is to make sure that taxpayers are properly treated by IRS employees (Code Sec. 7802(d)(5) as amended by the 1998 Act). The Board is also specifically required to be involved in strategic planning at the IRS. As part of its strategic planning role, the Board will review and approve the establishment of IRS strategic plans, including annual plans, long-range plans, and any other missions and objectives related to strategic planning. Performance standards related to any missions and objectives will also be subject to review (Code Sec. 7802(d)(1), as amended by the 1998 Act). The Board is to review and approve the Commissioner's plans for any reorganization of the Internal Revenue Service (Code Sec. 7802(d)(3)(C), as amended by the 1988 Act).

Comment. The Conference Report explains that the Board is expected to review and approve the IRS reorganization required by the 1998 Act (see ¶ 801). However, the conferees take into account that the Commissioner has already taken steps to develop and implement such a plan and state that these efforts should not be impeded. Thus, according to the Conference Report, the Commissioner need not wait until the Board is appointed to implement reorganization as intended under the 1998 Act.

Operational functions at the IRS will be subject to Board scrutiny. The Board is responsible for reviewing IRS plans for modernizing the tax system, outsourcing, managed competition and training and education (Code Sec. 7802(d)(2) as amended by the 1998 Act).

Part of the Board's role is to recommend candidates to fill high-level IRS positions, as well as evaluating whether these officers should be removed. The Board will recommend to the President candidates for IRS Commissioner, and may also recommend removal of the Commissioner (Code Sec. 7802(d)(3)(A) as amended by the 1998 Act).

Comment. The IRS Commissioner is one of the individuals designated to sit on the IRS Oversight Board (under Code Sec. 7802(b)(1)(C) as amended by the 1998 Act). The Commissioner is thus a member of the panel charged with evaluating his or her performance and recommending removal, if necessary.

Senior IRS executives are not specifically chosen by the Board; however, the Board is expected to review the Commissioner's selection, evaluation and compensation of IRS senior executives who have program management responsibilities over significant functions (Code Sec. 7804(d)(3)(E) as amended by the 1998 Act). The Treasury Secretary will consult with the Board and the Commissioner on the selection of the National Taxpayer Advocate; however, the Treasury Secretary has control over the candidates for that position (Code Sec. 7803(c)(1)(B)(ii), as amended by the 1998 Act).

Review of IRS Budget. The Board is also to be involved in the IRS budget-making process. The budget prepared by the IRS Commissioner is subject to review and approval by the Board. The Board is to ensure that the budget request supports the IRS's annual as well as long-range strategic plans. Once the budget is approved, the Board will submit the request to the Treasury Secretary (Code Sec. 7802(d)(4) as amended by the 1998 Act). The Secretary then submits the budget request to the President, who will submit the request without revision to Congress together with the President's annual budget request for the IRS (Code Sec. 7802(d), as amended by the 1998 Act).

Comment. The Oversight Board technically has no control over tax policy issues. However, as a guiding force in IRS budgetary decisions, the Board arguably has the power to influence tax policy by directing IRS resources to particular areas.

Limitations on Board authority. Express limitations on the responsibilities of the Board are designed to subdue fears that the Board will develop into a private, unaccountable tax authority serving a limited number of privileged constituents. The Board has no authority or responsibility to: (1) develop or formulate tax policy on existing or proposed tax laws, related statutes or tax conventions; (2) interfere in specific law enforcement activities of the IRS, including audits, collection activities or criminal investigations; (3) get involved in IRS procurement activities (such as choosing vendors in which a private Board member may have an interest); and (4) tangle with specific personnel issues, except for specific appointment and removal recommendations concerning IRS Commissioner and senior IRS executives (Code Sec. 7802(c)(2) as amended by the 1998 Act).

Quorum and Board meetings. In order to have a quorum, five members of the Oversight Board (out of the nine) must be present. A majority of members present and voting is thus required for any action of the Board (Code Sec.7802(c)(4) as amended by the 1998 Act). The Board must meet at least quarterly, but may meet at other times determined as appropriate by the Chair (Code Sec. 7802(f)(2) as amended by the 1998 Act).

Annual reports. Annual reports must be submitted to the President and Congress (specifically, the House Ways and Means Committee, Government Reform and Oversight Committee and Appropriations Committee and the Senate Finance Committee, Governmental Affairs and Appropriations Committee) concerning the activities of the Board. If the Oversight Board determines that the IRS is not fulfilling its mission, the Board must report this to the House Ways and Means Committee and the Senate Finance Committee (Code Sec. 7802(f)(3) as amended by the 1998 Act).

Ethical standards. During the term that a private-life member or the employee representative is on the Board, he or she is subject to the financial disclosure rules applicable to high-ranking government employees (as defined under Sec. 101(f) of the Ethics in Government Act of 1978, without regard to the number of days of service) (Code Sec. 7802(b)(3) as amended by the 1998 Act). This means that the Board member must file an annual public financial disclosure report. Post-employment restrictions are also imposed on private-life Board members and the employee representative.

Special conflict-of-interest restrictions may apply to a private-life or the employee representative Board member who is also a "special government employee," that is, a person who is not already an officer or employee of the Federal Government and who works for the government for less than 130 days during the year (18 USC § 202(a)). Special government employees on the Board may not:

(1) represent anyone before the Oversight Board or the IRS on any matter;

(2) represent a client before the Treasury Department on any matter concerning taxes or matters dealing with the IRS; or

(3) represent anyone in a Justice Department matter involving tax or other matters dealing with the IRS or Oversight Board.

The restrictions apply whether or not the Board members are compensated for such representation (Code Sec. 7802(b)(3)(C), as amended by the 1998 Act).

Waiver for employee representative. At the time that the President nominates the employee representative to the Oversight Board, the President has the authority to waive, for the term of such member, the conflict-of-interest provisions to the extent that the waiver is necessary to allow such member to participate in the decisions of the Board while continuing to serve as full-time Federal employee or employee (union) representative. Any such waiver shall not be effective unless a written intent of waiver to exempt such member (and actual waiver language) is submitted to the Senate with the nomination of the member (Code Sec. 7802(b)(3)(D) as amended by the 1998 Act). According to the Conference Report, it is not intended that waiver of restrictions on post-employment under the Act is necessary in order to allow the Federal employee or employee representative to participate in Board decisions while continuing to serve as an employee representative.

Removal of board member. The President is not restricted in his ability to remove a private-life or employee representative or Federal employee Board member from office. The IRS Commissioner and the Treasury Secretary (or the Deputy Treasury Secretary, if on the Board) are no longer on the Board when their terms of service expire (Code Sec. 7802(b)(5) as amended by the 1998 Act).

Personal liability rules. The private-life members of the Board and the employee representative have no personal liability under federal law with respect to any claim arising out of or resulting from any omission by the member within their scope of service as a Board member. Acts committed outside of the scope of service are not protected by this limitation, according to the Senate Committee Report. Other immunities and protections that are provided under any law for federal officers and employees, and any rules that limit or alter immunities that are available to federal officers and employees, are not affected (Code Sec. 7802(b)(6) as amended by the 1998 Act).

Compensation and other personnel matters. The private-life members of the Board (other than the Chairperson) will receive $30,000 per year as compensation.

¶ 826

The employee representative will also receive $30,000 if the representative is not a Federal officer or employee. The other members, i.e., the Commissioner and the Treasury Secretary (or his delegate) serve without compensation. The Chairperson of the Board will receive $50,000 per year (Code Sec. 7802(e)(1) as amended by the 1998 Act). Members will also be compensated for travel expenses (including per diem rates) incurred for the purpose of attending Board meetings. The Chairperson is required to provide advance approval of other expenses for traveling away from home or regular place of business for purposes of performing duties as Board members (Code Sec. 7802(e)(2) as amended by the 1998 Act). The Oversight Board is to include in its annual report information on the amount of travel expenses allowed (Code Sec. 7802(e)(2)(B), as amended by the 1998 Act).

The Board elects the chairperson from among the private-life Board members. The Chairperson serves a two-year term. Unless the Board votes otherwise, the Chairperson is responsible for establishing committees, setting meeting places and times, establishing meeting agendas and developing rules of conduct for the Board business (Code Sec. 7802(f)(1), as amended by the 1998 Act). The Chairperson can appoint and dismiss personnel in order to carry out Board functions. If the Chairperson requests, a government employee from another federal agency can be detailed to the Oversight Board. The Chair is also authorized to procure temporary and intermittent help (Code Sec. 7802(e)(3), as amended by the 1998 Act; Code Sec. 7802(e)(4), as amended by the 1998 Act).

Disclosure of return information. Private-life Board members, the Federal employee or employee representative Board member, and any employees of the Board are not entitled to receive confidential tax return information. Disclosure exceptions are provided in the case where a report is prepared for the Board's use by the Commissioner or Treasury Inspector General for Tax Administration and they determine that return information is necessary to enable the Board to act. Then, the return (or return information, without the taxpayer's identity revealed) can be disclosed. If a private-life member or the employee representative member contacts an IRS employee concerning a particular taxpayer or in pursuit of information that cannot be disclosed to the Board, the IRS employee must report it to the Treasury Secretary, the Treasury Inspector General for Tax Administration and the Joint Committee on Taxation (Code Sec. 6103(h)(5), as amended by the 1998 Act).

★ *Effective date.* The provisions are effective on the date of enactment. However, the names of the initial nominees to the Oversight Board are to be submitted by the President to the Senate not later than six months after the date of enactment (Act Sec. 1101(d) of the IRS Restructuring and Reform Act of 1998).

Act Sec. 1101(a), amending Code Sec. 7802; Act Sec. 1101(b), adding Code Sec. 6103(h)(5); Act Sec. 1101(c), amending Code Sec. 4946(c); Act Sec. 1101(d). Law at ¶ 5930, ¶ 6110 and ¶ 6850. Committee Report at ¶ 10,130.

Treasury Inspector General for Tax Administration

¶ 831

Background

The Treasury Office of Inspector General conducts independent audits within the Treasury Department. Special rules apply with respect to the Treasury Inspector General (Treasury IG) insofar as the Treasury IG does not have responsibility for IRS audit or inspection function of the IRS Chief Inspector. The Treasury IG can also investigate reports of IRS employee or executive misconduct. The IRS and the Treasury IG have agreements concerning the respective roles of each in investigating and overseeing the IRS. Moreover, the Treasury Secretary can prohibit the Treasury IG from conducting audits where confidential information is at issue. The IRS Chief Inspector, who reports directly to the Commissioner,

Background _____

is responsible for the integrity of the IRS and conducts its audits. Although the Treasury IG does have oversight responsibilities with respect to the conduct of the IRS Chief Inspector, Congress perceives that the IRS Office of Chief Inspector does not have sufficient structural and actual autonomy from the IRS, which it is supposed to monitor and oversee and that an independent office whose primary focus is to audit, evaluate and investigate will improve the quality and integrity of the IRS.

IRS Restructuring and Reform Impact

Independent Treasury IG for Tax Administration.—The Office of the Chief Inspector within the IRS is eliminated, and a new, independent office for oversight and inspection of the IRS is created. The Office of the Treasury Inspector General for Tax Administration exists in addition to the Office of Inspector General of the Department of the Treasury (5 USC App. § 2 (the Inspector General Act of 1978), as amended by Act Sec. 1103(a) of the IRS Restructuring and Reform Act of 1998). The Treasury IG's duties are defined as all duties and responsibilities of an Inspector General for the Department of the Treasury *other than* the duties and responsibilities exercised by the Treasury Inspector General for Tax Administration (5 USC App. § 8D(b), as amended by Act Sec. 1103(b) of the 1998 Act). Like all Inspector Generals, the Treasury IG for Tax Administration is to have a demonstrated ability in accounting, auditing, financial analysis, law, management analysis, public administration or investigations (5 USC App § 3(a)). In addition, the Treasury IG for Tax Administration should have demonstrated ability to lead a large and complex organization (5 USC App. § 8D(i), as added by the 1998 Act). Experience in tax administration is not a requirement.

Comment. The effective date of this provision is 180 days after the date of enactment of the IRS Restructuring And Reform Act of 1998, when the transfer of functions to the office has been enacted. At this time, the Office of Chief Inspector will be terminated (Act Sec. 1103(c) of the 1998 Act).

The Treasury Secretary has the responsibility for determining how the two Treasury IGs will handle audits and investigations in cases of overlapping jurisdiction. The Treasury Secretary is also to make sure that the two offices cooperate and are efficient and that their efforts are coordinated.

Taxpayer returns and return information are generally not available to the Treasury IG for Tax Administration unless the Secretary specifically authorizes such access (5 USC App. § 8(D)(e), the Inspector General Act of 1978, as amended by Act Sec. 1103(b)(3) of the 1998 Act).

Employment restrictions. An individual appointed to the position of Treasury Inspector General for Tax Administration may not be an employee of the IRS for the two years preceding the date of appointment and the five years following the appointment (5 USC App. § 8D(j), as added by Act Sec. 1103(b)(7) of the 1998 Act).

The Treasury IG for Tax Administration is required to appoint an Assistant Inspector General for Auditing and an Assistant General for Investigations (5 USC App. § 3(d)(2), the Inspector General Act of 1978). These persons are also subject to the two-year and five-year employment restriction rules (5 USC App. § 8(D)(j), as added by the 1998 Act).

Responsibilities. The Treasury IG for Tax Administration has the sole authority to conduct an audit or investigation of the IRS Oversight Board and the IRS Chief Counsel (5 USC App. § 8(d)(h), as added by Act Sec. 1103(b)(7) of the 1998 Act). The Treasury IG (or a designated employee) may enforce criminal proceedings pertaining to commodities (such as liquor or firearms) and may, for example, issue search and arrest warrants and carry firearms in pursuance of this duty. The Treasury IG for Tax Administration is responsible for protecting the IRS against external threats to corrupt or threaten employees but is not responsible for conducting background checks and providing physical security (5 USC App. § 8D(k)(1), as added by the 1998 Act).

If a law enforcement action is undertaken, the Treasury Inspector General for Tax Administration is to report to the Attorney General that there is reasonable ground to believe that a crime has been committed (5 USC App. § 8D(k)(2)(A), as added by Act Sec. 1103(b)(7) of the 1998 Act).

The Treasury IG is subject to semiannual reporting requirements set forth in section 5 of the Inspector General Act of 1978. If the Treasury IG submits any report required under this provision to the Treasury Secretary, submission to the IRS Oversight Board and the IRS Commissioner is also required (5 USC App. § 8D(g)(2), the Inspector General Act of 1998, as amended by the 1998 Act).

Request for IRS Audit. The Commissioner of Internal Revenue or the IRS Oversight Board may request, in writing, that the Treasury Inspector General for Tax Administration conduct an audit or investigation relating to the IRS. If the Treasury IG for Tax Administration decides not to conduct such audit or investigation, the Inspector General shall provide a written explanation for such determination to the person making the request (5 USC App. § 8D(l)(1), as added by the 1998 Act). The final audit report is to be timely submitted to the Commissioner and Oversight Board by the Treasury Inspector General.

The Treasury IG for Tax Administration is to report to the Board and Commissioner a list of investigations for which a final report has been completed by the Inspector General and to provide a copy of any such report upon the request of the Board or Commissioner.

The Treasury IG for Tax Administration is to conduct periodic audits of a statistically valid sample of the total number of denials of written requests to disclose information under the Freedom of Information Act or Code Sec. 6103. Taxpayers must be provided with a toll-free number to confidentially register complaints of IRS employee misconduct and incorporate this information in IRS Publication No. 1 (Code Sec. 7803(d)(3), as added by Act Sec. 1102(a) of the 1998 Act).

Transition issues. Certain internal audit personnel will be retained, even though the Office if Chief Inspector is terminated. The Commissioner is to designate and retain internal audit full-time equivalent positions necessary for management, but not in excess of 300 positions (Act Sec. 1103(c)(3) of the 1998 Act). In addition, effective 180 days after the date of enactment, the Treasury Secretary is required to transfer 21 full-time positions from the Office of the Inspector General of the Treasury Department to the newly-created office (Act Sec. 1103(c)(4) of the 1998 Act).

Additional reporting duties. The IG for Tax Administration must provide, in one of its semiannual reports to Congress, an evaluation of the IRS's compliance in the following areas: compliance with restrictions on use of tax enforcement results to evaluate or impose production quotas or goals (imposed under Act Sec. 1204 of the 1998 Act; see ¶ 981); compliance with restrictions on directly contacting taxpayers who have indicated they prefer their representatives be contacted; procedures for approval of a notice of lien under Code Sec. 6320; procedures for seizing property for tax collection purposes, including those pertaining to lien and levy approval; and compliance with restrictions on designating taxpayers as illegal tax protesters (see ¶ 891) (Code Sec. 7803(d)(1)(A), as added by the 1998 Act).

¶ 831

In addition, the Treasury IG for Tax Administration must provide a review and certification of whether or not the IRS is complying with the disclosure requirements for individuals filing a joint return as to collection activity involving the other individual on the return; information regarding extensions of the statute of limitations for assessing and collecting tax under Code Sec. 6501 and providing notice to taxpayers regarding extension requests; an evaluation of IRS technology as to whether it is adequate and secure; a report on termination and mitigation procedures enacted in the IRS Restructuring Act of 1998 (see ¶ 976); and information requiring improper denial of requests under the Freedom of Information Act or Code Sec. 6103 or the Fair Debt Collection provisions (Code Sec. 7803(d)(1)(B) through Code Sec. 7803(d)(1)(F), as added by the 1998 Act).

Each semiannual report must provide the number of taxpayer complaints during that period; the number of "serious" IRS employee misconduct and abuse allegations received by the IRS or the Treasury IG for Tax Administration from taxpayers, employees or other sources; and a summary of the status of such complaints and allegations, including any dispositions of such complaints (such as the outcome of any Department of Justice actions, monies paid as settlements, etc.) (Code Sec. 7803(d)(2), as amended by the 1998 Act).

★ *Effective date.* No specific effective date is provided by the Act. The provision is, therefore, considered effective on the date of enactment. However, the transfer of functions to the Office of the Treasury Inspector General, and the termination of the Office of Chief Inspector, is effective 180 days after the date of enactment of the 1998 IRS Reform and Restructuring Act (Act Sec. 1103(c)(1)(C) and Act Sec. 1103(c)(2) of the IRS Reform and Restructuring Act of 1998). Duties imposed under Code Sec. 7803(d) are effective on the date of enactment (Act Sec. 1102(f)(1) of the 1998 Act).

Act Sec. 1102(a), adding Code Sec. 7803(d); Act Sec. 1103(a), amending the Inspector General Act of 1978 (5 USC App.) § 2(3); Act Sec. 1103(b), amending the Inspector General Act of 1978 (5 USC App.) § 8D; Act Sec. 1103(c), amending the Inspector General Act of 1978 (5 USC App.) § 9(a)(1); Act Sec. 1103(d); Act Sec. 1103(e), amending the Inspector General Act of 1978 (5 USC App.) § 8D(a) and (b) and 8G; Act Sec. 1103(e)(4), amending Code Sec. 7608(b)(1); Act Sec. 1102(f)(1). Law at ¶ 6860, ¶ 8015 and ¶ 8020. Committee Report at ¶ 10,160.

Employee Plans and Exempt Organization Division

¶ 836

Background _____

Concomitant with the enactment of the Employee Retiree and Security Act of 1974 (ERISA), Congress created within the IRS an Office of Employee Plans and Exempt Organizations under the direction of an Assistant Commissioner. The Office was to oversee deferred compensation plans and tax-exempt organizations. To provide funding for the office, ERISA authorized amounts to be set aside from amounts collected from the Code Sec. 4940 excise tax on investment income under a funding formula contained in Code Sec. 7802(b)(2) (prior to amendment by the IRS Restructuring and Reform Act of 1998). These amounts have not been set aside, and general IRS funds are used for this office.

_____

IRS Restructuring and Reform Impact

Office of Employee Plans and Exempt Organizations eliminated.—The statutory establishment of an office of employee plans and exempt organizations is eliminated. The funding mechanism prescribed in former Code Sec. 7802(b)(2) is eliminated as well. The Senate Finance Committee Report indicates that it expects that a comparable structure will be created administratively to ensure that adequate resources within the IRS are devoted to the tax-exempt sector (see ¶ 801 for a discussion of the IRS reorganization provision). According to the Senate Committee Report, the funding mechanism was eliminated because, even if it were utilized, the funding level was unstable and perhaps inadequate for the sufficient exercise of responsibilities for the tax-exempt sector.

Comment. Prior to the 1998 Act, the office of employee plans and exempt reorganizations, as well as its funding, was authorized under Code Sec. 7802(b)(1) and (2). The 1998 Act replaced former Code Sec. 7802 with a new section outlining the rules concerning the IRS Commissioner, Chief Counsel, etc. The new section does not contain any provision for an office of employee plans and exempt organizations. Accordingly, the repeal of the office of employee plans and exempt organizations was accomplished by not including a provision for it under the 1998 Act.

★ *Effective date.* The provision is effective on the date of enactment (Act Sec. 1101(d)(1) of the IRS Restructuring and Reform Act of 1998).

Act Sec. 1101, amending Code Sec. 7802; Act Sec. 1102(e), amending 5 USC § 5109 and Code Sec. 7611(f)(1). Law at ¶ 6850. Committee Report at ¶ 10,135.

LEGISLATIVE PROCESS

IRS Participation in Drafting Legislation

¶ 841

Background

The complexity of the Internal Revenue Code directly impacts on the difficulty the IRS has in enforcing compliance. According to the IRS Restructuring Commission report, part of taxpayer frustration with the IRS stems from this complexity (A Vision for a New IRS: Report of the National Commission on Restructuring the Internal Revenue Service, June 25, 1997). The IRS does not participate in drafting legislation and is not formally consulted as to the administrative issues that might arise from legislation concerning the tax laws.

IRS Restructuring and Reform Impact

IRS participation in drafting legislation.—The Act includes a "sense of the Congress" provision that the IRS should provide Congress with an independent view of tax administration. Further, it is the sense of Congress that during the legislative process, frontline technical tax experts from the IRS should provide the tax writing committees with their opinion on the administrability of pending amendments to the Internal Revenue Code (Act Sec. 4021 of IRS Restructuring and Reform Act of 1998).

★ *Effective date.* No specific effective date is provided by the Act. The resolution is, therefore, considered effective on the date of enactment.

Act Sec. 4021. Law at ¶ 8215. Committee Report at ¶ 10,760.

Study of Tax Law Complexity

¶ 846

Background

Congress is not required to provide a formal complexity analysis when it makes changes to the tax laws. However, the IRS Restructuring Commission found a correlation among tax law complexity, difficulty of administration of the tax law,

Background

and taxpayer dissatisfaction with the tax system (A Vision for a New IRS: Report of the National Commission on Restructuring the Internal Revenue Service, June 25, 1997). Complexity leads to more involvement of taxpayers with the IRS in the form of increased calls, letters, and requests for rulings. Complexity also increases training costs for the IRS.

Frequent changes in the law add to uncertainty, and may lead to mistakes by the IRS as well as taxpayers. Senator Daniel Patrick Moynihan (D-NY) pointed out during consideration of the 1998 Act that the bill would be the 64th law to change the tax code since the Tax Reform Act of 1986. Most of these law changes have increased the complexity in the tax code rather than simplifying it. In light of this trend, the Restructuring Commission recommended measuring the success of new tax legislation in part by the cost to comply with and administer the law.

Support for a formal complexity analysis of proposed legislation has been mixed. The Joint Committee on Taxation has expressed support (in written testimony presented by former JCT Chief of Staff Kenneth J. Kies) for greater focus on the need for simplification. However, Kies also voiced the opinion that the ability to make a real difference lies in Congress and the Administration in the drafting process, and not in adding another layer of information to an already impressive array of paperwork. Information about complexity is also available in the form of hearing testimony, Congressional staff meetings with interested groups, and analyses already provided by the JCT as well as by the staffs of the House Ways and Means Committee and the Senate Finance Committee.

Counterarguments to the increased emphasis on attacking complexity have focused on the point that simplicity is only one of numerous goals of the tax system. Complexity should not be elevated over other concerns, such as fairness, flexibility, and economic benefits to taxpayers, under this line of reasoning. Often cited as an example, the home mortgage deduction adds to complexity and compliance costs, and yet these detractions are willingly overlooked by those who stand to benefit from the deduction.

IRS Restructuring and Reform Impact

Complexity analysis.—Both the Commissioner and Joint Committee on Taxation have been given responsibilities for analyzing the complexity of pending tax laws.

Commissioner study. The Commissioner is to conduct each year after 1998 an analysis of the sources of complexity in the administration of federal tax laws (Act Sec. 4022(a)(1) of the IRS Restructuring and Reform Act of 1998). Subjects to be analyzed may include the following:

(1) questions frequently asked by taxpayers with respect to return filing;

(2) common errors made by taxpayers in filling out returns;

(3) the areas of tax law which frequently result in disagreements between taxpayers and the IRS;

(4) major areas of the law in which there is no (or incomplete) published guidance or in which the law is uncertain;

(5) areas in which revenue officers make frequent errors interpreting or applying the law;

(6) the impact of recent legislation on complexity; and

(7) forms supplied by the IRS, including the time it takes for taxpayers to complete and review forms, the number of taxpayers who use each form and

how recent legislation has affected the time to complete and review forms (Act Sec. 4022(a)(1) of the 1988 Act).

The Commissioner's analysis for any year is due not later than March 1 of the following year. The Commissioner is to report on the results of the analysis to the House Ways and Means Committee and the Senate Finance Committee. The report is to include any recommendations for reducing the complexity of the administration of federal tax laws and for repeal or modification of any provision the Commissioner believes adds undue and unnecessary complexity to the administration of the federal tax laws (Act Sec. 4022(a)(2) of the 1998 Act).

Joint Committee analysis. The Joint Committee on Taxation, in consultation with the IRS and the Treasury Department, is to provide a "Tax Complexity Analysis" for each bill or joint resolution reported by the Senate Finance Committee, the House Ways and Means Committee, or any conference committee, if the legislation affects any provision of the Internal Revenue Code *and* it has widespread applicability to individuals or small businesses. This analysis is to be provided either in the Joint Committee Report to accompany the legislation or as soon as practicable after the report is filed (Act Sec. 4022(b)(1), as added by the 1998 Act). According to the Conference Committee Report, the complexity analysis should be included in committee or conference committee reports, to the extent possible.

Any Ways and Means Committee report on any bill or joint resolution containing a provision to amend the Internal Revenue Code must include the Tax Complexity Analysis prepared by the Joint Committee, unless the Ways and Means Committee causes the Complexity Analysis to be printed in the Congressional Record prior to the consideration of the legislation in the House or the Senate (as the case may be) (Act Sec. 4022(b)(3)(A) of the 1998 Act, amending Clause 2(l) of rule XI of the Rules of the House of Representatives).

Tax Complexity Analysis defined. A tax complexity analysis is defined as a report on the complexity and administrative difficulties of each tax law provision that has widespread applicability to individuals or small businesses. This analysis should include:

(1) an estimate of the number of taxpayers affected by the provision; and

(2) if applicable, the income level of taxpayers affected by the provision.

If it can be determined, the analysis should also contain information on: whether the IRS will need to revise tax forms or create new forms; the extent to which taxpayers would be required to keep additional records; the estimated cost to taxpayers to comply with the provision; the extent to which the IRS would have to develop or modify regulatory guidance; the extent to which the provision may result in disagreements between taxpayers and the IRS; any expected impact on the IRS as a result of the provision, including the impact on internal training, revision of the IRS manual, and reprogramming of computers; and the extent to which the IRS would have to divert or redirect resources as a response to the provision (Act Sec. 4022(b)(2) of the 1998 Act).

Point of order. The rules of the House of Representatives have been amended to conform with this provision. Neither the House nor the Senate is permitted to consider any legislation that requires a complexity analysis and does not have one (Act Sec. 4022(a) of the 1998 Act; Act Sec. 4022(b)(3) of 1998 Act, amending rules XI and XXVIII of the Rules of the House of Representatives). However, the point of order is subject to the right of each House of Congress to establish its own rules and procedures. Thus, the point of order can be changed at any time pursuant to the procedures of the House of Representatives.

¶ 846

★ *Effective date.* The provision applies to legislation considered on or after January 1, 1999 (Act Sec. 4022(b)(4) of the IRS Restructuring and Reform Act of 1998).

Act Sec. 4022(a); Act Sec. 4022(b)(1) and (2); Act Sec. 4022(b)(3)(A) and (B), amending rules XI and XXVIII of the Rules of the House of Representatives; Act Sec. 4022(b)(3)(C); Act Sec. 4022(b)(4). Law at ¶ 8220. Committee Report at ¶ 10,770.

IRS BUDGET AND FUNDING

Low-Income Taxpayer Clinics

¶ 851

Background

No federal law specifically provided for assistance to clinics that assist low-income taxpayers with their tax returns or tax controversies. Free tax services have been available largely through volunteer organizations that operate in cooperation with the IRS. These programs include the Volunteer Income Tax Assistance Program (VITA) and Tax Counseling for the Elderly (TCE). Return preparation and basic taxpayer education are the main objectives of VITA and TCE.

The TCE program is partially funded by IRS grants, which are used to reimburse volunteers for transportation and other expenses incurred in providing tax counseling. As part of the TCE program, the American Association of Retired Persons (AARP) offers a counseling program through which low- and moderate-income taxpayers age 60 and older can receive counseling from IRS certified volunteers.

In addition to these programs, the Student Tax Clinic Program (STCP) provides free tax counseling in audit, appeals, and tax court cases.

The Legal Services Corporation does not provide grants specifically for programs that assist low-income taxpayers. LSC is a private non-profit corporation created by Congress. It receives funds from Congress and makes grants to local programs that provide civil legal assistance to those otherwise unable to afford it.

The Chair of the ABA Section of Taxation noted in a statement before the IRS Restructuring Commission (Statement of Steven C. Salch, April 17, 1997) that, while return-preparation help was generally available, there was less organized help for low-income taxpayers once they entered the tax controversy stage. These taxpayers were faced with the choice of foregoing their rights to contest the IRS position or muddling through on their own.

IRS Restructuring and Reform Impact

Matching grants for low-income taxpayer clinics.—Up to $6,000,000 in matching grants will be available annually to fund taxpayer clinics for low-income and non-English-speaking clients. Each eligible clinic may receive up to $100,000 per year for development, expansion, or continuation of services for low-income and non-English-speaking taxpayers. Multi-year grants are available for terms of up to three years (Code Sec. 7526(c), as added by the IRS Restructuring and Reform Act of 1998).

Comment. The $6,000,000 aggregate limit on funds for low-income clinics is "subject to the availability of appropriated funds" (Code Sec. 7526(a), as added by the 1998 Act).

Qualified low-income taxpayer clinics. An eligible clinic can be either a clinical program operated by an accredited law school, business school or accounting school (in which students represent taxpayers), or a tax-exempt organization that represents taxpayers before the IRS or refers taxpayers to qualified outside representatives who will represent them (Code Sec. 7526(b)(2), as added by the 1998 Act). A qualified representative is any individual, whether or not an attorney, who is authorized to practice before the IRS or the applicable court (Code Sec. 7526(b)(3), as added by the 1998 Act).

Clinics eligible to receive matching funds must operate on a nominal-fee basis (excluding reimbursement of actual costs incurred). In addition, the clinic must either:

(1) represent low-income taxpayers in controversies with the IRS; or

(2) operate programs designed to inform individuals for whom English is a second language about their rights and duties under the tax laws (Code Sec. 7526(b)(1)(A), as added by the 1998 Act).

Low-income defined. A clinic's client base is considered low-income if at least 90 percent of the taxpayers represented by the clinic have incomes which are at or below 250 percent of the poverty level (determined by Office of Management and Budget criteria) (Code Sec. 7526(b)(1)(B)(i), as added by the 1998 Act). Under 1997 Census Bureau data, the weighted average poverty threshold for a family of four is $16,404. Thus, a four-member family falling within the Code Sec. 7526 guidelines as low-income would have a household income of less than $41,010 (for U.S. government poverty thresholds, see www.census.gov). Also, the amount in controversy for a given tax year cannot exceed the limit for small Tax Court cases under Code Sec. 7463, now $50,000 (Code Sec. 7526(b)(1)(B)(ii), as added by the 1998 Act; Code Sec. 7463, as amended by Act Sec. 3103(a) of the 1998 Act).

Criteria for awards. The IRS will consider the following criteria in determining whether to award a matching grant:

(1) the number of taxpayers who will be served by the clinic, including the number of taxpayers in the area for whom English is a second language;

(2) the existence of other low-income taxpayer clinics serving the same population;

(3) the quality of the program offered by the clinic, including the qualifications of the clinic's administrators and representatives as well as the clinic's record in providing service to low-income taxpayers; and

(4) alternative funding sources available to the clinic, such as amounts received from other grants and contributors and the endowment and resources of the school or institution sponsoring the clinic (Code Sec. 7526(c)(4), as added by the 1998 Act).

Clinic must match IRS grant. A clinic receiving grants under this provision must provide dollar-for-dollar matching funds. Matching funds may include the salaries of clinic employees and the cost of equipment used in the clinic (Code Sec. 7526(c)(5), as added by the 1998 Act). Indirect expenses, such as overhead of the organization sponsoring the clinic, do not count as matching funds.

PRACTICAL ANALYSIS. Robert McKenzie, of McKenzie & McKenzie PC, Chicago, Ill., comments that because of the complexity of current tax law, many people are only able to exercise their rights before the IRS with the assistance of a tax professional. Unfortunately, low-income taxpayers are unable to afford professional fees. In order to protect these taxpayers, Congress has chosen to provide for funding of low-income tax clinics. Protection of low-income taxpayers and their rights will also enhance protection of rights to all individuals. The more that taxpayers assert their rights, whether at the low- or high-income level, the more likely it is that the IRS will comply with proper procedures.

★ *Effective date.* The provision is effective on the date of enactment (Act Sec. 3601(c) of the IRS Restructuring and Reform Act of 1998).

Act Sec. 3601(a), adding Code Sec. 7526; Act Sec. 3601(b); Act Sec. 3601(c). Law at ¶ 6750. Committee Report at ¶ 10,625.

Year 2000 Date Change

¶ 856

Background————————————————————————————

The century-date-change issue relates to problems that most computer systems will have in referring to the calendar year 2000. Older computer programs were designed to use a two-digit representation of the year in which the first two digits are implied. When the calendar advances to January 1, 2000, these computer programs will interpret the date as January 1, 1900. The IRS has made the century date change its highest technology issue and has developed a plan to correct potential century date problems. The Restructuring Commission Report recommends that the century date change must remain the highest technology priority at the IRS and requests that Congress provide sufficient resources to address the problem (A Vision for a New IRS: Report of the National Commission on Restructuring the Internal Revenue Service, June 25, 1997). Sufficient funding is especially important in light of the fact that the cost of correcting century-date-change problems can increase with time. Also, since the century date change has diverted IRS technology managers from other modernization projects, more resources may be needed in order for other IRS database modernization efforts to continue.

The Restructuring Commission Report notes that the challenges faced by the IRS in confronting the century date change are largely managerial. While the technical aspects of the century-date-change plan are sound, risks remain in the implementation of the plan. The IRS must complete an inventory of its second- and third-tier programs and must recode, test, and implement programs in all three tiers. In order to monitor this process, the Commission suggests that the IRS should develop detailed schedules with intermediate milestones to be evaluated weekly between now and the program completion date. Contingency programs must also be developed in the event that certain milestones may not be met.

IRS Restructuring and Reform Impact

Century-date-change problems.—It is the sense of Congress that the IRS should place a high priority on resolving its century-date-change computing problems, and that the IRS efforts to resolve its century-date-change computing problems should be fully funded to provide for certain resolution of these problems. The Act does not require the IRS Commissioner to report to Congress on the impact of this legislation on the ability of the IRS to resolve its century-date-change problems.

★ *Effective date.* No specific effective date provision is provided by the Act. The provision is, therefore, considered effective on the date of enactment.

Act Sec. 4011. Law at ¶ 8210. Committee Report at ¶ 10,755.

Financial Management Advisory Group

¶ 861

Background————————————————————————————

The IRS has not had systematic input from the Treasury Department or the private sector on issues relating to IRS management, operations, and taxpayer services. As a result of Act Sec. 1001 of the IRS Restructuring and Reform Act of

Background _____

1998 (see ¶ 826), the IRS will benefit from an Oversight Board consisting of representatives from the private sector as well as government participants. As an extension of this concept, the House bill originally proposed creating a specific financial management advisory group for the Commissioner (Sec. 412 of H.R. 2676, as approved by the House 11/5/97). As proposed by the House, the advisory group would have consisted of both private and government sector members who would provide input on issues such as the partnership between the IRS and the General Accounting Office, the financial accounting aspects of the IRS's system modernization, the necessity of year-round auditing, and the IRS's plans for improving its financial management system.

IRS Restructuring and Reform Impact

Financial advisory group for IRS Commissioner.—The IRS Restructuring and Reform Act of 1998 does not contain legislation requiring the IRS Commissioner to convene a financial management advisory group. However, the Conference Report states that the conferees expect that the Chairman of the Oversight Board will consider establishing a financial management subcommittee to advise the Commissioner on financial management issues. The Commissioner's financial advisory group, if convened, will thus consist of members already serving on the IRS Oversight Board (see ¶ 826).

Committee Report at ¶ 11,590.

TAXPAYER CONFIDENTIALITY

Taxpayer Confidentiality Study

¶ 862

Background _____

Taxpayer return information is generally protected from disclosure under Code Sec. 6103. The Code contains over a dozen broad exceptions to the ban on disclosure, most of which relate to the administration and enforcement of tax laws. Return information can be disclosed to state and city tax officials for certain purposes; to persons having a material interest in the tax matter; to Congressional committees, the White House, and federal agencies; to the Justice department; and to various other agencies interested in the information for statistical or administrative purposes. No tax information may be furnished by the IRS to another agency (or state) unless the agency establishes satisfactory procedures for safeguarding the tax information it receives.

Unauthorized willful disclosure of taxpayer return information is a felony punishable by a fine up to $5,000, five years imprisonment, or both. Actions for civil damages may also be brought against employees who willfully disclose taxpayer information.

For unauthorized inspection of taxpayer return information by federal or state employees, the 1997 Taxpayer Browsing Protection Act (P.L. 105-35) added a new criminal penalty of up to $1,000 in fines, imprisonment up to one year, or both. Convicted federal employees will also lose their jobs. Civil damages for unauthorized inspection of tax returns are available if the inspection occurred either knowingly or by reason of negligence.

IRS Restructuring and Reform Impact

Studies on taxpayer confidentiality.—The Joint Committee on Taxation and the Secretary of the Treasury are required to conduct independent studies of the scope and use of provisions relating to taxpayer confidentiality (Act Sec. 3802 of the IRS Restructuring and Reform Act of 1998). Findings of the studies, with appropriate recommendations, are to be reported to Congress not later than 18 months after the date of enactment. The studies are required to examine:

(1) the present protections for taxpayer privacy;

(2) any need for third parties to use tax return information;

(3) whether greater levels of voluntary compliance may be achieved by allowing the public to know who is legally required to file tax returns, but does not file tax returns;

(4) the interrelationship of taxpayer confidentiality provisions under the Code with confidentiality provisions under other Federal laws (including the Freedom of Information Act (5 U.S.C. § 552a));

(5) the impact on taxpayer privacy of the sharing of tax return information for purposes of enforcing state and local laws, including the impact on privacy intended to be protected under the Taxpayer Browsing Protection Act of 1997 (P.L. 105-35); and

(6) whether the public interest would be served by greater disclosure of information relating to tax-exempt organizations described in Code Sec. 501.

The studies are being requested by Congress in order to evaluate possible changes to the existing confidentiality laws.

★ *Effective date.* No specific effective date is provided by the Act. The provision is, therefore, considered effective on the date of enactment. The findings of the study are to be reported to the Congress no later than 18 months after the date of enactment.

Act Sec. 3802. Law at ¶ 8195. Committee Report at ¶ 10,720.

Disclosure of Return Information by Whistle-Blowers

¶ 863

Background

The IRS is required to disclose taxpayer return information to the Chair of the Senate Finance Committee, House Ways and Means Committee, or Joint Committee on Taxation upon written request from the Chair (Code Sec. 6103(f)(1)). Information that directly or indirectly identifies a particular taxpayer may only be furnished to a committee sitting in closed session, unless the taxpayer consents in writing to making the information available in open committee meetings.

There was no avenue for average IRS employees to reveal return information in the course of reporting misconduct or taxpayer abuse to a congressional committee. One consequence of this rule was that employees were prevented by the taxpayer confidentiality provisions from reporting suspected politically motivated audits to the tax-writing committees, or from responding to congressional allegations that particular audits were politically motivated.

Testimony in IRS oversight hearings on abusive IRS management practices revealed several instances in which whistle-blowers faced retaliation for reporting managerial misconduct (CCH Tax Day Reports, May 1, 1998). In light of these allegations, increased protection for whistle-blowers was deemed desirable.

IRS Restructuring and Reform Impact

Disclosures in the course of alleging IRS employee misconduct or taxpayer abuse.—Any person with current or prior authorized access to taxpayer return information is permitted to disclose the information in the course of reporting IRS employee misconduct or taxpayer abuse to the House Ways and Means Committee, the Senate Finance Committee, or the Joint Committee on Taxation (Code Sec. 6103(f)(5), as added by the IRS Restructuring and Reform Act of 1998). Whistle-blower information may also be disclosed to any agents of these congressional committees or agents of the Chief of Staff of the Joint Committee on Taxation who are authorized to inspect return information under Code Sec. 6103(f)(4)(A). Disclosure is permissible if the person believes that the return information being disclosed may be related to possible misconduct, maladministration, or taxpayer abuse. Written approval from the committee chair is not needed prior to the disclosure.

★ *Effective date.* The provision is effective on the date of enactment (Act Sec. 3708(b) of the IRS Restructuring and Reform Act of 1998).

Act Sec. 3708(a), amending Code Sec. 6103(f); Act Sec. 3708(b). Law at ¶ 6110. Committee Report at ¶ 10,670.

Disclosure of Return Information by IRS

¶ 864

Background ————————————————————————————————————

Information gathered from taxpayers' returns is generally inaccessible to anyone other than IRS officials performing necessary duties. Federal employees are subject to criminal penalties for wrongfully disclosing return information (Code Sec. 7213) or even for inspecting taxpayer returns when they have no legitimate purpose for doing so (Code Sec. 7213A).

However, a growing number of exceptions in the Code permit access to confidential return information to various interested parties. Spouses, children, guardians, and certain business associates may be able to obtain information. State tax commissioners may obtain information to assist in their collection activities. Various federal agencies also now have access to return information for certain purposes, such as checking SBA loan applications, pursuing student loans in default, administering welfare programs, or pursuing delinquent owers of child support. Individual taxpayers are not notified when their return information is made available to state or other government officials under these Code Sec. 6103 rules.

The Joint Committee on Taxation releases an annual summary of the number and type of instances in which federal returns and return information were disclosed. The June 16, 1998, report reveals that the total number of federal return information disclosures for 1997 exceeded 3,201,710,000. Subsets of this very large number include: (1) nearly 1,814,861,000 disclosures to state tax officials administering state tax laws; (2) in excess of 335,615,000 disclosures to congressional committees and/or their agents, including General Accounting Office representatives; (3) nearly 171,924,000 disclosures to the Commerce Department's Bureau of the Census for statistical use; (4) approximately 1,643,000 disclosures to the Bureau of Economic Analysis; (5) around 857,200 disclosures to foreign governments with income tax conventions with the United States; and (6) nearly 4,300 disclosures as to whether prospective jurors in judicial tax proceedings have or have not been the subject of any tax investigation. Among others, the Drug Enforcement Agency, the Federal Bureau of Investigation, the Secret Service, the Small Business Administration, the Department of Labor, and assorted child support enforcement agencies may also legally request the disclosure of federal tax return information

Background _____

(JCT Disclosure Report for Public Inspection Pursuant to Internal Revenue Code Section 6103(p)(3)(C) for Calendar Year 1997, JCX-47-98).

_____

IRS Restructuring and Reform Impact

Confidentiality rules explained in tax form instruction booklets.—A plain language explanation of the return confidentiality rules must be included in any instruction booklets sent out to accompany individual income tax forms. The disclosure statement must include a concise statement of the situations in which the information reported on the tax form can be disclosed to a party outside of the IRS (including disclosure to a state, agency, body, commission, or legal representative of a commission). The statement must be printed in a conspicuous type size, in a noticeable place. The disclosure statement is to accompany instructions for forms 1040, 1040A, and 1040EZ (Act Sec. 3508 of the IRS Restructuring and Reform Act of 1998).

Comment. The conferees consider the statement already contained in the general tax forms instruction booklets to be sufficient to fulfill the requirement of this provision (Conference Committee Report). In the current Form 1040 instruction booklet, return confidentiality is mentioned on page 38 (of 41 pages) as part of the Privacy Act and Paperwork Reduction Act Notice. In the sixth paragraph, the return confidentiality statement reads as follows: "We may give the information to the Department of Justice and to other Federal agencies, as provided by law. We may also give it to cities, states, the District of Columbia, and U.S. commonwealths or possessions to carry out their tax laws. And we may give it to foreign governments because of tax treaties they have with the United States."

Comment. Floor discussion of the amendment to require clearer disclosures to taxpayers suggested that many taxpayers mistakenly believe their IRS files are extremely private and inscrutable (Senate floor debate, May 7, 1998). Citizens may be unaware that their files have been shared with state officials and administrators of federal loan programs. While tax return information is not openly shared with political individuals (governors and mayors), discussion in the Senate suggested that it might not be impossible for information to flow that way through the "good ole boy" channels. In the interest of fairness, the bill drafters thought that citizens should be made aware of the possible uses for the financial information they are required by law to provide.

★ *Effective date.* No specific effective date is provided by the Act. The provision is, therefore, considered effective on the date of enactment.

Act Sec. 3508. Law at ¶ 8155. Committee Report at ¶ 10,600.

Identification Number for Return Preparers

¶ 865

Background _____

Tax return preparers must provide an identifying number on tax returns or claims of refund that they prepare (Code Sec. 6109(a)(4)). As with any person required to make a return, statement or other document, the identifying number of the return preparer is his or her social security number.

_____

IRS Restructuring and Reform Impact

Return preparer's identifying number.—The 1998 Act authorizes the IRS to approve alternatives to social security numbers for use as identifying numbers by tax return preparers (Code Sec. 6109(a), as amended by the IRS Restructuring and Reform Act of 1998).

Comment. This change was made because a return preparer's social security number could be used for inappropriate purposes by anyone coming into contact with the return.

★ *Effective date.* The provision is effective on the date of enactment (Act Sec. 3710(b) of the IRS Restructuring and Reform Act of 1998).

Act Sec. 3710(a), amending Code Sec. 6109(a); Act Sec. 3710(b). Law at ¶ 6130. Committee Report at ¶ 10,680.

HEARINGS, REPORTS, AND RECORDS
General Accounting Office Investigations
¶ 866

Background ───────────────────────────────────────

General Accounting Office (GAO) investigations relating to the IRS have been traditionally allowed to proceed without approval by the Joint Committee on Taxation. However, some studies conducted by the GAO require access to return information that is protected under the Code Sec. 6103 confidentiality provisions. The GAO does not have blanket access to confidential return information under Code Sec. 6103. Under Code Sec. 6103(i)(7)(B), the Joint Committee on Taxation (JCT) must be notified within 90 days of the completion of an audit involving confidential return information. The Joint Committee can disapprove of the audit within 30 days of receiving the notification. As a practical matter, the Joint Committee has noted in its own commentary that the GAO generally seeks advance access to confidential return information from the Joint Committee before commencing an audit.

Investigations that require access to confidential return information include the annual GAO audit of IRS's financial statements (which might incidentally touch on confidential return information) as well as studies that require statistical samples of returns to determine the extent of a particular problem.

The Restructuring Committee recommended changes to the GAO investigation approval process based on its finding that the GAO conducts many audits of the IRS which may relate to minor matters and which are not integrated into a constructive, focused package (A Vision for a New IRS: Report of the National Commission on Restructuring the Internal Revenue Service, June 25, 1997). The House Committee Report notes that while GAO audits and reports are helpful as an oversight tool, they should be coordinated so as to ensure appropriate allocation of IRS and GAO resources. The Joint Committee could respond to requests by consolidating some GAO studies or by suggesting alternate solutions that would not require a special study.

IRS Restructuring and Reform Impact

Review of requests for General Accounting Office investigations.—The Joint Committee on Taxation is required to review all requests by the GAO for investigations of the IRS other than those originating from the chair or other ranking member of a House or Senate committee or subcommittee (Code Sec. 8021(e), as added by the IRS Restructuring and Reform Act of 1998). The conferees intend for the exception for congressional committee members to cover investigations required by statute and work initiated by the GAO under its basic statutory authorities, in addition to requests from the chair or ranking member of the committee (Conference Committee Report at ¶ 10,740). Appropriate requests will be approved. In reviewing requests, the JCT is directed to implement these objectives:

>   (1) eliminate overlapping investigations;

>   (2) ensure that the GAO has the capacity to handle the investigations; and

>   (3) ensure that investigations focus on areas of primary importance to tax administration (Code Sec. 8021(e), as added by the 1998 Act).

Comment. The review requirement does not apply to requests for GAO investigations that come from ranking members of House or Senate committees or subcommittees, whether or not the committee has jurisdiction over issues relating to the IRS. This exception covers a significant number of disclosures. For 1997, the Joint Committee tabulation of return information disclosures to Congressional committees exceeded 335 million (Joint Committee on Taxation, Disclosure Report for Public Inspection Pursuant to Internal Revenue Code Section 6103(p)(3)(C) for Calendar Year 1997 (JCX-47-98), June 16, 1998).

★ *Effective date.* The provision applies to requests for GAO investigations made after the date of enactment (Act Sec. 4001(b)(1) of the IRS Restructuring and Reform Act of 1998).

Act Sec. 4001(a), adding Code Sec. 8021(e); Act Sec. 4001(b)(1). Law at ¶ 6910. Committee Report at ¶ 10,740.

Annual Joint Congressional Review

¶ 871

Background _____

A number of different committees have jurisdiction over IRS oversight. Committees that share responsibility for IRS oversight include the House Committees on Ways and Means, Appropriations, Government Reform and Oversight; the Senate Committees on Finance, Appropriations, and Governmental Affairs; and the Joint Committee on Taxation. These committees typically act independently, have separate hearings, and make separate investigations of IRS matters. The National Commission on Restructuring the IRS found that the committees responsible for IRS oversight focused on different issues from year to year, and none of these issues involved high-level or strategic matters (A Vision for a New IRS: Report of the National Commission on Restructuring the Internal Revenue Service, June 25, 1997). Coordination of the different committee activities is desirable in order to improve the ability of Congress to set strategic direction and focus on long-term objectives.

The Restructuring Commission noted that the current structure is reactive rather than strategic. The IRS reacts to pressures applied by Congress from different oversight committees. The focus is often issue by issue, rather than taking an integrated and strategic direction. The traditional role of Congress has been to respond to specific complaints, rather than address core issues facing the IRS. In order to transform the reactive system into one that could reinforce change, the Commission suggested providing a structure in which Congress could give clear and consistent direction to the IRS on "macro" issues.

IRS Restructuring and Reform Impact

Joint congressional review of IRS.—A joint congressional review of the strategic plans and budget for the IRS will be held once a year as part of the effort to coordinate ongoing high-level oversight of the IRS. The joint review will be held at the call of the Chair of the Joint Committee on Taxation, before June 1 of each year from 1999 to 2003. Participants in the hearing will include three members (two majority and one minority) from each of the committees with shared jurisdiction over the IRS. The participating Senate committees are Finance, Appropriations, and Governmental Affairs. The participating House committees are Ways and Means, Appropriations, and Governmental Reform and Oversight (Code Sec. 8021(f)(2), as added by the IRS Reform and Restructuring Act of 1998).

The topics to be covered in the joint review, according to the Conference Committee Report, include: (1) IRS progress in meeting its objectives under its strategic and business plans; (2) IRS progress in improving taxpayer service and compliance; (3) IRS progress on technology modernization; and (4) the annual filing season. The topics to be addressed at this session are covered in the Joint Committee on Taxation report required by Code Sec. 8022(3)(C) (as added by Act Sec. 4022(a) of the 1998 Act) (see ¶ 873 for discussion of the reports to be filed by the Joint Committee).

The Chief of Staff of the Joint Committee on Taxation, as well as the Joint Committee staff, is directed to provide assistance as needed to facilitate these joint reviews (Code Sec. 8021(f)(1), as added by the 1998 Act).

The jurisdiction of the committees involved in the joint hearings is not modified. Ways and Means and Finance Committees retain jurisdiction over tax policy; and Appropriations committees retain jurisdiction over spending.

★ *Effective date.* The provision is effective on the date of enactment; however, the requirement for an annual joint review shall apply only for calendar years 1999—2003 (Act Sec. 4001(b)(2) of the IRS Restructuring and Reform Act of 1998).

Act Sec. 4001(a), adding Code Sec. 8021(f); Act Sec. 4001(b). Law at 6910. Committee Report at ¶ 10,745.

Annual Joint Committee Reports

¶ 873

Background————————————————————————

The statutory duties of the Joint Committee on Taxation are defined under Code Sec. 8022. The Joint Committee's official duties include investigating matters related to federal taxes, such as the operation and effects of the federal tax laws and the administration of taxes by the IRS. The Joint Committee is also directed to investigate methods for the simplification of income taxes, and to publish proposed measures for simplification from time to time. Reports to the Senate Finance Committee and House Ways and Means Committee on Joint Committee investigations, together with any recommendations the Joint Committee might have, may also be submitted from time to time. Reports to the rest of the House or Senate are permissible as the Joint Committee determines. Prior to the IRS Restructuring and Reform Act of 1998, the Joint Committee was not specifically required by statute to make annual reports to any House or Senate Committees.

IRS Restructuring and Reform Impact

Reports by the Joint Committee on Taxation.—The Joint Committee on Taxation will be required to make regularly scheduled reports to Congress, as well as discretionary reports that may be made from time to time. At least once each Congress, the Joint Committee is required to report to the Senate Finance Committee and the House Ways and Means Committee on the overall state of the federal tax system (Code Sec. 8022(3)(B), as added by the IRS Restructuring and Reform Act of 1998). The report is to include recommendations on proposals to simplify the tax system, as well as other matters relating to administration of the federal tax system as the Joint Committee deems advisable.

Comment. The Joint Committee's duty to report on the state of the federal tax system will not take effect unless funds necessary to carry out the requirement are specifically appropriated to the Joint Committee (Code Sec. 8022(3)(B), as added by the 1998 Act).

In addition to regular reports on the overall state of the federal tax system, the Joint Committee on Taxation will be required to produce an annual report covering the types of matters likely to be discussed as part of the joint congressional review of the IRS to be held each year under Code Sec. 8021(f)(2) (as added by the 1998 Act; see ¶ 871). This report will be directed to the committees with shared responsibility for IRS oversight that participate in the joint review: the Senate Committees on Finance, Appropriations, and Governmental Affairs, and the House Committees on Ways and Means, Appropriations, and Government Reform and Oversight. The topics covered in the report are the same as the topics likely to be covered by the joint IRS oversight sessions:

(1) IRS strategic and business plans;

(2) IRS progress in meeting its objectives;

(3) the IRS budget and whether it supports its objectives;

(4) IRS progress in improving taxpayer service and compliance;

(5) IRS progress on technology modernization; and

(6) the annual filing season (Code Sec. 8022(3)(C), as added by the 1998 Act).

The annual reports covering the joint congressional reviews of the IRS will be necessary only for years 1999 through 2003. The annual joint congressional reviews required under Code Sec. 8021(f)(2) (as added by the 1998 Act) are scheduled to cease after five years, in 2004.

Less regularly scheduled reports may be submitted from time to time to the Ways and Means and Finance Committees, at the discretion of the Joint Committee, to report on the results of any investigations undertaken by the JCT, as well as any recommendations that it may deem advisable (Code Sec. 8022(3)(A), as added by the 1998 Act). Discretionary reports were the only type of reports mentioned in the Code prior to the 1998 Act.

★ *Effective date.* The provision is effective on the date of enactment, however, the requirement for an annual report covering topics related to the joint IRS review shall apply only for calendar years 1999–2003 (Act Sec. 4002(b) of the IRS Restructuring and Reform Act of 1998).

Act Sec. 4002(a), amending Code Sec. 8022(3); Act Sec. 4002(b). Law at ¶ 6920. Committee Report at ¶ 10,750.

Study of Payments Made to Informants

¶ 876

The IRS is authorized to pay rewards for information relating to civil violations, as well as criminal violations (Code Sec. 7623). Rewards are paid out of the proceeds of amounts (other than interest) collected by reason of the information provided. An annual report on the rewards program is required under Act Sec. 1209(d) of Taxpayer Bill of Rights 2 (P.L. 104-168). The report is to include the amounts paid out during the year under Code Sec. 7623, as well as the amounts collected as a result of the information obtained from the informants.

IRS Restructuring and Reform Impact

Study of payments made to informants to detect underpayments.—The Secretary of the Treasury is required to conduct a study on the use of reward payments under Code Sec. 7623, which authorizes payments to be made to detect underpayments of tax and to bring to trial persons guilty of tax crimes (Act Sec. 3804 of the IRS Restructuring and Reform Act of 1998). The study must be conducted not later than one year after the date of enactment, and the results are to be reported to Congress. The study is to include:

(1) an analysis of the present use of rewards under Code Sec. 7623 and the results of the use of the rewards program;

(2) any legislative or administrative recommendations regarding the rewards provision and its application.

★ *Effective date.* No specific effective date is provided by the Act. The provison is, therefore, considered effective on the date of enactment. The study on the use of payments to informants shall be conducted not later than one year after the date of enactment.

Act Sec. 3804. Law at ¶ 8205. Committee Report at ¶ 10,730.

Taxpayer Noncompliance Study

¶ 877

Background

IRS Commissioner Charles Rossotti testified before the Senate Finance Committee that one of the ways the IRS should strive to serve taxpayers is by improving compliance levels. A fair tax system is one in which everyone pays their fair share. According to figures quoted by Rossotti, the average taxpayer pays $1,600 more in taxes each year as a result of their countrymen's failure to fully comply with their federal tax obligations. The belief by a growing number of Americans that more people get away with paying less taxes than they should also erodes confidence in the IRS and the tax system as a whole.

Rossotti specifically requested the Committee to requisition a study of willful noncompliance. The study was featured as one of the seven points in Rossotti's plan to improve the IRS Criminal Investigation Division (announced April 27, 1998, in IRS News Release IR-98-34). The review requested by the Commissioner would examine the sources and extent of taxpayer noncompliance and measures that would address the problem (Testimony before the Senate Finance Committee, May 1, 1998).

IRS Restructuring and Reform Impact

Study of taxpayer noncompliance with Internal Revenue laws.—A joint study conducted by the Secretary of the Treasury and the IRS Commissioner, in consultation with the Joint Committee on Taxation, will examine noncompliance by taxpayers. Willful noncompliance, as well as noncompliance due to tax law complexity or other factors, will be examined in the study. The findings of the study will be reported to Congress. The study is to be conducted within one year after the date of enactment of the IRS Restructuring and Reform Act of 1998 (Act Sec. 3803 of the 1998 Act).

★ *Effective date.* No specific effective date is provided by the Act. The provision is, therefore, considered effective on the date of enactment. The study on noncompliance must be conducted not more than one year after the date of enactment.

Act Sec. 3803. Law at ¶ 8200. Committee Report at ¶ 10,725.

Milwaukee and Waukesha IRS Offices

¶ 879

Background ——————————————————————————————————

The independent review of Milwaukee and Waukesha, Wisconsin, IRS offices proposed by Senator Herb Kohl (D-Wis) stems from a history of allegations of discrimination in these IRS offices. Senator Russell Feingold (D-Wis) cosponsored the Senate amendment to the IRS Restructuring and Reform Act of 1998 that would have required independent review of these issues.

Specific allegations of misconduct include the NAACP's accusation that the IRS stifled hiring and advancement opportunities for blacks at IRS offices in Milwaukee and Waukesha, Wisconsin. Complaints were also received by the offices of U.S. Senators from Wisconsin Russell Feingold and Herb Kohl.

The Midwest District office of the IRS (directed by Robert Brazzil) commissioned a study in January 1998 to investigate the allegations. The task force convened to conduct the study found widespread sentiment in the Milwaukee and Waukesha offices that employees from all ethnic groups and both genders felt that other groups were receiving favorable treatment. The study concluded that the offices suffered from a general lack of goodwill and trust.

The Milwaukee NAACP criticized the investigation and its report, noting that the independent investigation board was not independent because it was made up mostly of IRS officials. According to Milwaukee NAACP president Felmers Chaney, the study failed to address specific allegations of discrimination such as the use of racial slurs by an IRS manager.

In February 1998, Charles Fowler III, national director of equal employment opportunity and diversity for the IRS, spoke to a group of IRS managers from Wisconsin, Nebraska and Iowa at a Milwaukee hotel. Fowler urged the managers to support the IRS's commitment to equal opportunity and diversity programs.

IRS Restructuring and Reform Impact

Independent review of employment practices at IRS Wisconsin offices.—The Act does not specifically require the IRS to appoint an independent expert to review employment issues at the Wisconsin offices as proposed by the Senate amendment. Under the Senate amendment, the IRS would have been required to appoint an independent expert in employment and personnel matters to review the January 1998 study of equal opportunity processes in the IRS offices of Milwaukee and Waukesha, Wisconsin. Instead, the conference agreement states that the conferees intend for the task force initiated in January 1998 to continue its investigation to conclusion. The conferees also intend that the General Accounting Office will review the report of the task force and report to the House Ways and Means Committee and the Senate Finance Committee.

The independent review originally requested by Senators Kohl and Feingold would have included a determination of the accuracy and validity of the original investigation, and, if determined necessary by the expert, a further investigation of the Wisconsin offices relating to the equal employment opportunity process and any alleged discriminatory employment-related actions, including any alleged violations of federal law (Sec. 1106(a) of H.R. 2676, as approved by the Senate on May 7, 1998).

Committee Report at ¶ 11,575.

IRS Historical Archives

¶ 881

Background ————————————————————————————————————

The IRS has not historically adhered to a comprehensive recordkeeping program. All federal agencies are required to deposit significant and historical records with the National Archives and Records Administration (NARA). However, since Code Sec. 6103 prohibits the IRS from disclosing confidential return information, the IRS has denied access to its internal records to NARA. Instead, the IRS prescreens its own records and denies access to any records that the IRS determines might contain protected return information. In the interest of developing a history of the IRS through which taxpayers can hold the IRS accountable for its actions, the National Commission on Restructuring the IRS recommended that NARA be given access to all IRS records for purposes of evaluating their historical significance (A Vision for a New IRS: Report of the National Commission on Restructuring the Internal Revenue Service, June 25, 1997). NARA has expressed concern that the IRS may be using the Code Sec. 6103 disclosure provision to improperly conceal agency records with historical significance.

IRS Restructuring and Reform Impact

Disclosure of return information to National Archivist.—The IRS is required to disclose tax returns and return information to the National Archives and Records Administration for purposes of determining whether the records are worthy of archiving (Code Sec. 6103(l)(17), as added by the IRS Restructuring and Reform Act of 1998). Disclosure to NARA may not be denied on the basis of the IRS's duty to protect confidential return information under Code Sec. 6103.

Upon written request from the U.S. Archivist, officers and employees of NARA are permitted to examine returns and return information solely for the purpose of appraising the records for destruction or retention by NARA. Disclosure is permitted only to the extent necessary in performing this task.

NARA employees with access to tax return information are prohibited from disclosing the information to any person other than another NARA employee whose official duties require disclosure for purposes of appraising the records. Civil and criminal penalties may apply to employees who make unauthorized disclosures of confidential taxpayer return information in their possession (under Code Sec. 7213 and Code Sec. 7213A).

★ *Effective date.* The amendment applies to requests made by the Archivist of the United States after the date of enactment (Act Sec. 6703(c) of the IRS Restructuring and Reform Act of 1998).

Act Sec. 3702(a), amending Code Sec. 6103(l); Act Sec. 3702(b)(1), amending Code Sec. 6103(p)(3)(A); Act Sec. 3702(b)(2), amending Code Sec. 6103(p)(4); Act Sec. 3702(b)(3), amending Code Sec. 6103(p)(4)(F)(ii); Act Sec. 3702(c). Law at ¶ 6110. Committee Report at ¶ 10,640.

Records of Taxpayer Complaints

¶ 886

Background ————————————————————————————————————

The IRS is required to make an annual report to the House Ways and Means Committee and the Senate Finance Committee on all instances involving allegations of misconduct by IRS employees. This requirement was instituted in 1996 by the Taxpayer Bill of Rights 2 (P.L. 104-168, Act Sec. 1211). The report must identify categories of any misconduct allegations during the past year, the number

Background _____

of instances in each category, and the disposition during the year of any complaints, regardless of when the misconduct occurred. The report covers misconduct identified internally by the IRS as well as cases arising from taxpayer or third-party complaints.

The IRS has not been required to record allegations of misconduct against particular employees. In order to increase the public perception that the IRS is taking allegations of misconduct seriously, the House Committee Report for the IRS Restructuring and Reform Bill suggested requiring personnel details to be recorded. In the absence of records containing details about taxpayer complaints of misconduct against individual employees, the IRS would not be able to adequately investigate the allegations or properly prepare its report to Congress.

IRS Restructuring and Reform Impact

Records of complaints against individual IRS employees.—In collecting data for the IRS's annual report to Congress on allegations of IRS employee misconduct, the IRS is required to maintain records of taxpayer complaints on an individual-employee basis (Act Sec. 3701 of the IRS Restructuring and Reform Act of 1998). According to the House Committee Report, individual records are not to be listed in the IRS's annual report to Congress on instances of employee misconduct (this report is required by Act Sec. 1211 of the Taxpayer Bill of Rights 2, P.L. 104-168). However, according to the House Committee Report, records of misconduct relating to individual IRS employees are to be used in evaluating individual employee performance.

★ *Effective date.* No specific effective date is provided by the Act. The provision is, therefore, considered effective on the date of enactment. Individual records must be maintained beginning not later than January 1, 2000.

Act Sec. 3701. Law at ¶ 8160. Committee Report at ¶ 10,635.

Removal of "Illegal Tax Protestor" Designation

¶ 891

Background _____

Individuals who meet certain criteria are designated as "illegal tax protesters" in the IRS Master File. The process of receiving this designation starts in the IRS Service Centers, where return classifiers are responsible for reviewing returns according to their level of questionability. The Classification Handbook provides guidelines used to flag returns with tax protester or frivolous return potential. According to the guidelines, a return has potential for referral to the special examination program for tax protesters if it has these characteristics (Internal Revenue Manual Handbook 41(12)0, Section 840):

(1) contributions to unrecognized churches;

(2) refusals to include tax return information on a constitutional basis;

(3) reducing gross income because of the declining value of the dollar;

(4) vow of poverty statements;

(5) involvement with family estate trusts;

(6) reliance on the gold or silver standard;

(7) blank returns; or

(8) protest statements attached to the return.

Background ───────────────────────────────────

Illegal tax protester schemes are further defined in Internal Revenue Manual 4293.14. The IRS District Offices have special Tax Protester Coordinators who are responsible for further evaluation of returns for the Tax Protester Program. Once a return is classified as belonging under the special Illegal Tax Protester program, the taxpayer's record in the IRS Individual Master File will be marked "ITP." Much energy is expended by some taxpayers in challenging these file designations.

The Senate Finance Committee expressed concern that innocent taxpayers may be mislabeled as "illegal tax protesters."

IRS Restructuring and Reform Impact

Illegal Tax Protester designations to be removed.—The IRS is prohibited from designating taxpayers as illegal tax protesters (ITP) or any similar designation. The IRS is required to remove any existing tax protester designations from its Individual Master File (IMF) (Act Sec. 3708(a) of the IRS Restructuring and Reform Act of 1998). Any ITP designation in a place other than the Individual Master File is to be disregarded.

Nonfiler designations are still allowed in appropriate cases. A nonfiler designation must be removed once the taxpayer has filed income tax returns for two consecutive years and paid all taxes shown on the returns (Act Sec. 3707(b) of the 1998 Act).

Comment. Taxpayers who have made threats against IRS employees, have assaulted IRS employees, or who belong to a tax protestor group that advocates violence against IRS employees may be designated as "potentially dangerous taxpayers." This designation remains unchanged under the 1998 Act. The Conference agreement emphasizes that the provision is not intended to jeopardize the safety of IRS employees. If the IRS needs to implement additional procedures, including maintaining records, so as to ensure employees' safety, it has the authority to do so (Conference Committee Report).

PRACTICAL ANALYSIS. Robert McKenzie, of McKenzie & McKenzie PC, Chicago, Ill., comments that the IRS has had a policy over the years of identifying individuals presumed to be tax protesters and encoding its computer systems and all the files relative to those taxpayers with special "P" codes for protestor. That practice has resulted in individuals who have been identified as protestors receiving less courtesy and fewer rights than other individuals. The IRS's goal in establishing this policy was to discourage illegal tax protestors and to make it difficult for them to present their protestor arguments. Act Sec. 3707 prohibits the IRS from identifying individuals as protestors. Those taxpayers, therefore, will now not go through the remainder of their tax life with the scarlet letter "P." Taxpayers will be able to rehabilitate themselves without the stigma of having been identified as protestors. Unfortunately, this change of law will also encourage illegal tax protestors to continue making their spurious arguments. There will be less of a stigma attached to those arguments and IRS employees will be hard pressed to spot some protestor arguments. It is bad policy to create any system that encourages tax protestors to present their discredited arguments.

★ *Effective date.* The provision is effective on the date of enactment, however, removal of any existing ITP designations from the individual master file is not required to begin before January 1, 1999 (Act Sec. 3707(c) of the IRS Restructuring and Reform Act of 1998).

Act Sec. 3707(a); Act Sec. 3707(b); Act Sec. 3707(c). Law at ¶8180. Committee Report at ¶10,665.

OTHER

Public Inspection of Chief Counsel Advice

¶892

Background ————————————————————————————

Generally, all IRS written determinations, including private letter rulings, determination letters, and technical advice memoranda prepared pursuant to taxpayer requests (including any background file document relating to these), are open to public inspection once all identifying details and various commercial and financial information have been deleted (Code Sec. 6110). The disclosure requirements apply to all written determinations, including those issued before July 4, 1967, the effective date of the Freedom of Information Act (FOIA) (5 U.S.C. §552). However, special procedures and exceptions apply to disclosures of IRS written determinations issued pursuant to requests made before November 1, 1976. In addition, Code Sec. 6110(c) provides various exemptions from disclosure that are akin to the exemptions under the FOIA, including identifying details.

In recent years, the IRS has increasingly relied on communications with the Office of the Chief Counsel for general and taxpayer-specific advice. "Written determinations," as defined by Code Sec. 6110(b), prior to amendment by the IRS Restructuring and Reform Act of 1998, did not include unilateral advice issued by the Office of Chief Counsel to IRS field employees or regional or district employees of the Office of Chief Counsel. In 1997, however, pursuant to a not-for-profit publisher's FOIA request, the U.S. Court of Appeals for the District of Columbia upheld a federal district court order compelling the IRS to disclose field service advice memoranda (FSAs), which the IRS had been using to advise field personnel since 1988 (*Tax Analysts,* CA-DC, 97-2 USTC ¶50,529, 117 F3d 607). Although true return information, attorney work product, and matters within the scope of attorney-client privilege could be redacted from the FSAs, no blanket exemption applied to all of the FSAs. The discussions of tax law principles, legal analyses, and conclusions of law contained in the FSAs did not qualify as return information that was excepted from disclosure by Code Sec. 6103. According to the court, there was no difference, relevant to Code Sec. 6103, between FSAs and Technical Advice Memoranda. Both were means by which the Office of Chief Counsel provides field offices with advice about the tax law in response to questions regarding specific factual situations.

Although the decision in *Tax Analysts* resolved some issues, it left others unresolved. For example, there was no mechanism by which taxpayers could participate in the process of redacting information from documents or to resolve disagreements in court. What was clear, however, was that written documents issued by the Office of the Chief Counsel were not governed by Code Sec. 6110.

———

IRS Restructuring and Reform Impact

Public inspection of Chief Counsel advice.—The definition of "written determination" for purposes of Code Sec. 6110 (Public Release of Written Determinations) now includes Chief Counsel advice. As a result, Chief Counsel advice is open to public inspection (Code Sec. 6110(a), as amended by the IRS Restructuring and Reform Act of 1998).

Caution. The Conference Committee Report to the 1998 Act reiterates that Code Sec. 6110 is the exclusive means by which to obtain General Counsel advice for public inspection. Therefore, the FOIA, which was used to obtain field service advice prior to this amendment, may no longer be available to compel the IRS to release advice that originates in the Office of Chief Counsel. However, advice that is not encompassed within the definition of General Counsel advice may be subject to disclosure under the FOIA or other law.

Caution. Like rulings, determination letters, and technical advice memoranda, Chief Counsel advice cannot be relied upon as precedent.

Chief Counsel advice defined. Chief Counsel advice includes any written advice or instruction, under whatever name or designation, prepared and issued by any National Office component of the Office of Chief Counsel to IRS field employees or regional or district employees of the Office of Chief Counsel. Such advice conveys legal interpretations or the IRS or Chief Counsel position or policy concerning revenue provisions. Chief Counsel advice also includes any legal interpretation of state law, foreign law, or federal law that relates to the assessment or collection of liabilities under a revenue provision (Code Sec. 6110(i)(1)(A), as added by the 1998 Act). However, it does not include advice with respect to nontax matters, according to the Conference Committee Report to the 1998 Act. Thus, for example, Chief Counsel advice would not include written advice with respect to an employment law matter, a conflict-of-interest matter, or a procurement matter.

The term "revenue provision" includes, but is not limited to:

(1) the Internal Revenue Code;

(2) regulations;

(3) revenue rulings;

(4) revenue procedures;

(5) other administrative interpretations or guidance, whether published or unpublished (including, for example, other Chief Counsel advice); or

(6) tax treaties (Code Sec. 6110(i)(1)(b), as added by the 1998 Act).

The Conference Committee Report to the 1998 Act clarifies that court decisions and opinions are also encompassed within the definition of revenue provision.

Comment. The Conference Committee drafted this provision with field service advice in mind, as well as a broad spectrum of other possible advice produced by the Office of Chief Counsel. Thus, as provided in the Conference Report, the following existing categories of advice are subject to disclosure in addition to field service advice—technical assistance to the field, service center advice, litigation guideline memoranda, tax litigation bulletins, general litigation bulletins, and criminal tax bulletins. In addition, the IRS may, by regulation, identify additional advice or instruction that is subject to disclosure (Code Sec. 6110(i)(2), as added by the 1998 Act).

Comment. Chief Counsel advice encompasses advice from any National Office component of the Office of Chief Counsel. It may be either general or taxpayer-specific. As such, taxpayer-specific advice from the Associate Chief Counsel (Employee Benefits and Exempt Organizations), Associate Chief Counsel (International), and the Assistant Chief Counsel (Field Service), as well as any taxpayer-specific or nontaxpayer-specific written advice or instructions issued by the National Office of the Chief Counsel to field personnel, is subject to disclosure.

Comment. Code Sec. 6110(b)(2), addressing the scope of background file documents, is not amended and is not discussed in the Conference Committee Report to the 1998 Act. The provision nonetheless applies to Chief Counsel advice. The Conference Committee Report indicates, however, that Chief Counsel advice does not include written recordations of informal telephone advice and drafts of advice sent to the field for review.

Issuance of Chief Counsel advice. Chief Counsel advice is subject to disclosure when it is "issued." According to the Conference Committee Report to the 1998 Act, written advice is deemed to be issued after the following has occurred:

(1) the advice is approved within the National Office component from which the advice was proposed;

(2) the advice is signed by the person authorized to do so (usually the Assistant Chief Counsel or a Branch Chief); and

(3) the advice is sent to the field.

Further regulatory guidance is expected from the IRS with respect to when advice is deemed issued.

Redaction of Chief Counsel advice. Like rulings, determination letters, and technical advice memoranda, certain information in Chief Counsel advice will be redacted. Names, addresses, and other identifying details of taxpayers and other persons will be redacted pursuant to Code Sec. 6110(c)(1) (Code Sec. 6110(i)(3)(A), as added by the 1998 Act). However, new Code Sec. 6110(i)(3)(B) provides that any other information redacted will be determined by reference to subsections (b) and (c) of the FOIA. The information protected by those subsections includes, generally, the same information protected by Code Sec. 6110(c). But, the protected information also includes information related solely to internal personnel rules and practices, inter-agency or intra-agency memoranda or letters that would not be available by law to a party other than an agency in litigation with the agency, and records or information compiled for law enforcement purposes (subject to certain limitations that protect the enforcement process or individuals involved).

Comment. Even though the IRS had lost the battle over release of field service advice in *Tax Analysts,* the extent of the information to be released was still at issue. The Conference Committee recognized that the scope of Chief Counsel advice may involve sensitive matters beyond those discussed in private letter rulings, determination letters, and technical advice memoranda, and, therefore, has clearly distinguished Chief Counsel advice by allowing the IRS to redact information described by subsections (b) and (c) of the FOIA.

Comment. The Conference Committee Report to the 1998 Act indicates that, with respect to discretionary redactions such as those involving inter-agency or intra-agency memoranda or letters, it expects the Office of Chief Counsel to apply standards similar to the standards found in the Internal Revenue Manual Handbook (Internal Revenue Manual Handbook 1230, Internal Management Document System Handbook, § 293(2), CCH INTERNAL REVENUE MANUAL) and the Attorney General's October 4, 1993, Memorandum for Heads of Departments and Agencies.

Notice of intent to disclose. If Chief Counsel advice is written with respect to a specific taxpayer or a group of specific taxpayers, the IRS must mail a notice of intention to disclose (Code Sec. 6110(f)(1)) to each such taxpayer within 60 days of issuance of the advice, along with a copy of the advice with proposed redactions (Code Sec. 6110(i)(4)(B), as added by the 1998 Act). The IRS must, prior to notice, redact identifying information pertaining to other taxpayers (except for information for which the notified taxpayer was the source). The IRS may also redact information protected by the FOIA, as provided in Code Sec. 6110(i)(3), discussed above under the heading "Redaction of Chief Counsel advice." A taxpayer that disagrees with the proposed redaction may seek resolution in accordance with Code Sec. 6110(f), as amended by the 1998 Act.

If the Chief Counsel advice is written without reference to a specific taxpayer or group of specific taxpayers, the IRS must make redactions and make the advice publicly available within 60 days after issuance. The Code Sec. 6110(f) procedures for resolution of disputes do not apply (Code Sec. 6111(i)(4)(A), as added by the 1998 Act).

Civil remedies for improper disclosure—fees. The exclusive civil remedies of Code Sec. 6110 are extended to taxpayers who are the subject of Chief Counsel advice. As a result, a taxpayer may bring an action against the United States in the U.S. Court of Federal Claims if the IRS makes public any General Counsel advice without deleting any of the information required to be deleted under Code Sec. 6110(i)(4)(B). Actual damages (minimum $1,000) and costs may be assessed if the court determines that any IRS employee intentionally or willfully failed to follow the redaction procedures (Code Sec. 6110(j), as redesignated and amended by the 1998 Act). Also, like other written advice subject to public inspection under Code Sec. 6110, the IRS is authorized to collect the actual cost for duplication of the information made public, as well as the cost of making redactions (Code Sec. 6110(k), as redesignated and amended by the 1998 Act).

Electronic publication. The IRS is required to make any Chief Counsel advice that is issued more than 90 days after the date of enactment and is available for public inspection also available by computer telecommunications within one year after issuance (Act Sec. 3509(d)(4) of the 1998 Act).

★ *Effective date.* The amendments to Code Sec. 6110 generally apply to any Chief Counsel advice issued more than 90 days after the date of enactment (Act Sec. 3509(d) of the 1998 Act). See, however, "Special transition rules," below.

Special transition rules. The amendments apply to any Chief Counsel advice issued by the offices of the Associate Chief Counsel for Domestic, Employee Benefits and Exempt Organizations, and International after December 31, 1985, and before the 91st day after the date of enactment. Any such Chief Counsel advice will be treated as made available on a timely basis if it is made available for public inspection not later than:

(1) one year after the date of enactment, in the case of all litigation guideline memoranda, service center advice, tax litigation bulletins, criminal tax bulletins, and general bulletins;

(2) 18 months after the date of enactment, in the case of field service advice and technical assistance to the field issued on or after January 1, 1994;

(3) three years after the date of enactment, in the case of field service advice and technical assistance to the field issued on or after January 1, 1992, and before January 1, 1994; or

(4) six years after the date of enactment, in the case of any other Chief Counsel advice issued after December 31, 1985 (Act Sec. 3509(d)(2) of the 1998 Act).

Moreover, any additional advice or instruction issued by the Office of the Chief Counsel that is determined by IRS regulations to be Chief Counsel advice is to be made available in accordance with the effective date set forth in such regulation (Act Sec. 3509(d)(3) of the 1998 Act).

Act Sec. 3509(a), amending Code Sec. 6110(b)(1); Act Sec. 3509(b), redesignating Code Secs. 6110(i)–(l) as Code Secs. 6110(j)–(m), and adding new Code Sec. 6110(i); Act Sec. 3509(c), amending Code Secs. 6110(f)(1), 6110(j) and 6110(k)(1)(B), as redesignated. Act Sec. 3509(d). Law at ¶ 6140. Committee Report at ¶ 10,605.

Checks Payable to U.S. Treasury

¶ 893

Background

A check or money order in payment for federal taxes is made payable to the Internal Revenue Service (Reg. § 301.6311-1(a)(1)). The IRS is the collector of

Background

revenue for the federal government, and tax monies made payable to it by taxpayers are not kept within the agency itself.

IRS Restructuring and Reform Impact

Payment of taxes.—Checks or money orders for payment of federal taxes are now allowed to be made payable to the United States Treasury, under rules to be established by the Treasury Secretary or delegate (Act Sec. 3703 of the IRS Restructuring and Reform Act of 1998).

Comment. Making checks payable to the U.S. Treasury, rather than to the IRS, may improve the public's awareness of the IRS as merely the collector of revenue for the federal government.

★ *Effective date.* No specific effective date is provided by the Act. The provision is, therefore, considered effective on the date of enactment.

Act Sec. 3703. Law at ¶ 8165. Committee Report at ¶ 10,645.

Form of IRS Election Guidance

¶ 895

Background

Taxpayers are faced with a variety of choices in determining the amount of their tax. For example, a business taxpayer may claim a depreciation deduction for personal tangible property placed in service during the year or elect to expense at least a portion of the cost under what is called a "Section 179 election." Generally, elections taking their authority from the Internal Revenue Code must be made in the manner prescribed by a regulation or an IRS tax form (Code Sec. 7805(d), prior to amendment by the IRS Restructuring and Reform Act of 1998).

IRS Restructuring and Reform Impact

Authority to make elections.—The Act clarifies that the IRS may prescribe the manner of making any election by any reasonable means. The removal of the language "by regulations or forms" from Code Sec. 7805(d) is intended to eliminate any confusion over the manner in which elections may be prescribed (Code Sec. 7805(d), as amended by the IRS Restructuring and Reform Act of 1998).

★ *Effective date.* No specific effective date is provided by the Act. The provision is, therefore, considered effective as of the date of enactment.

Act Sec. 3704, amending Code Sec. 7805(d). Law at ¶ 6880. Committee Report at ¶ 10,650.

Chapter 9

Improvements in Personnel Flexibilities

GENERAL FLEXIBILITIES

Pay Authority

¶ 901

Background

The provisions found in Act Section 1201(a) and addressed in the following paragraphs (¶ 901-¶ 966) are intended to expand the range of options available to the IRS to motivate, reorient, and reward its employees and to attract highly-skilled individuals from the private sector to the IRS. These personnel flexibility provisions adopt an advancement philosophy based on performance and embrace the notion of individual accountability. They are consistent with IRS reform proposals and are aimed at raising IRS performance standards generally and, specifically, refocusing the IRS toward improved taxpayer assistance services.

IRS Restructuring and Reform Impact

Critical pay authority.—The Act provides specific authority to the Office of Management and Budget (OMB) to set a basic salary rate for certain positions deemed "critical pay positions" at levels higher than are currently authorized under Section 5377 of Title 5 of the United States Code, upon the Treasury Secretary's request (Section 9502 of Title 5 of the United States Code, as added by the IRS Restructuring and Reform Act of 1998). "Critical pay positions" are those highly-skilled technical, administrative and professional positions, other than those subject to streamlined authority (see "streamlined critical pay authority" below), that are considered critical to the IRS's successful execution of its task. The provision authorizes OMB to approve pay requests by the Treasury Secretary, notwithstanding Section 5377(d)(2) of Title 5 of the United States Code, at levels up to the rate of pay of the Vice President (*i.e.*, currently $175,400). Additional cash payments, awards, bonuses, allowances, and differentials to critical pay employees are prohibited if those payments would increase the employee's total annual compensation beyond the compensation of the Vice President (Section 9502 of Title 5 of the United States Code, as added by the IRS Restructuring and Reform Act of 1998).

Streamlined critical pay authority. In addition, the provision creates a streamlined process for the Treasury Secretary (or his delegate) to appoint and set the compensation for a maximum of 40 employees in senior-level management and technical positions if qualifying criteria are met. To utilize the streamlined procedure:

(1) the subject positions must require extremely high-level expertise in an administrative, professional or technical area that is critical to the functioning of the IRS;

(2) recruiting and retaining an individual who is exceptionally well qualified necessitates using streamlined procedures;

(3) there are no more than 40 such positions at any one time;

(4) the Secretary of the Treasury has approved the designation of the positions for streamlined procedures;

(5) the appointments are limited in duration to a maximum of four years;

(6) appointees were not IRS employees prior to June 1, 1998;

(7) the total annual compensation for the positions, including any performance bonuses, does not surpass the rate of pay of the Vice President (*i.e.,* currently $175,400, as per Section 104 of Title 3); and

(8) all such positions are excluded from the collective bargaining unit.

The Treasury Secretary's streamlined authorization runs for a period of 10 years (Section 9503 of Title 5 of the United States Code, as added by the IRS Restructuring and Reform Act of 1998).

★ *Effective date.* No specific effective date is provided by the Act. The provision is, therefore, considered effective on the date of enactment.

Act Sec. 1201(a), amending Part III of Title 5 of the United States Code by adding Section 9502 and Section 9503. Law at ¶ 8025. Committee Report at ¶ 10,185.

Recruitment, Retention, Relocation Incentives, and Relocation Expenses

¶ 931

Background

Under prior law, the payment of incentives was limited, under Sections 5753 and 5754 of Title 5 of the United States Code, to certain types of employees (*e.g.,* those with unusually high or unique qualifications, those who agreed to complete a specified period of employment with the IRS) in certain situations (*e.g.,* where filling a vacancy would be difficult absent a bonus, where there was a special need for the employee's services, where the agency determined that the employee would be likely to leave absent a retention allowance) and was restricted to a maximum amount of 25 percent of the employee's rate of basic pay.

IRS Restructuring and Reform Impact

Authority to offer incentives.—To improve the IRS's ability to recruit and retain talented employees, the Act provides the Secretary of the Treasury with enhanced flexibility to grant recruitment, retention and relocation incentives.

The Treasury Secretary is authorized under this provision to depart from the guidelines of Section 5753 and Section 5754 of Title 5 of the United States Code for a period of 10 years, subject to the approval of the Office of Personnel Management (OPM). Also, the Treasury Secretary is authorized, for a period of 10 years, to pay allowable relocation expenses under Section 5724a for employees who are transferred or reemployed and to pay allowable travel and transportation expenses under Section 5723 from appropriations made to the IRS for any new appointee appointed to a critical pay position (see ¶ 901) after June 1, 1998 (Section 9504 of

Title 5 of the United States Code, as added by the IRS Restructuring and Reform Act of 1998).

★ *Effective date.* The Act provides no specific effective date. The provision is, therefore, considered effective on the date of enactment.

Act Sec. 1201(a), amending Part III of Title 5 of the United States Code by adding Section 9504. Law at ¶ 8025. Committee Report at ¶ 10,185.

Performance Awards

¶ 936

Background

Under prior law, codified at Section 5384 of Title 5 of the United States Code, career appointees in the Senior Executive Service (SES) were eligible for performance awards only if their performance was deemed "fully successful" during their last performance appraisal. Further, the amount of an award was limited to 5 to 20 percent of the individual's rate of basic pay. An additional constraint on the availability of performance awards was the fact that Section 5384 limited the aggregate amount that the agency could pay in any fiscal year (equivalent to either three percent of the aggregate amount of basic pay for career appointees or 15 percent of the average of the annual rates of basic pay given to SES employees during the prior fiscal year, whichever was greater).

IRS Restructuring and Reform Impact

Senior Executive Service (SES).—The Act provides the Treasury Secretary with greater flexibility to pay bonuses to Senior Executive Service (SES) managers based on their performance. This is intended to encourage a shift in focus by IRS senior management toward aligning employees' performance with a broader set of IRS organizational objectives, such as improving taxpayer services and fostering personnel accountability.

While the awards are not restricted by prior criteria and salary percentage caps found at Section 5384(b)(2) of Title 5 of the United States Code, they are limited to the extent that they may not boost an employee's total annual compensation past the rate of pay of the Vice President (i.e., currently $175,400). In addition, an award in excess of 20 percent of an executive's rate of basic pay must be approved by the Treasury Secretary. A limitation is also placed on the aggregate amount of performance awards payable during any fiscal year (equivalent to five percent of the aggregate amount of basic pay paid to career senior executives in the IRS in the prior fiscal year). The Treasury Secretary's authorization to pay performance awards extends for 10 years (Section 9505 of Title 5 of the United States Code, as added by the IRS Restructuring and Reform Act of 1998).

Factors to be considered by the Secretary in determining whether to award a performance bonus include that manager's contribution toward attaining IRS goals under the Government Performance and Results Act of 1993, division E of the Clinger-Cohen Act of 1996 (P.L. 104-106), Revenue Procedure 64-22 (as in effect on July 30, 1997), taxpayer service surveys, and other performance criteria set by the IRS Oversight Board.

★ *Effective date.* No specific effective date is provided by the Act. The provision is, therefore, considered effective on the date of enactment.

Act Sec. 1201(a), amending Part III of Title 5, United States Code by adding Section 9505. Law at ¶ 8025. Committee Report at ¶ 10,185.

Performance Management System

¶941

Background _____

Under prior law, IRS employees were subject to a performance appraisal system authorized by Chapter 43 of Title 5 of the United States Code. As noted in the *Report of the National Commission on Restructuring the Internal Revenue Service* (June 25, 1997), the IRS's internal measurement systems (the Field Office Performance Index (FOPI), the Service Center Operations Index (SCOI), and the formal measurement system for evaluating employee performance) were viewed by employees as ineffective both with respect to assessing long-term quality performance and in influencing employee behavior. Employees tended to focus on meeting short-term performance and efficiency goals instead of trying to balance efficiency, quality and taxpayer service concerns, the report indicated. Consequently, the performance measures were not supporting the declared goals of the IRS.

IRS Restructuring and Reform Impact

Employee performance evaluations.—The new law authorizes the Treasury Secretary to depart from the current performance appraisal system, codified at Section 4302 of Title 5 of the United States Code, and create a new performance management system for the IRS in which individual accountability is stressed. The law calls upon the Treasury Secretary to establish this new system within one year of the enactment of this section.

The system should stress the need to achieve a balance between collection and enforcement results and improved taxpayer assistance services in evaluating performance. Consistent with broader plans for organizational restructuring at the IRS, periodic employee performance evaluations are required.

Individual accountability is to be maintained by:

(1) establishing one or more retention standards for each employee related to the work of the employee and expressed in terms of performance;

(2) providing for periodic performance evaluations to determine whether employees are meeting the applicable retention standards; and

(3) taking appropriate action, in accordance with applicable laws and regulations, with respect to any employee whose performance does not meet established retention standards. These actions include denial of increases in basic pay, promotions, and credit for performance, as well as reassignment, suspension, reduction in grade or pay, removal or other appropriate actions to redress a performance problem (Section 9508(a)(1) of Title 5 of the United States Code, as added by the IRS Restructuring and Reform Act of 1998).

The evaluations would determine pay adjustments, compliance with retention standards, cash awards, and other personnel actions. Further, the system would set objectives for individual, group or organizational performance to help create a more motivated work force.

Comment. According to a GAO report issued on March 12, 1998, it appears that the intention is to apply the new performance management system to Senior Executive Service (SES) employees and non-SES employees as well.

★ *Effective date.* No specific effective date is provided by the Act. The provision is, therefore, considered effective on the date of enactment.

Act Sec. 1201(a), amending Part III of Title 5 of the United States Code by adding Section 9508. Law at ¶ 8025. Committee Report at ¶ 10,185.

Classification and Pay

¶946

Under prior law, the IRS used a position-classification system, in accordance with Section 5102 of Title 5 of the United States Code, with jobs classified in various classes and grades according to the individual's duties, responsibilities, and qualifications.

IRS Restructuring and Reform Impact

General work force.—The provision authorizes the Treasury Secretary to restructure the job classification and pay systems to better accommodate the broader organizational restructuring that is envisioned in the Act's IRS restructuring and reform provisions. Specifically, the Secretary of the Treasury may combine grades and related ranges of salaries and create one or more "broad-banded systems" for all or any portion of the IRS work force (Section 9509 of Title 5 of the United States Code, as added by the IRS Restructuring and Reform Act of 1998). This system will be used for salary, performance tracking, and other purposes.

The new system will still be subject to criteria set by the Office of Personnel Management (OPM) including:

(1) ensuring that the concept of equal pay for substantially equal work is retained;

(2) fixing the minimum and maximum number of grades that may be merged into pay bands;

(3) setting requirements for minimum and maximum pay rates in each band;

(4) establishing pay adjustment rules within a pay band;

(5) setting requirements for the salaries of supervisory personnel within a pay band; and

(6) creating methods for converting the salaries of employees who are appointed to or move between a broad-banded system and another type of pay system.

★ *Effective date.* No specific effective date is provided by the Act. The provision is, therefore, considered effective on the date of enactment.

Act Sec. 1201(a), amending Part III of Title 5, United States Code by adding Section 9509. Law at ¶8025. Committee Report at ¶10,185.

Staffing

¶956

Under prior law, codified in Title 5 of the United States Code, the IRS was limited in its ability to hire, promote, reassign, and monitor its employees.

IRS Restructuring and Reform Impact

General work force staffing flexibilities.—The Act allows the IRS to fill certain permanent positions with temporary employees, establish category rating systems for evaluating job applications, and establish probation periods of up to three years.

Selection of temporary employees for general workforce permanent positions. To afford additional flexibility in filling permanent positions within the competitive service, the Act permits the IRS to select qualified temporary employees (using the generally applicable internal competitive promotion procedures). To qualify to compete for a permanent position in the general workforce, a temporary employee must have completed at least two years of continuous service under a term appointment or any combination of term appointments which were made under competitive procedures prescribed for permanent appointments. In addition, the employee's temporary job performance must meet the applicable retention standards (see ¶ 941). (For an employee not subject to these retention standards, the employee's performance must have been rated at the "fully successful" level or higher). Finally, the term appointment to the temporary position occupied by the employee must have stated that there was a potential for subsequent conversion to a permanent appointment (Section 9510(a) of Title 5 of the United States Code, as added by the IRS Restructuring and Reform Act of 1998).

Two-category rating system. The Act further permits the IRS to create a two-category rating system, in contrast to the individual numerical ratings in the competitive system (codified at Section 3302 of Title 5 of the United States Code) that previously applied, when evaluating IRS applicants. Under the two-category system, managers can choose any candidate from the highest quality category, irrespective of the candidate's individual rating. While the IRS would still have to list preference eligibles ahead of other individuals in each quality category, the appointing manager could select any candidate from the highest quality category if rules for passing over preference eligibles have been met.

Three-year probation period. Further, the Act creates a three-year probation for IRS employees when a shorter period is insufficient to properly evaluate an employee's proficiency at a given position.

Limited appointments in Senior Executive Service. The Act also extends the definition of "career reserved position" within the Senior Executive Service (SES) to include a limited term appointee or a limited emergency appointee (Section 9506 of Title 5 of the United States Code, as added by the IRS Restructuring and Reform Act of 1998). Now, not only would a career appointee qualify for these positions, but an individual who held a career or career-conditional appointment outside the SES immediately prior to assuming the career reserved position or one who had advance approval from the Office of Personnel Management would qualify as well. These positions are limited in number and may not exceed 10 percent of the total number of SES positions at the IRS. The appointments are also limited in duration, lasting only three years. The appointees may serve two three-year terms (plus any unexpired term that existed when the individual assumed the appointment).

★ *Effective date.* No specific effective date is provided by the Act. The provision, therefore, is considered effective on the date of enactment.

Act Sec. 1201(a), amending Part III of Title 5 of the United States Code by adding Section 9506 and Section 9510. Law at ¶ 8025. Committee Report at ¶ 10,185.

Demonstration Project Authority

¶ 961

Background ──

Under prior law, codified at Section 4703 of Title 5 of the United States Code, the Office of Personnel Management, or an agency under its supervision, had to comply with an extensive set of requirements in order to conduct a study to assess whether a proposed change in personnel management procedures or policies would, in fact, improve federal personnel management. These requirements included holding a public hearing on the proposed plan, providing notice to Congress and affected employees at least 180 days prior to the time that the plan would go into effect, issuing a report on the final version of the plan to Congress at least 90 days before the project took effect, conducting projects that involved less than 5,000 individuals, and limiting the number of active demonstration projects (*i.e.*, no more than 10 ongoing projects at one time).

IRS Restructuring and Reform Impact

Streamlined authority for demonstration projects.—Under the Act, the IRS may utilize a streamlined process in conducting research on employee performance and testing alternative management constructs (Section 9507(b) of Title 5 of the United States Code, as added by the IRS Restructuring and Reform Act of 1998).

The Secretary of the Treasury and the Office of Personnel Management (OPM) are also authorized to make a demonstration project permanent by waiving termination of the project. To accomplish this, 90 days prior to waiving the termination date, the OPM must:

(1) publish a notice of its intent in the *Federal Register*; and

(2) provide written notice of its intent to both Houses of Congress (Section 9507(c) of Title 5 of the United States Code, as added by the IRS Restructuring and Reform Act of 1998).

Comment. According to the controlling Senate Committee Report, the OPM is required to provide written notification to all concerned congressional committees (*e.g.*, the House Ways and Means Committee, the House Government Reform and Oversight Committee, the Senate Finance Committee, and the Senate Government Affairs Committee).

★ *Effective date.* No specific effective date is provided by the Act. The provision is, therefore, considered effective on the date of enactment.

Act Sec. 1201(a), amending Part III of Title 5 of the United States Code by adding Section 9507. Law at ¶ 8025. Committee Report at ¶ 10,185.

Effect of a Collective Bargaining Agreement

¶ 966

IRS Restructuring and Reform Impact

Limitation on application of personnel flexibility provisions.—Under the Act, IRS employees who are members of the employees' union will not be subject to personnel flexibilities regarding streamlined demonstration project authority, a general workforce performance management system, general workforce classification and pay rules, and general workforce staffing rules, as addressed in Sections 9507 through 9510 of Title 5 of the United States Code, as added by the Internal Revenue Service Restructuring and Reform Act of 1998 (see ¶ 941-¶ 961 for further details), unless a written agreement between the union representative and the IRS specifically provides for the proposed practices. In the event of a negotiating impasse in discussions between the union and the IRS, the Federal Services Impasse Panel may impose an agreement (Section 9501(c) of Title 5 of the United States Code, as added by the IRS Restructuring and Reform Act of 1998).

Additional limitations. In general, the IRS is required to exercise all of the new personnel flexibilities consistent with existing rules relating to merit system principles, prohibited personnel practices, and preference eligibles. Further, the Secretary of the Treasury must provide the Office of Personnel Management with any information the latter requires to carry out its responsibilities under this provision (Section 9501(a) and (b) of Title 5 of the United States Code, as added by the Internal Revenue Service Restructuring and Reform Act of 1998).

★ *Effective date.* No specific effective date is provided by the Act. The provision is, therefore, considered effective on the date of enactment.

Act Sec. 1201(a), amending Part III of Title 5 of the United States Code by adding Section 9501. Law at ¶ 8025. Committee Report at ¶ 10,185.

ADDITIONAL FLEXIBILITIES

Voluntary Separation Incentive Payments

¶ 971

Background

Section 5597 of Title 5, United States Code, and various noncodified provisions modeled after that section, grant the Department of Defense and other government agencies the authority to offer incentive payments, or "buyouts," to employees who voluntarily terminate their employment with the government. One of these noncodified provisions granted authority to executive agencies in general, including the IRS, to offer such buyouts for employees who left before December 31, 1997 (P.L. 104-208, Div. A, Title I, Sec. 101(f) [Title VI, Sec.663]).

Under authority of this provision, the IRS Commissioner offered to buyout as many as 2,900 IRS employees in December 1997. In his statement before the Senate Finance Committee on January 28, 1998, the Commissioner requested that Congress reauthorize the buyout authority so that he would have sufficient flexibility to reposition the IRS workforce to be more responsive to taxpayer needs.

IRS Restructuring and Reform Impact

Buyouts reauthorized: Terms of acceptance: Purpose.—The Commissioner is reauthorized to offer qualifying employees a cash incentive to voluntarily terminate their employment to the extent necessary to carry out the plan to reorganize the IRS as mandated by the Act (Act Sec. 1202(b)(1) of the IRS Restructuring and Reform Act of 1998) (see ¶ 801). Individuals who accept such a buyout will be discouraged from returning to government service for five years. Specifically, anyone accepting paid employment or a personal services contract with the U.S. government or any of its agencies within five years from the date of separation will have to return the entire amount of the buyout to the IRS. No proration is allowed (Act Sec. 1202(d) of the 1998 Act).

Voluntary separations are not necessarily intended to reduce the total number of full-time positions at the IRS. The IRS may use vacated, full-time positions to make other positions available to more critical locations or more critical occupations (Act Sec. 1202(e) of the 1998 Act).

Employees covered. Not all IRS employees qualify for buyouts. Employees must meet the definition of "employee" in 5 USC § 2105. Moreover, they must have been employed by the IRS for a continuous period of three years under an unlimited appointment. In addition, the following categories of employees are expressly excluded from receiving buyouts (Act Sec. 1202(a) of the 1998 Act):

(1) reemployed annuitants;

(2) employees with a disability who are or would be eligible for disability retirement;

(3) employees who have been notified they will be terminated for misconduct or poor performance;

(4) employees who, upon completing an additional period of service, would qualify for a voluntary separation incentive under the Federal Workforce Restructuring Act of 1994 (5 U.S.C.§ 5597);

(5) employees who previously received a voluntary separation incentive payment and have not repaid such amount;

(6) employees transferred to another organization who have a statutory right of reemployment; and

(7) employees who, within the past 24 months, have received a recruitment or relocation bonus or who, within the past 12 months, have received a retention allowance.

Payment form: Termination date. The buyout must be paid in a lump sum, from appropriations or funds available for payment of basic pay, and must not be greater than either (1) the amount of severance pay authorized by statute, or (2) an amount determined by the organization head, up to $25,000, whichever is less (Act Sec. 1202(b)(2) of the 1998 Act). The incentive payment would be independent of any other government benefit, including severance pay based on any other separation, to which the employee is entitled. Employees accepting such a payment must voluntarily terminate employment before January 1, 2003.

Example. Alice Grayson accepts an IRS buyout effective immediately. Grayson is a qualifying employee who is 43 years old and makes $800 in basic pay per week. She has been working with the IRS for 14 years and has no other government service. Her authorized severance is computed by adding one week's pay for each year of her first 10 years of service ($800 × 10 = $8,000), and two weeks' pay for every remaining year of service ($1,600 × 4 = $6,400). Her basic severance equals $14,400, to which is added an age adjustment equal to 10% of the basic severance for each year by which her age exceeds 40 ([$14,400 × 0.10 = $1,440] × 3 = $4,320). The statutory amount of severance to which Grayson is entitled equals $18,720 (the $14,400 basic severance plus a $4,320 age adjustment). Thus, Grayson's buyout payment will be either $18,720 or any lesser amount that her organization head may determine.

Comment. The current buyout provision closely follows P.L. 104-208, which provided authority for IRS buyouts prior to December 31, 1997, but with an important difference. Under the former provision the IRS had to reduce the total number of funded employee positions in the agency by the number of employees who accepted buyouts (P.L. 104-208, Div. A, Title I, Sec. 101(f), subsection (f)(1) [Title VI, Sec.663(f)(1)]). Under the current scheme, the IRS is expressly authorized to redeploy or use the full-time equivalent positions vacated by voluntary separations (Act Sec. 1202(e)(2) of the 1998 Act).

Additional retirement fund contribution. In addition to any other payment required by law, the IRS must pay to the Civil Service Retirement and Disability Fund an amount equal to 15 percent of the final basic pay of any qualifying employee accepting a buyout. For this purpose, final basic pay means the total basic pay the employee would receive for a year's service computed using the employee's final rate of basic pay (Act Sec. 1202(c) of the 1998 Act).

★ *Effective date.* The Act does not provide a specific effective date. The provision is, therefore, considered effective on the date of enactment.

Act Sec. 1202. Law at ¶ 8030. Committee Report at ¶ 10,190.

Termination of Employment for Misconduct

¶ 976

Background

Section 4303 of Title 5, United States Code, authorizes an agency to remove an employee for "unacceptable performance," as defined in Section 4301 of Title 5. In addition, Section 7513 of Title 5 authorizes an agency to discipline an employee (by applying specified sanctions ranging from furlough to removal, as set forth in Section 7512) only for such cause as will promote the efficiency of the IRS. In general, the courts have interpreted this provision to require a showing that (1) the employee is engaged in misconduct; and (2) there is a connection between such misconduct and the efficiency of the service. *See, King v. Frazier,* CA-DC, 77 F.3d 1361. However, the decision regarding whether to take, and the form of, any disciplinary action is largely left up to the particular agency.

Under both of these provisions, employees subject to removal are generally entitled to certain procedural safeguards including advance written notice, a hearing and a right of appeal.

IRS Restructuring and Reform Impact

Acts requiring termination.—The IRS must terminate an employee (absent direct intervention by the IRS Commissioner as explained below) if there is a final administrative or judicial determination that, in the course of his or her official duties, the employee:

(1) willfully failed to obtain the required approval signatures on documents authorizing the seizure of a taxpayer's home, personal belongings, or business assets;

(2) provided a false statement under oath with respect to a material matter involving a taxpayer or a taxpayer representative;

(3) violated the rights of a taxpayer, taxpayer representative or other employee of the IRS under the U.S. Constitution or under specified civil rights acts (see below);

(4) falsified or destroyed documents to conceal mistakes made by any employee with regard to a matter involving a taxpayer or taxpayer representative;

(5) assaulted or battered a taxpayer, taxpayer representative or other employee of the IRS, but only if there is a criminal conviction or a final civil judgment to that effect;

(6) violated the 1986 Code, Treasury regulations, or IRS policies (including the IRS Manual) for the purpose of retaliating against or harassing a taxpayer or other employee of the IRS;

(7) willfully misused the provisions of Code Sec. 6103 (regarding confidentiality of returns and return information) for the purpose of concealing information from congressional inquiry;

(8) willfully failed to file any tax return required under the Code on or before the required date, unless the failure is due to reasonable cause and not willful neglect;

(9) willfully understated federal tax liability, unless such understatement is due to reasonable cause and not willful neglect; or

(10) threatened to audit a taxpayer for the purpose of extracting personal gain or benefit (Act Sec. 1203(a) and (b) of the IRS Restructuring and Reform Act of 1998).

An employee who is terminated for any of the foregoing reasons will be considered removed for cause on charges of misconduct (Act Sec. 1203(a) of the 1998 Act).

The Conference Committee expanded paragraph (3) above to include constitutional violations in addition to violations of civil rights. Moreover, the prohibition against civil rights violations was clarified by reference to the following laws:

(i) Title VI or VII of the Civil Rights Act of 1964;

(ii) Title IX of the Education Amendments of 1972;

(iii) the Age Discrimination in Employment Act of 1967;

(iv) the Age Discrimination Act of 1975;

(v) Section 501 or 504 of the Rehabilitation Act of 1973; or

(vi) Title I of the Americans with Disabilities Act of 1990.

The Act also makes it clear that, for purposes of the provisions described in (i), (ii) and (iv) above, references to a program or activity receiving federal financial assistance or an education program or activity receiving federal financial assistance includes any IRS program or activity conducted for a taxpayer (Act Sec. 1203(d) of the 1998 Act).

Comment. This provision, defining specific acts of misconduct for which an IRS employee must be terminated, was subjected to several amendments before reaching its present form. Originating in the Senate version that was passed after the original House bill, Act Sec. 1203 initially listed only seven types of misconduct (Act Sec. 1203(b) of the Senate Bill (H.R.2676) as passed on May 7, 1998). However, an amendment proposed by Senator Phil Gramm, R-Tex., added paragraphs (8), (9) and (10) to subsection (b). And, an amendment proposed by Senator William V. Roth, Jr., R-Del., extended the scope of several provisions to include acts of misconduct against taxpayer representatives in addition to taxpayers. The Conference Committee made further changes, adding, for example, the word "willful" in paragraph (1) and clarifying that cases of assault or battery had to be supported by a court judgment. These changes, as well as statements made on the Senate floor, reflect a careful consideration of competing interests. While attempting to include as many instances of serious misconduct as possible, in an effort to change the culture of the IRS, Congress was aware that mandatory dismissal is a drastic measure. As such, it should only be required in clearly egregious or intentional cases of misconduct, not in questionable cases or in cases of negligence.

Discretion of the Commissioner.—As an additional safeguard, the Commissioner may decide to take a personnel action other than mandatory termination (Act Sec. 1203(c) of the 1998 Act). According to the Senate Finance Committee report, the purpose of this exception is to allow the Commissioner to take into account any mitigating factors. However, such a decision is at the sole discretion of the Commissioner and may not be delegated to any other officer. Moreover, the Commissioner's decision on this matter is final and may not be appealed in any administrative or judicial proceeding (Sec. 1203(c)(3) of the 1998 Act).

Comment. Although termination is mandatory in the instances cited, and there is no right of appeal from a decision of the Commissioner, the Act first requires a final administrative or judicial determination of misconduct (a criminal or civil court judgment in the case of assault or battery). Thus, an employee may be able to benefit from the safeguards afforded by the proceedings leading up to the final determination, including, possibly, the right of appeal. The extent to which such procedural safeguards apply, however, will depend in part on when a determination of misconduct becomes final. For example, an administrative determination of wrongdoing may be subject to judicial review, but might nevertheless result in immediate dismissal.

Comment. The grounds for terminating IRS employees in this section are in addition to those in Sections 4303 and 7513 of Title 5, applicable to government employees generally. Thus, there is a potential for conflict to the extent that an act of misconduct falls under this section and under another section of Title 5, especially regarding the procedural safeguards that may apply.

★ *Effective date.* The Act does not provide a specific effective date; the provision, therefore, is considered effective on the date of enactment.

Act Sec. 1203. Law at ¶ 8035. Committee Report at ¶ 10,195.

Basis for Evaluation of IRS Employees

¶ 981

Background ————————————————————————

Section 4302 of Title 5, United States Code, requires each agency to develop one or more performance appraisal systems that:

(1) provide for periodic appraisals of employee job performance;

(2) encourage employee participation in establishing performance standards; and

(3) use the results of such appraisals as a basis for training, rewarding, reassigning, promoting, reducing in grade, retaining and removing employees.

In September 1997, the Senate Finance Committee learned that certain IRS field offices relied on the use of enforcement statistics to measure collection personnel performance. A subsequent IRS audit revealed that the practice was especially widespread in group manager evaluations. The result was a work environment driven by statistical accomplishments that placed taxpayer rights and a fair employee evaluation system at risk (IRS Fact Sheet FS-98-4, January 1998, 98(16) CCH Standard Federal Tax Reports ¶ 46,248).

IRS Restructuring and Reform Impact

Evaluation criteria.—The IRS may not use records of tax enforcement results to evaluate employees or to impose or suggest production quotas or goals for such individuals (Act Sec. 1204(a) of the IRS Restructuring and Reform Act of 1998). Instead, it must use the fair and equitable treatment of taxpayers by IRS employees as one of the standards for evaluating employee performance (Act Sec. 1204(b) of the 1998 Act). Moreover, each quarter, supervisors will be required to certify in writing whether or not tax enforcement results are being used to evaluate employees or to impose or suggest production quotas or goals (Act Sec. 1204(c) of the 1998 Act).

Repeal of prior law. Sec. 6231 of the Technical and Miscellaneous Revenue Act of 1988 (P. L. 100-647) is repealed (Act Sec. 1204(d) of the 1998 Act).

Comment. The language of Act Sec. 1204 of the 1998 Act closely follows that of repealed Sec. 6231. Both provisions prohibit the IRS from using records of tax enforcement results to evaluate employees or to impose or suggest production quotas or goals with respect to such employees. In addition, they both require quarterly certification of compliance. Sec. 6231, however, applied only to employees who were directly involved in collection activities and their immediate supervisors, whereas Act Sec. 1204 extends the prohibition to all IRS employees. Ironically, Sec. 6231 as originally proposed applied to the evaluation of enforcement officers, appeals officers, and reviewers, but was amended in conference to cover only IRS employees directly involved in collection activities and their immediate supervisors.

★ *Effective date.* This provision applies to evaluations conducted on or after the date of enactment of the Act (Act Sec. 1204(e) of the IRS Restructuring and Reform Act of 1998).

Act Sec. 1204(a)-(c). Act Sec. 1204(d), repealing Act Sec. 6231 of the Technical and Miscellaneous Revenue Act of 1988 (P.L. 100-647). Act Sec.1204(e). Law at ¶ 8040. Committee Report at ¶ 10,200.

Employee Training Program

¶ 986

Background ————————————————————————

Section 4103 of Title 5, U. S. Code, directs the head of each agency to establish, operate, maintain and evaluate a program or programs, as well as a plan or plans thereunder, for the training of the agency's employees. Congressional hearings have revealed the need to change the internal culture of the IRS from one that is enforcement driven to one that is more responsive to taxpayer needs.

IRS Restructuring and Reform Impact

Training program: Report to Congress.—Congress has instructed the Commissioner to implement an employee training program to ensure adequate customer service training (Sec. 1205(a) of the IRS Restructuring and Reform Act of 1998). In addition, the Commissioner must submit an employee training plan to the Senate Finance Committee and to the House Ways and Means Committee which:

(1) provides details of the training plan;

(2) sets out the schedule for training and the fiscal years during which such training will occur;

(3) details the program's funding and otherwise demonstrates the priority and commitment of resources to the plan;

(4) reviews the organizational design of customer service;

(5) provides for the implementation of a performance development system; and

(6) provides for at least 16 hours of conflict management training during fiscal-year 1999 for employees conducting collection activities.

The IRS must comply with this provision not later than 180 days after the date of enactment of this Act (Act Sec. 1205(a) of the 1998 Act).

★ *Effective date.* The Act does not provide a specific effective date. The provision, therefore, is considered effective on the date of enactment.

Act Sec. 1205. Law at ¶ 8045. Committee Report at ¶ 10,205.

Chapter 10

Electronic Filing Initiatives

ELECTRONIC FILING

Electronic Filing of Tax and Information Returns

¶ 1001

Background

Under present law, the IRS permits the filing of "composite returns." These are returns that consist of electronically transmitted data and certain paper documents that cannot be electronically transmitted. Congress believes that there should be a comprehensive strategy to encourage electronic filing of tax and information returns. This should benefit taxpayers and make the processing of returns more efficient. For example, the error rate for paper returns is about 20 percent, half of which is attributable to the IRS and half to error in the taxpayer's returns. Because electronically filed returns usually are prepared using computer software programs with built-in accuracy checks, undergo pre-screening by the IRS, and experience no key punch errors, electronic returns have an error rate of less than one percent. Further, taxpayers who file electronic returns receive confirmation from the IRS that their return was received.

IRS Restructuring and Reform Impact

Promotion of electronic filing.—The Act states that the policy of Congress is to promote paperless filing, with a long-range goal of providing for the filing of at least 80 percent of all Federal tax and information returns in electronic form by the year 2007 (Act Sec. 2001(a) of the IRS Restructuring and Reform Act of 1998).

The IRS is required to establish a strategic plan to eliminate barriers, provide incentives, and use competitive market forces to increase taxpayer use of electronic filing while maintaining processing times for paper returns at 40 days. The plan must be established no later than 180 days after the date of enactment. Under the plan, all returns prepared in electronic form but filed as paper forms must be filed electronically, to the extent feasible, in tax years beginning after 2001 (Act Sec. 2001(b)(1) of the 1998 Act).

Advisory group. The Act requires the IRS to create an electronic commerce advisory group to insure that it receives input from the private sector regarding the implementation of the strategic plan to encourage electronic filing. The group is to include representatives from the small business community, the tax preparer, practitioner, and computerized tax processor communities, and other representatives from the electronic filing communities (Act Sec. 2001(b)(2) of the 1998 Act).

Administration programs. The IRS is authorized to promote the use of electronic tax administration programs as they become available. This promotion may include the payment of incentives for electronically filed returns (Code Sec. 6011(f), as added by the 1998 Act).

Report required. The chair of the IRS Oversight Board, the Secretary of the Treasury and the chair of the electronic commerce advisory group shall make an annual report to Congress not later than June 30th of every year after 1998. This report must include the progress of the IRS in meeting the goal of receiving 80 percent of tax and information returns electronically by 2007. The progress of the strategic plan and legislative changes necessary to assist the IRS in meeting its goal also must be reported (Act Sec. 2001(d), as added by the 1998 Act).

Comment. A last-minute addition to the Act requires the report to discuss the impact of filing tax and information returns electronically on small businesses and the self-employed.

Private sector cooperation. The Act provides that the IRS should cooperate with and encourage competition within the private sector to increase electronic filing (Act Sec. 2001(a)(3)).

Comment. The Conference Committee Report notes that disputes may arise between the IRS and the private sector on the question of whether services offered by the IRS inhibit competition or are appropriate services not reasonably available to taxpayers or tax preparers. In such cases, Congress expects that the electronic commerce advisory group will recommend an appropriate course of action to the IRS. The IRS is expected to continue to offer and improve its Telefile program and to make a similar program available on the Internet.

★ *Effective date.* No specific effective date is provided by the Act. The provision is, therefore, considered effective on the date of enactment.

Act Sec. 2001(a); Act Sec. 2001(b); Act Sec. 2001(c), redesignating Code Sec. 6011(f) as Code Sec. 6011(g) and adding new Code Sec. 6011(f); Act Sec. 2001(d); Act Sec. 2001(f). Law at ¶ 6020 and ¶ 8050. Committee Report at ¶ 10,215.

Due Date for Certain Information Returns

¶ 1005

Background _____

Information needed for filing taxes, such as dividend amounts, partnership distributions and interest paid during the calendar year, must be supplied to taxpayers by the payors by January 31 of the following calendar year. The payors must file an information return covering such payments with the IRS by February 28. The date is the same whether the filing is done with paper returns, on magnetic media, or electronically. Most of these information returns are filed on magnetic media with the tapes being physically shipped to the IRS.

IRS Restructuring and Reform Impact

Extension of due date for electronically filed information returns.— The Act provides an incentive to filers of information returns to use electronic filing by extending the due date for filing such returns from February 28 to March 31 (Code Sec. 6071(b), as amended by the IRS Restructuring and Reform Act of 1998).

The Act also requires the Department of the Treasury to issue a study evaluating the merits and disadvantages, if any, of extending the deadline for providing taxpayers with copies of information returns from January 31 to February 15. (Forms W-2 would still be required to be furnished by January 31.) The

IRS must report to Congress on the study by June 30, 1999 (Act Sec. 2002(b) of the 1998 Act).

★ *Effective date.* The extension for filing electronic returns from February 28 to March 31 is effective for returns required to be filed after December 31, 1999 (Act Sec. 2002(c) of the IRS Restructuring and Reform Act of 1998).

Act Sec. 2002(a), redesignating Code Sec. 6071(b) as Code Sec. 6071(c) and adding new Code Sec. 6071(b); Act Sec. 2002(b); Act Sec. 2002(c). Law at ¶ 6100 and ¶ 8055. Committee Report at ¶ 10,220.

Electronic Signatures

¶ 1009

Background ————————————————————————————————

Currently, the IRS will not accept an electronically filed return unless it has also received a Form 8453, "U. S. Individual Income Tax Declaration for Electronic Filing," which is a paper form that contains signature information of the filer (Code Sec. 6061). Thus, electronically filed returns cannot provide the maximum efficiency for taxpayers or the IRS under current rules requiring signature information to be filed on paper.

Taxpayers generally must authorize the disclosure of their return information by the IRS to other persons (Code Sec. 6103). Such authorization cannot be submitted electronically.

IRS Restructuring and Reform Impact

Electronic signatures.—The Act requires the IRS to develop procedures for the acceptance of signatures in digital or other electronic form. Until the procedures are in place, the Act authorizes the IRS to: (1) waive the requirement of a signature for designated types or classes of returns, declarations, statements, or other documents or (2) provide for alternative methods of signing these items.

Comment. The Act does not indicate when these procedures are required to be in place.

An alternative method of signature would be treated identically, for both civil and criminal purposes, as a signature on a paper form. The IRS must publish guidance to define and implement any signature waiver or alternative signature methods (Code Sec. 6061(b), as added by the IRS Restructuring and Reform Act of 1998).

Comment. Practitioners have indicated that Form 8453 is the most significant impediment to the efficient filing of electronic returns. Moreover, a significant portion of the IRS's cost of processing an electronic return is attributable to Form 8453.

Elimination of other paper returns filed by electronic filers. Further, the IRS must, to the extent practicable, develop procedures to eliminate any paper filing of any other information, statement, election or schedule required from a taxpayer filing an electronic return. These procedures should be made available for taxable periods beginning after December 31, 1998 (Act Sec. 2003(c) of the 1998 Act).

Electronic authorization of return disclosure to return preparer. The IRS is required to establish procedures allowing a taxpayer to authorize, on an electronically filed return, the disclosure of return information to the preparer of the return (Act Sec. 2003(e) of the 1998 Act).

¶ 1009

★ *Effective date.* The provision is effective on the date of enactment (Act Sec. 2003(f) of the IRS Restructuring and Reform Act of 1998).

Act Sec. 2003(a), amending Code Sec. 6061; Act Sec. 2003(c); Act Sec. 2003(e); Act Sec. 2003(f). Law at ¶ 6090 and ¶ 8060. Committee Report at ¶ 10,225.

Deemed Filing Date of Electronic Returns

¶ 1015

Background ——————————————————————————————

A return is considered timely filed if it is received by the IRS on or before the due date of the return (Code Sec. 7502). If certain requirements are met, timely mailing is treated as timely filing. For example, if the IRS receives a return, the postmark on the return is considered as the date of delivery. Registered and certified mail are considered postmarked and delivered on the date of registration or certification. However, because an electronically filed return is not mailed, the rules of Code Sec. 7502 do not apply. Thus, electronically filed returns place a taxpayer at a disadvantage under current rules because no similar safeguards apply in determining the filing and delivery date of an electronically filed return.

IRS Restructuring and Reform Impact

Filing date of electronic returns; electronic authorization of disclosure.—The IRS is authorized to issue regulations that extend to electronically filed returns rules similar to those that apply to paper returns sent by United States registered mail (Code Sec. 7502(c), as amended by the IRS Restructuring and Reform Act of 1998).

★ *Effective date.* The provision is effective on the date of enactment (Act Sec. 2003(f) of the IRS Restructuring and Reform Act of 1998).

Act Sec. 2003(b), amending Code Sec. 7502(c); Act Sec. 2003(f). Law at ¶ 6730. Committee Report at ¶ 10,225.

Return-Free Tax System

¶ 1019

Background ——————————————————————————————

A General Accounting Office Report released in October 1996 estimated that up to 51 million individuals would not need to file tax returns if the IRS adopted a "tax reconciliation system" similar to that in use in several European countries. Under such a system, the IRS would produce an account statement for individuals on the basis of income reported on information returns and information on filing status and dependents. Account statements, indicating a balance due or to be refunded, would be mailed to taxpayers.

IRS Restructuring and Reform Impact

IRS to develop return-free system for selected taxpayers.—The IRS must develop procedures for the implementation of a return-free tax system for "appropriate individuals." The system would be in place for tax years beginning after 2007. The IRS must report annually to the tax-writing committees of Congress on the progress of the development of such a system. The first report must be made by June 30, 2000. Each subsequent report is also due by June 30 (Act Sec. 2004 of the IRS Restructuring and Reform Act of 1998).

Each annual report must address the following issues:

(1) the additional resources needed by the IRS to implement the return-free system;

(2) changes to the Internal Revenue Code that could enhance the use of the return-free system;

(3) the procedures that have in fact been developed by the IRS to implement the return-free system; and

(4) the number and classes of taxpayers that would be permitted to use the return-free system procedures.

★ *Effective date.* No specific effective date is provided by the Act. The provision is, therefore, considered effective on the date of enactment.

Act Sec. 2004. Law at ¶ 8065. Committee Report at ¶ 10,230.

Access to Account Information

¶ 1025

Background

Although the banking industry offers "on line" customers the ability to review their account information from the privacy of their home, the IRS currently offers no similar feature to taxpayers, due largely to the fact that its data bases are not integrated.

IRS Restructuring and Reform Impact

Electronic review by electronic filers.— The IRS must develop procedures not later than December 31, 2006 under which a taxpayer filing returns electronically could review the taxpayer's account electronically. The ability to electronically review also should apply to anyone designated by a taxpayer under Code Sec. 6103(c). However, the December 31, 2006 target date is subject to the condition that all necessary privacy safeguards are also in place by that date (Act Sec. 2005(a) of the IRS Restructuring and Reform Act of 1998). The IRS must issue an interim report to the tax-writing committees of Congress no later than December 31, 2003 detailing the progress made in implementing this provision (Act Sec. 2005(b) of the 1998 Act).

★ *Effective date.* No specific effective date is provided by the Act. The provision is, therefore, considered effective on the date of enactment.

Act Sec. 2005. Law at ¶ 8070. Committee Report at ¶ 10,235.

Internet Access to Forms, Instructions, Publications

¶ 1027

Background

The IRS provides access to certain forms, instructions, and publications on its internet web page. There is no legal requirement, however, governing the types and timeliness of documents which the IRS makes available.

IRS Restructuring and Reform Impact

Internet access required for all forms, instructions, and publications.— The new law requires, in the case of taxable periods beginning after December 31, 1998, that the IRS establish procedures for all tax forms, instructions, and publications created in the most recent five-year period to be made available electronically on the internet in a searchable database. These items should be placed on the internet at approximately the same time that the paper versions are available to the public (Act Sec. 2003(d) of the IRS Restructuring and Reform Act of 1998).

The provision also requires the IRS to make "other taxpayer guidance" available electronically on the internet in a searchable database at approximately the same time such guidance is available to the public in paper form. Procedures for making these items available on the internet would also have to be established for taxable periods beginning after December 31, 1998 (Act Sec. 2003(d) of the 1998 Act).

Comment. The new law does not spell out what other types of taxpayer guidance need to be posted on the internet. Presumably, such guidance might include items typically found in the Internal Revenue Bulletin such as revenue procedures, revenue rulings, announcements, and notices.

★ *Effective date.* The provision is effective on the date of enactment (Act Sec. 2003(f) of the IRS Restructuring and Reform Act of 1998).

Act Sec. 2003(d); Act Sec. 2003(f). Law at ¶ 8060. Committee Report at ¶ 10,225.

Chapter 11
Taxpayer Rights—Examination Activities

AUDITS

Civil Damages for Unauthorized Collection Actions

¶1101

Background

With the enactment of Code Sec. 7433 in 1988 (relating to civil damages for certain unauthorized collection actions), the federal government waived a portion of its sovereign immunity in the area of federal tax collection. After some amendments enacted in 1996 (see below), the statute now generally provides that a taxpayer may sue the United States, in a federal district court, for up to $1 million of civil damages if an IRS officer or employee *recklessly or intentionally disregards* the provisions of the Internal Revenue Code or of the Treasury regulations. Except as provided in Code Sec. 7432 (relating to civil damages for failure to release a lien), this civil action constitutes the exclusive remedy for recovering damages resulting from such IRS abuses.

The Taxpayer Bill of Rights 2 (TBOR2) (P.L. 104-168), enacted in 1996, amended Code Sec. 7433 by raising the cap on the amount that a taxpayer could be awarded for damages caused by an unauthorized and unlawful collection action of an IRS officer or employee from $100,000 to $1 million. TBOR2 further amended Code Sec. 7433 to eliminate the jurisdictional requirement that a taxpayer first exhaust the administrative remedies available within the IRS before bringing suit for damages in a federal district court. However, a federal district court could reduce any damage award if the taxpayer failed to exhaust these administrative remedies. Rather than being a bar, a taxpayer's failure to exhaust IRS administrative remedies was only a factor in the judicial determination of damages.

TBOR2, however, did not alter the standard of liability originally expressed in the statute and, prior to the IRS Restructuring and Reform Act of 1998, a taxpayer could not recover any damages that occurred as a result of the *negligent disregard* of the Code or regulations by an officer or employee of the IRS in connection with a collection matter.

Furthermore, a taxpayer could not recover civil damages, pursuant to the Internal Revenue Code, that occurred as a result of an IRS officer's or employee's willful violation of certain protective provisions of the United States Bankruptcy Code. Although the Bankruptcy Code provided for the recovery of damages attributable to violations of an automatic stay, even the Bankruptcy Code itself failed to fully address the problem since it did not authorize an award of damages for violations of the discharge injunction. While the Bankruptcy Code provides that a discharge operates as an injunction against the commencement or continuation of a collection action (see below), sanctions for violations of the discharge injunction were at the discretion of the bankruptcy court.

Finally, third parties made subject to IRS collection actions could not recover damages for unauthorized collection actions that adversely affected these third parties.

IRS Restructuring and Reform Impact

Rights to civil damages extended.—Three new provisions now extend the rights of taxpayers and other impacted parties to sue and recover civil damages from the federal government for certain actions by IRS officers and employees in violation of the Internal Revenue Code, Treasury regulations and the federal Bankruptcy Code. One provision permits a taxpayer to recover civil damages caused by an IRS officer's or employee's negligent disregard of the Code or regulations in connection with the collection of federal tax from the taxpayer. Another provision authorizes a person other than the taxpayer to sue for civil damages if an IRS officer or employee disregards the Internal Revenue Code pursuant to an unauthorized IRS collection action and consequently injures that third party. The third provision enables a taxpayer to recover civil damages caused by an IRS officer's or employee's willful violation of certain Bankruptcy Code provisions in connection with the collection of federal tax from the taxpayer. These three significant changes are explained more comprehensively below.

Civil damages for negligent collection actions. A new provision permits a taxpayer to recover up to $100,000 in civil damages arising from an IRS officer's or employee's negligent disregard of any provision of the Internal Revenue Code or of the Treasury regulations in connection with the collection of federal tax from the taxpayer (Code Sec. 7433(a) and Code Sec. 7433(b), as amended by the IRS Restructuring and Reform Act of 1998).

Comment. Apparently, since a lower standard of liability is required for an aggrieved taxpayer to prevail in a negligence action, Congress limited the maximum amount that a successful taxpayer can recover to an amount significantly less than that amount recoverable by a taxpayer successfully proving an IRS officer's or employee's reckless and intentional disregard.

In a return to the law prior to TBOR2, another provision in the 1998 Act provides that a taxpayer will not be awarded a judgment for civil damages unless a federal district court determines that the plaintiff has exhausted the administrative remedies available to the plaintiff within the IRS (Code Sec. 7433(d)(1), as amended by the 1998 Act).

Comment. Reg. § 301.7433-1 currently provides that a taxpayer's administrative remedies are considered to be exhausted on the earlier of:

(1) the date that a decision is rendered by the IRS on an administrative claim for damages filed in accordance with the manner and form set forth in the regulations; or

(2) the date six months after the date that an administrative claim is filed in accordance with the manner and form set forth in the regulations.

Civil damages available to third parties. Persons other than the taxpayer who are inappropriately and adversely impacted by unauthorized IRS collection actions may now sue for civil damages if an IRS officer or employee disregards the Internal Revenue Code (Code Sec. 7426(h)(1), as added by the 1998 Act). Notwithstanding Code Sec. 7426(b) (which addresses the forms of relief that a federal district court can grant in civil actions by persons other than a taxpayer), if a federal district court determines that any officer or employee of the IRS recklessly or intentionally, or by reason of negligence, disregarded any provision of the Code, the federal government can be liable to the plaintiff in an amount equal to the lesser of $1 million ($100,000 in the case of negligence) or the sum of:

(1) the actual, direct economic damages sustained by the plaintiff as a proximate result of the reckless or intentional or negligent actions of the IRS officer or employee (reduced by any amount of such damages awarded under Code Sec. 7426(b)); and

(2) the costs of the action.

As is now true with an injured taxpayer, a third party adversely impacted by unauthorized IRS collection efforts cannot receive a judicial award for civil damages unless a federal district court determines that the plaintiff has exhausted the administrative remedies available to the plaintiff within the IRS (Code Sec. 7426(h)(2), as added by the 1998 Act). The Act further provides that the other rules of Code Sec. 7433(d), as amended, apply as well.

Thus, in addition to the applicability of new Code Sec. 7433(d)(1), which addresses the aforementioned requirement to exhaust administrative remedies, an injured third party has a duty to mitigate any damages (Code Sec. 7433(d)(2)) and must bring any action within two years after the date that the right of action accrues (Code Sec. 7433(d)(3)). Furthermore, any payments for claims pursuant to Code Sec. 7426(h) are payable out of those funds appropriated under section 1304 of Title 31 of the United States Code (Code Sec. 7426(h)(3), as added by the 1998 Act).

Civil damages for IRS violations of certain Bankruptcy Code provisions. A taxpayer may now recover up to $1 million in civil damages caused by an IRS officer or employee who willfully violates any provision of section 362 (relating to automatic stay) or section 524 (relating to the effect of discharge) of the U.S. Bankruptcy Code (Title 11, United States Code) (or any successor provision), or any regulation promulgated under these two sections, in connection with the collection of federal tax from the taxpayer. The adversely impacted taxpayer may now petition the bankruptcy court to recover applicable damages against the United States (Code Sec. 7433(e)(1), as added by the 1998 Act).

Notwithstanding section 105 of Title 11, this petition generally constitutes the exclusive remedy for recovering damages resulting from such IRS actions. However, this exclusive remedy provision does not apply to an action under section 362(h) of Title 11 for a violation of a stay provided by section 362 of such title, except that:

(1) administrative and litigation costs in connection with the action may only be awarded under Code Sec. 7430 (relating to the award of costs and certain fees); and

(2) administrative costs may be awarded only if incurred on or after the date that the bankruptcy petition is filed (Code Sec. 7433(e)(2), as added by the 1998 Act).

Comment. An "automatic stay," as defined by section 362(a) of the Bankruptcy Code, basically prevents the collection of debts from the debtor or the creation or enforcement of liens against the property of the estate or of the debtor. Section 362(h) provides that an individual injured by any willful violation of a stay can recover actual damages, including costs and attorneys' fees, and, in appropriate circumstances, may even recover punitive damages.

A violation of a stay is considered to be willful when a creditor acts intentionally with knowledge of the bankruptcy. A willful violation does not require any specific intent to violate the automatic stay. Rather, section 362(h) provides for damages upon a finding that the defendant knew of the automatic stay and that the defendant's actions which violated the stay were intentional. Note that knowledge of the bankruptcy filing is the legal equivalent of knowledge of the automatic stay provided under section 362.

Accordingly, the recording of a tax lien by the IRS in an effort to secure collection of a federal tax debt would be a violation of the automatic stay. The assessment of a tax would also constitute a significant violation of the automatic stay because it is the first step in the IRS's tax collection process and, thus, an act to collect a pre-petition debt.

Section 524(a)(2) of the Bankruptcy Code provides that a discharge operates as an injunction against the commencement or continuation of an action, the employment of process, or an act to collect, recover or offset any such debt as a personal liability of the debtor, whether or not the discharge of that debt is waived. Accordingly, the IRS can violate the discharge injunction by issuing notices of levy upon a taxpayer's wages, by entering into payroll deduction agreements with the taxpayer, by retaining a taxpayer's tax refunds, etc., after the taxpayer's personal liability has been discharged.

Comment. While Code Sec. 7433 has been expanded to provide greater remedies for taxpayers injured by IRS collection actions, taxpayer protections are far from complete. Note that the federal government has not waived its sovereign immunity in regard to the reckless or intentional or negligent disregard of the Code and regulations in connection with the *determination* of tax. Nor can a taxpayer bring an action against the IRS for a violation of its own Internal Revenue Manual, the compilation of the rules that IRS personnel are required to obey. Furthermore, while civil actions may be brought against the United States, no civil action may be brought against the offending IRS officer or employee, even though some critics of the IRS have advocated making wayward IRS personnel personally accountable for their improper tactics.

Code Sec. 7433 is also limited to the disregard of the Internal Revenue Code and Treasury regulations, and now to the disregard of two sections of the Bankruptcy Code and their applicable regulations. No other federal law or underlying regulation is included. Finally, a suit relating to an abusive IRS collection action may be brought only in a federal district court, and not in the Tax Court, which may require the advance payment of any disputed tax.

★ *Effective date.* These provisions are applicable to the actions of IRS officers or employees occurring after the date of enactment (Act Sec. 3102(d) of the IRS Restructuring and Reform Act of 1998).

Act Sec. 3102(a), amending Code Secs. 7433(a), (b) and (d)(1); Act Sec. 3102(b), amending Code Sec. 7426 by redesignating Code Sec. 7426(h) as Code Sec. 7426(i), and by adding new Code Sec. 7426(h); Act Sec. 3102(c),

¶ 1101

adding new Code Sec. 7433(e); Act Sec. 3102(d). Law at ¶ 6610 and ¶ 6650. Committee Report at ¶ 10,255.

Taxpayer Assistance Orders

¶ 1106

Background _____

Under prior law, when a taxpayer encountered a problem with the IRS and its administration of the Internal Revenue Code, the taxpayer first attempted to resolve the issue through interaction with the local problem resolution officer. However, if the problem remained unresolved, and the taxpayer faced a "significant hardship" as a consequence of a completed or pending IRS action, then the taxpayer could apply for a "taxpayer assistance order" (TAO). The Taxpayer Advocate, and local and regional problem resolution officers, could issue such TAOs.

Prior to amendment, Code Sec. 7811 provided that a taxpayer could request that the Taxpayer Advocate in the Internal Revenue Service issue a TAO if the taxpayer was suffering, or was about to suffer, a significant hardship as a result of the manner in which the IRS was administering the federal internal revenue laws. However, before the enactment of the IRS Restructuring and Reform Act of 1998, the meaning of "significant hardship" was much more of a subjective determination, although it was clear that a mere economic or personal inconvenience did not rise to the level of a significant hardship.

While a TAO could not, and cannot, override a provision of the Internal Revenue Code, a TAO may require that the IRS:

(1) release any property of the taxpayer that has been levied upon;

(2) cease any action, or take any action as permitted by law; or

(3) refrain from taking any action with respect to the taxpayer.

In general, a TAO provides the Taxpayer Advocate (after the 1998 Act, the "National Taxpayer Advocate") with additional time in which to review the taxpayer's case and to decide if the original IRS action was proper. However, the Taxpayer Advocate will not issue a TAO where there is no evidence of a significant hardship or where it appears that the taxpayer has applied for the TAO simply to delay IRS actions.

A taxpayer, or the taxpayer's duly authorized representative, can apply for relief by completing and filing the aptly-numbered Form 911, Application for Taxpayer Assistance Order to Relieve Hardship.

IRS Restructuring and Reform Impact

Factors to consider before issuing Taxpayer Assistance Orders.—The new law provides that, upon an application filed by a taxpayer with the Office of the Taxpayer Advocate (in such form, manner, and at such time as the Treasury Department might prescribe through future regulations), the National Taxpayer Advocate may issue a Taxpayer Assistance Order (TAO). The National Taxpayer Advocate may issue a TAO if he or she determines that the taxpayer is suffering, or is about to suffer, a significant hardship as a result of the manner in which the internal revenue laws are being administered by the IRS or if the taxpayer meets such other requirements as may be set forth in any future regulations (Code Sec. 7811(a)(1), as amended by the IRS Restructuring and Reform Act of 1998).

Comment. The Conference Committee Report provides that it is the intent of Congress that the circumstances set forth in these Treasury regulations be based upon considerations of equity.

Code Sec. 7811(a), as amended, now provides that the National Taxpayer Advocate must consider, among other things, the following four specific factors when determining whether there is a "significant hardship" and whether a TAO should be issued:

(1) whether there is an immediate threat of adverse action;

(2) whether there has been a delay of more than 30 days in resolving the taxpayer's account problems;

(3) whether the taxpayer will have to pay significant costs (including fees for professional representation) if relief is not granted; or

(4) whether the taxpayer will suffer irreparable injury, or a long-term adverse impact, if relief is not granted (Code Sec. 7811(a)(2), as amended by the 1998 Act).

Additionally, in cases where an IRS employee to whom the order would be issued is not following applicable published administrative guidance, including the Internal Revenue Manual, the National Taxpayer Advocate must construe the factors taken into account in determining whether to issue a TAO in the manner most favorable to the taxpayer (Code Sec. 7811(a)(3), as amended by the 1998 Act).

Comment. To a great extent, the IRS has already promoted the use of these four factors within its Internal Revenue Manual. However, these new statutory provisions make the IRS's own suggested considerations mandatory.

★ *Effective date.* These provisions are effective on the date of enactment (Act Sec. 1102(f) of the IRS Restructuring and Reform Act of 1998).

Act Sec. 1102(c), amending Code Sec. 7811(a); Act Sec. 1102(f). Law at ¶ 6890. Committee Report at ¶ 10,150.

Financial Status Audits

¶ 1111

Background _____

Prior to enactment of the IRS Restructuring and Reform Act of 1998, whenever an IRS agent encountered a low stated gross income on a personal tax return for a taxpayer obviously living well, the agent could ask assorted "financial status questions" to determine if there was any unreported income. While a traditional IRS audit principally focuses on books, records and other audit evidence directly related to the tax return and its preparation, in financial status auditing there was an immediate focus on unreported income at the very beginning of the audit. These financial status questions focused on the taxpayer's lifestyle, standard of living, and other elements *unrelated* to the specific preparation of the tax return. For example, an agent could ask a taxpayer the following types of questions:

(1) What is your educational background?

(2) Where do you go on vacation? How much do you spend?

(3) Where do your children go to school?

(4) How many automobiles do you own? What makes and models are they? What are the monthly payments?

(5) Do you own any large assets (over $10,000) besides automobiles and real estate? What are they? Where are they kept? Are they paid for? If not, what are the payments?

(6) What cash do you have on hand, personally or for business, that is not in a bank (i.e., at your home, in a safe deposit box, hidden somewhere, etc.)?

Background ———————————————————————————————————

(7) What is the largest amount of cash you ever had at any one time during the year?

(8) Have you made any significant home improvements? How were they paid for?

The IRS insisted that the financial status audit technique was not really new (it was formerly known as an "economic reality audit"), and that the technique came into play in only about 20 percent of all audits. However, the technique became controversial, even notorious, in 1995 when the IRS highlighted the use of this tool in its agent training modules.

Although many groups voiced their concern over the possible overuse and abuse of this technique, the American Institute of Certified Public Accountants (AICPA) took a leading role in expressing its dismay, asserting that overzealous IRS agents were using it to change a conventional search for possible unreported income into a criminal fraud inquiry. This caused great consternation in the accounting industry because, at the time, if the civil examination turned into a criminal one, a CPA did not enjoy any attorney-client privilege and, thus, could be compelled to testify against the client.

The AICPA argued that while its members were eminently qualified to represent a client at any IRS proceeding dealing with substantive tax law or return preparation, the only role for a CPA in a criminal tax fraud case was in support of an attorney who had expertise in criminal tax law, as well as the advantage of privileged communications with the taxpayer. For a CPA to stay involved as the primary taxpayer representative in such a criminal audit probe was tantamount to an invitation to a suit for malpractice.

Of the many "oppressive" aspects of the financial status audit, another component that drew the ire of taxpayers and their representatives was that the technique encouraged IRS agents to insist upon personal interviews with the taxpayer, often at the taxpayer's personal residence. The AICPA and other taxpayer-friendly groups found such an interview procedure to be overly intrusive and inconsistent with the taxpayer's statutory right to be represented by a qualified professional.

The AICPA asserted that the IRS educational program advocating the technique trained the agent to view a taxpayer representative as a hindrance, as someone impeding the audit process, or as an intermediary inappropriately protecting a guilty taxpayer. Accordingly, agents were allegedly bypassing valid powers of attorney and were requesting information and records directly from the taxpayer. The AICPA concluded that the financial status audit technique not only undermined a taxpayer's rights, but also undermined the legitimate role of the taxpayer's representative.

While acknowledging that the technique could be appropriate in certain IRS investigations, the AICPA and others insisted that the technique should not be utilized until a routine examination generated a reasonable suspicion or uncovered unreported income. Where there was no reasonable indication of unreported income not subject to information reporting (such as where the average wage earner's Forms W-2 and 1099s matched the individual income tax return), the agent should not be seeking intrusive, superfluous information relating to lifestyle. Rather, the agent in such a situation should only address those issues reported on the tax return. Apparently, some IRS agents were sending Form 4822 (Statement of Annual Estimated Personal and Family Expenses) with the *initial* contact letter and implying that completion of this form was mandatory. (This form basically breaks down a taxpayer's cost of living.)

¶ 1111

Background ————————————————————————————————

From a general policy standpoint, the AICPA and others also argued that the financial status audit technique instilled in an IRS agent the belief that most taxpayers are guilty of underreporting income, thus negatively influencing the agent's attitude towards the taxpayer, and increasing the confrontational atmosphere between an agent and the taxpayer.

IRS Restructuring and Reform Impact

Limitation on financial status audit technique.—Although the IRS is authorized, even required, to make the inquiries and determinations necessary to insure the proper assessment and payment of federal income taxes, Congress has determined that the financial status audit technique is unreasonable and overly intrusive, and should be limited to situations where the IRS already has indications of unreported income. Since several courts have upheld the use of financial status audits and economic reality examination techniques to determine the existence of unreported income in appropriate circumstances, Congress felt obliged to eliminate these techniques statutorily.

Accordingly, a new provision now prohibits the IRS from using financial status or economic reality examination techniques to determine the existence of unreported income of any taxpayer unless the IRS already has a reasonable indication that there is a likelihood of such unreported income.(Code Sec. 7602(d), as added by the IRS Restructuring and Reform Act of 1998).

★ *Effective date.* The Act provides no specific effective date. The provision, therefore, is considered effective on the date of enactment.

Act Sec. 3412, adding Code Sec. 7602(d). Law at ¶ 6760. Committee Report at ¶ 10,380.

Tip Reporting Audit Threats

¶ 1116

Background ————————————————————————————————

Code Sec. 6053 addresses an employee's obligation to report cash and charged tips to an employer for income tax purposes. Code Sec. 3111 and Code Sec. 3121(q) address an employer's liability for Federal Insurance Contribution Act taxes with respect to those tips. To help both tipped employees and their employers to comply with these reporting requirements, a restaurant, for example, may enter into a Tip Reporting Alternative Commitment (TRAC) agreement with the IRS. This agreement is part of a voluntary program developed by the IRS Office of Employment Tax Administration and Compliance and the restaurant industry as a means of improving tip reporting and ensuring greater compliance by employees of food and beverage establishments. The Tip Rate Determination Education Program, under which TRAC agreements are issued, is scheduled to end after May 31, 2000. (See the IRS's "Market Segment Understanding with the Food Service Industry—Tip Reporting Alternative Commitment," issued in connection with its Tip Rate Determination Education Program.)

In general, a restaurant that enters into a TRAC agreement with the IRS is obligated to:

(1) educate its employees on their tip reporting obligations;

(2) institute formal tip reporting procedures to ensure accurate tip reporting by its employees;

(3) fulfill all of the federal tax filing and recordkeeping requirements; and

Background

(4) pay and deposit all of the applicable employment taxes.

While a TRAC agreement is in effect, a participating restaurant must institute and maintain an educational program that trains and reminds employees of their tip reporting obligations. Such a restaurant must also file numerous federal forms, such as: Form 941, Employer's Quarterly Federal Tax Return; Form 8027, Employer's Annual Information Return of Tip Income and Allocated Tips; and Forms W-2 for each employee. All of these forms incorporate the employees' reported charged and cash tips. A restaurant signing a TRAC agreement must also fulfill numerous other recordkeeping and statistical data compilation responsibilities. Finally, the restaurant must pay the amount of any undisputed federal tax that is due and properly deposit such federal taxes.

In return for all of these educational, filing, recordkeeping and payment efforts, a participating restaurant receives the following IRS promise: the IRS will generally agree to base the restaurant's liability for employment taxes solely on the reported tips, and any unreported tips discovered during an IRS audit, of an employee (see Form 4137, Social Security and Medicare Tax on Unreported Tip Income, and Form 885-T, Adjustment of Social Security Tax on Tip Income Not Reported to Employer).

Although TRAC agreements help the IRS to monitor the tip reporting obligations of restaurant employees, reports arose that the IRS was compelling restaurants to accept TRAC agreements by intimating the possibility that the IRS might audit an "uncooperative" restaurant. Although the IRS has the authority to perform audits to ensure taxpayer compliance with the internal revenue laws, Congress found it to be inappropriate for the IRS to use the threat of an audit to induce a restaurant to participate in this voluntary program.

IRS Restructuring and Reform Impact

Threat of audit to coerce TRAC agreements prohibited.—The IRS Restructuring and Reform Act of 1998 requires the IRS to instruct its employees that they may not threaten to audit any taxpayer in an attempt to coerce the taxpayer to enter into a TRAC agreement.

PRACTICAL ANALYSIS. Robert McKenzie, of McKenzie & McKenzie PC, Chicago, Ill., notes that over the past several years the IRS has engaged in a program of attempting to seek greater tips compliance in the hotel, restaurant and entertainment industry by approaching employers to seek tip reporting commitment agreements. Unfortunately, the approach the IRS has taken has been to threaten the employer with audit if it did not force its employees to begin paying taxes on an agreed percentage of tips. The employer was confronted with the risk of an IRS audit or with the alternative of forcing each of its employees to agree to a certain percentage of presumed tips. Code Sec. 3414 specifically prohibits the IRS from engaging in its current arm twisting of employers. The provision appears to have been a clear concession to the entertainment, restaurant and casino industry.

★ *Effective date.* The Act does not provide a specific effective date. The provision is, therefore, considered effective on the date of enactment.

Act Sec. 3414. Law at ¶ 8090. Committee Report at ¶ 10,390.

Explanation of Interview Rights

¶ 1121

Background

Code Sec. 7521, enacted in 1988 by the first Taxpayer Bill of Rights (as part of the Technical and Miscellaneous Revenue Act of 1988 (P.L. 100-647)), addresses the power of the IRS to interview taxpayers for audit and tax collection purposes. Code Sec. 7521(b)(1) specifically provides that, prior to or at the initial in-person interview, an IRS officer or employee must provide the taxpayer with an explanation of the audit or collection process that is the subject of the interview. In addition, the IRS agent must also describe the taxpayer's rights under that process.

If the taxpayer clearly states at any time during the interview (other than in an interview initiated by an administrative summons) that the taxpayer wishes to consult with an attorney, certified public accountant, enrolled agent, enrolled actuary, or any other person permitted to represent the taxpayer before the IRS, the IRS agent must suspend the interview to allow the taxpayer a reasonable opportunity to consult with that representative. (Code Sec. 7521(c) addresses the requisite qualifications necessary to represent the taxpayer before the IRS.) Upon such a request, the interview must be suspended, even if the taxpayer has already answered one or more of the IRS agent's questions (Code Sec. 7521(b)(2)).

Once the taxpayer appoints a qualified representative and informs the IRS of that appointment, an IRS officer or employee cannot bypass the taxpayer's representative or require that the taxpayer accompany the representative, unless an administrative summons has been issued to the taxpayer. However, an IRS agent, with the consent of his or her immediate supervisor, may notify the taxpayer directly that the agent believes that the taxpayer's representative is responsible for unreasonable delay or is hindering the IRS's examination or investigation of the taxpayer. In such a case, the IRS may bypass the taxpayer's representative using the applicable IRS Manual procedures.

Note, however, that the provisions governing taxpayer interviews do not apply to criminal investigations or to investigations relating to the integrity of any IRS officer or employee (Code Sec. 7521(d)).

In an effort to more widely publicize these Code Sec. 7521 taxpayer interview rights, IRS Publication 1 ("Your Rights as a Taxpayer"), Part IV, provides that a taxpayer may represent himself or, with proper written authorization, may retain someone else to represent the taxpayer's interests. Part IV also provides that a taxpayer may be accompanied at the interview by another person. Furthermore, a taxpayer has the right to request that the interview take place at a reasonable time and place that is convenient for both the taxpayer and the IRS (IRS Publication 1, page 2).

IRS Restructuring and Reform Impact

Explanation of taxpayer's rights in interviews with the IRS.—Believing that taxpayers should be more fully informed of their Code Sec. 7521 rights to representation at IRS interviews, the IRS Restructuring and Reform Act of 1998 now requires the IRS to rewrite IRS Publication 1 ("Your Rights as a Taxpayer") to more clearly inform taxpayers of their rights:

(1) to be represented at interviews with the IRS by a representative authorized to practice before the IRS; and

(2) to suspend the interview pursuant to Code Sec. 7521(b)(2) (that is, the interview must be suspended once the taxpayer indicates that the tax-

payer wishes to consult with an attorney, accountant, enrolled agent, or other person permitted to represent the taxpayer before the IRS).

IRS Publication 1 must be revised and rewritten to more clearly inform taxpayers of these currently available interview rights as soon as practicable, but no later than 180 days after the date of enactment of the IRS Restructuring and Reform Act of 1998.

★ *Effective date.* The 1998 Act provides no specific effective date. The provision is, therefore, considered effective on the date of enactment. The revision of Publication 1 must be made no later than 180 days after the date of enactment.

Act Sec. 3502. Law at ¶ 8135. Committee Report at ¶ 10,570.

Disclosure of Audit Selection Criteria

¶ 1126

Background

The IRS annually examines, or "audits," numerous federal tax returns filed by individuals, corporations, etc., to ascertain whether these taxpayers have voluntarily complied with the applicable federal revenue laws and paid the proper amount of tax to the federal government. The IRS understandably believes that taxpayers are more likely to voluntarily comply with the tax laws if they believe that their return may be audited and that unpaid taxes may be identified. Code Sec. 7602 generally defines an "audit" as an examination of a taxpayer's books and records for the purpose of determining the correct tax liability. Note that there is currently no requirement that the federal government establish that it had probable cause to believe that a taxpayer has misstated the taxpayer's liability before initiating an audit of the taxpayer.

While the IRS has recently emphasized taxpayer education and assistance to encourage voluntary compliance, the IRS recognizes that the audit is one of its most effective tools in enforcing the voluntary compliance of taxpayers. However, to best utilize its limited audit resources, the IRS seeks to efficiently and effectively identify and audit those returns with the greatest likelihood of noncompliance. To do this, the IRS utilizes a variety of strategies, tools, programs and techniques. Although some estimates indicate that the IRS has at least 40 objective audit sources that it can use to select potentially noncompliant taxpayers' returns for audit, many of these strategies, tools, etc., remain unknown.

Nonetheless, one well-known investigative tool is the computerized classification system (i.e., the discriminant function ("DIF") system). This program selects returns for audit based on a computer score designed to predict those tax returns most likely to result in additional taxes if audited. This program has generated relatively less controversy than other IRS audit techniques because it examines objective, rather than subjective or random, factors in its selection methodology. Using the DIF system, the IRS has usually been able to avoid burdening compliant taxpayers with an audit.

The IRS has also capitalized on certain objective computer-matching techniques to coordinate the information returns filed by banks and other third-party recordkeepers with the returns filed by taxpayers.

Prior to its "elimination" from the IRS's toolbox, due to the significant burden imposed on those taxpayers included in the sample, revenue agents utilized the findings from the Taxpayer Compliance Measurement Program (TCMP) to make statistical determinations as to pockets of possible noncompliance. For example, among its many conclusions, the TCMP indicated that there was more taxpayer noncompliance in the western and southwestern areas of the United States, leading to a higher rate of audits of taxpayers in that geographical area.

Background

Occasionally, certain audit initiatives and compliance projects are generated by information indicating a high level of noncompliance by those taxpayers reporting a particular item on their return. For instance, the Treasury Department has estimated that about one-quarter of all filed earned income tax credit claims are made by nonqualifying individuals. Accordingly, such objectively determined abuses in the earned income credit area, as well as in the self-employment tax area, and in the promotion of certain tax shelters, have led to an increased number of audits of involved taxpayers.

The IRS also uses information offered by informants to determine whether a particular return is deserving of closer review. The IRS currently operates a program that pays informants up to 15 percent of the taxes, to a maximum reward of $2 million, recovered from their tips. Informants can call either a toll-free number or walk into any IRS district office. To receive a reward, an informant usually must complete Form 211, Application for Reward for Original Information. In 1996, the last year in which figures are available, 9,430 people sought rewards. Many of these informants were former spouses and fired employees. The IRS acted upon 650 of these tips and paid out rewards of $3.5 million on collected taxes of $103 million. In the three years prior to 1996, the IRS collected $797 million on approximately 2,000 tips. (For more information on this program, see Code Sec. 7623 and IRS Publication 733, Rewards for Information Provided by Individuals to the Internal Revenue Service.)

While audits of taxpayers generated by an evaluation of objective criteria have created some controversy among Congressional leaders and interested taxpayers, it is the utilization of random audits of taxpayers who are not suspected of any improper or illegal conduct that has recently created the most ire. In a recent General Accounting Office study, it was determined that:

(1) the IRS initiated at least six projects, covering tax years 1994 through 1996, that involved the performance of random audits on taxpayers;

(2) the IRS selected at least 7,421 taxpayers nationwide at random for audits and completed no less than 2,961 random audits of returns for tax years 1994 through 1996;

(3) more than 80 percent of all random audits completed covering tax years 1994 through 1996 were performed on low-income taxpayers earning $25,000 or less;

(4) nearly half of all these random audits occurred in 11 southern states; and

(5) four of the six IRS projects involving random audits were focused on small businesses or the self employed (see "Tax Administration: IRS's Use of Random Selection in Choosing Tax Returns for Audit" (GAO/GGD-98-40)).

Accordingly, any number of factors may come into play during the IRS's audit selection process. To help give taxpayers a greater understanding of the reasons for which they may be selected for an audit examination, Congress believes that taxpayers need to be better informed of the IRS's audit selection criteria, and that the IRS should more readily disclose certain nonconfidential, nonproprietary information relative to this topic.

IRS Restructuring and Reform Impact

Disclosure of criteria for examination selection.—A new provision enacted by the IRS Restructuring and Reform Act of 1998 generally instructs the IRS to add a statement to Publication 1 ("Your Rights as a Taxpayer") which sets forth, in simple and nontechnical terms, the criteria and procedures utilized by the IRS for selecting taxpayers for examination (Act Sec. 3503(a) of the IRS Restructuring and Reform Act of 1998).

However, recognizing the need to protect certain IRS investigative strategies, this statement need not include any information that would be detrimental to law enforcement if disclosed. Rather, the statement must specify the general procedures used by the IRS in selecting taxpayers for examination, including whether taxpayers are selected on the basis of information available in the media or on the basis of information provided to the IRS by informants.

Comment. Before final publication in Publication 1, drafts of the statement or proposed revisions to the statement must be submitted, on the same day, to the House Committee on Ways and Means and the Senate Committee on Finance (Act Sec. 3503(b) of the 1998 Act).

The IRS must revise Publication 1 to incorporate this statement addressing the disclosure of audit selection criteria as soon as practicable, but not later than 180 days after the date of enactment.

PRACTICAL ANALYSIS. Robert McKenzie, of McKenzie & McKenzie PC, Chicago, Ill., observes that the IRS uses many methods to select returns for examination. It uses a DIF scoring system that measures the variance from the norm of particular claimed exemptions and deductions. It also utilizes informants, document matches, media, other law enforcement agencies and special programs to select returns for examination. Act Sec. 3503 requires that the IRS inform the taxpayer of the method used to select his or her tax return for examination unless such information would be detrimental to law enforcement. The IRS must put these procedures into effect no later than 180 days after enactment of the provision. Taxpayers will now have greater clues as to the issues that the IRS might raise during an audit because they will be aware of the causes of that audit. Knowledge of the source of an audit should help reduce the fear generated by an audit and allow the taxpayer to better present a defense.

★ *Effective date.* No specific effective date is provided by the Act. The provision is, therefore, considered effective on the date of enactment.

Act Sec. 3503. Law at ¶ 8140. Committee Report at ¶ 10,575.

Executive Branch Audit Influence

¶ 1131

Background

Prior to enactment of the IRS Restructuring and Reform Act of 1998, the Internal Revenue Code did not explicitly prohibit high-level executive branch influence over taxpayer audits and collection activity. Although the Code Sec. 6103 prohibition on the disclosure of tax returns and return information was applicable to executive branch officials and employees, the legality of their exertion of influence over taxpayer audits and collection activity was unclear.

Accusations that the executive branch had exerted influence over the IRS to encourage it to engage in politically motivated tax examinations go back as far as 1975 when Congress investigated allegations that President Richard M. Nixon had used the IRS for political purposes. Recognizing that confidentiality is the foundation of the United States' voluntary compliance system, the enactment of the Code Sec. 6103 taxpayer confidentiality provisions soon followed.

Background _____

More recently, Congress has expressed concern regarding possible executive branch influence over the audits of conservative tax-exempt organizations. Although the audits of many of these groups may have been legitimately motivated by IRS concern that charitable assets were being utilized for partisan political purposes, some observers speculated that the audits were actually politically motivated. (Note that Code Sec. 501(c)(3) tax-exempt organizations are statutorily prohibited from intervening on behalf of candidates for public office. Political intervention on behalf of a candidate is a disqualifying event.) Whether or not any of these recent allegations are correct, such speculation encouraged Congress to specifically address the potential abuse of the IRS's audit power by the executive branch.

Although the IRS cannot legally publicly disclose which taxpayers it is or is not investigating, pursuant to Code Sec. 6103(f), a congressional committee, sitting in closed executive session, can inspect the IRS's list of current examination projects. Although this information may not be shared with the general public, the information obtained from such a review could possibly satisfy congressional concerns that some audits are politically targeted.

IRS Restructuring and Reform Impact

Prohibition on executive branch influence over taxpayer audits.—For requests made after the date of enactment, it is unlawful for "applicable persons" to request that any IRS officer or employee conduct or terminate an audit, or otherwise investigate or terminate the investigation of any taxpayer or the tax liability of such taxpayer (Code Sec. 7217(a), as added by the IRS Restructuring and Reform Act of 1998).

Comment. According to the Senate Finance Committee Report, Congress believes that the perception that it is possible for high-level executive branch officials and employees to exert influence over taxpayer audits and collection activity negatively impacts taxpayers' confidence in the federal tax system.

The prohibition on executive branch influence applies to both direct requests and to requests made through an intermediary. However, in the case of a law enforcement action authorized by the U.S. Attorney General, any discussions involving applicable persons with respect to that law enforcement action will not be considered requests made through an intermediary (see the Senate Finance Committee Report).

Exceptions. There are, however, three exceptions to the prohibition on executive branch influence on IRS audits and investigations.

Under the first exception, the prohibition does not apply to written requests made to an applicable person (as defined below) by or on behalf of a taxpayer that is then forwarded by the applicable person to the IRS (Code Sec. 7217(c)(1), as added by the 1998 Act).

According to the Senate Finance Committee Report, this exception is intended to cover the following two situations:

> (1) where a taxpayer (or a taxpayer's representative) writes to an applicable person seeking assistance in resolving a difficulty with the IRS; and

> (2) where there is an IRS audit or investigation of a presidential nominee.

Comment. The situation (1) exception permits the applicable person who receives such a request to forward it to the IRS for resolution without violating the general prohibition. The situation (2) exception applies to the "vetting" of presidential nominees to various federal posts. Under Code Sec. 6103(g), nominees for presidentially appointed positions must consent to the disclosure of their tax returns and return information so that appropriate background checks may be conducted. Sometimes an audit or other investigation is initiated as part of that requisite background check. The Senate Finance Committee Report clarifies that such an audit or investigation is intended to fall within this first exception.

The second exception applies to any written request made by an applicable person for the disclosure of a return or return information under Code Sec. 6103 (relating to the disclosure of return information) if that request is made pursuant to the Code Sec. 6103 disclosure requirements (Code Sec. 7217(c)(2), as added by the 1998 Act).

Finally, the third exception applies to any written request made by the Secretary of the Treasury as a result of implementing a change in tax policy (Code Sec. 7217(c)(3), as added by the 1998 Act).

Applicable person. For purposes of the prohibition on executive branch influence, an applicable person includes:

(1) the President;

(2) the Vice President;

(3) employees of the executive offices of either the President or Vice President; and

(4) any individual (other than the Attorney General of the United States) serving in a position specified in section 5312 of Title 5 of the United States Code (generally, a cabinet-level position) (Code Sec. 7217(e), as added by the 1998 Act).

Reporting requirement. Any IRS officer or employee who receives a request in violation of the prohibition must report this request to the Treasury Inspector General for Tax Administration (Code Sec. 7217(b), as added by the 1998 Act).

According to the Senate Finance Committee Report, the Treasury Inspector General has the authority to investigate any violations and to refer such violations to the Department of Justice for possible prosecution, as may be appropriate.

Penalty. Any applicable person who willfully violates the prohibition, or any IRS officer or employee who fails to report a request, can be punished, upon conviction, either by imprisonment (not to exceed five years) or by a fine (not to exceed $5,000), or by both. Upon conviction, that individual may also be liable for the costs of prosecution (Code Sec. 7217(d), as added by the 1998 Act).

★ *Effective date.* These provisions apply to requests made after the date of enactment (Act Sec. 1105(c) of the 1998 Act).

Act Sec. 1105, adding Code Sec. 7217. Law at ¶ 6580. Committee Report at ¶ 10,170.

Request to Give Up Right to Sue

¶ 1133

Background ————————————————————————————

Prior to the enactment of the IRS Restructuring and Reform Act of 1998, a knowledgeable officer or employee of the federal government could use his or her position of authority to persuade, even coerce, an unknowing, unrepresented taxpayer to waive that taxpayer's rights to bring a civil action against either the federal government or an officer or employee of the federal government. Prior to the 1998 Act, there was no restriction on the circumstances under which the federal government could request a taxpayer to waive that taxpayer's right to sue either the United States or one of its employees for any action taken in connection with the federal tax laws. Congress determined that no taxpayer should be subject to

Background

such influence unless the taxpayer had been sufficiently informed of his or her taxpayer rights and the consequences of such a waiver of those rights, or unless the taxpayer was competently assisted by counsel.

IRS Restructuring and Reform Impact

Prohibition on requests to taxpayers to waive their right to sue.—The new law generally provides that no officer or employee of the United States may request that a taxpayer waive the right to bring a civil action against either the federal government or any officer or employee of the federal government for any action taken in connection with the federal internal revenue laws (Act Sec. 3468(a) of the IRS Restructuring and Reform Act of 1998). However, this general rule will not apply in three specific situations:

(1) where the taxpayer knowingly and voluntarily waives the right to sue;

(2) where the request by the officer or employee is made in person and the taxpayer's attorney or other federally authorized tax practitioner (within the meaning of Code Sec. 7525(a)(3)(A)) is present; or

(3) where the request is made in writing to the taxpayer's attorney or other representative (Act Sec. 3468(b) of the 1998 Act).

Comment. The Conference Committee Report provides that the conferees do not intend this provision to apply to the waiver of claims for attorneys' fees or costs or to the waiver of one or more claims brought in the same administrative or judicial proceeding with other claims that are being settled.

★ *Effective date.* The Act provides no specific effective date. The provision is, therefore, considered effective on the date of enactment.

Act Sec. 3468(a); Act Sec. 3468(b). Law at ¶ 8125. Committee Report at ¶ 10,550.

Notification of Appointment of Tax Matters Partner

¶ 1136

Background

Code Sec. 6231(a)(7) provides that a partnership's tax matters partner (TMP) is either:

(1) the general partner who is specifically designated as the TMP by the partnership; or

(2) if no general partner has been so designated, the general partner who holds the largest profits interest in the partnership at the end of the tax year subject to audit. If two or more general partners hold an equally large profits interest, the general partner whose name would appear first in an alphabetical listing must assume the role of TMP.

The TMP, as the central figure in unified partnership audit and litigation proceedings, is the focal point for the service of all IRS notices, documents and orders. The TMP performs a myriad of other important duties as well, such as serving as the partnership's representative in an audit, and guiding the partnership through the various administrative and judicial proceedings that may follow.

The TMP is also responsible for keeping all of the other partners in the partnership informed of the progress of any administrative and judicial proceedings (Code Sec. 6223(g)). Furthermore, the TMP retains the authority to extend, on behalf of the entire partnership, the limitations period for tax assessments against partnership items. Accordingly, the TMP's initiative and skill during any adminis-

Background

trative and judicial proceeding, and in the execution of the TMP's statutory duties, has a substantial effect on the rights of all of the other partners in the partnership. Consequently, the proper selection of the TMP is crucial to all of the partners.

What makes the selection process all the more critical is that if the partnership fails to choose its own TMP, and if the IRS also determines that it is impracticable to appoint the general partner having the largest profits interest, then the IRS is statutorily authorized to select one of the partners of the partnership to serve as the TMP (Code Sec. 6231(a)(7)).

Note that the IRS may designate as the TMP for the applicable tax year any person who was a general partner at some point during the partnership's tax year, *even though that person is not a general partner at the time of the IRS's designation* (Reg. § 301.6231(a)(7)-1(b)(1)).

If the IRS makes a determination that it is impracticable to apply the largest-profits-interest rule, the IRS will notify the partnership by mail that, 30 days after the date of the notice, the IRS will select the TMP unless a prior designation is made by the partnership. This delay enables the partnership to designate its own TMP, thereby avoiding a selection made by the IRS. If the partnership fails to designate its own TMP within that 30-day period, the IRS will select a TMP for the partnership and will notify *both the selected partner and the partnership of its selection* (Reg. § 301.6231(a)(7)-1(r)).

Although this IRS regulation provides sufficient notice and opportunity for the partnership to appoint its own TMP, Congressional concern arose that in cases where the IRS designated the TMP, the *other partners* in the partnership may remain unaware of this strategically important designation.

IRS Restructuring and Reform Impact

IRS designation of tax matters partner.—The new law requires that, within 30 days of selecting a tax matters partner (TMP) for a partnership, the IRS must notify all of the partners entitled to receive notice under Code Sec. 6223(a) of the selected TMP's name and address (Code Sec. 6231(a)(7), as amended by the IRS Restructuring and Reform Act of 1998). Accordingly, within 30 days of selecting a TMP for a partnership, the IRS must notify all those partners with sufficient partnership interests whose names and addresses appear on the applicable partnership return, as well as all those partners with sufficient interests whose names and addresses have been timely furnished to the IRS through certain other prescribed methods.

Comment. The Senate Finance Committee report provides that the IRS must notify all partners of any resignation of the TMP that is required by the IRS and also notify the partners of any successor TMP.

★ *Effective date.* The provision applies to selections of tax matters partners made by the Secretary of the Treasury after the date of enactment (Act Sec. 3507(b) of the 1998 Act).

Act Sec. 3507(a), amending Code Sec. 6231(a)(7); Act Sec. 3507(b). Law at ¶ 6210. Committee Report at ¶ 10,595.

Tax-Exempt Status of Bond Issues

¶ 1137

Background

Generally, gross income does not include interest on debt incurred by state or local governments provided that the debt proceeds are used to carry out govern-

Background——————————————————————————————

mental functions of those entities and the debt is repaid with governmental funds (Code Sec. 103). However, interest on such governmental debt is taxable if the debt proceeds are used to finance activities of other persons whose funds are used to repay the debt (private activity bonds).

Whether interest on state or local government bonds is tax exempt is initially determined by the issuers when the bonds are issued. In determining the bonds' tax-exempt status, reference is made to how the bond proceeds are "to be used" (Code Sec. 141). Intentional acts after the date of issuance to use bond-financed property in a non-tax-exempt manner may render the bond interest taxable, retroactive to the date of issuance. The IRS, under regular examination procedures, may review or challenge the initial determination of tax-exempt status as well as issuer decisions relating to the effect of subsequent actions.

A state or local government seeking to issue tax-exempt bonds under Code Sec. 103 can request a ruling from the IRS regarding the bonds' tax-exempt status. Under Code Sec. 7478, the issuer can challenge the IRS determination (or the IRS's failure to make a timely determination) in a declaratory judgment proceeding in the Tax Court. However, issuers cannot directly litigate the tax-exempt status of the bonds after the bonds are issued because bondholders, not issuers, are the parties whose tax liability is affected.

IRS Restructuring and Reform Impact

Administrative appeal of tax-exempt bond status.—The IRS Restructuring and Reform Act of 1998 requires the IRS to amend its administrative procedures to allow tax-exempt bond issuers examined by the IRS to appeal any adverse examination determination (that is, a determination that interest on previously issued obligations of the issuer is not excludable from gross income under Code Sec. 103) to the Appeals Division of the IRS. This administrative appeal of right must be heard by a senior appeals officer because of the complexity of the issues involved.

The Conference Committee Report states the intent of the conferees that Congress should evaluate judicial remedies in the future, once the IRS's tax-exempt bond examination program has more fully developed and Congress is better able to ensure that any future measure protects all parties in interest to a bond status determination (such as issuers, bondholders, conduit borrowers, and the federal government).

Comment. Act Sec. 8001 of the 1998 Act identifies this provision as a limited tax benefit subject to the line item veto. This executive veto power, however, was recently declared unconstitutional by the U.S. Supreme Court. The line item veto is discussed at ¶ 30,025.

PRACTICAL ANALYSIS. David R. Brennan of Faegre & Benson, Minneapolis, MN (former Director, Tax Litigation Division, Chief Counsel's Office and former Treasury Acting General Counsel), comments that the bill as passed by the Senate would have provided the issuer of tax-exempt bonds with access to the Tax Court. It is unclear why it was dropped in conference. The Conference Report does indicate that Congress will continue to monitor the desirability of a judicial remedy as the IRS's bond audit program motive.

While access to the Appeals Division may be helpful, the inability of the issuer to litigate may frustrate the usefulness of an appeal.

There could be a question of whether the establishment of such a procedure will lead to reviewability by the issuer in the District Court under the Administrative Procedures Act.

★ *Effective date.* No specific effective date is provided by the Act. The provision is, therefore, considered effective on the date of enactment.

Act Sec. 3105. Law at ¶ 8075. Committee Report at ¶ 10,270.

PRIVILEGED COMMUNICATIONS

Confidentiality Privilege Extended to Nonattorneys

¶ 1141

Background ————————————————————————

Certain communications between an attorney and a client, or a prospective client, with respect to legal advice are protected by a common-law privilege of confidentiality. These protected communications must be based on facts that the client provides the attorney for the purpose of receiving the attorney's advice, legal opinion, legal services, or assistance in some legal proceeding. The confidentiality privilege applies only to advice on legal matters. The privilege does not apply if the attorney is acting in another capacity, such as where the attorney is engaged to prepare a tax return.

The attorney-client privilege exists only if it has not otherwise been waived and is not invoked for the purpose of committing a crime or a tort. Further, if information in the communication can be discovered from nonprivileged sources, the applicable communication will not be privileged (*Diversified Industries Inc. v. Meredith,* CA-8, 572 F.2d 596 (1978)).

Prior to the IRS Restructuring and Reform Act of 1998, the attorney-client privilege was limited to communications between a taxpayer and the taxpayer's attorney. No similar privilege was available for communications between a taxpayer and another professional, such as a certified public accountant or an enrolled agent.

The Supreme Court has ruled that no accountant-client privilege exists with respect to the workpapers prepared by an independent auditor (*A. Young & Co.,* SCt, 84-1 USTC ¶ 9305, 465 US 805). A claim of work-product immunity under an accountant-client privilege could not be invoked to bar enforcement of an IRS summons for workpapers prepared by an independent certified public accounting firm during an audit of its client corporation's finances. The Supreme Court stated that independent auditors that certify public reports on a corporation's finances serve the public's interest even more than their client's interests. The Court noted that, without an express statutory provision to the contrary, it could not accept the accounting work-product immunity doctrine in the face of strong congressional policy and statutory language favoring broad IRS summons authority.

While federal courts will protect documents under a work-product privilege, courts of appeal have split over the interpretation of the privilege. The second and seventh circuits protect documents prepared "because of" existing or expected litigation, while the fifth circuit protects documents that exist "primarily to assist in litigation."

The extension of confidentiality to nonattorneys has been characterized as a taxpayer rights issue by accountants who contend that a taxpayer's choice of a tax advisor should not be affected by whether communications will be privileged. A representative of the American Institute of Certified Public Accountants has testified that "as a matter of public policy, a taxpayer has the right to expect that if the tax advisor selected is authorized to practice before the IRS, all information

Background ————————————————————————————————

that the advisor has regarding the taxpayer's tax matters will be accorded the same protection of privacy, regardless of the specific professional classification of the advisor." Critics of this extension of confidentiality have countered that it would add little, except as a marketing tool for accountants.

Commentators have also suggested that the privilege should not be extended to public accounting firms, whose responsibilities to the public would be thus undermined. The American Bar Association (ABA) has written that "extension of the privilege to Certified Public Accountants responsible for independent audits of the same taxpayers for whom there is a privilege claim would be fundamentally contrary to the concept of independent audits and differing roles of the accounting and legal professions."

Critics of the proposal further contend that a noncompliant taxpayer could use the extension of confidentiality to shield abusive transactions. In addition, the Clinton administration has weighed in against creating a new evidentiary privilege for nonattorney communications. In a statement to the Senate, the Office of Management and Budget (OMB) urged the Senate to strike the provision from the proposed bill. The OMB expressed the FBI's and Department of Justice's view that creation of the privilege would impede the prosecution and investigation of fraud matters, and the existence of the privilege would inhibit the investigation of the types of civil tax matters that often lead to criminal tax referrals.

IRS Restructuring and Reform Impact

Confidentiality privilege extended to certain nonattorneys.—In any noncriminal tax proceeding before the IRS, a taxpayer is now entitled to the same common-law protections of confidentiality, with respect to the tax advice given by any "federally authorized tax practitioner," as the taxpayer would have if the advising individual were an attorney (Code Sec. 7525(a)(1), as added by the IRS Restructuring and Reform Act of 1998). The privilege also applies in any noncriminal tax proceeding in federal court brought by or against the United States (Code Sec. 7525(a)(2)(B), as added by the 1998 Act).

Comment. Note that the privilege may not be asserted to prevent the disclosure of information to any regulatory body other than the IRS. The ability of any other regulatory body to gain or compel information is unchanged by this provision.

Federally authorized tax practitioner. A "federally authorized tax practitioner" includes any nonattorney who is authorized to practice before the IRS under section 330 of Title 31 of the United States Code, such as an enrolled agent, an enrolled actuary or a certified public accountant (Code Sec. 7525(a)(3)(A), as added by the 1998 Act).

Tax advice. "Tax advice" is defined as advice given by an individual with respect to a matter that is within the scope of the individual's authority to practice before the IRS (Code Sec. 7525(a)(3)(B), as added by the 1998 Act).

Comment. The ABA has suggested that this would include any tax aspect of any matter, even if the tax component of the matter is very slight in relation to the overall content of the matter.

Tax shelters. The privilege does not apply to any written communication between a federally authorized tax practitioner and a director, shareholder, officer, employee, agent, or representative of a corporation in connection with the promotion of any Code Sec. 6662(d)(2)(C)(iii) tax shelter in which the corporation is a direct or indirect participant (Code Sec. 7525(b), as added by the 1998 Act).

¶ 1141

Comment. The Conference Committee Report states that a tax shelter is any partnership, entity, plan or arrangement a significant purpose of which is the avoidance or evasion of income tax. Tax shelters where there will be no privilege of confidentiality include those required to be registered as Code Sec. 6111(d) confidential corporate tax shelter arrangements. The report also states that since the promotion of tax shelters is not part of the routine relationship between a tax practitioner and a client, the tax shelter limitation should not adversely affect such routine relationships.

Waiver. The Conference Committee Report provides that the confidentiality privilege to nonattorneys may be waived in the same way, such as disclosure of information to third parties, as the attorney-client privilege.

Caution. It is as yet unclear whether this extension of the confidentiality privilege includes (1) work product prepared by a federally authorized practitioner, (2) an accountant's opinion on a taxpayer's financial statements or (3) audit workpapers. The remaining viability of the *Young* decision may need to be resolved in the courts. Further, the extension of the privilege does not protect communications related to private-party litigation, non-Title 26 matters, and those made to nonfederally authorized practitioners.

Comment. Since the provision applies to *noncriminal* proceedings before the IRS, the new law may encourage the IRS to increase *criminal* investigations and proceedings, and to use third-party summonses.

Comment. The common-law attorney-client privilege is based on judicial doctrine. In addition, the attorney-client privilege has been incorporated in Federal Rule of Evidence 501. The House Committee Report states that the extension of confidentiality to certain nonattorneys does not modify the attorney-client privilege. Accordingly, the same limitations that apply to the attorney-client privilege would apply to this expanded privilege. However, the Conference Committee Report followed the Senate, not the House, Report.

Applicability of state law. Tax advice given by the federally authorized tax practitioner must be in a manner consistent with state law for that individual's profession.

Caution. While some states already recognize an accountant-client privilege, many states do not. Approximately 17 states embrace a full accountant-client privilege, while numerous others permit some form of the privilege. Commentators have suggested that the extension of the confidentiality privilege will create a conflict between federal and state law.

PRACTICAL ANALYSIS. Lawrence M. Hill, head of Brown & Wood's Tax Litigation Practice, New York, New York, comments that the IRS Restructuring and Reform Act would extend the common law attorney-client privilege to tax advice provided by federally authorized tax practitioners (i.e., accountants and enrolled agents) in noncriminal tax proceedings before the IRS and in the federal courts, with respect to such noncriminal tax matters. Congress apparently intended the privilege to extend to such proceedings in the U.S. Tax Court, the U.S. Court of Federal Claims, and the U.S. federal district courts. It is unclear whether Congress intended the provision to apply in the federal bankruptcy courts, for example where these courts have the authority to determine a taxpayer's tax liability or in other federal court contexts. The language of the statute would arguably appear to protect this communication. The statute does not protect state tax advice. It also does not protect information from being obtained by regulatory bodies other than the IRS, such as the SEC, State Boards of Accountancy and the AICPA.

The Act does not modify the common law attorney-client privilege other than to extend it to other authorized professionals. The confidentiality protection, therefore, should not apply generally to the preparation of tax returns, tax accrual workpapers or the provision of business or accounting advice.

The Conference Agreement added a modification that did not appear in the House or Senate bills. The confidentiality privilege will not apply to any written communications between a federally authorized practitioner (nonlawyers) and certain corporate representatives in connection with the promotion of the direct or indirect participation of such corporation in any tax shelter. This creates a hole in the privilege umbrella and uncertainty given the expansive definition of "tax shelter" under Code Sec. 6662.

There are a number of questions that remain unresolved and can be expected to be the subject of future litigation, including: (1) What constitutes the scope of federally authorized tax advice of the nonlawyer? (2) When does a noncriminal tax proceeding become a criminal proceeding? (3) What happens when both nontax advice and tax advice are provided by the nonlawyer? (4) Under what circumstances does a waiver of the privileges occur? (5) Will the nonlawyer be held to a different ethical standard or to a higher standard of care than he or she is now held? (6) How will summons enforcement actions be affected when accountants fail to turn over documents claiming that they do not fall within the corporate tax shelter exception? Will the federal district courts have to determine whether the transaction is a shelter? If so, what preclusive effect, if any, would this have on subsequent Tax Court or refund litigation with respect to this issue?

Caution. While enhanced confidentiality protection is provided to nonlawyer communications, blanket protection is not provided. Nonlawyer practitioners should proceed with caution in communicating with their clients about the scope of protection afforded by this new provision. Careful attention to risk management and full and fair disclosure to clients is warranted. Training of nonlawyers as to the scope and application of the privilege also is strongly recommended. Accountants will have to grapple with these and other difficult issues, such as how to construct engagement letters; how mechanically to protect the privilege; how to address dual tax and nontax client engagements; how to handle dual tax compliance and tax consulting engagements; and how to protect the privilege when peer review is involved.

★ *Effective date.* The provision is applicable to communications made on or after the date of enactment (Act Sec. 3411(c) of the 1998 Act).

Act Sec. 3411(a), adding new Code Sec. 7525; Act Sec. 3411(b); Act Sec. 3411(c). Law at ¶ 6740. Committee Report at ¶ 10,375.

THIRD-PARTY SUMMONSES

Motion to Quash

¶ 1146

Background ————————————————————————————

Prior to the enactment of the IRS Restructuring and Reform Act of 1998, if the IRS issued a summons to a "third-party recordkeeper" that related to the business transactions or affairs of a taxpayer, the IRS was required to give notice

Background

of that summons to the affected taxpayer within three days, either by certified or registered mail (Code Sec. 7609). The taxpayer was then given up to 23 days in which to begin a proceeding in the applicable federal district court to quash the summons. If the taxpayer was successful in this effort, the taxpayer could prevent that third-party recordkeeper from divulging the financial information sought by the IRS. Generally, a third-party recordkeeper was defined as a person who held financial information about the taxpayer, such as a bank, consumer reporting agency, credit card company, broker, attorney and any enrolled agent.

Prior to amendment by the 1998 Act, the IRS was not required to notify the taxpayer if the IRS sought information relative to the taxpayer's tax liability from persons and institutions other than a third-party recordkeeper. Congress, however, determined that a taxpayer should be notified by the IRS any time that the IRS seeks information from others regarding the taxpayer and the taxpayer's tax liability.

IRS Restructuring and Reform Impact

Taxpayer notification of all IRS third-party summonses.—New provisions now expand the IRS notification requirement regarding the issuance of a summons from just "third-party recordkeepers" to almost all summonses issued to any third party (i.e., persons other than the taxpayer), including the production of any computer software code (Code Sec. 7609(a)(1), as amended by the IRS Restructuring and Reform Act of 1998).

Comment. This broader application of the IRS notification requirement will enable a taxpayer to protect himself from most inappropriate summonses that the IRS may issue.

Note, however, that nothing in Code Sec. 7609 (relating to special procedures for third-party summonses) should be construed as limiting the IRS's ability to obtain requisite information, other than by summons, through formal or informal procedures that are authorized by Code Sec. 7601 and Code Sec. 7602 (such as examining the taxpayer's own records) (Code Sec. 7609(j), as added by the 1998 Act).

In general, once a summons has been issued, the IRS must appropriately notify the taxpayer, and the taxpayer is entitled to bring an action in the applicable district court to quash the summons. Nonetheless, in certain situations, the IRS need not provide taxpayer notice of a third-party summons. Code Sec. 7609(c)(2), as amended by the 1998 Act, specifies several occasions where no IRS notice of a summons need be made. These exemptions include a summons—

(1) served on the person with respect to whose liability the summons is issued, or any officer or employee of the person;

(2) issued to determine whether or not records of the business transactions or affairs of an identified person have been made or kept; and

(3) issued by a criminal investigator of the IRS in connection with the investigation of an offense connected with the administration or enforcement of the revenue laws.

Comment. The new third-party notification provisions basically give a taxpayer notice just about any time that the IRS uses its summons power to gather information about the taxpayer and the taxpayer's liability. No inference, however, is intended with respect to (1) the applicability of prior law to IRS summonses to the taxpayer or (2) the scope of the IRS's authority to summons testimony, books, papers or other records.

PRACTICAL ANALYSIS. Robert McKenzie, of McKenzie & Mc-Kenzie PC, Chicago, Ill., points out that taxpayers are granted statutory authority to seek to quash third-party summonses. Although a right granted by this provision, the courts probably will liberally construe the IRS's right to gather information from third parties and it is unlikely that this provision will impede the IRS's ability to secure information from third parties. Code Sec. 3415 specifically excludes summonses issued to aid in the collection of an assessment or judgment entered against the person with respect to whose liability the summons was issued and the liability, at law or at equity, of the person for transfer or fiduciary liability. It also specifically excludes summonses issued by a criminal investigator in the IRS.

The IRS is now given specific authority to serve a third-party summons by mail. In the past the IRS was required to personally serve a summons.

★ *Effective date.* These provisions apply to summonses served after the date of enactment (Act Sec. 3415(d) of the 1998 Act).

Act Sec. 3415(a), amending Code Sec. 7609(a)(1); Act Sec. 3415(b), adding Code Sec. 7609(j); Act Sec. 3415(c)(1), amending Code Sec. 7609(a); Act Sec. 3415(c)(2), amending Code Sec. 7609(c); Act Sec. 3415(c)(3), amending Code Sec. 7609(e)(2); Act Sec. 3415(c)(4), amending Code Sec. 7609(f); Act Sec. 3415(c)(5), amending Code Sec. 7609(g); Act Sec. 3415(c)(6), amending Code Sec. 7609(i); Act Sec. 3415(d). Law at ¶ 6790. Committee Report at ¶ 10,395.

Service to Recordkeepers

¶ 1151

Background

A summons issued under Code Sec. 6420(e)(2) (relating to the examination of books and records with respect to gasoline used on farms), Code Sec. 6421(g)(2) (relating to the examination of books and witnesses with respect to gasoline used for certain nonhighway uses), Code Sec. 6427(j)(2) (relating to the examination of books and witnesses with respect to fuels not used for taxable purposes), and Code Sec. 7602 (relating to the examination of books and witnesses) must be served by delivering an attested copy by hand to the person to whom it is directed, or by leaving the copy at his or her last and usual place of abode (Code Sec. 7603).

IRS Restructuring and Reform Impact

Service of summons to third-party recordkeepers by mail permitted.— The IRS now has the option of serving a summons to third-party recordkeepers either in person or by certified or registered mail to the last known address of the recordkeeper (Code Sec. 7603, as amended by the IRS Restructuring and Reform Act of 1998).

Third-party recordkeeper defined. The term "third-party recordkeeper" includes:

¶ 1151

(1) any mutual savings bank, cooperative bank, domestic building and loan association, or other savings institution chartered and supervised as a savings and loan or similar association under federal or state law, any bank as defined in Code Sec. 581, or any credit union within the meaning of Code Sec. 501(c)(14)(A);

(2) any consumer reporting agency as defined in Sec. 603(f) of the Fair Credit Reporting Act (15 U.S.C. 1681a(f));

(3) any person extending credit through the use of credit cards or similar devices;

(4) any broker, as defined in Sec. 3(a)(4) of the Securities Exchange Act of 1934 (15 U.S.C. 78c(a)(4));

(5) any attorney;

(6) any accountant;

(7) any barter exchange as defined in Code Sec. 6045(c)(3);

(8) any regulated investment company (RIC), as defined in Code Sec. 851, and any agent of a RIC when acting as an agent of the RIC; and

(9) any enrolled agent.

Comment. The Senate Finance Committee Report indicates that the change was made because the personal appearance of an IRS official at a place of business could be unnecessarily disruptive. For a discussion of third-party recordkeepers with regard to computer software and source code, see ¶ 1161.

★ *Effective date.* The provision applies to summonses served after the date of enactment (Act Sec. 3416(b) of the 1998 Act).

Act Sec. 3416(a), adding new Code Sec. 7603(b); Act Sec. 3416(b). Law at ¶ 6770. Committee Report at ¶ 10,400.

Taxpayer Pre-notification

¶ 1156

Background

As part of its revenue collection and enforcement efforts, the IRS may contact third parties in connection with the examination of a taxpayer or the collection of any tax owed by a taxpayer. For example, the IRS may issue a summons to any person who has information or records that may be relevant to an IRS inquiry. Generally, the taxpayer must be notified of the service of a summons on the third party within three days of the date of service (Code Sec. 7609(a)). Although required to give notice of a summons after the fact, the IRS was not required to give prior notice to a taxpayer. Such lack of notice often led to a chilling effect on a taxpayer's business or damage to the taxpayer's reputation because taxpayers were denied the opportunity to resolve issues and volunteer information before the IRS contacted third parties for such information.

IRS Restructuring and Reform Impact

IRS prohibited from third-party contact without prior taxpayer notice.—The IRS is now required to provide reasonable notice in advance to a taxpayer before contacting third parties with respect to examination or collection activities regarding the taxpayer (Code Sec. 7602(c)(1), as amended by the IRS Restructuring and Reform Act of 1998). According to the Conference Committee Report, it is intended that this notice will be provided as part of an existing IRS notice provided to taxpayers. In addition, the IRS is also now required to periodically provide a taxpayer with a record of persons contacted during the period by the IRS with respect to the determination or collection of the taxpayer's tax liability. This record must also be provided upon the taxpayer's request (Code Sec. 7602(c)(2), as amended by the 1998 Act).

Caution. The prohibition on third-party contact by the IRS and the notice of specific contacts does not apply:

(1) to any contact that the taxpayer has authorized;

(2) if the IRS determines that the notice would jeopardize collection of any tax or such notice may involve reprisal against any person; or

(3) with respect to any pending criminal investigation (Code Sec. 7602(c)(3), as amended by the 1998 Act).

PRACTICAL ANALYSIS. Robert McKenzie, of McKenzie & McKenzie PC, Chicago, Ill., observes that this provision represents a substantial enhancement of taxpayer privacy rights. The IRS is now required to notify the taxpayer in advance of its intent to seek information from third parties. This will allow taxpayers several protections. First, the taxpayer will be able to better control the nature of the contact by informing third party record keepers of the potential contact by the IRS; and secondly, the taxpayer may be able to convince the IRS investigator that a better means to secure the information is available. The taxpayer might volunteer additional information in an effort to prevent the decision to seek third party information. The IRS retains the right to determine whether, for good cause shown, informing the taxpayer would jeopardize collection of any tax or involve reprisal against any person. The IRS also has the right to forego the notice in the event of a pending criminal investigation. Even with the rights to foreclose such notice granted to the IRS, the taxpayer's bargaining position is greatly enhanced by the new notice provisions.

Practitioners and taxpayers should be alert to opportunities to provide alternative information to the IRS to avoid contacts with third parties. Contacts to third parties by the IRS generally hurt a taxpayer's reputation and may severely damage business relationships. Therefore, the advance notice provisions should be used as an opportunity to prevent such contacts.

★ *Effective date.* The prohibition of IRS contact of third parties without prior taxpayer notice applies to contacts made after the 180th day after the date of enactment of the Act.

Act Sec. 3417(a), redesignating Code Sec. 7602(c) and (d), as added by Act Sec. 3412, as Code Sec. 7602(d) and (e), and adding new Code Sec. 7602(c); Act Sec. 3417(b). Law at ¶ 6760. Committee Report at ¶ 10,405.

Software Trade Secrets Protection

¶ 1161

Background

The IRS is authorized to examine any books, papers, records or other data that may be relevant to an inquiry into the correctness of a federal tax return (Code Sec. 7602(a)). In addition, the IRS may issue and serve summonses on certain third-party recordkeepers (Code Sec. 7609).

The IRS is considered to have made a prima facie case for the enforcement of a summons if the "*Powell* standards" are met (*M. Powell*, SCt, 64-2 USTC ¶ 9858,

Background———————————————————————————————

379 US 48). The *Powell* standards require that (1) the examination to which the summons relates be conducted for a legitimate purpose, (2) the summons seeks information that may be relevant to the examination, (3) the IRS does not already have the information, and (4) the administrative procedures of the Internal Revenue Code have been followed. However, there are no specific statutory restrictions on the ability of the IRS to demand the production of computer records, programs, source code or similar material from either the taxpayer or a third party.

Some commentators have complained that the IRS has abused its summons power in recent audits by obtaining the software source code of programs used to produce an audited tax return. According to these commentators, the intellectual property rights of developers and owners should be respected. They claim that the examination of computer source code could lead to the inadvertent disclosure of trade secrets.

IRS Restructuring and Reform Impact

IRS access to software source code limited.—In order to protect the intellectual and property rights of the developers and owners of computer programs used to produce a return, the IRS is generally prohibited from issuing a summons or enforcing a summons to produce or analyze any tax-related computer software and source code that is obtained by the IRS in the course of the examination of a taxpayer's return (Code Sec. 7612(a)(1), as added by the IRS Restructuring and Reform Act of 1998). In addition, the Act provides specific protections against the disclosure and improper use of trade secrets and other confidential information related to computer programs and source code in the possession of the IRS as a result of an examination of any taxpayer (Code Sec. 7612(a)(2), as added by the 1998 Act).

A summons, however, may be issued for tax-related computer source code if:

(1) the IRS cannot otherwise reasonably ascertain the accuracy of any item on a return from the taxpayer's records, or computer software program and related data which, when executed, produces the output to prepare the return;

(2) the IRS identifies with reasonable specificity the portion, item, or component of the source code needed to verify the correctness of a return item; and

(3) the IRS determines that the need for the source code outweighs the risk of an unauthorized disclosure of trade secrets (Code Sec. 7612(b)(1), as added by the 1998 Act).

The IRS will be treated as satisfying the first two conditions if it—

(1) determines that it is not feasible to determine the correctness of a return item without access to the computer software executable code and associated data; and

(2) formally asks both the taxpayer and the software owner (the term "owner" also includes the software developer (Code Sec. 7612(d)(4), as added by the 1998 Act)) for the code and the code is not provided within 180 days (Code Sec. 7612(b)(3), as added by the 1998 Act).

Exceptions. The limitation on the summons of tax-related computer software source code will not apply—

¶ 1161

(1) if the summons is issued in connection with an inquiry into any offense connected with the administration or enforcement of the internal revenue laws;

(2) to a summons of any tax-related computer software source code that was acquired or developed by the taxpayer or a related person primarily for internal use, rather than for commercial distribution, by the taxpayer or related person;

(3) to communications between the owner of the tax-related computer software source code and the taxpayer or related persons; or

(4) to any tax-related computer software source code that is required to be provided or made available under any other provision of the Internal Revenue Code (Code Sec. 7612(b)(2), as added by the 1998 Act).

Caution. The Conference Committee Report clarifies that a summons for third-party tax-related computer source code that meets the standards established by Code Sec. 7612 will not be enforced if it would not be enforced under current law. For example, if the IRS's purpose in issuing a summons is shown to be improper, the summons will not be enforced, even if the IRS otherwise met the new standards for the summons of computer software source code.

Caution. The limitations on the summons of tax-related computer software source code applies only with respect to computer software that is used for accounting, tax return preparation, tax compliance, or tax-planning purposes. The Conference Committee Report reiterates that software or source code that is required to be provided under current law must be provided. Thus, for example, computer software or source code that must be provided with respect to the registration of a confidential corporate tax shelter under Code Sec. 6111 would nevertheless be required without regard to Code Sec. 7612. The Code Sec. 6111 registration requirements cannot be avoided where the tax shelter benefits are discernible only from the operation of a computer program.

Summons enforcement proceedings. Any person summoned may contest the summons of computer source code in any proceeding brought under Code Sec. 7604 to enforce the summons (Code Sec. 7612(b)(4), as added by the 1998 Act). The court must, at the request of any party, hold an evidentiary hearing to determine whether the summons requirements have been met. Moreover, any court enforcing a summons may issue any order necessary to prevent disclosure of confidential information (Code Sec. 7612(c)(1), as added by the 1998 Act).

Safeguards. In addition to authorizing district courts to issue protective orders, other specific safeguards are in place to ensure protection against improper disclosure by the IRS of trade secrets and other confidential information. These safeguards include the following:

(1) computer software or source code may be examined only in connection with the examination of a taxpayer's return with which it was received;

(2) the IRS must provide the taxpayer and the software owner with a written list of the names of all persons who will analyze or otherwise have access to the software;

(3) the software must be maintained in a secure area;

(4) the computer source code may not be removed from the owner's place of business without the owner's consent, unless the owner permits, or a court orders, removal;

(5) the software may not be decompiled or disassembled;

(6) the software or source code may be copied only as necessary to perform the specific examination and the IRS must number all copies and provide written certification that no other copies have or will be made (at the

conclusion of the examination and related court proceedings, the copies must be accounted for and returned to the owner and permanently deleted from any hard drives);

(7) if an individual who is not an officer or employee of the United States examines the software, the individual must enter into a written agreement with the IRS that the individual (a) will not disclose the software to anyone other than IRS authorized agents and employees and (b) will not participate, for two years, in the development of software that is intended for a similar purpose; and

(8) computer software or source code that is obtained by the IRS in the course of the examination of a taxpayer's return will be treated as return information for the purposes of Code Sec. 6103 (relating to confidentiality and disclosure of returns and return information) (Code Sec. 7612(c), as added by the 1998 Act).

Penalty for unauthorized disclosure. Any person who willfully divulges or makes known to another person software that was obtained for the purpose of examining a taxpayer's return in violation of Code Sec. 7612 will be punished, upon conviction, either by imprisonment not to exceed five years or by a fine not to exceed $5,000, or by both. Such person may also be liable for the costs of prosecution (Code Sec. 7213(d), as added by the 1998 Act).

Third-party recordkeepers. The Code Sec. 7603 procedures for service of summons of third-party recordkeepers (see ¶ 1151) apply to any owners or developer of a computer software source code. The third-party summons procedures will apply only with respect to a summons requiring the production of computer source code, the computer software executable code, and associated data that produces the computer output (Code Sec. 7603(b)(2)(J), as added by the 1998 Act).

Software defined. For purposes of the prohibition on the summons of computer software, "software" includes computer software source code and computer executable code (Code Sec. 7612(d)(1), as added by the 1998 Act).

"Computer software source code" includes:

(1) the code written by a programmer using a programming language that is understandable to appropriately trained persons and is not capable of directly being used to give instructions to a computer;

(2) related programmers' notes, design documents and memoranda; and

(3) related customer communications (Code Sec. 7612(d)(2), as added by the 1998 Act).

"Computer software executable code" includes:

(1) any object code, machine code, or other code readable by a computer when loaded into its memory and used directly by the computer to execute instructions; and

(2) any related user manuals (Code Sec. 7612(d)(3), as added by the 1998 Act).

Tax-related computer software source code defined. "Tax-related computer software source code" means the computer source code for any computer software program that is used for accounting, tax return preparation, tax compliance, or tax planning purposes (Code Sec. 7612(d)(6), as added by the 1998 Act).

Related person defined. A person is treated as "related" to another person if they are related under Code Sec. 267 or Code Sec. 707(b) (Code Sec. 7612(d)(5)). Thus, for example, related persons include family members, two corporations that are members of the same controlled group, an individual and a corporation of which more than 50 percent in value of the outstanding stock is owned by or for that individual, and an individual and a partnership of which more than 50 percent of the capital interest or profits interest is owned by that individual.

★ *Effective date.* Generally, these provisions are effective for summonses issued, and software acquired, after the date of enactment of the Act. However, in the case of software acquired on or before the date of enactment of the Act, the provisions generally apply 90 days after the date of enactment of the Act (except for the Code Sec. 7612(c)(2)(G)(ii) requirement that the IRS enter into written agreements with non-U.S. employees) (Act Sec. 3413(e) of the 1998 Act).

Act Sec. 3413(a), redesignating Code Sec. 7612 as Code Sec. 7613 and adding new Code Sec. 7612; Act Sec. 3413(b), amending Code Sec. 7213 by redesignating Code Sec. 7213(d) as Code Sec. 7213(e) and adding new Code Sec. 7213(d); Act Sec. 3413(c), amending Code Sec. 7603(b)(2); Act Sec. 3413(d); Act Sec. 3413(e). Law at ¶ 6570, ¶ 6770, ¶ 6810 and ¶ 6820. Committee Report at ¶ 10,385.

ACCESS TO IRS

Notification of IRS Contact Person

¶ 1166

Background ——————————————————————————

Taxpayers receive many notices sent by the IRS. However, all of the notices do not indicate the name and telephone number of an IRS employee who the taxpayer may call if the taxpayer has any questions.

IRS Restructuring and Reform Impact

IRS employee contacts expanded.—In order to make the IRS more accessible to taxpayers, the IRS is required to: (1) include in all manually-generated correspondence the name, telephone number, and unique identifying number of the IRS employee that the taxpayer may contact regarding the correspondence; (2) include in other correspondence a telephone number that the taxpayer may call; and (3) provide a taxpayer, during a telephone or personal contact, the employee's name and unique identifying number. The name and number must be prominently disclosed (Act Sec. 3705(a) of the IRS Restructuring and Reform Act of 1998).

The IRS is also instructed to develop procedures under which, to the extent practicable and if advantageous to the taxpayer, one IRS employee is assigned to handle a taxpayer's matter until the matter is resolved (Act Sec. 3705(b) of the 1998 Act).

———————————————

PRACTICAL ANALYSIS. Robert McKenzie, of McKenzie & McKenzie PC, Chicago, Ill., notes that in the past, the IRS initiated many letters that did not contain an identifying number and telephone number for an IRS employee. Taxpayers were at a loss to properly respond to that correspondence. The problem was particularly difficult with respect to notices issued by service centers. Taxpayers who attempted to call a center were confronted with a bureaucracy and could not receive consistent resolution of their tax problems. Act Sec. 3705 requires the IRS to place specific phone numbers and identifying numbers on every piece of correspondence generated by the IRS. Once the taxpayer contacts the IRS, he or she is entitled to know the personal name and identifying number of an IRS employee. The provision also provides a requirement that the IRS develop a system so that the taxpayer can deal with one person during the process as opposed

to being shuffled from one person to another. The IRS is also required to establish help lines for Spanish speaking taxpayers. The IRS is required to provide the unique identifying number for each employee within six months of enactment.

★ *Effective date.* Generally, these provisions are effective 60 days after the date of enactment of the IRS Restructuring and Reform Act of 1998. The unique-identifying-number requirement is effective six months after the date of enactment of the Act.

Act Sec. 3705(a); Act Sec. 3705(b); Act Sec. 3705(e)(1) and (4). Law at ¶ 8170. Committee Report at ¶ 10,655.

Telephone Helpline Options

¶ 1167

Background ───────────────────────────────────

In an effort to improve its service and accessibility to the taxpaying public, the IRS currently affords taxpayers the ability to contact the IRS by the telephone. For example, toll-free telephone lines by which taxpayers can receive tax assistance and request tax forms are now open six days a week, 16 hours a day. While the IRS is endeavoring to improve its service and accessibility through both internal review and external management consulting services, Congress determined that it too should provide some advice and insight in these areas, especially that gleaned by congressional contact with various taxpaying constituencies.

Accordingly, Congress, recognizing the growing Spanish-speaking population in this country, believes that the IRS must be more attentive to the diverse needs of these taxpayers. Further, Congress recognizes that some taxpayers are unable and/or unwilling to deal with voice-mail and the other assorted telephone options now available to in-coming callers. Consequently, Congress believes that the IRS should provide all taxpayers with the opportunity to speak with an IRS employee in addition to hearing any pre-recorded messages. Currently, the IRS allows callers, during normal business hours, to communicate with a tax assistor in either English or Spanish.

IRS Restructuring and Reform Impact

IRS telephone helpline options expanded.—In order to expand its services and to make the IRS more accessible to non-English speaking taxpayers, the IRS will be required to provide all callers to the IRS telephone helplines with the option of having their questions answered in Spanish (Act Sec. 3705(c) of the IRS Restructuring and Reform Act of 1998).

Moreover, all callers to the IRS, during normal business hours, will have the option to talk to a live person, in addition to hearing any applicable recorded message. This helpline operator will then direct any of the taxpayer's telephone questions to other IRS personnel who can provide appropriate information that the taxpayer can understand (Act Sec. 3705(d) of the 1998 Act).

★ *Effective date.* Both the option that helpline questions be answered in Spanish and the requirement that all telephone helpline callers be able to talk to a live person are effective as of January 1, 2000 (Act Sec. 3705(e) of the IRS Restructuring and Reform Act of 1998).

Act Sec. 3705(c); Act Sec. 3705(d); Act Sec. 3705(e). Law at ¶ 8170. Committee Report at ¶ 10,655.

IRS Telephone Numbers and Addresses

¶ 1171

Background——————————————————————————————

The IRS is not required to publish the telephone number or address of its local offices, and generally does not do so.

IRS Restructuring and Reform Impact

Listing local IRS telephone numbers and addresses.—To make it easier for taxpayers and their advisors to contact the IRS, the IRS is now required to list the phone number and address of IRS local offices in local telephone books. The Conference Committee Report clarifies that it is intended that (1) the IRS is not required to publish in more than one directory in any local area and (2) publication in alternate language directories is permissible. The IRS is required to provide the listing as soon as practicable (Act Sec. 3709 of the IRS Restructuring and Reform Act of 1998). The Senate Finance Committee Report, however, indicates that the listing is required no later than 180 days after the date of enactment.

PRACTICAL ANALYSIS. Robert McKenzie, of McKenzie & McKenzie PC, Chicago, Ill., observes that it is very difficult to secure the phone number for local IRS offices. A review of the local phone directory generally will find a listing of an 800 number that does not connect directly to the local IRS office. For example, there is no general telephone number listed in the Chicago directory that allows someone to call directly to the local Chicago IRS office. Act Sec. 3709 requires that each district provide local phone numbers and addresses in local phone directories for the IRS offices in its area. This will allow taxpayers to locate local offices and to conduct business with them. IRS employees in distant offices do not have the same concerns with individual taxpayers as local employees. Experienced practitioners almost universally agree that the best results for IRS problems come with local contact with IRS officials. Therefore, the IRS will not be able to hide behind a structure that encourages the taxpayer to use an impersonal telephone system. The taxpayer will now be able to find a local office and go directly to that office to solve problems.

★ *Effective date.* The Act provides no specific effective date. The provision is, therefore, considered effective on the date of enactment.

Act Sec. 3709. Law at ¶ 8185. Committee Report at ¶ 10,675.

Use of Pseudonyms by IRS Employees

¶ 1176

Background——————————————————————————————

Under rules promulgated by the Federal Service Impasses Panel, an employee of the federal government may "register" a pseudonym if the employee believes that use of his or her last name only will identify the employee due to the unique nature of the employee's last name, and/or the nature of the office location. The pseudonym must be registered with the employee's supervisor.

IRS Restructuring and Reform Impact

IRS use of pseudonyms is limited.—The IRS Restructuring and Reform Act of 1998 clarifies that an IRS employee may use a pseudonym only if:

(1) the employee provides adequate justification for the use, such as personal safety; and

(2) use of the pseudonym is approved by the employee's supervisor prior to such use (Act Sec. 3706(a) of the IRS Restructuring and Reform Act of 1998).

According to the Senate Finance Committee Report, the new restrictions will help curb the use of pseudonyms in inappropriate circumstances.

★ *Effective date.* The provision applies to requests made after the date of enactment of the Act.

Act Sec. 3706(a); Act Sec. 3706(b). Law at ¶ 8175. Committee Report at ¶ 10,660.

Chapter 12

Taxpayer Rights—Collection Activities

LIENS AND LEVIES

Supervisor Approval

¶ 1201

Background

Persons liable for tax who do not make payment within 10 days after written notice and demand by the IRS are subject to having the IRS collect the tax by levy upon (i.e., seizure of) all property and rights to property belonging to the taxpayer, unless there is an explicit statutory prohibition from doing so (Code Sec. 6331(a)). The IRS may seize and sell property of the taxpayer subject to the levy no sooner than 30 days after sending the taxpayer a "Final Notice of Intent to Levy" (Code Sec. 6331(d)). Generally, under prior law, except in limited circumstances, revenue officers were not required to obtain supervisory approval of liens, levies and seizures.

IRS Restructuring and Reform Impact

Supervisory approval required for collection actions.—Revenue officers who seek to commence collection action against a taxpayer must now generally secure a supervisor's approval prior to issuing a notice of lien or levy with respect to a taxpayer's property, or levying or seizing a taxpayer's property.

Comment. Prior approval is required "where appropriate." The new law and controlling committee reports, however, do not provide guidance regarding situations in which prior approval would not be necessary. However, the Conference Report states that the IRS Commissioner shall have discretion in developing the approval procedures required by the Act to determine the circumstances under which supervisory approval of liens and levies issued by the automated collection system is or is not "appropriate." This issue will presumably be addressed in regulations.

The approval process requires the supervisor to review the taxpayer's information, verify the balance of the tax debt due and affirm that the collection action proposed is appropriate under the circumstances. The circumstances that the supervisor should take into consideration include the value of the asset subject to the seizure as it relates to the tax debt due (Act Sec. 3421(b) of the IRS Restructuring and Reform Act of 1998).

Comment. If the value of the property subject to seizure far exceeds the debt owed, then such a seizure would most likely be found to be inappropriate. However, if the value of the property to be seized is relatively small with respect to the outstanding liability, the seizure is likely to be appropriate, especially if such a seizure is part of a series of relatively "small value" seizures. It should be noted that the current regulations provide that property may not be seized if the proposed collection action is an "uneconomical levy," where the anticipated expenses with respect to the levy and sale of the seized property exceed the fair market value of the property (Reg. § 301.6331-2(b)(1)).

The revenue officer and/or supervisor are subject to disciplinary action for failure to adhere to the procedures for the supervisory approval and issuance of collection action notices (Act Sec. 3421(a)(2), as added by the 1998 Act).

Though not in the Act, the Senate Committee Report states that the Treasury Inspector General for Tax Administration is required to collect information regarding the approval process and annually report to the tax-writing committees.

PRACTICAL ANALYSIS. Robert McKenzie, of McKenzie & McKenzie PC, Chicago, Ill., comments that under current law, the IRS collection employees routinely file notices of lien and levy without discussion of the matter with supervisors. Revenue officers are routinely delegated the authority to levy upon bank accounts, wages and assets held by third parties without supervisory approval. Federal tax liens are routinely filed by the revenue officers without their supervisor's approval. Code Sec. 3421 imposes a duty upon IRS supervisory personnel to engage in specific reviews prior to the initiation of liens and levies. The supervisor must review the taxpayer's information and verify the balances due and confirm that an action proposed to be taken is appropriate considering the taxpayer's circumstances, the amount due and the value of the property.

McKenzie further notes that with respect to non-automated collection action, this provision takes effect immediately. However, with respect to automated collection actions, the provision will not take effect until December 31, 2000. The exclusion of Automated Collection System actions from the immediate impact of this provision is unfortunate. Most notices of levy and liens are served by the Automated Collection System. Only a small percentage of levies and liens are issued by revenue officers. Over the years more hardships have been visited on taxpayers by the Automated Collection System than revenue officers. Liens and levies

are issued in a rote fashion by a computer without human intervention via the Automatic Collection System. The system is ripe for errors and unintended harms to taxpayers. Given the current method of serving levies and liens by Automated Collection System, the IRS will face a substantial challenge to place a human element into the process. One must be alert to exercise the rights under Code Sec. 6330 to protect clients from potential abuses by the Automated Collection System during the period from enactment of this provision until December 31, 2000.

★ *Effective date.* The procedures for supervisory approval of collection actions (except for collection actions under the automated collection system) outlined by this provision are effective on the date of enactment (Act Sec. 3421(c)(1) of the IRS Restructuring and Reform Act of 1998). This provision applies to collection actions under an automated collection system initiated after December 31, 2000 (Act Sec. 3421(c)(2) of the IRS Restructuring and Reform Act of 1998).

Act Sec. 3421. Law at ¶ 8095. Committee Report at ¶ 10,415.

Jeopardy and Termination Levies

¶ 1206

Background ⎯⎯⎯⎯⎯⎯⎯⎯⎯⎯⎯⎯⎯⎯⎯⎯⎯⎯⎯⎯⎯⎯⎯⎯⎯⎯

Generally, the IRS is restricted from taking levy action on assessments until 30 days after sending the taxpayer a "Final Notice of Intent to Levy" pursuant to Code Sec. 6331(d)(2). When the IRS deems the collection of the tax to be at risk, however, the IRS may utilize special procedures under the Code to make jeopardy or termination assessments. If the taxpayer is leaving or removing property from the United States (Code Sec. 6851) or if assessment or collection would be jeopardized by delay (Code Secs. 6861 and 6862), the 30-day notice requirement of the intent to levy is effectively waived (Code Sec. 6331(a)).

Termination assessments apply to taxes in jeopardy for the current tax year or the immediately preceding tax year if the period for filing the return for such year has not passed. These assessments have the effect of closing the current tax year so that the amount of tax to be assessed and collected under the procedures can be determined. Jeopardy assessments are effective when the tax year is over.

The IRS considers the collection of tax liabilities in jeopardy when the following conditions exist:

(1) the taxpayer plans to avoid payment by concealing their person or property from the reach of the United States government by removing such property from the United States, dissipating it, or transferring it to others;

(2) the taxpayer plans to do any other act that would tend to prejudice collection proceedings actions or render such actions ineffective if the actions are not brought without delay; or

(3) the taxpayer's financial solvency appears to be imperiled unless the potential insolvency is due to the proposed assessment of tax and related penalties and interest (Code Sec. 6851(a); Reg. § 1.6851-1(a)(1)).

Since termination and jeopardy assessments have the same criteria for determining whether such assessments are appropriate in a particular circumstance, such assessments may be issued simultaneously against the same taxpayer.

Although the jeopardy collection actions often involve complex legal issues, the IRS is not required to obtain IRS Counsel review before jeopardy assessments, termination assessments and jeopardy levies are issued. Although IRS Counsel review for these types of collection actions is required by the Internal Revenue Service Manual and it is current IRS practice to obtain Counsel review for such actions, it is not a statutory requirement. Under Code Sec. 7429(g), the IRS bears

Background

the burden of proof with respect to the reasonableness of a termination or jeopardy assessment or a jeopardy levy.

IRS Restructuring and Reform Impact

IRS Counsel review of jeopardy and termination assessments required.—No jeopardy and termination assessments or jeopardy levy may be made without review and written approval by the IRS Chief Counsel or his delegate. Further, within five days of making the jeopardy or termination assessment or jeopardy levy, the IRS must provide the taxpayer with a written statement setting forth the basis on which the IRS relied in making the assessment or levy (Code Sec. 7429(a)(1), as amended by the IRS Restructuring and Reform Act of 1998).

The Senate Committee Report states that if prior IRS Counsel approval is not obtained, the taxpayer is entitled to an abatement of the assessment (Code Sec. 6201) or release of the levy (Code Sec. 6343(d)). If the IRS fails to offer such relief, the taxpayer may appeal to IRS Appeals under the new due process review procedure for IRS collections (see ¶ 1254) and then to court.

Comment. The requirement of an IRS Counsel review may lead to more intrusive and thorough IRS investigations because many approval decisions will be based on whether the IRS will be able to meet its burden of proof with respect to any administrative appeal or court action contesting a jeopardy or termination assessment or jeopardy levy.

Example. Anne Swanson, a revenue officer with the IRS, had been investigating Ray Nakamoto, an international art dealer, for income taxes for tax years 1999 and 2000. Following her meeting with Nakamoto on May 2, 2001, Swanson had reasonable cause to believe that Nakamoto was planning to leave the country and prepared to make a jeopardy assessment and levy for tax years 1999 and 2000 and a termination assessment for tax year 2001. After submitting her report to the IRS Chief Counsel for review and approval of the proposed collection actions, Swanson received a phone call from Nakamoto's wife that Nakamoto planned to divert funds from his domestic bank accounts to a small Colombian bank on May 4, 2001. Swanson feared that the Chief Counsel would not be able to approve the proposed collection action before Nakamoto's planned diversion of funds and immediately levied upon Nakamoto's domestic bank accounts. Since Chief Counsel approval was not received prior to the levy action, Nakamoto is entitled to an abatement of the assessment action and release of the levy. However, if the IRS does not grant Nakamoto relief, he would be able to seek relief first from the IRS Appeals office through the new due process procedures for IRS collections and then in a court proceeding.

★ *Effective date.* This provision is effective for taxes assessed and levies made after the date of enactment (Act Sec. 3434(b) of the IRS Restructuring and Reform Act of 1998).

Act Sec. 3434(a), amending Code Sec. 7429(a)(1); Act Sec. 3434(b). Law at ¶ 6620. Committee Report at ¶ 10,440.

Levy Exemption Amounts

¶ 1210

Background

The IRS is authorized to levy upon the property or rights to property held by delinquent taxpayers after notice (Code Sec. 6331). However, the IRS cannot levy

Background

upon all of the property of the taxpayer. Certain property is exempt from levy which allows the taxpayer sufficient assets to earn a living and pay for the necessities of life (Code Sec. 6334). Currently, Code Sec. 6334(a)(2) exempts from levy up to $2,500 in value of fuel, provisions, furniture and personal effects in the taxpayer's household. Code Sec. 6334(a)(3) exempts from levy up to $1,250 in the value of books and tools that is necessary for the trade, business or profession of the taxpayer.

IRS Restructuring and Reform Impact

Increased levy exemption amounts.—The $2,500 levy exemption amount stated in Code Sec. 6334(a)(2) and Reg. § 301.6334(a)(2) for the taxpayer's personal effects has been increased to $6,250. The $1,250 levy exemption amount stated in Code Sec. 6334(a)(3) and Reg. § 301.6334(a)(3) for the books and tools necessary for taxpayer's trade, business or profession has been increased to $3,125. Although the prior exemption amounts were increased in 1996 by the Taxpayer Bill of Rights 2 (P.L. 104-168), it was determined that the exemption amounts needed further adjustment in order to account for inflation and for the exemption to have a meaningful effect. For tax years beginning in 1999 or thereafter, the exemption amounts will be increased consistent with the applicable cost-of-living adjustment (COLA) amounts (Code Sec. 6334(g), as amended by IRS Restructuring and Reformation Act of 1998).

> **Example.** As of August 26, 1999, Mary Lambert, a taxpayer who had been served with a Final Notice of Intent to Levy on June 1, 1999, had household items and personal effects valued at $10,000. Lambert also had books and tools valued at $2,500 that she used in her consulting business. On August 27, 1999, the IRS executed its levy against Lambert's property. Under Code Sec. 6334(a)(2), the IRS would only be able to reach $3,750 ($10,000 − $6,250 exemption amount = $3,750) of the value of Lambert's household items and personal effects. Under Code Sec. 6334(a)(3), the IRS would not be able to seize any of the property used in Lambert's consulting business because the value of the property ($2,500) subject to seizure was less than the exemption amount ($3,125).

PRACTICAL ANALYSIS. Robert McKenzie, of McKenzie & Mc-Kenzie PC, Chicago, Ill., points out that the provision substantially increases the exemptions from levy available to taxpayers under Code Sec. 6334 of the Internal Revenue Code. The increases will have the practical effect of preventing seizure of books and tools in trade and personal effects from many lower income taxpayers. The prior exemptions were *de minimis* and allowed an opportunity for the IRS to take cars and other personal belongings from individuals with limited means. New exemptions will allow taxpayers to at least retain modest vehicles, personal items, books and tools of trade with reasonable value.

★ *Effective date.* The provision applies to levies issued after the date of enactment (Act Sec. 3431(d) of the IRS Restructuring and Reform Act of 1998).

Act Sec. 3431(a), amending Code Sec. 6334(a)(2); Act Sec. 3431(b), amending Code Sec. 6334(a)(3); Act Sec. 3431(c), amending Code Sec. 6334(g)(1); Act Sec. 3431(d). Law at ¶ 6290. Committee Report at ¶ 10,425.

Lien Exemption Amounts

¶ 1214

Background —————————————————————————

After a federal tax has been assessed and a demand for payment has been made, a federal tax lien attaches to all of a delinquent taxpayer's real and personal property until the tax is paid (Code Sec. 6321). The federal tax lien applies to property owned by the taxpayer during the lifetime of the lien, including property acquired after the lien arose (Reg. § 301.6321-1). However, federal tax liens are not valid against the 10 categories of "superpriority" interests enumerated in Code Sec. 6323(b).

Two of the superpriority interests are limited by a specific dollar amount. Code Sec. 6323(b)(4) provides that for casual sales for less than $250 with respect to household goods, personal effects or other tangible property, federal tax liens are not valid against a purchaser who does not have actual notice or knowledge of the existence of the lien or if the casual sale is not part of a series of related sales. Code Sec. 6323(b)(7) gives priority to mechanic's liens related to repairs or improvements to a taxpayer's owner-occupied personal residence for $1,000 or less. These dollar amounts have remained the same for decades.

Code Sec. 6323(10) provides that banks (Code Sec. 581) and savings and loans institutions (Code Sec. 591) have priority over federal tax liens with respect to "passbook" loans to the extent the institution made the loan without actual notice or knowledge of the federal tax lien. The institution must have been continuously in possession of the passbook from the time the loan was made. "Passbook" loans are loans made by banks and savings and loans to their savings account depositors. Such loans are secured by the borrower's savings deposit. Formerly, borrowers gave their passbooks to the lender as collateral, but under current banking practices, a "passbook" loan may be made without the use of an actual passbook.

IRS Restructuring and Reform Impact

Increase in dollar limits for superpriority lienholders.—The dollar limit for purchasers of personal property at a casual sale is increased from $250 to $1,000, and the dollar limit for mechanic's lienholders providing home improvement work on owner-occupied personal residences is increased from $1,000 to $5,000. For tax years beginning in 1999 or thereafter, the higher exemption amounts will be indexed annually for inflation (consistent with the cost-of-living adjustment (COLA) amounts for the applicable tax year) and rounded to the nearest multiple of $10 (Code Sec. 6323(b)(4), as amended by the IRS Restructuring and Reform Act of 1998 (the "1998 Act"); Code Sec. 6323(b)(7), as amended by the 1998 Act; and Code Sec. 6323(i)(4), as added by the 1998 Act).

For purposes of Code Sec. 6323(b)(10), passbook loans are referred to as "deposit-secured loans." Despite the change in terminology for these type of loans, such loans are still afforded the same treatment as passbook loans under prior law (Code Sec. 6323(b)(10), as amended by the IRS Restructuring and Reform Act of 1998).

★ *Effective date.* The amendments made by this provision take effect on the date of enactment (Act Sec. 3435(c) of the IRS Restructuring and Reform Act of 1998).

Act Sec. 3435(a)(1)(A), amending Code Sec. 6323(b)(4); Act Sec. 3435(a)(1)(B), amending Code Sec. 6323(b)(7); Act Sec. 3435(a)(2), adding Code Sec. 6323(i)(4); Act Sec. 3435(b), amending Code Sec. 6323(b)(10); Act Sec. 3435(c). Law at ¶ 6250. Committee Report at ¶ 10,445.

Release of Levy

¶ 1218

Background

The IRS is authorized to release levies upon all, or part of, the property or rights to property seized, including wages and salaries (Code Sec. 6343(a)). The IRS may release a wage levy once proof of uncollectibility is received by the taxpayer. However, some IRS critics have contended that after the receipt of the taxpayer's proof of uncollectibility, the IRS levies on one period of wages before releasing the levy.

IRS Restructuring and Reform Impact

Immediate release of levy upon agreement of uncollectibility.—Under the Act, the IRS must, as soon as it is practicable, release a wage levy once an agreement is made with the taxpayer that his outstanding tax liability is uncollectible (Code Sec. 6343(e), as added by the IRS Restructuring and Reform Act of 1998).

Comment. The new law and controlling committee reports do not provide specific guidance with respect to the level of effort required by the IRS in order to release wage levies once an agreement as to uncollectibility is reached. However, the Conference Committee Report states that the IRS must not intentionally delay until after one wage payment has been made and levied upon before releasing the levy.

Example. On June 4, 2000, Tracey Smith, who had been subject to a continuous wage levy since November 1999, reached an agreement with the IRS that her 1997 income tax debt was uncollectible. Tracey was due to receive wages from her employer on June 8, 2000. If it is practicable for the IRS to release the wage levy prior to June 8, then the IRS must not intentionally delay the release of the wage levy so that it can collect monies from the June 8th wage payment.

Caution. The release of a levy pursuant to Code Sec. 6343 does not prevent a subsequent levy on the same property (Code Sec. 6343(a)(3)). Thus, the IRS could levy a taxpayer's wages for the payment of other tax liabilities unrelated to the uncollectibility agreement.

PRACTICAL ANALYSIS. Robert McKenzie, of McKenzie & McKenzie PC, Chicago, Ill., notes that Internal Revenue Manual 5375 allows the IRS to declare an account currently not collectable. The IRS takes this step if, after reviewing the taxpayer's financial statement, it determines that he or she is unable to pay any tax liability at this time. Over the years the IRS has occasionally declared accounts uncollectable while continuing to levy upon a taxpayer's wages. This provision will prevent such action. If the IRS determines the account is uncollectable, it may not continue to take a taxpayer's wages.

The provision imposes a statutory mandate upon the IRS. In the past it was inconsistent for the IRS to determine the taxpayer could not pay a tax liability while at the same time continuing to seize that taxpayer's salary.

★ *Effective date.* This provision is effective for levies imposed after December 31, 1999 (Act Sec. 3432(b) of the IRS Restructuring and Reform Act of 1998).

Act Sec. 3432(a), adding Code Sec. 6343(e); Act Sec. 3432(b). Law at ¶ 6320. Committee Report at ¶ 10,430.

Prohibition During Refund Proceedings

¶ 1222

Background

The IRS may not assess a tax deficiency or take any collection action if the taxpayer has filed a timely petition with the Tax Court with respect to the deficiency. If a taxpayer files a claim for refund, however, there are certain circumstances in which the IRS is permitted to assess and collect tax while the taxpayer's liability is being litigated.

A taxpayer generally must pay the entire amount of a contested tax before filing a claim for refund. In the case of a "divisible tax," however, the taxpayer need only pay the tax for the applicable period before filing a claim. Divisible taxes are taxes that, by their nature, are paid periodically, such as employment taxes and trust fund recovery penalties under Code Sec. 6672. It is possible, therefore, that a taxpayer under the jurisdiction of a U.S. District Court or the U.S. Court of Federal Claims could be subjected to collection by levy with respect to the unpaid amount of tax at issue. Because the Tax Court does not have jurisdiction over most divisible taxes, taxpayers have no forum for contesting such taxes before they are paid.

IRS Restructuring and Reform Impact

IRS prohibited from taking levy action during pendency of refund suit.—The new law prohibits the IRS from collecting by levy any unpaid divisible tax while a refund proceeding in a proper federal trial court for the paid portion of such tax is pending. A proceeding is considered pending until a final judgment or order from which an appeal may be taken is entered (Code Sec. 6331(i)(6), as added by the IRS Restructuring and Reform Act of 1998). In order for the prohibition against levy actions to apply, a decision in the proceeding must be binding with respect to the unpaid tax, or the person against whom the collection proceeding would be brought must be collaterally estopped from contesting the unpaid tax (Code Sec. 6331(i)(1), as added by the 1998 Act). Divisible taxes are payroll taxes imposed by subtitle C of the Internal Revenue Code and the penalty imposed by Code Sec. 6672 for failure to collect and pay over tax or attempt to evade or defeat tax (Code Sec. 6331(i)(2), as added by the 1998 Act).

The prohibition against IRS collection by levy does not apply if the taxpayer files a written waiver with the IRS or the IRS finds that collection of the unpaid tax is in jeopardy. This prohibition also does not apply if the levy carries out a credit or refund under Code Sec. 6402 or the levy was first made before the applicable proceeding was begun (Code Sec. 6331(i)(3), as added by the 1998 Act).

IRS prohibited from beginning collection proceedings in court during pendency of refund suit. The IRS may not begin a court proceeding to collect any unpaid divisible tax while a refund proceeding for the paid portion of such tax is pending. If the IRS does begin such a proceeding, the anti-injunction provisions of Code Sec. 7421 do not apply. This prohibition does not apply to a proceeding that is a counterclaim or other proceeding related to the refund proceeding (Code Sec. 6331(i)(4), as added by 1998 Act). The Conference Report states that a proceeding related to a refund proceeding includes, but is not limited to, civil·actions brought by the United States or another person with respect to the same type of tax (or related taxes or penalties) for the same (or overlapping) tax periods. In other words, the IRS may institute a counterclaim against the taxpayer for the balance of the unpaid tax or may initiate an action against other persons assessed for trust fund recovery penalties for the same employment taxes.

Statute of limitations suspended. The 10-year period of limitations on collection of delinquent taxes after assessment (Code Sec. 6502) is suspended during the pendency of a refund proceeding court action during which the IRS is prohibited from collecting by levy (Code Sec. 6331(i)(5), as added by the 1998 Act).

Comment. The prohibition against IRS collection actions applies to levy actions and court proceedings. Accordingly, the IRS is not restricted in filing a Notice of Federal Tax Lien for the liability at issue.

PRACTICAL ANALYSIS. Robert McKenzie, of McKenzie & McKenzie PC, Chicago, Ill., observes that this provision adopts a policy of the IRS as a statutory protection. Policy 5-16 has provided since March 1, 1984, that the IRS would forbear collection regarding a devisable liability while a refund suit was pending. Unfortunately, the IRS has occasionally violated its own policies and the taxpayer was left without remedy. Most often this provision applies to a trust fund liability pursuant to Code Sec. 6672. Taxpayers are not required to pay the entire liability in order to file a refund claim. Taxpayers generally pay the amount of tax due for one employee for one period and then file a refund claim with a request for abatement of the remaining liability. If the IRS denies that claim, or six months expires, then the taxpayer is authorized to initiate a refund in U.S. District Court pursuant to Code Sec. 7421.

Unfortunately, notes McKenzie, the IRS occasionally continued to pursue collection measures even though the taxpayer had sought a refund in U.S. District Court. These courts were specifically prohibited from enjoining IRS collection efforts during the pendency of refund litigation concerning a devisable liability. Act Sec. 3433 grants specific authority to courts to enjoin IRS collection actions during the pendency of devisable liability disputes. This provision will prevent the abusive situation when a taxpayer disputes a liability, but faces draconian IRS collection actions, while at the same time pursuing legal rights before a federal court. The provision specifically provides for the suspension of the collection statute of limitations pursuant to Code Sec. 6502 during the pendency of a proceeding.

★ *Effective date.* This provision applies to unpaid tax attributable to tax periods beginning after December 31, 1998 (Act Sec. 3433(b) of the IRS Restructuring and Reform Act of 1998).

Act Sec. 3433(a), redesignating Code Sec. 6331(i) as (j) and adding new Code Sec. 6331(i); Act Sec. 3433(b). Law at ¶ 6280. Committee Report at ¶ 10,435.

Retirement Plans and IRAs

¶ 1226

Background

Generally, the IRS is authorized to levy upon all non-exempt property or rights to property belonging to a taxpayer (Code Sec. 6331). Qualified retirement plans and IRAs are not exempt from levy by the IRS. Moreover, distributions from a qualified plan or IRA are includible in the taxpayer's gross income to the extent that the distribution represents after-tax contributions or investments regardless of whether the plan or IRA is subject to levy. Further, the amount of the distribution included in the gross income of a taxpayer is subject to a 10-percent early withdrawal tax unless the distribution is made after the taxpayer reaches age 59½ or one of several other specifically enumerated exceptions applies (Code Sec. 72(t)(2)). Distributions made on account of an IRS levy are not listed as an exception to the early withdrawal tax (Code Sec. 72(t)(2)).

IRS Restructuring and Reform Impact

Early withdrawal tax does not apply to employer-sponsored retirement plan or IRA distributions on account of an IRS levy.—The 10-percent tax on early (pre-age 59½) withdrawals from employer-sponsored retirement plans or IRAs will not apply to distributions made on account of an IRS levy on a taxpayer's qualified retirement plan or IRA (Code Sec. 72(t)(2)(A)(vii), as added by the IRS Restructuring and Reform Act of 1998).

The Senate Committee Report emphasizes that this exception does not apply if there is no levy on the qualified plan or IRA. Thus, the exception does not apply when the IRS has not levied upon the taxpayer and the taxpayer withdraws funds to pay taxes in order avoid a levy, obtain the release of a levy on other interests, or in any other situation not specifically addressed by the statutory exceptions under Code Sec. 72(t)(2)(A). The exception becomes effective for distributions due to an IRS levy after December 31, 1999.

Example. On June 21, 2000, the IRS levied the IRA of Carol Navarro, a 57-year-old retiree. The amount levied was $230,000, of which $150,000 was from nondeductible contributions. Since the pre-age 59½ IRA distribution was due to an IRS levy, Navarro is not subject to the 10-percent early withdrawal penalty. However, since Navarro must still recognize income to the extent the IRA distribution represents pre-tax income, she will recognize $80,000 of the distribution as income in the tax year withdrawn ($230,000 − $150,000 = $80,000).

★ *Effective date.* This provision applies to levies made after December 31, 1999 (Act Sec. 3436(b) of the IRS Restructuring and Reform Act of 1998).

Act Sec. 3436(a), adding Code Sec. 72(t)(2)(A)(vii); Act Sec. 3436(b). Law at ¶ 5150. Committee Report at ¶ 10,450.

Erroneous Lien

¶ 1230

Prior to the Supreme Court's decision in *L.R. Williams* (SCt, 95-1 USTC ¶ 50,218, 115 SCt 1611 (1995)), the Internal Revenue Code provisions regarding refund suits were generally interpreted by the courts to mean that jurisdiction over such suits only applied to matters brought by the taxpayer against whom the tax was assessed. However, the Supreme Court held in *Williams* that a third party who paid another party's tax in order to remove an erroneously placed lien on her property was entitled to file a refund action against the United States. In *Williams*, the IRS had filed a nominee lien against the property owned by the former spouse of an assessed taxpayer that was under a contract for sale. The former spouse paid the taxpayer's liability under protest so that the sale could be completed and sued in the district court to recover the amount paid. The Supreme

Background

Court held that Code Sec. 1346(a)(1) authorizes suits against the United States by the person(s) the tax was collected from, in any civil action for the recovery of any erroneously or illegally assessed or collected tax without regard to whom the tax was assessed against. Moreover, the Court held that taxpayers forced to pay another taxpayer's liability under duress are authorized to bring refund suits because other judicial remedies are often inadequate.

IRS Restructuring and Reform Impact

Administrative procedure for release of erroneous lien.—The IRS Restructuring and Reform Act of 1998 creates an administrative procedure which provides that, as a matter of right, the third-party owner of property against which a federal tax lien has been filed may obtain a certificate of discharge with respect to the lien on such property. The certificate of discharge is issued if (1) the third-party owner deposits with the IRS an amount of money equal to the value of the United States' interest in the property as determined by the IRS or (2) the third-party owner posts a bond covering the United States' interest in the property in a form acceptable by the IRS. This procedural relief is not available to an owner of the property subject to the lien if that owner is the person whose unsatisfied liability gave rise to the lien (Code Sec. 6325(b)(4), as added by the 1998 Act).

If the IRS determines that (1) the liability to which the lien relates can be satisfied from other sources or (2) the value of the United States' interest in the property is less than the IRS's prior determination of the United States' interest in the property, then the IRS will refund (with interest at the same rate afforded to overpayments under Code Sec. 6621) the amount deposited and release the bond applicable to such property. Further, if no action is filed within the 120-day period prescribed under new Code Sec. 7426(a)(4), the IRS must, within 60 days after the 120-day period has elapsed, (1) apply the amount deposited or collect on the posted bond to the extent necessary to cover the unsatisfied liability secured by the lien and (2) refund (with interest at the same rate afforded to overpayments under Code Sec. 6621) any amount not used to satisfy such liability (Code Sec. 6324(b)(4)(C), as amended by the 1998 Act).

> **Example (1).** On August 1, 1999, Karin Harris and Jean Guth signed a contract to sell their townhouse to Kurt and Anne Jones for $275,000. On August 15, three days prior to the scheduled closing, the IRS placed a $130,000 lien on the townhouse for delinquent tax liabilities owed by Harris. After receiving assurances from Harris that the lien was placed on the townhouse in error, Guth posted a bond (acceptable to the IRS) in order to release the lien and the sale was completed as scheduled. The IRS issued a certificate of discharge from the lien and later determined that the $130,000 tax liability could be satisfied by levying upon Harris' IRA account. Since the IRS determined that the tax liability could be satisfied from another source, the IRS refunded the amount paid by Guth with interest and released the bond (Code Sec. 6325(b)(4)(B)(i), as amended by the 1998 Act).

Civil action to release erroneous lien. Within 120 days after a certificate of discharge is issued, the third-party owner may file a civil action against the United States in a U.S. District Court for a determination of whether the United States' interest in the property (if any) has less value than that determined by the IRS. If the court rules that the IRS's valuation exceeds the government's actual interest in the property, the court will order a refund of the deposited amount plus interest, and release of the bond. Interest on the refund is paid from the time the IRS received the deposited amount to the date the refund is made. However, if no action is filed within 120 days, the IRS, within 60 days after the prescribed

¶ 1230

120-day period has elapsed, must (1) apply the amount deposited or collect on the posted bond to the extent necessary to cover the unsatisfied liability secured by the lien and (2) refund (with interest at the same rate afforded to overpayments under Code Sec. 6621) any amount not used to satisfy such liability. This action is the exclusive remedy available to a third-party property owner seeking a determination- of the value of the government's interest in their property (Code Sec. 7426(a)(4) and (5), as added by the 1998 Act).

Example (2). On September, 15, 1999, Ken Brown and his sister Laurie, signed a contract to sell their jointly owned restaurant to Mike Martinez for $500,000. On September 20, a week before the scheduled closing, the IRS assessed Laurie $200,000 for delinquent taxes and placed a lien on the property to cover the liabilities. When Martinez threatened to pull out of the deal, Ken posted a money bond acceptable to the IRS to cover Laurie's tax liabilities and received a certificate of discharge of the lien on the property. On January 2, 2000, Ken filed suit in the U.S. District Court to contest the amount of the United States' interest in the property as determined by the IRS. The district court found that the United States' interest in the property was only $100,000. Accordingly, the court ordered a refund of $100,000 ($200,000 − $100,000 = $100,000) plus interest and release of the bond (Code Sec. 7426(a)(5), as added by the 1998 Act). However, if Ken waited until January 14, 2000, to file his action, the action would be disallowed because it would have been filed outside of the 120-day period after the certificate of discharge was issued (Code Sec. 7426(a)(4), as added by the 1998 Act).

Example (3). Assume the facts are the same as in Example (2), except that Ken did not file a civil action for a determination of the United States' interest in the property within the 120-day period. The IRS determined that an administrative mistake was made and that the value of the United States' interest in the property was only $150,000. Accordingly, within 60 days after the 120-day period has elapsed, the IRS will collect $150,000 on the bond and refund with interest, the $50,000 ($200,000 − $150,000 = $50,000), which was not used to satisfy the liability (Code Sec. 6325(b)(4)(C), as added by the 1998 Act).

PRACTICAL ANALYSIS. David R. Brennan of Faegre & Benson, Minneapolis, MN (former Director, Tax Litigation Division, Chief Counsel's Office and former Treasury Acting General Counsel), observes that this amendment is obviously of benefit only to an owner of property who also is not the taxpayer. A discharge of property owned by a taxpayer other than in conjunction with his sale of that property simply does not benefit him since the tax lien will immediately reattach to the property.

The statute seems to require that interest will be paid by the IRS on the amount deposited even though a deposit is generally not treated as an overpayment of tax to which Code Sec. 6621, relating to interest, would apply.

There may also be a question as to whether the determination of the Secretary that the tax cannot be satisfied from a source other than the property is subject to review judicially on an abuse of discretion basis.

Suspension of the running of statute of limitation. The 10-year statute of limitation for collection after assessment under Code Sec. 6502 is suspended from the date the IRS wrongfully seizes or receives a third party's property to 30 days *after* the earlier of (1) the date the IRS returns the property under Code Sec. 6343(b) or (2) the date on which a judgment secured pursuant to Code Sec. 7426 becomes final. Similarly, with respect to wrongful liens, the 10-year limitation period is suspended from the time the third-party owner is entitled to a certificate of discharge of lien until 30 days *after* the earlier of (1) the date that the IRS no longer holds any amount as a deposit or bond that was used to satisfy the unpaid liability, or that was refunded or released or (2) the date that the judgment in a civil action under Code Sec. 7426(b)(5) becomes final (Code Sec. 6503(f)(2), as added by the 1998 Act). The running of the statute of limitation under this provision is only suspended for the amount of the assessment that represents the United States' interest in the property plus any statutory additions such as interest or penalties (Code Sec. 6503(f), as amended by the 1998 Act).

PRACTICAL ANALYSIS. David R. Brennan of Faegre & Benson, Minneapolis, MN (former Director, Tax Litigation Division, Chief Counsel's Office and former Treasury Acting General Counsel), observes that, while the suspension of the statute is only for the portion of the assessment equal to the value of the interest of the United States in the property subject to the certificate, the statute nevertheless would appear to be open generally for the taxpayer on an *in persona* basis to such an extent and also open with respect to nontaxpayers owning property also subject to the federal tax lien in question to the extent of such value.

★ *Effective date.* The procedures for challenging an erroneous lien outlined by this provision are effective on the date of enactment (Act Sec. 3106(c) of the IRS Restructuring and Reform Act of 1998).

Act Sec. 3106(a), adding Code Sec. 6325(b)(4); Act Sec. 3106(b)(1), adding Code Sec. 7426(a)(4); Act Sec. 3106(b)(2)(A), adding Code Sec. 7426(b)(5); Act Sec. 3106(b)(2)(B), amending Code Sec. 7426(g) and adding Code Sec. 7426(g)(3); Act Sec. 3106(b)(3), amending Code Sec. 6503(f); Act Sec. 3106(c). Law at ¶ 6260, ¶ 6420, and ¶ 6610. Committee Report at ¶ 10,275.

SEIZURES AND SALES

Procedures for Seizures of Residences and Businesses

¶ 1234

Background

If a taxpayer does not pay any tax within 10 days after notice and demand, the IRS may levy (seize) property that the taxpayer owns or in which the taxpayer has an interest (Code Sec. 6331(a)). The seized property may then be sold in order to satisfy the unpaid tax liability. The IRS's authority to seize property is subject to certain procedural rules and limitations.

Principal residence. Unless collection of the tax is in jeopardy, the principal residence of a taxpayer may not be seized without approval of an IRS district or assistant district director (Code Sec. 6334(a)(13); Code Sec. 6334(e)). Code Sec. 121 applies in determining whether a residence is a principal residence. There is no restriction on the seizure of a residence used by persons other than the taxpayer, and there is no restriction on the seizure of even the taxpayer's principal residence to satisfy small tax deficiencies.

Going business. The policy of the IRS is to consider the facts of the case and alternative collection methods before seizing the assets of a going business (IRS Policy Statement P-5-34 (12-1-94)); however, this is not a statutory requirement.

IRS Restructuring and Reform Impact

Procedures for seizures of residences and businesses.—In order to prevent undue disruption to the occupants of any residence, the IRS may not seize any real property used as a residence by the taxpayer or any real property of the taxpayer (other than rented property) that is used as a residence by another person in order to satisfy a liability of $5,000 or less (including tax, penalties, and interest) (Code Sec. 6334(a)(13)(A), as amended by the IRS Restructuring and Reform Act of 1998).

In the case of the taxpayer's principal residence, the IRS may not seize the residence without written approval of a U.S. district court judge or magistrate (Code Sec. 6334(a)(13)(B) and Code Sec. 6334(e)(1), as amended by the 1998 Act).

Unless collection of tax is in jeopardy, tangible personal property or real property (other than rented real property) used in the taxpayer's trade or business may not be seized without written approval of an IRS district or assistant district director. Such approval may not be given unless it is determined that the taxpayer's other assets subject to collection are not sufficient to pay the amount due and the expenses of the proceedings. Act Sec. 3445(c) provides that "other assets" include future income that may be derived by a taxpayer from the commercial sale of fish or wildlife harvested under a state fish or wildlife permit (Code Sec. 6334(a)(13)(B) and Code Sec. 6334(e)(2), as amended by the 1998 Act).

Comment. The provision requiring the IRS to consider future income derived from the commercial sale of fish or wildlife harvested under a state permit before such a permit is seized was included at the request of Sen. Stevens of Alaska. He was primarily seeking protection for commercial fishermen in western Alaska whose livelihood depends on state-issued permits. Under the new provision, the IRS may not levy on state-issued fish and game permits if the future income from the permit would allow a taxpayer to pay the tax debt and procedural costs within the time allowed by law. The provision was identified as a limited tax benefit subject to the line item veto. This executive veto power, however, was recently declared unconstitutional by the U.S. Supreme Court. See ¶ 30,025 for more details.

PRACTICAL ANALYSIS. Robert McKenzie, of McKenzie & McKenzie PC, Chicago, Ill., comments that this provision imposes substantial constraints upon the seizure of residences and business assets. The provisions should substantially reduce the number of Internal Revenue seizures of residences and business assets.

Since 1977, the IRS has been required to secure the taxpayer's consent or writ of entry prior to entering into areas where the taxpayer had an expectation of privacy for the purposes of seizing assets (see *G.M. Leasing Corp.*, 429 US 338, 97 SCt 619 (1977)). Act Sec. 3445 does not prohibit ex parte actions by the IRS to secure judicial authority for seizure of tangible business assets or a personal residence. Therefore, the IRS probably will go before a judge to seek permission to seize such assets and the taxpayer may be forced to litigate the appropriateness of those actions after the seizure.

The protections provided by Act Sec. 3445 should also be viewed in context of the new protections regarding levy provided in Code Sec. 6330. The taxpayer now has the right to seek judicial review prior to any type of levy action by the IRS. But if we assume the taxpayer neglected to protest pursuant to Code Sec. 6330 when first given notice, the IRS would then be allowed to seek ex parte

authority to seize the personal residence or business assets of a taxpayer. The practitioner must be alert to take all steps to protect the taxpayer's rights pursuant to Code Secs. 6320 and 6330 at the first instance to avoid the potential that the IRS might later seek to exercise its authorities under Act Sec. 3445. At the insistence of an Alaskan Senator, Congress passed specific protections from seizure of state wildlife licenses. The IRS was specifically required to consider the future income available from such rights prior to seizure.

★ *Effective date.* This provision takes effect on the date of enactment (Act Sec. 3445(d) of the IRS Restructuring and Reform Act of 1998).

Act Sec. 3445(a), amending Code Sec. 6334(a)(13); Act Sec. 3445(b), amending Code Sec. 6334(e); Act. Sec. 3445(c); Act Sec. 3445(d). Law at ¶ 6290. Committee Report at ¶ 10,485.

Minimum Bid Requirement

¶ 1238

Background

Before property seized from a delinquent taxpayer is sold, the IRS must determine a minimum bid price for which the property shall be sold (Code Sec. 6335(e)(1)(A)(i)). The primary purpose of establishing a minimum bid price, which is fixed by the revenue officer in charge of the sale, is to avoid selling property at substantially less than the forced sale value of the taxpayer's interest in the property. In order to conserve the taxpayer's equity, the minimum bid price should ordinarily be at least 80 percent the forced sale value of the property less the amount of any encumbrances that have priority over the federal tax lien. However, the minimum bid price may not exceed the amount of the IRS's lien interest in the property plus expenses of sale (IRS Internal Revenue Manual IRM 56(13)5.1, 9-24-91, CCH INTERNAL REVENUE MANUAL—ADMINISTRATION; IRS Policy Statement P-5-35 (4-7-78)).

The revenue officer must advise the taxpayer of the minimum bid price and how it was computed and give the taxpayer 10 days to respond. The taxpayer may challenge the minimum bid price, provided it is below the upper limit of the sum of the tax liability and expenses of sale.

If the minimum bid price is not offered at the sale, the IRS may buy the property for such price (Code Sec. 6335(e)(1)(C)), or the property may be released to the owner (Code Sec. 6335(e)(1)(D)).

Although Code Sec. 6335(e)(1) did not suggest that seized property could be sold for less than the minimum bid price, it did not expressly prohibit a sale for a lesser amount.

IRS Restructuring and Reform Impact

Sale below minimum bid price prohibited.—The IRS is expressly prohibited from selling seized property for less than the minimum bid price. The sale of property for less than the minimum bid price is an unauthorized collection action with respect to which an affected person may sue for civil damages under Code Sec. 7433 (Code Sec. 6335(e), as amended by the IRS Restructuring and Reform Act of 1998).

★ *Effective date.* This provision is effective for sales made after the date of enactment (Act Sec. 3441(c) of the IRS Restructuring and Reform Act of 1998).

Act Sec. 3441(a), amending Code Sec. 6335(e)(1)(A)(i); Act Sec. 3441(b), adding Code Sec. 6335(e)(4); Act Sec. 3441(c). Law at ¶ 6300. Committee Report at ¶ 10,465.

Accounting for Sales

¶ 1242

Background ──

Certain statutory notice and recordkeeping requirements apply to the seizure and sale of a delinquent taxpayer's property. The Internal Revenue Code also prescribes how the sales proceeds must be applied, but there is no requirement that taxpayers be informed of how the proceeds are applied to their tax liability.

Notice requirements. The IRS must give written notice to the taxpayer at least 30 days before it seizes property (Code Sec. 6331(d)) and as soon as practicable after the seizure (Code Sec. 6335(a)). The IRS must also give notice of the sale of the seized property to the taxpayer and publish a public notice of the sale (Code Sec. 6335(b)). The property must be sold not less than 10 days nor more than 40 days after notice of the sale (Code Sec. 6335(d)).

Recordkeeping requirement. For sales of real property, the IRS must maintain records that indicate the delinquent tax, the dates of seizure and sale, the party assessed, the sale proceedings, the amount of expenses, the purchasers, and the date of the deed (Code Sec. 6340)).

Application of sales proceeds. Sales proceeds are applied first against levy and sale expenses, then against any specific tax liability on the seized property, and finally against any unpaid tax liability of the taxpayer. Surplus proceeds are credited to the taxpayer or other persons legally entitled to them (Code Sec. 6342).

IRS Restructuring and Reform Impact

Accounting requirement.—In order to provide a delinquent taxpayer with an accounting of the sales of seized property and how the sales proceeds are credited to the taxpayer's account, the recordkeeping provisions for sales of real property are extended to all types of property. Thus, for all sales, the IRS must keep records of the delinquent tax, seizure and sale dates, assessed party, sale proceedings, expenses, purchasers, and date of deed or certificate of sale of personal property (Code Sec. 6340(a), as amended by the IRS Restructuring and Reform Act of 1998). This record, other than the names of the purchasers, must be furnished to the delinquent taxpayer. The taxpayer must also be furnished with the amount of the sales proceeds applied to his or her tax liability and the balance of the liability (Code Sec. 6340(c), as added by the 1998 Act).

★ *Effective date.* This provision applies to seizures made after the date of enactment (Act Sec. 3442(b) of the IRS Restructuring and Reform Act of 1998).

Act Sec. 3442(a)(1), amending Code Sec. 6340(a); Act Sec. 3442(a)(2), adding Code Sec. 6340(c); Act Sec. 3442(b). Law at ¶ 6310. Committee Report at ¶ 10,470.

Uniform Asset Disposal System

¶ 1246

Background ──

The IRS must sell seized property either by public auction or by public sale under sealed bids (Code Sec. 6335(e)(2)). The revenue officer who is attempting to

Background —————————————————————————

collect the tax liability may also be conducting the sale. According to the Senate Committee Report, it is important for fairness and the appearance of propriety that revenue officers charged with collecting unpaid tax liabilities not be involved in the sale of property seized from taxpayers.

IRS Restructuring and Reform Impact

Creation of uniform asset disposal mechanism.—The IRS must implement a uniform asset disposal mechanism for sales of seized assets no later than two years after the date of enactment. The mechanism should be designed to remove any participation in such sales by IRS revenue officers. The IRS should consider outsourcing this function (Act Sec. 3443 of the IRS Restructuring and Reform Act of 1998).

PRACTICAL ANALYSIS. Robert McKenzie, of McKenzie & McKenzie PC, Chicago, Ill., comments that Congress has expressed its dissatisfaction with the current methods used to sell property by the IRS. Under the current procedures IRS sales are normally conducted by revenue officers. Some of the officers are skilled and able to secure the maximum price for property, while others have not exhibited skills for properly selling property. Act Sec. 3443 requires the IRS to establish a uniform system for disposing a property within two years of the date of enactment. It also expresses the desire that the IRS outsource auction sales. This provision will allow the involvement of professional auctioneers and should enhance the value recovered from the property. Unfortunately, the downside will be that the cost of the sale will be substantially increased for the taxpayer. Under the current system, the taxpayer is only charged for the cost of advertising and other necessary expenses of sale. Therefore, the cost of the labor performed by the revenue officer as an auctioneer is not included within the cost of sale. It would appear under the amendments that the taxpayer now would be faced with the additional cost of securing the services of an outside auctioneer. The provision could in fact reduce the net sale proceeds available to pay the taxpayer's tax obligation. Such a result would be unfortunate.

★ *Effective date.* No specific effective date is provided by the Act. The provision is, therefore, considered effective on the date of enactment.

Act Sec. 3443. Law at ¶ 8100. Committee Report at ¶ 10,475.

Codification of Administrative Procedures for Seizures

¶ 1250

Background —————————————————————————

The IRS provides guidelines for the collection of unpaid tax liabilities, including the seizure of property to satisfy such liabilities. Many of these guidelines provide protections to taxpayers. Guidelines that apply before property is seized include the following:

(1) The revenue officer must verify the taxpayer's liability (IRS Internal Revenue Manual IRM 56(12)5.1, 6-20-95, CCH INTERNAL REVENUE MANUAL—ADMINISTRATION).

Background ———————————————————————————

(2) The revenue officer must determine whether the estimated expenses of levy and sale exceed the fair market value of the property. If they do, the property should not be seized (Code Sec. 6331(f), IRS Internal Revenue Manual IRM 56(12)5.1, 6-20-95, CCH INTERNAL REVENUE MANUAL—ADMINISTRATION).

(3) The revenue office must determine whether the taxpayer has sufficient equity in the property to yield net proceeds from the sale to apply to unpaid tax liabilities. If it is determined that this is not the case and the property already has been seized, the revenue officer must immediately release the property (IRS Internal Revenue Manual IRM 56(12)2.1, 9-21-92, CCH INTERNAL REVENUE MANUAL—ADMINISTRATION).

(4) Before seizing the assets of a going business, the facts of the case and alternative collection methods must be thoroughly considered (IRS Policy Statement P-5-34 (12-1-94)). Reasonable forbearance should be exercised if a major disaster, such as flood, hurricane, drought, or fire, has affected the taxpayer's business and impaired the taxpayer's ability to pay the tax (IRS Policy Statement P-5-16 (3-1-84)).

IRS Restructuring and Reform Impact

Codification of administrative procedures.—In order to assure that the IRS follows its procedures uniformly, certain guidelines that apply before property is seized are codified. Thus, before property that is to be sold under Code Sec. 6335 is seized, a thorough investigation of the status of such property must be completed. Such an investigation must include the following:

(1) verification of the taxpayer's liability;

(2) analysis of whether the estimated expenses of levy and sale will exceed the fair market value of the property, as required by Code Sec. 6331(f);

(3) determination of whether the equity in the property is sufficient to yield net proceeds from the sale of the property to apply to the taxpayer's liability; and

(4) thorough consideration of alternative collection methods (Code Sec. 6331(j), as added by the IRS Restructuring and Reform Act of 1998).

★ *Effective date.* This provision takes effect on the date of enactment (Act Sec. 3444(b) of the IRS Restructuring and Reform Act of 1998).

Act Sec. 3444(a), redesignating Code Sec. 6331(j) as amended by Act Sec. 3433 as Code Sec. 6331(k) and adding new Code Sec. 6331(j); Act Sec. 3444(b). Law at ¶ 6280. Committee Report at ¶ 10,480.

COLLECTIONS

Due Process in Collection Activities

¶ 1254

Background ———————————————————————————

The Treasury Department reports that out of a total of 3.5 million notices of intent to levy issued annually, three million are computer-generated. Most levies involve seizures of bank and stock brokerage account balances, with about $1.5 billion collected annually. Only 10,000 levies involved seizures of tangible assets; however, witnesses at the recent congressional hearings on IRS abuses provided vivid testimony of IRS officials seizing taxpayers' personal property without warning.

¶ 1254

Background

The IRS's authority to seize property by levy arises when a federal tax lien has attached to the property. A lien arises automatically if the IRS has (1) made an assessment, (2) given the taxpayer notice of the assessment stating the amount of the tax liability and demanding payment, and (3) the taxpayer has failed to pay the amount within 10 days after the notice and demand for payment (Code Sec. 6321).

The IRS must give notice of its intent to enforce a lien by levy at least 30 days before the day of the levy. This period is increased to 90 days in the case of a levy against the cash value of an insurance contract. The levy notice must describe the IRS's intended levy procedure, the administrative appeals available to the taxpayer, alternatives that could prevent levy, and the procedures for redemption of the property and release of lien. However, the IRS may disregard the notice periods if the district director determines that tax collection is in jeopardy (Code Sec. 6331(a)).

IRS Restructuring and Reform Impact

Due process.—The IRS must notify any person subject to a lien of the existence of the lien within five days of the lien being filed. The notice of lien must be given in person, left at the taxpayer's home or place of business, or sent by certified or registered mail to the person's last known address. The notice must explain in simple, nontechnical terms (1) the amount of the unpaid tax, (2) the person's right to request a hearing during the 30-day period beginning on the sixth day after the lien is filed, (3) the available administrative appeals and their procedures, and (4) the procedures relating to the release of liens (Code Sec. 6320(a), as added by the IRS Restructuring and Reform Act of 1998).

Caution. The Conference Agreement states that the 30-day period during which the taxpayer may request a hearing begins running on the day the notice of lien is mailed or delivered. However, the Act specifies that the 30-day period begins running on the day after the five-day period during which the notice of lien must be delivered. Thus, the 1998 Act effectively provides for a 35-day period after receipt of the notice of lien during which the taxpayer may request a hearing (Code Sec. 6320(a)(3)(B), as added by the 1998 Act).

Notice and opportunity for hearing prior to levy. At least 30 days prior to levying on any person's property or right to property, the IRS must notify that person in writing of their right to a hearing. The notice must be given in person, left at the taxpayer's home or place of business, or sent by certified or registered mail to the person's last known address. Only one notice is required for each tax period to which the underlying tax liability relates (Code Sec. 6330(a), as added by the 1998 Act).

Caution. The right to a hearing prior to the IRS filing a notice of levy does not apply if the IRS has determined that collection of the tax liability is in jeopardy or if the IRS has served a levy on a state to collect federal tax from a state tax refund. In such case, the taxpayer has a right to a hearing within a reasonable amount of time after the levy (Code Sec. 6330(f), as added by the 1998 Act).

The notice of a right to a hearing must provide or explain in simple, nontechnical terms (1) the amount of unpaid tax, (2) the person's right to request a hearing during the 30-day period, and (3) the action proposed by the IRS and the rights held by the person with respect to such action. The notice must include a brief statement setting forth:

(a) the Internal Revenue Code provisions relating to levy and the sale of property;

(b) the procedures applicable to levy and sale of property;

(c) the administrative appeals (and their procedures) available in connection with levy and sale of property;

(d) the alternatives, such as an installment agreement, that could pre- ̄vent levy on property; and

(e) the Internal Revenue Code provisions and procedures relating to the redemption of property and release of lien (Code Sec. 6330(a)(3), as added by the 1998 Act).

Comment. An installment agreement under Code Sec. 6159 may provide a highly desirable alternative to losing one's property under a levy. The IRS must enter into installment agreements under certain circumstances (see ¶ 1274) (Code Sec. 6159(c), as amended by the 1998 Act).

Right to a fair hearing. Whether in connection with the notice of lien or notice of intent to levy, the hearing is to be held by the IRS Office of Appeals and conducted by an officer or employee who has no prior involvement with respect to the underlying tax liability. The taxpayer is entitled to only one hearing for the tax period covered by the lien. The right to an impartial hearing officer may be waived (Code Sec. 6320(b), as added by the 1998 Act, and Code Sec. 6330(b), as added by the 1998 Act).

Matters considered. The appeals officer presiding over the hearing must obtain verification from the IRS that all applicable laws and administrative procedures have been met. At the hearing, the taxpayer may raise any issue relevant to the appropriateness of the proposed collection activity. Thus, the taxpayer may request innocent spouse status, propose an offer-in-compromise, request an installment agreement or suggest which assets be used to satisfy the liability. No issue may be raised that was raised at a previous hearing in which the person seeking to raise the issue had a meaningful participation (Code Sec. 6320(c), as added by the 1998 Act, and Code Sec. 6330(c), as added by the 1998 Act).

Caution. Challenges to the underlying liability may be raised at the hearing only if the taxpayer did not receive any statutory notice of deficiency for such tax liability or did not otherwise have an opportunity to dispute such tax liability (Code Sec. 6320(c), as added by the 1998 Act, and Code Sec. 6330(c)(2)(B), as added by the 1998 Act).

After verifying that all applicable laws are satisfied and considering all issues raised by the taxpayer, the hearing officer must determine whether the proposed collection action balances efficient tax collection with the taxpayer's legitimate concerns (Code Sec. 6320(c), as added by the 1998 Act, and Code Sec. 6330(c)(3), as added by the 1998 Act).

Proceedings after hearing. The taxpayer has 30 days after the hearing determination to appeal the determination to the Tax Court. If the Tax Court lacks jurisdiction over the underlying tax liability, the taxpayer may appeal within the same 30-day period to a federal district court. If a court determines that the appeal was to an incorrect court, the taxpayer has 30 days after the court's determination to file an appeal to the correct court (Code Sec. 6020(c), as added by the 1998 Act, and Code Sec. 6030(d)(1), as added by the 1998 Act).

The IRS Office of Appeals retains jurisdiction over the determination with respect to any subsequent hearings requested by the taxpayer who originated the hearing. In the case of a hearing before a levy, the IRS Office of Appeals also retains jurisdiction over a claim of change in circumstance that the taxpayer may raise after exhausting all administrative remedies (Code Sec. 6320(c) as added by the 1998 Act, and Code Sec. 6330(d), as added by the 1998 Act).

Suspension of statute of limitations. Generally, when a taxpayer requests a hearing, the statute of limitations is suspended for the lien or levy action that is the subject of the hearing. In addition, the limitations periods under Code Sec. 6502 (relating to collection after assessment), Code Sec. 6531 (relating to criminal prosecutions), and Code Sec. 6532 (relating to other suits) are suspended during the pendency of the hearing and any related appeals. No limitations period may expire before 90 days after a final determination is made (Code Sec. 6320(c), as added by the 1998 Act, and Code Sec. 6330(e), as added by the 1998 Act).

Caution. The statute of limitations is not suspended in a levy action while an appeal is pending if the underlying tax liability is not at issue in the appeal and the court determines that the IRS has shown good cause not to suspend the levy (Code Sec. 6330(e)(2), as added by the 1998 Act).

Special trial judge. The chief judge of the Tax Court may assign any proceeding under new Code Sec. 6320 and Code Sec. 6330 to a special trial judge, as described under Code Sec. 7443A (Code Sec. 7443A(b)(4), as added by the 1998 Act).

PRACTICAL ANALYSIS. Robert McKenzie, of McKenzie & McKenzie PC, Chicago, Ill., observes that since February 12, 1996, the IRS has had a collection appeals program that allows taxpayers to appeal the filing of a lien. This protection however was not statutory. If the IRS chose not to follow its own procedures, there was no remedy available to the taxpayer (Internal Revenue Manual 8719.2).

Code Sec. 6320 provides statutory appeal rights to taxpayers who are subject to federal tax liens. The provision specifically provides for an impartial hearing officer (which may not have been the case in the past). In the past the IRS collection division engaged in substantial *ex parte* discussion with the Appeals Officer. Now there are specific statutory protections available to the taxpayer and specific guarantees of independence by the Appeals Officer. Because taxpayers will also have the right to seek judicial review of any determination of the Appeals Officer, the taxpayer is guaranteed to have better consideration at the appeals level. In the past, if an Appeals Officer ruled against you, the matter was referred back to the collection division and it proceeded to file the lien without further rights to the taxpayer. As case law develops in this area, Appeals Officers will also have guidelines from the courts as to appropriate reasons for foregoing liens and releasing liens.

Also since February 12, 1996, the IRS has had an appeals program that allowed taxpayers to appeal proposed or actual levies by the IRS. The unfortunate part of the program was that the taxpayers were not necessarily apprised of their rights to the appeals program. Revenue officers were not prone to tell taxpayers of appeal rights since that might encourage taxpayers to seek those rights. In addition, there was no statutory protection of appeal rights (Internal Revenue Manual 8719.2). Code Sec. 6330 now provides that the IRS must specifically inform taxpayers of their rights to appeal within 30 days of any proposed action by the IRS to levy upon the taxpayer's property. The taxpayer is specifically allowed to appeal the proposed levy and request that the IRS consider Code Sec. 6159 installment agreements. Under prior law a taxpayer who requested a payment plan could be legally denied his or

her payment plan and would have no further remedies. Code Sec. 6330(c)(2) specifically requires that the hearing officer consider spousal challenges to appropriateness of the collection actions and other collection alternatives which could include a bond, substitution of other assets, installment agreements or an offer in compromise. The prior administrative appeals procedure did not grant such broad authority to the Appeals Officer. The Appeals Officer was only allowed to look at the appropriateness of the IRS action even if another alternative would have been appropriate. The Appeals Division was not given the authority to find the best remedy for the taxpayer.

Code Sec. 6330(c)(2)(B) also authorizes the taxpayer to challenge the existence or the amount of the underlying tax liability for any tax period that the taxpayer did not receive statutory notice of deficiency for tax or did not otherwise have an opportunity to dispute such tax liability. The Appeals Officer is specifically directed to consider the following factors when considering a collection appeal: the verification presented, the issues raised by the taxpayer, and whether any proposed collection action balances the needs for collection of taxes with the legitimate concerns of the person that any collection action be no more intrusive than necessary.

The rights of taxpayers with respect to liens and levies are greatly extended by the waiver of sovereign immunity contained in Code Sec. 6330(d). A taxpayer who has exercised his rights to appeal under Code Sec. 6320 and/or Code Sec. 6330 with respect to liens and levies now has specific authority to seek judicial review of an adverse IRS decision. This provision represents a huge expansion of taxpayer rights. A basic presumption of all prior collection proceedings was the right of the IRS to take summary levy and lien actions without judicial intervention. The Tax Court has now been granted specific jurisdiction to hear matters concerning taxes under its jurisdiction. Generally those taxes would include income taxes, gift taxes, excise taxes and with the advent of Taxpayer Bill of Rights 3, Code Sec. 6672 penalties. Other taxes, including employment tax liabilities, would be subject to judicial review by a U.S. District Court. If the taxpayer chose the wrong jurisdiction, then the taxpayer will be allowed 30 days to seek review of an appeal before the proper court. While a judicial appeal is pending, the Appeals Officer will retain jurisdiction of the matter.

The addition of judicial rights to review IRS collection action could result in substantial delays in collection of taxes by the IRS. It might also encourage some recalcitrant taxpayers to prolong collection of taxes. Congress has chosen to balance protections of well-meaning taxpayers by providing the judicial remedies. One result however may be to encourage non-compliance by less dedicated taxpayers. The addition of judicial review provisions is a reaction to prior IRS abuses in collection matters. Many taxpayers who have legitimately sought payment arrangements and/or offers in compromise from the IRS have been confronted by inflexible collection employees. IRS policies including its allowable expense program (Internal Revenue Manual 5323, *et seq*) have imposed severe constraints on taxpayers who wish to repay their taxes. The IRS over the past several years has become increasingly inflexible in granting installment agreements. **In fact, for a period of time from 1994 to 1997, the IRS adopted severe restrictions on granting installment agreements with respect to employment tax liabilities (see Internal Revenue Manual 5331.54). The new collection appeals program will prevent the Service from imposing unreasonable restrictions on installment agreements. Taxpayers now have the right to seek independent review of a Collection Division decision. If the taxpayer is dissatisfied with that review, Code Sec. 6330(c) grants specific authority to seek judicial review of IRS determinations.**

A note of caution is merited here because, even though Code Sec. 6330(c) grants the authority for judicial review, there is no precedent as to the standards that the courts may apply. Although Code Sec. 6330(b) sets forth the standards for appeals review, there can be no certainty as to how those standards may be applied. One would hope that the courts will develop their own bright line tests so that practitioners may judge the appropriateness of judicial relief from IRS collection actions.

If a taxpayer exercises rights pursuant to the collection appeals process, the IRS is precluded from taking levy or lien action while the proceeding is pending except in the event of a jeopardy or a levy upon a state tax refund.

★ *Effective date.* These provisions are effective for collection actions initiated 180 days after the date of enactment (Act. Sec. 3401(d) of the IRS Restructuring and Reform Act of 1998).

Act Sec. 3401(a), adding Code Sec. 6320; Act Sec. 3401(b), adding Code Sec. 6330; Act Sec. 3401(c), redesignating Code Sec. 7443A(b)(4) as Code Sec. 7443A(b)(5) and inserting after Code Sec. 7443A(b)(3) new Code Sec. 7443A(b)(4); Act Sec. 3401(d). Law at ¶ 6240, ¶ 6270 and ¶ 6280. Committee Report at ¶ 10,365.

Appeal of Examination and Collections

¶ 1258

Background ————————————————————————————————

A variety of IRS regulations, rulings and publications describe the IRS's appeals procedures. The Statement of Procedural Rules (26 C.F.R., Part 601) outlines the appeals structure and function, noting that the IRS appeals operates through regional appeals offices, which are independent of the local District Director and Regional Commissioner's offices and have their own administrative hierarchy. The Office of Appeals has jurisdiction at both the pre- and post-assessment stages, providing the taxpayer with many opportunities to request Appeals Office consideration. For example, the Office of Appeals may consider a taxpayer's case after failing to reach agreement with the examination function and before filing a Tax Court petition, after rejection of a refund claim, or after proposed rejection of an offer in compromise (Reg. § 601.106(a)).

For auditing corporate taxpayers with assets over $250 million (over $1 billion in the case of financial institutions and utilities), the IRS developed the Coordinated Examination Program (CEP). The CEP uses a team of revenue agents with specialized skills in examining large organizations with complex business practices (Internal Revenue Manual 42(11)0). The Office of Appeals provides taxpayers subject to a CEP exam the opportunity to seek early referral of some issues while the examination is still pending on others (Rev. Proc. 96-9, 1996-1 CB 575). The

Background

early referral policy also applies to employment tax issues (Announcement 97-52, IRB 1997-21, 22).

The IRS's Alternative Dispute Resolution (ADR) process refers to a group of problem-solving methods designed to resolve disputes consensually before engaging in litigation. ADR is available only for cases in which the amount in dispute exceeds $10 million.

In 1996, the IRS began the Collections Appeals Program, which provided taxpayers who were subject to a lien, levy or seizure a right to appeal. Under this program, all such taxpayers received Publication 1660, "Collection Appeal Rights for Liens, Levies and Seizures," which explained appeal rights and procedures. In January 1997, the Taxpayer Bill of Rights 2 (P.L. 104-168) extended this appeals program to proposed terminations of installment agreements (Code Sec. 6159(c)).

IRS Restructuring and Reform Impact

Appeal of IRS examinations.—Current IRS procedures regarding the Office of Appeals are codified by the new law. Specifically, the IRS is required to develop procedures under which any taxpayer may request early referral of issues from the examination or collection division to the Office of Appeals. Additionally, procedures must be developed under which either a taxpayer or the Office of Appeals may request nonbinding mediation of any unresolved issue at the conclusion of the appeals procedure or an unsuccessful attempt to enter into a closing agreement under Code Sec. 7121 or an offer in compromise under Code Sec. 7122. A pilot program under which the Office of Appeals and the taxpayer may jointly request binding arbitration must also be developed. The Senate Committee Report states that the binding arbitration procedures should be extended to all taxpayers (Code Sec. 7123, as added by the IRS Restructuring and Reform Act of 1998).

The IRS must ensure that an appeals officer is regularly available within each state. It must also consider using videoconferencing techniques for conferences between appeals officers and taxpayers from rural areas seeking appeals (Act Sec. 3465(b) of the 1998 Act and Act Sec. 3465(c) of the 1998 Act).

PRACTICAL ANALYSIS. Robert McKenzie, of McKenzie & McKenzie PC, Chicago, Ill., notes that the IRS has had an early referral program for certain employment tax deficiencies for several years. This provision allowed for early referral of disputes regarding independent contractor employee status to the appeals division from the examination division. The provision allowed for a more rapid resolution of a large tax dispute. The IRS has now been directed to implement procedures to allow broader use of early appeals programs. The IRS has also been directed to establish procedures that will allow for alternative dispute resolution including mediation and arbitration.

In an effort to become more efficient, the IRS has reorganized over the past several years and now has reduced its total districts from sixty-three to thirty-three. This reorganization has resulted in some states being left without an individual appeals office. Act Sec 3465 specifically requires that the IRS maintain at least one appeals office in each state and that it consider the use of video conferences for taxpayers in remote areas.

¶ 1258

★ *Effective date.* No specific effective date is provided by the Act. The provision is, therefore, considered effective on the date of enactment.

Act Sec. 3465(a)(1), redesignating Code Sec. 7123 as Code Sec. 7124 and adding new Code Sec. 7123; Act Sec. 3465(a)(2) (conforming amendment); Act Sec. 3465(b); Act Sec. 3465(c). Law at ¶ 6550, ¶ 6560 and ¶ 8120. Committee Report at ¶ 10,535.

Fair Debt Collection Practices

¶ 1262

Background

Taxpayers may bring a damages action against the IRS if, in connection with a collections activity, an IRS employee recklessly or intentionally disregards any tax provision or regulation (Code Sec. 7433). However, the provisions of the Federal Debt Collection Practices Act (P.L. 95-109), which restrict various collection abuses and harassments in the private sector, generally do not apply to the federal government.

IRS Restructuring and Reform Impact

Restriction on collection abuses.—The new law requires the IRS to comply with certain provisions of the Fair Debt Collection Practices Act (P.L. 95-109) so that the treatment of tax debtors by tax collectors is at least equal to that required of private sector debt collectors. Thus, the IRS may not communicate with any taxpayer at any unusual or inconvenient time or place unless otherwise agreed to by the taxpayer. Unless otherwise agreed, the IRS is to assume that the convenient time for communicating with a taxpayer is between the hours of 8:00 a.m. and 9:00 p.m., as determined at the taxpayer's location. Further, the IRS may not communicate with the taxpayer if the IRS knows that the taxpayer has obtained representation from a person authorized to practice before the IRS and the IRS knows or can readily obtain the representative's name and address. This requirement is void if the representative consents to direct communication with the taxpayer or the representative fails to respond to IRS communications within a reasonable period of time. The IRS is also restricted from communicating with the taxpayer at the taxpayer's place of employment if the IRS knows or has reason to know that such communication is prohibited by the employer (Code Sec. 6304(a), as added by the IRS Restructuring and Reform Act of 1998).

Prohibitions on harassment and abuse. The IRS may not harass, oppress or abuse any person in connection with any tax collection activity or engage in any activity that would naturally lead to harassment, oppression or abuse. The following actions constitute violations of this provision (violations are not limited by this list):

(1) The threat or use of violence or other criminal means to harm the physical person, reputation or property of any person;

(2) The use of obscene, profane or abusive language either verbally or in writing;

(3) The use of a telephone with the intent to annoy, abuse or harass any person at the number called, whether through conversation or merely by repeated calling; and

(4) Except as provided under 15 USC § 1692b, placing telephone calls without meaningful disclosure of the caller's identity (Code Sec. 6304(b), as added by the 1998 Act).

Comment. Section 804 of the Fair Debt Collections Practices Act (15 USC § 1692b) contains rules regarding communications between the debt collector and persons other than the debtor for purposes of determining the debtor's location. These rules state that the debt collector may not identify his employer unless expressly requested to do so; may not reveal that the subject of the communication owes a debt; and may not communicate with any such person more than once unless it is determined that the information originally obtained was incomplete or erroneous. Presumably, the IRS will abide by similar rules to protect the privacy of the taxpayer.

PRACTICAL ANALYSIS. Robert McKenzie, of McKenzie & McKenzie PC, Chicago, Ill., points out that the collection division has been made subject to some of the protections provided to individuals from private bill collectors. The IRS is not allowed to contact the taxpayers at an unusual time or place which is known to be inconvenient to the taxpayer. The IRS specially is directed to deal with the taxpayer's authorized representative and not to deal with the taxpayer unless that representative fails to respond within a reasonable period of time. This provision provides additional protections for taxpayer by clearly delineating the right to be represented before the IRS by a CPA, enrolled agent or attorney.

The IRS is also prohibited from harassing or abusing the taxpayer and in some instances from calling the taxpayer on the job. If the IRS violates these provisions the taxpayer is authorized to pursue remedies pursuant to Code Sec. 7433 regarding negligent, reckless or intentional disregard of the Internal Revenue Code by IRS collection employees. Most employees of the IRS act in a professional manner but these additional protections will allow taxpayers specific rights to seek judicial damages as a result of improper conduct. In the past, the taxpayer had few remedies for abusive IRS conduct by incompetent or arrogant IRS employees. Now, the taxpayer has specific statutory rights. "Bad" IRS employees must change their collection approach to avoid judicial sanctions.

★ *Effective date.* The application of fair debt collection procedures to the IRS is effective on date of enactment (Act Sec. 3466(c) of the IRS Restructuring and Reform Act of 1998).

Act Sec. 3466(a), adding Code Sec. 6304; Act Sec. 3466(b); Act Sec. 3466(c). Law at ¶ 6220. Committee Report at ¶ 10,540.

Explanation of Appeal and Collection Process

¶ 1266

Background————————————————————————————

When sending a notice of deficiency to persons believed to owe tax, the IRS is under no obligation to concurrently inform the alleged tax debtor of the IRS's appeal procedures or of its examination and collection process.

IRS Restructuring and Reform Impact

Examination and collection procedure.—To increase taxpayer knowledge of the IRS's appeals and examination procedures, the IRS is now required to include an explanation of its entire examination and collection process with the first deficiency letter sent to a taxpayer. The explanation should accompany the first communication with respect to which the recipient taxpayer has an opportunity to obtain administrative review by the Office of Appeals. The explanation should include an overview of the assistance available from the National Taxpayer Advocate. The explanation is to be included with the first deficiency letter as soon as practicable, but no later than 180 days after the date of enactment (Act Sec. 3504 of the IRS Restructuring and Reform Act of 1998).

★ *Effective date.* No specific effective date is provided by the Act. The provision is, therefore, considered effective on the date of enactment.

Act Sec. 3504. Law at ¶ 8145. Committee Report at ¶ 10,580.

OFFERS IN COMPROMISE AND INSTALLMENT AGREEMENTS

Offers in Compromise

¶ 1270

Background

The IRS has authority to accept less than the full amount of liability owed in any civil or criminal case arising under the tax laws prior to the case's referral to the Justice Department. The basis for accepting a compromise may be either doubt as to liability or doubt as to collectability (or both). The basis of most offers in compromise is doubt as to collectibility.

An offer in compromise is a contractual agreement between the taxpayer and the IRS. In return for full settlement of tax liability, the taxpayer agrees to a 60-month suspension of the 10-year statute of limitations on collection and compliance with the tax laws during the 60-month period. To have an offer considered, the taxpayer must disclose detailed information regarding his or her assets and liabilities and must be willing to pay over the net value of such assets plus the present value of total net disposable income available over the 60-month suspension.

To aid in computing a taxpayer's net assets and disposable income, the IRS developed national standards for necessary living expenses and local standards for measuring the costs of housing, utilities and necessary transportation. Generally, assets or income above these standard amounts will be used to satisfy the tax liability at issue.

Critics of the IRS's offer-in-compromise program maintain that the local and national standards, which were created in part to increase the acceptance rate, removed revenue officers from case-by-case decision making. These critics recommend that revenue officers be given discretion to recognize education expenses as being necessary. They cite, for example, families who live in low-income urban areas who bear the expense of sending their children to parochial schools.

Other critics point to the prohibition against treating unsecured debt (except for court-ordered payments) as a necessary expense. They note that many middle- and low-income families have substantial unsecured debt on which they are paying a high rate of interest and argue that revenue agents' lack of discretion regarding unsecured debt eliminates the offer-in-compromise option for many taxpayers.

IRS Restructuring and Reform Impact

Offers in compromise.—The IRS Restructuring and Reform Act of 1998 requires the IRS to develop employee guidelines for determining whether a proposed offer in compromise is adequate and should be accepted to resolve a dispute. Thus, the legislation codifies the IRS's long-standing practices in this area. These guidelines must include national and local allowances under which IRS employees may determine the basic living expenses of a taxpayer entering into a compromise. However, the IRS is directed to determine, on the basis of the facts and circum-

¶ 1270

stances of each taxpayer, whether the use of the standard allowances is appropriate. Local and national standards are not to be used to the extent that they would result in a taxpayer not having adequate means to provide for basic living expenses (Code Sec. 7122(c)(1), as added by the 1998 Act, and Code Sec. 7122(c)(2), as added by the 1998 Act).

Under the offer-in-compromise guidelines, IRS employees may not reject an offer from a low-income employee solely on the basis of the amount of the offer. If an offer in compromise is based on doubt as to liability, the IRS may not reject an offer solely because the IRS cannot locate a taxpayer's return or return information for verification purposes. Moreover, anyone seeking an offer in compromise based on doubt as to liability is not required to provide a financial statement (Code Sec. 7122(c)(3), as added by the 1998 Act).

Comment. The Conference Agreement contemplates that the IRS will consider factors such as equity and hardship when determining whether to accept an offer in compromise. The conferees urge the IRS to be flexible in finding ways to work with taxpayers who are sincerely trying to meet their tax obligations. This could be accomplished by, for example, forgoing penalties and interest amounts that have accumulated while determinations of taxpayer liability were being made.

Levy prohibited. While a person has a compromise offer pending, the IRS may not levy against that person's property to satisfy the liability covered by the offer. If the offer is ultimately rejected, the levy prohibition remains in effect for 30 days after the rejection and during the pendency of any timely filed appeal of the rejection. An offer is pending from the date that it is accepted by the IRS for processing (Code Sec. 6331(k)(1), as added by the 1998 Act).

Similarly, the IRS may not levy on the property or rights to property of a person while that person has an installment agreement offer pending with the IRS. The prohibition extends for 30 days after an installment agreement offer is rejected by the IRS and during the pendency of any appeal of the rejection, providing the appeal is filed within 30 days of the rejection. Further, no levy may be made while an installment agreement is in effect. If the IRS terminates the installment agreement, no levy may be made for 30 days after the termination and during the pendency of any appeal of the rejection, providing the appeal is filed within 30 days of the rejection (Code Sec. 6331(k)(2), as added by the 1998 Act).

The prohibition does not apply to any unpaid tax if the taxpayer files a written notice waiving the levy prohibition. Moreover, the prohibition does not apply to any levy to carry out an offset under Code Sec. 6402 or to any levy predating the pendency of the compromise offer (Code Sec. 6331(i)(3), as added by the 1998 Act, and Code Sec. 6331(k)(3), as added by the 1998 Act).

Caution. The prohibition against levy does not apply if the IRS believes that collection of the liability is in jeopardy (Code Sec. 6331(i)(3)(A)(ii), as added by the 1998 Act, and Code Sec. 6331(k)(3), as added by the 1998 Act).

The IRS is also prohibited from initiating any court action with respect to the liability that is the subject of the compromise offer. However, this prohibition does not apply to any counterclaim with respect to the liability or any related proceeding (Code Sec. 6331(i)(4), as added by the 1998 Act, and Code Sec. 6331(k)(3), as added by the 1998 Act).

Caution. The 10-year statute of limitations on collection is suspended during the period the IRS is prohibited from making a levy or taking other collection measures against the liability that is subject to the compromise offer (Code Sec. 6331(i)(4), as added by the 1998 Act, and Code Sec. 6331(k)(3), as added by the 1998 Act).

Administrative review of rejections. The IRS must establish procedures for independent administrative review of any rejection of an offer in compromise or installment agreement. This review is to occur before the rejection is communicated to the taxpayer. The taxpayer must be allowed to appeal any rejection of any proposed offer in compromise or installment agreement to the IRS Office of Appeals (Code Sec. 6159(d)[(e)], as amended and redesignated by the 1998 Act, and Code Sec. 7122(d), as added by the 1998 Act).

Policy statement. The Treasury Department must prepare a statement setting forth the rights of the taxpayer and obligations of the IRS with regard to offers in compromise. This statement, which is to be written in simple, nontechnical terms, must:

(1) advise those who have entered into an offer-in-compromise contract of the advantages of promptly notifying the IRS of any change of address;

(2) inform married taxpayers who have entered into an offer-in-compromise contract that any noncompliant activity by one spouse or former spouse will not prevent the compliant individual from having the compromise reinstated, upon application; and

(3) notify taxpayers whose offer-in-compromise proposal was rejected that they have a right to appeal to the IRS Office of Appeals (Act Sec. 3462(d) of the 1998 Act).

PRACTICAL ANALYSIS. Robert McKenzie, of McKenzie & McKenzie PC, Chicago, Ill., observes that, since August 1995, the IRS has imposed specific standards for allowable expenses upon taxpayers who seek offers in compromise. In many cases, those standards are less than the actual expenses faced by the taxpayer. Although the Internal Revenue Manual provides authority for flexibility, most Internal Revenue Districts have been rather inflexible in applying the standards. The net result is that middle class individuals were not able to compromise their taxes because of the standards imposed by the IRS (Internal Revenue Manual 5323). Act Sec. 3462 imposes a duty upon the IRS to exercise much more flexibility in the use of its allowable expense standards. Revenue officers and employees of the collection division are not allowed to use the schedules to the extent that such use would result in the taxpayer not having adequate means to provide for basic living expenses.

This provision will be particularly important with respect to housing. Because the IRS uses the average cost of housing in a particular county in determining its current allowable expense standards, any taxpayer who recently purchased a home probably has housing expenses that exceed the IRS standard. It would appear that Act Sec. 3462 will require the IRS to look at the actual expenses of the taxpayer as opposed to its arbitrary determination of appropriate housing standards.

Some districts have imposed minimum offer standards for taxpayers. Therefore, a low-income taxpayer who offered a minimum amount might have the offer rejected even though it represented her maximum ability to pay. The IRS is now required to consider each offer submitted by a taxpayer on its individual merits, not based upon some minimal offer amount.

The IRS has had a policy since 1959 of foregoing collection during the pendency of an Offer in Compromise (Policy 5-9). Act Sec.

3462 prohibits levy while an Offer in Compromise is pending or an installment agreement pursuant to Code Sec. 6159 is pending. The provision also provides for suspension of collection while an appeal is pending. Although under the current protections of Policy 5-9 not many levies have taken place during the pendency of an Offer in Compromise, the taxpayer now has specific statutory protections against enforcement action by the IRS while attempting to settle his or her tax obligations.

Although the IRS currently provides for administrative review of Offers in Compromise by the Appeals Division, there has been no specific statutory requirement for such review. Act Sec. 3462(d) now enacts into law specific rights of independent review of Offers in Compromise by the IRS Office of Appeals.

Offers in Compromise contain within their terms the requirement that the taxpayer remain current during the five years subsequent to approval of an Offer in Compromise. One problem that has arisen is that married taxpayers who later divorce may face the possibility of default where one of the spouses fails to meet all of his or her tax obligation. As a result the IRS has occasionally attempted to default the Offer in Compromise with respect to both spouses. Act Sec 3462 now contains specific protections for an innocent spouse who has complied with all of his or her tax obligations notwithstanding any default by a spouse.

Another protection provided by Act Sec. 3462 is with respect to Offers in Compromise based on doubt as to liability. In the past the IRS has occasionally rejected offers with respect to doubt as to liability solely because it could not find its administrative file. The IRS is now prohibited from taking such action. The IRS has imposed additional duties upon taxpayers seeking compromise liabilities solely on the basis of doubt as to liability by requiring those taxpayers to submit financial statements. Many in the practitioner community believe that taxpayers with substantial means were prejudiced by this requirement because the IRS would consider the taxpayers substantial economic means when reviewing the underlying liability. The IRS is now specifically prohibited from requiring financial statements when offers are submitted based solely on doubt as to liability.

★ *Effective date.* Generally, these amendments apply to proposed offers in compromise and installment agreements submitted after the date of enactment. The amendment under Act Sec. 3462(b), relating to the suspension of collection by levy, applies to offers in compromise pending on or made after December 31, 1999 (Act Sec. 3462(e) of the IRS Restructuring and Reform Act of 1998).

Act Sec. 3462(a), adding Code Sec. 7122(c); Act Sec. 3462(b), redesignating Code Sec. 6331(k), as amended by Act Sec. 3433 and Act Sec. 3444, as Code Sec. 6331(l) and adding new Code Sec. 6331(k); Act Sec. 3462(c)(1), adding Code Sec. 7122(d); Act Sec. 3462(c)(2), adding Code Sec. 6159(d)[(e)] (conforming amendment); Act Sec. 3462(d); Act Sec. 3462(e). Law at ¶ 6150, ¶ 6280, ¶ 6540, and ¶ 8110. Committee Report at ¶ 10,520.

Guaranteed Availability of Installment Agreements

¶ 1274

Background ————————————————————————————

IRS district directors and certain other IRS officials are authorized to enter into a written agreement allowing a taxpayer to satisfy a tax liability through

Background

scheduled periodic payments. Taxpayers do not have an absolute right to an installment payment. The IRS director has discretion to accept or reject any installment payment proposal. An installment agreement does not reduce the tax liability, or any interest or penalty. However, during the installment payment period, other enforcement actions, such as liens and levies, are held in abeyance (Reg. § 301.6159-1(b)).

Streamlined installment agreement procedures exist for cases where the liability is $10,000 or less. The IRS generally approves installment payment requests falling under the $10,000 threshold and does not require verification of the taxpayer's financial background (IRS Internal Revenue Manual IRM 5331.31, 4-4-94, CCH INTERNAL REVENUE MANUAL—ADMINISTRATION). A $43 user fee is added to the liability if the installment agreement request is granted.

IRS Restructuring and Reform Impact

Guaranteed installment agreement availability.—In an effort to enhance taxpayer compliance, the new law requires the IRS, under certain conditions, to enter into an installment payment agreement with any individual requesting such an arrangement. The taxpayer requesting an installment payment arrangement must not owe more than $10,000 and over the previous five tax years must not have (1) failed to file any income tax return; (2) failed to pay any income tax; or (3) entered into any installment agreement for payment of any income tax (Code Sec. 6159(c), as added by the IRS Restructuring and Reform Act of 1998).

Caution. These three requirements also apply to the taxpayer's spouse if the liability proposed to be paid in installments relates to a joint return.

The right to an installment agreement only applies if the IRS determines that the taxpayer is unable to pay the liability in full when due. Further, the taxpayer must provide the IRS with all financial information necessary to make such determination. The liability must be paid in full within three years and the taxpayer must agree to abide by the income tax laws while the agreement is in effect (Code Sec. 6159(c), as added by the 1998 Act).

★ *Effective date.* The installment agreement provisions are effective on the date of enactment (Act Sec. 3467(b) of the IRS Restructuring and Reform Act of 1998).

Act Sec. 3467(a), redesignating Code Sec. 6159(c) as Code Sec. 6159(d) and inserting after Code Sec. 6159(b) new Code Sec. 6159(c); Act Sec. 3467(b). Law at ¶ 6150. Committee Report at ¶ 10,545.

Annual Installment Agreement Statement

¶ 1278

Background

Taxpayers seeking to satisfy their tax liability through an installment agreement with the IRS under Code Sec. 6159 generally must provide extensive financial background information. Once accepted, an installment agreement is subject to modification or termination by the IRS if a taxpayer fails to make an installment, pay any other tax liability or provide any requested financial information. The IRS has no obligation to provide the taxpayer with an annual accounting of the tax liability during the course of the installment payment period.

IRS Restructuring and Reform Impact

Annual Statement.—The 1998 Act requires the IRS to provide any taxpayer who has an installment agreement in effect with an annual statement setting forth the taxpayer's beginning of the year balance, all payments made during the year, and the remaining balance at year's end. The IRS must begin providing the installment agreement statements no later than July 1, 2000 (Act Sec. 3506 of the IRS Restructuring and Reform Act of 1998).

PRACTICAL ANALYSIS. Robert McKenzie, of McKenzie & McKenzie PC, Chicago, Ill., notes that taxpayers who have entered into installment agreements with the IRS pursuant to Code Sec. 6159 have not been provided with clear explanations of interest and penalties accruing on their tax liabilities. As a result, taxpayers who might be allowed to deduct accrued interest and taxes in certain situations have not been able to determine the proper amount without making specific requests for information from the IRS. Effective July 1, 2000, the IRS will be required to provide an annual statement to each taxpayer subject to an installment agreement with the accrued interest and penalties and balance due. This statement will allow individuals to provide information to their tax preparers. It will also allow taxpayers to clearly track their remaining outstanding liabilities to the IRS.

★ *Effective date.* No specific effective date is provided by the Act. The provision is, therefore, considered effective on the date of enactment.

Act Sec. 3506. Law at ¶ 8150. Committee Report at ¶ 10,590.

Limitation on Penalty

¶ 1282

Background

Taxpayers who fail to pay the tax shown on a return by the due date are subject to a penalty of 0.5 percent per month, up to a maximum penalty of 25 percent of the amount due (Code Sec. 6651(a)(2)). A failure-to-pay penalty is also imposed on unpaid amounts that are not shown on a return (Code Sec. 6651(a)(3)). The penalty begins to run on such an amount if it is not paid within a certain number of days after the IRS sends notice and demand for payment. If the amount demanded is less than $100,000, the penalty begins to run 22 calendar days after the date of notice and demand. If the amount demanded is more than $100,000, the penalty begins to run 11 business days after the date of notice and demand.

IRS Restructuring and Reform Impact

Penalty reduced during installment agreement.—For individuals, the penalty amount for failure to pay tax is limited by the Act to half the usual rate (0.25 percent rather than 0.5 percent) for any month in which an installment payment agreement with the IRS is in effect (Code Sec. 6651(h), as added by the IRS Restructuring and Reform Act of 1998).

Caution. The failure-to-pay penalty is reduced only if the individual timely filed (taking extensions into account) the return relating to the liability that is subject to the installment agreement.

Example. Sally Hayes timely filed her income tax return but was unable to pay the $10,000 tax liability. She successfully negotiated an installment agreement with the IRS under which she will pay off the $10,000 over the next three years. Since she timely filed the return, the one-half percent interest imposed under Code Sec. 6651(a)(2) is limited to 0.25 percent, decreasing her first month's installment by approximately $25 ($10,000 × .0025) (without taking into account compounding of interest).

★ *Effective date.* The provision applies in determining additions to tax for months beginning after December 31, 1999 (Act Sec. 3303(b) of the IRS Restructuring and Reformation Act of 1998).

Act Sec. 3303(a), adding Code Sec. 6651(h); Act Sec. 3303(b). Law at ¶ 6490. Committee Report at ¶ 10,325.

ASSESSMENT OF TAX

Statute of Limitations

¶ 1286

Background

The IRS generally has three years from the due date of a return to assess additional tax (Code Sec. 6501(a)). If tax has been assessed within the limitations period, the IRS generally has 10 years following the assessment to begin a proceeding to collect the tax by levy or in a court proceeding (Code Sec. 6502(a)(1)).

The IRS and a taxpayer may agree to an extension of time to assess all taxes (except estate taxes) imposed by the Code (Code Sec. 6501(c)(4)). To obtain an extension, the parties must execute a written consent before the initial period of assessment expires. Form 872, Consent to Extend the Time to Assess Tax, is used to extend the period of assessment to a specific date, which may be further extended by subsequent agreements within the most recent extension period. Form 872-A, Special Consent to Extend Time to Assess Tax, extends the assessment period indefinitely. It is common for the IRS to request audited taxpayers to agree to an extension of the three-year limitations period for assessment. Taxpayers may regard an extension as in their best interest if they believe the additional time will avoid forcing the hand of the IRS and permit a more reasonable resolution of the issues under discussion.

The 10-year limitations period for collecting assessed tax may also be extended by written agreement within the original 10-year limitations period or an extension thereof. Form 900, Tax Collection Waiver, is used for this purpose. The 10-year collections period may be extended even after it has expired if there has been a levy on any part of the taxpayer's property prior to the expiration and the extension is agreed to in writing before the levy is released (Code Sec. 6502(a)(2)).

IRS Restructuring and Reform Impact

Notification of taxpayer's rights.—In order to ensure that taxpayers are aware that they have the right to refuse to extend the limitations period for tax assessments, the IRS must notify the taxpayer of such right. More specifically, the IRS must notify the taxpayer that the taxpayer may (1) refuse to extend the period of limitations or (2) limit the extension to particular issues or to a particular period of time. This notice must be provided each time an extension is requested (Code Sec. 6501(c)(4), as amended by the IRS Restructuring and Reform Act of 1998).

Elimination of extension for collection of tax. In general, the 10-year limitations period on collections may not be extended if there has been no levy on any of the taxpayer's property. If the taxpayer entered into an installment agreement with the IRS, however, the 10-year limitations period may be extended for the period that the limitations period was extended under the original terms of the installment agreement plus 90 days (Code Sec. 6502(a)(2), as amended by the 1998 Act).

The collections period may continue to be extended after it has expired if there has been a levy on any of the taxpayer's property before the expiration and the extension is agreed to before the levy is released.

PRACTICAL ANALYSIS. Robert McKenzie, of McKenzie & McKenzie PC, Chicago, Ill., comments that the IRS is now prohibited from seeking extensions for statute of limitations pursuant to Code Sec. 6502 except in the case of granting an installment agreement. The IRS is allowed to solicit such extensions from corporations but not from individuals. The provision does not prohibit the IRS from taking enforcement action prior to the expiration of a statute of limitation. Therefore, the taxpayer could be close to the ten-year statute of limitations potential that he may no longer be required to pay the tax liability but might also be confronted by the IRS taking enforced collection measures.

The IRS also is not prohibited from suing the taxpayer in U.S. District Court. It may sue to reduce the tax claim to judgment that will then allow the IRS more time to collect the tax liability even though the taxpayer refused to sign an extension of the statute of limitations. Although such suits are rare, one might project that in the future more suits to reduce tax claims to judgment may be initiated by the IRS to protect its rights to collect taxes. This provision does not become effective except with respect to extensions requested after December 31, 1999. Therefore, during the next 18 months the IRS may continue to request extensions of statutes of limitations.

★ *Effective date.* This provision applies to requests to extend the applicable period of limitations made after December 31, 1999 (Act Sec. 3461(c)(1) of the IRS Restructuring and Reform Act of 1998). If, in any request made on or before December 31, 1999, a taxpayer agreed to extend the 10-year period of limitations on collections, the extension will expire on the latest of (1) the last day of the original 10-year limitations period, (2) December 31, 2002, or (3) in the case of an extension in connection with an installment agreement, the ninetieth day after the extension (Act Sec. 3461(c)(2) of the 1998 Act).

Act Sec. 3461(a), amending Code Sec. 6502(a); Act Sec. 3461(b), amending Code Sec. 6501(c)(4); Act Sec. 3461(c). Law at ¶ 6400 and ¶ 6410. Committee Report at ¶ 10,515.

INNOCENT SPOUSE

Innocent Spouse Relief and Separate Liability

¶ 1290

Background

Innocent spouse rule in general. For married taxpayers, joint and several liability is the obligation that accompanies the privilege of filing a joint return. Thus, one spouse may be subject to joint liability for the omissions from income or erroneous deductions of the other spouse. In some cases, one spouse intentionally has not reported income or has claimed false deductions and concealed the return errors from the other spouse. The question then becomes whether the innocent spouse, who merely signed a joint return, should be held liable for errors on the return attributable to the actions of the other spouse. The answer is especially critical if the couple has divorced and the innocent spouse is the only source of collection for the unpaid tax.

Code Sec. 6013(e) offered conditional relief to an innocent spouse. A spouse could qualify for relief from joint and several liability under Code Sec. 6013(e) if all of the following requirements were met:

(1) a joint return had been made for the tax year;

(2) there was a substantial understatement of tax attributable to grossly erroneous items of the other spouse on the return;

(3) the innocent spouse established that, in signing the return, he or she did not know or have reason to know of the substantial understatement; and

(4) under all the facts and circumstances, it would have been inequitable to hold the innocent spouse liable for the deficiency in tax resulting from the substantial understatement (Code Sec. 6013(e)(1)).

Grossly erroneous items. A grossly erroneous item with respect to a spouse is any item of gross income attributable to the spouse that is omitted from gross income, or any claim for deduction, credit, or basis by such spouse in an amount for which there is no basis in fact or law (Code Sec. 6013(e)(2)). Ordinarily, a deduction that has no basis in fact or law may be characterized as frivolous, fraudulent or phony. The fact that a deduction is disallowed does not prove that the deduction had no basis in fact or law. Generally, community property laws are disregarded in determining whether a grossly erroneous item is attributable to a spouse.

Substantial understatement of tax. Generally, a substantial understatement is an understatement exceeding $500 (Code Sec. 6013(e)(3)). However, for any understatement attributable to an unfounded claim for deduction, credit, or basis (as opposed to omissions from gross income), there is the additional requirement that the amount of the understatement must be greater than 10 percent of the innocent spouse's adjusted gross income (AGI) in the preadjustment year (the most recent tax year ending before the date the deficiency notice is mailed) if that spouse's AGI is $20,000 or less. If the innocent spouse's AGI in the preadjustment year is more than $20,000, then the understatement must exceed 25 percent of AGI (Code Sec. 6013(e)(4)).

Knowledge of understatement. The innocent spouse must establish that, in signing the return, he or she did not know or have reason to know of the substantial understatement. Courts have not consistently applied a single set of rules to determine whether a spouse had sufficient knowledge or had reason to know of an understatement to be disqualified from innocent spouse status. Stricter courts have ruled that knowledge of the facts of the transaction giving rise to the understatement precludes the purported innocent spouse from obtaining relief. Similar reasoning would always deny relief to a spouse signing a return with an erroneous deduction because the existence of the deduction is disclosed on the return. Other courts look at factors such as the business acumen or education level of the innocent spouse in order to rule that the spouse did not have knowledge of the understatement. The Code did not provide for partial relief based on a spouse's limited knowledge of the other spouse's affairs.

Taxpayers in community property states. A version of innocent spouse relief for married taxpayers in community property states protects married individuals who file separate returns (Code Sec. 66(c)).

IRS Restructuring and Reform Impact

Introduction.—The Act contains significant provisions designed to protect married taxpayers from the tax misdeeds of their spouses. With regard to innocent spouse relief, the requirements for obtaining such relief are made less stringent and relief is made available on an apportioned basis. A new requirement is that a taxpayer must elect innocent spouse relief within two years after tax collection activities are begun. The Act authorizes the IRS to provide equitable innocent spouse relief to spouses in community property states who do not file joint returns.

In the case of divorced taxpayers and married taxpayers who are legally separated or who have been living apart for at least one year, the Act permits such individuals to elect separate tax liability despite having filed a joint return.

The Act gives the Tax Court jurisdiction to review denials of innocent spouse relief and separate liability elections and restrains IRS collection efforts while a Tax Court procedure is pending.

In order to make married taxpayers more aware of the legal consequences of filing a joint return, the Act requires the IRS to notify joint filers of their joint and several liability (see ¶ 1294) and send any notice relating to a joint return separately to each individual on the return.

Innocent Spouse Relief Modified

Relief available for all understatements.—Innocent spouse relief applies to *all* understatements of tax attributable to erroneous items of the other spouse. It is no longer necessary for an understatement to be "substantial," which eliminates the $500 minimum and the minimums based on the innocent spouse's AGI. In addition, it is no longer necessary for the items of the other spouse to which an understatement is attributable to be "grossly" erroneous. This eliminates the hurdle of demonstrating that the understatement has no factual or legal basis (Code Sec. 6015(b)(1)(B), as added by the IRS Restructuring and Reform Act of 1998).

Comment. The easing of the restrictions on innocent spouse relief makes the determination of eligibility for such relief simpler and fairer. The minimum thresholds for innocent spouse relief were arbitrary and had a disproportionate impact on low income taxpayers. The grossly erroneous standard could be used by the IRS to deny relief even for understatements whose justification was very tenuous.

Partial relief available.—Innocent spouse relief continues to be available only if the spouse invoking such relief establishes that, in signing the return, he or she did not know, and had no reason to know, that there was an understatement of tax (Code Sec. 6015(b)(1)(C), as added by the 1998 Act). However, if the spouse establishes that, in signing the return, he or she did not know, and had no reason to know, the *extent* of the understatement, innocent spouse relief is available on an apportioned basis. In such a case, the spouse is relieved of liability to the extent it is attributable to the portion of the understatement that the spouse did not know or have reason to know (Code Sec. 6015(b)(2), as added by the 1998 Act).

Comment. In making innocent spouse relief available if a spouse was ignorant of the extent of an understatement, the Act suggests that partial relief may be available with respect to *one* item that is understated on a tax return. However, in summarizing the House Bill provision for apportioned relief, which the Conference Committee adopted, the Conference Committee Report notes that a spouse may be relieved of liability for a portion of an understatement even if the spouse knew or had reason to know of *other* understatements of tax on the same return. This could be read to imply that apportioned relief may not be available with respect to one item of income or one deduction.

¶ 1290

Election. Taxpayers must elect innocent spouse relief using an IRS form. Taxpayers are entitled to elect such relief up to two years *after* the date the IRS begins collection activities with respect to the electing taxpayer (Code Sec. 6015((b)(1)(E), as added by the 1998 Act). In reference to the separate liability election discussed below, the Senate Committee Report notes that the two-year period begins with collection activities that have the effect of notifying the electing spouse of the IRS's intention to collect from that spouse. Such activities would include garnishment of the electing spouse's wages and notice of levy against the electing spouse's property, but not notice of deficiency and demand for payment addressed to both spouses. Under the effective date provisions, this two-year period will not expire before two years after the date of the first collection activity that occurs after the date of enactment. The IRS must provide a form for such an election within 180 days after the date of enactment (Act Sec. 3201(c) of the 1998 Act).

Planning Note. In addition to electing innocent spouse relief, if an individual filing a joint return becomes divorced or separated, he or she may also be eligible to elect separate liability. As discussed below, the "actual knowledge" standard for separate liability is narrower than the "knew or should have known" standard for innocent spouse relief, which may make separate liability available under circumstances in which innocent spouse relief is not.

Equitable relief.—The requirement that, under all the facts and circumstances, it would be inequitable to hold the innocent spouse liable for a tax deficiency due to an understatement continues to be a requirement for innocent spouse relief (Code Sec. 6015(b)(1)(D), as added by the 1998 Act). The IRS is authorized, however, to provide equitable relief in cases in which innocent spouse relief is otherwise not available (Code Sec. 6015(f), as added by the 1998 Act).

The Conference Committee Report instructs the IRS to use its authority to grant equitable relief in tax underpayment situations. Thus, equitable relief is to be available to a spouse who did not know, and had no reason to know, that funds intended for paying tax were instead taken by the other spouse for the other spouse's benefit. The report emphasizes, however, that equitable relief should be available for both understatements and underpayments of tax.

Notice to other joint filer.—The IRS must issue regulations that give a joint filer notice of, and an opportunity to participate in, any administrative proceeding with respect to the other joint filer's election of innocent spouse relief (Code Sec. 6015(g)(2), as added by the 1998 Act).

Community property laws.—As under prior law, community property law is not taken into account in determining innocent spouse relief (Code Sec. 6015(a), as added by the 1998 Act).

Separate Liability Election

Despite filing a joint return for a tax year, certain taxpayers may elect to limit their liability for any deficiency assessed with respect to the return. In general, liability is limited to the amount of deficiency arising from items that would have been allocable to the electing taxpayer if he or she had filed a separate return for the tax year.

Eligibility for election.—A taxpayer may elect separate liability under a joint return if:

(1) at the time of the election, the taxpayer is no longer married to or is legally separated from the person with whom the taxpayer filed the joint return; or

(2) the taxpayer was not living in the same household as the person with whom the taxpayer filed the joint return at any time during the 12 months preceding the election (Code Sec. 6015(c)(3)(A)(i), as added by the 1998 Act).

The Conference Committee Report notes that, for purposes of determining eligibility for the election, a widowed taxpayer is treated as no longer married.

Election. Taxpayers are entitled to elect separate liability up to two years *after* the date the IRS begins collection activities with respect to the electing taxpayer (Code Sec. 6015(c)(3)(B), as added by the 1998 Act). The Senate Committee Report notes that the two-year period begins with collection activities that have the effect of notifying the electing taxpayer of the IRS's intention to collect from that taxpayer. Such activities would include garnishment of the electing taxpayer's wages and notice of levy against the electing taxpayer's property, but not notice of deficiency and demand for payment addressed to both spouses. Under the effective date provisions, this two-year period will not expire before two years after the date of the first collection activity that occurs after the date of enactment. The IRS must provide a form for such an election within 180 days after the date of enactment (Act Sec. 3201(c) of the 1998 Act).

Inappropriate elections prohibited.—An election to limit liability may be partially or completely ineffective due to the electing taxpayer's knowledge of an incorrect item on the joint return or transfers between the joint filers that are intended to avoid tax or are fraudulent.

Electing taxpayer's knowledge. An election to limit liability under a joint return is invalid with respect to a deficiency (or portion of a deficiency) if the IRS demonstrates that, at the time he or she signed the return, the taxpayer making the election had actual knowledge of any item giving rise to the deficiency (or portion thereof). An item of which the electing spouse had actual knowledge is allocable to both spouses. This provision does not apply if the electing taxpayer establishes that he or she signed the return under duress (Code Sec. 6015(c)(3)(C), as added by the 1998 Act).

> **Example.** Tony and Tina Orlando, who are separated, file a joint return for 1998 reporting $90,000 of wage income earned by Tony, $60,000 of wage income earned by Tina, and $30,000 of investment income on the couple's jointly owned assets. The IRS assesses a $4,800 tax deficiency for $12,000 of unreported investment income from assets held in Tony's name. Tina knew about a bank account in Tony's name that generated $1,000 of interest income but had no knowledge of Tony's other separate investments. Under the rules discussed below, the $12,000 of unreported income is fully allocable to Tony, and he is liable for the entire $4,800 deficiency. If Tina elects separate liability, she will not be liable for $4,400 of the deficiency. This is the amount of the deficiency attributable to the $11,000 of unreported income of which Tina had no actual knowledge ($4,800 × [$11,000 ÷ $12,000]). Tina will, however, be liable for $400, which is the amount of the deficiency attributable to the $1,000 of unreported interest income from the bank account ($4,800 × [$1,000 ÷ $12,000]).

The Senate and Conference Committee Reports state that "actual knowledge must be established by the evidence and shall not be inferred based on indications that the electing spouse had reason to know."

Comment. The standard of "actual" knowledge is much narrower than the standard of "known or should have known" that makes a taxpayer ineligible for innocent spouse relief. As the committee reports point out, knowledge of an erroneous item will not be imputed to a joint filer in determining that taxpayer's separate liability.

¶ 1290

Transfers to avoid tax. The liability of a joint filer electing separate liability is increased by the value of any "disqualified asset." A "disqualified asset" is any property or property right that is transferred by the other joint filer to the electing taxpayer for the principal purpose of avoiding tax or payment of tax. Any transfer by the other joint filer to the electing taxpayer within one year preceding the date on which the first letter of proposed deficiency is sent is presumed to have avoidance of tax or payment of tax as its principal purpose. This presumption can be rebutted by showing that the principal purpose of a transfer was not to avoid tax or payment of tax. In addition, the presumption does not apply to transfers made pursuant to a decree of divorce or separate maintenance (Code Sec. 6015(c)(4), as added by the 1998 Act).

Fraudulent transfers. An election is invalid, and joint and several liability continues to apply to the entire return, if the IRS demonstrates that the taxpayers filing the joint return transferred assets between themselves as part of a fraudulent scheme (Code Sec. 6015(c)(3)(A)(ii), as added by the 1998 Act).

Electing taxpayer's portion of deficiency.—An electing taxpayer's liability generally is limited to the portion of the deficiency that is attributable to items allocable to the taxpayer. An item giving rise to a deficiency generally is allocated in the manner it would had been allocated if the taxpayers had filed separate returns (Code Sec. 6015(d)(1) and Code Sec. 6015(d)(3)(A), as added by the 1998 Act).

Example (1). In 1998, Letta Thompson earns $30,000 from freelance work. She regards this income as her "play" money and does not tell her husband, Jerry, about it. The income is not reported on the Thompsons' joint return. Letta and Jerry get a divorce in 1999. If the IRS assesses a deficiency for the unreported income, Jerry may elect separate liability and owe none of the deficiency, regardless of the IRS's ability to collect the deficiency from Letta. Letta will be liable for the entire deficiency.

Example (2). Assume the same facts as in Example (1), except that on the couple's 1998 return Jerry claimed a $10,000 bad debt deduction for a loan he made to his cousin. The IRS assesses a deficiency attributable to $30,000 of unreported income and the $10,000 deduction, which it disallowed. If Jerry elects separate liability, his liability would be limited to 25% of the deficiency ($10,000 ÷ [$30,000 + $10,000]); if Letta elects separate liability, her liability would be limited to 75% of the deficiency. If either Jerry or Letta does not elect separate liability, the nonelecting spouse is liable for the entire deficiency unless it is reduced by innocent spouse relief or the IRS provides equitable relief.

The Senate Committee Report notes that, in general, items of income should be allocated according to which spouse earned the wages or owned the business or investment that produced the income. Income from a jointly owned business or investment should be allocated equally between each spouse unless there is clear and convincing evidence that supports a different allocation.

Burden of proof. A joint filer who elects separate liability bears the burden of proof in establishing his or her portion of the deficiency (Code Sec. 6015(c)(2), as added by the 1998 Act).

Allocation of deduction or credit. If a deficiency is attributable to the denial of a deduction or credit, the deficiency is allocated to the spouse to whom the deduction or credit is allocated. The Senate Committee Report explains that business deductions should be allocated according to ownership of the business. Personal deductions should be allocated equally between each spouse unless there is evidence that a different allocation is appropriate. For example, if one spouse produces evidence that an asset contributed to charity was the other spouse's property, a deficiency due to a valuation overstatement would be allocated to the other spouse.

*Comment.*The Conference Committee Report notes that disallowed miscellaneous itemized deductions will be allocated to a spouse even to the extent such deductions are disallowed because they do not exceed two percent of the spouse's AGI, as required by Code Sec. 67(a).

The Senate and Conference Committee Reports explain that that spouse's liability for the item is limited to the amount of income or tax that is allocated to the spouse and offset by the deduction or credit. The balance of the liability is allocated to the other spouse because income or tax allocated to the other spouse was offset by a portion of the disallowed deduction or credit.

> **Example (3).** Assume the same facts as in Example (2) and that Jerry and Letta each earn $75,000 in income. Because Jerry earned enough income to offset the entire $10,000 disallowed bad debt deduction, the entire deficiency attributable to the denied deduction is allocated to Jerry.

> **Example (4).** Assume the same facts as in Example (2) and that Letta earns $75,000 but Jerry has only $5,000 in income. The $10,000 disallowed deduction offsets Jerry's entire income, leaving a balance of $5,000, which offsets Letta's income. The deficiency attributable to the denied deduction is allocated to Jerry and Letta in proportion to the amount of each spouse's offset income. Thus, Jerry and Letta are each liable for one-half of the deficiency.

Separate treatment of disallowed credits and other taxes. If a deficiency (or portion of a deficiency) is attributable to the disallowance of a credit or a tax other than the income tax or alternative minimum tax (AMT) and the credit or tax is allocated to one spouse, the deficiency (or portion) is treated separately and allocated to that spouse (Code Sec. 6015(d)(2), as added by the 1998 Act). The Conference Committee Report explains this rule to mean that the portion of a deficiency attributable to a disallowed credit or tax other than the income tax or AMT is considered first.

> **Example (5).** Assume the same facts as in Example (2) and that, in addition to the income tax deficiency attributable to $30,000 of Letta's unreported income and Jerry's $10,000 disallowed deduction, the IRS assesses a $4,200 self-employment tax deficiency for Letta's unreported freelance income. The $4,200 self-employment tax deficiency is first allocated to Letta, and the income tax deficiency is allocated as in Example (2) (75% to Letta and 25% to Jerry).

Separate returns limitations disregarded. In determining a joint filer's separate liability, any provision disallowing a deduction or credit because a separate return is filed is disregarded. The deduction or credit is computed as if a joint return had been filed and appropriately allocated between the joint filers (Code Sec. 6015(d)(4), as added by the 1998 Act).

Child's tax liability. If a child's liability is included on a joint return, either joint filer's separate liability is first determined without regard to such liability. The child's liability is then allocated appropriately between the joint filers (Code Sec. 6015(d)(5), as added by the 1998 Act).

Allocation rule overridden in certain circumstances. The rule that an item giving rise to a deficiency generally is allocated in the manner it would have been allocated if the taxpayers had filed separately is subject to the following two exceptions:

> (1) Under rules to be prescribed by the IRS, an item otherwise allocable to one joint filer will be allocated to the other joint filer to the extent that the

item created a tax benefit on the joint return for the other filer (Code Sec. 6015(d)(3)(B), as added by the 1998 Act).

(2) The IRS may provide for a different manner of allocation if it establishes that such an allocation is appropriate due to fraud of one or both joint filers (Code Sec. 6015(d)(3)(C), as added by the 1998 Act).

Comment. The Senate Committee Report states that if the electing spouse establishes that he or she did not know, and had no reason to know, of an item and, considering the facts and circumstances, it is inequitable to hold the electing spouse responsible for any deficiency attributable to the item, the item may be equitably reallocated to the other spouse.

Community property laws. Community property law is not taken into account in determining separate liability (Code Sec. 6015(a), as added by the 1998 Act).

Equitable relief.—The IRS is authorized to provide equitable relief in cases in which relief under a separate liability election is otherwise not available (Code Sec. 6015(f), as added by the 1998 Act).

The Conference Committee Report instructs the IRS to use its authority to grant equitable relief in tax underpayment situations. Thus, equitable relief is to be available to a spouse who did not know, and had no reason to know, that funds intended for paying tax were instead taken by the other spouse for the other spouse's benefit. The report emphasizes, however, that equitable relief should be available for both understatements and underpayments of tax.

Notice to other joint filer.—The IRS must issue regulations that give a joint filer notice of, and an opportunity to participate in, any administrative proceeding with respect to the other joint filer's separate liability election (Code Sec. 6501(g)(2), as added by the 1998 Act).

Tax Court Review

If a joint filer is denied an election for innocent spouse relief or separate liability, the taxpayer may petition the Tax Court for review. The petition must be filed within 90 days following date on which the IRS mails a determination to the taxpayer or, if earlier, six months after the election was filed (Code Sec. 6015(e)(1)(A), as added by the 1998 Act).

Res judicata. A prior, final Tax Court decision is conclusive except with regard to the qualification of the petitioning taxpayer for innocent spouse relief or separate liability. The exception made for determining the taxpayer's qualification does not apply if the Tax Court determines that the petitioning taxpayer participated meaningfully in the prior proceeding (Code Sec. 6015(e)(3)(B), as added by the 1998 Act).

Suits for refund. The Tax Court cedes jurisdiction over a claim for innocent spouse relief or separate liability to a U.S. district court or the U.S. Court of Federal Claims that acquires jurisdiction for a refund suit with respect to the same tax years (Code Sec. 6015(e)(3)(C), as added by the 1998 Act).

Notice to other spouse. The Tax Court must establish rules for giving joint filers who do not make an innocent spouse or separate liability election adequate notice and an opportunity to become a party to a proceeding regarding either election (Code Sec. 6015(e)(4), as added by the 1998 Act).

Restrictions on collection activity. Except for termination and jeopardy assessments, the IRS may not begin or proceed with a levy or collection action for an assessment to which an election for innocent spouse relief or separate liability relates until the 90-day period for petitioning the Tax Court has expired or a Tax Court decision becomes final. A levy or collection proceeding begun during the period in which it is prohibited may be enjoined in the proper court. In order for the Tax Court to have jurisdiction to enjoin such actions, the taxpayer must have filed a timely petition to the court, and the court's jurisdiction is limited to the amount of the assessment to which the innocent spouse or separate liability election relates (Code Sec. 6015(e)(1)(B), as added by the 1998 Act). The period of limitations for collecting an assessment is suspended for the period during which the IRS is prohibited from collecting by levy or a court proceeding plus an additional 60 days (Code Sec. 6015(e)(2), as added by the 1998 Act).

Equitable Relief for Married Taxpayers in Community Property States

Married taxpayers residing in community property states may be liable for the income tax on the community property share of the other spouse's income even if they file separate returns. Such taxpayers are entitled to a form of innocent spouse relief under Code Sec. 66(c). In cases in which such relief is not available, the IRS is authorized to provide relief if failure to do so would be inequitable, taking into account all the facts and circumstances (Code Sec. 66(c), as amended by the 1998 Act).

PRACTICAL ANALYSIS. Denis J. Conlon, of Ernst & Young, LLP, Chicago, Illinois, observes that the Conference Agreement provides for significant relief with regard to the liability of spouses for taxes arising after the date of enactment and any liability for tax remaining unpaid as of that date. Taxes that are assessed and in collection status would be subject to the new procedure; however, taxpayers will need to file an election form within certain time limits or relief will not be available.

These provisions generally make innocent spouse relief easier to obtain. They eliminate the understatement thresholds, require only that the understatement be attributable to an erroneous (not just a *grossly erroneous*) item of the other spouse, and allow relief to be on an apportioned basis.

Under new Code Sec. 6015, an individual who made a joint return may seek relief under the new procedures by limiting their liability to a separate liability amount. Conlon points out that a new form must be developed for use by individuals in applying these new innocent spouse relief procedures.

The separate liability election, with respect to a deficiency in tax, is limited to individuals who are no longer married, are legally separated, or are not living with the other person who signed the joint tax return. Taxpayers, whether eligible or not to make the separate liability election, may still be granted innocent spouse relief where appropriate. In addition, some individuals are ineligible for relief because of the transfer of assets as a fraudulent scheme to evade payment of tax.

Tax Court review of the application of the relief provisions is provided for in the Conference Agreement, as well as provisions to prevent collection during the consideration of the matter by the Tax Court. The provisions also grant the Tax Court jurisdiction to review any denial of relief or failure to rule by the IRS and the authority to order refunds if it determines the spouse qualified for relief and an overpayment exists.

Equitable relief is provided for certain individuals not filing joint returns. This appears to be intended to deal with the community property implications of *Poe v. Seaborn*, 282 U.S. 101 (1930). This case stands for the rule that in community property states each spouse is liable for the tax on one half of the community income. This new provision appears to be intended to allow relief to a spouse who may be charged with income tax on items of income that are unknown to him or her and no joint return has been filed.

★ *Effective date.* These provisions apply to any tax liability arising after the date of enactment and any tax liability arising on or before the date of enactment but remaining unpaid as of the date of enactment (Act Sec. 3201(g)(1) of the IRS Restructuring and Reform Act of 1998). The two-year period for electing innocent spouse relief or separate liability will not expire before the date which is two years after the date of the first collection activity after the date of enactment (Act Sec. 3201(g)(2) of the 1998 Act).

Act Sec. 3201(a), adding Code Sec. 6015; Act Sec. 3201(b), amending Code Sec. 66(c); Act. Sec. 3201(c); Act Sec. 3201(d); Act Sec. 3201(e), deleting Code Sec. 6013(e); Act Sec. 3201(f); Act Sec. 3201(g). Law at ¶ 5140, ¶ 6030, ¶ 6040, ¶ 6200, ¶ 6590, and ¶ 8080. Committee Report at ¶ 10,285.

Explanation of Joint and Several Liability

¶ 1294

Background

Married taxpayers who file a joint tax return are fully responsible for the accuracy of the return and are fully liable for any tax payable under the return. Joint and several liability applies even though only one spouse may have earned the income shown on the return. Many married taxpayers, however, may not understand the legal consequences of signing a joint return. Married taxpayers who wish to avoid joint and several liability may file as a married person filing separately. Relief from joint and several liability is also available under the innocent spouse provisions.

IRS Restructuring and Reform Impact

Notice of joint and several liability and rights to limit liability.—The IRS must establish procedures to clearly alert married taxpayers of their joint and several liabilities on all appropriate publications and instructions (Act Sec. 3501(a) of the IRS Restructuring and Reform Act of 1998). The House and Senate Committee Reports note that the IRS is expected to make an appropriate cross-reference to such notifications near the signature line on appropriate tax forms.

The IRS also must establish procedures notifying taxpayers of their right to elect innocent spouse relief and/or separate liability under new Code Sec. 6015 (see ¶ 1290). Such notice must be included in IRS Publication 1 (Your Rights as a Taxpayer) and any collection-related notices (Act Sec. 3501(b) of the 1998 Act).

The IRS must establish these notification procedures as soon as practicable, but no later than 180 days after the date of enactment.

★ *Effective date.* No specific effective date is provided by the Act. The provision is, therefore, considered effective on the date of enactment.

Act Sec. 3501. Law at ¶ 8130. Committee Report at ¶ 10,565.

Disclosure to Authorized Representatives

¶ 1295

Background

If there is a deficiency with respect to a joint return but the individuals who filed the return are no longer living together or divorced, at the request of one of

¶ 1295

Background ———

the joint filers, the IRS may disclose to the joint filer making the request whether there has been an attempt to collect the deficiency from the other joint filer, the general nature of those collection activities, and the amount collected (Code Sec. 6103(e)(8)).

———

Technical Corrections Impact

Disclosure to taxpayer's authorized representatives.—The Act clarifies that the disclosure authorized by Code Sec. 6103(e)(8), regarding the IRS's collection activity with respect to a joint filer, may be made to the authorized representative of the joint filer requesting the disclosure (Code Sec. 6103(e)(6), as amended by the IRS Restructuring and Reform Act of 1998).

★ *Effective date.* This provision takes effect on the date of enactment (Act Sec. 6019(d) of the IRS Restructuring and Reform Act of 1998).

Act Sec. 6019(c), amending Code Sec. 6103(e)(6); Act Sec. 6019(d). Law at ¶ 6110. Committee Report at ¶ 11,360.

Chapter 13
Taxpayer Rights—Judicial Proceedings

TAX COURT
Estate Tax Refund Jurisdiction
¶ 1301

Background

The U.S. Court of Federal Claims and the federal district courts have jurisdiction over tax refund suits provided full payment of the assessed liability has been made (*W.W. Flora,* SCt, 60-1 USTC ¶ 9347, 362 US 145). Under Code Sec. 6166, if certain conditions are met, the executor of a decedent's estate may elect to pay the estate tax relating to certain closely held businesses over a 14-year period. Unless the entire estate tax liability has been paid, courts have held that the Court of Federal Claims and the federal district courts do not have jurisdiction over refund claims brought by taxpayers deferring estate tax payments. Further, timely payment of installments due prior to the bringing of an action is not sufficient to invoke jurisdiction (*J.G. Rocovich,* CA-FC, 91-1 USTC ¶ 60,072 and *L.C. Abruzzo,* 92-1 USTC ¶ 60,094, 24 ClsCt 668). The Tax Court, pursuant to Code Sec. 7479, has limited authority to provide declaratory judgments regarding initial or continuing eligibility for deferral under Code Sec. 6166.

IRS Restructuring and Reform Impact

Refund actions with respect to certain estates that have elected the installment method of payment.—The Act grants the Court of Federal Claims and the district courts jurisdiction to determine the correct amount of estate tax liability or refund in actions brought by taxpayers that defer estate tax payments provided certain conditions are met (Code Sec. 7422(j)(1), as added by the IRS Restructuring and Reform Act of 1998).

First, the estate must have made an election to pay the estate tax relating to certain closely held businesses over a 14-year period pursuant to Code Sec. 6166. Second, the estate must have fully paid each installment of principal and/or interest due as well as all non-Code Sec. 6166-related estate taxes due prior to filing suit. (Taxpayers are not relieved of the liability for making installment payments during the pendency of the suit.) Third, no portion of the payments due can have been accelerated. Fourth, there must be no suits for declaratory judgment under Code Sec. 7479 pending. Finally, no outstanding deficiency notices may exist against the estate (Code Sec. 7422(j)(2), as added by the 1998 Act).

Further, pursuant to the doctrine of res judicata, if the taxpayer has previously litigated its estate tax liability, the taxpayer may not use this provision. Also, once a final judgment has been entered by the Court of Federal Claims or a district court, the IRS may not collect any amount disallowed by the court. Any amounts paid by the taxpayer in excess of the amount the court finds due must be refunded (Code Sec. 7422(j)(3), as added by the 1998 Act).

The two-year statute of limitations for filing a refund action is suspended during the pendency of any action for declaratory judgment brought pursuant to Code Sec. 7479 to determine an estate's Code Sec. 6166 eligibility (Code Sec. 7479(c), as added by the 1998 Act).

PRACTICAL ANALYSIS. J. Earl Epstein of Epstein, Shapiro & Epstein, Philadelphia, PA, and former Attorney Adviser, U.S. Tax Court, comments that it is important to note that this additional jurisdiction is granted only when the lack of full payment is the sole reason why refund jurisdiction would have been denied under prior law.

★ *Effective date.* The provision is effective for refund claims filed after the date of enactment (Act Sec. 3104(c) of the IRS Restructuring and Reform Act of 1998).

Act Sec. 3104(a), adding Code Sec. 7422(j); Act Sec. 3104(b), adding Code Sec. 7479(c); Act Sec. 3104(c). Law at ¶ 6600 and ¶ 6710. Committee Report at ¶ 10,265.

Small Case Calendar

¶ 1316

Background _____

Taxpayers may chose to contest many tax disputes in the Tax Court. Code Sec. 7463 provides special small case procedures for taxpayers to apply to disputes involving $10,000 or less, if the taxpayer chooses to utilize these procedures (and the Tax Court concurs). Taxpayers are not required to use the small case procedures. Unless the case involves an issue that should be heard under normal procedures, the Tax Court usually concurs with a taxpayer's request to use the small case procedures. The Tax Court can order that the small case procedures be discontinued if (1) the amount in controversy will exceed $10,000 or (2) justice requires a change in procedure.

Proceedings for small tax cases are informal. Thus, briefs and oral arguments are not required and the strict rules of evidence are not applied. Although taxpayers may be represented by anyone admitted to practice before the Tax Court, taxpayers usually represent themselves in small tax cases. Decisions rendered under small case procedures may not be cited as precedent in future cases and may not be appealed by the government or the taxpayer.

A taxpayer can elect the small tax-case procedure by leaving blank the box at the end of the Petition, Form 2. Petition, Form 2, which is a simple printed form, is supplied by the Clerk of the Court, U. S. Tax Court, 400 Second St. N.W., Washington, D.C. 20217.

IRS Restructuring and Reform Impact

Increase in size of cases permitted on small case calendar.—The provision increases the cap for small case treatment from $10,000 to $50,000 (Code Sec. 7463, as amended by the IRS Restructuring and Reform Act of 1998). This increase in the cap may result in the inclusion of cases with significant precedential value in the small case procedure. Accordingly, the Conference Report comments that the conferees "anticipate" the Tax Court will carefully consider both (1) IRS objections to small case treatment based on potential precedential value and (2) the financial impact on the taxpayer, including additional legal fees and costs, of not continuing with small case treatment.

PRACTICAL ANALYSIS. J. Earl Epstein of Epstein, Shapiro & Epstein, Philadelphia, PA, and former Attorney Adviser, U.S. Tax Court, comments that the most obvious benefit of the small case procedure in the Tax Court is that the petition is an easy-to-complete printed form; that cases can comfortably be argued by the taxpayer without the need for an attorney; that the trial is conducted as informally as possible consistent with orderly procedure; that there is relaxed use of the rules of evidence; and that no written briefs or oral arguments are required. However, the downside of the procedure is that cases are normally decided by a brief statement by the Court, often orally, with only a summary of the reasons for the decision.

The small case procedure is initiated at the election of the taxpayer, but must be concurred with by the Court. The Court will usually agree to the taxpayer's election unless it appears that the dispute will exceed $50,000 or if the Court finds that justice requires that the case be heard by a regular division of the Court. An example would be where the issue involved is novel or where the decision would impact on other cases before the Court. In those situations, a full trial with written briefs and a complete, written opinion by the Court is considered preferable.

In deciding whether to elect the small case procedure, taxpayers should consider the complexity of the issue to be argued. In particular, one should consider whether a professional representative and a written brief would better serve the taxpayer's objectives.

PRACTICAL ANALYSIS. David R. Brennan of Faegre & Benson, Minneapolis, MN (former Director, Tax Litigation Division, Chief Counsel's Office and former Treasury Acting General Counsel), adds that the probability is that this provision will increase the number of motions being filed by the IRS to discontinue the small case procedure because of precedential issues. The Tax Court may discontinue a small case proceeding if justice so requires. The legislative history clearly contemplates an increase in the filing of such motions.

★ *Effective date.* The provision applies to proceedings commenced after the date of enactment (Act Sec. 3103(c) of the IRS Restructuring and Reform Act of 1998).

Act Sec. 3103, amending Code Sec. 7436(c)(1), Code Sec. 7443A(b)(3), and Code Sec. 7463. Law at ¶ 6670, ¶ 6690, and ¶ 6700. Committee Report at ¶ 10,260.

¶ 1316

Refund or Credit of Overpayments

¶ 1321

Background ———————————————————————————————

The IRS generally cannot take action to collect a deficiency during the period a taxpayer may petition the Tax Court. If a taxpayer petitions the Tax Court, no action to collect a deficiency can be taken until the Tax Court decision becomes final. Actions to collect a deficiency during this period may be enjoined, but there is no authority for ordering the refund of any amount collected by the IRS during the prohibited period.

If a taxpayer contests a deficiency in the Tax Court, no credit or refund of income tax for the contested tax year may be made, except in accordance with a Tax Court decision that has become final. Where the Tax Court determines that an overpayment has been made and a refund is due the taxpayer, no provision exists for the refund of any portion of any overpayment that is not contested on appeal.

IRS Restructuring and Reform Impact

Refund or credit of overpayments before final determination.—The Act provides that a proper court, including the Tax Court, has jurisdiction to order a refund of any amount that was collected within the period during which the IRS is prohibited from collecting by levy or through a court proceeding under Code Sec. 6213(a) (Code Sec. 6512(a)(5), as added by the IRS Restructuring and Reform Act of 1998).

The Tax Court is also authorized to refund or credit an overpayment that is not contested on appeal (Code Sec. 6512(b)(1), as amended by the 1998 Act; Code Sec. 6512(a)(6), as added by the 1998 Act).

★ *Effective date.* The provision takes effect on the date of enactment (Act Sec. 3464(d) of the IRS Restructuring and Reform Act of 1998).

Act Sec. 3464, amending Code Sec. 6213(a) and Code Sec. 6512(a) and (b)(1). Law at ¶ 6190 and ¶ 6440. Committee Report at ¶ 10,530.

Notification of Deadline for Filing Petition

¶ 1326

Background ———————————————————————————————

Taxpayers seeking a redetermination of their tax liability before the Tax Court must file a Tax Court petition within 90 days after the deficiency notice is mailed (within 150 days if the person is outside the United States). If the taxpayer fails to file a petition within that time period, the Tax Court lacks jurisdiction to consider the petition.

IRS Restructuring and Reform Impact

Notice of deficiency to specify deadlines for filing a Tax Court petition.—The IRS must include on each deficiency notice the date it determines to be the last day on which the taxpayer may file a petition with the Tax Court (Act Sec. 3463(a) of the IRS Restructuring and Reform Act of 1998). A petition filed with the Tax Court by that date is considered timely filed (Code Sec. 6213(a), as amended by the 1998 Act). Addition of the date will assist taxpayers in determining the time period within which they must file a petition in the Tax Court. Taxpayers may rely upon the date provided by the IRS.

Comment. If the IRS provides an erroneous date that would shorten the 90-day filing period, the taxpayer is not bound by the date provided by the IRS.

★ *Effective date.* The provision applies to notices mailed after December 31, 1998 (Act Sec. 3463(c) of the IRS Restructuring and Reform Act of 1998).

Act Sec. 3463(a); Act Sec. 3463(b), amending Code Sec. 6213(a); Act Sec. 3463(c). Law at ¶ 6190. Committee Report at ¶ 10,525.

BURDEN OF PROOF
Burden of Proof in Court Proceedings
¶ 1331

Background

Under Tax Court Rules, at trial, the taxpayer generally bears the burden of proof (Tax Court Rule 142); the Internal Revenue Code contains provisions only concerning when the taxpayer does not have the burden of proof. However, even without an Internal Revenue Code provision clearly placing the burden of proof on the taxpayer, the courts have long held that an IRS notice of deficiency enjoys a presumption of correctness, and that the taxpayer has the burden of proving it to be wrong (*T.H. Welch*, SCt, 3 USTC ¶ 1164). The presumption of correctness in favor of the IRS is a procedural device requiring the taxpayer to go forward with prima facie evidence to disprove the IRS's determination. In addition to rebutting the presumption, taxpayers have the burden of showing the merits of their claims by at least a preponderance of the evidence (*Danville Plywood Corp.*, CA-FC, 90-1 USTC ¶ 50,161).

Although the presumption of correctness is judicially based, there is considerable evidence that the presumption has been repeatedly considered and approved by Congress. This is evidenced by a number of Internal Revenue Code provisions that expressly place the burden of proof on the IRS. There are four exceptions provided in Tax Court Rule 142(b) through 142(e): fraud (Code Sec. 7422(e) and Code Sec. 7454(a)), foundation managers (Code Sec. 7454(b)), transferee liability (Code Sec. 6902(a)), or unreasonable accumulation of earnings and profits (Code Sec. 534).

In addition to the exceptions that are enumerated in Tax Court Rule 142, the Internal Revenue Code contains other provisions giving the IRS the burden of proof, such as in proceedings concerning required reasonable verification of information returns (Code Sec. 6201(d)), review of jeopardy levy or assessment procedures (Code Sec. 7429(g)(1)), property transferred in connection with performance of services (Code Sec. 83(d)(1)), illegal bribes, kickbacks and other payments (Code Sec. 162(c)(1) and (2)), golden parachute payments (Code Sec. 280G(b)(2)(B)), expatriation (Code Secs. 877(e), 2107(e), and 2501(a)(4)), public inspection of written determinations (Code Sec. 6110(f)(4)(A)), penalties for promoting abusive tax shelters (Code Sec. 6703(a)), income tax return preparer's penalty (Code Sec. 7427), and status as employees (pursuant to the safe harbor provisions of section 530 of the Revenue Act of 1978, P.L. 95-600).

Although a taxpayer has the burden of proving every claim made on his or her return, in all the exceptions above, the IRS is making a claim about the taxpayer's conduct: whether it is fraud, promoting abusive tax shelters or employee status. In such instances, the IRS, which should be in possession of evidence concerning the taxpayer's actions, bears the burden of proving its claim.

IRS Restructuring and Reform Impact
Burden of proof.—The new law shifts the burden of proof in a court proceeding with respect to a factual issue that is relevant to determining a

taxpayer's tax liability if the taxpayer presents credible evidence with respect to that issue *and* satisfies the applicable conditions discussed below (Code Sec. 7491, as added by the IRS Restructuring and Reform Act of 1998).

Condition one: compliance with substantiation and recordkeeping requirements. First, the taxpayer must comply with the substantiation and recordkeeping requirements of the Internal Revenue Code and regulations (Code Sec. 7491(a)(2)(A), as added by the 1998 Act; Code Sec. 7491(a)(2)(B), as added by the 1998 Act).

The Senate Finance Committee Report states that nothing in the provision "shall be construed to override any requirement under the Code or regulations to substantiate any item."

Further, the committee report adds that substantiation requirements must be met, whether generally or specifically imposed, and that the substantiation requirements include any requirement in the Code or regulations that a taxpayer establish an item to the IRS's satisfaction. If a taxpayer fails to substantiate any item, the taxpayer will not have satisfied all the conditions that are prerequisite to claiming an item on a tax return, and thus, the burden of proof provision will not apply.

The following examples of substantiation and recordkeeping requirements are specifically cited in the committee report:

(1) Code Sec. 6001 and Reg. § 1.6001-1 requiring taxpayers to keep such records as are prescribed by the IRS;

(2) Code Sec. 6038 and Code Sec. 6038A requiring a U.S. person to furnish information with respect to foreign businesses controlled by the U.S. person;

(3) Code Sec. 170(a)(1), Code Sec. 170(f)(8), and Reg. § 1.170A-13 relating to charitable contributions;

(4) Code Sec. 274(d) and Reg. § 1.274(d)-1, Temp. Reg. § 1.274-5T, and Reg. § 1.274-5A relating to traveling, entertainment, gifts, and certain other expenses; and

(5) Code Sec. 905(b) and Reg. § 1.905-2 requiring a taxpayer to provide all information deemed necessary by IRS for establishing the availability of the foreign tax credit.

Comment. If a taxpayer can demonstrate that he or she maintained the required substantiation but that it was destroyed or lost through no fault of the taxpayer, such as by fire or flood, existing tax rules regarding reconstruction of those records continue to apply, according to the Senate Committee Report.

Condition two: cooperation with IRS. The taxpayer must cooperate with reasonable requests by the IRS for witnesses, information, documents, meetings and interviews (Code Sec. 7491(a)(2)(B), as added by the 1998 Act).

The Senate Finance Committee Report clarifies that "cooperation" includes providing, within a reasonable period of time, access to and inspection of witnesses, information, and documents within the taxpayer's control, as reasonably requested by the IRS. It also indicates that "cooperation" includes reasonably assisting the IRS in obtaining access to and inspection of witnesses, information, and documents not within the taxpayer's control (including witnesses, information, and documents located in foreign countries) and exhausting all available administrative remedies, including any appeal rights provided by the IRS. However, the committee report indicates that cooperation does not include agreeing to extend the statute of limitations. Further, the taxpayer must establish the applicability of any privilege.

Comment. Cooperation includes providing English translations, as reasonably requested by the IRS.

¶ 1331

Condition three: net worth limitation for taxpayers other than individuals. Taxpayers other than individuals must meet the net worth limitations that apply for awarding attorneys' fees (Code Sec. 7491(a)(2)(C), as added by the 1998 Act). Corporations, trusts, and partnerships whose net worth exceeds $7,000,000 cannot benefit from this provision.

Comment. The taxpayer bears the burden of establishing that each of the three preceding conditions is satisfied.

Credible evidence defined. Before the burden of proof shifts to the IRS, the taxpayer must introduce credible evidence with respect to a factual issue that is necessary to determine the taxpayer's liability. Credible evidence, according to the Senate Finance Committee Report, refers to the quality of evidence that, after critical analysis, a court would find to be sufficient to serve as the basis for its decision on the issue, absent any contrary evidence. Implausible factual assertions, frivolous claims, and tax-protester-type arguments do not qualify as credible evidence. Further, evidence will not meet this standard if the court is not convinced that it is worthy of belief. If evidence from both sides has been introduced and it is equally balanced, the court should find that the IRS has not sustained its burden of proof.

Burden of proof where statistical information is used to reconstruct individual's income. In any court proceeding where the IRS solely uses statistical information from unrelated taxpayers to reconstruct an item of an *individual* taxpayer's income, such as the average income for taxpayers in the area in which the taxpayer lives, the burden of proof is on the IRS with respect to that item of income. This rule only applies to individual taxpayers (Code Sec. 7491(b), as added by the 1998 Act).

Burden of proof for penalties on individuals. Also, in any court proceeding, the IRS must initially come forward with evidence that it is appropriate to apply a penalty, addition to tax, or additional amount to an individual before the court can impose the penalty. Again, this rule only applies to individuals (Code Sec. 7491(c), as added by the 1998 Act).

According to the Senate committee report, it is the taxpayer's responsibility to introduce evidence of reasonable cause, substantial authority, or other similar penalty defense. The IRS, however, must initially come forward with evidence regarding the appropriateness of applying a particular penalty to the taxpayer.

PRACTICAL ANALYSIS. Lawrence M. Hill, head of Brown & Wood's Tax Litigation Practice, New York, New York, observes that this provision has far less utility to taxpayers than advertised. In fact, the costs to taxpayers associated with it may outweigh the potential benefits. Not only does the burden of producing credible evidence remain with the taxpayer, but the shift of the burden of proof to the IRS may increase the expenses of the taxpayer for the following reasons:

(1) The IRS is likely to be more intrusive at the administrative and trial level to satisfy its potential burden of proof.

(2) The taxpayer is required to exhaust every administrative remedy regardless of cost efficiency.

(3) Practitioners will be more likely to spend more time on cases to ensure that they fully cooperate with the IRS, so as not to expose themselves to malpractice claims in the event of a finding that the burden did not shift because of such lack of cooperation on their part.

(4) The taxpayer will be faced with increased litigation costs associated with trials within trials over the issue of whether the burden of proof has been shifted.

PRACTICAL ANALYSIS. J. Earl Epstein, of Epstein, Shapiro & Epstein, Philadelphia, PA, also foresees the shift in the burden of proof as potentially not particularly advantageous to many taxpayers for a number of reasons.

1. The requirement of exhaustion of administrative remedies would include use of all appeal rights at the administrative level, even though penalties and interest would continue to accrue during this period of time. Often, it is better to move directly to the Tax Court without using appeal rights. For example, where the position of the IRS is fixed and can only be overturned by a decision of the Court, there is little sense in wasting time in Appeals.

2. The IRS is likely to be more intrusive at the administrative and trial levels. This means that both practitioners and taxpayers will need to spend substantial time and effort to comply, and this will directly lead to more extensive costs and increased professional fees.

Example: The legislative history indicates that "cooperation" would include providing assistance to the IRS in obtaining access to and inspection of witnesses, information and documents that are not within the control of the taxpayer. Taxpayers who have control of information are often better off awaiting trial before disclosing this information and, where they do not have control of information, and the IRS cannot obtain that information on its own, they may find they are better served by doing nothing even though they would retain the burden of proof. .

Example: The Tax Court has always prided itself on the use of stipulation procedures to avoid long and costly discovery and trials. However, the new burden of proof provisions will encourage the IRS District Counsel to engage in substantial discovery in order for them to avoid having the burden of proof. It is understood that IRS Chief Counsel has already begun devising substantial interrogatories to be used for discovery purposes.

3. The efforts of practitioners to avoid malpractice claims will require that they spend the time and effort necessary to avoid causing the taxpayer to still bear the burden of proof.

Suggestion to Practitioners: Write a letter to clients informing them of the requirements of shifting the burden of proof to the IRS. Discuss the benefits of doing so compared with the costs and effort required. Have the taxpayer make the choice and sign off on that choice in writing.

Conclusion: The new burden of proof provisions could be a trap for taxpayers and practitioners. On the surface it seems like a benefit to taxpayers, but in practice it is likely to be a boon to the IRS because it gives them a club to use on taxpayers and permits them to become more intrusive than before.

★ *Effective date.* The provision applies to court proceedings arising in connection with examinations commencing after the date of enactment. If there was

¶ 1331

no examination, the provision applies to court proceedings arising in connection with the tax periods beginning or events occurring after the date of enactment. According to the Conference Report, an audit is not the only event that is considered to be an examination. The matching of an information return against amounts reported on a tax return is considered to be an examination, as is the review of a refund claim prior to issuing the refund (Act Sec. 3001(c) of the IRS Restructuring and Reform Act of 1998).

Act Sec. 3001, adding Code Sec. 7491. Law at ¶ 6720. Committee Report at ¶ 10,245.

COURT COSTS AND FEES

Authority to Award Expanded

¶ 1336

Background

Reasonable administrative and litigation costs may be awarded to a taxpayer who substantially prevails in an action by or against the United States in connection with the determination, collection, or refund of tax, interest, or penalty (Code Sec. 7430). Only an individual whose net worth does not exceed $2 million is eligible for an award. Further, corporations or partnerships that have net worth not exceeding $7 million are eligible for an award.

Reasonable administrative costs include: (1) any administrative fees or similar charges imposed by the IRS; and (2) expenses, costs and fees related to attorneys, expert witnesses, and studies or analyses necessary to prepare for the case (to the extent that such costs are incurred before the earlier of the date of the notice of decision by IRS Appeals or the date of the notice of deficiency). Reasonable litigation costs include reasonable fees paid or incurred for the services of attorneys. Generally, attorneys' fees will not be reimbursed at a rate in excess of $110 per hour (indexed for inflation). However, a higher rate may be justified if a special factor exists, such as the limited availability of qualified attorneys for the proceeding. Awards of reasonable litigation and administrative costs cannot exceed amounts paid or incurred.

Rule 68 of the Federal Rules of Civil Procedure provides that a party may recover costs if that party's offer for judgment was rejected and the subsequent court judgment was less favorable to the opposing party than the offer. The offering party's costs are limited to the costs (excluding attorneys' fees) incurred after the offer was made.

Civil damages may be awarded for the unauthorized inspection or disclosure of return information (Code Sec. 7431). The federal appellate courts are split over whether a party that substantially prevails over the United States in an action under Code Sec. 7431 is eligible for an award of reasonable fees and costs under Code Sec. 7430.

IRS Restructuring and Reform Impact

Expansion of authority to award costs and certain fees.—The provision moves the point in time after which reasonable administrative costs can be awarded to the earliest of (1) the date the taxpayer receives the notice of the decision of the IRS Appeals Division, (2) the date of the notice of deficiency, or (3) the date on which the first letter of proposed deficiency is sent that allows the taxpayer an opportunity for administrative review in the IRS Office of Appeals (Code Sec. 7430(c)(2), as amended by the IRS Restructuring and Reform Act of 1998).

Hourly fee cap raised; attorneys' fees for pro bono work. Further, hourly rate caps on awards of reasonable attorneys' fees are raised to $125 per hour (Code Sec. 7430(c)(1)(B), as amended by the 1998 Act). The new cap will continue to be indexed for inflation. The difficulty of the issues raised or the unavailability of local tax expertise are factors that may justify a higher rate. Reasonable attorneys' fees may also be awarded to specified persons who represent, on a pro bono basis or for a nominal fee, taxpayers who are prevailing parties. The award must be paid to the attorney or the attorney's employer (Code Sec. 7430(c)(3)(B), as amended by the 1998 Act).

Effect of ignoring Appellate Court precedent. The provision provides that, in determining whether the position of the United States was substantially justified, the court should take into account whether the government has won or lost in the court of appeals for other circuits on substantially similar issues (Code Sec. 7430(c)(4)(B)(iii), as amended by the 1998 Act).

Awards where court judgment less than taxpayer's offer. An award of fees and costs may be available if, after a taxpayer has a right to administrative review in the IRS Office of Appeals, the taxpayer makes a "qualified" offer that the IRS rejects and, then, the IRS obtains a judgment against the taxpayer in an amount that is equal to or less than the taxpayer's offer (without regard to interest). In this situation, the taxpayer should be treated as the prevailing party. This rule does not apply to judgments issued pursuant to a settlement or in a proceeding in which the amount of tax liability is not at issue, such as a declaratory judgment proceeding or a summons enforcement proceeding. (Code Sec. 7430(c)(4)(E), as amended by the 1998 Act).

Comment. The provision, which is similar to Rule 68 of the Federal Rules of Civil Procedure, provides an incentive for the IRS to settle taxpayers' cases for appropriate amounts.

A qualified offer is a written offer to the United States that specifies the offered amount of the taxpayer's liability (without regard to interest), is designated at the time that it is made as a qualified offer for purposes of this provision, and remains open during the period beginning on the date it is made and ending on the earliest of the date the offer is rejected, the date the trial begins, or the 90th day after the date the offer is made (Code Sec. 7430(g)(1), as added by the 1998 Act).

The qualified offer must be made during the "qualified offer period." This is the period that begins on the date on which the first letter of proposed deficiency that allows the taxpayer an opportunity for administrative review in the IRS Office of Appeals is sent and ends 30 days before the date the case is first set for trial (Code Sec. 7430(g)(2), as added by the 1998 Act).

The applicability of the provision is determined based on the amount of the taxpayer's last qualified offer made. Reasonable administrative and litigation costs only include costs incurred on or after the date of that last offer (Code Sec. 7430(c)(4)(E)(iii), as added by the 1998 Act).

Action for unauthorized inspection and disclosure. The Act allows the award of attorneys' fees in actions for civil damages for unauthorized inspection or disclosure of taxpayer returns and return information if the person filing the suit meets the Code Sec. 7430 net worth requirements. If the United States is the defendant, the plaintiff must also be the prevailing party as defined in Code Sec. 7430(c) (Code Sec. 7431(c)(3), as added by the 1998 Act).

PRACTICAL ANALYSIS. David R. Brennan of Faegre & Benson, Minneapolis, MN (former Director, Tax Litigation Division, Chief Counsel's Office and former Treasury Acting General Counsel) comments that the amendment to Code Sec. 7430 (and the comparable amendment to Code Sec. 7431) eliminates the former distinction between cases in which a taxpayer bypassed the Appeals Division and those cases in which the Appeals Division route was employed. In both situations, significant services could be performed in appearing before the Appeals Division, but only in the case in which the notice of deficiency had first been issued would the taxpayer have been entitled to attorneys' fees.

As a result of the amendment, there may be an increased sensitivity by the Examination Division to ensure that legitimate issues are being raised before a 30-day letter is issued.

The eligibility for administrative and litigation costs continues to be restricted to those persons eligible under 28 U.S.C. § 2412. An individual is eligible only if that person's net worth did not exceed $2 million at the time the action was filed. In the case of an owner of a business, a partnership, a corporation, an association, unit of local government, or other organization, eligibility exists if net worth did not exceed $7 million at the time the action was filed and that person did not have more than 500 employees at the time the action was filed. Section 501(c)(3) organizations and certain cooperatives are eligible regardless of the net worth limitations.

The increase of the hourly cap of $110 an hour to $125 an hour, coupled with the question of whether the case involved "difficult issues," will perpetuate litigation over fees.

The adoption of a pro bono provision should increase the numbers of pro bono representations in tax cases and lead to more effective representation of small taxpayers.

The provision requiring the Court to take into account the government's lack of success in other circuits on the same issue does not necessarily ensure the allowance of a fee. Nevertheless, if the issue has been relitigated often, it will tend to reinforce the allowance of fees as in such cases as *Allbritton v. Commissioner*, 37 F.3d 183 (5th Cir. 1994).

Brennan further comments that, by far, the most interesting provision within the Act's amendments to Code Sec. 7430 is the mandate that the taxpayer will be considered to have prevailed if the liability determined by the Court is equal to or less than the amount for which the taxpayer would have been prepared to settle the case. The offer must be made at any time during the time from the issuance of the 30-day letter to a date 30 days before the date the case is *first* set for trial. The offer must be in writing, must specify the amount of liability being offered (exclusive of interest), be designated as a qualified offer for purposes of Code Sec. 7430, and must remain open until the earliest of: (1) its rejection, (2) the date the trial begins, or (3) for a period of 90 days.

It appears that offers that do not "qualify" are ignored. Accordingly, when a series of offers may be made over time and only one is a "qualified" offer, it appears that the other offers are ignored for purposes of applying the statute. It is unclear how the statute will work if there are successive qualified offers. For example, if the IRS rejects qualified Offer #1 and the taxpayer comes back with qualified Offer #2 that is also rejected, will the Court conclude that the later offer is the one to be dispositive of the issue of substantial justification?

¶ 1336

If attorneys' fees are an objective, it places the premium upon the taxpayer to make a qualified offer before the case is first calendared for trial. Thus, in large cases or in multi-issue cases where a continuance is more than likely the first time the case is set for trial, there may be a premium on focusing on formal settlement offers before the case is first set for trial.

★ *Effective date.* The provision applies to costs incurred and services performed more than 180 days after the date of enactment (Act Sec. 3101(g) of the IRS Restructuring and Reform Act of 1988).

Act Sec. 3101, amending Code Sec. 7430(c) and Code Sec. 7431(c) and adding Code Sec. 7430(g). Law at ¶ 6630 and ¶ 6640. Committee Report at ¶ 10,250.

Chapter 14

Taxpayer Rights—Interest, Penalties, and Refunds

INTEREST

Suspension of Interest and Penalties for Failure to Send Notice Within 18 Months

¶ 1401

Background

Generally, interest and penalties accrue during periods for which taxes are unpaid, regardless of whether the taxpayer is aware that there is a tax due. As was made obvious during congressional hearings on IRS collection activities, interest and penalties can quickly increase a tax debt to the point that it becomes virtually impossible for a middle-class individual to clear the debt with the IRS without drastically compromising his or her lifestyle and financial goals.

IRS Restructuring and Reform Impact

Suspension of interest and penalties unless notice sent within 18 months.—The accrual of interest and penalties will be suspended after 18 months unless the IRS sends the taxpayer a notice within 18 months following the later of:

(1) the original due date of the return (without regard to extensions), or

(2) the date on which a timely return is filed (Code Sec. 6404(g), as added by the IRS Restructuring and Reform Act of 1998).

For tax years beginning on or after January 1, 2004, the 18-month period will be shortened to one year.

Comment. As originally drafted by the Senate, there was no provision for an 18-month period; the IRS's deadline for sending a notice was one year. However, there was concern whether it was possible for the IRS to review returns and determine deficiencies within the proposed one year, so the interim 18-month period was added.

The suspension of interest and penalties is available only for tax related to timely filed returns (i.e., returns filed by the original due date or by the extended due date) (Code Sec. 6404(g)(1)(A), as added by the 1998 Act).

The suspension begins on the day after the end of the 18-month period and ends on the day which is 21 days after the date on which the notice is provided by the IRS (Code Sec. 6404(g)(3), as added by the 1998 Act).

> **Example (1).** Jake Jones gets an automatic extension to file his 1998 return, and timely files on August 15, 1999. Jake inadvertently fails to include his receipt of $5,000 of interest on the return. The IRS sends Jake the required notice on July 1, 2001, and Jake pays the deficiency on September 1, 2001. Jake owes interest on the deficiency from April 15, 1999 (since a filing extension does not prevent the accrual of interest from the original filing date) through February 15, 2001. Interest is suspended from February 16, 2001 through July 21, 2001 (21 days after the date that the notice was provided). Interest again runs from July 22, 2001 until Jake pays the deficiency on September 1, 2001.

Affected items. The suspension is applied separately with respect to each item or adjustment (Code Sec. 6404(g)(1)(B), as added by the 1998 Act). Additionally, according to the Conference Committee Report, the provision does not apply where the taxpayer has self-assessed the tax.

> **Example (2).** Assume the same facts as in *Example (1).* In addition to the IRS notice relating to the interest payment Jake failed to include, the IRS sends a notice on August 1, 2001, relating to an adjustment based on an excessive deduction of real estate taxes on his 1998 return. The suspension period for interest and penalties attributable to the real estate taxes is calculated separately from the suspension period for the failure to include the $5,000 of interest.

Notice. In order for the IRS to continue the accrual of interest and penalties, the notice it provides to the taxpayer must specifically state the taxpayer's liability and the basis for the liability (Code Sec. 6404(g)(1)(A), as added by the 1998 Act). Interest and penalties resume 21 days after the IRS sends notice that meets these criteria.

Comment. As originally drafted by the Senate, notice would have been provided only by a notice of deficiency.

Restrictions. The suspension is contingent on a few restrictions. First, the provision is available only for individuals. Further, it applies only for income taxes (Code Sec. 1 through Code Sec. 1563); it does not apply to estate or gift taxes, employment taxes, etc. Finally, the suspension does not stop the accrual of:

> (1) the failure to pay and failure to file penalties (any penalty imposed by Code Sec. 6651);

> (2) any interest, penalty or other addition to tax in a case involving fraud (including, but not limited to, Code Sec. 6663);

> (3) any interest, penalty, addition to tax, or additional amount with respect to any tax liability shown on the return; or

> (4) any criminal penalty (Code Sec. 6404(g)(2), as added by the 1998 Act).

¶ 1401

★ *Effective date.* The suspension provision applies to tax years ending after the date of enactment (Act Sec. 3305(b), as added by the IRS Restructuring and Reform Act of 1998).

Act Sec. 3305(a), redesignating former Code Sec. 6404(g) as Code Sec. 6404(h), and adding Code Sec. 6404(g); Act Sec. 3305(b). Law at ¶6360. Committee Report at ¶10,335.

Interest Rate on Overlapping Underpayments and Overpayments

¶1406

Background——————————————————————————

Since 1986, taxpayers have paid higher interest rates on tax underpayments than the IRS has paid on tax overpayments. The specific rates are issued quarterly by the IRS, and are calculated as a set number of percentage points above the federal short-term rate:

Interest Rates

	Points Over Short-Term Rate
Underpayments	3
Overpayments	2
Large corporate underpayments (hot interest)	5
Corporate overpayments > $10,000	0.5

For periods when taxpayers have overlapping underpayments and overpayments, they could find that they owed the IRS to the extent of the spread between the underpayment and overpayment interest rates. In other words, taxpayers could owe interest at a rate equal to the difference between the underpayment and overpayment rates (as high as 4.5 percent for some corporations) on an underlying amount which netted out to zero; the IRS collected interest for periods during which the taxpayer did not have use of money that properly belonged to the IRS.

Prior to the Act, the IRS ameliorated the effect of the interest rate differential in two of the three situations in which it occurred:

(1) Annual interest netting. The IRS considers all increases and decreases in a taxpayer's liability *for the same tax period* before applying a single interest rate to the resulting net underpayment or overpayment (Rev. Proc. 94-60, 1994-2 CB 774). Thus, the taxpayer is charged only one interest rate depending on the net balance on the date of the adjustment.

(2) Offsetting. If the IRS credits an overpayment against any *outstanding* tax liability (under Code Sec. 6402(a) and Reg. §301.6402-1) *for a different tax period,* underpayment interest is not charged to the extent of the credit (Code Sec. 6601(f)). Thus, to the extent that an underpayment and an overpayment overlap in time and amount, the interest rate differential is zero. The IRS routinely offsets all types of tax liabilities (e.g., income tax overpayments are offset against employment or excise tax underpayments).

There was no clear authority for the IRS to net in a third situation: the IRS would not net an overpayment (of tax or interest) against an underpayment (of tax or interest) *for a different tax period* when either the overpayment or the deficiency had already been paid in full and *was not outstanding.* This situation is called "global interest netting." Global interest netting is similar to offsetting in that an overpayment of one tax liability decreases the underpayment of another tax liability. However, unlike offsetting, either the underpayment or the overpayment has already been satisfied and no further tax or interest is due on that amount from either the taxpayer or the IRS; the balance of one account is zero.

There are two basic methods or models that could be used to implement global interest netting: the credit/offset approach and the interest equalization approach.

Under the credit/offset approach, the IRS would implement global netting in essentially the same way it performs interest offsetting (under Code Sec. 6402). In the global interest netting situation, however, an overpayment would be credited to an underpayment regardless of whether the overpayment or underpayment existed at the time the global netting was performed. Thus, credits would be allowed as if the overpayment or underpayment were outstanding.

Alternatively, the IRS could implement global interest netting using the interest equalization method, which is the basis for annual interest netting (under Rev. Proc. 94-60). This approach does not rely on actual or deemed credit offsets. Instead, interest rates are equalized, i.e., no net interest is charged on either account to the extent that there are periods and amounts of overlapping indebtedness. Under this method, the effect of the interest rate differential is eliminated by netting tax accounts and paying or crediting the taxpayer with a "rate equalization amount" for the period of mutual indebtedness. The rate equalization amount is equal to the interest rate differential for the period and amount of mutual indebtedness. Under prior law, the problem with this approach was that the underpayment and overpayment rates required to be paid under the language of Code Sec. 6601 and Code Sec. 6611, respectively, were the rates prescribed by Code Sec. 6621. Thus, the IRS was not authorized to pay or impose an equalization rate.

The Treasury Department Office of Tax Policy Report to Congress on Netting of Interest on Tax Overpayments and Underpayments (April 1997), as ordered by Congress in Act Sec. 1208 of the Taxpayer Bill of Rights 2, advocated that Congress implement any global netting provision using the interest equalization approach. It would be substantially easier to administer than would a method based on the credit/offset approach and would allow the IRS to adjust taxpayer accounts in a way that is consistent with current procedures.

IRS authority for global interest netting. There has been disagreement as to whether the IRS could implement global interest netting using its administrative authority. Congress has long perceived the inequitable application of the interest rate differential and has repeatedly expressed its desire for a remedy, instructing the IRS to implement the most comprehensive netting procedures possible (see Notice 96-18, 1996-1 CB 370).

In 1996, the global interest netting issue received considerable attention when the Eighth Circuit handed down its opinion in *Northern States Power Co.* (96-1 USTC ¶ 50,022). In that case, the court concluded that the IRS was not required to perform global interest netting, costing NSP nearly $500,000 as a result of a one-percent difference between the underpayment and overpayment interest rates. The court reasoned that the IRS was entitled to net interest at its discretion (the IRS ... "*may* credit" an overpayment against any liability ... citing Code Sec. 6402(a)). Further, the liability to be netted had to be an outstanding liability ("*may* credit any overpayment of tax including interest thereon against any *outstanding* liability" ... citing Reg. § 301.6402-1). This reading made the most sense to the court "because only an outstanding liability can be 'satisfied' by a credit" (citing Code Sec. 6601(f)).

A few months after the Eighth Circuit decided *Northern States Power,* the Treasury Department issued the interest netting study mandated by Congress. The study concluded that global interest netting was not authorized under then-current law, but that a congressional mandate would be appropriate. The study recommended legislation providing for netting using the equalization method when taxpayers have overlapping periods and amounts of mutual indebtedness. It also requested congressional guidance on a number of issues that would arise in connection with a congressional mandate of global interest netting. These issues

Background

relate to calculation methodology, statutes of limitations, carryovers, and consolidated returns.

IRS Restructuring and Reform Impact

Global interest netting enacted.—Congress has essentially equalized the interest rate for overpayments and underpayments for any period of mutual indebtedness between a taxpayer and the IRS. No interest will be imposed to the extent that underpayment and overpayment interest run simultaneously on equal amounts (Code Sec. 6621(d), as added by the IRS Restructuring and Reform Act of 1998). The net interest rate of zero applies regardless of whether an underpayment otherwise would be subject to the increased interest rate imposed on large corporate underpayments (hot interest) or an overpayment otherwise would be subject to a reduced interest rate because it was a corporate overpayment in excess of $10,000.

> **Example.** On August 1, 2000, after an examination of its 1998 return, it is determined that BigCo overpaid its taxes by $10,000. Also during 2000, BigCo determines that it underpaid its 1999 taxes by $15,000; BigCo pays the 1999 underpayment, plus interest at the underpayment rate, on October 1, 2000. The statute of limitations has not run on either 1998 or 1999. In determining the amount owed to BigCo for its 1998 overpayment, the period for which the 1999 underpayment was outstanding must be taken into account. For the period that both the overpayment and the underpayment were outstanding (i.e., the due date of the 1999 return, March 15, 2000, until the underpayment was paid, October 1, 2000), the interest rate on the $10,000 overpayment and $10,000 of the underpayment must net out to zero. Interest on the $5,000 of the underpayment that is not offset (originally determined at the short-term federal rate plus three percentage points) is not affected.

Comment. Interestingly, the Act does not mention the specific situation in which underpayments and overpayments are not outstanding. Instead, the net interest rate is zero for interest "payable" on underpayments and "allowable" on overpayments. Further, Code Sec. 6601(f) (read by the court in *Northern States Power* to mean that only outstanding underpayments could be offset) explicitly is made inapplicable where the zero net interest rate applies. However, Congress anticipates that the IRS will take into account interest paid on previously determined deficiencies and refunds regardless of whether the underpayments or overpayments are currently outstanding (Conference Committee Report).

Taxpayers impacted. Global netting is not limited to specific categories of taxpayers. The Conference Committee Report states that it is intended that the zero net interest rate apply where interest is payable and allowable on an equivalent amount of underpayment and overpayment that is attributable to a taxpayer's interest in a pass-through entity.

Comment. A provision of the 1998 Act also raises the interest rate on the overpayments made by individuals to three percent over the short-term rate, equalizing it with the underpayment rate (see ¶ 1411), and mitigating the effect of the interest rate differential for individuals. Thus, the importance of the interest netting provision to individuals is decreased.

Types of taxes affected. Global netting is available for any type of tax imposed by the Internal Revenue Code (Code Sec. 6621(d), as amended by the 1998 Act). For example, income taxes can be netted against self-employment taxes, and employment taxes can be netted against excise taxes.

¶ 1406

Comment. Thus, regardless of the types of taxes at issue, the IRS may no longer make a distinction between liabilities that are outstanding and those that are not outstanding. It may not offset outstanding liabilities for different types of taxes under Code Sec. 6402(a) (which was not amended by the 1998 Act) as is current IRS practice, while using the new equalized (zero net) interest rate only for overlapping liabilities of the same type of tax.

Comment. The Treasury Study recommended that global netting be limited to income and self-employment taxes. The Study stated that opening up global netting to other types of taxes would significantly increase the administrative burden and require significant additional IRS resources to make the calculations.

Double counting. The Senate Committee Report states that each overpayment and underpayment "may be considered only once in determining whether equivalent amounts of overpayment and underpayment interest exist." Presumably, this is a stricture against double counting and not an indication that Congress intended the global netting computation to be available only once for any tax year.

Comment. Congress has left the implementation of the netting computation to the IRS. (In fact, the Senate Committee Report reiterates past committee reports, urging the IRS to implement the most comprehensive netting procedures that are consistent with sound administrative practice, and not only those affected by this provision.) Congress also anticipates that where interest is both payable from and allowable to an individual taxpayer for the same period, the IRS will make "all reasonable efforts" to offset the underpayments and overpayments, rather than process them separately using the zero net interest rate (Conference Committee Report).

A couple of indications as to the way that the global netting provision ultimately may be applied can be found in the Treasury Study. The Study recommends the following limitations and has indicated that the IRS has the administrative authority to realize them:

(1) Global netting should apply only to years that are not barred by statute. This limitation is justified by interests of finality, conserving IRS resources, and the fact that taxpayers can extend statutes of limitations for zero-balance tax years if they want to preserve an opportunity to net interest.

(2) The taxpayer should bear the burden of showing entitlement to any netted interest amount claimed. In this way, the IRS would require the taxpayer to perform the initial computation and submit the supporting documentation.

(3) The global netting computation should be available only once for any tax year.

PRACTICAL ANALYSIS. Jim Carlisle, Director, PricewaterhouseCoopers, Washington, DC, observes that this change—long sought by the business community—presents an immediate opportunity for taxpayers to apply the principles of interest netting to past periods of "mutual indebtedness" with the IRS. Companies with open tax years will want to consider a review of their accounts to identify overlapping tax overpayments and underpayments. While this review will be time-intensive and is inherently complex, the tax savings can be significant when you consider the interest rate differential (as high as 4.5 percent for large corporations) that otherwise applies. It is important to note that the new law requires taxpayers to take action by the end of 1999.

Going forward, the interest netting provision will remove an impediment to efforts to get current on audit cycles. In the past, the IRS's failure to perform interest netting has produced a strong incentive for taxpayers to keep overpayments and underpayments "outstanding" so as to allow these amounts to be offset against each other. For post-effective date interest periods, the provision will remove this consideration for taxpayers making deficiency payments and cashing refund checks.

Taxpayers should note that the provision applies to all types of taxes, including not only income taxes but also excise and employment taxes.

★ *Effective date.* The new interest netting rules apply to interest for periods beginning after the date of enactment. The rules also apply to interest for periods beginning before the date of enactment if the taxpayer:

(1) reasonably identifies and establishes the periods of underpayment and overpayment for which the zero net interest rate applies, and

(2) on or before December 31, 1999, requests the IRS to apply the zero net interest rate to those periods (Act Sec. 3301(c) of the IRS Restructuring and Reform Act of 1998).

Act Sec. 3301(a), adding Code Sec. 6621(d); Act Sec. 3301(b), amending Code Sec. 6601(f); Act Sec. 3301(c). Law at ¶ 6450 and ¶ 6470. Committee Report at ¶ 10,315.

Increase in Overpayment Rate

¶ 1411

Background ─────────────────────────────────

Since 1986, taxpayers have paid higher interest rates on underpayments of tax than the IRS has paid on tax overpayments. The specific rates are issued quarterly by the IRS, and are calculated as a set number of percentage points above the federal short-term interest rate (AFR). (The rates are provided at ¶ 1406.)

IRS Restructuring and Reform Impact

Interest rate differential eliminated for noncorporate taxpayers.—The rate at which the IRS pays interest on overpayments to noncorporate taxpayers has been increased to the AFR plus three percentage points (Code Sec. 6621(a)(1), as amended by the IRS Restructuring and Reform Act of 1998). Thus, the interest rate applicable to noncorporate taxpayers is now the same for underpayments and overpayments.

Comment. The Committee reports give no real explanation for the reason behind the elimination of the interest differential between the underpayment and overpayment rates. When the differential was enacted in 1986, both the House Committee Report and the Senate Committee Report explained that the purpose of the differential was to make the Treasury function more like a commercial financial institution in that it would lend money at a higher rate than that at which it borrowed money. By lending and borrowing at the same rate, the Treasury was distorting market forces and creating an incentive for taxpayers either to postpone paying taxes to take advantage of an underpayment rate that was lower than the rate they could earn by leaving the funds on deposit with a commercial lender or to overpay taxes to take advantage of an overpayment rate that was higher than the rate commercial lenders were paying.

At the same time that Congress enacted the interest rate differential, it began to express a desire that the IRS implement the most comprehensive interest netting procedures consistent with sound administrative practice. Interest netting essentially cancels out or equalizes interest on overlapping underpayments and overpayments, and directly ameliorates the impact of interest rate differentials during periods of mutual indebtedness. With the IRS Restructuring and Reform Act of 1998, Congress has enacted a comprehensive netting provision (see ¶ 1406), and it may be conforming other interest provisions to form a cohesive interest policy.

Another reason driving the equalization of the underpayment and the overpayment interest rates may be to ameliorate the interest netting problem for noncorporate taxpayers. By eliminating the differential, overlapping underpayments and overpayments need not be formally offset to generate the same monetary result (essentially eliminating the effect of an expired statute of limitations that prohibits formal netting).

★ *Effective date.* The increase in the overpayment rate applies to interest for the second and succeeding calendar quarters beginning after the date of enactment (Act Sec. 3302(b) of the IRS Restructuring and Reform Act of 1998).

Act Sec. 3302(a), amending Code Sec. 6621(a)(1); Act Sec. 3302(b). Law at ¶ 6470. Committee Report at ¶ 10,320.

Notice of Interest Charges

¶ 1416

Background ⸻

Taxpayers are required to pay interest on amounts they owe the IRS. The manner in which the IRS determines the amount of interest charged in a particular situation is not presented to a taxpayer in any notice or other document.

IRS Restructuring and Reform Impact

IRS must provide interest computation.—IRS notices that include interest that the IRS claims it is owed by an individual must include a detailed computation of the interest charged and the Code section under which the interest is imposed (Code Sec. 6631, as added by the IRS Restructuring and Reform Act of 1998).

Comment. A similar notification requirement is imposed for penalties. See ¶ 1436.

★ *Effective date.* Interest computations and the applicable Code section must be included with notices issued after December 31, 2000 (Act Sec. 3308(c) of the IRS Restructuring and Reform Act of 1998).

Act Sec. 3308(a), adding Code Sec. 6631; Act Sec. 3308(b), amending the Table of Subchapters for Chapter 67; Act Sec. 3308(c). Law at ¶ 6480. Committee Report at ¶ 10,350.

Interest Abatement in Disaster Areas

¶ 1417

Background ⸻

There is increasing recognition that a natural disaster creates a devastating situation for its victims. It seems that in each revenue act in the last several years some relief has been provided for the victims in a Presidentially declared disaster area. The due dates of tax returns and payments due in the months immediately following the disaster are commonly extended (Code Sec. 6081 and Code Sec. 6161, respectively).

Background _____

Under an amendment made by the Taxpayer Relief Act of 1997 (P.L. 105-34), if the IRS extends the due date of returns to be filed by individuals living in an area declared a disaster area by the President *during 1997*, no interest is charged for the duration of the extension as a result of the failure of an individual taxpayer to file an individual tax return, or to pay taxes shown on that return (Act Sec. 915, P.L. 105-34).

IRS Restructuring and Reform Impact

Interest payment exemption for disaster victims extended beyond 1997.—If the IRS extends the due date for filing income tax returns and for paying income tax for any taxpayer located in a Presidentially declared disaster area, the IRS will abate the interest that would otherwise accrue for the extension period. A Presidentially declared disaster area is an area which the President has determined needs federal government assistance under the Disaster Relief and Emergency Assistance Act (Code Sec. 6404(h), as added by the IRS Restructuring and Reform Act of 1998).

★ *Effective date.* The interest abatement provision applies to disaster areas declared after December 31, 1997, with respect to tax years beginning after December 31, 1997 (Act Sec. 3309(b) of the IRS Restructuring and Reform Act of 1998). This provision is designated as an emergency requirement for purposes of section 252(e) of the Budget and Emergency Deficit Control Act (related to funding), and the abatement provision will take effect only if the President transmits to Congress a message designating the provision as an emergency requirement pursuant to section 252(e) of the Balanced Budget and Emergency Deficit Control Act (Act Sec. 3309(c) of the 1998 Act).

The Conference Committee Report states that Congress intends that there be no gap between the interest abatement for 1997 disasters under P.L. 105-34 and the interest abatement under this provision.

Act Sec. 3309(a), redesignating Code Sec. 6404(h) (as redesignated by Act Sec. 3305) as Code Sec. 6404(i), and adding Code Sec. 6404(h); Act Sec. 3309(b); Act Sec. 3309(c). Law at ¶ 6360. Committee Report at ¶ 10,355.

PENALTIES

Mitigation of Failure to Deposit Penalty

¶ 1426

Background _____

A person that fails to timely deposit taxes is subject to a penalty that ranges from two to 15 percent of the underpayment, depending on the lateness of the deposit (Code Sec. 6656). The IRS applies any deposits received using a FIFO method: deposits are credited to the oldest past-due underdeposits within the same return period. Other credits to the taxpayer's account, such as an overpayment from a previous return period, are similarly applied (Rev. Proc. 90-58, 1990-2 CB 642).

The rationale underlying the FIFO application is that satisfaction of the oldest liability prevents the penalty rate on the underdeposit from increasing. However, if a taxpayer misses a deposit early in a return period but makes succeeding deposits on time, the result can be multiple failure-to-deposit penalties as payments are applied to old liabilities, causing a shortfall for the current deposit. These are known as cascading penalties.

Background _____

Beginning in 1998, the IRS provided some interim relief from cascading penalties. A taxpayer that receives multiple failure-to-deposit penalty notices as a result of a single failure to deposit may telephone the toll-free number provided on the penalty notice and the IRS will reduce the penalty if it deems relief is appropriate (Notice 98-14, I.R.B. 1998-8, 27).

Waiving the penalty for first-time depositors. For deposits required to be made after July 30, 1996, the IRS may waive the penalty for failure to deposit payroll taxes for a person's inadvertent failure to deposit any employment tax if:

(1) the failure to deposit occurs during the first quarter that the depositing entity was required to deposit any employment tax, and

(2) the depositing entity meets the net worth requirements applicable for an award of attorneys' fees (generally, net worth may not exceed $2 million for individuals and $7 million for corporations); and

(3) the employment tax return was filed on or before the due date (Code Sec. 6656(c)).

IRS Restructuring and Reform Impact

Taxpayers may designate periods to which payments apply.—Taxpayers may now designate the application of a deposit of taxes to a period or periods within the return period to which the deposit relates. The designation must be made during the 90 days immediately following the date of an IRS penalty notice (issued pursuant to Code Sec. 6656(a)) informing the taxpayer that a penalty has been imposed for the return period to which the deposit relates (Code Sec. 6656(e), as added by Act Sec. 3304(a) of the IRS Restructuring and Reform Act of 1998).

Comment. Designation under Code Sec. 6656(e) may not be made with the deposit. It is allowed only after a penalty notice is sent. The most common application of the new rules will be in the area of payroll taxes.

Example. SmallCo is required to deposit payroll taxes on a monthly basis and to report those deposits on Form 941, Employer's Quarterly Federal Tax Return. SmallCo timely deposits payroll taxes for July, August and September, 1999, and timely files Form 941 by October 31, 1999. Inadvertently, SmallCo's accountant transposed two numbers and remitted $12,000 instead of $21,000 for July. The IRS makes up the $9,000 shortfall for July (plus interest and penalties) from the $21,000 August deposit, and makes up the $9,000 shortfall for August (plus interest and penalties) with the $21,000 September deposit. On December 1, 1999, the IRS notifies SmallCo that Code Sec. 6656 penalties have been imposed for all three of the months covered by the third quarter return. SmallCo has 90 days from the date of the penalty notice to designate that the full $21,000 deposit for August be applied to payroll taxes due for that month, and that the full $21,000 deposit for September be applied to payroll taxes due for that month. SmallCo is left with a shortfall only for July.

Deposits after 2001: deposits automatically applied to most recent period. The IRS will apply any deposits required to be made after December 31, 2001, to the most recent period or periods within the specified tax period to which the deposit relates. This rule applies unless a taxpayer designates a different period or periods to which the deposit should be applied. Thus, beginning in 2002, the default rule for the application of deposits to the most recent liabilities will act to eliminate cascading penalties (Code Sec 6656(e)(1), as amended by Act Sec. 3304(c) of the 1998 Act, effective for deposits required to be made after December 31, 2001).

¶ 1426

Waiver for first-time depositors expanded. The IRS's ability to waive the failure-to-deposit penalty has been extended. Provided that the taxpayer meets the net worth requirement and files a timely employment tax return, the IRS may waive the penalty for the first deposit a taxpayer is required to make after the taxpayer is required to change the frequency of payroll deposits (Code Sec. 6656(c)(2), as amended by the 1998 Act).

★ *Effective date.* The amendments apply to deposits required to be made after the 180th day after the date of enactment. However, the rules providing that a deposit be automatically applied to the most recent period to which the deposit relates apply to deposits required to be made after December 31, 2001 (Act Sec. 3304(d) of the IRS Restructuring and Reform Act of 1998).

Act Sec. 3304(a), adding Code Sec. 6656(e); Act Sec. 3304(b), amending Code Sec. 6656(c)(2); Act Sec. 3304(c), amending Code Sec. 6656(e), as added by Act Sec. 3304(a); Act Sec. 3304(d). Law at ¶ 6500. Committee Report at ¶ 10,330.

Notice of Trust Fund Recovery Penalty

¶ 1431

Background

The trust fund recovery penalty, also known as the 100-percent penalty, is imposed on persons who are responsible for collecting and paying over employment taxes to the IRS, but who willfully fail to do so. The penalty equals 100 percent of the taxes that were not paid over. The taxpayer is personally liable for the penalty even if a corporation, other business entity, or another individual was also responsible for paying over the taxes (and even if that other person had primary or direct responsibility for making payment) (Code Sec. 6672).

Before the IRS can assess the trust fund recovery penalty, it must send a preliminary notice informing the responsible person of the proposed penalty. Notice and demand for the penalty may not be sent until 60 days after the preliminary notice is sent. The statute of limitations on assessments for the penalty does not expire earlier than 90 days after the date the notice is mailed. However, these restrictions do not apply if the IRS perceives that collection of the penalty is in jeopardy.

IRS Restructuring and Reform Impact

Preliminary notice may be delivered in person.—In addition to delivery by mail, the IRS now has the option of having the preliminary notice of the IRS's intent to assess the 100-percent penalty delivered in person to the responsible person (Code Sec. 6672(b), as amended by the IRS Restructuring and Reform Act of 1998). The Senate Committee Report indicates that Congress thinks that personal service of the preliminary notice may ensure that a greater percentage of responsible persons actually receive the notice, and thereby have a chance of resolving the issue before notice and demand for the penalty is made.

★ *Effective date.* Personal delivery of the preliminary notice is available as of the date of enactment (Act Sec. 3307(c) of the IRS Restructuring and Reform Act of 1998).

Act Sec. 3307(a), amending Code Sec. 6672(b)(1); Act Sec. 3307(b), amending Code Sec. 6672(b)(2) and Code Sec. 6672(b)(3); Act Sec. 3307(c). Law at ¶ 6510. Committee Report at ¶ 10,345.

Disclosure to Authorized Representatives of Persons Subject to the Trust Fund Recovery Penalty

¶ 1432

Background

The Taxpayer Bill of Rights 2 (P.L. 104-168) provided new protections for taxpayers from whom the IRS attempts to collect the trust fund recovery penalty (also known as the 100-percent penalty) for failure to pay over withheld employment taxes. One of these provisions granted the right of contribution to a responsible person who pays the penalty (Code Sec. 6672(d)). Thus, if more than one person is liable for the penalty, each person who actually paid the penalty is entitled to recover from the others who are liable for the penalty an amount equal to the excess of the amount paid by the person over the person's proportionate share of the penalty.

A companion provision requires the IRS to disclose the names of other taxpayers from whom it has attempted to collect the penalty. Specifically, upon the submission of a written request by a person that the IRS has determined to be liable for the penalty, the IRS must disclose in writing the identity of and collection efforts against any other person that the IRS has determined is a responsible person with respect to the same liability (Code Sec. 6103(e)(9)). Disclosure was authorized only to a person determined to be a responsible person, and not to the person's representatives.

IRS Restructuring and Reform Impact

Disclosure to authorized representatives.—The IRS may now disclose information regarding other responsible persons, upon written request, to an attorney in fact who provides the IRS with written authorization from the responsible person (Code Sec. 6103(e)(6), as amended by the IRS Restructuring and Reform Act of 1998). (A similar provision allowing disclosure to an attorney in fact was enacted with respect to the disclosure of collection activities in the case of joint returns. See ¶ 1295.)

★ *Effective date.* The provision allowing for the disclosure of information to a responsible person's authorized representative is effective on the date of enactment (Act Sec. 6019(d) of the IRS Restructuring and Reform Act of 1998).

Act Sec. 6019(c), amending Code Sec. 6013(e)(6); Act Sec. 6019(d). Law at ¶ 6110. Committee Report at ¶ 11,360.

Procedural Requirements for Imposition of Penalties

¶ 1436

Background

When the IRS sends a taxpayer a notice of penalty, it is not required to show how it has computed the penalties imposed upon the taxpayer. Further, penalties may be imposed without supervisory approval.

IRS Restructuring and Reform Impact

Notice must provide penalty computation.—The IRS must now include on each required notice of penalty the name of the penalty, the Code section that authorizes the penalty, and the computation that results in the penalty shown on the notice (Code Sec. 6751(a), as added by the IRS Restructuring and Reform Act of 1998). As used here, "penalty" includes any addition to tax or any additional amount (Code Sec. 6751(c), as added by the 1998 Act). The Senate Committee

Report expresses the congressional belief that taxpayers are entitled to an explanation of the penalties imposed upon them.

Further, penalties may not be assessed unless the initial determination of the assessment is personally approved, in writing, by the immediate supervisor of the individual making the determination (or a higher level official if the IRS so designates) (Code Sec. 6751(b)(1), as added by the 1998 Act).

Comment. This provision is intended to address the concern that penalties are often used as a bargaining chip by lower-level IRS employees who focus on collecting the maximum amount possible from taxpayers in order to satisfy any IRS collection-based performance goals. Presumably, there will be less artificial inflation of assessed penalties if prior supervisory approval and discernible computations are required.

Supervisory approval is not required prior to an assessment of an addition to tax for:

(1) failure to file or pay (any penalty imposed under Code Sec. 6651),

(2) failure to pay estimated tax (Code Sec. 6654 for individuals or Code Sec. 6655 for corporations), or

(3) any other penalty automatically computed through electronic means (Code Sec. 6751(b)(2), as added by the 1998 Act).

★ *Effective date.* The new procedural requirements apply to notices issued, and penalties assessed, after December 31, 2000 (Act Sec. 3306(c) of the IRS Restructuring and Reform Act of 1998).

Act Sec. 3306(a), adding Code Sec. 6751; Act Sec. 3306(b), conforming the Table of Subchapters for Chapter 68; Act Sec. 3306(c). Law at ¶ 6530. Committee Report at ¶ 10,340.

Penalty Administration Study

¶ 1441

Background

The interest and penalty provisions were restructured in 1989, making significant changes to consolidate and simplify the application of many Code penalties.

IRS Restructuring and Reform Impact

Studies to examine possible improvements.—The Joint Committee on Taxation and the Secretary of the Treasury are each required to undertake separate studies to review the administration and implementation by the IRS of the interest and penalty provisions of the Code (including the penalty reform provisions revised in 1989). Each report is to make any legislative and administrative recommendations that would simplify penalty or interest administration and reduce the burden on taxpayers (Act Sec. 3801 of the IRS Restructuring and Reform Act of 1998).

The Conference Committee Report states that Congress expects that the studies will examine whether the current interest and penalty provisions:

(1) encourage voluntary compliance,

(2) operate fairly,

(3) are effective deterrents to undesired behavior, and

(4) are designed in a manner that promotes efficient and effective administration of the provisions by the IRS.

¶ 1441

The Joint Committee and the Treasury department are instructed to consider comments from taxpayers and practitioners on relevant issues.

The studies are to be completed and submitted to the House Ways and Means Committee and the Senate Finance Committee no later than one year after the date of enactment.

Act Sec. 3801. Law at ¶ 8190. Committee Report at ¶ 10,715.

REFUNDS

Refund Offset for State Income Tax Debt

¶ 1446

Background

The IRS refund offset program enables the IRS to collect past-due child support and debts owed to other federal agencies from debtors who overpay federal taxes. The IRS subtracts the amount of the debt from the overpayment, pays the debt to the appropriate state (in the case of child support) or federal agency, and refunds or otherwise applies any remainder to the taxpayer. Past-due child support has priority for offset over debts to federal agencies. Both of these may be offset only after the taxpayer's federal tax liabilities are satisfied.

IRS Restructuring and Reform Impact

State income tax debts may be offset against federal tax refunds.—The IRS offset program will include past-due, legally enforceable state income tax debts that have been reduced to judgment (Code Sec. 6402(e)(1), as added by the IRS Restructuring and Reform Act of 1998). Various notifications, similar to those necessary for child support offset, are required.

(1) The state must notify the IRS that a qualifying state income tax judgment is outstanding.

(2) Upon offset, the IRS must notify the state of the taxpayer's name, taxpayer identification number (TIN), address, and the amount collected.

(3) The IRS must notify the taxpayer that the overpayment has been reduced by the amount necessary to satisfy the state's outstanding judgment. If the overpayment is made pursuant to a joint return, the notice must include identification of both filers (Code Sec. 6402(e)(1), as added by the 1998 Act).

Offset permitted against state resident. Unlike the child support offset, state tax judgments may be offset against federal tax overpayments only if the taxpayer who makes the overpayment has shown on the federal return for the year of the overpayment an address within the state seeking the offset (Code Sec. 6402(e)(2), as added by the 1998 Act).

Priority. Offsets are prioritized in the following order:

(1) any federal tax liability,

(2) past-due child support,

(3) past-due, legally enforceable debt owed to a federal agency

(4) past-due, legally enforceable state income tax debt, and

(5) future liability for federal tax.

If the IRS is notified of more than one legally enforceable debt owed to state agencies, it will apply any overpayment against the debts in the order in which the debts accrued (Code Sec. 6402(e)(3), as added by the 1998 Act).

Prerequisites to state notification of the IRS. Before a state may begin the offset process by notifying the IRS of an enforceable state income tax debt, it must take various steps to ensure that the debt is not collectible directly from the taxpayer. First, the taxpayer must be notified (by certified mail with return receipt) that the state proposes to collect the past-due state income tax liability by offset under Code Sec. 6402(e). The state must allow the taxpayer at least 60 days to provide evidence that all or part of the debt is not past due or is not legally enforceable, and must consider any evidence presented and its effect on the amount due. The IRS is authorized to prescribe other conditions to ensure that the state's determination is valid and that the state has made reasonable efforts to collect the debt (Code Sec. 6402(e)(4), as added by the 1998 Act). Congress intends that this include consideration of questions that may arise as a result of the taxpayer's being a Native American (Conference Committee Report).

The IRS is also authorized to issue regulations regarding the time, manner and contents of state notification to the IRS. The regulations may specify the types of state income taxes and minimum amount of debt to which the offset procedure applies. The regulations may require states to pay a fee to reimburse the IRS for the cost of providing the offset procedure (Code Sec. 6402(e)(6), as added by the 1998 Act).

Definition of past-due, legally enforceable state income tax obligation. A past-due, legally enforceable state income tax obligation is defined as a debt:

(1) which (a) resulted from a court judgment that has determined the amount of state income tax due, or a determination made after an administrative hearing which determined an amount of state income tax due, and (b) is no longer subject to judicial review; or

(2) which resulted from a state income tax which has been assessed but not collected, the time for redetermination of which has expired, and which has not been delinquent for more than ten years.

State income tax includes any local tax administered by the chief tax administration agency of the state (Code Sec. 6402(e)(5), as added by the 1998 Act).

Erroneous payments to states. If a state receives notification from the IRS that the IRS has made an erroneous payment to the state under the offset program, the state must repay that amount pursuant to regulations issued by the IRS. The repayment must be made without regard to whether any other amounts payable to the state under the offset program have actually been paid (Code Sec. 6402(e)(7), as added by the 1998 Act).

Information disclosure to states. As in the case of past-due child support and debts due to other federal agencies, the IRS may disclose information regarding its collection of past-due, legally enforceable state income tax debts to the agency seeking an offset. Disclosure is limited to information directly connected to the offset (Code Sec. 6103(l)(10), as amended by the 1998 Act).

★ *Effective date.* These amendments apply to refunds payable (under Code Sec. 6402) after December 31, 1999 (Act Sec. 3711(d) of the IRS Restructuring and Reform Act of 1998).

Act Sec. 3711(a), redesignating Code Sec. 6402(e) through Code Sec. 6402(j) (as amended by Act Sec. 3305) as Code Sec. 6402(f) through Code Sec. 6402(k), and adding Code Sec. 6402(e); Act Sec. 3711(b), amending Code Sec. 6103(l)(10); Act Sec. 3711(c), amending Code Sec. 6402(a), Code Sec. 6402(d)(2), redesignated Code Sec. 6402(f), and redesignated Code Sec. 6402(h); Act Sec. 3711(d). Law at ¶ 6110 and ¶ 6350. Committee Report at ¶ 10,685.

Statement of Reason for Refund Disallowance

¶ 1451

Background ———————————————————————

Claims for refund must be reviewed by the Examination Division of the IRS within 30 days after receipt. A claim is initially evaluated to see whether it should be disallowed because:

    (1) it was not timely filed,

    (2) it is based solely on the alleged unconstitutionality of the Revenue Acts,

    (3) there is evidence in the case file that the refund was waived as consideration for a settlement,

    (4) it covers a tax period in which the tax liability or specific issues were the subject of a final closing agreement or in which the tax liability was compromised, or

    (5) it relates to a return closed on the basis of a final court order. (Internal Revenue Manual (Text), 5(10)(82), revised 9-10-91).

If the claim can be denied for one of these reasons, the IRS issues a form letter stating that the claim can not be considered. If the claim can not be denied for one of these reasons, it is examined as soon as possible and if it is denied, the reasons for partial or total disallowance must be stated in the agent's report and sent to the taxpayer.

IRS Restructuring and Reform Impact

Explanation to be provided for all refund disallowances.—Taxpayers who are notified that a claim for refund has been disallowed must be provided with an explanation of the disallowance (Code Sec. 6402(j), as added by the IRS Restructuring and Reform Act of 1998). This expanded notice requirement applies in all cases where the refund claim was disallowed or partially disallowed. The Senate Committee Report explains that taxpayers are entitled to an explanation of the specific reasons for the disallowance so that they can appropriately respond to the disallowance.

★ *Effective date.* The requirement that an explanation of the reason for a refund disallowance be provided to taxpayers applies to disallowances after the 180th day after the date of enactment (Act Sec. 3505(b) of the IRS Restructuring and Reform Act of 1998).

Act Sec. 3505(a), adding Code Sec. 6402(j); Act Sec. 3505(b). Law at ¶ 6350. Committee Report at ¶ 10,585.

Suspension of Statute of Limitations During Period of Disability

¶ 1461

Background ———————————————————————

Usually, a taxpayer is required to file a claim for refund within three years after filing the return or within two years after paying the tax, whichever period expires later (Code Sec. 6511(a)).

Prior to the U.S. Supreme Court's decision in *M. Brockamp* (97-1 USTC ¶ 50,216), the Ninth Circuit stood alone in permitting the equitable tolling (stopping) of the statute of limitations period for filing refund claims in cases where taxpayers were in extreme need. In *Brockamp,* an elderly taxpayer, apparently senile, erroneously paid the IRS $7,000 and no timely refund claim was filed. In

Background ────────────────────────────────

the case consolidated with *Brockamp, N.T. Scott*, a taxpayer's alcoholism prevented him from timely filing a refund claim for overpaid taxes. In both cases, the Ninth Circuit relied on principles of equity and held that, although the period for filing refund claims had expired, it could be tolled to allow the taxpayers to pursue their refund claims. Similar requests for equitable tolling had been denied by the First, Fourth, Tenth, Eleventh, and Federal Circuits.

Although the appellate courts considering equitable tolling tended to produce lengthy discussions of the principles of equity and of the cases allowing equitable tolling in areas other than tax law, the Supreme Court's decision was unanimous and brief. The Court found no exception to the limitations on time and amount prescribed by Code Sec. 6511 for obtaining a tax refund. The decision made it clear that the principles of equity did not apply to override the statutory requirements.

Related limitations. In addition to the general statute of limitations on filing a refund claim, a limitations period also affects the amount of a refund. If a return is timely filed and a refund claim is made within the three-year period after filing, the amount of the refund may not exceed so much of the overpayment as was made during the period immediately preceding the filing of the refund claim equal to three years plus any extension of time for filing the return (Code Sec. 6511(b)).

Further, a taxpayer who agrees to extend the period for assessment gets an extension of the time in which to file a refund claim. The period within which such a taxpayer may file a claim for refund is extended by the length of the extension plus six months. The amount of the claim for refund in these cases may be limited (Code Sec. 6511(c)).

────────────────────────────────

IRS Restructuring and Reform Impact

Statute of limitations suspended during periods of disability.—The Act permits the suspension (tolling) of the statute of limitations on refund claims during any period that an individual is "financially disabled" (Code Sec. 6511(h)(1), as added by the IRS Restructuring and Reform Act of 1988).

Comment. Tolling applies to both the time and amount limitations (i.e., Code Sec. 6511(a), Code Sec. 6511(b), and Code Sec. 6511(c)).

Financially disabled. An individual is financially disabled if the individual is under a medically determinable medical or physical impairment that:

(1) can be expected to result in death or which has lasted or can be expected to last for a continuous period of not less than one year, and

(2) renders the person unable to manage his or her financial affairs.

An individual is not considered to be financially disabled unless the proper proof is provided to the IRS (the IRS will issue guidelines) (Code Sec. 6511(h)(2), as added by the 1998 Act). The House Committee Report states that in determining whether an impairment is medically determinable, the IRS will evaluate whether a medical opinion that a physical or mental impairment exists has been offered by a person qualified to do so with respect to the particular type of impairment.

Exception if there is a guardian. The suspension of the limitations period does not apply for any period during which the taxpayer's spouse or another person is authorized to act on behalf of the individual in financial matters.

Example. Michael Manning filed his tax return for 1994 on April 15, 1995. On March 15, 1998, Michael was in a car accident, the doctors didn't expect him to survive, and he was in a coma for seven months (until October 15, 1998). But for the accident and the resulting financial disability, Michael would have had to file any claim for a refund of 1994 tax by April 15, 1998. However, if he shows that he did not have a guardian during this period and he provides proof of the impairment as required by the IRS under the new law, the statute of limitations on Michael's 1994 refund claim would be extended by the seven-month duration of his disability, until November 15, 1998.

Comment. It would seem that, assuming adequate proof of a medically determinable impairment, both of the taxpayers in *Brockamp* had disabilities that could be eligible for suspension of the limitations period under the new law.

★ *Effective date.* The amendment applies to periods of disability before, on, or after the date of enactment, but does not apply to any claim for refund or credit that (without regard to the amendment) is barred by operation of any law or rule of law, including *res judicata,* as of the date of enactment (Act Sec. 3202(b) of the IRS Restructuring and Reform Act of 1998).

Act Sec. 3202(a), redesignating Code Sec. 6511(h) as Code Sec. 6511(i), and adding new Code Sec. 6511(h); Act Sec. 3202(b). **Law at ¶ 6430. Committee Report at ¶ 10,290.**

CODE SECTIONS ADDED, AMENDED OR REPEALED

[¶ 5000] INTRODUCTION

The law as amended by the Internal Revenue Service Restructuring and Reform Act of 1998 and the Surface Transportation Revenue Act of 1998 (P.L. 105-178) is shown in the following paragraphs. For your convenience, both laws are presented in one consolidated section. Amendments made by the Surface Transportation Revenue Act of 1998 are listed under the heading "P.L. 105-178 (ISTEA)" in the amendment notes following each subsection of the Code. All other amendments are from the IRS Restructuring and Reform Act of 1998.

[¶ 5001] CODE SEC. 1. TAX IMPOSED.

* * *

(g) CERTAIN UNEARNED INCOME OF MINOR CHILDREN TAXED AS IF PARENT'S INCOME.—

* * *

(3) ALLOCABLE PARENTAL TAX.—For purposes of this subsection—

* * *

(C) SPECIAL RULE WHERE PARENT HAS DIFFERENT TAXABLE YEAR.—Except as provided in regulations, if the parent does not have the same taxable year as the child, the allocable parental tax shall be determined on the basis of the taxable year of the parent ending in the child's taxable year.

* * *

Amendment Notes

Act Sec. 6007(f)(1) amended Code Sec. 1(g)(3) by striking subparagraph (C) and by redesignating subparagraph (D) as subparagraph (C). Prior to being stricken, Code Sec. 1(g)(3)(C) read as follows:

(C) COORDINATION WITH SECTION 644.—If tax is imposed under section 644(a)(1) with respect to the sale or exchange of any property of which the parent was the transferor, for purposes of applying subparagraph (A) to the taxable year of the parent in which such sale or exchange occurs—

(i) taxable income of the parent shall be increased by the amount treated as included in gross income under section 644(a)(2)(A)(i), and

(ii) the amount described in subparagraph (A)(ii) shall be increased by the amount of the excess referred to in section 644(a)(2)(A).

The above amendment is effective as if included in the provision of the Taxpayer Relief Act of 1997 (P.L. 105-34) to which it relates [effective for sales or exchanges after August 5, 1997.—CCH.].

(h) MAXIMUM CAPITAL GAINS RATE.—

(1) IN GENERAL.—If a taxpayer has a net capital gain for any taxable year, the tax imposed by this section for such taxable year shall not exceed the sum of—

(A) a tax computed at the rates and in the same manner as if this subsection had not been enacted on the greater of—

(i) taxable income reduced by the net capital gain, or

(ii) the lesser of—

(I) the amount of taxable income taxed at a rate below 28 percent, or

(II) taxable income reduced by the adjusted net capital gain,

(B) 10 percent of so much of the adjusted net capital gain (or, if less, taxable income) as does not exceed the excess (if any) of—

(i) the amount of taxable income which would (without regard to this paragraph) be taxed at a rate below 28 percent, over

(ii) the taxable income reduced by the adjusted net capital gain,

(C) 20 percent of the adjusted net capital gain (or, if less, taxable income) in excess of the amount on which a tax is determined under subparagraph (B),

(D) 25 percent of the excess (if any) of—

(i) the unrecaptured section 1250 gain (or, if less, the net capital gain), over

(ii) the excess (if any) of—

(I) the sum of the amount on which tax is determined under subparagraph (A) plus the net capital gain, over

(II) taxable income, and

(E) 28 percent of the amount of taxable income in excess of the sum of the amounts on which tax is determined under the preceding subparagraphs of this paragraph.

(2) REDUCED CAPITAL GAIN RATES FOR QUALIFIED 5-YEAR GAIN.—

(A) REDUCTION IN 10-PERCENT RATE.— In the case of any taxable year beginning after December 31, 2000, the rate under paragraph (1)(B) shall be 8 percent with respect to so much of the amount to which the 10-percent rate would otherwise apply as does not exceed qualified 5-year gain, and 10 percent with respect to the remainder of such amount.

(B) REDUCTION IN 20-PERCENT RATE.— The rate under paragraph (1)(C) shall be 18 percent with respect to so much of the amount to which the 20-percent rate would otherwise apply as does not exceed the lesser of—

(i) the excess of qualified 5-year gain over the amount of such gain taken into account under subparagraph (A) of this paragraph, or

(ii) the amount of qualified 5-year gain (determined by taking into account only property the holding period for which begins after December 31, 2000),

and 20 percent with respect to the remainder of such amount. For purposes of determining under the preceding sentence whether the holding period of property begins after December 31, 2000, the holding period of property acquired pursuant to the exercise of an option (or other right or obligation to acquire property) shall include the period such option (or other right or obligation) was held.

(3) NET CAPITAL GAIN TAKEN INTO ACCOUNT AS INVESTMENT INCOME.—For purposes of this subsection, the net capital gain for any taxable year shall be reduced (but not below zero) by the amount which the taxpayer takes into account as investment income under section 163(d)(4)(B)(iii).

(4) ADJUSTED NET CAPITAL GAIN.—For purposes of this subsection, the term "adjusted net capital gain" means net capital gain reduced (but not below zero) by the sum of—

(A) unrecaptured section 1250 gain, and

(B) 28-percent rate gain.

(5) 28-PERCENT RATE GAIN.—For purposes of this subsection, the term "28-percent rate gain" means the excess (if any) of—

(A) the sum of—

(i) collectibles gain, and

(ii) section 1202 gain, over

(B) the sum of—

(i) collectibles loss,

(ii) the net short-term capital loss, and

(iii) the amount of long-term capital loss carried under section 1212(b)(1)(B) to the taxable year.

(6) COLLECTIBLES GAIN AND LOSS.—For purposes of this subsection—

(A) IN GENERAL.—The terms "collectibles gain" and "collectibles loss" mean gain or loss (respectively) from the sale or exchange of a collectible (as defined in section 408(m) without regard to paragraph (3) thereof) which is a capital asset held for more than 1 year but only to the extent such gain is taken into account in computing gross income and such loss is taken into account in computing taxable income.

(B) PARTNERSHIPS, ETC.—For purposes of subparagraph (A), any gain from the sale of an interest in a partnership, S corporation, or trust which is attributable to unrealized appreciation in the value of collectibles shall be treated as gain from the sale or exchange of a collectible. Rules similar to the rules of section 751 shall apply for purposes of the preceding sentence.

(7) UNRECAPTURED SECTION 1250 GAIN.—For purposes of this subsection—

(A) IN GENERAL.—The term "unrecaptured section 1250 gain" means the excess (if any) of—

(i) the amount of long-term capital gain (not otherwise treated as ordinary income) which would be treated as ordinary income if section 1250(b)(1) included all depreciation and the applicable percentage under section 1250(a) were 100 percent, over

(ii) the excess (if any) of—

(I) the amount described in paragraph (5)(B), over

(II) the amount described in paragraph (5)(A).

(B) LIMITATION WITH RESPECT TO SECTION 1231 PROPERTY.—The amount described in subparagraph (A)(i) from sales, exchanges, and conversions described in section 1231(a)(3)(A) for any taxable year shall not exceed the net section 1231 gain (as defined in section 1231(c)(3)) for such year.

(8) SECTION 1202 GAIN.—For purposes of this subsection, the term "section 1202 gain" means an amount equal to the gain excluded from gross income under section 1202(a).

(9) QUALIFIED 5-YEAR GAIN.—For purposes of this subsection, the term "qualified 5-year gain" means the aggregate long-term capital gain from property held for more than 5 years. The determination under the preceding sentence shall be made without regard to collectibles gain, gain described in paragraph (7)(A)(i), and section 1202 gain.

(10) COORDINATION WITH RECAPTURE OF NET ORDINARY LOSSES UNDER SECTION 1231.—If any amount is treated as ordinary income under section 1231(c), such amount shall be allocated among the separate categories of net section 1231 gain (as defined in section 1231(c)(3)) in such manner as the Secretary may by forms or regulations prescribe.

(11) REGULATIONS.—The Secretary may prescribe such regulations as are appropriate (including regulations requiring reporting) to apply this subsection in the case of sales and exchanges by pass-thru entities and of interests in such entities.

(12) PASS-THRU ENTITY DEFINED.—For purposes of this subsection, the term "pass-thru entity" means—

(A) a regulated investment company,

(B) a real estate investment trust,

(C) an S corporation,

(D) a partnership,

(E) an estate or trust,

(F) a common trust fund,

(G) a foreign investment company which is described in section 1246(b)(1) and for which an election is in effect under section 1247, and

(H) a qualified electing fund (as defined in section 1295).

(13) SPECIAL RULES.—

(A) DETERMINATION OF 28-PERCENT RATE GAIN.—In applying paragraph (5)—

(i) the amount determined under subparagraph (A) of paragraph (5) shall include long-term capital gain (not otherwise described in such subparagraph)—

(I) which is properly taken into account for the portion of the taxable year before May 7, 1997, or

(II) from property held not more than 18 months which is properly taken into account for the portion of the taxable year after July 28, 1997, and before January 1, 1998,

(ii) the amount determined under subparagraph (B) of paragraph (5) shall include long-term capital loss (not otherwise described in such subparagraph)—

(I) which is properly taken into account for the portion of the taxable year before May 7, 1997, or

(II) from property held not more than 18 months which is properly taken into account for the portion of the taxable year after July 28, 1997, and before January 1, 1998, and

(iii) subparagraph (B) of paragraph (5) (as in effect immediately before the enactment of this clause) shall apply to amounts properly taken into account before January 1, 1998.

(B) DETERMINATION OF UNRECAPTURED SECTION 1250 GAIN.—The amount determined under paragraph (7)(A) shall not include gain—

(i) which is properly taken into account for the portion of the taxable year before May 7, 1997, or

(ii) from property held not more than 18 months which is properly taken into account for the portion of the taxable year after July 28, 1997, and before January 1, 1998.

(C) SPECIAL RULES FOR PASS-THRU ENTITIES.—In applying this paragraph with respect to any pass-thru entity, the determination of when gains and loss are properly taken into account shall be made at the entity level.

[CCH Explanation at ¶ 501, 502, 505, 506, 508, 510, 512, 515, 518, 521, and 524. Committee Reports at ¶ 10,785 and 10,915.]

Amendment Notes

Act Sec. 5001(a)(1) amended Code Sec. 1(h)(5) to read as above. Prior to amendment, Code Sec. 1(h)(5) read as follows:

(5) 28-PERCENT RATE GAIN.—For purposes of this subsection—

(A) IN GENERAL.—The term "28-percent rate gain" means the excess (if any) of—

(i) the sum of—

(I) the aggregate long-term capital gain from property held for more than 1 year but not more than 18 months,

(II) collectibles gain, and

(III) section 1202 gain, over

(ii) the sum of—

(I) the aggregate long-term capital loss (not described in subclause (IV)) from property referred to in clause (i)(I),

(II) collectibles loss,

(III) the net short-term capital loss, and

(IV) the amount of long-term capital loss carried under section 1212(b)(1)(B) to the taxable year.

(B) SPECIAL RULES.—

(i) SHORT SALE GAINS AND HOLDING PERIODS.—Rules similar to the rules of section 1233(b) shall apply where the substantially identical property has been held more than 1 year but not more than 18 months; except that, for purposes of such rules—

(I) section 1233(b)(1) shall be applied by substituting "18 months" for "1 year" each place it appears, and

(II) the holding period of such property shall be treated as being 1 year on the day before the earlier of the date of the closing of the short sale or the date such property is disposed of.

(ii) LONG-TERM LOSSES.—Section 1233(d) shall be applied separately by substituting "18 months" for "1 year" each place it appears.

(iii) OPTIONS.—A rule similar to the rule of section 1092(f) shall apply where the stock was held for more than 18 months.

(iv) SECTION 1256 CONTRACTS.— Amounts treated as long-term capital gain or loss under section 1256(a)(3) shall be treated as attributable to property held for more than 18 months.

Act Sec. 5001(a)(2) amended Code Sec. 1(h)(6)(A) by striking "18 months" and inserting "1 year".

Act Sec. 5001(a)(3) amended Code Sec. 1(h)(7)(A)(i) and (ii) to read as above. Prior to amendment, Code Sec. 1(h)(7)(A)(i)-(ii) read as follows:

(i) the amount of long-term capital gain (not otherwise treated as ordinary income) which would be treated as ordinary income if—

(I) section 1250(b)(1) included all depreciation and the applicable percentage under section 1250(a) were 100 percent, and

(II) only gain from property held for more than 18 months were taken into account, over

(ii) the excess (if any) of—

(I) the amount described in paragraph (5)(A)(ii), over

(II) the amount described in paragraph (5)(A)(i).

Act Sec. 5001(a)(4) amended so much of paragraph (13) of Code Sec. 1(h) as precedes subparagraph (C) to read as above. Prior to amendment, Code Sec. 1(h)(13) read as follows:

(13) SPECIAL RULES FOR PERIODS DURING 1997.—

(A) DETERMINATION OF 28-PERCENT RATE GAIN.—In applying paragraph (5)—

(i) the amount determined under subclause (I) of paragraph (5)(A)(i) shall include long-term capital gain (not otherwise described in paragraph (5)(A)(i)) which is properly taken into account for the portion of the taxable year before May 7, 1997,

(ii) the amounts determined under subclause (I) of paragraph (5)(A)(ii) shall include long-term capital loss (not otherwise described in paragraph (5)(A)(ii)) which is properly taken into account for the portion of the taxable year before May 7, 1997, and

(iii) clauses (i)(I) and (ii)(I) of paragraph (5)(A) shall be applied by not taking into account any gain and loss on property held for more than 1 year but not more than 18 months which is properly taken into account for the portion of the taxable year after May 6, 1997, and before July 29, 1997.

(B) OTHER SPECIAL RULES.—

(i) DETERMINATION OF UNRECAPTURED SECTION 1250 GAIN NOT TO INCLUDE PRE-MAY 7, 1997 GAIN.—The amount determined under paragraph (7)(A)(i) shall not include gain properly taken into account for the portion of the taxable year before May 7, 1997.

(ii) OTHER TRANSITIONAL RULES FOR 18-MONTH HOLDING PERIOD.—Paragraphs (6)(A) and (7)(A)(i)(II) shall be applied by substituting "1 year" for "18 months" with respect to gain properly taken into account for the portion of the taxable year after May 6, 1997, and before July 29, 1997.

The above amendments apply to tax years ending after December 31, 1997.

Act Sec. 6005(d)(1) amended Code Sec. 1(h) to read as above. Prior to amendment, Code Sec. 1(h) read as follows:

(h) MAXIMUM CAPITAL GAINS RATE.—

(1) IN GENERAL.—If a taxpayer has a net capital gain for any taxable year, the tax imposed by this section for such taxable year shall not exceed the sum of—

(A) a tax computed at the rates and in the same manner as if this subsection had not been enacted on the greater of—

(i) taxable income reduced by the net capital gain, or

(ii) the lesser of—

(I) the amount of taxable income taxed at a rate below 28 percent, or

(II) taxable income reduced by the adjusted net capital gain, plus

(B) 25 percent of the excess (if any) of—

(i) the unrecaptured section 1250 gain (or, if less, the net capital gain), over

(ii) the excess (if any) of—

(I) the sum of the amount on which tax is determined under subparagraph (A) plus the net capital gain, over

(II) taxable income, plus

(C) 28 percent of the amount of taxable income in excess of the sum of—

(i) the adjusted net capital gain, plus

(ii) the sum of the amounts on which tax is determined under subparagraphs (A) and (B), plus

(D) 10 percent of so much of the taxpayer's adjusted net capital gain (or, if less, taxable income) as does not exceed the excess (if any) of—

(i) the amount of taxable income which would (without regard to this paragraph) be taxed at a rate below 28 percent, over

(ii) the taxable income reduced by the adjusted net capital gain, plus

(E) 20 percent of the taxpayer's adjusted net capital gain (or, if less, taxable income) in excess of the amount on which a tax is determined under subparagraph (D).

(2) REDUCED CAPITAL GAIN RATES FOR QUALIFIED 5-YEAR GAIN.—

(A) REDUCTION IN 10-PERCENT RATE.—In the case of any taxable year beginning after December 31, 2000, the rate under paragraph (1)(D) shall be 8 percent with respect to so much of the amount to which the 10-percent rate would otherwise apply as does not exceed qualified 5-year gain, and 10 percent with respect to the remainder of such amount.

(B) REDUCTION IN 20-PERCENT RATE.—The rate under paragraph (1)(E) shall be 18 percent with respect to so much

of the amount to which the 20-percent rate would otherwise apply as does not exceed the lesser of—

(i) the excess of qualified 5-year gain over the amount of such gain taken into account under subparagraph (A) of this paragraph, or

(ii) the amount of qualified 5-year gain (determined by taking into account only property the holding period for which begins after December 31, 2000), and 20 percent with respect to the remainder of such amount. For purposes of determining under the preceding sentence whether the holding period of property begins after December 31, 2000, the holding period of property acquired pursuant to the exercise of an option (or other right or obligation to acquire property) shall include the period such option (or other right or obligation) was held.

(3) NET CAPITAL GAIN TAKEN INTO ACCOUNT AS INVESTMENT INCOME.—For purposes of this subsection, the net capital gain for any taxable year shall be reduced (but not below zero) by the amount which the taxpayer takes into account as investment income under section 163(d)(4)(B)(iii).

(4) ADJUSTED NET CAPITAL GAIN.—For purposes of this subsection, the term "adjusted net capital gain" means net capital gain determined without regard to—

(A) collectibles gain,

(B) unrecaptured section 1250 gain,

(C) section 1202 gain, and

(D) mid-term gain.

(5) COLLECTIBLES GAIN.—For purposes of this subsection—

(A) IN GENERAL.—The term "collectibles gain" means gain from the sale or exchange of a collectible (as defined in section 408(m) without regard to paragraph (3) thereof) which is a capital asset held for more than 1 year but only to the extent such gain is taken into account in computing gross income.

(B) PARTNERSHIPS, ETC.—For purposes of subparagraph (A), any gain from the sale of an interest in a partnership, S corporation, or trust which is attributable to unrealized appreciation in the value of collectibles shall be treated as gain from the sale or exchange of a collectible. Rules similar to the rules of section 751 shall apply for purposes of the preceding sentence.

(6) UNRECAPTURED SECTION 1250 GAIN.—For purposes of this subsection—

(A) IN GENERAL.—The term "unrecaptured section 1250 gain" means the amount of long-term capital gain which would be treated as ordinary income if—

(i) section 1250(b)(1) included all depreciation and the applicable percentage under section 1250(a) were 100 percent, and

(ii) in the case of gain properly taken into account after July 28, 1997, only gain from section 1250 property held for more than 18 months were taken into account.

(B) LIMITATION WITH RESPECT TO SECTION 1231 PROPERTY.—The amount of unrecaptured section 1250 gain from sales, exchanges, and conversions described in section 1231(a)(3)(A) for any taxable year shall not exceed the excess of the net section 1231 gain (as defined in section 1231(c)(3)) for such year over the amount treated as ordinary income under section 1231(c)(1) for such year.

(C) PRE-MAY 7, 1997, GAIN.—In the case of a taxable year which includes May 7, 1997, subparagraph (A) shall be applied by taking into account only the gain properly taken into account for the portion of the taxable year after May 6, 1997.

(7) SECTION 1202 GAIN.—For purposes of this subsection, the term "section 1202 gain" means an amount equal to the gain excluded from gross income under section 1202(a).

(8) MID-TERM GAIN.—For purposes of this subsection, the term "mid-term gain" means the amount which would be adjusted net capital gain for the taxable year if—

(A) adjusted net capital gain were determined by taking into account only the gain or loss properly taken into account after July 28, 1997, from property held for more than 1 year but not more than 18 months, and

(B) paragraph (3) and section 1212 did not apply.

(9) QUALIFIED 5-YEAR GAIN.—For purposes of this subsection, the term "qualified 5-year gain" means the amount of long-term capital gain which would be computed for the taxable year if only gains from the sale or exchange of property held by the taxpayer for more than 5 years were taken into account. The determination under the preceding sentence shall be made without regard to collectibles gain,

unrecaptured section 1250 gain (determined without regard to subparagraph (B) of paragraph (6)), section 1202 gain, or mid-term gain.

(10) PRE-EFFECTIVE DATE GAIN.—

(A) IN GENERAL.—In the case of a taxable year which includes May 7, 1997, gains and losses properly taken into account for the portion of the taxable year before May 7, 1997, shall be taken into account in determining mid-term gain as if such gains and losses were described in paragraph (8)(A).

(B) SPECIAL RULES FOR PASS-THRU ENTITIES.—In applying subparagraph (A) with respect to any pass-thru entity, the determination of when gains and loss are properly taken into account shall be made at the entity level.

(C) PASS-THRU ENTITY DEFINED.—For purposes of subparagraph (B), the term "pass-thru entity" means—

(i) a regulated investment company,

(ii) a real estate investment trust,

(iii) an S corporation,

(iv) a partnership,

(v) an estate or trust, and

(vi) a common trust fund.

(11) TREATMENT OF PASS-THRU ENTITIES.—The Secretary may prescribe such regulations as are appropriate (including regulations requiring reporting) to apply this subsection in the case of sales and exchanges by pass-thru entities (as defined in paragraph (10)(C)) and of interests in such entities.

The above amendment is effective as if included in the provision of the Taxpayer Relief Act of 1997 (P.L. 105-34) to which it relates [effective for tax years ending after May 6, 1997.—CCH.].

[¶ 5010] CODE SEC. 23. ADOPTION EXPENSES.
* * *

(b) LIMITATIONS.—
* * *

(2) INCOME LIMITATION.—

(A) IN GENERAL.—The amount allowable as a credit under subsection (a) for any taxable year *(determined without regard to subsection (c))* shall be reduced (but not below zero) by an amount which bears the same ratio to the amount so allowable (determined without regard to this paragraph but with regard to paragraph (1)) as—

(i) the amount (if any) by which the taxpayer's adjusted gross income exceeds $75,000, bears to

(ii) $40,000.
* * *

[CCH Explanation at ¶ 221. Committee Reports at ¶ 11,345.]

Amendment Notes

Act Sec. 6018(f)(1) amended Code Sec. 23(b)(2)(A) by inserting "(determined without regard to subsection (c))" after "for any taxable year".

The above amendment is effective as if included in the provision of the Small Business Job Protection Act of 1996 (P.L. 104-188) to which it relates [effective for tax years beginning after December 31, 1996.—CCH.].

(c) CARRYFORWARDS OF UNUSED CREDIT.—If the credit allowable under subsection (a) for any taxable year exceeds the limitation imposed by section 26(a) for such taxable year reduced by the sum of the credits allowable under this subpart (other than this section *and section 1400C*), such excess shall be carried to the succeeding taxable year and added to the credit allowable under subsection (a) for such taxable year. No credit may be carried forward under this subsection to any taxable year following the fifth taxable year after the taxable year in which the credit arose. For purposes of the preceding sentence, credits shall be treated as used on a first-in first-out basis.
* * *

[CCH Explanation at ¶ 577. Committee Reports at ¶ 11,060.]

Amendment Notes

Act Sec. 6008(d)(6) amended Code Sec. 23(c) by inserting "and section 1400C" after "other than this section".

The above amendment is effective as if included in the provision of the Taxpayer Relief Act of 1997 (P.L.

105-34) to which it relates [effective August 5, 1997.—CCH.].

[¶ 5020] CODE SEC. 24. CHILD TAX CREDIT.
* * *

(d) ADDITIONAL CREDIT FOR FAMILIES WITH 3 OR MORE CHILDREN.—

(1) IN GENERAL.—In the case of a taxpayer with 3 or more qualifying children for any taxable year, the aggregate credits allowed under subpart C shall be increased by the lesser of—

(A) the credit which would be allowed under this section without regard to this subsection and the limitation under section 26(a), or

(B) the amount by which the aggregate amount of credits allowed by this subpart (without regard to this subsection) would increase if the limitation imposed by section 26(a) were increased by the excess (if any) of—

(i) the taxpayer's social security taxes for the taxable year, over

(ii) the credit allowed under section 32 (determined without regard to subsection (n)) for the taxable year.

The amount of the credit allowed under this subsection shall not be treated as a credit allowed under this subpart and shall reduce the amount of credit otherwise allowable under subsection (a) without regard to section 26(a).

(2) *REDUCTION OF CREDIT TO TAXPAYER SUBJECT TO ALTERNATIVE MINIMUM TAX.—The credit determined under this subsection for the taxable year shall be reduced by the excess (if any) of—*

(A) *the amount of tax imposed by section 55 (relating to alternative minimum tax) with respect to such taxpayer for such taxable year, over*

(B) *the amount of the reduction under section 32(h) with respect to such taxpayer for such taxable year.*

(3) SOCIAL SECURITY TAXES.—For purposes of *paragraph (1)—*

* * *

[CCH Explanation at ¶ 201. Committee Reports at ¶ 10,815.]

Amendment Notes

Act Sec. 6003(a)(1)(A)-(C) amended Code Sec. 24(d) by striking paragraphs (3) and (4), by redesignating paragraph (5) as paragraph (3), and by striking paragraphs (1) and (2) and inserting new paragraphs (1) and (2) to read as above. Prior to amendment, Code Sec. 24(d)(1)-(4) read as follows:

(1) IN GENERAL.—In the case of a taxpayer with 3 or more qualifying children for any taxable year, the amount of the credit allowed under this section shall be equal to the greater of—

(A) the amount of the credit allowed under this section (without regard to this subsection and after application of the limitation under section 26), or

(B) the alternative credit amount determined under paragraph (2).

(2) ALTERNATIVE CREDIT AMOUNT.—For purposes of this subsection, the alternative credit amount is the amount of the credit which would be allowed under this section if the limitation under paragraph (3) were applied in lieu of the limitation under section 26.

(3) LIMITATION.—The limitation under this paragraph for any taxable year is the limitation under section 26 (without regard to this subsection)—

(A) increased by the taxpayer's social security taxes for such taxable year, and

(B) reduced by the sum of—

(i) the credits allowed under this part other than under subpart C or this section, and

(ii) the credit allowed under section 32 without regard to subsection (m) thereof.

(4) UNUSED CREDIT TO BE REFUNDABLE.—If the amount of the credit under paragraph (1)(B) exceeds the amount of the credit under paragraph (1)(A), such excess shall be treated as a credit to which subpart C applies. The rule of section 32(h) shall apply to such excess.

Act Sec. 6003(a)(2) amended Code Sec. 24(d)(3), as redesignated by Act Sec. 6003(a)(1), by striking "paragraph (3)" and inserting "paragraph (1)".

The above amendments are effective as if included in the provision of the Taxpayer Relief Act of 1997 (P.L. 105-34) to which they relate [effective for tax years beginning after December 31, 1997.—CCH.].

[¶ 5030] CODE SEC. 25. INTEREST ON CERTAIN HOME MORTGAGES.

* * *

(e) SPECIAL RULES AND DEFINITIONS.—For purposes of this section—

(1) CARRYFORWARD OF UNUSED CREDIT.—

* * *

(C) APPLICABLE TAX LIMIT.—For purposes of this paragraph, the term "applicable tax limit" means the limitation imposed by section 26(a) for the taxable year reduced by the sum of the credits allowable under this subpart (other than this section and *sections 23 and 1400C*).

* * *

[CCH Explanation at ¶ 577. Committee Reports at ¶ 11,060.]

Amendment Notes

Act Sec. 6008(d)(7) amended Code Sec. 25(e)(1)(C) by striking "section 23" and inserting "sections 23 and 1400C".

The above amendment is effective as if included in the provision of the Taxpayer Relief Act of 1997 (P.L.

105-34) to which it relates [effective August 5, 1997.—CCH.].

[¶ 5040] CODE SEC. 32. EARNED INCOME.

* * *

(c) DEFINITIONS AND SPECIAL RULES.—For purposes of this section—

(1) ELIGIBLE INDIVIDUAL.—

* * *

(F) IDENTIFICATION NUMBER REQUIREMENT.—*No credit shall be allowed under this section to an eligible individual who does not include on the return of tax for the taxable year—*

(i) such individual's taxpayer identification number, and

(ii) if the individual is married (within the meaning of section 7703), the taxpayer identification number of such individual's spouse.

(G) *INDIVIDUALS WHO DO NOT INCLUDE TIN, ETC., OF ANY QUALIFYING CHILD.—No credit shall be allowed under this section to any eligible individual who has 1 or more qualifying children if no qualifying child of such individual is taken into account under subsection (b) by reason of paragraph (3)(D).*

(2) EARNED INCOME.—

* * *

(B) For purposes of subparagraph (A)—

(i) the earned income of an individual shall be computed without regard to any community property laws,

(ii) no amount received as a pension or annuity shall be taken into account,

(iii) no amount to which section 871(a) applies (relating to income of nonresident alien individuals not connected with United States business) shall be taken into account,

(iv) no amount received for services provided by an individual while the individual is an inmate at a penal institution shall be taken into account, and

(v) no amount described in subparagraph (A) received for service performed in work activities as defined in paragraph (4) or (7) of section 407(d) of the Social Security Act to which the taxpayer is assigned under any State program under part A of title IV of such Act *shall be taken into account*, but only to the extent such amount is subsidized under such State program.

(3) QUALIFYING CHILD.—

(A) IN GENERAL.—The term "qualifying child" means, with respect to any taxpayer for any taxable year, an individual—

(i) who bears a relationship to the taxpayer described in subparagraph (B),

(ii) except as provided in subparagraph (B)(iii), who has the same principal place of abode as the taxpayer for more than one-half of such taxable year, *and*

(iii) who meets the age requirements of subparagraph (C).

* * *

(D) IDENTIFICATION REQUIREMENTS.—

(i) IN GENERAL.—A qualifying child shall not be taken into account under subsection (b) unless the taxpayer includes the name, age, and TIN of the qualifying child on the return of tax for the taxable year.

* * *

(5) MODIFIED ADJUSTED GROSS INCOME.—

(A) IN GENERAL.—The term "modified adjusted gross income" means adjusted gross income determined without regard to the amounts described in subparagraph (B) *and increased by the amounts described in subparagraph (C).*

(B) CERTAIN AMOUNTS DISREGARDED.—An amount is described in this subparagraph if it is—

(i) the amount of losses from sales or exchanges of capital assets in excess of gains from such sales or exchanges to the extent such amount does not exceed the amount under section 1211(b)(1),

(ii) the net loss from estates and trusts,

(iii) the excess (if any) of amounts described in subsection (i)(2)(C)(ii) over the amounts described in subsection (i)(2)(C)(i) (relating to nonbusiness rents and royalties), *or*

(iv) 75 percent of the net loss from the carrying on of trades or businesses, computed separately with respect to—

(I) trades or businesses (other than farming) conducted as sole proprietorships,

(II) trades or businesses of farming conducted as sole proprietorships, and

(III) other trades or businesses.

For purposes of clause (iv), there shall not be taken into account items which are attributable to a trade or business which consists of the performance of services by the taxpayer as an employee.

(C) CERTAIN AMOUNTS INCLUDED.—An amount is described in this subparagraph if it is—

(i) interest received or accrued during the taxable year which is exempt from tax imposed by this chapter, or

(ii) amounts received as a pension or annuity, and any distributions or payments received from an individual retirement plan, by the taxpayer during the taxable year to the extent not included in gross income.

Clause (ii) shall not include any amount which is not includible in gross income by reason of a trustee-to-trustee transfer or a rollover distribution.

* * *

[CCH Explanation at ¶ 211 and 216. Committee Reports at ¶ 11,215 and 11,375.]

Amendment Notes

Act Sec. 6010(p)(1)(A)-(C) amended Code Sec. 32(c)(5) by inserting before the period at the end of subparagraph (A) "and increased by the amounts described in subparagraph (C)", by adding "or" at the end of clause (iii) of subparagraph (B), and by striking all that follows subclause (II) of subparagraph (B)(iv) and inserting a new subclause (III) and a new subparagraph (C) to read as above. Prior to amendment, all that followed subclause (II) of Code Sec. 32(c)(5)(B)(iv) read as follows:

(III) other trades or businesses[,]

(v) interest received or accrued during the taxable year which is exempt from tax imposed by this chapter, and

(vi) amounts received as a pension or annuity, and any distributions or payments received from an individual retirement plan, by the taxpayer during the taxable year to the extent not included in gross income.

For purposes of clause (iv), there shall not be taken into account items which are attributable to a trade or business which consists of the performance of services by the taxpayer as an employee. Clause (vi) shall not include any amount which is not includible in gross income by reason of section 402(c), 403(a)(4), 403(b), 408(d)(3), (4), or (5), or 457(e)(10).

Act Sec. 6010(p)(2) amended Code Sec. 32(c)(2)(B)(v) by inserting "shall be taken into account" before ", but only".

The above amendments are effective as if included in the provision of the Taxpayer Relief Act of 1997 (P.L.

Code Sec. 32(c)   ¶ 5040

105-34) to which they relate [effective for tax years beginning after December 31, 1997.—CCH.].

Act Sec. 6021(a) amended Code Sec. 32(c)(1)(F) by striking "The term 'eligible individual' does not include any individual who does not include on the return of tax for the taxable year—" and inserting "No credit shall be allowed under this section to an eligible individual who does not include on the return of tax for the taxable year—".

The above amendment is effective as if included in the amendments made by Act Sec. 451 of the Personal Responsibility and Work Opportunity Reconciliation Act of 1996 (P.L. 104-193) [generally effective for returns due after September 21, 1996.—CCH.].

Act Sec. 6021(b)(1) amended Code Sec. 32(c)(3)(D)(i) to read as above. Prior to amendment, Code Sec. 32(c)(3)(D)(i) read as follows:

(i) IN GENERAL.—The requirements of this subparagraph are met if the taxpayer includes the name, age, and TIN of

each qualifying child (without regard to this subparagraph) on the return of tax for the taxable year.

Act Sec. 6021(b)(2) amended Code Sec. 32(c)(1) by adding at the end a new subparagraph (G) to read as above.

Act Sec. 6021(b)(3) amended Code Sec. 32(c)(3)(A) by inserting "and" at the end of clause (ii), by striking ", and" at the end of clause (iii) and inserting a period, and by striking clause (iv). Prior to being stricken, Code Sec. 32(c)(3)(A)(iv) read as follows:

(iv) with respect to whom the taxpayer meets the identification requirements of subparagraph (D).

The above amendments are effective as if included in the amendments made by Act Sec. 11111 of the Revenue Reconciliation Act of 1990 (P.L. 101-508) [effective for tax years beginning after December 31, 1990.—CCH.].

* * *

(n) SUPPLEMENTAL CHILD CREDIT.—

(1) IN GENERAL.—In the case of a taxpayer with respect to whom a credit is allowed under section 24(a) for the taxable year, the credit otherwise allowable under this section shall be increased by the lesser of—

(A) the excess of—

(i) the credits allowed under subpart A (determined after the application of section 26 and without regard to this subsection), over

(ii) the credits which would be allowed under subpart A after the application of section 26, determined without regard to section 24 and this subsection, or

(B) the excess of—

(i) the sum of the credits allowed under this part (determined without regard to sections 31, 33, and 34 and this subsection), over

(ii) the sum of the regular tax and the social security taxes (as defined in section 24(d)).

The credit determined under this subsection shall be allowed without regard to any other provision of this section, including subsection (d).

(2) COORDINATION WITH OTHER CREDITS.—The amount of the credit under this subsection shall reduce the amount of the credit otherwise allowable under subpart A for the taxable year (determined after the application of section 26), but the amount of the credit under this subsection (and such reduction) shall not be taken into account in determining the amount of any other credit allowable under this part.

[CCH Explanation at ¶ 206. Committee Reports at ¶ 10,820.]

Amendment Notes

Act Sec. 6003(b)(1) amended Code Sec. 32(m)[(n)] to read as above. Prior to amendment, Code Sec. 32(m)[(n)] read as follows:

(m) [(n)] SUPPLEMENTAL CHILD CREDIT.—

(1) IN GENERAL.—In the case of a taxpayer with respect to whom a credit is allowed under section 24 for the taxable year, there shall be allowed as a credit under this section an amount equal to the supplemental child credit (if any) determined for such taxpayer for such taxable year under paragraph (2). Such credit shall be in addition to the credit allowed under subsection (a).

(2) SUPPLEMENTAL CHILD CREDIT.—For purposes of this subsection, the supplemental child credit is an amount equal to the excess (if any) of—

(A) the amount determined under section 24(d)(1)(A), over

(B) the amount determined under section 24(d)(1)(B).

The amounts referred to in subparagraphs (A) and (B) shall be determined as if section 24(d) applied to all taxpayers.

(3) COORDINATION WITH SECTION 24.—The amount of the credit under section 24 shall be reduced by the amount of the credit allowed under this subsection.

The above amendment is effective as if included in the provision of the Taxpayer Relief Act of 1997 (P.L. 105-34) to which it relates [effective for tax years beginning after December 31, 1997.—CCH.].

[¶ 5050] CODE SEC. 34. CERTAIN USES OF GASOLINE AND SPECIAL FUELS.
* * *

(b) EXCEPTION.—Credit shall not be allowed under subsection (a) for any amount payable under section 6421 or 6427, if a claim for such amount is timely filed and, under *section 6421(i)* or 6427(k), is payable under such section.

[CCH Explanation at ¶ 30,050.]

Amendment Notes

Act Sec. 6023(24)(B) amended Code Sec. 34(b) by striking "section 6421(j)" and inserting "section 6421(i)".

The above amendment is effective on the date of the enactment of this Act.

[¶ 5060] CODE SEC. 39. CARRYBACK AND CARRYFORWARD OF UNUSED CREDITS.

(a) IN GENERAL.—

* * *

(2) AMOUNT CARRIED TO EACH YEAR.—

(A) ENTIRE AMOUNT CARRIED TO FIRST YEAR.—The entire amount of the unused credit for an unused credit year shall be carried to the earliest of the *21* taxable years to which (by reason of paragraph (1)) such credit may be carried.

(B) AMOUNT CARRIED TO OTHER *20* YEARS.—The amount of the unused credit for the unused credit year shall be carried to each of the other *20* taxable years to the extent that such unused credit may not be taken into account under section 38(a) for a prior taxable year because of the limitations of subsections (b) and (c).

* * *

Amendment Notes

Act Sec. 6010(n)(1)-(2) amended Act Sec. 1083(a)(2) of the Taxpayer Relief Act of 1997 (P.L. 105-34) by striking "21" and inserting "20", and by striking "22" and inserting "21". Thus, when this amendment is read in conjunction with Act Sec. 1083(a)(2) of P.L. 105-34, Code Sec. 39(a)(2) is amended by striking "18" each place it appears and inserting "21"

and by striking "17" each place it appears and inserting "20".

The above amendment is effective as if included in the provision of the Taxpayer Relief Act of 1997 (P.L. 105-34) to which it relates [effective for credits arising in tax years beginning after December 31, 1997.—CCH.].

[¶ 5065] CODE SEC. 40. ALCOHOL USED AS FUEL.

* * *

(e) TERMINATION.—

(1) IN GENERAL.—This section shall not apply to any sale or use—

(A) for any period after *December 31, 2007*, or

(B) for any period before *January 1, 2008*, during which the rates of tax under section 4081(a)(2)(A) are 4.3 cents per gallon.

* * *

[CCH Explanation at ¶ 760. Committee Reports at ¶ 15,035.]

Amendment Notes

P.L. 105-178 (ISTEA)

Act Sec. 9003(a)(3)(A)-(B) amended Code Sec. 40(e)(1) by striking "December 31, 2000" in subparagraph (A) and

inserting "December 31, 2007", and by striking "January 1, 2001" and inserting "January 1, 2008".

The above amendment is effective on January 1, 2001.

[Caution: Code Sec. 40(h), below, as amended by P.L. 105-178 (ISTEA), is effective on January 1, 2001.—CCH]

(h) *REDUCED CREDIT FOR ETHANOL BLENDERS.—*

(1) *IN GENERAL.—In the case of any alcohol mixture credit or alcohol credit with respect to any sale or use of alcohol which is ethanol during calendar years 2001 through 2007—*

(A) *subsections (b)(1)(A) and (b)(2)(A) shall be applied by substituting "the blender amount" for "60 cents",*

(B) *subsection (b)(3) shall be applied by substituting "the low-proof blender amount" for "45 cents" and "the blender amount" for "60 cents", and*

(C) *subparagraphs (A) and (B) of subsection (d)(3) shall be applied by substituting "the blender amount" for "60 cents" and "the low-proof blender amount" for "45 cents".*

(2) *AMOUNTS.—For purposes of paragraph (1), the blender amount and the low-proof blender amount shall be determined in accordance with the following table:*

In the case of any sale or use during calendar year:	The blender amount is:	The low-proof blender amount is:
2001 or 2002	53 cents	39.26 cents
2003 or 2004	52 cents	38.52 cents
2005, 2006, or 2007	51 cents	37.78 cents

[CCH Explanation at ¶ 760. Committee Reports at ¶ 15,035.]

Amendment Notes

P.L. 105-178 (ISTEA)

Act Sec. 9003(b)(1) amended Code Sec. 40(h) to read as above. Prior to amendment, Code Sec. 40(h) read as follows:

(h) REDUCED CREDIT FOR ETHANOL BLENDERS.—In the case of any alcohol mixture credit or alcohol credit with respect to any alcohol which is ethanol—

(1) subsections (b)(1)(A) and (b)(2)(A) shall be applied by substituting "54 cents" for "60 cents";

(2) subsection (b)(3) shall be applied by substituting "40 cents" for "45 cents" and "54 cents" for "60 cents"; and

(3) subparagraphs (A) and (B) of subsection (d)(3) shall be applied by substituting "54 cents" for "60 cents" and "40 cents" for "45 cents".

The above amendment is effective on January 1, 2001.

Code Sec. 40(h)   ¶ 5065

[¶ 5070] CODE SEC. 42. LOW-INCOME HOUSING CREDIT.
* * *

(j) RECAPTURE OF CREDIT.—
* * *

(4) SPECIAL RULES.—
* * *

(D) NO CREDITS AGAINST TAX.—Any increase in tax under this subsection shall not be treated as a tax imposed by this chapter for purposes of determining the amount of any credit under *this chapter.*
* * *

[CCH Explanation at ¶ 244. Committee Reports at ¶ 10,865.]

Amendment Notes

Act Sec. 6004(g)(5) amended Code Sec. 42(j)(4)(D) by striking "subpart A, B, D, or G of this part" and inserting "this chapter".

The above amendment is effective as if included in the provision of the Taxpayer Relief Act of 1997 (P.L. 105-34) to which it relates [effective for obligations issued after December 31, 1997.—CCH.].

[¶ 5080] CODE SEC. 45A. INDIAN EMPLOYMENT CREDIT.
* * *

(b) QUALIFIED WAGES; QUALIFIED EMPLOYEE HEALTH INSURANCE COSTS.—For purposes of this section—

(1) QUALIFIED WAGES.—
* * *

(B) COORDINATION WITH *WORK OPPORTUNITY CREDIT.*—The term "qualified wages" shall not include wages attributable to service rendered during the 1-year period beginning with the day the individual begins work for the employer if any portion of such wages is taken into account in determining the credit under section 51.
* * *

[CCH Explanation at ¶ 30,050.]

Amendment Notes

Act Sec. 6023(1) amended the heading for subparagraph (B) of Code Sec. 45A(b)(1) by striking "TARGETED JOBS CREDIT" and inserting "WORK OPPORTUNITY CREDIT".

The above amendment is effective on the date of the enactment of this Act.

[¶ 5090] CODE SEC. 49. AT-RISK RULES.
* * *

(b) INCREASES IN NONQUALIFIED NONRECOURSE FINANCING.—
* * *

(4) SPECIAL RULE.—Any increase in tax under paragraph (1) shall not be treated as tax imposed by this chapter for purposes of determining the amount of any credit allowable under *this chapter.*

[CCH Explanation at ¶ 244. Committee Reports at ¶ 10,865.]

Amendment Notes

Act Sec. 6004(g)(6) amended Code Sec. 49(b)(4) by striking "subpart A, B, D, or G" and inserting "this chapter".

The above amendment is effective as if included in the provision of the Taxpayer Relief Act of 1997 (P.L. 105-34) to which it relates [effective for obligations issued after December 31, 1997.—CCH.].

[¶ 5100] CODE SEC. 50. OTHER SPECIAL RULES.

(a) RECAPTURE IN CASE OF DISPOSITIONS, ETC.—Under regulations prescribed by the Secretary—
* * *

(5) DEFINITIONS AND SPECIAL RULES.—
* * *

(C) SPECIAL RULE.—Any increase in tax under paragraph (1) or (2) shall not be treated as tax imposed by this chapter for purposes of determining the amount of any credit allowable under *this chapter.*
* * *

[CCH Explanation at ¶ 244. Committee Reports at ¶ 10,865.]

Amendment Notes

Act Sec. 6004(g)(7) amended Code Sec. 50(a)(5)(C) by striking "subpart A, B, D, or G" and inserting "this chapter".

The above amendment is effective as if included in the provision of the Taxpayer Relief Act of 1997 (P.L. 105-34) to which it relates [effective for obligations issued after December 31, 1997.—CCH.].

[¶ 5110] CODE SEC. 55. ALTERNATIVE MINIMUM TAX IMPOSED.

* * *

(b) TENTATIVE MINIMUM TAX.—For purposes of this part—

* * *

(3) MAXIMUM RATE OF TAX ON NET CAPITAL GAIN OF NONCORPORATE TAXPAYERS.—The amount determined under the first sentence of paragraph (1)(A)(i) shall not exceed the sum of—

(A) the amount determined under such first sentence computed at the rates and in the same manner as if this paragraph had not been enacted on the taxable excess reduced by the lesser of—

(i) the net capital gain, or

(ii) the sum of—

(I) the adjusted net capital gain, plus

(II) the unrecaptured section 1250 gain, plus

(B) 10 percent of so much of the adjusted net capital gain (or, if less, taxable excess) as does not exceed the amount on which a tax is determined under section 1(h)(1)(B), plus

(C) 20 percent of the adjusted net capital gain (or, if less, taxable excess) in excess of the amount on which tax is determined under subparagraph (B), plus

(D) 25 percent of the amount of taxable excess in excess of the sum of the amounts on which tax is determined under the preceding subparagraphs of this paragraph.

In the case of taxable years beginning after December 31, 2000, rules similar to the rules of section 1(h)(2) shall apply for purposes of subparagraphs (B) and (C). Terms used in this paragraph which are also used in section 1(h) shall have the respective meanings given such terms by section 1(h) but computed with the adjustments under this part.

* * *

[CCH Explanation at ¶ 523. Committee Reports at ¶ 10,915.]

Amendment Notes

Act Sec. 6005(d)(2) amended Code Sec. 55(b)(3) to read as above. Prior to amendment, Code Sec. 55(b)(3) read as follows:

(3) MAXIMUM RATE OF TAX ON NET CAPITAL GAIN OF NONCORPORATE TAXPAYERS.—The amount determined under the first sentence of paragraph (1)(A)(i) shall not exceed the sum of—

(A) the amount determined under such first sentence computed at the rates and in the same manner as if this paragraph had not been enacted on the taxable excess reduced by the lesser of—

(i) the net capital gain, or

(ii) the sum of—

(I) the adjusted net capital gain, plus

(II) the unrecaptured section 1250 gain, plus

(B) 25 percent of the lesser of—

(i) the unrecaptured section 1250 gain, or

(ii) the amount of taxable excess in excess of the sum of—

(I) the adjusted net capital gain, plus

(II) the amount on which a tax is determined under subparagraph (A), plus

(C) 10 percent of so much of the taxpayer's adjusted net capital gain (or, if less, taxable excess) as does not exceed the amount on which a tax is determined under section 1(h)(1)(D), plus

(D) 20 percent of the taxpayer's adjusted net capital gain (or, if less, taxable excess) in excess of the amount on which tax is determined under subparagraph (C).

In the case of taxable years beginning after December 31, 2000, rules similar to the rules of section 1(h)(2) shall apply for purposes of subparagraphs (C) and (D). Terms used in this paragraph which are also used in section 1(h) shall have the respective meanings given such terms by section 1(h).

The above amendment is effective as if included in the provision of the Taxpayer Relief Act of 1997 (P.L. 105-34) to which it relates [effective for tax years ending after May 6, 1997.—CCH.].

(e) EXEMPTION FOR SMALL CORPORATIONS.—

(1) IN GENERAL.—

(A) $7,500,000 GROSS RECEIPTS TEST.—The tentative minimum tax of a corporation shall be zero for any taxable year if the corporation's average annual gross receipts for all 3-taxable-year periods ending before such taxable year does not exceed $7,500,000. For purposes of the preceding sentence, only taxable years beginning after December 31, 1993, shall be taken into account.

(B) $5,000,000 GROSS RECEIPTS TEST FOR FIRST 3-YEAR PERIOD.—Subparagraph (A) shall be applied by substituting "$5,000,000" for "$7,500,000" for the first 3-taxable-year period (or portion thereof) of the corporation which is taken into account under subparagraph (A).

(C) FIRST TAXABLE YEAR CORPORATION IN EXISTENCE.—If such taxable year that such corporation is in existence, the tentative minimum tax of such corporation for such year shall be zero.

(D) SPECIAL RULES.—For purposes of this paragraph, the rules of paragraphs (2) and (3) of section 448(c) shall apply.

* * *

[CCH Explanation at ¶ 566. Committee Reports at ¶ 10,945.]

Amendment Notes

Act Sec. 6006(a) amended Code Sec. 55(e)(1) to read as above. Prior to amendment, Code Sec. 55(e)(1) read as as follows:

(1) IN GENERAL.—The tentative minimum tax of a corporation shall be zero for any taxable year if—

(A) such corporation met the $5,000,000 gross receipts test of section 448(c) for its first taxable year beginning after December 31, 1996, and

(B) such corporation would meet such test for the taxable year and all prior taxable years beginning after such first taxable year if such test were applied by substituting "$7,500,000" for "$5,000,000".

The above amendment is effective as if included in the provision of the Taxpayer Relief Act of 1997 (P.L. 105-34) to which it relates [effective for tax years beginning after December 31, 1997.—CCH.].

[¶ 5120] CODE SEC. 57. ITEMS OF TAX PREFERENCE.

(a) GENERAL RULE.—For purposes of this part, the items of tax preference determined under this section are—

* * *

(7) EXCLUSION FOR GAINS ON SALE OF CERTAIN SMALL BUSINESS STOCK.—An amount equal to 42 percent of the amount excluded from gross income for the taxable year under section 1202. *In the case of stock the holding period of which begins after December 31, 2000 (determined with the application of the last sentence of section 1(h)(2)(B)), the preceding sentence shall be applied by substituting "28 percent" for "42 percent".*

* * *

[CCH Explanation at ¶ 523. Committee Reports at ¶ 10,915.]

Amendment Notes
Act Sec. 6005(d)(3) amended Code Sec. 57(a)(7) by adding at the end a new sentence to read as above.
The above amendment is effective as if included in the provision of the Taxpayer Relief Act of 1997 (P.L.

105-34) to which it relates [effective for tax years ending after May 6, 1997.—CCH.].

[¶ 5130] CODE SEC. 59. OTHER DEFINITIONS AND SPECIAL RULES.

(a) ALTERNATIVE MINIMUM TAX FOREIGN TAX CREDIT.—For purposes of this part—

* * *

(4) ELECTION TO USE SIMPLIFIED SECTION 904 LIMITATION.—

* * *

Amendment Notes
Act Sec. 6011(a) amended Code Sec. 59(a) by redesignating paragraph (3), as added by Act Sec. 1103 of the Taxpayer Relief Act of 1997 (P.L. 105-34), as paragraph (4).

The above amendment is effective as if included in the provision of the Taxpayer Relief Act of 1997 (P.L. 105-34) to which it relates [effective for tax years beginning after December 31, 1997.—CCH.].

(b) MINIMUM TAX NOT TO APPLY TO INCOME ELIGIBLE FOR *CREDITS UNDER SECTION 30A OR 936.*—In the case of any corporation for which a credit is allowable for the taxable year under section 30A or 936, alternative minimum taxable income shall not include any income with respect to which a credit is determined under section 30A or 936.

* * *

[CCH Explanation at ¶ 30,050.]

Amendment Notes
Act Sec. 6023(2) amended the heading for subsection (b) of Code Sec. 59 by striking "SECTION 936 CREDIT" and inserting "CREDITS UNDER SECTION 30A OR 936".

The above amendment is effective on the date of the enactment of this Act.

[¶ 5140] CODE SEC. 66. TREATMENT OF COMMUNITY INCOME.

* * *

(c) SPOUSE RELIEVED OF LIABILITY IN CERTAIN OTHER CASES.—Under regulations prescribed by the Secretary, if—

(1) an individual does not file a joint return for any taxable year,

(2) such individual does not include in gross income for such taxable year an item of community income properly includible therein which, in accordance with the rules contained in section 879(a), would be treated as the income of the other spouse,

(3) the individual establishes that he or she did not know of, and had no reason to know of, such item of community income, and

(4) taking into account all facts and circumstances, it is inequitable to include such item of community income in such individual's gross income,

then, for purposes of this title, such item of community income shall be included in the gross income of the other spouse (and not in the gross income of the individual). *Under procedures prescribed by the Secretary, if, taking into account all the facts and circumstances, it is inequitable to hold the individual liable for any unpaid tax or any deficiency (or any portion of either) attributable to any item for which relief is not available under the preceding sentence, the Secretary may relieve such individual of such liability.*

* * *

[CCH Explanation at ¶ 1290. Committee Reports at ¶ 10,285.]

Amendment Notes
Act Sec. 3201(b) amended Code Sec. 66(c) by adding at the end a new sentence to read as above.
The above amendment applies generally to any liability for tax arising after the date of the enactment of this

Act and any liability for tax arising on or before such date but remaining unpaid as of such date. However, for an exception, see Act Sec. 3201(g)(2), below.

Act Sec. 3201(g)(2) provides:

¶ 5120 Code Sec. 57(a)

(2) 2-YEAR PERIOD.—The 2-year period under subsection (b)(1)(E) or (c)(3)(B) of section 6015 of the Internal Revenue Code of 1986 shall not expire before the date which is 2 years after the date of the first collection activity after the date of the enactment of this Act.

[¶ 5150] CODE SEC. 72. ANNUITIES; CERTAIN PROCEEDS OF ENDOWMENT AND LIFE INSURANCE CONTRACTS.

* * *

(e) AMOUNTS NOT RECEIVED AS ANNUITIES.—

* * *

(9) EXTENSION OF PARAGRAPH (2)(B) TO QUALIFIED STATE TUITION PROGRAMS AND EDUCATIONAL INDIVIDUAL RETIREMENT ACCOUNTS.—*Notwithstanding any other provision of this subsection, paragraph (2)(B) shall apply to amounts received under a qualified State tuition program (as defined in section 529(b)) or under an education individual retirement account (as defined in section 530(b)). The rule of paragraph (8)(B) shall apply for purposes of this paragraph.*

* * *

[CCH Explanation at ¶ 228 and 236. Committee Reports at ¶ 10,845.]

Amendment Notes
Act Sec. 6004(d)(3)(B) amended Code Sec. 72(e) by inserting after paragraph (8) a new paragraph (9) to read as above.
The above amendment is effective as if included in the provision of the Taxpayer Relief Act of 1997 (P.L. 105-34) to which it relates [effective for tax years beginning after December 31, 1997.—CCH.].

(n) ANNUITIES UNDER RETIRED SERVICEMAN'S FAMILY PROTECTION PLAN OR SURVIVOR BENEFIT PLAN.—Subsection (b) shall not apply in the case of amounts received after December 31, 1965, as an annuity under chapter 73 of title 10 of the United States Code, but all such amounts shall be excluded from gross income until there has been so excluded (under section 122(b)(1) or this section, including amounts excluded before January 1, 1966) an amount equal to the consideration for the contract (as defined by section 122(b)(2)), plus any amount treated pursuant to section 101(b)(2)(D) *(as in effect on the day before the date of the enactment of the Small Business Job Protection Act of 1996)* as additional consideration paid by the employee. Thereafter all amounts so received shall be included in gross income.

* * *

[CCH Explanation at ¶ 30,050.]

Amendment Notes
Act Sec. 6023(3) amended Code Sec. 72(n) by inserting "(as in effect on the day before the date of the enactment of the Small Business Job Protection Act of 1996)" after "section 101(b)(2)(D)".
The above amendment is effective on the date of the enactment of this Act.

(t) 10-PERCENT ADDITIONAL TAX ON EARLY DISTRIBUTIONS FROM QUALIFIED RETIREMENT PLANS.—

* * *

(2) SUBSECTION NOT TO APPLY TO CERTAIN DISTRIBUTIONS.—Except as provided in paragraphs (3) and (4), paragraph (1) shall not apply to any of the following distributions:

[Caution: Code Sec. 72(t)(2)(A), below, as amended by Act Sec. 3436(a), applies to distributions after December 31, 1999.—CCH.]

(A) IN GENERAL.—Distributions which are—

(i) made on or after the date on which the employee attains age 59½,

(ii) made to a beneficiary (or to the estate of the employee) on or after the death of the employee,

(iii) attributable to the employee's being disabled within the meaning of subsection (m)(7),

(iv) part of a series of substantially equal periodic payments (not less frequently than annually) made for the life (or life expectancy) of the employee or the joint lives (or joint life expectancies) of such employee and his designated beneficiary,

(v) made to an employee after separation from service after attainment of age 55,

(vi) dividends paid with respect to stock of a corporation which are described in section 404(k), *or*

(vii) *made on account of a levy under section 6331 on the qualified retirement plan.*

* * *

(3) LIMITATIONS.—

(A) CERTAIN EXCEPTIONS NOT TO APPLY TO INDIVIDUAL RETIREMENT PLANS.—Subparagraphs *(A)(v)* and (C) of paragraph (2) shall not apply to distributions from an individual retirement plan.

* * *

(8) QUALIFIED FIRST-TIME HOMEBUYER DISTRIBUTIONS.—For purposes of paragraph (2)(F)—

* * *

(E) SPECIAL RULE WHERE DELAY IN ACQUISITION.—If any distribution from any individual retirement plan fails to meet the requirements of subparagraph (A) solely by reason of a delay or cancellation of the purchase or construction of the residence, the amount of the distribution may be contributed to an individual retirement plan as provided in section 408(d)(3)(A)(i) (determined by substituting *"120th day"* for *"60th day"* in such section), except that—

(i) section 408(d)(3)(B) shall not be applied to such contribution, and

(ii) such amount shall not be taken into account in determining whether section 408(d)(3)(B) applies to any other amount.

* * *

[CCH Explanation at ¶ 1226 and 30,050. Committee Reports at ¶ 10,450.]

Amendment Notes

Act Sec. 3436(a) amended Code Sec. 72(t)(2)(A) by striking "or" at the end of clauses (iv) and (v), by striking the period at the end of clause (vi) and inserting ", or", and by adding at the end a new clause (vii) to read as above.

The above amendment applies to distributions after December 31, 1999.

Act Sec. 6005(c)(1)(A)-(B) amended Code Sec. 72(t)(8)(E) by striking "120 days" and inserting "120th day", and by striking "60 days" and inserting "60th day".

The above amendment is effective as if included in the provision of the Taxpayer Relief Act of 1997 (P.L. 105-34) to which it relates [effective for distributions in tax years beginning after December 31, 1997.—CCH.].

Act Sec. 6023(4) amended Code Sec. 72(t)(3)(A) by striking "(A)(v)," and inserting "(A)(v)".

The above amendment is effective on the date of the enactment of this Act.

[¶ 5160] CODE SEC. 108. INCOME FROM DISCHARGE OF INDEBTEDNESS.

* * *

(f) STUDENT LOANS.—

* * *

(2) STUDENT LOAN.—For purposes of this subsection, the term "student loan" means any loan to an individual to assist the individual in attending an educational organization described in section 170(b)(1)(A)(ii) made by—

(A) the United States, or an instrumentality or agency thereof,

(B) a State, territory, or possession of the United States, or the District of Columbia, or any political subdivision thereof,

(C) a public benefit corporation—

(i) which is exempt from taxation under section 501(c)(3),

(ii) which has assumed control over a State, county, or municipal hospital, and

(iii) whose employees have been deemed to be public employees under State law, or

(D) any educational organization described in section 170(b)(1)(A)(ii) if such loan is made—

(i) pursuant to an agreement with any entity described in subparagraph (A), (B), or (C) under which the funds from which the loan was made were provided to such educational organization, or

(ii) pursuant to a program of such educational organization which is designed to encourage its students to serve in occupations with unmet needs or in areas with unmet needs and under which the services provided by the students (or former students) are for or under the direction of a governmental unit or an organization described in section 501(c)(3) and exempt from tax under section 501(a).

The term "student loan" includes any loan made by an educational organization described in section 170(b)(1)(A)(ii) or by an organization exempt from tax under section 501(a) to refinance a loan to an individual to assist the individual in attending any such educational organization but only if the refinancing loan is pursuant to a program of the refinancing organization which is designed as described in subparagraph (D)(ii).

(3) EXCEPTION FOR DISCHARGES ON ACCOUNT OF SERVICES PERFORMED FOR CERTAIN LENDERS.— Paragraph (1) shall not apply to the discharge of a loan made by an organization described in paragraph (2)(D) if the discharge is on account of services performed for either such organization.

* * *

[CCH Explanation at ¶ 241. Committee Reports at ¶ 10,860.]

Amendment Notes

Act Sec. 6004(f)(1) amended the last sentence of Code Sec. 108(f)(2) to read as above. Prior to amendment, the last sentence of Code Sec. 108(f)(2) read as follows:

The term "student loan" includes any loan made by an educational organization so described or by an organization exempt from tax under section 501(a) to refinance a loan meeting the requirements of the preceding sentence.

Act Sec. 6004(f)(2) amended Code Sec. 108(f)(3) by striking "(or by an organization described in paragraph (2)(E) from funds provided by an organization described in paragraph (2)(D))" following "paragraph (2)(D)".

The above amendments are effective as if included in the provisions of the Taxpayer Relief Act of 1997 (P.L. 105-34) to which they relate [effective for discharges of indebtedness after August 5, 1997.—CCH.].

[¶ 5170] CODE SEC. 119. MEALS OR LODGING FURNISHED FOR THE CONVENIENCE OF THE EMPLOYER.

* * *

(b) SPECIAL RULES.—For purposes of subsection (a)—

* * *

(4) MEALS FURNISHED TO EMPLOYEES ON BUSINESS PREMISES WHERE MEALS OF MOST EMPLOYEES ARE OTHERWISE EXCLUDABLE.—All meals furnished on the business premises of an employer to such employer's employees shall be treated as furnished for the convenience of the employer if, without regard to this paragraph, more than half of the employees to whom such meals are furnished on such premises are furnished such meals for the convenience of the employer.

* * *

[CCH Explanation at ¶ 593. Committee Reports at ¶ 10,790.]

Amendment Notes

Act Sec. 5002(a) amended Code Sec. 119(b) by adding at the end a new paragraph (4) to read as above.

The above amendment applies to tax years beginning before, on, or after the date of the enactment of this Act.

[¶ 5180] CODE SEC. 121. EXCLUSION OF GAIN FROM SALE OF PRINCIPAL RESIDENCE.

* * *

(b) LIMITATIONS.—

* * *

(2) SPECIAL RULES FOR JOINT RETURNS.—In the case of a husband and wife who make a joint return for the taxable year of the sale or exchange of the property—

(A) $500,000 LIMITATION FOR CERTAIN JOINT RETURNS.—Paragraph (1) shall be applied by substituting "$500,000" for "$250,000" if—

(i) either spouse meets the ownership requirements of subsection (a) with respect to such property,

(ii) both spouses meet the use requirements of subsection (a) with respect to such property, and

(iii) neither spouse is ineligible for the benefits of subsection (a) with respect to such property by reason of paragraph (3).

(B) OTHER JOINT RETURNS.—If such spouses do not meet the requirements of subparagraph (A), the limitation under paragraph (1) shall be the sum of the limitations under paragraph (1) to which each spouse would be entitled if such spouses had not been married. For purposes of the preceding sentence, each spouse shall be treated as owning the property during the period that either spouse owned the property.

* * *

[CCH Explanation at ¶ 248. Committee Reports at ¶ 10,920.]

Amendment Notes

Act Sec. 6005(e)(1) amended Code Sec. 121(b)(2) to read as above. Prior to amendment, Code Sec. 121(b)(2) read as follows:

(2) $500,000 LIMITATION FOR CERTAIN JOINT RETURNS.—Paragraph (1) shall be applied by substituting "$500,000" for "$250,000" if—

(A) a husband and wife make a joint return for the taxable year of the sale or exchange of the property,

(B) either spouse meets the ownership requirements of subsection (a) with respect to such property,

(C) both spouses meet the use requirements of subsection (a) with respect to such property, and

(D) neither spouse is ineligible for the benefits of subsection (a) with respect to such property by reason of paragraph (3).

The above amendment is effective as if included in the provision of the Taxpayer Relief Act of 1997 (P.L. 105-34) to which it relates [generally effective for sales and exchanges after May 6, 1997.—CCH.].

(c) EXCLUSION FOR TAXPAYERS FAILING TO MEET CERTAIN REQUIREMENTS.—

(1) IN GENERAL.—In the case of a sale or exchange to which this subsection applies, the ownership and use requirements of subsection (a), and subsection (b)(3), shall not apply; but the dollar limitation under paragraph (1) or (2) of subsection (b), whichever is applicable, shall be equal to—

(A) the amount which bears the same ratio to such limitation (determined without regard to this paragraph) as

(B)(i) the shorter of—

(I) the aggregate periods, during the 5-year period ending on the date of such sale or exchange, such property has been owned and used by the taxpayer as the taxpayer's principal residence, or

(II) the period after the date of the most recent prior sale or exchange by the taxpayer to which subsection (a) applied and before the date of such sale or exchange, bears to

(ii) 2 years.

* * *

[CCH Explanation at ¶ 246. Committee Reports at ¶ 10,925.]

Amendment Notes

Act Sec. 6005(e)(2) amended Code Sec. 121(c)(1) to read as above. Prior to amendment, Code Sec. 121(c)(1) read as follows:

(1) IN GENERAL.—In the case of a sale or exchange to which this subsection applies, the ownership and use requirements of subsection (a) shall not apply and subsection (b)(3) shall not apply; but the amount of gain excluded from gross

Code Sec. 121(c)   ¶ 5180

income under subsection (a) with respect to such sale or exchange shall not exceed—

(A) the amount which bears the same ratio to the amount which would be so excluded under this section if such requirements had been met, as

(B) the shorter of—

(i) the aggregate periods, during the 5-year period ending on the date of such sale or exchange, such property has been owned and used by the taxpayer as the taxpayer's principal residence, or

(ii) the period after the date of the most recent prior sale or exchange by the taxpayer to which subsection (a) applied and before the date of such sale or exchange,

bears to 2 years.

The above amendment is effective as if included in the provision of the Taxpayer Relief Act of 1997 (P.L. 105-34) to which it relates [generally effective for sales and exchanges after May 6, 1997.—CCH.].

[¶ 5185] CODE SEC. 132. CERTAIN FRINGE BENEFITS.
* * *

(f) QUALIFIED TRANSPORTATION FRINGE.—
* * *

[Caution: Code Sec. 132(f)(2), below, as amended by P.L. 105-178 (ISTEA), applies to tax years beginning after December 31, 1998.—CCH.]

(2) LIMITATION ON EXCLUSION.—The amount of the fringe benefits which are provided by an employer to any employee and which may be excluded from gross income under subsection (a)(5) shall not exceed—

(A) *$65* per month in the case of the aggregate of the benefits described in subparagraphs (A) and (B) of paragraph (1), and

(B) *$175* per month in the case of qualified parking.

[Caution: Code Sec. 132(f)(2), below, as amended by P.L. 105-178 (ISTEA), applies to tax years beginning after December 31, 2001.—CCH.]

(2) LIMITATION ON EXCLUSION.—The amount of the fringe benefits which are provided by an employer to any employee and which may be excluded from gross income under subsection (a)(5) shall not exceed—

(A) *$100* per month in the case of the aggregate of the benefits described in subparagraphs (A) and (B) of paragraph (1), and

(B) $175 per month in the case of qualified parking.
* * *

(4) *NO CONSTRUCTIVE RECEIPT.*—No amount shall be included in the gross income of an employee solely because the employee may choose between any qualified transportation fringe and compensation which would otherwise be includible in gross income of such employee.
* * *

[Caution: Code Sec. 132(f)(6), below, as amended by P.L. 105-178 (ISTEA), applies to tax years beginning after December 31, 1998.—CCH.]

(6) *INFLATION ADJUSTMENT.*—

(A) *IN GENERAL.*—In the case of any taxable year beginning in a calendar year after 1999, the dollar amounts contained in subparagraphs (A) and (B) of paragraph (2) shall be increased by an amount equal to—

(i) such dollar amount, multiplied by

(ii) the cost-of-living adjustment determined under section 1(f)(3) for the calendar year in which the taxable year begins, by substituting "calendar year 1998" for "calendar year 1992".

[Caution: The last sentence of Code Sec. 132(f)(6)(A), below, as amended by P.L. 105-178 (ISTEA), applies to tax years beginning after December 31, 2001.—CCH.]

In the case of any taxable year beginning in a calendar year after 2002, clause (ii) shall be applied by substituting "calendar year 2001" for "calendar year 1998" for purposes of adjusting the dollar amount contained in paragraph (2)(A).

(B) *ROUNDING.*—If any increase determined under subparagraph (A) is not a multiple of $5, such increase shall be rounded to the next lowest multiple of $5.
* * *

[CCH Explanation at ¶ 253. Committee Reports at ¶ 15,135.]

Amendment Notes
P.L. 105-178 (ISTEA)

Act Sec. 9010(a)(1) amended Code Sec. 132(f)(4) to read as above. Prior to amendment, Code Sec. 132(f)(4) read as follows:

(4) BENEFIT NOT IN LIEU OF COMPENSATION.—Subsection (a)(5) shall not apply to any qualified transportation fringe unless such benefit is provided in addition to (and not in lieu of) any compensation otherwise payable to the employee. This paragraph shall not apply to any qualified parking provided in lieu of compensation which otherwise would have been includible in gross income of the employee, and no amount shall be included in the gross income of the employee solely because the employee may choose between the qualified parking and compensation.

The above amendment applies to tax years beginning after December 31, 1997.

Act Sec. 9010(b)(1) amended Code Sec. 132(f)(6) to read as above. Prior to amendment, Code Sec. 132(f)(6) read as follows:

(6) INFLATION ADJUSTMENT.—In the case of any taxable year beginning in a calendar year after 1993, the dollar amounts contained in paragraph (2)(A) and (B) shall be increased by an amount equal to—

(A) such dollar amount, multiplied by

(B) the cost-of-living adjustment determined under section 1(f)(3) for the calendar year in which the taxable year begins. If any increase determined under the preceding sentence is not a multiple of $5, such increase shall be rounded to the next lowest multiple of $5.

Act Sec. 9010(b)(2)(A)-(B) amended Code Sec. 132(f)(2) by striking "$60" in subparagraph (A) and inserting "$65", and by striking "$155" in subparagraph (B) and inserting "$175".

The above amendments apply to tax years beginning after December 31, 1998.

Act Sec. 9010(c)(1) amended Code Sec. 132(f)(2)(A) by striking "$65" and inserting "$100".

Act Sec. 9010(c)(2) amended Code Sec. 132(f)(6)(A) by adding at the end a new flush sentence to read as above.

The above amendments apply to tax years beginning after December 31, 2001.

[¶ 5190] CODE SEC. 135. INCOME FROM UNITED STATES SAVINGS BONDS USED TO PAY HIGHER EDUCATION TUITION AND FEES.

* * *

(c) DEFINITIONS.—For purposes of this section—

* * *

(2) QUALIFIED HIGHER EDUCATION EXPENSES.—

* * *

(C) CONTRIBUTIONS TO QUALIFIED STATE TUITION PROGRAM *AND EDUCATION INDIVIDUAL RETIREMENT ACCOUNTS.*—Such term shall include any contribution to a qualified State tuition program (as defined in section 529) on behalf of a designated beneficiary (as defined in such section), or to an education individual retirement account (as defined in section 530) on behalf of an account beneficiary, who is an individual described in subparagraph (A); but there shall be no increase in the investment in the contract for purposes of applying *section 72* by reason of any portion of such contribution which is not includible in gross income by reason of this subparagraph.

(3) ELIGIBLE EDUCATIONAL INSTITUTION.—The term "eligible educational institution" has the meaning given such term by section 529(e)(5).

* * *

[CCH Explanation at ¶ 231. Committee Reports at ¶ 10,845.]

Amendment Notes

Act Sec. 6004(c)(1) amended Code Sec. 135(c)(3) to read as above. Prior to amendment, Code Sec. 135(c)(3) read as follows:

(3) ELIGIBLE EDUCATIONAL INSTITUTION.—The term "eligible educational institution" means—

(A) an institution described in section 1201(a) or subparagraph (C) or (D) of section 481(a)(1) of the Higher Education Act of 1965 (as in effect on October 21, 1988), and

(B) an area vocational education school (as defined in subparagraph (C) or (D) of section 521(3) of the Carl D.

Perkins Vocational Education Act) which is in any State (as defined in section 521(27) of such Act), as such sections are in effect on October 21, 1988.

Act Sec. 6004(d)(9)(A)-(B) amended Code Sec. 135(c)(2)(C) by inserting "AND EDUCATION INDIVIDUAL RETIREMENT ACCOUNTS" in the heading after "PROGRAM" and by striking "section 529(c)(3)(A)" and inserting "section 72".

The above amendments are effective as if included in the provisions of the Taxpayer Relief Act of 1997 (P.L. 105-34) to which they relate [generally effective for tax years beginning after December 31, 1997.—CCH.].

(d) SPECIAL RULES.—

* * *

(2) COORDINATION WITH OTHER HIGHER EDUCATION BENEFITS.—The amount of the qualified higher education expenses otherwise taken into account under subsection (a) with respect to the education of an individual shall be reduced (before the application of subsection (b)) by—

(A) the amount of such expenses which are taken into account in determining the credit allowable to the taxpayer or any other person under section 25A with respect to such expenses, and

(B) the amount of such expenses which are taken into account in determining the exclusion under section 530(d)(2).

* * *

[CCH Explanation at ¶ 231. Committee Reports at ¶ 10,845.]

Amendment Notes

Act Sec. 6004(d)(4) amended Code Sec. 135(d)(2) to read as above. Prior to amendment, Code Sec. 135(d)(2) read as follows:

(2) COORDINATION WITH HIGHER EDUCATION CREDIT.—The amount of the qualified higher education expenses otherwise taken into account under subsection (a) with respect to the education of an individual shall be reduced (before the

application of subsection (b)) by the amount of such expenses which are taken into account in determining the credit allowable to the taxpayer or any other person under section 25A with respect to such expenses.

The above amendment is effective as if included in the provision of the Taxpayer Relief Act of 1997 (P.L. 105-34) to which it relates [generally effective for tax years beginning after December 31, 1997.—CCH.].

[¶ 5200] CODE SEC. 142. EXEMPT FACILITY BOND.

* * *

(f) LOCAL FURNISHING OF ELECTRIC ENERGY OR GAS.—For purposes of subsection (a)(8)—

* * *

(3) TERMINATION OF FUTURE FINANCING.—For purposes of this section, no bond may be issued as part of an issue described in subsection (a)(8) with respect to a facility for the local furnishing of electric energy or gas on or after the date of the enactment of this paragraph unless—

(A) the facility will—

(i) be used by a person who is engaged in the local furnishing of that energy source on January 1, 1997, and

(ii) be used to provide service within the area served by such person on January 1, *1997* (or within a county or city any portion of which is within such area), or

(B) the facility will be used by a successor in interest to such person for the same use and within the same service area as described in subparagraph (A).

* * *

[CCH Explanation at ¶ 30,050.]

Amendment Notes

Act Sec. 6023(5) amended Code Sec. 142(f)(3)(A)(ii) by striking "1997, (" and inserting "1997 (".

The above amendment is effective on the date of the enactment of this Act.

[¶ 5205] CODE SEC. 162. TRADE OR BUSINESS EXPENSES.

(a) IN GENERAL.—There shall be allowed as a deduction all the ordinary and necessary expenses paid or incurred during the taxable year in carrying on any trade or business, including—

(1) a reasonable allowance for salaries or other compensation for personal services actually rendered;

(2) traveling expenses (including amounts expended for meals and lodging other than amounts which are lavish or extravagant under the circumstances) while away from home in the pursuit of a trade or business; and

(3) rentals or other payments required to be made as a condition to the continued use or possession, for purposes of the trade or business, of property to which the taxpayer has not taken or is not taking title or in which he has no equity.

For purposes of the preceding sentence, the place of residence of a Member of Congress (including any Delegate and Resident Commissioner) within the State, congressional district, or possession which he represents in Congress shall be considered his home, but amounts expended by such Members within each taxable year for living expenses shall not be deductible for income tax purposes in excess of $3,000. For purposes of paragraph (2), the taxpayer shall not be treated as being temporarily away from home during any period of employment if such period exceeds 1 year. The preceding sentence shall not apply to any Federal employee during any period for which such employee is certified by the Attorney General (or the designee thereof) as traveling on behalf of the United States in temporary duty status to *investigate or prosecute, or provide support services for the investigation or prosecution of, a Federal crime.*

* * *

[CCH Explanation at ¶ 256. Committee Reports at ¶ 11,255.]

Amendment Notes

Act Sec. 6012(a) amended Code Sec. 162(a) by striking "investigate" and all that follows and inserting "investigate or prosecute, or provide support services for the investigation or prosecution of, a Federal crime." in the last sentence. Prior to amendment, the last sentence of Code Sec. 162(a) read as follows:

The preceding sentence shall not apply to any Federal employee during any period for which such employee is

certified by the Attorney General (or the designee thereof) as traveling on behalf of the United States in temporary duty status to investigate, or provide support services for the investigation of, a Federal crime.

The above amendment is effective as if included in the provision of the Taxpayer Relief Act of 1997 (P.L. 105-34) to which it relates [effective for amounts paid or incurred with respect to tax years ending after August 5, 1997.—CCH.].

[¶ 5210] CODE SEC. 168. ACCELERATED COST RECOVERY SYSTEM.

* * *

(c) APPLICABLE RECOVERY PERIOD.—For purposes of this section, the applicable recovery period shall be determined in accordance with the following table:

In the case of:	The applicable recovery period is:
3-year property	3 years
5-year property	5 years
7-year property	7 years
10-year property	10 years
15-year property	15 years
20-year property	20 years
Water utility property	25 years
Residential rental property	27.5 years
Nonresidential real property	39 years
Any railroad grading or tunnel bore	50 years

(2) *[Stricken.]*

* * *

[CCH Explanation at ¶ 571. Committee Reports at ¶ 10,950.]

Amendment Notes

Act Sec. 6006(b)(1) amended Code Sec. 168(c) by striking paragraph (2). Prior to being stricken, Code Sec. 168(c)(2) read as follows:

(2) PROPERTY FOR WHICH 150 PERCENT METHOD ELECTED.— In the case of property to which an election under subsection (b)(2)(C) applies, the applicable recovery period shall be determined under the table contained in subsection (g)(2)(C).

Act Sec. 6006(b)(2) amended Code Sec. 168(c) by striking the portion of such subsection preceding the table in paragraph (1) and inserting new material to read as above. Prior

to amendment, the portion of Code Sec. 168(c) preceding the table in paragraph (1) read as follows:

(c) APPLICABLE RECOVERY PERIOD.—For purposes of this section—

(1) IN GENERAL.—Except as provided in paragraph (2), the applicable recovery period shall be determined in accordance with the following table:

The above amendments are effective as if included in the provisions of the Taxpayer Relief Act of 1997 (P.L. 105-34) to which they relate [effective August 5, 1997.— CCH.].

[¶ 5220] CODE SEC. 170. CHARITABLE, ETC., CONTRIBUTIONS AND GIFTS.

* * *

(e) CERTAIN CONTRIBUTIONS OF ORDINARY INCOME AND CAPITAL GAIN PROPERTY.—

* * *

(6) SPECIAL RULE FOR CONTRIBUTIONS OF COMPUTER TECHNOLOGY AND EQUIPMENT FOR ELEMENTARY OR SECONDARY SCHOOL PURPOSES.—

* * *

(B) QUALIFIED ELEMENTARY OR SECONDARY EDUCATIONAL CONTRIBUTION.—For purposes of this paragraph, the term "qualified elementary or secondary educational contribution" means a charitable contribution by a corporation of any computer technology or equipment, but only if—

* * *

(iv) substantially all of the use of the property by the donee is for use within the United States for educational purposes in any of the grades K-12 that are related to the purpose or function of the *donee,*

* * *

(vi) the property will fit productively into the *donee's* education plan, and

(vii) the *donee's* use and disposition of the property will be in accordance with the provisions of clauses (iv) and (v).

(C) CONTRIBUTION TO PRIVATE FOUNDATION.—A contribution by a corporation of any computer technology or equipment to a private foundation (as defined in section 509) shall be treated as a qualified elementary or secondary educational contribution for purposes of this paragraph if—

(i) the contribution to the private foundation satisfies the requirements of clauses (ii) and (v) of subparagraph (B), and

(ii) within 30 days after such contribution, the private foundation—

(I) contributes the property to *a donee* described in clause (i) of subparagraph (B) that satisfies the requirements of clauses (iv) through (vii) of subparagraph (B), and

(II) notifies the donor of such contribution.

* * *

(F) TERMINATION.—This paragraph shall not apply to any contribution made during any taxable year beginning after December 31, *2000.*

* * *

[CCH Explanation at ¶ 696. Committee Reports at ¶ 10,855.]

Amendment Notes

Act Sec. 6004(e)(1) amended Code Sec. 170(e)(6)(B)(vi) and (vii) by striking "entity's" and inserting "donee's".

Act Sec. 6004(e)(2) amended Code Sec. 170(e)(6)(B)(iv) by striking "organization or entity" and inserting "donee".

Act Sec. 6004(e)(3) amended Code Sec. 170(e)(6)(C)(ii)(I) by striking "an entity" and inserting "a donee".

Act Sec. 6004(e)(4) amended Code Sec. 170(e)(6)(F) by striking "1999" and inserting "2000".

The above amendments are effective as if included in the provisions of the Taxpayer Relief Act of 1997 (P.L. 105-34) to which they relate [effective for tax years beginning after December 31, 1997.—CCH.].

[¶ 5230] CODE SEC. 196. DEDUCTION FOR CERTAIN UNUSED BUSINESS CREDITS.

* * *

(c) QUALIFIED BUSINESS CREDITS.—For purposes of this section, the term "qualified business credits" means—

* * *

(6) the empowerment zone employment credit determined under section 1396(a),

(7) the Indian employment credit determined under section 45A(a), *and*

(8) the employer social security credit determined under section 45B(a).

* * *

[CCH Explanation at ¶ 586. Committee Reports at ¶ 11,365.]

Amendment Notes

Act Sec. 6020(a) amended Code Sec. 196(c) by striking "and" at the end of paragraph (6), by striking the period at the end of paragraph (7) and inserting ", and", and by adding at the end a new paragraph (8) to read as above.

The above amendment is effective as if included in the amendments made by Act Sec. 13443 of the Revenue Reconciliation Act of 1993 (P.L. 103-66) [effective for taxes paid after December 31, 1993.—CCH.].

[¶ 5240] CODE SEC. 219. RETIREMENT SAVINGS.

* * *

(g) LIMITATION ON DEDUCTION FOR ACTIVE PARTICIPANTS IN CERTAIN PENSION PLANS.—

(1) IN GENERAL.—If (for any part of any plan year ending with or within a taxable year) an individual *or the individual's spouse* is an active participant, each of the dollar limitations contained in subsections (b)(1)(A) and (c)(1)(A) for such taxable year shall be reduced (but not below zero) by the amount determined under paragraph (2).

* * *

(7) SPECIAL RULE FOR SPOUSES WHO ARE NOT ACTIVE PARTICIPANTS.—If this subsection applies to an individual for any taxable year solely because their spouse is an active participant, then, in applying this subsection to the individual (but not their spouse)—

(A) the applicable dollar amount under paragraph (3)(B)(i) shall be $150,000, and

(B) the amount applicable under paragraph (2)(A)(ii) shall be $10,000.

* * *

[CCH Explanation at ¶ 356. Committee Reports at ¶ 10,875.]

Amendment Notes

Act Sec. 6005(a)(1)(A)-(B) amended Code Sec. 219(g) by inserting "or the individual's spouse" after "individual" in paragraph (1), and by striking paragraph (7) and inserting a new paragraph (7) to read as above. Prior to being stricken, Code Sec. 219(g)(7) read as follows:

(7) SPECIAL RULE FOR CERTAIN SPOUSES.—In the case of an individual who is an active participant at no time during any plan year ending with or within the taxable year but whose spouse is an active participant for any part of any such plan year—

(A) the applicable dollar amount under paragraph (3)(B)(i) with respect to the taxpayer shall be $150,000, and

(B) the amount applicable under paragraph (2)(A)(ii) shall be $10,000.

The above amendment is effective as if included in the provision of the Taxpayer Relief Act of 1997 (P.L. 105-34) to which it relates [effective for tax years beginning after December 31, 1997.—CCH.].

[¶ 5250] CODE SEC. 221. INTEREST ON EDUCATION LOANS.

* * *

(d) LIMIT ON PERIOD DEDUCTION ALLOWED.—A deduction shall be allowed under this section only with respect to interest paid on any qualified education loan during the first 60 months (whether or not consecutive) in which interest payments are required. For purposes of this paragraph, any loan and all refinancings of such loan shall be treated as 1 loan. *Such 60 months shall be determined in the manner prescribed by the Secretary in the case of multiple loans which are refinanced by, or serviced as, a single loan and in the case of loans incurred before the date of the enactment of this section.*

[CCH Explanation at ¶ 242. Committee Reports at ¶ 10,840.]

Amendment Notes

Act Sec. 6004(b)(2) amended Code Sec. 221(d) by adding at the end a new sentence to read as above.

The above amendment is effective as if included in the provision of the Taxpayer Relief Act of 1997 (P.L.

105-34) to which it relates [effective for interest payments due and paid after December 31, 1997, and the portion of the 60-month period referred to in Code Sec. 221(d) after December 31, 1997.—CCH.].

(e) DEFINITIONS.—For purposes of this section—

(1) QUALIFIED EDUCATION LOAN.—The term "qualified education loan" means any indebtedness incurred *by the taxpayer solely* to pay qualified higher education expenses—

(A) which are incurred on behalf of the taxpayer, the taxpayer's spouse, or any dependent of the taxpayer as of the time the indebtedness was incurred,

(B) which are paid or incurred within a reasonable period of time before or after the indebtedness is incurred, and

(C) which are attributable to education furnished during a period during which the recipient was an eligible student.

Such term includes indebtedness used to refinance indebtedness which qualifies as a qualified education loan. The term "qualified education loan" shall not include any indebtedness owed to a person who is related (within the meaning of section 267(b) or 707(b)(1)) to the taxpayer.

* * *

[CCH Explanation at ¶ 242. Committee Reports at ¶ 10,840.]

¶ 5240   Code Sec. 219(g)

Amendment Notes

Act Sec. 6004(b)(1) amended Code Sec. 221(e)(1) by inserting "by the taxpayer solely" after "incurred" the first place it appears.

The above amendment is effective as if included in the provision of the Taxpayer Relief Act of 1997 (P.L. 105-34) to which it relates [effective for interest payments due and paid after December 31, 1997, and the portion of the 60-month period referred to in Code Sec. 221(d) after December 31, 1997.—CCH.].

[¶ 5260] CODE SEC. 264. CERTAIN AMOUNTS PAID IN CONNECTION WITH INSURANCE CONTRACTS.

(a) GENERAL RULE.—No deduction shall be allowed for—

* * *

(3) Except as provided in *subsection (d)*, any amount paid or accrued on indebtedness incurred or continued to purchase or carry a life insurance, endowment, or annuity contract (other than a single premium contract or a contract treated as a single premium contract) pursuant to a plan of purchase which contemplates the systematic direct or indirect borrowing of part or all of the increases in the cash value of such contract (either from the insurer or otherwise).

(4) Except as provided in *subsection (e)*, any interest paid or accrued on any indebtedness with respect to 1 or more life insurance policies owned by the taxpayer covering the life of any individual, or any endowment or annuity contracts owned by the taxpayer covering any individual.

* * *

[CCH Explanation at ¶ 556. Committee Reports at ¶ 11,205.]

Amendment Notes

Act Sec. 6010(o)(1) amended Code Sec. 264(a)(3) by striking "subsection (c)" and inserting "subsection (d)".

Act Sec. 6010(o)(2) amended Code Sec. 264(a)(4) by striking "subsection (d)" and inserting "subsection (e)".

The above amendments are effective as if included in the provisions of the Taxpayer Relief Act of 1997 (P.L. 105-34) to which they relate [effective for contracts issued after June 8, 1997, in tax years ending after such date.—CCH.].

(f) PRO RATA ALLOCATION OF INTEREST EXPENSE TO POLICY CASH VALUES.—

* * *

(4) EXCEPTION FOR CERTAIN POLICIES AND CONTRACTS.—

* * *

(E) MASTER CONTRACTS.—If coverage for each insured under a master contract is treated as a separate contract for purposes of sections 817(h), 7702, and 7702A, coverage for each such insured shall be treated as a separate contract for purposes of subparagraph (A). For purposes of the preceding sentence, the term "master contract" shall not include any group life insurance contract (as defined in section 848(e)(2)).

(5) EXCEPTION FOR POLICIES AND CONTRACTS HELD BY NATURAL PERSONS; TREATMENT OF PARTNERSHIPS AND S CORPORATIONS.—

(A) POLICIES AND CONTRACTS HELD BY NATURAL PERSONS.—

* * *

(iv) REPORTING.—The Secretary shall require such reporting from policyholders and issuers as is necessary to carry out clause (ii).

* * *

(8) AGGREGATION RULES.—

(A) IN GENERAL.—All members of a controlled group (within the meaning of *subsection (e)(5)(B))* shall be treated as 1 taxpayer for purposes of this subsection.

* * *

[CCH Explanation at ¶ 556. Committee Reports at ¶ 11,205.]

Amendment Notes

Act Sec. 6010(o)(3)(A) amended Code Sec. 264(f)(4) by adding at the end a new subparagraph (E) to read as above.

Act Sec. 6010(o)(4)(A) amended Code Sec. 264(f)(5)(A)(iv) by striking the second sentence. Prior to being stricken, the second sentence of Code Sec. 264(f)(5)(A)(iv) read as follows:

Any report required under the preceding sentence shall be treated as a statement referred to in section 6724(d)(1).

Act Sec. 6010(o)(5) amended Code Sec. 264(f)(8)(A) by striking "subsection (d)(5)(B)" and inserting "subsection (e)(5)(B)".

The above amendments are effective as if included in the provisions of the Taxpayer Relief Act of 1997 (P.L. 105-34) to which they relate [effective for contracts issued after June 8, 1997, in tax years ending after such date.—CCH.].

[¶ 5270] CODE SEC. 280F. LIMITATION ON DEPRECIATION FOR LUXURY AUTOMOBILES; LIMITATION WHERE CERTAIN PROPERTY USED FOR PERSONAL PURPOSES.

(a) LIMITATION ON AMOUNT OF DEPRECIATION FOR LUXURY AUTOMOBILES.—

(1) DEPRECIATION.—

* * *

(C) SPECIAL RULE FOR CERTAIN CLEAN-FUEL PASSENGER AUTOMOBILES.—

* * *

[Caution: Code Sec. 280F(aX1XCXii), below, as added by P.L. 105-34 and amended by Act Sec. 6009(c), applies to property placed in service after August 5, 1997, and before January 1, 2005.—CCH.]

(ii) PURPOSE BUILT PASSENGER VEHICLES.—In the case of a purpose built passenger vehicle (as defined in section 4001(a)(2)(C)(ii)), each of the annual limitations specified in *subparagraphs (A) and (B)* shall be tripled.

* * *

[CCH Explanation at ¶ 592. Committee Reports at ¶ 11,105.]

Amendment Notes
Act Sec. 6009(c) amended Code Sec. 280F(a)(1)(C)(ii) by striking "subparagraph (A)" and inserting "subparagraphs (A) and (B)".
The above amendment is effective as if included in the provision of the Taxpayer Relief Act of 1997 (P.L.

105-34) to which it relates [effective for property placed in service after August 5, 1997, and before January 1, 2005.—CCH.].

[¶ 5280] CODE SEC. 304. REDEMPTION THROUGH USE OF RELATED CORPORATIONS.

* * *

(b) SPECIAL RULES FOR APPLICATION OF SUBSECTION (a).—

* * *

(5) ACQUISITIONS BY FOREIGN CORPORATIONS.—

* * *

(B) REGULATIONS.—The Secretary shall prescribe such regulations as are appropriate to carry out the purposes of this paragraph.

(6) AVOIDANCE OF MULTIPLE INCLUSIONS, ETC.—In the case of any acquisition to which subsection (a) applies in which the acquiring corporation or the issuing corporation is a foreign corporation, the Secretary shall prescribe such regulations as are appropriate in order to eliminate a multiple inclusion of any item in income by reason of this subpart and to provide appropriate basis adjustments (including modifications to the application of sections 959 and 961).

* * *

[CCH Explanation at ¶ 631. Committee Reports at ¶ 11,155.]

Amendment Notes
Act Sec. 6010(d)(1) amended Code Sec. 304(b)(5) by striking subparagraph (B) and by redesignating subparagraph (C) as subparagraph (B). Prior to being stricken, Code Sec. 304(b)(5)(B) read as follows:
(B) APPLICATION OF SECTION 1248.—For purposes of subparagraph (A), the rules of section 1248(d) shall apply except to the extent otherwise provided by the Secretary.

Act Sec. 6010(d)(2) amended Code Sec. 304(b) by adding at the end a new paragraph (6) to read as above.

The above amendments are effective as if included in the provisions of the Taxpayer Relief Act of 1997 (P.L. 105-34) to which they relate [generally effective for distributions and acquisitions after June 8, 1997.—CCH.].

[¶ 5290] CODE SEC. 351. TRANSFER TO CORPORATION CONTROLLED BY TRANSFEROR.

* * *

(c) SPECIAL RULES WHERE DISTRIBUTION TO SHAREHOLDERS.—

(1) IN GENERAL.—In determining control for purposes of this section, the fact that any corporate transferor distributes part or all of the stock in the corporation which it receives in the exchange to its shareholders shall not be taken into account.

(2) SPECIAL RULE FOR SECTION 355.—If the requirements of section 355 (or so much of section 356 as relates to section 355) are met with respect to a distribution described in paragraph (1), then, solely for purposes of determining the tax treatment of the transfers of property to the controlled corporation by the distributing corporation, the fact that the shareholders of the distributing corporation dispose of part or all of the distributed stock shall not be taken into account in determining control for purposes of this section.

* * *

[CCH Explanation at ¶ 601. Committee Reports at ¶ 11,150.]

Amendment Notes
Act Sec. 6010(c)(3)(A) amended Code Sec. 351(c) to read as above. Prior to amendment, Code Sec. 351(c) read as follows:
(c) SPECIAL RULES WHERE DISTRIBUTION TO SHAREHOLDERS.—In determining control for purposes of this section—
(1) the fact that any corporate transferor distributes part or all of the stock in the corporation which it receives in the exchange to its shareholders shall not be taken into account, and
(2) if the requirements of section 355 are met with respect to such distribution, the shareholders shall be treated as in

control of such corporation immediately after the exchange if the shareholders own (immediately after the distribution) stock possessing—
(A) more than 50 percent of the total combined voting power of all classes of stock of such corporation entitled to vote, and
(B) more than 50 percent of the total value of shares of all classes of stock of such corporation.
The above amendment is effective as if included in the provision of the Taxpayer Relief Act of 1997 (P.L. 105-34) to which it relates [generally effective for transfers after August 5, 1997.—CCH.].

(g) NONQUALIFIED PREFERRED STOCK NOT TREATED AS STOCK.—

(1) IN GENERAL.—In the case of a person who transfers property to a corporation and receives nonqualified preferred stock—

(A) subsection (a) shall not apply to such transferor, *and*

(B) *if (and only if) the transferor receives stock other than nonqualified preferred stock—*

(i) *subsection (b) shall apply to such transferor, and*

(ii) *such nonqualified preferred stock shall be treated as other property for purposes of applying subsection (b).*

* * *

[CCH Explanation at ¶ 616. Committee Reports at ¶ 11,160.]

Amendment Notes

Act Sec. 6010(e)(1) amended Code Sec. 351(g)(1) by adding "and" at the end of subparagraph (A) and by striking subparagraphs (B) and (C) and inserting a new subparagraph (B) to read as above. Prior to being stricken, Code Sec. 351(g)(1)(B)-(C) read as follows:

(B) subsection (b) shall apply to such transferor, and

(C) such nonqualified preferred stock shall be treated as other property for purposes of applying subsection (b).

The above amendment is effective as if included in the provision of the Taxpayer Relief Act of 1997 (P.L. 105-34) to which it relates [generally effective for transactions after June 8, 1997.—CCH.].

[¶ 5300] CODE SEC. 354. EXCHANGES OF STOCK AND SECURITIES IN CERTAIN REORGANIZATIONS.

(a) GENERAL RULE.—

* * *

(2) LIMITATIONS.—

* * *

(C) NONQUALIFIED PREFERRED STOCK.—

* * * .

(ii) RECAPITALIZATIONS OF FAMILY-OWNED CORPORATIONS.—

* * *

(III) *EXTENSION OF STATUTE OF LIMITATIONS.—The statutory period for the assessment of any deficiency attributable to a corporation failing to be a family-owned corporation shall not expire before the expiration of 3 years after the date the Secretary is notified by the corporation (in such manner as the Secretary may prescribe) of such failure, and such deficiency may be assessed before the expiration of such 3-year period notwithstanding the provisions of any other law or rule of law which would otherwise prevent such assessment.*

* * *

[CCH Explanation at ¶ 621. Committee Reports at ¶ 11,165.]

Amendment Notes

Act Sec. 6010(e)(2) amended Code Sec. 354(a)(2)(C)(ii) by adding at the end a new subclause (III) to read as above.

The above amendment is effective as if included in the provision of the Taxpayer Relief Act of 1997 (P.L

105-34) to which it relates [generally effective for transactions after June 8, 1997.—CCH.].

[¶ 5310] CODE SEC. 355. DISTRIBUTION OF STOCK AND SECURITIES OF A CONTROLLED CORPORATION.

* * *

(e) RECOGNITION OF GAIN ON CERTAIN DISTRIBUTIONS OF STOCK OR SECURITIES IN CONNECTION WITH ACQUISITIONS.—

* * *

(3) SPECIAL RULES RELATING TO ACQUISITIONS.—

(A) CERTAIN ACQUISITIONS NOT TAKEN INTO ACCOUNT.—Except as provided in regulations, the following acquisitions *shall not be taken into account in applying* paragraph (2)(A)(ii):

(i) The acquisition of stock in any controlled corporation by the distributing corporation.

(ii) The acquisition by a person of stock in any controlled corporation by reason of holding stock or securities in the distributing corporation.

(iii) The acquisition by a person of stock in any successor corporation of the distributing corporation or any controlled corporation by reason of holding stock or securities in such distributing or controlled corporation.

(iv) *The acquisition of stock in the distributing corporation or any controlled corporation to the extent that the percentage of stock owned directly or indirectly in such corporation by each person owning stock in such corporation immediately before the acquisition does not decrease.*

Code Sec. 355(e)   ¶ 5310

This subparagraph shall not apply to any acquisition if the stock held before the acquisition was acquired pursuant to a plan (or series of related transactions) described in paragraph (2)(A)(ii).

* * *

[CCH Explanation at ¶ 601. Committee Reports at ¶ 11,150.]

Amendment Notes

Act Sec. 6010(c)(2)(A)-(B) amended Code Sec. 355(e)(3)(A) by striking "shall not be treated as described in" and inserting "shall not be taken into account in applying", and by striking clause (iv) and inserting a new clause (iv) to read as above. Prior to being stricken, Code Sec. 355(e)(3)(A)(iv) read as follows:

(iv) The acquisition of stock in a corporation if shareholders owning directly or indirectly stock possessing—

(I) more than 50 percent of the total combined voting power of all classes of stock entitled to vote, and

(II) more than 50 percent of the total value of shares of all classes of stock,

in the distributing corporation or any controlled corporation before such acquisition own directly or indirectly stock possessing such vote and value in such distributing or controlled corporation after such acquisition.

The above amendment is effective as if included in the provision of the Taxpayer Relief Act of 1997 (P.L. 105-34) to which it relates [generally effective for distributions after April 16, 1997.—CCH.].

[¶ 5320] CODE SEC. 368. DEFINITIONS RELATING TO CORPORATE REORGANIZATIONS.

(a) REORGANIZATION.—

* * *

(2) SPECIAL RULES RELATING TO PARAGRAPH (1).—

* * *

(H) SPECIAL RULES FOR DETERMINING WHETHER CERTAIN TRANSACTIONS ARE QUALIFIED UNDER PARAGRAPH (1)(D).—For purposes of determining whether a transaction qualifies under paragraph (1)(D)—

(i) in the case of a transaction with respect to which the requirements of subparagraphs (A) and (B) of section 354(b)(1) are met, the term "control" has the meaning given such term by section 304(c), and

(ii) in the case of a transaction with respect to which the requirements of section 355 (or so much of section 356 as relates to section 355) are met, the fact that the shareholders of the distributing corporation dispose of part or all of the distributed stock shall not be taken into account.

* * *

[CCH Explanation at ¶ 601. Committee Reports at ¶ 11,150.]

Amendment Notes

Act Sec. 6010(c)(3)(B) amended Code Sec. 368(a)(2)(H)(ii) to read as above. Prior to amendment, Code Sec. 368(a)(2)(H)(ii) read as follows:

(ii) in the case of a transaction with respect to which the requirements of section 355 are met, the shareholders described in paragraph (1)(D) shall be treated as having control of the corporation to which the assets are transferred if such shareholders own (immediately after the distribution) stock possessing—

(I) more than 50 percent of the total combined voting power of all classes of stock of such corporation entitled to vote, and

(II) more than 50 percent of the total value of shares of all classes of stock of such corporation.

The above amendment is effective as if included in the provision of the Taxpayer Relief Act of 1997 (P.L. 105-34) to which it relates [generally effective for transfers after August 5, 1997.—CCH.].

[¶ 5330] CODE SEC. 402. TAXABILITY OF BENEFICIARY OF EMPLOYEES' TRUST.

* * *

(c) RULES APPLICABLE TO ROLLOVERS FROM EXEMPT TRUSTS.—

* * *

[Caution: Code Sec. 402(c)(4), below, as amended by Act Sec. 6005(c)(2)(A), applies to distributions after December 31, 1998.—CCH.]

(4) ELIGIBLE ROLLOVER DISTRIBUTION.—For purposes of this subsection, the term "eligible rollover distribution" means any distribution to an employee of all or any portion of the balance to the credit of the employee in a qualified trust; except that such term shall not include—

(A) any distribution which is one of a series of substantially equal periodic payments (not less frequently than annually) made—

(i) for the life (or life expectancy) of the employee or the joint lives (or joint life expectancies) of the employee and the employee's designated beneficiary, or

(ii) for a specified period of 10 years or more,

(B) any distribution to the extent such distribution is required under section 401(a)(9), *and*

(C) any hardship distribution described in section 401(k)(2)(B)(i)(IV).

* * *

[CCH Explanation at ¶ 361. Committee Reports at ¶ 10,895.]

Amendment Notes

Act Sec. 6005(c)(2)(A) amended Code Sec. 402(c)(4) by striking "and" at the end of subparagraph (A), by striking

the period at the end of subparagraph (B) and inserting ", and", and by inserting at the end a new subparagraph (C) to read as above.

The above amendment applies to distributions after December 31, 1998.

[¶ 5340] CODE SEC. 403. TAXATION OF EMPLOYEE ANNUITIES.
* * *

(b) TAXABILITY OF BENEFICIARY UNDER ANNUITY PURCHASED BY SECTION 501(c)(3) ORGANIZATION OR PUBLIC SCHOOL.—
* * *

(8) ROLLOVER AMOUNTS.—
* * *

[Caution: Code Sec. 403(b)(8)(B), below, as amended by Act Sec. 6005(c)(2)(B), applies to distributions after December 31, 1998.—CCH.]

(B) CERTAIN RULES MADE APPLICABLE.—Rules similar to the rules of paragraphs (2) through (7) of section 402(c) *(including paragraph (4)(C) thereof)* shall apply for purposes of subparagraph (A).
* * *

[CCH Explanation at ¶ 361. Committee Reports at ¶ 10,895.]

Amendment Notes

Act Sec. 6005(c)(2)(B) amended Code Sec. 403(b)(8)(B) by inserting "(including paragraph (4)(C) thereof)" after "section 402(c)".

The above amendment applies to distributions after December 31, 1998.

[¶ 5350] CODE SEC. 404. DEDUCTION FOR CONTRIBUTIONS OF AN EMPLOYER TO AN EMPLOYEES' TRUST OR ANNUITY PLAN AND COMPENSATION UNDER A DEFERRED-PAYMENT PLAN.

(a) GENERAL RULE.—If contributions are paid by an employer to or under a stock bonus, pension, profit-sharing, or annuity plan, or if compensation is paid or accrued on account of any employee under a plan deferring the receipt of such compensation, such contributions or compensation shall not be deductible under this chapter; but if they would otherwise be deductible, they shall be deductible under this section, subject, however, to the following limitations as to the amounts deductible in any year:
* * *

(9) CERTAIN CONTRIBUTIONS TO EMPLOYEE STOCK OWNERSHIP PLANS.—
* * *

(D) QUALIFIED GRATUITOUS TRANSFERS.—A qualified gratuitous transfer (as defined in section 664(g)(1)) shall have no effect on the amount or amounts otherwise deductible under paragraph (3) or (7) or under this paragraph.
* * *

(11) DETERMINATIONS RELATING TO DEFERRED COMPENSATION.—For purposes of determining under this section—

(A) whether compensation of an employee is deferred compensation, and

(B) when deferred compensation is paid,

no amount shall be treated as received by the employee, or paid, until it is actually received by the employee.
* * *

[CCH Explanation at ¶ 591. Committee Reports at ¶ 11,515.]

Amendment Notes

Act Sec. 6015(d) amended Code Sec. 404(a)(9) by redesignating subparagraph (C) as added by Act Sec. 1530(c)(2) of the Taxpayer Relief Act of 1997 (P.L. 105-34) as subparagraph (D) and by striking "A qualified" and inserting "QUALIFIED GRATUITOUS TRANSFERS.—A qualified".

The above amendment is effective as if included in the provision of the Taxpayer Relief Act of 1997 (P.L. 105-34) to which it relates [effective for transfers made by trusts to, or for the use of, an employee stock ownership plan after August 5, 1997.—CCH.].

Act Sec. 7001(a) amended Code Sec. 404(a) by adding at the end a new paragraph (11) to read as above.

The above amendment is generally applicable to tax years ending after the date of the enactment of this Act. For a special rule, see Act Sec. 7001(b)(2)(A)-(C), below.

Act Sec. 7001(b)(2)(A)-(C) provides:

(2) CHANGE IN METHOD OF ACCOUNTING.—In the case of any taxpayer required by the amendment made by subsection (a) to change its method of accounting for its first taxable year ending after the date of the enactment of this Act—

(A) such change shall be treated as initiated by the taxpayer,

(B) such change shall be treated as made with the consent of the Secretary of the Treasury, and

(C) the net amount of the adjustments required to be taken into account by the taxpayer under section 481 of the Internal Revenue Code of 1986 shall be taken into account ratably over the 3-taxable year period beginning with such first taxable year.

[¶ 5360] CODE SEC. 408. INDIVIDUAL RETIREMENT ACCOUNTS.
* * *

(d) TAX TREATMENT OF DISTRIBUTIONS.—
* * *

(7) SPECIAL RULES FOR SIMPLIFIED EMPLOYEE PENSIONS *OR SIMPLE RETIREMENT ACCOUNTS.*—
* * *

(B) CERTAIN EXCLUSIONS TREATED AS DEDUCTIONS.—For purposes of paragraphs (4) and (5) and section 4973, any amount excludable or excluded from gross income under section 402(h) *or 402(k)* shall be treated as an amount allowable or allowed as a deduction under section 219.
* * *

[CCH Explanation at ¶ 369.]

Amendment Notes

Act Sec. 6018(b)(1)-(2) amended Code Sec. 408(d)(7) by inserting "or 402(k)" after "section 402(h)" in subparagraph (B), and by inserting "OR SIMPLE RETIREMENT ACCOUNTS" after "PENSIONS" in the heading.

The above amendment is effective as if included in the provision of the Small Business Job Protection Act of 1996 (P.L. 104-188) to which it relates [effective for tax years beginning after December 31, 1996.—CCH.].

(p) SIMPLE RETIREMENT ACCOUNTS.—
* * *

(2) QUALIFIED SALARY REDUCTION ARRANGEMENT.—
* * *

(C) DEFINITIONS.—For purposes of this subsection—
(i) ELIGIBLE EMPLOYER.—
* * *

(II) 2-YEAR GRACE PERIOD.—An eligible employer who establishes and maintains a plan under this subsection for 1 or more years and who fails to be an eligible employer for any subsequent year shall be treated as an eligible employer for the 2 years following the last year the employer was an eligible employer. If such failure is due to any acquisition, disposition, or similar transaction involving an eligible employer, *the preceding sentence shall not apply.*
* * *

(D) ARRANGEMENT MAY BE ONLY PLAN OF EMPLOYER.—
(i) IN GENERAL.—An arrangement shall not be treated as a qualified salary reduction arrangement for any year if the employer (or any predecessor employer) maintained a qualified plan with respect to which contributions were made, or benefits were accrued, for service in any year in the period beginning with the year such arrangement became effective and ending with the year for which the determination is being made. If only individuals other than employees described in subparagraph (A) of section 410(b)(3) are eligible to participate in such arrangement, then the preceding sentence shall be applied without regard to any qualified plan in which only employees so described are eligible to participate.
* * *

(9) MATCHING CONTRIBUTIONS ON BEHALF OF SELF-EMPLOYED INDIVIDUALS NOT TREATED AS ELECTIVE EMPLOYER CONTRIBUTIONS.—Any matching contribution described in paragraph (2)(A)(iii) which is made on behalf of a self-employed individual (as defined in section 401(c)) shall not be treated as an elective employer contribution to a simple retirement account for purposes of this title.

(10) *SPECIAL RULES FOR ACQUISITIONS, DISPOSITIONS, AND SIMILAR TRANSACTIONS.—*
(A) IN GENERAL.—An employer which fails to meet any applicable requirement by reason of an acquisition, disposition, or similar transaction shall not be treated as failing to meet such requirement during the transition period if—
(i) the employer satisfies requirements similar to the requirements of section 410(b)(6)(C)(i)(II), and
(ii) the qualified salary reduction arrangement maintained by the employer would satisfy the requirements of this subsection after the transaction if the employer which maintained the arrangement before the transaction had remained a separate employer.
(B) APPLICABLE REQUIREMENT.—For purposes of this paragraph, the term "applicable requirement" means—
(i) the requirement under paragraph (2)(A)(i) that an employer be an eligible employer,
(ii) the requirement under paragraph (2)(D) that an arrangement be the only plan of an employer, and
(iii) the participation requirements under paragraph (4).
(C) TRANSITION PERIOD.—For purposes of this paragraph, the term "transition period" means the period beginning on the date of any transaction described in subparagraph (A) and ending on the last day of the second calendar year following the calendar year in which such transaction occurs.
* * *

[CCH Explanation at ¶ 366 and 368. Committee Reports at ¶ 11,325.]

¶ 5360   Code Sec. 408(p)

Amendment Notes

Act Sec. 6015(a) amended Code Sec. 408(p) by redesignating paragraph (8), as added by Act Sec. 1501(b) of the Taxpayer Relief Act of 1997 (P.L. 105-34), as paragraph (9).

Act Sec. 6016(a)(1)(A) amended Code Sec. 408(p)(2)(D)(i) by striking "or (B)" after "subparagraph (A)" in the last sentence.

Act Sec. 6016(a)(1)(B) amended Code Sec. 408(p) by adding at the end a new paragraph (10) to read as above.

Act Sec. 6016(a)(1)(C)(i)-(ii) amended Code Sec. 408(p)(2) by striking "the preceding sentence shall apply only in accordance with rules similar to the rules of section 410(b)(6)(C)(i)" in the last sentence of subparagraph (C)(i)(II) and inserting "the preceding sentence shall not

apply", and by striking clause (iii) of subparagraph (D). Prior to being stricken, Code Sec. 408(p)(2)(D)(iii) read as follows:

(iii) GRACE PERIOD.—In the case of an employer who establishes and maintains a plan under this subsection for 1 or more years and who fails to meet any requirement of this subsection for any subsequent year due to any acquisition, disposition, or similar transaction involving another such employer, rules similar to the rules of section 410(b)(6)(C) shall apply for purposes of this subsection.

The above amendments are effective as if included in the provisions of the Taxpayer Relief Act of 1997 (P.L. 105-34) to which they relate [effective for tax years beginning after December 31, 1996.—CCH.].

[¶ 5370] CODE SEC. 408A. ROTH IRAS.

* * *

(c) TREATMENT OF CONTRIBUTIONS.—

* * *

(3) LIMITS BASED ON MODIFIED ADJUSTED GROSS INCOME.—

(A) DOLLAR LIMIT.—The amount determined under paragraph (2) for any taxable year *shall not exceed an amount equal to the amount determined under paragraph (2)(A) for such taxable year, reduced* (but not below zero) by the amount which bears the same ratio to such amount as—

(i) the excess of—

(I) the taxpayer's adjusted gross income for such taxable year, over

(II) the applicable dollar amount, bears to

(ii) $15,000 ($10,000 in the case of a joint return *or a married individual filing a separate return).*

The rules of subparagraphs (B) and (C) of section 219(g)(2) shall apply to any reduction under this subparagraph.

(B) ROLLOVER FROM IRA.—A taxpayer shall not be allowed to make a qualified rollover contribution to a Roth IRA from an individual retirement plan other than a Roth IRA during any taxable year if, *for the taxable year of the distribution to which such contribution relates—*

(i) the taxpayer's adjusted gross income exceeds $100,000, or

(ii) the taxpayer is a married individual filing a separate return

(C) DEFINITIONS.—For purposes of this paragraph—

[Caution: Code Sec. 408A(c)(3)(C)(i), below, as amended by Act Sec. 7004(a), applies to tax years beginning after December 31, 2004.—CCH.]

(i) adjusted gross income shall be determined in the same manner as under section 219(g)(3), except that—

(I) any amount included in gross income under subsection (d)(3) shall not be taken into account, and

(II) any amount included in gross income by reason of a required distribution under a provision described in paragraph (5) shall not be taken into account for purposes of subparagraph (B)(i). [, and]

(ii) the applicable dollar amount is—

(I) in the case of a taxpayer filing a joint return, $150,000,

(II) in the case of any other taxpayer (other than a married individual filing a separate return), $95,000, or

(III) in the case of a married individual filing a separate return, zero.

* * *

[CCH Explanation at ¶ 321, 323, 325 and 331. Committee Reports at ¶ 10,880, 10,885, ¶ 10,890 and 11,545.]

Amendment Notes

Act Sec. 6005(b)(1) amended Code Sec. 408A(c)(3)(A) by striking "shall be reduced" and inserting "shall not exceed an amount equal to the amount determined under paragraph (2)(A) for such taxable year, reduced".

Act Sec. 6005(b)(2)(A)-(C) amended Code Sec. 408A(c)(3) by inserting "or a married individual filing a separate return" after "joint return" in subparagraph (A)(ii), by inserting ", for the taxable year of the distribution to which such contribution relates" after "if" in subparagraph (B), by striking "for such taxable year" after "gross income" in clause (i) of subparagraph (B), and by striking "and the

deduction under section 219 shall be taken into account" before ", and" in subparagraph (C)(i).

The above amendments are effective as if included in the provisions of the Taxpayer Relief Act of 1997 (P.L. 105-34) to which they relate [effective for tax years beginning after December 31, 1996.—CCH.].

Act Sec. 7004(a) amended Code Sec. 408A(c)(3)(C)(i) to read as above. Prior to amendment, Code Sec. 408A(c)(3)(C)(i) read as follows:

(i) adjusted gross income shall be determined in the same manner as under section 219(g)(3), except that any amount included in gross income under subsection (d)(3) shall not be taken into account, and

The above amendment is applicable to tax years
beginning after December 31, 2004.

(d) DISTRIBUTION RULES.—For purposes of this title—

(1) EXCLUSION.—*Any qualified distribution from a Roth IRA shall not be includible in gross income.*

(2) QUALIFIED DISTRIBUTION.—For purposes of this subsection—

* * *

(B) DISTRIBUTIONS WITHIN NONEXCLUSION PERIOD.—*A payment or distribution from a Roth IRA shall not be treated as a qualified distribution under subparagraph (A) if such payment or distribution is made within the 5-taxable year period beginning with the 1st taxable year for which the individual made a contribution to a Roth IRA (or such individual's spouse made a contribution to a Roth IRA) established for such individual.*

(C) DISTRIBUTIONS OF EXCESS CONTRIBUTIONS AND EARNINGS.—*The term "qualified distribution" shall not include any distribution of any contribution described in section 408(d)(4) and any net income allocable to the contribution.*

(3) ROLLOVERS FROM AN IRA OTHER THAN A ROTH IRA.—

(A) IN GENERAL.—Notwithstanding section 408(d)(3), in the case of any distribution to which this paragraph applies—

(i) there shall be included in gross income any amount which would be includible were it not part of a qualified rollover contribution,

(ii) section 72(t) shall not apply, and

(iii) *unless the taxpayer elects not to have this clause apply for any taxable year, any amount required to be included in gross income for such taxable year by reason of this paragraph for any distribution before January 1, 1999, shall be so included ratably over the 4-taxable year period beginning with such taxable year.*

Any election under clause (iii) for any distributions during a taxable year may not be changed after the due date for such taxable year.

* * *

(D) ADDITIONAL REPORTING REQUIREMENTS.—Trustees of Roth IRAs, trustees of individual retirement plans, or both, whichever is appropriate, shall include such additional information in reports required under section 408(i) as the Secretary may require to ensure that amounts required to be included in gross income under subparagraph (A) are so included.

(E) SPECIAL RULES FOR CONTRIBUTIONS TO WHICH 4-YEAR AVERAGING APPLIES.—*In the case of a qualified rollover contribution to a Roth IRA of a distribution to which subparagraph (A)(iii) applied, the following rules shall apply:*

(i) ACCELERATION OF INCLUSION.—

(I) IN GENERAL.—*The amount required to be included in gross income for each of the first 3 taxable years in the 4-year period under subparagraph (A)(iii) shall be increased by the aggregate distributions from Roth IRAs for such taxable year which are allocable under paragraph (4) to the portion of such qualified rollover contribution required to be included in gross income under subparagraph (A)(i).*

(II) LIMITATION ON AGGREGATE AMOUNT INCLUDED.—*The amount required to be included in gross income for any taxable year under subparagraph (A)(iii) shall not exceed the aggregate amount required to be included in gross income under subparagraph (A)(iii) for all taxable years in the 4-year period (without regard to subclause (I)) reduced by amounts included for all preceding taxable years.*

(ii) DEATH OF DISTRIBUTEE.—

(I) IN GENERAL.—*If the individual required to include amounts in gross income under such subparagraph dies before all of such amounts are included, all remaining amounts shall be included in gross income for the taxable year which includes the date of death.*

(II) SPECIAL RULE FOR SURVIVING SPOUSE.—*If the spouse of the individual described in subclause (I) acquires the individual's entire interest in any Roth IRA to which such qualified rollover contribution is properly allocable, the spouse may elect to treat the remaining amounts described in subclause (I) as includible in the spouse's gross income in the taxable years of the spouse ending with or within the taxable years of such individual in which such amounts would otherwise have been includible. Any such election may not be made or changed after the due date for the spouse's taxable year which includes the date of death.*

(F) SPECIAL RULE FOR APPLYING SECTION 72.—

(i) IN GENERAL.—*If—*

(I) *any portion of a distribution from a Roth IRA is properly allocable to a qualified rollover contribution described in this paragraph, and*

(II) such distribution is made within the 5-taxable year period beginning with the taxable year in which such contribution was made,

then section 72(t) shall be applied as if such portion were includible in gross income.

(ii) LIMITATION.—Clause (i) shall apply only to the extent of the amount of the qualified rollover contribution includible in gross income under subparagraph (A)(i).

(4) AGGREGATION AND ORDERING RULES.—

(A) AGGREGATION RULES.—Section 408(d)(2) shall be applied separately with respect to Roth IRAs and other individual retirement plans.

(B) ORDERING RULES.—For purposes of applying this section and section 72 to any distribution from a Roth IRA, such distribution shall be treated as made—

(i) from contributions to the extent that the amount of such distribution, when added to all previous distributions from the Roth IRA, does not exceed the aggregate contributions to the Roth IRA, and

(ii) from such contributions in the following order:

(I) Contributions other than qualified rollover contributions to which paragraph (3) applies.

(II) Qualified rollover contributions to which paragraph (3) applies on a first-in, first-out basis.

Any distribution allocated to a qualified rollover contribution under clause (ii)(II) shall be allocated first to the portion of such contribution required to be included in gross income.

* * *

(6) TAXPAYER MAY MAKE ADJUSTMENTS BEFORE DUE DATE.—

(A) IN GENERAL.—Except as provided by the Secretary, if, on or before the due date for any taxable year, a taxpayer transfers in a trustee-to-trustee transfer any contribution to an individual retirement plan made during such taxable year from such plan to any other individual retirement plan, then, for purposes of this chapter, such contribution shall be treated as having been made to the transferee plan (and not the transferor plan).

(B) SPECIAL RULES.—

(i) TRANSFER OF EARNINGS.—Subparagraph (A) shall not apply to the transfer of any contribution unless such transfer is accompanied by any net income allocable to such contribution.

(ii) NO DEDUCTION.—Subparagraph (A) shall apply to the transfer of any contribution only to the extent no deduction was allowed with respect to the contribution to the transferor plan.

(7) DUE DATE.—For purposes of this subsection, the due date for any taxable year is the date prescribed by law (including extensions of time) for filing the taxpayer's return for such taxable year.

* * *

[CCH Explanation at ¶ 301, 305, 311 and 315. Committee Reports at ¶ 10,890.]

Amendment Notes

Act Sec. 6005(b)(3)(A) amended Code Sec. 408A(d)(2) by striking subparagraph (B) and inserting a new subparagraph (B) to read as above. Prior to being stricken, Code Sec. 408(d)(2)(B) read as follows:

(B) CERTAIN DISTRIBUTIONS WITHIN 5 YEARS.—A payment or distribution shall not be treated as a qualified distribution under subparagraph (A) if—

(i) it is made within the 5-taxable year period beginning with the 1st taxable year for which the individual made a contribution to a Roth IRA (or such individual's spouse made a contribution to a Roth IRA) established for such individual, or

(ii) in the case of a payment or distribution properly allocable (as determined in the manner prescribed by the Secretary) to a qualified rollover contribution from an individual retirement plan other than a Roth IRA (or income allocable thereto), it is made within the 5-taxable year period beginning with the taxable year in which the rollover contribution was made.

Act Sec. 6005(b)(3)(B) amended Code Sec. 408A(d)(2) by adding at the end a new subparagraph (C) to read as above.

Act Sec. 6005(b)(4)(A)-(B) amended Code Sec. 408A(d)(3) by striking clause (iii) of subparagraph (A) and inserting a new clause (iii) and the new material that follows to read as above, and by adding at the end new subparagraphs (F) and (G) to read as above. Prior to being stricken, Code Sec. 408A(d)(3)(A)(iii) read as follows:

(iii) in the case of a distribution before January 1, 1999, any amount required to be included in gross income by reason of this paragraph shall be so included ratably over the

4-taxable year period beginning with the taxable year in which the payment or distribution is made.

Act Sec. 6005(b)(5)(A) amended Code Sec. 408A(d)(4) to read as above. Prior to amendment, Code Sec. 408A(d)(4) read as follows:

(4) COORDINATION WITH INDIVIDUAL RETIREMENT ACCOUNTS.—Section 408(d)(2) shall be applied separately with respect to Roth IRAs and other individual retirement plans.

Act Sec. 6005(b)(5)(B) amended Code Sec. 408A(d)(1) to read as above. Prior to amendment, Code Sec. 408A(d)(1) read as follows:

(1) GENERAL RULES.—

(A) EXCLUSIONS FROM GROSS INCOME.—Any qualified distribution from a Roth IRA shall not be includible in gross income.

(B) NONQUALIFIED DISTRIBUTIONS.—In applying section 72 to any distribution from a Roth IRA which is not a qualified distribution, such distribution shall be treated as made from contributions to the Roth IRA to the extent that such distribution, when added to all previous distributions from the Roth IRA, does not exceed the aggregate amount of contributions to the Roth IRA.

Act Sec. 6005(b)(6)(A) amended Code Sec. 408A(d) by adding at the end a new paragraph (6) to read as above.

Act Sec. 6005(b)(6)(B) amended Code Sec. 408A(d)(3), as amended by Act Sec. 6005(b), by striking subparagraph (D) and by redesignating subparagraphs (E), (F), and (G) as subparagraphs (D), (E), and (F), respectively. Prior to being stricken, Code Sec. 408A(d)(3)(D) read as follows:

(D) CONVERSION OF EXCESS CONTRIBUTIONS.—If, no later than the due date for filing the return of tax for any taxable year (without regard to extensions), an individual transfers, from an individual retirement plan (other than a Roth IRA), contributions for such taxable year (and any earnings allocable thereto) to a Roth IRA, no such amount shall be includible in gross income to the extent no deduction was allowed with respect to such amount.

Act Sec. 6005(b)(7) amended Code Sec. 408A(d), as amended by Act Sec. 6005(b)(6), by adding at the end a new paragraph (7) to read as above.

The above amendments are effective as if included in the provisions of the Taxpayer Relief Act of 1997 (P.L. 105-34) to which they relate [effective for tax years beginning after December 31, 1997.—CCH.].

(f) *INDIVIDUAL RETIREMENT PLAN.—For purposes of this section—*

(1) *a simplified employee pension or a simple retirement account may not be designated as a Roth IRA, and*

(2) *contributions to any such pension or account shall not be taken into account for purposes of subsection (c)(2)(B).*

[CCH Explanation at ¶ 331. Committee Reports at ¶ 10,880.]

Amendment Notes

Act Sec. 6005(b)(9) amended Code Sec. 408A by adding at the end a new subsection (f) to read as above.

The above amendment is effective as if included in the provision of the Taxpayer Relief Act of 1997 (P.L.

105-34) to which it relates [effective for tax years beginning after December 31, 1997.—CCH.].

[¶ 5380] CODE SEC. 475. MARK TO MARKET ACCOUNTING METHOD FOR DEALERS IN SECURITIES.

* * *

(c) DEFINITIONS.—For purposes of this section—

* * *

(4) *SPECIAL RULES FOR CERTAIN RECEIVABLES.—*

(A) *IN GENERAL.—Paragraph (2)(C) shall not include any nonfinancial customer paper.*

(B) *NONFINANCIAL CUSTOMER PAPER.— For purposes of subparagraph (A), the term "nonfinancial customer paper" means any receivable which—*

(i) *is a note, bond, debenture, or other evidence of indebtedness,*

(ii) *arises out of the sale of nonfinancial goods or services by a person the principal activity of which is the selling or providing of nonfinancial goods or services, and*

(iii) *is held by such person (or a person who bears a relationship to such person described in section 267(b) or 707(b)) at all times since issue.*

* * *

[CCH Explanation at ¶ 554. Committee Reports at ¶ 11,535.]

Amendment Notes

Act Sec. 7003(a) amended Code Sec. 475(c) by adding at the end a new paragraph (4) to read as above.

The above amendment generally applies to tax years ending after the date of the enactment of this Act. For a special rule, see Act Sec. 7003(c)(2)(A)-(C), below.

Act Sec. 7003(c)(2)(A)-(C) provides:

(2) CHANGE IN METHOD OF ACCOUNTING.—In the case of any taxpayer required by the amendments made by this section to change its method of accounting for its first taxable year ending after the date of the enactment of this Act—

(A) such change shall be treated as initiated by the taxpayer,

(B) such change shall be treated as made with the consent of the Secretary of the Treasury, and

(C) the net amount of the adjustments required to be taken into account by the taxpayer under section 481 of the Internal Revenue Code of 1986 shall be taken into account ratably over the 4-taxable year period beginning with such first taxable year.

(f) ELECTION OF MARK TO MARKET FOR TRADERS IN SECURITIES OR COMMODITIES.—

(1) TRADERS IN SECURITIES.—

* * *

(D) OTHER RULES TO APPLY.—Rules similar to the rules of subsections (b)(4) and (d) shall apply to securities held by a person in any trade or business with respect to which an election under this paragraph is in effect. *Subsection (d)(3) shall not apply under the preceding sentence for purposes of applying sections 1402 and 7704.*

* * *

[CCH Explanation at ¶ 551. Committee Reports at ¶ 11,135.]

Amendment Notes

Act Sec. 6010(a)(3) amended Code Sec. 475(f)(1)(D) by adding at the end a new sentence to read as above.

The above amendment is effective as if included in the provision of the Taxpayer Relief Act of 1997 (P.L.

105-34) to which it relates [generally effective for tax years ending fter August 5, 1997.—CCH.].

(g) REGULATORY AUTHORITY.—The Secretary shall prescribe such regulations as may be necessary or appropriate to carry out the purposes of this section, including rules—

(1) to prevent the use of year-end transfers, related parties, or other arrangements to avoid the provisions of this section,

(2) to provide for the application of this section to any security which is a hedge which cannot be identified with a specific security, position, right to income, or liability, *and*

(3) *to prevent the use by taxpayers of subsection (c)(4) to avoid the application of this section to a receivable that is inventory in the hands of the taxpayer (or a person who bears a relationship to the taxpayer described in sections 267(b) of [or] 707(b)).*

[CCH Explanation at ¶ 554. Committee Reports at ¶ 11,535.]

Amendment Notes

Act Sec. 7003(b) amended Code Sec. 475(g) by striking "and" at the end of paragraph (1), by striking the period at the end of paragraph (2) and inserting ", and", and by adding at the end a new paragraph (3) to read as above.

The above amendment generally applies to tax years ending after the date of the enactment of this Act. For a special rule, see Act Sec. 7003(c)(2)(A)-(C), below.

Act Sec. 7003(c)(2)(A)-(C) provides:

(2) CHANGE IN METHOD OF ACCOUNTING.—In the case of any taxpayer required by the amendments made by this section to change its method of accounting for its first taxable year ending after the date of the enactment of this Act—

(A) such change shall be treated as initiated by the taxpayer,

(B) such change shall be treated as made with the consent of the Secretary of the Treasury, and

(C) the net amount of the adjustments required to be taken into account by the taxpayer under section 481 of the Internal Revenue Code of 1986 shall be taken into account ratably over the 4-taxable year period beginning with such first taxable year.

[¶ 5390] CODE SEC. 501. EXEMPTION FROM TAX ON CORPORATIONS, CERTAIN TRUSTS, ETC.

* * *

(n) CHARITABLE RISK POOLS.—

* * *

(3) ORGANIZATIONAL REQUIREMENTS.—An organization (hereinafter in this subsection referred to as the "risk pool") meets the organizational requirements of this paragraph if—

(A) such risk pool is organized as a nonprofit organization under State law provisions authorizing risk pooling arrangements for charitable organizations,

(B) such risk pool is exempt from any income tax imposed by the State (or will be so exempt after such pool qualifies as an organization exempt from tax under this title),

(C) such risk pool has obtained at least $1,000,000 in startup capital from nonmember charitable organizations,

(D) such risk pool is controlled by a board of directors elected by its members, and

(E) the organizational documents of such risk pool require that—

(i) each member of such pool shall at all times be an organization described in subsection (c)(3) and exempt from tax under subsection (a),

(ii) any member which receives a final determination that it no longer qualifies as an organization described in subsection (c)(3) shall immediately notify the pool of such determination and the effective date of such determination, and

(iii) each policy of insurance issued by the risk pool shall provide that such policy will not cover the insured with respect to events occurring after the date such final determination was issued to the insured.

An organization shall not cease to qualify as a qualified charitable risk pool solely by reason of the failure of any of its members to continue to be an organization described in subsection (c)(3) if, within a reasonable period of time after such pool is notified as required under *subparagraph (E)(ii),* such pool takes such action as may be reasonably necessary to remove such member from such pool.

* * *

[CCH Explanation at ¶ 30,050.]

Amendment Notes

Act Sec. 6023(6) amended the last sentence of paragraph (3) of Code Sec. 501(n) by striking "subparagraph (C)(ii)" and inserting "subparagraph (E)(ii)".

The above amendment is effective on the date of the enactment of this Act.

(o) TREATMENT OF HOSPITALS PARTICIPATING IN PROVIDER-SPONSORED ORGANIZATIONS.—An organization shall not fail to be treated as organized and operated exclusively for a charitable purpose for purposes of subsection (c)(3) solely because a hospital which is owned and operated by such organization participates in a provider-sponsored organization (as defined in *section 1855(d)* of the Social Security Act), whether or not the provider-sponsored organization is exempt from tax. For purposes of subsection (c)(3), any person with a material financial interest in such a provider-sponsored organization shall be treated as a private shareholder or individual with respect to the hospital.

* * *

[CCH Explanation at ¶ 30,050.]

Amendment Notes

Act Sec. 6023(7) amended Code Sec. 501(o) by striking "section 1853(e)" and inserting "section 1855(d)".

The above amendment is effective on the date of the enactment of this Act.

[¶ 5400] CODE SEC. 512. UNRELATED BUSINESS TAXABLE INCOME.

* * *

(b) MODIFICATIONS.—The modifications referred to in subsection (a) are the following:

* * *

(13) SPECIAL RULES FOR CERTAIN AMOUNTS RECEIVED FROM CONTROLLED ENTITIES.—

(A) IN GENERAL.—If an organization (in this paragraph referred to as the "controlling organization") receives *or accrues* (directly or indirectly) a specified payment from another entity which it controls (in this paragraph referred to as the "controlled entity"), notwithstanding paragraphs (1), (2), and (3), the controlling organization shall include such payment as an item of gross income derived from an unrelated trade or business to the extent such payment reduces the net unrelated income of the controlled entity (or increases any net unrelated loss of the controlled entity). There shall be allowed all deductions of the controlling organization directly connected with amounts treated as derived from an unrelated trade or business under the preceding sentence.

(B) NET UNRELATED INCOME OR LOSS.—For purposes of this paragraph—

(i) NET UNRELATED INCOME.—The term "net unrelated income" means—

(I) in the case of a controlled entity which is not exempt from tax under section 501(a), the portion of such entity's taxable income which would be unrelated business taxable income if such entity were exempt from tax under section 501(a) and had the same exempt purposes as the controlling organization, or

* * *

(17) TREATMENT OF CERTAIN AMOUNTS DERIVED FROM FOREIGN CORPORATIONS.—

* * *

(B) EXCEPTION.—

* * *

(ii) AFFILIATE.—For purposes of this subparagraph—

* * *

(II) SPECIAL *RULE*.—Two or more organizations (and any affiliates of such organizations) shall be treated as affiliates if such organizations are colleges or universities described in section 170(b)(1)(A)(ii) or organizations described in section 170(b)(1)(A)(iii) and participate in an insurance arrangement that provides for any profits from such arrangement to be returned to the policyholders in their capacity as such.

* * *

[CCH Explanation at ¶ 686 and 30,050. Committee Reports at ¶ 11,190.]

Amendment Notes

Act Sec. 6010(j)(1) amended Code Sec. 512(b)(13)(A) by inserting "or accrues" after "receives".

Act Sec. 6010(j)(2) amended Code Sec. 512(b)(13)(B)(i)(I) by striking "(as defined in section 513A(a)(5)(A))" after "purposes".

The above amendments are effective as if included in the provisions of the Taxpayer Relief Act of 1997 (P.L.

105-34) to which they relate [generally effective for tax years beginning after August 5, 1997.—CCH.].

Act Sec. 6023(8) amended the heading for Code Sec. 512(b)(17)(B)(ii)(II) by striking "RULE" and inserting "RULE".

The above amendment is effective on the date of the enactment of this Act.

[¶ 5410] CODE SEC. 529. QUALIFIED STATE TUITION PROGRAMS.

* * *

(c) TAX TREATMENT OF DESIGNATED BENEFICIARIES AND CONTRIBUTORS.—

* * *

(3) DISTRIBUTIONS.—

(A) IN GENERAL.—Any distribution under a qualified State tuition program shall be includible in the gross income of the distributee in the manner as provided under *section 72* to the extent not excluded from gross income under any other provision of this chapter.

* * *

[CCH Explanation at ¶ 228. Committee Reports at ¶ 10,850.]

Amendment Notes

Act Sec. 6004(c)(2) amended Code Sec. 529(c)(3)(A) by striking "section 72(b)" and inserting "section 72".

The above amendment is effective as if included in the provision of the Taxpayer Relief Act of 1997 (P.L.

105-34) to which it relates [generally effective January 1, 1998.—CCH.].

(e) OTHER DEFINITIONS AND SPECIAL RULES.—For purposes of this section—

* * *

(2) MEMBER OF FAMILY.—The term "member of the family" means, with respect to any designated beneficiary—

(A) the spouse of such beneficiary,

(B) an individual who bears a relationship to such beneficiary which is described in paragraphs (1) through (8) of section 152(a), and

(C) the spouse of any individual described in subparagraph (B).

* * *

[CCH Explanation at ¶ 228. Committee Reports at ¶ 10,850.]

Amendment Notes

Act Sec. 6004(c)(3) amended Code Sec. 529(e)(2) to read as above. Prior to amendment, Code Sec. 529(e)(2) read as follows:

(2) MEMBER OF FAMILY.—The term "member of the family" means—

(A) an individual who bears a relationship to another individual which is a relationship described in paragraphs (1) through (8) of section 152(a), and

(B) the spouse of any individual described in subparagraph (A).

The above amendment is effective as if included in the provision of the Taxpayer Relief Act of 1997 (P.L. 105-34) to which it relates [generally effective January 1, 1998.—CCH.].

[¶ 5420] CODE SEC. 530. EDUCATION INDIVIDUAL RETIREMENT ACCOUNTS.

* * *

(b) DEFINITIONS AND SPECIAL RULES.—For purposes of this section—

(1) EDUCATION INDIVIDUAL RETIREMENT ACCOUNT.—The term "education individual retirement account" means a trust created or organized in the United States exclusively for the purpose of paying the qualified higher education expenses of *an individual who is* the designated beneficiary of the trust (and designated as an education individual retirement account at the time created or organized), but only if the written governing instrument creating the trust meets the following requirements:

* * *

(E) Except as provided in subsection (d)(7), any balance to the credit of the designated beneficiary on the date on which the beneficiary attains age 30 shall be distributed within 30 days after such date to the beneficiary or, if the beneficiary dies before attaining age 30, shall be distributed within 30 days after the date of death of such beneficiary.

* * *

[CCH Explanation at ¶ 236. Committee Reports at ¶ 10,845.]

Amendment Notes

Act Sec. 6004(d)(1) amended Code Sec. 530(b)(1) by inserting "an individual who is" before "the designated beneficiary" in the material preceding subparagraph (A).

Act Sec. 6004(d)(2)(A) amended Code Sec. 530(b)(1)(E) to read as above. Prior to amendment, Code Sec. 530(b)(1)(E) read as follows:

(E) Upon the death of the designated beneficiary, any balance to the credit of the beneficiary shall be distributed

within 30 days after the date of death to the estate of such beneficiary.

The above amendments are effective as if included in the provisions of the Taxpayer Relief Act of 1997 (P.L. 105-34) to which they relate [effective for tax years beginning after December 31, 1997.—CCH.].

(d) TAX TREATMENT OF DISTRIBUTIONS.—

(1) IN GENERAL.—Any distribution shall be includible in the gross income of the distributee in the manner as provided in *section 72.*

(2) DISTRIBUTIONS FOR QUALIFIED HIGHER EDUCATION EXPENSES.—

* * *

(D) DISALLOWANCE OF EXCLUDED AMOUNTS AS CREDIT OR DEDUCTION.—No deduction or credit shall be allowed to the taxpayer under any other section of this chapter for any qualified education expenses to the extent taken into account in determining the amount of the exclusion under this paragraph.

* * *

(4) ADDITIONAL TAX FOR DISTRIBUTIONS NOT USED FOR EDUCATIONAL EXPENSES.—

* * *

(B) EXCEPTIONS.—Subparagraph (A) shall not apply if the payment or distribution is—

(i) made to a beneficiary (or to the estate of the designated beneficiary) on or after the death of the designated beneficiary,

(ii) attributable to the designated beneficiary's being disabled (within the meaning of section 72(m)(7)),

(iii) made on account of a scholarship, allowance, or payment described in section 25A(g)(2) received by the account holder to the extent the amount of the payment or distribution does not exceed the amount of the scholarship, allowance, or payment, *or*

(iv) an amount which is includible in gross income solely because the taxpayer elected under paragraph (2)(C) to waive the application of paragraph (2) for the taxable year.

(C) CONTRIBUTIONS RETURNED BEFORE DUE DATE OF RETURN.—Subparagraph (A) shall not apply to the distribution of any contribution made during a taxable year on behalf of the designated beneficiary if—

(i) such distribution is made on or before the day prescribed by law (including extensions of time) for filing the beneficiary's return of tax for the taxable year or, if the beneficiary is not required to file such a return, the 15th day of the 4th month of the taxable year following the taxable year, and

(ii) such distribution is accompanied by the amount of net income attributable to such excess contribution.

Any net income described in clause (ii) shall be included in gross income for the taxable year in which such excess contribution was made.

(5) ROLLOVER CONTRIBUTIONS.—*Paragraph (1) shall not apply to any amount paid or distributed from an education individual retirement account to the extent that the amount received is paid, not later than the 60th day after the date of such payment or distribution, into another education individual retirement account for the benefit of the same beneficiary or a member of the family (within the meaning of section 529(e)(2)) of such beneficiary who has not attained age 30 as of such date.* The preceding sentence shall not apply to any payment or distribution if it applied to any prior payment or, distribution during the 12-month period ending on the date of the payment or distribution.

(6) CHANGE IN BENEFICIARY.—Any change in the beneficiary of an education individual retirement account shall not be treated as a distribution for purposes of paragraph (1) if the new beneficiary is a member of the family (as so defined) of the old beneficiary *and has not attained age 30 as of the date of such change.*

(7) SPECIAL RULES FOR DEATH AND DIVORCE.—Rules similar to the rules of paragraphs (7) and (8) of section 220(f) shall apply. *In applying the preceding sentence, members of the family (as so defined) of the designated beneficiary shall be treated in the same manner as the spouse under such paragraph (8).*

(8) *DEEMED DISTRIBUTION ON REQUIRED DISTRIBUTION DATE.—In any case in which a distribution is required under subsection (b)(1)(E), any balance to the credit of a designated beneficiary as of the close of the 30-day period referred to in such subsection for making such distribution shall be deemed distributed at the close of such period.*

* * *

[CCH Explanation at ¶ 236. Committee Reports at ¶ 10,845.]

Amendment Notes

Act Sec. 6004(d)(2)(B) amended Code Sec. 530(d)(7) by inserting at the end a new sentence to read as above.

Act Sec. 6004(d)(2)(C) amended Code Sec. 530(d) by adding at the end a new paragraph (8) to read as above.

Act Sec. 6004(d)(3)(A) amended Code Sec. 530(d)(1) by striking "section 72(b)" and inserting "section 72".

Act Sec. 6004(d)(5) amended Code Sec. 530(d)(2) by adding at the end a new subparagraph (D) to read as above.

Act Sec. 6004(d)(6) amended Code Sec. 530(d)(4)(B) by striking "or" at the end of clause (ii), by striking the period at the end of clause (iii) and inserting ", or", and by adding at the end a new clause (iv) to read as above.

Act Sec. 6004(d)(7) amended so much of Code Sec. 530(d)(4)(C) as precedes clause (ii) to read as above. Prior to amendment, so much of Code Sec. 530(d)(4)(C) as preceded clause (ii) read as follows:

(C) EXCESS CONTRIBUTIONS RETURNED BEFORE DUE DATE OF RETURN.—Subparagraph (A) shall not apply to the distribution of any contribution made during a taxable year on behalf of a designated beneficiary to the extent that such contribution exceeds $500 if—

(i) such distribution is received on or before the day prescribed by law (including extensions of time) for filing such contributor's return for such taxable year, and

Act Sec. 6004(d)(8)(A) amended Code Sec. 530(d)(5) by striking the first sentence and inserting a new sentence to read as above. Prior to amendment, the first sentence of Code Sec. 530(d)(5) read as follows:

Paragraph (1) shall not apply to any amount paid or distributed from an education individual retirement account to the extent that the amount received is paid into another education individual retirement account for the benefit of the same beneficiary or a member of the family (within the meaning of section 529(e)(2)) of such beneficiary not later than the 60th day after the date of such payment or distribution.

Act Sec. 6004(d)(8)(B) amended Code Sec. 530(d)(6) by inserting "and has not attained age 30 as of the date of such change" before the period.

The above amendments are effective as if included in the provisions of the Taxpayer Relief Act of 1997 (P.L. 105-34) to which they relate [effective for tax years beginning after December 31, 1997.—CCH.].

[¶ 5430] CODE SEC. 543. PERSONAL HOLDING COMPANY INCOME.

* * *

(d) ACTIVE BUSINESS COMPUTER SOFTWARE ROYALTIES.—

* * *

(5) DIVIDENDS MUST EQUAL OR EXCEED EXCESS OF PERSONAL HOLDING COMPANY INCOME OVER 10 PERCENT OF ORDINARY GROSS INCOME.—

(A) IN GENERAL.—The requirements of this paragraph are met if the sum of—

(i) the dividends paid during the taxable year (determined under section 562),

(ii) the dividends considered as paid on the last day of the taxable year under *section 563(d)* (as limited by the second sentence of section 563(b)), and

(iii) the consent dividends for the taxable year (determined under section 565),

equals or exceeds the amount, if any, by which the personal holding company income for the taxable year exceeds 10 percent of the ordinary gross income of such corporation for such taxable year.

* * *

[CCH Explanation at ¶ 30,050.]

Amendment Notes

Act Sec. 6023(9) amended Code Sec. 543(d)(5)(A)(ii) by striking "section 563(c)" and inserting "section 563(d)".

The above amendment is effective on the date of the enactment of this Act.

[¶ 5440] CODE SEC. 641. IMPOSITION OF TAX.
* * *

(c) SPECIAL RULES FOR TAXATION OF ELECTING SMALL BUSINESS TRUSTS.—
* * *

Amendment Notes

Act Sec. 6007(f)(2) amended Code Sec. 641 by striking subsection (c) and by redesignating subsection (d) as subsection (c). Prior to being stricken, Code Sec. 641(c) read as follows:

(c) EXCLUSION OF INCLUDIBLE GAIN FROM TAXABLE INCOME.—

(1) GENERAL RULE.—For purposes of this part, the taxable income of a trust does not include the amount of any includible gain as defined in section 644(b) reduced by any deductions properly allocable thereto.

(2) CROSS REFERENCE.—

For the taxation of any includible gain, see section 644.

The above amendment is effective as if included in the provision of the Taxpayer Relief Act of 1997 (P.L. 105-34) to which it relates [effective for sales or exchanges after August 5, 1997.—CCH.].

[¶ 5450] CODE SEC. 645. CERTAIN REVOCABLE TRUSTS TREATED AS PART OF ESTATE.
* * *

[CCH Explanation at ¶ 433. Committee Reports at ¶ 11,275.]

Amendment Notes

Act Sec. 6013(a)(1) redesignated Code Sec. 646 as Code Sec. 645.

The above amendment is effective as if included in the provision of the Taxpayer Relief Act of 1997 (P.L. 105-34) to which it relates [effective for estates of decedents dying after August 5, 1997.—CCH.].

[¶ 5470] CODE SEC. 664. CHARITABLE REMAINDER TRUSTS.
* * *

(d) DEFINITIONS.—

(1) CHARITABLE REMAINDER ANNUITY TRUST.—For purposes of this section, a charitable remainder annuity trust is a trust—

(A) from which a sum certain (which is not less than 5 percent nor more than 50 percent of the initial net fair market value of all property placed in trust) is to be paid, not less often than annually, to one or more persons (at least one of which is not an organization described in section 170(c) and, in the case of individuals, only to an individual who is living at the time of the creation of the trust) for a term of years (not in excess of 20 years) or for the life or lives of such individual or individuals,

(B) from which no amount other than the payments described in subparagraph (A) and other than qualified gratuitous transfers described in subparagraph (C) may be paid to or for the use of any person other than an organization described in section 170(c),

(C) following the termination of the payments described in subparagraph (A), the remainder interest in the trust is to be transferred to, or for the use of, an organization described in section 170(c) or is to be retained by the trust for such a use or, to the extent the remainder interest is in qualified employer securities (as defined in subsection (g)(4)), all or part of such securities are to be transferred to an employee stock ownership plan (as defined in section 4975(e)(7)) in a qualified gratuitous transfer (as defined by subsection (g)), *and*

(D) the value (determined under section 7520) of such remainder interest is at least 10 percent of the initial net fair market value of all property placed in the trust.

(2) CHARITABLE REMAINDER UNITRUST.—For purposes of this section, a charitable remainder unitrust is a trust—

(A) from which a fixed percentage (which is not less than 5 percent nor more than 50 percent) of the net fair market value of its assets, valued annually, is to be paid, not less often than annually, to one or more persons (at least one of which is not an organization described in section 170(c) and, in the case of individuals, only to an individual who is living at the time of the creation of the trust) for a term of years (not in excess of 20 years) or for the life or lives of such individual or individuals,

(B) from which no amount other than the payments described in subparagraph (A) and other than qualified gratuitous transfers described in subparagraph (C) may be paid to or for the use of any person other than an organization described in section 170(c),

(C) following the termination of the payments described in subparagraph (A), the remainder interest in the trust is to be transferred to, or for the use of, an organization described in section 170(c) or is to be retained by the trust for such a use or, to the extent the remainder interest is in qualified employer securities (as defined in subsection (g)(4)), all or part of such securities are to be transferred to an employee stock ownership plan (as defined in section 4975(e)(7)) in a qualified gratuitous transfer (as defined by subsection (g)), *and*

(D) with respect to each contribution of property to the trust, the value (determined under section 7520) of such remainder interest in such property is at least 10 percent of the net fair market value of such property as of the date such property is contributed to the trust.

* * *

Amendment Notes
Act Sec. 6010(r) amended Code Sec. 664(d)(1)(C) and (2)(C) by adding ", and" at the end.
The above amendment is effective as if included in the provision of the Taxpayer Relief Act of 1997 (P.L. 105-34) to which it relates [generally effective for transfers in trust after July 28, 1997.—CCH.].

[¶ 5480] CODE SEC. 672. DEFINITIONS AND RULES.

* * *

(f) Subpart Not to Result in Foreign Ownership.—

* * *

(3) Special Rules.—Except as otherwise provided in regulations prescribed by the Secretary—

(A) a controlled foreign corporation (as defined in section 957) shall be treated as a domestic corporation for purposes of paragraph (1), and

(B) paragraph (1) shall not apply for purposes of applying *section 1297.*

* * *

Amendment Notes
Act Sec. 6011(c)(1) amended Code Sec. 672(f)(3)(B) by striking "section 1296" and inserting "section 1297".
The above amendment is effective as if included in the provision of the Taxpayer Relief Act of 1997 (P.L. 105-34) to which it relates [effective for tax years of U.S. persons beginning after December 31, 1997, and tax years of foreign corporations ending with or within such tax years of U.S. persons.—CCH.].

[¶ 5490] CODE SEC. 685. TREATMENT OF FUNERAL TRUSTS.

* * *

(b) Qualified Funeral Trust.—For purposes of this subsection, the term "qualified funeral trust" means any trust (other than a foreign trust) if—

(1) the trust arises as a result of a contract with a person engaged in the trade or business of providing funeral or burial services or property necessary to provide such services,

(2) the sole purpose of the trust is to hold, invest, and reinvest funds in the trust and to use such funds solely to make payments for such services or property for the benefit of the beneficiaries of the trust,

(3) the only beneficiaries of such trust are individuals with respect to whom such services or property are to be provided at their death under contracts described in paragraph (1),

(4) the only contributions to the trust are contributions by or for the benefit of such beneficiaries,

(5) the trustee elects the application of this subsection, and

(6) the trust would (but for the election described in paragraph (5)) be treated as owned under subpart E by the purchasers of the contracts described in paragraph (1).

A trust shall not fail to be treated as meeting the requirement of paragraph (6) by reason of the death of an individual but only during the 60-day period beginning on the date of such death.

* * *

[CCH Explanation at ¶ 456. Committee Reports at ¶ 11,280.]

Amendment Notes
Act Sec. 6013(b)(1) amended Code Sec. 685(b) by adding at the end a new flush sentence to read as above.
The above amendment is effective as if included in the provision of the Taxpayer Relief Act of 1997 (P.L. 105-34) to which it relates [effective for tax years ending after August 5, 1997.—CCH.].

(f) Simplified Reporting.—The Secretary may prescribe rules for simplified reporting of all trusts having a single trustee *and of trusts terminated during the year.*

[CCH Explanation at ¶ 456. Committee Reports at ¶ 11,280.]

Amendment Notes
Act Sec. 6013(b)(2) amended Code Sec. 685(f) by inserting before the period at the end "and of trusts terminated during the year".
The above amendment is effective as if included in the provision of the Taxpayer Relief Act of 1997 (P.L. 105-34) to which it relates [effective for tax years ending after August 5, 1997.—CCH.].

[¶ 5500] CODE SEC. 751. UNREALIZED RECEIVABLES AND INVENTORY ITEMS.

* * *

(c) Unrealized Receivables.—For purposes of this subchapter, the term "unrealized receivables" includes, to the extent not previously includible in income under the method of accounting used by the partnership, any rights (contractual or otherwise) to payment for—

(1) goods delivered, or to be delivered, to the extent the proceeds therefrom would be treated as amounts received from the sale or exchange of property other than a capital asset, or

(2) services rendered, or to be rendered.

For purposes of this section and, sections *731, 732,* and 741 (but not for purposes of section 736), such term also includes mining property (as defined in section 617(f)(2)), stock in a DISC (as described in section 992(a)), section 1245 property (as defined in section 1245(a)(3)), stock in certain foreign corporations (as described in section 1248), section 1250 property (as defined in section 1250(c)), farm land (as defined in section 1252(a)), franchises, trademarks, or trade names (referred to in section 1253(a)), and an oil, gas, or geothermal property (described in section 1254) but only to the extent of the amount which would be treated as gain to which section 617(d)(1), 995(c), 1245(a), 1248(a), 1250(a), 1252(a), 1253(a) or 1254(a) would apply if (at the time of the transaction described in this section or section *731, 732,* or 741, as the case may be) such property had been sold by the partnership at its fair market value. For purposes of this section and, sections *731, 732,* and 741 (but not for purposes of section 736), such term also includes any market discount bond (as defined in section 1278) and any short-term obligation (as defined in section 1283) but only to the extent of the amount which would be treated as ordinary income if (at the time of the transaction described in this section or section *731, 732,* or 741, as the case may be) such property had been sold by the partnership.

* * *

[CCH Explanation at ¶ 681. Committee Reports at ¶ 11,200.]

Amendment Notes

Act Sec. 6010(m) amended Code Sec. 751(c) by striking "731" each place it appears and inserting "731, 732,".

The above amendment is effective as if included in the provision of the Taxpayer Relief Act of 1997 (P.L.

105-34) to which it relates [effective for distributions after August 5, 1997.—CCH.].

[¶ 5510] CODE SEC. 774. OTHER MODIFICATIONS.

* * *

(d) PARTNERSHIP ENTITLED TO CERTAIN CREDITS.—The following shall be allowed to an electing large partnership and shall not be taken into account by the partners of such partnership:

(1) The credit provided by section 34.

(2) Any credit or refund under section 852(b)(3)(D) *or 857(b)(3)(D).*

* * *

Amendment Notes

Act Sec. 6012(c) amended Code Sec. 774(d)(2) by inserting before the period "or 857(b)(3)(D)".

The above amendment is effective as if included in the provision of the Taxpayer Relief Act of 1997 (P.L.

105-34) to which it relates [effective for partnership tax years beginning after December 31, 1997.—CCH.].

[¶ 5520] CODE SEC. 853. FOREIGN TAX CREDIT ALLOWED TO SHAREHOLDERS.

* * *

(c) NOTICE TO SHAREHOLDERS.—The amounts to be treated by the shareholder, for purposes of subsection (b) (2), as his proportionate share of—

(1) taxes paid to any foreign country or possession of the United States, and

(2) gross income derived from sources within any foreign country or possession of the United States,

shall not exceed the amounts so designated by the company in a written notice mailed to its shareholders not later than 60 days after the close of its taxable year.

* * *

[CCH Explanation at ¶ 666. Committee Reports at ¶ 11,195.]

Amendment Notes

Act Sec. 6010(k)(2) amended Code Sec. 853(c) by striking the last sentence. Prior to being stricken, the last sentence of Code Sec. 853(c) read as follows:

Such notice shall also include the amount of such taxes which (without regard to the election under this section)

would not be allowable as a credit under section 901(a) to the regulated investment company by reason of section 901(k).

The above amendment is effective as if included in the provision of the Taxpayer Relief Act of 1997 (P.L. 105-34) to which it relates [effective for dividends paid or accrued after September 4, 1997.—CCH.].

(e) *TREATMENT OF TAXES NOT ALLOWED AS A CREDIT UNDER SECTION 901(k).—This section shall not apply to any tax with respect to which the regulated investment company is not allowed a credit under section 901 by reason of section 901(k).*

[CCH Explanation at ¶ 666. Committee Reports at ¶ 11,195.]

Amendment Notes

Act Sec. 6010(k)(1) amended Code Sec. 853 by redesignating subsection (e) as subsection (f) and by inserting after subsection (d) a new subsection (e) to read as above.

The above amendment is effective as if included in the provision of the Taxpayer Relief Act of 1997 (P.L. 105-34) to which it relates [effective for dividends paid or accrued after September 4, 1997.—CCH.].

(f) CROSS REFERENCES.—

* * *

[CCH Explanation at ¶ 666. Committee Reports at ¶ 11,195.]

Amendment Notes

Act Sec. 6010(k)(1) amended Code Sec. 853 by redesignating subsection (e) as subsection (f).

The above amendment is effective as if included in the provision of the Taxpayer Relief Act of 1997 (P.L. 105-34) to which it relates [effective for dividends paid or accrued after September 4, 1997.—CCH.].

[¶ 5530] CODE SEC. 857. TAXATION OF REAL ESTATE INVESTMENT TRUSTS AND THEIR BENEFICIARIES.

* * *

(d) EARNINGS AND PROFITS.—

* * *

(3) DISTRIBUTIONS TO MEET REQUIREMENTS OF SUBSECTION (a)(2)(B).—Any distribution which is made in order to comply with the requirements of subsection (a)(2)(B)—

(A) shall be treated for purposes of this subsection and subsection (a)(2)(B) as made from the *earliest earnings and profits accumulated in any taxable year to which the provisions of this part did not apply* rather than the most recently accumulated earnings and profits, and

(B) to the extent treated under subparagraph (A) as made from accumulated earnings and profits, shall not be treated as a distribution for purposes of subsection (b)(2)(B).

* * *

[CCH Explanation at ¶ 661. Committee Reports at ¶ 11,270.]

Amendment Notes

Act Sec. 6012(g) amended Code Sec. 857(d)(3)(A) by striking "earliest accumulated earnings and profits (other than earnings and profits to which subsection (a)(2)(A) applies)" and inserting "earliest earnings and profits accumulated in any taxable year to which the provisions of this part did not apply".

The above amendment is effective as if included in the provision of the Taxpayer Relief Act of 1997 (P.L. 105-34) to which it relates [effective for tax years beginning after August 5, 1997.—CCH.].

Act Sec. 7002 provides:

SEC. 7002. TERMINATION OF EXCEPTION FOR CERTAIN REAL ESTATE INVESTMENT TRUSTS FROM THE TREATMENT OF STAPLED ENTITIES.

(a) IN GENERAL.—Notwithstanding paragraph (3) of section 136(c) of the Tax Reform Act of 1984 (relating to stapled stock; stapled entities), the REIT gross income provisions shall be applied by treating the activities and gross income of members of the stapled REIT group properly allocable to any nonqualified real property interest held by the exempt REIT or any stapled entity which is a member of such group (or treated under subsection (c) as held by such REIT or stapled entity) as the activities and gross income of the exempt REIT in the same manner as if the exempt REIT and such group were 1 entity.

(b) NONQUALIFIED REAL PROPERTY INTEREST.— For purposes of this section—

(1) IN GENERAL.—The term "nonqualified real property interest" means, with respect to any exempt REIT, any interest in real property acquired after March 26, 1998, by the exempt REIT or any stapled entity.

(2) EXCEPTION FOR BINDING CONTRACTS, ETC.—Such term shall not include any interest in real property acquired after March 26, 1998, by the exempt REIT or any stapled entity if—

(A) the acquisition is pursuant to a written agreement (including a put option, buy-sell agreement, and an agreement relating to a third party default) which was binding on such date and at all times thereafter on such REIT or stapled entity, or

(B) the acquisition is described on or before such date in a public announcement or in a filing with the Securities and Exchange Commission.

(3) IMPROVEMENTS AND LEASES.—

(A) IN GENERAL.—Except as otherwise provided in this paragraph, the term "nonqualified real property interest" shall not include—

(i) any improvement to land owned or leased by the exempt REIT or any member of the stapled REIT group, and

(ii) any repair to, or improvement of, any improvement owned or leased by the exempt REIT or any member of the stapled REIT group,

if such ownership or leasehold interest is a qualified real property interest.

(B) LEASES.—The term "nonqualified real property interest" shall not include—

(i) any lease of a qualified real property interest if such lease is not otherwise such an interest, or

(ii) any renewal of a lease which is a qualified real property interest,

but only if the rent on any lease referred to in clause (i) or any renewal referred to in clause (ii) does not exceed an arm's length rate.

(C) TERMINATION WHERE CHANGE IN USE.—

(i) IN GENERAL.—Subparagraph (A) shall not apply to any improvement placed in service after December 31, 1999, which is part of a change in the use of the property to which such improvement relates unless the cost of such improvement does not exceed 200 percent of—

(I) the cost of such property, or

(II) if such property is substituted basis property (as defined in section 7701(a)(42) of the Internal Revenue Code of 1986), the fair market value of the property at the time of acquisition.

(ii) BINDING CONTRACTS.—For purposes of clause (i), an improvement shall be treated as placed in service before January 1, 2000, if such improvement is placed in service before January 1, 2004, pursuant to a binding contract in effect on December 31, 1999, and at all times thereafter.

(4) EXCEPTION FOR PERMITTED TRANSFERS, ETC.—The term "nonqualified real property interest" shall not include any interest in real property acquired solely as a result of a direct or indirect contribution, distribution, or other transfer of such interest from the exempt REIT or any member of the stapled REIT group to such REIT or any such member, but only to the extent the aggregate of the interests of the exempt REIT and all stapled entities in such interest in real property (determined in accordance with subsection (c)(1)) is not increased by reason of the transfer.

(5) TREATMENT OF ENTITIES WHICH ARE NOT STAPLED, ETC. ON MARCH 26, 1998.—Notwithstanding any other provision of this section, all interests in real property held by an exempt REIT or any stapled entity with respect to such REIT (or treated under subsection (c) as held by such REIT or stapled entity) shall be treated as nonqualified real property interests unless—

(A) such stapled entity was a stapled entity with respect to such REIT as of March 26, 1998, and at all times thereafter, and

(B) as of March 26, 1998, and at all times thereafter, such REIT was a real estate investment trust.

(6) QUALIFIED REAL PROPERTY INTEREST.— The term "qualified real property interest" means any interest in real property other than a non-qualified real property interest.

(c) TREATMENT OF PROPERTY HELD BY 10-PERCENT SUBSIDIARIES.—For purposes of this section—

(1) IN GENERAL.—Any exempt REIT and any stapled entity shall be treated as holding their proportionate shares of each interest in real property held by any 10-percent subsidiary entity of the exempt REIT or stapled entity, as the case may be.

(2) PROPERTY HELD BY 10-PERCENT SUBSIDIARIES TREATED AS NONQUALIFIED.—

(A) IN GENERAL.—Except as provided in subparagraph (B), any interest in real property held by a 10-percent subsidiary entity of an exempt REIT or stapled entity shall be treated as a nonqualified real property interest.

(B) EXCEPTION FOR INTERESTS IN REAL PROPERTY HELD ON MARCH 26, 1998, ETC.—In the case of an entity which was a 10-percent subsidiary entity of an exempt REIT or stapled entity on March 26, 1998, and at all times thereafter, an interest in real property held by such subsidiary entity shall be treated as a qualified real property interest if such interest would be so treated if held or acquired directly by the exempt REIT or the stapled entity.

(3) REDUCTION IN QUALIFIED REAL PROPERTY INTEREST IF INCREASE IN OWNERSHIP OF SUBSIDIARY.—If, after March 26, 1998, an exempt REIT or stapled entity increases its ownership interest in a subsidiary entity to which paragraph (2)(B) applies above its ownership interest in such subsidiary entity as of such date, the additional portion of each interest in real property which is treated as held by the exempt REIT or stapled entity by reason of such increased ownership shall be treated as a nonqualified real property interest.

(4) SPECIAL RULES FOR DETERMINING OWNERSHIP.—For purposes of this subsection—

(A) percentage ownership of an entity shall be determined in accordance with subsection (e)(4),

(B) interests in the entity which are acquired by an exempt REIT or a member of the stapled REIT group in any acquisition described in an agreement, announcement, or filing described in subsection (b)(2) shall be treated as acquired on March 26, 1998, and

(C) except as provided in guidance prescribed by the Secretary, any change in proportionate ownership which is attributable solely to fluctuations in the relative fair market values of different classes of stock shall not be taken into account.

(5) TREATMENT OF 60-PERCENT PARTNERSHIPS.—

(A) IN GENERAL.—If, as of March 26, 1998—

(i) an exempt REIT or stapled entity held directly or indirectly at least 60 percent of the capital or profits interest in a partnership, and

(ii) 90 percent or more of the capital interests and 90 percent or more of the profits interests in such partnership (other than interests held directly or indirectly by the exempt REIT or stapled entity) are, or will be, redeemable or exchangeable for consideration the amount of which is determined by reference to the value of shares of stock in the exempt REIT or stapled entity (or both),

paragraph (3) shall not apply to such partnership, and such REIT or entity shall be treated for all purposes of this section as holding all of the capital and profits interests in such partnership.

(B) LIMITATION TO 1 PARTNERSHIP.—If, as of January 1, 1999, more than 1 partnership owned by any exempt REIT or stapled entity meets the requirements of subparagraph (A), only the largest such partnership on such date (determined by aggregate asset bases) shall be treated as meeting such requirements.

(C) MIRROR ENTITY.—For purposes of subparagraph (A), an interest in a partnership formed after March 26, 1998, shall be treated as held by an exempt REIT or stapled entity on March 26, 1998, if such partnership is formed to mirror the stapling of an exempt REIT and a stapled entity in connection with an acquisition agreed to or announced on or before March 26, 1998.

(d) TREATMENT OF PROPERTY SECURED BY MORTGAGE HELD BY EXEMPT REIT OR MEMBER OF STAPLED REIT GROUP.—

(1) IN GENERAL.—In the case of any nonqualified obligation held by an exempt REIT or any member of the stapled REIT group, the REIT gross income provisions shall be applied by treating the exempt REIT as having impermissible tenant service income equal to—

(A) the interest income from such obligation which is properly allocable to the property described in paragraph (2), and

(B) the income of any member of the stapled REIT group from services described in paragraph (2) with respect to such property. If the income referred to in subparagraph (A) or (B) is of a 10-percent subsidiary entity, only the portion of such income which is properly allocable to the exempt REIT's or the stapled entity's interest in the subsidiary entity shall be taken into account.

(2) NONQUALIFIED OBLIGATION.—Except as otherwise provided in this subsection, the term "nonqualified obligation" means any obligation secured by a mortgage on an interest in real property if the income of any member of the stapled REIT group for services furnished with respect to such property would be impermissible tenant service income were such property held by the exempt REIT and such services furnished by the exempt REIT.

(3) EXCEPTION FOR CERTAIN MARKET RATE OBLIGATIONS.—Such term shall not include any obligation—

(A) payments under which would be treated as interest if received by a REIT, and

(B) the rate of interest on which does not exceed an arm's length rate.

(4) EXCEPTION FOR EXISTING OBLIGATIONS.— Such term shall not include any obligation—

(A) which is secured on March 26, 1998, by an interest in real property, and

(B) which is held on such date by the exempt REIT or any entity which is a member of the stapled REIT group on such date and at all times thereafter,

but only so long as such obligation is secured by such interest, and the interest payable on such obligation is not changed to a rate which exceeds an arm's length rate unless such change is pursuant to the terms of the obligation in effect on March 26, 1998. The preceding sentence shall not cease to apply by reason of the refinancing of the obligation if (immediately after the refinancing) the principal amount of the obligation resulting from the refinancing does not exceed the principal amount of the refinanced obligation (immediately before the refinancing) and the interest payable on such refinanced obligation does not exceed an arm's length rate.

(5) TREATMENT OF ENTITIES WHICH ARE NOT STAPLED, ETC. ON MARCH 26, 1998.—A rule similar to the rule of subsection (b)(5) shall apply for purposes of this subsection.

(6) INCREASE IN AMOUNT OF NONQUALIFIED OBLIGATIONS IF INCREASE IN OWNERSHIP OF SUBSIDIARY.—A rule similar to the rule of subsection (c)(3) shall apply for purposes of this subsection.

(7) COORDINATION WITH SUBSECTION (a).— This subsection shall not apply to the portion of any interest in real property that the exempt REIT or stapled entity holds or is treated as holding under this section without regard to this subsection.

(e) DEFINITIONS.—For purposes of this section—

(1) REIT GROSS INCOME PROVISIONS.—The term "REIT gross income provisions" means—

(A) paragraphs (2), (3), and (6) of section 856(c) of the Internal Revenue Code of 1986, and

(B) section 857(b)(5) of such Code.

(2) EXEMPT REIT.—The term "exempt REIT" means a real estate investment trust to which section 269B of the Internal Revenue Code of 1986 does not apply by reason of paragraph (3) of section 136(c) of the Tax Reform Act of 1984.

(3) STAPLED REIT GROUP.—The term "stapled REIT group" means, with respect to an exempt REIT, the group consisting of—

(A) all entities which are stapled entities with respect to the exempt REIT, and

(B) all entities which are 10-percent subsidiary entities of the exempt REIT or any such stapled entity.

(4) 10-PERCENT SUBSIDIARY ENTITY.—

(A) IN GENERAL.—The term "10-percent subsidiary entity" means, with respect to any exempt REIT or stapled entity, any entity in which the exempt REIT or stapled entity (as the case may be) directly or indirectly holds at least a 10-percent interest.

(B) EXCEPTION FOR CERTAIN C CORPORATION SUBSIDIARIES OF REITS.—A corporation which would, but for this subparagraph, be treated as a 10-percent subsidiary of an exempt REIT shall not be so treated if such corporation is taxable under section 11 of the Internal Revenue Code of 1986.

(C) 10-PERCENT INTEREST.—The term "10-percent interest" means—

(i) in the case of an interest in a corporation, ownership of 10 percent (by vote or value) of the stock in such corporation,

(ii) in the case of an interest in a partnership, ownership of 10 percent of the capital or profits interest in the partnership, and

(iii) in any other case, ownership of 10 percent of the beneficial interests in the entity.

(5) OTHER DEFINITIONS.—Terms used in this section which are used in section 269B or section 856 of such Code shall have the respective meanings given such terms by such section.

(f) GUIDANCE.—The Secretary may prescribe such guidance as may be necessary or appropriate to carry out the purposes of this section, including guidance to prevent the avoidance of such purposes and to prevent the double counting of income.

(g) EFFECTIVE DATE.—This section shall apply to taxable years ending after March 26, 1998.

[¶ 5540] CODE SEC. 871. TAX ON NONRESIDENT ALIEN INDIVIDUALS.
* * *

(f) CERTAIN ANNUITIES RECEIVED UNDER QUALIFIED PLANS—
* * *

(2) EXCLUSION.—Income received during the taxable year which would be excluded from gross income under this subsection but for the requirement of paragraph (1)(B) shall not be included in gross income if—

(A) the recipient's country of residence grants a substantially equivalent exclusion to residents and citizens of the United States; or

(B) the recipient's country of residence is a beneficiary developing country under title V of the Trade Act of 1974 [( ]*19 U.S.C. 2461 et seq.).*
* * *

[CCH Explanation at ¶ 30,050.]

Amendment Notes

Act Sec. 6023(10) amended Code Sec. 871(f)(2)(B) by striking "(19 U.S.C. 2462)" and inserting "19 U.S.C. 2461 et seq.)".

The above amendment is effective on the date of the enactment of this Act.

[¶ 5550] CODE SEC. 901. TAXES OF FOREIGN COUNTRIES AND OF POSSESSIONS OF UNITED STATES.
* * *

(k) MINIMUM HOLDING PERIOD FOR CERTAIN TAXES.—
* * *

(4) EXCEPTION FOR CERTAIN TAXES PAID BY SECURITIES DEALERS.—

(A) IN GENERAL.—Paragraphs (1) and (2) shall not apply to any qualified tax with respect to any security held in the active conduct in a foreign country of a *business as a securities dealer* of any person—

(i) who is registered as a securities broker or dealer under section 15(a) of the Securities Exchange Act of 1934,

(ii) who is registered as a Government securities broker or dealer under section 15C(a) of such Act, or

(iii) who is licensed or authorized in such foreign country to conduct securities activities in such country and is subject to bona fide regulation by a securities regulating authority of such country.
* * *

[CCH Explanation at ¶ 668. Committee Reports at ¶ 11,195.]

Amendment Notes

Act Sec. 6010(k)(3) amended Code Sec. 901(k)(4)(A) by striking "securities business" and inserting "business as a securities dealer".

The above amendment is effective as if included in the provision of the Taxpayer Relief Act of 1997 (P.L. 105-34) to which it relates [effective for dividends paid or accrued after September 4, 1997.—CCH.].

[¶ 5560] CODE SEC. 991. TAXATION OF A DOMESTIC INTERNATIONAL SALES CORPORATION.

For purposes of the taxes imposed by this subtitle upon a DISC (as defined in section 992(a)), a DISC shall not be subject to the taxes imposed by this subtitle.

Amendment Notes

Act Sec. 6011(e)(1) amended Code Sec. 991 by striking "except for the tax imposed by chapter 5" before the period.

The above amendment is effective as if included in the provision of the Taxpayer Relief Act of 1997 (P.L. 105-34) to which it relates [effective August 5, 1997.—CCH.].

[¶ 5570] CODE SEC. 1017. DISCHARGE OF INDEBTEDNESS.

(a) GENERAL RULE.—If—

(1) an amount is excluded from gross income under subsection (a) of section 108 (relating to discharge of indebtedness), and

(2) under subsection *(b)(2)(E)*, (b)(5), or (c)(1) of section 108, any portion of such amount is to be applied to reduce basis,

then such portion shall be applied in reduction of the basis of any property held by the taxpayer at the beginning of the taxable year following the taxable year in which the discharge occurs.

* * *

[CCH Explanation at ¶ 30,050.]

Amendment Notes

Act Sec. 6023(11) amended Code Sec. 1017(a)(2) by striking "(b)(2)(D)" and inserting "(b)(2)(E)".

The above amendment is effective on the date of the enactment of this Act.

[¶ 5580] CODE SEC. 1045. ROLLOVER OF GAIN FROM QUALIFIED SMALL BUSINESS STOCK TO ANOTHER QUALIFIED SMALL BUSINESS STOCK.

(a) NONRECOGNITION OF GAIN.—In the case of any sale of qualified small business stock held by *a taxpayer other than a corporation* for more than 6 months and with respect to which *such taxpayer* elects the application of this section, gain from such sale shall be recognized only to the extent that the amount realized on such sale exceeds—

(1) the cost of any qualified small business stock purchased by the taxpayer during the 60-day period beginning on the date of such sale, reduced by

(2) any portion of such cost previously taken into account under this section.

This section shall not apply to any gain which is treated as ordinary income for purposes of this title.

[CCH Explanation at ¶ 531. Committee Reports at ¶ 10,935.]

Amendment Notes

Act Sec. 6005(f)(1)(A)-(B) amended Code Sec. 1045(a) by striking "an individual" and inserting "a taxpayer other than a corporation", and by striking "such individual" and inserting "such taxpayer".

The above amendment is effective as if included in the provision of the Taxpayer Relief Act of 1997 (P.L. 105-34) to which it relates [effective for sales after August 5, 1997.—CCH.].

(b) DEFINITIONS AND SPECIAL RULES.—For purposes of this section—

* * *

(5) *CERTAIN RULES TO APPLY.—Rules similar to the rules of subsections (f), (g), (h), (i), (j), and (k) of section 1202 shall apply.*

[CCH Explanation at ¶ 531. Committee Reports at ¶ 10,935.]

Amendment Notes

Act Sec. 6005(f)(2) amended Code Sec. 1045(b) by adding at the end a new paragraph (5) to read as above.

The above amendment is effective as if included in the provision of the Taxpayer Relief Act of 1997 (P.L.

105-34) to which it relates [effective for sales after August 5, 1997.—CCH.].

[¶ 5590] CODE SEC. 1059. CORPORATE SHAREHOLDER'S BASIS IN STOCK REDUCED BY NONTAXED PORTION OF EXTRAORDINARY DIVIDENDS.

* * *

(g) REGULATIONS.—The Secretary shall prescribe such regulations as may be appropriate to carry out the purposes of this section, including regulations—

(1) providing for the application of this section in the case of stock dividends, stock splits, reorganizations, and other similar transactions, *in the case of stock held by pass-thru entities, and in the case of consolidated groups,* and

(2) providing that the rules of subsection (f) shall apply in the case of stock which is not preferred as to dividends in cases where stock is structured to avoid the purposes of this section.

[CCH Explanation at ¶ 626. Committee Reports at ¶ 11,145.]

Amendment Notes

Act Sec. 6010(b) amended Code Sec. 1059(g)(1) by striking "and in the case of stock held by pass-thru entities" and inserting ", in the case of stock held by pass-thru entities, and in the case of consolidated groups".

The above amendment is effective as if included in the provision of the Taxpayer Relief Act of 1997 (P.L. 105-34) to which it relates [generally effective for distributions after May 3, 1995.—CCH.].

[¶ 5600] CODE SEC. 1223. HOLDING PERIOD OF PROPERTY.

For purposes of this subtitle—

* * *

(11) In the case of a person acquiring property from a decedent or to whom property passed from a decedent (within the meaning of section 1014(b)), if—

(A) the basis of such property in the hands of such person is determined under section 1014, and

(B) such property is sold or otherwise disposed of by such person within *1 year* after the decedent's death,

then such person shall be considered to have held such property for more than *1 year.*

(12) If—

(A) property is acquired by any person in a transfer to which section 1040 applies,

(B) such property is sold or otherwise disposed of by such person within *1 year* after the decedent's death, and

(C) such sale or disposition is to a person who is a qualified heir (as defined in section 2032A(e)(1)) with respect to the decedent,

then the person making such sale or other disposition shall be considered to have held such property for more than *1 year.*

* * *

[CCH Explanation at ¶ 502 and 503. Committee Reports at ¶ 10,785 and 10,915.]

Amendment Notes

Act Sec. 5001(a)(5) amended Code Sec. 1223(11)-(12) by striking "18 months" each place it appears and inserting "1 year".

The above amendment is effective on January 1, 1998.

Act Sec. 6005(d)(4) amended Code Sec. 1223(11)-(12), prior to amendment by Act Sec. 5001(a)(5), by striking "1 year" each place it appears and inserting "18 months".

The above amendment is effective as if included in the provision of the Taxpayer Relief Act of 1997 (P.L. 105-34) to which it relates [effective for tax years anding after May 6, 1997.—CCH.].

[¶ 5605] CODE SEC. 1235. SALE OR EXCHANGE OF PATENTS.

(a) GENERAL.—A transfer (other than by gift, inheritance, or devise) of property consisting of all substantial rights to a patent, or an undivided interest therein which includes a part of all such rights, by any holder shall be considered the sale or exchange of a capital asset held for more than *1 year,* regardless of whether or not payments in consideration of such transfer are—

(1) payable periodically over a period generally coterminous with the transferee's use of the patent, or

(2) contingent on the productivity, use, or disposition of the property transferred.

* * *

[CCH Explanation at ¶ 502 and 503. Committee Reports at ¶ 10,785 and 10,915.]

Amendment Notes

Act Sec. 5001(a)(5) amended Code Sec. 1235(a) by striking "18 months" and inserting "1 year".

The above amendment is effective on January 1, 1998.

Act Sec. 6005(d)(4) amended Code Sec. 1235(a), prior to amendment by Act Sec. 5001(a)(5), by striking "1 year" and inserting "18 months".

The above amendment is effective as if included in the provision of the Taxpayer Relief Act of 1997 (P.L. 105-34) to which it relates [effective for tax years ending after May 6, 1997.—CCH.].

[¶ 5610] CODE SEC. 1250. GAIN FROM DISPOSITIONS OF CERTAIN DEPRECIABLE REALTY.

* * *

(d) EXCEPTIONS AND LIMITATIONS.—

* * *

(4) LIKE KIND EXCHANGES; INVOLUNTARY CONVERSIONS, ETC.—

* * *

(D) BASIS OF PROPERTY ACQUIRED.—In the case of property purchased by the taxpayer in a transaction described in section 1033(a)(2), in applying [*the last sentence of*] *section 1033(b)(2),* such sentence shall be applied—

(i) first solely to section 1250 properties and to the amount of gain not taken into account under subsection (a) by reason of this paragraph, and

(ii) then to all purchased properties to which such sentence applies and to the remaining gain not recognized on the transaction as if the cost of the section 1250 properties were the basis of such properties computed under clause (i).

In the case of property acquired in any other transaction to which this paragraph applies, rules consistent with the preceding sentence shall be applied under regulations prescribed by the Secretary.

* * *

[CCH Explanation at ¶ 30,050.]

Amendment Notes

Act Sec. 6023(12) amended Code Sec. 1250(d)(4)(D) by striking "the last sentence of section 1033(b)" and inserting "[the last sentence of] section 1033(b)(2)".

The above amendment is effective on the date of the enactment of this Act.

[¶ 5620] CODE SEC. 1259. CONSTRUCTIVE SALES TREATMENT FOR APPRECIATED FINANCIAL POSITIONS.

* * *

(b) APPRECIATED FINANCIAL POSITION.—For purposes of this section—

* * *

(2) EXCEPTIONS.—The term "appreciated financial position" shall not include—

(A) any position with respect to debt if—

(i) the *position* unconditionally entitles the holder to receive a specified principal amount,

(ii) the interest payments (or other similar amounts) with respect to such *position* meet the requirements of clause (i) of section 860G(a)(1)(B), and

(iii) such *position* is not convertible (directly or indirectly) into stock of the issuer or any related person,

(B) any hedge with respect to a position described in subparagraph (A), and

(C) any position which is marked to market under any provision of this title or the regulations thereunder.

* * *

[CCH Explanation at ¶ 536. Committee Reports at ¶ 11,125.]

Amendment Notes

Act Sec. 6010(a)(1)(A)-(C) amended Code Sec. 1259(b)(2) by striking "debt" each place it appears in clauses (i), (ii), and (iii) of subparagraph (A) and inserting "position", by striking "and" at the end of subparagraph (A), and by redesignating subparagraph (B) as subparagraph (C) and by inserting after subparagraph (A) a new subparagraph (B) to read as above.

The above amendment is effective as if included in the provision of the Taxpayer Relief Act of 1997 (P.L. 105-34) to which it relates [generally effective for constructive sales after June 8, 1997.—CCH.].

(d) OTHER DEFINITIONS.—For purposes of this section—

(1) FORWARD CONTRACT.—The term "forward contract" means a contract to deliver a substantially fixed amount of property *(including cash)* for a substantially fixed price.

* * *

[CCH Explanation at ¶ 541. Committee Reports at ¶ 11,130.]

Amendment Notes

Act Sec. 6010(a)(2) amended Code Sec. 1259(d)(1) by inserting "(including cash)" after "property".

The above amendment is effective as if included in the provision of the Taxpayer Relief Act of 1997 (P.L. 105-34) to which it relates [generally effective for constructive sales after June 8, 1997 —CCH.]

[¶ 5630] CODE SEC. 1291. INTEREST ON TAX DEFERRAL.

* * *

(d) COORDINATION WITH SUBPARTS B AND C.—

(1) IN GENERAL.—This section shall not apply with respect to any distribution paid by a passive foreign investment company, or any disposition of stock in a passive foreign investment company, if such company is a qualified electing fund with respect to the taxpayer for each of its taxable years—

(A) which begins after December 31, 1986, and for which such company is a passive foreign investment company, and

(B) which includes any portion of the taxpayer's holding period.

Except as provided in section 1296(j), this section also shall not apply if an election under section 1296(k) is in effect for the taxpayer's taxable year. *In the case of stock which is marked to market under section 475 or any other provision of this chapter, this section shall not apply, except that rules similar to the rules of section 1296(j) shall apply.*

* * *

[CCH Explanation at ¶ 651. Committee Reports at ¶ 11,235.]

Amendment Notes

Act Sec. 6011(c)(2) amended Code Sec. 1291(d)(1) by adding at the end a new sentence to read as above.

The above amendment is effective as if included in the provision of the Taxpayer Relief Act of 1997 (P.L. 105-34) to which it relates [effective for tax years of U.S. persons beginning after December 31, 1997 and tax years of foreign corporations ending with or within such tax years of U.S. persons.—CCH.].

[¶ 5640] CODE SEC. 1296. ELECTION OF MARK TO MARKET FOR MARKETABLE STOCK.

* * *

(d) UNREVERSED INCLUSIONS.—For purposes of this section, the term "unreversed inclusions" means, with respect to any stock in a passive foreign investment company, the excess (if any) of—

(1) the amount included in gross income of the taxpayer under subsection (a)(1) with respect to such stock for prior taxable years, over

(2) the amount allowed as a deduction under subsection (a)(2) with respect to such stock for prior taxable years.

The amount referred to in paragraph (1) shall include any amount which would have been included in gross income under subsection (a)(1) with respect to such stock for any prior taxable year but for section 1291. *In the case of a regulated investment company which elected to mark to market the stock held by such company as of the last day of the taxable year preceding such company's first taxable year for which such company elects the application of this section, the amount referred to in paragraph (1) shall include amounts included in gross income under such mark to market with respect to such stock for prior taxable years.*

* * *

[CCH Explanation at ¶ 646. Committee Reports at ¶ 11,240.]

Amendment Notes
Act Sec. 6011(c)(3) amended Code Sec. 1296(d) by adding at the end a new sentence to read as above.
The above amendment is effective as if included in the provision of the Taxpayer Relief Act of 1997 (P.L.

105-34) to which it relates [effective for tax years of U.S. persons beginning after December 31, 1997 and tax years of foreign corporations ending with or within such tax years of U.S. persons.—CCH.].

[¶ 5650] CODE SEC. 1297. PASSIVE FOREIGN INVESTMENT COMPANY.

* * *

(e) EXCEPTION FOR UNITED STATES SHAREHOLDERS OF CONTROLLED FOREIGN CORPORATIONS.—

* * *

(4) TREATMENT OF HOLDERS OF OPTIONS.—Paragraph (1) shall not apply to stock treated as owned by a person by reason of section 1298(a)(4) (relating to the treatment of a person that has an option to acquire stock as owning such stock) unless such person establishes that such stock is owned (within the meaning of section 958(a)) by a United States shareholder (as defined in section 951(b)) who is not exempt from tax under this chapter.

[CCH Explanation at ¶ 641. Committee Reports at ¶ 11,225.]

Amendment Notes
Act Sec. 6011(b)(1) amended Code Sec. 1297(e) by adding at the end a new paragraph (4) to read as above.
The above amendment is effective as if included in the provision of the Taxpayer Relief Act of 1997 (P.L.

105-34) to which it relates [effective for tax years of U.S. persons beginning after December 31, 1997 and tax years of foreign corporations ending with or within such tax years of U.S. persons.—CCH.].

(f) METHODS FOR MEASURING ASSETS.—

* * *

Amendment Notes
Act Sec. 6011(d) amended Code Sec. 1297 by redesignating subsection (e), as added by Act Sec. 1123 of the Taxpayer Relief Act of 1997 (P.L. 105-34), as subsection (f).
The above amendment is effective as if included in the provision of the Taxpayer Relief Act of 1997 (P.L.

105-34) to which it relates [effective for tax years of U.S. persons beginning after December 31, 1997 and tax years of foreign corporations ending with or within such tax years of U.S. persons.—CCH.].

[¶ 5660] CODE SEC. 1298. SPECIAL RULES.

(a) ATTRIBUTION OF OWNERSHIP.—For purposes of this part—

* * *

(2) CORPORATIONS.—

* * *

(B) 50-PERCENT LIMITATION NOT TO APPLY TO PFIC.—For purposes of determining whether a shareholder of a passive foreign investment company is treated as owning stock owned directly or indirectly by or for such company, subparagraph (A) shall be applied without regard to the 50-percent limitation contained therein. *Section 1297(e) shall not apply in determining whether a corporation is a passive foreign investment company for purposes of this subparagraph.*

* * *

[CCH Explanation at ¶ 636. Committee Reports at ¶ 11,230.]

Amendment Notes
Act Sec. 6011(b)(2) amended Code Sec. 1298(a)(2)(B) by adding at the end a new sentence to read as above.
The above amendment is effective as if included in the provision of the Taxpayer Relief Act of 1997 (P.L.

105-34) to which it relates [effective for tax years of U.S. persons beginning after December 31, 1997 and tax years of foreign corporations ending with or within such tax years of U.S. persons.—CCH.].

[¶ 5670] CODE SEC. 1361. S CORPORATION DEFINED.

* * *

(e) ELECTING SMALL BUSINESS TRUST DEFINED.—

* * *

(4) CROSS REFERENCE.—For special treatment of electing small business trusts, see *section 641(c).*

Amendment Notes

Act Sec. 6007(f)(3) amended Code Sec. 1361(e)(4) by striking "section 641(d)" and inserting "section 641(c)".

The above amendment is effective as if included in the provision of the Taxpayer Relief Act of 1997 (P.L. 105-34) to which it relates [effective for sales or exchanges after August 5, 1997.—CCH.].

[¶ 5690] CODE SEC. 1397E. CREDIT TO HOLDERS OF QUALIFIED ZONE ACADEMY BONDS.

* * *

(d) QUALIFIED ZONE ACADEMY BOND.—For purposes of this section—

* * *

(4) QUALIFIED ZONE ACADEMY.—

* * *

(B) ELIGIBLE LOCAL EDUCATION AGENCY.—The term "eligible local education agency" means any *local educational agency as defined* in section 14101 of the Elementary and Secondary Education Act of 1965.

* * *

[CCH Explanation at ¶ 244. Committee Reports at ¶ 10,685.]

Amendment Notes

Act Sec. 6004(g)(2) amended Code Sec. 1397E(d)(4)(B) by striking "local education agency as defined" and inserting "local educational agency as defined".

The above amendment is effective as if included in the provision of the Taxpayer Relief Act of 1997 (P.L. 105-34) to which it relates [effective for obligations issued after December 31, 1997.—CCH.].

(g) CREDIT INCLUDED IN GROSS INCOME.—Gross income includes the amount of the credit allowed to the taxpayer under this section *(determined without regard to subsection (c)).*

[CCH Explanation at ¶ 244. Committee Reports at ¶ 10,685.]

Amendment Notes

Act Sec. 6004(g)(4) amended Code Sec. 1397E(g) by inserting "(determined without regard to subsection (c))" after "section".

The above amendment is effective as if included in the provision of the Taxpayer Relief Act of 1997 (P.L. 105-34) to which it relates [effective for obligations issued after December 31, 1997.—CCH.].

(h) CREDIT TREATED AS ALLOWED UNDER PART IV OF SUBCHAPTER A.—For purposes of subtitle F, the credit allowed by this section shall be treated as a credit allowable under part IV of subchapter A of this chapter.

[CCH Explanation at ¶ 244. Committee Reports at ¶ 10,685.]

Amendment Notes

Act Sec. 6004(g)(3) amended Code Sec. 1397E by adding at the end a new subsection (h) to read as above.

The above amendment is effective as if included in the provision of the Taxpayer Relief Act of 1997 (P.L. 105-34) to which it relates [effective for obligations issued after December 31, 1997.—CCH.].

[¶ 5700] CODE SEC. 1400. ESTABLISHMENT OF DC ZONE.

* * *

(b) APPLICABLE DC AREA.—For purposes of subsection (a), the term "applicable DC area" means the area consisting of—

(1) the census tracts located in the District of Columbia which are part of an enterprise community designated under subchapter U before the date of the enactment of this subchapter, and

(2) all other census tracts—

(A) which are located in the District of Columbia, and

(B) for which the poverty rate is not less than than 20 percent *as determined on the basis of the 1990 census.*

* * *

[CCH Explanation at ¶ 574. Committee Reports at ¶ 11,045.]

Amendment Notes

Act Sec. 6008(a) amended Code Sec. 1400(b)(2)(B) by inserting "as determined on the basis of the 1990 census" after "percent".

The above amendment is effective as if included in the provision of the Taxpayer Relief Act of 1997 (P.L. 105-34) to which it relates [effective August 5, 1997.—CCH.].

[¶ 5710] CODE SEC. 1400A. TAX-EXEMPT ECONOMIC DEVELOPMENT BONDS.

(a) IN GENERAL.—In the case of the District of Columbia Enterprise Zone, subparagraph (A) of section 1394(c)(1) (relating to limitation on amount of bonds) shall be applied by substituting "$15,000,000" for "$3,000,000" *and section 1394(b)(3)(B)(iii) shall be applied without regard to the employee residency requirement.*

* * *

[CCH Explanation at ¶ 580. Committee Reports at ¶ 11,050.]

Amendment Notes

Act Sec. 6008(b) amended Code Sec. 1400A(a) by inserting before the period "and section 1394(b)(3)(B)(iii) shall be applied without regard to the employee residency requirement".

The above amendment is effective as if included in the provision of the Taxpayer Relief Act of 1997 (P.L. 105-34) to which it relates [effective August 5, 1997.—CCH.].

[¶ 5720] CODE SEC. 1400B. ZERO PERCENT CAPITAL GAINS RATE.

* * *

(b) DC ZONE ASSET.—For purposes of this section—

* * *

(5) TREATMENT OF DC ZONE TERMINATION.—The termination of the designation of the DC Zone shall be disregarded for purposes of determining whether any property is a DC Zone asset.

(6) TREATMENT OF SUBSEQUENT PURCHASERS, ETC.—The term "DC Zone asset" includes any property which would be a DC Zone asset but for paragraph (2)(A)(i), (3)(A), or *(4)(A)(i) or (ii)* in the hands of the taxpayer if such property was a DC Zone asset in the hands of a prior holder.

* * *

[CCH Explanation at ¶ 580. Committee Reports at ¶ 11,055.]

Amendment Notes

Act Sec. 6008(c)(1) amended Code Sec. 1400B(b) by inserting after paragraph (4) a new paragraph (5) to read as above.

Act Sec. 6008(c)(2) amended Code Sec. 1400B(b)(6) by striking "(4)(A)(ii)" and inserting "(4)(A)(i) or (ii)".

The above amendments are effective as if included in the provisions of the Taxpayer Relief Act of 1997 (P.L. 105-34) to which they relate [effective August 5, 1997.—CCH.].

(c) DC ZONE BUSINESS.—For purposes of this section, the term "DC Zone business" means any enterprise zone business (as defined in section 1397B), determined—

(1) after the application of section 1400(e),

(2) by substituting "80 percent" for "50 percent" in subsections (b)(2) and (c)(1) of section 1397B, and

(3) by treating no area other than the DC Zone as an empowerment zone or enterprise community.

[CCH Explanation at ¶ 574. Committee Reports at ¶ 11,055.]

Amendment Notes

Act Sec. 6008(c)(3) amended Code Sec. 1400B(c) by striking "entity which is an" before "enterprise zone business".

The above amendment is effective as if included in the provision of the Taxpayer Relief Act of 1997 (P.L.

105-34) to which it relates [effective August 5, 1997.—CCH.].

(d) TREATMENT OF ZONE AS INCLUDING CENSUS TRACTS WITH 10 PERCENT POVERTY RATE.—For purposes of applying this section (and for purposes of applying this subchapter and subchapter U with respect to this section), the DC Zone shall be treated as including all census tracts—

(1) which are located in the District of Columbia, and

(2) for which the poverty rate is not less than 10 percent *as determined on the basis of the 1990 census.*

* * *

[CCH Explanation at ¶ 583. Committee Reports at ¶ 11,055.]

Amendment Notes

Act Sec. 6008(c)(4) amended Code Sec. 1400B(d)(2) by inserting "as determined on the basis of the 1990 census" after "percent".

The above amendment is effective as if included in the provision of the Taxpayer Relief Act of 1997 (P.L. 105-34) to which it relates [effective August 5, 1997.—CCH.].

[¶ 5730] CODE SEC. 1400C. FIRST-TIME HOMEBUYER CREDIT FOR DISTRICT OF COLUMBIA.

* * *

(b) LIMITATION BASED ON MODIFIED ADJUSTED GROSS INCOME.—

(1) IN GENERAL.—The amount allowable as a credit under subsection (a) (determined without regard to this subsection *and subsection (d)*) for the taxable year shall be reduced (but not below zero) by the amount which bears the same ratio to the credit so allowable as—

(A) the excess (if any) of—

(i) the taxpayer's modified adjusted gross income for such taxable year, over

(ii) $70,000 ($110,000 in the case of a joint return), bears to

(B) $20,000.

* * *

[CCH Explanation at ¶ 577. Committee Reports at ¶ 11,060.]

Amendment Notes ·

Act Sec. 6008(d)(1) amended Code Sec. 1400C(b)(1) by inserting "and subsection (d)" after "this subsection".

The above amendment is effective as if included in the provision of the Taxpayer Relief Act of 1997 (P.L. 105-34) to which it relates [effective August 5, 1997.—CCH.].

(c) FIRST-TIME HOMEBUYER.—For purposes of this section—.

(1) IN GENERAL.—*The term "first-time homebuyer" means any individual if such individual (and if married, such individual's spouse) had no present ownership interest in a principal residence in the District of Columbia during the 1-year period ending on the date of the purchase of the principal residence to which this section applies.*

* * *

[CCH Explanation at ¶ 577. Committee Reports at ¶ 11,060.]

Amendment Notes

Act Sec. 6008(d)(2) amended Code Sec. 1400C(c)(1) to read as above. Prior to amendment, Code Sec. 1400C(c)(1) read as follows:

(1) IN GENERAL.—The term "first-time homebuyer" has the same meaning as when used in section 72(t)(8)(D)(i), except that "principal residence in the District of Columbia

during the 1-year period" shall be substituted for "principal residence during the 2-year period" in subclause (I) thereof.

The above amendment is effective as if included in the provision of the Taxpayer Relief Act of 1997 (P.L. 105-34) to which it relates [effective August 5, 1997.— CCH.].

(e) SPECIAL RULES.—For purposes of this section—

* * *

(2) PURCHASE.—

* * *

(B) CONSTRUCTION.—A residence which is constructed by the taxpayer shall be treated as purchased by the taxpayer *on the date the taxpayer first occupies such residence.*

(3) PURCHASE PRICE.—The term "purchase price" means the adjusted basis of the principal residence *on the date such residence is purchased.*

* * *

[CCH Explanation at ¶ 577. Committee Reports at ¶ 11,060.]

Amendment Notes

Act Sec. 6008(d)(3) amended Code Sec. 1400C(e)(2)(B) by inserting before the period "on the date the taxpayer first occupies such residence".

Act Sec. 6008(d)(4) amended Code Sec. 1400C(e)(3) by striking all that follows "principal residence" and inserting "on the date such residence is purchased." Prior to amendment, Code Sec. 1400C(e)(3) read as follows:

(3) PURCHASE PRICE.—The term "purchase price" means the adjusted basis of the principal residence on the date of acquisition (within the meaning of section 72(t)(8)(D)(iii)).

The above amendments are effective as if included in the provisions of the Taxpayer Relief Act of 1997 (P.L. 105-34) to which they relate [effective August 5, 1997.— CCH.].

(i) APPLICATION OF SECTION.—*This section shall apply to property purchased after August 4, 1997, and before January 1, 2001.*

[CCH Explanation at ¶ 577. Committee Reports at ¶ 11,060.]

Amendment Notes

Act Sec. 6008(d)(5) amended Code Sec. 1400C(i) to read as above. Prior to amendment, Code Sec. 1400C(i) read as follows:

(i) TERMINATION.—This section shall not apply to any property purchased after December 31, 2000.

The above amendment is effective as if included in the provision of the Taxpayer Relief Act of 1997 (P.L. 105-34) to which it relates [effective August 5, 1997.— CCH.].

[¶ 5740] CODE SEC. 2001. IMPOSITION AND RATE OF TAX.

* * *

(f) VALUATION OF GIFTS.—

(1) IN GENERAL—*If the time has expired under section 6501 within which a tax may be assessed under chapter 12 (or under corresponding provisions of prior laws) on—*

(A) *the transfer of property by gift made during a preceding calendar period (as defined in section 2502(b)), or*

(B) *an increase in taxable gifts required under section 2701(d),*

the value thereof shall, for purposes of computing the tax under this chapter, be the value as finally determined for purposes of chapter 12.

(2) FINAL DETERMINATION.—*For purposes of paragraph (1), a value shall be treated as finally determined for purposes of chapter 12 if—*

(A) *the value is shown on a return under such chapter and such value is not contested by the Secretary before the expiration of the time referred to in paragraph (1) with respect to such return,*

(B) *in a case not described in subparagraph (A), the value is specified by the Secretary and such value is not timely contested by the taxpayer, or*

(C) *the value is determined by a court or pursuant to a settlement agreement with the Secretary.*

[CCH Explanation at ¶ 446. Committee Reports at ¶ 11,030.]

a statement attached to the return, in a manner adequate to apprise the Secretary of the nature of such gift, the value of such gift shall, for purposes of computing the tax under this chapter, be the value of such gift as finally determined for purposes of chapter 12.

The above amendment is effective as if included in the provision of the Taxpayer Relief Act of 1997 (P.L. 105-34) to which it relates [effective for gifts made after August 5, 1997.—CCH.].

[¶ 5750] CODE SEC. 2031. DEFINITION OF GROSS ESTATE.

* * *

(c) ESTATE TAX WITH RESPECT TO LAND SUBJECT TO A QUALIFIED CONSERVATION EASEMENT.—

* * *

(6) ELECTION.—The election under this subsection shall be made *on or before the due date (including extensions) for filing the return of tax imposed by section 2001 and shall be made on such return.*

* * *

(9) *TREATMENT OF EASEMENTS GRANTED AFTER DEATH.*—*In any case in which the qualified conservation easement is granted after the date of the decedent's death and on or before the due date (including extensions) for filing the return of tax imposed by section 2001, the deduction under section 2055(f) with respect to such easement shall be allowed to the estate but only if no charitable deduction is allowed under chapter 1 to any person with respect to the grant of such easement.*

(10) APPLICATION OF THIS SECTION TO INTERESTS IN PARTNERSHIPS, CORPORATIONS, AND TRUSTS.— This section shall apply to an interest in a partnership, corporation, or trust if at least 30 percent of the entity is owned (directly or indirectly) by the decedent, as determined under the rules described in section 2033A(e)(3).

* * *

[CCH Explanation at ¶ 451. Committee Reports at ¶ 11,035.]

[¶ 5770] *CODE SEC. 2057. FAMILY-OWNED BUSINESS INTERESTS.*

(a) *GENERAL RULE.—*

(1) *ALLOWANCE OF DEDUCTION.—For purposes of the tax imposed by section 2001, in the case of an estate of a decedent to which this section applies, the value of the taxable estate shall be determined by deducting from the value of the gross estate the adjusted value of the qualified family-owned business interests of the decedent which are described in subsection (b)(2).*

(2) *MAXIMUM DEDUCTION.—The deduction allowed by this section shall not exceed $675,000.*

(3) *COORDINATION WITH UNIFIED CREDIT.—*

(A) *IN GENERAL.—Except as provided in subparagraph (B), if this section applies to an estate, the applicable exclusion amount under section 2010 shall be $625,000.*

(B) *INCREASE IN UNIFIED CREDIT IF DEDUCTION IS LESS THAN $675,000.—If the deduction allowed by this section is less than $675,000, the amount of the applicable exclusion amount under section 2010 shall be increased (but not above the amount which would apply to the estate without regard to this section) by the excess of $675,000 over the amount of the deduction allowed.*

[CCH Explanation at ¶ 401 and 406. Committee Reports at ¶ 10,975 and 10,980.]

(b) Estates to Which Section Applies.—

* * *

(2) Includible qualified family-owned business interests.—The qualified family-owned business interests described in this paragraph are the interests which—

(A) are included in determining the value of the gross estate, and

(B) are acquired by any qualified heir from, or passed to any qualified heir from, the decedent (within the meaning of section 2032A(e)(9)).

(3) Includible gifts of interests.—The amount of the gifts of qualified family-owned business interests determined under this paragraph is the sum of—

(A) the amount of such gifts from the decedent to members of the decedent's family taken into account under section 2001(b)(1)(B), plus

(B) the amount of such gifts otherwise excluded under section 2503(b),

to the extent such interests are continuously held by members of such family (other than the decedent's spouse) between the date of the gift and the date of the decedent's death.

[CCH Explanation at ¶ 401 and 411. Committee Reports at ¶ 10,975 and 10,985.]

Amendment Notes

Act Sec. 6007(b)(1)(A) amended Code Sec. 2033A by moving it to the end of part IV of subchapter A of chapter 11 and redesignating it as Code Sec. 2057.

Act Sec. 6007(b)(1)(C) amended Code Sec. 2057(b)(2)(A) (as redesignated) by striking "(without regard to this section)" after "the value of the gross estate".

Act Sec. 6007(b)(2) amended Code Sec. 2057(b)(3) (as redesignated) to read as above. Prior to amendment, Code Sec. 2057(b)(3) read as follows:

(3) Includible gifts of interests.—The amount of the gifts of qualified family-owned business interests determined under this paragraph is the excess of—

(A) the sum of—

(i) the amount of such gifts from the decedent to members of the decedent's family taken into account under subsection 2001(b)(1)(B), plus

(ii) the amount of such gifts otherwise excluded under section 2503(b),

to the extent such interests are continuously held by members of such family (other than the decedent's spouse) between the date of the gift and the date of the decedent's death, over

(B) the amount of such gifts from the decedent to members of the decedent's family otherwise included in the gross estate.

The above amendments are effective as if included in the provisions of the Taxpayer Relief Act of 1997 (P.L. 105-34) to which they relate [effective for estates of decedents dying after December 31, 1997.—CCH.].

(c) Adjusted Gross Estate.—For purposes of this section, the term "adjusted gross estate" means the value of the gross estate—

(1) reduced by any amount deductible under paragraph (3) or (4) of section 2053(a), and

(2) increased by the excess of—

(A) the sum of—

(i) the amount of gifts determined under subsection (b)(3), plus

(ii) the amount (if more than de minimis) of other transfers from the decedent to the decedent's spouse (at the time of the transfer) within 10 years of the date of the decedent's death, plus

(iii) the amount of other gifts (not included under clause (i) or (ii)) from the decedent within 3 years of such date, other than gifts to members of the decedent's family otherwise excluded under section 2503(b), over

(B) the sum of the amounts described in clauses (i), (ii), and (iii) of subparagraph (A) which are otherwise includible in the gross estate.

For purposes of the preceding sentence, the Secretary may provide that de minimis gifts to persons other than members of the decedent's family shall not be taken into account.

* * *

[CCH Explanation at ¶ 401. Committee Reports at ¶ 10,975.]

Amendment Notes

Act Sec. 6007(b)(1)(A) amended Code Sec. 2033A by moving it to the end of part IV of subchapter A of chapter 11 and redesignating it as Code Sec. 2057.

Act Sec. 6007(b)(1)(D) amended Code Sec. 2057(c) (as redesignated) by striking "(determined without regard to this section)" after "the value of the gross estate".

The above amendments are effective as if included in the provisions of the Taxpayer Relief Act of 1997 (P.L. 105-34) to which they relate [effective for estates of decedents dying after December 31, 1997.—CCH.].

(e) Qualified Family-Owned Business Interest.—

(1) In general.—For purposes of this section, the term "qualified family-owned business interest" means—

(A) an interest as a proprietor in a trade or business carried on as a proprietorship, or

(B) an interest in an entity carrying on a trade or business, if—

(i) at least—

(I) 50 percent of such entity is owned (directly or indirectly) by the decedent and members of the decedent's family,

(II) 70 percent of such entity is so owned by members of 2 families, or

(III) 90 percent of such entity is so owned by members of 3 families, and

(ii) for purposes of subclause (II) or (III) of clause (i), at least 30 percent of such entity is so owned by the decedent and members of the decedent's family.

For purposes of the preceding sentence, a decedent shall be treated as engaged in a trade or business if any member of the decedent's family is engaged in such trade or business.

(2) LIMITATION.—Such term shall not include—

(A) any interest in a trade or business the principal place of business of which is not located in the United States,

(B) any interest in an entity, if the stock or debt of such entity or a controlled group (as defined in section 267(f)(1)) of which such entity was a member was readily tradable on an established securities market or secondary market (as defined by the Secretary) at any time within 3 years of the date of the decedent's death,

(C) any interest in a trade or business not described in section 542(c)(2), if more than 35 percent of the adjusted ordinary gross income of such trade or business for the taxable year which includes the date of the decedent's death would qualify as personal holding company income *(as defined in section 543(a) without regard to paragraph (2)(B) thereof) if such trade or business were a corporation,*

(D) that portion of an interest in a trade or business that is attributable to—

(i) cash or marketable securities, or both, in excess of the reasonably expected day-to-day working capital needs of such trade or business, and

(ii) any other assets of the trade or business (other than assets used in the active conduct of a trade or business described in section 542(c)(2)), which produce, or are held for the production of, *personal holding company income (as defined in subparagraph (C)) or income described* in section 954(c)(1) (determined without regard to subparagraph (A) thereof and by substituting "trade or business" for "controlled foreign corporation").

In the case of a lease of property on a net cash basis by the decedent to a member of the decedent's family, income from such lease shall not be treated as personal holding company income for purposes of subparagraph (C), and such property shall not be treated as an asset described in subparagraph (D)(ii), if such income and property would not be so treated if the lessor had engaged directly in the activities engaged in by the lessee with respect to such property.

* * *

[CCH Explanation at ¶ 401. Committee Reports at ¶ 10,975.]

Amendment Notes

Act Sec. 6007(b)(1)(A) amended Code Sec. 2033A by moving it to the end of part IV of subchapter A of chapter 11 and redesignating it as Code Sec. 2057.

Act Sec. 6007(b)(3)(A) amended Code Sec. 2057(e)(2)(C) (as redesignated) by striking "(as defined in section 543(a))" and inserting "(as defined in section 543(a) without regard to paragraph (2)(B) thereof) if such trade or business were a corporation".

Act Sec.. 6007(b)(3)(B) amended Code Sec. 2057(e)(2)(D)(ii) (as redesignated) by striking "income of which is described in section 543(a) or" and inserting "per-

sonal holding company income (as defined in subparagraph (C)) or income described".

Act Sec. 6007(b)(3)(C) amended Code Sec. 2057(e)(2) (as redesignated) by adding at the end a new flush sentence to read as above.

Act Sec. 6007(b)(5)(A) amended Code Sec. 2057(e)(1) (as redesignated) by adding at the end a new flush sentence to read as above.

The above amendments are effective as if included in the provisions of the Taxpayer Relief Act of 1997 (P.L. 105-34) to which they relate [effective for estates of decedents dying after December 31, 1997.—CCH.].

(f) TAX TREATMENT OF FAILURE TO MATERIALLY PARTICIPATE IN BUSINESS OR DISPOSITIONS OF INTERESTS.—

* * *

(2) ADDITIONAL ESTATE TAX.—

(A) IN GENERAL.—The amount of the additional estate tax imposed by paragraph (1) shall be equal to—

(i) the applicable percentage of the adjusted tax difference attributable to the qualified family-owned business interest, plus

(ii) interest on the amount determined under clause (i) at the underpayment rate established under section 6621 for the period beginning on the date the estate tax liability was due under this chapter and ending on the date such additional estate tax is due.

* * *

(C) ADJUSTED TAX DIFFERENCE.—For purposes of subparagraph (A)—

(i) IN GENERAL.—The adjusted tax difference attributable to a qualified family-owned business interest is the amount which bears the same ratio to the adjusted tax difference with respect to the estate (determined under clause (ii)) as the value of such interest bears to the value of all qualified family-owned business interests described in subsection (b)(2).

(ii) ADJUSTED TAX DIFFERENCE WITH RESPECT TO THE ESTATE.—For purposes of clause (i), the term "adjusted tax difference with respect to the estate" means the excess of what would have

been the estate tax liability but for the election under this section over the estate tax liability. For purposes of this clause, the term "estate tax liability" means the tax imposed by section 2001 reduced by the credits allowable against such tax.

(3) USE IN TRADE OR BUSINESS BY FAMILY MEMBERS.—A qualified heir shall not be treated as disposing of an interest described in subsection (e)(1)(A) by reason of ceasing to be engaged in a trade or business so long as the property to which such interest relates is used in a trade or business by any member of such individual's family.

[CCH Explanation at ¶ 401 and 421. Committee Reports at ¶ 10,975 and 10,995.]

Amendment Notes

Act Sec. 6007(b)(1)(A) amended Code Sec. 2033A by moving it to the end of part IV of subchapter A of chapter 11 and redesignating it as Code Sec. 2057.

Act Sec. 6007(b)(4)(A)-(B) amended Code Sec. 2057(f)(2) (as redesignated) by striking "(as determined under rules similar to the rules of section 2032A(c)(2)(B))" before ", plus", and by adding at the end a new subparagraph (C) to read as above.

Act Sec. 6007(b)(5)(B) amended Code Sec. 2057(f) (as redesignated) by adding at the end a new paragraph (3) to read as above.

The above amendments are effective as if included in the provisions of the Taxpayer Relief Act of 1997 (P.L. 105-34) to which they relate [effective for estates of decedents dying after December 31, 1997.—CCH.].

(g) SECURITY REQUIREMENTS FOR NONCITIZEN QUALIFIED HEIRS.—

(1) IN GENERAL.—Except upon the application of subparagraph (F) of subsection (i)(3), if a qualified heir is not a citizen of the United States, any interest under this section passing to or acquired by such heir (including any interest held by such heir at a time described in subsection (f)(1)(C)) shall be treated as a qualified family-owned business interest only if the interest passes or is acquired (or is held) in a qualified trust.

* * *

[CCH Explanation at ¶ 401, 416 and 426. Committee Reports at ¶ 10,975, 10,990 and 11,015.]

Amendment Notes

Act Sec. 6007(b)(1)(A) amended Code Sec. 2033A by moving it to the end of part IV of subchapter A of chapter 11 and redesignating it as Code Sec. 2057.

Act Sec. 6007(b)(6) amended Code Sec. 2057(g)(1) (as redesignated) by striking "or (M)" after "subparagraph (F)".

The above amendments are effective as if included in the provisions of the Taxpayer Relief Act of 1997 (P.L. 105-34) to which they relate [effective for estates of decedents dying after December 31, 1997.—CCH.].

(i) OTHER DEFINITIONS AND APPLICABLE RULES.—For purposes of this section—
* * *

(3) APPLICABLE RULES.—Rules similar to the following rules shall apply.
* * *

(L) Section 2032A(g) (relating to application to interests in partnerships, corporations, and trusts).

(M) Subsections (h) and (i) of section 2032A.

(N) Section 6166(b)(3) (relating to farmhouses and certain other structures taken into account).

(O) Subparagraphs (B), (C), and (D) of section 6166(g)(1) (relating to acceleration of payment).

(P) Section 6324B (relating to special lien for additional estate tax).

[CCH Explanation at ¶ 401 and 426. Committee Reports at ¶ 10,975 and 10,990.]

Amendment Notes

Act Sec. 6007(b)(1)(A) amended Code Sec. 2033A by moving it to the end of part IV of subchapter A of chapter 11 and redesignating it as Code Sec. 2057.

Act Sec. 6007(b)(7) amended Code Sec. 2057(i)(3) (as redesignated) by redesignating subparagraphs (L), (M), and (N) as subparagraphs (N), (O), and (P), respectively, and by

inserting after subparagraph (K) new subparagraphs (L) and (M) to read as above.

The above amendments are effective as if included in the provisions of the Taxpayer Relief Act of 1997 (P.L. 105-34) to which they relate [effective for estates of decedents dying after December 31, 1997.—CCH.].

[¶ 5780] CODE SEC. 2504. TAXABLE GIFTS FOR PRECEDING CALENDAR PERIODS.
* * *

(c) VALUATION OF GIFTS.—If the time has expired under section 6501 within which a tax may be assessed under this chapter 12 (or under corresponding provisions of prior laws) on—

(1) the transfer of property by gift made during a preceding calendar period (as defined in section 2502(b)), or

(2) an increase in taxable gifts required under section 2701(d),

the value thereof shall, for purposes of computing the tax under this chapter, be the value as finally determined (within the meaning of section 2001(f)(2)) for purposes of this chapter.
* * *

[CCH Explanation at ¶ 446. Committee Reports at ¶ 11,030.]

Amendment Notes

Act Sec. 6007(e)(2)(B)[(C)] amended Code Sec. 2504(c) to read as above. Prior to amendment, Code Sec. 2504(c) read as follows:

(c) VALUATION OF CERTAIN GIFTS FOR PRECEDING CALENDAR PERIODS.—If the time has expired within which a tax may be assessed under this chapter or under corresponding provisions of prior laws on the transfer of property by gift made during a preceding calendar period, as defined in section 2502(b), the value of such gift made in such preceding calendar period shall, for purposes of computing the tax under this chapter for any calendar year, be the value of such gift which was used in computing the tax for the last preceding calendar period for which a tax under this chapter or under corresponding provisions of prior laws was assessed or paid.

The above amendment is effective as if included in the provision of the Taxpayer Relief Act of 1997 (P.L. 105-34) to which it relates [effective for gifts made after August 5, 1997.—CCH.].

[¶ 5790] CODE SEC. 2631. GST EXEMPTION.

* * *

(c) INFLATION ADJUSTMENT.—

(1) IN GENERAL.—In the case of any calendar year after 1998, the $1,000,000 amount contained in subsection (a) shall be increased by an amount equal to—

(A) $1,000,000, multiplied by

(B) the cost-of-living adjustment determined under section 1(f)(3) for such calendar year by substituting "calendar year 1997" for "calendar year 1992" in subparagraph (B) thereof.

If any amount as adjusted under the preceding sentence is not a multiple of $10,000, such amount shall be rounded to the next lowest multiple of $10,000.

(2) ALLOCATION OF INCREASE.—Any increase under paragraph (1) for any calendar year shall apply only to generation-skipping transfers made during or after such calendar year; except that no such increase for calendar years after the calendar year in which the transferor dies shall apply to transfers by such transferor.

[CCH Explanation at ¶ 431. Committee Reports at ¶ 10,970.]

Amendment Notes

Act Sec. 6007(a)(1) amended Code Sec. 2631(c) to read as above. Prior to amendment, Code Sec. 2631(c) read as follows:

(c) INFLATION ADJUSTMENT.—In the case of an individual who dies in any calendar year after 1998, the $1,000,000 amount contained in subsection (a) shall be increased by an amount equal to—

(1) $1,000,000, multiplied by

(2) the cost-of-living adjustment determined under section 1(f)(3) for such calendar year by substituting "calendar year 1997" for "calendar year 1992" in subparagraph (B) thereof.

If any amount as adjusted under the preceding sentence is not a multiple of $10,000, such amount shall be rounded to the next lowest multiple of $10,000.

The above amendment is effective as if included in the provision of the Taxpayer Relief Act of 1997 (P.L. 105-34) to which it relates [effective for generation-skipping transfers made after December 31, 1998.—CCH.].

[¶ 5800] CODE SEC. 2652. OTHER DEFINITIONS.

* * *

(b) TRUST AND TRUSTEE.—

(1) TRUST.—The term "trust" includes any arrangement (other than an estate) which, although not a trust, has substantially the same effect as a trust.

* * *

[CCH Explanation at ¶ 433. Committee Reports at ¶ 11,275.]

Amendment Notes

Act Sec. 6013(a)(3) amended Code Sec. 2652(b)(1) by striking "section 646" and inserting "section 645".

Act Sec. 6013(a)(4)(A) amended Code Sec. 2652(b)(1) [as amended by Act Sec. 6013(a)(3)] by striking the second sentence. Prior to being stricken, the second sentence of Code Sec. 2652(b)(1) read as follows:

Such term shall not include any trust during any period the trust is treated as part of an estate under section 645.

The above amendments are effective as if included in the provisions of the Taxpayer Relief Act of 1997 (P.L. 105-34) to which they relate [effective for estates of decedents dying after August 5, 1997.—CCH.].

[¶ 5810] CODE SEC. 2654. SPECIAL RULES.

* * *

(b) CERTAIN TRUSTS TREATED AS SEPARATE TRUSTS.—For purposes of this chapter—

(1) the portions of a trust attributable to transfers from different transferors shall be treated as separate trusts, and

(2) substantially separate and independent shares of different beneficiaries in a trust shall be treated as separate trusts.

Except as provided in the preceding sentence, nothing in this chapter shall be construed as authorizing a single trust to be treated as 2 or more trusts. *For purposes of this subsection, a trust shall be treated as part of an estate during any period that the trust is so treated under section 645.*

* * *

[CCH Explanation at ¶ 433. Committee Reports at ¶ 11,275.]

Amendment Notes

Act Sec. 6013(a)(4)(B) amended Code Sec. 2654(b) by adding at the end a new sentence to read as above.

The above amendment is effective as if included in the provision of the Taxpayer Relief Act of 1997 (P.L. 105-34) to which it relates [effective for estates of decedents dying after August 5, 1997.—CCH.].

[¶ 5820] CODE SEC. 3121. DEFINITIONS.

(a) WAGES.—For purposes of this chapter, the term "wages" means all remuneration for employment, including the cash value of all remuneration (including benefits) paid in any medium other than cash; except that such term shall not include—

* * *

(5) any payment made to, or on behalf of, an employee or his beneficiary—

(A) from or to a trust described in section 401(a) which is exempt from tax under section 501(a) at the time of such payment unless such payment is made to an employee of the trust as remuneration for services rendered as such employee and not as a beneficiary of the trust,

(B) under or to an annuity plan which, at the time of such payment, is a plan described in section 403(a),

(C) under a simplified employee pension (as defined in section 408(k)(1)), other than any contributions described in section 408(k)(6),

(D) under or to an annuity contract described in section 403(b), other than a payment for the purchase of such contract which is made by reason of a salary reduction agreement (whether evidenced by a written instrument or otherwise),

(E) under or to an exempt governmental deferred compensation plan (as defined in subsection (v)(3)),

(F) to supplement pension bnefits under a plan or trust described in any of the foregoing provisions of this paragraph to take into account some portion or all of the increase in the cost of living (as determined by the Secretary of Labor) since retirement but only if such supplemental payments are under a plan which is treated as a welfare plan under section 3(2)(B)(ii) of the Employee Retirement Income Security Act of 1974,

(G) under a cafeteria plan (within the meaning of section 125) if such payment would not be treated as wages without regard to such plan and it is reasonable to believe that (if section 125 applied for purposes of this section) section 125 would not treat any wages as constructively received,

(H) under an arrangement to which section 408(p) applies, other than any elective contributions under paragraph (2)(A)(i) thereof, or

(I) under a plan described in section 457(e)(11)(A)(ii) and maintained by an eligible employer (as defined in section 457(e)(1));

* * *

[CCH Explanation at ¶ 30,050.]

Amendment Notes

Act Sec. 6023(13)(A)-(C) amended Code Sec. 3121(a)(5) by striking the semicolon at the end of subparagraph (F) and inserting a comma, by striking "or" at the end of subpara- graph (G), and by striking the period at the end of subparagraph (I) and inserting a semicolon.

The above amendment is effective on the date of the enactment of this Act.

[¶ 5830] CODE SEC. 3401. DEFINITIONS.

(a) WAGES.—For purposes of this chapter, the term "wages" means all remuneration (other than fees paid to a public official) for services performed by an employee for his employer, including the cash value of all remuneration (including benefits) paid in any medium other than cash; except that such term shall not include remuneration paid—

* * *

(19) *for* any benefit provided to or on behalf of an employee if at the time such benefit is provided it is reasonable to believe that the employee will be able to exclude such benefit from income under section 74(c), 117 or 132;

(20) for any medical care reimbursement made to or for the benefit of an employee under a self-insured medical reimbursement plan (within the meaning of section 105(h)(6)); or

(21) *for* any payment made to or for the benefit of an employee if at the time of such payment it is reasonable to believe that the employee will be able to exclude such payment from income under section 106(b).

* * *

[CCH Explanation at ¶ 30,050.]

Amendment Notes

Act Sec. 6023(14) amended Code Sec. 3401(a)(19) by inserting "for" before "any benefit provided to".

Act Sec. 6023(15) amended Code Sec. 3401(a)(21) by inserting "for" before "any payment made".

The above amendments are effective on the date of the enactment of this Act.

[¶ 5840] CODE SEC. 4041. IMPOSITION OF TAX.

(a) DIESEL FUEL AND SPECIAL MOTOR FUELS.—

(1) TAX ON DIESEL FUEL IN CERTAIN CASES.—

* * *

(C) RATE OF TAX.—

(i) IN GENERAL.—Except as otherwise provided in this subparagraph, the rate of the tax imposed by this paragraph shall be the rate of tax specified in section 4081(a)(2)(A) on diesel fuel which is in effect at the time of such sale or use.

(ii) RATE OF TAX ON TRAINS.—In the case of any sale for use, or use, of diesel fuel in a train, the rate of tax imposed by this paragraph shall be—

(I) 6.8 cents per gallon after September 30, 1993, and before October 1, 1995,

(II) 5.55 cents per gallon after September 30, 1995, and before *November 1, 1998*, and

(III) 4.3 cents per gallon after *October 31, 1998*.

(iii) RATE OF TAX ON CERTAIN BUSES.—

(I) IN GENERAL.—Except as provided in subclause (II), in the case of fuel sold for use or used in a use described in section 6427(b)(1) (after the application of section 6427(b)(3)), the rate of tax imposed by this paragraph shall be 7.3 cents per gallon (4.3 cents per gallon after September 30, *2005*).

* * *

(2) SPECIAL MOTOR FUELS.—

* * *

(B) RATE OF TAX.—The rate of the tax imposed by this paragraph shall be—

(i) except as otherwise provided in this subparagraph, the rate of tax specified in section 4081(a)(2)(A)(i) which is in effect at the time of such sale or use,

(ii) 13.6 cents per gallon in the case of liquefied petroleum gas, and

(iii) 11.9 cents per gallon in the case of liquefied natural gas.

In the case of any sale or use after September 30, *2005*, clause (ii) shall be applied by substituting "3.2 cents" for "13.6 cents", and clause (iii) shall be applied by substituting "2.8 cents" for "11.9 cents".

* * *

[CCH Explanation at ¶ 727 and 750. Committee Reports at ¶ 15,015 and 15,095.]

Amendment Notes
P.L. 105-178 (ISTEA)
Act Sec. 9002(a)(1)(A) amended Code Sec. 4041(a)(1)(C)(iii)(I) by striking "1999" and inserting "2005".
Act Sec. 9002(a)(1)(B) amended Code Sec. 4041(a)(2)(B) by striking "1999" and inserting "2005".

Act Sec. 9006(a)(1)-(2) amended Code Sec. 4041(a)(1)(C)(ii) by striking "October 1, 1999" in subclause (II) and inserting "November 1, 1998", and by striking "September 30, 1999" in subclause (III) and inserting "October 31, 1998".

The above amendments are effective on June 9, 1998.

(b) EXEMPTION FOR OFF-HIGHWAY BUSINESS USE; REDUCTION IN TAX FOR QUALIFIED METHANOL AND ETHANOL FUEL.—

* * *

[Caution: Code Sec. 4041(b)(2), below, as amended by P.L. 105-178 (ISTEA), is effective on January 1, 2001.—CCH.]

(2) QUALIFIED METHANOL AND ETHANOL FUEL.—

(A) IN GENERAL.—In the case of any qualified methanol or ethanol fuel—

(i) the rate applicable under subsection (a)(2) shall be *the applicable blender rate* per gallon less than the otherwise applicable rate (6 cents per gallon in the case of a mixture none of the alcohol in which consists of ethanol), and

(ii) subsection (d)(1) shall be applied by substituting "0.05 cent" for "0.1 cent" with respect to the sales and uses to which clause (i) applies.

(B) QUALIFIED METHANOL OR ETHANOL FUEL.—The term "qualified methanol or ethanol fuel" means any liquid at least 85 percent of which consists of methanol, ethanol, or other alcohol produced from a substance other than petroleum or natural gas.

(C) APPLICABLE BLENDER RATE.—For purposes of subparagraph (A)(i), the applicable blender rate is—

(i) except as provided in clause (ii), 5.4 cents, and

(ii) for sales or uses during calendar years 2001 through 2007, 1/10 of the blender amount applicable under section 40(h)(2) for the calendar year in which the sale or use occurs.

(D) TERMINATION.—On and after October 1, *2007*, subparagraph (A) shall not apply.

* * *

[CCH Explanation at ¶ 760. Committee Reports at ¶ 15,035.]

¶ 5840   Code Sec. 4041(b)

Amendment Notes
P.L. 105-178 (ISTEA)
Act Sec. 9003(a)(1)(A) amended Code Sec. 4041(b)(2)(C) by striking "2000" and inserting "2007".

Act Sec. 9003(b)(2)(A)(i)-(ii) amended Code Sec. 4041(b)(2) by striking "5.4 cents" in subparagraph (A)(i)

and inserting "the applicable blender rate", and by redesignating subparagraph (C), as amended by Act Sec. 9003(a)(1)(A), as subparagraph (D) and inserting after subparagraph (B) a new subparagraph (C) to read as above.

The above amendments are effective on January 1, 2001.

(k) FUELS CONTAINING ALCOHOL.—

* * *

(3) TERMINATION.—Paragraph (1) shall not apply to any sale or use after September 30, *2007*.

[CCH Explanation at ¶ 760. Committee Reports at ¶ 15,035.]

Amendment Notes
P.L. 105-178 (ISTEA)
Act Sec. 9003(a)(1)(B) amended Code Sec. 4041(k)(3) by striking "2000" and inserting "2007".

The above amendment is effective on January 1, 2001.

(l) EXEMPTION FOR CERTAIN USES.—No tax shall be imposed under this section on any liquid sold for use in, or used in, a helicopter or a fixed-wing aircraft for purposes of providing transportation with respect to which the requirements of *subsection (f) or (g)* of section 4261 are met.

Amendment Notes
Act Sec. 6010(g)(1) amended Code Sec. 4041(l) by striking "subsection (e) or (f)" and inserting "subsection (f) or (g)".

The above amendment is effective as if included in the provision of the Taxpayer Relief Act of 1997 (P.L. 105-34) to which it relates [effective October 1, 1997.—CCH.].

(m) CERTAIN ALCOHOL FUELS.—

(1) IN GENERAL.—In the case of the sale or use of any partially exempt methanol or ethanol fuel—

(A) the rate of the tax imposed by subsection (a)(2) shall be—

(i) after September 30, 1997, and before October 1, *2005*—

(I) in the case of fuel none of the alcohol in which consists of ethanol, 9.15 cents per gallon, and

(II) in any other case, 11.3 cents per gallon, and

(ii) after September 30, *2005*—

(I) in the case of fuel none of the alcohol in which consists of ethanol, 2.15 cents per gallon, and

(II) in any other case, 4.3 cents per gallon, and

(B) the rate of the tax imposed by subsection (c)(1) shall be the comparable rate under section 4091(c)(1).

[CCH Explanation at ¶ 750. Committee Reports at ¶ 15,015.]

Amendment Notes
P.L. 105-178 (ISTEA)
Act Sec. 9002(a)(1)(C) amended Code Sec. 4041(m)(1)(A) by striking "1999" each place it appears and inserting "2005".

The above amendment is effective on June 9, 1998.

[¶ 5845] CODE SEC. 4051. IMPOSITION OF TAX ON HEAVY TRUCKS AND TRAILERS SOLD AT RETAIL.

* * *

(c) TERMINATION.—On and after October 1, *2005*, the taxes imposed by this section shall not apply.

* * *

[CCH Explanation at ¶ 750. Committee Reports at ¶ 15,015.]

Amendment Notes
P.L. 105-178 (ISTEA)
Act Sec. 9002(a)(1)(D) amended Code Sec. 4051(c) by striking "1999" and inserting "2005".

The above amendment is effective on June 9, 1998.

[¶ 5850] CODE SEC. 4052. DEFINITIONS AND SPECIAL RULES.

* * *

(f) CERTAIN REPAIRS AND MODIFICATIONS NOT TREATED AS MANUFACTURE.—

* * *

(2) EXCEPTION.—Paragraph (1) shall not apply if the article (as repaired or modified) would, if new, be taxable under section 4051 and the article when new was not taxable under *such section* or the corresponding provision of prior law.

* * *

Amendment Notes
Act Sec. 6014(c) amended Code Sec. 4052(f)(2) by striking "this section" and inserting "such section".
The above amendment is effective as if included in the provision of the Taxpayer Relief Act of 1997 (P.L.

105-34) to which it relates [effective January 1, 1998.—CCH.].

[¶ 5853] CODE SEC. 4071. IMPOSITION OF TAX.
* * *

(d) TERMINATION.—On and after October 1, *2005*, the taxes imposed by subsection (a) shall not apply.
* * *

[CCH Explanation at ¶ 750. Committee Reports at ¶ 15,015.]

Amendment Notes
P.L. 105-178 (ISTEA)
Act Sec. 9002(a)(1)(E) amended Code Sec. 4071(d) by striking "1999" and inserting "2005".

The above amendment is effective on June 9, 1998.

[¶ 5857] CODE SEC. 4081. IMPOSITION OF TAX.
* * *

(c) TAXABLE FUELS MIXED WITH ALCOHOL.—Under regulations prescribed by the Secretary—
* * *

(4) ALCOHOL MIXTURE RATES FOR GASOLINE MIXTURES.—For purposes of this subsection—

[Caution: Code Sec. 4081(c)(4)(A), below, as amended by Act Sec. 9003(b)(2)(B) of P.L. 105-178 (ISTEA), is effective on January 1, 2001.—CCH.]

(A) GENERAL RULES.—

(i) MIXTURES CONTAINING ETHANOL.—Except as provided in clause (ii), in the case of a qualified alcohol mixture which contains gasoline, the alcohol mixture rate is the excess of the rate which would (but for this paragraph) be determined under subsection (a) over—

(I) in the case of 10 percent gasohol, the applicable blender rate (as defined in section 4041(b)(2)(C)) per gallon,

(II) in the case of 7.7 percent gasohol, the number of cents per gallon equal to 77 percent of such applicable blender rate, and

(III) in the case of 5.7 percent gasohol, the number of cents per gallon equal to 57 percent of such applicable blender rate.

(ii) MIXTURES NOT CONTAINING ETHANOL.—In the case of a qualified alcohol mixture which contains gasoline and none of the alcohol in which consists of ethanol, the alcohol mixture rate is the excess of the rate which would (but for this paragraph) be determined under subsection (a) over—

(I) in the case of 10 percent gasohol, 6 cents per gallon,

(II) in the case of 7.7 percent gasohol, 4.62 cents per gallon, and

(III) in the case of 5.7 percent gasohol, 3.42 cents per gallon.
* * *

[Caution: Code Sec. 4081(c)(5), below, as amended by Act Sec. 9003(b)(2)(C) of P.L. 105-178 (ISTEA), is effective on January 1, 2001.—CCH.]

(5) ALCOHOL MIXTURE RATE FOR DIESEL FUEL MIXTURES.—The alcohol mixture rate for a qualified alcohol mixture which does not contain gasoline is the excess of the rate which would (but for this paragraph) be determined under subsection (a) over *the applicable blender rate (as defined in section 4041(b)(2)(C))* per gallon (6 cents per gallon in the case of a qualified alcohol mixture none of the alcohol in which consists of ethanol).
* * *

(8) TERMINATION.—Paragraphs (1) and (2) shall not apply to any removal, entry, or sale after September 30, *2007*.

[CCH Explanation at ¶ 760. Committee Reports at ¶ 15,035.]

Amendment Notes
P.L. 105-178 (ISTEA)
Act Sec. 9003(a)(1)(C) amended Code Sec. 4081(c)(8) by striking "2000" and inserting "2007".
The above amendment is effective on June 9, 1998.
Act Sec. 9003(b)(2)(B) amended Code Sec. 4081(c)(4)(A) to read as above. Prior to amendment, Code Sec, 4081(c)(4)(A) read as follows:
(A) IN GENERAL.—The alcohol mixture rate for a qualified alcohol mixture which contains gasoline is the excess of the rate which would (but for this paragraph) be determined under subsection (a) over—

(i) 5.4 cents per gallon for 10 percent gasohol,
(ii) 4.158 cents per gallon for 7.7 percent gasohol, and
(iii) 3.078 cents per gallon for 5.7 percent gasohol.
In the case of a mixture none of the alcohol in which consists of ethanol, clauses (i), (ii), and (iii) shall be applied by substituting "6 cents" for "5.4 cents", "4.62 cents" for "4.158 cents", and "3.42 cents" for "3.078 cents".
Act Sec. 9003(b)(2)(C) amended Code Sec. 4081(c)(5) by striking "5.4 cents" and inserting "the applicable blender rate (as defined in section 4041(b)(2)(C))".
The above amendments are effective on January 1, 2001.

(d) TERMINATION.—

(1) IN GENERAL.—The rates of tax specified in clauses (i) and (iii) of subsection (a)(2)(A) shall be 4.3 cents per gallon after September 30, *2005.*

* * *

[CCH Explanation at ¶ 750. Committee Reports at ¶ 15,015.]

Amendment Notes

P.L. 105-178 (ISTEA)

Act Sec. 9002(a)(1)(F) amended Code Sec. 4081(d)(1) by striking "1999" and inserting "2005".

The above amendment is effective **on June 9, 1998.**

[¶ 5860] CODE SEC. 4082. EXEMPTIONS FOR DIESEL FUEL AND KEROSENE.

* * *

(d) ADDITIONAL EXCEPTIONS TO DYEING REQUIREMENTS FOR KEROSENE.—

(1) AVIATION-GRADE KEROSENE.—Subsection (a)(2) shall not apply to aviation-grade kerosene (as determined under regulations prescribed by the Secretary) which the Secretary determines is destined for use as a fuel in an aircraft.

* * *

(3) WHOLESALE DISTRIBUTORS.—To the extent provided in regulations, subsection (a)(2) shall not apply to *kerosene received by* a wholesale distributor of kerosene if such distributor—

(A) is registered under section 4101 with respect to the tax imposed by section 4081 on kerosene, and

(B) sells kerosene exclusively to ultimate vendors described in section 6427(l)(5)(B) with respect to kerosene.

* * *

[CCH Explanation at ¶ 725 and 726. Committee Reports at ¶ 11,178.]

Amendment Notes

Act Sec. 6010(h)(3) amended Code Sec. 4082(d)(1) to read as above. Prior to amendment, Code Sec. 4082(d)(1) read as follows:

(1) AVIATION-GRADE KEROSENE.—Subsection (a)(2) shall not apply to a removal, entry, or sale of aviation-grade kerosene (as determined under regulations prescribed by the Secretary) if the person receiving the kerosene is registered under section 4101 with respect to the tax imposed by section 4091.

Act Sec. 6010(h)(4) amended Code Sec. 4082(d)(3) by striking "a removal, entry, or sale of kerosene to" and inserting "kerosene received by".

The above amendments are effective **as if included in the provisions of the Taxpayer Relief Act of 1997 (P.L. 105-34) to which they relate [effective July 1, 1998.—CCH.].**

[¶ 5870] CODE SEC. 4091. IMPOSITION OF TAX.

(a) TAX ON SALE.—

* * *

(2) USE TREATED AS SALE.—For purposes of paragraph (1), if any producer uses aviation fuel (other than for a nontaxable use as defined in section 6427(l)(2)(B)) on which no tax has been imposed under such paragraph *or on which tax has been credited or refunded,* then such use shall be considered a sale.

* * *

[CCH Explanation at ¶ 716.]

Amendment Notes

Act Sec. 6014(d) amended Code Sec. 4091(a)(2) by inserting "or on which tax has been credited or refunded" after "such paragraph".

The above amendment is effective **as if included in the provision of the Taxpayer Relief Act of 1997 (P.L. 105-34) to which it relates [effective for fuel acquired by the producer after September 30, 1997.—CCH.].**

[Caution: Code Sec. 4091(c)(1), below, as amended by Act Sec. 9003(b)(2)(D) of P.L. 105-178 (ISTEA), is effective on January 1, 2001.—CCH.]

(c) REDUCED RATE OF TAX FOR AVIATION FUEL IN ALCOHOL MIXTURE, ETC.—Under regulations prescribed by the Secretary—

(1) IN GENERAL.—The rate of tax under subsection (a) shall be reduced by *the applicable blender amount* per gallon in the case of the sale of any mixture of aviation fuel if—

(A) at least 10 percent of such mixture consists of alcohol (as defined in section 4081(c)(3)), and

(B) the aviation fuel in such mixture was not taxed under paragraph (2).

In the case of such a mixture none of the alcohol in which is ethanol, the preceding sentence shall be applied by substituting "14 cents" for *"the applicable blender amount". For purposes of this paragraph, the term "applicable blender amount" means 13.3 cents in the case of any sale or use during 2001 or 2002, 13.2 cents in the case of any sale or use during 2003 or 2004, 13.1 cents in the case of any sale or use during 2005, 2006, or 2007, and 13.4 cents in the case of any sale or use during 2008 or thereafter.*

* * *

(5) TERMINATION.—Paragraphs (1) and (2) shall not apply to any sale after September 30, *2007.*

* * *

[CCH Explanation at ¶ 760. Committee Reports at ¶ 15,035.]

Amendment Notes
P.L. 105-178 (ISTEA)
Act Sec. 9003(a)(1)(D) amended Code Sec. 4091(c)(5) by striking "2000" each place it appears and inserting "2007".
Act Sec. 9003(b)(2)(D) amended Code Sec. 4091(c)(1) by striking "13.4 cents" each place it appears and inserting "the

applicable blender amount" and by adding new material at the end to read as above.
The above amendments are effective on January 1, 2001.

[¶ 5880] CODE SEC. 4092. EXEMPTIONS.

* * *

(b) NO EXEMPTION FROM CERTAIN TAXES ON FUEL USED IN COMMERCIAL AVIATION.—In the case of fuel sold for use in commercial aviation (other than supplies for vessels or aircraft within the meaning of section 4221(d)(3)), subsection (a) shall not apply to so much of the tax imposed by section 4091 as is attributable to—

(1) the Leaking Underground Storage Tank Trust Fund financing rate imposed by such section, and

(2) in the case of fuel sold after September 30, 1995, 4.3 cents per gallon of the rate specified in section 4091(b)(1).

For purposes of the preceding sentence, the term "commercial aviation" means any use of an aircraft other than in noncommercial aviation (as defined in *section 4041(c)(2))*.

* * *

[CCH Explanation at ¶ 30,050.]

Amendment Notes
Act Sec. 6023(16) amended Code Sec. 4092(b) by striking "section 4041(c)(4)" and inserting "section 4041(c)(2)".

The above amendment is effective on the date of the enactment of this Act.

[¶ 5890] CODE SEC. 4101. REGISTRATION AND BOND.

* * *

(e) CERTAIN APPROVED TERMINALS OF REGISTERED PERSONS REQUIRED TO OFFER DYED DIESEL FUEL AND KEROSENE FOR NONTAXABLE PURPOSES.—

(1) IN GENERAL.—A terminal for kerosene or diesel fuel may not be an approved facility for storage of non-tax-paid diesel fuel or kerosene under this section unless the operator of such terminal offers *such fuel in a dyed form* for removal for nontaxable use in accordance with section 4082(a).

* * *

[CCH Explanation at ¶ 724. Committee Reports at ¶ 11,180.]

Amendment Notes
Act Sec. 6010(h)(5) amended Code Sec. 4101(e)(1) by striking "dyed diesel fuel and kerosene" and inserting "such fuel in a dyed form."

The above amendment is effective as if included in the provision of the Taxpayer Relief Act of 1997 (P.L. 105-34) to which it relates [effective July 1, 2000.—CCH.].

[¶ 5900] CODE SEC. 4221. CERTAIN TAX-FREE SALES.

(a) GENERAL RULE.—Under regulations prescribed by the Secretary, no tax shall be imposed under this chapter (other than under section 4121, 4081, or 4091) on the sale by the manufacturer (or under subchapter A or C of chapter 31 on the first retail sale) of an article—

* * *

(5) to a nonprofit educational organization for its exclusive use,

but only if such exportation or use is to occur before any other use. Paragraphs (4) and (5) shall not apply to the tax imposed by section 4064. In the case of taxes imposed by section 4051 or 4071, paragraphs (4) and (5) shall not apply on and after October 1, *2005.* In the case of the tax imposed by section 4131, paragraphs (3), (4), and (5) shall not apply and paragraph (2) shall apply only if the use of the exported vaccine meets such requirements as the Secretary may by regulations prescribe. In the case of taxes imposed by subchapter A of chapter 31, paragraphs (1), (3), (4), and (5) shall not apply.

* * *

[CCH Explanation at ¶ 750. Committee Reports at ¶ 15,015.]

Amendment Notes
P.L. 105-178 (ISTEA)
Act Sec. 9002(b)(1) amended Code Sec. 4221(a) by striking "1999" and inserting "2005".

The above amendment is effective on June 9, 1998.

(c) MANUFACTURER RELIEVED FROM LIABILITY IN CERTAIN CASES.—In the case of any article sold free of tax under this section (other than a sale to which subsection (b) applies), and in the case of any article sold free of tax under section 4001(c), 4001(d), or *4053(6)*, if the manufacturer in good faith accepts a certification by the purchaser that the article will be used in accordance with the applicable provisions of law, no tax shall thereafter be imposed under this chapter in respect of such sale by such manufacturer

* * *

[CCH Explanation at ¶ 30,050.]

Amendment Notes

Act Sec. 6023(17) amended Code Sec. 4221(c) by striking "4053(a)(6)" and inserting "4053(6)".

The above amendment is effective on the date of the enactment of this Act.

[¶ 5910] CODE SEC. 4222. REGISTRATION.

* * *

(d) REGISTRATION IN THE CASE OF CERTAIN OTHER EXEMPTIONS.—The provisions of this section may be extended to, and made applicable with respect to, the exemptions provided by sections 4001(c), 4001(d), *4053(6)*, 4064(b)(1)(C), 4101, and 4182(b), and the exemptions authorized under section 4293 in respect of the taxes imposed by this chapter, to the extent provided by regulations prescribed by the Secretary.

* * *

[CCH Explanation at ¶ 30,050.]

Amendment Notes

Act Sec. 6023(17) amended Code Sec. 4222(d) by striking "4053(a)(6)" and inserting "4053(6)".

The above amendment is effective on the date of the enactment of this Act.

[¶ 5920] CODE SEC. 4251. IMPOSITION OF TAX.

* * *

(d) TREATMENT OF PREPAID TELEPHONE CARDS.—

* * *

(3) PREPAID TELEPHONE CARD.—For purposes of this subsection, the term "prepaid telephone card" means any card *or any other similar arrangement* which permits its holder to obtain communications services and pay for such services in advance.

[CCH Explanation at ¶ 746. Committee Reports at ¶ 11,185.]

Amendment Notes

Act Sec. 6010(i) amended Code Sec. 4251(d)(3) by striking 'other similar arrangement" and inserting "any other similar arrangement".

The above amendment is effective as if included in the provision of the Taxpayer Relief Act of 1997 (P.L.

105-34) to which it relates [effective for amounts paid in calendar months beginning after October 4, 1997.—CCH.]

[¶ 5923] CODE SEC. 4481. IMPOSITION OF TAX

* * *

(e) PERIOD TAX IN EFFECT.—The tax imposed by this section shall apply only to use before October 1, *2005*.

[CCH Explanation at ¶ 750. Committee Reports at ¶ 15,015.]

Amendment Notes

P.L. 105-178 (ISTEA)

Act Sec. 9002(a)(1)(G) amended Code Sec. 4481(e) by striking "1999" and inserting "2005".

The above amendment is effective on June 9, 1998.

[¶ 5925] CODE SEC. 4482. DEFINITIONS.

* * *

(c) OTHER DEFINITIONS AND SPECIAL RULE.—For purposes of this subchapter—

* * *

(4) TAXABLE PERIOD.—The term "taxable period" means any year beginning before July 1, *2005*, and the period which begins on July 1, *2005*, and ends at the close of September 30, *2005*.

* * *

[CCH Explanation at ¶ 750. Committee Reports at ¶ 15,015.]

Amendment Notes

P.L. 105-178 (ISTEA)

Act Sec. 9002(a)(1)(H) amended Code Sec. 4482(c)(4) by striking "1999" and inserting "2005".

The above amendment is effective on June 9, 1998.

(d) SPECIAL RULE FOR TAXABLE PERIOD IN WHICH TERMINATION DATE OCCURS.—In the case of the taxable period which ends on September 30, *2005*, the amount of the tax imposed by section 4481 with respect to any highway motor vehicle shall be determined by reducing each dollar amount in the table contained in section 4481(a) by 75 percent.

[CCH Explanation at ¶ 750. Committee Reports at ¶ 15,015.]

Amendment Notes   The above amendment is effective on June 9, 1998.
P.L. 105-178 (ISTEA)
Act Sec. 9002(a)(1)(I) amended Code Sec. 4482(d) by striking "1999" and inserting "2005".

[¶ 5927] CODE SEC. 4483. EXEMPTIONS.

* * *

(g) TERMINATION OF EXEMPTIONS.—Subsections (a) and (c) shall not apply on and after October 1, *2005.*

[CCH Explanation at ¶ 750. Committee Reports at ¶ 15,015.]

Amendment Notes   The above amendment is effective on June 9, 1998.
P.L. 105-178 (ISTEA)
Act Sec. 9002(b)(2) amended Code Sec. 4483(g) by striking "1999" and inserting "2005".

[¶ 5930] CODE SEC. 4946. DEFINITIONS AND SPECIAL RULES.

* * *

(c) GOVERNMENT OFFICIAL.—For purposes of subsection (a)(1)(I) and section 4941, the term "government official" means, with respect to an act of self-dealing described in section 4941, an individual who, at the time of such act, holds any of the following offices or positions (other than as a "special Government employee", as defined in section 202(a) of title 18, United States Code):

(1) an elective public office in the executive or legislative branch of the Government of the United States,

(2) an office in the executive or judicial branch of the Government of the United States, appointment to which was made by the President,

(3) a position in the executive, legislative, or judicial branch of the Government of the United States—

(A) which is listed in schedule C of rule VI of the Civil Service Rules, or

(B) the compensation for which is equal to or greater than the lowest rate of compensation prescribed for GS-16 of the General Schedule under section 5332 of title 5, United States Code,

(4) a position under the House of Representatives or the Senate of the United States held by an individual receiving gross compensation at an annual rate of $15,000 or more,

(5) an elective or appointive public office in the executive, legislative, or judicial branch of the government of a State, possession of the United States, or political subdivision or other area of any of the foregoing, or of the District of Columbia, held by an individual receiving gross compensation at an annual rate of $20,000 or more,

(6) a position as personal or executive assistant or secretary to any of the foregoing, *or*

(7) a member of the Internal Revenue Service Oversight Board.

* * *

[CCH Explanation at ¶ 826. Committee Reports at ¶ 10,130.]

Amendment Notes

Act Sec. 1101(c)(1) amended Code Sec. 4946(c) by striking "or" at the end of paragraph (5), by striking the period at the end of paragraph (6) and inserting ", or", and by adding at the end a new paragraph (7) to read as above.

The above amendment is effective on the date of the enactment of this Act. For a special rule, see Act Sec. 1101(d)(2)-(3), below.

Act Sec. 1101(d)(2)-(3) provides:

(2) INITIAL NOMINATIONS TO INTERNAL REVENUE SERVICE OVERSIGHT BOARD.—The President shall submit the initial

nominations under section 7802 of the Internal Revenue Code of 1986, as added by this section, to the Senate not later than 6 months after the date of the enactment of this Act.

(3) EFFECT ON ACTIONS PRIOR TO APPOINTMENT OF OVERSIGHT BOARD.—Nothing in this section shall be construed to invalidate the actions and authority of the Internal Revenue Service prior to the appointment of the members of the Internal Revenue Service Oversight Board.

[¶ 5940] CODE SEC. 4973. *TAX ON EXCESS CONTRIBUTIONS TO CERTAIN TAX-FAVORED ACCOUNTS AND ANNUITIES.*

* * *

(b) EXCESS CONTRIBUTIONS.—For purposes of this section, in the case of individual retirement accounts, or individual retirement annuities the term "excess contributions" means the sum of—

(1) the excess (if any) of—

(A) the amount contributed for the taxable year to the accounts or for the annuities or bonds (other than *a contribution to a Roth IRA or* a rollover contribution described in section 402(c), 403(a)(4), 403(b)(8), or 408(d)(3)), over

(B) the amount allowable as a deduction under section 219 for such contributions, and

(2) the amount determined under this subsection for the preceding taxable year, reduced by the sum of—

(A) the distributions out of the account for the taxable year which were included in the gross income of the payee under section 408(d)(1),

(B) the distributions out of the account for the taxable year to which section 408(d)(5) applies, and

(C) the excess (if any) of the maximum amount allowable as a deduction under section 219 for the taxable year over the amount contributed (determined without regard to section 219(f)(6)) to the accounts or for the annuities *(including the amount contributed to a Roth IRA)* or bonds for the taxable year.

For purposes of this subsection, any contribution which is distributed from the individual retirement account or the individual retirement annuity in a distribution to which section 408(d)(4) applies shall be treated as an amount not contributed. For purposes of paragraphs (1)(B) and (2)(C), the amount allowable as a deduction under section 219 shall be computed without regard to section 219(g).

* * *

[CCH Explanation at ¶ 331 and 30,050. Committee Report at ¶ 10,880.]

Amendment Notes

Act Sec. 6005(b)(8)(B)(i)-(ii) amended Code Sec. 4973(b) by inserting "a contribution to a Roth IRA or" after "other than" in paragraph (1)(A), and by inserting "(including the amount contributed to a Roth IRA)" after "annuities" in paragraph (2)(C).

The above amendment is effective as if included in the provision of the Taxpayer Relief Act of 1997 (P.L. 105-34) to which it relates [effective for tax years beginning after December 31, 1997.—CCH.].

Act Sec. 6023(18)(A) amended the heading of Code Sec. 4973 to read as above. Prior to amendment, the heading of Code Sec. 4973 read as follows:

SEC. 4973. TAX ON EXCESS CONTRIBUTIONS TO INDIVIDUAL RETIREMENT ACCOUNTS, MEDICAL SAVINGS ACCOUNTS, CERTAIN SECTION 403(b) CONTRACTS, AND CERTAIN INDIVIDUAL RETIREMENT ANNUITIES.

The above amendment is effective on the date of the enactment of this Act.

(e) EXCESS CONTRIBUTIONS TO EDUCATION INDIVIDUAL RETIREMENT ACCOUNTS.—For purposes of this section—

(1) IN GENERAL.—In the case of education individual retirement accounts maintained for the benefit of any 1 beneficiary, the term "excess contributions" means the sum of—

(A) the amount by which the amount contributed for the taxable year to such accounts exceeds $500 (or, if less, the sum of the maximum amounts permitted to be contributed under section 530(c) by the contributors to such accounts for such year),

(B) if any amount is contributed (other than a contribution described in section 530(b)(2)(B)) during such year to a qualified State tuition program for the benefit of such beneficiary, any amount contributed to such accounts for such taxable year, and

(C) the amount determined under this subsection for the preceding taxable year, reduced by the sum of—

(i) the distributions out of the accounts for the taxable year (other than rollover distributions), and

(ii) the excess (if any) of the maximum amount which may be contributed to the accounts for the taxable year over the amount contributed to the accounts for the taxable year.

(2) SPECIAL RULES.—For purposes of paragraph (1), the following contributions shall not be taken into account:

(A) Any contribution which is distributed out of the education individual retirement account in a distribution to which section 530(d)(4)(C) applies.

(B) Any rollover contribution.

[CCH Explanation at ¶ 236. Committee Reports at ¶ 10,845.]

Amendment Notes

Act Sec. 6004(d)(10)(A) amended Code Sec. 4973(e)(1) to read as above. Prior to amendment, Code Sec. 4973(e)(1) read as follows:

(1) IN GENERAL.—In the case of education individual retirement accounts maintained for the benefit of any 1 beneficiary, the term "excess contributions" means—

(A) the amount by which the amount contributed for the taxable year to such accounts exceeds $500, and

(B) any amount contributed to such accounts for any taxable year if any amount is contributed during such year to a qualified State tuition program for the benefit of such beneficiary.

Act Sec. 6004(d)(10)(B) amended Code Sec. 4973(e)(2) by striking subparagraph (B) and by redesignating subparagraph (C) as subparagraph (B). Prior to amendment, Code Sec. 4973(e)(2)(B) read as follows:

(B) Any contribution described in section 530(b)(2)(B) to a qualified State tuition program.

The above amendments are effective as if included in the provisions of the Taxpayer Relief Act of 1997 (P.L. 105-34) to which they relate [effective for tax years beginning after December 31, 1997.—CCH.].

(f) EXCESS CONTRIBUTIONS TO ROTH IRAs.—For purposes of this section, in the case of contributions to a Roth IRA (within the meaning of section 408A(b)), the term "excess contributions" means the sum of—

(1) the excess (if any) of—

(A) the amount contributed for the taxable year to *Roth IRAs* (other than a qualified rollover contribution described in section 408A(e)), over

Code Sec. 4973(f) ¶ 5940

(B) the amount allowable as a contribution under sections 408A (c)(2) and (c)(3), and

(2) the amount determined under this subsection for the preceding taxable year, reduced by the sum of—

(A) the distributions out of the accounts for the taxable year, and

(B) the excess (if any) of the maximum amount allowable as a contribution under sections 408A (c)(2) and (c)(3) for the taxable year over the amount contributed *by the individual to all individual retirement plans* for the taxable year.

For purposes of this subsection, any contribution which is distributed from a Roth IRA in a distribution described in section 408(d)(4) shall be treated as an amount not contributed.

[CCH Explanation at ¶ 331. Committee Reports at ¶ 10,880.]

Amendment Notes

Act Sec. 6005(b)(8)(A)(i)-(ii) amended Code Sec. 4973(f) by striking "such accounts" in paragraph (1)(A) and inserting "Roth IRAs", and by striking "to the accounts" in paragraph (2)(B) and inserting "by the individual to all individual retirement plans".

The above amendment is effective as if included in the provision of the Taxpayer Relief Act of 1997 (P.L. 105-34) to which it relates [effective for tax years beginning after December 31, 1997.—CCH.].

[¶ 5950] CODE SEC. 4975. TAX ON PROHIBITED TRANSACTIONS.

* * *

(c) PROHIBITED TRANSACTION.—

* * *

(3) SPECIAL RULE FOR INDIVIDUAL RETIREMENT ACCOUNTS.—An individual for whose benefit an individual retirement account is established and his beneficiaries shall be *exempt from the tax* imposed by this section with respect to any transaction concerning such account (which would otherwise be taxable under this section) if, with respect to such transaction, the account ceases to be an individual retirement account by reason of the application of section 408(e)(2)(A) or if section 408(e)(4) applies to such account.

* * *

[CCH Explanation at ¶ 30,050.]

Amendment Notes

Act Sec. 6023(19)(A) amended Code Sec. 4975(c)(3) by striking "exempt for the tax" and inserting "exempt from the tax".

The above amendment is effective on the date of the enactment of this Act.

(i) CROSS REFERENCE.—

For provisions concerning coordination procedures between Secretary of Labor and *Secretary of the Treasury* with respect to application of tax imposed by this section and for authority to waive imposition of the tax imposed by subsection (b), see section 3003 of the Employee Retirement Income Security Act of 1974.

[CCH Explanation at ¶ 30,050.]

Amendment Notes

Act Sec. 6023(19)(B) amended Code Sec. 4975(i) by striking "Secretary of Treasury" and inserting "Secretary of the Treasury".

The above amendment is effective on the date of the enactment of this Act.

[¶ 5960] CODE SEC. 5041. IMPOSITION AND RATE OF TAX.

* * *

(b) RATES OF TAX.—

* * *

(6) On hard cider *which is a still wine* derived primarily from apples or apple concentrate and water, containing no other fruit product, and containing at least one-half of 1 percent and less than 7 percent alcohol by volume, 22.6 cents per wine gallon.

* * *

[CCH Explanation at ¶ 731. Committee Reports at ¶ 11,095.]

Amendment Notes

Act Sec. 6009(a) amended Code Sec. 5041(b)(6) by inserting "which is a still wine" after "hard cider".

The above amendment is effective as if included in the provision of the Taxpayer Relief Act of 1997 (P.L.

105-34) to which it relates [effective October 1, 1997.—CCH.].

[¶ 5970] CODE SEC. 5043. COLLECTION OF TAXES ON WINES.

(a) PERSONS LIABLE FOR PAYMENT.—The taxes on wine provided for in this subpart shall be paid—

* * *

(2) FOREIGN WINE.—In the case of foreign wines *which are not transferred to a bonded wine cellar free of tax under section 5364*, by the importer thereof.

[CCH Explanation at ¶ 732. Committee Reports at ¶ 11,285.]

Amendment Notes
Act Sec. 6014(b)(1) amended Code Sec. 5043(a)(2) by inserting "which are not transferred to a bonded wine cellar free of tax under section 5364" after "foreign wines".

The above amendment is effective as if included in the provision of the Taxpayer Relief Act of 1997 (P.L. 105-34) to which it relates [effective April 1, 1998.—CCH.].

[¶ 5980] CODE SEC. 5044. REFUND OF TAX ON WINE.

(a) GENERAL.—In the case of any wine *removed from a bonded wine cellar* and returned to bond under section 5361—

(1) any tax imposed by section 5041 shall, if paid, be refunded or credited, without interest, to the proprietor of the bonded wine cellar to which such wine is delivered; or

(2) if any tax so imposed has not been paid, the person liable for the tax may be relieved of liability therefor,

under such regulations as the Secretary may prescribe. Such regulations may provide that claim for refund or credit under paragraph (1), or relief from liability under paragraph (2), may be made only with respect to minimum quantities specified in such regulations. The burden of proof in all such cases shall be on the applicant.

* * *

[CCH Explanation at ¶ 733. Committee Reports at ¶ 11,290.]

Amendment Notes
Act Sec. 6014(b)(2) amended Code Sec. 5044(a) by striking "produced in the United States" and inserting "removed from a bonded wine cellar".

The above amendment is effective as if included in the provision of the Taxpayer Relief Act of 1997 (P.L. 105-34) to which it relates [effective April 1, 1998.—CCH.].

[¶ 5990] CODE SEC. 5054. DETERMINATION AND COLLECTION OF TAX ON BEER.

(a) TIME OF DETERMINATION.—

(1) BEER PRODUCED IN THE UNITED STATES; *CERTAIN IMPORTED BEER.*—Except as provided in paragraph (3), the tax imposed by section 5051 on beer produced in the United States, *or imported into the United States and transferred to a brewery free of tax under section 5418,* shall be determined at the time it is removed for consumption or sale, and shall be paid by the brewer thereof in accordance with section 5061.

(2) BEER IMPORTED INTO THE UNITED STATES.—Except as provided in paragraph (4), the tax imposed by section 5051 on beer imported into the United States *and not transferred to a brewery free of tax under section 5418* shall be determined at the time of the importation thereof, or, if entered for warehousing, at the time of removal from the 1st such warehouse.

* * *

[CCH Explanation at ¶ 743. Committee Reports at ¶ 11,285.]

Amendment Notes
Act Sec. 6014(a)(1)(A)-(B) amended Code Sec. 5054(a)(1) by inserting ", or imported into the United States and transferred to a brewery free of tax under section 5418," after "produced in the United States," in the text, and by inserting "; CERTAIN IMPORTED BEER" after "PRODUCED IN THE UNITED STATES" in the heading.

Act Sec. 6014(a)(2) amended Code Sec. 5054(a)(2) by inserting "and not transferred to a brewery free of tax under section 5418" after "United States".

The above amendments are effective as if included in the provisions of the Taxpayer Relief Act of 1997 (P.L. 105-34) to which they relate [effective April 1, 1998.—CCH.].

[¶ 6000] CODE SEC. 5056. REFUND AND CREDIT OF TAX, OR RELIEF FROM LIABILITY.

(a) BEER RETURNED OR VOLUNTARILY DESTROYED.—Any tax paid by any brewer on beer *removed for consumption or sale* may be refunded or credited to the brewer, without interest, or if the tax has not been paid, the brewer may be relieved of liability therefor, under such regulations as the Secretary may prescribe, if such beer is returned to any brewery of the brewer or is destroyed under the supervision required by such regulations. In determining the amount of tax due on beer removed on any day, the quantity of beer returned to the same brewery from which removed shall be allowed, under such regulations as the Secretary may prescribe, as an offset against or deduction from the total quantity of beer removed from that brewery on the day of such return.

[CCH Explanation at ¶ 743. Committee Reports at ¶ 11,290.]

Amendment Notes
Act Sec. 6014(a)(3) amended Code Sec. 5056 by striking "produced in the United States" and inserting "removed for consumption or sale".

The above amendment is effective as if included in the provision of the Taxpayer Relief Act of 1997 (P.L. 105-34) to which it relates [effective April 1, 1998.—CCH.].

(b) BEER LOST BY FIRE, CASUALTY, OR ACT OF GOD.—Subject to regulations prescribed by the Secretary, the tax paid by any brewer on beer *removed for consumption or sale* may be refunded or credited to the brewer, without interest, or if the tax has not been paid, the brewer may be relieved of liability therefor, if such beer is lost, whether by theft or otherwise, or is destroyed or otherwise rendered unmerchantable by fire, casualty, or act of God before the transfer of title thereto to any other person. In any case in which beer is lost or destroyed, whether by theft or otherwise, the Secretary may require the brewer to file a claim for relief from the tax and submit proof as to the cause of such loss. In every case where it appears that the loss was by theft, the first sentence shall not apply unless the brewer establishes to the satisfaction of the Secretary that such theft occurred before removal from the brewery and occurred without connivance, collusion, fraud, or negligence on the part of the brewer, consignor, consignee, bailee, or carrier, or the employees or agents of any of them.

[CCH Explanation at ¶ 743. Committee Reports at ¶ 11,290.]

Amendment Notes	
Act Sec. 6014(a)(3) amended Code Sec. 5056 by striking "produced in the United States" and inserting "removed for consumption or sale".	The above amendment is effective as if included in the provision of the Taxpayer Relief Act of 1997 (P.L. 105-34) to which it relates [effective April 1, 1998.—CCH.].

(c) BEER RECEIVED AT A DISTILLED SPIRITS PLANT.—Any tax paid by any brewer on beer *removed for consumption or sale* may be refunded or credited to the brewer, without interest, or if the tax has not been paid, the brewer may be relieved of liability therefor, under regulations as the Secretary may prescribe, if such beer is received on the bonded premises of a distilled spirits plant pursuant to the provisions of section 5222(b)(2), for use in the production of distilled spirits.

* * *

[CCH Explanation at ¶ 743. Committee Reports at ¶ 11,290.]

Amendment Notes	
Act Sec. 6014(a)(3) amended Code Sec. 5056 by striking "produced in the United States" and inserting "removed for consumption or sale".	The above amendment is effective as if included in the provision of the Taxpayer Relief Act of 1997 (P.L. 105-34) to which it relates [effective April 1, 1998.—CCH.].

[¶ 6010] CODE SEC. 5364. WINE IMPORTED IN BULK.

Natural wine (as defined in section 5381) imported or brought into the United States in bulk containers may, under such regulations as the Secretary may prescribe, be withdrawn from customs custody and transferred in such bulk containers to the premises of a bonded wine cellar without payment of the internal revenue tax imposed on such wine. The proprietor of a bonded wine cellar to which such wine is transferred shall become liable for the tax on the wine withdrawn from customs custody under this section upon release of the wine from customs custody, and the importer, or the person bringing such wine into the United States, shall thereupon be relieved of the liability for such tax.

[CCH Explanation at ¶ 741. Committee Reports at ¶ 11,295.]

Amendment Notes	
Act Sec. 6014(b)(3) amended Code Sec. 5364 by striking "Wine imported or brought into" and inserting "Natural wine (as defined in section 5381) imported or brought into".	The above amendment is effective as if included in the provision of the Taxpayer Relief Act of 1997 (P.L. 105-34) to which it relates [effective April 1, 1998.—CCH.].

[¶ 6020] CODE SEC. 6011. GENERAL REQUIREMENT OF RETURN, STATEMENT, OR LIST.

* * *

(f) PROMOTION OF ELECTRONIC FILING.—

(1) IN GENERAL.—*The Secretary is authorized to promote the benefits of and encourage the use of electronic tax administration programs, as they become available, through the use of mass communications and other means.*

(2) INCENTIVES.—*The Secretary may implement procedures to provide for the payment of appropriate incentives for electronically filed returns.*

[CCH Explanation at ¶ 1001. Committee Reports at ¶ 10,215.]

Amendment Notes

Act Sec. 2001(c) amended Code Sec. 6011 by redesignating subsection (f) as subsection (g) and by inserting after subsection (e) a new subsection (f) to read as above.

The above amendment is effective on the date of the enactment of this Act.

Act Sec. 2001(a)-(b) and (d) provides:

(a) IN GENERAL.—It is the policy of Congress that—

(1) paperless filing should be the preferred and most convenient means of filing Federal tax and information returns,

(2) it should be the goal of the Internal Revenue Service to have at least 80 percent of all such returns filed electronically by the year 2007, and

(3) the Internal Revenue Service should cooperate with and encourage the private sector by encouraging competition to increase electronic filing of such returns.

(b) STRATEGIC PLAN.—

(1) IN GENERAL.—Not later than 180 days after the date of the enactment of this Act, the Secretary of the Treasury or the Secretary's delegate (hereafter in this section referred to as the "Secretary") shall establish a plan to eliminate barriers, provide incentives, and use competitive market forces to increase electronic filing gradually over the next 10 years while maintaining processing times for paper returns at 40 days. To the extent practicable, such plan shall provide that

all returns prepared electronically for taxable years beginning after 2001 shall be filed electronically.

(2) ELECTRONIC COMMERCE ADVISORY GROUP.—To ensure that the Secretary receives input from the private sector in the development and implementation of the plan required by paragraph (1), the Secretary shall convene an electronic commerce advisory group to include representatives from the small business community and from the tax practitioner, preparer, and computerized tax processor communities and other representatives from the electronic filing industry.

* * *

(d) ANNUAL REPORTS.—Not later than June 30 of each calendar year after 1998, the Chairperson of the Internal Revenue Service Oversight Board, the Secretary of the Treasury, and the Chairperson of the electronic commerce advisory group established under subsection (b)(2) shall report to the Committees on Ways and Means, Appropriations, Government Reform and Oversight, and Small Business of the House of Representatives and the Committees on Finance, Appropriations, Governmental Affairs, and Small Business of the Senate on—

(1) the progress of the Internal Revenue Service in meeting the goal of receiving electronically 80 percent of tax and information returns by 2007;

(2) the status of the plan required by subsection (b);

(3) the legislative changes necessary to assist the Internal Revenue Service in meeting such goal; and

(4) the effects on small businesses and the self-employed of electronically filing tax and information returns.

Act Sec. 2003(c)-(e) provides:

(c) ESTABLISHMENT OF PROCEDURES FOR OTHER INFORMATION.—In the case of taxable periods beginning after December 31, 1999, the Secretary of the Treasury or the Secretary's delegate shall, to the extent practicable, establish procedures to accept, in electronic form, any other information, statements, elections, or schedules, from taxpayers filing returns electronically, so that such taxpayers will not be required to file any paper.

(d) INTERNET AVAILABILITY.—In the case of taxable periods beginning after December 31, 1998, the Secretary of the Treasury or the Secretary's delegate shall establish procedures for all tax forms, instructions, and publications created in the most recent 5-year period to be made available electronically on the Internet in a searchable database at approximately the same time such records are available to the public in paper form. In addition, in the case of taxable periods beginning after December 31, 1998, the Secretary of the Treasury or the Secretary's delegate shall, to the extent practicable, establish procedures for other taxpayer guidance to be made available electronically on the Internet in a searchable database at approximately the same time such guidance is available to the public in paper form.

(e) PROCEDURES FOR AUTHORIZING DISCLOSURE ELECTRONICALLY.—The Secretary shall establish procedures for any taxpayer to authorize, on an electronically filed return, the Secretary to disclose information under section 6103(c) of the Internal Revenue Code of 1986 to the preparer of the return.

(g) INCOME, ESTATE, AND GIFT TAXES.—

For requirement that returns of income, estate, and gift taxes be made whether or not there is tax liability, see subparts B and C.

[CCH Explanation at ¶ 1001. Committee Reports at ¶ 10,215.]

Amendment Notes

Act Sec. 2001(c) amended Code Sec. 6011 by redesignating subsection (f) as subsection (g).

The above amendment is effective on the date of the enactment of this Act.

[¶ 6030] CODE SEC. 6013. JOINT RETURNS OF INCOME TAX BY HUSBAND AND WIFE.

* * *

(e) *[Stricken.]*

* * *

[CCH Explanation at ¶ 1290. Committee Reports at ¶ 10,285.]

Amendment Notes

Act Sec. 3201(e)(1) amended Code Sec. 6013 by striking subsection (e). Prior to being stricken, Code Sec. 6013(e) read as follows:

(e) SPOUSE RELIEVED OF LIABILITY IN CERTAIN CASES.—

(1) IN GENERAL.—Under regulations prescribed by the Secretary, if—

(A) a joint return has been made under this section for a taxable year,

(B) on such return there is a substantial understatement of tax attributable to grossly erroneous items of one spouse,

(C) the other spouse establishes that in signing the return he or she did not know, and had no reason to know, that there was such substantial understatement, and

(D) taking into account all the facts and circumstances, it is inequitable to hold the other spouse liable for the deficiency in tax for such taxable year attributable to such substantial understatement,

then the other spouse shall be relieved of liability for tax (including interest, penalties, and other amounts) for such taxable year to the extent such liability is attributable to such substantial understatement.

(2) GROSSLY ERRONEOUS ITEMS.—For purposes of this subsection, the term "grossly erroneous items" means, with respect to any spouse—

(A) any item of gross income attributable to such spouse which is omitted from gross income, and

(B) any claim of a deduction, credit, or basis by such spouse in an amount for which there is no basis in fact or law.

(3) SUBSTANTIAL UNDERSTATEMENT.—For purposes of this subsection, the term "substantial understatement" means any understatement (as defined in section 6662(d)(2)(A)) which exceeds $500.

(4) UNDERSTATEMENT MUST EXCEED SPECIFIED PERCENTAGE OF SPOUSE'S INCOME.—

(A) ADJUSTED GROSS INCOME OF $20,000 OR LESS.—If the spouse's adjusted gross income for the preadjustment year is $20,000 or less, this subsection shall apply only if the liability described in paragraph (1) is greater than 10 percent of such adjusted gross income.

(B) ADJUSTED GROSS INCOME OF MORE THAN $20,000.—If the spouse's adjusted gross income for the preadjustment year is more than $20,000, subparagraph (A) shall be applied by substituting "25 percent" for "10 percent".

(C) PREADJUSTMENT YEAR.—For purposes of this paragraph, the term "preadjustment year" means the most recent taxable year of the spouse ending before the date the deficiency notice is mailed.

(D) COMPUTATION OF SPOUSE'S ADJUSTED GROSS INCOME.—If the spouse is married to another spouse at the close of the preadjustment year, the spouse's adjusted gross income shall include the income of the new spouse (whether or not they file a joint return).

(E) EXCEPTION FOR OMISSIONS FROM GROSS INCOME.—This paragraph shall not apply to any liability attributable to the omission of an item from gross income.

(5) SPECIAL RULE FOR COMMUNITY PROPERTY INCOME.—For purposes of this subsection, the determination of the spouse to whom items of gross income (other than gross income from property) are attributable shall be made without regard to community property laws.

The above amendment applies to any liability for tax arising after the date of the enactment of this Act and any liability for tax arising on or before such date but remaining unpaid as of such date. For a special rule, see Act Sec. 3201(g)(2), below.

Act Sec. 3201(g)(2) provides:

(2) 2-YEAR PERIOD.—The 2-year period under subsection (b)(1)(E) or (c)(3)(B) of section 6015 of the Internal Revenue Code of 1986 shall not expire before the date which is 2 years after the date of the first collection activity after the date of the enactment of this Act.

(g) ELECTION TO TREAT NONRESIDENT ALIEN INDIVIDUAL AS RESIDENT OF THE UNITED STATES.—

(1) IN GENERAL.—A nonresident alien individual with respect to whom this subsection is in effect for the taxable year shall be treated as a resident of the United States—

(A) for purposes of *chapter 1* for all of such taxable year, and

(B) for purposes of chapter 24 (relating to wage withholding) for payments of wages made during such taxable year.

* * *

(5) TERMINATION BY SECRETARY.—The Secretary may terminate any election under this subsection for any taxable year if he determines that either spouse has failed—

(A) to keep such books and records,

(B) to grant such access to such books and records, or

(C) to supply such other information,

as may be reasonably necessary to ascertain the amount of liability for taxes under *chapter 1* of either spouse for such taxable year.

* * *

<table>
<tr><td>

Amendment Notes

Act Sec. 6011(e)(2) amended Code Sec. 6013 by striking "chapters 1 and 5" each place it appears in paragraphs (1)(A) and (5) of subsection (g) and inserting "chapter 1".

</td><td>

The above amendment is effective as if included in the provision of the Taxpayer Relief Act of 1997 (P.L. 105-34) to which it relates [effective August 5, 1997.— CCH.].

</td></tr>
</table>

(h) JOINT RETURN, ETC., FOR YEAR IN WHICH NONRESIDENT ALIEN BECOMES RESIDENT OF UNITED STATES.—

(1) IN GENERAL.—If—

(A) any individual is a nonresident alien individual at the beginning of any taxable year but is a resident of the United States at the close of such taxable year,

(B) at the close of such taxable year, such individual is married to a citizen or resident of the United States, and

(C) both individuals elect the benefits of this subsection at the time and in the manner prescribed by the Secretary by regulation,

then the individual referred to in subparagraph (A) shall be treated as a resident of the United States for purposes of *chapter 1* for all of such taxable year, and for purposes of chapter 24 (relating to wage withholding) for payments of wages made during such taxable year.

* * *

<table>
<tr><td>

Amendment Notes

Act Sec. 6011(e)(2) amended Code Sec. 6013 by striking "chapters 1 and 5" in subsection (h)(1) and inserting "chapter 1".

</td><td>

The above amendment is effective as if included in the provision of the Taxpayer Relief Act of 1997 (P.L. 105-34) to which it relates [effective August 5, 1997.— CCH.].

</td></tr>
</table>

[¶ 6040] *CODE SEC. 6015. RELIEF FROM JOINT AND SEVERAL LIABILITY ON JOINT RETURN.*

(a) *IN GENERAL.—Notwithstanding section 6013(d)(3)—*

(1) an individual who has made a joint return may elect to seek relief under the procedures prescribed under subsection (b), and

(2) if such individual is eligible to elect the application of subsection (c), such individual may, in addition to any election under paragraph (1), elect to limit such individual's liability for any deficiency with respect to such joint return in the manner prescribed under subsection (c).

Any determination under this section shall be made without regard to community property laws.

(b) *PROCEDURES FOR RELIEF FROM LIABILITY APPLICABLE TO ALL JOINT FILERS.—*

(1) IN GENERAL.—Under procedures prescribed by the Secretary, if—

(A) a joint return has been made for a taxable year,

(B) on such return there is an understatement of tax attributable to erroneous items of 1 individual filing the joint return,

(C) the other individual filing the joint return establishes that in signing the return he or she did not know, and had no reason to know, that there was such understatement,

(D) taking into account all the facts and circumstances, it is inequitable to hold the other individual liable for the deficiency in tax for such taxable year attributable to such understatement, and

(E) the other individual elects (in such form as the Secretary may prescribe) the benefits of this subsection not later than the date which is 2 years after the date the Secretary has begun collection activities with respect to the individual making the election,

then the other individual shall be relieved of liability for tax (including interest, penalties, and other amounts) for such taxable year to the extent such liability is attributable to such understatement.

(2) APPORTIONMENT OF RELIEF.—If an individual who, but for paragraph (1)(C), would be relieved of liability under paragraph (1), establishes that in signing the return such individual did not know, and had no reason to know, the extent of such understatement, then such individual shall be relieved of liability for tax (including interest, penalties, and other amounts) for such taxable year to the extent that such liability is attributable to the portion of such understatement of which such individual did not know and had no reason to know.

(3) UNDERSTATEMENT.—For purposes of this subsection, the term "understatement" has the meaning given to such term by section 6662(d)(2)(A).

(c) PROCEDURES TO LIMIT LIABILITY FOR TAXPAYERS NO LONGER MARRIED OR TAXPAYERS LEGALLY SEPARATED OR NOT LIVING TOGETHER.—

(1) IN GENERAL.—Except as provided in this subsection, if an individual who has made a joint return for any taxable year elects the application of this subsection, the individual's liability for any deficiency which is assessed with respect to the return shall not exceed the portion of such deficiency properly allocable to the individual under subsection (d).

(2) BURDEN OF PROOF.—Except as provided in subparagraph (A)(ii) or (C) of paragraph (3), each individual who elects the application of this subsection shall have the burden of proof with respect to establishing the portion of any deficiency allocable to such individual.

(3) ELECTION.—

(A) INDIVIDUALS ELIGIBLE TO MAKE ELECTION.—

(i) IN GENERAL.—An individual shall only be eligible to elect the application of this subsection if—

(I) at the time such election is filed, such individual is no longer married to, or is legally separated from, the individual with whom such individual filed the joint return to which the election relates, or

(II) such individual was not a member of the same household as the individual with whom such joint return was filed at any time during the 12-month period ending on the date such election is filed.

(ii) CERTAIN TAXPAYERS INELIGIBLE TO ELECT.—If the Secretary demonstrates that assets were transferred between individuals filing a joint return as part of a fraudulent scheme by such individuals, an election under this subsection by either individual shall be invalid (and section 6013(d)(3) shall apply to the joint return).

(B) TIME FOR ELECTION.—An election under this subsection for any taxable year shall be made not later than 2 years after the date on which the Secretary has begun collection activities with respect to the individual making the election.

(C) ELECTION NOT VALID WITH RESPECT TO CERTAIN DEFICIENCIES.—If the Secretary demonstrates that an individual making an election under this subsection had actual knowledge, at the time such individual signed the return, of any item giving rise to a deficiency (or portion thereof) which is not allocable to such individual under subsection (d), such election shall not apply to such deficiency (or portion). This subparagraph shall not apply where the individual with actual knowledge establishes that such individual signed the return under duress.

(4) LIABILITY INCREASED BY REASON OF TRANSFERS OF PROPERTY TO AVOID TAX.—

(A) IN GENERAL.—Notwithstanding any other provision of this subsection, the portion of the deficiency for which the individual electing the application of this subsection is liable (without regard to this paragraph) shall be increased by the value of any disqualified asset transferred to the individual.

(B) DISQUALIFIED ASSET.—For purposes of this paragraph—

(i) IN GENERAL.—The term "disqualified asset" means any property or right to property transferred to an individual making the election under this subsection with respect to a joint return by the other individual filing such joint return if the principal purpose of the transfer was the avoidance of tax or payment of tax.

(ii) PRESUMPTION.—

(I) IN GENERAL.—For purposes of clause (i), except as provided in subclause (II), any transfer which is made after the date which is 1 year before the date on which the 1st letter of proposed deficiency which allows the taxpayer an opportunity for administrative review in the Internal Revenue Service Office of Appeals is sent shall be presumed to have as its principal purpose the avoidance of tax or payment of tax.

(II) EXCEPTIONS.—Subclause (I) shall not apply to any transfer pursuant to a decree of divorce or separate maintenance or a written instrument incident to such a decree or to any transfer which an individual establishes did not have as its principal purpose the avoidance of tax or payment of tax.

(d) ALLOCATION OF DEFICIENCY.—For purposes of subsection (c)—

(1) IN GENERAL.—The portion of any deficiency on a joint return allocated to an individual shall be the amount which bears the same ratio to such deficiency as the net amount of items taken into account in computing the deficiency and allocable to the individual under paragraph (3) bears to the net amount of all items taken into account in computing the deficiency.

(2) SEPARATE TREATMENT OF CERTAIN ITEMS.—If a deficiency (or portion thereof) is attributable to—

(A) the disallowance of a credit, or

(B) any tax (other than tax imposed by section 1 or 55) required to be included with the joint return, and such item is allocated to 1 individual under paragraph (3), such deficiency (or portion) shall be allocated to such individual. Any such item shall not be taken into account under paragraph (1).

(3) ALLOCATION OF ITEMS GIVING RISE TO THE DEFICIENCY.—For purposes of this subsection—

(A) IN GENERAL.—Except as provided in paragraphs (4) and (5), any item giving rise to a deficiency on a joint return shall be allocated to individuals filing the return in the same manner as it would have been allocated if the individuals had filed separate returns for the taxable year.

(B) EXCEPTION WHERE OTHER SPOUSE BENEFITS.—Under rules prescribed by the Secretary, an item otherwise allocable to an individual under subparagraph (A) shall be allocated to the other individual filing the joint return to the extent the item gave rise to a tax benefit on the joint return to the other individual.

(C) EXCEPTION FOR FRAUD.—The Secretary may provide for an allocation of any item in a manner not prescribed by subparagraph (A) if the Secretary establishes that such allocation is appropriate due to fraud of 1 or both individuals.

(4) LIMITATIONS ON SEPARATE RETURNS DISREGARDED.—If an item of deduction or credit is disallowed in its entirety solely because a separate return is filed, such disallowance shall be disregarded and the item shall be computed as if a joint return had been filed and then allocated between the spouses appropriately. A similar rule shall apply for purposes of section 86.

(5) CHILD'S LIABILITY.—If the liability of a child of a taxpayer is included on a joint return, such liability shall be disregarded in computing the separate liability of either spouse and such liability shall be allocated appropriately between the spouses.

(e) PETITION FOR REVIEW BY TAX COURT.—

(1) IN GENERAL.—In the case of an individual who elects to have subsection (b) or (c) apply—

(A) IN GENERAL.—The individual may petition the Tax Court (and the Tax Court shall have jurisdiction) to determine the appropriate relief available to the individual under this section if such petition is filed during the 90-day period beginning on the date on which the Secretary mails by certified or registered mail a notice to such individual of the Secretary's determination of relief available to the individual. Notwithstanding the preceding sentence, an individual may file such petition at any time after the date which is 6 months after the date such election is filed with the Secretary and before the close of such 90-day period.

(B) RESTRICTIONS APPLICABLE TO COLLECTION OF ASSESSMENT.—

(i) IN GENERAL.—Except as otherwise provided in section 6851 or 6861, no levy or proceeding in court shall be made, begun, or prosecuted against the individual making an election under subsection (b) or (c) for collection of any assessment to which such election relates until the expiration of the 90-day period described in subparagraph (A), or, if a petition has been filed with the Tax Court, until the decision of the Tax Court has become final. Rules similar to the rules of section 7485 shall apply with respect to the collection of such assessment.

(ii) AUTHORITY TO ENJOIN COLLECTION ACTIONS.—Notwithstanding the provisions of section 7421(a), the beginning of such levy or proceeding during the time the prohibition under clause (i) is in force may be enjoined by a proceeding in the proper court, including the Tax Court. The Tax Court shall have no jurisdiction under this subparagraph to enjoin any action or proceeding unless a timely petition has been filed under subparagraph (A) and then only in respect of the amount of the assessment to which the election under subsection (b) or (c) relates.

(2) SUSPENSION OF RUNNING OF PERIOD OF LIMITATIONS.—The running of the period of limitations in section 6502 on the collection of the assessment to which the petition under paragraph (1)(A) relates shall be suspended for the period during which the Secretary is prohibited by paragraph (1)(B) from collecting by levy or a proceeding in court and for 60 days thereafter.

(3) APPLICABLE RULES.—

(A) ALLOWANCE OF CREDIT OR REFUND.—Except as provided in subparagraph (B), notwithstanding any other law or rule of law (other than section 6512(b), 7121, or 7122), credit or refund shall be allowed or made to the extent attributable to the application of this section.

(B) RES JUDICATA.—In the case of any election under subsection (b) or (c), if a decision of the Tax Court in any prior proceeding for the same taxable year has become final, such decision shall be conclusive except with respect to the qualification of the individual for relief which was not an issue in such proceeding. The exception contained in the preceding sentence shall not apply if the Tax Court determines that the individual participated meaningfully in such prior proceeding.

(C) LIMITATION ON TAX COURT JURISDICTION.—If a suit for refund is begun by either individual filing the joint return pursuant to section 6532—

(i) the Tax Court shall lose jurisdiction of the individual's action under this section to whatever extent jurisdiction is acquired by the district court or the United States Court of Federal Claims over the taxable years that are the subject of the suit for refund, and

(ii) the court acquiring jurisdiction shall have jurisdiction over the petition filed under this subsection.

(4) NOTICE TO OTHER SPOUSE.—The Tax Court shall establish rules which provide the individual filing a joint return but not making the election under subsection (b) or (c) with adequate notice and an opportunity to become a party to a proceeding under either such subsection.

(f) EQUITABLE RELIEF.—Under procedures prescribed by the Secretary, if—

(1) taking into account all the facts and circumstances, it is inequitable to hold the individual liable for any unpaid tax or any deficiency (or any portion of either), and

(2) relief is not available to such individual under subsection (b) or (c),

the Secretary may relieve such individual of such liability.

(g) REGULATIONS.—The Secretary shall prescribe such regulations as are necessary to carry out the provisions of this section, including—

(1) regulations providing methods for allocation of items other than the methods under subsection (d)(3), and

(2) regulations providing the opportunity for an individual to have notice of, and an opportunity to participate in, any administrative proceeding with respect to an election made under subsection (b) or (c) by the other individual filing the joint return.

[CCH Explanation at ¶ 1290. Committee Reports at ¶ 10,285.]

Amendment Notes

Act Sec. 3201(a) amended subpart B of part II of subchapter A of chapter 61 by inserting after Code Sec. 6014 a new Code Sec. 6015 to read as above.

The above amendment generally applies to any liability for tax arising after the date of the enactment of this Act and any liability for tax arising on or before such date but remaining unpaid as of such date. For a special rule, see Act Sec. 3201(c)-(d) and (g)(2), below.

Act Sec. 3201(c)-(d) and (g)(2) provides:

(c) SEPARATE FORM FOR APPLYING FOR SPOUSAL RELIEF.—Not later than 180 days after the date of the enactment of this Act, the Secretary of the Treasury shall develop a separate form with instructions for use by taxpayers in applying for relief under section 6015(a) of the Internal Revenue Code of 1986, as added by this section.

(d) SEPARATE NOTICE TO EACH FILER.—The Secretary of the Treasury shall, wherever practicable, send any notice relating to a joint return under section 6013 of the Internal Revenue Code of 1986 separately to each individual filing the joint return.

* * *

(g) EFFECTIVE DATES.—

* * *

(2) 2-YEAR PERIOD.—The 2-year period under subsection (b)(1)(E) or (c)(3)(B) of section 6015 of the Internal Revenue Code of 1986 shall not expire before the date which is 2 years after the date of the first collection activity after the date of the enactment of this Act.

[¶ 6050] CODE SEC. 6038. INFORMATION REPORTING WITH RESPECT TO CERTAIN FOREIGN CORPORATIONS AND PARTNERSHIPS.

(a) REQUIREMENT.—

* * *

(2) PERIOD FOR WHICH INFORMATION IS TO BE FURNISHED, ETC.—The information required under paragraph (1) shall be furnished for the annual accounting period of the foreign business entity ending with or within the United States person's taxable year. The information so required shall be furnished at such time and in such manner as the Secretary shall prescribe.

(3) LIMITATION.—No information shall be required to be furnished under this subsection with respect to any foreign business entity for any annual accounting period unless *the Secretary has prescribed the furnishing of such information on or before the first day of such annual accounting period.*

* * *

[CCH Explanation at ¶ 683. Committee Reports at ¶ 11,245.]

Amendment Notes

Act Sec. 6011(f)(1) amended Code Sec. 6038(a)(2) by striking "by regulations" following "Secretary shall".

Act Sec. 6011(f)(2) amended Code Sec. 6038(a)(3) by striking "such information" and all that follows through the period and inserting "the Secretary has prescribed the furnishing of such information on or before the first day of such annual accounting period." Prior to amendment, Code Sec. 6038(a)(3) read as follows:

(3) LIMITATION.—No information shall be required to be furnished under this subsection with respect to any foreign

business entity for any annual accounting period unless such information was required to be furnished under regulations in effect on the first day of such annual accounting period.

The above amendments are effective as if included in the provisions of the Taxpayer Relief Act of 1997 (P.L. 105-34) to which they relate [effective for annual accounting periods beginning after August 5, 1997.— CCH.].

(e) DEFINITIONS.—For purposes of this section—

* * *

(4) ANNUAL ACCOUNTING PERIOD.—The annual accounting period of a foreign business entity is the annual period on the basis of which such *foreign business entity* regularly computes its income in keeping its books. In the case of a specified foreign business entity (as defined in section 898), the taxable year of such *foreign business entity* shall be treated as its annual accounting period.

* * *

Code Sec. 6038(e)   ¶ 6050

[CCH Explanation at ¶ 683. Committee Reports at ¶ 11,245.]

Amendment Notes	
Act Sec. 6011(f)(3) amended Code Sec. 6038(e)(4) by striking "corporation" and inserting "foreign business entity" each place it appears.	The above amendment is effective as if included in the provision of the Taxpayer Relief Act of 1997 (P.L. 105-34) to which it relates [effective for annual accounting periods beginning after August 5, 1997.—CCH.].

[¶ 6060] CODE SEC. 6039. INFORMATION REQUIRED IN CONNECTION WITH CERTAIN OPTIONS.

(a) FURNISHING OF INFORMATION.—Every corporation—

(1) which in any calendar year transfers *to any person* a share of stock pursuant to such person's exercise of an incentive stock option, or

(2) which in any calendar year records (or has by its agent recorded) a transfer of the legal title of a share of stock acquired by the transferor pursuant to his exercise of an option described in section 423(c) (relating to special rule where option price is between 85 percent and 100 percent of value of stock),

shall (on or before January 31 of the following calendar year) furnish to such person a written statement in such manner and setting forth such information as the Secretary may by regulations prescribe.

* * *

[CCH Explanation at ¶ 30,050.]

Amendment Notes	
Act Sec. 6023(20) amended Code Sec. 6039(a)(1) by inserting "to any person" after "transfers".	The above amendment is effective on the date of the enactment of this Act.

[¶ 6070] CODE SEC. 6050R. RETURNS RELATING TO CERTAIN PURCHASES OF FISH.

* * *

(b) RETURN.—A return is described in this subsection if such return—

(1) is in such form as the Secretary may prescribe, and

(2) contains—

(A) the name, address, and TIN of each person to whom a payment described in subsection (a)(2) was made during the calendar year,

(B) the aggregate amount of such payments made to such person during such calendar year and the date and amount of each such payment, and

(C) such other information as the Secretary may require.

* * *

[CCH Explanation at ¶ 30,050.]

Amendment Notes	
Act Sec. 6023(21) amended Code Sec. 6050R(b)(2)(A) by striking the semicolon at the end thereof and inserting a comma.	The above amendment is effective on the date of the enactment of this Act.

[¶ 6080] CODE SEC. 6050S. RETURNS RELATING TO HIGHER EDUCATION TUITION AND RELATED EXPENSES.

(a) IN GENERAL.—Any person—

(1) which is an eligible educational institution—

(A) which receives payments for qualified tuition and related expenses with respect to any individual for any calendar year, or

(B) which makes reimbursements or refunds (or similar amounts) to any individual of qualified tuition and related expenses,

(2) which is engaged in a trade or business of making payments to any individual under an insurance arrangement as reimbursements or refunds (or similar amounts) of qualified tuition and related expenses, or

(3) except as provided in regulations, which is engaged in a trade or business and, in the course of which, receives from any individual interest aggregating $600 or more for any calendar year on 1 or more qualified education loans,

shall make the return described in subsection (b) with respect to the individual at such time as the Secretary may by regulations prescribe.

[CCH Explanation at ¶ 226. Committee Reports at ¶ 10,835.]

Amendment Notes	
Act Sec. 6004(a)(2) amended Code Sec. 6050S(a) to read as above. Prior to amendment, Code Sec. 6050S(a) read as follows: (a) IN GENERAL.—Any person—	(1) which is an eligible educational institution which receives payments for qualified tuition and related expenses with respect to any individual for any calendar year, or (2) which is engaged in a trade or business and, in the course of such trade or business— (A) makes payments during any calendar year to any individual which constitutes reimbursements or refunds (or

similar amounts) of qualified tuition and related expenses of such individual, or

(B) except as provided in regulations, receives from any individual interest aggregating $600 or more for any calendar year on 1 or more qualified education loans,

shall make the return described in subsection (b) with respect to the individual at such time as the Secretary may by regulations prescribe.

The above amendment is effective as if included in the provision of the Taxpayer Relief Act of 1997 (P.L. 105-34) to which it relates [effective for expenses paid after December 31, 1997 (in tax years ending after such date), for education furnished in academic periods beginning after such date.—CCH.].

(b) FORM AND MANNER OF RETURNS.—A return is described in this subsection if such return—

(1) is in such form as the Secretary may prescribe,

(2) contains—

* * *

(C) the—

(i) aggregate amount of payments for qualified tuition and related expenses received with respect to the individual described in subparagraph (A) during the calendar year,

[Caution: Code Sec. 6050S(b)(2)(C)(ii)-(iv), below, as amended by Act Sec. 3712(a)(1)-(3), applies to returns required to be filed with respect to tax years beginning after December 31, 1998.—CCH.]

(ii) the amount of any grant received by such individual for payment of costs of attendance and processed by the person making such return during such calendar year,

(iii) aggregate amount of reimbursements or refunds (or similar amounts) paid to such individual during the calendar year *by the person making such return,* and

(iv) aggregate amount of interest received for the calendar year from such individual, *and*

(D) such other information as the Secretary may prescribe.

[CCH Explanation at ¶ 226. Committee Reports at ¶ 10,690.]

Amendment Notes

Act Sec. 3712(a)(1) amended Code Sec. 6050S(b)(2)(C) by redesignating clauses (ii) and (iii) as clauses (iii) and (iv), respectively, and by inserting after clause (i) a new clause (ii) to read as above.

Act Sec. 3712(a)(2) amended Code Sec. 6050S(b)(2)(C)(iii), as redesignated by Act Sec. 3712(a)(1), by inserting "by the person making such return" after "year".

Act Sec. 3712(a)(3) amended Code Sec. 6050S(b)(2)(C)(iv), as redesignated by Act Sec. 3712(a)(1), by inserting "and" at the end.

The above amendments apply to returns required to be filed with respect to tax years beginning after December 31, 1998.

(d) STATEMENTS TO BE FURNISHED TO INDIVIDUALS WITH RESPECT TO WHOM INFORMATION IS REQUIRED.—Every person required to make a return under subsection (a) shall furnish to each individual whose name is required to be set forth in such return under subparagraph (A) or (B) of subsection (b)(2) a written statement showing—

(1) the name, address, and phone number of the information contact of the person required to make such return, and

[Caution: Code Sec. 6050S(d)(2), below, as amended by Act Sec. 3712(b)(1), applies to returns required to be filed with respect to tax years beginning after December 31, 1998.—CCH.]

(2) the amounts described in subparagraph (C) of subsection (b)(2).

The written statement required under the preceding sentence shall be furnished on or before January 31 of the year following the calendar year for which the return under subsection (a) was required to be made.

[CCH Explanation at ¶ 226. Committee Reports at ¶ 10,690.]

Amendment Notes

Act Sec. 3712(b)(1) amended Code Sec. 6050S(d)(2) by striking "aggregate" before "amounts".

The above amendment applies to returns required to be filed with respect to tax years beginning after December 31, 1998.

[Caution: Code Sec. 6050S(e), below, as amended by Act Sec. 3712(b)(2), applies to returns required to be filed with respect to tax years beginning after December 31, 1998.—CCH.]

(e) DEFINITIONS.—For purposes of this section, the terms "eligible educational institution" and "qualified tuition and related expenses" have the meanings given such terms by section 25A *(without regard to subsection (g)(2) thereof),* and except as provided in regulations, the term "qualified education loan" has the meaning given such term by section 221(e)(1).

* * *

[CCH Explanation at ¶ 226. Committee Reports at ¶ 10,690.]

Code Sec. 6050S(e)   ¶ 6080

Amendment Notes
Act Sec. 3712(b)(2) amended Code Sec. 6050S(e) by inserting "(without regard to subsection (g)(2) thereof)" after "section 25A".

The above amendment applies to returns required to be filed with respect to tax years beginning after December 31, 1998.

[¶ 6090] CODE SEC. 6061. SIGNING OF RETURNS AND OTHER DOCUMENTS.

(a) GENERAL RULE.—Except as otherwise provided by subsection (b) and sections 6062 and 6063, any return, statement, or other document required to be made under any provision of the internal revenue laws or regulations shall be signed in accordance with forms or regulations prescribed by the Secretary.

[CCH Explanation at ¶ 1009. Committee Reports at ¶ 10,225.]

Amendment Notes
Act Sec. 2003(a)(1) amended Code Sec. 6061 by striking "Except as otherwise provided by" and inserting "(a) GENERAL RULE.—Except as otherwise provided by subsection (b) and".

The above amendment is effective on the date of the enactment of this Act.

(b) ELECTRONIC SIGNATURES.—

(1) IN GENERAL.—The Secretary shall develop procedures for the acceptance of signatures in digital or other electronic form. Until such time as such procedures are in place, the Secretary may—

(A) waive the requirement of a signature for, or

(B) provide for alternative methods of signing or subscribing,

a particular type or class of return, declaration, statement, or other document required or permitted to be made or written under internal revenue laws and regulations.

(2) TREATMENT OF ALTERNATIVE METHODS.—Notwithstanding any other provision of law, any return, declaration, statement, or other document filed and verified, signed, or subscribed under any method adopted under paragraph (1)(B) shall be treated for all purposes (both civil and criminal, including penalties for perjury) in the same manner as though signed or subscribed.

(3) PUBLISHED GUIDANCE.—The Secretary shall publish guidance as appropriate to define and implement any waiver of the signature requirements or any method adopted under paragraph (1).

[CCH Explanation at ¶ 1009. Committee Reports at ¶ 10,225.]

Amendment Notes
Act Sec. 2003(a)(2) amended Code Sec. 6061 by adding at the end a new subsection (b) to read as above.
The above amendment is effective on the date of the enactment of this Act.
Act Sec. 2003(c)-(e) provides:
(c) ESTABLISHMENT OF PROCEDURES FOR OTHER INFORMATION.—In the case of taxable periods beginning after December 31, 1999, the Secretary of the Treasury or the Secretary's delegate shall, to the extent practicable, establish procedures to accept, in electronic form, any other information, statements, elections, or schedules, from taxpayers filing returns electronically, so that such taxpayers will not be required to file any paper.
(d) INTERNET AVAILABILITY.—In the case of taxable periods beginning after December 31, 1998, the Secretary of the Treasury or the Secretary's delegate shall establish procedures for all tax forms, instructions, and publications created in the most recent 5-year period to be made available electronically on the Internet in a searchable database at approximately the same time such records are available to the public in paper form. In addition, in the case of taxable periods beginning after December 31, 1998, the Secretary of the Treasury or the Secretary's delegate shall, to the extent practicable, establish procedures for other taxpayer guidance to be made available electronically on the Internet in a searchable database at approximately the same time such guidance is available to the public in paper form.

(e) PROCEDURES FOR AUTHORIZING DISCLOSURE ELECTRONICALLY.—The Secretary shall establish procedures for any taxpayer to authorize, on an electronically filed return, the Secretary to disclose information under section 6103(c) of the Internal Revenue Code of 1986 to the preparer of the return.

[¶ 6100] CODE SEC. 6071. TIME FOR FILING RETURNS AND OTHER DOCUMENTS.
* * *

[Caution: Code Sec. 6071(b), below, as added by Act Sec. 2002(a), applies to returns required to be filed after December 31, 1999.—CCH.]

(b) ELECTRONICALLY FILED INFORMATION RETURNS.—Returns made under subparts B and C of part III of this subchapter which are filed electronically shall be filed on or before March 31 of the year following the calendar year to which such returns relate.

[CCH Explanation at ¶ 1005. Committee Reports at ¶ 10,220.]

Amendment Notes
Act Sec. 2002(a) amended Code Sec. 6071 by redesignating subsection (b) as subsection (c) and by inserting after subsection (a) a new subsection (b) to read as above.
The above amendment applies to returns required to be filed after December 31, 1999.
Act Sec. 2002(b)(1)-(2) provides:
(1) IN GENERAL.—The Secretary of the Treasury shall conduct a study evaluating the effect of extending the deadline for providing statements to persons with respect to whom information is required to be furnished under subparts B and C of part III of subchapter A of chapter 61 of the Internal Revenue Code of 1986 (other than section 6051 of such Code) from January 31 to February 15 of the year in which the return to which the statement relates is required to be filed.

(2) REPORT.—Not later than June 30, 1999, the Secretary of the Treasury shall submit a report on the study under paragraph (1) to the Committee on Ways and Means of the House of Representatives and the Committee on Finance of the Senate.

(c) SPECIAL TAXES.—

For payment of special taxes before engaging in certain trades and businesses, see section 4901 and section 5142.

[CCH Explanation at ¶ 1005. Committee Reports at ¶ 10,220.]

Amendment Notes

Act Sec. 2002(a) amended Code Sec. 6071 by redesignating subsection (b) as subsection (c).

The above amendment applies to returns required to be filed after December 31, 1999.

[¶ 6110] CODE SEC. 6103. CONFIDENTIALITY AND DISCLOSURE OF RETURNS AND RETURN INFORMATION.
* * *

(d) DISCLOSURE TO STATE TAX OFFICIALS AND STATE AND LOCAL LAW ENFORCEMENT AGENCIES.—
* * *

(5) DISCLOSURE FOR CERTAIN COMBINED REPORTING PROJECT.—The Secretary shall disclose taxpayer identities and signatures for purposes of the demonstration project described in *section 976 of the Taxpayer Relief Act of 1997. Subsections (a)(2) and (p)(4) and sections 7213 and 7213A shall not apply with respect to disclosures or inspections made pursuant to this paragraph.*

[CCH Explanation at ¶ 589. Committee Reports at ¶ 11,110.]

Amendment Notes

Act Sec. 6009(d) amended Code Sec. 6103(d)(5) by striking "section 967 of the Taxpayer Relief Act of 1997." and inserting "section 976 of the Taxpayer Relief Act of 1997. Subsections (a)(2) and (p)(4) and sections 7213 and 7213A shall not apply with respect to disclosures or inspections made pursuant to this paragraph."

The above amendment is effective as if included in the provision of the Taxpayer Relief Act of 1997 (P.L. 105-34) to which it relates [effective August 5, 1997.— CCH.].

(e) DISCLOSURE TO PERSONS HAVING MATERIAL INTEREST.—

(1) IN GENERAL.—The return of a person shall, upon written request, be open to inspection by or disclosure to—

(A) in the case of the return of an individual—

(i) that individual,

(ii) the spouse of that individual if the individual and such spouse have signified their consent to consider a gift reported on such return as made one-half by him and one-half by the spouse pursuant to the provisions of section 2513, or

(iii) the child of that individual (or such child's legal representative) to the extent necessary to comply with the provisions of section (1)(g);
* * *

(6) ATTORNEY IN FACT.—Any return to which this subsection applies shall, upon written request, also be open to inspection by or disclosure to the attorney in fact duly authorized in writing by any of the persons described in paragraph (1), (2), (3), (4), *(5), (8), or (9)* to inspect the return or receive the information on his behalf, subject to the conditions provided in such paragraphs.
* * *

[CCH Explanation at ¶ 1295 and 1432. Committee Reports at ¶ 11,360.]

Amendment Notes

Act Sec. 6007(f)(4) amended Code Sec. 6103(e)(1)(A) by striking clause (ii) and by redesignating clauses (iii) and (iv) as clauses (ii) and (iii), respectively. Prior to being stricken, Code Sec. 6103(e)(1)(A)(ii) read as follows:
(ii) if property transferred by that individual to a trust is sold or exchanged in a transaction described in section 644, the trustee or trustees, jointly or separately, of such trust to the extent necessary to ascertain any amount of tax imposed upon the trust by section 644,

The above amendment is effective as if included in the provision of the Taxpayer Relief Act of 1997 (P.L. 105-34) to which it relates [effective for sales or exchanges after August 5, 1997.—CCH.].

Act Sec. 6019(c) amended Code Sec. 6103(e)(6) by striking "or (5)" and inserting "(5), (8), or (9)".

The above amendment is effective on the date of the enactment of this Act.

(f) DISCLOSURE TO COMMITTEES OF CONGRESS.—
* * *

(5) DISCLOSURE BY WHISTLEBLOWER.—*Any person who otherwise has or had access to any return or return information under this section may disclose such return or return information to a committee referred to in paragraph (1) or any individual authorized to receive or inspect information under paragraph (4)(A) if such person believes such return or return information may relate to possible misconduct, maladministration, or taxpayer abuse.*
* * *

[CCH Explanation at ¶ 863. Committee Reports at ¶ 10,670.]

Amendment Notes

Act Sec. 3708(a) amended Code Sec. 6103(f) by adding at the end a new paragraph (5) to read as above.

The above amendment is effective on the date of the enactment of this Act.

(h) DISCLOSURE TO CERTAIN FEDERAL OFFICERS AND EMPLOYEES FOR PURPOSES OF TAX ADMINISTRATION, ETC.—

* * *

(4) DISCLOSURE IN JUDICIAL AND ADMINISTRATIVE TAX PROCEEDINGS.—A return or return information may be disclosed in a Federal or State judicial or administrative proceeding pertaining to tax administration, but only—

(A) *if* the taxpayer is a party to the proceeding, or the proceeding arose out of, or in connection with, determining the taxpayer's civil or criminal liability, or the collection of such civil liability, in respect of any tax imposed under this title;

* * *

(5)[(6)] INTERNAL REVENUE SERVICE OVERSIGHT BOARD.— ʹ

(A) IN GENERAL.—Notwithstanding paragraph (1), and except as provided in subparagraph (B), no return or return information may be disclosed to any member of the Oversight Board described in subparagraph (A) or (D) of section 7802(b)(1) or to any employee or detailee of such Board by reason of their service with the Board. Any request for information not permitted to be disclosed under the preceding sentence, and any contact relating to a specific taxpayer, made by any such individual to an officer or employee of the Internal Revenue Service shall be reported by such officer or employee to the Secretary, the Treasury Inspector General for Tax Administration, and the Joint Committee on Taxation.

(B) EXCEPTION FOR REPORTS TO THE BOARD.—If—

(i) the Commissioner or the Treasury Inspector General for Tax Administration prepares any report or other matter for the Oversight Board in order to assist the Board in carrying out its duties, and

(ii) the Commissioner or such Inspector General determines it is necessary to include any return or return information in such report or other matter to enable the Board to carry out such duties, such return or return information (other than information regarding taxpayer identity) may be disclosed to members, employees, or detailees of the Board solely for the purpose of carrying out such duties.

* * *

[CCH Explanation at ¶ 826 and 30,050. Committee Reports at ¶ 10,130.]

Amendment Notes

Act Sec. 1101(b) amended Code Sec. 6103(h) by adding at the end a new paragraph (5)[(6)] to read as above.

The above amendment is effective on the date of the enactment of this Act. For a special rule, see Act Sec. 1101(d)(2)-(3), below.

Act Sec. 1101(d)(2)-(3) provides:

(2) INITIAL NOMINATIONS TO INTERNAL REVENUE SERVICE OVERSIGHT BOARD.—The President shall submit the initial nominations under section 7802 of the Internal Revenue Code of 1986, as added by this section, to the Senate not later than 6 months after the date of the enactment of this Act.

(3) EFFECT ON ACTIONS PRIOR TO APPOINTMENT OF OVERSIGHT BOARD.—Nothing in this section shall be construed to invalidate the actions and authority of the Internal Revenue Service prior to the appointment of the members of the Internal Revenue Service Oversight Board.

Act Sec. 6023(22) amended Code Sec. 6103(h)(4)(A) by inserting "if" before "the taxpayer is a party to".

The above amendment is effective on the date of the enactment of this Act.

(k) DISCLOSURE OF CERTAIN RETURNS AND RETURN INFORMATION FOR TAX ADMINISTRATION PURPOSES.—

* * *

(9) DISCLOSURE OF INFORMATION TO ADMINISTER SECTION 6311.—The Secretary may disclose returns or return information to financial institutions and others to the extent the Secretary deems necessary for the administration of section 6311. Disclosures of information for purposes other than to accept payments by checks or money orders shall be made only to the extent authorized by written procedures promulgated by the Secretary.

Amendment Notes

Act Sec. 6012(b)(2) amended Code Sec. 6103(k) by redesignating paragraph (8) (as added by Act Sec. 1205(c)(1) of the Taxpayer Relief Act of 1997 (P.L. 105-34)) as paragraph (9).

The above amendment is effective as if included in the provision of the Taxpayer Relief Act of 1997 (P.L. 105-34) to which it relates [effective May 5, 1998.—CCH.].

(l) DISCLOSURE OF RETURNS AND RETURN INFORMATION FOR PURPOSES OTHER THAN TAX ADMINISTRATION.—

* * *

[*Caution: Code Sec. 6103(l)(10), below, as amended by Act Sec. 3711(b)(1)-(2), applies to refunds payable under Code Sec. 6402 after December 31, 1999.—CCH.*]

(10) DISCLOSURE OF CERTAIN INFORMATION TO AGENCIES REQUESTING A REDUCTION UNDER SUBSECTION *(c), (d), OR (e) OF SECTION 6402.—*

(A) RETURN INFORMATION FROM INTERNAL REVENUE SERVICE.—The Secretary may, upon receiving a written request, disclose to officers and employees of any agency seeking a reduction under subsection *(c), (d), or (e)* of section 6402 and to officers and employees of the Department of the Treasury in connection with such reduction—

(i) taxpayer identity information with respect to the taxpayer against whom such a reduction was made or not made and with respect to any other person filing a joint return with such taxpayer,

(ii) the fact that a reduction has been made or has not been made under such subsection with respect to such taxpayer,

(iii) the amount of such reduction,

(iv) whether such taxpayer filed a joint return, and

(v) the fact that a payment was made (and the amount of the payment) to the spouse of the taxpayer on the basis of a joint return.

(B) RESTRICTION ON USE OF DISCLOSED INFORMATION.—Any officers and employees of an agency receiving return information under subparagraph (A) shall use such information only for the purposes of, and to the extent necessary in, establishing appropriate agency records, locating any person with respect to whom a reduction under subsection *(c), (d), or (e)* of section 6402 is sought for purposes of collecting the debt with respect to which the reduction is sought, or in the defense of any litigation or administrative procedure ensuing from a reduction made under subsection *(c), (d), or (e)* of section 6402.

* * *

(17) DISCLOSURE TO NATIONAL ARCHIVES AND RECORDS ADMINISTRATION.—The Secretary shall, upon written request from the Archivist of the United States, disclose or authorize the disclosure of returns and return information to officers and employees of the National Archives and Records Administration for purposes of, and only to the extent necessary in, the appraisal of records for destruction or retention. No such officer or employee shall, except to the extent authorized by subsections (f), (i)(7), or (p), disclose any return or return information disclosed under the preceding sentence to any person other than to the Secretary, or to another officer or employee of the National Archives and Records Administration whose official duties require such disclosure for purposes of such appraisal

* * *

[CCH Explanation at ¶ 881 and 1446. Committee Reports at ¶ 10,640 and 10,685.]

Amendment Notes

Act Sec. 3702(a) amended Code Sec. 6103(l) by adding at the end a new paragraph (17) to read as above.

The above amendment applies to requests made by the Archivist of the United States after the date of the enactment of this Act.

Act Sec. 3711(b)(1) amended Code Sec. 6103(l)(10) by striking "(c) or (d)" each place it appears and inserting "(c), (d), or (e)".

Act Sec. 3711(b)(2) amended the paragraph heading of Code Sec. 6103(l)(10) by striking "SECTION 6402(c) OR 6402(d)" and inserting "SUBSECTION (c), (d), OR (e) OF SECTION 6402".

The above amendments apply to refunds payable under Code Sec. 6402 after December 31, 1999.

(p) PROCEDURE AND RECORDKEEPING.—

* * *

(3) RECORDS OF INSPECTION AND DISCLOSURE.—

(A) SYSTEM OF RECORDKEEPING.—Except as otherwise provided by this paragraph, the Secretary shall maintain a permanent system of standardized records or accountings of all requests for inspection or disclosure of returns and return information (including the reasons for and dates of such requests) and of returns and return information inspected or disclosed under this section. Notwithstanding the provisions of section 552a(c) of title 5, United States Code, the Secretary shall not be required to maintain a record or accounting of requests for inspection or disclosure of returns and return information, or of returns and return information inspected or disclosed, under the authority of subsections (c), (e), (h)(1), (3)(A), or (4), (i)(4), or (7)(A)(ii), (k)(1), (2), (6), *(8), or (9)*, (l)(1), (4)(B), (5), (7), (8), (9), (10), (11), (12), (13)[,] (14), (15), *(16), or (17)*, (m), or (n). The records or accountings required to be maintained under this paragraph shall be available for examination by the Joint Committee on Taxation or the Chief of Staff of such joint committee. Such record or accounting shall also be available for examination by such person or persons as may be, but only to the extent, authorized to make such examination under section 552a(c)(3) of title 5, United States Code.

* * *

(4) SAFEGUARDS.—Any Federal agency described in subsection (h)(2), (h)(5), (i)(1), (2), (3), or (5), (j)(1) or (2), (k)(8), (l)(1), (2), (3), (5), (10), (11), (13), *(14), or (17)* or (o)(1), the General Accounting Office, or any agency, body, or commission described in subsection (d), (i)(3)(B)(i), or

(l)(6), (7), (8), (9), (12), or[sic] (15), or (16), or any other person described in subsection (l)(16) shall, as a condition for receiving returns or return information—

* * *

(F) upon completion of use of such returns or return information—

* * *

(i) in the case of an agency, body, or commission described in subsection (d), (i)(3)(B)(i), or (l)(6), (7), (8), (9), or (16), or any other person described in subsection (l)(16) return to the Secretary such returns or return information (along with any copies made therefrom) or make such returns or return information undisclosable in any manner and furnish a written report to the Secretary describing such manner,

(ii) in the case of an agency described in subsections (h)(2), (h)(5), (i)(1), (2), (3), or (5), (j)(1) or (2), (k)(8), (l)(1), (2), (3), (5), (10), (11), (12), (13), (14), *(15), or 17*, or (o)(1), or the General Accounting Office, either—

(I) return to the Secretary such returns or return information (along with any copies made therefrom),

(II) otherwise make such returns or return information undisclosable, or

(III) to the extent not so returned or made undisclosable, ensure that the conditions of subparagraphs (A), (B), (C), (D), and (E) of this paragraph continue to be met with respect to such returns or return information, and

* * *

[CCH Explanation at ¶ 881. Committee Reports at ¶ 10,640.]

Amendment Notes

Act Sec. 3702(b)(1) amended Code Sec. 6103(p)(3)(A) by striking "or (16)" and inserting "(16), or (17)".

Act Sec. 3702(b)(2) amended Code Sec. 6103(p)(4) by striking "or (14)" and inserting ", (14), or (17)".

Act Sec. 3702(b)(3) amended Code Sec. 6103(p)(4)(F)(ii) by striking "or (15)" and inserting ", (15), or (17)".

The above amendments apply to requests made by the Archivist of the United States after the date of the enactment of this Act.

Act Sec. 6012(b)(4) provides that Act Sec. 1205(c)(3) of the Taxpayer Relief Act of 1997 (P.L. 105-34) shall be applied as if the amendment to Code Sec. 6103(p)(3)(A) struck "or (8)" and inserted "(8), or (9)".

The above amendment is effective as if included in the provision of the Taxpayer Relief Act of 1997 (P.L. 105-34) to which it relates [effective May 5, 1998.— CCH.].

Act Sec. 2003(e) provides:

(e) PROCEDURES FOR AUTHORIZING DISCLOSURE ELECTRONICALLY.—The Secretary shall establish procedures for any taxpayer to authorize, on an electronically filed return, the Secretary to disclose information under section 6103(c) of the Internal Revenue Code of 1986 to the preparer of the return.

Act Sec. 2005 provides:

SEC. 2005. ACCESS TO ACCOUNT INFORMATION.

(a) IN GENERAL.—Not later than December 31, 2006, the Secretary of the Treasury or the Secretary's delegate shall develop procedures under which a taxpayer filing returns electronically (and their designees under section 6103(c) of the Internal Revenue Code of 1986) would be able to review the taxpayer's account electronically, but only if all necessary safeguards to ensure the privacy of such account information are in place.

(b) REPORT.—Not later than December 31, 2003, the Secretary of the Treasury shall report on the progress the Secretary is making on the development of procedures under subsection (a) to the Committee on Ways and Means of the House of Representatives and the Committee on Finance of the Senate.

Act Sec. 3508 provides:

SEC. 3508. DISCLOSURE TO TAXPAYERS.

The Secretary of the Treasury or the Secretary's delegate shall ensure that any instructions booklet accompanying an individual Federal income tax return form (including forms 1040, 1040A, 1040EZ, and any similar or successor forms) shall include, in clear language, in conspicuous print, and in a conspicuous place, a concise description of the conditions under which return information may be disclosed to any party outside the Internal Revenue Service, including disclosure to any State or agency, body, or commission (or legal representative) thereof.

[¶ 6120] CODE SEC. 6104. PUBLICITY OF INFORMATION REQUIRED FROM CERTAIN EXEMPT ORGANIZATIONS AND CERTAIN TRUSTS.

* * *

(b) INSPECTION OF ANNUAL INFORMATION RETURNS.—The information required to be furnished by sections 6033, 6034, and 6058, together with the names and addresses of such organizations and trusts, shall be made available to the public at such times and in such places as the Secretary may prescribe. Nothing in this subsection shall authorize the Secretary to disclose the name or address of any contributor to any organization or trust (other than a private foundation, as defined in section 509(a)) which is required to furnish such information. *In the case of an organization described in section 501(d), this subsection shall not apply to copies referred to in section 6031(b) with respect to such organization.*

* * *

[CCH Explanation at ¶ 691. Committee Reports at ¶ 11,355.]

Amendment Notes

Act Sec. 6019(a) amended Code Sec. 6104(b) by adding at the end a new sentence to read as above.

The above amendment is effective on the date of the enactment of this Act.

(e) PUBLIC INSPECTION OF CERTAIN ANNUAL RETURNS AND APPLICATIONS FOR EXEMPTION.—

(1) ANNUAL RETURNS.—

* * *

(C) NONDISCLOSURE OF CONTRIBUTORS.—Subparagraph (A) shall not require the disclosure of the name or address of any contributor to the organization. *In the case of an organization described in section 501(d), subparagraph (A) shall not require the disclosure of the copies referred to in section 6031(b) with respect to such organization.*

* * *

[CCH Explanation at ¶ 691. Committee Reports at ¶ 11,355.]

Amendment Notes	The above amendment is effective on the date of the
Act Sec. 6019(b) amended Code Sec. 6104(e)(1)(C) by adding at the end a new sentence to read as above.	enactment of this Act.

[¶ 6130] CODE SEC. 6109. IDENTIFYING NUMBERS.

(a) SUPPLYING OF IDENTIFYING NUMBERS.—When required by regulations prescribed by the Secretary:

* * *

For purposes of paragraphs (1), (2), and (3), the identifying number of an individual (or his estate) shall be such individual's social security account number.

* * *

[CCH Explanation at ¶ 865. Committee Reports at ¶ 10,680.]

Amendment Notes	The above amendment is effective on the date of the
Act Sec. 3710(a) amended the last sentence of Code Sec. 6109(a) by striking "For purposes of this subsection" and inserting "For purposes of paragraphs (1), (2), and (3)".	enactment of this Act.

[¶ 6140] CODE SEC. 6110. PUBLIC INSPECTION OF WRITTEN DETERMINATIONS.

* * *

(b) DEFINITIONS.—For purposes of this section—

(1) WRITTEN DETERMINATION.—The term "written determination" means a ruling, determination letter, *technical advice memorandum, or Chief Counsel advice.*

* * *

[CCH Explanation at ¶ 892. Committee Reports at ¶ 10,605.]

Amendment Notes

Act Sec. 3509(a) amended Code Sec. 6110(b)(1) by striking "or technical advice memorandum" and inserting "technical advice memorandum, or Chief Counsel advice".

The above amendment applies to any Chief Counsel advice issued more than 90 days after the date of the enactment of this Act. For transition rules, see Act Sec. 3509(d)(2)-(4), below.

Act Sec. 3509(d)(2)-(4) provides:

(2) TRANSITION RULES.—The amendments made by this section shall apply to any Chief Counsel advice issued after December 31, 1985, and before the 91st day after the date of the enactment of this Act by the offices of the associate chief counsel for domestic, employee benefits and exempt organizations, and international, except that any such Chief Counsel advice shall be treated as made available on a timely basis if such advice is made available for public inspection not later than the following dates:

(A) One year after the date of the enactment of this Act, in the case of all litigation guideline memoranda, service center advice, tax litigation bulletins, criminal tax bulletins, and general litigation bulletins.

(B) Eighteen months after such date of enactment, in the case of field service advice and technical assistance to the field issued on or after January 1, 1994.

(C) Three years after such date of enactment, in the case of field service advice and technical assistance to the field issued on or after January 1, 1992, and before January 1, 1994.

(D) Six years after such date of enactment, in the case of any other Chief Counsel advice issued after December 31, 1985.

(3) DOCUMENTS TREATED AS CHIEF COUNSEL ADVICE.—If the Secretary of the Treasury by regulation provides pursuant to section 6110(i)(2) of the Internal Revenue Code of 1986, as added by this section, that any additional advice or instruction issued by the Office of Chief Counsel shall be treated as Chief Counsel advice, such additional advice or instruction shall be made available for public inspection pursuant to section 6110 of such Code, as amended by this section, only in accordance with the effective date set forth in such regulation.

(4) CHIEF COUNSEL ADVICE TO BE AVAILABLE ELECTRONICALLY.—The Internal Revenue Service shall make any Chief Counsel advice issued more than 90 days after the date of the enactment of this Act and made available for public inspection pursuant to section 6110 of such Code, as amended by this section, also available by computer telecommunications within 1 year after issuance.

(f) RESOLUTION OF DISPUTES RELATING TO DISCLOSURE.—

(1) NOTICE OF INTENTION TO DISCLOSE.—*Except as otherwise provided by subsection (i), the Secretary* shall upon issuance of any written determination, or upon receipt of a request for a background file document, mail a notice of intention to disclose such determination or document to any person to whom the written determination pertains (or a successor in interest, executor, or other person authorized by law to act for or on behalf of such person).

* * *

[CCH Explanation at ¶ 892. Committee Reports at ¶ 10,605.]

Amendment Notes	The above amendment applies to any Chief Counsel
Act Sec. 3509(c)(1) amended Code Sec. 6110(f)(1) by striking "The Secretary" and inserting "Except as otherwise provided by subsection (i), the Secretary".	advice issued more than 90 days after the date of the enactment of this Act. For transition rules, see Act Sec.

3509(d)(2)-(4) under the amendment notes to subsection (b), above.

(i) SPECIAL RULES FOR DISCLOSURE OF CHIEF COUNSEL ADVICE.—

(1) CHIEF COUNSEL ADVICE DEFINED.—

(A) IN GENERAL.—For purposes of this section, the term "Chief Counsel advice" means written advice or instruction, under whatever name or designation, prepared by any national office component of the Office of Chief Counsel which—

(i) is issued to field or service center employees of the Service or regional or district employees of the Office of Chief Counsel, and

(ii) conveys—

(I) any legal interpretation of a revenue provision,

(II) any Internal Revenue Service or Office of Chief Counsel position or policy concerning a revenue provision, or

(III) any legal interpretation of State law, foreign law, or other Federal law relating to the assessment or collection of any liability under a revenue provision.

(B) REVENUE PROVISION DEFINED.—For purposes of subparagraph (A), the term "revenue provision" means any existing or former internal revenue law, regulation, revenue ruling, revenue procedure, other published or unpublished guidance, or tax treaty, either in general or as applied to specific taxpayers or groups of specific taxpayers.

(2) ADDITIONAL DOCUMENTS TREATED AS CHIEF COUNSEL ADVICE.—The Secretary may by regulation provide that this section shall apply to any advice or instruction prepared and issued by the Office of Chief Counsel which is not described in paragraph (1).

(3) DELETIONS FOR CHIEF COUNSEL ADVICE.—In the case of Chief Counsel advice open to public inspection pursuant to this section—

(A) paragraphs (2) through (7) of subsection (c) shall not apply, but

(B) the Secretary may make deletions of material in accordance with subsections (b) and (c) of section 552 of title 5, United States Code, except that in applying subsection (b)(3) of such section, no statutory provision of this title shall be taken into account.

(4) NOTICE OF INTENTION TO DISCLOSE.—

(A) NONTAXPAYER-SPECIFIC CHIEF COUNSEL ADVICE.—In the case of Chief Counsel advice which is written without reference to a specific taxpayer or group of specific taxpayers—

(i) subsection (f)(1) shall not apply, and

(ii) the Secretary shall, within 60 days after the issuance of the Chief Counsel advice, complete any deletions described in subsection (c)(1) or paragraph (3) and make the Chief Counsel advice, as so edited, open for public inspection.

(B) TAXPAYER-SPECIFIC CHIEF COUNSEL ADVICE.—In the case of Chief Counsel advice which is written with respect to a specific taxpayer or group of specific taxpayers, the Secretary shall, within 60 days after the issuance of the Chief Counsel advice, mail the notice required by subsection (f)(1) to each such taxpayer. The notice shall include a copy of the Chief Counsel advice on which is indicated the information that the Secretary proposes to delete pursuant to subsection (c)(1). The Secretary may also delete from the copy of the text of the Chief Counsel advice any of the information described in paragraph (3), and shall delete the names, addresses, and other identifying details of taxpayers other than the person to whom the advice pertains, except that the Secretary shall not delete from the copy of the Chief Counsel advice that is furnished to the taxpayer any information of which that taxpayer was the source.

[CCH Explanation at ¶ 892. Committee Reports at ¶ 10,605.]

Amendment Notes
Act Sec. 3509(b) amended Code Sec. 6110 by redesignating subsections (i), (j), (k), and (l) as subsections (j), (k), (l), and (m), respectively, and by inserting after subsection (h) a new subsection (i) to read as above.

The above amendment applies to any Chief Counsel advice issued more than 90 days after the date of the enactment of this Act. For transition rules, see Act Sec. 3509(d)(2)-(4) in the amendment notes to subsection (b), above.

(j) CIVIL REMEDIES.—

(1) CIVIL ACTION.—Whenever the Secretary—

(A) fails to make deletions required in accordance with subsection (c), or

(B) fails to follow the procedures in subsection (g) or (i)(4)(B), the recipient of the written determination or any person identified in the written determination shall have as an exclusive civil remedy an action against the Secretary in the United States Claims Court, which shall have jurisdiction to hear any action under this paragraph.

(2) DAMAGES.—In any suit brought under the provisions of paragraph (1)(A) in which the Court determines that an employee of the Internal Revenue Service intentionally or willfully failed to delete in accordance with subsection (c), or in any suit brought under subparagraph (1)(B) in which the Court determines that an employee intentionally or willfully failed to act in accordance with

subsection (g) or (i)(4)(B), the United States shall be liable to the person in an amount equal to the sum of—

(A) actual damages sustained by the person but in no case shall a person be entitled to receive less than the sum of $1,000, and

(B) the costs of the action together with reasonable attorney's fees as determined by the Court.

[CCH Explanation at ¶ 892. Committee Reports at ¶ 10,605.]

Amendment Notes

Act Sec. 3509(b) amended Code Sec. 6110 by redesignating subsection (i) as subsection (j).

Act Sec. 3509(c)(2) amended Code Sec. 6110(j)(1)(B) and (2), as redesignated, by striking " subsection (g)" each place it appears and inserting "subsection (g) or (i)(4)(B)".

The above amendments apply to any Chief Counsel advice issued more than 90 days after the date of the enactment of this Act. For transition rules, see Act Sec. 3509(d)(2)-(4) in the amendment notes to subsection (b), above.

(k) SPECIAL PROVISIONS.—

(1) FEES.—The Secretary is authorized to assess actual costs—

(A) for duplication of any written determination or background file document made open or available to the public under this section, and

(B) incurred in searching for and making deletions required under *subsection (c)(1) or (i)(3)* from any written determination or background file document which is available to public inspection only upon written request.

The Secretary shall furnish any written determination or background file document without charge or at a reduced charge if he determines that waiver or reduction of the fee is in the public interest because furnishing such determination or background file document can be considered as primarily benefiting the general public.

* * *

[CCH Explanation at ¶ 892. Committee Reports at ¶ 10,605.]

Amendment Notes

Act Sec. 3509(b) amended Code Sec. 6110 by redesignating subsection (j) as subsection (k).

Act Sec. 3509(c)(3) amended Code Sec. 6110(k)(1)(B), as redesignated, by striking " subsection (c)" and inserting "subsection (c)(1) or (i)(3)".

The above amendments apply to any Chief Counsel advice issued more than 90 days after the date of the enactment of this Act. For transition rules, see Act Sec. 3509(d)(2)-(4) in the amendment notes to subsection (b), above.

(l) SECTION NOT TO APPLY.—This section shall not apply to—

(1) any matter to which section 6104 applies, or

(2) any—

(A) written determination issued pursuant to a request made before November 1, 1976, with respect to the exempt status under section 501(a) of an organization described in section 501(c) or (d), the status of an organization as a private foundation under section 509(a), or the status of an organization as an operating foundation under section 4942(j)(3),

(B) written determination described in subsection (g)(5)(B) issued pursuant to a request made before November 1, 1976,

(C) determination letter not otherwise described in subparagraph (A), (B), or (E) issued pursuant to a request made before November 1, 1976,

(D) background file document relating to any general written determination issued before July 5, 1967, or

(E) letter or other document described in section 6104(a)(1)(B)(iv) issued before September 2, 1974.

[CCH Explanation at ¶ 892. Committee Reports at ¶ 10,605.]

Amendment Notes

Act Sec. 3509(b) amended Code Sec. 6110 by redesignating subsection (k) as subsection (l).

The above amendment applies to any Chief Counsel advice issued more than 90 days after the date of the

enactment of this Act. For transition rules, see Act Sec. 3509(d)(2)-(4) in the amendment notes to subsection (b), above.

(m) EXCLUSIVE REMEDY.—Except as otherwise provided in this title, or with respect to a discovery order made in connection with a judicial proceeding, the Secretary shall not be required by any Court to make any written determination or background file document open or available to public inspection, or to refrain from disclosure of any such documents.

[CCH Explanation at ¶ 892. Committee Reports at ¶ 10,605.]

Amendment Notes

Act Sec. 3509(b) amended Code Sec. 6110 by redesignating subsection (l) as subsection (m).

The above amendment applies to any Chief Counsel advice issued more than 90 days after the date of the enactment of this Act. For transition rules, see Act Sec. 3509(d)(2)-(4) in the amendment notes to subsection (b), above.

Code Sec. 6110(m)   ¶ 6140

[¶ 6145] CODE SEC. 6156. INSTALLMENT PAYMENTS OF TAX ON USE OF HIGHWAY MOTOR VEHICLES.

* * *

(e) SECTION INAPPLICABLE TO CERTAIN LIABILITIES.—This section shall not apply to any liability for tax incurred in—

(1) April, May, or June of any year, or

(2) July, August, or September of *2005*.

[CCH Explanation at ¶ 750.]

Amendment Notes

P.L. 105-178 (ISTEA)
Act Sec. 9002(a)(2)(B) amended Code Sec. 6156(e)(2) by striking "1999" and inserting "2005".

The above amendment is effective on June 9, 1998.

[¶ 6150] CODE SEC. 6159. AGREEMENTS FOR PAYMENT OF TAX LIABILITY IN INSTALLMENTS.

* * *

(c) SECRETARY REQUIRED TO ENTER INTO INSTALLMENT AGREEMENTS IN CERTAIN CASES.—In the case of a liability for tax of an individual under subtitle A, the Secretary shall enter into an agreement to accept the payment of such tax in installments if, as of the date the individual offers to enter into the agreement—

(1) the aggregate amount of such liability (determined without regard to interest, penalties, additions to the tax, and additional amounts) does not exceed $10,000,

(2) the taxpayer (and, if such liability relates to a joint return, the taxpayer's spouse) has not, during any of the preceding 5 taxable years—

(A) failed to file any return of tax imposed by subtitle A,

(B) failed to pay any tax required to be shown on any such return, or

(C) entered into an installment agreement under this section for payment of any tax imposed by subtitle A,

(3) the Secretary determines that the taxpayer is financially unable to pay such liability in full when due (and the taxpayer submits such information as the Secretary may require to make such determination),

(4) the agreement requires full payment of such liability within 3 years, and

(5) the taxpayer agrees to comply with the provisions of this title for the period such agreement is in effect.

[CCH Explanation at ¶ 1274. Committee Reports at ¶ 10,545.]

Amendment Notes
Act Sec. 3467(a) amended Code Sec. 6159 by redesignating subsection (c) as subsection (d) and by inserting after subsection (b) a new subsection (c) to read as above.
The above amendment is effective on the date of the enactment of this Act.

Act Sec. 3506 provides:
SEC. 3506. STATEMENTS REGARDING IN-STALLMENT AGREEMENTS.
The Secretary of the Treasury or the Secretary's delegate shall, beginning not later than July 1, 2000, provide each taxpayer who has an installment agreement in effect under section 6159 of the Internal Revenue Code of 1986 an annual statement setting forth the initial balance at the beginning of the year, the payments made during the year, and the remaining balance as of the end of the year.

(d) ADMINISTRATIVE REVIEW.—The Secretary shall establish procedures for an independent administrative review of terminations of installment agreements under this section for taxpayers who request such a review.

[CCH Explanation at ¶ 1274. Committee Reports at ¶ 10,545.]

Amendment Notes
Act Sec. 3467(a) amended Code Sec. 6159 by redesignating subsection (c) as subsection (d).

The above amendment is effective on the date of the enactment of this Act.

(d) [(e)] CROSS REFERENCE.—

For rights to administrative review and appeal, see section 7122(d).

[CCH Explanation at ¶ 1270. Committee Reports at ¶ 10,520.]

Amendment Notes
Act Sec. 3462(c)(2) amended Code Sec. 6159 by adding at the end a new subsection (d) [(e)] to read as above.

The above amendment applies to proposed offers-in-compromise and installment agreements submitted after the date of the enactment of this Act.

[¶ 6160] CODE SEC. 6166. EXTENSION OF TIME FOR PAYMENT OF ESTATE TAX WHERE ESTATE CONSISTS LARGELY OF INTEREST IN CLOSELY HELD BUSINESS.

* * *

(b) DEFINITIONS AND SPECIAL RULES.—

* * *

(7) PARTNERSHIP INTERESTS AND STOCK WHICH IS NOT READILY TRADABLE.—

(A) IN GENERAL.—If the executor elects the benefits of this paragraph (at such time and in such manner as the Secretary shall by regulations prescribe), then—

(i) for purposes of paragraph (1)(B)(i) or (1)(C)(i) (whichever is appropriate) and for purposes of subsection (c), any capital interest in a partnership and any non-readily-tradable stock which (after the application of paragraph (2)) is treated as owned by the decedent shall be treated as included in determining the value of the decedent's gross estate,

(ii) the executor shall be treated as having selected under subsection (a)(3) the date prescribed by section 6151(a), and

(iii) *for purposes of applying section 6601(j), the 2-percent portion (as defined in such section) shall be treated as being zero.*

* * *

(8) STOCK IN HOLDING COMPANY TREATED AS BUSINESS COMPANY STOCK IN CERTAIN CASES.—

(A) IN GENERAL.—If the executor elects the benefits of this paragraph, then—

* * *

(iii) *2-PERCENT INTEREST RATE NOT TO APPLY.—For purposes of applying section 6601(j), the 2-percent portion (as defined in such section) shall be treated as being zero.*

* * *

[CCH Explanation at ¶ 436. Committee Reports at ¶ 11,020.]

Amendment Notes

Act Sec. 6007(c)(1) amended Code Sec. 6166(b)(7)(A)(iii) to read as above. Prior to amendment, Code Sec. 6166(b)(7)(A)(iii) read as follows:

(iii) section 6601(j) (relating to 2-percent rate of interest) shall not apply.

Act Sec. 6007(c)(2) amended Code Sec. 6166(b)(8)(A)(iii) to read as above. Prior to amendment, Code Sec. 6166(b)(8)(A)(iii) read as follows:

(iii) 2-PERCENT INTEREST RATE NOT TO APPLY.—Section 6601(j) (relating to 2-percent rate of interest) shall not apply.

The above amendments are effective as if included in the provisions of the Taxpayer Relief Act of 1997 (P.L. 105-34) to which they relate [effective for estates of decedents dying after December 31, 1997.—CCH.].

[¶ 6170] CODE SEC. 6211. DEFINITION OF A DEFICIENCY.

* * *

(c) COORDINATION WITH *SUBCHAPTERS C AND D.*—In determining the amount of any deficiency for purposes of this subchapter, adjustments to partnership items shall be made only as provided in *subchapters C and D.*

Amendment Notes

Act Sec. 6012(f)(1) and (2) amended Code Sec. 6211(c) by striking "SUBCHAPTER C" in the heading and inserting "SUBCHAPTERS C AND D", and by striking "subchapter C" in the text and inserting "subchapters C and D".

The above amendment is effective as if included in the provision of the Taxpayer Relief Act of 1997 (P.L. 105-34) to which it relates [effective for partnership tax years ending after August 5, 1997.—CCH.].

[¶ 6180] CODE SEC. 6212. NOTICE OF DEFICIENCY.

(a) IN GENERAL.—If the Secretary determines that there is a deficiency in respect of any tax imposed by subtitle A or B or chapter 41, 42, 43, or 44, he is authorized to send notice of such deficiency to the taxpayer by certified mail or registered mail. *Such notice shall include a notice to the taxpayer of the taxpayer's right to contact a local office of the taxpayer advocate and the location and phone number of the appropriate office.*

* * *

[CCH Explanation at ¶ 821. Committee Reports at ¶ 10,150.]

Amendment Notes

Act Sec. 1102(b) amended Code Sec. 6212(a) by adding at the end a new sentence to read as above.

The above amendment is effective on the date of the enactment of this Act. For a special rule, see Act Sec. 1102(f)(3)-(4), below.

Act Sec. 1102(f)(3)-(4) provides:

(3) NATIONAL TAXPAYER ADVOCATE.—Notwithstanding section 7803(c)(1)(B)(iv) of such Code, as added by this section, in appointing the first National Taxpayer Advocate after the date of the enactment of this Act, the Secretary of the Treasury—

(A) shall not appoint any individual who was an officer or employee of the Internal Revenue Service at any time during the 2-year period ending on the date of appointment, and

(B) need not consult with the Internal Revenue Service Oversight Board if the Oversight Board has not been appointed.

(4) CURRENT OFFICERS.—

(A) In the case of an individual serving as Commissioner of Internal Revenue on the date of the enactment of this Act who was appointed to such position before such date, the 5-year term required by section 7803(a)(1) of such Code, as added by this section, shall begin as of the date of such appointment.

(B) Clauses (ii), (iii), and (iv) of section 7803(c)(1)(B) of such Code, as added by this section, shall not apply to the individual serving as Taxpayer Advocate on the date of the enactment of this Act.

Act Sec. 3463(a) provides:

SEC. 3463. NOTICE OF DEFICIENCY TO SPECIFY DEADLINES FOR FILING TAX COURT PETITION.

(a) IN GENERAL.—The Secretary of the Treasury or the Secretary's delegate shall include on each notice of deficiency under section 6212 of the Internal Revenue Code of 1986 the date determined by such Secretary (or delegate) as the last day on which the taxpayer may file a petition with the Tax Court.

[*Caution: Code Sec. 6213(a), below, as amended by Act Sec. 3463(b), applies to notices mailed after December 31, 1998.—CCH.*]

[¶ 6190] CODE SEC. 6213. RESTRICTIONS APPLICABLE TO DEFICIENCIES; PETITION TO TAX COURT.

(a) TIME FOR FILING PETITION AND RESTRICTION ON ASSESSMENT.—Within 90 days, or 150 days if the notice is addressed to a person outside the United States, after the notice of deficiency authorized in section 6212 is mailed (not counting Saturday, Sunday, or a legal holiday in the District of Columbia as the last day), the taxpayer may file a petition with the Tax Court for a redetermination of the deficiency. Except as otherwise provided in section 6851, 6852, or 6861 no assessment of a deficiency in respect of any tax imposed by subtitle A or B, chapter 41, 42, 43, or 44 and no levy or proceeding in court for its collection shall be made, begun, or prosecuted until such notice has been mailed to the taxpayer, nor until the expiration of such 90-day or 150-day period, as the case may be, nor, if a petition has been filed with the Tax Court, until the decision of the Tax Court has become final. Notwithstanding the provisions of section 7421(a), the making of such assessment or the beginning of such proceeding or levy during the time such prohibition is in force may be enjoined by a proceeding in the proper court, *including the Tax Court, and a refund may be ordered by such court of any amount collected within the period during which the Secretary is prohibited from collecting by levy or through a proceeding in court under the provisions of this subsection.* The Tax Court shall have no jurisdiction *to enjoin any action or proceeding or order any refund* under this subsection unless a timely petition for a redetermination of the deficiency has been filed and then only in respect of the deficiency that is the subject of such petition. *Any petition filed with the Tax Court on or before the last date specified for filing such petition by the Secretary in the notice of deficiency shall be treated as timely filed.*

* * *

[CCH Explanation at ¶ 1321 and 1326. Committee Reports at ¶ 10,525 and 10,530.]

Amendment Notes
Act Sec. 3463(b) amended Code Sec. 6213(a) by adding at the end a new sentence to read as above.
The above amendment applies to notices mailed after December 31, 1998.
Act Sec. 3464(a)(1)-(2) amended Code Sec. 6213(a) by striking ", including the Tax Court." and inserting ", including the Tax Court, and a refund may be ordered by such

court of any amount collected within the period during which the Secretary is prohibited from collecting by levy or through a proceeding in court under the provisions of this subsection.", and by striking "to enjoin any action or proceeding" and inserting "to enjoin any action or proceeding or order any refund".
The above amendment is effective on the date of the enactment of this Act.

[¶ 6200] CODE SEC. 6230. ADDITIONAL ADMINISTRATIVE PROVISIONS.

* * *

(c) CLAIMS ARISING OUT OF ERRONEOUS COMPUTATIONS, ETC.—

* * *

(5) RULES FOR SEEKING INNOCENT SPOUSE RELIEF.—

(A) IN GENERAL.—The spouse of a partner may file a claim for refund on the ground that the Secretary failed to relieve the spouse under *section 6015* from a liability that is attributable to an adjustment to a partnership item (including any liability for any penalties, additions to tax, or additional amounts relating to such adjustment).

* * *

[CCH Explanation at ¶ 1290. Committee Reports at ¶ 10,285.]

Amendment Notes
Act Sec. 3201(e)(2) amended Code Sec. 6230(c)(5)(A) by striking "section 6013(e)" and inserting "section 6015".
The above amendment applies to any liability for tax arising after the date of the enactment of this Act and

any liability for tax arising on or before such date but remaining unpaid as of such date.

[¶ 6210] CODE SEC. 6231. DEFINITIONS AND SPECIAL RULES.

(a) DEFINITIONS.—For purposes of this subchapter—

* * *

(7) TAX MATTERS PARTNER.—The tax matters partner of any partnership is—

(A) the general partner designated as the tax matters partner as provided in regulations, or

(B) if there is no general partner who has been so designated, the general partner having the largest profits interest in the partnership at the close of the taxable year involved (or, where there is more than 1 such partner, the 1 of such partners whose name would appear first in an alphabetical listing).

If there is no general partner designated under subparagraph (A) and the Secretary determines that it is impracticable to apply subparagraph (B), the partner selected by the Secretary shall be treated as the tax matters partner. *The Secretary shall, within 30 days of selecting a tax matters partner under the preceding sentence, notify all partners required to receive notice under section 6223(a) of the name and address of the person selected.*

* * *

[CCH Explanation at ¶ 1136. Committee Reports at ¶ 10,595.]

Amendment Notes

Act Sec. 3507(a) amended Code Sec. 6231(a)(7) by adding at the end a new sentence to read as above

The above amendment applies to selections of tax matters partners made by the Secretary of the Treasury after the date of the enactment of this Act.

[¶ 6220] *CODE SEC. 6304. FAIR TAX COLLECTION PRACTICES.*

(a) COMMUNICATION WITH THE TAXPAYER.—*Without the prior consent of the taxpayer given directly to the Secretary or the express permission of a court of competent jurisdiction, the Secretary may not communicate with a taxpayer in connection with the collection of any unpaid tax—*

(1) at any unusual time or place or a time or place known or which should be known to be inconvenient to the taxpayer;

(2) if the Secretary knows the taxpayer is represented by any person authorized to practice before the Internal Revenue Service with respect to such unpaid tax and has knowledge of, or can readily ascertain, such person's name and address, unless such person fails to respond within a reasonable period of time to a communication from the Secretary or unless such person consents to direct communication with the taxpayer; or

(3) at the taxpayer's place of employment if the Secretary knows or has reason to know that the taxpayer's employer prohibits the taxpayer from receiving such communication.

In the absence of knowledge of circumstances to the contrary, the Secretary shall assume that the convenient time for communicating with a taxpayer is after 8 a.m. and before 9 p.m., local time at the taxpayer's location.

(b) PROHIBITION OF HARASSMENT AND ABUSE.—*The Secretary may not engage in any conduct the natural consequence of which is to harass, oppress, or abuse any person in connection with the collection of any unpaid tax. Without limiting the general application of the foregoing, the following conduct is a violation of this subsection:*

(1) The use or threat of use of violence or other criminal means to harm the physical person, reputation, or property of any person.

(2) The use of obscene or profane language or language the natural consequence of which is to abuse the hearer or reader.

(3) Causing a telephone to ring or engaging any person in telephone conversation repeatedly or continuously with intent to annoy, abuse, or harass any person at the called number.

(4) Except as provided under rules similar to the rules in section 804 of the Fair Debt Collection Practices Act (15 U.S.C. 1692b), the placement of telephone calls without meaningful disclosure of the caller's identity.

(c) CIVIL ACTION FOR VIOLATIONS OF SECTION.—

For civil action for violations of this section, see section 7433

[CCH Explanation at ¶ 1262. Committee Reports at ¶ 10,540.]

Amendment Notes

Act Sec. 3466(a) amended subchapter A of chapter 64 by inserting after Code Sec. 6303 a new Code Sec. 6304 to read as above.

The above amendment is effective on the date of the enactment of this Act.

[¶ 6230] CODE SEC. 6311. PAYMENT OF TAX BY COMMERCIALLY ACCEPTABLE MEANS.

* * *

(e) CONFIDENTIALITY OF INFORMATION.—

(1) IN GENERAL.—Except as otherwise authorized by this subsection, no person may use or disclose any information relating to credit or debit card transactions obtained pursuant to *section 6103(k)(9)* other than for purposes directly related to the processing of such transactions, or the billing or collection of amounts charged or debited pursuant thereto.

* * *

Amendment Notes

Act Sec. 6012(b)(1) amended Code Sec. 6311(e)(1) by striking "section 6103(k)(8)" and inserting "section 6103(k)(9)"

The above amendment is effective as if included in the provision of the Taxpayer Relief Act of 1997 (P.L. 105-34) to which it relates [effective May 5, 1998.—CCH.].

Code Sec. 6311(e)   ¶ 6230

[Caution: Code Sec. 6320, below, as added by Act Sec. 3401(a), applies to collection actions initiated after the date which is 180 days after the date of the enactment of this Act.—CCH.]

[¶ 6240] CODE SEC. 6320. NOTICE AND OPPORTUNITY FOR HEARING UPON FILING OF NOTICE OF LIEN.

(a) REQUIREMENT OF NOTICE.—

*(1) IN GENERAL.—*The Secretary shall notify in writing the person described in section 6321 of the filing of a notice of lien under section 6323.

*(2) TIME AND METHOD FOR NOTICE.—*The notice required under paragraph (1) shall be—

(A) given in person,

(B) left at the dwelling or usual place of business of such person, or

(C) sent by certified or registered mail to such person's last known address,

not more than 5 business days after the day of the filing of the notice of lien.

*(3) INFORMATION INCLUDED WITH NOTICE.—*The notice required under paragraph (1) shall include in simple and nontechnical terms—

(A) the amount of unpaid tax,

(B) the right of the person to request a hearing during the 30-day period beginning on the day after the 5-day period described in paragraph (2),

(C) the administrative appeals available to the taxpayer with respect to such lien and the procedures relating to such appeals, and

(D) the provisions of this title and procedures relating to the release of liens on property.

(b) RIGHT TO FAIR HEARING.—

*(1) IN GENERAL.—*If the person requests a hearing under subsection (a)(3)(B), such hearing shall be held by the Internal Revenue Service Office of Appeals.

*(2) ONE HEARING PER PERIOD.—*A person shall be entitled to only one hearing under this section with respect to the taxable period to which the unpaid tax specified in subsection (a)(3)(A) relates.

*(3) IMPARTIAL OFFICER.—*The hearing under this subsection shall be conducted by an officer or employee who has had no prior involvement with respect to the unpaid tax specified in subsection (a)(3)(A) before the first hearing under this section or section 6330. A taxpayer may waive the requirement of this paragraph.

*(4) COORDINATION WITH SECTION 6330.—*To the extent practicable, a hearing under this section shall be held in conjunction with a hearing under section 6330.

*(c) CONDUCT OF HEARING; REVIEW; SUSPENSIONS.—*For purposes of this section, subsections (c), (d) (other than paragraph (2)(B) thereof), and (e) of section 6330 shall apply.

[CCH Explanation at ¶ 1254. Committee Reports at ¶ 10,365.]

Amendment Notes	
Act Sec. 3401(a) amended subchapter C of chapter 64 by inserting a new Code Sec. 6320 to read as above.	The above amendment applies to collection actions initiated after the date which is 180 days after the date of the enactment of this Act.

[¶ 6250] CODE SEC. 6323. VALIDITY AND PRIORITY AGAINST CERTAIN PERSONS.

* * *

(b) PROTECTION FOR CERTAIN INTERESTS EVEN THOUGH NOTICE FILED.—Even though notice of a lien imposed by section 6321 has been filed, such lien shall not be valid—

* * *

(4) PERSONAL PROPERTY PURCHASED IN CASUAL SALE.—With respect to household goods, personal effects, or other tangible personal property described in section 6334(a) purchased (not for resale) in a casual sale for less than *$1,000*, as against the purchaser, but only if such purchaser does not have actual notice or knowledge (A) of the existence of such lien, or (B) that this sale is one of a series of sales.

* * *

(7) RESIDENTIAL PROPERTY SUBJECT TO A MECHANIC'S LIEN FOR CERTAIN REPAIRS AND IMPROVEMENTS.—With respect to real property subject to a lien for repair or improvement of a personal residence (containing not more than four dwelling units) occupied by the owner of such residence, as against a mechanic's lienor, but only if the contract price on the contract with the owner is not more than *$5,000*.

* * *

(10) DEPOSIT-SECURED LOANS.—With respect to a savings deposit, share, or other account, with an institution described in section 581 or 591, to the extent of any loan made by such institution without actual notice or knowledge of the existence of such lien, as against such institution, if such loan is secured by such account.

* * *

[CCH Explanation at ¶ 1214. Committee Reports at ¶ 10,445.]

¶ 6240   Code Sec. 6320(a)

Act Sec. 3435(a)(1)(A)-(B) amended Code Sec. 6323(b) by striking "$250" and inserting "$1,000" in paragraph (4), and by striking "$1,000" and inserting "$5,000" in paragraph (7).

Act Sec. 3435(b)(1)-(3) amended Code Sec. 6323(b)(10) by striking "PASSBOOK LOANS" in the heading and inserting "DEPOSIT-SECURED LOANS", by striking ", evidenced by a passbook,", and by striking all that follows "secured by such account" and inserting a period. Prior to amendment, Code Sec. 6323(b)(10) read as follows:

(10) PASSBOOK LOANS.—With respect to a savings deposit, share, or other account, evidenced by a passbook, with an institution described in section 581 or 591, to the extent of any loan made by such institution without actual notice or knowledge of the existence of such lien, as against such institution, if such loan is secured by such account and if such institution has been continuously in possession of such passbook from the time the loan is made.

The above amendments are effective on the date of the enactment of this Act.

(i) SPECIAL RULES.—

* * *

(4) COST-OF-LIVING ADJUSTMENT.—In the case of notices of liens imposed by section 6321 which are filed in any calendar year after 1998, each of the dollar amounts under paragraph (4) or (7) of subsection (b) shall be increased by an amount equal to—

(A) such dollar amount, multiplied by

(B) the cost-of-living adjustment determined under section 1(f)(3) for the calendar year, determined by substituting "calendar year 1996" for "calendar year 1992" in subparagraph (B) thereof.

If any amount as adjusted under the preceding sentence is not a multiple of $10, such amount shall be rounded to the nearest multiple of $10.

[CCH Explanation at ¶ 1214. Committee Reports at ¶ 10,445.]

Act Sec. 3435(a)(2) amended Code Sec. 6323(i) by adding at the end a new paragraph (4) to read as above.

The above amendment is effective on the date of the enactment of this Act.

(j) WITHDRAWAL OF NOTICE IN CERTAIN CIRCUMSTANCES.—

(1) IN GENERAL.—The Secretary may withdraw a notice of a lien filed under this section and this chapter shall be applied as if the withdrawn notice had not been filed, if the Secretary determines that—

(A) the filing of such notice was premature or otherwise not in accordance with administrative procedures of the Secretary,

(B) the taxpayer has entered into an agreement under section 6159 to satisfy the tax liability for which the lien was imposed by means of installment payments, unless such agreement provides otherwise,

(C) the withdrawal of such notice will facilitate the collection of the tax liability, or

(D) with the consent of the taxpayer or the *National Taxpayer Advocate*, the withdrawal of such notice would be in the best interests of the taxpayer (as determined by the *National Taxpayer Advocate*) and the United States. Any such withdrawal shall be made by filing notice at the same office as the withdrawn notice. A copy of such notice of withdrawal shall be provided to the taxpayer.

* * *

[CCH Explanation at ¶ 821. Committee Reports at ¶ 10,150.]

Act Sec. 1102(d)(1)(A) amended Code Sec. 6323(j)(1)(D) by striking "Taxpayer Advocate" each place it appears and inserting "National Taxpayer Advocate".

The above amendment is effective on the date of the enactment of this Act. For special rules, see Act Sec. 1102(f)(3)-(4) in the amendment notes following Code Sec. 7803.

[¶ 6260] CODE SEC. 6325. RELEASE OF LIEN OR DISCHARGE OF PROPERTY.
* * *

(b) DISCHARGE OF PROPERTY.—

* * *

(4) RIGHT OF SUBSTITUTION OF VALUE.—

(A) IN GENERAL.—At the request of the owner of any property subject to any lien imposed by this chapter, the Secretary shall issue a certificate of discharge of such property if such owner—

(i) deposits with the Secretary an amount of money equal to the value of the interest of the United States (as determined by the Secretary) in the property, or

(ii) furnishes a bond acceptable to the Secretary in a like amount.

(B) REFUND OF DEPOSIT WITH INTEREST AND RELEASE OF BOND.—The Secretary shall refund the amount so deposited (and shall pay interest at the overpayment rate under section 6621), and shall release such bond, to the extent that the Secretary determines that—

(i) the unsatisfied liability giving rise to the lien can be satisfied from a source other than such property, or

(ii) the value of the interest of the United States in the property is less than the Secretary's prior determination of such value.

Code Sec. 6325(b)   ¶ 6260

(C) Use of Deposit, etc., if Action to Contest Lien Not Filed.—If no action is filed under section 7426(a)(4) within the period prescribed therefor, the Secretary shall, within 60 days after the expiration of such period—

(i) apply the amount deposited, or collect on such bond, to the extent necessary to satisfy the unsatisfied liability secured by the lien, and

(ii) refund (with interest as described in subparagraph (B)) any portion of the amount deposited which is not used to satisfy such liability.

(D) Exception.—Subparagraph (A) shall not apply if the owner of the property is the person whose unsatisfied liability gave rise to the lien.

* * *

[CCH Explanation at ¶ 1230. Committee Reports at ¶ 10,275.]

Amendment Notes

Act Sec. 3106(a) amended Code Sec. 6325(b) by adding at the end a new paragraph (4) to read as above.

The above amendment is effective on the date of the enactment of this Act.

[Caution: Code Sec. 6330, below, as added by Act Sec. 3401(b), applies to collection actions initiated after the date which is 180 days after the date of the enactment of this Act.—CCH.]

[¶ 6270] *CODE SEC. 6330. NOTICE AND OPPORTUNITY FOR HEARING BEFORE LEVY.*

(a) Requirement of Notice Before Levy.—

(1) In General.—No levy may be made on any property or right to property of any person unless the Secretary has notified such person in writing of their right to a hearing under this section before such levy is made. Such notice shall be required only once for the taxable period to which the unpaid tax specified in paragraph (3)(A) relates.

(2) Time and Method for Notice.—The notice required under paragraph (1) shall be—

(A) given in person,

(B) left at the dwelling or usual place of business of such person, or

(C) sent by certified or registered mail, return receipt requested, to such person's last known address,

not less than 30 days before the day of the first levy with respect to the amount of the unpaid tax for the taxable period.

(3) Information Included with Notice.—The notice required under paragraph (1) shall include in simple and nontechnical terms—

(A) the amount of unpaid tax,

(B) the right of the person to request a hearing during the 30-day period under paragraph (2), and

(C) the proposed action by the Secretary and the rights of the person with respect to such action, including a brief statement which sets forth—

(i) the provisions of this title relating to levy and sale of property,

(ii) the procedures applicable to the levy and sale of property under this title,

(iii) the administrative appeals available to the taxpayer with respect to such levy and sale and the procedures relating to such appeals,

(iv) the alternatives available to taxpayers which could prevent levy on property (including installment agreements under section 6159), and

(v) the provisions of this title and procedures relating to redemption of property and release of liens on property.

(b) Right to Fair Hearing.—

(1) In General.—If the person requests a hearing under subsection (a)(3)(B), such hearing shall be held by the Internal Revenue Service Office of Appeals.

(2) One Hearing per Period.—A person shall be entitled to only one hearing under this section with respect to the taxable period to which the unpaid tax specified in subsection (a)(3)(A) relates.

(3) Impartial Officer.—The hearing under this subsection shall be conducted by an officer or employee who has had no prior involvement with respect to the unpaid tax specified in subsection (a)(3)(A) before the first hearing under this section or section 6320. A taxpayer may waive the requirement of this paragraph.

(c) Matters Considered at Hearing.—In the case of any hearing conducted under this section—

(1) Requirement of Investigation.—The appeals officer shall at the hearing obtain verification from the Secretary that the requirements of any applicable law or administrative procedure have been met.

(2) Issues at Hearing.—

(A) IN GENERAL.—The person may raise at the hearing any relevant issue relating to the unpaid tax or the proposed levy, including—

(i) appropriate spousal defenses,

(ii) challenges to the appropriateness of collection actions, and

(iii) offers of collection alternatives, which may include the posting of a bond, the substitution of other assets, an installment agreement, or an offer-in-compromise.

(B) UNDERLYING LIABILITY.—The person may also raise at the hearing challenges to the existence or amount of the underlying tax liability for any tax period if the person did not receive any statutory notice of deficiency for such tax liability or did not otherwise have an opportunity to dispute such tax liability.

(3) BASIS FOR THE DETERMINATION.—The determination by an appeals officer under this subsection shall take into consideration—

(A) the verification presented under paragraph (1),

(B) the issues raised under paragraph (2), and

(C) whether any proposed collection action balances the need for the efficient collection of taxes with the legitimate concern of the person that any collection action be no more intrusive than necessary.

(4) CERTAIN ISSUES PRECLUDED.—An issue may not be raised at the hearing if—

(A) the issue was raised and considered at a previous hearing under section 6320 or in any other previous administrative or judicial proceeding, and

(B) the person seeking to raise the issue participated meaningfully in such hearing or proceeding.

This paragraph shall not apply to any issue with respect to which subsection (d)(2)(B) applies.

(d) PROCEEDING AFTER HEARING.—

(1) JUDICIAL REVIEW OF DETERMINATION.—The person may, within 30 days of a determination under this section, appeal such determination—

(A) to the Tax Court (and the Tax Court shall have jurisdiction to hear such matter), or

(B) if the Tax Court does not have jurisdiction of the underlying tax liability, to a district court of the United States.

If a court determines that the appeal was to an incorrect court, a person shall have 30 days after the court determination to file such appeal with the correct court.

(2) JURISDICTION RETAINED AT IRS OFFICE OF APPEALS.—The Internal Revenue Service Office of Appeals shall retain jurisdiction with respect to any determination made under this section, including subsequent hearings requested by the person who requested the original hearing on issues regarding—

(A) collection actions taken or proposed with respect to such determination, and

(B) after the person has exhausted all administrative remedies, a change in circumstances with respect to such person which affects such determination.

(e) SUSPENSION OF COLLECTIONS AND STATUTE OF LIMITATIONS.—

(1) IN GENERAL.—Except as provided in paragraph (2), if a hearing is requested under subsection (a)(3)(B), the levy actions which are the subject of the requested hearing and the running of any period of limitations under section 6502 (relating to collection after assessment), section 6531 (relating to criminal prosecutions), or section 6532 (relating to other suits) shall be suspended for the period during which such hearing, and appeals therein, are pending. In no event shall any such period expire before the 90th day after the day on which there is a final determination in such hearing.

(2) LEVY UPON APPEAL.—Paragraph (1) shall not apply to a levy action while an appeal is pending if the underlying tax liability is not at issue in the appeal and the court determines that the Secretary has shown good cause not to suspend the levy.

(f) JEOPARDY AND STATE REFUND COLLECTION.—If—

(1) the Secretary has made a finding under the last sentence of section 6331(a) that the collection of tax is in jeopardy, or

(2) the Secretary has served a levy on a State to collect a Federal tax liability from a State tax refund,

this section shall not apply, except that the taxpayer shall be given the opportunity for the hearing described in this section within a reasonable period of time after the levy.

[CCH Explanation at ¶ 1254. Committee Reports at ¶ 10,365.]

Amendment Notes

Act Sec. 3401(b) amended subchapter D of chapter 64 by inserting a new Code Sec. 6330.

The above amendment applies to collection actions initiated after the date which is 180 days after the date of the enactment of this Act.

[¶ 6280] CODE SEC. 6331. LEVY AND DISTRAINT.
* * *

(h) CONTINUING LEVY ON CERTAIN PAYMENTS.—

(1) IN GENERAL.—*If the Secretary approves a levy under this subsection, the effect of such levy* on specified payments to or received by a taxpayer shall be continuous from the date such levy is first made until such levy is released. Notwithstanding section 6334, such continuous levy shall attach to up to 15 percent of any specified payment due to the taxpayer.
* * *

[CCH Explanation at ¶ 266. Committee Reports at ¶ 11,170.]

Amendment Notes

Act Sec. 6010(f) amended Code Sec. 6331(h)(1) by striking "The effect of a levy" and inserting "If the Secretary approves a levy under this subsection, the effect of such levy".

The above amendment is effective as if included in the provision of the Taxpayer Relief Act of 1997 (P.L. 105-34) to which it relates [effective for levies issued after August 5, 1997.—CCH.].

Act Sec. 3421 provides:

SEC. 3421. APPROVAL PROCESS FOR LIENS, LEVIES, AND SEIZURES.

(a) IN GENERAL.—The Commissioner of Internal Revenue shall develop and implement procedures under which—

(1) a determination by an employee to file a notice of lien or levy with respect to, or to levy or seize, any property or right to property would, where appropriate, be required to be reviewed by a supervisor of the employee before the action was taken, and

(2) appropriate disciplinary action would be taken against the employee or supervisor where the procedures under paragraph (1) were not followed.

(b) REVIEW PROCESS.—The review process under subsection (a)(1) may include a certification that the employee has—

(1) reviewed the taxpayer's information,

(2) verified that a balance is due, and

(3) affirmed that the action proposed to be taken is appropriate given the taxpayer's circumstances, considering the amount due and the value of the property or right to property.

(c) EFFECTIVE DATES.—

(1) IN GENERAL.—Except as provided in paragraph (2), this section shall take effect on the date of the enactment of this Act.

(2) AUTOMATED COLLECTION SYSTEM ACTIONS.—In the case of any action under an automated collection system, this section shall apply to actions initiated after December 31, 2000.

[*Caution: Code Sec. 6331(i), below, as added by Act Sec. 3433(a), applies to unpaid tax attributable to taxable periods beginning after December 31, 1998.—CCH.*]

(i) *NO LEVY DURING PENDENCY OF PROCEEDINGS FOR REFUND OF DIVISIBLE TAX.—*

(1) *IN GENERAL.*—No levy may be made under subsection (a) on the property or rights to property of any person with respect to any unpaid divisible tax during the pendency of any proceeding brought by such person in a proper Federal trial court for the recovery of any portion of such divisible tax which was paid by such person if—

(A) the decision in such proceeding would be res judicata with respect to such unpaid tax, or

(B) such person would be collaterally estopped from contesting such unpaid tax by reason of such proceeding.

(2) *DIVISIBLE TAX.*—For purposes of paragraph (1), the term "divisible tax" means—

(A) any tax imposed by subtitle C, and

(B) the penalty imposed by section 6672 with respect to any such tax.

(3) *EXCEPTIONS.—*

(A) *CERTAIN UNPAID TAXES.*—This subsection shall not apply with respect to any unpaid tax if—

(i) the taxpayer files a written notice with the Secretary which waives the restriction imposed by this subsection on levy with respect to such tax, or

(ii) the Secretary finds that the collection of such tax is in jeopardy.

(B) *CERTAIN LEVIES.*—This subsection shall not apply to—

(i) any levy to carry out an offset under section 6402, and

(ii) any levy which was first made before the date that the applicable proceeding under this subsection commenced.

(4) *LIMITATION ON COLLECTION ACTIVITY; AUTHORITY TO ENJOIN COLLECTION.—*

(A) *LIMITATION ON COLLECTION.*—No proceeding in court for the collection of any unpaid tax to which paragraph (1) applies shall be begun by the Secretary during the pendency of a proceeding under such paragraph. This subparagraph shall not apply to—

(i) any counterclaim in a proceeding under such paragraph, or

(ii) any proceeding relating to a proceeding under such paragraph.

(B) *AUTHORITY TO ENJOIN.*—Notwithstanding section 7421(a), a levy or collection proceeding prohibited by this subsection may be enjoined (during the period such prohibition is in force) by the court in which the proceeding under paragraph (1) is brought.

(5) *SUSPENSION OF STATUTE OF LIMITATIONS ON COLLECTION.*—The period of limitations under section 6502 shall be suspended for the period during which the Secretary is prohibited under this subsection from making a levy.

¶ 6280   Code Sec. 6331(h)

(6) PENDENCY OF PROCEEDING.—For purposes of this subsection, a proceeding is pending beginning on the date such proceeding commences and ending on the date that a final order or judgment from which an appeal may be taken is entered in such proceeding.

[CCH Explanation at ¶ 1222. Committee Reports at ¶ 10,435.]

Amendment Notes	
Act Sec. 3433(a) amended Code Sec. 6331 by redesignating subsection (i) as subsection (j) and by inserting after subsection (h) a new subsection (i) to read as above.	The above amendment applies to unpaid tax attributable to taxable periods beginning after December 31, 1998.

(j) NO LEVY BEFORE INVESTIGATION OF STATUS OF PROPERTY.—

(1) IN GENERAL.—For purposes of applying the provisions of this subchapter, no levy may be made on any property or right to property which is to be sold under section 6335 until a thorough investigation of the status of such property has been completed.

(2) ELEMENTS IN INVESTIGATION.—For purposes of paragraph (1), an investigation of the status of any property shall include—

(A) a verification of the taxpayer's liability,

(B) the completion of an analysis under subsection (f),

(C) the determination that the equity in such property is sufficient to yield net proceeds from the sale of such property to apply to such liability, and

(D) a thorough consideration of alternative collection methods.

[CCH Explanation at ¶ 1250. Committee Reports at ¶ 10,480.]

Amendment Notes	
Act Sec. 3444(a) amended Code Sec. 6331, as amended by Act Sec. 3433, by redesignating subsection (j) as subsection (k) and by inserting after subsection (i) a new subsection (j) to read as above.	The above amendment is effective on the date of the enactment of this Act.

[*Caution: Code Sec. 6331(k), below, as added by Act Sec. 3462(b), applies to offers-in-compromise pending on or made after December 31, 1999.—CCH.*]

(k) NO LEVY WHILE CERTAIN OFFERS PENDING OR INSTALLMENT AGREEMENT PENDING OR IN EFFECT.—

(1) OFFER-IN-COMPROMISE PENDING.—No levy may be made under subsection (a) on the property or rights to property of any person with respect to any unpaid tax—

(A) during the period that an offer-in-compromise by such person under section 7122 of such unpaid tax is pending with the Secretary, and

(B) if such offer is rejected by the Secretary, during the 30 days thereafter (and, if an appeal of such rejection is filed within such 30 days, during the period that such appeal is pending).

For purposes of subparagraph (A), an offer is pending beginning on the date the Secretary accepts such offer for processing.

(2) INSTALLMENT AGREEMENTS.—No levy may be made under subsection (a) on the property or rights to property of any person with respect to any unpaid tax—

(A) during the period that an offer by such person for an installment agreement under section 6159 for payment of such unpaid tax is pending with the Secretary,

(B) if such offer is rejected by the Secretary, during the 30 days thereafter (and, if an appeal of such rejection is filed within such 30 days, during the period that such appeal is pending),

(C) during the period that such an installment agreement for payment of such unpaid tax is in effect, and

(D) if such agreement is terminated by the Secretary, during the 30 days thereafter (and, if an appeal of such termination is filed within such 30 days, during the period that such appeal is pending).

(3) CERTAIN RULES TO APPLY.—Rules similar to the rules of paragraphs (3), (4), and (5) of subsection (i) shall apply for purposes of this subsection.

[CCH Explanation at ¶ 1270. Committee Reports at ¶ 10,520.]

Amendment Notes	
Act Sec. 3462(b) amended Code Sec. 6331, as amended by Act Secs. 3433 and 3444, by redesignating subsection (k) as subsection (l) and by inserting after subsection (j) a new subsection (k) to read as above.	The above amendment applies to offers-in-compromise pending on or made after December 31, 1999.

(l) CROSS REFERENCES.—

* * *

[CCH Explanation at ¶ 1222, 1250 and 1270. Committee Reports at ¶ 10,435, 10,480 and 10,520.]

Amendment Notes	
Act Sec. 3433(a) amended Code Sec. 6331 by redesignating subsection (i) as subsection (j).	The above amendment applies to unpaid tax attributable to taxable periods beginning after December 31, 1998.

Code Sec. 6331(l)   ¶6280

Act Sec. 3444(a) amended Code Sec. 6331, as amended by Act Sec. 3433, by redesignating subsection (j) as subsection (k).

The above amendment is effective on the date of the enactment of this Act.

Act Sec. 3462(b) amended Code Sec. 6331, as amended by Act Secs. 3433 and 3444, by redesignating subsection (k) as subsection (l).

The above amendment applies to offers-in-compromise pending on or made after December 31, 1999.

[¶ 6290] CODE SEC. 6334. PROPERTY EXEMPT FROM LEVY.

(a) ENUMERATION.—There shall be exempt from levy—

* * *

(2) FUEL, PROVISIONS, FURNITURE, AND PERSONAL EFFECTS.—So much of the fuel, provisions, furniture, and personal effects in the taxpayer's household, and of the arms for personal use, livestock, and poultry of the taxpayer, as does not exceed *$6,250* in value;

(3) BOOKS AND TOOLS OF A TRADE, BUSINESS, OR PROFESSION.—So many of the books and tools necessary for the trade, business, or profession of the taxpayer as do not exceed in the aggregate *$3,125* in value.

* * *

(13) RESIDENCES EXEMPT IN SMALL DEFICIENCY CASES AND PRINCIPAL RESIDENCES AND CERTAIN BUSINESS ASSETS EXEMPT IN ABSENCE OF CERTAIN APPROVAL OR JEOPARDY.—

(A) RESIDENCES IN SMALL DEFICIENCY CASES.—If the amount of the levy does not exceed $5,000—

(i) any real property used as a residence by the taxpayer, or

(ii) any real property of the taxpayer (other than real property which is rented) used by any other individual as a residence.

(B) PRINCIPAL RESIDENCES AND CERTAIN BUSINESS ASSETS.—Except to the extent provided in subsection (e)—

(i) the principal residence of the taxpayer (within the meaning of section 121), and

(ii) tangible personal property or real property (other than real property which is rented) used in the trade or business of an individual taxpayer.

* * *

[CCH Explanation at ¶ 1210 and 1234. Committee Reports at ¶ 10,425 and 10,485.]

Amendment Notes

Act Sec. 3431(a) amended Code Sec. 6334(a)(2) by striking "$2,500" and inserting "$6,250".

Act Sec. 3431(b) amended Code Sec. 6334(a)(3) by striking "$1,250" and inserting "$3,125".

The above amendments are effective with respect to levies issued after the date of the enactment of this Act.

Act Sec. 3445(a) amended Code Sec. 6334(a)(13) to read as above. Prior to amendment, Code Sec. 6334(a)(13) read as follows:

(13) PRINCIPAL RESIDENCE EXEMPT IN ABSENCE OF CERTAIN APPROVAL OR JEOPARDY.—Except to the extent provided in subsection (e), the principal residence of the taxpayer (within the meaning of section 121).

The above amendment is effective on the date of the enactment of this Act.

(e) LEVY ALLOWED ON PRINCIPAL RESIDENCES AND CERTAIN BUSINESS ASSETS IN CERTAIN CIRCUMSTANCES.—

(1) PRINCIPAL RESIDENCES.—

(A) APPROVAL REQUIRED.—A principal residence shall not be exempt from levy if a judge or magistrate of a district court of the United States approves (in writing) the levy of such residence.

(B) JURISDICTION.—The district courts of the United States shall have exclusive jurisdiction to approve a levy under subparagraph (A).

(2) CERTAIN BUSINESS ASSETS.—Property (other than a principal residence) described in subsection (a)(13)(B) shall not be exempt from levy if—

(A) a district director or assistant district director of the Internal Revenue Service personally approves (in writing) the levy of such property, or

(B) the Secretary finds that the collection of tax is in jeopardy.

An official may not approve a levy under subparagraph (A) unless the official determines that the taxpayer's other assets subject to collection are insufficient to pay the amount due, together with expenses of the proceedings.

* * *

[CCH Explanation at ¶ 1234. Committee Reports at ¶ 10,485.]

Amendment Notes

Act Sec. 3445(b) amended Code Sec. 6334(e) to read as above. Prior to amendment, Code Sec. 6334(e) read as follows:

(e) LEVY ALLOWED ON PRINCIPAL RESIDENCE IN CASE OF JEOPARDY OR CERTAIN APPROVAL.—Property described in subsection (a)(13) shall not be exempt from levy if—

(1) a district director or assistant district director of the Internal Revenue Service personally approves (in writing) the levy of such property, or

(2) the Secretary finds that the collection of tax is in jeopardy.

The above amendment is effective on the date of the enactment of this Act.

Act Sec. 3445(c)(1)-(2) provides:

(1) IN GENERAL.—With respect to permits issued by a State and required under State law for the harvest of fish or wildlife in the trade or business of an individual taxpayer, the term "other assets" as used in section 6334(e)(2) of the Internal Revenue Code of 1986 shall include future income

which may be derived by such taxpayer from the commercial sale of fish or wildlife under such permit.

(2) CONSTRUCTION.—Paragraph (1) shall not be construed to invalidate or in any way prejudice any assertion that the privilege embodied in permits described in paragraph (1) is not property or a right to property under the Internal Revenue Code of 1986.

(g) INFLATION ADJUSTMENT.—

(1) IN GENERAL.—In the case of any calendar year beginning after *1999*, each dollar amount referred to in paragraphs (2) and (3) of subsection (a) shall be increased by an amount equal to—

(A) such dollar amount, multiplied by

(B) the cost-of-living adjustment determined under section 1(f)(3) for such calendar year, by substituting "calendar year *1998*" for "calendar year 1992" in subparagraph (B) thereof.

* * *

[CCH Explanation at ¶ 1210. Committee Reports at ¶ 10,425.]

Amendment Notes

Act Sec. 3431(c)(1) amended Code Sec. 6334(g)(1) by striking "1997" and inserting "1999".

Act Sec. 3431(c)(2) amended Code Sec. 6334(g)(1)(B) by striking "1996" and inserting "1998".

The above amendments are effective with respect to levies issued after the date of the enactment of this Act.

[¶ 6300] CODE SEC. 6335. SALE OF SEIZED PROPERTY.

* * *

(e) MANNER AND CONDITIONS OF SALE.—

(1) IN GENERAL.—

(A) DETERMINATIONS RELATING TO MINIMUM PRICE.—Before the sale of property seized by levy, the Secretary shall determine—

(i) *a minimum price below which such property shall not be sold* (taking into account the expense of making the levy and conducting the sale), and

(ii) whether, on the basis of criteria prescribed by the Secretary, the purchase of such property by the United States at such minimum price would be in the best interest of the United States.

* * *

(4) CROSS REFERENCE.—

For provision providing for civil damages for violation of paragraph (1)(A)(i), see section 7433.

* * *

[CCH Explanation at ¶ 1238. Committee Reports at ¶ 10,465.]

Amendment Notes

Act Sec. 3441(a) amended Code Sec. 6335(e)(1)(A)(i) by striking "a minimum price for which such property shall be sold" and inserting "a minimum price below which such property shall not be sold".

Act Sec. 3441(b) amended Code Sec. 6335(e) by adding a new paragraph (4) to read as above.

The above amendments apply to sales made after the date of the enactment of this Act.

Act Sec. 3443 provides:

SEC. 3443. UNIFORM ASSET DISPOSAL MECHANISM.

Not later than the date which is 2 years after the date of the enactment of this Act, the Secretary of the Treasury or the Secretary's delegate shall implement a uniform asset disposal mechanism for sales under section 6335 of the Internal Revenue Code of 1986. The mechanism should be designed to remove any participation in such sales by revenue officers of the Internal Revenue Service and should consider the use of outsourcing.

[¶ 6310] CODE SEC. 6340. RECORDS OF SALE.

(a) REQUIREMENT.—The Secretary shall, for each internal revenue district, keep a record of all sales of property under section 6335 and of redemptions of such property. The record shall set forth the tax for which any such sale was made, the dates of seizure and sale, the name of the party assessed and all proceedings in making such sale, the amount of expenses, the names of the purchasers, and the date of the deed *or certificate of sale of personal property.*

* * *

[CCH Explanation at ¶ 1242. Committee Reports at ¶ 10,470.]

Amendment Notes

Act Sec. 3442(a)(1)(A)-(B) amended Code Sec. 6340(a) by striking "real" after "sales of", and by inserting "or certificate of sale of personal property" after "deed".

The above amendment applies to seizures occurring after the date of the enactment of this Act.

(c) ACCOUNTING TO TAXPAYER.—The taxpayer with respect to whose liability the sale was conducted or who redeemed the property shall be furnished—

(1) the record under subsection (a) (other than the names of the purchasers),

(2) the amount from such sale applied to the taxpayer's liability, and

(3) the remaining balance of such liability.

[CCH Explanation at ¶ 1242. Committee Reports at ¶ 10,470.]

Amendment Notes
Act Sec. 3442(a)(2) amended Code Sec. 6340 by adding at the end a new subsection (c) to read as above.

The above amendment applies to seizures occurring after the date of the enactment of this Act.

[¶ 6320] CODE SEC. 6343. AUTHORITY TO RELEASE LEVY AND RETURN PROPERTY.

* * *

(d) RETURN OF PROPERTY IN CERTAIN CASES.—If—

(1) any property has been levied upon, and

(2) the Secretary determines that—

(A) the levy on such property was premature or otherwise not in accordance with administrative procedures of the Secretary,

(B) the taxpayer has entered into an agreement under section 6159 to satisfy the tax liability for which the levy was imposed by means of installment payments, unless such agreement provides otherwise,

(C) the return of such property will facilitate the collection of the tax liability, or

(D) with the consent of the taxpayer or the *National Taxpayer Advocate*, the return of such property would be in the best interests of the taxpayer (as determined by the *National Taxpayer Advocate*) and the United States,

the provisions of subsection (b) shall apply in the same manner as if such property had been wrongly levied upon, except that no interest shall be allowed under subsection (c).

[CCH Explanation at ¶ 821. Committee Reports at ¶ 10,150.]

Amendment Notes
Act Sec. 1102(d)(1)(B) amended Code Sec. 6343(d)(2)(D) by striking "Taxpayer Advocate" each place it appears and inserting "National Taxpayer Advocate".

The above amendment is effective on the date of the enactment of this Act. For a special rule, see Act Sec 1102 (f)(3)-(4), below.

Act Sec. 1102(f)(3)-(4) provides:

(3) NATIONAL TAXPAYER ADVOCATE.—Notwithstanding section 7803(c)(1)(B)(iv) of such Code, as added by this section, in appointing the first National Taxpayer Advocate after the date of the enactment of this Act, the Secretary of the Treasury—

(A) shall not appoint any individual who was an officer or employee of the Internal Revenue Service at any time during the 2-year period ending on the date of appointment, and

(B) need not consult with the Internal Revenue Service Oversight Board if the Oversight Board has not been appointed.

(4) CURRENT OFFICERS.—

(A) In the case of an individual serving as Commissioner of Internal Revenue on the date of the enactment of this Act who was appointed to such position before such date, the 5-year term required by section 7803(a)(1) of such Code, as added by this section, shall begin as of the date of such appointment.

(B) Clauses (ii), (iii), and (iv) of section 7803(c)(1)(B) of such Code, as added by this section, shall not apply to the individual serving as Taxpayer Advocate on the date of the enactment of this Act.

[*Caution: Code Sec. 6343(e), below, as added by Act Sec. 3432(a), applies to levies imposed after December 31, 1999.—CCH.*]

(e) *RELEASE OF LEVY UPON AGREEMENT THAT AMOUNT IS NOT COLLECTIBLE.—In the case of a levy on the salary or wages payable to or received by the taxpayer, upon agreement with the taxpayer that the tax is not collectible, the Secretary shall release such levy as soon as practicable.*

[CCH Explanation at ¶ 1218. Committee Reports at ¶ 10,430.]

Amendment Notes
Act Sec. 3432(a) amended Code Sec. 6343 by adding at the end a new subsection (e) to read as above.

The above amendment applies to levies imposed after December 31, 1999.

[¶ 6330] CODE SEC. 6344. CROSS REFERENCES.

* * *

(b) DELINQUENT COLLECTION OFFICERS.—For distraint proceedings against delinquent internal revenue officers, see *section 7804(c).*

* * *

[CCH Explanation at ¶ 817. Committee Reports at ¶ 10,165.]

Amendment Notes
Act Sec. 1104(b)(1) amended Code Sec. 6344(b) by striking "section 7803(d)" and inserting "section 7804(c)".

The above amendment is effective on the date of the enactment of this Act.

[¶ 6340] CODE SEC. 6401. AMOUNTS TREATED AS OVERPAYMENTS.

* * *

(b) EXCESSIVE CREDITS.—

(1) IN GENERAL.—If the amount allowable as credits under subpart C of part IV of subchapter A of chapter 1 (relating to refundable credits) exceeds the tax imposed by subtitle A (reduced by the credits allowable under subparts A, B, *D, and G* of such part IV), the amount of such excess shall be considered an overpayment.

* * *

[CCH Explanation at ¶ 224.]

Amendment Notes

Act Sec. 6022(a) amended Code Sec. 6401(b)(1) by striking "and D" and inserting ''D, and G".

The above amendment is effective as if included in the amendments made by Act Sec. 701(b) of the Tax Reform Act of 1986 (P.L. 99-514) [generally effective for tax years beginning after December 31, 1986.—CCH.].

[¶ 6350] CODE SEC. 6402. AUTHORITY TO MAKE CREDITS OR REFUNDS.

[Caution: Code Sec. 6402(a), below, as amended by Act Sec. 3711(c)(1), applies to refunds payable under Code Sec. 6402 after December 31, 1999.—CCH.]

(a) GENERAL RULE.—In the case of any overpayment, the Secretary, within the applicable period of limitations, may credit the amount of such overpayment, including any interest allowed thereon, against any liability in respect of an internal revenue tax on the part of the person who made the overpayment and shall, subject to subsections *(c), (d), and (e)* refund any balance to such person.

* * *

[CCH Explanation at ¶ 1446. Committee Reports at ¶ 10,685.]

Amendment Notes

Act Sec. 3711(c)(1) amended Code Sec. 6402(a) by striking "(c) and [or] (d)" and inserting "(c), (d), and (e)".

The above amendment applies to refunds payable under Code Sec. 6402 after December 31, 1999.

[Caution: Code Sec. 6402(d)(2), below, as amended by Act Sec. 3711(c)(2), applies to refunds payable under Code Sec. 6402 after December 31, 1999.—CCH.]

(d) COLLECTION OF DEBTS OWED TO FEDERAL AGENCIES.—

* * *

(2) PRIORITIES FOR OFFSET.—Any overpayment by a person shall be reduced pursuant to this subsection after such overpayment is reduced pursuant to subsection (c) with respect to past-due support collected pursuant to an assignment under section 402(a)(26) of the Social Security Act *and before such overpayment is reduced pursuant to subsection (e) and before such overpayment is* credited to the future liability for tax of such person pursuant to subsection (b). If the Secretary receives notice from a Federal agency or agencies of more than one debt subject to paragraph (1) that is owed by a person to such agency or agencies, any overpayment by such person shall be applied against such debts in the order in which such debts accrued.

* * *

[CCH Explanation at ¶ 1446. Committee Reports at ¶ 10,685.]

Amendment Notes

Act Sec. 3711(c)(2) amended Code Sec. 6402(d)(2) by striking "and before such overpayment" and inserting "and before such overpayment is reduced pursuant to subsection (e) and before such overpayment".

The above amendment applies to refunds payable under Code Sec. 6402 after December 31, 1999.

[Caution: Code Sec. 6402(e), below, as added by Act Sec. 3711(a), applies to refunds payable under Code Sec. 6402 after December 31, 1999.—CCH.]

(e) COLLECTION OF PAST-DUE, LEGALLY ENFORCEABLE STATE INCOME TAX OBLIGATIONS.—

(1) IN GENERAL.—Upon receiving notice from any State that a named person owes a past-due, legally enforceable State income tax obligation to such State, the Secretary shall, under such conditions as may be prescribed by the Secretary—

(A) reduce the amount of any overpayment payable to such person by the amount of such State income tax obligation;

(B) pay the amount by which such overpayment is reduced under subparagraph (A) to such State and notify such State of such person's name, taxpayer identification number, address, and the amount collected; and

(C) notify the person making such overpayment that the overpayment has been reduced by an amount necessary to satisfy a pastdue, legally enforceable State income tax obligation.

If an offset is made pursuant to a joint return, the notice under subparagraph (B) shall include the names, taxpayer identification numbers, and addresses of each person filing such return.

(2) OFFSET PERMITTED ONLY AGAINST RESIDENTS OF STATE SEEKING OFFSET.—Paragraph (1) shall apply to an overpayment by any person for a taxable year only if the address shown on the Federal return for such taxable year of the overpayment is an address within the State seeking the offset.

(3) PRIORITIES FOR OFFSET.—Any overpayment by a person shall be reduced pursuant to this subsection—

(A) after such overpayment is reduced pursuant to—

(i) subsection (a) with respect to any liability for any internal revenue tax on the part of the person who made the overpayment,

(ii) subsection (c) with respect to past-due support, and

(iii) subsection (d) with respect to any past-due, legally enforceable debt owed to a Federal agency, and

(B) before such overpayment is credited to the future liability for any Federal internal revenue tax of such person pursuant to subsection (b).

If the Secretary receives notice from 1 or more agencies of the State of more than 1 debt subject to paragraph (1) that is owed by such person to such an agency, any overpayment by such person shall be applied against such debts in the order in which such debts accrued.

(4) NOTICE; CONSIDERATION OF EVIDENCE.— No State may take action under this subsection until such State—

(A) notifies by certified mail with return receipt the person owing the past-due State income tax liability that the State proposes to take action pursuant to this section,

(B) gives such person at least 60 days to present evidence that all or part of such liability is not past-due or not legally enforceable,

(C) considers any evidence presented by such person and determines that an amount of such debt is past-due and legally enforceable, and

(D) satisfies such other conditions as the Secretary may prescribe to ensure that the determination made under subparagraph (C) is valid and that the State has made reasonable efforts to obtain payment of such State income tax obligation.

(5) PAST-DUE, LEGALLY ENFORCEABLE STATE INCOME TAX OBLIGATION.—For purposes of this subsection, the term "past-due, legally enforceable State income tax obligation" means a debt—

(A)(i) which resulted from—

(I) a judgment rendered by a court of competent jurisdiction which has determined an amount of State income tax to be due, or

(II) a determination after an administrative hearing which has determined an amount of State income tax to be due, and

(ii) which is no longer subject to judicial review, or

(B) which resulted from a State income tax which has been assessed but not collected, the time for redetermination of which has expired, and which has not been delinquent for more than 10 years.

For purposes of this paragraph, the term "State income tax" includes any local income tax administered by the chief tax administration agency of the State.

(6) REGULATIONS.—The Secretary shall issue regulations prescribing the time and manner in which States must submit notices of past-due, legally enforceable State income tax obligations and the necessary information that must be contained in or accompany such notices. The regulations shall specify the types of State income taxes and the minimum amount of debt to which the reduction procedure established by paragraph (1) may be applied. The regulations may require States to pay a fee to reimburse the Secretary for the cost of applying such procedure. Any fee paid to the Secretary pursuant to the preceding sentence shall be used to reimburse appropriations which bore all or part of the cost of applying such procedure.

(7) ERRONEOUS PAYMENT TO STATE.—Any State receiving notice from the Secretary that an erroneous payment has been made to such State under paragraph (1) shall pay promptly to the Secretary, in accordance with such regulations as the Secretary may prescribe, an amount equal to the amount of such erroneous payment (without regard to whether any other amounts payable to such State under such paragraph have been paid to such State).

[CCH Explanation at ¶ 1446. Committee Reports at ¶ 10,685.]

Amendment Notes
Act Sec. 3711(a) amended Code Sec. 6402, as amended by Act Sec. 3505(a), by redesignating subsections (e) through (j) as subsections (f) through (k), respectively, and by inserting after subsection (d) a new subsection (e) to read as above.

The above amendment applies to refunds payable under Code Sec. 6402 after December 31, 1999.

[Caution: Code Sec. 6402(f), below, as amended by Act Sec. 3711(c)(3)(A)-(B), applies to refunds payable under Code Sec. 6402 after December 31, 1999.—CCH.]

(f) REVIEW OF REDUCTIONS.—No court of the United States shall have jurisdiction to hear any action, whether legal or equitable, brought to restrain or review a reduction authorized by subsection (c), (d), or (e). No such reduction shall be subject to review by the Secretary in an administrative proceeding. No action brought against the United States to recover the amount of any such reduction shall be considered to be a suit for refund of tax. This subsection does not preclude any legal, equitable, or administrative action against the Federal agency or State to which the amount of such reduction was paid or any such action against the Commissioner of Social Security which is otherwise available with respect to recoveries of overpayments of benefits under section 204 of the Social Security Act.

[CCH Explanation at ¶ 1446. Committee Reports at ¶ 10,685.]

¶ 6350   Code Sec. 6402(f)

Amendment Notes
Act Sec. 3711(a) amended Code Sec. 6402 by redesignating subsection (e) as subsection (f).
Act Sec. 3711(c)(3)(A)-(B) amended Code Sec. 6402(f), as redesignated by Act Sec. 3711(a), by striking "(c) or (d)" and inserting "(c), (d), or (e)", and by striking "Federal agency" and inserting "Federal agency or State".

The above amendment applies to refunds payable under Code Sec. 6402 after December 31, 1999.

(g) FEDERAL AGENCY.—For purposes of this section, the term "Federal agency" means a department, agency, or instrumentality of the United States, and includes a Government corporation (as such term is defined in section 103 of title 5, United States Code).

[CCH Explanation at ¶ 1446. Committee Reports at ¶ 10,685.]

Amendment Notes
Act Sec. 3711(a) amended Code Sec. 6402 by redesignating subsection (f) as subsection (g).

The above amendment applies to refunds payable under Code Sec. 6402 after December 31, 1999.

[*Caution: Code Sec. 6402(h), below, as amended by Act Sec. 3711(c)(4), applies to refunds payable under Code Sec. 6402 after December 31, 1999.—CCH.*]

(h) TREATMENT OF PAYMENTS TO STATES.—The Secretary may provide that, for purposes of determining interest, the payment of any amount withheld under *subsection (c) or (e)* to a State shall be treated as a payment to the person or persons making the overpayment.

[CCH Explanation at ¶ 1446. Committee Reports at ¶ 10,685.]

Amendment Notes
Act Sec. 3711(a) amended Code Sec. 6402 by redesignating subsection (g) as subsection (h).

Act Sec. 3711(c)(4) amended Code Sec. 6402(h), as redesignated by Act Sec. 3711(a), by striking "subsection (c)" and inserting "subsection (c) or (e)".
The above amendment applies to refunds payable under Code Sec. 6402 after December 31, 1999.

(i) CROSS REFERENCE.—For procedures relating to agency notification of the Secretary, see section 3721 of title 31, United States Code.

[CCH Explanation at ¶ 1446. Committee Reports at ¶ 10,685.]

Amendment Notes
Act Sec. 3711(a) amended Code Sec. 6402 by redesignating subsection (h) as subsection (i).

The above amendment applies to refunds payable under Code Sec. 6402 after December 31, 1999.

(j) REFUNDS TO CERTAIN FIDUCIARIES OF INSOLVENT MEMBERS OF AFFILIATED GROUPS.— Notwithstanding any other provision of law, in the case of an insolvent corporation which is a member of an affiliated group of corporations filing a consolidated return for any taxable year and which is subject to a statutory or court-appointed fiduciary, the Secretary may by regulation provide that any refund for such taxable year may be paid on behalf of such insolvent corporation to such fiduciary to the extent that the Secretary determines that the refund is attributable to losses or credits of such insolvent corporation.

[CCH Explanation at ¶ 1446. Committee Reports at ¶ 10,685.]

Amendment Notes
Act Sec. 3711(a) amended Code Sec. 6402 by redesignating subsection (i) as subsection (j).

The above amendment applies to refunds payable under Code Sec. 6402 after December 31, 1999.

[*Caution: Code Sec. 6402(j), below, as added by Act Sec. 3505(a) and redesignated as (k) by Act Sec. 3711(a), applies to disallowances after the 180th day after the date of the enactment of this Act.—CCH.*]

(k) EXPLANATION OF REASON FOR REFUND DISALLOWANCE.—In the case of a disallowance of a claim for refund, the Secretary shall provide the taxpayer with an explanation for such disallowance.

[CCH Explanation at ¶ 1451. Committee Reports at ¶ 10,585.]

Amendment Notes
Act Sec. 3505(a) amended Code Sec. 6402 by adding at the end a new subsection (j) to read as above.
The above amendment applies to disallowances after the 180th day after the date of the enactment of this Act.
Act Sec. 3711(a) amended Code Sec. 6402(j), as added by Act Sec. 3505(a), by redesignating subsection (j) as subsection (k).

The above amendment applies to refunds payable under Code Sec. 6402 after December 31, 1999.

[¶ 6360] CODE SEC. 6404. ABATEMENTS.

* * *

(g) SUSPENSION OF INTEREST AND CERTAIN PENALTIES WHERE SECRETARY FAILS TO CONTACT TAXPAYER.—

(1) SUSPENSION.—

(A) IN GENERAL.—In the case of an individual who files a return of tax imposed by subtitle A for a taxable year on or before the due date for the return (including extensions), if the Secretary does not provide a notice to the taxpayer specifically stating the taxpayer's liability and the basis for the liability before the close of the 1-year period (18-month period in the case of taxable years beginning before January 1, 2004) beginning on the later of—

(i) the date on which the return is filed, or

(ii) the due date of the return without regard to extensions, *the Secretary shall suspend the imposition of any interest, penalty, addition to tax, or additional amount with respect to any failure relating to the return which is computed by reference to the period of time the failure continues to exist and which is properly allocable to the suspension period.*

(B) SEPARATE APPLICATION.—This paragraph shall be applied separately with respect to each item or adjustment.

(2) EXCEPTIONS.—Paragraph (1) shall not apply to—

(A) any penalty imposed by section 6651,

(B) any interest, penalty, addition to tax, or additional amount in a case involving fraud,

(C) any interest, penalty, addition to tax, or additional amount with respect to any tax liability shown on the return, or

(D) any criminal penalty.

(3) SUSPENSION PERIOD.—For purposes of this subsection, the term "suspension period" means the period—

(A) beginning on the day after the close of the 1-year period (18-month period in the case of taxable years beginning before January 1, 2004) under paragraph (1), and

(B) ending on the date which is 21 days after the date on which notice described in paragraph (1)(A) is provided by the Secretary.

[CCH Explanation at ¶ 1401. Committee Reports at ¶ 10,335.]

<table>
<tr><td>

Amendment Notes

Act Sec. 3305(a) amended Code Sec. 6404 by redesignating subsection (g) as subsection (h) and by inserting after subsection (f) a new subsection (g) to read as above.
</td><td>

The above amendment applies to tax years ending after the date of the enactment of this Act.
</td></tr>
</table>

(h) ABATEMENT OF INTEREST ON UNDERPAYMENTS BY TAXPAYERS IN PRESIDENTIALLY DECLARED DISASTER AREAS.—

(1) IN GENERAL.—If the Secretary extends for any period the time for filing income tax returns under section 6081 and the time for paying income tax with respect to such returns under section 6161 for any taxpayer located in a Presidentially declared disaster area, the Secretary shall abate for such period the assessment of any interest prescribed under section 6601 on such income tax.

(2) PRESIDENTIALLY DECLARED DISASTER AREA.—For purposes of paragraph (1), the term "Presidentially declared disaster area" means, with respect to any taxpayer, any area which the President has determined warrants assistance by the Federal Government under the Disaster Relief and Emergency Assistance Act.

[CCH Explanation at ¶ 1417. Committee Reports at ¶ 10,355.]

<table>
<tr><td>

Amendment Notes

Act Sec. 3309(a) amended Code Sec. 6404, as amended by Act Sec. 3305(a), by redesignating subsection (h) as subsection (i) and by inserting after subsection (g) a new subsection (h) to read as above.

The above amendment applies to disasters declared after December 31, 1997, with respect to tax years beginning after December 31, 1997. For a special rule, see Act Sec. 3309(c)(1)-(2), below.

Act Sec. 3309(c)(1)-(2) provides:
</td><td>

(1) For the purposes of section 252(e) of the Balanced Budget and Emergency Deficit Control Act, Congress designates the provisions of this section as an emergency requirement.

(2) The amendments made by subsections (a) and (b) of this section shall only take effect upon the transmittal by the President to the Congress of a message designating the provisions of subsections (a) and (b) as an emergency requirement pursuant to section 252(e) of the Balanced Budget and Emergency Deficit Control Act.
</td></tr>
</table>

(i) REVIEW OF DENIAL OF REQUEST FOR ABATEMENT OF INTEREST.—

* * *

[CCH Explanation at ¶ 1417. Committee Reports at ¶ 10,355.]

<table>
<tr><td>

Amendment Notes

Act Sec. 3309(a) amended Code Sec. 6404, as amended by Act Sec. 3305(a), by redesignating subsection (h) as subsection (i).

The above amendment applies to disasters declared after December 31, 1997, with respect to tax years beginning after December 31, 1997. For a special rule, see Act Sec. 3309(c)(1)-(2), below.

Act Sec. 3309(c)(1)-(2) provides:

(1) For the purposes of section 252(e) of the Balanced Budget and Emergency Deficit Control Act, Congress
</td><td>

designates the provisions of this section as an emergency requirement.

(2) The amendments made by subsections (a) and (b) of this section shall only take effect upon the transmittal by the President to the Congress of a message designating the provisions of subsections (a) and (b) as an emergency requirement pursuant to section 252(e) of the Balanced Budget and Emergency Deficit Control Act.
</td></tr>
</table>

[¶ 6365] CODE SEC. 6412. FLOOR STOCKS REFUNDS.

(a) IN GENERAL.—

(1) TIRES AND TAXABLE FUEL.—Where before October 1, *2005,* any article subject to the tax imposed by section 4071 or 4081 has been sold by the manufacturer, producer, or importer and on such date is held by a dealer and has not been used and is intended for sale, there shall be credited or refunded (without interest) to the manufacturer, producer, or importer an amount equal to the difference between the tax paid by such manufacturer, producer, or importer on his sale of the article and the amount of tax made applicable to such article on and after October 1, *2005,* if claim for such

credit or refund is filed with the Secretary on or before March 31, *2006*, based upon a request submitted to the manufacturer, producer, or importer before January 1, *2006*, by the dealer who held the article in respect of which the credit or refund is claimed, and, on or before March 31, *2006*, reimbursement has been made to such dealer by such manufacturer, producer, or importer for the tax reduction on such article or written consent has been obtained from such dealer to allowance of such credit or refund. No credit or refund shall be allowable under this paragraph with respect to taxable fuel in retail stocks held at the place where intended to be sold at retail, nor with respect to taxable fuel held for sale by a producer or importer of taxable fuel.

* * *

[CCH Explanation at ¶ 750.]

Amendment Notes

P.L. 105-178 (ISTEA)

Act Sec. 9002(a)(2)(A)(i)-(ii) amended Code Sec. 6412(a)(1) by striking "1999" each place it appears and inserting "2005", and by striking "2000" each place it appears and inserting "2006".

The above amendment is effective on June 9, 1998.

[¶ 6370] CODE SEC. 6416. CERTAIN TAXES ON SALES AND SERVICES.

* * *

(b) SPECIAL CASES IN WHICH TAX PAYMENTS CONSIDERED OVERPAYMENTS.—Under regulations prescribed by the Secretary, credit or refund (without interest) shall be allowed or made in respect of the overpayments determined under the following paragraphs:

* * *

(5) RETURN OF CERTAIN INSTALLMENT ACCOUNTS.—If—

(A) tax was paid under *section 4216(d)(1)* in respect of any installment account,

(B) such account is, under the agreement under which the account was sold, returned to the person who sold such account, and

(C) the consideration is readjusted as provided in such agreement,

the part of the tax paid under *section 4216(d)(1)* allocable to the part of the consideration repaid or credited to the purchaser of such account shall be deemed to be an overpayment.

* * *

[CCH Explanation at ¶ 30,050.]

Amendment Notes

Act Sec. 6023(23) amended Code Sec. 6416(b)(5) by striking "section 4216(e)(1)" each place it appears and inserting "section 4216(d)(1)".

The above amendment is effective on the date of the enactment of this Act.

[¶ 6380] CODE SEC. 6421. GASOLINE USED FOR CERTAIN NONHIGHWAY PURPOSES, USED BY LOCAL TRANSIT SYSTEMS, OR SOLD FOR CERTAIN EXEMPT PURPOSES.

(a) NONHIGHWAY USES.—Except as provided in *subsection (i)*, if gasoline is used in an off-highway business use, the Secretary shall pay (without interest) to the ultimate purchaser of such gasoline an amount equal to the amount determined by multiplying the number of gallons so used by the rate at which tax was imposed on such gasoline under section 4081. Except as provided in paragraph (2) of subsection (f) of this section, in the case of gasoline used as a fuel in an aircraft, the Secretary shall pay (without interest) to the ultimate purchaser of such gasoline an amount equal to the amount determined by multiplying the number of gallons of gasoline so used by the rate at which tax was imposed on such gasoline under section 4081.

[CCH Explanation at ¶ 30,050.]

Amendment Notes

Act Sec. 6023(24)(C) amended Code Sec. 6421(a) by striking "subsection (j)" and inserting "subsection (i)".

The above amendment is effective on the date of the enactment of this Act.

(b) INTERCITY, LOCAL, OR SCHOOL BUSES.—

(1) ALLOWANCE.—Except as provided in paragraph (2) and *subsection (i)*, if gasoline is used in an automobile bus while engaged in—

(A) furnishing (for compensation) passenger land transportation available to the general public, or

(B) the transportation of students and employees of schools (as defined in the last sentence of section 4221(d)(7)(C)),

the Secretary shall pay (without interest) to the ultimate purchaser of such gasoline an amount equal to the product of the number of gallons of gasoline so used multiplied by the rate at which tax was imposed on such gasoline by section 4081.

* * *

[CCH Explanation at ¶ 30,050.]

Amendment Notes
Act Sec. 6023(24)(C) amended Code Sec. 6421(b) by striking "subsection (j)" and inserting "subsection (i)".

The above amendment is effective on the date of the enactment of this Act.

(c) EXEMPT PURPOSES.—If gasoline is sold to any person for any purpose described in paragraph (2), (3), (4), or (5) of section 4221(a), the Secretary shall pay (without interest) to such person an amount equal to the product of the number of gallons of gasoline so sold multiplied by the rate at which tax was imposed on such gasoline by section 4081. The preceding sentence shall apply notwithstanding paragraphs *(2)* and (3) of subsection (f). *Subsection (a) shall not apply to gasoline to which this subsection applies.*

[CCH Explanation at ¶ 701. Committee Reports at ¶ 11,175.]

Amendment Notes
Act Sec. 6010(g)(3)(A)-(B) amended Code Sec. 6421(c) by striking "(2)(A)" and inserting "(2)", and by adding at the end a new sentence to read as above.
The above amendment is effective as if included in the provision of the Taxpayer Relief Act of 1997 (P.L.

105-34) to which it relates [effective October 1, 1997.— CCH.].

(d) TIME FOR FILING CLAIMS; PERIOD COVERED.—
* * *

(2) EXCEPTION.—For payments per quarter based on aggregate amounts payable under this section and section 6427, see section 6427(i)(2).
* * *

[CCH Explanation at ¶ 729. Committee Reports at ¶ 15,125.]

Amendment Notes
P.L. 105-178 (ISTEA)
Act Sec. 9009(b)(3) amended Code Sec. 6421(d)(2) to read as above. Prior to amendment, Code Sec. 6421(d)(2) read as follows:
(2) EXCEPTION.—If $1,000 or more is payable under this section to any person with respect to gasoline used during

any of the first three quarters of his taxable year, a claim may be filed under this section by such person with respect to gasoline used during such quarter. No claim filed under this paragraph shall be allowed unless filed on or before the last day of the first quarter following the quarter for which the claim is filed.
The above amendment is effective October 1, 1998.

(f) EXEMPT SALES; OTHER PAYMENTS OR REFUNDS AVAILABLE.—
* * *

(3) GASOLINE USED IN TRAINS.—In the case of gasoline used as a fuel in a train, this section shall not apply with respect to—
* * *

(B) so much of the rate specified in section 4081(a)(2)(A) as does not exceed—
(i) 6.8 cents per gallon after September 30, 1993, and before October 1, 1995,
(ii) 5.55 cents per gallon after September 30, 1995, and before *November 1, 1998*, and
(iii) 4.3 cents per gallon after *October 31, 1998.*
* * *

[CCH Explanation at ¶ 727. Committee Reports at ¶ 15,095.]

Amendment Notes
P.L. 105-178 (ISTEA)
Act Sec. 9006(b)(1)(A)-(B) amended Code Sec. 6421(f)(3)(B) by striking "October 1, 1999" in clause (ii) and

inserting "November 1, 1998", and by striking "September 30, 1999" in subclause (iii) and inserting "October 31, 1998".
The above amendment is effective June 9, 1998.

(i) INCOME TAX CREDIT IN LIEU OF PAYMENT.—
* * *

[CCH Explanation at ¶ 30,050.]

Amendment Notes
Act Sec. 6023(24)(A) amended Code Sec. 6421 by redesignating subsections (j) and (k) as subsections (i) and (j), respectively.

The above amendment is effective on the date of the enactment of this Act.

(j) CROSS REFERENCES.—
* * *

[CCH Explanation at ¶ 30,050.]

Amendment Notes
Act Sec. 6023(24)(A) amended Code Sec. 6421 by redesignating subsection (k) as subsection (j).

The above amendment is effective on the date of the enactment of this Act.

[¶ 6390] CODE SEC. 6427. FUELS NOT USED FOR TAXABLE PURPOSES.
* * *

(d) USE BY CERTAIN AIRCRAFT MUSEUMS OR IN CERTAIN *OTHER AIRCRAFT USES.*—Except as provided in subsection (k), if—
(1) any gasoline on which tax is imposed by section 4081, or
(2) any fuel on the sale of which tax was imposed under section 4041,

is used by an aircraft museum (as defined in section 4041(h)(2)) in an aircraft or vehicle owned by such museum and used exclusively for purposes set forth in section 4041(h)(2)(C), or is used in a helicopter *or a fixed-wing aircraft* for a purpose described in section 4041(1), the Secretary shall pay (without interest) to the ultimate purchaser of such gasoline or fuel an amount equal to the aggregate amount of the tax imposed on such gasoline or fuel.

[CCH Explanation at ¶ 721.]

Amendment Notes

Act Sec. 6016(b)(1)-(2) amended Code Sec. 6427(d) by striking "HELICOPTERS" in the heading and inserting "OTHER AIRCRAFT USES", and by inserting "or a fixed-wing aircraft" after "helicopter".

The above amendment is effective as if included in the provision of the Taxpayer Relief Act of 1997 (P.L. 105-34) to which it relates [generally effective August 27, 1996.—CCH.].

(f) GASOLINE, DIESEL FUEL, KEROSENE, AND AVIATION FUEL USED TO PRODUCE CERTAIN ALCOHOL FUELS.—

* * *

(3) COORDINATION WITH OTHER REPAYMENT PROVISIONS.—No amount shall be payable under paragraph (1) with respect to any gasoline, diesel fuel, kerosene, or aviation fuel with respect to which an amount is payable under subsection (d) or (1) of this section or under section 6420 or 6421.

(4) TERMINATION.—This subsection shall not apply with respect to any mixture sold or used after September 30, *2007.*

* * *

[CCH Explanation at ¶ 760 and 30,050. Committee Reports at ¶ 15,035.]

Amendment Notes

Act Sec. 6023(25) amended Code Sec. 6427(f)(3) by striking ", (e)," after "(d)".

The above amendment is effective on the date of the enactment of this Act.

P.L. 105-178 (ISTEA)

Act Sec. 9003(a)(2) amended Code Sec. 6427(f)(4), as amended by the Taxpayer Relief Act of 1997 (P.L. 105-34), by striking "1999" and inserting "2007".

The above amendment is effective on June 9, 1998.

(i) TIME FOR FILING CLAIMS; PERIOD COVERED.—

(1) GENERAL RULE.—Except as otherwise provided in this subsection, not more than one claim may be filed under subsection (a), (b), (d), (h), (1), or (o) by any person with respect to fuel used during his taxable year; and no claim shall be allowed under this paragraph with respect to fuel used during any taxable year unless filed by the purchaser not later than the time prescribed by law for filing a claim for credit or refund of overpayment of income tax for such taxable year. For purposes of this paragraph, a person's taxable year shall be his taxable year for purposes of subtitle A

(2) EXCEPTIONS.—

(A) IN GENERAL.—If, at the close of any quarter of the taxable year of any person, at least $750 is payable in the aggregate under subsections (a), (b), (d), (h), (1), and (o) of this section and section 6421 to such person with respect to fuel used during—

(i) such quarter, or

(ii) any prior quarter (for which no other claim has been filed) during such taxable year,

a claim may be filed under this section with respect to such fuel.

(B) TIME FOR FILING CLAIM.—No claim filed under this paragraph shall be allowed unless filed during the 1st quarter following the last quarter included in the claim * * *

(4) SPECIAL RULE FOR VENDOR REFUNDS.—

(A) IN GENERAL.—A claim may be filed under subsection (1)(5) by any person with respect to fuel sold by such person for any period—

(i) for which $200 or more ($100 or more in the case of kerosene) is payable under subsection (1)(5), and

(ii) which is not less than 1 week.

Notwithstanding subsection (1)(1), paragraph (3)(B) shall apply to claims filed under the preceding sentence.

(B) TIME FOR FILING CLAIM.—No claim filed under this paragraph shall be allowed unless filed on or before the last day of the first quarter following the earliest quarter included in the claim.

* * *

[CCH Explanation at ¶ 729 and 30,050. Committee Reports at ¶ 15,125.]

Amendment Notes

Act Sec. 6017(a) amended Code Sec. 6427(i)(2)(B) to read as above. Prior to amendment, Code Sec. 6427(i)(2)(B) read as follows:

(B) TIME FOR FILING CLAIM.—No claim filed under this paragraph shall be allowed unless filed on or before the last

day of the first quarter following the quarter for which the claim is filed.

The above amendment is effective as if included in the amendments made by Act Sec. 9009 of the Transportation Equity Act for the 21st Century (P.L. 105-178) [effective October 1, 1998.—CCH.].

Code Sec. 6427(i)   ¶ 6390

Act Sec. 6023(26)(B) amended Code Sec. 6427(i)(1) and (2)(A) by striking "(q)" and inserting "(o)".

The above amendment is effective on the date of the enactment of this Act.

P.L. 105-178 (ISTEA)

Act Sec. 9009(a) amended Code Sec. 6427(i)(2)(A) to read as above. Prior to amendment, Code Sec. 6427(i)(2)(A) read as follows:

(A) IN GENERAL.—If $1,000 or more is payable under subsections (a), (b), (d), (h), and (q) to any person with respect to fuel used, during any of the first 3 quarters of his taxable year, a claim may be filed under this section with respect to fuel used, during such quarter.

Act Sec. 9009(b)(1) amended Code Sec. 6427(i) by striking paragraph (4) and by redesignating paragraph (5) as para-

graph (4). Prior to being stricken, Code Sec. 6427(4) read as follows:

(4) SPECIAL RULE FOR REFUNDS UNDER SUBSECTION (l).—

(A) IN GENERAL.—If at the close of any of the 1st 3 quarters of the taxable year of any person, at least $750 is payable under subsection (l) to such person with respect to fuel used during such quarter or any prior quarter during the taxable year (and for which no other claim has been filed), a claim may be filed under subsection (l) with respect to such fuel.

(B) TIME FOR FILING CLAIM.—No claim filed under this paragraph shall be allowed unless filed during the 1st quarter following the last quarter included in the claim.

The above amendments are effective on October 1, 1998.

(k) INCOME TAX CREDIT IN LIEU OF PAYMENT.—

* * *

(2) EXCEPTION.—Paragraph (1) shall not apply to a payment of a claim filed under paragraph (2), (3), or (4) of subsection (i).

* * *

[CCH Explanation at ¶ 729. Committee Reports at ¶ 15,125.]

Amendment Notes

P.L. 105-178 (ISTEA)

Act Sec. 9009(b)(2) amended Code Sec. 6427(k)(2) to read as above. Prior to amendment, Code Sec. 6427(k)(2) read as follows:

(2) EXCEPTION.—Paragraph (1) shall not apply to a payment of a claim filed under paragraph (2), (3) [,] (4), or (5) of subsection (i).

The above amendment is effective on October 1, 1998.

(l) NONTAXABLE USES OF DIESEL FUEL, KEROSENE AND AVIATION FUEL.—

* * *

(3) REFUND OF CERTAIN TAXES ON FUEL USED IN DIESEL-POWERED TRAINS.—For purposes of this subsection, the term "nontaxable use" includes fuel used in a diesel-powered train. The preceding sentence shall not apply with respect to—

(A) the Leaking Underground Storage Tank Trust Fund financing rate under sections 4041 and 4081, and

(B) so much of the rate specified in section 4081(a)(2)(A) as does not exceed—

(i) 6.8 cents per gallon after September 30, 1993, and before October 1, 1995,

(ii) 5.55 cents per gallon after September 30, 1995, and before *November 1, 1998*, and

(iii) 4.3 cents per gallon after *October 31, 1998.*

The preceding sentence shall not apply in the case of fuel sold for exclusive use by a State or any political subdivision thereof.

* * *

[CCH Explanation at ¶ 727. Committee Reports at ¶ 15,095.]

Amendment Notes

P.L. 105-178 (ISTEA)

Act Sec. 9006(b)(2)(A)-(B) amended Code Sec. 6427(l)(3)(B) by striking "October 1, 1999" in clause (ii) and

inserting "November 1, 1998", and by striking "September 30, 1999" in clause (iii) and inserting "October 31, 1998".

The above amendment is effective on June 9, 1998.

(m) REGULATIONS.—The Secretary may by regulations prescribe the conditions, not inconsistent with the provisions of this section, under which payments may be made under this section.

[CCH Explanation at ¶ 30,050.]

Amendment Notes

Act Sec. 6023(26)(A) amended Code Sec. 6427, as amended by Act Sec. 6023(16), by redesignating subsections (n), (p), (q), and (r) as subsections (m), (n), (o), and (p), respectively.

The above amendment is effective on the date of the enactment of this Act.

(n) PAYMENTS FOR TAXES IMPOSED BY SECTION 4041(d).—For purposes of subsections (a), (b), and (c), the taxes imposed by section 4041(d) shall be treated as imposed by section 4041(a).

[CCH Explanation at ¶ 30,050.]

Amendment Notes

Act Sec. 6023(26)(A) amended Code Sec. 6427 by redesignating subsection (p) as subsection (n).

The above amendment is effective on the date of the enactment of this Act.

(o) GASOHOL USED IN NONCOMMERCIAL AVIATION.—Except as provided in subsection (k), if—

(1) any tax is imposed by section 4081 at a rate determined under subsection (c) thereof on gasohol (as defined in such subsection), and

(2) such gasohol is used as a fuel in any aircraft in noncommercial aviation (as defined in *section 4041(c)(2)),*

the Secretary shall pay (without interest) to the ultimate purchaser of such gasohol an amount equal to 1.4 cents (2 cents in the case of a mixture none of the alcohol in which consists of ethanol) multiplied by the number of gallons of gasohol so used.

[CCH Explanation at ¶ 30,050.]

Amendment Notes

Act Sec. 6023(16) amended Code Sec. 6427(q)(2) by striking "section 4041(c)(4)" and inserting "section 4041(c)(2)".

Act Sec. 6023(26)(A) amended Code Sec. 6427, as amended by Act Sec. 6023(16), by redesignating subsection (q) as subsection (o).

The above amendments are effective on the date of the enactment of this Act.

(p) CROSS REFERENCES.—

* * *

[CCH Explanation at ¶ 30,050.]

Amendment Notes

Act Sec. 6023(26)(A) amended Code Sec. 6427 by redesignating subsection (r) as subsection (p).

The above amendment is effective on the date of the enactment of this Act.

[¶ 6400] CODE SEC. 6501. LIMITATIONS ON ASSESSMENT AND COLLECTION.

* * *

(c) EXCEPTIONS.—

* * *

[*Caution: Code Sec. 6501(c)(4), below, as amended by Act Sec. 3461(b)(1)-(2), generally applies to requests to extend the period of limitations made after December 31, 1999.— CCH.*]

(4) EXTENSION BY AGREEMENT.—

(A) IN GENERAL.—Where before the expiration of the time prescribed in this section for the assessment of any tax imposed by this title, except the estate tax provided in chapter 11, both the Secretary and the taxpayer have consented in writing to its assessment after such time, the tax may be assessed at any time prior to the expiration of the period agreed upon. The period so agreed upon may be extended by subsequent agreements in writing made before the expiration of the period previously agreed upon.

(B) NOTICE TO TAXPAYER OF RIGHT TO REFUSE OR LIMIT EXTENSION.—The Secretary shall notify the taxpayer of the taxpayer's right to refuse to extend the period of limitations, or to limit such extension to particular issues or to a particular period of time, on each occasion when the taxpayer is requested to provide such consent.

* * *

(9) GIFT TAX ON CERTAIN GIFTS NOT SHOWN ON RETURN.—If any gift of property the value of which (or any increase in taxable gifts required under section 2701(d) which) is required to be shown on a return of tax imposed by chapter 12 (without regard to section 2503(b)), and is not shown on such return, any tax imposed by chapter 12 on such gift may be assessed, or a proceeding in court for the collection of such tax may be begun without assessment, at any time. The preceding sentence shall not apply to any item which is disclosed in such return, or in a statement attached to the return, in a manner adequate to apprise the Secretary of the nature of such item.

* * *

[CCH Explanation at ¶ 446 and 1286. Committee Reports at ¶ 10,515 and 11,030.]

Amendment Notes

Act Sec. 3461(b)(1)-(2) amended Code Sec. 6501(c)(4) by striking "Where" and inserting "(A) IN GENERAL.—Where", and by adding at the end a new subparagraph (B) to read as above.

The above amendment applies to requests to extend the period of limitations made after December 31, 1999. For a special rule, see Act Sec. 3461(c)(2), below.

Act Sec. 3461(c)(2) provides:

(2) PRIOR REQUEST.—If, in any request to extend the period of limitations made on or before December 31, 1999, a taxpayer agreed to extend such period beyond the 10-year period referred to in section 6502(a) of the Internal Revenue Code of 1986, such extension shall expire on the latest of—

(A) the last day of such 10-year period,

(B) December 31, 2002, or

(C) in the case of an extension in connection with an installment agreement, the 90th day after the end of the period of such extension.

Act Sec. 6007(e)(2)(A) amended Code Sec. 6501(c)(9) by striking the last sentence. Prior to being stricken, the last sentence of Code Sec. 6501(c)(9) read as follows:

The value of any item which is so disclosed may not be redetermined by the Secretary after the expiration of the period under subsection (a).

The above amendment is effective as if included in the provision of the Taxpayer Relief Act of 1997 (P.L. 105-34) to which it relates [effective for gifts made in calendar years ending after August 5, 1997.—CCH.].

(m) DEFICIENCIES ATTRIBUTABLE TO ELECTION OF CERTAIN CREDITS.—The period for assessing a deficiency attributable to any *election under section 30(d)(4), 40(f), 43, 45B, 45C(d)(4), or 51(j) (or any* revocation thereof) shall not expire before the date 1 year after the date on which the Secretary is notified of such election (or revocation).

* * *

[CCH Explanation at ¶ 30,050.]

Amendment Notes

Act Sec. 6023(27) amended Code Sec. 6501(m) by striking "election under" and all that follows through "(or any" and inserting "election under section 30(d)(4), 40(f), 43, 45B, 45C(d)(4), or 51(j) (or any". Prior to amendment, Code Sec. 6501(m) read as follows:

(m) DEFICIENCIES ATTRIBUTABLE TO ELECTION OF CERTAIN CREDITS.—The period for assessing a deficiency attributable

to any election under section 30(d)(4), 40(f), 43, 45B, or 51(j) (or any revocation thereof) shall not expire before the date 1 year after the date on which the Secretary is notified of such election (or revocation).

The above amendment is effective on the date of the enactment of this Act.

[¶ 6410] CODE SEC. 6502. COLLECTION AFTER ASSESSMENT.

[*Caution: Code Sec. 6502(a), below, as amended by Act Sec. 3461(a)(1)-(2), generally applies to requests to extend the period of limitations made after December 31, 1999.— CCH.*]

(a) LENGTH OF PERIOD.—Where the assessment of any tax imposed by this title has been made within the period of limitation properly applicable thereto, such tax may be collected by levy or by a proceeding in court, but only if the levy is made or the proceeding begun—

(1) within 10 years after the assessment of the tax, or

(2) if—

(A) there is an installment agreement between the taxpayer and the Secretary, prior to the date which is 90 days after the expiration of any period for collection agreed upon in writing by the Secretary and the taxpayer at the time the installment agreement was entered into, or

(B) there is a release of levy under section 6343 after such 10-year period, prior to the expiration of any period for collection agreed upon in writing by the Secretary and the taxpayer before such release.

If a timely proceeding in court for the collection of a tax is commenced, the period during which such tax may be collected by levy shall be extended and shall not expire until the liability for the tax (or a judgment against the taxpayer arising from such liability) is satisfied or becomes unenforceable.

* * *

[CCH Explanation at ¶ 1286. Committee Reports at ¶ 10,515.]

Amendment Notes

Act Sec. 3461(a)(1)-(2) amended Code Sec. 6502(a) by striking paragraph (2) and inserting a new paragraph (2) to read as above, and by striking the first sentence in the matter following paragraph (2). Prior to amendment, Code Sec. 6502(a)(2) and the first sentence in the matter following paragraph (2) read as follows:

(2) prior to the expiration of any period for collection agreed upon in writing by the Secretary and the taxpayer before the expiration of such 10-year period (or, if there is a release of levy under section 6343 after such 10-year period, then before such release).

The period so agreed upon may be extended by subsequent agreements in writing made before the expiration of the period previously agreed upon.

The above amendment applies to requests to extend the period of limitations made after December 31, 1999. For a special rule, see Act Sec. 3461(c)(2), below.

Act Sec. 3461(c)(2) provides:

(2) PRIOR REQUEST.—If, in any request to extend the period of limitations made on or before December 31, 1999, a taxpayer agreed to extend such period beyond the 10-year period referred to in section 6502(a) of the Internal Revenue Code of 1986, such extension shall expire on the latest of—

(A) the last day of such 10-year period,

(B) December 31, 2002, or

(C) in the case of an extension in connection with an installment agreement, the 90th day after the end of the period of such extension.

[¶ 6420] CODE SEC. 6503. SUSPENSION OF RUNNING OF PERIOD OF LIMITATION.

* * *

(f) WRONGFUL SEIZURE OF OR LIEN ON PROPERTY OF THIRD PARTY.—

(1) WRONGFUL SEIZURE.—The running of the period under section 6502 shall be suspended for a period equal to the period from the date property (including money) of a third party is wrongfully seized or received by the Secretary to the date the Secretary returns property pursuant to section 6343(b) or the date on which a judgment secured pursuant to section 7426 with respect to such property becomes final, and for 30 days thereafter. The running of such period shall be suspended under this paragraph only with respect to the amount of such assessment equal to the amount of money or the value of specific property returned.

(2) WRONGFUL LIEN.—In the case of any assessment for which a lien was made on any property, the running of the period under section 6502 shall be suspended for a period equal to the period beginning on the date any person becomes entitled to a certificate under section 6325(b)(4) with respect to such property and ending on the date which is 30 days after the earlier of—

(A) the earliest date on which the Secretary no longer holds any amount as a deposit or bond provided under section 6325(b)(4) by reason of such deposit or bond being used to satisfy the unpaid tax or being refunded or released, or

(B) the date that the judgment secured under section 7426(b)(5) becomes final.

¶ 6410   Code Sec. 6502(a)

The running of such period shall be suspended under this paragraph only with respect to the amount of such assessment equal to the value of the interest of the United States in the property plus interest, penalties, additions to the tax, and additional amounts attributable thereto.

* * *

[CCH Explanation at ¶ 1230. Committee Reports at ¶ 10,275.]

Amendment Notes

Act Sec. 3106(b)(3) amended Code Sec. 6503(f) to read as above. Prior to amendment, Code Sec. 6503(f) read as follows:

(f) WRONGFUL SEIZURE OF PROPERTY OF THIRD PARTY.— The running of the period of limitations on collection after assessment prescribed in section 6502 shall be suspended for a period equal to the period from the date property (including money) of a third party is wrongfully seized or received by the Secretary to the date the Secretary returns property

pursuant to section 6343(b) or the date on which a judgment secured pursuant to section 7426 with respect to such property becomes final, and for 30 days thereafter. The running of the period of limitations on collection after assessment shall be suspended under this subsection only with respect to the amount of such assessment equal to the amount of money or the value of specific property returned.

The above amendment is effective on the date of the enactment of this Act.

[¶ 6430] CODE SEC. 6511. LIMITATIONS ON CREDIT OR REFUND.

* * *

(h) RUNNING OF PERIODS OF LIMITATION SUSPENDED WHILE TAXPAYER IS UNABLE TO MANAGE FINANCIAL AFFAIRS DUE TO DISABILITY.—

(1) IN GENERAL.—In the case of an individual, the running of the periods specified in subsections (a), (b), and (c) shall be suspended during any period of such individual's life that such individual is financially disabled.

(2) FINANCIALLY DISABLED.—

(A) IN GENERAL.—For purposes of paragraph (1), an individual is financially disabled if such individual is unable to manage his financial affairs by reason of a medically determinable physical or mental impairment of the individual which can be expected to result in death or which has lasted or can be expected to last for a continuous period of not less than 12 months. An individual shall not be considered to have such an impairment unless proof of the existence thereof is furnished in such form and manner as the Secretary may require.

(B) EXCEPTION WHERE INDIVIDUAL HAS GUARDIAN, ETC.—An individual shall not be treated as financially disabled during any period that such individual's spouse or any other person is authorized to act on behalf of such individual in financial matters.

[CCH Explanation at ¶ 1461. Committee Reports at ¶ 10,290.]

Amendment Notes

Act Sec. 3202(a) amended Code Sec. 6511 by redesignating subsection (h) as subsection (i) and by inserting after subsection (g) a new subsection (h) to read as above.

The above amendment applies to periods of disability before, on, or after the date of the enactment of this Act

but does not apply to any claim for credit or refund which (without regard to such amendment) is barred by the operation of any law or rule of law (including res judicata) as of the date of the enactment of this Act.

(i) CROSS REFERENCES.—

* * *

[CCH Explanation at ¶ 1461. Committee Reports at ¶ 10,290.]

Amendment Notes

Act Sec. 3202(a) amended Code Sec. 6511 by redesignating subsection (h) as subsection (i).

The above amendment applies to periods of disability before, on, or after the date of the enactment of this Act

but does not apply to any claim for credit or refund which (without regard to such amendment) is barred by the operation of any law or rule of law (including res judicata) as of the date of the enactment of this Act.

[¶ 6440] CODE SEC. 6512. LIMITATIONS IN CASE OF PETITION TO TAX COURT.

(a) EFFECT OF PETITION TO TAX COURT.—If the Secretary has mailed to the taxpayer a notice of deficiency under section 6212(a) (relating to deficiencies of income, estate, gift, and certain excise taxes) and if the taxpayer files a petition with the Tax Court within the time prescribed in section 6213(a) (or 7481(c) with respect to a determination of statutory interest or section 7481(d) solely with respect to a determination of estate tax by the Tax Court), no credit or refund of income tax for the same taxable year, of gift tax for the same calendar year or calendar quarter, of estate tax in respect of the taxable estate of the same decedent, or of tax imposed by chapter 41, 42, 43, or 44 with respect to any act (or failure to act) to which such petition relates, in respect of which the Secretary has determined the deficiency shall be allowed or made and no suit by the taxpayer for the recovery of any part of the tax shall be instituted in any court except—

(1) As to overpayments determined by a decision of the Tax Court which has become final; and

(2) As to any amount collected in excess of an amount computed in accordance with the decision of the Tax Court which has become final; and

(3) As to any amount collected after the period of limitation upon the making of levy or beginning a proceeding in court for collection has expired; but in any such claim for credit or refund

or in any such suit for refund the decision of the Tax Court which has become final, as to whether such period has expired before the notice of deficiency was mailed, shall be conclusive, and [sic]

(4) As to overpayments attributable to partnership items, in accordance with subchapter C of chapter 63, *and*

(5) As to any amount collected within the period during which the Secretary is prohibited from making the assessment or from collecting by levy or through a proceeding in court under the provisions of section 6213(a), and

(6) As to overpayments the Secretary is authorized to refund or credit pending appeal as provided in subsection (b).

[CCH Explanation at ¶ 1321. Committee Reports at ¶ 10,530.]

Amendment Notes

Act Sec. 3464(b) amended Code Sec. 6512(a) by striking the period at the end of paragraph (4) and inserting ", and", and by inserting after paragraph (4) new paragraphs (5) and (6) to read as above.

The above amendment is effective on the date of the enactment of this Act.

(b) Overpayment Determined by Tax Court.—

(1) Jurisdiction to determine.—Except as provided by paragraph (3) and by section 7463, if the Tax Court finds that there is no deficiency and further finds that the taxpayer has made an overpayment of income tax for the same taxable year, of gift tax for the same calendar year or calendar quarter, of estate tax in respect of the taxable estate of the same decedent, or of tax imposed by chapter 41, 42, 43, or 44 with respect to any act (or failure to act) to which such petition relates for the same taxable period, in respect of which the Secretary determined the deficiency, or finds that there is a deficiency but that the taxpayer has made an overpayment of such tax, the Tax Court shall have jurisdiction to determine the amount of such overpayment, and such amount shall, when the decision of the Tax Court has become final, be credited or refunded to the taxpayer. *If a notice of appeal in respect of the decision of the Tax Court is filed under section 7483, the Secretary is authorized to refund or credit the overpayment determined by the Tax Court to the extent the overpayment is not contested on appeal.*

* * *

[CCH Explanation at ¶ 1321. Committee Reports at ¶ 10,530.]

Amendment Notes

Act Sec. 3464(c) amended Code Sec. 6512(b)(1) by adding at the end a new sentence to read as above.

The above amendment is effective on the date of the enactment of this Act.

[¶ 6450] CODE SEC. 6601. INTEREST ON UNDERPAYMENT, NONPAYMENT, OR EXTENSIONS OF TIME FOR PAYMENT, OF TAX.

* * *

(f) Satisfaction by Credits.—If any portion of a tax is satisfied by credit of an overpayment, then no interest shall be imposed under this section on the portion of the tax so satisfied for any period during which, if the credit had not been made, interest would have been allowable with respect to such overpayment. *The preceding sentence shall not apply to the extent that section 6621(d) applies.*

* * *

[CCH Explanation at ¶ 1406. Committee Reports at ¶ 10,315.]

Amendment Notes

Act Sec. 3301(b) amended Code Sec. 6601(f) by adding at the end a new sentence to read as above.

The above amendment generally applies to interest for periods beginning after the date of the enactment of this Act. For a special rule, see Act Sec. 3301(c)(2), below.

Act Sec. 3301(c)(2) provides:

(2) Special rule.—The amendments made by this section shall apply to interest for periods beginning before the date of the enactment of this Act if the taxpayer—

(A) reasonably identifies and establishes periods of such tax overpayments and under-payments for which the zero rate applies, and

(B) not later than December 31, 1999, requests the Secretary of the Treasury to apply section 6621(d) of the Internal Revenue Code of 1986, as added by subsection (a), to such periods.

[¶ 6460] CODE SEC. 6611. INTEREST ON OVERPAYMENTS.

* * *

(g) No Interest Until Return in Processible Form.—

(1) For purposes of subsections (b)(3), *and (e)*, a return shall not be treated as filed until it is filed in processible form.

* * *

Amendment Notes

Act Sec. 6010(l) amended Code Sec. 6611(g)(1) by striking "(e), and (h)" and inserting "and (e)".

The above amendment is effective as if included in the provision of the Taxpayer Relief Act of 1997 (P.L. 105-34) to which it relates [effective for foreign tax credit carrybacks arising in tax years beginning after August 5, 1997.—CCH.].

[¶ 6470] CODE SEC. 6621. DETERMINATION OF RATE OF INTEREST.

(a) GENERAL RULE.—

(1) OVERPAYMENT RATE.—The overpayment rate established under this section shall be the sum of—

(A) the Federal short-term rate determined under subsection (b), plus

(B) *3 percentage points (2 percentage points in the case of a corporation).*

To the extent that an overpayment of tax by a corporation for any taxable period (as defined in subsection (c)(3), applied by substituting "overpayment" for "underpayment") exceeds $10,000, subparagraph (B) shall be applied by substituting "0.5 percentage point" for "2 percentage points".

* * *

[CCH Explanation at ¶ 1411. Committee Reports at ¶ 10,320.]

Amendment Notes

Act Sec. 3302(a) amended Code Sec. 6621(a)(1)(B) to read as above. Prior to amendment, Code Sec. 6621(a)(1)(B) read as follows:

(B) 2 percentage points.

The above amendment applies to interest for the second and succeeding calendar quarters beginning after the date of the enactment of this Act.

(d) *ELIMINATION OF INTEREST ON OVERLAPPING PERIODS OF TAX OVERPAYMENTS AND UNDERPAYMENTS.—To the extent that, for any period, interest is payable under subchapter A and allowable under subchapter B on equivalent underpayments and overpayments by the same taxpayer of tax imposed by this title, the net rate of interest under this section on such amounts shall be zero for such period.*

[CCH Explanation at ¶ 1406. Committee Reports at ¶ 10,315.]

Amendment Notes

Act Sec. 3301(a) amended Code Sec. 6621 by adding at the end a new subsection (d) to read as above.

The above amendment generally applies to interest for periods beginning after the date of the enactment of this Act. For a special rule, see Act Sec. 3301(c)(2), below.

Act Sec. 3301(c)(2) provides:

(2) SPECIAL RULE.—The amendments made by this section shall apply to interest for periods beginning before the date of the enactment of this Act if the taxpayer—

(A) reasonably identifies and establishes periods of such tax overpayments and under-payments for which the zero rate applies, and

(B) not later than December 31, 1999, requests the Secretary of the Treasury to apply section 6621(d) of the Internal Revenue Code of 1986, as added by subsection (a), to such periods.

[Caution: Code Sec. 6631, below, as added by Act Sec. 3308(a), applies to notices issued after December 31, 2000.—CCH.]

[¶ 6480] *CODE SEC. 6631. NOTICE REQUIREMENTS.*

The Secretary shall include with each notice to an individual taxpayer which includes an amount of interest required to be paid by such taxpayer under this title information with respect to the section of this title under which the interest is imposed and a computation of the interest.

[CCH Explanation at ¶ 1416. Committee Reports at ¶ 10,350.]

Amendment Notes

Act Sec. 3308(a) amended chapter 67 by adding at the end a new subchapter D (Code Sec. 6631) to read as above.

The above amendment applies to notices issued after December 31, 2000.

[¶ 6490] CODE SEC. 6651. FAILURE TO FILE TAX RETURN OR TO PAY TAX.

* * *

[Caution: Code Sec. 6651(h), below, as added by Act Sec. 3303(a), applies for purposes of determining additions to the tax for months beginning after December 31, 1999.— CCH.]

(h) *LIMITATION ON PENALTY ON INDIVIDUAL'S FAILURE TO PAY FOR MONTHS DURING PERIOD OF INSTALLMENT AGREEMENT.— In the case of an individual who files a return of tax on or before the due date for the return (including extensions), paragraphs (2) and (3) of subsection (a) shall each be applied by substituting "0.25" for "0.5" each place it appears for purposes of determining the addition to tax for any month during which an installment agreement under section 6159 is in effect for the payment of such tax.*

[CCH Explanation at ¶ 1282. Committee Reports at ¶ 10,325.]

Amendment Notes

Act Sec. 3303(a) amended Code Sec. 6651 by adding at the end a new subsection (h) to read as above.

The above amendment applies for purposes of determining additions to the tax for months beginning after December 31, 1999.

[¶ 6500] CODE SEC. 6656. FAILURE TO MAKE DEPOSIT OF TAXES.

* * *

(c) EXCEPTION FOR FIRST-TIME DEPOSITORS OF EMPLOYMENT TAXES.—The Secretary may waive the penalty imposed by subsection (a) on a person's inadvertent failure to deposit any employment tax if—

(1) such person meets the requirements referred to in section 7430(c)(4)(A)(ii),

Code Sec. 6656(c) ¶ 6500

[*Caution: Code Sec. 6656(c)(2), below, as amended by Act Sec. 3304(b)(1), applies to deposits required to be made after the 180th day after the date of the enactment of this Act.—CCH.*]

(2) such failure—

(A) occurs during the 1st quarter that such person was required to deposit any employment tax, or

(B) if such person is required to change the frequency of deposits of any employment tax, relates to the first deposit to which such change applies, and

(3) the return of such tax was filed on or before the due date.

For purposes of this subsection, the term "employment taxes" means the taxes imposed by subtitle C.

* * *

[CCH Explanation at ¶ 1426. Committee Reports at ¶ 10,330.]

Amendment Notes

Act Sec. 3304(b)(1) amended Code Sec. 6656(c)(2) to read as above. Prior to amendment, Code Sec. 6656(c)(2) read as follows:

(2) such failure occurs during the 1st quarter that such person was required to deposit any employment tax, and

The above amendment applies to deposits required to be made after the 180th day after the date of the enactment of this Act.

(e) DESIGNATION OF PERIODS TO WHICH DEPOSITS APPLY.—

[*Caution: Code Sec. 6656(e)(1), below, as added by Act Sec. 3304(a), but prior to amendment by Act Sec. 3304(c), applies to deposits required to be made after the 180th day after the date of the enactment of this Act and before January 1, 2002.—CCH.*]

(1) IN GENERAL.—A person may, with respect to any deposit of tax to be reported on such person's return for a specified tax period, designate the period or periods within such specified tax period to which the deposit is to be applied for purposes of this section.

[*Caution: Code Sec. 6656(e)(1), below, as amended by Act Sec. 3304(c), applies to deposits required to be made after December 31, 2001.—CCH.*]

(1) IN GENERAL.—A deposit made under this section shall be applied to the most recent period or periods within the specified tax period to which the deposit relates, unless the person making such deposit designates a different period or periods to which such deposit is to be applied.

(2) TIME FOR MAKING DESIGNATION.—A person may make a designation under paragraph (1) only during the 90-day period beginning on the date of a notice that a penalty under subsection (a) has been imposed for the specified tax period to which the deposit relates.

[CCH Explanation at ¶ 1426. Committee Reports at ¶ 10,330.]

Amendment Notes

Act Sec. 3304(a) amended Code Sec. 6656 by adding at the end a new subsection (e) to read as above.

The above amendment applies to deposits required to be made after the 180th day after the date of the enactment of this Act.

Act Sec. 3304(c) amended Code Sec. 6656(e)(1), as added by Act Sec. 3304(a), to read as above. Prior to amendment, Code Sec. 6656(e)(1) read as follows:

(1) IN GENERAL.—A person may, with respect to any deposit of tax to be reported on such person's return for a specified tax period, designate the period or periods within such specified tax period to which the deposit is to be applied for purposes of this section.

The above amendment applies to deposits required to be made after December 31, 2001.

[¶ 6510] CODE SEC. 6672. FAILURE TO COLLECT AND PAY OVER TAX, OR ATTEMPT TO EVADE OR DEFEAT TAX.

* * *

(b) PRELIMINARY NOTICE REQUIREMENT.—

(1) IN GENERAL.—No penalty shall be imposed under subsection (a) unless the Secretary notifies the taxpayer in writing by mail to an address as determined under section 6212(b) *or in person* that the taxpayer shall be subject to an assessment of such penalty.

(2) TIMING OF NOTICE.—The mailing of the notice described in paragraph (1) *(or, in the case of such a notice delivered in person, such delivery)* shall precede any notice and demand of any penalty under subsection (a) by at least 60 days.

(3) STATUTE OF LIMITATIONS.—If a notice described in paragraph (1) with respect to any penalty is mailed *or delivered in person* before the expiration of the period provided by section 6501 for the assessment of such penalty (determined without regard to this paragraph), the period provided by such section for the assessment of such penalty shall not expire before the later of—

(A) the date 90 days after the date on which such notice was mailed *or delivered in person,* or

(B) if there is a timely protest of the proposed assessment, the date 30 days after the Secretary makes a final administrative determination with respect to such protest.

* * *

[CCH Explanation at ¶ 1431. Committee Reports at ¶ 10,345.]

Amendment Notes

Act Sec. 3307(a) amended Code Sec. 6672(b)(1) by inserting "or in person" after "section 6212(b)".

Act Sec. 3307(b)(1) amended Code Sec. 6672(b)(2) by inserting "(or, in the case of such a notice delivered in person, such delivery)" after "paragraph (1)"

Act Sec. 3307(b)(2) amended Code Sec. 6672(b)(3) by inserting "or delivered in person" after "mailed" each place it appears.

The above amendments are effective on the date of the enactment of this Act.

[¶ 6520] CODE SEC. 6724. WAIVER; DEFINITIONS AND SPECIAL RULES.

* * *

(c) SPECIAL RULE FOR FAILURE TO MEET MAGNETIC MEDIA REQUIREMENTS.—No penalty shall be imposed under section 6721 solely by reason of any failure to comply with the requirements of the regulations prescribed under section 6011(e)(2), except to the extent that such a failure occurs with respect to more than 250 information returns *(more than 100 information returns in the case of a partnership having more than 100 partners)*.

[CCH Explanation at ¶ 682. Committee Reports at ¶ 11,260.]

Amendment Notes

Act Sec. 6012(d) amended Code Sec. 6724(c) by inserting before the period "(more than 100 information returns in the case of a partnership having more than 100 partners)".

The above amendment is effective as if included in the provision of the Taxpayer Relief Act of 1997 (P.L. 105-34) to which it relates [effective for partnership tax years beginning after December 31, 1997.—CCH.].

(d) DEFINITIONS.—For purposes of this part—

(1) INFORMATION RETURN.—The term "information return" means—

* * *

(B) any return required by—

* * *

(xv) section 4101(d) (relating to information reporting with respect to fuels taxes)[,]

(xvi) subparagraph (C) of section 338(h)(10) (relating to information required to be furnished to the Secretary in case of elective recognition of gain or loss), *or*

(xvii) section 264(f)(5)(A)(iv) (relating to reporting with respect to certain life insurance and annuity contracts).

* * *

(2) PAYEE STATEMENT.—The term "payee statement" means any statement required to be furnished under—

* * *

(Y) section 6047(d) (relating to reports by plan administrators) to any person other than the Secretary with respect to the amount of payments made to such person,

(Z) section 6050S(d) (relating to returns relating to qualified tuition and related expenses) *or*

(AA) section 264(f)(5)(A)(iv) (relating to reporting with respect to certain life insurance and annuity contracts).

* * *

[CCH Explanation at ¶ 561. Committee Reports at ¶ 11,210.]

Amendment Notes

Act Sec. 6010(o)(4)(B) amended Code Sec. 6724(d)(1)(B) by striking "or" at the end of clause (xv), by striking the period at the end of clause (xvi) and inserting ", or", and by adding a new clause (xvii) to read as above.

Act Sec. 6010(o)(4)(C) amended Code Sec. 6724(d)(2) by striking "or" at the end of subparagraph (Y), by striking the period at the end of subparagraph (Z) and inserting "or",

and by adding at the end a new subparagraph (AA) to read as above.

The above amendments are effective as if included in the provisions of the Taxpayer Relief Act of 1997 (P.L 105-34) to which they relate [effective for contracts issued after June 8, 1997, in tax years ending after such date.—CCH.].

[Caution: Code Sec. 6751, below, as added by Act Sec. 3306(a), applies to notices issued, and penalties assessed, after December 31, 2000.—CCH.]

[¶ 6530] *CODE SEC. 6751. PROCEDURAL REQUIREMENTS.*

(a) COMPUTATION OF PENALTY INCLUDED IN NOTICE.—The Secretary shall include with each notice of penalty under this title information with respect to the name of the penalty, the section of this title under which the penalty is imposed, and a computation of the penalty.

(b) APPROVAL OF ASSESSMENT.—

(1) IN GENERAL.—No penalty under this title shall be assessed unless the initial determination of such assessment is personally approved (in writing) by the immediate supervisor of the individual making such determination or such higher level official as the Secretary may designate.

(2) EXCEPTIONS.—Paragraph (1) shall not apply to—

(A) any addition to tax under section 6651, 6654, or 6655, or

(B) any other penalty automatically calculated through electronic means.

(c) PENALTIES.—*For purposes of this section, the term "penalty" includes any addition to tax or any additional amount.*

[CCH Explanation at ¶ 1436. Committee Reports at ¶ 10,340.]

Amendment Notes

Act Sec. 3306(a) amended chapter 68 by adding at the end a new subchapter C (Code Sec. 6751) to read as above.

The above amendment applies to notices issued, and penalties assessed, after December 31, 2000.

[¶ 6540] CODE SEC. 7122. COMPROMISES.

* * *

(c) STANDARDS FOR EVALUATION OF OFFERS.—

(1) IN GENERAL.—*The Secretary shall prescribe guidelines for officers and employees of the Internal Revenue Service to determine whether an offer-in-compromise is adequate and should be accepted to resolve a dispute.*

(2) ALLOWANCES FOR BASIC LIVING EXPENSES.—

(A) IN GENERAL.—*In prescribing guidelines under paragraph (1), the Secretary shall develop and publish schedules of national and local allowances designed to provide that taxpayers entering into a compromise have an adequate means to provide for basic living expenses.*

(B) USE OF SCHEDULES.—*The guidelines shall provide that officers and employees of the Internal Revenue Service shall determine, on the basis of the facts and circumstances of each taxpayer, whether the use of the schedules published under subparagraph (A) is appropriate and shall not use the schedules to the extent such use would result in the taxpayer not having adequate means to provide for basic living expenses.*

(3) SPECIAL RULES RELATING TO TREATMENT OF OFFERS.—*The guidelines under paragraph (1) shall provide that—*

(A) an officer or employee of the Internal Revenue Service shall not reject an offer-in-compromise from a low-income taxpayer solely on the basis of the amount of the offer, and

(B) in the case of an offer-in-compromise which relates only to issues of liability of the taxpayer—

(i) such offer shall not be rejected solely because the Secretary is unable to locate the taxpayer's return or return information for verification of such liability, and

(ii) the taxpayer shall not be required to provide a financial statement.

[CCH Explanation at ¶ 1270. Committee Reports at ¶ 10,520.]

Amendment Notes

Act Sec. 3462(a) amended Code Sec. 7122 by adding at the end a new subsection (c) to read as above.

The above amendment applies to proposed offers-in-compromise and installment agreements submitted after the date of the enactment of this Act.

(d) ADMINISTRATIVE REVIEW.—*The Secretary shall establish procedures—*

(1) for an independent administrative review of any rejection of a proposed offer-in-compromise or installment agreement made by a taxpayer under this section or section 6159 before such rejection is communicated to the taxpayer, and

(2) which allow a taxpayer to appeal any rejection of such offer or agreement to the Internal Revenue Service Office of Appeals.

[CCH Explanation at ¶ 1270. Committee Reports at ¶ 10,520.]

Amendment Notes

Act Sec. 3462(c)(1) amended Code Sec. 7122, as amended by Act Sec. 3462(a), by adding at the end a new subsection (d) to read as above.

The above amendment applies to proposed offers-in-compromise and installment agreements submitted after the date of the enactment of this Act.

Act Sec. 3462(d)(1)-(3) provides:

(d) PREPARATION OF STATEMENT RELATING TO OFFERS-IN-COMPROMISE.—The Secretary of the Treasury shall prepare a statement which sets forth in simple, non-technical terms the rights of a taxpayer and the obligations of the Internal Revenue Service relating to offers-in-compromise. Such statement shall—

(1) advise taxpayers who have entered into a compromise of the advantages of promptly notifying the Internal Revenue Service of any change of address or marital status,

(2) provide notice to taxpayers that in the case of a compromise terminated due to the actions of 1 spouse or former spouse, the Internal Revenue Service will, upon application, reinstate such compromise with the spouse or former spouse who remains in compliance with such compromise, and

(3) provide notice to the taxpayer that the taxpayer may appeal the rejection of an offer-in-compromise to the Internal Revenue Service Office of Appeals.

[¶ 6550] *CODE SEC. 7123. APPEALS DISPUTE RESOLUTION PROCEDURES.*

(a) EARLY REFERRAL TO APPEALS PROCEDURES.—*The Secretary shall prescribe procedures by which any taxpayer may request early referral of 1 or more unresolved issues from the examination or collection division to the Internal Revenue Service Office of Appeals.*

(b) ALTERNATIVE DISPUTE RESOLUTION PROCEDURES.—

(1) MEDIATION.—*The Secretary shall prescribe procedures under which a taxpayer or the Internal Revenue Service Office of Appeals may request non-binding mediation on any issue unresolved at the conclusion of—*

¶ 6540   Code Sec. 7122(c)

(A) appeals procedures, or

(B) unsuccessful attempts to enter into a closing agreement under section 7121 or a compromise under section 7122.

(2) ARBITRATION.—The Secretary shall establish a pilot program under which a taxpayer and the Internal Revenue Service Office of Appeals may jointly request binding arbitration on any issue unresolved at the conclusion of—

(A) appeals procedures, or

(B) unsuccessful attempts to enter into a closing agreement under section 7121 or a compromise under section 7122.

[CCH Explanation at ¶ 1258. Committee Reports at ¶ 10,535.]

Amendment Notes
Act Sec. 3465(a)(1) amended chapter 74 by redesignating Code Sec. 7123 as Code Sec. 7124 and by inserting after Code Sec. 7122 a new Code Sec. 7123 to read as above.
The above amendment is effective on the date of the enactment of this Act.

Act Sec. 3465(b)-(c) provides:
(b) APPEALS OFFICERS IN EACH STATE.—The Commissioner of Internal Revenue shall ensure that an appeals officer is regularly available within each State.
(c) APPEALS VIDEOCONFERENCING ALTERNATIVE FOR RURAL AREAS.—The Commissioner of Internal Revenue shall consider the use of the videoconferencing of appeals conferences between appeals officers and taxpayers seeking appeals in rural or remote areas.

[¶ 6560] CODE SEC. 7124. CROSS REFERENCES.

For criminal penalties for concealment of property, false statement, or falsifying and destroying records, in connection with any closing agreement, compromise, or offer of compromise, see section 7206.

[CCH Explanation at ¶ 1258. Committee Reports at ¶ 10,535.]

Amendment Notes
Act Sec. 3465(a)(1) amended chapter 74 by redesignating Code Sec. 7123 as Code Sec. 7124.

The above amendment is effective on the date of the enactment of this Act.

[¶ 6570] CODE SEC. 7213. UNAUTHORIZED DISCLOSURE OF INFORMATION.
* * *

(d) DISCLOSURE OF SOFTWARE.—Any person who willfully divulges or makes known software (as defined in section 7612(d)(1)) to any person in violation of section 7612 shall be guilty of a felony and, upon conviction thereof, shall be fined not more than $5,000, or imprisoned not more than 5 years, or both, together with the costs of prosecution.

[CCH Explanation at ¶ 1161. Committee Reports at ¶ 10,385.]

Amendment Notes
Act Sec. 3413(b) amended Code Sec. 7213 by redesignating subsection (d) as subsection (e) and by inserting after subsection (c) a new subsection (d) to read as above.
The above amendment generally applies to summonses issued, and software acquired, after the date of the enactment of this Act. For a special rule, see Act Sec. 3413(e)(2), below.

Act Sec. 3413(e)(2) provides:
(2) SOFTWARE PROTECTION.—In the case of any software acquired on or before such date of enactment, the requirements of section 7612(a)(2) of the Internal Revenue Code of 1986 (as added by such amendments) shall apply after the 90th day after such date. The preceding sentence shall not apply to the requirement under section 7612(c)(2)(G)(ii) of such Code (as so added).

(e) CROSS REFERENCES.—

* * *

[CCH Explanation at ¶ 1161. Committee Reports at ¶ 10,385.]

Amendment Notes
Act Sec. 3413(b) amended Code Sec. 7213 by redesignating subsection (d) as subsection (e).
The above amendment applies to summonses issued, and software acquired, after the date of the enactment of

this Act. For a special rule, see Act Sec. 3413(e)(2) in the amendment notes following Code Sec. 7213(d).

[¶ 6580] CODE SEC. 7217. PROHIBITION ON EXECUTIVE BRANCH INFLUENCE OVER TAXPAYER AUDITS AND OTHER INVESTIGATIONS.

(a) PROHIBITION.—It shall be unlawful for any applicable person to request, directly or indirectly, any officer or employee of the Internal Revenue Service to conduct or terminate an audit or other investigation of any particular taxpayer with respect to the tax liability of such taxpayer.

(b) REPORTING REQUIREMENT.—Any officer or employee of the Internal Revenue Service receiving any request prohibited by subsection (a) shall report the receipt of such request to the Treasury Inspector General for Tax Administration.

(c) EXCEPTIONS.—Subsection (a) shall not apply to any written request made—

(1) to an applicable person by or on behalf of the taxpayer and forwarded by such applicable person to the Internal Revenue Service,

(2) by an applicable person for disclosure of return or return information under section 6103 if such request is made in accordance with the requirements of such section, or

(3) by the Secretary of the Treasury as a consequence of the implementation of a change in tax policy.

(d) PENALTY.—Any person who willfully violates subsection (a) or fails to report under subsection (b) shall be punished upon conviction by a fine in any amount not exceeding $5,000, or imprisonment of not more than 5 years, or both, together with the costs of prosecution.

(e) APPLICABLE PERSON.—For purposes of this section, the term "applicable person" means—

(1) the President, the Vice President, any employee of the executive office of the President, and any employee of the executive office of the Vice President, and

(2) any individual (other than the Attorney General of the United States) serving in a position specified in section 5312 of title 5, United States Code.

[CCH Explanation at ¶ 1131. Committee Reports at ¶ 10,170.]

Amendment Notes

Act Sec. 1105(a) amended part I of subchapter A of chapter 75 by adding after Code Sec. 7216 a new Code Sec. 7217 to read as above.

The above amendment applies to requests made after the date of the enactment of this Act.

[¶ 6590] CODE SEC. 7421. PROHIBITION OF SUITS TO RESTRAIN ASSESSMENT OR COLLECTION.

(a) TAX.—Except as provided in sections *6015(d),* 6212(a) and (c), 6213(a), 6225(b), 6246(b), 6672(b), 6694(c), 7426(a) and (b)(1), 7429(b), and 7436, no suit for the purpose of restraining the assessment or collection of any tax shall be maintained in any court by any person, whether or not such person is the person against whom such tax was assessed.

* * *

[CCH Explanation at ¶ 1290. Committee Reports at ¶ 10,285.]

Amendment Notes

Act Sec. 3201(e)(3) amended Code Sec. 7421(a) by inserting "6015(d)," after "sections".

The above amendment applies to any liability for tax arising after the date of the enactment of this Act and

any liability for tax arising on or before such date but remaining unpaid as of such date.

[¶ 6600] CODE SEC. 7422. CIVIL ACTIONS FOR REFUND.

* * *

(j) SPECIAL RULE FOR ACTIONS WITH RESPECT TO ESTATES FOR WHICH AN ELECTION UNDER SECTION 6166 IS MADE.—

(1) IN GENERAL.—The district courts of the United States and the United States Court of Federal Claims shall not fail to have jurisdiction over any action brought by the representative of an estate to which this subsection applies to determine the correct amount of the estate tax liability of such estate (or for any refund with respect thereto) solely because the full amount of such liability has not been paid by reason of an election under section 6166 with respect to such estate.

(2) ESTATES TO WHICH SUBSECTION APPLIES.—This subsection shall apply to any estate if, as of the date the action is filed—

(A) no portion of the installments payable under section 6166 have been accelerated,

(B) all such installments the due date for which is on or before the date the action is filed have been paid,

(C) there is no case pending in the Tax Court with respect to the tax imposed by section 2001 on the estate and, if a notice of deficiency under section 6212 with respect to such tax has been issued, the time for filing a petition with the Tax Court with respect to such notice has expired, and

(D) no proceeding for declaratory judgment under section 7479 is pending.

(3) PROHIBITION ON COLLECTION OF DISALLOWED LIABILITY.—If the court redetermines under paragraph (1) the estate tax liability of an estate, no part of such liability which is disallowed by a decision of such court which has become final may be collected by the Secretary, and amounts paid in excess of the installments determined by the court as currently due and payable shall be refunded.

[CCH Explanation at ¶ 1301. Committee Reports at ¶ 10,265.]

Amendment Notes

Act Sec. 3104(a) amended Code Sec. 7422 by redesignating subsection (j) as subsection (k) and by inserting after subsection (i) a new subsection (j) to read as above.

The above amendment applies to any claim for refund filed after the date of the enactment of this Act.

(k) CROSS REFERENCES.—

* * *

[CCH Explanation at ¶ 1301. Committee Reports at ¶ 10,265.]

Amendment Notes

Act Sec. 3104(a) amended Code Sec. 7422 by redesignating subsection (j) as subsection (k).

The above amendment applies to any claim for refund filed after the date of the enactment of this Act.

[¶ 6610] CODE SEC. 7426. CIVIL ACTIONS BY PERSONS OTHER THAN TAXPAYERS.
(a) ACTIONS PERMITTED.—

* * *

(4) SUBSTITUTION OF VALUE.—If a certificate of discharge is issued to any person under section 6325(b)(4) with respect to any property, such person may, within 120 days after the day on which such certificate is issued, bring a civil action against the United States in a district court of the United States for a determination of whether the value of the interest of the United States (if any) in such property is less than the value determined by the Secretary. No other action may be brought by such person for such a determination.

[CCH Explanation at ¶ 1230. Committee Reports at ¶ 10,275.]

Amendment Notes
Act Sec. 3106(b)(1) amended Code Sec. 7426(a) by adding at the end a new paragraph (4) to read as above.

The above amendment is effective on the date of the enactment of this Act.

(b) ADJUDICATION.—The district court shall have jurisdiction to grant only such of the following forms of relief as may be appropriate in the circumstances:

* * *

(5) SUBSTITUTION OF VALUE.—If the court determines that the Secretary's determination of the value of the interest of the United States in the property for purposes of section 6325(b)(4) exceeds the actual value of such interest, the court shall grant a judgment ordering a refund of the amount deposited, and a release of the bond, to the extent that the aggregate of the amounts thereof exceeds such value determined by the court.

* * *

[CCH Explanation at ¶ 1230. Committee Reports at ¶ 10,275.]

Amendment Notes
Act Sec. 3106(b)(2)(A) amended Code Sec. 7426(b) by adding at the end a new paragraph (5) to read as above.

The above amendment is effective on the date of the enactment of this Act.

(g) INTEREST.—Interest shall be allowed at the overpayment rate established under section 6621—
(1) in the case of a judgment pursuant to subsection (b)(2)(B), from the date the Secretary receives the money wrongfully levied upon to the date of payment of such judgment;
(2) in the case of a judgment pursuant to subsection (b)(2)(C), from the date of the sale of the property wrongfully levied upon to the date of payment of such judgment; *and*
(3) in the case of a judgment pursuant to subsection (b)(5) which orders a refund of any amount, from the date the Secretary received such amount to the date of payment of such judgment.

[CCH Explanation at ¶ 1230. Committee Reports at ¶ 10,275.]

Amendment Notes
Act Sec. 3106(b)(2)(B) amended Code Sec. 7426(g) by striking "and" at the end of paragraph (1), by striking the period at the end of paragraph (2) and inserting "; and", and by adding at the end a new paragraph (3) to read as above

The above amendment is effective on the date of the enactment of this Act.

(h) RECOVERY OF DAMAGES PERMITTED IN CERTAIN CASES.—
(1) IN GENERAL.—Notwithstanding subsection (b), if, in any action brought under this section, there is a finding that any officer or employee of the Internal Revenue Service recklessly or intentionally, or by reason of negligence, disregarded any provision of this title the defendant shall be liable to the plaintiff in an amount equal to the lesser of $1,000,000 ($100,000 in the case of negligence) or the sum of—
(A) actual, direct economic damages sustained by the plaintiff as a proximate result of the reckless or intentional or negligent disregard of any provision of this title by the officer or employee (reduced by any amount of such damages awarded under subsection (b)), and
(B) the costs of the action.
(2) REQUIREMENT THAT ADMINISTRATIVE REMEDIES BE EXHAUSTED; MITIGATION; PERIOD.—The rules of section 7433(d) shall apply for purposes of this subsection.
(3) PAYMENT AUTHORITY.—Claims pursuant to this section shall be payable out of funds appropriated under section 1304 of title 31, United States Code.

[CCH Explanation at ¶ 1101. Committee Reports at ¶ 10,255.]

Amendment Notes
Act Sec. 3102(b) amended Code Sec. 7426 by redesignating subsection (h) as subsection (i) and by adding after subsection (g) a new subsection (h) to read as above.

The above amendment applies to actions of officers or employees of the Internal Revenue Service after the date of the enactment of this Act.

(i) CROSS REFERENCE.—
For period of limitation, see section 6532(c).

[CCH Explanation at ¶ 1101. Committee Reports at ¶ 10,255.]

Amendment Notes

Act Sec. 3102(b) amended Code Sec. 7426 by redesignating subsection (h) as subsection (i).

The above amendment applies to actions of officers or employees of the Internal Revenue Service after the date of the enactment of this Act.

[¶ 6620] CODE SEC. 7429. REVIEW OF JEOPARDY LEVY OR ASSESSMENT PROCEDURES.

(a) ADMINISTRATIVE REVIEW.—

(1) *ADMINISTRATIVE REVIEW.*—

(A) *PRIOR APPROVAL REQUIRED.*—*No assessment may be made under section 6851(a), 6852(a), 6861(a), or 6862, and no levy may be made under section 6331(a) less than 30 days after notice and demand for payment is made, unless the Chief Counsel for the Internal Revenue Service (or such Counsel's delegate) personally approves (in writing) such assessment or levy.*

(B) *INFORMATION TO TAXPAYER.*—*Within 5 days after the day on which such an assessment or levy is made, the Secretary shall provide the taxpayer with a written statement of the information upon which the Secretary relied in making such assessment or levy.*

* * *

[CCH Explanation at ¶ 1206. Committee Reports at ¶ 10,440.]

Amendment Notes

Act Sec. 3434(a) amended Code Sec. 7429(a)(1) to read as above. Prior to amendment, Code Sec. 7429(a)(1) read as follows:

(1) INFORMATION TO TAXPAYER.—Within 5 days after the day on which an assessment is made under section 6851(a), 6852(a), 6861(a), or 6862, or levy is made under section 6331(a) less than 30 days after notice and demand for payment is made under section 6331(a), the Secretary shall provide the taxpayer with a written statement of the information upon which the Secretary relies in making such assessment or levy.

The above amendment applies to taxes assessed and levies made after the date of the enactment of this Act.

[¶ 6630] CODE SEC. 7430. AWARDING OF COSTS AND CERTAIN FEES.

* * *

(b) LIMITATIONS.—

* * *

(4) PERIOD FOR APPLYING TO IRS FOR ADMINISTRATIVE COSTS.—An award may be made under subsection (a) by the Internal Revenue Service for reasonable administrative costs only if the prevailing party files an application with the Internal Revenue Service for such costs before the 91st day after the date on which the final decision of the Internal Revenue Service as to the determination of the tax, interest, or penalty is mailed to such party.

Amendment Notes

Act Sec. 6012(h) amended Code Sec. 7430(b) by redesignating paragraph (5) as paragraph (4).

The above amendment is effective as if included in the provision of the Taxpayer Relief Act of 1997 (P.L.

105-34) to which it relates [effective for civil actions or proceedings commenced after August 5, 1997.—CCH.].

(c) DEFINITIONS.—For purposes of this section—

[*Caution: Code Sec. 7430(c)(1)-(2), below, as amended by Act Sec. 3101(a)-(b), applies to costs incurred more than 180 days after the date of the enactment of this Act.—CCH.*]

(1) REASONABLE LITIGATION COSTS.—The term "reasonable litigation costs" includes—

(A) reasonable court costs, and

(B) based upon prevailing market rates for the kind or quality of services furnished—

(i) the reasonable expenses of expert witnesses in connection with a court proceeding, except that no expert witness shall be compensated at a rate in excess of the highest rate of compensation for expert witnesses paid by the United States,

(ii) the reasonable cost of any study, analysis, engineering report, test, or project which is found by the court to be necessary for the preparation of the party's case, and

(iii) reasonable fees paid or incurred for the services of attorneys in connection with the court proceeding, except that such fees shall not be in excess of *$125* per hour unless the court determines that an increase in the cost of living or a special factor, such as the limited availability of qualified attorneys for such proceeding, *the difficulty of the issues presented in the case, or the local availability of tax expertise,* justifies a higher rate.

In the case of any calendar year beginning after 1996, the dollar amount referred to in clause (iii) shall be increased by an amount equal to such dollar amount multiplied by the cost-of-living adjustment determined under section 1(f)(3) for such calendar year, by substituting "calendar year 1995" for "calendar year 1992" in subparagraph (B) thereof. If any dollar amount after being increased under the preceding sentence is not a multiple of $10, such dollar amount shall be rounded to the nearest multiple of $10.

(2) REASONABLE ADMINISTRATIVE COSTS.—The term "reasonable administrative costs" means—

(A) any administrative fees or similar charges imposed by the Internal Revenue Service, and

(B) expenses, costs, and fees described in paragraph (1)(B), except that any determination made by the court under clause (ii) or (iii) thereof shall be made by the Internal Revenue Service in cases where the determination under paragraph (4)(C) of the awarding of reasonable administrative costs is made by the Internal Revenue Service.

Such term shall only include costs incurred on or after whichever of the following is the earliest: (i) the date of the receipt by the taxpayer of the notice of the decision of the Internal Revenue Service Office of Appeals, (ii) the date of the notice of deficiency, or (iii) the date on which the 1st letter of proposed deficiency which allows the taxpayer an opportunity for administrative review in the Internal Revenue Service Office of Appeals is sent.

[Caution: Code Sec. 7430(c)(3), below, as amended by Act Sec. 3101(c), applies to costs incurred and services performed more than 180 days after the date of the enactment of this Act.—CCH.]

(3) ATTORNEYS FEES.—

(A) IN GENERAL.—For purposes of paragraphs (1) and (2), fees for the services of an individual (whether or not an attorney) who is authorized to practice before the Tax Court or before the Internal Revenue Service shall be treated as fees for the services of an attorney.

(B) PRO BONO SERVICES.—The court may award reasonable attorneys fees under subsection (a) in excess of the attorneys fees paid or incurred if such fees are less than the reasonable attorneys fees because an individual is representing the prevailing party for no fee or for a fee which (taking into account all the facts and circumstances) is no more than a nominal fee. This subparagraph shall apply only if such award is paid to such individual or such individual's employer.

(4) PREVAILING PARTY.—

* * *

(B) EXCEPTION IF UNITED STATES ESTABLISHES THAT ITS POSITION WAS SUBSTANTIALLY JUSTIFIED.—

* * *

[Caution: Code Sec. 7430(c)(4)(B)(iii)-(iv), below, as amended by Act Sec. 3101(d), applies to costs incurred more than 180 days after the date of the enactment of this Act.—CCH.]

(iii) EFFECT OF LOSING ON SUBSTANTIALLY SIMILAR ISSUES.—In determining for purposes of clause (i) whether the position of the United States was substantially justified, the court shall take into account whether the United States has lost in courts of appeal for other circuits on substantially similar issues.

(iv) APPLICABLE PUBLISHED GUIDANCE.—For purposes of clause (ii), the term "applicable published guidance" means—

(I) regulations, revenue rulings, revenue procedures, information releases, notices, and announcements, and

(II) any of the following which are issued to the taxpayer: private letter rulings, technical advice memoranda, and determination letters.

* * *

(D) SPECIAL RULES FOR APPLYING NET WORTH REQUIREMENT.—In applying the requirements of section 2412(d)(2)(B) of title 28, United States Code, for purposes of *subparagraph (A)(ii)* of this paragraph—

(i) the net worth limitation in clause (i) of such section shall apply to—

(I) an estate but shall be determined as of the date of the decedent's death, and

(II) a trust but shall be determined as of the last day of the taxable year involved in the proceeding, and

(ii) individuals filing a joint return shall be treated as separate individuals for purposes of clause (i) of such section.

[Caution: Code Sec. 7430(c)(4)(E), below, as added by Act Sec. 3101(e)(1), applies to costs incurred more than 180 days after the date of the enactment of this Act.—CCH.]

(E) SPECIAL RULES WHERE JUDGMENT LESS THAN TAXPAYER'S OFFER.—

(i) IN GENERAL.—A party to a court proceeding meeting the requirements of subparagraph (A)(ii) shall be treated as the prevailing party if the liability of the taxpayer pursuant to the judgment in the proceeding (determined without regard to interest) is equal to or less than the liability of the taxpayer which would have been so determined if the United States had accepted a qualified offer of the party under subsection (g).

(ii) EXCEPTIONS.—This subparagraph shall not apply to—

Code Sec. 7430(c)   ¶ 6630

(I) any judgment issued pursuant to a settlement, or

(II) any proceeding in which the amount of tax liability is not in issue, including any declaratory judgment proceeding, any proceeding to enforce or quash any summons issued pursuant to this title, and any action to restrain disclosure under section 6110(f).

(iii) SPECIAL RULES.—If this subparagraph applies to any court proceeding—

(I) the determination under clause (i) shall be made by reference to the last qualified offer made with respect to the tax liability at issue in the proceeding, and

(II) reasonable administrative and litigation costs shall only include costs incurred on and after the date of such offer.

(iv) COORDINATION.—This subparagraph shall not apply to a party which is a prevailing party under any other provision of this paragraph.

* * *

[CCH Explanation at ¶ 1336. Committee Reports at ¶ 10,250.]

Amendment Notes

Act Sec. 3101(a)(1) amended Code Sec. 7430(c)(1)(B)(iii) by striking "$110" and inserting "$125".

Act Sec. 3101(a)(2) amended Code Sec. 7430(c)(1)(B)(iii) by inserting "the difficulty of the issues presented in the case, or the local availability of tax expertise," before "justifies a higher rate".

Act Sec. 3101(b) amended Code Sec. 7430(c)(2) by striking the last sentence and inserting a new flush sentence to read as above. Prior to being stricken, the last sentence of Code Sec. 7430(c)(2) read as follows:

Such term shall only include costs incurred on or after the earlier of (i) the date of the receipt by the taxpayer of the notice of the decision of the Internal Revenue Service Office of Appeals, or (ii) the date of the notice of deficiency.

The above amendments apply to costs incurred more than 180 days after the date of the enactment of this Act.

Act Sec. 3101(c) amended Code Sec. 7430(c)(3) to read as above. Prior to amendment, Code Sec. 7430(c)(3) read as follows:

(3) ATTORNEY'S FEES.—For purposes of paragraphs (1) and (2), fees for the services of an individual (whether or not an attorney) who is authorized to practice before the Tax Court or before the Internal Revenue Service shall be treated as fees for the services of an attorney.

The above amendment applies to costs incurred and services performed more than 180 days after the date of the enactment of this Act.

Act Sec. 3101(d) amended Code Sec. 7430(c)(4)(B) by redesignating clause (iii) as clause (iv) and by inserting after clause (ii) a new clause (iii) to read as above.

Act Sec. 3101(e)(1) amended Code Sec. 7430(c)(4) by adding at the end a new subparagraph (E) to read as above.

The above amendments apply to costs incurred more than 180 days after the date of the enactment of this Act.

Act Sec. 6014(e) amended Code Sec. 7430(c)(4)(D) by striking "subparagraph (A)(iii)" and inserting "subparagraph (A)(ii)".

The above amendment is effective as if included in the provision of the Taxpayer Relief Act of 1997 (P.L. 105-34) to which it relates [effective for proceedings commenced after August 5, 1997.—CCH.].

[Caution: Code Sec. 7430(g), below, as added by Act Sec. 3101(e)(2), applies to costs incurred more than 180 days after the date of the enactment of this Act.—CCH.]

(g) QUALIFIED OFFER.—For purposes of subsection (c)(4)—

(1) IN GENERAL.—The term "qualified offer" means a written offer which—

(A) is made by the taxpayer to the United States during the qualified offer period,

(B) specifies the offered amount of the taxpayer's liability (determined without regard to interest),

(C) is designated at the time it is made as a qualified offer for purposes of this section, and

(D) remains open during the period beginning on the date it is made and ending on the earliest of the date the offer is rejected, the date the trial begins, or the 90th day after the date the offer is made.

(2) QUALIFIED OFFER PERIOD.—For purposes of this subsection, the term "qualified offer period" means the period—

(A) beginning on the date on which the 1st letter of proposed deficiency which allows the taxpayer an opportunity for administrative review in the Internal Revenue Service Office of Appeals is sent, and

(B) ending on the date which is 30 days before the date the case is first set for trial.

[CCH Explanation at ¶ 1336. Committee Reports at ¶ 10,250.]

Amendment Notes

Act Sec. 3101(e)(2) amended Code Sec. 7430 by adding at the end a new subsection (g) to read as above.

The above amendment applies to costs incurred more than 180 days after the date of the enactment of this Act.

[¶ 6640] CODE SEC. 7431. CIVIL DAMAGES FOR UNAUTHORIZED INSPECTION OR DISCLOSURE OF RETURNS AND RETURN INFORMATION.
* * *

[Caution: Code Sec. 7431(c), below, as amended by Act Sec. 3101(f), applies to costs incurred more than 180 days after the date of the enactment of this Act.—CCH.]

(c) DAMAGES.—In any action brought under subsection (a), upon a finding of liability on the part of the defendant, the defendant shall be liable to the plaintiff in an amount equal to the sum of—

(1) the greater of—

(A) $1,000 for each act of unauthorized inspection or disclosure of a return or return information with respect to which such defendant is found liable, or

(B) the sum of—

(i) the actual damages sustained by the plaintiff as a result of such unauthorized inspection or disclosure, plus

(ii) in the case of a willful inspection or disclosure or an inspection or disclosure which is the result of gross negligence, punitive damages, plus

(2) the costs of the action, *plus*

(3) in the case of a plaintiff which is described in section 7430(c)(4)(A)(ii), reasonable attorneys fees, except that if the defendant is the United States, reasonable attorneys fees may be awarded only if the plaintiff is the prevailing party (as determined under section 7430(c)(4)).
* * *

[CCH Explanation at ¶ 1336. Committee Reports at ¶ 10,250.]

Amendment Notes

Act Sec. 3101(f) amended Code Sec. 7431(c) by striking the period at the end of paragraph (2) and inserting ", plus", and by adding at the end a new paragraph (3) to read as above.

The above amendment applies to costs incurred more than 180 days after the date of the enactment of this Act.

(h) SPECIAL RULE FOR INFORMATION OBTAINED UNDER SECTION 6103(k)*(9)*.—For purposes of this section, any reference to section 6103 shall be treated as including a reference to section 6311(e).

Amendment Notes

Act Sec. 6012(b)(3) amended Code Sec. 7431 by redesignating subsection (g), as added by Act Sec. 1205 of the Taxpayer Relief Act of 1997 (P.L. 105-34), as subsection (h) and by striking "(8)" and inserting "(9)" in the heading.

The above amendment is effective as if included in the provision of the Taxpayer Relief Act of 1997 (P.L. 105-34) to which it relates [effective May 5, 1998.— CCH.]

[¶ 6650] CODE SEC. 7433. CIVIL DAMAGES FOR CERTAIN UNAUTHORIZED COLLECTION ACTIONS.

(a) IN GENERAL.—If, in connection with any collection of Federal tax with respect to a taxpayer, any officer or employee of the Internal Revenue Service recklessly or intentionally, *or by reason of negligence,* disregards any provision of this title, or any regulation promulgated under this title, such taxpayer may bring a civil action for damages against the United States in a district court of the United States. Except as provided in section 7432, such civil action shall be the exclusive remedy for recovering damages resulting from such actions.

[CCH Explanation at ¶ 1101. Committee Reports at ¶ 10,255.]

Amendment Notes

Act Sec. 3102(a)(1)(A) amended Code Sec. 7433(a) by inserting ", or by reason of negligence," after "recklessly or intentionally"

The above amendment applies to actions of officers or employees of the Internal Revenue Service after the date of the enactment of this Act.

(b) DAMAGES.—In any action brought under subsection (a) *or petition filed under subsection (e),* upon a finding of liability on the part of the defendant, the defendant shall be liable to the plaintiff in an amount equal to the lesser of $1,000,000 *($100,000, in the case of negligence)* or the sum of—

(1) actual, direct economic damages sustained by the plaintiff as a proximate result of the reckless or intentional *or negligent* actions of the officer or employee, and

(2) the costs of the action.
* * *

[CCH Explanation at ¶ 1101. Committee Reports at ¶ 10,255.]

Amendment Notes

Act Sec. 3102(a)(1)(B)(i)-(ii) amended Code Sec. 7433(b), in the matter preceding paragraph (1), by inserting "($100,000, in the case of negligence)" after "$1,000,000", and in paragraph (1), by inserting "or negligent" after "reckless or intentional".

Act Sec. 3102(c)(2) amended Code Sec. 7433(b) by inserting "or petition filed under subsection (e)" after "subsection (a)".

The above amendments apply to actions of officers or employees of the Internal Revenue Service after the date of the enactment of this Act.

(d) LIMITATIONS.—

(1) REQUIREMENT THAT ADMINISTRATIVE REMEDIES BE EXHAUSTED.—A judgment for damages shall not be awarded under subsection (b) unless the court determines that the plaintiff has exhausted the administrative remedies available to such plaintiff within the Internal Revenue Service.

* * *

[CCH Explanation at ¶ 1101. Committee Reports at ¶ 10,255.]

Amendment Notes

Act Sec. 3102(a)(2) amended Code Sec. 7433(d)(1) to read as above. Prior to amendment, Code Sec. 7433(d)(1) read as follows:

(1) AWARD FOR DAMAGES MAY BE REDUCED IF ADMINISTRATIVE REMEDIES NOT EXHAUSTED.—The amount of damages awarded under subsection (b) may be reduced if the court determines that the plaintiff has not exhausted the administrative remedies available to such plaintiff within the Internal Revenue Service.

The above amendment applies to actions of officers or employees of the Internal Revenue Service after the date of the enactment of this Act.

(e) ACTIONS FOR VIOLATIONS OF CERTAIN BANKRUPTCY PROCEDURES.—

(1) IN GENERAL.—If, in connection with any collection of Federal tax with respect to a taxpayer, any officer or employee of the Internal Revenue Service willfully violates any provision of section 362 (relating to automatic stay) or 524 (relating to effect of discharge) of title 11, United States Code (or any successor provision), or any regulation promulgated under such provision, such taxpayer may petition the bankruptcy court to recover damages against the United States.

(2) REMEDY TO BE EXCLUSIVE.—

(A) IN GENERAL.—Except as provided in subparagraph (B), notwithstanding section 105 of such title 11, such petition shall be the exclusive remedy for recovering damages resulting from such actions.

(B) CERTAIN OTHER ACTIONS PERMITTED.—Subparagraph (A) shall not apply to an action under section 362(h) of such title 11 for a violation of a stay provided by section 362 of such title; except that—

(i) administrative and litigation costs in connection with such an action may only be awarded under section 7430, and

(ii) administrative costs may be awarded only if incurred on or after the date that the bankruptcy petition is filed.

[CCH Explanation at ¶ 1101. Committee Reports at ¶ 10,255.]

Amendment Notes

Act Sec. 3102(c)(1) amended Code Sec. 7433 by adding at the end a new subsection (e) to read as above

The above amendment applies to actions of officers or employees of the Internal Revenue Service after the date of the enactment of this Act.

[¶ 6660] CODE SEC. 7434. CIVIL DAMAGES FOR FRAUDULENT FILING OF INFORMATION RETURNS.

* * *

(b) DAMAGES.—In any action brought under subsection (a), upon a finding of liability on the part of the defendant, the defendant shall be liable to the plaintiff in an amount equal to the greater of $5,000 or the sum of—

(1) any actual damages sustained by the plaintiff as a proximate result of the filing of the fraudulent information return (including any costs attributable to resolving deficiencies asserted as a result of such filing),

(2) the costs of the action, and

(3) in the court's discretion, reasonable *attorneys' fees.*

* * *

[CCH Explanation at ¶ 30,050.]

Amendment Notes

Act Sec. 6023(29) amended Code Sec. 7434(b)(3) by striking "attorneys fees" and inserting "attorneys' fees".

The above amendment is effective on the date of the enactment of this Act.

[¶ 6670] CODE SEC. 7436. PROCEEDINGS FOR DETERMINATION OF EMPLOYMENT STATUS.

* * *

(c) SMALL CASE PROCEDURES.—

(1) IN GENERAL.—At the option of the petitioner, concurred in by the Tax Court or a division thereof before the hearing of the case, proceedings under this section may (notwithstanding the provisions of section 7453) be conducted subject to the rules of evidence, practice, and procedure applicable under section 7463 if the amount of employment taxes placed in dispute is *$50,000 or less* for each calendar quarter involved.

* * *

[CCH Explanation at ¶ 1316. Committee Reports at ¶ 10,260.]

Amendment Notes
Act Sec. 3103(b)(1) amended Code Sec. 7436(c)(1) by striking "$10,000" and inserting "$50,000".

The above amendment applies to proceedings commenced after the date of the enactment of this Act.

[¶ 6690] CODE SEC. 7443A. SPECIAL TRIAL JUDGES.

* * *

(b) PROCEEDINGS WHICH MAY BE ASSIGNED TO SPECIAL TRIAL JUDGES.—The chief judge may assign—

* * *

[Caution: Code Sec. 7443[A](b)(3)-(5), below, as amended by Act Sec. 3401(c)(1), applies to collection actions initiated after the date which is 180 days after the date of the enactment of this Act.—CCH.]

(3) any proceeding where neither the amount of the deficiency placed in dispute (within the meaning of section 7463) nor the amount of any claimed overpayment exceeds *$50,000,*

(4) *any proceeding under section 6320 or 6330,* and

(5) *any other proceeding which the chief judge may designate,*

to be heard by the special trial judges of the court.

[CCH Explanation at ¶ 1316. Committee Reports at ¶ 10,260.]

Amendment Notes
Act Sec. 3103(b)(1) amended Code Sec. 7443A(b)(3) by striking "$10,000" and inserting "$50,000".
The above amendment applies to proceedings commencing after the date of the enactment of this Act.
Act Sec. 3401(c)(1) amended Code Sec. 7443[A](b) by striking "and" at the end of paragraph (3), by redesignating

paragraph (4) as paragraph (5), and by inserting after paragraph (3) a new paragraph (4) to read as above.

The above amendment applies to collection actions initiated after the date which is 180 days after the date of the enactment of this Act.

[Caution: Code Sec. 7443[A](c), below, as amended by Act Sec. 3401(c)(2), applies to collection actions initiated after the date which is 180 days after the date of the enactment of this Act.—CCH.]

(c) AUTHORITY TO MAKE COURT DECISIONS.—The court may authorize a special trial judge to make the decision of the court with respect to any proceeding described in paragraph (1), (2), *(3), or (4)* of subsection (b), subject to such conditions and review as the court may provide.

* * *

[CCH Explanation at ¶ 1254. Committee Reports at ¶ 10,365.]

Amendment Notes
Act Sec. 3401(c)(2) amended Code Sec. 7443[A](c) by striking "or (3)" and inserting "(3), or (4)".

The above amendment applies to collection actions initiated after the date which is 180 days after the date of the enactment of this Act.

[¶ 6700] CODE SEC. 7463. DISPUTES INVOLVING *$50,000* OR LESS.

(a) IN GENERAL.—In the case of any petition filed with the Tax Court for a redetermination of a deficiency where neither the amount of the deficiency placed in dispute, nor the amount of any claimed overpayment, exceeds—

(1) *$50,000* for any one taxable year, in the case of the taxes imposed by subtitle A,

(2) *$50,000,* in the case of the tax imposed by chapter 11,

(3) *$50,000* for any one calendar year, in the case of the tax imposed by chapter 12, or

(4) *$50,000* for any 1 taxable period (or, if there is no taxable period, taxable event) in the case of any tax imposed by subtitle D which is described in section 6212(a) (relating to a notice of deficiency),

at the option of the taxpayer concurred in by the Tax Court or a division thereof before the hearing of the case, proceedings in the case shall be conducted under this section. Notwithstanding the provisions of section 7453, such proceedings shall be conducted in accordance with such rules of evidence, practice, and procedure as the Tax Court may prescribe. A decision, together with a brief summary of the reasons therefor, in any such case shall satisfy the requirements of sections 7459(b) and 7460.

* * *

[CCH Explanation at ¶ 1316. Committee Reports at ¶ 10,260.]

Amendment Notes
Act Sec. 3103(a) amended Code Sec. 7463 by striking "$10,000" each place it appears (including the section heading) and inserting "$50,000".

The above amendment applies to proceedings commenced after the date of the enactment of this Act.

[¶ 6710] CODE SEC. 7479. DECLARATORY JUDGMENTS RELATING TO ELIGIBILITY OF ESTATE WITH RESPECT TO INSTALLMENT PAYMENTS UNDER SECTION 6166.

(a) CREATION OF REMEDY.—In a case of actual controversy involving a determination by the Secretary of (or a failure by the Secretary to make a determination with respect to)—

(1) whether an election may be made under section 6166 (relating to extension of time for payment of estate tax where estate consists largely of interest in closely held business) with respect to *an estate (or with respect to any property included therein),* or

(2) whether the extension of time for payment of tax provided in section 6166(a) has ceased to apply with respect to *an estate (or with respect to any property included therein,*

upon the filing of an appropriate pleading, the Tax Court may make a declaration with respect to whether such election may be made or whether such extension has ceased to apply. Any such declaration shall have the force and effect of a decision of the Tax Court and shall be reviewable as such.

* * *

[CCH Explanation at ¶ 441. Committee Reports at ¶ 11,025.]

Amendment Notes

Act Sec. 6007(d) amended Code Sec. 7479(a)(1)-(2) by striking "an estate," and inserting "an estate (or with respect to any property included therein),".

The above amendment is effective as if included in the provision of the Taxpayer Relief Act of 1997 (P.L. 105-34) to which it relates [effective for estates of decedents dying after August 5, 1997.—CCH.].

(c) EXTENSION OF TIME TO FILE REFUND SUIT.—The 2-year period in section 6532(a)(1) for filing suit for refund after disallowance of a claim shall be suspended during the 90-day period after the mailing of the notice referred to in subsection (b)(3) and, if a pleading has been filed with the Tax Court under this section, until the decision of the Tax Court has become final.

[CCH Explanation at ¶ 1301. Committee Reports at ¶ 10,265.]

Amendment Notes

Act Sec. 3104(b) amended Code Sec. 7479 by adding at the end a new subsection (c) to read as above.

The above amendment applies to any claim for refund filed after the date of the enactment of this Act.

[¶ 6720] *CODE SEC. 7491. BURDEN OF PROOF.*

(a) BURDEN SHIFTS WHERE TAXPAYER PRODUCES CREDIBLE EVIDENCE.—

(1) GENERAL RULE.—If, in any court proceeding, a taxpayer introduces credible evidence with respect to any factual issue relevant to ascertaining the liability of the taxpayer for any tax imposed by subtitle A or B, the Secretary shall have the burden of proof with respect to such issue.

(2) LIMITATIONS.—Paragraph (1) shall apply with respect to an issue only if—

(A) the taxpayer has complied with the requirements under this title to substantiate any item,

(B) the taxpayer has maintained all records required under this title and has cooperated with reasonable requests by the Secretary for witnesses, information, documents, meetings, and interviews, and

(C) in the case of a partnership, corporation, or trust, the taxpayer is described in section 7430(c)(4)(A)(ii).

(3) COORDINATION.—Paragraph (1) shall not apply to any issue if any other provision of this title provides for a specific burden of proof with respect to such issue.

(b) USE OF STATISTICAL INFORMATION ON UNRELATED TAXPAYERS.—In the case of an individual taxpayer, the Secretary shall have the burden of proof in any court proceeding with respect to any item of income which was reconstructed by the Secretary solely through the use of statistical information on unrelated taxpayers.

(c) PENALTIES.—Notwithstanding any other provision of this title, the Secretary shall have the burden of production in any court proceeding with respect to the liability of any individual for any penalty, addition to tax, or additional amount imposed by this title.

[CCH Explanation at ¶ 1331. Committee Reports at ¶ 10,245.]

Amendment Notes

Act Sec. 3001(a) amended Chapter 76 by adding at the end a new Code Sec. 7491 to read as above.

The above amendment generally applies to court proceedings arising in connection with examinations commencing after the date of the enactment of this Act. For a special rule, see Act Sec. 3001(c)(2), below.

Act Sec. 3001(c)(2) provides:

(2) TAXABLE PERIODS OR EVENTS AFTER DATE OF ENACTMENT.—In any case in which there is no examination, such amendments shall apply to court proceedings arising in connection with taxable periods or events beginning or occurring after such date of enactment.

[¶ 6730] CODE SEC. 7502. TIMELY MAILING TREATED AS TIMELY FILING AND PAYING.

* * *

(c) REGISTERED AND CERTIFIED MAILING; ELECTRONIC FILING.—

(1) REGISTERED MAIL.—For purposes of this section, if any return, claim, statement, or other document, or payment, is sent by United States registered mail—

(A) such registration shall be prima facie evidence that the return, claim, statement, or other document was delivered to the agency, officer, or office to which addressed, and

(B) the date of registration shall be deemed the postmark date.

(2) CERTIFIED MAIL: ELECTRONIC FILING.—The Secretary is authorized to provide by regulations the extent to which the provisions of paragraph (1) with respect to prima facie evidence of delivery and the postmark date shall apply to certified mail and electronic filing.

* * *

[CCH Explanation at ¶ 1015. Committee Reports at ¶ 10,225.]

¶ 6720   Code Sec. 7491(a)

Amendment Notes

Act Sec. 2003(b) amended Code Sec. 7502(c) to read as above. Prior to amendment, Code Sec. 7502(c) read as follows:

(c) REGISTERED AND CERTIFIED MAILING.—

(1) REGISTERED MAIL.—For purposes of this section, if any such return, claim, statement, or other document, or payment, is sent by United States registered mail—

(A) such registration shall be prima facie evidence that the return, claim, statement, or other document was delivered to the agency, officer, or office to which addressed, and

(B) the date of registration shall be deemed the postmark date.

(2) CERTIFIED MAIL.—The Secretary is authorized to provide by regulations the extent to which the provisions of paragraph (1) of this subsection with respect to prima facie evidence of delivery and the postmark date shall apply to certified mail.

The above amendment is effective on the date of the enactment of this Act.

[¶ 6740] *CODE SEC. 7525. CONFIDENTIALITY PRIVILEGES RELATING TO TAXPAYER COMMUNICATIONS.*

(a) UNIFORM APPLICATION TO TAXPAYER COMMUNICATIONS WITH FEDERALLY AUTHORIZED PRACTITIONERS.—

(1) GENERAL RULE.—With respect to tax advice, the same common law protections of confidentiality which apply to a communication between a taxpayer and an attorney shall also apply to a communication between a taxpayer and any federally authorized tax practitioner to the extent the communication would be considered a privileged communication if it were between a taxpayer and an attorney.

(2) LIMITATIONS.—Paragraph (1) may only be asserted in—

(A) any noncriminal tax matter before the Internal Revenue Service, and

(B) any noncriminal tax proceeding in Federal court brought by or against the United States.

(3) DEFINITIONS.—For purposes of this subsection—

(A) FEDERALLY AUTHORIZED TAX PRACTITIONER.—The term "federally authorized tax practitioner" means any individual who is authorized under Federal law to practice before the Internal Revenue Service if such practice is subject to Federal regulation under section 330 of title 31, United States Code.

(B) TAX ADVICE.—The term "tax advice" means advice given by an individual with respect to a matter which is within the scope of the individual's authority to practice described in subparagraph (A).

(b) SECTION NOT TO APPLY TO COMMUNICATIONS REGARDING CORPORATE TAX SHELTERS.—The privilege under subsection (a) shall not apply to any written communication between a federally authorized tax practitioner and a director, shareholder, officer, or employee, agent, or representative of a corporation in connection with the promotion of the direct or indirect participation of such corporation in any tax shelter (as defined in section 6662(d)(2)(C)(iii)).

[CCH Explanation at ¶ 1141. Committee Reports at ¶ 10,375.]

Amendment Notes

Act Sec. 3411(a) amended Chapter 77 by adding at the end a new Code Sec. 7525 to read as above.

The above amendment applies to communications made on or after the date of the enactment of this Act. Act Sec. 3468 provides:

SEC. 3468. PROHIBITION ON REQUESTS TO TAXPAYERS TO GIVE UP RIGHTS TO BRING ACTIONS.

(a) PROHIBITION.—No officer or employee of the United States may request a taxpayer to waive the taxpayer's right to bring a civil action against the United States or any officer

or employee of the United States for any action taken in connection with the internal revenue laws.

(b) EXCEPTIONS.—Subsection (a) shall not apply in any case where—

(1) a taxpayer waives the right described in subsection (a) knowingly and voluntarily, or

(2) the request by the officer or employee is made in person and the taxpayer's attorney or other federally authorized tax practitioner (within the meaning of section 7525(a)(3)(A) of the Internal Revenue Code of 1986) is present, or the request is made in writing to the taxpayer's attorney or other representative.

[¶ 6750] *CODE SEC. 7526. LOW INCOME TAXPAYER CLINICS.*

(a) IN GENERAL.—The Secretary may, subject to the availability of appropriated funds, make grants to provide matching funds for the development, expansion, or continuation of qualified low income taxpayer clinics.

(b) DEFINITIONS.—For purposes of this section—

(1) QUALIFIED LOW INCOME TAXPAYER CLINIC.—

(A) IN GENERAL.—The term "qualified low income taxpayer clinic" means a clinic that—

(i) does not charge more than a nominal fee for its services (except for reimbursement of actual costs incurred), and

(ii)(I) represents low income taxpayers in controversies with the Internal Revenue Service, or

(II) operates programs to inform individuals for whom English is a second language about their rights and responsibilities under this title.

(B) REPRESENTATION OF LOW INCOME TAXPAYERS.—A clinic meets the requirements of subparagraph (A)(ii)(I) if—

(i) at least 90 percent of the taxpayers represented by the clinic have incomes which do not exceed 250 percent of the poverty level, as determined in accordance with criteria established by the Director of the Office of Management and Budget, and

(ii) the amount in controversy for any taxable year generally does not exceed the amount specified in section 7463.

(2) CLINIC.—The term "clinic" includes—

(A) a clinical program at an accredited law, business, or accounting school in which students represent low income taxpayers in controversies arising under this title, and

(B) an organization described in section 501(c) and exempt from tax under section 501(a) which satisfies the requirements of paragraph (1) through representation of taxpayers or referral of taxpayers to qualified representatives.

(3) QUALIFIED REPRESENTATIVE.—The term "qualified representative" means any individual (whether or not an attorney) who is authorized to practice before the Internal Revenue Service or the applicable court.

(c) SPECIAL RULES AND LIMITATIONS.—

(1) AGGREGATE LIMITATION.—Unless otherwise provided by specific appropriation, the Secretary shall not allocate more than $6,000,000 per year (exclusive of costs of administering the program) to grants under this section.

(2) LIMITATION ON ANNUAL GRANTS TO A CLINIC.—The aggregate amount of grants which may be made under this section to a clinic for a year shall not exceed $100,000.

(3) MULTI-YEAR GRANTS.—Upon application of a qualified low income taxpayer clinic, the Secretary is authorized to award a multi-year grant not to exceed 3 years.

(4) CRITERIA FOR AWARDS.—In determining whether to make a grant under this section, the Secretary shall consider—

(A) the numbers of taxpayers who will be served by the clinic, including the number of taxpayers in the geographical area for whom English is a second language,

(B) the existence of other low income taxpayer clinics serving the same population,

(C) the quality of the program offered by the low income taxpayer clinic, including the qualifications of its administrators and qualified representatives, and its record, if any, in providing service to low income taxpayers, and

(D) alternative funding sources available to the clinic, including amounts received from other grants and contributions, and the endowment and resources of the institution sponsoring the clinic.

(5) REQUIREMENT OF MATCHING FUNDS.—A low income taxpayer clinic must provide matching funds on a dollar for dollar basis for all grants provided under this section. Matching funds may include—

(A) the salary (including fringe benefits) of individuals performing services for the clinic, and

(B) the cost of equipment used in the clinic.

Indirect expenses, including general overhead of the institution sponsoring the clinic, shall not be counted as matching funds.

[CCH Explanation at ¶ 851. Committee Reports at ¶ 10,625.]

Amendment Notes

Act Sec. 3601(a) amended chapter 77, as amended by Act Sec. 3411, by adding at the end a new Code Sec. 7526 to read as above.

The above amendment is effective on the date of the enactment of this Act.

[¶ 6760] CODE SEC. 7602. EXAMINATION OF BOOKS AND WITNESSES.

* * *

[*Caution: Code Sec. 7602(c), below, as added by Act Sec. 3417(a), applies to contacts made after the 180th day after the day of the enactment of this Act.—CCH.*]

(c) NOTICE OF CONTACT OF THIRD PARTIES.—

(1) GENERAL NOTICE.—An officer or employee of the Internal Revenue Service may not contact any person other than the taxpayer with respect to the determination or collection of the tax liability of such taxpayer without providing reasonable notice in advance to the taxpayer that contacts with persons other than the taxpayer may be made.

(2) NOTICE OF SPECIFIC CONTACTS.—The Secretary shall periodically provide to a taxpayer a record of persons contacted during such period by the Secretary with respect to the determination or collection of the tax liability of such taxpayer. Such record shall also be provided upon request of the taxpayer.

(3) EXCEPTIONS.—This subsection shall not apply—

(A) to any contact which the taxpayer has authorized,

(B) if the Secretary determines for good cause shown that such notice would jeopardize collection of any tax or such notice may involve reprisal against any person, or

(C) with respect to any pending criminal investigation.

[CCH Explanation at ¶ 1156. Committee Reports at ¶ 10,405.]

Amendment Notes

Act Sec. 3417(a) amended Code Sec. 7602, as amended by Act Sec. 3412, by redesignating subsections (c) and (d) as subsections (d) and (e), respectively, and by inserting after subsection (b) a new subsection (c) to read as above.

The above amendment applies to contacts made after the 180th day after the day of the enactment of this Act.

(d) No Administrative Summons When There Is Justice Department Referral.—

* * *

[CCH Explanation at ¶ 1156. Committee Reports at ¶ 10,405.]

Amendment Notes

Act Sec. 3417(a) amended Code Sec. 7602, as amended by Act Sec. 3412, by redesignating subsection (c) as subsection (d).

The above amendment applies to contacts made after the 180th day after the day of the enactment of this Act.

(e) Limitation on Examination on Unreported Income.—The Secretary shall not use financial status or economic reality examination techniques to determine the existence of unreported income of any taxpayer unless the Secretary has a reasonable indication that there is a likelihood of such unreported income.

[CCH Explanation at ¶ 1111 and 1156. Committee Reports at ¶ 10,380 and 10,405.]

Amendment Notes

Act Sec. 3412 amended Code Sec. 7602 by adding at the end a new subsection (d) to read as above.

The above amendment is effective on the date of the enactment of this Act.

Act Sec. 3417(a) amended Code Sec. 7602, as amended by Act Sec. 3412, by redesignating subsection (d) as subsection (e).

The above amendment applies to contacts made after the 180th day after the day of the enactment of this Act.

[¶ 6770] CODE SEC. 7603. SERVICE OF SUMMONS.

(a) *In General.—A summons issued* under section 6420(e)(2), 6421(g)(2), 6427(j)(2), or 7602 shall be served by the Secretary, by an attested copy delivered in hand to the person to whom it is directed, or left at his last and usual place of abode; and the certificate of service signed by the person serving the summons shall be evidence of the facts it states on the hearing of an application for the enforcement of the summons. When the summons requires the production of books, papers, records, or other data, it shall be sufficient if such books, papers, records, or other data are described with reasonable certainty.

[CCH Explanation at ¶ 1151. Committee Reports at ¶ 10,400.]

Amendment Notes

Act Sec. 3416(a) amended Code Sec. 7603 by striking "A summons issued" and inserting "(a) In General.—A summons issued".

The above amendment applies to summonses served after the date of the enactment of this Act.

(b) Service by Mail to Third-Party Recordkeepers.—

(1) In General.—A summons referred to in subsection (a) for the production of books, papers, records, or other data by a third-party recordkeeper may also be served by certified or registered mail to the last known address of such recordkeeper.

(2) Third-Party Recordkeeper.—For purposes of paragraph (1), the term "third-party recordkeeper" means—

(A) any mutual savings bank, cooperative bank, domestic building and loan association, or other savings institution chartered and supervised as a savings and loan or similar association under Federal or State law, any bank (as defined in section 581), or any credit union (within the meaning of section 501(c)(14)(A));

(B) any consumer reporting agency (as defined under section 603(f) of the Fair Credit Reporting Act (15 U.S.C. 1681a(f)));

(C) any person extending credit through the use of credit cards or similar devices;

(D) any broker (as defined in section 3(a)(4) of the Securities Exchange Act of 1934 (15 U.S.C. 78c(a)(4)));

(E) any attorney;

(F) any accountant;

(G) any barter exchange (as defined in section 6045(c)(3));

(H) any regulated investment company (as defined in section 851) and any agent of such regulated investment company when acting as an agent thereof,

(I) any enrolled agent, and

(J) any owner or developer of a computer software source code (as defined in section 7612(d)(2)).

Subparagraph (J) shall apply only with respect to a summons requiring the production of the source code referred to in subparagraph (J) or the program and data described in section 7612(b)(1)(A)(ii) to which such source code relates.

Code Sec. 7603(b)   ¶ 6770

[CCH Explanation at ¶ 1151 and 1161. Committee Reports at ¶ 10,385 and 10,400.]

Amendment Notes

Act Sec. 3413(c) amended Code Sec. 7603(b)(2), as amended by Act Sec. 3416(a), by striking "and" at the end of subparagraph (H), by striking a period at the end of subparagraph (I) and inserting ", and", and by adding at the end a new subparagraph (J) to read as above.

The above amendment generally applies to summonses issued, and software acquired, after the date of the enactment of this Act. For a special rule, see Act Sec. 3413(e)(2), below.

Act Sec. 3413(e)(2) provides:

(2) SOFTWARE PROTECTION.—In the case of any software acquired on or before such date of enactment, the requirements of section 7612(a)(2) of the Internal Revenue Code of 1986 (as added by such amendments) shall apply after the 90th day after such date. The preceding sentence shall not apply to the requirement under section 7612(c)(2)(G)(ii) of such Code (as so added).

Act Sec. 3416(a) amended Code Sec. 7603 by adding at the end a new subsection (b) to read as above.

The above amendment applies to summonses served after the date of the enactment of this Act.

[¶ 6780] CODE SEC. 7608. AUTHORITY OF INTERNAL REVENUE ENFORCEMENT OFFICERS.

* * *

(b) ENFORCEMENT OF LAWS RELATING TO INTERNAL REVENUE OTHER THAN SUBTITLE E.—

(1) Any criminal investigator of the Intelligence Division of the Internal Revenue Service whom the Secretary charges with the duty of enforcing any of the criminal provisions of the internal revenue laws, any other criminal provisions of law relating to internal revenue for the enforcement of which the Secretary is responsible, or any other law for which the Secretary has delegated investigatory authority to the Internal Revenue Service, is, in the performance of his duties, authorized to perform the functions described in paragraph (2).

* * *

[CCH Explanation at ¶ 831. Committee Reports at ¶ 10,160.]

Amendment Notes

Act Sec. 1103(e)(4) amended Code Sec. 7608(b)(1) by striking "or of the Internal Security Division" after "of the Intelligence Division".

The above amendment is effective on the date of the enactment of this Act.

[¶ 6790] CODE SEC. 7609. SPECIAL PROCEDURES FOR THIRD-PARTY SUMMONSES.

(a) NOTICE.—

(1) IN GENERAL.—If any summons to which this section applies requires the giving of testimony on or relating to, the production of any portion of records made or kept on or relating to, or the production of any computer software source code (as defined in 7612(d)(2)) with respect to, any person (other than the person summoned) who is identified in the summons, then notice of the summons shall be given to any person so identified within 3 days of the day on which such service is made, but no later than the 23rd day before the day fixed in the summons as the day upon which such records are to be examined. Such notice shall be accompanied by a copy of the summons which has been served and shall contain an explanation of the right under subsection (b)(2) to bring a proceeding to quash the summons.

* * *

(3) NATURE OF SUMMONS.—Any summons to which this subsection applies (and any summons in aid of collection described in subsection (c)(2)(D)) shall identify the taxpayer to whom the summons relates or the other person to whom the records pertain and shall provide such other information as will enable the person summoned to locate the records required under the summons.

* * *

[CCH Explanation at ¶ 1146. Committee Reports at ¶ 10,395.]

Amendment Notes

Act Sec. 3415(a) amended Code Sec. 7609(a)(1) by striking so much of such paragraph as precedes "notice of the summons" and inserting new material to read as above. Prior to amendment, Code Sec. 7609(a)(1) read as follows:

(1) IN GENERAL.—If—

(A) any summons described in subsection (c) is served on any person who is a third-party recordkeeper, and

(B) the summons requires the production of any portion of records made or kept of the business transactions or affairs of any person (other than the person summoned) who is identified in the description of the records contained in the summons,

then notice of the summons shall be given to any person so identified within 3 days of the day on which such service is made, but no later than the 23rd day before the day fixed in the summons as the day upon which such records are to be examined. Such notice shall be accompanied by a copy of the summons which has been served and shall contain an explanation of the right under subsection (b)(2) to bring a proceeding to quash the summons.

Act Sec. 3415(c)(1) amended Code Sec. 7609(a) by striking paragraphs (3) and (4), by redesignating paragraph (5) as paragraph (3), and by striking in paragraph (3) (as so redesignated) "subsection (c)(2)(B)" and inserting "subsection (c)(2)(D)". Prior to being stricken, Code Sec. 7609(a)(3)-(4) read as follows:

(3) THIRD-PARTY RECORDKEEPER DEFINED.—For purposes of this subsection, the term "third-party recordkeeper" means—

(A) any mutual savings bank, cooperative bank, domestic building and loan association, or other savings institution chartered and supervised as a savings and loan or similar association under Federal or State law, any bank (as defined in section 581), or any credit union (within the meaning of section 501(c)(14)(A));

(B) any consumer reporting agency (as defined under section 603(d) of the Fair Credit Reporting Act (15 U.S.C. 1681a(f)));

(C) any person extending credit through the use of credit cards or similar devices;

(D) any broker (as defined in section 3(a)(4) of the Securities Exchange Act of 1934 (15 U.S.C. 78c(a)(4)));

(E) any attorney;

(F) any accountant;

(G) any barter exchange (as defined in section 6045(c)(3));

(H) any regulated investment company (as defined in section 851) and any agent of such regulated investment company when acting as an agent thereof; and

(I) any enrolled agent.

(4) EXCEPTIONS.—Paragraph (1) shall not apply to any summons—

(A) served on the person with respect to whose liability the summons is issued, or any officer or employee of such person,

(B) to determine whether or not records of the business transactions or affairs of an identified person have been made or kept, or

(C) described in subsection (f).

The above amendments apply to summonses served after the date of the enactment of this Act.

(c) SUMMONS TO WHICH SECTION APPLIES.—

(1) IN GENERAL.—Except as provided in paragraph (2), this section shall apply to any summons issued under paragraph (2) of section 7602(a) or under section 6420(e)(2), 6421(g)(2), 6427(j)(2), or 7612.

(2) EXCEPTIONS.—This section shall not apply to any summons—

(A) served on the person with respect to whose liability the summons is issued, or any officer or employee of such person,

(B) issued to determine whether or not records of the business transactions or affairs of an identified person have been made or kept,

(C) issued solely to determine the identity of any person having a numbered account (or similar arrangement) with a bank or other institution described in section 7603(b)(2)(A),

(D) issued in aid of the collection of—

(i) an assessment made or judgment rendered against the person with respect to whose liability the summons is issued, or

(ii) the liability at law or in equity of any transferee or fiduciary of any person referred to in clause (i),

(E)(i) issued by a criminal investigator of the Internal Revenue Service in connection with the investigation of an offense connected with the administration or enforcement of the internal revenue laws, and

(ii) served on any person who is not a third-party recordkeeper (as defined in section 7603(b)), or

(F) described in subsection (f) or (g).

(3) RECORDS.—For purposes of this section, the term "records" includes books, papers, and other data.

* * *

[CCH Explanation at ¶ 1146. Committee Reports at ¶ 10,395.]

Amendment Notes

Act Sec. 3415(c)(2) amended Code Sec. 7609(c) to read as above. Prior to amendment, Code Sec. 7609(c) read as follows:

(c) SUMMONS TO WHICH SECTION APPLIES.—

(1) IN GENERAL.—Except as provided in paragraph (2), a summons is described in this subsection if it is issued under paragraph (2) of section 7602(a) or under section 6420(e)(2), 6421(g)(2), or 6427(j)(2) and requires the production of records.

(2) EXCEPTIONS.—A summons shall not be treated as described in this subsection if—

(A) it is solely to determine the identity of any person having a numbered account (or similar arrangement) with a bank or other institution described in subsection (a)(3)(A), or

(B) it is in aid of the collection of—

(i) the liability of any person against whom an assessment has been made or judgment rendered, or

(ii) the liability at law or in equity of any transferee or fiduciary of any person referred to in clause (i).

(3) RECORDS; CERTAIN RELATED TESTIMONY.—For purposes of this section—

(A) the term "records" includes books, papers, or other data, and

(B) a summons requiring the giving of testimony relating to records shall be treated as a summons requiring the production of such records.

The above amendment applies to summonses served after the date of the enactment of this Act.

(e) SUSPENSION OF STATUTE OF LIMITATIONS.—

* * *

(2) SUSPENSION AFTER 6 MONTHS OF SERVICE OF SUMMONS.—In the absence of the resolution of the summoned party's response to the summons, the running of any period of limitations under section 6501 or under section 6531 with respect to any person with respect to whose liability the summons is issued (other than a person taking action as provided in subsection (b)) shall be suspended for the period—

(A) beginning on the date which is 6 months after the service of such summons, and

(B) ending with the final resolution of such response.

[CCH Explanation at ¶ 1146. Committee Reports at ¶ 10,395.]

Amendment Notes

Act Sec. 3415(c)(3) amended Code Sec. 7609(e)(2) by striking "third-party recordkeeper's" and all that follows through "subsection (f)" and inserting "summoned party's response to the summons". Prior to amendment, Code Sec. 7609(e)(2) read as follows:

(2) SUSPENSION AFTER 6 MONTHS OF SERVICE OF SUMMONS.— In the absence of the resolution of the third-party recordkeeper's response to the summons described in subsection (c), or the summoned party's response to a summons described in subsection (f), the running of any period of limitations under section 6501 or under section 6531 with respect to any person with respect to whose liability the

Code Sec. 7609(e)   ¶ 6790

summons is issued (other than a person taking action as provided in subsection (b)) shall be suspended for the period—

(A) beginning on the date which is 6 months after the service of such summons, and

(B) ending with the final resolution of such response.

The above amendment applies to summonses served after the date of the enactment of this Act.

(f) ADDITIONAL REQUIREMENT IN THE CASE OF A JOHN DOE SUMMONS.—*Any summons described in subsection (c)(1)* which does not identify the person with respect to whose liability the summons is issued may be served only after a court proceeding in which the Secretary establishes that—

(1) the summons relates to the investigation of a particular person or ascertainable group or class of persons,

(2) there is a reasonable basis for believing that such person or group or class of persons may fail or may have failed to comply with any provision of any internal revenue law, and

(3) the information sought to be obtained from the examination of the records *or testimony* (and the identity of the person or persons with respect to whose liability the summons is issued) is not readily available from other sources.

[CCH Explanation at ¶ 1146. Committee Reports at ¶ 10,395.]

Amendment Notes

Act Sec. 3415(c)(4)(A) amended Code Sec. 7609(f) by striking "described in subsection (c)" and inserting "described in subsection (c)(1)".

Act Sec. 3415(c)(4)(B) amended Code Sec. 7609(f)(3) by inserting "or testimony" after "records".

The above amendments apply to summonses served after the date of the enactment of this Act.

(g) SPECIAL EXCEPTION FOR CERTAIN SUMMONSES.—*A summons is described in this subsection if,* upon petition by the Secretary, the court determines, on the basis of the facts and circumstances alleged, that there is reasonable cause to believe the giving of notice may lead to attempts to conceal, destroy, or alter records relevant to the examination, to prevent the communication of information from other persons through intimidation, bribery, or collusion, or to flee to avoid prosecution, testifying, or production of records.

* * *

[CCH Explanation at ¶ 1146. Committee Reports at ¶ 10,395.]

Amendment Notes

Act Sec. 3415(c)(5) amended Code Sec. 7609(g) by striking "In the case of any summons described in subsection (c), the provisions of subsections (a)(1) and (b) shall not apply if" and inserting "A summons is described in this subsection if"

The above amendment applies to summonses served after the date of the enactment of this Act.

(i) DUTY OF SUMMONED PARTY.—

(1) RECORDKEEPER MUST ASSEMBLE RECORDS AND BE PREPARED TO PRODUCE RECORDS.—On receipt of a summons *to which this section applies for the production of records, the summoned party* shall proceed to assemble the records requested, or such portion thereof as the Secretary may prescribe, and shall be prepared to produce the records pursuant to the summons on the day on which the records are to be examined.

(2) SECRETARY MAY GIVE *SUMMONED PARTY* CERTIFICATE.—The Secretary may issue a certificate to *the summoned party* that the period prescribed for beginning a proceeding to quash a summons has expired and that no such proceeding began within such period, or that the taxpayer consents to the examination.

(3) *PROTECTION FOR SUMMONED PARTY WHO DISCLOSES.—Any summoned party, or agent or employee thereof, making a disclosure of records or testimony pursuant to this section in good faith reliance on the certificate of the Secretary or an order of a court requiring production of records or the giving of such testimony shall not be liable to any customer or other person for such disclosure.*

* * *

[CCH Explanation at ¶ 1146. Committee Reports at ¶ 10,395.]

Amendment Notes

Act Sec. 3415(c)(6)(A) amended Code Sec. 7609(i) by striking "THIRD-PARTY RECORDKEEPER AND" after "DUTY OF" in the subsection heading.

Act Sec. 3415(c)(6)(B) amended Code Sec. 7609(i)(1) by striking "described in subsection (c), the third-party recordkeeper" and inserting "to which this section applies for the production of records, the summoned party".

Act Sec. 3415(c)(6)(C)(i)-(ii) amended Code Sec. 7609(i)(2) by striking "RECORDKEEPER" in the heading and inserting "SUMMONED PARTY", and by striking "the third-party recordkeeper" and inserting "the summoned party".

Act Sec. 3415(c)(6)(D) amended Code Sec. 7609(i)(3) to read as above. Prior to amendment, Code Sec. 7609(i)(3) read as follows:

(3) PROTECTION FOR RECORDKEEPER WHO DISCLOSES.—Any third-party recordkeeper, or agent or employee thereof, making a disclosure of records pursuant to this section in good-faith reliance on the certificate of the Secretary or an order of a court requiring production of records shall not be liable to any customer or other person for such disclosure.

The above amendments apply to summonses served after the date of the enactment of this Act.

(j) USE OF SUMMONS NOT REQUIRED.—*Nothing in this section shall be construed to limit the Secretary's ability to obtain information, other than by summons, through formal or informal procedures authorized by sections 7601 and 7602.*

[CCH Explanation at ¶ 1146. Committee Reports at ¶ 10,395.]

Amendment Notes

Act Sec. 3415(b) amended Code Sec. 7609 by adding at the end a new subsection (j) to read as above.

The above amendment applies to summonses served after the date of the enactment of this Act.

[¶ 6800] CODE SEC. 7611. RESTRICTIONS ON CHURCH TAX INQUIRIES AND EXAMINATIONS.

* * *

(f) LIMITATIONS ON ADDITIONAL INQUIRIES AND EXAMINATIONS.—

(1) IN GENERAL.—If any church tax inquiry or examination with respect to any church is completed and does not result in—

(A) a revocation, notice of deficiency, or assessment described in subsection (d)(1), or

(B) a request by the Secretary for any significant change in the operational practices of the church (including the adequacy of accounting practices),

no other church tax inquiry or examination may begin with respect to such church during the applicable 5-year period unless such inquiry or examination is approved in writing by the *Secretary* or does not involve the same or similar issues involved in the preceding inquiry or examination. For purposes of the preceding sentence, an inquiry or examination shall be treated as completed not later than the expiration of the applicable period under paragraph (1) of subsection (c).

* * *

[CCH Explanation at ¶ 821. Committee Reports at ¶ 10,150.]

Amendment Notes

Act Sec. 1102(e)(3) amended Code Sec. 7611(f)(1) by striking "Assistant Commissioner for Employee Plans and Exempt Organizations of the Internal Revenue Service" and inserting "Secretary".

The above amendment is generally effective on the date of the enactment of this Act. For a special rule, see Act Sec. 1102(f)(3)-(4), below.

Act Sec. 1102(f)(3)-(4) provides:

(3) NATIONAL TAXPAYER ADVOCATE.—Notwithstanding section 7803(c)(1)(B)(iv) of such Code, as added by this section, in appointing the first National Taxpayer Advocate after the date of the enactment of this Act, the Secretary of the Treasury—

(A) shall not appoint any individual who was an officer or employee of the Internal Revenue Service at any time during the 2-year period ending on the date of appointment, and

(B) need not consult with the Internal Revenue Service Oversight Board if the Oversight Board has not been appointed.

(4) CURRENT OFFICERS.—

(A) In the case of an individual serving as Commissioner of Internal Revenue on the date of the enactment of this Act who was appointed to such position before such date, the 5-year term required by section 7803(a)(1) of such Code, as added by this section, shall begin as of the date of such appointment.

(B) Clauses (ii), (iii), and (iv) of section 7803(c)(1)(B) of such Code, as added by this section, shall not apply to the individual serving as Taxpayer Advocate on the date of the enactment of this Act.

[¶ 6810] *CODE SEC. 7612. SPECIAL PROCEDURES FOR SUMMONSES FOR COMPUTER SOFTWARE.*

(a) *GENERAL RULE.—For purposes of this title—*

(1) except as provided in subsection (b), no summons may be issued under this title, and the Secretary may not begin any action under section 7604 to enforce any summons to produce or analyze any tax-related computer software source code, and

(2) any software and related materials which are provided to the Secretary under this title shall be subject to the safeguards under subsection (c).

(b) *CIRCUMSTANCES UNDER WHICH COMPUTER SOFTWARE SOURCE CODE MAY BE PROVIDED.—*

(1) IN GENERAL.—Subsection (a)(1) shall not apply to any portion, item, or component of tax-related computer software source code if—

(A) the Secretary is unable to otherwise reasonably ascertain the correctness of any item on a return from—

(i) the taxpayer's books, papers, records, or other data, or

(ii) the computer software executable code (and any modifications thereof) to which such source code relates and any associated data which, when executed, produces the output to ascertain the correctness of the item,

(B) the Secretary identifies with reasonable specificity the portion, item, or component of such source code needed to verify the correctness of such item on the return, and

(C) the Secretary determines that the need for the portion, item, or component of such source code with respect to such item outweighs the risks of unauthorized disclosure of trade secrets.

(2) EXCEPTIONS.—Subsection (a)(1) shall not apply to—

(A) any inquiry into any offense connected with the administration or enforcement of the internal revenue laws,

Code Sec. 7612(b)   ¶ 6810

(B) any tax-related computer software source code acquired or developed by the taxpayer or a related person primarily for internal use by the taxpayer or such person rather than for commercial distribution,

(C) any communications between the owner of the tax-related computer software source code and the taxpayer or related persons, or

(D) any tax-related computer software source code which is required to be provided or made available pursuant to any other provision of this title.

(3) COOPERATION REQUIRED.—For purposes of paragraph (1), the Secretary shall be treated as meeting the requirements of subparagraphs (A) and (B) of such paragraph if—

(A) the Secretary determines that it is not feasible to determine the correctness of an item without access to the computer software executable code and associated data described in paragraph (1)(A)(ii),

(B) the Secretary makes a formal request to the taxpayer for such code and data and to the owner of the computer software source code for such executable code, and

(C) such code and data is not provided within 180 days of such request.

(4) RIGHT TO CONTEST SUMMONS.—In any proceeding brought under section 7604 to enforce a summons issued under the authority of this subsection, the court shall, at the request of any party, hold a hearing to determine whether the applicable requirements of this subsection have been met.

(c) SAFEGUARDS TO ENSURE PROTECTION OF TRADE SECRETS AND OTHER CONFIDENTIAL INFORMATION.—

(1) ENTRY OF PROTECTIVE ORDER.—In any court proceeding to enforce a summons for any portion of software, the court may receive evidence and issue any order necessary to prevent the disclosure of trade secrets or other confidential information with respect to such software, including requiring that any information be placed under seal to be opened only as directed by the court.

(2) PROTECTION OF SOFTWARE.—Notwithstanding any other provision of this section, and in addition to any protections ordered pursuant to paragraph (1), in the case of software that comes into the possession or control of the Secretary in the course of any examination with respect to any taxpayer—

(A) the software may be used only in connection with the examination of such taxpayer's return, any appeal by the taxpayer to the Internal Revenue Service Office of Appeals, any judicial proceeding (and any appeals therefrom), and any inquiry into any offense connected with the administration or enforcement of the internal revenue laws,

(B) the Secretary shall provide, in advance, to the taxpayer and the owner of the software a written list of the names of all individuals who will analyze or otherwise have access to the software,

(C) the software shall be maintained in a secure area or place, and, in the case of computer software source code, shall not be removed from the owner's place of business unless the owner permits, or a court orders, such removal,

(D) the software may not be copied except as necessary to perform such analysis, and the Secretary shall number all copies made and certify in writing that no other copies have been (or will be) made,

(E) at the end of the period during which the software may be used under subparagraph (A)—

(i) the software and all copies thereof shall be returned to the person from whom they were obtained and any copies thereof made under subparagraph (D) on the hard drive of a machine or other mass storage device shall be permanently deleted, and

(ii) the Secretary shall obtain from any person who analyzes or otherwise had access to such software a written certification under penalty of perjury that all copies and related materials have been returned and that no copies were made of them,

(F) the software may not be decompiled or disassembled,

(G) the Secretary shall provide to the taxpayer and the owner of any interest in such software, as the case may be, a written agreement, between the Secretary and any person who is not an officer or employee of the United States and who will analyze or otherwise have access to such software, which provides that such person agrees not to—

(i) disclose such software to any person other than persons to whom such information could be disclosed for tax administration purposes under section 6103, or

(ii) participate for 2 years in the development of software which is intended for a similar purpose as the software examined, and

(H) the software shall be treated as return information for purposes of section 6103.

For purposes of subparagraph (C), the owner shall make available any necessary equipment or materials for analysis of computer software source code required to be conducted on the owner's premises. The owner of any interest in the software shall be considered a party to any agreement described in subparagraph (G).

(d) DEFINITIONS.—For purposes of this section—

(1) SOFTWARE.—The term "software" includes computer software source code and computer software executable code.

(2) COMPUTER SOFTWARE SOURCE CODE.—The term "computer software source code" means—

(A) the code written by a programmer using a programming language which is comprehensible to appropriately trained persons and is not capable of directly being used to give instructions to a computer,

(B) related programmers' notes, design documents, memoranda, and similar documentation, and

(C) related customer communications.

(3) COMPUTER SOFTWARE EXECUTABLE CODE.—The term "computer software executable code" means—

(A) any object code, machine code, or other code readable by a computer when loaded into its memory and used directly by such computer to execute instructions, and

(B) any related user manuals.

(4) OWNER.—The term "owner" shall, with respect to any software, include the developer of the software.

(5) RELATED PERSON.—A person shall be treated as related to another person if such persons are related persons under section 267 or 707(b).

(6) TAX-RELATED COMPUTER SOFTWARE SOURCE CODE.—The term "tax-related computer software source code" means the computer source code for any computer software program intended for accounting, tax return preparation or compliance, or tax planning.

[CCH Explanation at ¶ 1161. Committee Reports at ¶ 10,385.]

Amendment Notes

Act Sec. 3413(a) amended Subchapter A of chapter 78 by redesignating Code Sec. 7612 as Code Sec. 7613 and by inserting after Code Sec. 7611 a new Code Sec. 7612 to read as above.

The above amendment generally applies to summonses issued, and software acquired, after the date of the enactment of this Act. For a special rule, see Act Sec. 3413(e)(2), below.

Act Sec. 3413(e)(2) provides:

(2) SOFTWARE PROTECTION.—In the case of any software acquired on or before such date of enactment, the requirements of section 7612(a)(2) of the Internal Revenue Code of 1986 (as added by such amendments) shall apply after the 90th day after such date. The preceding sentence shall not apply to the requirement under section 7612(c)(2)(G)(ii) of such Code (as so added).

[¶ 6820] CODE SEC. *7613*. CROSS REFERENCES.

* * *

[CCH Explanation at ¶ 1161. Committee Reports at ¶ 10,385.]

Amendment Notes

Act Sec. 3413(a) amended subchapter A of chapter 78 by redesignating Code Sec. 7612 as Code Sec. 7613

The above amendment generally applies to summonses issued, and software acquired, after the date of the enactment of this Act.

[¶ 6830] CODE SEC. 7702B. TREATMENT OF QUALIFIED LONG-TERM CARE INSURANCE.

* * *

(e) TREATMENT OF COVERAGE PROVIDED AS PART OF A LIFE INSURANCE CONTRACT.—Except as otherwise provided in regulations prescribed by the Secretary, in the case of any long-term care insurance coverage (whether or not qualified) provided by a rider on or as part of a life insurance contract—

(1) IN GENERAL.—This section shall apply as if the portion of the contract providing such coverage is a separate contract.

(2) APPLICATION OF *SECTION* 7702.—Section 7702(c)(2) (relating to the guideline premium limitation) shall be applied by increasing the guideline premium limitation with respect to a life insurance contract, as of any date—

(A) by the sum of any charges (but not premium payments) against the life insurance contract's cash surrender value (within the meaning of section 7702(f)(2)(A)) for such coverage made to that date under the contract, less

(B) any such charges the imposition of which reduces the premiums paid for the contract (within the meaning of section 7702(f)(1)).

* * *

[CCH Explanation at ¶ 30,050.]

Amendment Notes

Act Sec. 6023(28) amended the paragraph heading of paragraph (2) of Code Sec. 7702B(e) by inserting "SECTION" after "APPLICATION OF".

The above amendment is effective on the date of the enactment of this Act.

[¶ 6840] **CODE SEC. 7704. CERTAIN PUBLICLY TRADED PARTNERSHIPS TREATED AS CORPORATIONS.**
* * *

(g) EXCEPTION FOR ELECTING 1987 PARTNERSHIPS.—
* * *

(3) ADDITIONAL TAX ON ELECTING PARTNERSHIPS.—
* * *

(C) TREATMENT OF TAX.—*For purposes of this title, the tax imposed by this paragraph shall be treated as imposed by chapter 1 other than for purposes of determining the amount of any credit allowable under chapter 1 and shall be paid by the partnership. Section 6655 shall be applied to such partnership with respect to such tax in the same manner as if the partnership were a corporation, such tax were imposed by section 11, and references in such section to taxable income were references to the gross income referred to in subparagraph (A).*
* * *

[CCH Explanation at ¶ 676. Committee Reports at ¶ 11,100.]

Amendment Notes

Act Sec. 6009(b)(1) amended Code Sec. 7704(g)(3)(C) by striking the period at the end and inserting "and shall be paid by the partnership. Section 6655 shall be applied to such partnership with respect to such tax in the same manner as if the partnership were a corporation, such tax were imposed by

section 11, and references in such section to taxable income were references to the gross income referred to in subparagraph (A)."

The above amendment applies to tax years beginning after the date of the enactment of this Act.

[¶ 6850] **CODE SEC. 7802. *INTERNAL REVENUE SERVICE OVERSIGHT BOARD.***

(a) ESTABLISHMENT.—*There is established within the Department of the Treasury the Internal Revenue Service Oversight Board (hereafter in this subchapter referred to as the "Oversight Board").*

(b) MEMBERSHIP.—

(1) COMPOSITION.—*The Oversight Board shall be composed of 9 members, as follows:*

(A) *6 members shall be individuals who are not otherwise Federal officers or employees and who are appointed by the President, by and with the advice and consent of the Senate.*

(B) *1 member shall be the Secretary of the Treasury or, if the Secretary so designates, the Deputy Secretary of the Treasury.*

(C) *1 member shall be the Commissioner of Internal Revenue.*

(D) *1 member shall be an individual who is a full-time Federal employee or a representative of employees and who is appointed by the President, by and with the advice and consent of the Senate.*

(2) QUALIFICATIONS AND TERMS.—

(A) QUALIFICATIONS.—*Members of the Oversight Board described in paragraph (1)(A) shall be appointed without regard to political affiliation and solely on the basis of their professional experience and expertise in 1 or more of the following areas:*

(i) *Management of large service organizations.*

(ii) *Customer service.*

(iii) *Federal tax laws, including tax administration and compliance.*

(iv) *Information technology.*

(v) *Organization development.*

(vi) *The needs and concerns of taxpayers.*

(vii) *The needs and concerns of small businesses.*

In the aggregate, the members of the Oversight Board described in paragraph (1)(A) should collectively bring to bear expertise in all of the areas described in the preceding sentence.

(B) TERMS.—*Each member who is described in subparagraph (A) or (D) of paragraph (1) shall be appointed for a term of 5 years, except that of the members first appointed under paragraph (1)(A)—*

(i) *2 members shall be appointed for a term of 3 years,*

(ii) *2 members shall be appointed for a term of 4 years, and*

(iii) *2 members shall be appointed for a term of 5 years.*

(C) REAPPOINTMENT.—*An individual who is described in subparagraph (A) or (D) of paragraph (1) may be appointed to no more than two 5-year terms on the Oversight Board.*

(D) VACANCY.—*Any vacancy on the Oversight Board shall be filled in the same manner as the original appointment. Any member appointed to fill a vacancy occurring before the expiration of the term for which the member's predecessor was appointed shall be appointed for the remainder of that term.*

(3) ETHICAL CONSIDERATIONS.—

(A) FINANCIAL DISCLOSURE.—*During the entire period that an individual appointed under subparagraph (A) or (D) of paragraph (1) is a member of the Oversight Board, such individual shall be treated as serving as an officer or employee referred to in section 101(f) of the Ethics in Government Act of 1978 for purposes of title I of such Act, except that section 101(d) of such Act shall apply without regard to the number of days of service in the position.*

(B) RESTRICTIONS ON POST-EMPLOYMENT.—For purposes of section 207(c) of title 18, United States Code, an individual appointed under subparagraph (A) or (D) of paragraph (1) shall be treated as an employee referred to in section 207(c)(2)(A)(i) of such title during the entire period the individual is a member of the Board, except that subsections (c)(2)(B) and (f) of section 207 of such title shall not apply.

(C) MEMBERS WHO ARE SPECIAL GOVERNMENT EMPLOYEES.—If an individual appointed under subparagraph (A) or (D) of paragraph (1) is a special Government employee, the following additional rules apply for purposes of chapter 11 of title 18, United States Code:

(i) RESTRICTION ON REPRESENTATION.—In addition to any restriction under section 205(c) of title 18, United States Code, except as provided in subsections (d) through (i) of section 205 of such title, such individual (except in the proper discharge of official duties) shall not, with or without compensation, represent anyone to or before any officer or employee of—

(I) the Oversight Board or the Internal Revenue Service on any matter,

(II) the Department of the Treasury on any matter involving the internal revenue laws or involving the management or operations of the Internal Revenue Service, or

(III) the Department of Justice with respect to litigation involving a matter described in subclause (I) or (II).

(ii) COMPENSATION FOR SERVICES PROVIDED BY ANOTHER.—For purposes of section 203 of such title—

(I) such individual shall not be subject to the restrictions of subsection (a)(1) thereof for sharing in compensation earned by another for representations on matters covered by such section, and

(II) a person shall not be subject to the restrictions of subsection (a)(2) thereof for sharing such compensation with such individual.

(D) WAIVER.—The President may, only at the time the President nominates the member of the Oversight Board described in paragraph (1)(D), waive for the term of the member any appropriate provision of chapter 11 of title 18, United States Code, to the extent such waiver is necessary to allow such member to participate in the decisions of the Board while continuing to serve as a full-time Federal employee or a representative of employees. Any such waiver shall not be effective unless a written intent of waiver to exempt such member (and actual waiver language) is submitted to the Senate with the nomination of such member.

(4) QUORUM.—5 members of the Oversight Board shall constitute a quorum. A majority of members present and voting shall be required for the Oversight Board to take action.

(5) REMOVAL.—

(A) IN GENERAL.—Any member of the Oversight Board appointed under subparagraph (A) or (D) of paragraph (1) may be removed at the will of the President.

(B) SECRETARY AND COMMISSIONER.— An individual described in subparagraph (B) or (C) of paragraph (1) shall be removed upon termination of service in the office described in such subparagraph.

(6) CLAIMS.—

(A) IN GENERAL.—Members of the Oversight Board who are described in subparagraph (A) or (D) of paragraph (1) shall have no personal liability under Federal law with respect to any claim arising out of or resulting from an act or omission by such member within the scope of service as a member.

(B) EFFECT ON OTHER LAW.—This paragraph shall not be construed—

(i) to affect any other immunities and protections that may be available to such member under applicable law with respect to such transactions,

(ii) to affect any other right or remedy against the United States under applicable law, or

(iii) to limit or alter in any way the immunities that are available under applicable law for Federal officers and employees.

(c) GENERAL RESPONSIBILITIES.—

(1) OVERSIGHT.—

(A) IN GENERAL.—The Oversight Board shall oversee the Internal Revenue Service in its administration, management, conduct, direction, and supervision of the execution and application of the internal revenue laws or related statutes and tax conventions to which the United States is a party.

(B) MISSION OF IRS.—As part of its oversight functions described in subparagraph (A), the Oversight Board shall ensure that the organization and operation of the Internal Revenue Service allows it to carry out its mission.

(C) CONFIDENTIALITY.—The Oversight Board shall ensure that appropriate confidentiality is maintained in the exercise of its duties.

(2) EXCEPTIONS.—The Oversight Board shall have no responsibilities or authority with respect to—

(A) the development and formulation of Federal tax policy relating to existing or proposed internal revenue laws, related statutes, and tax conventions,

(B) specific law enforcement activities of the Internal Revenue Service, including specific compliance activities such as examinations, collection activities, and criminal investigations,

(C) specific procurement activities of the Internal Revenue Service, or

(D) except as provided in subsection (d)(3), specific personnel actions.

(d) SPECIFIC RESPONSIBILITIES.—The Oversight Board shall have the following specific responsibilities.

(1) STRATEGIC PLANS.—To review and approve strategic plans of the Internal Revenue Service, including the establishment of—

(A) mission and objectives, and standards of performance relative to either, and

(B) annual and long-range strategic plans.

(2) OPERATIONAL PLANS.—To review the operational functions of the Internal Revenue Service, including—

(A) plans for modernization of the tax system,

(B) plans for outsourcing or managed competition, and

(C) plans for training and education.

(3) MANAGEMENT.—To—

(A) recommend to the President candidates for appointment as the Commissioner of Internal Revenue and recommend to the President the removal of the Commissioner,

(B) review the Commissioner's selection, evaluation, and compensation of Internal Revenue Service senior executives who have program management responsibility over significant functions of the Internal Revenue Service, and

(C) review and approve the Commissioner's plans for any major reorganization of the Internal Revenue Service.

(4) BUDGET.—To—

(A) review and approve the budget request of the Internal Revenue Service prepared by the Commissioner,

(B) submit such budget request to the Secretary of the Treasury, and

(C) ensure that the budget request supports the annual and long-range strategic plans.

(5) TAXPAYER PROTECTION.—To ensure the proper treatment of taxpayers by the employees of the Internal Revenue Service.

The Secretary shall submit the budget request referred to in paragraph (4)(B) for any fiscal year to the President who shall submit such request, without revision, to Congress together with the President's annual budget request for the Internal Revenue Service for such fiscal year.

(e) BOARD PERSONNEL MATTERS.—

(1) COMPENSATION OF MEMBERS.—

(A) IN GENERAL.—Each member of the Oversight Board who—

(i) is described in subsection (b)(1)(A), or

(ii) is described in subsection (b)(1)(D) and is not otherwise a Federal officer or employee,

shall be compensated at a rate of $30,000 per year. All other members shall serve without compensation for such service.

(B) CHAIRPERSON.—In lieu of the amount specified in subparagraph (A), the Chairperson of the Oversight Board shall be compensated at a rate of $50,000 per year.

(2) TRAVEL EXPENSES.—

(A) IN GENERAL.—The members of the Oversight Board shall be allowed travel expenses, including per diem in lieu of subsistence, at rates authorized for employees of agencies under subchapter I of chapter 57 of title 5, United States Code, to attend meetings of the Oversight Board and, with the advance approval of the Chairperson of the Oversight Board, while otherwise away from their homes or regular places of business for purposes of duties as a member of the Oversight Board.

(B) REPORT.—The Oversight Board shall include in its annual report under subsection (f)(3)(A) information with respect to the travel expenses allowed for members of the Oversight Board under this paragraph.

(3) STAFF.—

(A) IN GENERAL.—The Chairperson of the Oversight Board may appoint and terminate any personnel that may be necessary to enable the Board to perform its duties.

(B) DETAIL OF GOVERNMENT EMPLOYEES.—Upon request of the Chairperson of the Oversight Board, a Federal agency shall detail a Federal Government employee to the Oversight Board without reimbursement. Such detail shall be without interruption or loss of civil service status or privilege.

(4) PROCUREMENT OF TEMPORARY AND INTERMITTENT SERVICES.—The Chairperson of the Oversight Board may procure temporary and intermittent services under section 3109(b) of title 5, United States Code

(f) ADMINISTRATIVE MATTERS.—

(1) CHAIR.—

(A) TERM.—The members of the Oversight Board shall elect for a 2-year term a chairperson from among the members appointed under subsection (b)(1)(A).

(B) POWERS.—Except as otherwise provided by a majority vote of the Oversight Board, the powers of the Chairperson shall include—

(i) establishing committees,

(ii) setting meeting places and times,

(iii) establishing meeting agendas, and

(iv) developing rules for the conduct of business.

(2) MEETINGS.—The Oversight Board shall meet at least quarterly and at such other times as the Chairperson determines appropriate.

(3) REPORTS.—

(A) ANNUAL.—The Oversight Board shall each year report with respect to the conduct of its responsibilities under this title to the President, the Committees on Ways and Means, Government Reform and Oversight, and Appropriations of the House of Representatives and the Committees on Finance, Governmental Affairs, and Appropriations of the Senate.

(B) ADDITIONAL REPORT.—Upon a determination by the Oversight Board under subsection (c)(1)(B) that the organization and operation of the Internal Revenue Service are not allowing it to carry out its mission, the Oversight Board shall report such determination to the Committee on Ways and Means of the House of Representatives and the Committee on Finance of the Senate.

[CCH Explanation at ¶ 826 and 836. Committee Reports at ¶ 10,130 and 10,135.]

Amendment Notes

Act Sec. 1101(a) amended Code Sec. 7802 to read as above. Prior to amendment, Code Sec. 7802 read as follows:

SEC. 7802. COMMISSIONER OF INTERNAL REVENUE; ASSISTANT COMMISSIONERS; TAXPAYER ADVOCATE.

(a) COMMISSIONER OF INTERNAL REVENUE.—There shall be in the Department of the Treasury a Commissioner of Internal Revenue, who shall be appointed by the President, by and with the advice and consent of the Senate. The Commissioner of Internal Revenue shall have such duties and powers as may be prescribed by the Secretary of the Treasury.

(b) ASSISTANT COMMISSIONER FOR EMPLOYEE PLANS AND EXEMPT ORGANIZATIONS.—

(1) ESTABLISHMENT OF OFFICE.—There is established within the Internal Revenue Service an office to be known as the "Office of Employee Plans and Exempt Organizations" to be under the supervision and direction of an Assistant Commissioner of Internal Revenue. As head of the Office, the Assistant Commissioner shall be responsible for carrying out such functions as the Secretary may prescribe with respect to organizations exempt from tax under section 501(a) and with respect to plans to which part I of subchapter D of chapter 1 applies (and with respect to organizations designed to be exempt under such section and plans designed to be plans to which such part applies).

(2) AUTHORIZATION OF APPROPRIATIONS.—There is authorized to be appropriated to the Department of the Treasury to carry out the functions of the Office an amount equal to the sum of—

(A) so much of the collections from taxes imposed under section 4940 (relating to excise tax based on investment income) as would have been collected if the rate of tax under such section was 2 percent during the second preceding fiscal year; and

(B) the greater of—

(i) an amount equal to the amount described in paragraph (A); or

(ii) $30,000,000.

(c) ASSISTANT COMMISSIONER (TAXPAYER SERVICES).—There is established within the Internal Revenue Service an office to be known as the "Office for Taxpayer Services" to be under the supervision and direction of an Assistant Commissioner of Internal Revenue. The Assistant Commissioner shall be responsible for taxpayer services such as telephone, walk-in, and taxpayer educational services, and the design and production of tax and informational forms

(d) OFFICE OF TAXPAYER ADVOCATE.

(1) IN GENERAL.—There is established in the Internal Revenue Service an office to be known as the "Office of the Taxpayer Advocate". Such office shall be under the supervision and direction of an official to be known as the "Taxpayer Advocate" who shall be appointed by and report directly to the Commissioner of Internal Revenue. The Taxpayer Advocate shall be entitled to compensation at the same rate as the highest level official reporting directly to the Deputy Commissioner of the Internal Revenue Service

(2) FUNCTIONS OF OFFICE.—

(A) IN GENERAL.—It shall be the function of the Office of Taxpayer Advocate to—

(i) assist taxpayers in resolving problems with the Internal Revenue Service,

(ii) identify areas in which taxpayers have problems in dealings with the Internal Revenue Service,

(iii) to the extent possible, propose changes in the administrative practices of the Internal Revenue Service to mitigate problems identified under clause (ii), and

(iv) identify potential legislative changes which may be appropriate to mitigate such problems.

(B) ANNUAL REPORTS.—

(i) OBJECTIVES.—Not later than June 30 of each calendar year after 1995, the Taxpayer Advocate shall report to the Committee on Ways and Means of the House of Representatives and the Committee on Finance of the Senate on the objectives of the Taxpayer Advocate for the fiscal year beginning in such calendar year. Any such report shall contain full and substantive analysis, in addition to statistical information.

(ii) ACTIVITIES.—Not later than December 31 of each calendar year after 1995, the Taxpayer Advocate shall report to the Committee on Ways and Means of the House of Representatives and the Committee on Finance of the Senate on the activities of the Taxpayer Advocate during the fiscal year ending during such calendar year. Any such report shall contain full and substantive analysis, in addition to statistical information, and shall—

(I) identify the initiatives the Taxpayer Advocate has taken on improving taxpayer services and Internal Revenue Service responsiveness,

(II) contain recommendations received from individuals with the authority to issue Taxpayer Assistance Orders under section 7811,

(III) contain a summary of at least 20 of the most serious problems encountered by taxpayers, including a description of the nature of such problems,

(IV) contain an inventory of the items described in subclauses (I), (II), and (III) for which action has been taken and the result of such action,

(V) contain an inventory of the items described in subclauses (I), (II), and (III) for which action remains to be completed and the period during which each item has remained on such inventory,

(VI) contain an inventory of the items described in subclauses (II) and (III) for which no action has been taken, the period during which each item has remained on such inventory, the reasons for the inaction, and identify any Internal Revenue Service official who is responsible for such inaction,

(VII) identify any Taxpayer Assistance Order which was not honored by the Internal Revenue Service in a timely manner, as specified under section 7811(b),

(VIII) contain recommendations for such administrative and legislative action as may be appropriate to resolve problems encountered by taxpayers,

(IX) describe the extent to which regional problem resolution officers participate in the selection and evaluation of local problem resolution officers, and

(X) include such other information as the Taxpayer Advocate may deem advisable.

(iii) REPORT TO BE SUBMITTED DIRECTLY.—Each report required under this subparagraph shall be provided directly to the Committees referred to in clauses (i) and (ii) without any prior review or comment from the Commissioner, the Secretary of the Treasury, any other officer or employee of the Department of the Treasury, or the Office of Management and Budget.

(3) RESPONSIBILITIES OF COMMISSIONER.—The Commissioner of Internal Revenue shall establish procedures requiring a formal response to all recommendations submitted to the Commissioner by the Taxpayer Advocate within 3 months after submission to the Commissioner.

The above amendment is effective on the date of the enactment of this Act.

Act Sec. 1101(d)(2)-(3) provides:

(2) INITIAL NOMINATIONS TO INTERNAL REVENUE SERVICE OVERSIGHT BOARD.—The President shall submit the initial nominations under section 7802 of the Internal Revenue Code of 1986, as added by this section, to the Senate not later than 6 months after the date of the enactment of this Act.

(3) EFFECT ON ACTIONS PRIOR TO APPOINTMENT OF OVERSIGHT BOARD.—Nothing in this section shall be construed to invalidate the actions and authority of the Internal Revenue Service prior to the appointment of the members of the Internal Revenue Service Oversight Board.

[¶ 6860] CODE SEC. 7803. *COMMISSIONER OF INTERNAL REVENUE; OTHER OFFICIALS.*

(a) *COMMISSIONER OF INTERNAL REVENUE.—*

(1) *APPOINTMENT.—*

(A) *IN GENERAL.—There shall be in the Department of the Treasury a Commissioner of Internal Revenue who shall be appointed by the President, by and with the advice and consent of the Senate, to a 5-year term. Such appointment shall be made from individuals who, among other qualifications, have a demonstrated ability in management.*

(B) *VACANCY.—Any individual appointed to fill a vacancy in the position of Commissioner occurring before the expiration of the term for which such individual's predecessor was appointed shall be appointed only for the remainder of that term.*

(C) *REMOVAL.—The Commissioner may be removed at the will of the President.*

(D) *REAPPOINTMENT.—The Commissioner may be appointed to more than one 5-year term.*

(2) *DUTIES.—The Commissioner shall have such duties and powers as the Secretary may prescribe, including the power to—*

(A) *administer, manage, conduct, direct, and supervise the execution and application of the internal revenue laws or related statutes and tax conventions to which the United States is a party, and*

(B) *recommend to the President a candidate for appointment as Chief Counsel for the Internal Revenue Service when a vacancy occurs, and recommend to the President the removal of such Chief Counsel.*

If the Secretary determines not to delegate a power specified in subparagraph (A) or (B), such determination may not take effect until 30 days after the Secretary notifies the Committees on Ways and Means, Government Reform and Oversight, and Appropriations of the House of Representatives and the Committees on Finance, Governmental Affairs, and Appropriations of the Senate.

(3) *CONSULTATION WITH BOARD.—The Commissioner shall consult with the Oversight Board on all matters set forth in paragraphs (2) and (3) (other than paragraph (3)(A)) of section 7802(d).*

(b) *CHIEF COUNSEL FOR THE INTERNAL REVENUE SERVICE.—*

(1) *APPOINTMENT.—There shall be in the Department of the Treasury a Chief Counsel for the Internal Revenue Service who shall be appointed by the President, by and with the consent of the Senate.*

(2) *DUTIES.—The Chief Counsel shall be the chief law officer for the Internal Revenue Service and shall perform such duties as may be prescribed by the Secretary, including the duty—*

(A) *to be legal advisor to the Commissioner and the Commissioner's officers and employees,*

(B) *to furnish legal opinions for the preparation and review of rulings and memoranda of technical advice,*

(C) *to prepare, review, and assist in the preparation of proposed legislation, treaties, regulations, and Executive orders relating to laws which affect the Internal Revenue Service,*

(D) *to represent the Commissioner in cases before the Tax Court, and*

(E) *to determine which civil actions should be litigated under the laws relating to the Internal Revenue Service and prepare recommendations for the Department of Justice regarding the commencement of such actions.*

¶ 6860   Code Sec. 7803(a)

If the Secretary determines not to delegate a power specified in subparagraph (A), (B), (C), (D), or (E), such determination may not take effect until 30 days after the Secretary notifies the Committees on Ways and Means, Government Reform and Oversight, and Appropriations of the House of Representatives and the Committees on Finance, Governmental Affairs, and Appropriations of the Senate.

(3) PERSONS TO WHOM CHIEF COUNSEL REPORTS.—The Chief Counsel shall report directly to the Commissioner of Internal Revenue, except that—

(A) the Chief Counsel shall report to both the Commissioner and the General Counsel for the Department of the Treasury with respect to—

(i) legal advice or interpretation of the tax law not relating solely to tax policy, and

(ii) tax litigation, and

(B) the Chief Counsel shall report to the General Counsel with respect to legal advice or interpretation of the tax law relating solely to tax policy.

If there is any disagreement between the Commissioner and the General Counsel with respect to any matter jointly referred to them under subparagraph (A), such matter shall be submitted to the Secretary or Deputy Secretary for resolution.

(4) CHIEF COUNSEL PERSONNEL.—All personnel in the Office of Chief Counsel shall report to the Chief Counsel.

(c) OFFICE OF THE TAXPAYER ADVOCATE.—

(1) ESTABLISHMENT.—

(A) IN GENERAL.—There is established in the Internal Revenue Service an office to be known as the "Office of the Taxpayer Advocate".

(B) NATIONAL TAXPAYER ADVOCATE.—

(i) IN GENERAL.—The Office of the Taxpayer Advocate shall be under the supervision and direction of an official to be known as the "National Taxpayer Advocate". The National Taxpayer Advocate shall report directly to the Commissioner of Internal Revenue and shall be entitled to compensation at the same rate as the highest rate of basic pay established for the Senior Executive Service under section 5382 of title 5, United States Code, or, if the Secretary of the Treasury so determines, at a rate fixed under section 9503 of such title.

(ii) APPOINTMENT.—The National Taxpayer Advocate shall be appointed by the Secretary of the Treasury after consultation with the Commissioner of Internal Revenue and the Oversight Board and without regard to the provisions of title 5, United States Code, relating to appointments in the competitive service or the Senior Executive Service.

(iii) QUALIFICATIONS.—An individual appointed under clause (ii) shall have—

(I) a background in customer service as well as tax law, and

(II) experience in representing individual taxpayers.

(iv) RESTRICTION ON EMPLOYMENT.—An individual may be appointed as the National Taxpayer Advocate only if such individual was not an officer or employee of the Internal Revenue Service during the 2-year period ending with such appointment and such individual agrees not to accept any employment with the Internal Revenue Service for at least 5 years after ceasing to be the National Taxpayer Advocate. Service as an officer or employee of the Office of the Taxpayer Advocate shall not be taken into account in applying this clause.

(2) FUNCTIONS OF OFFICE.—

(A) IN GENERAL.—It shall be the function of the Office of the Taxpayer Advocate to—

(i) assist taxpayers in resolving problems with the Internal Revenue Service,

(ii) identify areas in which taxpayers have problems in dealings with the Internal Revenue Service,

(iii) to the extent possible, propose changes in the administrative practices of the Internal Revenue Service to mitigate problems identified under clause (ii), and

(iv) identify potential legislative changes which may be appropriate to mitigate such problems.

(B) ANNUAL REPORTS.—

(i) OBJECTIVES.—Not later than June 30 of each calendar year, the National Taxpayer Advocate shall report to the Committee on Ways and Means of the House of Representatives and the Committee on Finance of the Senate on the objectives of the Office of the Taxpayer Advocate for the fiscal year beginning in such calendar year. Any such report shall contain full and substantive analysis, in addition to statistical information.

(ii) ACTIVITIES.—Not later than December 31 of each calendar year, the National Taxpayer Advocate shall report to the Committee on Ways and Means of the House of Representatives and the Committee on Finance of the Senate on the activities of the Office of the Taxpayer Advocate during the fiscal year ending during such calendar year. Any

Code Sec. 7803(c)   ¶ 6860

such report shall contain full and substantive analysis, in addition to statistical information, and shall—

(I) identify the initiatives the Office of the Taxpayer Advocate has taken on improving taxpayer services and Internal Revenue Service responsiveness,

(II) contain recommendations received from individuals with the authority to issue Taxpayer Assistance Orders under section 7811,

(III) contain a summary of at least 20 of the most serious problems encountered by taxpayers, including a description of the nature of such problems,

(IV) contain an inventory of the items described in subclauses (I), (II), and (III) for which action has been taken and the result of such action,

(V) contain an inventory of the items described in subclauses (I), (II), and (III) for which action remains to be completed and the period during which each item has remained on such inventory,

(VI) contain an inventory of the items described in subclauses (I), (II), and (III) for which no action has been taken, the period during which each item has remained on such inventory, the reasons for the inaction, and identify any Internal Revenue Service official who is responsible for such inaction,

(VII) identify any Taxpayer Assistance Order which was not honored by the Internal Revenue Service in a timely manner, as specified under section 7811(b),

(VIII) contain recommendations for such administrative and legislative action as may be appropriate to resolve problems encountered by taxpayers,

(IX) identify areas of the tax law that impose significant compliance burdens on taxpayers or the Internal Revenue Service, including specific recommendations for remedying these problems,

(X) identify the 10 most litigated issues for each category of taxpayers, including recommendations for mitigating such disputes, and

(XI) include such other information as the National Taxpayer Advocate may deem advisable.

(iii) REPORT TO BE SUBMITTED DIRECTLY.—Each report required under this subparagraph shall be provided directly to the committees described in clause (i) without any prior review or comment from the Commissioner, the Secretary of the Treasury, the Oversight Board, any other officer or employee of the Department of the Treasury, or the Office of Management and Budget.

(iv) COORDINATION WITH REPORT OF TREASURY INSPECTOR GENERAL FOR TAX ADMINISTRATION.—To the extent that information required to be reported under clause (ii) is also required to be reported under paragraph (1) or (2) of subsection (d) by the Treasury Inspector General for Tax Administration, the National Taxpayer Advocate shall not contain such information in the report submitted under such clause.

(C) OTHER RESPONSIBILITIES.—The National Taxpayer Advocate shall—

(i) monitor the coverage and geographic allocation of local offices of taxpayer advocates,

(ii) develop guidance to be distributed to all Internal Revenue Service officers and employees outlining the criteria for referral of taxpayer inquiries to local offices of taxpayer advocates,

(iii) ensure that the local telephone number for each local office of the taxpayer advocate is published and available to taxpayers served by the office, and

(iv) in conjunction with the Commissioner, develop career paths for local taxpayer advocates choosing to make a career in the Office of the Taxpayer Advocate.

(D) PERSONNEL ACTIONS.—

(i) IN GENERAL.—The National Taxpayer Advocate shall have the responsibility and authority to—

(I) appoint local taxpayer advocates and make available at least 1 such advocate for each State, and

(II) evaluate and take personnel actions (including dismissal) with respect to any employee of any local office of a taxpayer advocate described in subclause (I).

(ii) CONSULTATION.—The National Taxpayer Advocate may consult with the appropriate supervisory personnel of the Internal Revenue Service in carrying out the National Taxpayer Advocate's responsibilities under this subparagraph.

(3) RESPONSIBILITIES OF COMMISSIONER.— The Commissioner shall establish procedures requiring a formal response to all recommendations submitted to the Commissioner by the National Taxpayer Advocate within 3 months after submission to the Commissioner.

(4) OPERATION OF LOCAL OFFICES.—

(A) IN GENERAL.—Each local taxpayer advocate—

(i) shall report to the National Taxpayer Advocate or delegate thereof,

(ii) may consult with the appropriate supervisory personnel of the Internal Revenue Service regarding the daily operation of the local office of the taxpayer advocate,

(iii) shall, at the initial meeting with any taxpayer seeking the assistance of a local office of the taxpayer advocate, notify such taxpayer that the taxpayer advocate offices operate independently of any other Internal Revenue Service office and report directly to Congress through the National Taxpayer Advocate, and

(iv) may, at the taxpayer advocate's discretion, not disclose to the Internal Revenue Service contact with, or information provided by, such taxpayer.

(B) MAINTENANCE OF INDEPENDENT COMMUNICATIONS.—Each local office of the taxpayer advocate shall maintain a separate phone, facsimile, and other electronic communication access, and a separate post office address.

(d) ADDITIONAL DUTIES OF THE TREASURY INSPECTOR GENERAL FOR TAX ADMINISTRATION.—

(1) ANNUAL REPORTING.—The Treasury Inspector General for Tax Administration shall include in one of the semiannual reports under section 5 of the Inspector General Act of 1978—

(A) an evaluation of the compliance of the Internal Revenue Service with—

(i) restrictions under section 1204 of the Internal Revenue Service Restructuring and Reform Act of 1998 on the use of enforcement statistics to evaluate Internal Revenue Service employees,

(ii) restrictions under section 7521 on directly contacting taxpayers who have indicated that they prefer their representatives be contacted,

(iii) required procedures under section 6320 upon the filing of a notice of a lien,

(iv) required procedures under subchapter D of chapter 64 for seizure of property for collection of taxes, including required procedures under section 6330 regarding levies, and

(v) restrictions under section 3707 of the Internal Revenue Service Restructuring and Reform Act of 1998 on designation of taxpayers,

(B) a review and a certification of whether or not the Secretary is complying with the requirements of section 6103(e)(8) to disclose information to an individual filing a joint return on collection activity involving the other individual filing the return,

(C) information regarding extensions of the statute of limitations for assessment and collection of tax under section 6501 and the provision of notice to taxpayers regarding requests for such extension,

(D) an evaluation of the adequacy and security of the technology of the Internal Revenue Service,

(E) any termination or mitigation under section 1203 of the Internal Revenue Service Restructuring and Reform Act of 1998,

(F) information regarding improper denial of requests for information from the Internal Revenue Service identified under paragraph (3)(A), and

(G) information regarding any administrative or civil actions with respect to violations of the fair debt collection provisions of section 6304, including—

(i) a summary of such actions initiated since the date of the last report, and

(ii) a summary of any judgments or awards granted as a result of such actions.

(2) SEMIANNUAL REPORTS.—

(A) IN GENERAL.—The Treasury Inspector General for Tax Administration shall include in each semiannual report under section 5 of the Inspector General Act of 1978—

(i) the number of taxpayer complaints during the reporting period;

(ii) the number of employee misconduct and taxpayer abuse allegations received by the Internal Revenue Service or the Inspector General during the period from taxpayers, Internal Revenue Service employees, and other sources;

(iii) a summary of the status of such complaints and allegations; and

(iv) a summary of the disposition of such complaints and allegations, including the outcome of any Department of Justice action and any monies paid as a settlement of such complaints and allegations.

(B) Clauses (iii) and (iv) of subparagraph (A) shall only apply to complaints and allegations of serious employee misconduct.

(3) OTHER RESPONSIBILITIES.—The Treasury Inspector General for Tax Administration shall—

(A) conduct periodic audits of a statistically valid sample of the total number of determinations made by the Internal Revenue Service to deny written requests to disclose information to taxpayers on the basis of section 6103 of this title or section 552(b)(7) of title 5, United States Code, and

(B) establish and maintain a toll-free telephone number for taxpayers to use to confidentially register complaints of misconduct by Internal Revenue Service employees and *incorporate the telephone number in the statement required by section 6227 of the Omnibus Taxpayer Bill of Rights (Internal Revenue Service Publication No. 1).*

[CCH Explanation at ¶ 811, 816, 821 and 831. Committee Reports at ¶ 10,140, 10,145, 10,150 and 10,160.]

Amendment Notes

Act Sec. 1102(a) amended Code Sec. 7803 to read as above. Prior to amendment, Code Sec. 7803 read as follows:

SEC. 7803. OTHER PERSONNEL.

(a) APPOINTMENT AND SUPERVISION.—The Secretary is authorized to employ such number of persons as the Secretary deems proper for the administration and enforcement of the internal revenue laws, and the Secretary shall issue all necessary directions, instructions, orders, and rules applicable to such persons.

(b) POSTS OF DUTY OF EMPLOYEES IN FIELD SERVICE OR TRAVELING.—

(1) DESIGNATION OF POST OF DUTY.—The Secretary shall determine and designate the posts of duty of all such persons engaged in field work or traveling on official business outside of the District of Columbia.

(2) DETAIL OF PERSONNEL FROM FIELD SERVICE.—The Secretary may order any such person engaged in field work to duty in the District of Columbia, for such periods as the Secretary may prescribe, and to any designated post of duty outside the District of Columbia upon the completion of such duty.

(c) DELINQUENT INTERNAL REVENUE OFFICERS AND EMPLOYEES.—If any officer or employee of the Treasury Department acting in connection with the internal revenue laws fails to account for and pay over any amount of money or property collected or received by him in connection with the internal revenue laws, the Secretary shall issue notice and demand to such officer or employee for payment of the amount which he failed to account for and pay over, and, upon failure to pay the amount demanded within the time specified in such notice, the amount so demanded shall be deemed imposed upon such officer or employee and assessed upon the date of such notice and demand, and the provisions of chapter 64 and all other provisions of law relating to the

collection of assessed taxes shall be applicable in respect of such amount.

The above amendment is generally effective on the date of the enactment of this Act. For a special rule, see Act Sec. 1102(f)(2)-(4), below.

Act Sec. 1102(f)(2)-(4) provides:

(2) CHIEF COUNSEL.—Section 7803(b)(3) of the Internal Revenue Code of 1986, as added by this section, shall take effect on the date that is 90 days after the date of the enactment of this Act.

(3) NATIONAL TAXPAYER ADVOCATE.—Notwithstanding section 7803(c)(1)(B)(iv) of such Code, as added by this section, in appointing the first National Taxpayer Advocate after the date of the enactment of this Act, the Secretary of the Treasury—

(A) shall not appoint any individual who was an officer or employee of the Internal Revenue Service at any time during the 2-year period ending on the date of appointment, and

(B) need not consult with the Internal Revenue Service Oversight Board if the Oversight Board has not been appointed.

(4) CURRENT OFFICERS.—

(A) In the case of an individual serving as Commissioner of Internal Revenue on the date of the enactment of this Act who was appointed to such position before such date, the 5-year term required by section 7803(a)(1) of such Code, as added by this section, shall begin as of the date of such appointment.

(B) Clauses (ii), (iii), and (iv) of section 7803(c)(1)(B) of such Code, as added by this section, shall not apply to the individual serving as Taxpayer Advocate on the date of the enactment of this Act.

[¶ 6870] CODE SEC. 7804. *OTHER PERSONNEL.*

(a) APPOINTMENT AND SUPERVISION.—Unless otherwise prescribed by the Secretary, the Commissioner of Internal Revenue is authorized to employ such number of persons as the Commissioner deems proper for the administration and enforcement of the internal revenue laws, and the Commissioner shall issue all necessary directions, instructions, orders, and rules applicable to such persons.

(b) POSTS OF DUTY OF EMPLOYEES IN FIELD SERVICE OR TRAVELING.—Unless otherwise prescribed by the Secretary—

(1) DESIGNATION OF POST OF DUTY.—The Commissioner shall determine and designate the posts of duty of all such persons engaged in field work or traveling on official business outside of the District of Columbia.

(2) DETAIL OF PERSONNEL FROM FIELD SERVICE.—The Commissioner may order any such person engaged in field work to duty in the District of Columbia, for such periods as the Commissioner may prescribe, and to any designated post of duty outside the District of Columbia upon the completion of such duty.

(c) DELINQUENT INTERNAL REVENUE OFFICERS AND EMPLOYEES.—If any officer or employee of the Treasury Department acting in connection with the internal revenue laws fails to account for and pay over any amount of money or property collected or received by him in connection with the internal revenue laws, the Secretary shall issue notice and demand to such officer or employee for payment of the amount which he failed to account for and pay over, and, upon failure to pay the amount demanded within the time specified in such notice, the amount so demanded shall be deemed imposed upon such officer or employee and assessed upon the date of such notice and demand, and the provisions of chapter 64 and all other provisions of law relating to the collection of assessed taxes shall be applicable in respect of such amount.

[CCH Explanation at ¶ 817. Committee Reports at ¶ 10,165.]

Amendment Notes

Act Sec. 1104(a) amended Code Sec. 7804 to read as above. Prior to amendment, Code Sec. 7804 read as follows:

SEC. 7804. EFFECT OF REORGANIZATION PLANS.

(a) APPLICATION.—The provisions of Reorganization Plan Numbered 26 of 1950 and Reorganization Plan Numbered 1 of 1952 shall be applicable to all functions vested by this title, or by any act amending this title (except as otherwise expressly provided in such amending act), in any officer, employee, or agency, of the Department of the Treasury.

(b) PRESERVATION OF EXISTING RIGHTS AND REMEDIES.—Nothing in Reorganization Plan Numbered 26 of 1950 or Reorganization Plan Numbered 1 of 1952 shall be considered to impair any right or remedy, including trial by jury, to recover any internal revenue tax alleged to have been erroneously or illegally assessed or collected, or any penalty claimed to have been collected without authority, or any sum alleged to have been excessive or in any manner wrongfully collected under the internal revenue laws. For the purpose of any action to recover any such tax, penalty, or sum, all statutes, rules, and regulations referring to the collector of internal revenue, the principal officer for the internal revenue district, or the Secretary, shall be deemed to refer to the officer whose act or acts referred to in the preceding sentence gave rise to such action. The venue of any such action shall be the same as under existing law.

The above amendment is effective on the date of the enactment of this Act.

[¶ 6880] CODE SEC. 7805. RULES AND REGULATIONS.

* * *

(d) MANNER OF MAKING ELECTIONS PRESCRIBED BY SECRETARY.—Except to the extent otherwise provided by this title, any election under this title shall be made at such time and in such manner as the Secretary shall prescribe.

* * *

[CCH Explanation at ¶ 895. Committee Reports at ¶ 10,650.]

Amendment Notes

Act Sec. 3704 amended Code Sec. 7805(d) by striking "by regulations or forms" after "Secretary shall".

The above amendment is effective on the date of the enactment of this Act.

[¶ 6890] CODE SEC. 7811. TAXPAYER ASSISTANCE ORDERS.

(a) AUTHORITY TO ISSUE.—

(1) IN GENERAL.—*Upon application filed by a taxpayer with the Office of the Taxpayer Advocate (in such form, manner, and at such time as the Secretary shall by regulations prescribe), the National Taxpayer Advocate may issue a Taxpayer Assistance Order if—*

(A) *the National Taxpayer Advocate determines the taxpayer is suffering or about to suffer a significant hardship as a result of the manner in which the internal revenue laws are being administered by the Secretary, or*

(B) *the taxpayer meets such other requirements as are set forth in regulations prescribed by the Secretary.*

(2) DETERMINATION OF HARDSHIP.—*For purposes of paragraph (1), a significant hardship shall include—*

(A) *an immediate threat of adverse action,*

(B) *a delay of more than 30 days in resolving taxpayer account problems,*

(C) *the incurring by the taxpayer of significant costs (including fees for professional representation) if relief is not granted, or*

(D) *irreparable injury to, or a long-term adverse impact on, the taxpayer if relief is not granted.*

(3) STANDARD WHERE ADMINISTRATIVE GUIDANCE NOT FOLLOWED.—*In cases where any Internal Revenue Service employee is not following applicable published administrative guidance (including the Internal Revenue Manual), the National Taxpayer Advocate shall construe the factors taken into account in determining whether to issue a taxpayer assistance order in the manner most favorable to the taxpayer.*

[CCH Explanation at ¶ 1106. Committee Reports at ¶ 10,150.]

Amendment Notes

Act Sec. 1102(c) amended Code Sec. 7811(a) to read as above. Prior to amendment, Code Sec. 7811(a) read as follows:

(a) AUTHORITY TO ISSUE.—Upon application filed by a taxpayer with the Office of the Taxpayer Advocate (in such form, manner, and at such time as the Secretary shall by regulations prescribe), the Taxpayer Advocate may issue a Taxpayer Assistance Order if, in the determination of the Taxpayer Advocate, the taxpayer is suffering or about to suffer a significant hardship as a result of the manner in which the internal revenue laws are being administered by the Secretary.

The above amendment is effective on the date of the enactment of this Act.

(b) TERMS OF A TAXPAYER ASSISTANCE ORDER.—The terms of a Taxpayer Assistance Order may require the Secretary within a specified time period—

(1) to release property of the taxpayer levied upon, or

(2) to cease any action, take any action as permitted by law, or refrain from taking any action, with respect to the taxpayer under—

(A) chapter 64 (relating to collection),

(B) subchapter B of chapter 70 (relating to bankruptcy and receiverships),

(C) chapter 78 (relating to discovery of liability and enforcement of title), or

(D) any other provision of law which is specifically described by the *National Taxpayer Advocate* in such order.

[CCH Explanation at ¶ 821. Committee Reports at ¶ 10,150.]

Amendment Notes

Act Sec. 1102(d)(1)(C) amended Code Sec. 7811(b)(2)(D) by striking "Taxpayer Advocate" and inserting "National Taxpayer Advocate".

The above amendment is effective on the date of the enactment of this Act.

(c) AUTHORITY TO MODIFY OR RESCIND.—Any Taxpayer Assistance Order issued by the *National Taxpayer Advocate* under this section may be modified or rescinded—

(1) only by the *National Taxpayer Advocate*, the Commissioner of Internal Revenue, or the Deputy Commissioner of Internal Revenue, and

(2) only if a written explanation of the reasons for the modification or rescission is provided to the *National Taxpayer Advocate*.

[CCH Explanation at ¶ 821. Committee Reports at ¶ 10,150.]

Amendment Notes
Act Sec. 1102(d)(1)(D) amended Code Sec. 7811(c) by striking "Taxpayer Advocate" each place it appears and inserting "National Taxpayer Advocate".

The above amendment is effective on the date of the enactment of this Act.

(d) SUSPENSION OF RUNNING OF PERIOD OF LIMITATION.—The running of any period of limitation with respect to any action described in subsection (b) shall be suspended for—

(1) the period beginning on the date of the taxpayer's application under subsection (a) and ending on the date of the *National Taxpayer Advocate's* decision with respect to such application, and

(2) any period specified by the *National Taxpayer Advocate* in a Taxpayer Assistance Order issued pursuant to such application.

[CCH Explanation at ¶ 821. Committee Reports at ¶ 10,150.]

Amendment Notes
Act Sec. 1102(d)(1)(E) amended Code Sec. 7811(d)(2) by striking "Taxpayer Advocate" and inserting "National Taxpayer Advocate".
Act Sec. 1102(d)(2) amended Code Sec. 7811(d)(1) by striking "Taxpayer Advocate's" and inserting "National Taxpayer Advocate's".

The above amendments are effective on the date of the enactment of this Act.

(e) INDEPENDENT ACTION OF *NATIONAL TAXPAYER ADVOCATE*.—Nothing in this section shall prevent the *National Taxpayer Advocate* from taking any action in the absence of an application under subsection (a).

[CCH Explanation at ¶ 821. Committee Reports at ¶ 10,150.]

Amendment Notes
Act Sec. 1102(d)(1)(F) amended Code Sec. 7811(e) by striking "Taxpayer Advocate" and inserting "National Taxpayer Advocate".
Act Sec. 1102(d)(3) amended the heading of subsection (e) of Code Sec. 7811 by striking "TAXPAYER ADVOCATE" and inserting "NATIONAL TAXPAYER ADVOCATE".

The above amendments are effective on the date of the enactment of this Act

(f) *NATIONAL TAXPAYER ADVOCATE*.—For purposes of this section, the term *"National Taxpayer Advocate"* includes any designee of the *National Taxpayer Advocate*.

[CCH Explanation at ¶ 821. Committee Reports at ¶ 10,150.]

Amendment Notes
Act Sec. 1102(d)(1)(G) amended Code Sec. 7811(f) by striking "Taxpayer Advocate" and inserting "National Taxpayer Advocate".
Act Sec. 1102(d)(3) amended the heading of subsection (f) of Code Sec. 7811 by striking "TAXPAYER ADVOCATE" and inserting "NATIONAL TAXPAYER ADVOCATE".

The above amendments are effective on the date of the enactment of this Act.

[¶ 6900] CODE SEC. 7872. TREATMENT OF LOANS WITH BELOW-MARKET INTEREST RATES.

* * *

(f) OTHER DEFINITIONS AND SPECIAL RULES.—For purposes of this section—

* * *

(2) APPLICABLE FEDERAL RATE.—

* * *

(B) DEMAND LOANS.—In the case of a demand loan, the applicable Federal rate shall be the Federal short-term rate in effect under section 1274(d) for the period for which the amount of *forgone* interest is being determined, compounded semiannually.

* * *

[CCH Explanation at ¶ 30,050.]

Amendment Notes
Act Sec. 6023(30) amended Code Sec. 7872(f)(2)(B) by striking "foregone" and inserting "forgone".

The above amendment is effective on the date of the enactment of this Act.

¶ 6900   Code Sec. 7872(f)

[¶ 6910] CODE SEC. 8021. POWERS.

* * *

(e) INVESTIGATIONS.—The Joint Committee shall review all requests (other than requests by the chairman or ranking member of a Committee or Subcommittee) for investigations of the Internal Revenue Service by the General Accounting Office, and approve such requests when appropriate, with a view towards eliminating overlapping investigations, ensuring that the General Accounting Office has the capacity to handle the investigation, and ensuring that investigations focus on areas of primary importance to tax administration.

[CCH Explanation at ¶ 866.]

Amendment Notes

Act Sec. 4001(a) amended Code Sec. 8021 by adding at the end a new subsection (e) to read as above.

The above amendment applies to requests made after the date of the enactment of this Act.

(f) RELATING TO JOINT REVIEWS.—

(1) IN GENERAL.—The Chief of Staff, and the staff of the Joint Committee, shall provide such assistance as is required for joint reviews described in paragraph (2).

(2) JOINT REVIEWS.—Before June 1 of each calendar year after 1998 and before 2004, there shall be a joint review of the strategic plans and budget for the Internal Revenue Service and such other matters as the Chairman of the Joint Committee deems appropriate. Such joint review shall be held at the call of the Chairman of the Joint Committee and shall include two members of the majority and one member of the minority from each of the Committees on Finance, Appropriations, and Governmental Affairs of the Senate, and the Committees on Ways and Means, Appropriations, and Government Reform and Oversight of the House of Representatives.

[CCH Explanation at ¶ 871.]

Amendment Notes

Act Sec. 4001(a) amended Code Sec. 8021 by adding at the end a new subsection (f) to read as above

The above amendment is effective on the date of the enactment of this Act

[¶ 6920] CODE SEC. 8022. DUTIES.

It shall be the duty of the Joint Committee—

* * *

(3) REPORTS.—

(A) To report, from time to time, to the Committee on Finance and the Committee on Ways and Means, and, in its discretion, to the Senate or House of Representatives, or both, the results of its investigations, together with such recommendations as it may deem advisable.

(B) Subject to amounts specifically appropriated to carry out this subparagraph, to report, at least once each Congress, to the Committee on Finance and the Committee on Ways and Means on the overall state of the Federal tax system, together with recommendations with respect to possible simplification proposals and other matters relating to the administration of the Federal tax system as it may deem advisable.

(C) To report, for each calendar year after 1998 and before 2004, to the Committees on Finance, Appropriations, and Governmental Affairs of the Senate, and to the Committees on Ways and Means, Appropriations, and Government Reform and Oversight of the House of Representatives, with respect to—

(i) strategic and business plans for the Internal Revenue Service;

(ii) progress of the Internal Revenue Service in meeting its objectives,

(iii) the budget for the Internal Revenue Service and whether it supports its objectives,

(iv) progress of the Internal Revenue Service in improving taxpayer service and compliance;

(v) progress of the Internal Revenue Service on technology modernization; and

(vi) the annual filing season.

* * *

[CCH Explanation at ¶ 873. Committee Reports at ¶ 10,750.]

Amendment Notes

Act Sec. 4002(a) amended Code Sec. 8022(3) to read as above. Prior to amendment, Code Sec. 8022(3) read as follows:

(3) REPORTS.—To report, from time to time, to the Committee on Finance and the Committee on Ways and Means,

and, in its discretion, to the Senate or the House of Representatives, or both, the results of its investigations, together with such recommendations as it may deem advisable.

The above amendment is effective on the date of the enactment of this Act.

[¶ 6930] CODE SEC. 9502. AIRPORT AND AIRWAY TRUST FUND.

* * *

(b) TRANSFERS TO AIRPORT AND AIRWAY TRUST FUND.—There are hereby appropriated to the Airport and Airway Trust Fund amounts equivalent to—

(1) the taxes received in the Treasury under—

(A) subsections (c) and (e) of section 4041 (relating to aviation fuels),

(B) sections 4261 and 4271 (relating to transportation by air),

(C) section 4081 (relating to gasoline) with respect to aviation gasoline, and

(D) section 4091 (relating to aviation fuel), and

(2) the amounts determined by the Secretary of the Treasury to be equivalent to the amounts of civil penalties collected under section 47107(n) of title 49, United States Code.

There shall not be taken into account under paragraph (1) so much of the taxes imposed by sections 4081 and 4091 as are determined at the rates specified in section 4081(a)(2)(B) or 4091(b)(2).

* * *

[CCH Explanation at ¶ 701. Committee Reports at ¶ 11,175.]

Amendment Notes

Act Sec. 6010(g)(2) amended Code Sec. 9502(b) by moving the sentence added by Act Sec. 1031(d)(1)(C) of the Taxpayer Relief Act of 1997 (P.L. 105-34) at the end of paragraph (1) to the end of the subsection.

The above amendment is effective as if included in the provision of the Taxpayer Relief Act of 1997 (P.L. 105-34) to which it relates [effective for taxes received on and after October 1, 1997.—CCH.].

(e) CERTAIN TAXES ON ALCOHOL MIXTURES TO REMAIN IN GENERAL FUND.—For purposes of this section, the amounts which would (but for this subsection) be required to be appropriated under subparagraphs (A), (C), and (D) of subsection (b)(1) shall be reduced by—

(1) 0.6 cent per gallon in the case of taxes imposed on any mixture at least 10 percent of which is alcohol (as defined in section 4081(c)(3)) if any portion of such alcohol is ethanol, and

(2) 0.67 cent per gallon in the case of fuel used in producing a mixture described in paragraph (1).

[CCH Explanation at ¶ 30,050.]

Amendment Notes

Act Sec. 6023(31) amended Code Sec. 9502(e) to read as above. Prior to amendment, Code Sec. 9502(e) read as follows:

(e) SPECIAL RULES FOR TRANSFERS INTO TRUST FUND.—

(1) INCREASES IN TAX REVENUES BEFORE 1993 TO REMAIN IN GENERAL FUND.—In the case of taxes imposed before January 1, 1993, the amounts required to be appropriated under paragraphs (1), (2), and (3) of subsection (b) shall be determined without regard to any increase in a rate of tax enacted by the Revenue Reconciliation Act of 1990.

(2) CERTAIN TAXES ON ALCOHOL MIXTURES TO REMAIN IN GENERAL FUND.—For purposes of this section, the amounts

which would (but for this paragraph) be required to be appropriated under paragraphs (1), (2), and (3) of subsection (b) shall be reduced by—

(A) 0.6 cent per gallon in the case of taxes imposed on any mixture at least 10 percent of which is alcohol (as defined in section 4081(c)(3)) if any portion of such alcohol is ethanol, and

(B) 0.67 cent per gallon in the case of fuel used in producing a mixture described in subparagraph (A).

The above amendment is effective on the date of the enactment of this Act.

[¶ 6940] CODE SEC. 9503. HIGHWAY TRUST FUND.

* * *

(b) TRANSFER TO HIGHWAY TRUST FUND OF AMOUNTS EQUIVALENT TO CERTAIN TAXES.—

(1) IN GENERAL.—There are hereby appropriated to the Highway Trust Fund amounts equivalent to the taxes received in the Treasury before October 1, *2005*, under the following provisions—

(A) section 4041 (relating to taxes on diesel fuels and special motor fuels),

(B) section 4051 (relating to retail tax on heavy trucks and trailers),

(C) section 4071 (relating to tax on tires),

(D) section 4081 (relating to tax on gasoline, diesel fuel, and kerosene), and

(E) section 4481 (relating to tax on use of certain vehicles).

(2) LIABILITIES INCURRED BEFORE OCTOBER 1, *2005*.—There are hereby appropriated to the Highway Trust Fund amounts equivalent to the taxes which are received in the Treasury after September 30, *2005*, and before July 1, *2006*, and which are attributable to liability for tax incurred before October 1, *2005*, under the provisions described in paragraph (1).

* * *

(4) CERTAIN TAXES NOT TRANSFERRED TO HIGHWAY TRUST FUND.—For purposes of paragraphs (1) and (2), there shall not be taken into account the taxes imposed by—

(A) section 4041(d),

(B) section 4081 to the extent attributable to the rate specified in section 4081(a)(2)(B),

(C) section 4041 or 4081 to the extent attributable to fuel used in a train,

(D) in the case of gasoline and special motor fuels used as described in paragraph (4)(D) or (5)(B) of subsection (c), section 4041 or 4081 with respect to so much of the rate of tax as exceeds—

(i) 11.5 cents per gallon with respect to taxes imposed before October 1, 2001,

(ii) 13 cents per gallon with respect to taxes imposed after September 30, 2001, and before October 1, 2003, and

(iii) 13.5 cents per gallon with respect to taxes imposed after September 30, 2003, and before October 1, 2005,

(E) in the case of fuels described in section 4041(b)(2)(A), 4041(k), or 4081(c), section 4041 or 4081 before October 1, *2005*, with respect to a rate equal to 2.5 cents per gallon, or

(F) in the case of fuels described in section 4081(c)(2), such section before October 1, *2005*, with respect to a rate equal to 2.8 cents per gallon.

* * *

(6) LIMITATION ON TRANSFERS TO HIGHWAY TRUST FUND.—

(A) IN GENERAL.—Except as provided in subparagraph (B), no amount may be appropriated to the Highway Trust Fund on and after the date of any expenditure from the Highway Trust Fund which is not permitted by this section. The determination of whether an expenditure is so permitted shall be made without regard to—

(i) any provision of law which is not contained or referenced in this title or in a revenue Act, and

(ii) whether such provision of law is a subsequently enacted provision or directly or indirectly seeks to waive the application of this paragraph.

(B) EXCEPTION FOR PRIOR OBLIGATIONS.—Subparagraph (A) shall not apply to any expenditure to liquidate any contract entered into (or for any amount otherwise obligated) before October 1, 2003, in accordance with the provisions of this section.

[CCH Explanation at ¶ 750, 751, 752, 753 and 5185. Committee Reports at ¶ 15,025, 15,075 and 15,145.]

Amendment Notes

P.L. 105-178 (ISTEA)

Act Sec. 9002(c)(1)(A)-(B) amended Code Sec. 9503(b) by striking "1999" each place it appears and inserting "2005", and by striking "2000" each place it appears and inserting "2006".

Act Sec. 9002(f)(1) amended Code Sec. 9503(b)(1) by striking subparagraph (C), by striking "and tread rubber" following "tires" in subparagraph (D), and by redesignating subparagraphs (D), (E), and (F) as subparagraphs (C), (D), and (E), respectively. Prior to being stricken, Code Sec. 9503(b)(1)(C) read as follows:

(C) section 4061 (relating to tax on trucks and truck parts),

Act Sec. 9004(c) amended Code Sec. 9503(b) by adding at the end a new paragraph (6) to read as above.

Act Sec. 9005(a)(1) amended Code Sec. 9503(b)(4)(D), as amended by Act Sec. 9011(b)(2), by striking "exceeds 11.5 cents per gallon," and inserting new material following "rate of tax as" to read as above.

Act Sec. 9011(b)(2) amended Code Sec. 9503(b)(4)(D) to read as above. Prior to amendment, Code Sec. 9503(b)(4)(D) read as follows:

(D) in the case of fuels used as described in paragraph (4)(D), (5)(B), or (6)(D) of subsection (c), section 4041 or 4081—

(i) with respect to so much of the rate of tax on gasoline or special motor fuels as exceeds 11.5 cents per gallon, and

(ii) with respect to so much of the rate of tax on diesel fuel or kerosene as exceeds 17.5 cents per gallon,

The above amendments are effective on June 9, 1998.

(c) EXPENDITURES FROM HIGHWAY TRUST FUND.—

(1) FEDERAL-AID HIGHWAY PROGRAM.—Except as provided in subsection (e), amounts in the Highway Trust Fund shall be available, as provided by appropriation Acts, for making expenditures before October 1, *2003*, to meet those obligations of the United States heretofore or hereafter incurred which are—

(A) authorized by law to be paid out of the Highway Trust Fund established by section 209 of the Highway Revenue Act of 1956,

(B) authorized to be paid out of the Highway Trust Fund under title I or II of the Surface Transportation Assistance Act of 1982,

(C) authorized to be paid out of the Highway Trust Fund under the Surface Transportation and Uniform Relocation Assistance Act of 1987,

(D) authorized to be paid out of the Highway Trust Fund under the Intermodal Surface Transportation Efficiency Act of *1991, or*

(E) authorized to be paid out of the Highway Trust Fund under the Transportation Equity Act for the 21st Century.

In determining the authorizations under the Acts referred to in the preceding subparagraphs, such Acts shall be applied as in effect on the date of the enactment of the TEA 21 Restoration Act.

(2) TRANSFERS FROM HIGHWAY TRUST FUND FOR CERTAIN REPAYMENTS AND CREDITS.—

(A) IN GENERAL.—The Secretary shall pay from time to time from the Highway Trust Fund into the general fund of the Treasury amounts equivalent to—

(i) the amounts paid before July 1, *2006*, under—

(I) section 6420 (relating to amounts paid in respect of gasoline used on farms),

(II) section 6421 (relating to amounts paid in respect of gasoline used for certain nonhighway purposes or by local transit systems), *and*

(III) section 6427 (relating to fuels not used for taxable purposes), on the basis of claims filed for periods ending before October 1, *2005*, and

(ii) the credits allowed under section 34 (relating to credit for certain uses of *fuel)* with respect to *fuel* used before October 1, *2005*.

The amounts payable from the Highway Trust Fund under this subparagraph or paragraph (3) shall be determined by taking into account only the portion of the taxes which are deposited into the Highway Trust Fund.

* * *

(3) *FLOOR STOCKS REFUNDS.*—The Secretary shall pay from time to time from the Highway Trust Fund into the general fund of the Treasury amounts equivalent to the floor stocks refunds made before July 1, *2006*, under section 6412(a).

(4) TRANSFERS FROM THE TRUST FUND FOR MOTORBOAT FUEL TAXES.—

(A) TRANSFER TO BOAT SAFETY ACCOUNT.—

(i) IN GENERAL.—The Secretary shall pay from time to time from the Highway Trust Fund into the Boat Safety Account in the Aquatic Resources Trust Fund amounts (as determined by him) equivalent to the motorboat fuel taxes received on or after October 1, 1980, and before October 1, *2005*.

(ii) LIMITATIONS.—

(I) LIMIT ON TRANSFERS DURING ANY FISCAL YEAR.—The aggregate amount transferred under this subparagraph during any fiscal year shall not exceed $60,000,000 for each of fiscal years 1989 and 1990 and $70,000,000 for each fiscal year thereafter.

(II) LIMIT ON AMOUNT IN FUND.—No amount shall be transferred under this subparagraph if the Secretary determines that such transfer would result in increasing the amount in the Boat Safety Account to a sum in excess of $60,000,000 for Fiscal Year 1987 only and $45,000,000 for each fiscal year thereafter.

In making the determination under subclause (II) for any fiscal year, the Secretary shall not take into account any amount appropriated from the Boat Safety Account in any preceding fiscal year but not distributed.

* * *

(5) TRANSFERS FROM THE TRUST FUND FOR SMALL-ENGINE FUEL TAXES.—

(A) IN GENERAL.—The Secretary shall pay from time to time from the Highway Trust Fund into the Sport Fish Restoration Account in the Aquatic Resources Trust Fund amounts (as determined by him) equivalent to the small-engine fuel taxes received on or after December 1, 1990, and before October 1, *2005*.

(6) *[Stricken.]*

(7) *[Stricken.]*

* * *

[CCH Explanation at ¶ 750, 751, 752 and 753. Committee Reports at ¶ 11,560, 15,025, 15,055, 15,075 and 15,145.]

Amendment Notes

Act Sec. 9015(a) amended Act Sec. 9002(f) of the Transportation Equity Act for the 21st Century (P.L. 105-178) by adding at the end of such Act section a new paragraph (4). The effect of this amendment is to strike "the date of enactment of the Transportation Equity Act for the 21st Century" and insert "the date of the enactment of the TEA 21 Restoration Act" in the last sentence of Code Sec. 9503(c)(1), as amended by Act Sec. 9002(d)(1) of the Transportation Equity Act of the 21st Century (P.L. 105-178).

For the effective date of the above amendment, see Act Sec. 9016, below.

Act Sec. 9016 provides:

SEC. 9016. EFFECTIVE DATE.

This title and the amendments made by this title shall take effect simultaneously with the enactment of the Transportation Equity Act for the 21st Century. For purposes of all Federal laws, the amendments made by this title shall be treated as being included in the Transportation Equity Act for the 21st Century at the time of the enactment of such Act, and the provisions of such Act (including the amendments made by such Act) (as is effect on the day before the date of enactment of this Act) that are amended by this title shall be treated as not being enacted.

P.L. 105-178 (ISTEA)

Act Sec. 9002(c)(1)(A)-(B) amended Code Sec. 9503(c)(2)-(3) by striking "1999" each place it appears and inserting "2005", and by striking "2000" each place it appears and inserting "2006".

Act Sec. 9002(c)(2)(A) amended Code Sec. 9503(c)(4)(A)(i) and (5)(A) by striking "1998" and inserting "2005".

Act Sec. 9002(c)(3) amended the heading for Code Sec. 9503(c)(3) to read as above. Prior to amendment, the heading read as follows:

(3) 1988 FLOOR STOCKS REFUNDS.—.

Act Sec. 9002(d)(1)(A) amended Code Sec. 9503(c)(1) by striking "1998" and inserting "2003".

Act Sec. 9002(d)(1)(B)(i)-(ii) amended Code Sec. 9503(c)(1) by striking "or" at the end of subparagraph (C), by striking "1991." in subparagraph (D) and all that follows through the end of paragraph (1) and inserting "1991, or", and by adding a new subparagraph (E) and flush sentence to read as above. Prior to amendment, the flush sentence at the end of Code Sec. 9503(c)(1) read as follows:

In determining the authorizations under the Acts referred to in the preceding subparagraphs, such Acts shall be applied as in effect on the date of the enactment of this sentence.

Act Sec. 9002(f)(2) amended Code Sec. 9503(c)(2)(A)(i) by adding "and" at the end of subclause (II), by striking subclause (III), and by redesignating subclause (IV) as subclause (III). Prior to amendment, Code Sec 9503(c)(2)(A)(i)(III) read as follows:

(III) section 6424 (relating to amounts paid in respect of lubricating oil used for certain nontaxable purposes), and

Act Sec. 9002(f)(3) amended Code Sec. 9503(c)(2)(A)(ii) by striking "gasoline, special fuels, and lubricating oil" each place it appears and inserting "fuel".

The above amendments are effective on June 9, 1998.

Act Sec. 9004(b)(1) amended Code Sec. 9503(c) by striking paragraph (7). Prior to being stricken, paragraph (7) read as follows:

(7) LIMITATION ON EXPENDITURES.—Notwithstanding any other provision of law, in calculating amounts under section 157(a) of title 23, United States Code, and sections 1013(c), 1015(a), and 1015(b) of the Intermodal Surface Transportation Efficiency Act of 1991 (Public Law 102-240; 105 Stat. 1914), deposits in the Highway Trust Fund resulting from the amendments made by the Taxpayer Relief Act of 1997 shall not be taken into account.

¶ 6940   Code Sec. 9503(c)

The above amendment is effective as if included in the amendments made by section 901 of the Taxpayer Relief Act of 1997 (P.L. 105-34) [applicable to taxes received in the Treasury after September 30, 1997.—CCH.].

Act Sec. 9005(a)(2) amended Code Sec. 9503(c)(4)(A)(ii) by adding at the end a new flush sentence to read as above.

Act Sec. 9011(b)(1) amended Code Sec. 9503(c) by striking paragraph (6). Prior to being stricken, Code Sec. 9503(c)(6) read as follows:

(6) TRANSFERS FROM TRUST FUND OF CERTAIN RECREATIONAL FUEL TAXES, ETC.—

(A) IN GENERAL.—The Secretary shall pay from time to time from the Highway Trust Fund into the National Recreational Trails Trust Fund amounts (as determined by him) equivalent to 0.3 percent (as adjusted under subparagraph (C)) of the total Highway Trust Fund receipts for the period for which the payment is made.

(B) LIMITATION.—The amount paid into the National Recreational Trails Trust Fund under this paragraph during any fiscal year shall not exceed the amount obligated under section 1302 of the Intermodal Surface Transportation Efficiency Act of 1991 (as in effect on the date of the enactment of this paragraph) for such fiscal year to be expended from such Trust Fund.

(C) ADJUSTMENT OF PERCENTAGE.—

(i) FIRST YEAR.—Within 1 year after the date of the enactment of this paragraph, the Secretary shall adjust the percentage contained in subparagraph (A) so that it corresponds to the revenues received by the Highway Trust Fund from nonhighway recreational fuel taxes.

(ii) SUBSEQUENT YEARS.—Not more frequently than once every 3 years, the Secretary may increase or decrease the percentage established under clause (i) to reflect, in the Secretary's estimation, changes in the amount of revenues received in the Highway Trust Fund from nonhighway recreational fuel taxes.

(iii) AMOUNT OF ADJUSTMENT.—Any adjustment under clause (ii) shall be not more than 10 percent of the percentage in effect at the time the adjustment is made.

(iv) USE OF DATA.—In making the adjustments under clauses (i) and (ii), the Secretary shall take into account data on off-highway recreational vehicle registrations and use.

(D) NONHIGHWAY RECREATIONAL FUEL TAXES.—For purposes of this paragraph, the term "nonhighway recreational fuel taxes" means taxes under section 4041 and 4081 (to the extent deposited into the Highway Trust Fund) with respect to—

(i) fuel used in vehicles on recreational trails or back country terrain (including vehicles registered for highway use when used on recreational trails, trail access roads not eligible for funding under title 23, United States Code, or back country terrain), and

(ii) fuel used in campstoves and other non-engine uses in outdoor recreational equipment.

Such term shall not include small-engine fuel taxes (as defined by paragraph (5)) and taxes which are credited or refunded.

(E) TERMINATION.—No amount shall be paid under this paragraph after September 30, 1998.

The above amendments are effective on June 9, 1998.

(e) ESTABLISHMENT OF MASS TRANSIT ACCOUNT.—

* * *

(2) TRANSFERS TO MASS TRANSIT ACCOUNT.—The Secretary of the Treasury shall transfer to the Mass Transit Account the mass transit portion of the amounts appropriated to the Highway Trust Fund under subsection (b) which are attributable to taxes under sections 4041 and 4081 imposed after March 31, 1983. *For purposes of the preceding sentence, the term "mass transit portion" means, for any fuel with respect to which tax was imposed under section 4041 or 4081 and otherwise deposited into the Highway Trust Fund, the amount determined at the rate of—*

(A) except as otherwise provided in this sentence, 2.86 cents per gallon,

(B) 1.43 cents per gallon in the case of any partially exempt methanol or ethanol fuel (as defined in section 4041(m)) none of the alcohol in which consists of ethanol,

(C) 1.86 cents per gallon in the case of liquefied natural gas,

(D) 2.13 cents per gallon in the case of liquefied petroleum gas, and

(E) 9.71 cents per MCF (determined at standard temperature and pressure) in the case of compressed natural gas.

[Caution: Code Sec. 9503(e)(3), below, as amended by P.L. 105-130, is effective on October 1, 1997. However, this amendment cannot be reconciled with the amendment made to Code Sec. 9503(e)(3) by Act Sec. 1 of P.L. 105-102.—CCH.]

(3) EXPENDITURES FROM ACCOUNT.—Amounts in the Mass Transit Account shall be available, as provided by appropriation Acts, for making capital or capital-related expenditures before October 1, 2003 (including capital expenditures for new projects) in accordance with—

(A) section 5338(a)(1) or (b)(1) of title 49,

(B) the Intermodal Surface Transportation Efficiency Act of 1991, *or*

(C) *the Transportation Equity Act for the 21st Century,*

as such section and Acts are in effect on the date of the enactment of the TEA 21 Restoration Act.

(4) LIMITATION.—*Rules similar to the rules of subsection (d) shall apply to the Mass Transit Account.*

* * *

[CCH Explanation at ¶ 750 and 751. Committee Reports at ¶ 11,560, 15,025 and 15,055.]

Amendment Notes

Act Sec. 9015(a) amended Act Sec. 9002(f) of the Transportation Equity Act for the 21st Century (P.L. 105-178) by adding at the end a new paragraph (5). The effect of this amendment is to strike "the date of enactment of the Transportation Equity Act for the 21st Century" and insert "the date of the enactment of the TEA 21 Restoration Act" in Code Sec. 9503(e)(3), as amended by Act Sec. 9002(d)(2) of the Transportation Equity Act for the 21st Century (P.L. 105-178).

For the effective date of the above amendment, see Act Sec. 9016, below.

Act Sec. 9016. provides:

SEC. 9016. EFFECTIVE DATE.

This title and the amendments made by this title shall take effect simultaneously with the enactment of the Transportation Equity Act for the 21st Century. For purposes of all Federal laws, the amendments made by this title shall be treated as being included in the Transportation Equity Act for the 21st Century at the time of the enactment of such Act, and the provisions of such Act (including the amendments made by such Act) (as is effect on the day before the date of enactment of this Act) that are amended by this title shall be treated as not being enacted.

P.L. 105-178 (ISTEA)

Act Sec. 9002(d)(2)(A) amended Code Sec. 9503(e)(3) by striking "1998" and inserting "2003".

Act Sec. 9002(d)(2)(B)(i)-(iii) amended Code Sec. 9503(e)(3) by striking "or" at the end of subparagraph (A), by adding "or" at the end of subparagraph (B), and by striking all that follows subparagraph (B) and inserting a new subparagraph (C) and flush text to read as above. Prior to amendment, all that followed subparagraph (B) read as follows:

as section 5338(a)(1) or (b)(1) and the Intermodal Surface Transportation Efficiency Act of 1991 were in effect on December 18, 1991.

The above amendments are effective on June 9, 1998.

Act Sec. 9002(e)(1) amended Code Sec. 9503(e)(2) by striking the last sentence and inserting new material to read

as above. Prior to amendment, the last sentence read as follows:

For purposes of the preceding sentence, the term "mass transit portion" means an amount determined at the rate of 2.85 cents for each gallon with respect to which tax was imposed under section 4041 or 4081.

The above amendment is effective as if included in the amendment made by section 901(b) of the Taxpayer Relief Act of 1997 (P.L. 105-34) [applicable to taxes received in the Treasury after September 30, 1997.— CCH.].

Act Sec. 9004(d) amended Code Sec. 9503(e)(4) to read as above. Prior to amendment, Code Sec. 9503(e)(4) read as follows:

(4) LIMITATION.—Rules similar to the rules of subsection (d) shall apply to the Mass Transit Account except that subsection (d)(1) shall be applied by substituting "12-month" for "24-month".

The above amendment is effective on June 9, 1998.

(f) DETERMINATION OF TRUST FUND BALANCES AFTER SEPTEMBER 30, 1998.—For purposes of determining the balances of the Highway Trust Fund and the Mass Transit Account after September 30, 1998—

> *(1) the opening balance of the Highway Trust Fund (other than the Mass Transit Account) on October 1, 1998, shall be $8,000,000,000, and*

> *(2) no interest accruing after September 30, 1998, on any obligation held by such Fund shall be credited to such Fund.*

The Secretary shall cancel obligations held by the Highway Trust Fund to reflect the reduction in the balance under this subsection.

[CCH Explanation at ¶ 751. Committee Reports at ¶ 15,055.]

Amendment Notes

P.L. 105-178 (ISTEA)

Act Sec. 9004(a)(1) amended Code Sec. 9503 by adding at the end a new subsection (f) to read as above.

The above amendment is effective on October 1, 1998.

[¶ 6950] CODE SEC. 9504. AQUATIC RESOURCES TRUST FUND.

* * *

(b) SPORT FISH RESTORATION ACCOUNT.—

* * *

(2) EXPENDITURES FROM ACCOUNT.—Amounts in the Sport Fish Restoration Account shall be available, as provided by appropriation Acts, for making expenditures—

> (A) to carry out the purposes of the Act entitled "An Act to provide that the United States shall aid the States in fish restoration and management projects, and for other purposes", approved August 9, 1950 (as in effect on *the date of the enactment of the TEA 21 Restoration Act),*

> (B) to carry out the purposes of *section 7404(d) of the Transportation Equity Act for the 21st Century (as in effect on the date of the enactment of the TEA 21 Restoration Act), and*

> (C) to carry out the purposes of the Coastal Wetlands Planning Protection and Restoration Act (as in effect on *the date of the enactment of the TEA 21 Restoration Act).*

Amounts transferred to such account under section 9503(c)(5) may be used only for making expenditures described in subparagraph (B) of this paragraph.

[Committee Reports at ¶ 11,560.]

Amendment Notes

Act Sec. 9015(b) amended Act Sec. 9005 of the Transportation Equity Act for the 21st Century (P.L. 105-178) by adding at the end a new subsection (f). The effect of this amendment is to strike "the date of the enactment of the Transportation Equity Act for the 21st Century" and insert "the date of the enactment of the TEA 21 Restoration Act" in Code Sec. 9504(b)(2)(A), to strike "such Act" and insert "the TEA 21 Restoration Act" in Code Sec. 9504(b)(2)(B) and to strike "the date of the enactment of the Transportation Equity Act for the 21st Century" and insert "the date of the enactment of the TEA 21 Restoration Act" in Code Sec. 9504(b)(2)(C).

For the effective date of the above amendments, see Act Sec. 9016, below.

Act Sec. 9016 provides:

SEC. 9016. EFFECTIVE DATE.

This title and the amendments made by this title shall take effect simultaneously with the enactment of the Trans-

portation Equity Act for the 21st Century. For purposes of all Federal laws, the amendments made by this title shall be treated as being included in the Transportation Equity Act for the 21st Century at the time of the enactment of such Act, and the provisions of such Act (including the amendments made by such Act) (as is effect on the day before the date of enactment of this Act) that are amended by this title shall be treated as not being enacted.

P.L. 105-178 (ISTEA)

Act Sec. 9005(b)(1)-(3) amended Code Sec. 9504(b)(2) by striking "October 1, 1988), and" and inserting "the date of the enactment of the Transportation Equity Act for the 21st Century)," in subparagraph (A), by striking "November 29, 1990" and inserting "the date of the enactment of the Transportation Equity Act for the 21st Century" in subparagraph (B), and by redesignating subparagraph (B) as subparagraph (C) and by inserting after subparagraph (A) a new subparagraph (B) to read as above.

The above amendment is effective on June 9, 1998.

(c) EXPENDITURES FROM BOAT SAFETY ACCOUNT.—Amounts in the Boat Safety Account shall be available, as provided by appropriation Acts, for making expenditures before October 1, *2003,* to carry out the purposes of section 13106 of title 46, United States Code (as in effect on *the date of the enactment of the TEA 21 Restoration Act).*

[Committee Reports at ¶ 11,560.]

Amendment Notes

Act Sec. 9015(b) amended Act Sec. 9005 of the Transportation Equity Act for the 21st Century (P.L. 105-178) by adding at the end a new subsection (f). The effect of this amendment is to strike "the date of enactment of the Transportation Equity Act for the 21st Century" and insert "the date of the enactment of the TEA 21 Restoration Act" in Code Sec. 9504(c).

For the effective date of the above amendment, see Act Sec. 9016, below.

Act Sec. 9016 provides:

SEC. 9016. EFFECTIVE DATE.

This title and the amendments made by this title shall take effect simultaneously with the enactment of the Trans-

portation Equity Act for the 21st Century. For purposes of all Federal laws, the amendments made by this title shall be treated as being included in the Transportation Equity Act for the 21st Century at the time of the enactment of such Act, and the provisions of such Act (including the amendments made by such Act) (as is effect on the day before the date of enactment of this Act) that are amended by this title shall be treated as not being enacted.

P.L. 105-178 (ISTEA)

Act Sec. 9005(c)(1)-(2) amended Code Sec. 9504(c) by striking "1998" and inserting "2003", and by striking "October 1, 1988" and inserting "the date of the enactment of the Transportation Equity Act for the 21st Century".

The above amendment is effective on June 9, 1998.

(d) LIMITATION OF TRANSFERS TO AQUATIC RESOURCES TRUST FUND.—

(1) IN GENERAL.—Except as provided in paragraph (2), no amount may be appropriated or paid to any Account in the Aquatic Resources Trust Fund on and after the date of any expenditure from any such Account which is not permitted by this section. The determination of whether an expenditure is so permitted shall be made without regard to—

(A) any provision of law which is not contained or referenced in this title or in a revenue Act, and

(B) whether such provision of law is a subsequently enacted provision or directly or indirectly seeks to waive the application of this subsection.

(2) EXCEPTION FOR PRIOR OBLIGATIONS.—Paragraph (1) shall not apply to any expenditure to liquidate any contract entered into (or for any amount otherwise obligated) before October 1, 2003, in accordance with the provisions of this section.

[CCH Explanation at ¶ 752. Committee Reports at ¶ 15,075.]

Amendment Notes

P.L. 105-178 (ISTEA)

Act Sec. 9005(d) amended Code Sec. 9504 by redesignating subsection (d) as subsection (e) and by inserting after subsection (c) a new subsection (d) to read as above.

The above amendment is effective on June 9, 1998.

(e) CROSS REFERENCE.—

For provision transferring motorboat fuels taxes to Boat Safety Account and Sport Fish Restoration Account, see section 9503(c)(4).

Amendment Notes

[CCH Explanation at ¶ 752. Committee Reports at ¶ 15,075.]

Amendment Notes

P.L. 105-178 (ISTEA)

Act Sec. 9005(d) amended Code Sec. 9504 by redesignating subsection (d) as subsection (e).

The above amendment is effective on June 9, 1998.

[¶ 6955] CODE SEC. 9511. *[Repealed.]*
[CCH Explanation at ¶ 752. Committee Reports at ¶ 15,145.]

Amendment Notes

P.L. 105-178 (ISTEA)

Act Sec. 9011(a) repealed Code Sec. 9511. Prior to repeal, Code Sec. 9511 read as follows:

SEC. 9511. NATIONAL RECREATIONAL TRAILS TRUST FUND.

(a) CREATION OF TRUST FUND.—There is established in the Treasury of the United States a trust fund to be known as the "National Recreational Trails Trust Fund", consisting of such amounts as may be credited or paid to such Trust Fund as provided in this section, section 9503(c)(6), or section 9602(b).

(b) CREDITING OF CERTAIN UNEXPENDED FUNDS.—There shall be credited to the National Recreational Trails Trust Fund amounts returned to such Trust Fund under section 1302(e)(8) of the Intermodal Surface Transportation Efficiency Act of 1991.

(c) EXPENDITURES FROM TRUST FUND.—Amounts in the National Recreational Trails Trust Fund shall be available, as provided in appropriation Acts, for making expenditures before October 1, 1998, to carry out the purposes of sections 1302 and 1303 of the Intermodal Surface Transportation Efficiency Act of 1991, as in effect on the date of the enactment of such Act.

The above amendment is effective on June 9, 1998.

[¶ 6960] CODE SEC. 9811. STANDARDS RELATING TO BENEFITS FOR MOTHERS AND NEWBORNS.

* * *

(e) PREEMPTION; EXCEPTION FOR HEALTH INSURANCE COVERAGE IN CERTAIN STATES.—The requirements of this section shall not apply with respect to health insurance coverage if there is a State law (including a decision, rule, regulation, or other State action having the effect of law) for a State that regulates such coverage that is described in any of the following paragraphs:

(1) Such State law requires such coverage to provide for at least a 48-hour hospital length of stay following a normal vaginal delivery and at least a 96-hour hospital length of stay following a caesarean section.

(2) Such State law requires such coverage to provide for maternity and pediatric care in accordance with guidelines established by the American College of Obstetricians and Gynecologists, the American Academy of Pediatrics, or other established professional medical associations.

(3) Such State law requires, in connection with such coverage for maternity care, that the hospital length of stay for such care is left to the decision of (or required to be made by) the attending provider in consultation with the mother.

Amendment Notes

Act Sec. 6015(e) amended Code Sec. 9811 by redesignating subsection (f), as added by Act Sec. 1531 of the Taxpayer Relief Act of 1997 (P.L. 105-34), as subsection (e).

The above amendment is effective as if included in the provision of the Taxpayer Relief Act of 1997 (P.L. 105-34) to which it relates [effective for group health plans for plan years beginning on or after January 1, 1998.—CCH.].

ACT SECTIONS NOT AMENDING CODE SECTIONS
IRS RESTRUCTURING AND REFORM ACT OF 1998

[¶ 8001] ACT SEC. 1. SHORT TITLE; AMENDMENT OF 1986 CODE; WAIVER OF ESTIMATED TAX PENALTIES; TABLE OF CONTENTS.

(a) SHORT TITLE.—This Act may be cited as the "Internal Revenue Service Restructuring and Reform Act of 1998".

(b) AMENDMENT OF 1986 CODE.—Except as otherwise expressly provided, whenever in this Act an amendment or repeal is expressed in terms of an amendment to, or repeal of, a section or other provision, the reference shall be considered to be made to a section or other provision of the Internal Revenue Code of 1986.

(c) WAIVER OF ESTIMATED TAX PENALTIES.—No addition to tax shall be made under section 6654 or 6655 of the Internal Revenue Code of 1986 with respect to any underpayment of an installment required to be paid on or before the 30th day after the date of the enactment of this Act to the extent such underpayment was created or increased by any provision of this Act.

* * *

TITLE I—REORGANIZATION OF STRUCTURE AND MANAGEMENT OF THE INTERNAL REVENUE SERVICE

Subtitle A—Reorganization of the Internal Revenue Service

[¶ 8005] ACT SEC. 1001. REORGANIZATION OF THE INTERNAL REVENUE SERVICE.

(a) IN GENERAL.—The Commissioner of Internal Revenue shall develop and implement a plan to reorganize the Internal Revenue Service. The plan shall—

(1) supersede any organization or reorganization of the Internal Revenue Service based on any statute or reorganization plan applicable on the effective date of this section;

(2) eliminate or substantially modify the existing organization of the Internal Revenue Service which is based on a national, regional, and district structure;

(3) establish organizational units serving particular groups of taxpayers with similar needs, and

(4) ensure an independent appeals function within the Internal Revenue Service, including the prohibition in the plan of ex parte communications between appeals officers and other Internal Revenue Service employees to the extent that such communications appear to compromise the independence of the appeals officers.

(b) SAVINGS PROVISIONS.—

(1) PRESERVATION OF SPECIFIC TAX RIGHTS AND REMEDIES.—Nothing in the plan developed and implemented under subsection (a) shall be considered to impair any right or remedy, including trial by jury, to recover any internal revenue tax alleged to have been erroneously or illegally assessed or collected, or any penalty claimed to have been collected without authority, or any sum alleged to have been excessive or in any manner wrongfully collected under the internal revenue laws. For the purpose of any action to recover any such tax, penalty, or sum, all statutes, rules, and regulations referring to the collector of internal revenue, the principal officer for the internal revenue district, or the Secretary, shall be deemed to refer to the officer whose act or acts referred to in the preceding sentence gave rise to such action. The venue of any such action shall be the same as under existing law.

(2) CONTINUING EFFECT OF LEGAL DOCUMENTS.—All orders, determinations, rules, regulations, permits, agreements, grants, contracts, certificates, licenses, registrations, privileges, and other administrative actions—

(A) which have been issued, made, granted, or allowed to become effective by the President, any Federal agency or official thereof, or by a court of competent jurisdiction, in the performance of any function transferred or affected by the reorganization of the Internal Revenue Service or any other administrative unit of the Department of the Treasury under this section, and

(B) which are in effect at the time this section takes effect, or were final before the effective date of this section and are to become effective on or after the effective date of this section,

shall continue in effect according to their terms until modified, terminated, superseded, set aside, or revoked in accordance with law by the President, the Secretary of the Treasury, the Commissioner of Internal Revenue, or other authorized official, a court of competent jurisdiction, or by operation of law.

(3) PROCEEDINGS NOT AFFECTED.—The provisions of this section shall not affect any proceedings, including notices of proposed rulemaking, or any application for any license, permit, certificate, or financial assistance pending before the Department of the Treasury (or any administrative unit of the Department, including the Internal Revenue Service) at the time this section takes effect, with respect to functions transferred or affected by the reorganization under this section but such proceedings and applications shall continue. Orders shall be issued in such proceedings, appeals shall be taken therefrom, and payments shall be made pursuant to such orders, as if this section had not been enacted, and orders issued in any such proceedings shall continue in effect until modified, terminated, superseded, or revoked by a duly authorized official, by a court of competent jurisdiction, or by operation of law. Nothing in this paragraph shall be deemed to prohibit the discontinuance or modification of any such proceeding under the same terms and conditions and to the same extent that such proceeding could have been discontinued or modified if this section had not been enacted.

(4) SUITS NOT AFFECTED.—The provisions of this section shall not affect suits commenced before the effective date of this section, and in all such suits, proceedings shall be had, appeals taken, and judgments rendered in the same manner and with the same effect as if this section had not been enacted.

(5) NONABATEMENT OF ACTIONS.—No suit, action, or other proceeding commenced by or against the Department of the Treasury (or any administrative unit of the Department, including the Internal Revenue Service), or by or against any individual in the official capacity of such individual as an officer of the Department of the Treasury, shall abate by reason of the enactment of this section.

(6) ADMINISTRATIVE ACTIONS RELATING TO PROMULGATION OF REGULATIONS.—Any administrative action relating to the preparation or promulgation of a regulation by the Department of the Treasury (or any administrative unit of the Department, including the Internal Revenue Service) relating to a function transferred or affected by the reorganization under this section may be continued by the Department of the Treasury through any appropriate administrative unit of the Department, including the Internal Revenue Service with the same effect as if this section had not been enacted.

(c) EFFECTIVE DATE.—This section shall take effect on the date of the enactment of this Act.

[CCH Explanation at ¶ 801. Committee Reports at ¶ 10,115.]

[¶ 8010] ACT SEC. 1002. IRS MISSION TO FOCUS ON TAXPAYERS' NEEDS.

The Internal Revenue Service shall review and restate its mission to place a greater emphasis on serving the public and meeting taxpayers' needs.

[CCH Explanation at ¶ 806. Committee Reports at ¶ 10,120.]

Subtitle B—Executive Branch Governance and Senior Management
* * *

[¶ 8015] ACT SEC. 1102. COMMISSIONER OF INTERNAL REVENUE; OTHER OFFICIALS.
* * *

(e) ADDITIONAL CONFORMING AMENDMENTS.—
* * *

(2) Section 5109 of title 5, United States Code, is amended by striking subsection (b) and redesignating subsection (c) as subsection (b).
* * *

(f) EFFECTIVE DATE.—

¶ 8010   Act Sec. 1002

(1) IN GENERAL.—Except as provided in paragraph (2), the amendments made by this section shall take effect on the date of the enactment of this Act.

* * *

(3) NATIONAL TAXPAYER ADVOCATE.—Notwithstanding section 7803(c)(1)(B)(iv) of such Code, as added by this section, in appointing the first National Taxpayer Advocate after the date of the enactment of this Act, the Secretary of the Treasury—

(A) shall not appoint any individual who was an officer or employee of the Internal Revenue Service at any time during the 2-year period ending on the date of appointment, and

(B) need not consult with the Internal Revenue Service Oversight Board if the Oversight Board has not been appointed.

(4) CURRENT OFFICERS.—

(A) In the case of an individual serving as Commissioner of Internal Revenue on the date of the enactment of this Act who was appointed to such position before such date, the 5-year term required by section 7803(a)(1) of such Code, as added by this section, shall begin as of the date of such appointment.

(B) Clauses (ii), (iii), and (iv) of section 7803(c)(1)(B) of such Code, as added by this section, shall not apply to the individual serving as Taxpayer Advocate on the date of the enactment of this Act.

[CCH Explanation at ¶ 811 and 831. Committee Reports at ¶ 10,160.]

[¶ 8020] ACT SEC. 1103. TREASURY INSPECTOR GENERAL FOR TAX ADMINISTRATION.

(a) ESTABLISHMENT OF 2 INSPECTORS GENERAL IN THE DEPARTMENT OF THE TREASURY.—Section 2 of the Inspector General Act of 1978 (5 U.S.C. App.) is amended by striking the matter following paragraph (3) and inserting the following:

"there is established—

"(A) in each of such establishments an office of Inspector General, subject to subparagraph (B); and

"(B) in the establishment of the Department of the Treasury—

"(i) an Office of Inspector General of the Department of the Treasury; and

"(ii) an Office of Treasury Inspector General for Tax Administration."

(b) AMENDMENTS TO SECTION 8D OF THE INSPECTOR GENERAL ACT OF 1978.—

(1) LIMITATION ON AUTHORITY OF INSPECTOR GENERAL.—Section 8D(a) of the Inspector General Act of 1978 (5 U.S.C. App.) is amended by adding at the end the following new paragraph:

"(4) The Secretary of the Treasury may not exercise any power under paragraph (1) or (2) with respect to the Treasury Inspector General for Tax Administration."

(2) DUTIES OF INSPECTOR GENERAL OF THE DEPARTMENT OF THE TREASURY; RELATIONSHIP TO THE TREASURY INSPECTOR GENERAL FOR TAX ADMINISTRATION.—Section 8D(b) of such Act is amended—

(A) by inserting "(1)" after "(b)"; and

(B) by adding at the end the following new paragraphs:

"(2) The Inspector General of the Department of the Treasury shall exercise all duties and responsibilities of an Inspector General for the Department of the Treasury other than the duties and responsibilities exercised by the Treasury Inspector General for Tax Administration.

"(3) The Secretary of the Treasury shall establish procedures under which the Inspector General of the Department of the Treasury and the Treasury Inspector General for Tax Administration will—

"(A) determine how audits and investigations are allocated in cases of overlapping jurisdiction, and

"(B) provide for coordination, cooperation, and efficiency in the conduct of such audits and investigations."

(3) ACCESS TO RETURNS AND RETURN INFORMATION.—Section 8D(e) of such Act is amended—

(A) in paragraph (1), by striking "Inspector General" and inserting "Treasury Inspector General for Tax Administration";

(B) in paragraph (2), by striking all beginning with "(2)" through subparagraph (B);

(C)(i) by redesignating subparagraph (C) of paragraph (2) as paragraph (2) of such subsection; and

(ii) in such redesignated paragraph (2), by striking "Inspector General" and inserting "Treasury Inspector General for Tax Administration"; and

(D)(i) by redesignating subparagraph (D) of such paragraph as paragraph (3) of such subsection; and

(ii) in such redesignated paragraph (3), by striking "Inspector General" and inserting "Treasury Inspector General for Tax Administration".

(4) EFFECT ON CERTAIN FINAL DECISIONS OF THE SECRETARY.—Section 8D(f) of such Act is amended by striking "Inspector General" and inserting "Inspector General of the Department of the Treasury or the Treasury Inspector General for Tax Administration".

(5) REPEAL OF LIMITATION ON REPORTS TO THE ATTORNEY GENERAL.—Section 8D of such Act is amended by striking subsection (g).

(6) TRANSMISSION OF REPORTS.—Section 8D(h) of such Act is amended—

(A) by striking "(h)" and inserting "(g)(1)";

(B) by striking "and the Committees on Government Operations and Ways and Means of the House of Representatives" and inserting "and the Committees on Government Reform and Oversight and Ways and Means of the House of Representatives"; and

(C) by adding at the end the following new paragraph:

"(2) Any report made by the Treasury Inspector General for Tax Administration that is required to be transmitted by the Secretary of the Treasury to the appropriate committees or subcommittees of Congress under section 5(d) shall also be transmitted, within the 7-day period specified under such subsection, to the Internal Revenue Service Oversight Board and the Commissioner of Internal Revenue."

(7) TREASURY INSPECTOR GENERAL FOR TAX ADMINISTRATION.—Section 8D of the Act is amended by adding at the end the following new subsections:

"(h) The Treasury Inspector General for Tax Administration shall exercise all duties and responsibilities of an Inspector General of an establishment with respect to the Department of the Treasury and the Secretary of the Treasury on all matters relating to the Internal Revenue Service. The Treasury Inspector General for Tax Administration shall have sole authority under this Act to conduct an audit or investigation of the Internal Revenue Service Oversight Board and the Chief Counsel for the Internal Revenue Service.

"(i) In addition to the requirements of the first sentence of section 3(a), the Treasury Inspector General for Tax Administration should have demonstrated ability to lead a large and complex organization.

"(j) An individual appointed to the position of Treasury Inspector General for Tax Administration, the Assistant Inspector General for Auditing of the Office of the Treasury Inspector General for Tax Administration under section 3(d)(1), the Assistant Inspector General for Investigations of the Office of the Treasury Inspector General for Tax Administration under section 3(d)(2), or any position of Deputy Inspector General of the Office of the Treasury Inspector General for Tax Administration may not be an employee of the Internal Revenue Service—

"(1) during the 2-year period preceding the date of appointment to such position; or

"(2) during the 5-year period following the date such individual ends service in such position.

"(k)(1) In addition to the duties and responsibilities exercised by an inspector general of an establishment, the Treasury Inspector General for Tax Administration—

"(A) shall have the duty to enforce criminal provisions under section 7608(b) of the Internal Revenue Code of 1986;

"(B) in addition to the functions authorized under section 7608(b)(2) of such Code, may carry firearms;

"(C) shall be responsible for protecting the Internal Revenue Service against external attempts to corrupt or threaten employees of the Internal Revenue Service, but shall not be responsible for the conducting of background checks and the providing of physical security; and

"(D) may designate any employee in the Office of the Treasury Inspector General for Tax Administration to enforce such laws and perform such functions referred to under subparagraphs (A), (B), and (C).

"(2)(A) In performing a law enforcement function under paragraph (1), the Treasury Inspector General for Tax Administration shall report any reasonable grounds to believe there has been a violation of Federal criminal law to the Attorney General at an appropriate time as determined by the Treasury Inspector General for Tax Administration, notwithstanding section 4(d).

"(B) In the administration of section 5(d) and subsection (g)(2) of this section, the Secretary of the Treasury may transmit the required report with respect to the Treasury Inspector General for Tax Administration at an appropriate time as determined by the Secretary, if the problem, abuse, or deficiency relates to—

"(i) the performance of a law enforcement function under paragraph (1); and

"(ii) sensitive information concerning matters under subsection (a)(1)(A) through (F).

"(3) Nothing in this subsection shall be construed to affect the authority of any other person to carry out or enforce any provision specified in paragraph (1).

"(l)(1) The Commissioner of Internal Revenue or the Internal Revenue Service Oversight Board may request, in writing, the Treasury Inspector General for Tax Administration to conduct an audit or investigation relating to the Internal Revenue Service. If the Treasury Inspector General for Tax Administration determines not to conduct such audit or investigation, the Inspector General shall timely provide a written explanation for such determination to the person making the request.

"(2)(A) Any final report of an audit conducted by the Treasury Inspector General for Tax Administration shall be timely submitted by the Inspector General to the Commissioner of Internal Revenue and the Internal Revenue Service Oversight Board.

"(B) The Treasury Inspector General for Tax Administration shall periodically submit to the Commissioner and Board a list of investigations for which a final report has been completed by the Inspector General and shall provide a copy of any such report upon request of the Commissioner or Board.

"(C) This paragraph applies regardless of whether the applicable audit or investigation is requested under paragraph (1)."

(c) TRANSFER OF FUNCTIONS.—

(1) IN GENERAL.—Section 9(a)(1) of the Inspector General Act of 1978 (5 U.S.C. App.) is amended in subparagraph (L)—

(A) by inserting "(i)" after "(L)";

(B) by inserting "and" after the semicolon; and

(C) by adding at the end the following new clause:

"(ii) of the Treasury Inspector General for Tax Administration, effective 180 days after the date of the enactment of the Internal Revenue Service Restructuring and Reform Act of 1998, the Office of Chief Inspector of the Internal Revenue Service,".

(2) TERMINATION OF OFFICE OF CHIEF INSPECTOR.—Effective upon the transfer of functions under the amendment made by paragraph (1), the Office of Chief Inspector of the Internal Revenue Service is terminated.

(3) RETENTION OF CERTAIN INTERNAL AUDIT PERSONNEL.—In making the transfer under the amendment made by paragraph (1), the Commissioner of Internal Revenue shall designate and retain an appropriate number (not in excess of 300) of internal audit full-time equivalent employee positions necessary for management relating to the Internal Revenue Service.

(4) ADDITIONAL PERSONNEL TRANSFERS.—Effective 180 days after the date of the enactment of this Act, the Secretary of the Treasury shall transfer 21 full-time equivalent positions from the Office of the Inspector General of the Department of the Treasury to the Office of the Treasury Inspector General for Tax Administration.

(d) AUDITS AND REPORTS OF AGENCY FINANCIAL STATEMENTS.—Subject to section 3521(g) of title 31, United States Code—

(1) the Inspector General of the Department of the Treasury shall, subject to paragraph (2)—

(A) audit each financial statement in accordance with section 3521(e) of such title; and

(B) prepare and submit each report required under section 3521(f) of such title; and

(2) the Treasury Inspector General for Tax Administration shall—

(A) audit that portion of each financial statement referred to under paragraph (1)(A) that relates to custodial and administrative accounts of the Internal Revenue Service; and

(B) prepare that portion of each report referred to under paragraph (1)(B) that relates to custodial and administrative accounts of the Internal Revenue Service.

(e) TECHNICAL AND CONFORMING AMENDMENTS.—

(1) TRANSFER OF FUNCTIONS.—Section 8D(b) of the Inspector General Act of 1978 (5 U.S.C. App.) is amended by striking "and the internal audits and internal investigations performed by the Office of Assistant Commissioner (Inspection) of the Internal Revenue Service".

(2) AMENDMENTS RELATING TO REFERENCES TO THE INSPECTOR GENERAL OF THE DEPARTMENT OF THE TREASURY.—

(A) LIMITATION ON AUTHORITY.—Section 8D(a) of the Inspector General Act of 1978 (5 U.S.C. App.) is amended—

(i) in the first sentence of paragraph (1), by inserting "of the Department of the Treasury" after "Inspector General";

(ii) in paragraph (2), by inserting "of the Department of the Treasury" after "prohibit the Inspector General"; and

(iii) in paragraph (3)—

(I) in the first sentence, by inserting "of the Department of the Treasury" after "notify the Inspector General"; and

(II) in the second sentence, by inserting "of the Department of the Treasury" after "notice, the Inspector General".

(B) DUTIES.—Section 8D(b) of such Act is amended in the second sentence by inserting "of the Department of the Treasury" after "Inspector General".

(C) AUDITS AND INVESTIGATIONS.—Section 8D (c) and (d) of such Act are amended by inserting "of the Department of the Treasury" after "Inspector General" each place it appears.

(3) REFERENCES.—The second section 8G of the Inspector General Act of 1978 (relating to rule of construction of special provisions) is amended—

(A) by striking "SEC. 8G" and inserting "SEC. 8H";

(B) by striking "or 8E" and inserting "8E or 8F"; and

(C) by striking "section 8F(a)" and inserting "section 8G(a)".

* * *

[CCH Explanation at ¶ 831. Committee Reports at ¶ 10,160.]

Subtitle C—Personnel Flexibilities

[¶ 8025] ACT SEC. 1201. IMPROVEMENTS IN PERSONNEL FLEXIBILITIES.

(a) IN GENERAL.—Part III of title 5, United States Code, is amended by adding at the end the following new subpart:

"Subpart I—Miscellaneous

"CHAPTER 95—PERSONNEL FLEXIBILITIES RELATING TO THE INTERNAL REVENUE SERVICE

"Sec.

"9501. Internal Revenue Service personnel flexibilities.

"9502. Pay authority for critical positions.

"9503. Streamlined critical pay authority.

"9504. Recruitment, retention, relocation incentives, and relocation expenses.

"9505. Performance awards for senior executives.

"9506. Limited appointments to career reserved Senior Executive Service positions.

"9507. Streamlined demonstration project authority.

"9508. General workforce performance management system.

"9509. General workforce classification and pay.

"9510. General workforce staffing.

"§ 9501. Internal Revenue Service personnel flexibilities

"(a) Any flexibilities provided by sections 9502 through 9510 of this chapter shall be exercised in a manner consistent with—

"(1) chapter 23 (relating to merit system principles and prohibited personnel practices);

"(2) provisions relating to preference eligibles;

"(3) except as otherwise specifically provided, section 5307 (relating to the aggregate limitation on pay);

"(4) except as otherwise specifically provided, chapter 71 (relating to labor-management relations); and

"(5) subject to subsections (b) and (c) of section 1104, as though such authorities were delegated to the Secretary of the Treasury under section 1104(a)(2).

"(b) The Secretary of the Treasury shall provide the Office of Personnel Management with any information that Office requires in carrying out its responsibilities under this section.

"(c) Employees within a unit to which a labor organization is accorded exclusive recognition under chapter 71 shall not be subject to any flexibility provided by sections 9507 through 9510 of this chapter unless the exclusive representative and the Internal Revenue Service have entered into a written agreement which specifically provides for the exercise of that flexibility. Such written agreement may be imposed by the Federal Services Impasses Panel under section 7119.

"§ 9502. Pay authority for critical positions

"(a) When the Secretary of the Treasury seeks a grant of authority under section 5377 for critical pay for 1 or more positions at the Internal Revenue Service, the Office of Management and Budget may fix the rate of basic pay, notwithstanding sections 5377(d)(2) and 5307, at any rate up to the salary set in accordance with section 104 of title 3.

"(b) Notwithstanding section 5307, no allowance, differential, bonus, award, or similar cash payment may be paid to any employee receiving critical pay at a rate fixed under subsection (a), in any calendar year if, or to the extent that, the employee's total annual compensation will exceed the maximum amount of total annual compensation payable at the salary set in accordance with section 104 of title 3.

"§ 9503. Streamlined critical pay authority

"(a) Notwithstanding section 9502, and without regard to the provisions of this title governing appointments in the competitive service or the Senior Executive Service and chapters 51 and 53 (relating to classification and pay rates), the Secretary of the Treasury may, for a period of 10 years after the date of enactment of this section, establish, fix the compensation of, and appoint individuals to, designated critical administrative, technical, and professional positions needed to carry out the functions of the Internal Revenue Service, if—

"(1) the positions—

"(A) require expertise of an extremely high level in an administrative, technical, or professional field; and

"(B) are critical to the Internal Revenue Service's successful accomplishment of an important mission;

"(2) exercise of the authority is necessary to recruit or retain an individual exceptionally well qualified for the position;

"(3) the number of such positions does not exceed 40 at any one time;

"(4) designation of such positions are approved by the Secretary of the Treasury;

"(5) the terms of such appointments are limited to no more than 4 years;

"(6) appointees to such positions were not Internal Revenue Service employees prior to June 1, 1998;

"(7) total annual compensation for any appointee to such positions does not exceed the highest total annual compensation payable at the rate determined under section 104 of title 3; and

"(8) all such positions are excluded from the collective bargaining unit.

"(b) Individuals appointed under this section shall not be considered to be employees for purposes of subchapter II of chapter 75.

"§ 9504. Recruitment, retention, relocation incentives, and relocation expenses

"(a) For a period of 10 years after the date of enactment of this section and subject to approval by the Office of Personnel Management, the Secretary of the Treasury may provide for variations from sections 5753 and 5754 governing payment of recruitment, relocation, and retention incentives.

"(b) For a period of 10 years after the date of enactment of this section, the Secretary of the Treasury may pay from appropriations made to the Internal Revenue Service allowable relocation expenses under section 5724a for employees transferred or reemployed and allowable travel and transportation expenses under section 5723 for new appointees appointed to a position for which pay is fixed under section 9502 or 9503 after June 1, 1998.

"§ 9505. Performance awards for senior executives

"(a) For a period of 10 years after the date of enactment of this section, Internal Revenue Service senior executives who have program management responsibility over significant functions of the Internal Revenue Service may be paid a performance bonus without regard to the limitation in section 5384(b)(2) if the Secretary of the Treasury finds such award warranted based on the executive's performance.

"(b) In evaluating an executive's performance for purposes of an award under this section, the Secretary of the Treasury shall take into account the executive's contributions toward the successful accomplishment of goals and objectives established under the Government Performance and Results Act of 1993, division E of the ClingerCohen Act of 1996 (Public Law 104-106; 110 Stat. 679), Revenue Procedure 64-22 (as in effect on July 30, 1997), taxpayer service surveys, and other performance metrics or plans established in consultation with the Internal Revenue Service Oversight Board.

"(c) Any award in excess of 20 percent of an executive's rate of basic pay shall be approved by the Secretary of the Treasury.

"(d) Notwithstanding section 5384(b)(3), the Secretary of the Treasury shall determine the aggregate amount of performance awards available to be paid during any fiscal year under this section and section 5384 to career senior executives in the Internal Revenue Service. Such amount may not exceed an amount equal to 5 percent of the aggregate amount of basic pay paid to career senior executives in the Internal Revenue Service during the preceding fiscal year. The Internal Revenue Service shall not be included in the determination under section 5384(b)(3) of the aggregate amount of performance awards payable to career senior executives in the Department of the Treasury other than the Internal Revenue Service.

"(e) Notwithstanding section 5307, a performance bonus award may not be paid to an executive in a calendar year if, or to the extent that, the executive's total annual compensation will exceed the maximum amount of total annual compensation payable at the rate determined under section 104 of title 3.

"§ 9506. Limited appointments to career reserved Senior Executive Service positions

"(a) In the application of section 3132, a 'career reserved position' in the Internal Revenue Service means a position designated under section 3132(b) which may be filled only by—

"(1) a career appointee, or

"(2) a limited emergency appointee or a limited term appointee—

"(A) who, immediately upon entering the career reserved position, was serving under a career or career-conditional appointment outside the Senior Executive Service; or

"(B) whose limited emergency or limited term appointment is approved in advance by the Office of Personnel Management.

"(b)(1) The number of positions described under subsection (a) which are filled by an appointee as described under paragraph (2) of such subsection may not exceed 10 percent of the total number of Senior Executive Service positions in the Internal Revenue Service.

"(2) Notwithstanding section 3132—

"(A) the term of an appointee described under subsection (a)(2) may be for any period not to exceed 3 years; and

"(B) such an appointee may serve—

"(i) 2 such terms; or

"(ii) 2 such terms in addition to any unexpired term applicable at the time of appointment.

"§ 9507. Streamlined demonstration project authority

"(a) The exercise of any of the flexibilities under sections 9502 through 9510 shall not affect the authority of the Secretary of the Treasury to implement for the Internal Revenue Service a demonstration project subject to chapter 47, as provided in subsection (b).

"(b) In applying section 4703 to a demonstration project described in section 4701(a)(4) which involves the Internal Revenue Service—

"(1) section 4703(b)(1) shall be deemed to read as follows:

" '(1) develop a plan for such project which describes its purpose, the employees to be covered, the project itself, its anticipated outcomes, and the method of evaluating the project;';

"(2) section 4703(b)(3) shall not apply;

"(3) the 180-day notification period in section 4703(b)(4) shall be deemed to be a notification period of 30 days;

"(4) section 4703(b)(6) shall be deemed to read as follows:

" '(6) provides each House of Congress with the final version of the plan.';

"(5) section 4703(c)(1) shall be deemed to read as follows:

" '(1) subchapter V of chapter 63 or subpart G of part III of this title;';

"(6) the requirements of paragraphs (1)(A) and (2) of section 4703(d) shall not apply; and

"(7) notwithstanding section 4703(d)(1)(B), based on an evaluation as provided in section 4703(h), the Office of Personnel Management and the Secretary of the Treasury, except as otherwise provided by this subsection, may waive the termination date of a demonstration project under section 4703(d).

"(c) At least 90 days before waiving the termination date under subsection (b)(7), the Office of Personnel Management shall publish in the Federal Register a notice of its intention to waive the termination date and shall inform in writing both Houses of Congress of its intention.

"§ 9508. General workforce performance management system

"(a) In lieu of a performance appraisal system established under section 4302, the Secretary of the Treasury shall, within 1 year after the date of enactment of this section, establish for the Internal Revenue Service a performance management system that—

"(1) maintains individual accountability by—

"(A) establishing 1 or more retention standards for each employee related to the work of the employee and expressed in terms of individual performance, and communicating such retention standards to employees;

"(B) making periodic determinations of whether each employee meets or does not meet the employee's established retention standards; and

"(C) taking actions, in accordance with applicable laws and regulations, with respect to any employee whose performance does not meet established retention standards, including denying any increases in basic pay, promotions, and credit for performance under section 3502, and taking 1 or more of the following actions:

"(i) Reassignment.

"(ii) An action under chapter 43 or chapter 75 of this title.

"(iii) Any other appropriate action to resolve the performance problem; and

"(2) except as provided under section 1204 of the Internal Revenue Service Restructuring and Reform Act of 1998, strengthens the system's effectiveness by—

"(A) establishing goals or objectives for individual, group, or organizational performance (or any combination thereof), consistent with the Internal Revenue Service's performance planning procedures, including those established under the Government Performance and Results Act of 1993, division E of the Clinger-Cohen Act of 1996 (Public Law 104-106; 110 Stat. 679), Revenue Procedure 64-22 (as in effect on July 30, 1997), and taxpayer service surveys, and communicating such goals or objectives to employees;

"(B) using such goals and objectives to make performance distinctions among employees or groups of employees; and

"(C) using performance assessments as a basis for granting employee awards, adjusting an employee's rate of basic pay, and other appropriate personnel actions, in accordance with applicable laws and regulations.

"(b)(1) For purposes of subsection (a)(2), the term 'performance assessment' means a determination of whether or not retention standards established under subsection (a)(1)(A) are met, and any additional performance determination made on the basis of performance goals and objectives established under subsection (a)(2)(A).

"(2) For purposes of this title, the term 'unacceptable performance' with respect to an employee of the Internal Revenue Service covered by a performance management system established under this section means performance of the employee which fails to meet a retention standard established under this section.

"(c)(1) The Secretary of the Treasury may establish an awards program designed to provide incentives for and recognition of organizational, group, and individual achievements by providing for granting awards to employees who, as individuals or members of a group, contribute to meeting the performance goals and objectives established under this chapter by such means as a superior individual or group accomplishment, a documented productivity gain, or sustained superior performance.

"(2) A cash award under subchapter I of chapter 45 may be granted to an employee of the Internal Revenue Service without the need for any approval under section 4502(b).

"(d)(1) In applying sections 4303(b)(1)(A) and 7513(b)(1) to employees of the Internal Revenue Service, '30 days' may be deemed to be '15 days'.

"(2) Notwithstanding the second sentence of section 5335(c), an employee of the Internal Revenue Service shall not have a right to appeal the denial of a periodic step increase under section 5335 to the Merit Systems Protection Board.

"**§ 9509. General workforce classification and pay**

"(a) For purposes of this section, the term 'broad-banded system' means a system for grouping positions for pay, job evaluation, and other purposes that is different from the system established under chapter 51 and subchapter III of chapter 53 as a result of combining grades and related ranges of rates of pay in 1 or more occupational series.

"(b)(1)(A) The Secretary of the Treasury may, subject to criteria to be prescribed by the Office of Personnel Management, establish 1 or more broad-banded systems covering all or any portion of the Internal Revenue Service workforce.

"(B) With the approval of the Office of Personnel Management, a broad-banded system established under this section may either include or consist of positions that otherwise would be subject to subchapter IV of chapter 53 or section 5376.

"(2) The Office of Personnel Management may require the Secretary of the Treasury to submit information relating to broad-banded systems at the Internal Revenue Service.

"(3) Except as otherwise provided under this section, employees under a broad-banded system shall continue to be subject to the laws and regulations covering employees under the pay system that otherwise would apply to such employees.

"(4) The criteria to be prescribed by the Office of Personnel Management shall, at a minimum—

"(A) ensure that the structure of any broad-banded system maintains the principle of equal pay for substantially equal work;

"(B) establish the minimum and maximum number of grades that may be combined into pay bands;

"(C) establish requirements for setting minimum and maximum rates of pay in a pay band;

"(D) establish requirements for adjusting the pay of an employee within a pay band;

"(E) establish requirements for setting the pay of a supervisory employee whose position is in a pay band or who supervises employees whose positions are in pay bands; and

"(F) establish requirements and methodologies for setting the pay of an employee upon conversion to a broad-banded system, initial appointment, change of position or type of appointment (including promotion, demotion, transfer, reassignment, reinstatement, placement in another pay band, or movement to a different geographic location), and movement between a broad-banded system and another pay system.

"(c) With the approval of the Office of Personnel Management and in accordance with a plan for implementation submitted by the Secretary of the Treasury, the Secretary may, with respect to Internal Revenue Service employees who are covered by a broad-banded system established under this section, provide for variations from the provisions of subchapter VI of chapter 53.

"**§ 9510. General workforce staffing**

"(a)(1) Except as otherwise provided by this section, an employee of the Internal Revenue Service may be selected for a permanent appointment in the competitive service in the Internal Revenue Service through internal competitive promotion procedures if—

"(A) the employee has completed, in the competitive service, 2 years of current continuous service under a term appointment or any combination of term appointments;

"(B) such term appointment or appointments were made under competitive procedures prescribed for permanent appointments;

"(C) the employee's performance under such term appointment or appointments met established retention standards, or, if not covered by a performance management system established under section 9508, was rated at the fully successful level or higher (or equivalent thereof); and

"(D) the vacancy announcement for the term appointment from which the conversion is made stated that there was a potential for subsequent conversion to a permanent appointment.

"(2) An appointment under this section may be made only to a position in the same line of work as a position to which the employee received a term appointment under competitive procedures.

"(b)(1) Notwithstanding subchapter I of chapter 33, the Secretary of the Treasury may establish category rating systems for evaluating applicants for Internal Revenue Service positions in the competitive service under which qualified candidates are divided into 2 or more quality categories on the basis of relative degrees of merit, rather than assigned individual numerical ratings.

"(2) Each applicant who meets the minimum qualification requirements for the position to be filled shall be assigned to an appropriate category based on an evaluation of the applicant's knowledge, skills, and abilities relative to those needed for successful performance in the position to be filled.

"(3) Within each quality category established under paragraph (1), preference eligibles shall be listed ahead of individuals who are not preference eligibles. For other than scientific and professional positions at or higher than GS-9 (or equivalent), preference eligibles who have a compensable service-connected disability of 10 percent or more, and who meet the minimum qualification standards, shall be listed in the highest quality category.

"(4) An appointing authority may select any applicant from the highest quality category or, if fewer than 3 candidates have been assigned to the highest quality category, from a merged category consisting of the highest and second highest quality categories.

"(5) Notwithstanding paragraph (4), the appointing authority may not pass over a preference eligible in the same or higher category from which selection is made unless the requirements of section 3317(b) or 3318(b), as applicable, are satisfied.

"(c) The Secretary of the Treasury may detail employees among the offices of the Internal Revenue Service without regard to the 120-day limitation in section 3341(b).

"(d) Notwithstanding any other provision of law, the Secretary of the Treasury may establish a probationary period under section 3321 of up to 3 years for Internal Revenue Service positions if the Secretary of the Treasury determines that the nature of the work is such that a shorter period is insufficient to demonstrate complete proficiency in the position.

"(e) Nothing in this section exempts the Secretary of the Treasury from—

"(1) any employment priority established under direction of the President for the placement of surplus or displaced employees; or

"(2) any obligation under a court order or decree relating to the employment practices of the Internal Revenue Service or the Department of the Treasury."

* * *

[CCH Explanation at ¶ 901, 931, 936, 941, 946, 956, 961 and 966. Committee Reports at ¶ 10,185.]

[¶ 8030] ACT SEC. 1202. VOLUNTARY SEPARATION INCENTIVE PAYMENTS.

(a) DEFINITION.—In this section, the term "employee" means an employee (as defined by section 2105 of title 5, United States Code) who is employed by the Internal Revenue Service serving under an appointment without time limitation, and has been currently employed for a continuous period of at least 3 years, but does not include—

(1) a reemployed annuitant under subchapter III of chapter 83 or chapter 84 of title 5, United States Code, or another retirement system;

(2) an employee having a disability on the basis of which such employee is or would be eligible for disability retirement under the applicable retirement system referred to in paragraph (1);

(3) an employee who is in receipt of a specific notice of involuntary separation for misconduct or unacceptable performance;

(4) an employee who, upon completing an additional period of service as referred to in section 3(b)(2)(B)(ii) of the Federal Workforce Restructuring Act of 1994 (5 U.S.C. 5597 note), would qualify for a voluntary separation incentive payment under section 3 of such Act;

(5) an employee who has previously received any voluntary separation incentive payment by the Federal Government under this section or any other authority and has not repaid such payment;

(6) an employee covered by statutory reemployment rights who is on transfer to another organization; or

(7) any employee who, during the 24-month period preceding the date of separation, has received a recruitment or relocation bonus under section 5753 of title 5, United States Code, or who, within the 12-month period preceding the date of separation, received a retention allowance under section 5754 of title 5, United States Code.

(b) AUTHORITY TO PROVIDE VOLUNTARY SEPARATION INCENTIVE PAYMENTS.—

(1) IN GENERAL.—The Commissioner of Internal Revenue may pay voluntary separation incentive payments under this section to any employee to the extent necessary to carry out the plan to reorganize the Internal Revenue Service under section 1001.

(2) AMOUNT AND TREATMENT OF PAYMENTS.— A voluntary separation incentive payment—

(A) shall be paid in a lump sum after the employee's separation;

(B) shall be paid from appropriations or funds available for the payment of the basic pay of the employees;

(C) shall be equal to the lesser of—

(i) an amount equal to the amount the employee would be entitled to receive under section 5595(c) of title 5, United States Code; or

(ii) an amount determined by an agency head not to exceed $25,000;

(D) may not be made except in the case of any qualifying employee who voluntarily separates (whether by retirement or resignation) before January 1, 2003;

(E) shall not be a basis for payment, and shall not be included in the computation, of any other type of Government benefit; and

(F) shall not be taken into account in determining the amount of any severance pay to which the employee may be entitled under section 5595 of title 5, United States Code, based on any other separation.

(c) ADDITIONAL INTERNAL REVENUE SERVICE CONTRIBUTIONS TO THE RETIREMENT FUND.—

(1) IN GENERAL.—In addition to any other payments which it is required to make under subchapter III of chapter 83 of title 5, United States Code, the Internal Revenue Service shall remit to the Office of Personnel Management for deposit in the Treasury of the United States to the credit of the Civil Service Retirement and Disability Fund an amount equal to 15 percent of the final basic pay of each employee who is covered under subchapter III of chapter 83 or chapter 84 of title 5, United States Code, to whom a voluntary separation incentive has been paid under this section.

(2) DEFINITION.—In paragraph (1), the term "final basic pay", with respect to an employee, means the total amount of basic pay which would be payable for a year of service by such employee, computed using the employee's final rate of basic pay, and, if last serving on other than a full-time basis, with appropriate adjustment therefor.

(d) EFFECT OF SUBSEQUENT EMPLOYMENT WITH THE GOVERNMENT.—An individual who has received a voluntary separation incentive payment under this section and accepts any employment for compensation with the Government of the United States, or who works for any agency of the United States Government through a personal services contract, within 5 years after the date of the separation on which the payment is based shall be required to pay, prior to the individual's first day of employment, the entire amount of the incentive payment to the Internal Revenue Service.

(e) EFFECT ON INTERNAL REVENUE SERVICE EMPLOYMENT LEVELS.—

(1) INTENDED EFFECT.—Voluntary separations under this section are not intended to necessarily reduce the total number of full-time equivalent positions in the Internal Revenue Service.

(2) USE OF VOLUNTARY SEPARATIONS.—The Internal Revenue Service may redeploy or use the full-time equivalent positions vacated by voluntary separations under this section to make other positions available to more critical locations or more critical occupations.

[CCH Explanation at ¶ 971. Committee Reports at ¶ 10,190.]

[¶ 8035] ACT SEC. 1203. TERMINATION OF EMPLOYMENT FOR MISCONDUCT.

(a) IN GENERAL.—Subject to subsection (c), the Commissioner of Internal Revenue shall terminate the employment of any employee of the Internal Revenue Service if there is a final administrative or judicial determination that such employee committed any act or omission described under subsection (b) in the performance of the employee's official duties. Such termination shall be a removal for cause on charges of misconduct.

(b) ACTS OR OMISSIONS.—The acts or omissions referred to under subsection (a) are—

(1) willful failure to obtain the required approval signatures on documents authorizing the seizure of a taxpayer's home, personal belongings, or business assets;

(2) providing a false statement under oath with respect to a material matter involving a taxpayer or taxpayer representative;

(3) with respect to a taxpayer, taxpayer representative, or other employee of the Internal Revenue Service, the violation of—

(A) any right under the Constitution of the United States; or

(B) any civil right established under—

(i) title VI or VII of the Civil Rights Act of 1964;

(ii) title IX of the Education Amendments of 1972;

(iii) the Age Discrimination in Employment Act of 1967;

(iv) the Age Discrimination Act of 1975;

(v) section 501 or 504 of the Rehabilitation Act of 1973; or

(vi) title I of the Americans with Disabilities Act of 1990;

(4) falsifying or destroying documents to conceal mistakes made by any employee with respect to a matter involving a taxpayer or taxpayer representative;

(5) assault or battery on a taxpayer, taxpayer representative, or other employee of the Internal Revenue Service, but only if there is a criminal conviction, or a final judgment by a court in a civil case, with respect to the assault or battery;

(6) violations of the Internal Revenue Code of 1986, Department of Treasury regulations, or policies of the Internal Revenue Service (including the Internal Revenue Manual) for the purpose of retaliating against, or harassing, a taxpayer, taxpayer representative, or other employee of the Internal Revenue Service;

(7) willful misuse of the provisions of section 6103 of the Internal Revenue Code of 1986 for the purpose of concealing information from a congressional inquiry,

(8) willful failure to file any return of tax required under the Internal Revenue Code of 1986 on or before the date prescribed therefor (including any extensions), unless such failure is due to reasonable cause and not to willful neglect,

(9) willful understatement of Federal tax liability, unless such understatement is due to reasonable cause and not to willful neglect, and

(10) threatening to audit a taxpayer for the purpose of extracting personal gain or benefit.

(c) DETERMINATION OF COMMISSIONER.—

(1) IN GENERAL.—The Commissioner of Internal Revenue may take a personnel action other than termination for an act or omission under subsection (a).

(2) DISCRETION.—The exercise of authority under paragraph (1) shall be at the sole discretion of the Commissioner of Internal Revenue and may not be delegated to any other officer. The Commissioner of Internal Revenue, in his sole discretion, may establish a procedure which will be used to determine whether an individual should be referred to the Commissioner of Internal Revenue for a determination by the Commissioner under paragraph (1).

(3) NO APPEAL.—Any determination of the Commissioner of Internal Revenue under this subsection may not be appealed in any administrative or judicial proceeding.

(d) DEFINITION.—For purposes of the provisions described in clauses (i), (ii), and (iv) of subsection (b)(3)(B), references to a program or activity receiving Federal financial assistance or an education program or activity receiving Federal financial assistance shall include any program or activity conducted by the Internal Revenue Service for a taxpayer.

[CCH Explanation at ¶ 976. Committee Reports at ¶ 10,195.]

[¶ 8040] ACT SEC. 1204. BASIS FOR EVALUATION OF INTERNAL REVENUE SERVICE EMPLOYEES.

(a) IN GENERAL.—The Internal Revenue Service shall not use records of tax enforcement results—

(1) to evaluate employees; or

(2) to impose or suggest production quotas or goals with respect to such employees.

(b) TAXPAYER SERVICE.—The Internal Revenue Service shall use the fair and equitable treatment of taxpayers by employees as one of the standards for evaluating employee performance.

(c) CERTIFICATION.—Each appropriate supervisor shall certify quarterly by letter to the Commissioner of Internal Revenue whether or not tax enforcement results are being used in a manner prohibited by subsection (a).

(d) TECHNICAL AND CONFORMING AMENDMENT.—Section 6231 of the Technical and Miscellaneous Revenue Act of 1988 (Public Law 100-647; 102 Stat. 3734) is repealed.

● ● *TAMRA 1988 Act Sec. 6231 before repeal*

SEC. 6231. BASIS FOR EVALUATION OF INTERNAL REVENUE SERVICE EMPLOYEES.

(a) IN GENERAL.—The Internal Revenue Service shall not use records of tax enforcement results—

(1) to evaluate employees directly involved in collection activities and their immediate supervisors, or

(2) to impose or suggest production quotas or goals with respect to individuals described in clause (i).

(b) APPLICATION OF IRS POLICY STATEMENT.—The Internal Revenue Service shall not be treated as failing to meet the requirements of subsection (a) if the Service follows the policy statement of the Service regarding employee evaluation (as in effect on the date of the enactment of this Act) in a manner which does not violate subsection (a).

(c) CERTIFICATION.—Each district director shall certify quarterly by letter to the Commissioner of Internal Revenue that tax enforcement results are not used in a manner prohibited by subsection (a).

(d) EFFECTIVE DATE.—The provisions of this section shall apply to evaluations conducted on or after January 1, 1989.

(e) EFFECTIVE DATE.—This section shall apply to evaluations conducted on or after the date of the enactment of this Act.

[CCH Explanation at ¶ 981. Committee Reports at ¶ 10,200.]

[¶ 8045] ACT SEC. 1205. EMPLOYEE TRAINING PROGRAM.

(a) IN GENERAL.—Not later than 180 days after the date of the enactment of this Act, the Commissioner of Internal Revenue shall implement an employee training program and shall submit an employee training plan to the Committee on Finance of the Senate and the Committee on Ways and Means of the House of Representatives.

(b) CONTENTS.—The plan submitted under subsection (a) shall—

(1) detail a comprehensive employee training program to ensure adequate customer service training;

(2) detail a schedule for training and the fiscal years during which the training will occur;

(3) detail the funding of the program and relevant information to demonstrate the priority and commitment of resources to the plan;

(4) review the organizational design of customer service;

(5) provide for the implementation of a performance development system; and

(6) provide for at least 16 hours of conflict management training during fiscal year 1999 for employees conducting collection activities.

[CCH Explanation at ¶ 986. Committee Reports at ¶ 10,205.]

TITLE II—ELECTRONIC FILING

[¶ 8050] ACT SEC. 2001. ELECTRONIC FILING OF TAX AND INFORMATION RETURNS.

(a) IN GENERAL.—It is the policy of Congress that—

(1) paperless filing should be the preferred and most convenient means of filing Federal tax and information returns,

(2) it should be the goal of the Internal Revenue Service to have at least 80 percent of all such returns filed electronically by the year 2007, and

(3) the Internal Revenue Service should cooperate with and encourage the private sector by encouraging competition to increase electronic filing of such returns.

(b) STRATEGIC PLAN.—

(1) IN GENERAL.—Not later than 180 days after the date of the enactment of this Act, the Secretary of the Treasury or the Secretary's delegate (hereafter in this section referred to as the "Secretary") shall establish a plan to eliminate barriers, provide incentives, and use competitive market forces to increase electronic filing gradually over the next 10 years while maintaining processing times for paper returns at 40 days. To the extent practicable, such plan shall provide that all returns prepared electronically for taxable years beginning after 2001 shall be filed electronically.

(2) ELECTRONIC COMMERCE ADVISORY GROUP.—To ensure that the Secretary receives input from the private sector in the development and implementation of the plan required by paragraph (1), the Secretary shall convene an electronic commerce advisory group to include representatives from the small business community and from the tax practitioner, preparer, and computerized tax processor communities and other representatives from the electronic filing industry.

* * *

(d) ANNUAL REPORTS.—Not later than June 30 of each calendar year after 1998, the Chairperson of the Internal Revenue Service Oversight Board, the Secretary of the Treasury, and the Chairperson of the electronic commerce advisory group established under subsection (b)(2) shall report to the Committees on Ways and Means, Appropriations, Government Reform and Oversight, and Small Business of the House of Representatives and the Committees on Finance, Appropriations, Governmental Affairs, and Small Business of the Senate on—

(1) the progress of the Internal Revenue Service in meeting the goal of receiving electronically 80 percent of tax and information returns by 2007;

(2) the status of the plan required by subsection (b);

(3) the legislative changes necessary to assist the Internal Revenue Service in meeting such goal; and

(4) the effects on small businesses and the self-employed of electronically filing tax and information returns.

[CCH Explanation at ¶ 1001. Committee Reports at ¶ 10,215.]

[¶ 8055] ACT SEC. 2002. DUE DATE FOR CERTAIN INFORMATION RETURNS.

* * *

(b) STUDY RELATING TO TIME FOR PROVIDING NOTICE TO RECIPIENTS.—

(1) IN GENERAL.—The Secretary of the Treasury shall conduct a study evaluating the effect of extending the deadline for providing statements to persons with respect to whom information is required to be furnished under subparts B and C of part III of subchapter A of chapter 61 of the Internal Revenue Code of 1986 (other than section 6051 of such Code) from January 31 to February 15 of the year in which the return to which the statement relates is required to be filed.

(2) REPORT.—Not later than June 30, 1999, the Secretary of the Treasury shall submit a report on the study under· paragraph (1) to the Committee on Ways and Means of the House of Representatives and the Committee on Finance of the Senate.

* * *

[CCH Explanation at ¶ 1005. Committee Reports at ¶ 10,220.]

[¶ 8060] ACT SEC. 2003. PAPERLESS ELECTRONIC FILING.

* * *

(c) ESTABLISHMENT OF PROCEDURES FOR OTHER INFORMATION.—In the case of taxable periods beginning after December 31, 1999, the Secretary of the Treasury or the Secretary's delegate shall, to the extent practicable, establish procedures to accept, in electronic form, any other information, statements, elections, or schedules, from taxpayers filing returns electronically, so that such taxpayers will not be required to file any paper.

(d) INTERNET AVAILABILITY.—In the case of taxable periods beginning after December 31, 1998, the Secretary of the Treasury or the Secretary's delegate shall establish procedures for all tax forms, instructions, and publications created in the most recent 5-year period to be made available electronically on the Internet in a searchable database at approximately the same time such records are available to the public in paper form. In addition, in the case of taxable periods beginning after December 31, 1998, the Secretary of the Treasury or the Secretary's delegate shall, to the extent practicable, establish procedures for other taxpayer guidance to be made available electronically on the Internet in a searchable database at approximately the same time such guidance is available to the public in paper form.

(e) PROCEDURES FOR AUTHORIZING DISCLOSURE ELECTRONICALLY.—The Secretary shall establish procedures for any taxpayer to authorize, on an electronically filed return, the Secretary to disclose information under section 6103(c) of the Internal Revenue Code of 1986 to the preparer of the return.

* * *

[CCH Explanation at ¶ 1009 and 1027. Committee Reports at ¶ 10,225.]

[¶ 8065] ACT SEC. 2004. RETURN-FREE TAX SYSTEM.

(a) IN GENERAL.—The Secretary of the Treasury or the Secretary's delegate shall develop procedures for the implementation of a return-free tax system under which appropriate individuals would be permitted to comply with the Internal Revenue Code of 1986 without making the return required under section 6012 of such Code for taxable years beginning after 2007.

(b) REPORT.—Not later than June 30 of each calendar year after 1999, the Secretary shall report to the Committee on Ways and Means of the House of Representatives and the Committee on Finance of the Senate on—

(1) what additional resources the Internal Revenue Service would need to implement such a system,

(2) the changes to the Internal Revenue Code of 1986 that could enhance the use of such a system,

(3) the procedures developed pursuant to subsection (a), and

(4) the number and classes of taxpayers that would be permitted to use the procedures developed pursuant to subsection (a).

[CCH Explanation at ¶ 1019. Committee Reports at ¶ 10,230.]

[¶ 8070] ACT SEC. 2005. ACCESS TO ACCOUNT INFORMATION.

(a) IN GENERAL.—Not later than December 31, 2006, the Secretary of the Treasury or the Secretary's delegate shall develop procedures under which a taxpayer filing returns electronically (and their designees under section 6103(c) of the Internal Revenue Code of 1986) would be able to review the taxpayer's account electronically, but only if all necessary safeguards to ensure the privacy of such account information are in place.

(b) REPORT.—Not later than December 31, 2003, the Secretary of the Treasury shall report on the progress the Secretary is making on the development of procedures under subsection (a) to the Committee on Ways and Means of the House of Representatives and the Committee on Finance of the Senate.

[CCH Explanation at ¶ 1025. Committee Reports at ¶ 10,235.]

TITLE III—TAXPAYER PROTECTION AND RIGHTS

[¶ 8071] ACT SEC. 3000. SHORT TITLE.

This title may be cited as the "Taxpayer Bill of Rights 3".

* * *

Subtitle B—Proceedings by Taxpayers

* * *

[¶ 8075] ACT SEC. 3105. ADMINISTRATIVE APPEAL OF ADVERSE IRS DETERMINATION OF TAX-EXEMPT STATUS OF BOND ISSUE.

The Internal Revenue Service shall amend its administrative procedures to provide that if, upon examination, the Internal Revenue Service proposes to an issuer that interest on previously issued obligations of such issuer is not excludable from gross income under section 103(a) of the Internal Revenue Code of 1986, the issuer of such obligations shall have an administrative appeal of right to a senior officer of the Internal Revenue Service Office of Appeals.

* * *

[CCH Explanation at ¶ 1137. Committee Reports at ¶ 10,270.]

Subtitle C—Relief for Innocent Spouses and for Taxpayers Unable To Manage Their Financial Affairs Due to Disabilities

[¶ 8080] ACT SEC. 3201. RELIEF FROM JOINT AND SEVERAL LIABILITY ON JOINT RETURN.

* * *

(c) SEPARATE FORM FOR APPLYING FOR SPOUSAL RELIEF.—Not later than 180 days after the date of the enactment of this Act, the Secretary of the Treasury shall develop a separate form with instructions for use by taxpayers in applying for relief under section 6015(a) of the Internal Revenue Code of 1986, as added by this section.

(d) SEPARATE NOTICE TO EACH FILER.—The Secretary of the Treasury shall, wherever practicable, send any notice relating to a joint return under section 6013 of the Internal Revenue Code of 1986 separately to each individual filing the joint return.

* * *

[CCH Explanation at ¶ 1290. Committee Reports at ¶ 10,285.]

Subtitle D—Provisions Relating to Interest and Penalties

* * *

[¶ 8085] ACT SEC. 3309. ABATEMENT OF INTEREST ON UNDERPAYMENTS BY TAXPAYERS IN PRESIDENTIALLY DECLARED DISASTER AREAS.

* * *

(c) EMERGENCY DESIGNATION.—

(1) For the purposes of section 252(e) of the Balanced Budget and Emergency Deficit Control Act, Congress designates the provisions of this section as an emergency requirement.

* * *

[CCH Explanation at ¶ 1417. Committee Reports at ¶ 10,355.]

Subtitle E—Protections for Taxpayers Subject to Audit or Collection Activities

* * *

PART II—EXAMINATION ACTIVITIES

* * *

[¶ 8090] ACT SEC. 3414. THREAT OF AUDIT PROHIBITED TO COERCE TIP REPORTING ALTERNATIVE COMMITMENT AGREEMENTS.

The Secretary of the Treasury or the Secretary's delegate shall instruct employees of the Internal Revenue Service that they may not threaten to audit any taxpayer in an attempt to coerce the taxpayer into entering into a Tip Reporting Alternative Commitment Agreement.

* * *

[CCH Explanation at ¶ 1116. Committee Reports at ¶ 10,390.]

PART III—COLLECTION ACTIVITIES

Subpart A—Approval Process

[¶ 8095] ACT SEC. 3421. APPROVAL PROCESS FOR LIENS, LEVIES, AND SEIZURES.

(a) IN GENERAL.—The Commissioner of Internal Revenue shall develop and implement procedures under which—

(1) a determination by an employee to file a notice of lien or levy with respect to, or to levy or seize, any property or right to property would, where appropriate, be required to be reviewed by a supervisor of the employee before the action was taken, and

(2) appropriate disciplinary action would be taken against the employee or supervisor where the procedures under paragraph (1) were not followed.

(b) REVIEW PROCESS.—The review process under subsection (a)(1) may include a certification that the employee has—

(1) reviewed the taxpayer's information,

(2) verified that a balance is due, and

(3) affirmed that the action proposed to be taken is appropriate given the taxpayer's circumstances, considering the amount due and the value of the property or right to property.

(c) EFFECTIVE DATES.—

(1) IN GENERAL.—Except as provided in paragraph (2), this section shall take effect on the date of the enactment of this Act.

(2) AUTOMATED COLLECTION SYSTEM ACTIONS.—In the case of any action under an automated collection system, this section shall apply to actions initiated after December 31, 2000.

* * *

[CCH Explanation at ¶ 1201. Committee Reports at ¶ 10,415.]

Subpart C—Seizures

* * *

[¶ 8100] ACT SEC. 3443. UNIFORM ASSET DISPOSAL MECHANISM.

Not later than the date which is 2 years after the date of the enactment of this Act, the Secretary of the Treasury or the Secretary's delegate shall implement a uniform asset disposal mechanism for sales under section 6335 of the Internal Revenue Code of 1986. The mechanism should be designed to remove any participation in such sales by revenue officers of the Internal Revenue Service and should consider the use of outsourcing.

* * *

[CCH Explanation at ¶ 1246. Committee Reports at ¶ 10,475.]

PART IV—PROVISIONS RELATING TO EXAMINATION AND COLLECTION ACTIVITIES
* * *

[¶ 8110] ACT SEC. 3462. OFFERS-IN-COMPROMISE.
* * *

(d) PREPARATION OF STATEMENT RELATING TO OFFERS-IN-COMPROMISE.—The Secretary of the Treasury shall prepare a statement which sets forth in simple, non-technical terms the rights of a taxpayer and the obligations of the Internal Revenue Service relating to offers-in-compromise. Such statement shall—

(1) advise taxpayers who have entered into a compromise of the advantages of promptly notifying the Internal Revenue Service of any change of address or marital status,

(2) provide notice to taxpayers that in the case of a compromise terminated due to the actions of 1 spouse or former spouse, the Internal Revenue Service will, upon application, reinstate such compromise with the spouse or former spouse who remains in compliance with such compromise, and

(3) provide notice to the taxpayer that the taxpayer may appeal the rejection of an offer-in-compromise to the Internal Revenue Service Office of Appeals.

* * *

[CCH Explanation at ¶ 1270. Committee Reports at ¶ 10,520.]

[¶ 8115] ACT SEC. 3463. NOTICE OF DEFICIENCY TO SPECIFY DEADLINES FOR FILING TAX COURT PETITION.

(a) IN GENERAL.—The Secretary of the Treasury or the Secretary's delegate shall include on each notice of deficiency under section 6212 of the Internal Revenue Code of 1986 the date determined by such Secretary (or delegate) as the last day on which the taxpayer may file a petition with the Tax Court.

* * *

(c) EFFECTIVE DATE.—Subsection (a) and the amendment made by subsection (b) shall apply to notices mailed after December 31, 1998.

* * *

[CCH Explanation at ¶ 1326. Committee Reports at ¶ 10,525.]

[¶ 8120] ACT SEC. 3465. IRS PROCEDURES RELATING TO APPEALS OF EXAMINATIONS AND COLLECTIONS.
* * *

(b) APPEALS OFFICERS IN EACH STATE.—The Commissioner of Internal Revenue shall ensure that an appeals officer is regularly available within each State.

(c) APPEALS VIDEOCONFERENCING ALTERNATIVE FOR RURAL AREAS.—The Commissioner of Internal Revenue shall consider the use of the videoconferencing of appeals conferences between appeals officers and taxpayers seeking appeals in rural or remote areas.

* * *

[CCH Explanation at ¶ 1258. Committee Reports at ¶ 10,535.]

[¶ 8125] ACT SEC. 3468. PROHIBITION ON REQUESTS TO TAXPAYERS TO GIVE UP RIGHTS TO BRING ACTIONS.

(a) PROHIBITION.—No officer or employee of the United States may request a taxpayer to waive the taxpayer's right to bring a civil action against the United States or any officer or employee of the United States for any action taken in connection with the internal revenue laws.

(b) EXCEPTIONS.—Subsection (a) shall not apply in any case where—

(1) a taxpayer waives the right described in subsection (a) knowingly and voluntarily, or

(2) the request by the officer or employee is made in person and the taxpayer's attorney or other federally authorized tax practitioner (within the meaning of section 7525(a)(3)(A) of the Internal Revenue Code of 1986) is present, or the request is made in writing to the taxpayer's attorney or other representative.

[CCH Explanation at ¶ 1133. Committee Reports at ¶ 10,550.]

Subtitle F—Disclosures to Taxpayers

[¶ 8130] ACT SEC. 3501. EXPLANATION OF JOINT AND SEVERAL LIABILITY.

(a) IN GENERAL.—The Secretary of the Treasury or the Secretary's delegate shall, as soon as practicable, but not later than 180 days after the date of the enactment of this Act, establish procedures to clearly alert married taxpayers of their joint and several liabilities on all appropriate publications and instructions.

(b) RIGHT TO LIMIT LIABILITY.—The procedures under subsection (a) shall include requirements that notice of an individual's right to relief under section 6015 of the Internal Revenue Code of 1986 shall be included in the statement required by section 6227 of the Omnibus Taxpayer Bill of Rights (Internal Revenue Service Publication No. 1) and in any collection-related notices.

[CCH Explanation at ¶ 1294. Committee Reports at ¶ 10,565.]

[¶ 8135] ACT SEC. 3502. EXPLANATION OF TAXPAYERS' RIGHTS IN INTERVIEWS WITH THE INTERNAL REVENUE SERVICE.

The Secretary of the Treasury or the Secretary's delegate shall, as soon as practicable, but not later than 180 days after the date of the enactment of this Act, revise the statement required by section 6227 of the Omnibus Taxpayer Bill of Rights (Internal Revenue Service Publication No. 1) to more clearly inform taxpayers of their rights—

(1) to be represented at interviews with the Internal Revenue Service by any person authorized to practice before the Internal Revenue Service, and

(2) to suspend an interview pursuant to section 7521(b)(2) of the Internal Revenue Code of 1986.

[CCH Explanation at ¶ 1121. Committee Reports at ¶ 10,570.]

[¶ 8140] ACT SEC. 3503. DISCLOSURE OF CRITERIA FOR EXAMINATION SELECTION.

(a) IN GENERAL.—The Secretary of the Treasury or the Secretary's delegate shall, as soon as practicable, but not later than 180 days after the date of the enactment of this Act, incorporate into the statement required by section 6227 of the Omnibus Taxpayer Bill of Rights (Internal Revenue Service Publication No. 1) a statement which sets forth in simple and nontechnical terms the criteria and procedures for selecting taxpayers for examination. Such statement shall not include any information the disclosure of which would be detrimental to law enforcement, but shall specify the general procedures used by the Internal Revenue Service, including whether taxpayers are selected for examination on the basis of information available in the media or on the basis of information provided to the Internal Revenue Service by informants.

(b) TRANSMISSION TO COMMITTEES OF CONGRESS.—The Secretary shall transmit drafts of the statement required under subsection (a) (or proposed revisions to any such statement) to the Committee on Ways and Means of the House of Representatives and the Committee on Finance of the Senate on the same day.

[CCH Explanation at ¶ 1126. Committee Reports at ¶ 10,575.]

[¶ 8145] ACT SEC. 3504. EXPLANATIONS OF APPEALS AND COLLECTION PROCESS.

The Secretary of the Treasury or the Secretary's delegate shall, as soon as practicable, but not later than 180 days after the date of the enactment of this Act, include with any 1st letter of proposed deficiency which allows the taxpayer an opportunity for administrative review in the Internal Revenue Service Office of Appeals an explanation of the entire process from examination through collection with respect to such proposed deficiency, including the assistance available to the taxpayer from the National Taxpayer Advocate at various points in the process.

* * *

[CCH Explanation at ¶ 1266. Committee Reports at ¶ 10,580.]

[¶ 8150] ACT SEC. 3506. STATEMENTS REGARDING INSTALLMENT AGREEMENTS.

The Secretary of the Treasury or the Secretary's delegate shall, beginning not later than July 1, 2000, provide each taxpayer who has an installment agreement in effect under section 6159 of the Internal Revenue Code of 1986 an annual statement setting forth the initial balance at the beginning of the year, the payments made during the year, and the remaining balance as of the end of the year.

* * *

[CCH Explanation at ¶ 1278. Committee Reports at ¶ 10,590.]

[¶ 8155] ACT SEC. 3508. DISCLOSURE TO TAXPAYERS.

The Secretary of the Treasury or the Secretary's delegate shall ensure that any instructions booklet accompanying an individual Federal income tax return form (including forms 1040, 1040A, 1040EZ, and any similar or successor forms) shall include, in clear language, in conspicuous print, and in a conspicuous place, a concise description of the conditions under which return information may be disclosed to any party outside the Internal Revenue Service, including disclosure to any State or agency, body, or commission (or legal representative) thereof.

* * *

[CCH Explanation at ¶ 864. Committee Reports at ¶ 10,600.]

Subtitle H—Other Matters

[¶ 8160] ACT SEC. 3701. CATALOGING COMPLAINTS.

In collecting data for the report required under section 1211 of Taxpayer Bill of Rights 2 (Public Law 104-168), the Secretary of the Treasury or the Secretary's delegate shall, not later than January 1, 2000, maintain records of taxpayer complaints of misconduct by Internal Revenue Service employees on an individual employee basis.

* * *

[CCH Explanation at ¶ 886. Committee Reports at ¶ 10,635.]

[¶ 8165] ACT SEC. 3703. PAYMENT OF TAXES.

The Secretary of the Treasury or the Secretary's delegate shall establish such rules, regulations, and procedures as are necessary to allow payment of taxes by check or money order made payable to the United States Treasury.

* * *

[CCH Explanation at ¶ 893. Committee Reports at ¶ 10,645.]

[¶ 8170] ACT SEC. 3705. IRS EMPLOYEE CONTACTS.

(a) NOTICE.—The Secretary of the Treasury or the Secretary's delegate shall provide that—

(1) any manually generated correspondence received by a taxpayer from the Internal Revenue Service shall include in a prominent manner the name, telephone number, and unique identifying number of an Internal Revenue Service employee the taxpayer may contact with respect to the correspondence,

(2) any other correspondence or notice received by a taxpayer from the Internal Revenue Service shall include in a prominent manner a telephone number that the taxpayer may contact, and

(3) an Internal Revenue Service employee shall give a taxpayer during a telephone or personal contact the employee's name and unique identifying number.

(b) SINGLE CONTACT.—The Secretary of the Treasury or the Secretary's delegate shall develop a procedure under which, to the extent practicable and if advantageous to the taxpayer, one Internal Revenue Service employee shall be assigned to handle a taxpayer's matter until it is resolved.

Act Sec. 3705(b) ¶ 8170

(c) TELEPHONE HELPLINE IN SPANISH.—The Secretary of the Treasury or the Secretary's delegate shall provide, in appropriate circumstances, that taxpayer questions on telephone helplines of the Internal Revenue Service are answered in Spanish.

(d) OTHER TELEPHONE HELPLINE OPTIONS.—The Secretary of the Treasury or the Secretary's delegate shall provide, in appropriate circumstances, on telephone helplines of the Internal Revenue Service an option for any taxpayer to talk to an Internal Revenue Service employee during normal business hours. The person shall direct phone questions of the taxpayer to other Internal Revenue Service personnel who can provide assistance to the taxpayer.

(e) EFFECTIVE DATES.—

(1) IN GENERAL.—Except as otherwise provided in this subsection, this section shall take effect 60 days after the date of the enactment of this Act.

(2) SUBSECTION (c).—Subsection (c) shall take effect on January 1, 2000.

(3) SUBSECTION (d).—Subsection (d) shall take effect on January 1, 2000.

(4) UNIQUE IDENTIFYING NUMBER.—Any requirement under this section to provide a unique identifying number shall take effect 6 months after the date of the enactment of this Act.

[CCH Explanation at ¶ 1166 and 1167. Committee Reports at ¶ 10,655.]

[¶ 8175] ACT SEC. 3706. USE OF PSEUDONYMS BY IRS EMPLOYEES.

(a) IN GENERAL.—Any employee of the Internal Revenue Service may use a pseudonym only if—

(1) adequate justification for the use of a pseudonym is provided by the employee, including protection of personal safety, and

(2) such use is approved by the employee's supervisor before the pseudonym is used.

(b) EFFECTIVE DATE.—Subsection (a) shall apply to requests made after the date of the enactment of this Act.

[CCH Explanation at ¶ 1176. Committee Reports at ¶ 10,660.]

[¶ 8180] ACT SEC. 3707. ILLEGAL TAX PROTESTER DESIGNATION.

(a) PROHIBITION.—The officers and employees of the Internal Revenue Service—

(1) shall not designate taxpayers as illegal tax protesters (or any similar designation), and

(2) in the case of any such designation made on or before the date of the enactment of this Act—

(A) shall remove such designation from the individual master file, and

(B) shall disregard any such designation not located in the individual master file.

(b) DESIGNATION OF NONFILERS ALLOWED.—An officer or employee of the Internal Revenue Service may designate any appropriate taxpayer as a nonfiler, but shall remove such designation once the taxpayer has filed income tax returns for 2 consecutive taxable years and paid all taxes shown on such returns.

(c) EFFECTIVE DATE.—The provisions of this section shall take effect on the date of the enactment of this Act, except that the removal of any designation under subsection (a)(2)(A) shall not be required to begin before January 1, 1999.

* * *

[CCH Explanation at ¶ 891. Committee Reports at ¶ 10,665.]

[¶ 8185] ACT SEC. 3709. LISTING OF LOCAL IRS TELEPHONE NUMBERS AND ADDRESSES.

The Secretary of the Treasury or the Secretary's delegate shall, as soon as practicable, provide that the local telephone numbers and addresses of Internal Revenue Service offices located in any particular area be listed in a telephone book for that area.

* * *

[CCH Explanation at ¶ 1171. Committee Reports at ¶ 10,675.]

¶ 8175 Act Sec. 3706(a)

Subtitle I—Studies

[¶ 8190] SEC. 3801. ADMINISTRATION OF PENALTIES AND INTEREST.

The Joint Committee on Taxation and the Secretary of the Treasury shall each conduct a separate study—

(1) reviewing the administration and implementation by the Internal Revenue Service of the interest and penalty provisions of the Internal Revenue Code of 1986 (including the penalty reform provisions of the Omnibus Budget Reconciliation Act of 1989), and

(2) making any legislative and administrative recommendations the Committee or the Secretary deems appropriate to simplify penalty or interest administration and reduce taxpayer burden.

Such studies shall be submitted to the Committee on Ways and Means of the House of Representatives and the Committee on Finance of the Senate not later than 1 year after the date of the enactment of this Act.

[CCH Explanation at ¶ 1441. Committee Reports at ¶ 10,715.]

[¶ 8195] SEC. 3802. CONFIDENTIALITY OF TAX RETURN INFORMATION.

The Joint Committee on Taxation and the Secretary of the Treasury shall each conduct a separate study of the scope and use of provisions regarding taxpayer confidentiality, and shall report the findings of such study, together with such recommendations as the Committee or the Secretary deems appropriate, to the Congress not later than 18 months after the date of the enactment of this Act. Such study shall examine—

(1) the present protections for taxpayer privacy,

(2) any need for third parties to use tax return information,

(3) whether greater levels of voluntary compliance may be achieved by allowing the public to know who is legally required to file tax returns, but does not file tax returns,

(4) the interrelationship of the taxpayer confidentiality provisions in the Internal Revenue Code of 1986 with such provisions in other Federal law, including section 552a of title 5, United States Code (commonly known as the "Freedom of Information Act"),

(5) the impact on taxpayer privacy of the sharing of income tax return information for purposes of enforcement of State and local tax laws other than income tax laws, and including the impact on the taxpayer privacy intended to be protected at the Federal, State, and local levels under Public Law 105-35, the Taxpayer Browsing Protection Act of 1997, and

(6) whether the public interest would be served by greater disclosure of information relating to tax exempt organizations described in section 501 of the Internal Revenue Code of 1986.

[CCH Explanation at ¶ 862. Committee Reports at ¶ 10,720.]

[¶ 8200] SEC. 3803. STUDY OF NONCOMPLIANCE WITH INTERNAL REVENUE LAWS BY TAXPAYERS.

Not later than 1 year after the date of the enactment of this Act, the Secretary of the Treasury and the Commissioner of Internal Revenue shall conduct jointly a study, in consultation with the Joint Committee on Taxation, of the noncompliance with internal revenue laws by taxpayers (including willful noncompliance and noncompliance due to tax law complexity or other factors) and report the findings of such study to Congress.

[CCH Explanation at ¶ 877. Committee Reports at ¶ 10,725.]

[¶ 8205] SEC. 3804. STUDY OF PAYMENTS MADE FOR DETECTION OF UNDERPAYMENTS AND FRAUD.

Not later than 1 year after the date of the enactment of this Act, the Secretary of the Treasury shall conduct a study and report to Congress on the use of section 7623 of the Internal Revenue Code of 1986 including—

(1) an analysis of the present use of such section and the results of such use, and

(2) any legislative or administrative recommendations regarding the provisions of such section and its application.

* * *

Code Sec. 3804   ¶ 8205

[CCH Explanation at ¶ 876. Committee Reports at ¶ 10,730.]

TITLE IV—CONGRESSIONAL ACCOUNTABILITY FOR THE INTERNAL REVENUE SERVICE

* * *

Subtitle B—Century Date Change

[¶ 8210] ACT SEC. 4011. CENTURY DATE CHANGE.

It is the sense of Congress that—

(1) the Internal Revenue Service should place a high priority on resolving the century date change computing problems, and

(2) the Internal Revenue Service efforts to resolve the century date change computing problems should be funded fully to provide for certain resolution of such problems.

[CCH Explanation at ¶ 856. Committee Reports at ¶ 10,755.]

Subtitle C—Tax Law Complexity

[¶ 8215] ACT SEC. 4021. ROLE OF THE INTERNAL REVENUE SERVICE.

It is the sense of Congress that the Internal Revenue Service should provide Congress with an independent view of tax administration, and that during the legislative process, the tax writing committees of Congress should hear from front-line technical experts at the Internal Revenue Service with respect to the administrability of pending amendments to the Internal Revenue Code of 1986.

[CCH Explanation at ¶ 841. Committee Reports at ¶ 10,761.]

[¶ 8220] ACT SEC. 4022. TAX LAW COMPLEXITY ANALYSIS.

(a) COMMISSIONER STUDY.—

(1) IN GENERAL.—The Commissioner of Internal Revenue shall conduct each year after 1998 an analysis of the sources of complexity in administration of the Federal tax laws. Such analysis may include an analysis of—

(A) questions frequently asked by taxpayers with respect to return filing,

(B) common errors made by taxpayers in filling out their returns,

(C) areas of law which frequently result in disagreements between taxpayers and the Internal Revenue Service,

(D) major areas of law in which there is no (or incomplete) published guidance or in which the law is uncertain,

(E) areas in which revenue officers make frequent errors interpreting or applying the law,

(F) the impact of recent legislation on complexity, and

(G) forms supplied by the Internal Revenue Service, including the time it takes for taxpayers to complete and review forms, the number of taxpayers who use each form, and how recent legislation has affected the time it takes to complete and review forms.

(2) REPORT.—The Commissioner shall not later than March 1 of each year report the results of the analysis conducted under paragraph (1) for the preceding year to the Committee on Ways and Means of the House of Representatives and the Committee on Finance of the Senate. The report shall include any recommendations—

(A) for reducing the complexity of the administration of Federal tax laws, and

(B) for repeal or modification of any provision the Commissioner believes adds undue and unnecessary complexity to the administration of the Federal tax laws.

(b) ANALYSIS TO ACCOMPANY CERTAIN LEGISLATION.—

(1) IN GENERAL.—The Joint Committee on Taxation, in consultation with the Internal Revenue Service and the Department of the Treasury, shall include a tax complexity analysis in each report for legislation, or provide such analysis to members of the committee reporting the legislation as soon as practicable after the report is filed, if—

(A) such legislation is reported by the Committee on Finance in the Senate, the Committee on Ways and Means of the House of Representatives, or any committee of conference, and

(B) such legislation includes a provision which would directly or indirectly amend the Internal Revenue Code of 1986 and which has widespread applicability to individuals or small businesses.

(2) TAX COMPLEXITY ANALYSIS.—For purposes of this subsection, the term "tax complexity analysis" means, with respect to any legislation, a report on the complexity and administrative difficulties of each provision described in paragraph (1)(B) which—

(A) includes—

(i) an estimate of the number of taxpayers affected by the provision, and

(ii) if applicable, the income level of taxpayers affected by the provision, and

(B) should include (if determinable)—

(i) the extent to which tax forms supplied by the Internal Revenue Service would require revision and whether any new forms would be required,

(ii) the extent to which taxpayers would be required to keep additional records,

(iii) the estimated cost to taxpayers to comply with the provision,

(iv) the extent to which enactment of the provision would require the Internal Revenue Service to develop or modify regulatory guidance,

(v) the extent to which the provision may result in disagreements between taxpayers and the Internal Revenue Service, and

(vi) any expected impact on the Internal Revenue Service from the provision (including the impact on internal training, revision of the Internal Revenue Manual, reprogramming of computers, and the extent to which the Internal Revenue Service would be required to divert or redirect resources in response to the provision).

(3) LEGISLATION SUBJECT TO POINT OF ORDER IN HOUSE OF REPRESENTATIVES.—

(A) LEGISLATION REPORTED BY COMMITTEE ON WAYS AND MEANS.—Clause 2(1) of rule XI of the Rules of the House of Representatives is amended by adding at the end the following new subparagraph:

"(8) The report of the Committee on Ways and Means on any bill or joint resolution containing any provision amending the Internal Revenue Code of 1986 shall include a Tax Complexity Analysis prepared by the Joint Committee on Taxation in accordance with section 4022(b) of the Internal Revenue Service Restructuring and Reform Act of 1998 unless the Committee on Ways an d Means causes to have such Analysis printed in the Congressional Record prior to the consideration of the bill or joint resolution."

(B) CONFERENCE REPORTS.—Rule XXVIII of the Rules of the House of Representatives is amended by adding at the end the following new clause:

"7. It shall not be in order to consider the report of a committee of conference which contains any provision amending the Internal Revenue Code of 1986 unless—

"(a) the accompanying joint explanatory statement contains a Tax Complexity Analysis prepared by the Joint Committee on Taxation in accordance with section 4022(b) of the Internal Revenue Service Restructuring and Reform Act of 1998, or

"(b) such Analysis is printed in the Congressional Record prior to the consideration of the report."

(C) RULES OF HOUSE OF REPRESENTATIVES.—This paragraph is enacted by the House of Representatives—

(i) as an exercise of the rulemaking power of the House of Representatives, and as such it is deemed a part of the Rules of the House, and it supersedes other rules only to the extent that it is inconsistent therewith; and

(ii) with full recognition of the constitutional right of the House to change its rules at any time, in the same manner and to the same extent as in the case of any other rule of the House.

(4) EFFECTIVE DATE.—This subsection shall apply to legislation considered on and after January 1, 1999.

Act Sec. 4022(b)   ¶ 8220

[CCH Explanation at ¶ 846. Committee Reports at ¶ 10,770.]

TITLE V—ADDITIONAL PROVISIONS
* * *

[¶ 8225] ACT SEC. 5003. CLARIFICATION OF DESIGNATION OF NORMAL TRADE RELATIONS.

(a) FINDINGS AND POLICY.—

(1) FINDINGS.—The Congress makes the following findings:

(A) Since the 18th century, the principle of nondiscrimination among countries with which the United States has trade relations, commonly referred to as "most-favored-nation" treatment, has been a cornerstone of United States trade policy.

(B) Although the principle remains firmly in place as a fundamental concept in United States trade relations, the term "most-favored-nation" is a misnomer which has led to public misunderstanding.

(C) It is neither the purpose nor the effect of the most-favored-nation principle to treat any country as "most favored". To the contrary, the principle reflects the intention to confer on a country the same trade benefits that are conferred on any other country, that is, the intention not to discriminate among trading partners.

(D) The term "normal trade relations" is a more accurate description of the principle of nondiscrimination as it applies to the tariffs applicable generally to imports from United States trading partners, that is, the general rates of duty set forth in column 1 of the Harmonized Tariff Schedule of the United States.

(2) POLICY.—It is the sense of the Congress that—

(A) the language used in United States laws, treaties, agreements, executive orders, directives, and regulations should more clearly and accurately reflect the underlying principles of United States trade policy; and

(B) accordingly, the term "normal trade relations" should, where appropriate, be substituted for the term "most-favored-nation".

(b) CHANGE IN TERMINOLOGY.—

(1) TRADE EXPANSION ACT OF 1962.—The heading for section 251 of the Trade Expansion Act of 1962 (19 U.S.C. 1881) is amended to read as follows: "**NORMAL TRADE RELATIONS**".

(2) TRADE ACT OF 1974.—(A) Section 402 of the Trade Act of 1974 (19 U.S.C. 2432) is amended by striking "(most-favored-nation treatment)" each place it appears and inserting "(normal trade relations)".

(B) Section 601(9) of the Trade Act of 1974 (19 U.S.C. 2481(9)) is amended by striking "most-favored-nation treatment" and inserting "trade treatment based on normal trade relations (known under international law as most-favored-nation treatment)".

(3) CFTA.—Section 302(a)(3)(C) of the United States Canada Free-Trade Agreement Implementation Act of 1988 (19 U.S.C. 2112 note) is amended by striking "the most-favored-nation rate of duty" each place it appears and inserting "the general subcolumn of the column 1 rate of duty set forth in the Harmonized Tariff Schedule of the United States".

(4) NAFTA.—Section 202(n) of the North American Free Trade Agreement Implementation Act (19 U.S.C. 3332(n)) is amended by striking "most-favored-nation".

(5) URUGUAY ROUND AGREEMENTS ACT.—Section 135(a)(2) of the Uruguay Round Agreements Act (19 U.S.C. 3555(a)(2)) is amended by striking "most-favored-nation" and inserting "normal trade relations".

(6) SEED ACT.—Section 2(c)(11) of the Support for East European Democracy (SEED) Act of 1989 (22 U.S.C. 5401(c)(11)) is amended—

(A) by striking "(commonly referred to as 'most favored nation status')", and

(B) by striking "MOST FAVORED NATION TRADE STATUS" in the heading and inserting "NORMAL TRADE RELATIONS".

¶ 8225   Act Sec. 5003(a)

(7) United States-Hong Kong Policy Act of 1992.—Section 103(4) of the United States-Hong Kong Policy Act of 1992 (22 U.S.C. 5713(4)) is amended by striking "(commonly referred to as 'most-favored-nation status')".

(c) Savings Provisions.—Nothing in this section shall affect the meaning of any provision of law, Executive order, Presidential proclamation, rule, regulation, delegation of authority, other document, or treaty or other international agreement of the United States relating to the principle of "most-favored-nation" (or "most favored nation") treatment. Any Executive order, Presidential proclamation, rule, regulation, delegation of authority, other document, or treaty or other international agreement of the United States that has been issued, made, granted, or allowed to become effective and that is in effect on the effective date of this Act, or was to become effective on or after the effective date of this Act, shall continue in effect according to its terms until modified, terminated, superseded, set aside, or revoked in accordance with law.

[Committee Reports at ¶ 10,795.]

TITLE VI—TECHNICAL CORRECTIONS

[¶ 8230] ACT SEC. 6001. SHORT TITLE; COORDINATION WITH OTHER TITLES.

(a) Short Title.—This title may be cited as the "Tax Technical Corrections Act of 1998".

(b) Coordination With Other Titles.—For purposes of applying the amendments made by any title of this Act other than this title, the provisions of this title shall be treated as having been enacted immediately before the provisions of such other titles.

[¶ 8235] ACT SEC. 6002. DEFINITIONS.

For purposes of this title—

(1) 1986 Code.—The term "1986 Code" means the Internal Revenue Code of 1986.

(2) 1997 Act.—The term "1997 Act" means the Taxpayer Relief Act of 1997.

* * *

[¶ 8239] ACT SEC. 6004. AMENDMENTS RELATED TO TITLE II OF 1997 ACT.

(a) Amendments Related to Section 201 of 1997 Act.—

* * *

(3) Subparagraph (A) of section 201(c)(2) of the 1997 Act is amended to read as follows:

"(A) Subparagraph (B) of section 6724(d)(1) (relating to definitions) is amended by redesignating clauses (x) through (xv) as clauses (xi) through (xvi), respectively, and by inserting after clause (ix) the following new clause:

" '(x) section 6050S (relating to returns relating to payments for qualified tuition and related expenses),' ".

● ● *Taxpayer Relief Act of 1997 Act Sec. 201(c)(2)(A) before amendment*

ACT SEC. 201. HOPE AND LIFETIME LEARNING CREDITS.

* * *

(c) Returns Relating to Tuition and Related Expenses.—

* * *

(2) Assessable penalties.—

(A) Subparagraph (B) of section 6724(d)(1) (relating to definitions) is amended by redesignating clauses (ix) through (xiv) as clauses (x) through (xv), respectively, and by inserting after clause (viii) the following new clause:

"(ix) section 6050S (relating to returns relating to payments for qualified tuition and related expenses),".

* * *

* * *

(g) Amendments Related to Section 226 of 1997 Act.—

Act Sec. 6004(g) ¶ 8239

(1) Section 226(a) of the 1997 Act is amended by striking "section 1397E" and inserting "section 1397D".

● ● *Taxpayer Relief Act of 1997 Act Sec. 226(a) as amended*

ACT SEC. 226. INCENTIVES FOR EDUCATION ZONES.

(a) IN GENERAL.—Subchapter U of chapter 1 (relating to additional incentives for empowerment zones) is amended by redesignating part IV as part V, by redesignating *section 1397D* as section 1397F, and by inserting after part III the following new part:

* * *

* * *

[CCH Explanation at ¶ 226 and 244. Committee Reports at ¶ 10,835 and 10,865.]

[¶ 8240] ACT SEC. 6005. AMENDMENTS RELATED TO TITLE III OF 1997 ACT.

(a) AMENDMENTS RELATED TO SECTION 301 OF 1997 ACT.—

* * *

(2) Paragraph (2) of section 301(a) of the 1997 Act is amended by inserting "after '$10,000' " before the period.

● ● *Taxpayer Relief Act of 1997 Act Sec. 301(a)(2) as amended*

ACT SEC. 301. RESTORATION OF IRA DEDUCTION FOR CERTAIN TAXPAYERS.

(a) INCREASE IN INCOME LIMITS APPLICABLE TO ACTIVE PARTICIPANTS.—

* * *

(2) INCREASE IN PHASE-OUT RANGE FOR JOINT RETURNS.—Clause (ii) of section 219(g)(2)(A) is amended by inserting "($20,000 in the case of a joint return for a taxable year beginning after December 31, 2006)" *after "$10,000".*

* * *

* * *

(b) AMENDMENTS RELATED TO SECTION 302 OF 1997 ACT.—

* * *

(8) * * *

(C) Section 302(b) of the 1997 Act is amended by striking "Section 4973(b)" and inserting "Section 4973".

● ● *Taxpayer Relief Act of 1997 Act Sec. 302(b) as amended*

ACT SEC. 302. ESTABLISHMENT OF NONDEDUCTIBLE TAX-FREE INDIVIDUAL RETIREMENT ACCOUNTS.

* * *

(b) EXCESS CONTRIBUTIONS.—*Section 4973*, as amended by title II, is amended by adding at the end the following new subsection:

"(f) EXCESS CONTRIBUTIONS TO ROTH IRAS.— * * *

* * *

* * *

(e) AMENDMENTS RELATED TO SECTION 312 OF 1997 ACT.—

* * *

(3) Section 312(d)[e](2) of the 1997 Act (relating to sales before date of the enactment) is amended by inserting "on or" before "before" each place it appears in the text and heading.

● ● *Taxpayer Relief Act of 1997 Act Sec. 312(d)[e](2) as amended*

ACT SEC. 312. EXEMPTION FROM TAX FOR GAIN ON SALE OF PRINCIPAL RESIDENCE.

* * *

(d)[e] EFFECTIVE DATE.—

* * *

(2) SALES *ON OR* BEFORE DATE OF ENACTMENT.—At the election of the taxpayer, the amendments made by this section shall not apply to any sale or exchange *on or* before the date of the enactment of this Act.

* * *

* * *

[CCH Explanation at ¶ 251. Committee Reports at ¶ 10,930.]

[¶ 8245] ACT SEC. 6007. AMENDMENTS RELATED TO TITLE V OF 1997 ACT.

(a) AMENDMENTS RELATED TO SECTION 501 OF 1997 ACT.—

* * *

(2) Subsection (f) of section 501 of the 1997 Act is amended by inserting "(other than the amendment made by subsection (d))" after "this section".

● ● *Taxpayer Relief Act of 1997 Act Sec. 501(f) as amended*

ACT SEC. 501. COST-OF-LIVING ADJUSTMENTS RELATING TO ESTATE AND GIFT TAX PROVISIONS.

* * *

(f) EFFECTIVE DATE.—The amendments made by this section *(other than the amendment made by subsection (d))* shall apply to the estates of decedents dying, and gifts made, after December 31, 1997.

* * *

(e) AMENDMENTS RELATED TO SECTION 506 OF THE 1997 ACT.—

(1) Paragraph (1) of section 506(e) of the 1997 Act is amended by striking "and (c)" and inserting ", (c), and (d)".

● ● *Taxpayer Relief Act of 1997 Act Sec. 506(e)(1) as amended*

ACT SEC. 506. GIFTS MAY NOT BE REVALUED FOR ESTATE TAX PURPOSES AFTER EXPIRATION OF STATUTE OF LIMITATIONS.

* * *

(e) EFFECTIVE DATES.—

(1) IN GENERAL.—The amendments made by subsections (a), *(c), and (d)* shall apply to gifts made after the date of the enactment of this Act.

* * *

* * *

[CCH Explanation at ¶ 446. Committee Reports at ¶ 11,030.]

[¶ 8250] ACT SEC. 6009. AMENDMENTS RELATED TO TITLE IX OF 1997 ACT.

* * *

(e) AMENDMENT RELATED TO SECTION 977 OF 1997 ACT.—Paragraph (2) of section 977(e) of the 1997 Act is amended to read as follows:

"(2) NON-AMTRAK STATE.—The term 'non-Amtrak State' means any State which is not receiving intercity passenger rail service from the Corporation as of the date of the enactment of this Act."

Act Sec. 6009(e)   ¶ 8250

● ● *Taxpayer Relief Act of 1997 Act Sec. 977(e)(2) before amendment*⎯⎯⎯⎯

ACT SEC. 977. ELECTIVE CARRYBACK OF EXISTING CARRYOVERS OF NATIONAL RAILROAD PASSENGER CORPORATION.

* * *

(e) DEFINITIONS.—For purposes of this section—

* * *

(2) NON-AMTRAK STATE.—The term "non-Amtrak State" means, with respect to any payment, any State which does not receive intercity passenger rail service from the Corporation at any time during the period beginning on the date of the enactment of this Act and ending on the date of the payment.

* * *

[CCH Explanation at ¶ 694. Committee Reports at ¶ 11,115.]

[¶ 8255] ACT SEC. 6010. AMENDMENTS RELATED TO TITLE X OF 1997 ACT.

(a) AMENDMENTS RELATED TO SECTION 1001 OF 1997 ACT.—

* * *

(4) Subparagraph (C) of section 1001(d)(3) of the 1997 Act is amended by striking "within the 30-day period beginning on" and inserting "before the close of the 30th day after".

● ● *Taxpayer Relief Act of 1997 Act Sec. 1001(d)(3)(C) as amended*⎯⎯⎯⎯

ACT SEC. 1001. CONSTRUCTIVE SALES TREATMENT FOR APPRECIATED FINANCIAL POSITIONS.

* * *

(d) EFFECTIVE DATES.—

(3) SPECIAL RULE.—In the case of a decedent dying after June 8, 1997, if—

(A) there was a constructive sale on or before such date of any appreciated financial position,

(B) the transaction resulting in such constructive sale of such position remains open (with respect to the decedent or any related person)—

(i) for not less than 2 years after the date of such transaction (whether such period is before or after June 8, 1997), and

(ii) at any time during the 3-year period ending on the date of the decedent's death, and

(C) such transaction is not closed *before the close of the 30th day after* the date of the enactment of this Act,

then, for purposes of such Code, such position (and the transaction resulting in such constructive sale) shall be treated as property constituting rights to receive an item of income in respect of a decedent under section 691 of such Code. Section 1014(c) of such Code shall not apply to so much of such position's or property's value (as included in the decedent's estate for purposes of chapter 11 of such Code) as exceeds its fair market value as of the date such transaction is closed.

* * *

* * *

(c) AMENDMENTS RELATED TO SECTION 1012 OF 1997 ACT.—

(1) Paragraph (1) of section 1012(d) of the 1997 Act is amended by striking "1997, pursuant" and inserting "1997; except that the amendment made by subsection (a) shall apply to such distributions only if pursuant".

● ● *Taxpayer Relief Act of 1997 Act Sec. 1012(d)(1) as amended*

ACT SEC. 1012. APPLICATION OF SECTION 355 TO DISTRIBUTIONS IN CONNECTION WITH ACQUISITIONS AND TO INTRAGROUP TRANSACTIONS.

* * *

(d) EFFECTIVE DATES.—

(1) SECTION 355 RULES.—The amendments made by subsections (a) and (b) shall apply to distributions after April 16, *1997; except that the amendment made by subsection (a) shall apply to such distributions only if pursuant* to a plan (or series of related transactions) which involves an acquisition described in section 355(e)(2)(A)(ii) of the Internal Revenue Code of 1986 occurring after such date.

* * *

* * *

(h) AMENDMENTS RELATED TO SECTION 1032 OF 1997 ACT.—

(1) Section 1032(a) of the 1997 Act is amended by striking "Subsection (a) of section 4083" and inserting "Paragraph (1) of section 4083(a)".

● ● *Taxpayer Relief Act of 1997 Act Sec. 1032(a) as amended*

ACT SEC. 1032. KEROSENE TAXED AS DIESEL FUEL.

(a) IN GENERAL.—*Paragraph (1) of section 4083(a)* (defining taxable fuel) is amended by striking "and" at the end of subparagraph (A), by striking the period at the end of subparagraph (B) and inserting ", and", and by adding at the end the following new subparagraph:

"(C) kerosene.".

* * *

(2) Section 1032(e)(12)(A) of the 1997 Act shall be applied as if "gasoline, diesel fuel," were the material proposed to be stricken.

* * *

(j) AMENDMENTS RELATED TO SECTION 1041 OF 1997 ACT.—

* * *

(3) Paragraph (2) of section 1041(b) of the 1997 Act is amended to read as follows:

"(2) BINDING CONTRACTS.—The amendments made by this section shall not apply to any amount received or accrued during the first 2 taxable years beginning on or after the date of the enactment of this Act if such amount is received or accrued pursuant to a written binding contract in effect on June 8, 1997, and at all times thereafter before such amount is received or accrued. The preceding sentence shall not apply to any amount which would (but for the exercise of an option to accelerate payment of such amount) be received or accrued after such 2 taxable years."

● ● *Taxpayer Relief Act of 1997 Act Sec. 1041(b)(2) before amendment*

ACT SEC. 1041. EXPANSION OF LOOK-THRU RULE FOR INTEREST, ANNUITIES, ROYALTIES, AND RENTS DERIVED BY SUBSIDIARIES OF TAX-EXEMPT ORGANIZATIONS.

* * *

(b) EFFECTIVE DATE.—

* * *

(2) BINDING CONTRACTS.—The amendments made by this section shall not apply to any payment made during the first 2 taxable years beginning on or after the date of the enactment of this Act if such payment is made pursuant to a written binding contract in effect on June 8, 1997, and at all times thereafter before such payment.

* * *

Act Sec. 6010(j)   ¶ 8255

(o) AMENDMENTS RELATED TO SECTION 1084 OF 1997 ACT.—

* * *

(3) * * *

* * *

(B) The second sentence of section 1084(d) of the 1997 Act is amended by striking "but" and all that follows and inserting "except that, in the case of a master contract (within the meaning of section 264(f)(4)(E) of the Internal Revenue Code of 1986), the addition of covered lives shall be treated as a new contract only with respect to such additional covered lives."

● ● *Taxpayer Relief Act of 1997 Act Sec. 1084(d) before amendment*

ACT SEC. 1084. EXPANSION OF DENIAL OF DEDUCTION FOR CERTAIN AMOUNTS PAID IN CONNECTION WITH INSURANCE.

* * *

(d) EFFECTIVE DATE.—The amendments made by this section shall apply to contracts issued after June 8, 1997, in taxable years ending after such date. For purposes of the preceding sentence, any material increase in the death benefit or other material change in the contract shall be treated as a new contract but the addition of covered lives shall be treated as a new contract only with respect to such additional covered lives. For purposes of this subsection, an increase in the death benefit under a policy or contract issued in connection with a lapse described in section 501(d)(2) of the Health Insurance Portability and Accountability Act of 1996 shall not be treated as a new contract.

* * *

(p) AMENDMENTS RELATED TO SECTION 1085 OF 1997 ACT.—

* * *

(3) The text of paragraph (3) of section 1085(a) of the 1997 Act is amended to read as follows: "Paragraph (2) of section 6213(g) (relating to the definition of mathematical or clerical errors) is amended by striking "and" at the end of subparagraph (I), by striking the period at the end of subparagraph (J) and inserting ", and", and by inserting after subparagraph (J) the following new subparagraph:

"(K) an omission of information required by section 32(k)(2) (relating to taxpayers making improper prior claims of earned income credit)."

● ● *Taxpayer Relief Act of 1997 Act Sec. 1085(a)(3) before amendment*

ACT SEC. 1085. IMPROVED ENFORCEMENT OF THE APPLICATION OF THE EARNED INCOME CREDIT.

(a) RESTRICTIONS ON AVAILABILITY OF EARNED INCOME CREDIT FOR TAXPAYERS WHO IMPROPERLY CLAIMED CREDIT IN PRIOR YEAR.—

* * *

(3) EXTENSION PROCEDURES APPLICABLE TO MATHEMATICAL OR CLERICAL ERRORS.— Paragraph (2) of section 6213(g) (relating to the definition of mathematical or clerical errors) is amended by striking "and" at the end of subparagraph (H), by striking the period at the end of subparagraph (I) and inserting ", and", and by inserting after subparagraph (I) the following new subparagraph:

"(J) an omission of information required by section 32(k)(2) (relating to taxpayers making improper prior claims of earned income credit).".

* * *

(q) AMENDMENT RELATED TO SECTION 1088 OF 1997 ACT.—Section 1088(b)(2)(C) of the 1997 Act is amended by inserting "more than 1 year" before "after".

● ● *Taxpayer Relief Act of 1997 Act Sec. 1088(b)(2)(C) as amended*_____

ACT SEC. 1088. TREATMENT OF EXCEPTION FROM INSTALLMENT SALES RULES FOR SALES OF PROPERTY BY A MANUFACTURER TO A DEALER.

* * *

(b) EFFECTIVE DATE.—

* * *

(2) COORDINATION WITH SECTION 481.—In the case of any taxpayer required by this section to change its method of accounting for any taxable year—

(A) such changes shall be treated as initiated by the taxpayer,

(B) such changes shall be treated as made with the consent of the Secretary of the Treasury, and

(C) the net amount of the adjustments required to be taken into account under section 481(a) of the Internal Revenue Code of 1986 shall be taken into account ratably over the 4 taxable year period beginning with the first taxable year beginning *more than 1 year* after the date of the enactment of this Act.

* * *

[CCH Explanation at ¶ 211, 546, 553, 556, 601 and 686. Committee Reports at ¶ 11,140, 11,150, 11,190, 11,205 and 11,215.]

[¶ 8260] **ACT SEC. 6011. AMENDMENTS RELATED TO TITLE XI OF 1997 ACT.**

* * *

(g) AMENDMENT RELATED TO SECTION 1144 OF 1997 ACT.—Paragraphs (1) and (2) of section 1144(c) of the 1997 Act are each amended by striking "6038B(b)" and inserting "6038B(c) (as redesignated by subsection (b))".

● ● *Taxpayer Relief Act of 1997 Act Sec. 1144(c)(1)-(2) as amended*_____

ACT SEC. 1144. TRANSFERS OF PROPERTY TO FOREIGN PARTNERSHIPS SUBJECT TO INFORMATION REPORTING COMPARABLE TO INFORMATION REPORTING FOR SUCH TRANSFERS TO FOREIGN CORPORATIONS.

* * *

(c) MODIFICATION OF PENALTY APPLICABLE TO FOREIGN CORPORATIONS AND PARTNERSHIPS.—

(1) IN GENERAL.—Paragraph (1) of section *6038B(c) (as redesignated by subsection (b))* is amended by striking "equal to" and all that follows and inserting "equal to 10 percent of the fair market value of the property at the time of the exchange (and, in the case of a contribution described in subsection (a)(1)(B), such person shall recognize gain as if the contributed property had been sold for such value at the time of such contribution).".

(2) LIMIT ON PENALTY.—Section *6038B(c) (as redesignated by subsection (b))* is amended by adding at the end the following new paragraph:

"(3) LIMIT ON PENALTY.—The penalty under paragraph (1) with respect to any exchange shall not exceed $100,000 unless the failure with respect to such exchange was due to intentional disregard.".

* * *

[CCH Explanation at ¶ 683. Committee Reports at ¶ 11,245.]

[¶ 8265] **ACT SEC. 6012. AMENDMENTS RELATED TO TITLE XII OF 1997 ACT.**

* * *

(b) AMENDMENTS RELATED TO SECTION 1205 OF 1997 ACT.—

* * *

(5) Section 1213(b) of the 1997 Act is amended by striking "section 6724(d)(1)(A)" and inserting "section 6724(d)(1)".

● ● *Taxpayer Relief Act of 1997 Act Sec. 1213(b) as amended*_____

ACT SEC. 1213. QUALIFIED LESSEE CONSTRUCTION ALLOWANCES FOR SHORT-TERM LEASES.

* * *

(b) TREATMENT AS INFORMATION RETURN.—Subparagraph (A) of *section 6724(d)(1)* is amended by striking "or" at the end of clause (vii), by adding "or" at the end of clause (viii), and by adding at the end the following new clause:

"(ix) section 110(d) (relating to qualified lessee construction allowances for short-term leases),".

* * *

* * *

(e) AMENDMENT RELATED TO SECTION 1226 OF 1997 ACT.—Section 1226 of the 1997 Act is amended by striking "ending on or" and inserting "beginning".

● ● *Taxpayer Relief Act of 1997 Act Sec. 1226 as amended*_____

ACT SEC. 1226. EFFECTIVE DATE.

The amendments made by this part shall apply to partnership taxable years *beginning* after December 31, 1997.

* * *

[CCH Explanation at ¶ 671. Committee Reports at ¶ 11,265.]

[¶ 8270] ACT SEC. 6015. AMENDMENTS RELATED TO TITLE XV OF 1997 ACT.
* * *

(b) AMENDMENT RELATED TO SECTION 1505 OF 1997 ACT.—Section 1505(d)(2) of the 1997 Act is amended by striking "(b)(12)" and inserting "(b)(12)(A)(i)".

● ● *Taxpayer Relief Act of 1997 Act Sec. 1505(d)(2) as amended*_____

ACT SEC. 1505. EXTENSION OF MORATORIUM ON APPLICATION OF CERTAIN NONDISCRIMINATION RULES TO STATE AND LOCAL GOVERNMENTS.

* * *

(d) EFFECTIVE DATE.—

* * *

(2) TREATMENT FOR YEARS BEGINNING BEFORE DATE OF ENACTMENT.—A governmental plan (within the meaning of section 414(d) of the Internal Revenue Code of 1986) maintained by a State or local government or political subdivision thereof (or agency or instrumentality thereof) shall be treated as satisfying the requirements of sections 401(a)(3), 401(a)(4), 401(a)(26), 401(k), 401(m), 403 (b)(1)(D) and *(b)(12)(A)(i)*, and 410 of such Code for all taxable years beginning before the date of enactment of this Act.

(c) AMENDMENTS RELATED TO SECTION 1529 OF 1997 ACT.—

(1) Section 1529(a) of the 1997 Act is amended to read as follows:

"(a) GENERAL RULE.—Amounts to which this section applies which are received by an individual (or the survivors of the individual) as a result of hypertension or heart disease of the individual shall be excludable from gross income under section 104(a)(1) of the Internal Revenue Code of 1986."

(2) Section 1529(b)(1)(B) of the 1997 Act is amended to read as follows:

"(B) under—

"(i) a State law (as amended on May 19, 1992) which irrebuttably presumed that heart disease and hypertension are work-related illnesses but only for employees hired before July 1, 1992, or

"(ii) any other statute, ordinance, labor agreement, or similar provision as a disability pension payment or in the nature of a disability pension payment attributable to employment as a police officer or fireman, but only if the individual is referred to in the State law described in clause (i); and".

● ● *TRA 1997 Act Sec. 1529(a), (b)(1)(B) before amendment*

ACT SEC. 1529. TREATMENT OF CERTAIN DISABILITY BENEFITS RECEIVED BY FORMER POLICE OFFICERS OR FIREFIGHTERS.

(a) GENERAL RULE.—For purposes of determining whether any amount to which this section applies is excludable from gross income under section 104(a)(1) of the Internal Revenue Code of 1986, the following conditions shall be treated as personal injuries or sickness in the course of employment:

(1) Heart disease.

(2) Hypertension.

(b) AMOUNTS TO WHICH SECTION APPLIES.—This section shall apply to any amount—

(1) which is payable—

* * *

(B) under a State law (as amended on May 19, 1992) which irrebuttably presumed that heart disease and hypertension were work-related illnesses but only for employees separating from service before July 1, 1992; and

* * *

* * *

[CCH Explanation at ¶ 261. Committee Reports at ¶ 11,315.]

[¶ 8275] ACT SEC. 6016. AMENDMENTS RELATED TO TITLE XVI OF 1997 ACT.

(a) AMENDMENTS RELATED TO SECTION 1601(d) OF 1997 ACT.—

* * *

(2) AMENDMENT TO SECTION 1601(d)(4).—Section 1601(d)(4)(A) of the 1997 Act is amended—

(A) by striking "Section 403(b)(11)" and inserting "Paragraphs (7)(A)(ii) and (11) of section 403(b)", and

(B) by striking "403(b)(1)" in clause (ii) and inserting "403(b)(10)".

● ● *Taxpayer Relief Act of 1997 Act Sec. 1601(d)(4)(A) as amended*

ACT SEC. 1601. AMENDMENTS RELATED TO SMALL BUSINESS JOB PROTECTION ACT OF 1996.

* * *

(d) AMENDMENTS RELATED TO SUBTITLE D.—

* * *

(4) CLARIFICATION OF SECTION 1450.—

(A) *Paragraphs (7)(A)(ii) and (11) of section 403(b)* of the Internal Revenue Code of 1986 shall not apply with respect to a distribution from a contract described in section 1450(b)(1) of such Act to the extent that such distribution is not includible in income by reason of—

(i) in the case of distributions before January 1, 1998, section 403 (b)(8) or (b)(10) of such Code (determined after the application of section 1450(b)(2) of such Act), and

(ii) in the case of distributions on and after such date, such section *403(b)(10).*

* * *

* * *

[CCH Explanation at ¶ 371. Committee Reports at ¶ 11,330.]

[¶ 8280] ACT SEC. 6018. AMENDMENTS RELATED TO SMALL BUSINESS JOB PROTECTION ACT OF 1996.

(a) AMENDMENT RELATING TO SECTION 1116.— Subparagraph (C) of section 1116(b)(2) of the Small Business Job Protection Act of 1996 is amended by striking "chapter 68" and inserting "chapter 61".

● ● *Small Business Act of 1996 Act Sec. 1116(b)(2)(C) as amended*

> **ACT SEC. 1116. CLARIFICATION OF EMPLOYMENT TAX STATUS OF CERTAIN FISHERMEN.**
>
> * * *
>
> (b) INFORMATION REPORTING.—
>
> * * *
>
> (2) TECHNICAL AMENDMENTS.—
>
> * * *
>
> (C) The table of sections for subpart B of part III of subchapter A of *chapter 61* is amended by inserting after the item relating to 6050Q the following new item:
> "Sec. 6050R. Returns relating to certain purchases of fish.".
>
> * * *

* * *

(c) AMENDMENT RELATING TO SECTION 1431.— Subparagraph (E) of section 1431(c)(1) of the Small Business Job Protection Act of 1996 is amended to read as follows:

"(E) Section 414(q)(5), as redesignated by subparagraph (A), is amended by striking 'under paragraph (4) or the number of officers taken into account under paragraph (5)' ".

● ● *Small Business Act of 1996 Act Sec. 1431(c)(1)(E) before amendment*

> **ACT SEC. 1431. DEFINITION OF HIGHLY COMPENSATED EMPLOYEES; REPEAL OF FAMILY AGGREGATION.**
>
> * * *
>
> (c) CONFORMING AMENDMENTS.—
>
> (1) * * *
>
> * * *
>
> (E) Section 414(q)(5), as redesignated by subparagraph (A), is amended by striking "under paragraph (4), or the number of officers taken into account under paragraph (5)".
>
> * * *

(d) AMENDMENT RELATING TO SECTION 1604.— Paragraph (3) of section 1604(b) of such Act is amended—

(1) by striking "such Code" and inserting "the Internal Revenue Code of 1986", and

(2) by striking "such date of enactment" and inserting "the date of the enactment of this Act".

● ● *Small Business Act of 1996 Act Sec. 1604(b)(3) as amended*

> **ACT SEC. 1604. DEPRECIATION UNDER INCOME FORECAST METHOD.**
> * * *
>
> (b) EFFECTIVE DATE.—
>
> * * *
>
> (3) UNDERPAYMENTS OF INCOME TAX.—No addition to tax shall be made under section 6662 of *the Internal Revenue Code of 1986* as a result of the application of subsection (d) of that section (relating to substantial understatements of income tax) with respect to any underpayment of income tax for any taxable year ending before *the date of the enactment of this Act*, to the extent such underpayment was created or increased by the amendments made by subsection (a).

(e) AMENDMENT RELATING TO SECTION 1609.— Paragraph (1) of section 1609(h) of such Act is amended by striking "paragraph (3)(A)(i)" and inserting "paragraph (3)(A)".

¶ 8280 Act Sec. 6018(a)

● ● *Small Business Act of 1996 Act Sec. 1609(h)(1) as amended*_____

ACT SEC. 1609. EXTENSION OF AIRPORT AND AIRWAY TRUST FUND EXCISE TAXES.

* * *

(h) FLOOR STOCKS TAXES ON AVIATION FUEL.—

(1) IMPOSITION OF TAX.—In the case of aviation fuel on which tax was imposed under section 4091 of the Internal Revenue Code of 1986 before the tax-increase date described in *paragraph (3)(A)* and which is held on such date by any person, there is hereby imposed a floor stocks tax of 17.5 cents per gallon.

* * *

(f) AMENDMENTS RELATING TO SECTION 1807.—

* * *

(2) Paragraph (3) of section 1807(c) of the Small Business Job Protection Act of 1996 is amended by striking "Clause (i)" and inserting "Clause (ii)".

● ● *Small Business Act of 1996 Act Sec. 1807(c)(3) as amended*_____

ACT SEC. 1807. ADOPTION ASSISTANCE.

* * *

(c) CONFORMING AMENDMENTS.—

* * *

(3) *Clause (ii)* of section 219(g)(3)(A) is amended by inserting ", 137," before "and 911".

* * *

(g) AMENDMENT RELATING TO SECTION 1903.— Subsection (b) of section 1903 of such Act shall be applied as if "or" in the material proposed to be stricken were capitalized.

(h) EFFECTIVE DATE.—The amendments made by this section shall take effect as if included in the provisions of the Small Business Job Protection Act of 1996 to which they relate.

* * *

[CCH Explanation at ¶ 221. Committee Reports at ¶ 11,345.]

[¶ 8283] ACT SEC. 6024. EFFECTIVE DATE.

Except as otherwise provided in this title, the amendments made by this title shall take effect as if included in the provisions of the Taxpayer Relief Act of 1997 to which they relate.

TITLE VII—REVENUE PROVISIONS

* * *

[¶ 8285] ACT SEC. 7002. TERMINATION OF EXCEPTION FOR CERTAIN REAL ESTATE INVESTMENT TRUSTS FROM THE TREATMENT OF STAPLED ENTITIES.

(a) IN GENERAL.—Notwithstanding paragraph (3) of section 136(c) of the Tax Reform Act of 1984 (relating to stapled stock; stapled entities), the REIT gross income provisions shall be applied by treating the activities and gross income of members of the stapled REIT group properly allocable to any nonqualified real property interest held by the exempt REIT or any stapled entity which is a member of such group (or treated under subsection (c) as held by such REIT or stapled entity) as the activities and gross income of the exempt REIT in the same manner as if the exempt REIT and such group were 1 entity.

(b) NONQUALIFIED REAL PROPERTY INTEREST.— For purposes of this section—

(1) IN GENERAL.—The term "nonqualified real property interest" means, with respect to any exempt REIT, any interest in real property acquired after March 26, 1998, by the exempt REIT or any stapled entity.

Act Sec. 7002(b)   ¶ 8285

(2) EXCEPTION FOR BINDING CONTRACTS, ETC.—Such term shall not include any interest in real property acquired after March 26, 1998, by the exempt REIT or any stapled entity if—

(A) the acquisition is pursuant to a written agreement (including a put option, buy-sell agreement, and an agreement relating to a third party default) which was binding on such date and at all times thereafter on such REIT or stapled entity, or

(B) the acquisition is described on or before such date in a public announcement or in a filing with the Securities and Exchange Commission.

(3) IMPROVEMENTS AND LEASES.—

(A) IN GENERAL.—Except as otherwise provided in this paragraph, the term "nonqualified real property interest" shall not include—

(i) any improvement to land owned or leased by the exempt REIT or any member of the stapled REIT group, and

(ii) any repair to, or improvement of, any improvement owned or leased by the exempt REIT or any member of the stapled REIT group,

if such ownership or leasehold interest is a qualified real property interest.

(B) LEASES.—The term "nonqualified real property interest' shall not include—

(i) any lease of a qualified real property interest if such lease is not otherwise such an interest, or

(ii) any renewal of a lease which is a qualified real property interest,

but only if the rent on any lease referred to in clause (i) or any renewal referred to in clause (ii) does not exceed an arm's length rate.

(C) TERMINATION WHERE CHANGE IN USE.—

(i) IN GENERAL.—Subparagraph (A) shall not apply to any improvement placed in service after December 31, 1999, which is part of a change in the use of the property to which such improvement relates unless the cost of such improvement does not exceed 200 percent of—

(I) the cost of such property, or

(II) if such property is substituted basis property (as defined in section 7701(a)(42) of the Internal Revenue Code of 1986), the fair market value of the property at the time of acquisition.

(ii) BINDING CONTRACTS.—For purposes of clause (i), an improvement shall be treated as placed in service before January 1, 2000, if such improvement is placed in service before January 1, 2004, pursuant to a binding contract in effect on December 31, 1999, and at all times thereafter.

(4) EXCEPTION FOR PERMITTED TRANSFERS, ETC.—The term "nonqualified real property interest" shall not include any interest in real property acquired solely as a result of a direct or indirect contribution, distribution, or other transfer of such interest from the exempt REIT or any member of the stapled REIT group to such REIT or any such member, but only to the extent the aggregate of the interests of the exempt REIT and all stapled entities in such interest in real property (determined in accordance with subsection (c)(1)) is not increased by reason of the transfer.

(5) TREATMENT OF ENTITIES WHICH ARE NOT STAPLED, ETC. ON MARCH 26, 1998.—Notwithstanding any other provision of this section, all interests in real property held by an exempt REIT or any stapled entity with respect to such REIT (or treated under subsection (c) as held by such REIT or stapled entity) shall be treated as nonqualified real property interests unless—

(A) such stapled entity was a stapled entity with respect to such REIT as of March 26, 1998, and at all times thereafter, and

(B) as of March 26, 1998, and at all times thereafter, such REIT was a real estate investment trust.

(6) QUALIFIED REAL PROPERTY INTEREST.— The term "qualified real property interest" means any interest in real property other than a non-qualified real property interest.

(c) TREATMENT OF PROPERTY HELD BY 10-PERCENT SUBSIDIARIES.—For purposes of this section—

(1) IN GENERAL.—Any exempt REIT and any stapled entity shall be treated as holding their proportionate shares of each interest in real property held by any 10-percent subsidiary entity of the exempt REIT or stapled entity, as the case may be.

(2) PROPERTY HELD BY 10-PERCENT SUBSIDIARIES TREATED AS NONQUALIFIED.—

(A) IN GENERAL.—Except as provided in subparagraph (B), any interest in real property held by a 10-percent subsidiary entity of an exempt REIT or stapled entity shall be treated as a nonqualified real property interest.

(B) EXCEPTION FOR INTERESTS IN REAL PROPERTY HELD ON MARCH 26, 1998, ETC.—In the case of an entity which was a 10-percent subsidiary entity of an exempt REIT or stapled entity on March 26, 1998, and at all times thereafter, an interest in real property held by such subsidiary entity shall be treated as a qualified real property interest if such interest would be so treated if held or acquired directly by the exempt REIT or the stapled entity.

(3) REDUCTION IN QUALIFIED REAL PROPERTY INTERESTS IF INCREASE IN OWNERSHIP OF SUBSIDIARY.—If, after March 26, 1998, an exempt REIT or stapled entity increases its ownership interest in a subsidiary entity to which paragraph (2)(B) applies above its ownership interest in such subsidiary entity as of such date, the additional portion of each interest in real property which is treated as held by the exempt REIT or stapled entity by reason of such increased ownership shall be treated as a nonqualified real property interest.

(4) SPECIAL RULES FOR DETERMINING OWNERSHIP.—For purposes of this subsection—

(A) percentage ownership of an entity shall be determined in accordance with subsection (e)(4),

(B) interests in the entity which are acquired by an exempt REIT or a member of the stapled REIT group in any acquisition described in an agreement, announcement, or filing described in subsection (b)(2) shall be treated as acquired on March 26, 1998, and

(C) except as provided in guidance prescribed by the Secretary, any change in proportionate ownership which is attributable solely to fluctuations in the relative fair market values of different classes of stock shall not be taken into account.

(5) TREATMENT OF 60-PERCENT PARTNERSHIPS.—

(A) IN GENERAL.—If, as of March 26, 1998—

(i) an exempt REIT or stapled entity held directly or indirectly at least 60 percent of the capital or profits interest in a partnership, and

(ii) 90 percent or more of the capital interests and 90 percent or more of the profits interests in such partnership (other than interests held directly or indirectly by the exempt REIT or stapled entity) are, or will be, redeemable or exchangeable for consideration the amount of which is determined by reference to the value of shares of stock in the exempt REIT or stapled entity (or both),

paragraph (3) shall not apply to such partnership, and such REIT or entity shall be treated for all purposes of this section as holding all of the capital and profits interests in such partnership.

(B) LIMITATION TO 1 PARTNERSHIP.—If, as of January 1, 1999, more than 1 partnership owned by any exempt REIT or stapled entity meets the requirements of subparagraph (A), only the largest such partnership on such date (determined by aggregate asset bases) shall be treated as meeting such requirements.

(C) MIRROR ENTITY.—For purposes of subparagraph (A), an interest in a partnership formed after March 26, 1998, shall be treated as held by an exempt REIT or stapled entity on March 26, 1998, if such partnership is formed to mirror the stapling of an exempt REIT and a stapled entity in connection with an acquisition agreed to or announced on or before March 26, 1998.

(d) TREATMENT OF PROPERTY SECURED BY MORTGAGE HELD BY EXEMPT REIT OR MEMBER OF STAPLED REIT GROUP.—

(1) IN GENERAL.—In the case of any nonqualified obligation held by an exempt REIT or any member of the stapled REIT group, the REIT gross income provisions shall be applied by treating the exempt REIT as having impermissible tenant service income equal to—

(A) the interest income from such obligation which is properly allocable to the property described in paragraph (2), and

Act Sec. 7002(d)　¶8285

(B) the income of any member of the stapled REIT group from services described in paragraph (2) with respect to such property.

If the income referred to in subparagraph (A) or (B) is of a 10-percent subsidiary entity, only the portion of such income which is properly allocable to the exempt REIT's or the stapled entity's interest in the subsidiary entity shall be taken into account.

(2) NONQUALIFIED OBLIGATION.—Except as otherwise provided in this subsection, the term "nonqualified obligation" means any obligation secured by a mortgage on an interest in real property if the income of any member of the stapled REIT group for services furnished with respect to such property would be impermissible tenant service income were such property held by the exempt REIT and such services furnished by the exempt REIT.

(3) EXCEPTION FOR CERTAIN MARKET RATE OBLIGATIONS.—Such term shall not include any obligation—

(A) payments under which would be treated as interest if received by a REIT, and

(B) the rate of interest on which does not exceed an arm's length rate.

(4) EXCEPTION FOR EXISTING OBLIGATIONS.— Such term shall not include any obligation—

(A) which is secured on March 26, 1998, by an interest in real property, and

(B) which is held on such date by the exempt REIT or any entity which is a member of the stapled REIT group on such date and at all times thereafter,

but only so long as such obligation is secured by such interest, and the interest payable on such obligation is not changed to a rate which exceeds an arm's length rate unless such change is pursuant to the terms of the obligation in effect on March 26, 1998. The preceding sentence shall not cease to apply by reason of the refinancing of the obligation if (immediately after the refinancing) the principal amount of the obligation resulting from the refinancing does not exceed the principal amount of the refinanced obligation (immediately before the refinancing) and the interest payable on such refinanced obligation does not exceed an arm's length rate.

(5) TREATMENT OF ENTITIES WHICH ARE NOT STAPLED, ETC. ON MARCH 26, 1998.—A rule similar to the rule of subsection (b)(5) shall apply for purposes of this subsection.

(6) INCREASE IN AMOUNT OF NONQUALIFIED OBLIGATIONS IF INCREASE IN OWNERSHIP OF SUBSIDIARY.—A rule similar to the rule of subsection (c)(3) shall apply for purposes of this subsection.

(7) COORDINATION WITH SUBSECTION (a).— This subsection shall not apply to the portion of any interest in real property that the exempt REIT or stapled entity holds or is treated as holding under this section without regard to this subsection.

(e) DEFINITIONS.—For purposes of this section—

(1) REIT GROSS INCOME PROVISIONS.—The term "REIT gross income provisions" means—

(A) paragraphs (2), (3), and (6) of section 856(c) of the Internal Revenue Code of 1986, and

(B) section 857(b)(5) of such Code.

(2) EXEMPT REIT.—The term "exempt REIT" means a real estate investment trust to which section 269B of the Internal Revenue Code of 1986 does not apply by reason of paragraph (3) of section 136(c) of the Tax Reform Act of 1984.

(3) STAPLED REIT GROUP.—The term "stapled REIT group" means, with respect to an exempt REIT, the group consisting of—

(A) all entities which are stapled entities with respect to the exempt REIT, and

(B) all entities which are 10-percent subsidiary entities of the exempt REIT or any such stapled entity.

(4) 10-PERCENT SUBSIDIARY ENTITY.—

(A) IN GENERAL.—The term "10-percent subsidiary entity" means, with respect to any exempt REIT or stapled entity, any entity in which the exempt REIT or stapled entity (as the case may be) directly or indirectly holds at least a 10-percent interest.

(B) EXCEPTION FOR CERTAIN C CORPORATION SUBSIDIARIES OF REITS.—A corporation which would, but for this subparagraph, be treated as a 10-percent subsidiary of an exempt REIT shall not be so treated if such corporation is taxable under section 11 of the Internal Revenue Code of 1986.

(C) 10-PERCENT INTEREST.—The term "10-percent interest" means—

(i) in the case of an interest in a corporation, ownership of 10 percent (by vote or value) of the stock in such corporation,

(ii) in the case of an interest in a partnership, ownership of 10 percent of the capital or profits interest in the partnership, and

(iii) in any other case, ownership of 10 percent of the beneficial interests in the entity

(5) OTHER DEFINITIONS.—Terms used in this section which are used in section 269B or section 856 of such Code shall have the respective meanings given such terms by such section.

(f) GUIDANCE.—The Secretary may prescribe such guidance as may be necessary or appropriate to carry out the purposes of this section, including guidance to prevent the avoidance of such purposes and to prevent the double counting of income.

(g) EFFECTIVE DATE.—This section shall apply to taxable years ending after March 26, 1998.

* * *

[CCH Explanation at ¶ 655. Committee Reports at ¶ 11,525.]

TITLE VIII—IDENTIFICATION OF LIMITED TAX BENEFITS SUBJECT TO LINE ITEM VETO

[¶ 8290] ACT SEC. 8001. IDENTIFICATION OF LIMITED TAX BENEFITS SUBJECT TO LINE ITEM VETO.

Section 1021(a)(3) of the Congressional Budget and Impoundment Control Act of 1974 shall only apply to—

(1) section 3105 (relating to administrative appeal of adverse IRS determination of tax-exempt status of bond issue), and

(2) section 3445(c) (relating to State fish and wildlife permits).

[CCH Explanation at ¶ 1137, 1234 and 30,025. Committee Reports at ¶ 11,555.]

TITLE IX—TECHNICAL CORRECTIONS TO TRANSPORTATION EQUITY ACT FOR THE 21ST CENTURY

[¶ 8295] ACT SEC. 9001. SHORT TITLE.

This title may be cited as the "TEA 21 Restoration Act". [NOTE: The corrections made by Title IX of the IRS Restructuring and Reform Act of 1998 to the Transportation Equity Act for the 21st Century (P.L. 105-178) do not relate to any tax provisions. Thus, this title is not reproduced.—CCH.]

* * *

SURFACE TRANSPORTATION REVENUE ACT OF 1998

[¶ 8375] ACT SEC. 1. SHORT TITLE; TABLE OF CONTENTS.

(a) SHORT TITLE.—This Act may be cited as the "Transportation Equity Act for the 21st Century".

(b) TABLE OF CONTENTS.—The table of contents of this Act is as follows:

* * *

[¶ 8380] ACT SEC. 2. DEFINITIONS.

In this Act, the following definitions apply:

(1) INTERSTATE SYSTEM.—The term "Interstate System" has the meaning such term has under section 101 of title 23, United States Code.

(2) SECRETARY.—The term "Secretary" means the Secretary of Transportation.

* * *

TITLE IX—AMENDMENTS OF INTERNAL REVENUE CODE OF 1986

[¶ 8385] ACT SEC. 9001. SHORT TITLE; AMENDMENT OF 1986 CODE.

(a) SHORT TITLE.—This title may be cited as the "Surface Transportation Revenue Act of 1998".

(b) AMENDMENT OF 1986 CODE.—Except as otherwise expressly provided, whenever in this title an amendment or repeal is expressed in terms of an amendment to, or repeal of, a section or other provision, the reference shall be considered to be made to a section or other provision of the Internal Revenue Code of 1986.

* * *

[¶ 8387] ACT SEC. 9002. EXTENSION OF HIGHWAY-RELATED TAXES AND TRUST FUND.

* * *

(c) EXTENSION OF DEPOSITS INTO, AND CERTAIN TRANSFERS FROM, TRUST FUND.—

* * *

(2) MOTORBOAT AND SMALL-ENGINE FUEL TAX TRANSFERS.—

* * *

(B) CONFORMING AMENDMENTS TO LAND AND WATER CONSERVATION FUND.—Section 201(b) of the Land and Water Conservation Fund Act of 1965 (16 U.S.C. 460l-11(b)) is amended—

(i) by striking "1997" and inserting "2003", and

(ii) by striking "1998" each place it appears and inserting "2004".

* * *

[CCH Explanation at ¶ 750. Committee Reports at ¶ 15,025.]

[¶ 8390] ACT SEC. 9003. EXTENSION AND MODIFICATION OF TAX BENEFITS FOR ALCOHOL FUELS.

* * *

(a) EXTENSION OF TAX BENEFITS.—

* * *

(4) TARIFF SCHEDULE.—Headings 9901.00.50 and 9901.00.52 of the Harmonized Tariff Schedule of the United States (19 U.S.C. 3007) are each amended in the effective period column by striking "10/1/2000" each place it appears and inserting "10/1/2007".

* * *

[CCH Explanation at ¶ 760. Committee Reports at ¶ 15,035.]

[¶ 8392] ACT SEC. 9007. ADDITIONAL QUALIFIED EXPENSES AVAILABLE TO NONAMTRAK STATES.

(a) IN GENERAL.—Section 977(e)(1)(B) of the Taxpayer Relief Act of 1997 (defining qualified expenses) is amended—

(1) by striking "and" at the end of clause (iii), and

(2) by striking clause (iv) and inserting the following:

"(iv) capital expenditures related to State-owned rail operations in the State,

"(v) any project that is eligible to receive funding under section 5309, 5310, or 5311 of title 49, United States Code,

"(vi) any project that is eligible to receive funding under section 103, 130, 133, 144, 149, or 152 of title 23, United States Code,

"(vii) the upgrading and maintenance of intercity primary and rural air service facilities, and the purchase of intercity air service between primary and rural airports and regional hubs,

"(viii) the provision of passenger ferryboat service within the State,

"(ix) the provision of harbor improvements within the State, and

"(x) the payment of interest and principal on obligations incurred for such acquisition, upgrading, maintenance, purchase, expenditures, provision, and projects.".

● ● *Taxpayer Relief Act of 1997 Act Sec. 977(e)(1)(B) before amendment*

ACT SEC. 977. ELECTIVE CARRYBACK OF EXISTING CARRYOVERS OF NATIONAL RAILROAD PASSENGER CORPORATION.

* * *

(e) DEFINITIONS.—For purposes of this section—

(1) QUALIFIED EXPENSES.—The term "qualified expenses" means expenses incurred for—

* * *

(B) in the case of a non-Amtrak State—

(i) the acquisition of equipment, rolling stock, and other capital improvements, the upgrading of maintenance facilities, and the maintenance of existing equipment, in intercity passenger rail service,

(ii) the acquisition of equipment, rolling stock, and other capital improvements, the upgrading of maintenance facilities, and the maintenance of existing equipment, in intercity bus service,

(iii) the purchase of intercity passenger rail services from the Corporation, and

(iv) the payment of interest and principal on obligations incurred for such acquisition, upgrading, maintenance, and purchase.

In the case of a non-Amtrak State which provides its own intercity passenger rail service on the date of the enactment of this paragraph, subparagraph (B) shall be applied by only taking into account clauses (i) and (iv).

* * *

(b) EFFECTIVE DATE.—The amendments made by this section shall take effect as if included in the enactment of section 977 of the Taxpayer Relief Act of 1997.

[CCH Explanation at ¶ 694. Committee Reports at ¶ 15,105.]

[¶ 8395] ACT SEC. 9008. DELAY IN EFFECTIVE DATE OF NEW REQUIREMENT FOR APPROVED DIESEL OR KEROSENE TERMINALS.

Subsection (f) of section 1032 of the Taxpayer Relief Act of 1997 is amended to read as follows:

"(f) EFFECTIVE DATES.—

"(1) Except as provided in paragraph (2), the amendments made by this section shall take effect on July 1, 1998.

"(2) The amendment made by subsection (d) shall take effect on July 1, 2000.".

● ● *Taxpayer Relief Act of 1997 Act Sec. 1032(f) before amendment*

ACT SEC. 1032. KEROSENE TAXED AS DIESEL FUEL.

* * *

(f) EFFECTIVE DATE.—The amendments made by this section shall take effect on July 1, 1998.

* * *

* * *

[CCH Explanation at ¶ 723. Committee Reports at ¶ 15,115.]

[¶ 8400] ACT SEC. 9012. IDENTIFICATION OF LIMITED TAX BENEFITS SUBJECT TO LINE ITEM VETO.

For purposes of part C of title X of the Congressional Budget and Impoundment Control Act of 1974 (relating to line item veto), the Joint Committee on Taxation has determined that this title does not contain any limited tax benefit (as defined in such part).

[Committee Reports at ¶ 15,155.]

Committee Reports
IRS Restructuring and Reform Act of 1998
Introduction

[¶ 10,001]

The IRS Restructuring and Reform Act of 1998 was introduced in the House on October 21, 1997 as H.R. 2676. H.R. 2676 was reported by the House Ways and Means Committee on October 31, 1997 (H.R. REP. NO. 105-364, pt. 1). The Tax Technical Corrections Bill (H.R. 2645) as reported by the House Ways and Means Committee on October 29, 1997 (H.R. REP. NO. 105-356) was incorporated into H.R. 2676 on November 4, 1997 as new Title VI, pursuant to H. Res. 303 (H.R. REP. NO. 105-380 (Committee on Rules)). The bill, as amended, was then passed by the House on November 5, 1997.

An amendment in the nature of a substitute for H.R. 2676 was reported by the Senate Finance Committee on April 22, 1998 (S. REP. NO. 105-174). The bill was considered by the Senate on May 4-7, 1998, and the provisions of the bill as amended on the Senate floor, were incorporated in the Senate-passed version on May 7, 1998. A conference report on H.R. 2676 was filed in the House on June 24, 1998 (H.R. CONF. REP. NO. 105-599), and the House agreed to the conference report on June 25, 1998.

This section includes the pertinent texts of the controlling committee reports that explain the changes enacted in the Internal Revenue Service Restructuring and Reform Act of 1998. The following material is the official wording of the relevant House, Senate and Conference Committee Reports in Act Sec. order. The Joint Committee on Taxation Description of the Roth Financing Amendment (Amendment No. 2339) and excerpts from the Congressional Record's account of the Senate Floor Debate on May 6-7, 1998, have also been included as background for Senate Floor Amendments that were passed after the Senate Finance Committee was released. Headings have been added for convenience in locating the committee reports. Any omission of text is indicated by asterisks (* * *). References are following to the official reports:

● Internal Revenue Service Restructuring and Reform Bill of 1997 (H.R. 2676) House Ways and Means Committee Report, reported on October 31, 1997, and issued as CCH Special 2, STANDARD FEDERAL TAX REPORTS NO. 48, November 13, 1997, is referred to as **House Committee Report (H.R. REP. NO. 105-364, pt. 1)**.

● Tax Technical Corrections Bill of 1997 (H.R. 2645) House Ways and Means Committee Report, reported on October 29, 1997, is referred to as **House Committee Report (H.R. REP. NO. 105-356)**.

● Internal Revenue Service Restructuring and Reform Bill of 1998 (H.R. 2676) Senate Finance Committee Report, reported on April 22, 1998, and issued as CCH Special 3, STANDARD FEDERAL TAX REPORTS NO. 17 (Extra Issue), April 29, 1998, is referred to as **Senate Committee Report (S. REP. NO. 105-174)**.

● Joint Committee on Taxation Description of Roth Financing Amendment to the "Internal Revenue Service Restructuring and Reform Act of 1998" as Reported by the Senate Committee on Finance, JCX-31-98, May 5, 1998, issued as part of CCH Special 4, STANDARD FEDERAL TAX REPORTS NO. 21, May 21, 1998, is referred to as **JCT Description of Roth Financing Amendment (JCX-31-98)**.

● Congressional Record recitation of selected May 6-7, 1998, Senate Floor Debate for amendments made to Senate Finance Committee version of H.R. 2676, is referred to as **Senate Floor Debate**. The relevant amendment number is included along with the citation to the page in the Congressional Record where the discussion of the particular amendment begins.

● IRS Restructuring and Reform Bill of 1998 Conference Report as released on June 24, 1998, issued as a CCH Special, STANDARD FEDERAL TAX REPORTS, is referred to as **Conference Committee Report (H.R. CONF. REP. NO. 105-599).**

[¶ 10,115]   Act Sec. 1001.   IRS mission and restructuring (reorganization of the IRS)

Senate Committee Report (S. REP. NO. 105-174)

[Act Sec. 1001]

Present Law
* * *

IRS organizational plan

Under Reorganization Plan No. 1 of 1952, the Internal Revenue Service ("IRS") is organized into a 3-tier geographic structure with a multifunctional National Office, Regional Offices, and District Offices. A number of IRS reorganizations have occurred since then, but no major changes have been made to the basic 3-tier structure. Presently, as a result of a 1995 reorganization, there is a Regional Commissioner, a Regional Counsel and a Regional Director of Appeals for each of the following 4 regions: (1) the Northeast Region (headquartered in New York); (2) the Southeast Region (Atlanta); (3) the Midstates Region (Dallas); and (4) the Western Region (San Francisco). There are 33 District Offices, 10 service centers, and 3 computing centers.

Reasons for Change

The Committee believes that a key reason for taxpayer frustration with the IRS is the lack of appropriate attention to taxpayer needs. At a minimum, taxpayers should be able to receive from the IRS the same level of service expected from the private sector. For example, taxpayer inquiries should be answered promptly and accurately; taxpayers should be able to obtain timely resolutions of problems and information regarding activity on their accounts; and taxpayers should be treated fairly and courteously at all times. The Commissioner of Internal Revenue has indicated his interest in improving customer service. The Committee believes that taxpayer service is of such importance that the Committee should not only support the Commissioner's efforts, but also mandate that a key part of the IRS mission must be taxpayer service.

The Commissioner has announced a broad outline of a plan to reorganize the structure of the IRS in order to help make the IRS more oriented toward assisting taxpayers and providing better taxpayer service. Under this plan, the present regional structure would be replaced with a structure based on units that serve particular groups of taxpayers with similar needs. The Commissioner has currently identified four different groups of taxpayers with similar needs: individual taxpayers, small businesses, large businesses, and the tax-exempt sector (including employee plans, exempt organizations and State and local governments). Under this structure, each unit would be charged with end-to-end responsibility for serving a particular group of taxpayers. The Commissioner believes that this type of structure will solve many of the problems taxpayers encounter now with the IRS. For example, each of the 33 district offices and 10 service centers are now required to deal with every kind of taxpayer and every type of issue. The proposed plan would enable IRS personnel to understand the needs and problems affecting particular groups of taxpayers, and better address those issues. The present-law structure also impedes continuity and accountability. For example, if a taxpayer moves, the responsibility for the taxpayer's account moves to another geographical area. Further, every taxpayer is serviced by both a service center and at least one district. Thus, many taxpayers have to deal with different IRS offices on the same issues. The proposed structure would eliminate many of these problems.

The Committee believes that the current IRS organizational structure is one of the factors contributing to the inability of the IRS to properly serve taxpayers and the proposed structure would help enable the IRS to better serve taxpayers and provide the necessary level of services and accountability to taxpayers. The Committee supports the Commissioner in his efforts to modernize and update the IRS and believes it appropriate to provide statutory direction for the reorganization of the IRS.

Explanation of Provision
* * *

The IRS Commissioner is directed to restructure the IRS by eliminating or substantially modifying the present-law three-tier geographic structure and replacing it with an organizational structure that features operating units serving particular groups of taxpayers with similar needs. The plan is also required to ensure an independent appeals function within the IRS. As part of ensuring an independent appeals function, the reorganization plan is to prohibit ex parte communications between appeals officers and other IRS employees to the extent such communications appear to compromise the independence of the appeals officers. The legality of IRS actions will not be affected pending further appropriate statutory changes relating to such a reorganization (e.g., eliminating statutory references to obsolete positions).

Effective Date

The provision is effective on the date of enactment.

Conference Committee Report (H.R. CONF. REP. NO. 105-599)

The conference agreement follows the Senate amendment.

Effective Date

The provision is effective on the date of enactment.

[Law at ¶ 8005. CCH Explanation at ¶ 801.]

[¶ 10,120]   Act Sec. 1002.   IRS mission and restructuring (IRS mission)

Senate Committee Report (S. REP. NO. 105-174)

[Act Sec. 1002]
Present Law
IRS mission statement

The IRS mission statement provides that:

The purpose of the Internal Revenue Service is to collect the proper amount of tax revenue at the least cost; serve the public by continually improving the quality of our products and services; and perform in a manner warranting the highest degree of public confidence in our integrity and fairness.
* * *

Reasons for Change

The Committee believes that a key reason for taxpayer frustration with the IRS is the lack of appropriate attention to taxpayer needs. At a minimum, taxpayers should be able to receive from the IRS the same level of service expected from the private sector. For example, taxpayer inquiries should be answered promptly and accu-

rately; taxpayers should be able to obtain timely resolutions of problems and information regarding activity on their accounts; and taxpayers should be treated fairly and courteously at all times. The Commissioner of Internal Revenue has indicated his interest in improving customer service. The Committee believes that taxpayer service is of such importance that the Committee should not only support the Commissioner's efforts, but also mandate that a key part of the IRS mission must be taxpayer service.
* * *

Explanation of Provision

The IRS is directed to revise its mission statement to provide greater emphasis on serving the public and meeting the needs of taxpayers.
* * *

Effective Date

The provision is effective on the date of enactment.

Conference Committee Report (H.R. CONF. REP. NO. 105-599)

The conference agreement follows the Senate amendment.

Effective Date

The provision is effective on the date of enactment.

[Law at ¶ 8010. CCH Explanation at ¶ 806.]

[¶ 10,130]   Act Sec. 1101.   Establishment and duties of IRS Oversight Board

House Committee Report (H.R. REP. NO. 105-364, pt. 1)

[Code Sec. 7802]
Present Law

Under present law, the administration and enforcement of the internal revenue laws are performed by or under the supervision of the Secretary of the Treasury.[3]

Present law imposes standards of ethical conduct on Federal employees in order to avoid conflicts of interest. Criminal penalties are imposed on violations of these standards. In some cases, less strict standards apply to special government employees than to regular, full-time Federal government employees. In general, a special government employee is an individual who is expected to serve no more than 130 days during any 365-day period.

In general, the ethical conduct rules (1) prohibit a Federal employee from accepting compensation for representing clients before the agency in which the employee serves or against the United States;[4] (2) prohibit a Federal employee from acting as agent or attorney for anyone in a claim against the United States;[5] (3) impose post-employment restrictions on senior employees in order to prohibit the unfair use of prior Government employment;[6] and (4) prohibit a Federal employee from participating personally and substantially in matters that affect his or her own financial interest or that of persons with certain relationships to the employee.[7]

In the case of a special government employee who serves less than 60 days in the preceding 365 days, the restrictions in (1) and (2) above only

---

[3] Code sec. 780(a).
[4] 18 U.S.C. sec. 203.
[5] 18 U.S.C. sec. 205.
[6] 18 U.S.C. sec. 207.
[7] 18 U.S.C. sec. 208.

Act Sec. 1101   ¶ 10,130

apply with respect to matters in which the special government employee personally and substantially participated in his or her official capacity.

One of the post-employment restrictions prohibits senior government employees from representing parties other than the United States before their former department or agency for one year after employment. This restriction does not apply to special government employees who serve less than 60 days in the final 1-year period of service.

Federal government employees compensated at certain pay grades are subject to public financial disclosure requirements. Special government employees who serve less than 60 days in a year are not subject to the public financial disclosure requirements, but are subject to confidential financial disclosure requirements.

Reasons for Change

The Committee believes that a well-run IRS is critical to the operation of our tax system. Public confidence in the IRS must be restored so that our system of voluntary compliance will not be compromised. The Committee believes that most Americans are willing to pay their fair share of taxes, and that public faith in the IRS is key to maintaining that willingness.

The National Commission on Restructuring the IRS (the "Restructuring Commission"), which conducted a year-long study of the IRS, found that a number of factors contribute to current IRS management problems, including the following. While the Treasury is responsible for IRS oversight, it has generally provided little consistent strategic oversight or guidance to the IRS. The Secretary and Deputy Secretary have many other broad responsibilities, and generally leave the IRS largely independent. The average tenure of an IRS Commissioner is under 3 years, as is the average tenure of senior Treasury officials responsible for IRS oversight. Many of the issues that need to be addressed by the IRS will require expertise in various areas, particularly management and technology.

The Restructuring Commission concluded that "problems throughout the IRS cannot be solved without focus, consistency and direction from the top. The current structure, which includes Congress, the President, the Department of the Treasury, and the IRS itself, does not allow the IRS to set and maintain consistent long-term strategy and priorities, nor to develop and execute focused plans for improvement. Additionally, the structure does not ensure that the IRS budget, staffing and technology are targeted toward achieving organizational success."

The Committee shares the concerns of the Commission, and agrees that fundamental change in IRS management and oversight is essential. The Committee believes that a new management structure that will bring greater expertise in more areas, focus, and continuity will help the IRS on the path toward becoming an efficient, responsive, and respected agency that always acts appropriately in carrying out its functions.

The Committee believes that private sector input is a necessary part of any new management structure. The Committee believes that the ethics rules applicable to special government employees (without regard to exceptions for length of service or pay grade) should be applied to the private sector members of the new IRS management. These rules will enhance the ability of such members to demonstrate impartiality in the performance of their duties, while not unduly restricting the available pool of potential candidates.

The Committee is aware that the taxpaying public may never relish contacts with the agency responsible for collecting taxes. Nevertheless, by establishing a new management structure that will better enable the IRS to develop and fulfill long-term goals, the Committee believes that the IRS will be able to gain public support, and will make contacts with the IRS as infrequent and as pleasant as possible. The Committee is also aware that changes being made to IRS management structure are not the final step, and that continued oversight of the IRS, by Congress as well as the Administration, is necessary in order to ensure long-term progress.

Explanation of Provision

* * *

Compensation of Board members
* * *

The members of the Board will be entitled to travel expenses for purposes of attending meetings of the Board.
* * *

Effective Date

The provisions of the bill relating to the Board are effective on the date of enactment. The President is directed to submit nominations for Board members to the Senate within 6 months of the date of enactment.

Senate Committee Report (S. Rep. No. 105-174)

[This committee report does not reflect changes made by Senate Floor Amendment No. 2347. Selected portions of the Senate Floor Debate are reproduced below.—CCH.]

Present Law

Under present law, the administration and enforcement of the internal revenue laws are performed by or under the supervision of the Secretary of the Treasury.[3] The Secretary has delegated the responsibility to administer and enforce the Internal Revenue laws to the Commissioner. The Commissioner has the final authority of the IRS concerning the substantive interpretation of the tax laws as reflected in legislative and regulatory proposals, revenue rulings, letter rulings, and technical advice memoranda. Under present law, the duties of the Chief Counsel of the IRS are prescribed by the Secretary. The Secretary has delegated authority over the Chief Counsel to General Counsel of the Treasury. The General Counsel has delegated authority to serve

---

[3] Code sec. 7801(a).

as the legal adviser to the Commissioner to the Chief Counsel.

Federal employees are subject to rules designed to prevent conflicts of interest or the appearance of conflicts of interest. The rules applicable to any particular employee depend in part on whether the employee is a regular, full-time Federal Government employee or a special government employee, the length of service of the employee and the pay grade of the employee. A "special government employee" is, in general, an officer or employee of the executive or legislative branch of the U.S. government who is appointed or employed to perform (with or without compensation) for not to exceed 130 days during any period of 365 days, temporary duties either on a full-time or intermittent basis. Violations of the ethical conduct rules are generally punishable by imprisonment for up to 1 year (5 years in the case of wilful conduct), a civil fine, or both. The amount of the fine with respect to each violation cannot exceed the greater of $50,000 or the compensation received by the employee in connection with the prohibited conduct.

Under the ethical conduct rules, all Federal Government employees (including special government employees) are precluded from participating in a matter in which the employee (or a related party) has a financial interest. In addition, special government employees cannot represent a party (whether or not for compensation) or receive compensation for representation of a party[4] in relation to a matter (1) in which the employee has at any time participated personally and substantially, or (2) which is pending in the department or agency of the Government in which the special government employee is serving. In the case of a special government employee who has served in a department no more than 60 days during the immediately preceding 365 days, item (2) does not apply. Thus, for example, such an individual can receive compensation for representational services with respect to matters pending in the department in which the employee serves, as long as it is not a matter involving parties in which the employee personally and substantially participated.[5]

The conflict of interest rules also impose restrictions on what a Federal Government employee can do after leaving the Government. Under these rules, senior level officers and employees (including special government employees) who served at least 60 days cannot represent anyone other than the United States before the individual's former department or agency for 1 year after terminating employment. Whether an employee is a senior level officer or employee is determined by pay grade. The one-year post employment restriction does not apply to special government employees who serve less than 60 days during the 365-day period before termination of employment.[6]

Federal employees with pay grades above certain levels (and who have at least 60 days of service) are required to file annually public financial disclosures.

Reasons for Change

The Committee believes that a well-run IRS is critical to the operation of our tax system. Public confidence in the IRS must be restored so that our system of voluntary compliance will not be compromised. The Committee believes that most Americans are willing to pay their fair share of taxes, and that public confidence in the IRS is key to maintaining that willingness.

The National Commission on Restructuring the IRS (the "Restructuring Commission") conducted a year-long study of the IRS and found that a number of factors contribute to current IRS management problems. The Restructuring Commission found that, while the Treasury is responsible for IRS oversight, it has generally provided little consistent strategic oversight or guidance to the IRS. The Secretary and Deputy Secretary have many other broad responsibilities and generally leave the IRS largely independent. The average tenure of an IRS Commissioner is under 3 years, as is the average tenure of senior Treasury officials responsible for IRS oversight. Many of the issues that need to be addressed by the IRS require expertise in various areas, particularly management and technology.

The Restructuring Commission concluded the following:

> problems throughout the IRS cannot be solved without focus, consistency and direction from the top. The current structure, which includes Congress, the President, the Department of the Treasury, and the IRS itself, does not allow the IRS to set and maintain consistent long-term strategy and priorities, nor to develop and execute focused plans for improvement. Additionally, the structure does not ensure that the IRS budget, staffing and technology are targeted toward achieving organizational success.

The Committee shares the concerns of the Commission, and believes that fundamental change in IRS management and oversight is essential. The Committee believes that a new management

---

[4] The prohibition on receipt of compensation applies regardless of whether the services are performed by the Federal employee or someone else. For example, it would preclude a Federal employee from sharing in the compensation received by a partner of the Federal employee with respect to covered matters.

[5] More stringent rules apply to regular Federal Government employees. Such employees cannot receive compensation for representational services (whether rendered by the individual or another) in matters in which the United States is a party or has a direct and substantial interest before any department, agency or court. In addition, a Federal Government employee cannot act as agent or attorney (whether or not for compensation) for prosecuting any claim against the United States or act as agent or attorney for anyone before any department, agency, or court in which the United States is a party or has a direct and substantial interest.

[6] All Federal Government employees are permanently prohibited from representing a party other than the government in connection with a particular matter (1) in which the government is a party or has an interest, (2) in which the individual participated personally and substantially, and (3) which involved a specific party or parties at the time of their participation. In addition, Federal employees cannot, within 2 years after terminating employment, represent any person other than the United States in connection with any matter (1) in which the government is a party or has a direct and substantial interest, (2) which the person knows or reasonably should know was actually pending under his or her official responsibility within one year before termination of employment, and (3) which involved a specific party or parties at the time it was pending[.]

structure that will bring greater expertise in needed areas, and more focus and continuity will help the IRS to become an efficient, responsive, and respected agency that acts appropriately in carrying out its functions.

The Committee believes that private sector input is a necessary part of any new management structure. The Committee believes that appropriate ethics rules should be applied to the private sector members of the new IRS management in order to enhance the ability of such members to demonstrate impartiality in the performance of their duties, while not unduly restricting the available pool of potential candidates.

The Committee is aware that the taxpaying public does not relish contacts with the agency responsible for collecting taxes. Nevertheless, by establishing a new management structure that will better enable the IRS to develop and fulfill long-term goals, the Committee believes the IRS will provide better service and reduce IRS contact with taxpayers. The Committee is also aware that changes being made to IRS management structure are not the final step, and that continued oversight of the IRS, by Congress as well as the Administration, is necessary in order to ensure long-term progress.

Explanation of Provision
Duties, responsibilities, and powers of the IRS Oversight Board

The bill provides for the establishment within the Treasury Department of the Internal Revenue Service Oversight Board (referred to as the "Board"). The general responsibilities of the Board are to oversee the IRS in the administration, management, conduct, direction, and supervision of the execution and application of the internal revenue laws. As part of its oversight responsibilities, the Board has the responsibility to ensure that the organization and operation of the IRS allows it to carry out its mission. The Board will sunset September 30, 2008.

The Board has the following specific responsibilities: (1) to review and approve strategic plans of the IRS, including the establishment of mission and objectives (and standards of performance) and annual and long-range strategic plans; (2) to review the operational functions of the IRS, including plans for modernization of the tax administration system, outsourcing or managed competition, and training and education; (3) to review and approve the Commissioner's plans for major reorganization of the IRS (except that the approval authority does not apply to the reorganization provided for under the bill); and (4) to review operations of the IRS in order to ensure the proper treatment of taxpayers. The Board also has the following specific responsibilities relating to management: (1) to recommend to the President candidates for Commissioner (and to recommend the removal of the Commissioner); (2) taking into account the recommendations, if any, of the Commissioner, to recommend to the Secretary 3 candidates for appointment as the National Taxpayer Advocate from individuals who have a background in customer service and tax law, and expe-

rience representing individual taxpayers (and to recommend the removal of the National Taxpayer Advocate); (3) to review the Commissioner's selection, evaluation, and compensation of IRS senior executives who have program management responsibility over significant functions of the IRS; (4) and to review procedures of the IRS relating to financial audits.

In addition, the Board will review and approve the budget request of the IRS prepared by the Commissioner, submit such budget request to the Secretary, and ensure that the budget request supports the annual and long-range strategic plans of the IRS. The Secretary is required to submit the budget request approved by the Board to the President, who is required to submit such request, without revision, to the Congress together with the President's annual budget request for the IRS. The bill does not affect the ability of the President to include, in addition, his own budget request relating to the IRS.

It is intended that the Board will reach a formal decision on all matters subject to its review. With respect to those matters over which the Board has approval authority, the Board's decisions will be determinative.

The Board has no responsibilities or authority with respect to the development and formulation of Federal tax policy relating to existing or proposed internal revenue laws. In addition, the Board has no authority (1) to intervene in specific taxpayer cases, including compliance activities involving specific taxpayers such as criminal investigations, examinations, and collection activities, (2) to engage in specific procurement activities of the IRS (e.g., selecting vendors or awarding contracts), or (3) to intervene in specific individual personnel matters.

Board members would have limited access to confidential tax return and return information under section 6103. This limited access would permit the Board to receive such information (i.e., information that has not been redacted to remove confidential tax return and return information) from the Treasury IG for Tax Administration or the Commissioner in connection with reports made to the Board. This access to section 6103 information does not include the taxpayer's name, address, or taxpayer or employer identification number. The Board members are subject to the anti-browsing rules applicable to IRS employees under present law.[7]

In exercising its duties, it is expected that the members of the Board shall maintain appropriate confidentiality (e.g., regarding enforcement matters).

The Board is required to report each year regarding the conduct of its responsibilities. The annual report shall be provided to the President and the House Committees on Ways and Means, Government Reform and Oversight, and Appropriations and the Senate Committees on Finance, Governmental Affairs, and Appropriations. In addition, the Board is required to report to the Ways and Means and Finance Committees if the IRS does not address problems identified by the Board.

---

[7] The provision does not affect the Secretary's (or Deputy Secretary's) or the Commissioner's access to section 6103 information or the application of the anti-browsing rules to the Secretary (or Deputy Secretary) or the Commissioner.

It is expected that the Treasury Department will no longer utilize the IRS Management Board once the new Board created by the bill is in place, as the functions of the IRS Management Board would be taken over by the new Board.

Composition of the Board

The Board is composed of 9 members. Six of the members are so-called "private-life" members who are not otherwise Federal officers or employees. These private-life members are appointed by the President, with the advice and consent of the Senate. The other members are: (1) the Secretary (or, if the Secretary so designates, the Deputy Secretary); (2) the Commissioner; and (3) a representative from an employee organization that represents a substantial number of IRS employees and who is appointed by the President, with the advice and consent of the Senate. In appointing the representative of an employee organization, the President is not required to choose an individual recommended by the employee organization, but may choose whoever the President determines to be an appropriate representative of the employee organization.

The private-life members of the Board will be appointed without regard to political affiliation and based solely on their expertise in the following areas: (1) management of large service organizations; (2) customer service; (3) the Federal tax laws, including administration and compliance; (4) information technology; (5) organization development; and (6) the needs and concerns of taxpayers. In the aggregate, the private-life members of the Board should collectively bring to bear expertise in these enumerated areas.

A private-life Board member and the employee representative Board member may be removed at the will of the President. In addition, the Secretary (or Deputy Secretary) and the IRS Commissioner are automatically removed from the Board upon his or her termination of employment as such.

Compensation of Board members

The private-life members of the Board will be compensated at a rate of $30,000 per year, except that the Chair would be compensated at a rate of $50,000 a year. The other Board members will receive no compensation for their services as a Board member. All members of the Board are entitled to travel expenses for purposes of attending Board meetings or visiting IRS offices in connection with Board functions.

Ethical conduct rules

Private-life members

Under the bill, the private-life Board members are subject to the public financial disclosure rules applicable to Federal government employees above certain pay grades and who have at least 60 days of service. Thus, the private-life Board members are required to file a public financial disclosure report for purposes of confirmation, annually during their tenure on the Board, and upon termination of appointment.

The ethical conduct rules applicable to private-life Board members depend on whether or not such members are determined to be "special government employees" under the present-law rules. It is expected that they generally will be. In that case, they will be subject, at a minimum, to the ethical conduct rules applicable to special government employees. In addition, during their term as a Board member, a private-life Board member cannot represent any party (whether or not for compensation) with respect to (1) any matter before the Board or the IRS, (2) any tax-related matter before the Treasury Department or (3) any court proceeding with respect to a matter described in (1) or (2). Thus, for example, the day after appointment to the Board, a private-life Board member could not meet with representatives of the IRS or Treasury on behalf of a client or the Board member's corporate employer with respect to proposed tax regulations. On the other hand, the Board member could, for example, represent clients before the U.S. Customs Service. The special rules applicable to private-life Board members generally do not preclude the Board member from sharing in compensation from representation of clients by another person (e.g., a partner of the Board member) before the IRS or Treasury.[8]

In addition, private-life Board members are subject to the 1-year post employment restriction applicable to individuals above certain pay grades and who have served at least 60 days (whether or not the members are special government employees under the present-law rules).

If the Board members are determined not to be special government employees under the present-law rules, then they will be subject to the ethical conduct rules relating to regular Federal Government employees.

Representative of employee organization

In general, the bill provides that the employee representative or Board member is subject to the same ethical conduct rules as the private-life Board members. However, the bill modifies the otherwise applicable ethical conduct rules so that they do not preclude the employee representative from carrying out his or her duties as a Board member and his or her duties with respect to the employee organization. In particular, the employee representative is not prohibited from (1) representing the interests of the employee organization before the Federal Government on any matter, or (2) acting on a Board matter because the employee organization has a financial interest in the matter. In addition, the employee representative can continue to receive his or her compensation from the employee organization.[9]

The employee representative is subject to the same public financial disclosure rules as the private-life Board members. In addition, the employee organization is required to provide an annual financial report with the House Ways and Means Committee and the Senate Finance Com-

---

[8] Certain limitations to this exception to the otherwise applicable ethical rules would apply. For example, this exception would not apply if the matter was one in which the Board member personally and substantially participated. Similarly, the Board member could not act with respect to a matter in which he or she has a personal financial interest, including the potential to receive a share in compensation as a result of another's representation.

[9] Certain limitations on this exception would apply. For example, the rules relating to bribery would continue to apply. In addition, the employee representative would be precluded from acting on a matter in which he or she has a financial interest.

Act Sec. 1101   ¶ 10,130

mittee. Such report is required to include the compensation paid to the individual serving on the Board, the compensation of individuals employed by the employee organization, and membership dues collected by the organization.

The employee representative is subject to the same 1-year post employment restriction applicable to the private-life Board members, except to the extent the representative is acting in his capacity as a representative of the employee organization.

Administrative matters

Term of appointments

The 6 private-life Board members will be appointed for 5-year terms. The private-life members may serve no more than two 5-year terms. Board member terms will be staggered, as a result of a special rule providing that some private-life members first appointed to the Board would serve terms of less than 5 years. Under this rule, 2 members first appointed will have a term of 2 years, 2 for a term of 4 years, and 2 for a term of 5 years. The terms of the initial Board members will run from the date of employment. Subsequent terms will run from expiration of the previous term. A Board member appointed to fill a vacancy before the expiration of a term will be appointed to the remainder of the term. Of course, such a member could be appointed to subsequent 5-year term.

Chair of the Board

The members of the Board are to elect a Chair from the private-life members for a 2-year term. Except as otherwise provided by a majority of the Board, the authority of the Chair includes the authority to hire appropriate staff, call meetings, establish committees, establish the agenda for meetings, and develop rules for the conduct of business.

Meetings

The Board is required to meet on a regular basis (as determined necessary by the Chair), but no less frequently than quarterly. The Board can meet privately, and is not subject to public disclosure laws.

A quorum of 5 members is required in order for the Board to conduct business. Actions of the Board can be taken by a majority vote of those members present and voting.

Staffing

The Chair is authorized to hire (and terminate) such personnel as the Chair finds necessary to enable the Board to carry out its duties. In addition, the Board will have such staff as detailed by the Commissioner or from another Federal agency at the request of the Chair of the Board. The Chair can procure temporary and intermittent services under section 3109(b) of title 5 of the U.S. Code.

Claims against Board members

The private-life members of the Board have no personal liability under Federal law with respect to any claim arising out of or resulting form an act or omission by the Board member within the scope of service as a Board member. The bill does not limit personal liability for criminal acts or omissions, wilful or malicious conduct, acts or omissions for private gain, or any other act or omission outside the scope of service as a Board member. The bill does not affect any other immunities and protections that may be available under applicable law or any other right or remedy against the United States under applicable law, or limit or alter the immunities that are available under applicable law for Federal officers and employees.

Effective Date

The provision relating to the Board is effective on the date of enactment. The President is directed to submit nominations for Board members to the Senate within 6 months of the date of enactment. The legality of the actions of the IRS are not affected pending appointment of the Board.

Senate Floor Debate for Amendment No. 2347 (144 CONG. REC. 55, S4406)

* * *

Mr. GRAHAM.— * * * The legislation is written so that three of the members of the nine-member oversight board are ex officio—the Secretary of the Treasury, the IRS Commissioner, and a representative of IRS employees. The other six appointees are Presidential appointments, and according to the current draft of the legislation these six appointees must possess expertise in the following areas: management of large service organizations, customer service. Federal tax laws, information technology, organization development, and needs and concerns of taxpayers.

The amendment that I am offering will add an additional category of expertise to be represented among the six Presidential appointees and that is the needs and concerns of small business. It is the

expectation that the President would appoint six individuals, and his responsibility would be to assure that those six had a sufficient range of backgrounds that they would be able to cover the six and, if this amendment is added, the seventh requirement.

I think it is extremely important that among the six people who are appointed as Presidential appointees to the oversight board for the Internal Revenue Service there be represented in that six one or more individuals who understand the needs and concerns of small businesses of America and can assure that those concerns are effectively communicated to the management and administration of the Internal Revenue Service and, if necessary, the Congress, for appropriate changes in the law. * * *

Conference Committee Report (H.R. CONF. REP. NO. 105-599)

Duties, responsibilities, and powers of the IRS Oversight Board

General responsibilities of the Board

The conference agreement follows the Senate amendment.

Specific responsibilities of the Board

Under the conference agreement, the specific responsibilities of the Board are the same as under the Senate amendment, except that they do not include the responsibility (1) to recommend to the Secretary (taking into account the recommendations, if any, of the Commissioner) 3 candidates for appointment as the National Taxpayer Advocate; or (2) to review procedures of the IRS relating to financial audits. However, the conferees intend that the Chairman of the Board will consider establishing a financial management subcommittee.

Consistent with the Board's responsibility to review and approve plans for major reorganizations, the conferees intend for the Board to have the authority to review and approve the reorganization plan that is contained in Title I of this legislation. However, to the extent that the Commissioner has already taken measures to develop and implement such a plan, the conferees do not want to impede such efforts. Thus, the conferees do not intend in any way that the Commissioner should be precluded from moving ahead with such planning and implementation prior to the appointment of the Board.

Composition of the Board

The conference agreement follows the Senate amendment, except that in lieu of a Board member who is a representative of an organization that represents a substantial number of IRS employees, the conference agreement provides for an individual who is a full-time Federal employee or a representative of employees ("employee representative").

Section 6103 authority

The conference agreement follows the Senate amendment.

Qualifications of Board members

The conference agreement follows the Senate amendment.

Ethical standards for private-life members

The conference agreement follows the Senate amendment with respect to the application of the ethics rules to the private-life Board members regarding representational activities and compensation matters, post-employment restrictions, and financial disclosure requirements.

Ethical standards for employee representative

Under the conference agreement, the same ethics rules applicable to the private-life members regarding the representational activities and compensation matters apply to the employee representative if the individual is a special Government employee (i.e., the individual is not already an officer or employee of the Federal Government). In addition, the same post-employment restrictions and the financial disclosure requirements applicable to the private-life members apply to the employee representative. The conference agreement does not include the Senate amendment requirement for filing annual financial reports that applies to the organization representing a substantial number of IRS employees, a representative of which is a Board member.

The conference agreement does not include the Senate amendment provision for waiver of the conflict-of-interest laws. Instead, the conference agreement grants the President the authority to waive, at the time the President nominates the employee representative to the Board, for the term of the member, any appropriate provisions of chapter 11 of title 18 of the United States Code, to the extent such waiver is necessary to allow such member to participate in the decisions of the Board while continuing to serve as an employee representative. Any such waiver is not effective unless a written intent of waiver to exempt the member (and the actual waiver language) is submitted to the Senate with the nomination of the member. It is not intended that waiver of the restrictions on post-employment provided under the conference agreement be necessary to allow such member to participate in the decisions of the Board while continuing to serve as an employee representative.

Administrative matters

Term of appointments

The conference agreement follows the Senate amendment, with modifications. First, the staggered term of the initial Board shall be as follows: 2 members first appointed will have a term of 3 years, 2 members shall have a term of 4 years, and 2 members shall have a term of 5 years. In addition, the limitation of the Senate amendment that private-life members may serve no more than two five-year terms also applies to the employee representative under the conference agreement.

Chair of the Board

The conference agreement follows the Senate amendment.

Meetings and quorum

The conference agreement follows the Senate amendment.

Staffing

The conference agreement follows the Senate amendment. However, the conferees intend that the size of the staff be limited to a small number, and the Board is encouraged to use outside consultants whenever necessary.

Compensation and travel expenses

The conference agreement follows the Senate amendment with respect to compensation of Board members, with a modification. The employee representative member of the Board will be compensated at a rate of $30,000 per year unless the individual is already an officer or employee of the Federal Government.

The conference agreement follows the House bill provision on travel expenses, with a modification. Travel expenses other than those incurred to attend Board meetings are allowed if approved in advance by the Chair, and the Board shall report annually to Congress the amount of travel expenditures incurred by the Board.

Reports

The conference agreement follows the Senate amendment, with a modification providing that the Board is to include in its annual report information on travel expenses allowed.

Effective Date

The conference agreement follows the House bill. The conference agreement does not include the Senate amendment provision for termination of the Board on September 30, 2008. The conference agreement provides that the provisions relating to the Board are not to be construed to invalidate the actions and authority of the IRS prior to the appointment of members of the Board.

[Law at ¶ 5930, ¶ 6110 and ¶ 6850. CCH Explanation at ¶ 826.] .

[¶ 10,135]   Act Sec. 1101.   Structure and funding of the Employee Plans and Exempt Organizations division ("EP/EO")

Senate Committee Report (S. REP. NO. 105-174)

[Repealed Code Sec. 7802(b)]

Present Law

Prior to 1974, no one specific office in the IRS had primary responsibility for employee plans and tax-exempt organizations. As part of the reforms contained in the Employee Retirement Income Security Act of 1974 ("ERISA"), Congress statutorily created the Office of Employee Plans and Exempt Organizations ("EP/EO") under the direction of an Assistant Commissioner.[13] EP/EO was created to oversee deferred compensation plans governed by sections 401-414 of the Code and organizations exempt from tax under Code section 501(a).

In general, EP/EO was established in response to concern about the level of IRS resources devoted to oversight of employee plans and exempt organizations. The legislative history of Code section 7802(b) states that, with respect to administration of laws relating to employee plans and exempt organizations, "the natural tendency is for the Service to emphasize those areas that produce revenue rather than those areas primarily concerned with maintaining the integrity and carrying out the purposes of exemption provisions."[14]

To provide funding for the new EP/EO office, ERISA authorized the appropriation of an amount equal to the sum of the section 4940 excise tax on investment income of private foundations (assuming a rate of 2 percent) as would have been collected during the second preceding year plus the greater of the same amount or $30 million.[15] However, amounts raised by the section 4940 excise tax have never been dedicated to the administration of EP/EO, but are transferred instead to general revenues. Thus, the level of EP/EO funding, like that of the rest of the IRS, is dependent on annual Congressional appropriations to the Treasury Department.

Reasons for Change

To facilitate the reorganization of the IRS along functional lines, the Committee believes that the statutory provision requiring the establishment of the Office of Employee Plans and Exempt Organizations under the direction of an Assistant Commissioner should be eliminated. In addition, because the funding formula for EP/EO set forth in section 7802(b)(2) would, if utilized, result in an unstable level of funding that may bear little or no relation to the amount of financial resources actually required by the EP/EO division, the Committee believes that it is appropriate to repeal the funding mechanism.

Explanation of Provision

The bill eliminates the statutory requirement contained in section 7802(b) that there be an "Office of Employee Plans and Exempt Organizations" under the supervision and direction of an Assistant Commissioner. The Committee intends that a comparable structure be created administratively to ensure that adequate resources within the IRS are devoted to oversight of the tax-exempt sector.

In addition, because the funding formula for EP/EO set forth in section 7802(b)(2) would, if utilized, result in an unstable level of funding that may bear little or no relation to the amount of financial resources actually required by the EP/EO division, the bill repeals the funding mechanism. Thus, the appropriate level of funding for EP/EO is, consistent with current practice, subject to annual Congressional appropriations, as are other functions within the IRS. In this regard, however, the Committee believes that, given the magnitude of the sectors EP/EO is charged with regulating, as well as the unique nature of its mandate, an adequately funded EP/EO is extremely important to the efficient and fair administration of the Federal tax system. Accordingly, financial resources for EP/EO should not be constrained on the basis that EP/EO is a "non-core" IRS function; rather, EP/EO, like all functions of the IRS, should be funded so as to promote the efficient and fair administration of the Federal tax system.

For example, it is important to allocate sufficient funds for EP/EO staffing adequately to monitor and assist businesses in establishing and maintaining retirement plans. Recently, in Revenue Procedure 98-22, the IRS announced the expansion of the self-correction programs it offers employers to encourage companies to identify and correct errors without incurring significant penalties. These changes are welcomed, and it is not intended that the elimination of the statutory requirement contained in section 7802(b)(1) or the self-funding mechanism described in section 7802(b)(2) impede the implementation of these

---

[13]Code section 7802(b).
[14]S. Rept. 98-383, 108 (1973). See also H. Rept. 93-807, 104 (1974).

[15]Code section 7802(b)(2).

and EP/EO's other programs and activities. Rather, it is intended that there be adequate funding for EP/EO, including these self-correction programs that will encourage the establishment and continuation of retirement plans to increase coverage of American workers while protecting the rights of employees to benefits under

these plans and maintaining the integrity and purposes of the exemption provisions.

Effective Date

The provision is effective on the date of enactment.

Conference Committee Report (H.R. CONF. REP. NO. 105-599)

The conference agreement follows the Senate amendment.

[CCH Explanation at ¶ 836.]

[¶ 10,140] Act Sec. 1102(a). IRS Commissioner and other personnel (Commissioner of Internal Revenue)

House Committee Report (H.R. REP. NO. 105-364, pt. 1)

[Code Sec. 7803(a)]

Present Law

Within the Department of the Treasury is a Commissioner of Internal Revenue, who is appointed by the President, with the advice and consent of the Senate. The Commissioner has such duties and powers as may be prescribed by the Secretary.[12] The Secretary has delegated to the Commissioner the administration and enforcement of the internal revenue laws.[13] The Commissioner generally does not have authority with respect to policy matters.[14]

The Secretary is authorized to employ such persons as the Secretary deems appropriate for the administration and enforcement of the internal revenue laws and to assign posts of duty.

Reasons for Change

The Committee believes that the duties and responsibilities of the Commissioner are of such significance that the Commissioner should continue to be appointed by the President.[15] However, the frequency with which the Commissioner changes—the average tenure in office is under 3 years—is one of the factors contributing to lack of

IRS management continuity. The Committee believes (as did the National Commission on Restructuring the IRS) that providing a statutory term for the Commissioner to serve would help ensure greater continuity of IRS management.

The Committee believes that it is appropriate to preserve the present-law structure under which the duties of the Commissioner are delegated by the Secretary of the Treasury. Modifying this structure may unnecessarily interfere with the operations of the IRS and other agencies within the Treasury. In order to enable the Congress to properly fulfill its oversight responsibilities with respect to the IRS, the Committee believes that the Congress should be notified of changes in the delegation of authority to the Commissioner.

* * *

Effective Date

The provisions of the bill relating to the Commissioner generally are effective on the date of enactment. The provision relating to the 5-year term of office applies to the Commissioner in office on the date of enactment. This 5-year term runs from the date of appointment.

Senate Committee Report (S. REP. NO. 105-174)

Present Law

Within the Department of the Treasury is a Commissioner of Internal Revenue, who is appointed by the President, with the advice and consent of the Senate. The Commissioner has such duties and powers as may be prescribed by the Secretary.[10] The Secretary has delegated to the Commissioner the administration and enforcement of the internal revenue laws.[11] The Commissioner generally does not have authority with respect to tax policy matters.[12]

The Secretary is authorized to employ such persons as the Secretary deems appropriate for the administration and enforcement of the internal revenue laws and to assign posts of duty.

Explanation of Provision

As under present law, the Commissioner is appointed by the President, with the advice and consent of the Senate, and may be removed at will by the President. Under the bill, one of the qualifications of the Commissioner is demonstrated ability in management. The Commissioner is ap-

---

[12] Code sec. 7802(a).
[13] Treasury Order 150-10 (April 22, 1982).
[14] See, e.g., Treasury Order 111-2 March 16, 1981), which delegates to the Assistant Secretary (Tax Policy) the exclusive authority to make the final determination of the Treasury Department's position with respect to issues of tax policy arising in connection with regulations, published Revenue Rulings and Revenue Procedures, and tax return forms and to determine the time, form and manner for the public communication of such position.
[15] Retaining present law also eliminates any constitutional issues that may arise if the Commissioner is appointed by someone other than the President, such as by the

Board, as suggested by the National Commission on Restructuring the IRS.
[10] Code sec. 7802(a).
[11] Treasury Order 150-10 (April 22, 1982).
[12] See, e.g., Treasury Order 111-2 (March 16, 1981), which delegates to the Assistant Secretary (Tax Policy) the exclusive authority to make the final determination of the Treasury Department's position with respect to issues of tax policy arising in connection with regulations, published Revenue Rulings and Revenue Procedures, and tax return forms and to determine the time, form and manner for the public communication of such position.

pointed to a 5-year term, beginning with the date of appointment. The Commissioner may be reappointed for more than one 5-year term. The Board recommends candidates to the President for the position of Commissioner; however, the President is not required to nominate for Commissioner a candidate recommended by the Board. The Board has the authority to recommend the removal of the Commissioner.

The Commissioner has such duties and powers as prescribed by the Secretary. Unless otherwise specified by the Secretary, such duties and powers include the power to administer, manage, conduct, direct, and supervise the execution and application of the internal revenue laws or related statutes and tax conventions to which the United States is a party, to exercise the IRS' final authority concerning the substantive interpretation of the tax laws, to recommend to the President a candidate for Chief Counsel (and recommend the removal of the Chief Counsel), and to recommend candidates for the position of National Taxpayer

Advocate to the IRS Board. If the Secretary determines not to delegate such specified duties to the Commissioner, such determination will not take effect until 30 days after the Secretary notifies the House Committees on Ways and Means, Government Reform and Oversight, and Appropriations, and the Senate Committees on Finance, Governmental Affairs, and Appropriations. The Commissioner is to consult with the Board on all matters within the Board's authority (other than the recommendation of candidates for Commissioner and the recommendation to remove the Commissioner).

* * *

Effective Date

The provisions relating to the Commissioner are effective on the date of enactment. The provision relating to the 5-year term of office applies to the Commissioner in office on the date of enactment. The 5-year term runs from the date of appointment.

Conference Committee Report (H.R. CONF. REP. NO. 105-599)

The conference agreement follows the Senate amendment, with a modification. Instead of the Senate amendment provision relating to the duty of the Commissioner to recommend candidates for the position of National Taxpayer Advocate to the IRS Board, the conference agreement provides that the Treasury Secretary is to consult with the

Commissioner and the Board before selecting the National Taxpayer Advocate.

Effective Date

The conference agreement follows the Senate amendment and the House bill.

[Law at ¶ 6860. CCH Explanation at ¶ 811.]

[¶ 10,145]   Act Sec. 1102(a).   IRS Chief Counsel

Senate Committee Report (S. REP. NO. 105-174)

[Code Sec. 7803(b)]

Present Law

The President is authorized to appoint, by and with the consent of the Senate, an Assistant General Counsel of the Treasury, who is the Chief Counsel of the IRS. The Chief Counsel is the chief law officer for the IRS and has such duties as may be prescribed by the Secretary. The Secretary has delegated authority over the Chief Counsel to the Treasury General Counsel. The Chief Counsel does not report to the Commissioner, but to the Treasury General Counsel. As delegated by the Treasury General Counsel, the duties of the Chief Counsel include: (1) to be the legal advisor to the Commissioner and his or her officers and employees; (2) to furnish such legal opinions as may be required in the preparation and review of rulings and memoranda of technical advice and the performance of other duties delegated to the Chief Counsel; (3) to prepare, review, or assist in the preparation of proposed legislation, treaties, regulations and Executive Orders relating to laws affecting the IRS; (4) to represent the Commissioner in cases before the Tax Court; (5) to determine what civil actions should be brought in the courts under the laws affecting the IRS and to prepare recommendations to the Department

of Justice for the commencement of such actions and to authorize or sanction commencement of such actions.

Explanation of Provision

As under present law, the Chief Counsel is appointed by the President, with the advice and consent of the Senate. Under the bill, the Chief Counsel is not an Assistant General Counsel of the Treasury and reports directly to the Commissioner.

The Chief Counsel has such duties and powers as prescribed by the Secretary. Unless otherwise specified by the Secretary, these duties include the duties currently delegated to the Chief Counsel as described above. If the Secretary determined not to delegate such specified duties to the Chief Counsel, such determination is subject to the same notice requirement applicable to changes in the delegation of authority with respect to the Commissioner.

Effective Date

The provision is generally effective on the date of enactment. The provision providing that the Chief Counsel reports directly to the Commissioner is effective 90 days after the date of enactment.

Conference Committee Report (H.R. CONF. REP. NO. 105-599)

The conference agreement follows the Senate amendment, with modifications. Under the conference agreement, the Chief Counsel is to report directly to the Commissioner, with two exceptions.

First, the Chief Counsel is to report to both the Commissioner and the General Counsel of the Treasury Department with respect to (1) legal advice or interpretation of the tax law not relating solely to tax policy, and (2) tax litigation. Under this rule, the conferees intend that the Chief Counsel's dual reporting to the Commissioner and to the General Counsel include reporting with respect to legal advice or interpretation of the tax law set forth in regulations, revenue rulings and revenue procedures, technical advice and other similar memoranda, private letter rulings, and published guidance not described in the foregoing.

Second, the Chief Counsel is to report to the General Counsel with respect to legal advice or interpretation of the tax law relating solely to tax policy. Under this rule, the conferees intend that the Chief Counsel's reporting to the General Counsel include proposed legislation and international tax treaties.

The conference agreement provides that if there is any disagreement between the Commissioner and the General Counsel with respect to any matter on which the Chief Counsel has dual reporting to both the Commissioner and the General Counsel, the matter is to be submitted to the Secretary or the Deputy Secretary of the Treasury for resolution.

The conferees intend that under the general rule, the Chief Counsel's reporting directly to the Commissioner include reporting with respect to budget, organizational structure and reorganizations, mission and strategic plans. In addition, the conferees intend that the Chief Counsel's reporting directly to the Commissioner include reporting with respect to all matters relating to the day-to-day operations of the IRS, such as management of the IRS and procurement.

The conference agreement provides that all personnel in the Office of the Chief Counsel are to report to the Chief Counsel (and not to any person at the IRS or elsewhere within the Treasury Department).

[Law at ¶ 6860. CCH Explanation at ¶ 816.]

[¶ 10,150]   Act Sec. 1102(a) 1102(c) and 1102(d).   Taxpayer Advocate and Taxpayer Assistance Orders

Senate Committee Report (S. REP. NO. 105-174)

[Code Sec. 7803(c) and Code Sec. 7811(a)]

[*This committee report does not reflect changes made by Senate Floor Amendment No. 2382. Senate Floor Amendment No. 2382 (144 Cong. Rec. 56, S4517) was passed with nominal debate.—CCH.*]

Present Law

Taxpayer Advocate

In 1996, the Taxpayer Bill of Rights 2 ("TBOR 2") established the position of Taxpayer Advocate, which replaced the position of Taxpayer Ombudsman, created in 1979 by the IRS. The Taxpayer Advocate is appointed by and reports directly to the IRS Commissioner.

TBOR 2 also created the Office of the Taxpayer Advocate. The functions of the office are (1) to assist taxpayers in resolving problems with the IRS, (2) to identify areas in which taxpayers have problems in dealings with the IRS, (3) to propose changes (to the extent possible) in the administrative practices of the IRS that will mitigate those problems, and (4) to identify potential legislative changes that may mitigate those problems.

Taxpayer assistance orders

Taxpayers can request that the Taxpayer Advocate issue a taxpayer assistance order ("TAO") if the taxpayer is suffering or about to suffer a significant hardship as a result of the manner in which the internal revenue laws are being administered. A TAO may require the IRS to release property of the taxpayer that has been levied upon, or to cease any action, take any action as

permitted by law, or refrain from taking any action with respect to the taxpayer.

Under present law, the direct point of contact for taxpayers seeking taxpayer assistance orders is a problem resolution officer appointed by a District Director or a Regional Director of Appeals The Taxpayer Advocate has designated the authority to issue taxpayer assistance orders to the local and regional problem resolution officers.

Reports of the Taxpayer Advocate

The Taxpayer Advocate is required to report annually to the House Committee on Ways and Means and the Senate Finance Committee on the objectives of the Taxpayer Advocate for the upcoming fiscal year. This report is required to be provided no later than June 30 of each calendar year and is to contain full and substantive analysis, in addition to statistical information.

The Taxpayer Advocate is also required to report annually to the House Committee on Ways and Means and the Senate Finance Committee on the activities of the Taxpayer Advocate during the most recently ended fiscal year. This report is required to be provided no later than December 31 of each calendar year, and is to contain full and substantive analysis, in addition to statistical information. This report is also required to: (1) identify the initiatives the Taxpayer Advocate has taken on improving taxpayer services and IRS responsiveness; (2) contain recommendations received from individuals with the authority to issue TAOs; (3) contain a summary of at least 20 of the most serious problems encountered by taxpayers, including a description of the nature of

Act Sec. 1102(a)   ¶ 10,150

such problems; (4) contain an inventory of the items described in (1), (2), and (3) for which action has been taken and the result of such action; (5) contain an inventory of the items described in (1), (2), and (3) for which action remains to be completed and the period during which each item has remained on such inventory; (6) contain an inventory of the items described in (1), (2) and (3) for which no action has been taken, the period during which the item has remained on the inventory, the reasons for the inaction, and identify any IRS official who is responsible for the inaction; (7) identify any TAO that was not honored by the IRS in a timely manner; (8) contain recommendations for such administrative and legislative action as may be appropriate to resolve problems encountered by taxpayers; (9) describe the extent to which regional problem resolution officers participate in the selection and evaluation of local problem resolution officers, and (10) include such other information as the Taxpayer Advocate deems advisable.

The reports of the Taxpayer Advocate are to be submitted directly to the Congressional Committees without prior review or comment from the Commissioner, Secretary, any other officer or employee of the Treasury, or the Office of Management and Budget.

Reasons for Change

The Committee believes that the Taxpayer Advocate serves an important role within the IRS in terms of preserving taxpayer rights and solving problems that taxpayers encounter in their dealings with the IRS. To that end, it is appropriate that the IRS Oversight Board have input in the selection of the Taxpayer Advocate. Due to the enhanced powers of the Taxpayer Advocate in TBOR2 and this bill, the Committee has been advised that the Taxpayer Advocate should be appointed by the Secretary to avoid constitutional problems. In addition, the Committee believes that the Taxpayer Advocate should have experience appropriate to the position and that the Taxpayer Advocate's objectivity would be best preserved by limiting prior and future employment with the IRS. The Committee also believes that the reporting requirements of the Taxpayer Advocate should be targeted not only towards solving problems with the IRS but also towards preventing problems before they arise.

The Committee believes that the Taxpayer Advocate must have broad discretion to provide relief to taxpayers. In determining whether a taxpayer assistance order should be issued, the Taxpayer Advocate should consider certain factors as constituting a "significant hardship" for the taxpayer. In addition to providing relief if the taxpayer is about to suffer a significant hardship, the Taxpayer Assistance Order should be issued in other appropriate situations, such as if there is an immediate threat of adverse action, if there has been a delay of more than 30 days in resolving the taxpayer's account problems, the taxpayer will have to pay significant costs if relief is not granted, or the taxpayer will suffer irreparable injury, or long-term adverse impact, if relief is not granted. The Committee believes that the Taxpayer Advocate should have flexibility to issue a

TAO under any appropriate circumstances, not only when one of the listed factors exists.

Explanation of Provision
National Taxpayer Advocate

The bill renames the Taxpayer Advocate the "National Taxpayer Advocate." * * * The Secretary is required to choose a National Taxpayer Advocate from among the individuals recommended by the Oversight Board. An individual may be appointed as the National Taxpayer Advocate only if the individual was not an officer or employee of the IRS during the 2-year period ending with such appointment and the individual agrees not to accept employment with the IRS for at least 5 years after ceasing to be the National Taxpayer Advocate.

The bill replaces the present-law problem resolution system with a system of local Taxpayer Advocates who report directly to the National Taxpayer Advocate and who will be employees of the Taxpayer Advocate's Office, independent from the IRS examination, collection, and appeals functions. The National Taxpayer Advocate has the responsibility to evaluate and take personnel actions (including dismissal) with respect to any local Taxpayer Advocate or any employee in the Office of the National Taxpayer Advocate. In conjunction with the Commissioner, the National Taxpayer Advocate is required to develop career paths for local Taxpayer Advocates.

The National Taxpayer Advocate is required to monitor the coverage and geographical allocation of the local Taxpayer Advocates, develop guidance to be distributed to all IRS officers and employees outlining the criteria for referral of taxpayer inquires to local taxpayer advocates, ensure that the local telephone number for the local taxpayer advocate is published and available to taxpayers.

Each local Taxpayer Advocate may consult with the appropriate supervisory personnel of the IRS regarding the daily operation of the office of the Taxpayer Advocate. At the initial meeting with any taxpayer seeking the assistance of the Office of the Taxpayer Advocate, the local taxpayer advocate is required to notify the taxpayer that the Office operated independently of any other IRS office and reports directly to Congress through the National Taxpayer Advocate. At the discretion of the local taxpayer advocate, the advocate shall not disclose to the IRS any contact with or information provided by the taxpayer. Each local office of the Taxpayer Advocate is to maintain a separate phone, facsimile, and other electronic communication access, and a separate post office address.

The IRS would be required to publish the taxpayer's right to contact the local Taxpayer Advocate on the statutory notice of deficiency.

Taxpayer assistance orders

The provision expands the circumstances under which a TAO may be issued. The bill provides that a "significant hardship" is deemed to occur if one of the following four factors exists: (1) there is an immediate threat of adverse action; (2) there has been a delay of more than 30 days in resolving the taxpayer's account problems; (3) the taxpayer will have to pay significant costs (including fees for professional services) if relief is not granted; or (4) the taxpayer will suffer irreparable injury, or a long-term adverse impact, if relief is not granted. These factors are not an exclusive list of what constitutes a significant hardship; a TAO may also be issued in other circumstances in which it is determined that the taxpayer is or will suffer a significant hardship. * * *

In determining whether to issue a TAO in cases in which the IRS failed to follow applicable published guidance (including procedures set forth in the Internal Revenue Manual), the Taxpayer Advocate is to construe the matter in a manner most favorable to the taxpayer.

Reports of the National Taxpayer Advocate

The provision requires the annual report regarding the activities of the National Taxpayer Advocate for the most recently ended fiscal year to (in addition to the information required under present law): (1) identify areas of the tax law that impose significant compliance burdens on taxpayers or the IRS, including specific recommenda-tions for remedying such problems; and (2) identify the 10 most litigated issues for each category of taxpayers, including recommendations for mitigating such disputes.

Effective Date

The provision is generally effective on the date of enactment. During the period before the appointment of the IRS Oversight Board, the National Taxpayer Advocate shall be appointed by the Secretary (taking into consideration individuals nominated by the Commissioner) from among individuals who have a background in customer service as well as tax law and experience in representing individual taxpayers. The provision providing that the Taxpayer Advocate reports directly to the Commissioner, the provision providing that the Taxpayer Advocate is appointed by the Secretary, and the restrictions on previous and subsequent employment of the Taxpayer Advocate do not apply to the individual serving as the Taxpayer Advocate on the date of enactment.

Conference Committee Report (H.R. CONF. REP. NO. 105-599)

Senate Amendment

National Taxpayer Advocate

The Senate amendment renames the Taxpayer Advocate the "National Taxpayer Advocate." The Senate amendment provides that the IRS Oversight Board is to recommend to the Secretary 3 candidates for National Taxpayer Advocate from among individuals with a background in customer service as well as tax law and with experience representing individual taxpayers. The Secretary is required to choose a National Taxpayer Advocate from among the individuals recommended by the Oversight Board. An individual may be appointed as the National Taxpayer Advocate only if the individual was not an officer or employee of the IRS during the 2-year period ending with such appointment and the individual agrees not to accept employment with the IRS for at least 5 years after ceasing to be the National Taxpayer Advocate.

The Senate amendment replaces the present-law problem resolution system with a system of local Taxpayer Advocates who report directly to the National Taxpayer Advocate and who will be employees of the Taxpayer Advocate's Office, independent from the IRS examination, collection, and appeals functions. The National Taxpayer Advocate has the responsibility to evaluate and take personnel actions (including dismissal) with respect to any local Taxpayer Advocate or any employee in the Office of the National Taxpayer Advocate. In conjunction with the Commissioner, the National Taxpayer Advocate is required to develop career paths for local Taxpayer Advocates.

The National Taxpayer Advocate is required to monitor the coverage and geographical allocation of the local Taxpayer Advocates, develop guidance to be distributed to all IRS officers and employees outlining the criteria for referral of taxpayer inquires to local taxpayer advocates, ensure that the local telephone number for the local taxpayer advocate is published and available to taxpayers.

Each local Taxpayer Advocate may consult with the appropriate supervisory personnel of the IRS regarding the daily operation of the office of the Taxpayer Advocate. At the initial meeting with any taxpayer seeking the assistance of the Office of the Taxpayer Advocate, the local taxpayer advocate is required to notify the taxpayer that the Office operated independently of any other IRS office and reports directly to Congress through the National Taxpayer Advocate. At the discretion of the local taxpayer advocate, the advocate shall not disclose to the IRS any contact with or information provided by the taxpayer. Each local office of the Taxpayer Advocate is to maintain a separate phone, facsimile, and other electronic communication access, and a separate post office address.

The IRS would be required to publish the taxpayer's right to contact the local Taxpayer Advocate on the statutory notice of deficiency.

Under the Senate amendment, the National Taxpayer Advocate is to appoint a counsel in the Office of the Taxpayer Advocate to report directly to the National Taxpayer Advocate.

Taxpayer assistance orders

The provision expands the circumstances under which a TAO may be issued. The Senate amendment provides that a "significant hardship" is deemed to occur if one of the following four factors exists: (1) there is an immediate threat of adverse action; (2) there has been a delay of more than 30 days in resolving the taxpayer's account problems; (3) the taxpayer will have to pay significant costs (including fees for professional services) if relief is not granted; or (4) the taxpayer will suffer irreparable injury, or a long-term adverse impact, if relief is not granted. These factors are not an exclusive list of what constitutes a significant hardship; a TAO may also be issued in other circumstances in which it is determined that the taxpayer is or will suffer a significant hard-

Act Sec. 1102(a) ¶ 10,150

ship. The Taxpayer Advocate is also authorized to issue a TAO in any circumstances that the Taxpayer Advocate considers appropriate for the issuance of a TAO.

In determining whether to issue a TAO in cases in which the IRS failed to follow applicable published guidance (including procedures set forth in the Internal Revenue Manual), the Taxpayer Advocate is to construe the matter in a manner most favorable to the taxpayer.

Reports of the National Taxpayer Advocate

The provision requires the annual report regarding the activities of the National Taxpayer Advocate for the most recently ended fiscal year to (in addition to the information required under present law): (1) identify areas of the tax law that impose significant compliance burdens on taxpayers or the IRS, including specific recommendations for remedying such problems; and (2) identify the 10 most litigated issues for each category of taxpayers, including recommendations for mitigating such disputes.

Effective Date

The Senate amendment provision is generally effective on the date of enactment. During the period before the appointment of the IRS Oversight· Board, the National Taxpayer Advocate shall be appointed by the Secretary (taking into consideration individuals nominated by the Commissioner) from among individuals who have a background in customer service as well as tax law and experience in representing individual taxpayers. The provision providing that the Taxpayer Advocate reports directly to the Commissioner, the provision providing that the Taxpayer Advocate is appointed by the Secretary, and the restrictions on previous and subsequent employment of the Taxpayer Advocate do not apply to the individual serving as the Taxpayer Advocate on the date of enactment.

Conference Agreement

National Taxpayer Advocate

The conference agreement follows the Senate amendment, with modifications. The conference agreement does not include the Senate amendment provision that the IRS Oversight Board is to recommend to the Secretary 3 candidates for National Taxpayer Advocate; instead, the conference agreement provides that the National Taxpayer Advocate is appointed by the Secretary after consultation with the Commissioner and the Board (without regard to the provisions of Title 5 of the U.S. Code, relating to appointments in the competitive service or the Senior Executive Service). The conference agreement modifies the Senate amendment provision that an individual may be appointed as the National Taxpayer Advocate only if the individual was not an officer or employee of the IRS during the 2-year period ending with such appointment and the individual agrees not to accept employment with the IRS for at least 5 years after ceasing to be the National Taxpayer Advocate. The conference agreement

provides that service as an officer or employee of the Office of the Taxpayer Advocate is not taken into account, for purposes of these 2-year and 5-year rules. The conference agreement also clarifies that the National Taxpayer Advocate's compensation is to be at the highest rate of basic pay established for the Senior Executive Service, or, if the Treasury Secretary so determines, at a rate fixed under 5 U.S.Code section 9503.

The conferees intend that the National Taxpayer Advocate's responsibility to appoint local taxpayer advocates and make available at least one local taxpayer advocate for each State means that a local taxpayer advocate will be available to taxpayers in each State.

The conference agreement does not include the Senate amendment provision that the National Taxpayer ·Advocate has the responsibility and authority to appoint· a counsel in the Office of the Taxpayer Advocate to report directly to the National Taxpayer Advocate. The conferees intend that the National Taxpayer Advocate be able to hire and consult counsel as appropriate.

The conference agreement provides that each local taxpayer advocate reports to the National Taxpayer Advocate or his delegate. The committees intend that a delegate mean the taxpayer advocate for the appropriate organizational unit. It is not intended that a local taxpayer advocate report to a District Director of the IRS, for example. Providing reporting to a delegate of the National Taxpayer Advocate under the conference agreement is intended to provide reporting flexibility sufficient to take into account the necessities of any reorganization of the IRS.

Taxpayer assistance orders

The conference agreement follows the Senate amendment, except that the conference agreement does not include the Senate amendment provision that the Taxpayer Advocate is authorized to issue a TAO in any circumstances that the Taxpayer Advocate considers appropriate for the issuance of a TAO. Instead, the conference agreement provides that the National Taxpayer Advocate may issue a TAO if the taxpayer meets requirements set forth in regulations. It is intended that the circumstances set forth in regulations be based on considerations of equity.

Effective Date

The conference agreement follows the Senate amendment, with modifications. Under the conference agreement, the provisions are effective on date of enactment, except that in appointing the first National Taxpayer Advocate after date, of enactment, the Treasury Secretary may not appoint anyone who was an officer or employee of the IRS at any time during the 2-year period ending on the date of appointment, and the Treasury Secretary need not consult with the Board if the Board has not been appointed.

[Law at ¶ 6250, ¶ 6320, ¶ 6860, and ¶ 6890. CCH Explanation at ¶ 821, and ¶ 1106.]

[¶ 10,160] Act Sec. 1103. Treasury Office of Inspector General; IRS Office of the Chief Inspector

Senate Committee Report (S. REP. NO. 105-174)

[Code Sec. 7803(d) and Act Sec. 1103]
Present Law
Treasury Inspector General

The Treasury Office of Inspector General ("Treasury IG") was established in 1988 and charged with conducting independent audits, investigations and review to help the Department of Treasury accomplish its mission, improve its programs and operations, promote economy, efficiency and effectiveness, and prevent and detect fraud and abuse. The Treasury IG derives its statutory authority under the Inspector General Act of 1978, as amended ("IG Act of 1978").

Appointment and qualifications

The IG Act of 1978 provides that the Treasury IG is selected by the President, with the advice and consent of the Senate, without regard to political affiliation and solely on the basis of integrity and demonstrated ability in accounting, auditing, financial analysis, law, management analysis, public administration, or investigations. The Treasury IG can be removed from office by the President. The President must communicate the reasons for such removal to both Houses of Congress.

Duties and responsibilities

The Treasury IG generally is authorized to conduct, supervise and coordinate internal audits and investigations relating to the programs and operations of the Treasury, including all of its bureaus and offices.[16] Special rules apply, however, with respect to the Treasury IG's jurisdiction over ATF, Customs, the Secret Service and the IRS—the four so-called "law enforcement bureaus." Upon its establishment, the Treasury IG assumed the internal audit functions previously performed by the offices of internal affairs of ATF, Customs and the Secret Service. Although the Treasury IG was granted oversight responsibility for the internal investigations performed by the Office of Internal Affairs of ATF, the Office of Internal Affairs of Customs, and the Office of Inspections of the Secret Service, the internal investigation or inspection functions of these offices remained with the respective bureaus. The Treasury IG did not assume responsibility for either the internal audit or inspection functions of the IRS Office of the Chief Inspector. However, it was directed to oversee the internal audits and internal investigations performed by the IRS Office of the Chief Inspector.

The Commissioner and the Treasury IG have entered into two Memorandums of Understanding

("MOUs")[17] to clarify the respective roles of the IRS Office of the Chief Inspector and the Treasury IG in two primary areas: (1) the investigation of allegations of wrongdoing by IRS executives and employees in situations where the independence of the Office of the Chief Inspector could be questioned, and (2) oversight by the Treasury IG of the IRS Office of the Chief Inspector.[18] Pursuant to the 1990 MOU, the Commissioner agreed to transfer 21 FTEs and $1.9 million from the IRS appropriation to the Treasury IG appropriation to be used for the following purposes: (1) oversight of the operations of the Office of the Chief Inspector; (2) conduct of special reviews of IRS operations; (3) investigation of allegations of misconduct concerning the Commissioner, the Senior Deputy Commissioner, and employees of the IRS Office of the Chief Inspector; and (4) investigation of allegations of misconduct where the independence of the IRS Office of the Chief Inspector might be questioned. With respect to item (4), the Commissioner and Treasury IG agreed that all allegations of misconduct involving IRS executives and managers (Grade 15 and above), as well as any other allegation involving "significant or notorious" matters were to be referred to the Treasury IG, and that investigations arising out of such referrals generally would be conducted by the Treasury IG.

In general, under the IG Act of 1978, Inspectors General are instructed to report expeditiously to the Attorney General whenever the Inspector General has reasonable grounds to believe there has been a violation of Federal criminal law. However, in matters involving criminal violations of the Internal Revenue Code, the Treasury IG may report to the Attorney General only those offenses under section 7214 of the Code (unlawful acts of revenue officers or agents, including extortion, bribery and fraud) without the consent of the Commissioner.

Authority

The Treasury IG reports to and is under the general supervision of the Secretary of Treasury, acting through the Deputy Secretary. In general, the Secretary cannot prevent or prohibit the Treasury IG from initiating, carrying out, or completing any audit or investigation or from issuing any subpoena during the course of any audit or investigation.

However, section 8D of the IG Act of 1978 grants the Secretary authority to prohibit audits or investigations by the Treasury IG under certain circumstances. In particular, the Treasury

---

[16] The Treasury Department organization includes the Departmental offices as well as the Bureau of Alcohol, Tobacco and Firearms ("ATF"), the Office of the Comptroller of the Currency ("OCC"), the U.S. Customs Service ("Customs"), the Bureau of Engraving and Printing, the Federal Law Enforcement Training Center, the Financial Management Service, the U.S. Mint, the Bureau of the Public Debt, the U.S. Secret Service ("Secret Service"), the Office of Thrift Supervision, and the IRS.
[17] The first MOU was entered into in 1990 and the second in 1994.

[18] Treasury Directive 40-01 (September 21, 1992) reiterates that the Treasury IG is responsible for investigating alleged misconduct on the part of IRS employees at the grade 15 level and above, all employees of the Office of the Chief Inspector. In addition, Treasury Directive 40-01 states that the Treasury IG is responsible for investigating alleged misconduct on the part of Office of Chief Counsel employees (excluding employees of the National Director, Office of Appeals).

IG is under the authority, direction, and control of the Secretary with respect to audits or investigations, or the issuance of subpoenas, which require access to sensitive information concerning: (1) ongoing criminal investigations or proceedings; (2) undercover operations; (3) the identity of confidential sources, including protected witnesses; (4) deliberations and decisions on policy matters, including documented information used as a basis for making policy decisions, the disclosure of which could reasonably be expected to have a significant influence on the economy or market behavior; (5) intelligence or counterintelligence matters; (6) other matters the disclosure of which would constitute a serious threat to national security or to the protection of certain persons. With respect to audits, investigations or subpoenas that require access to the above-listed information, the Secretary may prohibit the Treasury IG from carrying out such audit, investigation or subpoena if the Secretary determines that such prohibition is necessary to prevent the disclosure of such information or to prevent significant impairment to the national interests of the United States. The Secretary must provide written notice of such a prohibition to the Treasury IG, who must, in turn, transmit a copy of such notice to the Committees on Government Reform and Oversight and Ways and Means of the House and the Committees on Governmental Affairs and Finance of the Senate.

Access to taxpayer returns and return information

The Treasury IG has access to taxpayer returns and return information under section 6103(h)(1) of the Code. However, such access is subject to certain special requirements, including the requirement that the Treasury IG notify the IRS Office of the Chief Inspector (or the Deputy Commissioner in certain circumstances) of its intent to access returns and return information.

Reporting requirements

Under the IG Act of 1978, the Treasury IG reports to the Congress semiannually on its activities. Reports from the Treasury IG are transmitted to the Committees on Government Reform and Oversight and Ways and Means of the House and the Committees on Governmental Affairs and Finance of the Senate.

Resources

For fiscal year 1997, the Treasury IG had 296 FTEs and total funding of $29.7 million. 174 FTEs were assigned to the Treasury IG's audit function and 61 were assigned to the investigative function. The remaining FTEs were divided among the following functions: evaluations, legal, program, technology and administrative support. Of the total Treasury IG FTEs, approximately 23 were used for IRS oversight activities in fiscal year 1997.

IRS Office of Chief Inspector

The IRS Office of the Chief Inspector (also known as the "Inspection Service") was established on October 1, 1951, in response to publicity revealing widespread corruption in the IRS. At the time of its creation, President Harry S. Truman stated, "A strong, vigorous inspection service will be established and will be made completely independent of the rest of the Internal Revenue Service."

Appointment of the Chief Inspector

In 1952, the Office of the Assistant Commissioner (Inspection) was established. The office was redesignated as the Office of the Chief Inspector on March 25, 1990. The Chief Inspector is appointed by the Commissioner. In this regard, pursuant to Treasury Director 40-01, the Commissioner must consult with the Treasury IG before selecting candidates for the position of Chief Inspector (and all other senior executive service ("SES") positions in the Office of the Chief Inspector). The Commissioner must also consult with the Treasury IG regarding annual performance appraisals for the Chief Inspector and other SES officials.

The Office of the Chief Inspector consists of a National Office and the offices of the Regional Inspectors. The offices of the Regional Inspectors are located in the same cities and have the same geographic boundaries as the offices of the four IRS Regional Commissioners. The Regional Inspectors report directly to the Chief Inspector.

Duties and responsibilities

The Office of the Chief Inspector generally is responsible for carrying out internal audits and investigations that: (1) promote the economic, efficient, and effective administration of the nation's tax laws; (2) detect and deter fraud and abuse in IRS programs and operations; and (3) protect the IRS against external attempts to corrupt or threaten its employees. The Chief Inspector reports directly to the Commissioner and Deputy Commissioner of the IRS.

The IRS Inspection Service is divided into three functions: Internal Security, Internal Audit, and Integrity Investigations and Activities. Internal Security's responsibilities include criminal investigations (employee conduct, bribery, assault and threat and investigations of non-IRS employees for acts such as impersonation, theft, enrolled agent misconduct, disclosure, and anti-domestic terrorism) investigative support activities (including forensic lab, computer investigative support, and maintenance of law enforcement equipment), protection, and background investigations.

Internal Audit is responsible for providing IRS management with independent reviews and appraisals of all IRS activities and operations. In addition, Internal Audit makes recommendations to improve the efficiency and effectiveness of programs and to assist IRS officials in carrying out their program and operational responsibilities. In this regard, Internal Audit generally conducts performance reviews (program audits, system development audits, internal control audits) and financial reviews (financial statement audits and financial related reviews).

Integrity Investigations and Activities are joint internal audit and internal security operations undertaken as a proactive effort to detect and deter fraud and abuse within the IRS. Integrity Investigations and Activities also includes the UNAX Central Case Development Center. The Center was developed in October, 1997, in response to the Taxpayer Browsing Protection Act of 1997. Its purpose is to detect unauthorized accesses to IRS computer systems by IRS employees and to refer such instances to Internal Security investigators for further investigation.

Authority

The Chief Inspector derives specific and general authority from delegation by the Commissioner and Deputy Commissioner. In addition, under section 7608(b) of the Code, the Chief Inspector is authorized to perform certain functions in connection with the duty of enforcing any of the criminal provisions of the Code, including executing and serving search and arrest warrants, serving subpoenas and summonses, making arrests without warrant, carrying firearms, and seizing property subject to forfeiture under the Code.

Access to taxpayer returns and return information

The Office of the Chief Inspector has full access to taxpayer returns and return information.

Reporting requirements

The Office of the Chief Inspector reports facts developed through its internal audit and internal security activities to IRS management officials, who are charged with the responsibility of reviewing IRS activities. The results of the Chief Inspector's internal audit and internal security activities also are reported to the Treasury IG and are included in the Treasury IG's semiannual reports to Congress.

Internal audit reports prepared by the Office of the Chief Inspector are provided monthly to the Government Accounting Office, as well as to the House and Senate Appropriations Committees. In addition, a monthly list of Internal Audit reports is provided to Treasury and the Office of Management and Budget. Reports of Investigation regarding criminal conduct are referred to the Department of Justice for prosecution.

Resources

The IRS Office of the Chief Inspector had 1,202 FTEs for 1997 and total funding of $100.1 million. Of these FTEs, approximately 442 performed Internal Audit functions, 511 performed Internal Security functions, and 94 performed Integrity Investigations and Activities. Of the remaining FTEs, approximately 95 were dedicated to information technology functions and 60 staffed the offices of the Chief Inspector and the Regional Inspectors.

Reasons for Change

The Committee believes that the current IRS Office of the Chief Inspector lacks sufficient structural and actual autonomy from the agency it is charged with monitoring and overseeing. Further, the current relationship between the Treasury IG and the IRS Office of the Chief Inspector does not foster appropriate oversight over the IRS. The Committee believes that the establishment of an independent Inspector General within the Department of Treasury whose primary focus and responsibility will be to audit, investigate, and evaluate IRS programs will improve the quality as well as the credibility of IRS oversight.

Explanation of Provision

In general

The bill establishes a new, independent, Treasury Inspector General for Tax Administration ("Treasury IG for Tax Administration") within the Department of Treasury. The IRS Office of the Chief Inspector is eliminated, and all of its powers and responsibilities are transferred to the Treasury IG for Tax Administration. The Treasury IG for Tax Administration has the powers and responsibilities generally granted to Inspectors General under the IG Act of 1978, without the limitations that currently apply to the Treasury IG under section D of the Act. The role of the existing Treasury IG is redefined to exclude responsibility for the IRS. The Treasury IG for Tax Administration is under the supervision of the Secretary of Treasury, with certain additional reporting to the Board and the Congress.

Appointment and qualifications of Treasury IG for Tax Administration

The Treasury IG for Tax Administration is selected by the President, with the advice and consent of the Senate. The Treasury IG for Tax Administration can be removed from office by the President. The President must communicate the reasons for such removal to both Houses of Congress.

The Treasury IG for Tax Administration must be selected without regard to political affiliation and solely on the basis of integrity and demonstrated ability in accounting, auditing, financial analysis, law, management analysis, public administration, or investigations. In addition, however, the Treasury IG for Tax Administration should have experience in tax administration and demonstrated ability to lead a large and complex organization. The Treasury IG for Tax Administration may not be employed by the IRS within the two years preceding and the five years following his or her appointment.

The Treasury IG for Tax Administration is required to appoint an Assistant Inspector General for Auditing and an Assistant Inspector for Inspections. Under the bill, such appointees, as well as any Deputy Inspector General(s) appointed by the Treasury IG for Tax Administration, may not be employed by the IRS within the two years preceding and the five years following their appointments.

Duties and responsibilities of Treasury IG for Tax Administration

The Treasury IG for Tax Administration has the present-law duties and responsibilities currently delegated to the Treasury IG with respect to the IRS. In addition, the Treasury IG for Tax Administration assumes all of the duties and responsibilities currently delegated to the IRS Office of the Chief Inspector. The Treasury IG for Tax Administration has jurisdiction over IRS matters, as well as matters involving the Board.

Accordingly, the Treasury IG for Tax Administration is charged with conducting audits, investigations, and evaluations of IRS programs and operations (including the Board) to promote the economic, efficient and effective administration of the nation's tax laws and to detect and deter fraud and abuse in IRS programs and operations. In this regard, the Treasury IG for Tax Administration specifically is directed to evaluate the adequacy and security of IRS technology on an ongoing basis. In addition, the Treasury IG for Tax Administration is responsible for protecting the IRS against external attempts to corrupt or threaten its employees. The Treasury IG for Tax Administration is charged with investigating allegations of criminal misconduct (e.g., Code sections 7212, 7213, 7214, 7216 and new section 7217), as well as administrative misconduct (e.g., violations of the Taxpayer Bill of Rights and the Taxpayer Bill of Rights 2, the Office of Government Ethics Standards of Ethical Conduct and the IRS Supplemental Standards of Ethical Conduct).

In addition, the bill directs the Treasury IG for Tax Administration to implement a program periodically to audit at least one percent of all determinations (identified through a random selection process) where the IRS has asserted either section 6103 (directly or in connection with the Freedom of Information Act or the Privacy Act) or law enforcement considerations (i.e., executive privilege) as a rationale for refusing to disclose requested information. The program must be implemented within 6 months after establishment of the Treasury IG for Tax Administration. The Treasury IG for Tax Administration is directed to report any findings of improper assertion of section 6103 or law enforcement considerations to the Board.

Further, the Treasury IG for Tax Administration is directed to establish a toll-free confidential telephone number for taxpayers to register complaints of misconduct by IRS employees and to publish the telephone number in IRS Publication 1.

There are no restrictions on the Treasury IG for Tax Administration's ability to refer matters to the Department of Justice. Thus, the Treasury IG for Tax Administration is required to report to the Attorney General whenever the Treasury IG for Tax Administration has reasonable grounds to believe that there has been a violation of Federal criminal law.

Authority of Treasury IG for Tax Administration

The Treasury IG for Tax Administration reports to and is under the general supervision of the Secretary of Treasury. Under the bill, the Secretary cannot prevent or prohibit the Treasury IG for Tax Administration from initiating, carrying out, or completing any audit or investigation or from issuing any subpoena during the course of any audit or investigation.

Under the bill, the Treasury IG for Tax Administration must provide to the Board all reports regarding IRS matters on a timely basis and conduct audits or investigations requested by the Board. The Treasury IG for Tax Administration also must, in a timely manner, conduct such audits or investigations and provide such reports as may be requested by the Commissioner.

In carrying out the duties and responsibilities described above, the Treasury IG for Tax Administration has the present-law authority generally granted to Inspectors General under the IG Act of 1978. The limitations on the authority of the Treasury IG under such Act do not apply to the Treasury IG for Tax Administration. In addition, the Treasury IG for Tax Administration has the authority granted to the IRS Office of the Chief Inspector under present-law Code section 7608, including the right to execute and serve search and arrest warrants, to serve subpoenas and summonses, to make arrests without warrant, to carry firearms, and to seize property subject to forfeiture under the Code.

Resources

To ensure that the Treasury IG for Tax Administration has sufficient resources to carry out his or her duties and responsibilities under the bill, all but 300 FTEs from the IRS Office of the Chief Inspector are transferred to the Treasury IG for Tax Administration. Such FTEs include all of the FTEs performing investigative functions in the Office of the Chief Inspector Internal Security and Integrity Investigations and Activities. In addition, the 21 FTEs previously transferred from Inspection to Treasury IG pursuant to the 1990 MOU to perform oversight of the IRS are transferred to the Treasury IG for Tax Administration.

The Commissioner will retain approximately 300 FTEs from the IRS Office of the Chief Inspector to staff an audit function (including support staff) for internal IRS management purposes. Like other IRS functions, however, this audit function is subject to oversight and review by the Treasury IG for Tax Administration.

Access to taxpayer returns and return information

Taxpayer returns and return information are available for inspection by the Treasury IG for Tax Administration pursuant to section 6103(h)(1). Thus, the Treasury IG for Tax Administration has the same access to taxpayer returns and return information as does the Chief Inspector under present law.

Reporting requirements

The Treasury IG for Tax Administration is subject to the semiannual reporting requirements set forth in section 5 of the IG Act of 1978. As under present law, reports are made to the Committees on Government Reform and Oversight and Ways and Means of the House and the Committees on Governmental Affairs and Finance of the Senate. The reports must contain the information that is required to be reported by the Treasury IG with respect to the IRS under present law, as well as information regarding the source, nature and status of taxpayer complaints and allegations of serious misconduct by IRS employees received by the IRS or by the Treasury IG for Tax Administration. In addition, the Treasury IG for Tax Administration is required to report annually on certain additional information (e.g., regarding the use of enforcement statistics in evaluating IRS employees, the implementation of various taxpayer rights protections, and IRS employee terminations and mitigations) required by the bill.

Treasury IG

The Treasury IG generally continues to have its present-law responsibilities and authority with respect to all Treasury functions other than the IRS and the Board. However, the Treasury IG generally does not have access to taxpayer returns and return information under section 6103 (unless the Secretary specifically authorizes such access).

The Treasury IG for Tax Administration operates independently of the Treasury IG. The Secretary of Treasury is directed to establish procedures pursuant to which the Treasury IG for

Tax Administration and the Treasury IG shall coordinate audits and investigations in cases involving overlapping jurisdiction.

The Treasury IG continues to have responsibility for providing an opinion on the Department of Treasury's consolidated financial statement as required under the Chief Financial Officer Act. The Treasury IG for Tax Administration is responsible for rendering an opinion on the IRS custodial and administrative accounts (to the extent the Government Accounting Office does not exercise its option to preempt under the CFO Act).

Effective Date

The provision is effective 180 days after the date of enactment.

Conference Committee Report (H.R. CONF. REP. NO. 105-599)

The conference agreement follows the Senate amendment, except as follows. The conference agreement provides that experience in tax administration is not among the qualifications applicable to the Treasury IG for Tax Administration. With respect to the authority of the Treasury IG for Tax Administration, the conference agreement provides that the Commissioner or the Oversight Board may request the Treasury IG for Tax Administration to conduct an audit or investigation relating to the IRS. If the Treasury IG for Tax Administration determines not to conduct an audit or investigation requested by the Commissioner or the Oversight Board, the Treasury IG for Tax Administration shall timely provide the requesting party with a written explanation of its determination. In this regard, the conferees intend that the Treasury IG for Tax Administration shall make all reasonable efforts to be responsive to the requests of the Commissioner and the Oversight Board. In addition, the conference agreement modifies the duties and responsibilities of the Treasury IG for Tax Administration by providing that the responsibility for (1) protecting IRS employees and (2) investigating the backgrounds of prospective IRS employees shall not be transferred to the Treasury IG for Tax Administration, but rather shall remain with the IRS.

[Law at ¶ 6780 and ¶ 8020. CCH Explanation at ¶ 831.]

[¶ 10,165] Act Sec. 1104. IRS Commissioner and other personnel (other personnel)

House Committee Report (H.R. REP. NO. 105-364, pt. 1)

[Code Sec. 7804]

Present Law

Within the Department of the Treasury is a Commissioner of Internal Revenue, who is appointed by the President, with the advice and consent of the Senate. The Commissioner has such duties and powers as may be prescribed by the Secretary.[12] The Secretary has delegated to the Commissioner the administration and enforcement of the internal revenue laws.[13] The Commissioner generally does not have authority with respect to policy matters.[14]

The Secretary is authorized to employ such persons as the Secretary deems appropriate for the administration and enforcement of the internal revenue laws and to assign posts of duty.

Reasons for Change

The Committee believes that the duties and responsibilities of the Commissioner are of such significance that the Commissioner should continue to be appointed by the President.[15] However, the frequency with which the Commissioner changes—the average tenure in office is under 3 years—is one of the factors contributing to lack of IRS management continuity. The Committee believes (as did the National Commission on Restructuring the IRS) that providing a statutory term for the Commissioner to serve would help ensure greater continuity of IRS management.

The Committee believes that it is appropriate to preserve the present-law structure under which the duties of the Commissioner are delegated by the Secretary of the Treasury. Modifying this structure may unnecessarily interfere with the operations of the IRS and other agencies within the Treasury. In order to enable the Congress to properly fulfill its oversight responsibilities with respect to the IRS, the Committee believes that the Congress should be notified of changes in the delegation of authority to the Commissioner.

Explanation of Provision
* * *

Effective Date

The provisions of the bill relating to the Commissioner generally are effective on the date of enactment. * * *

---

[12] Code sec. 7802(a).

[13] Treasury Order 150-10 (April 22, 1982).

[14] See, e.g., Treasury Order 111-2 March 16, 1981), which delegates to the Assistant Secretary (Tax Policy) the exclusive authority to make the final determination of the Treasury Department's position with respect to issues of tax policy arising in connection with regulations, published Revenue Rulings and Revenue Procedures, and tax return forms and to determine the time, form and manner for the public communication of such position.

[15] Retaining present law also eliminates any constitutional issues that may arise if the Commissioner is appointed by someone other than the President, such as by the Board, as suggested by the National Commission on Restructuring the IRS.

Senate Committee Report (S. REP. NO. 105-174)

Present Law

Within the Department of the Treasury is a Commissioner of Internal Revenue, who is appointed by the President, with the advice and consent of the Senate. The Commissioner has such duties and powers as may be prescribed by the Secretary.[10] The Secretary has delegated to the Commissioner the administration and enforcement of the internal revenue laws.[11] The Commissioner generally does not have authority with respect to tax policy matters.[12]

The Secretary is authorized to employ such persons as the Secretary deems appropriate for the administration and enforcement of the internal revenue laws and to assign posts of duty.

Explanation of Provision

* * *

Unless otherwise specified by the Secretary, the Commissioner is authorized to employ such persons as the Commissioner deems proper for the administration and enforcement of the internal revenue laws and is required to issue all necessary directions, instructions, orders, and rules applicable to such persons. Unless otherwise provided by the Secretary, the Commissioner will determine and designate the posts of duty.

Effective Date

The provisions relating to the Commissioner are effective on the date of enactment. * * *

Conference Committee Report (H.R. CONF. REP. NO. 105-599)

The conference agreement follows the Senate amendment, with a modification. Instead of the Senate amendment provision relating to the duty of the Commissioner to recommend candidates for the position of National Taxpayer Advocate to the IRS Board, the conference agreement provides that the Treasury Secretary is to consult with the

Commissioner and the Board before selecting the National Taxpayer Advocate.

Effective Date

The conference agreement follows the Senate amendment and the House bill.

[Law at ¶ 6870. CCH Explanation at ¶ 817.]

[¶ 10,170]   Act Sec. 1105.   Prohibition on Executive Branch influence over taxpayer audits

Senate Committee Report (S. REP. NO. 105-174)

[Code Sec. 7217]

Present Law

There is no explicit prohibition in the Code on high-level Executive Branch influence over taxpayer audits and collection activity.

The Internal Revenue Code prohibits disclosure of tax returns and return information, except to the extent specifically authorized by the Internal Revenue Code (sec. 6103). Unauthorized disclosure is a felony punishable by a fine not exceeding $5,000 or imprisonment of not more than five years, or both (sec. 7213). An action for civil damages also may be brought for unauthorized disclosure (sec. 7431).

Reasons for Change

The Committee believes that the perception that it is possible that high-level Executive Branch influence over taxpayer audits and collection activity could occur has a negative influence on taxpayers' views of the tax system. Accordingly, the Committee believes that it is appropriate to prohibit such influence.

Explanation of Provision

The bill makes it unlawful for a specified person to request that any officer or employee of the IRS conduct or terminate an audit or otherwise investigate or terminate the investigation of any particular taxpayer with respect to the tax liability of that taxpayer. The prohibition applies to

the President, the Vice President, and employees of the executive offices of either the President or Vice President, as well as any individual (except the Attorney General) serving in a position specified in section 5312 of Title 5 of the United States Code (these are generally Cabinet-level positions). The prohibition applies to both direct requests and requests made through an intermediary. In the case of a law enforcement action authorized by the Attorney General, discussions involving specified persons with respect to that law enforcement action shall not be considered to be requests made through an intermediary.

Any request made in violation of this rule must be reported by the IRS employee to whom the request was made to the Chief Inspector of the IRS. The Chief Inspector has the authority to investigate such violations and to refer any violations to the Department of Justice for possible prosecution, as appropriate. Anyone convicted of violating this provision will be punished by imprisonment of not more than 5 years or a fine not exceeding $5,000 (or both).

Three exceptions to the general prohibition apply. First, the prohibition does not apply to a request made to a specified person by or on behalf of a taxpayer that is forwarded by the specified person to the IRS. This exception is intended to cover two types of situations. The first situation is where a taxpayer (or a taxpayer's representative)

---

[10] Code sec. 7802(a).
[11] Treasury Order 150-10 (April 22, 1982).
[12] See, e.g., Treasury Order 111-2 (March 16, 1981), which delegates to the Assistant Secretary (Tax Policy) the exclusive authority to make the final determination of the

Treasury Department's position with respect to issues of tax policy arising in connection with regulations, published Revenue Rulings and Revenue Procedures, and tax return forms and to determine the time, form and manner for the public communication of such position.

writes to a specified person seeking assistance in resolving a difficulty with the IRS. This exception permits the specified person who receives such a request to forward it to the IRS for resolution without violating the general prohibition. The second situation that this first exception is intended to cover is an audit or investigation by the IRS of a Presidential nominee. Under present law (sec. 6103(c)), nominees for Presidentially appointed positions consent to disclosure of their tax returns and return information so that background checks may be conducted. Sometimes an audit or other investigation is initiated as part of that background check. The Committee anticipates that any such audit or investigation that is part of

such a background check will be encompassed within this first exception.

The second exception to the general prohibition applies to requests for disclosure of returns or return information under section 6103 if the request is made in accordance with the requirements of section 6103.

The third exception to the general prohibition applies to requests made by the Secretary of the Treasury as a consequence of the implementation of a change in tax policy.

Effective Date

The provision applies to violations occurring after the date of enactment.

Conference Committee Report (H.R. CONF. REP. NO. 105-599)

The conference agreement follows the Senate amendment.

[Law at ¶ 6580. CCH Explanation at ¶ 1131.]

[¶ 10,185]   Act Sec. 1201(a).   IRS personnel flexibilities (improvements in personnel flexibilities)

Senate Committee Report (S. REP. NO. 105-174)

Present Law

The IRS is subject to the personnel rules and procedures set forth in title 5, United States Code. Under these rules, IRS employees generally are classified under the General Schedule or the Senior Executive Service.

Reasons for Change

The Committee believes that as part of restructuring the IRS, the Commissioner should have the ability to bring in experts and the flexibility to revitalize the current IRS workforce. The current hiring practices often inhibit the ability of the Commissioner to change the IRS' institutional culture. Commissioner Rossotti has indicated that in order to maximize efforts to transform the IRS into an efficient, modern and responsive agency, the ability to recruit and retain a top-notch leadership and technical team is critical.

The Committee believes the IRS needs the flexibility to recruit employees from the private sector, to redesign its salary and incentive structures to reward employees who meet their objectives, and to hold non-performers accountable. Personnel and pay flexibilities are necessary prerequisites for larger fundamental changes in the IRS.

The Committee wants to support the Commissioner's initiatives to reposition the current IRS workforce as part of implementing a new organization designed around the needs of taxpayers.

Explanation of Provision

In general

The bill amends title 5 of the United States Code to provide certain personnel flexibilities to the IRS. In general, the bill provides that the IRS exercise the personnel flexibilities consistently with existing rules relating to merit system principles, prohibited personnel practices, and preference eligibles. In those cases where the exercise of personnel flexibilities would affect members of the employees' union, such employees' will not be subject to the exercise of any flexibility unless there is a written agreement between the IRS and the employees' union. Negotiation impasses be-

tween the IRS and the employees' union may be appealed to the Federal Services Impasse Panel.

Senior management and technical positions

Streamlined critical pay authority

The bill provides a streamlined process for the Secretary of the Treasury, or his delegate, to fix the compensation of, and appoint up to 40 individuals to, designated critical technical and professional positions, provided that: (1) the positions require expertise of an extremely high level in a technical, administrative or professional field and are critical to the IRS; (2) exercise of the authority is necessary to recruit or retain an individual exceptionally well qualified for the position; (3) designation of such positions is approved by the Secretary; (4) the terms of such appointments are limited to no more than four years; (5) appointees to such positions are not IRS employees immediately prior to such appointment; and (6) the total annual compensation for any position (including performance bonuses) does not exceed the rate of pay of the Vice President (currently $175,400).

These appointments are not subject to the otherwise applicable requirements under title 5. All such appointments will be excluded from the collective bargaining unit and the appointments will not be subject to approval of the Office of Management and Budget ("OMB") or the Office of Personnel Management ("OPM").

The streamlined authority will be limited to a period of 10 years.

Critical pay authority

The bill provides OMB with authority to set the pay for certain critical pay positions requested by the Secretary under section 5377 of title 5 of the United States Code at levels higher than authorized under current law. These critical pay positions would be critical, technical, administrative and professional positions other than those designated under the streamlined authority. Under the bill, OMB is authorized to approve requests for critical position pay up to the rate of pay of the Vice President (currently $175,400).

Recruitment, retention and relocation incentives

The bill authorizes the Secretary to vary from the existing provisions governing recruitment, retention and relocation incentives. The authority will be for a period of 10 years and will be subject to OPM approval.

Career-reserve Senior Executive Service ("SES") positions

The bill broadens the definition of a "career reserved position" in the SES to include a limited emergency appointee or a limited term appointee who, immediately upon entering the career-reserved position, was serving under a career or a career-conditional appointment outside the SES or whose limited emergency or limited term appointment is approved in advance by OPM. The number of appointments to these SES positions will be limited to up to 10 percent of the total number of SES positions available to the IRS. These positions will be limited to a 3 year term, with the option of extending the term for 2 more 3-year terms.

Variable compensation

The bill provides the Secretary with the authority to provide performance bonus awards to IRS senior executives of up to one-third of the individual's annual compensation. The bonus award would be based on meeting preset performance goals established by the IRS. An individual's total annual compensation, including the bonus, can not exceed the rate of pay of the Vice President. The authority will not be subject to OPM approval.

It is anticipated that the bonuses will not be available to more than 25 IRS senior executives annually.

General workforce
Performance management system

The bill permits the Secretary to establish a new performance management system which will maintain individual accountability by: (1) establishing one or more retention standards for each employee related to the work of the employee and expressed in terms of performance; (2) providing for periodic performance evaluations to determine whether employees are meeting the applicable retention standard; and (3) taking appropriate action, in accordance with applicable laws, with respect to any employee whose performance does not meet established retention standards.

The bill requires that the performance management system provide for: (1) establishing goals or objectives for individual, group or organizational performance and taxpayer service surveys; (2) communicating such goals or objectives to employees; and (3) using such goals or objectives to make performance distinctions among employees or groups of employees.

It is intended that in no event will performance measures be used which rank employees or groups of employees based on enforcement results, establish dollar goals for assessments or collections, or otherwise undermine fair treatment of taxpayers.

Awards

The bill provides the Secretary the authority to establish an awards program for IRS employees. The program will be designed to provide incentives for and recognition of individual, group and organizational achievements. The Secretary will

have the authority to provide awards between $10,000 and $25,000 without OPM approval.

These awards will be based on performance under the new performance management system, and in no case will awards be made (or performance measured) based on tax enforcement results.

Workforce classification and pay banding

The bill provides the Secretary with authority to establish one or more broad band pay systems covering all or any portion of the IRS workforce, subject to OPM criteria. At a minimum, the OPM criteria will have to: (1) ensure that the pay band system maintain the concept of equal pay for substantially equal work; (2) establish the minimum and maximum number of grades that may be combined into pay bands; (3) establish requirements for setting minimum and maximum rates of pay in a pay band; (4) establish requirements for adjusting the pay of an employee within a pay band; (5) establish requirements for setting the pay of a supervisory employee in a pay band; and (6) establish requirements and methodologies for setting the pay of an employee upon conversion to a broad-banded system, initial appointment, change of position or type of appointment and movement between a broad-banded system and another pay system.

Workforce staffing

The bill provides the IRS with flexibility in filling certain permanent appointments with qualified temporary employees. A qualified temporary employee is defined as a temporary employee of the IRS with at least two years of continuous service, who has met all applicable retention standards and who meets the minimum qualifications for the vacant position.

The bill authorizes the IRS to establish category rating systems for evaluating job applicants, under which qualified candidates are divided into two or more quality categories on the basis of relative degrees of merit, rather than assigned individual numerical ratings. Managers will be authorized to select any candidate from the highest quality category, and will not be limited to the three highest ranked candidates. In administering these category rating systems, the IRS generally will be required to list preference eligibles ahead of other individuals within each quality category. The appointing authority, however, could select any candidate from the highest quality category, as long as existing requirements relating to passing over preference eligibles are satisfied.

The bill authorizes the IRS to establish probation periods for IRS employees of up to 3 years, when it is determined that a shorter period will not be sufficient for an employee to demonstrate proficiency in a position.

* * *

Demonstration projects

The bill provides the IRS with authority to conduct one or more demonstration projects through a streamlined process. The authority will enable the IRS to test new approaches to Human Resource Management. The bill provides authority to the Secretary and OPM to waive the termination of a demonstration project, thereby making it permanent. At least 90 days prior to waiving the termination date OPM will be required to publish a notice of such intent in the Federal Register and inform the appropriate Committees (including the House Ways and Means Committee, the House Government Reform and Oversight Committee, the Senate Finance Committee and the Senate Governmental Affairs Committee) of both Houses of Congress in writing.

* * *

Effective Date

The provision, other than the IRS employee training program provision, is effective on the date of enactment. * * *

Conference Committee Report (H.R. CONF. REP. NO. 105-599)

The conference agreement follows the Senate amendment, with modifications. The conference agreement includes the House bill provision requiring the IRS to establish a new performance management system within one year from the date of enactment.

The conferees intend to give the IRS flexibility to establish a new performance management system. The conferees expect that this will refocus the IRS' personnel system on the overall mission of the IRS and how each employee's performance relates to that mission. Although the new performance standards are premised on the notion of retention, such standards should go beyond simply establishing a retention/non-retention or pass-fail performance system. At a minimum, the conferees believe that there should be at least one standard above the retention standard. This will enable managers to make meaningful distinctions among employees based on performance, to encourage employees to perform at a higher level and to reward superior performance.

The conference agreement permits the Secretary to appoint an individual, who was appointed an IRS employee on or after June 1, 1998, to a critical pay position under the streamlined critical pay authority.

The conference agreement also authorizes the IRS to pay certain relocation expenses for individuals appointed to critical pay positions after June 1, 1998. This authority is for a period of 10 years after the date of enactment.

The provision (in particular the written agreement requirement) is not intended to expand the jurisdiction of the Federal Service Impasses Panel.

* * *

[Law at ¶ 8025. CCH Explanation at ¶ 901, ¶ 931, ¶ 936, ¶ 941, ¶ 946, ¶ 956, ¶ 961 and ¶ 966.]

[¶ 10,190]   Act Sec. 1202.   IRS personnel flexibilities (voluntary separation incentive payments)

Senate Committee Report (S. REP. NO. 105-174)

[Act Sec. 1202]

Present Law

The IRS is subject to the personnel rules and procedures set forth in title 5, United States Code. Under these rules, IRS employees generally are classified under the General Schedule or the Senior Executive Service.

Reasons for Change

The Committee believes that as part of restructuring the IRS, the Commissioner should have the ability to bring in experts and the flexibility to revitalize the current IRS workforce. The current hiring practices often inhibit the ability of the Commissioner to change the IRS' institutional culture. Commissioner Rossotti has indicated that in order to maximize efforts to transform the IRS into an efficient, modern and responsive agency, the ability to recruit and retain a top-notch leadership and technical team is critical.

The Committee believes the IRS needs the flexibility to recruit employees from the private sector, to redesign its salary and incentive structures

to reward employees who meet their objectives, and to hold non-performers accountable. Personnel and pay flexibilities are necessary prerequisites for larger fundamental changes in the IRS.

The Committee wants to support the Commissioner's initiatives to reposition the current IRS workforce as part of implementing a new organization designed around the needs of taxpayers.

Explanation of Provision
* * *

Voluntary separation incentives

The bill provides authority to the IRS to use Voluntary Separation Incentive Pay ("buyouts") through December 31, 2002. The use of voluntary separation incentive is not intended to necessarily reduce the total number of Full Time Equivalents ("FTE") positions in the IRS.

* * *

Effective Date

The provision, other than the IRS employee training program provision, is effective on the date of enactment. * * *

Conference Committee Report (H.R. CONF. REP. NO. 105-599)

The conference agreement follows the Senate amendment, with modifications. * * *

[Law at ¶ 8030. CCH Explanation at ¶ 971.]

[¶ 10,195]   Act Sec. 1203.   IRS personnel flexibilities (termination of employment for misconduct)

Senate Committee Report (S. REP. NO. 105-174)

[*This committee report does not reflect changes made by Senate Floor Amendment Nos. 2376 and 2382. Senate Floor Amendment No. 2382 (144 Cong. Rec. 56, S4517) was passed with nominal debate. However, selected portions of the Senate Floor Debate for Amendment No. 2376 are reproduced below.—CCH.*]

Present Law

The IRS is subject to the personnel rules and procedures set forth in title 5, United States Code. Under these rules, IRS employees generally are classified under the General Schedule or the Senior Executive Service.

Reasons for Change

The Committee believes that as part of restructuring the IRS, the Commissioner should have the ability to bring in experts and the flexibility to revitalize the current IRS workforce. The current hiring practices often inhibit the ability of the Commissioner to change the IRS' institutional culture. Commissioner Rossotti has indicated that in order to maximize efforts to transform the IRS into an efficient, modern and responsive agency, the ability to recruit and retain a top-notch leadership and technical team is critical.

The Committee believes the IRS needs the flexibility to recruit employees from the private sector, to redesign its salary and incentive structures to reward employees who meet their objectives, and to hold non-performers accountable. Personnel and pay flexibilities are necessary prerequisites for larger fundamental changes in the IRS.

The Committee wants to support the Commissioner's initiatives to reposition the current IRS workforce as part of implementing a new organization designed around the needs of taxpayers.

Explanation of Provision
* * *

Violations for which IRS employees may be terminated

The bill requires the IRS to terminate an employee for certain proven violations committed by the employee in connection with the performance of official duties. The violations include: (1) failure to obtain the required approval signatures on documents authorizing the seizure of a taxpayer's home, personal belongings, or business assets; (2) providing a false statement under oath material to a matter involving a taxpayer; (3) falsifying or destroying documents to avoid uncovering mistakes made by the employee with respect to a matter involving a taxpayer; (4) assault or battery on a taxpayer or other IRS employee; (5) violation of the civil rights of a taxpayer or other IRS employee; (6) violations of the Internal Revenue Code, Treasury Regulations, or policies of the IRS (including the Internal Revenue Manual) for the purpose of retaliating or harassing a taxpayer or other IRS employee; and (7) wilful misuse of section 6103 for the purpose of concealing data from a Congressional inquiry.

The bill provides non-delegable authority to the Commissioner to determine that mitigating factors exist, that, in the Commissioner's sole discretion, mitigate against terminating the employee. The bill also provides that the Commissioner, in his sole discretion, may establish a procedure which will be used to determine whether an individual should be referred for such a determination by the Commissioner. The Treasury IG is required to track employee terminations and terminations that would have occurred had the Commissioner not determined that there were mitigation factors and include such information in the IG's annual report.

* * *

Effective Date

The provision, other than the IRS employee training program provision, is effective on the date of enactment. * * *

Senate Floor Debate for Amendment No. 2376 (144 CONG. REC. 56, S4486)

* * * Mr. GRAMM.—* * * Basically, we have in the bill a list of offenses for which an employee of the Internal Revenue Service may be terminated. In light of concerns that have arisen since we had the bill before the committee. I want to add two offenses to the list.

One has to do with testimony we heard where members of the Internal Revenue Service were said to be threatening to audit people for personal gain. We heard an assertion that a police officer had stopped an IRS agent and was going to write him a ticket, and the IRS agent allegedly had told the officer that if he wrote the ticket, he was going to get audited.

The second provision has to do with a knowing and willful failure of an IRS agent to file a tax return or pay taxes or declare income. Both of these fit, I think, perfectly into the list of very strong offenses that we have in the bill. * * *

Mr. KERRY.—Mr. President, the National Restructuring Commission included this provision in our bill. It is in the House bill, or at least provisions in it that dictate that an employee who does a number of things would be automatically terminated.

What the Senator from Texas has done is identified some additional things that ought to be on the list and once again has carefully drawn it—I believe the language is "willful" and—what was the other word, I ask the Senator? "Willful" and "intentionally."

This would not be a situation where an individual accidentally underpays taxes or misses a deadline or something like that. This is a much higher standard, a much more difficult standard. And I think it is a quite reasonable provision to add to the list of things that would force and require automatic termination.

In general, this legislation is attempting to change the culture by saying here are some things that, if you do it, there are going to be severe penalties. This is obviously a severe penalty. Punitive damages for damages, we have an expanded right for legal fees.

What we are trying to do is change the culture so that there is a new seriousness given to actions taken by the IRS. And all of us understand the penalty needs to be sufficient to meet the offense. I think the amendment of the distinguished Senator from Texas is a reasonable one and I urge its adoption.

* * *

Conference Committee Report (H.R. CONF. REP. NO. 105-599)

Senate Amendment
* * *

Mandatory employee terminations

The Senate amendment requires the IRS to terminate an employee for certain proven violations committed by the employee in connection with the performance of official duties. The violations include: (1) failure to obtain the required approval signatures on documents authorizing the seizure of a taxpayer's home, personal belongings, or business assets; (2) providing a false statement under oath material to a matter involving a taxpayer; (3) falsifying or destroying documents to avoid uncovering mistakes made by the employee with respect to a matter involving a taxpayer; (4) assault or battery on a taxpayer or other IRS employee; (5) violation of the civil rights of a taxpayer or other IRS employee; (6) violations of the Internal Revenue Code, Treasury Regulations, or policies of the IRS (including the Internal Revenue Manual) for the purpose of retaliating or harassing a taxpayer or other IRS employee; (7) willful misuse of section 6103 for the purpose of concealing data from a Congressional inquiry; (8) willful failure to file any tax return required under the Code on or before the due date (including extensions) unless failure is due to reasonable cause; (9) willful understatement of Federal tax liability, unless such understatement is due to reasonable cause; and (10) threatening to audit a taxpayer for the purpose of extracting personal gain or benefit.

The Senate amendment provides non-delegable authority to the Commissioner to determine that mitigating factors exist, that, in the Commissioner's sole discretion, mitigate against terminating the employee. The Senate amendment also provides that the Commissioner, in his sole discretion, may establish a procedure which will be used to determine whether an individual should be referred for such a determination by the Commissioner. The Treasury IG is required to track employee terminations and terminations that would have occurred had the Commissioner not determined that there were mitigation factors and include such information in the IG's annual report.

* * *

Conference Agreement

The conference agreement follows the Senate amendment, with modifications. * * *

With respect to mandatory terminations of employees for certain proven violations committed by the employee in connection with the performance of official duties, the conference agreement modifies the definitions of some of the violations. The definitions of the other violations are the same as the Senate amendment. The modified definitions are: (1) willful failure to obtain the required approval signatures on documents authorizing the seizure of a taxpayer's home, personal belongings, or business assets; (2) assault or battery on a taxpayer or other IRS employee, but only if there is a criminal conviction or a final judgment by a court in a civil case, with respect to the assault or battery; (3) falsifying or destroying documents to conceal mistakes made by any employee with respect to a matter involving a taxpayer or taxpayer representative; and (4) with respect to a taxpayer, taxpayer representative, or other IRS employee, the violation of any right under the U.S. Constitution, or any civil right established under titles VI or VII of the Civil Rights Act of 1964, title IX of the Educational Amendments of 1972, the Age Discrimination in Employment Act of 1967, the Age Discrimination Act of 1975, sections 501 or 504 of the Rehabilitation Act of 1973 and title I of the Americans with Disabilities Act of 1990.

* * *

[Law at ¶ 8035. CCH Explanation at ¶ 976.]

[¶ 10,200] Act Sec. 1204. IRS personnel flexibilities (basis for evaluation of IRS employees)

Senate Committee Report (S. REP. NO. 105-174)

[*This committee report does not reflect changes made by Senate Floor Amendment No. 2382. Senate Floor Amendment No. 2382 (144 Cong. Rec. 56, S4517) was passed with nominal debate.—CCH.*]

[Act Sec. 1204]

Present Law

The IRS is subject to the personnel rules and procedures set forth in title 5, United States Code. Under these rules, IRS employees generally are classified under the General Schedule or the Senior Executive Service.

Reasons for Change

The Committee believes that as part of restructuring the IRS, the Commissioner should have the ability to bring in experts and the flexibility to revitalize the current IRS workforce. The current hiring practices often inhibit the ability of the Commissioner to change the IRS' institutional culture. Commissioner Rossotti has indicated that in order to maximize efforts to transform the IRS into an efficient, modern and responsive agency, the ability to recruit and retain a top-notch leadership and technical team is critical.

The Committee believes the IRS needs the flexibility to recruit employees from the private sector, to redesign its salary and incentive structures to reward employees who meet their objectives, and to hold non-performers accountable. Personnel and pay flexibilities are necessary prerequisites for larger fundamental changes in the IRS.

The Committee wants to support the Commissioner's initiatives to reposition the current IRS workforce as part of implementing a new organization designed around the needs of taxpayers.

Explanation of Provision
* * *

Performance measures

The IRS is directed to develop employee performance measures that favor taxpayer service and prohibit awarding merit pay or bonuses that are based on enforcement quotas, goals, or statistics.
* * *

Effective Date

The provision, other than the IRS employee training program provision, is effective on the date of enactment. * * *

Conference Committee Report (H.R. CONF. REP. NO. 105-599)

The conference agreement follows the Senate amendment, with modifications. * * *

[Law at ¶ 8040. CCH Explanation at ¶ 981.]

[¶ 10,205] Act Sec. 1205. IRS personnel flexibilities (IRS employee training program)

Senate Committee Report (S. REP. NO. 105-174)

[Act Sec. 1205]

Present Law

The IRS is subject to the personnel rules and procedures set forth in title 5, United States Code. Under these rules, IRS employees generally are classified under the General Schedule or the Senior Executive Service.

Reasons for Change

The Committee believes that as part of restructuring the IRS, the Commissioner should have the ability to bring in experts and the flexibility to revitalize the current IRS workforce. The current hiring practices often inhibit the ability of the Commissioner to change the IRS' institutional culture. Commissioner Rossotti has indicated that in order to maximize efforts to transform the IRS into an efficient, modern and responsive agency, the ability to recruit and retain a top-notch leadership and technical team is critical.

The Committee believes the IRS needs the flexibility to recruit employees from the private sector, to redesign its salary and incentive structures to reward employees who meet their objectives, and to hold non-performers accountable. Personnel and pay flexibilities are necessary prerequisites for larger fundamental changes in the IRS.

The Committee wants to support the Commissioner's initiatives to reposition the current IRS workforce as part of implementing a new organization designed around the needs of taxpayers.

Explanation of Provision
* * *

IRS employee training program

The bill requires the IRS to place a high priority on employee training and to adequately fund employee training programs. The bill also requires the IRS to provide to the Congressional tax writing committees a comprehensive multi-year plan to: (1) ensure adequate customer service training; (2) review the organizational design of customer service; (3) implement a performance development system; and (4) provide, in fiscal year 1999, sixteen to twenty-four hours of conflict management training for collection employees.

Effective Date

* * * The provision relating to the IRS employee training program is effective 90 days after the date of enactment.

Conference Committee Report (H.R. CONF. REP. NO. 105-599)

The conference agreement follows the Senate amendment, with modifications. * * *

The conference agreement also provides that the Commissioner is to implement an employee training program no later than 180 days after enactment.

[Law at ¶ 8045. CCH Explanation at ¶ 986.]

[¶ 10,215]   Act Sec. 2001.   Electronic filing of tax and information returns

Senate Committee Report (S. REP. NO. 105-174)

[Act Sec. 2001]

[*This committee report does not reflect changes made by Senate Floor Amendment Nos. 2361 and 2373. Senate Floor Amendment No. 2361 (144 Cong. Rec. 56, S4460) was passed with nominal debate. However, selected portions of the Senate Floor Debate for Amendment No. 2373 are reproduced below. —CCH.*]

Present Law

Treasury Regulations section 1.6012-5 provides that the Commissioner may authorize a taxpayer to elect to file a composite return in lieu of a paper return. An electronically filed return is a composite return consisting of electronically transmitted data and certain paper documents that cannot be electronically transmitted.

The IRS periodically publishes a list of the forms and schedules that may be electronically transmitted, as well as a list of forms, schedules, and other information that cannot be electronically filed.

During the 1997 tax filing season, the IRS received approximately 20 million individual income tax returns electronically.

Reasons for Change

The Committee believes that the implementation of a comprehensive strategy to encourage electronic filing of tax and information returns holds significant potential to benefit taxpayers and make the IRS returns processing function more efficient. For example, the error rate associated with processing paper tax returns is approximately 20 percent, half of which is attributable to the IRS and half to error in taxpayer data. Because electronically-filed returns usually are prepared using computer software programs with built-in accuracy checks, undergo pre-screening by the IRS, and experience no key punch errors, electronic returns have an error rate of less than one percent. Thus, the Committee believes that an expansion of electronic filing will significantly reduce errors (and the resulting notices that are triggered by such errors). In addition, taxpayers who file their returns electronically receive confirmation from the IRS that their return was received.

Explanation of Provision

The provision states that the policy of Congress is to promote paperless filing, with a long-range goal of providing for the filing of at least 80 percent of all tax returns in electronic form by the year 2007. The provision requires the Secretary of the Treasury to establish a strategic plan to eliminate barriers, provide incentives, and use competitive market forces to increase taxpayer use of electronic filing. The provision requires all returns prepared in electronic form but filed in paper form to be filed electronically, to the extent feasible, by the year 2002.

The provision requires the Secretary to create an electronic commerce advisory group and to report annually to the tax-writing committees on the IRS's progress in implementing its plan to meet the goal of 80 percent electronic filing by 2007.

Effective Date

The provision is effective on the date of enactment.

Senate Floor Debate for Amendment No. 2373 (144 CONG. REC. 56, S4483)

* * *Mr. Bond.—* * * The bill we are now considering contains far-reaching provisions that will encourage the Internal Revenue Service to expand the use of electronic filing. My amendment improves those provisions in two ways. First, my amendment makes it absolutely clear that electronic filing of tax returns should be voluntary— not another burdensome government mandate on American taxpayers. While the bill calls on the IRS to make electronic filing the "preferred and most convenient means for filing," it also establishes a goal of 80 percent electronic filing of tax returns by 2007. Without a clear statement of congressional intent, it will be too easy for the IRS to interpret those provisions as requiring electronic filing by certain taxpayers or in certain circumstances.

As the Chairman of the Committee on Small Business, I have heard over the past 2 years from hundreds of small businesses about a similar government mandate—the Electronic Federal Tax Payment System or EFTPS. Under the statute establishing this system, the Treasury is required to collect certain percentages of tax electronically each year. To implement that requirement, the IRS established thresholds based on a business' past employment tax deposits. Regrettably, the IRS established the thresholds to serve its convenience rather than the taxpayer's. As a result, it now appears that far more taxpayers are required to pay their taxes electronically than the law requires.

While EFTPS deals with electronic payment of taxes, as opposed to filing of tax returns as we are addressing in this bill, it is a clear example of how the intent of Congress can be misinterpreted and result in an onerous mandate, in this case on America's small businesses. My amendment outs that misunderstanding off at the pass. As the IRS develops new programs and procedures for electronic filing, they must not be forced down the throats of the country's taxpayers. If they are truly convenient and cost effective, taxpayers will volunteer in droves to file their tax returns electronically, just as they have with the IRS' TeleFile program. And those taxpayers who, for one reason or another, decide that electronic filing is not practical, should be permitted to continue filing paper returns.

Second, my amendment expands the reporting requirements under the bill to ensure that the IRS pays particular attention to electronic-filing issues pertaining to small business. The bill currently requires that the Treasury Secretary, the IRS Commissioner, and the advisory group on electronic filing to report annually to the Congress on the progress made in expanding the use of electronic filing.

I commend the distinguished Chairman of the Finance Committee for including representatives of small business on the advisory group as I proposed. My amendment capitalizes on that small business voice, by requiring that the report to Congress include an analysis of the effects of electronic filing on small enterprises. If we are to prevent another burdensome program like EFTPS, I believe we must require the IRS to focus on how electronic-filing programs will affect small business. It will be of little benefit to the government if new electronic-filing programs include new requirements, like a substantial investment in new equipment, since most small businesses will not be able to participate. In addition, if the IRS pays particular attention to the issues facing small businesses in this areas, the agency will be better equipped to market and promote the benefits of electronic filing—a 100 percent improvement over the agency's initial efforts to encourage small firms to use EFTPS.

* * *

Conference Committee Report (H.R. CONF. REP. NO. 105-599)

Senate Amendment

Same as the House bill, except as follows. The Senate amendment also states that it is the policy of Congress that electronic filing should be a voluntary option for taxpayers. The Senate amendment also requires that the annual report discuss the effects on small businesses and the self-employed of electronically filing tax and information returns.

In addition, the Senate amendment states that the policy of Congress is that the IRS should cooperate with the private sector by encouraging competition to increase electronic filing.

Effective Date
Same as the House bill.

Conference Agreement
The conference agreement generally follows the Senate amendment, except that the provision in the Senate amendment that states that it is the policy of Congress that electronic filing should be a voluntary option for taxpayers is deleted.[1] The

provision on private sector cooperation is clarified to provide that the IRS should cooperate with and encourage the private sector by encouraging competition to increase electronic filing of returns. The intent of the conferees with respect to this provision is for the IRS and Treasury to press for robust private sector competition. When disputes arise between the IRS and the private sector on the question of whether services offered by the IRS inhibit competition or are appropriate services not reasonably available to taxpayers or tax preparers, the Electronic Commerce Advisory Group shall recommend to the IRS Commissioner an appropriate course of action. Those recommendations shall also be made available to the Congress. Notwithstanding the previous sentence, the conferees also intend that the IRS should continue to offer and improve its Telefile program and make available a comparable program on the Internet.

[Law at ¶ 8050. CCH Explanation at ¶ 1001.]

[¶ 10,220]   Act Sec. 2002.   Due date for certain information returns

Senate Committee Report (S. REP. NO. 105-174)

[Code Sec. 6071 and Act Sec. 2002]
Present Law
Information such as the amount of dividends, partnership distributions, and interest paid during the calendar year must be supplied to taxpayers by the payors by January 31 of the following calendar year. The payors must file an information return with the IRS with the information by February 28 of the year following the calendar year for which the return must be filed. Under present law, the due date for filing information returns with the IRS is the same whether such

returns are filed on paper, on magnetic media, or electronically. Most information returns are filed on magnetic media (such as computer tapes), which are physically shipped to the IRS.

Reasons for Change
The Committee believes that encouraging information return filers to file electronically will substantially increase the efficiency of the tax system by avoiding the need to convert the information from magnetic media or paper to electronic form before return matching.

---

[1] No inference is intended by this deletion. Present law (section 6011(e)(1) of the Code) already states that returns of any tax imposed by subtitle A (income taxes and self-employment taxes) on individuals, estates and trusts may not be required to be filed in any format (such as by electronic means) other than on paper forms supplied by the IRS.

Explanation of Provision

The provision provides an incentive to filers of information returns to use electronic filing by extending the due date for filing such returns from February 28 (under present law) to March 31 of the year following the calendar year to which the return relates.

The provision also requires the Treasury to issue a study evaluating the merits and disadvantages, if any, of extending the deadline for providing taxpayers with copies of information returns from January 31 to February 15 (Forms W-2 would still be required to be furnished by January 31).

Effective Date

The extension of the due date for filing returns applies to information returns required to be filed after December 31, 1999. The Treasury study is due by December 31, 1998.

Conference Committee Report (H.R. CONF. REP. NO. 105-599)

The conference agreement follows the Senate amendment, except that the Treasury study is due by June 30, 1999.

[Law at ¶ 6100 and ¶ 8055. CCH Explanation at ¶ 1005.]

[¶ 10,225]   Act Sec. 2003.   Paperless electronic filing

Senate Committee Report (S. REP. NO. 105-174)

[*This committee report does not reflect changes made by Senate Floor Amendment Nos. 2343 and 2348. Selected portions of the Senate Floor Debate for Amendment Nos. 2343 and 2348 are reproduced below.—CCH.*]

[Code Sec. 6061]
Present Law

Code section 6061 requires that tax forms be signed as required by the Secretary. The IRS will not accept an electronically filed return unless it has also received a Form 8453, which is a paper form that contains signature information of the filer.

A return generally is considered timely filed when it is received by the IRS on or before the due date of the return. If the requirements of Code section 7502 are met, timely mailing is treated as timely filing. If the return is mailed by registered mail, the dated registration statement is prima facie evidence of delivery. As an electronically filed return is not mailed, section 7502 does not apply.

The IRS periodically publishes a list of the forms and schedules that may be electronically transmitted, as well as a list of forms, schedules, and other information that cannot be electronically filed.

Reasons for Change

Electronically filed returns cannot provide the maximum efficiency for taxpayers and the IRS under current rules that require signature information to be filed on paper. Also, taxpayers need to know how the IRS will determine the filing date of a return filed electronically. The Committee believes that more types of returns could be filed electronically if proper procedures were in place. Also, as the IRS shifts to a paperless tax return system, the Committee intends for the IRS to assist taxpayers in shifting to paperless record retention.

Explanation of Provision

The provision requires the Secretary to develop procedures that would eliminate the need to file a paper form relating to signature information. Until the procedures are in place, the provision authorizes the Secretary to provide for alternative methods of signing all returns, declarations, statements, or other documents. An alternative method of signature would be treated identically, for both civil and criminal purposes, as a signature on a paper form.

The provision also provides rules for determining when electronic returns are deemed filed and to make it possible for taxpayers to authorize, on electronically filed returns, persons (such as return preparers) to whom information may be disclosed pursuant to section 6103.

The provision requires the Secretary to establish procedures, to the extent practicable, to receive all forms electronically for taxable periods beginning after December 31, 1998.

Effective Date

The provision is effective on the date of enactment.

Senate Floor Debate for Amendment No. 2343 (144 CONG. REC. 55, S4401)

* * * Mr. LEAHY.—* * * Today, Senator Ashcroft and I are offering an amendment to H.R. 2676 based on the Taxpayers Internet Assistance Act of 1998, S. 1901. Our bipartisan legislation requires the IRS to provide taxpayers with speedy access to tax forms, publications and other published guidance via the Internet.

Mr. President, I want to praise the Senate Finance Committee, Chairman Roth, Senator Moynihan, Senator Kerrey and Senator Grassley for their leadership in moving the IRS reform legislation to the full Senate. I strongly support the bill approved by the Finance Committee.

As the Senate prepares to debate IRS reforms, we must use technology to make the IRS more effective for all taxpayers. What better way to do that then to require the IRS to maintain online access to the latest tax information. Every citizen in the United States, no matter if he or she lives in a small town or big city, should be able to receive electronically the latest published tax guidance or download the most up-to-date tax form.

The IRS web page at >http://irs.ustreas.gov< provides timely service to taxpayers by increasing electronic access to some tax forms and publications. I commend the IRS for its use of Internet technology to improve its services. More information and services should be offered online and not just as a passing fad. Our legislation is needed to build on this electronic start and lock into the law for today and tomorrow comprehensive online taxpayer services.

For Tax Forms, Instructions and Publications, our legislation provides for online posting of docu-

ments created during the most recent five years, the same period of time that the IRS now keeps these documents on CD-ROM for Congressional offices. With these common sense requirements, the IRS will be able to enhance its web page with comprehensive tax guidance in a matter of days at little cost to taxpayers under our bipartisan bill. In fact, the Congressional Budget Office has scored our legislation as adding no new direct spending.

* * *

Senate Floor Debate for Amendment No. 2348 (144 CONG. REC. 55, S4429)

* * * Mr. ASHCROFT.—Mr. President, the amendment which I have just sent to the desk, known as the Ashcroft-Leahy amendment, would strike a one-sentence provision that holds taxpayers as guilty until proven innocent. The IRS would deem a minimum level of security of a personal identification number code assigned each taxpayer for purposes of electronic filing as actually more binding than an analog signature.

Let me just sort of put that in ordinary language. Ordinarily, it is the responsibility of the IRS in seeking to act upon a tax return to prove that the signature is actually the signature of the person who purportedly signed it. For those individuals signing electronically, this provision would be reversed so that a person who signs electronically would be discriminated against as compared to an individual who signs in analog form.

That is a problem, but it is really not nearly the problem that comes when you just open the door to the legal nightmare for taxpayers who might be victims of electronic identity theft, where their identity is stolen electronically, whose pin codes or real electronic signature is fraudulently used. And secondly, not only does it subject people to that kind of risk, but it makes very bad technology policy. As we begin to welcome the use of technology to alleviate the kind of burden that is both on taxpayers and on the individuals in the bureaucracy. it is time for us to welcome the kind of technology which would provide valid authentication but not to switch to individuals who provide their tax returns via the Internet or via electronic

filing a kind of discrimination which would be a disincentive for them to use the program.

The IRS is wedded to technology that is decades old. The kind of things they are talking about, the PIN code system would only make matters worse. A PIN code that anyone can type is not a secure means of authenticating documents. As we proceed into the future of electronic signatures with the use of a wide variety of technologies that will provide for authentication, it is important that we not, in the law, place this prejudice against the use of technology.

Currently, the Internal Revenue Service plans to implement electronic filing by means of a taxpayer PIN code that would actually be more authoritative than a written signature, so the person filing with a written signature would not undertake some of the responsibilities and liabilities people do with the electronic filing. That disparity in the way people are treated is not reasonable, it is not appropriate, and it is counterproductive. The IRS should use the best technology available for protection of such sensitive information and help to ensure the future of electronic commerce.

So we offer this Ashcroft-Leahy amendment which simply would strike the one-sentence provision that reverses, in terms of signatures on the Internet, the normal burdens of proof and the normal responsibility of the person proving up the document to prove the authenticity of the signature.

* * *

Conference Committee Report (H.R. CONF. REP. NO. 105-599)

The conference agreement follows the Senate amendment, except as follows. The Secretary is permitted to waive the signature requirement, but only returns signed or subscribed under alternative methods prescribed by the Secretary (not including waiver) are entitled to be treated as though signed or subscribed. The provision that requires the Secretary, to the extent practicable,

to receive all forms electronically applies to taxable periods after December 31, 1999. The provision relating to authorizing return preparers to communicate with the IRS on matters included on electronically filed returns is clarified.

[Law at ¶ 6090, ¶ 6730 and ¶ 8060. CCH Explanation at ¶ 1009, ¶ 1015 and ¶ 1027.]

[¶ 10,230]   Act Sec. 2004.   Return-free tax system

House Committee Report (H.R. REP. NO. 105-364, pt. 1)

[Act Sec. 2004]
Present Law
Under present law, taxpayers are required to calculate their own tax liabilities and submit returns showing their calculations.

Reasons for Change
The Committee believes that it would benefit taxpayers to be relieved, to the extent feasible, from the burden of determining tax liability and filing returns.

Explanation of Provision
The bill requires the Secretary or his delegate to study the feasibility of and develop procedures for the implementation of a return-free tax system for taxable years beginning after 2007. The Secretary is required annually to report to the tax-writing committees on the progress of the development of such system, including what additional resources the IRS would need to implement the system, the changes to the Internal Revenue Code that would facilitate the system, the procedures developed to date, and the number and classes of taxpayers who would be permitted to use such a system. The Secretary is required to make the first report on the development of the return-free filing system to the tax-writing committees on June 30, 1999. It is contemplated that the return-free filing system would initially be targeted at taxpayers who had taxable income from wages, interest, dividends, pensions, and unemployment compensation; did not itemize deductions; and did not take any tax credits other than the earned income tax credit.[25]

Effective Date
The provision is effective on the date of enactment.

Conference Committee Report (H.R. CONF. REP. NO. 105-599)

Senate Amendment
Same as the House bill.

Conference Agreement
The conference agreement follows the House bill and the Senate amendment.

[Law at ¶ 8065. CCH Explanation at ¶ 1019.]b

[¶ 10,235]   Act Sec. 2005.   Access to account information

Senate Committee Report (S. REP. NO. 105-174)

[Act Sec. 2005]
Present Law
Taxpayers who file their returns electronically cannot review their accounts electronically.

Reasons for Change
The Committee believes that it would be desirable for a taxpayer (or the taxpayer's designee) to be able to review that taxpayer's account electronically, but only if all necessary privacy safeguards are in place.

Explanation of Provision
The provision requires the Secretary to develop procedures not later than December 31, 2006, under which a taxpayer filing returns electronically (or the taxpayer's designee under section 6103(c)) could review the taxpayer's own account electronically, but only if all necessary privacy safeguards are in place by that date. The Secretary is required to issue an interim progress report to the tax-writing committees by December 31, 2003.

Effective Date
The provision is effective on the date of enactment.

Conference Committee Report (H.R. CONF. REP. NO. 105-599)

The conference agreement follows the Senate amendment.

[Law at ¶ 8070. CCH Explanation at ¶ 1025.]

---

[25] See "The President's Tax Proposals to Congress for Fairness, Growth, and Simplicity," at 115 (May 1985) and The GAO Report on Tax Administration Alternative Filing Systems (October 1996).

[¶ 10,245] Act Sec. 3001. Burden of proof

Senate Committee Report (S. REP. NO. 105-174)

[Code Sec. 7491]

[*This committee report does not reflect changes made by Senate Floor Amendment No. 2374. See selected excerpts from Senate Floor Debate below.—CCH.*]

Present Law

Under present law, a rebuttable presumption exists that the Commissioner's determination of tax liability is correct.[19] "This presumption in favor of the Commissioner is a procedural device that requires the plaintiff to go forward with prima facie evidence to support a finding contrary to the Commissioner's determination. Once this procedural burden is satisfied, the taxpayer must still carry the ultimate burden of proof or persuasion on the merits. Thus, the plaintiff not only has the burden of proof of establishing that the Commissioner's determination was incorrect, but also of establishing the merit of its claims by a preponderance of the evidence".[20]

The general rebuttable presumption that the Commissioner's determination of tax liability is correct is a fundamental element of the structure of the Internal Revenue Code. Although this presumption is judicially based, rather than legislatively based, there is considerable evidence that the presumption has been repeatedly considered and approved by the Congress. This is the case because the Internal Revenue Code contains a number of civil provisions that explicitly place the burden of proof on the Commissioner in specifically designated circumstances. The Congress would have enacted these provisions only if it recognized and approved of the general rule of presumptive correctness of the Commissioner's determination. A list of these civil provisions follows.

(1) *Fraud.*—Any proceeding involving the issue of whether the taxpayer has been guilty of fraud with intent to evade tax (secs. 7454(a) and 7422(e)).

(2) *Required reasonable verification of information returns.*—In any court proceeding, if a taxpayer asserts a reasonable dispute with respect to any item of income reported on an information returned filed with the Secretary by a third party and the taxpayer has fully cooperated with the Secretary (including providing, within a reasonable period of time, access to and inspection of all witnesses, information, and documents within the control of the taxpayer as reasonably requested by the Secretary), the Secretary has the burden of producing reasonable and probative information concerning such deficiency in addition to such information return (sec. 6201(d)).

(3) *Foundation managers.*—Any proceeding involving the issue of whether a foundation manager has knowingly participated in prohibited transactions (sec. 7454(b)).

(4) *Transferee liability.*—Any proceeding in the Tax Court to show that a petitioner is liable as a transferee of property of a taxpayer (sec. 6902(a)).

(5) *Review of jeopardy levy or assessment procedures.*—Any proceeding to review the reasonableness of a jeopardy levy or jeopardy assessment (sec. 7429(g)(1)).

(6) *Property transferred in connection with performance of services.*—In the case of property subject to a restriction that by its terms will never lapse and that allows the transferee to sell only at a price determined under a formula, the price is deemed to be fair market value unless established to the contrary by the Secretary (sec. 83(d)(1)).

(7) *Illegal bribes, kickbacks, and other payments.*—As to whether a payment constitutes an illegal bribe, illegal kickback, or other illegal payment (sec. 162(c)(1) and (2)).

(8) *Golden parachute payments.*—As to whether a payment is a parachute payment on account of a violation of any generally enforced securities laws or regulations (sec. 280G(b)(2)(B)).

(9) *Unreasonable accumulation of earnings and profits.*—In any Tax Court proceeding as to whether earnings and profits have been permitted to accumulate beyond the reasonable needs of the business, provided that the Commissioner has not fulfilled specified procedural requirements (sec. 534).

(10) *Expatriation.*—As to whether it is reasonable to believe that an individual's loss of citizenship would result in a substantial reduction in the individual's income taxes or transfer taxes (secs. 877(e), 2107(e), 2501(a)(4)).

(11) *Public inspection of written determinations.*—In any proceeding seeking additional disclosure of information (sec. 6110(f)(4)(A)).

(12) *Penalties for promoting abusive tax shelters, aiding and abetting the understatement of tax liability, and filing a frivolous income return.*—As to whether the person is liable for the penalty (sec. 6703(a)).

(13) *Income tax return preparers' penalty.*—As to whether a preparer has willfully attempted to understate tax liability (sec. 7427).

(14) *Status as employees.*—As to whether individuals are employees for purposes of employment taxes (pursuant to the safe harbor provisions of section 530 of the Revenue Act of 1978).[21]

Reasons for Change

The Committee is concerned that individual and small business taxpayers frequently are at a disadvantage when forced to litigate with the Internal Revenue Service. The Committee believes that the present burden of proof rules contribute to that disadvantage. The Committee believes that, all other things being equal, facts asserted by individual and small business taxpayers who cooperate with the IRS and satisfy relevant recordkeeping and substantiation requirements should be accepted. The Committee

---

[19] *Welch v. Helvering,* 290 U.S. 111, 115 (1933).
[20] *Danville Plywood Corp. v. U.S.,* U.S. Cl. Ct., 63 AFTR 2d 89-1036, 1043 (1989); citations omitted.

[21] Public Law 95-600 (November 6, 1978), as amended by section 1122 of the Small Business Job Protection Act of 1996 (Public Law 104-188; August 20, 1996).

believes that shifting the burden of proof to the Secretary in such circumstances will create a better balance between the IRS and such taxpayers, without encouraging tax avoidance.

The Committee believes that it is inappropriate for the IRS to rely solely on statistical information on unrelated taxpayers to reconstruct unreported income of an individual taxpayer. The Committee also believes that, in a court proceeding, the IRS should not be able to rest on its presumption of correctness if it does not provide any evidence whatsoever relating to penalties.

Explanation of Provision

The provision provides that the Secretary shall have the burden of proof in any court proceeding with respect to a factual issue if the taxpayer introduces credible evidence with respect to the factual issue relevant to ascertaining the taxpayer's income tax liability. Four conditions apply. First, the taxpayer must comply with the requirements of the Internal Revenue Code and the regulations issued thereunder to substantiate any item (as under present law). Second, the taxpayer must maintain records required by the Code and regulations (as under present law). Third, the taxpayer must cooperate with reasonable requests by the Secretary for meetings, interviews, witnesses, information, and documents (including providing, within a reasonable period of time, access to and inspection of witnesses, information, and documents within the control of the taxpayer, as reasonably requested by the Secretary). Cooperation also includes providing reasonable assistance to the Secretary in obtaining access to and inspection of witnesses, information, or documents not within the control of the taxpayer (including any witnesses, information, or documents located in foreign countries[22]). A necessary element of cooperating with the Secretary is that the taxpayer must exhaust his or her administrative remedies (including any appeal rights provided by the IRS). The taxpayer is not required to agree to extend the statute of limitations to be considered to have cooperated with the Secretary. Cooperating also means that the taxpayer must establish the applicability of any privilege. Fourth, taxpayers other than individuals must meet the net worth limitations that apply for awarding attorney's fees (accordingly, no net worth limitation would be applicable to individuals). Corporations, trusts, and partnerships whose net worth exceeds $7 million are not eligible for the benefits of the provision. The taxpayer has the burden of proving that it meets each of these conditions, because they are necessary prerequisites to establishing that the burden of proof is on the Secretary.

The burden will shift to the Secretary under this provision only if the taxpayer first introduces credible evidence with respect to a factual issue relevant to ascertaining the taxpayer's income tax liability. Credible evidence is the quality of evidence which, after critical analysis, the court would find sufficient upon which to base a decision on the issue if no contrary evidence were submitted (without regard to the judicial presumption of IRS correctness). A taxpayer has not produced credible evidence for these purposes if the taxpayer merely makes implausible factual assertions, frivolous claims, or tax protestor-type arguments. The introduction of evidence will not meet this standard if the court is not convinced that it is worthy of belief. If after evidence from both sides, the court believes that the evidence is equally balanced, the court shall find that the Secretary has not sustained his burden of proof.

Nothing in the provision shall be construed to override any requirement under the Code or regulations to substantiate any item. Accordingly, taxpayers must meet applicable substantiation requirements, whether generally imposed[23] or imposed with respect to specific items, such as charitable contributions[24] or meals, entertainment, travel, and certain other expenses.[25] Substantiation requirements include any requirement of the Code or regulations that the taxpayer establish an item to the satisfaction of the Secretary.[26] Taxpayers who fail to substantiate any item in accordance with the legal requirement of substantiation will not have satisfied the legal conditions that are prerequisite to claiming the item on the taxpayer's tax return and will accordingly be unable to avail themselves of this provision regarding the burden of proof. Thus, if a taxpayer required to substantiate an item fails to do so in the manner required (or destroys the substantiation), this burden of proof provision is inapplicable.[27]

The provision also provides that in any instance in which the Secretary uses statistical information from unrelated taxpayers solely to reconstruct an individual taxpayer's income (such as average income for taxpayers in the area in which the taxpayer lives), the burden of proof is on the Secretary with respect to the item of income that was reconstructed by the Secretary.

Further, the provision provides that, in any court proceeding, the Secretary must initially come forward with evidence that it is appropriate to apply a particular penalty to the taxpayer before the court can impose the penalty. This provision is not intended to require the Secretary to introduce evidence of elements such as reasonable cause or substantial authority. Rather, the Secretary must come forward initially with evi-

---

[22] Cooperation also includes providing English translations, as reasonably requested by the Secretary.
[23] See e.g., Sec. 6001 and Treas. Reg. sec. 1.6001-1 requiring every person liable for any tax imposed by this Title to keep such records as the Secretary may from time to time prescribe, and secs. 6038 and 6038A requiring United States persons to furnish certain information the Secretary may prescribe with respect to foreign businesses controlled by the U.S. person.
[24] Sec. 170(a)(1) and (f)(8) and Treas. Reg. sec. 1.170A-13.
[25] See e.g., Sec. 274(d) and Treas. Reg. sec. 1.274(d)-1, 1.274-5T, and 1.274-5A.

[26] For example, sec. 905(b) of the Code provides that foreign tax credits shall be allowed only if the taxpayer establishes to the satisfaction of the Secretary all information necessary for the verification and computation of the credit. Instructions for meeting that requirement are set forth in Treas. Reg. sec. 1.905-2.

[27] If, however, the taxpayer can demonstrate that he had maintained the required substantiation but that it was destroyed or lost through no fault of the taxpayer, such as by fire or flood, existing tax rules regarding reconstruction of those records would continue to apply.

dence regarding the appropriateness of applying a particular penalty to the taxpayer; if the taxpayer believes that, because of reasonable cause, substantial authority, or a similar provision, it is inappropriate to impose the penalty, it is the taxpayer's responsibility (and not the Secretary's obligation) to raise those issues.

Effective Date

The provision applies to court proceedings arising in connection with examinations commencing after the date of enactment.

Senate Floor Debate for Amendment No. 2374 (144 CONG. REC. 56, S4484)

* * * Mr. GRAMM.—Mr. President, this is a very simple amendment. We have a provision in the bill, a very important provision, that sets up a set of criteria where, if the taxpayer meets a test of keeping prudent records and of turning those records over to the IRS on a timely basis, that once that transfer of records has occurred and the other requirements have been met, then the burden of proof shifts to the Internal Revenue Service when someone is accused of having violated the IRS code by not being in compliance on their income taxes.

This was a provision that was included in the bill under the leadership of the chairman. We, I think, generally wanted to extend it to all tax cases but because of revenue constraints we were unable to do it. I have constructed this amendment in a fashion which does permit the expanded burden of proof transfer. It delays the expansion for 6 months and sunsets it at the end of 5 years, so it fits within the revenue cap we have.

I believe that once we provide this protection that we will end up not taking it back or allowing it to expire. I think this is an important protection, because on gift and estate issues, we have the same problem as income taxes, where the Internal Revenue Service enters into a dispute with the taxpayer and, in a system unlike any other system in American society, under existing law, you are guilty until you prove yourself innocent.

This amendment would simply say that if you keep all the records that a prudent person could be expected to keep, and if you turn those substantiation records over to the Internal Revenue Service so there is no question about the fact that you have shared the information you have with them, at that point the burden of proof shifts from the taxpayer to the IRS not only in cases dealing with income tax disputes but in all other types of tax cases as well. * * *

Conference Committee Report (H.R. CONF. REP. NO. 105-599)

The conference agreement follows the Senate amendment, except as follows. The provision applies to income,[15] estate, gift, and generation-skipping transfer taxes, permanently (i.e., without the June 1, 2001 termination of some taxes as under the Senate amendment). The effective date is clarified by adding that in any case in which there is no examination, the provision applies to court proceedings arising in connection with taxable periods or events beginning or occurring after the date of enactment. An audit is not the only

event that would be considered an examination for purposes of this provision. For example, the matching of an information return against amounts reported on a tax return is intended to be an examination for purposes of this provision. Similarly, the review of a claim for refund prior to issuing that refund is also intended to be an examination for purposes of this provision.

[Law at ¶ 6720. CCH Explanation at ¶ 1331.]

[¶ 10,250]   Act Sec. 3101.   Expansion of authority to award costs and certain fees

House Committee Report (H.R. REP. NO. 105-364, pt. 1)

[Code Sec. 7430 and Code Sec. 7431]

Present Law

Any person who substantially prevails in any action by or against the United States in connection with the determination, collection, or refund of any tax, interest, or penalty may be awarded reasonable administrative costs incurred before the IRS and reasonable litigation costs incurred in connection with any court proceeding. In general, only an individual whose net worth does not exceed $2 million is eligible for an award, and only a corporation or partnership whose net worth does not exceed $7 million is eligible for an award.

Reasonable litigation costs include reasonable fees paid or incurred for the services of attorneys, except that the attorney's fees will not be reimbursed at a rate in excess of $110 per hour (indexed for inflation) unless the court determines that a special factor, such as the limited availability of qualified attorneys for the proceeding, justifies a higher rate. Awards of reasonable litigation costs and reasonable administrative costs cannot exceed amounts paid or incurred.

Once a taxpayer has substantially prevailed over the IRS in a tax dispute, the IRS has the burden of proof to establish that it was substantially justified in maintaining its position against

---

[15] For this purpose, self-employment taxes are treated as income taxes.

the taxpayer. A rebuttable presumption exists that provides that the position of the United States is not considered to be substantially justified if the IRS did not follow in the administrative proceeding (1) its published regulations, revenue rulings, revenue procedures, information releases, notices, or announcements, or (2) a private letter ruling, determination letter, or technical advice memorandum issued to the taxpayer.

Reasons for Change

The Committee believes that taxpayers should be allowed to recover the reasonable administrative costs they incur where the IRS takes a position against the taxpayer that is not substantially justified, beginning at the time that the IRS establishes its initial position by issuing a letter of proposed deficiency which allows the taxpayer an opportunity for administrative review in the IRS Office of Appeals. In determining what constitutes reasonable costs, the Committee believes that either the difficulty of issues or the limited local availability of tax expertise may justify the payment of higher hourly rates.

The Committee believes that the pro bono publicum representation of taxpayers should be encouraged and the value of the legal services rendered in these situations should be recognized. Where the IRS takes positions that are not substantially justified, it should not be relieved of its obligation to bear reasonable administrative and litigation costs because representation was provided the taxpayer on a pro bono basis.

The Committee is concerned that the IRS may continue to litigate issues that have previously been decided in favor of taxpayers in other circuits. The Committee believes that this places an undue burden on taxpayers that are required to litigate such issues. Accordingly, the Committee believes it is important that the court take into account whether the IRS has lost in the courts of appeals of other circuits on similar issues in determining whether the IRS has taken a position that is not substantially justified and thus liable for reasonable administrative and litigation costs.

Explanation of Provision

The bill: (1) provides that the difficulty of the issues presented or the unavailability of local tax expertise can be used to justify an award of attorney's fees of more than the statutory limit of $110 per hour; * * *

Effective Date

The provision applies to costs incurred and services performed more than 180 days after the date of enactment.

Senate Committee Report (S. Rep. No. 105-174)

Present Law

Any person who substantially prevails in any action by or against the United States in connection with the determination, collection, or refund of any tax, interest, or penalty may be awarded reasonable administrative costs incurred before the IRS and reasonable litigation costs incurred in connection with any court proceeding. Reasonable administrative costs are defined as (1) any administrative fees or similar charges imposed by the IRS and (2) expenses, costs and fees related to attorneys, expert witnesses, and studies or analyses necessary for preparation of the case, to the extent that such costs are incurred before earlier of the date of the notice of decision by IRS Appeals or the notice of deficiency (sec. 7430(c)(2)). Net worth limitations apply.

Reasonable litigation costs include reasonable fees paid or incurred for the services of attorneys, except that the attorney's fees will not be reimbursed at a rate in excess of $110 per hour (indexed for inflation) unless the court determines that a special factor, such as the limited availability of qualified attorneys for the proceeding, justifies a higher rate.

Rule 68 of the Federal Rules of Civil Procedure (FRCP) provides a procedure under which a party may recover costs if the party's offer for judgment was rejected and the subsequent court judgment was less favorable to the opposing party than the offer. The offering party's costs are limited to costs (excluding attorney's fees) incurred after the offer was made. The FRCP generally apply to tax litigation in the district courts and the United States Court of Federal Claims.

Code section 7431 permits the award of civil damages for unauthorized inspection or disclosure of return information. The Federal appellate courts are split over whether a party who substantially prevails over the United States in an action under Code section 7431 is eligible for an award of fees and reasonable costs.[28]

Reasons for Change

The Committee believes that taxpayers should be allowed to recover the reasonable administrative costs they incur where the IRS takes a position against the taxpayer that is not substantially justified, beginning at the time that the IRS establishes its initial position by issuing a letter of proposed deficiency which allows the taxpayer an opportunity for administrative review by the IRS Office of Appeals.

The Committee believes that the pro bono publicum representation of taxpayers should be encouraged and the value of the legal services rendered in these situations should be recognized. Where the IRS takes positions that are not substantially justified, it should not be relieved of its obligation to bear reasonable administrative and litigation costs because representation was provided the taxpayer on a pro bono basis.

The Committee is concerned that the IRS may continue to litigate issues that have previously been decided in favor of taxpayers in other circuits. The Committee believes that this places an undue burden on taxpayers that are required to litigate such issues. Accordingly, the Committee

---

[28] See *McLarty v. United States*, 6 F.2d 545 (8th Cir. 1993) (holding that the taxpayer may not recover fees and costs) and *Huckaby v. United States Department of Trea-* sury, 804 F.2d 297 (5th Cir. 1986) (holding that the taxpayer may recover fees and costs).

believes it is important that the court take into account whether the IRS has lost in the courts of appeals of other circuits on similar issues in determining whether the IRS has taken a position that is not substantially justified and thus liable for reasonable administrative and litigation costs.

The Committee believes that settlement of tax cases should be encouraged whenever possible. Accordingly, the Committee believes that the application of a rule similar to FRCP 68 is appropriate to provide an incentive for the IRS to settle taxpayers' cases for appropriate amounts, by requiring reimbursement of taxpayer's costs when the IRS fails to do so.

The Committee believes that when the IRS violates taxpayer's right to privacy by engaging in unauthorized inspection or disclosure activities, it is appropriate to reimburse taxpayers for the costs of their damages.

Explanation of Provision

The provision:

(1) moves the point in time after which reasonable administrative costs can be awarded to the date on which the first letter of proposed deficiency which allows the taxpayer an opportunity for administrative review in the IRS Office of Appeals is sent;

* * *

(3) permits the award of reasonable attorney's fees to specified persons who represent for no more than a nominal fee a taxpayer who is a prevailing party;

(4) provides that in determining whether the position of the United States was substantially justified, the court shall take into account whether the United States has lost in other courts of appeal on substantially similar issues;

(5) provides that if a taxpayer makes an offer after the taxpayer has a right to administrative review in the IRS Office of Appeals, the IRS rejects the offer, and later the IRS obtains a judgment[29] against the taxpayer in an amount that is equal to or less than the taxpayer's offer for the amount of the tax liability (excluding interest), reasonable costs and attorney's fees from the date of the offer would be awarded; and

(6) permits the award of attorney's fees in actions for civil damages for unauthorized inspection or disclosure of taxpayer returns and return information.

The above rules for making awards apply subject to the same net worth limitations as under present law.

Effective Date

The provision applies to eligible costs and services incurred more than 180 days after the date of enactment.

Conference Committee Report (H.R. CONF. REP. NO. 105-599)

The conference agreement follows the Senate amendment, except that the conference agreement follows the House bill with respect to the hourly rate caps, with the following modification. The hourly rate is raised to $125 per hour, which parallels the rate utilized under the Equal Access to Justice Act (the statute that authorizes the awarding of attorney's fees in non-tax Federal cases). This new cap will continue to be indexed for inflation (as under present law). With respect to the award of attorney's fees in unauthorized inspection and disclosure cases, the conferees wish to clarify that fees are payable by the United States only when the United States is the defendant and the plaintiff is a prevailing party. Also, individual defendants (such as State employees or contractors) may be liable for attorneys' fees and costs in cases where the United States is not a party, whenever they are found to have made a wrongful disclosure.

[Law at ¶ 6630 and ¶ 6640. CCH Explanation at ¶ 1336.]

[¶ 10,255] Act Sec. 3102. Civil damages for collection actions

Senate Committee Report (S. REP. NO. 105-174)

[Code Sec. 7426 and Code Sec. 7433]

Present Law

A taxpayer may sue the United States for up to $1 million of civil damages caused by an officer or employee of the IRS who recklessly or intentionally disregards provisions of the Internal Revenue Code or Treasury regulations in connection with the collection of Federal tax with respect to the taxpayer.

Reasons for Change

The Committee believes that taxpayers should also be able to recover economic damages they incur as a result of the negligent disregard of the Code or regulations by an officer or employee of the IRS in connection with a collection matter.

The Committee also believes that taxpayers should be able to recover civil damages they incur as a result of a willful violation of the Bankruptcy Code by an officer or employee of the IRS. As third parties may also be subject to IRS collection actions, the Committee believes that it is appropriate to afford them the opportunity to recover damages for unauthorized collection actions.

Explanation of Provision

The provision permits (1) up to $100,000 in civil damages caused by an officer or employee of the IRS who negligently disregards provisions of the Internal Revenue Code or Treasury regulations in connection with the collection of Federal tax with respect to the taxpayer, and (2) up to $1

---

[29] A judgment pursuant to a stipulation or a settlement will not be treated as a judgment for this purpose.

million in civil damages caused by an officer or employee of the IRS who willfully violates provisions of the Bankruptcy Code relating to automatic stays or discharges. The provision also provides that persons other than the taxpayer may sue for civil damages for unauthorized collection actions. No person is entitled to seek civil damages in a court of law without first exhausting administrative remedies.

Effective Date

The provision is effective with respect to actions of officers or employees of the IRS occurring after the date of enactment.

Conference Committee Report (H.R. CONF. REP. NO. 105-599)

The conference agreement follows the Senate amendment.

[Law at ¶ 6610 and ¶ 6650. CCH Explanation at ¶ 1101.]

[¶ 10,260]   Act Sec. 3103.   Increase in size of cases permitted on small case calendar

Senate Committee Report (S. REP. NO. 105-174)

[Code Sec. 7436, Code Sec. 7443A and Code Sec. 7463]

Present Law

Taxpayers may choose to contest many tax disputes in the Tax Court. Special small case procedures apply to disputes involving $10,000 or less, if the taxpayer chooses to utilize these procedures (and the Tax Court concurs) (sec. 7463). The IRS cannot require the taxpayer to use the small case procedures. The Tax Court generally concurs with the taxpayer's request to use the small case procedures, unless it decides that the case involves an issue that should be heard under the normal procedures. After the case has commenced, the Tax Court may order that the small case procedures should be discontinued only if (1) there is reason to believe that the amount in controversy will exceed $10,000 or (2) justice would require the change in procedure.

Small tax cases are conducted as informally as possible. Neither briefs nor oral arguments are required and strict rules of evidence are not applied. Most taxpayers represent themselves in small tax cases, although they may be represented by anyone admitted to practice before the Tax Court. Decisions in a case conducted under small case procedures are neither precedent for future cases nor reviewable upon appeal by either the government or the taxpayer.

Reasons for Change

The Committee believes that use of the small case procedures should be expanded.

Explanation of Provision

The provision increases the cap for small case treatment from $10,000 to $50,000. The Committee recognizes that an increase of this size may encompass a small number of cases of significant precedential value. Accordingly, the Committee anticipates that the Tax Court will carefully consider IRS objections to small case treatment, such as objections based upon the potential precedential value of the case.

Effective Date

The provision applies to proceedings commenced after the date of enactment.

Conference Committee Report (H.R. CONF. REP. NO. 105-599)

The conference agreement follows the Senate amendment. The conferees recognize that an increase of this size may encompass a small number of cases of significant precedential value. Accordingly, the conferees anticipate that the Tax Court will carefully consider (1) IRS objections to small case treatment, such as objections based upon the potential precedential value of the case, as well as (2) the financial impact on the taxpayer, including additional legal fees and costs, of not utilizing small case treatment.

[Law at ¶ 6670, ¶ 6690 and ¶ 6700. CCH Explanation at ¶ 1316.]

[¶ 10,265]   Act Sec. 3104.   Actions for refund with respect to certain estates which have elected the installment method of payment

Senate Committee Report (S. REP. NO. 105-174)

[Code Sec. 7422 and Code Sec. 7479]

Present Law

In general, the U.S. Court of Federal Claims and the U.S. district courts have jurisdiction over suits for the refund of taxes, as long as full payment of the assessed tax liability has been made. *Flora v. United States*, 357 U.S. 63 (1958), aff'd on reh'g, 362 U.S. 145 (1960). Under Code section 6166, if certain conditions are met, the executor of a decedent's estate may elect to pay the estate tax attributable to certain closely-held businesses over a 14-year period. Courts have held that U.S. district courts and the U.S. Court of Federal Claims do not have jurisdiction over claims for refunds by taxpayers deferring estate tax payments pursuant to section 6166 unless the entire estate tax liability has been paid (i.e., timely payment of the installments due prior to the bringing of an action is not sufficient to invoke jurisdiction). See, e.g., *Rocovich v. United States*, 933 F.2d 991 (Fed. Cir. 1991), *Abruzzo v. United States*, 24 Ct. Cl. 668 (1991). Under section 7479, the U.S. Tax

Court has limited authority to provide declaratory judgments regarding initial or continuing eligibility for deferral under section 6166.

Reasons for Change

The Committee believes that the refund jurisdiction of the U.S. Court of Federal Claims and the U.S. district courts should apply without regard to whether the taxpayer has elected, and the Secretary accepted, the payment of that tax in installments.

Explanation of Provision

The provision grants the U.S. Court of Federal Claims and the U.S. district courts jurisdiction to determine the correct amount of estate tax liability (or refund) in actions brought by taxpayers deferring estate tax payments under section 6166, as long certain conditions are met. In order to qualify for the provision, (1) the estate must have made an election pursuant to section 6166, (2) the estate must have fully paid each installment of principal and/or interest due (and all non-6166-related estate taxes due) before the date the suit is filed, (3) no portion of the payments due may have been accelerated, (4) there must be no suits for declaratory judgment pursuant to section 7479 pending, and (5) there must be no

outstanding deficiency notices against the estate. In general, to the extent that a taxpayer has previously litigated its estate tax liability, the taxpayer would not be able to take advantage of this procedure under principles of res judicata. Taxpayers are not relieved of the liability to make any installment payments that become due during the pendency of the suit (i.e., failure to make such payments would subject the taxpayer to the existing provisions of section 6166(g)(3)).

The provision further provides that once a final judgment has been entered by a district court or the U.S. Court of Federal Claims, the IRS is not permitted to collect any amount disallowed by the court, and any amounts paid by the taxpayer in excess of the amount the court finds to be currently due and payable are refunded to the taxpayer, with interest. Lastly, the provision provides that the two-year statute of limitations for filing a refund action is suspended during the pendency of any action brought by a taxpayer pursuant to section 7479 for a declaratory judgment as to an estate's eligibility for section 6166.

Effective Date

The provision is effective with respect to claims for refunds filed after the date of enactment.

Conference Committee Report (H.R. CONF. REP. NO. 105-599)

The conference agreement follows the Senate amendment.

[Law at ¶ 6600 and ¶ 6710. CCH Explanation at ¶ 1301.]

[¶ 10,270]   Act Sec. 3105.   Tax Court jurisdiction to review an adverse IRS determination of a bond issue's tax-exempt status

Conference Committee Report (H.R. CONF. REP. NO. 105-599)

[Act Sec. 3105]
Present Law

Interest on debt incurred by States or local governments generally is excluded from gross income if the proceeds of the borrowing are used to carry out governmental functions of those entities and the debt is repaid with governmental funds.

A State or local government that seeks to issue bonds, the interest on which is intended to be excludable from gross income, can request a ruling from the IRS regarding the eligibility of such bonds for tax-exemption. The prospective issuer can challenge the IRS's determination (or failure to make a timely determination) in a declaratory judgment proceeding in the Tax Court. Because bondholders, not issuers, are the parties whose tax liability is affected, issuers are not allowed to litigate the tax-exempt status of the bonds directly after the bonds are issued.

House Bill

No provision.

Senate Amendment

The Senate amendment expands the declaratory judgment procedures currently applicable to prospective bond issuers to allow issuers to litigate in the Tax Court issues related to the tax-exempt status of outstanding bonds. In such cases, the issuer must provide adequate notice to outstanding bondholders, and the bondholders are authorized to intervene in court proceedings brought

under this provision. The statute of limitations on assessment and collection of the tax liability of the bondholders is suspended during the pendency of the proceeding.

Effective Date

Determinations of tax-exempt status made after the date of enactment. In the case of a determination under a technical advice memorandum the public release of which occurred within one year of the date of enactment, a pleading may be filed not later than 90 days after the date of enactment.

Conference Agreement

In lieu of the Senate amendment provision, the conference agreement directs the Internal Revenue Service to modify its administrative procedures to allow tax-exempt bond issuers examined by the IRS to appeal adverse examination determinations to the Appeals Division of the IRS as a matter of right. Because of the complexity of the issues involved, the IRS is directed to provide that these appeals will be heard by senior appeals officers having experience in resolving complex cases.

The conferees further express their intent that Congress will evaluate judicial remedies in future legislation once the IRS's tax-exempt bond examination program has developed more fully and the Congress is better able to ensure that any such future measure protects all parties in interest to these determinations (i.e., issuers, bondholders, conduit borrowers, and the Federal Government).

Effective Date

The direction to the IRS is effective on the date of enactment.

[Law at ¶ 8075. CCH Explanation at ¶ 1137.]

[¶ 10,275]   Act Sec. 3106.   Civil action for release of erroneous lien

Senate Committee Report (S. REP. NO. 105-174)

[Code Sec. 6325 and Code Sec. 7426]

Present Law

Prior to 1995, the provisions governing jurisdiction over refund suits had generally been interpreted to apply only if an action was brought by the taxpayer against whom tax was assessed. Remedies for third parties from whom tax was collected (rather than assessed) were found in other provisions of the Internal Revenue Code. The Supreme Court held in *Williams v. United States*, 115 S.Ct. 1611 (1995), however, that a third party who paid another person's tax under protest to remove a lien on the third party's property could bring a refund suit, because she had no other adequate administrative or judicial remedy. In *Williams*, the IRS had filed a nominee lien against property that was owned by the taxpayer's former spouse and that was under a contract for sale. In order to complete the sale, the former spouse paid the amount of the lien under protest, and then sued in district court to recover the amount paid. The Supreme Court held that parties who are forced to pay another's tax under duress could bring a refund suit, because no other judicial remedy was adequate.

Reasons for Change

The Committee believes that third parties should have a mechanism to release an erroneous tax lien. Accordingly, the Committee believes it is appropriate to provide relief similar to that provided to third parties who are subject to wrongful levy of property.

Explanation of Provision

The provision creates an administrative procedure similar to the wrongful levy remedy for third parties in section 7426. Under this procedure, a record owner of property against which a Federal tax lien had been filed could obtain a certificate of discharge of property from the lien as a matter of right. The third party would be required to apply to the Secretary of the Treasury for such a certificate and either to deposit cash or to furnish a bond sufficient to protect the lien interest of the United States. Although the Secretary would determine the amount of the bond necessary to protect the Government's lien interest, the Secretary would have no discretion to refuse to issue a certificate of discharge if this procedure was followed, thus curing the defect in this remedy that the Supreme Court found in *Williams*. A certificate of discharge of property from a lien issued pursuant to the procedure would enable the record owner to sell the property free and clear of the Federal tax lien in all circumstances. The provision also authorizes the refund of all or part of the amount deposited, plus interest at the same rate that would be made on an overpayment of tax by the taxpayer, or the release of all or part of the bond, if the tax liability is satisfied or the Secretary determines that the United States does not have a lien interest or has a lesser lien interest than the amount initially determined.

The provision also establishes a judicial cause of action for third parties challenging a lien that is similar to the wrongful levy remedy in section 7426. The period within which such an action must be commenced would be 120 days after the date the certificate of discharge is issued to ensure an early resolution of the parties' interests. Upon conclusion of the litigation, the IRS would be authorized to apply the deposit or bond to the assessed liability and to refund to the third party any amount in excess of the liability, plus interest, or to release the bond. Actions to quiet title under 28 U.S.C. § 2410 would still be available to persons who did not seek the expedited review permitted under the new statutory procedure.

Effective Date

The provision is effective on the date of enactment.

Conference Committee Report (H.R. CONF. REP. NO. 105-599)

The conference agreement follows the Senate amendment.

[Law at ¶ 6260, ¶ 6420 and ¶ 6610. CCH Explanation at ¶ 1230.]

[¶ 10,285]   Act Sec. 3201.   Relief for innocent spouses

House Committee Report (H.R. REP. NO. 105-364, pt. 1)

[Code Sec. 6015 and Act Sec. 3201]

Present Law

Spouses who file a joint tax return are each fully responsible for the accuracy of the return and for the full tax liability. This is true even though only one spouse may have earned the wages or income which is shown on the return. This is "joint and several" liability. A spouse who wishes to avoid joint liability may file as a "married person filing separately."

Relief from liability for tax, interest and penalties is available for "innocent spouses" in certain limited circumstances. To qualify for such relief, the innocent spouse must establish: (1) that a joint return was made; (2) that an understatement of tax, which exceeds the greater of $500 or a specified percentage of the innocent spouse's adjusted gross income for the preadjustment (most recent) year, is attributable to a grossly erroneous item[36] of the other spouse; (3) that in signing the return, the innocent spouse did not know, and had no reason to know, that there was an understatement of tax; and (4) that taking into account all the facts and circumstances, it is inequitable to hold the innocent spouse liable for the deficiency in tax. The specified percentage of adjusted gross income is 10 percent if adjusted gross income is $20,000 or less. Otherwise, the specified percentage is 25 percent.

It is unclear under present law whether a court may grant partial innocent spouse relief. The Ninth Circuit Court of Appeals in *Wiksell v. Commissioner*[37] has allowed partial innocent spouse relief where the spouse did not know, and had no reason to know, the magnitude of the understatement of tax, even though the spouse knew that the return may have included some understatement.

The proper forum for contesting a denial by the Secretary of innocent spouse relief is determined by whether an underpayment is asserted or the taxpayer is seeking a refund of overpaid taxes. Accordingly, the Tax Court may not have jurisdiction to review all denials of innocent spouse relief.

No form is currently provided to assist taxpayers in applying for innocent spouse relief.

Reasons for Change

The Committee is concerned that the innocent spouse provisions of present law are inadequate. The Committee believes it is inappropriate to limit innocent spouse relief only to the most egregious cases where the understatement is large and the tax position taken is grossly erroneous. The Committee also believes that partial innocent spouse relief should be considered in appropriate circumstances, and that all taxpayers should have access to the Tax Court in resolving disputes concerning their status as an innocent spouse. Finally, the Committee believes that taxpayers need to be better informed of their right to apply for innocent spouse relief in appropriate cases and that the IRS is the best source of that information.

Explanation of Provision

The bill generally makes innocent spouse status easier to obtain. The bill eliminates all of the understatement thresholds and requires only that the understatement of tax be attributable to an erroneous (and not just a grossly erroneous) item of the other spouse.

The bill provides that innocent spouse relief may be provided on an apportioned basis. That is, the spouse may be relieved of liability as an innocent spouse to the extent the liability is attributable to the portion of an understatement of tax which such spouse did not know of and had no reason to know of.

The bill specifically provides that the Tax Court has jurisdiction to review any denial (or failure to rule) by the Secretary regarding an application for innocent spouse relief. The Tax Court may order refunds as appropriate where it determines the spouse qualifies for relief and an overpayment exists as a result of the innocent spouse qualifying for such relief. The taxpayer must file his or her petition for review with the Tax Court during the 90-day period that begins on the earlier of (1) 6 months after the date the taxpayer filed his or her claim for innocent spouse relief with the Secretary or (2) the date a notice denying innocent spouse relief was mailed by the Secretary. Except for termination and jeopardy assessments (secs. 6851, 6861), the Secretary may not levy or proceed in court to collect any tax from a taxpayer claiming innocent spouse status with regard to such tax until the expiration of the 90-day period in which such taxpayer may petition the Tax Court or, if the Tax Court considers such petition, before the decision of the Tax Court has become final. The running of the statute of limitations is suspended in such situations with respect to the spouse claiming innocent spouse status.

The bill also requires the Secretary of the Treasury to develop a separate form with instructions for taxpayers to use in applying for innocent spouse relief within 180 days from the date of enactment. An innocent spouse seeking relief under this provision must claim innocent spouse status with regard to any assessment not later than two years after the date of such assessment.

Effective Date

The provision is effective for understatements with respect to taxable years beginning after the date of enactment.

Senate Committee Report (S. REP. NO. 105-174)

[*This committee report does not reflect changes made by Senate Floor Amendment No. 2369. Selected portions of the Senate Floor Debate are reproduced below.—CCH.*]

* * *

Explanation of Provision

In general

The bill modifies the innocent spouse provisions to permit a spouse to elect to limit his or her liability for unpaid taxes on a joint return to the spouse's separate liability amount. In the case of a deficiency arising from a joint return, a spouse would be liable only to the extent items giving rise to the deficiency are allocable to the spouse. Special rules apply to prevent the inappropriate use of the election.

Items are generally allocated between spouses in the same manner as they would have been allocated had the spouses filed separate returns. The Secretary may prescribe other methods of allocation by regulation. The allocation of items is to be accomplished without regard to community property laws.

---

[36] Grossly erroneous items include items of gross income that are omitted from reported income and claims of deductions, credits or basis in an amount for which there is no basis in fact of law (code sec. 6013(e)(2)).

[37] 90 F.3d 1459 (9th Cir. 1997).

The election applies to all unpaid taxes under subtitle A of the Internal Revenue Code, including the income tax and the self-employment tax. The election may be made at any time not later than 2 years after collection activities begin with respect to the electing spouse. The Committee intends that 2 year period not begin until collection activities have been undertaken against the electing spouse that have the effect of giving the spouse notice of the IRS' intention to collect the joint liability from such spouse. For example, garnishment of wages, a notice of intent to levy against the property of the electing spouse would constitute collection activity against the electing spouse. The mailing of a notice of deficiency and demand for payment to the last known address of the electing spouse, addressed to both spouses, would not.

The Tax Court has jurisdiction of disputes arising from the separate liability election. For example, a spouse who makes the separate liability election may petition the Tax Court to determine the limits on liability applicable under this provision. The Tax Court is authorized to establish rules that would allow the Secretary of the Treasury and the electing spouse to require, with adequate notice, the other spouse to become a party to any proceeding before the Tax Court. The Secretary of the Treasury is required to develop a separate form with instructions for taxpayers to use in electing to limit liability.

Allocations of items

Under the bill, allocation of items of income and deduction follows the present-law rules determining which spouse is responsible for reporting an item when the spouses use the married, filing separate filing status. The Secretary of the Treasury is granted authority to prescribe regulations providing simplified methods of allocating items.

In general, apportionment of items of income are expected to follow the source of the income. Wage income is allocated to the spouse performing the job and receiving the Form W-2. Business and investment income (including any capital gains) is allocated in the same proportion as the ownership of the business or investment that produces the income. Where ownership of the business or investment is held by both spouses as joint tenants, it is expected that any income is allocated equally to each spouse, in the absence of clear and convincing evidence supporting a different allocation.

The allocation of business deductions is expected to follow the ownership of the business. Personal deduction items are expected to be allocated equally between spouses, unless the evidence shows that a different allocation is appropriate. For example, a charitable contribution normally would be allocated equally to both spouses. However, if the wife provides evidence that the deduction relates to the contribution of an asset that was the sole property of the husband, any deficiency assessed because it is later determined that the value of the property was overstated would be allocated to the husband.

Items of loss or deduction are allocated to a spouse only to the extent that income attributable to the spouse was offset by the deduction or loss. Any remainder is allocated to the other spouse.

Income tax withholding is allocated to the spouse from whose paycheck the tax was withheld. Estimated tax payments are generally expected to be allocated to the spouse who made the payments. If the payments were made jointly, the payments are expected to be allocated equally to each spouse, in the absence of evidence supporting a different allocation.

The allocation of items is to be made without regard to the community property laws of any jurisdiction.

If the electing spouse establishes that he or she did not know, and had no reason to know, of an item and, considering all the facts and circumstances, it is inequitable to hold the electing spouse responsible for any unpaid tax or deficiency attributable to such item, the item may be equitably reallocated to the other spouse. In cases where the IRS proves fraud, the IRS may distribute, apportion, or allocate any item between spouses.

Tax deficiencies

If a spouse makes the separate liability election, the liability for deficiencies determined after a joint return is filed is allocated to the spouse whose item gives rise to the deficiency. For example, if a deficiency is assessed after an IRS audit that relates to the husband's income that he failed to report on the return, the entire deficiency is allocated to the husband. If the wife elects separate liability, she owes none of the deficiency. The deficiency is the sole responsibility of the husband who failed to report the income.

If the deficiency relates to the items of both spouses, the separate liability for the deficiency is allocated between the spouses in the same proportion as the net items taken into account in determining the deficiency. If the deficiency arises as a result of the denial of an item of deduction or credit, the amount of the deficiency allocated to the spouse to whom the item of deduction or credit is allocated is limited to the amount of income or tax allocated to such spouse that was offset by the deduction or credit. The remainder of the liability is allocated to the other spouse to reflect the fact that income or tax allocated to that spouse was originally offset by a portion of the disallowed deduction or credit.

For example, a married couple files a joint return with wage income of $100,000 allocable to the wife and $30,000 of self employment income allocable to the husband. On examination, a $20,000 deduction allocated to the husband is disallowed, resulting in a deficiency of $5,600. Under the provision, the liability is allocated in proportion to the items giving rise to the deficiency. Since the only item giving rise to the deficiency is allocable to the husband, and because he reported sufficient income to offset the item of deduction, the entire deficiency is allocated to the husband and the wife has no liability with regard to the deficiency, regardless of the ability of the IRS to collect the deficiency from the husband.

If the joint return had shown only $15,000 (instead of $30,000) of self employment income for the husband, the income offset limitation rule discussed above would apply. In this case, the disallowed $20,000 deduction entirely offsets the

$15,000 of income of the husband, and $5,000 remains. This remaining $5,000 of the disallowed deduction offsets income of the wife. The liability for the deficiency is therefore divided in proportion to the amount of income offset for each spouse. In this example, the husband is liable for 3/4 of the deficiency ($4,200), and the wife is liable for the remaining 1/4 ($1,400).

The rule that the election will not apply to the extent any deficiency is attributable to an item the electing spouse had actual knowledge of is expected to be applied by treating the item as fully allocable to both spouses. For example a married couple files a joint return with wage income of $150,000 allocable to the wife and $30,000 of self employment income allocable to the husband. On examination, an additional $20,000 of the husband's self employment income is discovered, resulting in a deficiency of $9,000. The IRS proves that the wife had actual knowledge that $5,000 of this additional self employment income, but had no knowledge of the remaining $15,000. In this case, the husband would be liable for the full amount of the deficiency, since the item giving rise to the deficiency is fully allocable to him. In addition, the wife would be liable for the amount that would have been calculated as the deficiency based on the $5,000 of unreported income of which she had actual knowledge. The IRS would be allowed to collect that amount from either spouse, while the remainder of the deficiency could be collected from only the husband.

Tax shown on a return, but not paid

The separate liability election also applies in situations where the tax shown on a joint return is not paid with the return. In this case, the amount determined under the separate liability election equals the amount that would have been reported by the electing spouse on a separate return. However, if any item of credit or deduction would be disallowed solely because a separate return is filed, the item of credit or deduction will be computed without regard to such prohibition[31]. Similarly, a base amount and an adjusted base amount will be allowed in the determination of the taxable portion of social security and tier 1 railroad retirement benefits without regard to the rule in section 86(c). The calculation of the tax that would be shown on the separate return does not constitute the filing of a separate return. Other actions whose character may have been dependent upon the joint filing status of the taxpayer (for example, the making of a deductible IRA contribution under section 219) are unaffected by the election.

The separate liability election may not be used to create a refund, or to direct a refund to a particular spouse.

Special rules

Special rules apply to prevent the inappropriate use of the election.

First, if the IRS demonstrates that assets were transferred between the spouses in a fraudulent scheme joined in by both spouses, neither spouse is eligible to make the election under the provision (and consequently joint and several liability applies to both spouses).

Second, if the IRS proves that the electing spouse had actual knowledge that an item on a return is incorrect, the election will not apply to the extent any deficiency is attributable to such item. Such actual knowledge must be established by the evidence and shall not be inferred based on indications that the electing spouse had a reason to know.

Third, the limitation on the liability of an electing spouse is increased by the value of any disqualified assets received from the other spouse. Disqualified assets include any property or right to property that was transferred to an electing spouse if the principle purpose of the transfer is the avoidance of tax (including the avoidance of payment of tax). A rebuttable presumption exists that a transfer is made for tax avoidance purposes if the transfer was made less than one year before the earlier of the payment due date or the date of the notice of proposed deficiency. The rebuttable presumption does not apply to transfers pursuant to a decree of divorce or separate maintenance. The presumption may be rebutted by a showing that the principal purpose of the transfer was not the avoidance of tax or the payment of tax.

Notification of taxpayers

The Internal Revenue Service is required to notify all taxpayers who have filed joint returns of their rights to elect to limit their joint and several liability under this provision. It is expected that notice will appear in appropriate IRS publications, including IRS Publication 1, and in collection related notices sent to taxpayers.

The Internal Revenue Service should, whenever practicable, send appropriate notifications separately to each spouses. For example, where notifications are being sent by registered mail, it is expected a separate notice will be sent by registered mail to each spouse. This is intended to increase the likelihood that separated or divorced spouses will each receive such notices, as well as increase the likelihood that the Internal Revenue Service will be made aware of address changes that apply to one, but not both spouses.

Effective Date

The provision applies to any liability for tax arising after the date of enactment and any liability for tax arising on or before such date, but remaining unpaid as of such date.

The period in which an election may be made under the provision will not expire before the date that is 2 years after the date of the first collection action undertaken against the electing spouse on or after the date of enactment that has the effect of giving the spouse notice of the IRS' intention to collect the joint liability from the spouse. However, this rule does not extend the statute of limitations.

---

[31] For example, provisions requiring the filing of a joint return in order to claim a credit such as section 21(e)(2) (dependent care credit), section 22(e)(1) (credit for the elderly and permanently disabled), section 23(f)(1) (adoption credit), section 25A(f)(6) (Hope and lifetime learning credits) and section 32(d) (earned income credit) would not apply under this provision. Section 221(f)(2) (deductions for interest on education loans) would be an example of a rule disallowing a deduction that would not apply

An individual may elect under the provision without regard to whether such individual has previously been denied innocent spouse relief under present law.

Senate Floor Debate for Amendment No. 2369 (144 CONG. REC. 56, S4473)

* * *Mr. GRAHAM.—Mr. President, the amendment that I am offering, joined by our colleagues, Senator D'Amato and Senator Feinstein, makes two modifications to the innocent spouse provision which is in this legislation.

Background: Under the current tax law, if a husband and wife jointly sign a return, they are jointly responsible for any deficiency that might subsequently be found to have been the result of that filling.

A typical case is that after a husband and wife have had marital discord and are divorced, the husband may have left town and is difficult to find, the IRS locates the custodial parent, typically the wife, who is more easily accessible, and then the becomes responsible for 100 percent of the tax deficiency that was the result of a filing while the marriage was in place.

Under the current law, there is a provision called "innocent spouse" in which a spouse can theoretically avoid that responsibility. I emphasize the word "theoretically," because the testimony we heard before the Finance Committee was that it is virtually impossible for the standards of that innocent spouse provision to be met and that, in fact, there are some 50,000 women, generally ex-spouses, who are caught up in this 100-percent responsibility for a tax return.

In the Finance Committee hearings, we were impressed with a recommendation made by the American Bar Association as to a different approach to this issue. That approach was essentially an accounting approach which said that instead of using joint and several responsibility, it would be an individual responsibility.

If, for instance, the husband was responsible for 60 percent of the income, which went into the tax return, and the wife, 40 percent, then those percentages would define responsibility in a subsequent deficiency.

That basic approach was adopted by the Finance Committee, but there were some exceptions to that filing for proportional responsibility. The primary exception was that if the Secretary of the Treasury could demonstrate—and the burden is on the Secretary of the Treasury to demonstrate—that an individual making this election to be taxed only for their proportional share of the deficiency of the return, that if they had actual knowledge of the conditions within that return which led to this deficiency, then they would be 100 percent responsible. So actual knowledge would override the ability to elect only partial responsibility.

This amendment makes two modifications to that provision. The first is the question of when is that knowledge relevant. The language that we are inserting into the legislation which is currently before the Senate is that the actual knowledge has to be "at the time such individual" — that is, the individual who is seeking to pay only a proportionate share of a deficiency— "signed the return." So the key question is what did you know at the time you signed the return.

The second issue is an unfortunate reality where we had testimony that some spouses signed the joint return, and may even have had actual knowledge of its contents, but did so under duress, including under physical duress. So we have provided a second provision which says that even if you had actual knowledge at the time you signed the return, that you would not be denied the right to apply for this proportioning of responsibility if you, the individual, can establish that the return was signed under duress.

The burden of proof is on the taxpayer to establish that even though they had actual knowledge of the circumstances in the return that led to the deficiency, but still want to secure the benefits of less than joint and several responsibility, because they were under duress, coerced into signing, it is their responsibility to carry the burden of proof that, in fact, those circumstances existed. * * *

Conference Committee Report (H.R. CONF. REP. NO. 105-599)

In general

The conference agreement follows the Senate amendment with respect to deficiencies of a taxpayer who is no longer married to, is legally separated from, or has been living apart for at least 12 months from the person with whom the taxpayer originally filed the joint return. The conference agreement also includes the provision in the House bill expanding the circumstances in which innocent spouse relief is available. Taxpayers, whether or not eligible to make the separate liability election, may be granted innocent spouse relief where appropriate. In addition, the conference agreement authorizes the Secretary to provide equitable relief in appropriate situations. The con-ference agreement follows the House bill and the Senate amendment in establishing jurisdiction in the Tax Court over disputes arising in this area.

Deficiencies of certain taxpayers

The conference agreement follows the Senate amendment with respect to deficiencies of a tax payer who, at the time of election, is no longer married [16] to, is legally separated from, or has been living apart for at least 12 months from the person with whom the taxpayer originally filed the joint return. Such taxpayers may elect to limit their liability for any deficiency limited to the portion of the deficiency that is attributable to items allocable to the taxpayer.

---

[16] For the purpose of this rule, a taxpayer is no longer married if he or she is widowed

For example, a deficiency is assessed after IRS audit of a joint return. The deficiency relates to income earned by the husband that was not reported on the return. If the spouses who joined in the return are no longer married, are legally separated, or have lived apart for at least 12 months, either may elect limited liability under this provision. If the wife elects, she would owe none of the deficiency. The deficiency would be the sole responsibility of the husband whose income gave rise to the deficiency.

If the deficiency relates to the items of both spouses, the separate liability for the deficiency is allocated between the spouses in the same proportion as the net items taken into account in determining the deficiency. For example, a deficiency is assessed that is attributable to $70,000 of unreported income allocable to the husband and the disallowance of a $30,000 miscellaneous itemized deduction allocable to the wife. If the spouses who joined in the return are no longer married, are legally separated, or have lived apart for at least 12 months, either may elect limited liability under this provision. If either the husband and wife elect, the husband's liability would be limited to 70 percent of the deficiency (if he elects) and the wife's liability limited to 30 percent (if she elects). This would be the case even if a portion of the miscellaneous itemized deductions had been disallowed under section 67(a). The election is required in order to limit liability. If either spouse fails to elect, that spouse would be liable for the full amount of the deficiency, unless reduced by innocent spouse relief or pursuant to the grant of authority to the Secretary to provide equitable relief.

If the deficiency arises as a result of the denial of an item of deduction or credit, the amount of the deficiency allocated to the spouse to whom the item of deduction or credit is allocated is limited to the amount of income or tax allocated to such spouse that was offset by the deduction or credit. The remainder of the liability is allocated to the other spouse to reflect the fact that income or tax allocated to that spouse was originally offset by a portion of the disallowed deduction or credit.

For example, a married couple files a joint return with wage income of $100,000 allocable to the wife and $30,000 of self employment income allocable to the husband. On examination, a $20,000 deduction allocated to the husband is disallowed, resulting in a deficiency of $5,600. Under the provision, the liability is allocated in proportion to the items giving rise to the deficiency. Since the only item giving rise to the deficiency is allocable to the husband, and because he reported sufficient income to offset the item of deduction, the entire deficiency is allocated to the husband and the wife has no liability with regard to the deficiency, regardless of the ability of the IRS to collect the deficiency from the husband.

If the joint return had shown only $15,000 (instead of $30,000) of self employment income for the husband, the income offset limitation rule discussed above would apply. In this case, the disallowed $20,000 deduction entirely offsets the $15,000 of income of the husband, and $5,000 remains. This remaining $5,000 of the disallowed deduction offsets income of the wife. The liability for the deficiency is therefore divided in proportion to the amount of income offset for each spouse. In this example, the husband is liable for 3/4 of the deficiency ($4,200), and the wife is liable for the remaining 1/4 ($1,400).

Where a deficiency is attributable to the disallowance of a credit, or to any tax other than regular or alternative minimum income tax, the portion of the deficiency attributable to such credit or other tax is considered first. For example, on examination a deficiency of $10,000 ($2,800 of self-employment tax and $7,200 of income tax) is determined to be attributable to $20,000 of unreported self-employment income of the husband and a disallowed itemized deduction of $5,000 allocable to the wife. The $2,800 of deficient self-employment taxes is first allocated to the husband, and the remaining $7,200 of income tax deficiency is allocated 80 percent to the husband and 20 percent to the wife.

The special rules included in the Senate bill to prevent the inappropriate use of the election are included in the conference agreement.

First, if the IRS demonstrates that assets were transferred between the spouses in a fraudulent scheme joined in by both spouses, neither spouse is eligible to make the election under the provision (and consequently joint and several liability applies to both spouses).

Second, if the IRS proves that the electing spouse had actual knowledge that an item on a return is incorrect, the election will not apply to the extent any deficiency is attributable to such item. Such actual knowledge must be established by the evidence and shall not be inferred based on indications that the electing spouse had a reason to know.

The rule that the election will not apply to the extent any deficiency is attributable to an item the electing spouse had actual knowledge of is expected to be applied by treating the item as fully allocable to both spouses. For example a married couple files a joint return with wage income of $150,000 allocable to the wife and $30,000 of self employment income allocable to the husband. On examination, an additional $20,000 of the husband's self-employment income is discovered, resulting in a deficiency of $9,000. The IRS proves that the wife had actual knowledge that $5,000 of this additional self-employment income, but had no knowledge of the remaining $15,000. In this case, the husband would be liable for the full amount of the deficiency, since the item giving rise to the deficiency is fully allocable to him. In addition, the wife would be liable for the amount that would have been calculated as the deficiency based on the $5,000 of unreported income of which she had actual knowledge. The IRS would be allowed to collect that amount from either spouse, while the remainder of the deficiency could be collected from only the husband.

Third, the portion of the deficiency for which the electing spouse is liable is increased by the value of any disqualified assets received from the other spouse. Disqualified assets include any property or right to property that was transferred to an electing spouse if the principle purpose of the transfer is the avoidance of tax (including the avoidance of payment of tax). A rebuttable presumption exists that a transfer is made for tax avoidance purposes if the transfer was made less than one year before the earlier of the payment due date or the date of the notice of proposed deficiency. The rebuttable presumption does not apply to transfers pursuant to a decree of divorce or separate maintenance. The presumption may be rebutted by a showing that the principal purpose of the transfer was not the avoidance of tax or the payment of tax.

Other deficiencies

The conference agreement also includes the provision in the House bill modifying innocent spouse relief. Taxpayers who do not make the separate liability election may be eligible for innocent spouse relief. For example, a taxpayer may be ineligible to make the separate liability election for a deficiency because he or she is not widowed, divorced, legally separated, or living apart (for at least 12 months) from the person with whom the taxpayer originally joined in filing the joint return. Such a taxpayer may apply for relief of any deficiency that is attributable to an erroneous item of the other spouse, provided he or she did not know or have reason to know of the understatement of tax and it would be inequitable to hold the taxpayer responsible for the deficiency. The election is required to be made no later than the date that is two years after the Secretary has begun collection actions with respect to the individual. The rule in the House bill allowing innocent spouse relief to be provided on an apportioned basis is included in the conference agreement.

Other circumstances, including tax shown on a return but not paid

The conference agreement does not include the portion of the Senate amendment that could provide relief in situations where tax was shown on a joint return, but not paid with the return. The conferees intend that the Secretary will consider using the grant of authority to provide equitable relief in appropriate situations to avoid the inequitable treatment of spouses in such situations. For example, the conferees intend that equitable relief be available to a spouse that does not know, and had no reason to know, that funds intended for the payment of tax were instead taken by the other spouse for such other spouse's benefit.

The conferees do not intend to limit the use of the Secretary's authority to provide equitable relief to situations where tax is shown on a return but not paid. The conferees intend that such authority be used where, taking into account all the facts and circumstances, it is inequitable to hold an individual liable for all or part of any unpaid tax or deficiency arising from a joint return. The conferees intend that relief be available where there is both an understatement and an underpayment of tax.

Procedural rules

The conference agreement follows the House bill and the Senate amendment with respect to procedural rules, including the jurisdiction of the Tax Court to review matters relating to this provision. The conference agreement also follows the Senate amendment in requiring the IRS to notify taxpayers of their rights under this provision, and, whenever practicable, to send notifications separately to each spouse.

Effective Date

The conference agreement follows the Senate amendment. The separate liability election, expanded innocent spouse relief and authority to provide equitable relief all apply to liabilities for tax arising after the date of enactment, as well as any liability for tax arising on or before the date of enactment that remains unpaid on the date of enactment. The applicable 2-year election periods do not expire before the date that is two years after the first collection activity taken by the IRS after the date of enactment. The Secretary is required to develop a separate form for electing innocent spouse relief within 180 days after the date of enactment.

[Law at ¶ 5140, ¶ 6030, ¶ 6040, ¶ 6200, ¶ 6590 and ¶ 8080. CCH Explanation at ¶ 1290.]

[¶ 10,290]   Act Sec. 3202.   Suspension of statute of limitations on filing refund claims during periods of disability

House Committee Report (H.R. REP. NO. 105-364, pt. 1)

[Code Sec. 6511]
Present Law

In general, a taxpayer must file a refund claim within three years of the filing of the return or within two years of the payment of the tax, whichever period expires later (if no return is filed, the two-year limit applies) (sec. 6511(a)). A refund claim that is not filed within these time periods is rejected as untimely.

There is no explicit statutory rule providing for equitable tolling of the statute of limitations. Several courts have considered whether equitable tolling implicitly exists. The First, Third, Fourth, and Eleventh Circuits have rejected equitable tolling with respect to tax refund claims. The Ninth Circuit has permitted equitable tolling. However, the U.S. Supreme Court has reversed the Ninth Circuit in *U.S. v. Brockamp*,[38] holding that Congress did not intend the equitable tolling doctrine to apply to the statutory limitations of section 6511 on the filing of tax refund claims.

Reasons for Change

The Committee believes that, in cases of severe disability, equitable tolling should be considered in the application of the statutory limitations on the filing of tax refund claims.

---

[38] 117 S.Ct. 849 (1997), reversing 67 F.3d 260 and 70 F.3d 120.

Explanation of Provision

The bill permits equitable tolling of the statute of limitations for refund claims of an individual taxpayer during any period of the individual's life in which he or she is unable to manage his or her financial affairs by reason of a medically determinable physical or mental impairment that can be expected to result in death or to last for a continuous period of not less than 12 months. Proof of the existence of the impairment must be furnished in the form and manner required by the Secretary. It is anticipated that, in applying the medically determinable test, the Secretary will evaluate whether a medical opinion that a physical or

mental impairment exists has been offered by a person qualified to do so with respect to that particular type of impairment. Tolling does not apply during periods in which the taxpayer's spouse or another person is authorized to act on the taxpayer's behalf in financial matters.

Effective Date

The provision applies to periods of disability before, on, or after the date of enactment but would not apply to any claim for refund or credit which (without regard to the provision) is barred by the statute of limitations as of January 1, 1998.

Conference Committee Report (H.R. CONF. REP. NO. 105-599)

Senate Amendment
Same as the House bill.

Conference Agreement
The conference agreement follows the House bill and the Senate amendment.

Effective Date
The provision applies to periods of disability before, on, or after the date of enactment but does

not apply to any claim for refund or credit that (without regard to the provision) is barred by the operation of any law, including the statute of limitations, as of the date of enactment.

[Law at ¶ 6430. CCH Explanation at ¶ 1461.]

[¶ 10,315]   Act Sec. 3301.   Elimination of interest differential on overlapping periods of interest on income tax overpayments and underpayments

Senate Committee Report (S. REP. NO. 105-174)

[Code Sec. 6621]

[*This committee report does not reflect changes made by Senate Floor Amendment No. 2383. Senate Floor Amendment No. 2383 (144 Cong. Rec. 56, S4518) was passed with nominal debate.—CCH.*]

Present Law

A taxpayer that underpays its taxes is required to pay interest on the underpayment at a rate equal to the Federal short term interest rate plus three percentage points. A special "hot interest" rate equal to the Federal short term interest rate plus five percentage points applies in the case of certain large corporate underpayments.

A taxpayer that overpays its taxes receives interest on the overpayment at a rate equal to the Federal short term interest rate plus two percentage points. In the case of corporate overpayments in excess of $10,000, this is reduced to the Federal short term interest rate plus one-half of a percentage point.

If a taxpayer has an underpayment of tax from one year and an overpayment of tax from a different year that are outstanding at the same time, the IRS will typically offset the overpayment against the underpayment and apply the appropriate interest to the resulting net underpayment or overpayment. However, if either the underpayment or overpayment has been satisfied, the IRS

will not typically offset the two amounts, but rather will assess or credit interest on the full underpayment or overpayment at the underpayment or overpayment rate. This has the effect of assessing the underpayment at the higher underpayment rate and crediting the overpayment at the lower overpayment rate. This results in the taxpayer being assessed a net interest charge, even if the amounts of the overpayment and underpayment are the same.

The Secretary has the authority to credit the amount of any overpayment against any liability under the Code.[32] Congress has previously directed the Internal Revenue Service to implement procedures for "netting" overpayments and underpayments to the extent a portion of tax due is satisfied by a credit of an overpayment.[33]

Reasons for Change

The Committee believes that taxpayers should be charged interest only on the amount they actually owe, taking into account overpayments and underpayments from all open years. The Committee does not believe that the different interest rates provided for overpayments and underpayments were ever intended to result in the charging of the differential on periods of mutual indebtedness.

The Committee is also concerned that current practices provide an incentive to taxpayers to

---

[32] Code sec. 6402
[33] Pursuant to TBOR2 (1996), the Secretary conducted a study of the manner in which the IRS has implemented the netting of interest on overpayments and underpayments and the policy and administrative implications of global netting. The legislative history to the General Agreement on

Trade and Tariffs (GATT) (1994) stated that the Secretary should implement the most comprehensive crediting procedures that are consistent with sound administrative practice, and should do so as rapidly as is practicable. A similar statement was included in the Conference Report to the Omnibus Budget Reconciliation Act of 1990.

delay the payment of underpayments they do not contest, so that the underpayments will be available to offset any overpayments that are later determined. The Committee believes that this is contrary to sound tax administrative practice and that taxpayers should not be disadvantaged solely because they promptly pay their tax bills.

Explanation of Provision

The provision establishes a net interest rate of zero on equivalent amounts of overpayment and underpayment that exist for any period. Each overpayment and underpayment is considered only once in determining whether equivalent amounts of overpayment and underpayment exist. The special rules that increase the interest rate paid on large corporate underpayments and decrease the interest rate received on corporate underpayments in excess of $10,000 do not prevent the application of the net zero rate. The provision applies to income taxes and self-employment taxes.

Effective Date

The provision applies to interest for calendar quarters beginning after the date of enactment. Until such time as procedures are implemented that allow for the automatic application of this provision by the IRS, the Committee expects that the Secretary will promptly and carefully consider any taxpayer's request to have interest charges recalculated in accordance with this provision. It is expected that the Secretary will extend the statute of limitations on assessment where necessary to allow for the consideration of such requests.

In light of past Congressional statements urging the Secretary to eliminate interest rate differentials in these circumstances, and taking into consideration Congress' belief that the Secretary may do so, the Committee continues to expect that the Secretary will implement the most comprehensive interest netting procedures that are consistent with sound administrative practice, and not only those affected by this provision.

Conference Committee Report (H.R. CONF. REP. NO. 105-599)

Senate Amendment

Generally same as the House bill, except that the Senate amendment applies where interest is payable and allowable on equivalent amounts of overpayment and underpayment of any taxes imposed by Title 26 (the Internal Revenue Code), and not only income taxes.

Conference Agreement

The conference agreement follows the Senate amendment. It is anticipated that the Secretary will take into account interest paid on previously determined deficiencies or refunds for the purpose of determining the rate of interest under this provision without regard to whether the under-

payments or overpayments are currently outstanding. It is also anticipated that where interest is both payable from and allowable to an individual taxpayer for the same period, the Secretary will take all reasonable efforts to offset the liabilities, rather than process them separately using the net interest rate of zero. Where interest is payable and allowable on an equivalent amount of underpayment and overpayment that is attributable to a taxpayer's interest in a pass-thru entity (e.g., a partnership), the conferees intend that the benefits of the provision apply.

[Law at ¶ 6450 and ¶ 6470. CCH Explanation at ¶ 1406.]

[¶ 10,320]   Act Sec. 3302.   Increase in overpayment rate payable to taxpayers other than corporations

Senate Committee Report (S. REP. NO. 105-174)

[Code Sec. 6621(a)(1)]

[*This committee report does not reflect changes made by Senate Floor Amendment No. 2380. Selected portions of the Senate Floor Debate are reproduced below.—CCH.*]

Present Law

A taxpayer that underpays its taxes is required to pay interest on the underpayment at a rate equal to the Federal short-term interest rate (AFR) plus three percentage points. A taxpayer that overpays its taxes receives interest on the overpayment at a rate equal to the Federal short-term interest rate (AFR) plus two percentage points.

Reasons for Change

The Committee believes that the interest differential for noncorporate taxpayers should be eliminated.

Explanation of Provision

The provision provides that the overpayment interest rate will be AFR plus three percentage points, except that for corporations, the rate remains at AFR plus two percentage points.

Effective Date

The provision applies to interest for calendar quarters beginning after the date of enactment.

Senate Floor Debate for Amendment No. 2380 (144 CONG. REC. 56, S4510)

* * *

Mr. MOYNIHAN.—* * * Mr. President, it was with these challenges in mind that Senator Kerrey and I offered this amendment to briefly delay some of the effective dates in the Finance Committee's IRS Restructuring legislation in order to

allow time for the Y2K conversion to be completed. This amendment has been drafted based on Commissioner Rossotti's recommendations, and has been modified after consultations with the Majority.

Act Sec. 3302   ¶ 10,320

The amendment would delay the effective date on a list of provisions from date of enactment until after the century date change.

* * *

Conference Committee Report (H.R. CONF. REP. NO. 105-599)

The conference agreement follows the Senate amendment.

[Law at ¶ 6470. CCH Explanation at ¶ 1411.]

[¶ 10,325] Act Sec. 3303. Mitigation of penalty for individual's failure to pay during period of installment agreement

Senate Committee Report (S. REP. NO. 105-174)

[Code Sec. 6651]

[This committee report does not reflect changes made by Senate Floor Amendment No. 2380. Selected portions of the Senate Floor Debate are reproduced below.—CCH.]

Present Law

Taxpayers who fail to pay their taxes are subject to a penalty of one-half percent per month on the unpaid amount, up to a maximum of 25 percent (sec. 6651(a)). If the liability is shown on the return, the penalty begins to accrue on the date prescribed for payment of the tax (with regard to extensions (sec. 6651(a)(2)). If the liability should have been shown on the return but was not, the penalty generally begins to accrue after the date that is 21 days from the date of the IRS notice and demand for payment with respect to such liability (sec. 6651(a)(3)). Taxpayers who make installment payments pursuant to an agreement with the IRS (under sec. 6159) are also subject to this penalty (Treas. reg. sec. 301.6159-1(f) and sec. 6601(b)).

Reasons for Change

The Committee believes that it is inappropriate to apply the penalty for failure to pay taxes to taxpayers who are in fact paying their taxes through an installment agreement.

Explanation of Provision

The provision provides that the penalty for failure to pay taxes is not imposed with respect to the tax liability of an individual for any month in which an installment payment agreement with the IRS (under sec. 6159) is in effect, provided that the individual filed the tax return in a timely manner (including extensions).

Effective Date

The provision is effective for installment agreement payments made after the date of enactment.

Senate Floor Debate for Amendment No. 2380 (144 CONG. REC. 56, S4510)

* * *

Mr. MOYNIHAN.—* * * Mr. President, it was with these challenges in mind that Senator Kerrey and I offered this amendment to briefly delay some of the effective dates in the Finance Committee's IRS Restructuring legislation in order to allow time for the Y2K conversion to be completed. This amendment has been drafted based on Commissioner Rossotti's recommendations, and has been modified after consultations with the Majority.

The amendment would delay the effective date on a list of provisions from date of enactment until after the century date change.

* * *

Conference Committee Report (H.R. CONF. REP. NO. 105-599)

The conference agreement follows the Senate amendment, except that the rate of the penalty is half the usual rate (0.25 percent instead of 0.5 percent) for any month in which an installment payment agreement with the IRS is in effect.

[Law at ¶ 6490. CCH Explanation at ¶ 1282.]

[¶ 10,330] Act Sec. 3304. Mitigation of failure to deposit penalty

Senate Committee Report (S. REP. NO. 105-174)

[Code Sec. 6656(c) and Code Sec. 6656(e)]

Present Law

Deposits of payroll taxes are allocated to the earliest period for which such a deposit is due. If a taxpayer misses or makes an insufficient deposit, later deposits will first be applied to satisfy the shortfall for the earlier period; the remainder is then applied to satisfy the obligation for the current period. If the depositor is not aware this is taking place, cascading penalties may result as payments that would otherwise be sufficient to satisfy current liabilities are applied to satisfy earlier shortfalls.

Code section 6656(c) authorizes the Secretary to waive the failure to make deposit penalty for inadvertent failures by first-time depositors of employment taxes.

Reasons for Change

The Committee believes that the cascading penalty effect is unfair and that depositors should be able to designate payments to minimize its effect.

Explanation of Provision

The provision allows the taxpayer to designate the period to which each deposit is applied. The designation must be made no later than 90 days of the related IRS penalty notice. The provision also extends the authorization to waive the failure to deposit penalty to the first deposit a taxpayer is required to make after the taxpayer is required to change the frequency of the taxpayer's deposits.

Effective Date

The provision applies to deposits made more than 180 days after the date of enactment.

Conference Committee Report (H.R. CONF. REP. NO. 105-599)

The conference agreement follows the Senate amendment, with technical modifications. Also, the designation must be made during the 90 days immediately following the sending of the related IRS penalty notice. The conference agreement also provides that, for deposits required to be made after December 31, 2001, any deposit is to be applied to the most recent period to which the deposit relates, unless the taxpayer explicitly designates otherwise.

[Law at ¶ 6500. CCH Explanation at ¶ 1426.]

[¶ 10,335] Act Sec. 3305. Suspension of interest and certain penalties if Secretary fails to contact individual taxpayer

Senate Committee Report (S. REP. NO. 105-174)

[Code Sec. 6404(g)]

Present Law

In general, interest and penalties accrue during periods for which taxes are unpaid without regard to whether the taxpayer is aware that there is tax due.

Reasons for Change

The Committee believes that the IRS should promptly inform taxpayers of their obligations with respect to tax deficiencies and amounts due. In addition, the Committee is concerned that accrual of interest and penalties absent prompt resolution of tax deficiencies may lead to the perception that the IRS is more concerned about collecting revenue than in resolving taxpayer's problems.

Explanation of Provision

The provision suspends the accrual of penalties and interest after 1 year if the IRS has not sent the taxpayer a notice of deficiency within 1 year following the date which is the later of (1) the original due date of the return or (2) the date on which the individual taxpayer timely filed the return. The suspension only applies to taxpayers who file a timely tax return. The provision applies only to individuals and does not apply to the failure to pay penalty, in the case of fraud, or with respect to criminal penalties. Interest and penalties resume 21 days after the IRS sends a notice and demand for payment to the taxpayer.

Effective Date

The provision is effective for taxable years ending after the date of enactment.

Conference Committee Report (H.R. CONF. REP. NO. 105-599)

The conference agreement follows the Senate amendment, with the following modifications. With respect to taxable years beginning before January 1, 2004, the 1-year period is increased to 18 months. Interest and penalties are suspended if the IRS fails to send a notice specifically stating the taxpayer's liability and the basis for the liability within the specified period. Interest and penalties resume 21 days after the IRS sends that notice to the taxpayer. The provision is applied separately with respect to each item or adjustment. The provision does not apply where a taxpayer has self-assessed the tax.

For example, if the IRS sends a math error notice to a taxpayer 2 months after the return is filed and also sends a notice of deficiency related to a different item 2 years later, the provision applies to the item reflected on the second notice (notwithstanding that the first notice was sent within the applicable time period).

[Law at ¶ 6360. CCH Explanation at ¶ 1401.]

[¶ 10,340] Act Sec. 3306. Procedural requirements for imposition of penalties and additions to tax

Senate Committee Report (S. REP. NO. 105-174)

[Code Sec. 6751]

Present Law

Present law does not require the IRS to show how penalties are computed on the notice of penalty. In some cases, penalties may be imposed without supervisory approval.

Reasons for Change

The Committee believes that taxpayers are entitled to an explanation of the penalties imposed upon them. The Committee believes that penalties should only be imposed where appropriate and not as a bargaining chip.

Explanation of Provision

Each notice imposing a penalty is required to include the name of the penalty, the code section imposing the penalty, and a computation of the penalty.

The provision also requires the specific approval of IRS management to assess all non-computer generated penalties unless excepted. This provision does not apply to failure to file penalties, failure to pay penalties, or to penalties for failure to pay estimated tax.

Effective Date

The provision applies to notices issued, and penalties assessed, more than 180 days after the date of enactment.

Conference Committee Report (H.R. CONF. REP. NO. 105-599)

The conference agreement follows the Senate amendment.

Effective Date

Notices issued, and penalties assessed after December 31, 2000.

[Law at ¶ 6530. CCH Explanation at ¶ 1436.]

[¶ 10,345]   Act Sec. 3307.   Personal delivery of notice of penalty under section 6672

Senate Committee Report (S. REP. NO. 105-174)

[Code Sec. 6672(b)]

Present Law

Any person who is required to collect, truthfully account for, and pay over any tax imposed by the Internal Revenue Code who willfully fails to do so is liable for a penalty equal to the amount of the tax (Code sec. 6672(a)). Before the IRS may assess any such "100-percent penalty," it must mail a written preliminary notice informing the person of the proposed penalty to that person's last known address. The mailing of such notice must precede any notice and demand for payment of the penalty by at least 60 days. The statute of limitations on assessments shall not expire before the date 90 days after the date on which the notice was mailed. These restrictions do not apply if the Secretary finds the collection of the penalty is in jeopardy.

Reasons for Change

The imposition of the 100-percent penalty is a serious matter. The Committee believes that permitting personal service of the preliminary notice required under Code section 6672 may afford taxpayers the opportunity to resolve cases involving the 100-percent penalty at an earlier stage.

Explanation of Provision

The provision permits in person delivery, as an alternative to delivery by mail, of a preliminary notice that the IRS intends to assess a 100-percent penalty. (In some cases, personal delivery may better assure that the recipient actually receives notice.)

Effective Date

The provision is effective on the date of enactment.

Conference Committee Report (H.R. CONF. REP. NO. 105-599)

The conference agreement follows the Senate amendment.

[Law at ¶ 6510. CCH Explanation at ¶ 1431.]

[¶ 10,350]   Act Sec. 3308.   Notice of interest charges

Senate Committee Report (S. REP. NO. 105-174)

[Code Sec. 6631]

Present Law

Taxpayer generally must pay interest on amounts due to the IRS.

Reasons for Change

The Committee believes that taxpayers should be provided the detail to support the amount of interest charged by the IRS. The computation of interest is a complex calculation, often involving multiple interest rates. The Committee believes that it is appropriate to require the IRS to give notice to the taxpayer that interest is being charged, how it is calculated, and the total amount of the interest.

Explanation of Provision

The provision requires every IRS notice that includes an amount of interest required to be paid by the taxpayer that is sent to an individual taxpayer to include a detailed computation of the interest charged and a citation to the Code section under which such interest is imposed.

Effective Date

The provision applies to notices issued after June 30, 2000.

Conference Committee Report (H.R. CONF. REP. NO. 105-599)

The conference agreement follows the Senate amendment.

Effective Date

Notices issued after December 31, 2000.

[Law at ¶ 6480. CCH Explanation at ¶ 1416.]

[¶ 10,355] Act Sec. 3309. Abatement of interest on underpayments by taxpayers in Presidentially declared disaster areas

Conference Committee Report (H.R. CONF. REP. NO. 105-599)

[Code Sec. 6406]

Present Law

In the case of a Presidentially declared disaster, the Secretary of the Treasury has the authority to postpone some tax-related deadlines, but there is no authority to abate interest.

Under a provision of the Taxpayer Relief Act of 1997, if the Secretary of the Treasury extends the filing date of an individual tax return for individuals living in an area that has been declared a disaster area by the President during 1997, no interest is charged as a result of the failure of the individual taxpayer to file an individual tax return, or to pay the taxes shown on such return, during the extension.

Senate [Floor] Amendment [No. 2379]

The Senate amendment provides that taxpayers located in a Presidentially declared disaster area do not have to pay interest on taxes due for the length of any extension for filing their tax returns granted by the Secretary of the Treasury.

Effective Date

Disasters declared after December 31, 1996, with respect to taxable years beginning after December 31, 1996.

Conference Agreement

The conference agreement follows the Senate amendment.

This provision is designated as emergency legislation under section 252(e) of the Balanced Budget and Emergency Deficit Control Act.

Effective Date

Disasters declared after December 31, 1997, with respect to taxable years beginning after December 31, 1997. The conferees have modified the effective date because section 915 of The Taxpayer Relief Act of 1997 already applies to 1997 disasters. The conferees intend that no gap between the two provisions exists.

[Law at ¶ 6360. CCH Explanation at ¶ 1417.]

[¶ 10,365] Act Sec. 3401. Due process in IRS collection actions

Senate Committee Report (S. REP. NO. 105-174)

[Code Sec. 6320 and Code Sec. 6330]

Present Law

Levy is the IRS's administrative authority to seize a taxpayer's property to pay the taxpayer's tax liability. The IRS is entitled to seize a taxpayer's property by levy if the Federal tax lien has attached to such property. The Federal tax lien arises automatically where (1) a tax assessment has been made; (2) the taxpayer has been given notice of the assessment stating the amount and demanding payment; and (3) the taxpayer has failed to pay the amount assessed within ten days after the notice and demand.

The IRS may collect taxes by levy upon a taxpayer's property or rights to property (including accrued salary and wages) if the taxpayer neglects or refuses to pay the tax within 10 days after notice and demand that the tax be paid. Notice of the IRS's intent to collect taxes by levy must be given no less than 30 days (90 days in the case of a life insurance contract) before the day of the levy. The notice of levy must describe the procedures that will be used, the administrative appeals available to the taxpayer and the procedures relating to such appeals, the alternatives available to the taxpayer that could prevent levy, and the procedures for redemption of property and release of liens.

The effect of a levy on salary or wages payable to or received by a taxpayer is continuous from the date the levy is first made until it is released.

If the IRS district director finds that the collection of any tax is in jeopardy, collection by levy may be made without regard to either notice period. A similar rule applies in the case of termination assessments.

Reasons for Change

The Committee believes that taxpayers are entitled to protections in dealing with the IRS that are similar to those they would have in dealing with any other creditor. Accordingly, the Committee believes that the IRS should afford taxpayers adequate notice of collection activity and a meaningful hearing before the IRS deprives them of their property. When collection of tax is in jeopardy, the Committee believes it is appropriate to provide notice and a hearing promptly after the deprivation of property. The Committee believes that following procedures designed to afford taxpayers due process in collections will increase fairness to taxpayers.

Explanation of Provision

The provision establishes formal procedures designed to insure due process where the IRS seeks to collect taxes by levy (including by seizure). The due process procedures also apply after the Federal tax lien attaches, but before the notice of the Federal tax lien has been given to the taxpayer.

Act Sec. 3401 ¶ 10,365

As under present law, notice of the intent to levy must be given at least 30 days (90 days in the case of a life insurance contract) before property can be seized or salary and wages garnished. During the 30-day (90-day) notice period, the taxpayer may demand a hearing to take place before an appeals officer who has had no prior involvement in the taxpayer's case. If the taxpayer demands a hearing within that period, the proposed collection action may not proceed until the hearing has concluded and the appeals officer has issued his or her determination.

During the hearing, the IRS is required to verify that all statutory, regulatory, and administrative requirements for the proposed collection action have been met. IRS verifications are expected to include (but not be limited to) showings that:

(1) the revenue officer recommending the collection action has verified the taxpayer's liability;

(2) the estimated expenses of levy and sale will not exceed the value of the property to be seized;

(3) the revenue officer has determined that there is sufficient equity in the property to be seized to yield net proceeds from sale to apply to the unpaid tax liabilities; and

(4) with respect to the seizure of the assets of a going business, the revenue officer recommending the collection action has thoroughly considered the facts of the case, including the availability of alternative collection methods, before recommending the collection action.

The taxpayer (or affected third party) is allowed to raise any relevant issue at the hearing. Issues eligible to be raised include (but are not limited to):

(1) challenges to the underlying liability as to existence or amount;

(2) appropriate spousal defenses;

(3) challenges to the appropriateness of collection actions; and

(4) collection alternatives, which could include the posting of a bond, substitution of other assets, an installment agreement or an offer-in-compromise.

Once the taxpayer has had a hearing with respect to an issue, the taxpayer would not be permitted to raise the same issue in another hearing.

The determination of the appeals officer is to address whether the proposed collection action

balances the need for the efficient collection of taxes with the legitimate concern of the taxpayer that the collection action be no more intrusive than necessary. A proposed collection action should not be approved solely because the IRS shows that it has followed appropriate procedures.

The taxpayer may contest the determination of the appellate officer in Tax Court by filing a petition within 30 days of the date of the determination. The Tax Court is expected to review the appellate officer's determination for abuse of discretion and also may consider procedural issues, as under present law. The IRS may not take any collection action pursuant to the determination during such 30 day period or while the taxpayer's contest is pending in Tax Court.

IRS Appeals would retain jurisdiction over its determinations. IRS Appeals could enter an order requiring the IRS collection division to adhere to the original determination. In addition, the taxpayer would be allowed to return to IRS Appeals to seek a modification of the original determination based on any change of circumstances.

In the case of a continuous levy, the due process procedures would apply to the original imposition of the levy. Except in jeopardy and termination cases, continuous levy would not be allowed to begin without notice and an opportunity for a hearing. A determination allowing the continuous levy to proceed that is entered at the conclusion of a hearing would be subject to post-determination adjustment on application by the taxpayer. Thus, taxpayers would have the right to have IRS Appeals review any continuous levy and take any changes in circumstances into account.

This provision does not apply in the case of jeopardy and termination assessments. Jeopardy and termination assessments would be subject to post-seizure review as part of the Appeals determination hearing as well as through any existing judicial procedure. A jeopardy or termination assessment must be approved by the IRS District Counsel responsible for the case. Failure to obtain District Counsel approval would render the jeopardy or termination assessment void.

Effective Date

The due process procedures apply to collection actions initiated more than six months after the date of enactment.

Conference Committee Report (H.R. CONF. REP. NO. 105-599)

Liens

The conference agreement generally follows the Senate amendment, except that taxpayers would have a right to a hearing after the Notice of Lien is filed. The IRS would be required to notify the taxpayer that a Notice of Lien had been filed within 5 days after filing. During the 30-day period beginning with the mailing or delivery of such notification, the taxpayer may demand a hearing before an appeals officer who has had no prior involvement with the taxpayer's case. In general, any issue relevant to the appropriateness

of the proposed collection against the taxpayer can be raised at this hearing. For example, the taxpayer can request innocent spouse status, make an offer-in-compromise, request an installment agreement or suggest which assets should be used to satisfy the tax liability. However, the validity of the tax liability can be challenged only if the taxpayer did not actually receive the statutory notice of deficiency or has not otherwise had an opportunity to dispute the liability. This hearing right applies only after the first Notice of Lien with regard to each tax liability is filed.

Levies

The conference agreement includes a modified form of the Senate amendment. The IRS would be required to provide the taxpayer with a "Notice of Intent to Levy," formally stating its intention to collect a tax liability by levy against the taxpayer's property or rights to property. The conferees intend that the Secretary have the discretion to provide the Notice of Intent to Levy in combination with the notice required by present law under section 6331(d). Service by registered or certified mail, return receipt requested would be required. The Notice of Intent to Levy would not be required to itemize the property the Secretary seeks to levy on.

Subject to the exceptions noted below, no levy could occur within the 30-day period beginning with the mailing of the "Notice of Intent to Levy." During that 30-day period, the taxpayer may demand a hearing before an appeals officer who has had no prior involvement with the taxpayer's case, other than in connection with a hearing after the filing of a notice of tax lien. If a hearing is requested within the 30-day period, no levy could occur until a determination by the appeals officer is rendered. In general, any issue that is relevant to the appropriateness of the proposed collection against the taxpayer can be raised at the pre-levy hearing. For example, the taxpayer can request innocent spouse status, make an offer-in-compromise, request an installment agreement or suggest which assets should be used to satisfy the tax liability. However, the validity of the tax liability can be challenged only if the taxpayer did not actually receive the statutory notice of deficiency or has not otherwise had an opportunity to dispute the liability.

If a return receipt is not returned, the Secretary may proceed to levy on the taxpayer's property or rights to property 30 days after the Notice of Intent to Levy was mailed. The Secretary must provide a hearing equivalent to the pre-levy hearing if later requested by the taxpayer. However, the Secretary is not required to suspend the levy process pending the completion of a hearing that is not requested within 30 days of the mailing of the Notice. If the taxpayer did not receive the required notice and requests a hearing after collection activity has begun, then collection shall be suspended and a hearing provided to the taxpayer.

The conferees anticipate that the IRS will combine Notice of Intent to Levy and Notice of Lien hearings whenever possible. If multiple hearings are held, it is expected that, to the extent practicable, the same appellate officer will hear the taxpayer with regard to both lien and levy issues. If the taxpayer requests a hearing following receipt of a Notice of Lien or Notice of Intent to Levy and, prior to the date of the hearing, receives the other notice, the scheduled hearing will serve for both purposes and the taxpayer is obligated to raise all relevant issues at such hearing.

Judicial review

The conferees expect the appeals officer will prepare a written determination addressing the issues presented by the taxpayer and considered at the hearing. The determination of the appeals officer may be appealed to Tax Court or, where appropriate, the Federal district court. Where the validity of the tax liability was properly at issue in the hearing, and where the determination with regard to the tax liability is a part of the appeal, no levy may take place during the pendency of the appeal. The amount of the tax liability will in such cases be reviewed by the appropriate court on a de novo basis. Where the validity of the tax liability is not properly part of the appeal, the taxpayer may challenge the determination of the appeals officer for abuse of discretion. In such cases, the appeals officer's determination as to the appropriateness of collection activity will be reviewed using an abuse of discretion standard of review. Levies will not be suspended during the appeal if the Secretary shows good cause why the levy should be allowed to proceed.

No further hearings are provided under this provision as a matter of right. It is the responsibility of the taxpayer to raise all relevant issues at the time of the pre-levy hearing. A taxpayer could apply for consideration of new information, make an offer-in-compromise, request an installment agreement, or raise other considerations at any time before, during, or after the Notice of Intent to Levy hearing. However, after the 30 day period had expired, the IRS is not required to provide a hearing or delay any levy or sale of levied property. Nothing in this provision is intended to limit any remedy that is otherwise available under present law.

An exception to the general rule prohibiting levies during the 30-day period would apply in the case of state tax offset procedures, and in the case of jeopardy or termination assessments.

Prior judicial approval required for seizures of principal residences

No seizure of a dwelling that is the principal residence of the taxpayer or the taxpayer's spouse, former spouse, or minor child would be allowed without prior judicial approval. Notice of the judicial hearing must be provided to the taxpayer and family members residing in the property. At the judicial hearing, the Secretary would be required to demonstrate (1) that the requirements of any applicable law or administrative procedure relevant to the levy have been met, (2) that the liability is owed, and (3) that no reasonable alternative for the collection of the taxpayer's debt exists.

Effective Date

The provision is effective for collection actions initiated more than 180 days after the date of enactment.

[Law at ¶ 6240, ¶ 6270 and ¶ 6680. CCH Explanation at ¶ 1254.]

Act Sec. 3401   ¶ 10,365

[¶ 10,375]   Act Sec. 3411.   Uniform application of confidentiality privilege to taxpayer communications with federally authorized practitioners

Senate Committee Report (S. REP. NO. 105-174)

[Code Sec. 7525]

Present Law

A common law privilege of confidentiality exists for communications between an attorney and client with respect to the legal advice the attorney gives the client. Communications protected by the attorney-client privilege must be based on facts of which the attorney is informed by the taxpayer, without the presence of strangers, for the purpose of securing the advice of the attorney. The privilege may not be claimed where the purpose of the communication is the commission of a crime or tort. The taxpayer must either be a client of the attorney or be seeking to become a client of the attorney.

The privilege of confidentiality applies only where the attorney is advising the client on legal matters. It does not apply in situations where the attorney is acting in other capacities. Thus, a taxpayer may not claim the benefits of the attorney-client privilege simply by hiring an attorney to perform some other function. For example, if an attorney is retained to prepare a tax return, the attorney-client privilege will not automatically apply to communications and documents generated in the course of preparing the return.

The privilege of confidentiality also does not apply where an attorney that is licensed to practice another profession is performing such other profession. For example, if a taxpayer retains an attorney who is also licensed as a certified public accountant (CPA), the taxpayer may not assert the attorney-client privilege with regard to communications made and documents prepared by the attorney in his role as a CPA.

The attorney-client privilege is limited to communications between taxpayers and attorneys. No equivalent privilege is provided for communications between taxpayers and other professionals authorized to practice before the Internal Revenue Service, such as accountants or enrolled agents.

Reasons for Change

The Committee believes that a right to privileged communications between a taxpayer and his or her advisor should be available in noncriminal proceedings before the IRS and in noncriminal proceedings in Federal courts with respect to such matters where the IRS is a party, so long as the advisor is authorized to practice before the IRS. A right to privileged communications in such situations should not depend upon whether the advisor is also licensed to practice law.

Explanation of Provision

The provision extends the present law attorney-client privilege of confidentiality to tax advice that is furnished to a client-taxpayer (or potential

client-taxpayer) by any individual who is authorized under Federal law to practice before the IRS if such practice is subject to regulation under section 330 of Title 31, United States Code. Individuals subject to regulation under section 330 of Title 31, United States Code include attorneys, certified public accountants, enrolled agents and enrolled actuaries. Tax advice means advice that is within the scope of authority for such individual's practice with respect to matters under Title 26 (the Internal Revenue Code). The privilege of confidentiality may be asserted in any noncriminal tax proceeding before the IRS, as well as in noncriminal tax proceedings in the Federal Courts where the IRS is a party to the proceeding.

The provision allows taxpayers to consult with other qualified tax advisors in the same manner they currently may consult with tax advisors that are licensed to practice law. The provision does not modify the attorney-client privilege of confidentiality, other than to extend it to other authorized practitioners. The privilege established by the provision applies only to the extent that communications would be privileged if they were between a taxpayer and an attorney. Accordingly, the privilege does not apply to any communication between a certified public accountant, enrolled agent, or enrolled actuary and such individual's client (or prospective client) if the communication would not have been privileged between an attorney and the attorney's client or prospective client. For example, information disclosed to an attorney for the purpose of preparing a tax return is not privileged under present law. Such information would not be privileged under the provision whether it was disclosed to an attorney, certified public accountant, enrolled agent or enrolled actuary.

The privilege granted by the provision may only be asserted in noncriminal tax proceedings before the IRS and in the Federal Courts with regard to such noncriminal tax matters in proceedings where the IRS is a party. The privilege may not be asserted to prevent the disclosure of information to any regulatory body other than the IRS. The ability of any other regulatory body, including the Securities and Exchange Commission (SEC), to gain or compel information is unchanged by the provision. No privilege may be asserted under this provision by a taxpayer in dealings with such other regulatory bodies in an administrative or court proceeding.

Effective Date

The provision is effective with regard to communications made on or after the date of enactment.

Conference Committee Report (H.R. CONF. REP. NO. 105-599)

The conference agreement follows the Senate amendment with a modification. The privilege of confidentiality created by this provision will not apply to any written communication between a federally authorized tax practitioner and any director, shareholder, officer, employee, agent, or representative of a corporation in connection with the promotion of the direct or indirect participation of such corporation in any tax shelter (as defined in section 6662(d)(2)(C)(iii)).

A tax shelter for this purpose is any partnership, entity, plan, or arrangement a significant purpose of which is the avoidance or evasion of income tax. Tax shelters for which no privilege of confidentiality will apply include, but are not limited to, those required to be registered as confidential corporate tax shelter arrangements under section 6111(d). The Conferees do not understand the promotion of tax shelters to be part of the routine relationship between a tax practitioner and a client. Accordingly, the Conferees do not anticipate that the tax shelter limitation will adversely affect such routine relationships.

The privilege created by this provision may be waived in the same manner as the attorney-client privilege. For example, if a taxpayer or federally authorized tax practitioner discloses to a third party the substance of a communication protected by the privilege, the privilege for that communication and any related communications is considered to be waived to the same extent and in the same manner as the privilege would be waived if the disclosure related to an attorney-client communication.

The conference agreement also clarifies that the privilege created by this provision may be asserted in noncriminal tax proceedings before the IRS and in the Federal courts with regard to a noncriminal tax proceeding where the United States is a party.

This provision relates only to matters of privileged communications. No inference is intended as to whether aspects of federal tax practice covered by the new privilege constitute the authorized or unauthorized practice of law under various State laws.

Effective Date

The provision is effective with regard to communications made on or after the date of enactment.

[Law at ¶ 6740. CCH Explanation at ¶ 1141.]

[¶ 10,380]   Act Sec. 3412.   Limitation on financial status audit techniques

House Committee Report (H.R. REP. NO. 105-364, pt. 1)

[Code Sec. 7602]
Present Law
The IRS examines Federal tax returns to determine the correct liability of taxpayers. The IRS selects returns to be audited in a number of ways, such as through a computerized classification system (the discriminant function ("DIF") system).
Reasons for Change
The Committee believes that financial status audit techniques are intrusive, and that their use should be limited to situations where the IRS already has indications of unreported income.

Explanation of Provision
The bill prohibits IRS from using financial status or economic reality examination techniques to determine the existence of unreported income of any taxpayer unless the IRS has a reasonable indication that there is a likelihood of unreported income.

Effective Date
The provision is effective on the date of enactment.

Conference Committee Report (H.R. CONF. REP. NO. 105-599)

Senate Amendment
Same as the House bill.
Conference Agreement
The conference agreement follows the House bill and the Senate amendment.

[Law at ¶ 6760. CCH Explanation at ¶ 1111.]

[¶ 10,385]   Act Sec. 3413.   Software trade secrets protection

House Committee Report (H.R. REP. NO. 105-364, pt. 1)

[Code Sec. 7612]
Present Law
The Secretary of the Treasury is authorized to examine any books, papers, records, or other data that may be relevant or material to an inquiry into the correctness of any Federal tax return. The Secretary may issue and serve summonses necessary to obtain such data, including summonses on certain third-party record keepers. There are no specific statutory restrictions on the ability of the Secretary to demand the production of computer records, programs, code or similar materials.
Reasons for Change
The Committee believes that the intellectual property rights of the developers and owners of

computer programs should be respected and is concerned that the examination of third-party tax-related computer source code by the IRS could lead to the diminution of those rights through the inadvertent disclosure of trade secrets. The Committee also believes that the indiscriminate examination of computer source code by the IRS to identify issues on a taxpayer's return would be inappropriate. Accordingly, the Committee believes that a summons for the production of third-party tax-related computer source code should only be issued where the IRS has not otherwise been able to ascertain through reasonable efforts the manner in which a taxpayer has arrived at the entry on a return and has identified with specificity the portion of the computer source code it seeks to examine.

Explanation of Provision

The Secretary is generally prohibited from issuing (or beginning an action to enforce) a summons in a civil action for any portion of any third-party tax-related computer source code unless (1) the Secretary is unable to otherwise reasonably ascertain the correctness of an item on a return from the taxpayer's other books, papers, records, other data, or the computer software program and associated data itself and (2) the Secretary first identifies with reasonable specificity the portion of the computer source code to be used to verify the correctness of the item.

The Secretary would be considered to have satisfied these requirements with regard to the identified portion of the source code if the Secretary makes a formal request for such materials to both the taxpayer and the owner or developer of the software that is not satisfied within 90 days. Such formal request must clearly state that one of the consequences of failure to respond to the request will be the waiver of any prohibition on the summons of tax-related computer source code that might otherwise apply.

The Secretary's determination that the identified portion of the third-party tax-related computer source code may be summoned may be contested in any proceeding to enforce the summons, by any person to whom the summons is addressed. For this purpose, the special procedures for third-party summonses[42] will apply. In any such proceeding, the court may issue any order that is necessary to prevent the disclosure of trade secrets or other confidential information.

* * *

The prohibition applies only in the case of tax-related computer software that is intended for commercial distribution. Source code related to computer software that was developed by, or primarily for the benefit of, the taxpayer or a related person (within the meaning of section 267 or 707(b)) for the internal use of the taxpayer or such related person may continue to be summonsed by the Secretary to the extent allowed under present law.

Effective Date

The provision is effective for summonses issued more than 90 days after the date of enactment. It is expected that the Secretary will not use the 90 day period between the date of enactment and the effective date in a manner that would circumvent the intent of the provision.

Senate Committee Report (S. REP. NO. 105-174)

Present Law

The Secretary of the Treasury is authorized to examine any books, papers, records, or other data that may be relevant or material to an inquiry into the correctness of any Federal tax return. The Secretary may issue and serve summonses necessary to obtain such data, including summonses on certain third-party record keepers. There are no specific statutory restrictions on the ability of the Secretary to demand the production of computer records, programs, code or similar materials.

Reasons for Change

The Committee believes that the intellectual property rights of the developers and owners of computer programs should be respected. The Committee is concerned that the examination of computer programs and source code by the IRS could lead to the diminution of those rights through the inadvertent disclosure of trade secrets and believes that special protection against such inadvertent disclosure should be established.

The Committee also believes that the indiscriminate examination of computer source code by the IRS is inappropriate. Accordingly, the Committee believes that a summons for the production of certain computer source code should only be issued where the IRS is not otherwise able to ascer-

tain through reasonable efforts the manner in which a taxpayer has arrived at an item on a return, identifies with specificity the portion of the computer source code it seeks to examine, and determines that the need to see the source code outweighs the risk of unauthorized disclosure of trade secrets.

Explanation of Provision

Discovery of computer source code

The provision generally prohibits the Secretary from issuing a summons in a Federal tax matter for any portion of computer source code. Exceptions to the general rule are provided for inquiries into any criminal offense connected with the administration or enforcement of the internal revenue laws and for computer software source code that was developed by the taxpayer or a related person for internal use by the taxpayer or related person. Computer software source code is considered to have been developed for internal use by the taxpayer or a related person if the software is primarily used in the taxpayer or related person's trade or business, as opposed to being held for sale or license to others. Software is considered to be used in a trade or business if it is used in the provision of services to others. It is anticipated that software that was originally developed for internal use by the taxpayer or a related person

---

[42] Sec. 7609.

will continue to be subject to the exception, even if the software is later transferred to another. For example, software may have originally been developed by the taxpayer to administer the taxpayer's employee benefits system. If that function and the software necessary to perform it is later transferred to an unrelated third party, the software would continue to be subject to the exception.

In addition, the prohibition of the general rule would not apply, and the Secretary would be allowed to summons computer source code if the Secretary: (1) is unable to otherwise reasonably ascertain the correctness of an item on a return from the taxpayer's books and records, or the computer software program and any associated data; (2) identifies with reasonable specificity the portion of the computer source code to be used to verify the correctness of the item; and (3) determines that the need for the source code outweighs the risks of disclosure of the computer source code. No inference is intended as to whether software is included in the definition of a taxpayer's books and records.

It is expected that the Secretary will make a good faith and significant effort to ascertain the correctness of an item prior to seeking computer source code. The portion of the computer source code to be used would be considered identified with reasonable specificity where, for example, the Secretary requests the portion of the code that is used to determine a particular item on the return, that otherwise is necessary to the determination of an item on the return, or that implements an accounting or other method.

The Committee is aware that the refusal of the taxpayer or the owner of the software to cooperate could, in certain situations, prevent the Secretary from establishing the factors necessary to support the summons of computer source code. Accordingly, the requirement that the Secretary be unable to otherwise reasonably ascertain the correctness of an item on a return from the taxpayer's books and records, or from the computer software program and any associated data, and the requirement that the Secretary have identified with reasonable specificity the portion of the computer source code requested, will be deemed to be satisfied where (1) the Secretary makes a good faith determination that it is not feasible to determine the correctness of the return item in question without access to the computer software program and associated data, (2) the Secretary makes a formal request for such program and any data from the taxpayer and requests such program from the owner of the source code after reaching such determination, and (3) the Secretary has not received such program and data within 180 days of making the formal request. In the case of requests to the taxpayer, the Committee expects that a formal request will take the form of an Information Document Request (IDR), summons, or similar document. The Committee intends that the Secretary actively pursue the recovery of such program and any data from the taxpayer before seeking to have the normal requirements deemed satisfied under this rule.

Additional protections against disclosure of computer software and source code

The provision establishes a number of protections against the disclosure and improper use of trade secrets and confidential information incident to the examination by the Secretary of any computer software program or source code that comes into the possession or control of the Secretary in the course of any examination with respect to any taxpayer. These protections include the following:

(1) Such software or source code may be examined only in connection with the examination of the taxpayer's return with regard to which it was received. It is expected that the taxpayer will be informed of any alternative data or settings to be used in the examination of the software. However, the Committee does not intend to provide the taxpayer with the right to monitor the examination of the software by the IRS on a key stroke by key stroke or similar basis.

(2) Such software or source code must be maintained in a secure area.

(3) Such source code may not be removed from the owner's place of business without the owner's consent unless such removal is pursuant to a court order. If the owner does not consent to the removal of source code from its place of business, the owner must make available the necessary equipment to review the source code. The owner shall have the right to require the use of equipment that is configured to prevent electronic communication outside the owner's place of business.

(4) Such software or source code may not be decompiled or disassembled.

(5) Such software or source code may only be copied as necessary to perform the specific examination. The owner of the software must be informed of any copies that are made, such copies must be numbered, and at the conclusion of the examination and any related court proceedings, all such copies must be accounted for and returned to the owner, permanently deleted, or destroyed. The Secretary must provide the owner of such software or source code with the names of any individuals who will have access to such software or source code. Source code may be copied (by the use of a scanner or otherwise) from written to machine readable form. However, any such machine readable copies shall be treated as separate copies and must be numbered, accounted for and returned or destroyed at the conclusion of the examination.

(6) If an individual who is not an officer or employee of the U.S. Government will examine the software or source code, such individual must enter into a written agreement with the Secretary that such individual will not disclose such software or source code to any person other than authorized employees or agents of the Secretary at any time, and that such individual will not participate in the development of software that is intended for a similar purpose as the summoned software for a period of two years.

Act Sec. 3413 ¶ 10,385

Computer source code is the code written by a programmer using a programming language that is comprehensible to an appropriately trained person, is not machine readable, and is not capable of directly being used to give instructions to a computer. Computer source code also includes any related programmer's notes, design documents, memoranda and similar documentation and customer communications regarding the operation of the program (other than communications with the taxpayer or any person related to the taxpayer).

The Secretary's determination may be contested in any proceeding to enforce the summons, by any person to whom the summons is addressed. In any such proceeding, the court may issue any order that is necessary to prevent the disclosure of confidential information, including (but not limited to) the enforcement of the protections established by this provision.

Criminal penalties are provided where any person willfully divulges or makes known software that was obtained (whether or not by summons) for the purpose of examining a taxpayer's return in violation of this provision.

Effective Date

The provision is effective for summons issued and software acquired after the date of enactment. In addition, 90 days after the date of enactment, the protections against the disclosure and improper use of trade secrets and confidential information added by the provision (except for the requirement that the Secretary provide a written agreement from non-U.S. government officers and employees) apply to software and source code acquired on or before the date of enactment.

Conference Committee Report (H.R. CONF. REP. NO. 105-599)

The conference agreement generally follows the Senate amendment with regard to the safeguards for protection of computer software and source code that is obtained by the IRS in the course of the examination of a taxpayer's return. The conference agreement specifically provides that computer software or source code that is obtained by the IRS in the course of the examination of a taxpayer's return will be treated as return information for the purposes of section 6103. The conference agreement follows the Senate amendment with regard to the standards the Secretary must meet in order to summons certain types of computer source code. The conference agreement follows the House bill in limiting the higher standards for a summons to third-party tax-related computer source code.

Under the conference agreement, no summons may be issued for tax-related computer software source code unless (1) the Secretary is unable otherwise to ascertain the correctness of any item on a return from the taxpayer's books and records or the computer software program and associated data, (2) the Secretary identifies with reasonable specificity the portion of the computer source code needed to verify the correctness of the item and (3) the Secretary determines that the need for the source code outweighs the risk of unauthorized disclosure of trade secrets. The Secretary is considered to have satisfied the first two of these requirements if the Secretary makes a formal request for such materials to both the taxpayer and the owner of the software that is not satisfied within 180 days.

This limitation on the summons of tax-related computer software source code does not apply if the summons is issued in connection with an inquiry into any offense connected with the administration or enforcement of the internal revenue laws. The limitation also does not apply to a summons of computer software source code that was acquired or developed by the taxpayer or a related person primarily for internal use by the taxpayer or such person rather than for commercial distribution. A finding that computer software source code was developed for internal use, and thus not eligible for the limitation in

summons authority in this provision, is not intended to be dispositive of whether such software was intended for internal use for any other purpose of this title.

Communications between the owner of the tax-related computer software source code and the taxpayer are not protected from summons by this provision. Communications between the owner of the tax-related source code and persons not related to the taxpayer that are related to the functioning and operation of the software may be treated as a part of the computer software source code.

The provision does not change or eliminate any other requirement of the Code. A summons for third-party tax-related computer source code that meets the standards established by the provision will not be enforced if it would not be enforced under present law. For example, if the Secretary's purpose in issuing the summons is shown to be improper, the summons would not be enforced, even if the Secretary otherwise met the standards for the summons of computer source code established by the provision. The limitations on the summons of tax-related computer software source code apply only with respect to computer software that is used for accounting tax return preparation, tax compliance or tax planning purposes. No inference is intended with respect to computer software used for all other purposes. In such cases, current law will continue to apply, subject to the protections against the disclosure and improper use of trade secrets and other confidential information added by this provision.

Software or source code that is required to be provided under present law must be provided without regard to this provision. For example, computer software or source code that is required to be provided in connection with the registration of a confidential corporate tax shelter arrangements under section 6111 would continue to be required to be provided without regard to this provision. Thus, the registration requirement of section 6111 cannot be avoided where the tax benefits of the shelter are discernible only from the operation of a computer program.

The conference agreement includes the protections against the disclosure and improper use of trade secrets and confidential information contained in the Senate amendment. The requirement that software or source code obtained by the Secretary in the course of an examination be used only in connection with that examination is intended to prevent the Secretary from using the software for the purpose of examining other, unrelated taxpayers. The requirement is not intended to prevent the Secretary from using knowledge it obtains in the course of the examination, so long as such use does not result in the disclosure of tax return information (including the software or source code) or the violation of any statutory protection or judicial order.

Effective Date

The conference agreement follows the Senate effective date.

[Law at ¶ 6570, ¶ 6770, ¶ 6810 and ¶ 6820. CCH Explanation at ¶ 1161.]

[¶ 10,390]   Act Sec. 3414.   Threat of audit prohibited to coerce tip reporting alternative commitment agreements

House Committee Report (H.R. REP. NO. 105-364, pt. 1)

[Act Sec. 3414]

Present Law

Restaurants may enter into Tip Reporting Alternative Commitment (TRAC) agreements. A restaurant entering into a TRAC agreement is obligated to educate its employees on their tip reporting obligations, to institute formal tip reporting procedures, to fulfill all filing and record keeping requirements, and to pay and deposit taxes. In return, the IRS agrees to base the restaurant's liability for employment taxes solely on reported tips and any unreported tips discovered during an IRS audit of an employee.

Reasons for Change

The Committee believes that it is inappropriate for the Secretary to use the threat of an Internal Revenue Service audit to induce participation in voluntary programs.

Explanation of Provision

The bill requires the IRS to instruct its employees that they may not threaten to audit any taxpayer in an attempt to coerce the taxpayer to enter into a TRAC agreement.

Effective Date

The provision is effective on the date of enactment.

Conference Committee Report (H.R. CONF. REP. NO. 105-599)

Senate Amendment

Same as the House bill

Conference Agreement

The conference agreement follows the House bill and the Senate amendment

[Law at ¶ 8090. CCH Explanation at ¶ 1116.]

[¶ 10,395]   Act Sec. 3415.   Taxpayers allowed motion to quash all third party summonses

Senate Committee Report (S. REP. NO. 105-174)

[Code Sec. 7609(a)]

Present Law

When the IRS issues a summons to a "third-party recordkeeper" relating to the business transactions or affairs of a taxpayer, Code section 7609 requires that notice of the summons be given to the taxpayer within three days by certified or registered mail. The taxpayer is thereafter given up to 23 days to begin a court proceeding to quash the summons. If the taxpayer does so, third-party recordkeepers are prohibited from complying with the summons until the court rules on the taxpayer's petition or motion to quash, but the statute of limitations for assessment and collection with respect to the taxpayer is stayed during the pendency of such a proceeding. Third-party recordkeepers are generally persons who hold financial information about the taxpayer, such as banks, brokers, attorneys, and accountants.

Reasons for Change

The Committee believes that a taxpayer should have notice when the IRS uses its summons power to gather information in an effort to determine the taxpayer's liability. Expanding notice requirement to cover all third party summonses will ensure that taxpayer will receive notice and an opportunity to contest any summons issued to a third party in connection with the determination of their liability.

Explanation of Provision

The provision generally expands the current "third-party recordkeeper" procedures to apply to summonses issued to persons other than the taxpayer. Thus, the taxpayer whose liability is being investigated receives notice of the summons and is entitled to bring an action in the appropriate U.S. District Court to quash the summons. As under the current third-party recordkeeper provision, the statute of limitations on assessment and collection is stayed during the litigation, and certain kinds of summonses specified under current law are not subject to these requirements. No inference is intended with respect to the applicability of present law to summonses to the taxpayer or the scope of the authority to summons testimony, books, papers, or other records.

Effective Date

The provision is effective for summonses served after the date of enactment.

Conference Committee Report (H.R. CONF. REP. NO. 105-599)

The conference agreement follows the Senate amendment with a clarification that nothing in section 7609 of the Code (relating to special procedures for third-party summonses) shall be construed to limit the ability of the IRS to obtain information (other than by summons) through formal or informal procedures authorized by the Code.

[**Law at ¶ 6790. CCH Explanation at ¶ 1146.**]

[¶ 10,400]   Act Sec. 3416.   Service of summonses to third-party recordkeepers permitted by mail

Senate Committee Report (S. REP. NO. 105-174)

[Code Sec. 7603]

Present Law

Code section 7603 requires that a summons shall be served "by an attested copy delivered in hand to the person to whom it is directed or left at his last and usual place of abode." By contrast, if a third-party recordkeeper summons is served, section 7609 permits the IRS to give the taxpayer notice of the summons via certified or registered mail. Moreover, Rule 4 of the Federal Rules of Civil Procedure permits service of process by mail even in summons enforcement proceedings.

Reasons for Change

The Committee is concerned that, in certain cases, the personal appearance of an IRS official at a place of business for the purpose of serving a summons may be unnecessarily disruptive. The Committee believes that it is appropriate to permit service of summons, as well as notice of summons, by mail.

Explanation of Provision

The provision allows the IRS the option of serving any summons either in person or by mail.

Effective Date

The provision is effective for summonses served after the date of enactment.

Conference Committee Report (H.R. CONF. REP. NO. 105-599)

The conference agreement follows the Senate amendment.

[**Law at ¶ 6770. CCH Explanation at ¶ 1151.**]

[¶ 10,405]   Act Sec. 3417.   Notice of IRS contact of third parties

Conference Committee Report (H.R. CONF. REP. NO. 105-599)

[Code Sec. 7602]

Present Law

Third parties may be contacted by the IRS in connection with the examination of a taxpayer or the collection of the tax liability of the taxpayer. The IRS has the right to summon third-party recordkeepers. In general, the taxpayer must be notified of the service of summons on a third party within three days of the date of service. The IRS also has the right to seize property of the taxpayer that is held in the hands of third parties. Except in jeopardy situations, the Internal Revenue Manual provides that IRS will personally contact the taxpayer and inform the taxpayer that seizure of the asset is planned.

House Bill

No provision.

Senate Amendment

The Senate amendment requires the IRS to notify the taxpayer before contacting third parties regarding examination or collection activities (including summonses) with respect to the taxpayer. Contacts with government officials relating to matters such as the location of assets or the taxpayer's current address are not restricted by this provision. The provision does not apply to criminal tax matters, if the collection of the tax liability is in jeopardy, or if the taxpayer authorized the contact.

Effective Date

Contacts made after 180 days after the date of enactment.

Conference Agreement

The conference agreement provides that the IRS may not contact any person other than the taxpayer with respect to the determination or collection of the tax liability of the taxpayer without providing reasonable notice in advance to the taxpayer that the IRS may contact persons other than the taxpayer. It is intended that in general this notice will be provided as part of an existing IRS notice provided to taxpayers. The conference agreement also requires the IRS to provide periodically to the taxpayer a record of persons previously contacted during that period by the IRS with respect to the determination or collection of that taxpayer's tax liability. This record shall also be provided upon request of the taxpayer. The provision does not apply to criminal tax matters, if the collection of the tax liability is in jeopardy, if the Secretary determines for good cause shown that disclosure may involve reprisal against any person, or if the taxpayer authorized the contact.

Effective Date

Contacts made after 180 days after the date of enactment.

[Law at ¶ 6760. CCH Explanation at ¶ 1156.]

[¶ 10,415]   Act Sec. 3421.   Approval process for liens, levies, and seizures

Senate Committee Report (S. REP. NO. 105-174)

[Act Sec. 3421]

[*This committee report does not reflect changes made by Senate Floor Amendment No. 2380. Selected portions of the Senate Floor Debate are reproduced below.—CCH.*]

Present Law

Supervisory approval of liens, levies or seizures is only required under certain circumstances. For example, a levy on a taxpayer's principal residence is only permitted upon the written approval of the District Director or Assistant District Director (sec. 6334(e)).

Reasons for Change

The Committee believes that the imposition of liens, levies, and seizures may impose significant hardships on taxpayers. Accordingly, the Committee believes that extra protection in the form of an administrative approval process is appropriate.

Explanation of Provision

The provision requires the IRS to implement an approval process under which any lien, levy or seizure would be approved by a supervisor, who would review the taxpayer's information, verify that a balance is due, and affirm that a lien, levy or seizure is appropriate under the circumstances. Circumstances to be considered include the amount due and the value of the asset. Failure to follow such procedures should result in disciplinary action against the supervisor and/or revenue officer.

In addition, the Treasury Inspector General for Tax Administration is required to collect information on the approval process and annually report to the tax-writing committees.

Effective Date

The provision is effective for collection actions commenced after date of enactment.

Senate Floor Debate for Amendment No. 2380 (144 CONG. REC. 56, S4510)

* * *

Mr. MOYNIHAN.—* * *Mr. President, it was with these challenges in mind that Senator Kerrey and I offered this amendment to briefly delay some of the effective dates in the Finance Committee's IRS Restructuring legislation in order to allow time for the Y2K conversion to be completed. This amendment has been drafted based

on Commissioner Rossotti's recommendations, and has been modified after consultations with the Majority.

The amendment would delay the effective date on a list of provisions from date of enactment until after the century date change.

* * *

Conference Committee Report (H.R. CONF. REP. NO. 105-599)

The conference agreement follows the Senate amendment. The conferees intend that the Commissioner have discretion in promulgating the procedures required by this provision to determine the circumstances under which supervisory review of liens or levies issued by the automated collection system is or is not appropriate.

Effective Date

Collection actions commenced after date of enactment, except in the case of any action under the automated collection system, the provision applies to actions initiated after December 31, 2000.

[Law at ¶ 8095. CCH Explanation at ¶ 1201.]

[¶ 10,425]   Act Sec. 3431.   Modifications to certain levy exemption amounts

Conference Committee Report (H.R. CONF. REP. NO. 105-599)

[Code Sec. 6334]

Present Law

IRS may levy on all non-exempt property of the taxpayer. Property exempt from levy includes up to $2,500 in value of fuel, provisions, furniture, and personal effects in the taxpayer's household and up to $1,250 in value of books and tools necessary for the trade, business or profession of the taxpayer.

House Bill

No provision.

Senate Amendment

The Senate amendment increases the value of personal effects exempt from levy to $10,000 and the value of books and tools exempt from levy to $5,000. These amounts are indexed for inflation.

Effective Date

Levies issued after date of enactment.

Conference Agreement

The conference agreement increases the value of personal effects exempt from levy to $6,250 and the value of books and tools exempt from levy to $3,125. These amounts are indexed for inflation.

Effective Date

Levies issued after date of enactment.

[Law at ¶ 6290. CCH Explanation at ¶ 1210.]

[¶ 10,430]   Act Sec. 3432.   Release of levy upon agreement that amount is uncollectible

Senate Committee Report (S. REP. NO. 105-174)

[Code Sec. 6343]

[*This committee report does not reflect changes made by Senate Floor Amendment No. 2380. Selected portions of the Senate Floor Debate are reproduced below.—CCH.*]

Present Law

Some have contended that the IRS does not release a wage levy immediately upon receipt of proof that the taxpayer is unable to pay the tax, but instead, the IRS levies on one period's wage payment before releasing the levy.

Reasons for Change

Congress believes that taxpayers should not have collection activity taken against them once the IRS has determined that the amounts are uncollectible.

Explanation of Provision

The IRS is required to immediately release a wage levy upon agreement with the taxpayer that the tax is not collectible.

Effective Date

The provision is effective for levies imposed after date of enactment.

Senate Floor Debate for Amendment No. 2380 (144 CONG. REC. 56, S4510)

* * *

Mr. MOYNIHAN.—* * * Mr. President, it was with these challenges in mind that Senator Kerrey and I offered this amendment to briefly delay some of the effective dates in the Finance Committee's IRS Restructuring legislation in order to allow time for the Y2K conversion to be completed. This amendment has been drafted based on Commissioner Rossotti's recommendations, and has been modified after consultations with the Majority.

The amendment would delay the effective date on a list of provisions from date of enactment until after the century date change.

* * *

Conference Committee Report (H.R. CONF. REP. NO. 105-599)

The conference agreement follows the Senate amendment, with a clarification that the release is to occur as soon as practicable. The IRS is not to intentionally delay until after one wage payment has been made and levied upon before releasing the levy.

[Law at ¶ 6320. CCH Explanation at ¶ 1218.]

[¶ 10,435]   Act Sec. 3433.   Levy prohibited during pendency of refund proceedings

Senate Committee Report (S. REP. NO. 105-174)

[Code Sec. 6331]

Present Law

The IRS is prohibited from making a tax assessment (and thus prohibited from collecting payment) with respect to a tax liability while it is being contested in Tax Court. However, the IRS is permitted to assess and collect tax liabilities during the pendency of a refund suit relating to such tax liabilities, under the circumstances described below.

Generally, full payment of the tax at issue is a prerequisite to a refund suit. However, if the tax is divisible (such as employment taxes or the trust fund penalty under Code section 6672), the taxpayer need only pay the tax for the applicable period before filing a refund claim. Most divisible taxes are not within the Tax Court's jurisdiction; accordingly, the taxpayer has no pre-payment forum for contesting such taxes. In the case of divisible taxes, it is possible that the taxpayer could be properly under the refund jurisdiction of the District Court or the U.S. Court of Federal Claims and still be subject to collection by levy with respect to the entire amount of the tax at issue. The IRS's policy is generally to exercise forbearance with respect to collection while the refund suit is pending, so long as the interests of the Government are adequately protected (e.g., by the filing of a notice of Federal tax lien) and collection is not in jeopardy. Any refunds due the taxpayer may be credited to the unpaid portion of the liability pending the outcome of the suit.

Reasons for Change

The Committee believes that taxpayers who are litigating a refund action over divisible taxes should be protected from collection of the full assessed amount, because the court considering the refund suit may ultimately determine that the taxpayer is not liable.

Explanation of Provision

The provision requires the IRS to withhold collection by levy of liabilities that are the subject of a refund suit during the pendency of the litigation. This will only apply when refund suits can be brought without the full payment of the tax, i.e., in the case of divisible taxes. Collection by levy would be withheld unless jeopardy exists or the taxpayer waives the suspension of collection in writing (because collection will stop the running of interest and penalties on the tax liability). This provision will not affect the IRS's ability to collect other assessments that are not the subject of the refund suit, to offset refunds, to counterclaim in a refund suit or related proceeding, or to file a notice of Federal tax lien. The statute of limitations on collection is stayed for the period during which the IRS is prohibited from collecting by levy.

Effective Date

The provision is effective for refund suits brought with respect to tax years beginning after December 31, 1998.

Conference Committee Report (H.R. CONF. REP. NO. 105-599)

The conference agreement follows the Senate amendment, with a technical modification. The conferees wish to clarify that proceedings related to a proceeding[20] under this provision include, but are not limited to, civil actions or third-party complaints initiated by the United States or another person with respect to the same kinds of tax (or related taxes or penalties) for the same (or overlapping) tax periods. For example, if a taxpayer brings a suit for a refund of a portion of a penalty that the taxpayer has paid under section 6672, the United States could, consistent with this provision, counterclaim against the taxpayer for the balance of the penalty or initiate related claims against other persons assessed penalties under section 6672 for the same employment taxes.

[Law at ¶ 6280. CCH Explanation at ¶ 1222.]

[¶ 10,440]   Act Sec. 3434.   Approval required for jeopardy and termination assessments and jeopardy levies

Senate Committee Report (S. REP. NO. 105-174)

[Code Sec. 7429(a)]
Present Law

In general, a 30-day waiting period is imposed after assessment of all types of taxes. In certain circumstances, the waiting period puts the collection of taxes at risk. The Code provides special procedures that allow the IRS to make jeopardy assessments or termination assessments in certain extraordinary circumstances, such as if the taxpayer is leaving or removing property from the United States (sec. 6851), or if assessment or collection would be jeopardized by delay (secs. 6861 and 6862). In jeopardy or termination situations, a levy may be made without the 30-days' notice of intent to levy that is ordinarily required by section 6331(d)(2). Jeopardy assessments apply when the tax year is over. Termination assessments apply to the current taxable year or the immediately preceding taxable year if the filing date has not yet passed. A termination assessment serves to terminate the taxable year for the purpose of computing the tax to be assessed and collected under the termination assessment procedure. Under both the jeopardy and termination assessment procedures, the IRS can assess the tax and immediately begin collection if any one of the following situations exists: (1) the taxpayer is or appears to be planning to depart the United States or to go into hiding; (2) the taxpayer is or appears to be planning to place property beyond the reach of the IRS by removing it from the country, hiding it, dissipating it, or by transfer-

ring it to other persons; or (3) the taxpayer's financial solvency is or appears to be imperiled. Because the same criteria apply to jeopardy and termination assessments, jeopardy and termination assessments are often entered at the same time against the same taxpayer.

The Code and regulations do not presently require Counsel to review jeopardy assessments, termination assessments, or jeopardy levies, although the Internal Revenue Manual does require Counsel review before such actions and it is current practice to make such a review. The IRS bears the burden of proof with respect to the reasonableness of a jeopardy or termination assessment or a jeopardy levy (sec. 7429(g)).

Reasons for Change

The Committee believes that it is appropriate to require Counsel review and approval of jeopardy and termination levies, because such actions often involve difficult legal issues.

Explanation of Provision

The provision requires IRS Counsel review and approval before the IRS could make a jeopardy assessment, a termination assessment, or a jeopardy levy. If Counsel's approval was not obtained, the taxpayer would be entitled to obtain abatement of the assessment or release of the levy, and, if the IRS failed to offer such relief, to appeal first to IRS Appeals under the new due process procedure for IRS collections (described in E. 1, above) and then to court.

---

[20] For purposes of new section 6331(i)(4)(A)(ii) of the Code.

Effective Date

The provision is effective with respect to taxes assessed and levies made after the date of enactment.

Conference Committee Report (H.R. CONF. REP. NO. 105-599)

The conference agreement follows the Senate amendment.

[Law at ¶ 6620. CCH Explanation at ¶ 1206.]

[¶ 10,445]   Act Sec. 3435.   Increase in amount of certain property on which lien not valid

Senate Committee Report (S. REP. NO. 105-174)

[Code Sec. 6323]

Present Law

The Federal tax lien attaches to all property and rights in property of the taxpayer, if the taxpayer fails to pay the assessed tax liability after notice and demand (sec. 6321). However, the Federal tax lien is not valid as to certain "superpriority" interests as defined in section 6323(b).

Two of these interests are limited by a specific dollar amount. Under section 6323(b)(4), purchasers of personal property at a casual sale are presently protected against a Federal tax lien attached to such property to the extent the sale is for less than $250. Section 6323(b)(7) provides protection to mechanic's lienors with respect to the repairs or improvements made to owner—occupied personal residences, but only to the extent that the contract for repair or improvement is for not more than $1,000.

In addition, a superpriority is granted under section 6323(b)(10) to banks and building and loan associations which make passbook loans to their customers, provided that those institutions retain the passbooks in their possession until the loan is completely paid off.

Reasons for Change

The Committee believes that it is appropriate to increase the dollar limits on the superpriority amounts because the dollar limits have not been increased for decades and do not reflect current prices or values.

Explanation of Provision

The provision increases the dollar limit in section 6323(b)(4) for purchasers at a casual sale from $250 to $1,000, and further increases the dollar limit in section 6323(b)(7) from $1,000 to $5,000 for mechanics lienors providing home improvement work for owner-occupied personal residences. The provision indexes these amounts for inflation. The provision also clarifies section 6323(b)(10) to reflect present banking practices, where a passbook-type loan may be made even though an actual passbook is not used.

Effective Date

The provision is effective on the date of enactment.

Conference Committee Report (H.R. CONF. REP. NO. 105-599)

The conference agreement follows the Senate amendment.

[Law at ¶ 6250. CCH Explanation at ¶ 1214.]

[¶ 10,450]   Act Sec. 3436.   Waiver of early withdrawal tax for IRS levies on employer-sponsored retirement plans or IRAs

Senate Committee Report (S. REP. NO. 105-174)

[Code Sec. 72(t)(2)(A)]

[This committee report does not reflect changes made by Senate Floor Amendment No. 2380. Selected portions of the Senate Floor Debate are reproduced below.—CCH.]

Present Law

Under present law, a distribution of benefits from any employer-sponsored retirement plan or an individual retirement arrangement ("IRA") generally is includible in gross income in the year it is paid or distributed, except to the extent the amount distributed represents the employee's after-tax contributions or investment in the contract (i.e., basis). Special rules apply to certain lump-sum distributions from qualified retirement plans, distributions rolled over to an IRA or em-

ployer-sponsored retirement plan, and lump-sum distributions of employer securities.

Distributions from qualified plans and IRAs prior to attainment of age 59-1/2 that are includible in income generally are subject to a 10-percent early withdrawal tax, unless an exception to the tax applies. An exception to the tax applies if the withdrawal is due to death or disability, is made in the form of certain periodic payments, or is used to pay medical expenses in excess of 7.5 percent of adjusted gross income ("AGI"). Certain additional exceptions to the tax apply separately to withdrawals from IRAs and qualified plans. Distributions from IRAs for education expenses, for up to $10,000 of first-time homebuyer expenses, or to unemployed individuals to purchase

¶ 10,445   Act Sec. 3435

health insurance are not subject to the 10-percent early withdrawal tax. A distribution from a qualified plan made by an employee after separation from service after attainment of age 55 is not subject to the 10-percent early withdrawal tax.

Under present law, the IRS is authorized to levy on all non-exempt property of the taxpayer. Benefits under employer-sponsored retirement plans (including section 403(b) and 457 plans) and IRAs are not exempt from levy by the IRS.

Under present law, distributions from employer-sponsored retirement plans or IRAs made on account of an IRS levy are includible in the gross income of the individual, except to the extent the amount distributed represents after-tax contributions. In addition, the amount includible in income is subject to the 10-percent early withdrawal tax, unless an exception described above applies.

Reasons for Change

The Committee believes that the imposition of the 10-percent early withdrawal tax on amounts distributed from employer-sponsored retirement plans or IRAs on account of an IRS levy may impose significant hardships on taxpayers. Accordingly, the Committee believes such distributions should be exempt from the 10-percent early withdrawal tax.

Explanation of Provision

The provision provides an exception from the 10-percent early withdrawal tax for amounts withdrawn from any employer-sponsored retirement plan or an IRA that are subject to a levy by the IRS. The exception applies only if the plan or IRA is levied; it does not apply, for example, if the taxpayer withdraws funds to pay taxes in the absence of a levy, in order to release a levy on other interests, or in any other situation not addressed by the express statutory exceptions to the 10-percent early withdrawal tax.

Effective Date

The provision is effective for withdrawals after the date of enactment.

Senate Floor Debate for Amendment No. 2380 (144 CONG. REC. 144, S4510)

Mr. MOYNIHAN.—* * * Mr. President, it was with these challenges in mind that Senator Kerrey and I offered this amendment to briefly delay some of the effective dates in the Finance Committee's IRS Restructuring legislation in order to allow time for the Y2K conversion to be completed. This amendment has been drafted based on Commissioner Rossotti's recommendations, and has been modified after consultations with the Majority.

The amendment would delay the effective date on a list of provisions from date of enactment until after the century date change. * * *

Conference Committee Report (H.R. CONF. REP. NO. 105-599)

The conference agreement follows the Senate amendment, with a modification to the effective date. The provision is effective for distributions after December 31, 1999.

[Law at ¶ 5150. CCH Explanation at ¶ 1226.]

[¶ 10,465] Act Sec. 3441. Prohibition of sales of seized property at less than minimum bid

Senate Committee Report (S. REP. NO. 105-174)

[Code Sec. 6335(e)]

Present Law

Section 6335(e) requires that a minimum bid price be established for seized property offered for sale. To conserve the taxpayer's equity, the minimum bid price should normally be computed at 80 percent or more of the forced sale value of the property less encumbrances having priority over the Federal tax lien. If the group manager concurs, the minimum sales price may be set at less than 80 percent. The taxpayer is to receive notice of the minimum bid price within 10 days of the sale. The taxpayer has the opportunity to challenge the minimum bid price, which cannot be more than the tax liability plus the expenses of sale. Accordingly, if the minimum bid price is set at the tax liability plus the expenses of sale, the taxpayer's concurrence is not required. IRM 56(13)5.1.(4). Section 6335 does not contemplate a sale of the seized property at less than the minimum bid price. Rather, if no person offers the minimum bid price, the IRS may buy the property at the minimum bid price or the property may be released to the owner. Code section 7433 provides civil damages for certain unauthorized collection actions.

Reasons for Change

The Committee believes that strengthening provisions regarding the minimum bid price, including preventing the IRS from selling the taxpayer's property for less than the minimum bid price, are appropriate to preserve taxpayers' rights.

Explanation of Provision

The provision prohibits the IRS from selling seized property for less than the minimum bid price. The provision provides that the sale of property for less than the minimum bid price would constitute an unauthorized collection action, which would permit an affected person to sue for civil damages pursuant to section 7433.

Effective Date

The provision is effective for sales occurring after the date of enactment.

Act Sec. 3441   ¶ 10,465

Conference Committee Report (H.R. CONF. REP. NO. 105-599)

The conference agreement follows the Senate amendment.

[Law at ¶ 6300. CCH Explanation at ¶ 1238.]

[¶ 10,470]   Act Sec. 3442.   Accounting of sales of seized property

Senate Committee Report (S. REP. NO. 105-174)

[Code Sec. 6340]

Present Law

The IRS is authorized to seize and sell a taxpayer's property to satisfy an unpaid tax liability (sec. 6331(b)). The IRS is required to give written notice to the taxpayer before seizure of the property (sec. 6331(d)). The IRS must also give written notice to the taxpayer at least 10 days before the sale of the seized property.

The IRS is required to keep records of all sales of real property (sec. 6340). The records must set forth all proceeds and expenses of the sale. The IRS is required to apply the proceeds first against the expenses of the sale, then against a specific tax liability on the seized property, if any, and finally against any unpaid tax liability of the taxpayer (sec. 6342(a)). Any surplus proceeds are credited to the taxpayer or persons legally entitled to the proceeds.

Reasons for Change

The Committee believes that taxpayers are entitled to know how proceeds from the sale of their property seized by the IRS are applied to their tax liability.

Explanation of Provision

The provision requires the IRS to provide a written accounting of all sales of seized property, whether real or personal, to the taxpayer. The accounting must include a receipt for the amount credited to the taxpayer's account.

Effective Date

The provision is effective for seizures occurring after the date of enactment.

Conference Committee Report (H.R. CONF. REP. NO. 105-599)

The conference agreement follows the Senate amendment.

[Law at ¶ 6310. CCH Explanation at ¶ 1242.]

[¶ 10,475]   Act Sec. 3443.   Uniform asset disposal mechanism

Senate Committee Report (S. REP. NO. 105-174)

[Act Sec. 3443]

Present Law

The IRS must sell property seized by levy either by public auction or by public sale under sealed bids (sec. 6335(e)(2)(A)). These are often conducted by the revenue officer charged with collecting the tax liability.

Reasons for Change

The Committee believes that it is important for fairness and the appearance of propriety that revenue officers charged with collecting unpaid tax liability are not personally involved with the sale of seized property.

Explanation of Provision

The provision requires the IRS to implement a uniform asset disposal mechanism for sales of seized property. The disposal mechanism should be designed to remove any participation in the sale of seized assets by revenue officers. The provision authorizes the consideration of out sourcing of the disposal mechanism.

Effective Date

The provision requires a uniform asset disposal system to be implemented within two years from the date of enactment.

Conference Committee Report (H.R. CONF. REP. NO. 105-599)

The conference agreement follows the Senate amendment.

[Law at ¶ 8100. CCH Explanation at ¶ 1246.]

[¶ 10,480]   Act Sec. 3444.   Codification of IRS administrative procedures for seizure of taxpayer's property

Senate Committee Report (S. REP. NO. 105-174)

[Code Sec. 6331]

Present Law

The IRS provides guidelines for revenue officers engaged in the collection of unpaid tax liabilities. The Internal Revenue Manual (IRM) 56(12)5.1 provides general guidelines for seizure actions: (1) the revenue officer must first verify the tax-payer's liability; (2) no levy may be made if the estimated expenses of levy and sale will exceed the fair market value of the property to be sized (sec. 6331(f)); (3) no levy may be made on the date of an appearance in response to an administrative summons, unless jeopardy exists (sec. 6331(g)); (4) the taxpayer should have an opportunity to read the levy form; (5) the revenue officer must attach a sufficient number of warning notices on the property to clearly identify the property to be seized; (6) the revenue officer must inventory the property to be seized; and (7) a revenue officer may not use force in the seizure of property.

Prior to the levy action, the revenue officer must determine that there is sufficient equity in the property to be seized to yield net proceeds from the sale to apply to unpaid tax liabilities. If it is determined after seizure that the taxpayer's equity is insufficient to yield net proceeds from sale to apply to the unpaid tax, the revenue officer will immediately release the seized property. See IRM 56(12)2.1.

IRS Policy Statement P-5-34 states that the facts of a case and alternative collection methods must be thoroughly considered before deciding to seize the assets of a going business. IRS Policy Statement P-5-16 advises reasonable forbearance on collection activity when the taxpayer's business has been affected by a major disaster such as flood, hurricane, drought, fire, etc., and whose ability to pay has been impaired by such disaster

Reasons for Change

The Committee believes that the IRS procedures on collections provide important protections to taxpayers. Accordingly, the Committee believes that it is appropriate to codify those procedures to ensure that they are uniformly followed by the IRS.

Explanation of Provision

The provision codifies the IRS administrative procedures which require the IRS to investigate the status of property prior to levy. The Treasury Inspector General for Tax Administration would be required to review IRS compliance with seizure procedures and report annually to Congress.

Effective Date

The provision is effective on the date of enactment.

Conference Committee Report (H.R. CONF. REP. NO. 105-599)

The conference agreement follows the Senate amendment, with a technical modification applying the investigation requirement only to property to be sold pursuant to section 6335.

[Law at ¶ 6280. CCH Explanation at ¶ 1250.]

[¶ 10,485]   Act Sec. 3445.   Procedures for seizure of residences and businesses

Senate Committee Report (S. REP. NO. 105-174)

[Code Sec. 6334(a)(13)]

[*This committee report does not reflect changes made by Senate Floor Amendment No. 2384. Selected portions of the Senate Floor Debate are reproduced below.—CCH.*]

Present Law

Subject to certain procedural rules and limitations, the Secretary may seize the property of the taxpayer who neglects or refuses to pay any tax within 10 days after notice and demand. The IRS may not levy on the personal residence of the taxpayer unless the District Director (or the assistant District Director) personally approves in writing or in cases of jeopardy. There are no special rules for property that is used as a residence by parties other than the taxpayer.

IRS Policy Statement P-5-34 states that the facts of a case and alternative collection methods must be thoroughly considered before deciding to seize the assets of a going business.

Reasons for Change

The Committee is concerned that seizure of the taxpayer's principal residence is particularly disruptive for the taxpayer as well as the taxpayer's family. The seizure of any residence is disruptive to the occupants, and is not justified in the case of a small deficiency. In the case of seizure of a business, the seizure not only disrupts the taxpayer's life but also may adversely impact the taxpayer's ability to enter into an installment agreement or otherwise to continue to pay off the tax liability. Accordingly, the Committee believes that the taxpayer's principal residence or business should only be seized to satisfy tax liability as a last resort, and that any property used by any person as a residence should not be seized for a small deficiency.

Explanation of Provision

The provision prohibits the IRS from seizing real property that is used as a residence (by the taxpayer or another person) to satisfy an unpaid liability of $5,000 or less, including penalties and interest.

The provision requires the IRS to exhaust all other payment options before seizing the taxpayer's business or principal residence. The provision does not prohibit the seizure of a business or a principal residence, but would treat such seizure as a payment option of last resort. The provision does not apply in cases of jeopardy. It is anticipated that the IRS would consider installment agreements, offer-in-compromise, and seizure of other assets of the taxpayer before taking collection action against the taxpayer's business or principal residence.

Effective Date

The provision is effective on the date of enactment.

Senate Floor Debate for Amendment No. 2384 (144 CONG. REC. 56, S4518)

* * *

Mr. STEVENS.—Mr. President, I have a reasonable amendment to this bill relating to a very unique "tool of the trade" in the fishing industry of Alaska, the bill already would increase the cap for the value of tools of the trade exempted from IRS levy to $5,000, up from $1,250.

My amendment addresses a class of tools—State-issued permits that give their holder the privilege to commercially harvest fish or game in our State.

The State of Alaska has never conceded that these permits are property that may be seized by IRS. Yet, the IRS seizes them, without giving any consideration to the unique circumstances in Alaska, particularly western Alaska.

In those villages, commercial fishing is the only industry. If you don't have a fishing job, you do not have a job.

When a fisherman in that area fails to pay taxes on time, the IRS never gives any consideration to the fact that without the fishing permit, the taxpayer would have no way to pay back taxes.

In addition, he or she will then have no way to support their children, their family, pay child support, or buy heating oil for their house, or face other problems.

We do have a problem in western Alaska—the IRS estimates that commercial fishermen owe over $20 million in back taxes. That is not much, nationally. But as one IRS agent visiting rural

Alaska pointed out, they have in some cases been trying to collect taxes from people who did not even know the IRS existed.

There are positive changes, in the bill with respect to IRS collection procedures, but the language and cultural barriers, and isolation of vast areas of Alaska still lead to results that people in the rest of the country find hard to believe.

Instead of exempting State permits entirely from IRS levies, I have accepted a compromise. Under section 3445 of the bill, the IRS will be required, before seizing the assets of a small business, to first determine that the business owner's "other assets" are not sufficient to pay the back taxes and expenses of IRS proceedings.

My compromise would require the IRS to consider future income from State-issued fish and game permits as "other income" in its determination before making a levy on such permits. This means the IRS must consider whether the future income from the permit would allow the fishermen to pay the tax debt and procedural expenses before the maximum time possible for repayment under law has occurred.

In treating these permits as an asset used in a trade or business, Congress does not intend to determine whether such permits are property or a right to property. We only mean to say that as long as the IRS asserts that the permits are property or a right to property, the holder should have the added protection of having future income considered.

Conference Committee Report (H.R. CONF. REP. NO. 105-599)

The conference agreement follows the Senate amendment, except as follows. The prohibition on seizing a residence to satisfy an unpaid liability of $5,000 or less is clarified to apply to any real property used as a residence by the taxpayer or any nonrental real property of the taxpayer used by any other individual as a residence. The definition of business assets is clarified to apply to tangible personal property or real property used

in the trade or business of an individual taxpayer (other than real property that is rented). The conference agreement provides that a levy is permitted on a principal residence only if a judge or magistrate of a United States district court approves (in writing) of the levy.

[Law at ¶ 6290. CCH Explanation at ¶ 1234.]

[¶ 10,515]   Act Sec. 3461.   Procedures relating to extensions of statute of limitations by agreement

Senate Committee Report (S. REP. NO. 105-174)

[Code Sec. 6502(a)]

[This committee report does not reflect changes made by Senate Floor Amendment No. 2380. Selected portions of the Senate Floor Debate are reproduced below.—CCH.]

Present Law

The statute of limitations within which the IRS may assess additional taxes is generally three years from the date a return is filed (sec. 6501).[34] Prior to the expiration of the statute of limitations, both the taxpayer and the IRS may agree in writing to extend the statute, using Form 872 or

872-A. An extension may be for either a specified period or an indefinite period. The statute of limitations within which a tax may be collected after assessment is 10 years after assessment (sec. 6502). Prior to the expiration of the statute of limitations, both the taxpayer and the IRS may agree in writing to extend the statute, using Form 900.

Reasons for Change

The Committee believes that taxpayers should be fully informed of their rights with respect to the statute of limitations on assessment. The

---

[34] For this purpose, a return filed before the due date is considered to be filed on the due date.

Committee is concerned that in some cases taxpayer have not been fully aware of their rights to refuse to extend the statute of limitations, and have felt that they had no choice but to agree to extend the statute of limitations upon the request of the IRS.

Moreover, the Committee believes that the IRS should collect all taxes within 10 years, and that such statute of limitation should not be extended.

Explanation of Provision
The provision eliminates the provision of present law that allows the statute of limitations on collections to be extended by agreement between the taxpayer and the IRS.

The provision also requires that, on each occasion on which the taxpayer is requested by the IRS to extend the statute of limitations on assessment, the IRS must notify the taxpayer of the taxpayer's right to refuse to extend the statute of limitations or to limit the extension to particular issues.

Effective Date
The provision applies to requests to extend the statute of limitations made after the date of enactment and to all extensions of the statute of limitations on collection that are open 180 days after the date of enactment.

Senate Floor Debate for Amendment No. 2380 (144 CONG. REC. 56, S4510)

* * *

Mr. MOYNIHAN.—* * *Mr. President, it was with these challenges in mind that Senator Kerrey and I offered this amendment to briefly delay some of the effective dates in the Finance Committee's IRS Restructuring legislation in order to allow time for the Y2K conversion to be completed. This amendment has been drafted based on Commissioner Rossotti's recommendations, and has been modified after consultations with the Majority.

The amendment would delay the effective date on a list of provisions from date of enactment until after the century date change.

* * *

Conference Committee Report (H.R. CONF. REP. NO. 105-599)

The conference agreement follows the Senate amendment, except that extensions of the statute of limitations on collection may be made in connection with an installment agreement; the extension is only for the period for which the waiver of the statute of limitations entered in connection with the original written terms of the installment agreement extends beyond the end of the otherwise applicable 10-year period, plus 90 days.

Effective Date.
Requests to extend the statute of limitations made after December 31, 1999. If, in any request

to extend the period of limitations made on or before December 31, 1999, a taxpayer agreed to extend that period beyond the 10-year statute of limitations on collection, that extension shall expire on the latest of: the last day of such 10-year period, December 31, 2002, or, in the case of an extension in connection with an installment agreement, the 90th day after the end of the period of such extension.

[Law at ¶ 6400 and ¶ 6410. CCH Explanation at ¶ 1286.]

[¶ 10,520]   Act Sec. 3462.   Offers-in-compromise

Senate Committee Report (S. REP. NO. 105-174)

[Code Sec. 7122]
[*This committee report does not reflect changes made by Senate Floor Amendment No. 2380. Selected portions of the Senate Floor Debate are reproduced below.—CCH.*]

Present Law
Section 7122 of the Code permits the IRS to compromise a taxpayer's tax liability. An offer-in-compromise is a provision by the taxpayer to settle unpaid tax accounts for less than the full amount of the assessed balance due. An offer-in-compromise may be submitted for all types of taxes, as well as interest and penalties, arising under the Internal Revenue Code.

There are two bases on which an offer can be made: doubt as to liability for the amount owed and doubt as to ability to pay the amount owed.

A compromise agreement based on doubt as to ability to pay requires the taxpayer to file returns and pay taxes for five years from the date the IRS

accepts the offer. Failure to do so permits the IRS to begin immediate collection actions for the original amount of the liability. The Internal Revenue Manual[35] provides guidelines for revenue officers to determine whether an offer-in-compromise is adequate. An offer is adequate if it reasonably reflects collection potential. Although the revenue officer is instructed to consider the taxpayer's assets and future and present income, the IRM advises that rejection of an offer solely based on narrow asset and income evaluations should be avoided.

Pursuant to the IRM, collection normally is withheld during the period an offer-in-compromise is pending, unless it is determined that the offer is a delaying tactic and collection is in jeopardy.

Reasons for Change
The Committee believes that the ability to compromise tax liability and to make payments of tax liability by installment enhances taxpayer compli-

---

[35] IRM 57(10)(10).1

ance. In addition, the Committee believes that the IRS should be flexible in finding ways to work with taxpayers who are sincerely trying to meet their obligations and remain in the tax system. Accordingly, the Committee believes that the IRS should make it easier for taxpayers to enter into offer-in-compromise agreements, and should do more to educate the taxpaying public about the availability of such agreements.

Explanation of Provision

Rights of taxpayers entering into offers-in-compromise

The provision requires the IRS to develop and publish schedules of national and local allowances that will provide taxpayers entering into an offer-in-compromise with adequate means to provide for basic living expenses. The IRS also will be required to consider the facts and circumstances of a particular taxpayer's case in determining whether the national and local schedules are adequate for that particular taxpayer. If the facts indicate that use of scheduled allowances would be inadequate under the circumstances, the taxpayer would not be limited by the national or local allowances.

The provision prohibits the IRS from rejecting an offer-in-compromise from a low—income taxpayer solely on the basis of the amount of the offer.[36] The provision provides that, in the case of an offer-in-compromise submitted solely on the basis of doubt as to liability, the IRS may not reject the offer merely because the IRS cannot locate the taxpayer's file. The provision prohibits the IRS from requesting a financial statement if the taxpayer makes an offer-in-compromise based solely on doubt as to liability.

Suspend collection by levy while offer-in-compromise is pending

The provision prohibits the IRS from collecting a tax liability by levy (1) during any period that a taxpayer's offer-in-compromise for that liability is being processed, (2) during the 30 days following rejection of an offer, and (3) during any period in which an appeal of the rejection of an offer is being considered. Taxpayers whose offers are rejected and who made good faith revisions of their offers and resubmitted them within 30 days of the rejection or return would be eligible for a continuous period of relief from collection by levy. This prohibition on collection by levy would not apply if the IRS determines that collection is in jeopardy or that the offer was submitted solely to delay collection. The provision provides that the statute of limitations on collection would be tolled for the period during which collection by levy is barred.

Procedures for reviews of rejections of offers-in-compromise and installment agreements

The provision requires that the IRS implement procedures to review all proposed IRS rejections of taxpayer offers-in-compromise and requests for installment agreements prior to the rejection being communicated to the taxpayer. The provision requires the IRS to allow the taxpayer to appeal any rejection of such offer or agreement to the IRS Office of Appeals. The IRS must notify taxpayers of their right to have an appeals officer review a rejected offer-in-compromise on the application form for an offer-in-compromise.

Publication of taxpayer's rights with respect to offers-in-compromise

The provision requires the IRS to publish guidance on the rights and obligations of taxpayers and the IRS relating to offers in compromise, including a compliant spouse's right to apply to reinstate an agreement that would otherwise be revoked due to the nonfiling or nonpayment of the other spouse, providing all payments required under the compromise agreement are current.

Liberal acceptance policy

It is anticipated that the IRS will adopt a liberal acceptance policy for offers-in-compromise to provide an incentive for taxpayers to continue to file tax returns and continue to pay their taxes.

Effective Date

The provision is generally effective for offers-in-compromise submitted after the date of enactment. The provision suspending levy is effective with respect to offers-in-compromise pending on or made after the 60th day after the date of enactment.

Senate Floor Debate for Amendment No. 2380 (144 CONG. REC. 56, S4510)

* * *

Mr. MOYNIHAN.—* * * Mr. President, it was with these challenges in mind that Senator Kerrey and I offered this amendment to briefly delay some of the effective dates in the Finance Committee's IRS Restructuring legislation in order to allow time for the Y2K conversion to be completed. This amendment has been drafted based on Commissioner Rossotti's recommendations, and has been modified after consultations with the Majority.

The amendment would delay the effective date on a list of provisions from date of enactment until after the century date change.

* * *

Conference Committee Report (H.R. CONF. REP. NO. 105-599)

The conference agreement follows the Senate amendment, with the following additions. First, the provision suspending collection by levy while an offer-in-compromise is pending is also expanded to apply while an installment agreement is pending.

Second, the provision authorizes the Secretary to prescribe guidelines for the IRS to determine whether an offer-in-compromise is adequate and

---

[36] This provision does not affect the ability of the IRS to reject an offer in compromise made by a taxpayer (other than a low-income taxpayer) because the amount offered is too low.

should be accepted to resolve a dispute. Accordingly, the conferees expect that the present regulations will be expanded so as to permit the IRS, in certain circumstances, to consider additional factors (i.e., factors other than doubt as to liability or collectibility) in determining whether to compromise the income tax liabilities of individual taxpayers. For example, the conferees anticipate that the IRS will take into account factors such as equity, hardship, and public policy where a compromise of an individual taxpayer's income tax liability would promote effective tax administration. The conferees anticipate that, among other situations, the IRS may utilize this new authority to resolve longstanding cases by forgoing penalties and interest which have accumu-

lated as a result of delay in determining the taxpayer's liability. The conferees believe that the ability to compromise tax liability and to make payments of tax liability by installment enhances taxpayer compliance. In addition, the conferees believe that the IRS should be flexible in finding ways to work with taxpayers who are sincerely trying to meet their obligations and remain in the tax system. Accordingly, the conferees believe that the IRS should make it easier for taxpayers to enter into offer-in-compromise agreements, and should do more to educate the taxpaying public about the availability of such agreements.

[Law at ¶ 6150, ¶ 6280 and ¶ 6540. CCH Explanation at ¶ 1270.]

[¶ 10,525]   Act Sec. 3463.   Notice of deficiency to specify deadlines for filing Tax Court petition

House Committee Report (H.R. REP. NO. 105-364, pt. 1)

[Code Sec. 6213]
Present Law
Taxpayers must file a petition with the Tax Court within 90 days after the deficiency notice is mailed (150 days if the person is outside the United States) (sec. 6213). If the petition is not filed within that time period, the Tax Court does not have jurisdiction to consider the petition.

Reasons for Change
The Committee believes that taxpayers should receive assistance in determining the time period within which they must file a petition in the Tax Court and that taxpayers should be able to rely on the computation of that period by the IRS.

Explanation of Provision
The bill requires that the IRS include on each deficiency notice the date determined by the IRS as the last day on which the taxpayer may file a petition with the Tax Court. It is expected that the last day on which a taxpayer who is outside the United States may file a petition with the Tax Court will be shown as an alternative. The bill provides that a petition filed with the Tax Court by this date shall be treated as timely filed.

Effective Date
The provision would apply to notices mailed after December 31, 1998.

Conference Committee Report (H.R. CONF. REP. NO. 105-599)

Senate Amendment
Same as the House bill.
Conference Agreement
The conference agreement follows the House bill and the Senate amendment.

[Law at ¶ 6190. CCH Explanation at ¶ 1326.]

[¶ 10,530]   Act Sec. 3464.   Refund or credit of overpayments before final determination

House Committee Report (H.R. REP. NO. 105-364, pt. 1)

[Code Sec. 6213 and Code Sec. 6512]
Present Law
A taxpayer may petition the Tax Court for a redetermination of a deficiency within 90 days (150 days if the notice is addressed to a person outside the United States) from the date the notice of deficiency is mailed by the IRS. Generally, the Secretary may not make any assessment or commence any levy or other proceeding to collect the deficiency during such period or, if the taxpayer petitions the Tax Court, until the decision of the Tax Court has become final. The making of any such assessment, or the commencing of any proceeding or levy, during the prohibited period may be enjoined by a proceeding in the proper court (including the Tax Court). However, no authority is provided for ordering the refund of any amount collected within the prohibited period.

If a taxpayer contests a deficiency in the Tax Court, no credit or refund of income tax for the contested taxable year generally may be made, except in accordance with a decision of the Tax Court that has become final. Where the Tax Court determines that an overpayment has been made and a refund is due the taxpayer, and a party appeals a portion of the decision of the Tax Court, no provision exists for the refund of any portion of any overpayment that is not contested in the appeal.

Reasons for Change
The Committee believes that the Secretary should be allowed to refund the uncontested portion of an overpayment of taxes, without regard to whether other portions of the overpayment are contested.

Act Sec. 3464   ¶ 10,530

Explanation of Provision

The bill provides that where a timely petition in respect of a deficiency is filed in the Tax Court, the proper court (including the Tax Court) may order a refund of any amount that was collected within the period during which the Secretary is prohibited from collecting the deficiency by levy or other proceeding.

The bill also allows the refund of that portion of any overpayment determined by the Tax Court to the extent the overpayment is not contested on appeal.

Effective Date

The provision applies on the date of enactment.

Conference Committee Report (H.R. CONF. REP. NO. 105-599)

Senate Amendment

Same as the House bill.

Conference Agreement

The conference agreement follows the House bill and the Senate amendment.

[Law at ¶ 6190 and ¶ 6440. CCH Explanation at ¶ 1321.]

[¶ 10,535] Act Sec. 3465. IRS procedures relating to appeal of examinations and collections

Senate Committee Report (S. REP. NO. 105-174)

[Code Sec. 7123]

Present Law

IRS Appeals operates through regional Appeals offices which are independent of the local District Director and Regional Commissioner's offices. The regional Directors of Appeals report to the National Director of Appeals of the IRS, who reports directly to the Commissioner and Deputy Commissioner. In general, IRS Appeals offices have jurisdiction over both pre-assessment and post-assessment cases. The taxpayer generally has an opportunity to seek Appeals jurisdiction after failing to reach agreement with the Examination function and before filing a petition in Tax Court, after filing a petition in Tax Court (but before litigation), after assessment of certain penalties, after a claim for refund has been rejected by the District Director's office, and after a proposed rejection of an offer-in-compromise in a collection case (Treas. Reg. sec. 601.106(a)(1)).

In certain cases under Coordinated Examination Program procedures, the taxpayer has an opportunity to seek early Appeals jurisdiction over some issues while an examination is still pending on other issues (Rev. Proc. 96-9, 1996-1 C.B. 575). The early referral procedures also apply to employment tax issues on a limited basis (Announcement 97-52).

A mediation or alternative dispute resolution (ADR) process is also available in certain cases. ADR is used at the end of the administrative process as a final attempt to resolve a dispute before litigation. ADR is currently only available for cases with more than $10 million in dispute. ADR processes are also available in bankruptcy cases and cases involving a competent authority determination.

In April 1996, the IRS implemented a Collections Appeals Program within the Appeals function, which allows taxpayers to appeal lien, levy, or seizure actions proposed by the IRS. In January 1997, appeals for installment agreements proposed for termination were added to the program.

The local IRS Offices of Appeals are generally located in the same area as the District Director's Offices. The IRS has videoconferencing capability. The IRS does not have any program to provide for Appeals conferences by videoconferencing techniques.

Reasons for Change

The Committee believes that the IRS should be statutorily bound to follow the procedures that the IRS has developed to facilitate settlement in the IRS Office of Appeals. The Committee also believes that mediation, binding arbitration, early referral to Appeals, and other procedures would foster more timely resolution of taxpayers' problems with the IRS.

In addition, the Committee believes that the ADR process is valuable to the IRS and taxpayers and should be extended to all taxpayers.

The Committee believes that all taxpayers should enjoy convenient access to Appeals, regardless of their locality.

Explanation of Provision

The provision codifies existing IRS procedures with respect to early referrals to Appeals and the Collections Appeals Process. The provision also codifies the existing ADR procedures, as modified by eliminating the dollar threshold.

In addition, the IRS is required to establish a pilot program of binding arbitration for disputes of all sizes. Under the pilot program, binding arbitration must be agreed to by both the taxpayer and the IRS.

The provision requires the IRS to make Appeals officers available on a regular basis in each State, and consider videoconferencing of Appeals conferences for taxpayers seeking appeals in rural or remote areas.

Effective Date

The provision is effective as of the date of enactment.

Conference Committee Report (H.R. CONF. REP. NO. 105-599)

The conference agreement follows the Senate amendment.

[Law at ¶ 6550, ¶ 6560 and ¶ 8120. CCH Explanation at ¶ 1258.]

[¶ 10,540]   Act Sec. 3466.   Application of certain fair debt collection practices

Senate Committee Report (S. REP. NO. 105-174)

[Code Sec. 6304]

[This committee report does not reflect changes made by Senate Floor Amendment No. 2359. Selected portions of the Senate Floor Debate are reproduced below.—CCH]

Present Law

The Fair Debt Collection Practices Act provides a number of rules relating to debt collection practices. Among these are restrictions on communication with the consumer, such as a general prohibition on telephone calls outside the hours of 8:00 a.m. to 9:00 p.m. local time, and prohibitions on harassing or abusing the consumer. In general, these provisions do not apply to the Federal Government.

Reasons for Change

The Committee believes that the IRS should be at least as considerate to taxpayers as private creditors are required to be with their customers.

Accordingly, the Committee believes that it is appropriate to require the IRS to comply with applicable portions of the Fair Debt Collection Practices Act, so that both taxpayers and the IRS are fully aware of these requirements.

Explanation of Provision

The provision makes the restrictions relating to communication with the taxpayer/debtor and the prohibitions on harassing or abusing the debtor applicable to the IRS by incorporating these provisions into the Internal Revenue Code. The restrictions relating to communication with the taxpayer/debtor are not intended to hinder the ability of the IRS to respond to taxpayer inquiries (such as answering telephone calls from taxpayers).

Effective Date

The provision is effective on the date of enactment.

Senate Floor Debate for Amendment No. 2359 (144 CONG. REC. 56, S4455)

* * *

Mr. KERREY.—* * * The second amendment came as a consequence of a witness that we had in the hearings that the chairman held. Mr. Earl Epstein of Philadelphia. He was talking about putting teeth in the provision dealing with violations of· fair debt collection practices. And at the chairman's suggestion, what we have asked for in this study is that the new Treasury inspector general for tax administration also look at this and provide Congress with a report, an annual report outlining any violations of the fair debt collection practices that we have included in this bill.

Mr. Epstein notes, this is likely to result in better attention being paid to collection abuses as "no Commissioner would be happy to report significant abuses, to say nothing of awards for damages [or] for failures to enforce proper authority over collection agents." It is an important amendment. I appreciate the source of it was the chairman's hearings, and I appreciate a chance to work with the chairman to get this worked out.

* * *

Conference Committee Report (H.R. CONF. REP. NO. 105-599)

The conference agreement follows the Senate amendment.

[Law at ¶ 6220. CCH Explanation at ¶ 1262.]

[¶ 10,545]   Act Sec. 3467.   Guaranteed availability of installment agreements

Senate Committee Report (S. REP. NO. 105-174)

[Code Sec. 6159]

Present Law

Section 6159 of the Code authorizes the IRS to enter into written agreements with any taxpayer under which the taxpayer is allowed to pay taxes owed, as well as interest and penalties, in installment payments if the IRS determines that doing so will facilitate collection of the amounts owed. An installment agreement does not reduce the amount of taxes, interest, or penalties owed. However, it does provide for a longer period during which payments may be made during which other

IRS enforcement actions (such as levies or seizures) are held in abeyance. Many taxpayers can request an installment agreement by filing form 9465. This form is relatively simple and does not require the submission of detailed financial statements. The IRS in most instances readily approves these requests if the amounts involved are not large (in general, below $10,000) and if the taxpayer has filed tax returns on time in the past. Some taxpayers are required to submit background information to the IRS substantiating their application. If the request for an installment agreement is approved by the IRS, a user fee of $43 is charged. This user fee is in addition to the tax, interest, and penalties that are owed.

Reasons for Change

The Committee believes that the ability to make payments of tax liability by installment enhances taxpayer compliance. In addition, the Committee believes that the IRS should be flexible in finding ways to work with taxpayers who are sincerely trying to meet their obligations. Accordingly, the Committee believes that the IRS should make it easier for taxpayers to enter into installment agreements.

Explanation of Provision

The provision requires the Secretary to enter an installment agreement, at the taxpayer's option, if:

(1) the liability is $10,000, or less (excluding penalties and interest);

(2) within the previous 5 years, the taxpayer has not failed to file or to pay, nor entered an installment agreement under this provision;

(3) if requested by the Secretary, the taxpayer submits financial statements, and the Secretary determines that the taxpayer is unable to pay the tax due in full;

(4) the installment agreement provides for full payment of the liability within 3 years; and

(5) the taxpayer agrees to continue to comply with the tax laws and the terms of the agreement for the period (up to 3 years) that the agreement is in place.

Effective Date

The provision is effective on the date of enactment.

Conference Committee Report (H.R. CONF. REP. NO. 105-599)

The conference agreement follows the Senate amendment.

[Law at ¶ 6150. CCH Explanation at ¶ 1274.]

[¶ 10,550]   Act Sec. 3468.   Prohibition on requests to taxpayers to waive rights to bring actions

Conference Committee Report (H.R. CONF. REP. NO. 105-599)

[Act Sec. 3468]
Present Law

There is no restriction on the circumstances under which the Government may request a taxpayer to waive the taxpayer's right to sue the United States or one of its employees for any action taken in connection with the tax laws.

House Bill

No provision.

Senate [Floor] Amendment [No. 2375]

The Senate amendment provides that the Government may not request a taxpayer to waive the taxpayer's right to sue the United States or one of its employees for any action taken in connection with the tax laws, unless (1) the taxpayer know-

ingly and voluntarily waives that right, or (2) the request is made to the taxpayer's attorney or other representative.

Effective Date

Date of enactment.

Conference Agreement

The conference agreement follows the Senate amendment. The conferees do not intend this provision to apply to the waiver of claims for attorneys' fees or costs or to the waiver of one or more claims brought in the same administrative or judicial proceeding with other claims that are being settled.

[Law at ¶ 8125. CCH Explanation at ¶ 1133.]

[¶ 10,565]   Act Sec. 3501.   Explanation of joint and several liability

Senate Committee Report (S. REP. NO. 105-174)

[Act Sec. 3501]
Present Law

In general, spouses who file a joint tax return are each fully responsible for the accuracy of the tax return and for the full liability. Spouses who wish to avoid such joint and several liability may file as married persons filing separately. Special rules apply in the case of innocent spouses pursuant to section 6013(e).

Reasons for Change

The Committee believes that married taxpayers need to clearly understand the legal implications of signing a joint return and that it is appropriate for the IRS to provide the information necessary for that understanding.

Explanation of Provision

The provision requires that, no later than 180 days after the date of enactment, the IRS must establish procedures clearly to alert married taxpayers of their joint and several liability on all appropriate tax publications and instructions and of the availability of electing separate liability. It is anticipated that the IRS will make an appropriate cross-reference to these statements near the signature line on appropriate tax forms.

Effective Date

The provision requires that the procedures be established as soon as practicable, but no later than 180 days after the date of enactment.

Conference Committee Report (H.R. CONF. REP. NO. 105-599)

The conference agreement follows the Senate amendment, except that notification must be given of an individual's right to relief under new section 6015 of the Code.

[Law at ¶ 8130. CCH Explanation at ¶ 1294.]

[¶ 10,570] Act Sec. 3502. Explanation of taxpayers' rights in interviews with the IRS

House Committee Report (H.R. REP. NO. 105-364, pt. 1)

[Act Sec. 3502]
Present Law
Prior to or at initial in-person audit interviews, the IRS must explain to taxpayers the audit process and taxpayers' rights under that process (sec. 7521). In addition, prior to or at initial in-person collection interviews, the IRS must explain the collection process and taxpayers' rights under that process. If a taxpayer clearly states during an interview with the IRS that the taxpayer wishes to consult with the taxpayers' representative, the interview must be suspended to afford the taxpayer a reasonable opportunity to consult with the representative.

Reasons for Change
The Committee believes that taxpayers should be more fully informed of their rights to representation in dealings with the IRS and that those rights should be respected.

Explanation of Provision

The bill requires that the IRS rewrite Publication 1 ("Your Rights as a Taxpayer") to more clearly inform taxpayers of their rights (1) to be represented by a representative and (2) if the taxpayer is so represented, that the interview may not proceed without the presence of the representative unless the taxpayer consents.

Effective Date

The addition to Publication 1 must be made not later than 180 days after the date of enactment.

Conference Committee Report (H.R. CONF. REP. NO. 105-599)

Senate Amendment
Same as the House bill.
Conference Agreement
The conference agreement follows the House bill and the Senate amendment.

[Law at ¶ 8135. CCH Explanation at ¶ 1121.]

[¶ 10,575] Act Sec. 3503. Disclosure of criteria for examination selection

House Committee Report (H.R. REP. NO. 105-364, pt. 1)

[Act Sec. 3503]
Present Law
The IRS examines Federal tax returns to determine the correct liability of taxpayers. The IRS selects returns to be audited in a number of ways, such as through a computerized classification system (the discriminant function ("DIF") system).

Reasons for Change
The Committee believes it is important that taxpayers understand the reasons they may be selected for examination.

Explanation of Provision
The bill requires that IRS add to Publication 1 ("Your Rights as a Taxpayer") a statement which sets forth in simple and nontechnical terms the criteria and procedures for selecting taxpayers for examination. The statement must not include any information the disclosure of which would be detrimental to law enforcement. The statement must specify the general procedures used by the IRS, including whether taxpayers are selected for examination on the basis of information in the media or from informants. Drafts of the statement or proposed revisions to the statement are required to be submitted to the House Committee on Ways and Means, the Senate Committee on Finance, and the Joint Committee on Taxation.

Effective Date
The addition to Publication 1 must be made not later than 180 days after the date of enactment.

Conference Committee Report (H.R. CONF. REP. NO. 105-599)

Senate Amendment
Same as the House bill.
Conference Agreement
The conference agreement follows the House bill and the Senate amendment.

[Law at ¶ 8140. CCH Explanation at ¶ 1126.]

Act Sec. 3503 ¶ 10,575

[¶ 10,580] Act Sec. 3504.   Explanation of the appeals and collection process

Senate Committee Report (S. REP. NO. 105-174)

[Act Sec. 3504]

Present Law

There is no statutory requirement that specific notices be given to taxpayers along with the first letter of proposed deficiency that allows the taxpayer an opportunity for administrative review in the IRS Office of Appeals.

Reasons for Change

The Committee believes it is important that taxpayers understand they have a right to have any assessment reviewed by the IRS Office of Appeals, as well as be informed of the steps they must take to obtain that review.

Explanation of Provision

The provision requires that, no later than 180 days after the date of enactment, a description of the entire process from examination through collections, including the assistance available to taxpayers from the Taxpayer Advocate at various points in the process, be provided with the first letter of proposed deficiency that allows the taxpayer an opportunity for administrative review in the IRS Office of Appeals.

Effective Date

The provision requires that the explanation be included as soon as practicable, but no later than 180 days after the date of enactment.

Conference Committee Report (H.R. CONF. REP. NO. 105-599)

The conference agreement follows the Senate amendment.

[Law at ¶ 8145. CCH Explanation at ¶ 1266.]

[¶ 10,585] Act Sec. 3505.   Explanation of reason for refund disallowance

Senate Committee Report (S. REP. NO. 105-174)

[Code Sec. 6402(j)]

Present Law

The Examination Division of the IRS examines claims for refund submitted by taxpayers. The Internal Revenue Manual requires examination or other audit action on refund claims within 30 days after receipt of the claims. The refund claim is preliminarily examined to determine if it should be disallowed because it (1) was untimely filed, (2) was based solely on alleged unconstitutionality of the Revenue Acts, (3) was already waived by the taxpayer as consideration for a settlement, (4) covers a taxable year and issues which were the subject of a final closing agreement or an offer in compromise, or (5) relates to a return closed on the basis of a final order of the Tax Court. In those cases, the taxpayer will receive a form from the IRS stating that the claim for refund cannot be considered. Other cases will be examined as quickly as possible and the disposition of the case, including the reasons for the disallowance or partial disallowance of the refund claim, must be stated in the portion of the revenue agent's report that is sent to the taxpayer.

Reasons for Change

The Committee believes that taxpayers are entitled to an explanation of the reason for the disallowance or partial disallowance of a refund claim so that the taxpayer may appropriately respond to the IRS.

Explanation of Provision

The provision requires the IRS to notify the taxpayer of the specific reasons for the disallowance (or partial disallowance) of the refund claim.

Effective Date

The provision is effective 180 days after the date of enactment.

Conference Committee Report (H.R. CONF. REP. NO. 105-599)

The conference agreement follows the Senate amendment, with technical modifications.

[Law at ¶ 6350. CCH Explanation at ¶ 1451.]

[¶ 10,590]   Act Sec. 3506.   Statements to taxpayers with installment agreements

Senate Committee Report (S. REP. NO. 105-174)

[Act Sec. 3506]
Present Law

A taxpayer entering into an installment agreement to pay tax liabilities due to the IRS must complete a Form 433-D which sets forth the installment amounts to be paid monthly and the total amount of tax due. The IRS does not provide the taxpayer with an annual statement reflecting the amounts paid and the amount due remaining.

Reasons for Change

The Committee believes that taxpayers who enter into an installment agreement should be kept informed of amounts applied towards the outstanding tax liability and amounts remaining due.

Explanation of Provision

The provision requires the IRS to send every taxpayer in an installment agreement an annual statement of the initial balance owed, the payments made during the year, and the remaining balance.

Effective Date

The provision is effective no later than 180 days after the date of enactment.

Conference Committee Report (H.R. CONF. REP. NO. 105-599)

The conference agreement follows the Senate amendment.

Effective Date

July 1, 2000.
[Law at ¶ 8150. CCH Explanation at ¶ 1278.]

[¶ 10,595]   Act Sec. 3507.   Notification of change in tax matters partner

Senate Committee Report (S. REP. NO. 105-174)

[Code Sec. 6231(a)(7)]
Present Law

In general, the tax treatment of items of partnership income, loss, deductions and credits are determined at the partnership level in a unified partnership proceeding rather than in separate proceedings with each partner. In providing notice to taxpayers with respect to partnership proceedings, the IRS relies on information furnished by a party designated as the tax matters partner (TMP) of the partnership. The TMP is required to keep each partner informed of all administrative and judicial proceedings with respect to the partnership (sec. 6233(g)). Under certain circumstances, the IRS may require the resignation of the incumbent TMP and designate another partner as the TMP of a partnership (sec. 6231(a)(7)).

Reasons for Change

The Committee is concerned that, in cases where the IRS designates the TMP, that the other partners may be unaware of such designation.

Explanation of Provision

The provision requires the IRS to notify all partners of any resignation of the tax matters partner that is required by the IRS, and to notify the partners of any successor tax matters partner.

Effective Date

The provision applies to selections of tax matters partners made by the Secretary after the date of enactment.

Conference Committee Report (H.R. CONF. REP. NO. 105-599)

The conference agreement follows the Senate amendment.

[Law at ¶ 6210. CCH Explanation at ¶ 1136.]

[¶ 10,600]   Act Sec. 3508.   Conditions under which taxpayers' returns may be disclosed

Conference Committee Report (H.R. CONF. REP. NO. 105-599)

[Act Sec. 3508]
Present Law

There is no requirement that the general tax forms instruction booklets include a description of conditions under which tax return information may be disclosed outside the IRS (including to States).

House Bill

No provision.

Senate [Floor] Amendment [No. 2377]

The Senate amendment requires that general tax forms instruction booklets include a description of conditions under which tax return information may be disclosed outside the IRS (including to States).

Effective Date

Date of enactment.

Act Sec. 3508   ¶ 10,600

Conference Agreement

The conference agreement follows the Senate amendment with technical modifications; the conferees consider the statement currently contained in the general tax forms instruction booklets to be sufficient to fulfill the requirements of this provision.

[Law at ¶ 8155. CCH Explanation at ¶ 864.]

[¶ 10,605]   Act Sec. 3509.   Disclosure of Chief Counsel advice

Conference Committee Report (H.R. CONF. REP. NO. 105-599)

[Code Sec. 6110]
Present Law

Section 6110 of the Code provides for the public inspection of written determinations, i.e., rulings, determination letters, and technical advice memoranda. The IRS issues annual revenue procedures setting forth the procedures for requests for these various forms of written determinations and participation in the formulation of such determinations.[21] Under section 6110 and the regulations promulgated thereunder, the taxpayer who is the subject of a written determination can participate in the redaction of the documents to ensure that the taxpayer's privacy is protected and that sensitive private information is removed before the determination is publicly disclosed. In the event there is disagreement as to the information to be deleted, the section provides for litigation in the courts to resolve such disagreements.

One of the Office of Chief Counsel's major roles is to advise Internal Revenue Service personnel on legal matters at all stages of case development. The Office of Chief Counsel thus issues various forms of written legal advice to field agents of the IRS and to its own field attorneys that do not fall within the current definition of "written determination" under section 6110. Traditionally, field Counsel offices provided most of the assistance to the IRS, usually at IRS field offices, but since 1988, the National Office of Chief Counsel has been rendering more assistance to field Counsel and IRS offices. National Office of Chief Counsel assistance in taxpayer-specific cases is generally called "field service advice." The taxpayers who are the subject of field service advice generally do not participate in the process, leading some tax commentators to express concern that the field service advice process was displacing the technical advice process.

There has been controversy as to whether the Office of Chief Counsel must release forms of advice other than written determinations pursuant to the Freedom of Information Act (FOIA). In Tax Analysts v. IRS,[22] the D.C. Circuit held that the legal analysis portions of field service advice created in the context of specific taxpayers' cases are not "return information," as defined by section 6103(b)(2), and must be released under FOIA. The court also found that portions of field service advice issued in docketed cases may be withheld as privileged attorney work product. However, some issues remain outstanding. Although the extent to which such materials must be released is still in dispute, it is clear that they are not expressly covered by section 6110. As a consequence, there exists no mechanism by which taxpayers may participate in the administrative process of redacting their private information from such documents or to resolve disagreements in court.

House Bill

No provision.

Senate Amendment

No provision.

Conference Agreement

In general

The conferees believe that written documents issued by the National Office of Chief Counsel to its field components and field agents of the IRS should be subject to public release in a manner similar to technical advice memoranda or other written determinations. In this way, all taxpayers can be assured of access to the "considered view of the Chief Counsel's national office on significant tax issues."[23] Creating a structured mechanism by which these types of legal memoranda are open to public inspection will increase the public's confidence that the tax system operates fairly and in an even-handed manner with respect to all taxpayers.

As part of making these documents public, however, the privacy of the taxpayer who is the subject of the advice must be protected. Any procedure for making such advice public must therefore include adequate safeguards for taxpayers whose privacy interests are implicated. There should be a mechanism for taxpayer participation in the deletion of any private information. There should also be a process whereby appropriate governmental privileges may be asserted by the IRS and contested by the public or the taxpayer.

The provision amends section 6110 of the Code, establishing a structured process by which the IRS will make certain work products, designated as "Chief Counsel Advice," open to public inspection on an ongoing basis. It is designed to protect taxpayer privacy while allowing the public inspection of these documents in a manner generally consistent with the mechanism of section 6110 for the public inspection of written determinations. In general, the provision operates by establishing that Chief Counsel Advice are written determinations subject to the public inspection provisions of section 6110.

Definition of Chief Counsel Advice

For purposes of this provision, Chief Counsel Advice is written advice or instruction prepared and issued by any national office component of the Office of Chief Counsel to field employees of the Service or the Office of Chief Counsel that convey certain legal interpretations or positions of the IRS or the Office of Chief Counsel concerning existing or former revenue provisions. For these

---

[21] See e.g., Rev. Procs. 98-1 and 98-2.
[22] 117 F.3d 607 (D.C. Cir. 1997).

[23] 117 F.3d at 617.

purposes, the term "revenue provisions" includes, without limitation: the Internal Revenue Code itself; regulations, revenue rulings, revenue procedures, or other administrative interpretations or guidance, whether published or unpublished (including, for example, other Chief Counsel Advice); tax treaties; and court decisions and opinions. Chief Counsel Advice also includes legal interpretations of State law, foreign law, or other federal law relating to the assessment or collection of liabilities under revenue provisions.

Chief Counsel Advice may interpret or set forth policies concerning the internal revenue laws either in general or as applied to specific taxpayers or groups of specific taxpayers. The definition is, however, not meant to include advice written with respect to nontax matters, including but not limited to employment law, conflicts of interest, or procurement matters.

The new statutory category of written determination encompasses certain existing categories of advisory memoranda or instructions written by the National Office of Chief Counsel to field personnel of either the IRS or the Office of Chief Counsel. Specifically, Chief Counsel Advice includes field service advice, technical assistance to the field, service center advice, litigation guideline memoranda, tax litigation bulletins, general litigation bulletins, and criminal tax bulletins. The definition applies not only to the case-specific field service advice issued from the offices of the Associate Chief Counsel (International), Associate Chief Counsel (Employee Benefits and Exempt Organizations), and the Assistant Chief Counsel (Field Service), which were at issue in the Tax Analysts decision, but any case-specific or non-case-specific written advice or instructions issued by the National Office of Chief Counsel to field personnel of either the IRS or the Office of Chief Counsel.

Moreover, Chief Counsel Advice includes any documents created subsequent to the enactment of this provision that satisfy the general statutory definition, regardless of their name or designation. Chief Counsel Advice also includes any such advice or instruction even if the organizations currently issuing them are reorganized or reconstituted as part of any IRS restructuring.

The new subsection covers written advice "issued" to field personnel of either the IRS or the Office of Chief Counsel in its final form. With respect to Chief Counsel Advice, issuance occurs when the Chief Counsel Advice has been approved within the national office component of the office of Chief Counsel in which the Chief Counsel Advice was proposed, signed by the person authorized to do so (usually the Assistant Chief Counsel or a Branch Chief), and sent to the field. Chief Counsel Advice does not include written recordations of informal telephonic advice by the National Office of Chief Counsel to field personnel of either the IRS or the Office of Chief Counsel. Drafts of Chief Counsel Advice sent to the field for review, criticism, or comment prior to approval within the National Office also need not be made public. However, Chief Counsel Advice may be treated as issued even if supplemental advice is contemplated. The Secretary is expected to issue regulations to clarify the distinction between issuance as it applies to Chief Counsel Advice and as it applies to other documents disclosed under section 6110.

The provision also allows the Secretary to promulgate regulations providing that additional types of advice or instruction issued by the Office of Chief Counsel (or components of the Office of Chief Counsel, such as regional or local Counsel offices) will be treated as Chief Counsel Advice and subject to public inspection pursuant to this provision. No inference shall be drawn from the failure of the Secretary to treat additional types of advice or instruction as Chief Counsel Advice in determining whether such advice or instruction is to be disclosed under FOIA.

As with other written determinations, Chief Counsel Advice may not be used or cited as precedent, except as the Secretary otherwise establishes by regulation.

Redaction process

Under this provision, Chief Counsel Advice will be redacted prior to their public release in a manner similar to that provided for private letter rulings, technical advice memoranda, and determination letters. Specific taxpayers or groups of specific taxpayers who are the subject of Chief Counsel Advice will be afforded the opportunity to participate in the process of redacting the Chief Counsel Advice prior to their public release.

In addition, the new provision affords additional protection for certain governmental interests implicated by Chief Counsel Advice. Information may be redacted from Chief Counsel Advice under subsections (b) and (c) of the Freedom of Information Act, 5 U.S.C. sec. 552 (except, with respect to 5 U.S.C. sec. 552(b)(3), only material required to be withheld under a Federal statute, other than title 26, may be redacted), as those provisions have been, or shall be, interpreted by the courts of the United States. For those deletions that are discretionary, such as those under FOIA section 552(b)(5), it is expected that the Office of Chief Counsel and the IRS will apply any discretionary standards applicable to federal agencies in general or the Chief Counsel or the IRS in particular.[24]

Under new section 6110(i), as with current section 6110(c)(1), identifying details consisting of names, addresses, and any other information that the Secretary determines could identify any person, including the taxpayer's representative, will be redacted, after the participation of the taxpayer in the redaction process. In some situations, information included in a Chief Counsel Advice (other than a name or address) may not identify a person as of the time the advice is made open to public inspection, but that information, together with information that is expected to be disclosed by another source at a later date, will serve to identify a person. Consequently, in deciding whether a Chief Counsel Advice contains identify-

---

[24] The current standards for the exercise of such discretion are set forth in the Internal Revenue Manual (part 1230, section 293(2)) and the Attorney General's October 4, 1993, Memorandum for Heads of Departments and Agencies.

Act Sec. 3509 ¶ 10,605

ing information, the Secretary is to take into account information that is available to the public at the time that the advice is made open to public inspection as well as information that is expected to be publicly available from other sources within a reasonable time after the Chief Counsel Advice is made open to public inspection. Generally, it is intended that the standard the IRS is to use in determining whether information will identify a person is a standard of a reasonable person generally knowledgeable with respect to the appropriate community. The standard is not, however, to be one of a person with inside knowledge of the particular taxpayer.

As under current section 6110, taxpayers who are the subject of Chief Counsel Advice, as well as members of the public, will be afforded the opportunity to challenge judicially the redaction determinations by the Secretary.

Relation to present law

The public inspection of Chief Counsel Advice is to be accomplished only pursuant to the rules and procedures set forth in section 6110, as amended, and not under those of any other provision of law, such as FOIA. This provision is not intended to affect the disclosure under FOIA, or under any other provision of law, of any documents not included within the definition of Chief Counsel Advice in new sections 6110(i)(1) and (i)(2). The only FOIA exemption affected by this provision is 5 U.S.C. section 552(b)(3), to the extent that it incorporates section 6103 of the

Code. The timetable and the manner in which existing Chief Counsel Advice may ultimately be open to public inspection shall be governed by this provision, except that the provision is inapplicable to Chief Counsel Advice that any federal district court has, prior to the date of enactment, ordered be disclosed. Disclosure of any documents that are subject to such a court order is to proceed pursuant to the order rather than this provision. Finally, no inference is intended with respect to the disclosure, under FOIA or any other provision of law, of any other documents produced by the Office of Chief Counsel that are not included in the definition of Chief Counsel Advice.

Effective Date

The provision applies to Chief Counsel Advice issued more than ninety days after enactment. In addition, the provision contains certain rules governing disclosure of any document fitting the definition of Chief Counsel Advice issued after 1985 and before 90 days after the date of enactment by the offices of the associate chief counsel for domestic, employee benefits and exempt organizations, and international. It sets forth a schedule for the IRS to release such Chief Counsel Advice over a six year period after the date of enactment. Finally, additional advice or instruction that the Secretary determines by regulations to treat as Chief Counsel Advice shall be made public pursuant to this provision in accordance with the effective dates set forth in such regulations.

[Law at ¶ 6140. CCH Explanation at ¶ 892.]

[¶ 10,625] Act Sec. 3601. Low-income taxpayer clinics

House Committee Report (H.R. REP. NO. 105-364, pt. 1)

[Code Sec. 7526]

Present Law

There are no provisions in present law providing for assistance to clinics that assist low-income taxpayers.

Reasons for Change

The Committee believes that the provision of tax services by accredited nominal fee clinics to low-income individuals and those for whom English is a second language will improve compliance with the Federal tax laws and should be encouraged.

Explanation of Provision

The Secretary shall make matching grants for the development, expansion, or continuation of certain low-income taxpayer clinics. Eligible clinics are those that charge no more than a nominal fee to either represent low-income taxpayers in controversies with the IRS or provide tax information to individuals for whom English is a second language. The term "clinic" includes (1) a clinical program at an accredited law school in which students represent low-income taxpayers, and (2) an organization exempt from tax under Code section 501(c) which either represents low-income taxpayers or provides referral to qualified representatives.

A clinic is treated as representing low-income taxpayers if at least 90 percent of the taxpayers represented by the clinic have incomes which do not exceed 250 percent of the poverty level and amounts in controversy of $25,000 or less.

The aggregate amount of grants to be awarded each year is limited to $3,000,000. No taxpayer clinic could receive more than $100,000 per year. The clinic must provide matching funds on a dollar-for-dollar basis. Matching funds may include the allocable portion of both the salary (including fringe benefits) of individuals performing services for the clinic and clinic equipment costs, but not general institutional overhead.

The following criteria are to be considered in making awards: (1) number of taxpayers served by the clinic, including the number of taxpayers in the geographical area for whom English is a second language; (2) the existence of other taxpayer clinics serving the same population; (3) the quality of the program; and (4) alternative funding sources available to the clinic.

Effective Date

The provision is effective on the date of enactment.

¶ 10,625   Act Sec. 3601

Conference Committee Report (H.R. Conf. Rep. No. 105-599)

The conference agreement follows the House bill, except that the overall limit is $6,000,000 and clinical programs at accredited business schools or accounting schools would be eligible for grants.

[Law at ¶ 6750. CCH Explanation at ¶ 851.]

[¶ 10,635]   Act Sec. 3701.   Cataloging complaints

House Committee Report (H.R. Rep. No. 105-364, pt. 1)

[Act Sec. 3701]
Present Law

The IRS is required to make an annual report to the Congress, beginning in 1997, on all categories of instances involving allegations of misconduct by IRS employees, arising either from internally identified cases or from taxpayer or third-party initiated complaints.[44] The report must identify the nature of the misconduct or complaint, the number of instances received by category, and the disposition of the complaints.

Reasons for Change

The Committee believes that all allegations of misconduct by IRS employees must be carefully investigated. The Committee also believes that the annual report to Congress will help develop a public perception that the IRS takes such allegations of misconduct seriously. The Committee is concerned that, in the absence of records detailing taxpayer complaints of misconduct on an individual employee basis, the IRS will not be able to adequately investigate such allegations or properly prepare the required report.

Explanation of Provision

The bill requires that, in collecting data for this report, records of taxpayer complaints of misconduct by IRS employees shall be maintained on an individual employee basis. These individual records are not to be listed in the report, but they will be useful in preparing the report. The Committee intends that these records be used in evaluating individual employees.

Effective Date

The requirement is effective on the date of enactment.

Conference Committee Report (H.R. Conf. Rep. No. 105-599)

Senate Amendment
Same as the House bill.

Conference Agreement
The conference agreement follows the House bill and the Senate amendment.

Effective Date
January 1, 2000.
[Law at ¶ 8160. CCH Explanation at ¶ 886.]

[¶ 10,640]   Act Sec. 3702.   Archive of records of Internal Revenue Service

House Committee Report (H.R. Rep. No. 105-364, pt. 1)

[Code Sec. 6103]
Present Law

The IRS is obligated to transfer agency records to the National Archives and Records Administration ("NARA") for retention or disposal. The IRS is also obligated to protect confidential taxpayer records from disclosure. These two obligations have created conflict between NARA and the IRS. Under present law, the IRS determines whether records contain taxpayer information. Once the IRS has made that determination, NARA is not permitted to examine those records. NARA has expressed concern that the IRS may be using the disclosure prohibition to improperly conceal agency records with historical significance.

IRS obligation to archive records

The IRS, like all other Federal agencies, must create, maintain, and preserve agency records in accordance with section 3101 of title 44 of the United States Code. NARA is the Government agency responsible for overseeing the management of the records of the Federal government.[45] Federal agencies are required to deposit significant and historical records with NARA.[46] The head of each Federal agency must also establish safeguards against the removal or loss of records.[47]

Authority of NARA

NARA is authorized, under the Federal Records Act, to establish standards for the selective retention of records of continuing value.[48] NARA has the statutory authority to inspect records management practices of Federal agencies and to make recommendations for improvement.[49] The head of each Federal agency must submit to NARA a list of records to be destroyed and a schedule for such destruction.[50] NARA examines

---

[44] Section 1211 of the Taxpayer Bill of Rights 2 (Public Law 104-168; July 30, 1996).
[45] 44 U.S.C. sec. 2904.
[46] 5 U.S.C. sec. 552a(b)(6).

[47] 44 U.S.C. sec. 3105.
[48] 44 U.S.C. sec. 2905.
[49] 44 U.S.C. sec. 2904(c)(7).
[50] 44 U.S.C. sec. 3303.

the list to determine if any of the records on the list have sufficient administrative, legal research, or other value to warrant their continued preservation. In many cases, the description of the record on the list is sufficient for NARA to make the determination. For example, NARA does not need to inspect Presidential tax returns to determine that they have historical value and should be retained. In some cases, NARA may find it helpful to examine a particular record. NARA has general authority to inspect records solely for the purpose of making recommendations for the improvement of records management practices.[51] However, tax returns and return information can only be disclosed under the authority provided in section 6103 of the Internal Revenue Code. There is no exception to the disclosure prohibition for records management inspection by NARA.[52]

In connection with its evaluation of the records management system of the IRS, NARA noted several instances where the disclosure prohibitions of Code section 6103 complicated their review of many IRS records.

NARA is also responsible for the custody, use and withdrawal of records transferred to it.[53] Statutory provisions that restrict public access to the records in the hands of the agency from which the records were transferred also apply to NARA. Thus, if a confidential record, such as a Presidential tax return, is transferred to NARA for archival storage, NARA is not permitted to disclose it. In general, the application of such restrictions to records in the hands of NARA expire after the records have been in existence for 30 years.[54] The issue of whether the specific disclosure prohibition of section 6103 takes precedence over the general 30-year expiration of restrictions generally applicable to records in the hands of NARA has not been addressed by a court, but an informal advisory opinion from the Office of Legal Counsel of the Attorney General concluded that the 30-year expiration provision would not reach records subject to section 6103.[55]

Confidentiality requirements

The IRS must preserve the confidentiality of taxpayer information contained in Federal income tax returns. Such information may not be disclosed except as authorized under Code section 6103. Section 6103 was substantially revised in 1976 to address Congress' concern that tax information was being used by Federal agencies in pursuit of objectives unrelated to administration and enforcement of the tax laws. Congress believed that the widespread use of tax information by agencies other than the IRS could adversely affect the willingness of taxpayers to comply vol-untarily with the tax laws and could undermine the country's self-assessment tax system.[56] Section 6103 does not authorize the disclosure of confidential return information to NARA.

Section 6103 restricts the disclosure of returns and return information only. Return means any tax or information return, declaration of estimated tax, or claim for refund, including schedules and attachments thereto, filed with the IRS. Return information includes the taxpayer's name; nature and source or amount of income; and whether the taxpayer's return is under investigation. Section 6103(b)(2) provides that "nothing in any other provision of law shall be construed to require the disclosure of standards used or to be used for the selection of returns for examination, or data used or to be used for determining such standards, if the Secretary determines that such disclosure will seriously impair assessment, collection, or enforcement under the internal revenue laws." Section 6103 does not restrict the disclosure of other records required to be maintained by the IRS, such as records documenting agency policy, programs and activities, and agency histories. Such records are required to be made available to the public under the Freedom of Information Act ("FOIA").[57]

The Internal Revenue Code prohibits disclosure of tax returns and return information, except to the extent specifically authorized by the Internal Revenue Code (sec. 6103). Unauthorized disclosure is a felony punishable by a fine not exceeding $5,000 or imprisonment of not more than five years, or both (sec. 7213). An action for civil damages also may be brought for unauthorized disclosure (sec. 7431).

Reasons for Change

The Committee believes that it is appropriate to permit disclosure to NARA for purposes of scheduling records for destruction or retention, while at the same time preserving the confidentiality of taxpayer information in those documents.

Explanation of Provision

The bill provides an exception to the disclosure rules to require IRS to disclose IRS records to officers or employees of NARA, upon written request from the Archivist, for purposes of the appraisal of such records for destruction or retention in the National Archives. The present-law prohibitions on and penalties for disclosure of tax information will generally apply to NARA.

Effective Date

The provision is effective for requests made by the Archivist after the date of enactment.

---

[51] 44 U.S.C. sec. 2906.

[52] *American Friends Service Committee v. Webster*, 720 F.2d 29 (D.C. Cir. 1983).

[53] 44 U.S.C. sec. 2108.

[54] 44 U.S.C. sec. 2108.

[55] Department of Justice, Office of Legal Counsel, Memorandum to Richard K. Willard, Assistant Attorney General (Civil Division) (February 27, 1986).

[56] S. Rept. 94-938, p. 317 (1976).

[57] FOIA does not require disclosure of records or information that would frustrate law enforcement efforts. 5 U.S.C sec. 552(b)(7).

Conference Committee Report (H.R. CONF. REP. NO. 105-599)

Senate Amendment
Same as the House bill.

Conference Agreement
The conference agreement follows the House bill and the Senate amendment.

[Law at ¶ 6110. CCH Explanation at ¶ 881.]

[¶ 10,645]   Act Sec. 3703.   Payment of taxes

House Committee Report (H.R. REP. NO. 105-364, pt. 1)

[Act Sec. 3703]
Present Law

The Code provides that it is lawful for the Secretary to accept checks or money orders as payment for taxes, to the extent and under the conditions provided in regulations prescribed by the Secretary (sec. 6311). Those regulations[58] state that checks or money orders should be made payable to the Internal Revenue Service.

Reasons for Change

The Committee believes that it more appropriate that checks be made payable to the United States Treasury.

Explanation of Provision

The bill requires the Secretary or his delegate to establish such rules, regulations, and procedures as are necessary to allow payment of taxes by check or money order to be made payable to the United States Treasury

Effective Date

The provision is effective on the date of enactment.

Conference Committee Report (H.R. CONF. REP. NO. 105-599)

Senate Amendment
Same as the House bill.

Conference Agreement
The conference agreement follows the House bill and the Senate amendment.

[Law at ¶ 8165. CCH Explanation at ¶ 893.]

[¶ 10,650]   Act Sec. 3704.   Clarification of authority of Secretary relating to the making of elections

House Committee Report (H.R. REP. NO. 105-364, pt. 1)

[Code Sec. 7805(d)]
Present Law

Except as otherwise provided, elections provided by the Code are to be made in such manner as the Secretary shall by regulations or forms prescribe.

Reasons for Change

The Committee wishes to eliminate any confusion over the type of guidance in which the Secretary may prescribe the manner of making any election.

Explanation of Provision

The provision clarifies that, except as otherwise provided, the Secretary may prescribe the manner of making of any election by any reasonable means.

Effective Date

The provision is effective as of the date of enactment.

Conference Committee Report (H.R. CONF. REP. NO. 105-599)

Senate Amendment
Same as the House bill.

Conference Agreement
The conference agreement follows the House bill and the Senate amendment.

[Law at ¶ 6880. CCH Explanation at ¶ 895.]

---

[58] Treas. Reg. Sec. 301.6311-1(a)(1)

[¶ 10,655]   Act Sec. 3705.   IRS employee contacts

Senate Committee Report (S. REP. NO. 105-174)

[Act Sec. 3705]

[*This committee report does not reflect changes made by Senate Floor Amendment Nos. 2370 and 2371. Senate Floor Amendment No. 2370 (144 Cong. Rec. 56, S4474) and Senate Floor Amendment No. 2371 (144 Cong. Rec. 56, S4474) were passed with nominal debate.—CCH.*]

Present Law

The IRS sends many different notices to taxpayers. Some (but not all) of these notices contain a name and telephone number of an IRS employee who the taxpayer may call if the taxpayer has any questions.

Reasons for Change

The Committee believes that it is important that taxpayers receive prompt answers to their questions about their tax liability. Many taxpayers report frustration because they cannot determine the appropriate IRS employee to contact for information.

Explanation of Provision

The provision requires that all IRS notices and correspondence contain a name and telephone number of an IRS employee whom the taxpayer may call. In addition, to the extent practicable and where it is advantageous to the taxpayer, the IRS should assign one employee to handle a matter with respect to a taxpayer until that matter is resolved.

Effective Date

The provision is effective 60 days after the date of enactment.

Conference Committee Report (H.R. CONF. REP. NO. 105-599)

Senate Amendment

The Senate amendment requires that all IRS notices and correspondence contain a name and telephone number of an IRS employee whom the taxpayer may call. In addition, to the extent practicable and advantageous to the taxpayer, the IRS should assign one employee to handle a matter with respect to a taxpayer until that matter is resolved.

The Senate amendment also requires that all IRS telephone helplines provide an option for any taxpayer questions to be answered in Spanish.

Further, the Senate amendment requires that all IRS telephone helplines provide an option for any taxpayer to talk to a live person in addition to hearing a recorded message. That person can then direct the taxpayer to other IRS personnel who can provide understandable information to the taxpayer.

Effective Date

Effective January 1, 2000.

Conference Agreement

The conference agreement generally follows the Senate amendment, with modifications. Any manually generated correspondence received by a taxpayer from the IRS must include in a prominent manner the name, telephone number, and unique identifying number of an IRS employee the taxpayer may contact with respect to the correspondence. Any other correspondence or notice received by a taxpayer from the IRS must include in a prominent manner a telephone number that the taxpayer may contact. An IRS employee must give a taxpayer during a telephone or personal contact the employee's name and unique identifying number. The requirements pertaining to a unique identifying number are effective six months after the date of enactment.

[Law at ¶ 8170. CCH Explanation at ¶ 1166 and ¶ 1167.]

[¶ 10,660]   Act Sec. 3706.   Use of pseudonyms by IRS employees

Senate Committee Report (S. REP. NO. 105-174)

[Act Sec. 3706]

Present Law

The Federal Service Impasses Panel has ruled that if an employee believes that use of the employee's last name only will identify the employee due to the unique nature of the employee's last name, and/or nature of the office locale, then the employee may "register" a pseudonym with the employee's supervisor.

Reasons for Change

The Committee is concerned that IRS employees may use pseudonyms in inappropriate circumstances.

Explanation of Provision

The provision provides that an IRS employee may use a pseudonym only if (1) adequate justification, such as protecting personal safety, for using the pseudonym was provided by the employee as part of the employee's request and (2) management has approved the request to use the pseudonym prior to its use.

Effective Date

The provision is effective with respect to requests made after the date of enactment.

Conference Committee Report (H.R. CONF. REP. NO. 105-599)

The conference agreement follows the Senate amendment.

[Law at ¶ 8175. CCH Explanation at ¶ 1176.]

[¶ 10,665]   Act Sec. 3707.   Illegal tax protester designations

Senate Committee Report (S. REP. NO. 105-174)

[Act Sec. 3707]

[*This committee report does not reflect changes made by Senate Floor Amendment No. 2380. Selected portions of the Senate Floor Debate are reproduced below.—CCH.*]

Present Law

The IRS designates individuals who meet certain criteria as "illegal tax protesters" in the IRS Master File.

Reasons for Change

The Committee is concerned that taxpayers may be stigmatized by a designation as an "illegal tax protester."

Explanation of Provision

The provision prohibits the use by the IRS of the "illegal tax protester" designation. Any extant designation in the individual master file (the main computer file) must be removed and any other extant designation (such as on paper records that have been archived) must be disregarded. The IRS is, however, permitted to designate appropriate taxpayers as nonfilers. The IRS must remove the nonfiler designation once the taxpayer has filed valid tax returns for two consecutive years and paid all taxes shown on those returns.

Effective Date

The provision is effective on the date of enactment.

Senate Floor Debate for Amendment No. 2380 (144 CONG. REC. 56, S4510)

* * *

Mr. MOYNIHAN.—* * * Mr. President, it was with these challenges in mind that Senator Kerrey and I offered this amendment to briefly delay some of the effective dates in the Finance Committee's IRS Restructuring legislation in order to allow time for the Y2K conversion to be completed. This amendment has been drafted based on Commissioner Rossotti's recommendations, and has been modified after consultations with the Majority.

The amendment would delay the effective date on a list of provisions from date of enactment until after the century date change.

* * *

Conference Committee Report (H.R. CONF. REP. NO. 105-599)

The conference agreement follows the Senate amendment. While this provision prohibits the use by the IRS of the "illegal tax protester" designation, it does allow the IRS to continue its current practice of tracking "potentially dangerous taxpayers." The conferees recognize the potential hazards connected with the assessment and collection of taxes, and this provision is not intended to jeopardize the safety of IRS employees. Accordingly, if the IRS needs to implement additional procedures, such as the maintenance of appropriate records, in connection with this provision so as to ensure IRS employees' safety, it has the authority to do so.

[Law at ¶ 8180. CCH Explanation at ¶ 891.]

[¶ 10,670]   Act Sec. 3708.   Provision of confidential information to Congress by whistleblowers

Senate Committee Report (S. REP. NO. 105-174)

[Code Sec. 6103(f)]

Present Law

Tax return information generally may not be disclosed, except as specifically provided by statute. The Secretary of the Treasury may furnish tax return information to the Committee on Finance, the Committee on Ways and Means and the Joint Committee on Taxation upon a written request from the chairmen of such committees. If the information can be associated with, or otherwise identify, directly or indirectly, a particular taxpayer, the information may by furnished to the committee only while sitting in closed executive session unless such taxpayer otherwise consents in writing to such disclosure.

Reasons for Change

The Committee believes that it is appropriate to have the opportunity to receive tax return information directly from whistleblowers.

Explanation of Provision

The provision allows any person who is (or was) authorized to receive confidential tax return information to disclose tax return information directly to the Chairman of the Senate Committee on Finance, the Chairman of the House Committee on Ways and Means or the Chief of Staff of the

Joint Committee on Taxation provided: (1) such disclosure is for the purpose of disclosing an incident of IRS employee or taxpayer abuse, and (2) the Chairman of the committee to which the information will be disclosed gives prior approval for the disclosure in writing.

Effective Date

The provision is effective on the date of enactment.

Conference Committee Report (H.R. CONF. REP. NO. 105-599)

The conference agreement provides that any person (i.e., a whistleblower) who otherwise has or had access to any return or return information under section 6103 may disclose such return or return information to the House Ways and Means Committee, the Senate Finance Committee, or the Joint Committee on Taxation or to any individual authorized by one of those committees to receive or inspect any return or return information if such person (the whistleblower) believes such return or return information may relate to evidence of possible misconduct, maladministration, or taxpayer abuse. Disclosure to one of these committees could be made either to the Chairman or to the full committee (sitting in closed executive session), but would not be permitted to be made to an individual Member of Congress (unless explicitly authorized as an agent). No inference is intended that such whistleblower disclosures are not permitted under present law.

Effective Date

Date of enactment.

[Law at ¶ 6110. CCH Explanation at ¶ 863.]

[¶ 10,675] Act Sec. 3709. Listing of local IRS telephone numbers and addresses

Senate Committee Report (S. REP. NO. 105-174)

[Act Sec. 3709]
Present Law

The IRS is not statutorily required to publish the local telephone number or address of its local offices, and generally does not do so.

Reasons for Change

The Committee believes that every taxpayer should have convenient access to the IRS.

Explanation of Provision

The provision requires the IRS, as soon as is practicable but no later than 180 days after the date of enactment, to publish addresses and local telephone numbers of local IRS offices in appropriate local telephone directories.

Effective Date

The provision is effective on the date of enactment.

Conference Committee Report (H.R. CONF. REP. NO. 105-599)

The conference agreement generally follows the Senate amendment. The conferees intend that (1) the IRS not be required to publish in more than one directory in any local area and (2) publication in alternate language directories is permissible.

Effective Date

As soon as is practicable.

[Law at ¶ 8185. CCH Explanation at ¶ 1171.]

[¶ 10,680] Act Sec. 3710. Identification of return preparers

Senate Committee Report (S. REP. NO. 105-174)

[Code Sec. 6109(a)]
Present Law
Any return or claim for refund prepared by an income tax return preparer must bear the social security number of the return preparer, if such preparer is an individual (sec. 6109(a)).

Reasons for Change
The Committee is concerned that inappropriate use might be made of a preparer's social security number.

Explanation of Provision

The provision authorizes the IRS to approve alternatives to Social Security numbers to identify tax return preparers.

Effective Date

The provision is effective on the date of enactment.

Conference Committee Report (H.R. CONF. REP. NO. 105-599)

The conference agreement follows the Senate amendment.

[Law at ¶ 6130. CCH Explanation at ¶ 865.]

[¶ 10,685]   Act Sec. 3711.   Offset of past-due, legally enforceable State income tax obligations against overpayments

Senate Committee Report (S. REP. NO. 105-174)

[Code Sec. 6402(e)]

[This committee report does not reflect changes made by Senate Floor Amendment No. 2368. Senate Floor Amendment No. 2368 (144 Cong. Rec. 56, S4468) was passed with nominal debate.—CCH.]

Present Law

Overpayments of Federal tax may be used to pay past-due child support and debts owed to Federal agencies (sec. 6402), without the consent of the taxpayer. Such amount for past-due child support may be paid directly to a State. Present law provides that offsets are made in the following priority: (1) child support; and (2) other Federal debts, in the order in which such debts accrued.

Reasons for Change

The Committee believes that it is appropriate to permit States to collect past-due, legally enforceable income tax debts that have been re-duced to judgment from Federal tax overpayments.

Explanation of Provision

The provision permits States to participate in the IRS refund offset program for past-due, legally enforceable State income tax debts that have been reduced to judgment, providing the person making the Federal tax overpayment has shown on the return establishing the overpayment an address that is within the State seeking the tax offset. The offset applies after the offsets provided in present law for internal revenue tax liabilities, past-due support, and past-due, legally enforceable obligations owed a Federal agency. The offset occurs before the designation of any refund toward future Federal tax liability.

Effective Date

The provision applies to Federal income tax refunds payable after December 31, 1998.

Conference Committee Report (H.R. CONF. REP. NO. 105-599)

Senate Amendment

The Senate amendment permits States to participate in the IRS refund offset program for specified past-due, legally enforceable State income tax debts, providing the person making the Federal tax overpayment has shown on the Federal return for the taxable year of the overpayment an address that is within the State seeking the tax offset. The offset applies after the offsets provided in present law for internal revenue tax liabilities, past-due support, and past-due, legally enforceable obligations owed a Federal agency. The offset occurs before the designation of any refund toward future Federal tax liability.

Effective Date

Federal income tax refunds payable after December 31, 1998.

Conference Agreement

The conference agreement follows the Senate amendment, with technical modifications. The provision permits the Secretary to prescribe additional conditions (pursuant to new section 6402(e)(4)(D)) to ensure that the determination is valid that the State or local income tax liability is past-due and legally enforceable. The conferees intend that this include consideration of questions that may arise as a result of the taxpayer being a Native American.

Effective Date

Federal income tax refunds payable after December 31, 1999.

[Law at ¶ 6110 and ¶ 6350. CCH Explanation at ¶ 1446.]

[¶ 10,690]   Act Sec. 3712.   Reporting requirements relating to education tax credits

Conference Committee Report (H.R. CONF. REP. NO. 105-599)

[Code Sec. 6050S]

Present Law

Individual taxpayers are allowed to claim a nonrefundable HOPE credit against Federal income taxes up to $1,500 per student per year for qualified tuition and related expenses paid for the first two years of the student's post-secondary education in a degree program. A Lifetime Learning credit against Federal income taxes equal to 20 percent of qualified expenses (up to a maximum credit of $1,000 per taxpayer return for 1998 through 2002 and $2,000 per taxpayer return after 2002) is also available. Qualified tuition and related expenses do not include expenses covered by educational assistance that is not required to be included in the gross income of either the student or the taxpayer claiming the credit (e.g., scholarship or fellowship grants).

Code section 6050S requires information reporting by eligible educational institutions which receive payments for qualified tuition and related expenses, and certain other persons who make reimbursement or refunds of qualified tuition and related expenses, in order to assist students, their parents, and the IRS in calculating the amount of the HOPE and Lifetime Learning credits potentially available. Section 6050S(b) provides that the annual information report to the Secretary must be in the form prescribed by the Secretary and must contain the following: (1) the name, address, and taxpayer identification number (TIN) of the individual which respect to whom the qualified tuition and related expenses were received or the reimbursement or refund was paid; (2) the name, address, and TIN of any individual certified by the student as the taxpayer who will claim that student as a dependent for purposes of the deduction under section 151 for any taxable years ending with or within the year for which the information return is filed; (3) the aggregate amount of payments of qualified tuition and related expenses received by the eligible educational institution and the aggregate amount of reimbursements or refunds (or similar amounts) paid during the calendar year with respect to the student; and (4) such other information as the Secretary may prescribe. Under section 6050S(d), an educational institution also must provide to each person identified on the information return submitted to the Secretary (e.g., the student and his or her parent(s)) a written statement showing the name, address, and phone number of the reporting person's information contact, and the amounts set forth in (3) above.

On December 22, 1997, the Department of Treasury issued Notice 97-73 setting forth the information reporting requirements under section 6050S for 1998. Notice 97-73 describes who must report information and the nature of the information that must be reported for 1998. In general, the required reporting under Notice 97-73 is more limited than that which will ultimately be required under section 6050S upon the issuance of final regulations. Accordingly, for 1998, educational institutions must report the following information: (1) the name, address, and TIN of the educational institution; (2) the name, address, and TIN of the student with respect to whom payments of qualified tuition and related expenses were received during 1998; (3) an indication as to whether the student was enrolled for at least half the full-time academic workload during any academic period commencing in 1998; and (4) an indication as to whether the student was enrolled exclusively in a program or programs leading to a graduate-level degree, graduate-level certificate, or other recognized graduate-level educational credential. Educational institutions must provide to students the information listed above, as well as the phone number of the information contact at the school. Information returns must be provided to students by February 1, 1999 and filed with the IRS by March 1, 1999. Notice 97-73 states that until final regulations are adopted, no penalties will be imposed under sections 6721 and 6722 for failure to file correct information returns or to furnish correct statements to the individuals with respect to whom information reporting is required under section 6050S. In addition, Notice 97-73 states that, even after final regulations are adopted, no penalties will be imposed under sections 6721 and 6722 for 1998 if the institution made a good faith effort to file information returns and furnish statements in accordance with Notice 97-73.

House Bill

No provision.

Senate [Floor] Amendment [No. 2381]

The Senate amendment modifies the information reporting requirements under section 6050S. In addition to reporting the aggregate amount of payments for qualified tuition and related expenses received by the educational institution with respect to a student, the institution must report any grant amount received by the student and processed through the institution during the applicable calendar year. The institution is not required to report on grant aid that is paid directly to the student and is not processed through the institution. In addition, an educational institution is required to report only the aggregate amount of reimbursements or refunds paid to a student by the institution (and not by any other party).

Effective Date

The provision applies to returns required to be filed with respect to taxable years beginning after December 31, 1998.

Conference Agreement

The conference agreement follows the Senate amendment, but includes certain additional clarifications intended to minimize the reporting burdens imposed on educational institutions while preserving the ability of the IRS to monitor compliance with respect to the HOPE Scholarship and Lifetime Learning credits. In particular, the conference agreement clarifies that the definition of the term "qualified tuition and related expenses" shall be as set forth in section 25A, determined without regard to section 25A(g)(2) (which requires adjustments for certain scholarships). Eligible educational institutions that receive payments of qualified tuition and related expenses (or reimburse or refund such payments) are required separately to report the following items with respect to each student under section 6050S(b)(2)(C): (1) the aggregate amount of qualified tuition and related expenses (not including certain expenses relating to sports, games, or hobbies, or nonacademic fees); (2) any grant amount (whether or not excludable from income) received by such individual for payment of costs of attendance and processed through the institution during the applicable calendar year; and (3) the aggregate amount of reimbursements or refunds (or similar amounts) paid to such individual during the calendar year by the institution.

The conferees understand that the Department of Treasury is in the process of issuing regulatory guidance with respect to the education credit reporting requirements. In developing such guidance, the conferees urge Treasury to minimize the reporting burdens imposed on educational institutions in connection with the HOPE Scholarship and Lifetime Learning credits. For example, section 472(1) of the Higher Education Act contains a definition of tuition and fees that is used in calculating a student's total "cost of attendance." The conferees urge Treasury to conform the definition of "qualified tuition and related expenses" for purposes of the HOPE Scholarship and Lifetime Learning credits to the definition set forth in section 472(1) to the extent possible, so as to minimize the additional reporting burden on educational institutions.

In general, the conferees expect that the regulatory guidance regarding the education credit reporting requirements will have an effective date that will provide educational institutions with sufficient time, after any notice and comment period, to implement additional required reporting. In addition, although the provision generally applies to taxable years beginning after December 31, 1998, the conferees intend that no reporting beyond the reporting currently required in Notice 97-73 would be required of educational institutions until such final regulatory guidance is available.

In furtherance of the objective of minimizing the reporting burden on educational institutions, the conferees note that, pursuant to the regulatory authority granted in section 25A(i), Treasury may exempt educational institutions from the reporting requirements with respect to certain categories of students, such as non-degree students enrolled in a course for which academic credit is not granted by the institution, provided that such exemptions do not undermine the overall compliance objectives of the provision. The conferees further expect that Treasury will provide clarification regarding the reasonable cause exception contained in section 6724(a) as it may apply to the education information reporting requirements. Finally, the conferees urge that any update and modernization of IRS computer systems incorporate the capacity to match a dependent's TIN with the return filed by the person claiming the individual as a dependent.

[Law at ¶ 6080. CCH Explanation at ¶ 226.]

[¶ 10,715]   Act Sec. 3801.   Administration of penalties and interest

Senate Committee Report (S. REP. NO. 105-174)

[Act Sec. 3801]
Present Law
The last major comprehensive revision of the overall penalty structure in the Internal Revenue Code was the "Improved Penalty Administration and Compliance Tax Act," enacted as part of the Omnibus Budget Reconciliation Act of 1989.

Reasons for Change
The Committee believes that it is appropriate to undertake a study of penalty and interest administration, which will provide the Committee with legislative and administrative recommendations for improvement of the current penalty and interest structure.

Explanation of Provision
The provision requires the Joint Committee on Taxation and the Treasury to each conduct a separate study reviewing the interest and penalty provisions of the Code (including the administration and implementation of the penalty reform provisions of the Omnibus Budget Reconciliation Act of 1989), and making any legislative and administrative recommendations it deems appropriate to simplify penalty administration and reduce taxpayer burden. The studies must also include an analysis of the interest provisions in the Code, including legislative and administrative recommendations deemed appropriate to simplify the administration of the interest provisions and to reduce taxpayer burden.

Effective Date
The reports must be provided not later than nine months after the date of enactment.

Conference Committee Report (H.R. CONF. REP. NO. 105-599)

The conference agreement follows the Senate amendment. The conferees expect that the Joint Committee on Taxation and the Treasury Department studies will examine whether the current penalty and interest provisions encourage voluntary compliance. The studies should also consider whether the provisions operate fairly, whether they are effective deterrents to undesired behavior, and whether they are designed in a manner that promotes efficient and effective administration of the provisions by the IRS. The conferees expect that the Joint Committee on Taxation and the Treasury Department will consider comments from taxpayers and practitioners on issues relevant to the studies.

Effective Date
The reports must be provided not later than one year after the date of enactment.

[Law at ¶ 8190. CCH Explanation at ¶ 1441.]

[¶ 10,720]   Act Sec. 3802.   Confidentiality of tax return information

Senate Committee Report (S. REP. NO. 105-174)

[Act Sec. 3802]
[*This committee report does not reflect changes made by Senate Floor Amendment No. 2378. Senate Floor Amendment No. 2378 (144 Cong. Rec. 56, S4487) was passed with nominal debate.—CCH.*]

Present Law
The Internal Revenue Code prohibits disclosure of tax returns and return information, except to the extent specifically authorized by the Internal Revenue Code (sec. 6103). Unauthorized disclosure is a felony punishable by a fine not exceeding $5,000 or imprisonment of not more than five years, or both (sec. 7213). An action for civil damages also may be brought for unauthorized disclosure (sec. 7431). No tax information may be furnished by the IRS to another agency unless the other agency establishes procedures satisfactory to the IRS for safeguarding the tax information it receives (sec. 6103(p)).

Reasons for Change
The Committee believes that a study of the confidentiality provisions will be useful in assisting the Committee in determining whether improvements can be made to these provisions.

Explanation of Provision
The provision requires the Joint Committee on Taxation and Treasury to each conduct a separate

study on provisions regarding taxpayer confidentiality. The studies are to examine present-law protections of taxpayer privacy, the need, if any, for third parties to use tax return information, whether greater levels of voluntary compliance can be achieved by allowing the public to know who is legally required to file tax returns but does not do so, and the interrelationship of the taxpayer confidentiality provisions in the Internal Revenue Code with those elsewhere in the United States Code (such as the Freedom of Information Act).

Effective Date

The findings of the studies, along with any recommendations, are required to be reported to the Congress no later than one year after the date of enactment.

Conference Committee Report (H.R. CONF. REP. NO. 105-599)

The conference agreement generally follows the Senate amendment. The conference agreement adds to the study an examination of whether the public interest would be served by greater disclosure of information relating to tax-exempt organizations (described in section 501 of the Code). The conference agreement deletes from the study an examination of whether return information should be disclosed to a State unless the State has first notified personally in advance each person with respect to whom information has been requested.

Effective Date

The findings of the study, along with any recommendations, are required to be reported to the Congress no later than 18 months after the date of enactment.

[Law at ¶ 8195. CCH Explanation at ¶ 862.]

[¶ 10,725] Act Sec. 3803. Noncompliance with internal revenue laws by taxpayers

Conference Committee Report (H.R. CONF. REP. NO. 105-599)

[Act Sec. 3803]

Present Law

No provision.

House Bill

No provision.

Senate [Floor] Amendment [No. 2358]

The Senate amendment provides that the Joint Committee on Taxation, the Secretary of the Treasury and the Commissioner of the Internal Revenue Service must jointly conduct a study of taxpayers' willful noncompliance with the tax law. The study must be reported to the Congress within one year of the date of enactment.

Effective Date

Date of enactment.

Conference Agreement

The conference agreement follows the Senate amendment, with clarifications that the study is to examine noncompliance with the internal revenue laws by taxpayers (including willful noncompliance and noncompliance due to tax law complexity or other factors). Treasury and IRS are to conduct the study, in consultation with the Joint Committee on Taxation.

[Law at ¶ 8200. CCH Explanation at ¶ 877.]

[¶ 10,730] Act Sec. 3804. Payments for informants

Conference Committee Report (H.R. CONF. REP. NO. 105-599)

[Act Sec. 3804]

Present Law

Under present law, rewards may be paid for information relating to civil violations, as well as criminal violations. Present law also provides that the rewards are paid out of the proceeds of amounts (other than interest) collected by reason of the information provided. An annual report on the rewards program is required.

House Bill

No provision.

Senate Amendment

The Senate amendment requires a study and report by Treasury to the Congress (within one year of the date of enactment) of the present-law reward program (including results) and any legislative or administrative recommendations regarding the program and its application.

Effective Date

Date of enactment.

Conference Agreement

The conference agreement follows the Senate amendment.

[Law at ¶ 8205. CCH Explanation at ¶ 876.]

[¶ 10,740] Act Sec. 4001. Review of requests for GAO investigations of the IRS

House Committee Report (H.R. REP. NO. 105-364, pt. 1)

[Code Sec. 8021(e)]
Present Law
There is presently no specific statutory requirement that requests for investigations by the General Accounting Office ("GAO") relating to the IRS be reviewed by the Joint Committee on Taxation (the "Joint Committee"). However, some of the studies that GAO conducts relating to taxation and oversight of the IRS require access under section 6103 of the Code to confidential tax returns and return information. Under section 6103, the GAO may inform the Joint Committee of its initiation of an audit of the IRS and obtain access to confidential taxpayer information unless, within 30 days, three-fifths of the Members of the Joint Committee disapprove of the audit. This provision has not been utilized; the GAO generally seeks advance access to confidential taxpayer return information from the Joint Committee.

Reasons for Change
The Restructuring Commission recommended changes to the approval process for GAO reports based on its findings that the GAO conducts myriad audits of the IRS, many of which relate to lesser matters and which are not integrated into a constructive, focused package. The Committee believes that GAO audits and reports can be helpful as an oversight tool, but that they should be coordinated so as to ensure appropriate allocation of resources, both of the IRS and the GAO.

Explanation of Provision
Under the bill, the Joint Committee on Taxation reviews all requests (other than requests by the chair or ranking member of a Committee or Subcommittee of the Congress) for investigations of the IRS by the GAO and approves such requests when appropriate. In reviewing such requests, the Joint Committee is to eliminate overlapping investigations, ensure that the GAO has the capacity to handle the investigation, and ensure that investigations focus on areas of primary importance to tax administration.

The provision does not change the present-law rules under section 6103.

Effective Date
The provision is effective with respect to requests for GAO investigations made after the date of enactment.

Conference Committee Report (H.R. CONF. REP. NO. 105-599)

The conference agreement follows the House bill. The conferees intend that the provision exclude requests made by the chairman or ranking member of a committee or subcommittee, investigations required by statute, and work initiated by GAO under its basic statutory authorities.

Effective Date
Same as the House bill.
[Law at ¶ 6910. CCH Explanation at ¶ 866.]

[¶ 10,745] Act Sec. 4001. Joint congressional hearings and coordinated oversight reports (joint congressional hearings)

House Committee Report (H.R. REP. NO. 105-364, pt. 1)

[Code Sec. 8021(f)]
Present Law
Under the present Congressional committee structure, a number of committees have jurisdiction with respect to IRS oversight. The committees most responsible for IRS oversight are the House Committees on Ways and Means, Appropriations, Government Reform and Oversight, the corresponding Senate Committees on Finance, Appropriations, and Governmental Affairs, and the Joint Committee on Taxation. While these Committees have a shared interest in IRS matters, they typically act independently, and have separate hearings and make separate investigations into IRS matters. Each committee also has jurisdiction over certain issues. For example, the House Ways and Means Committee and the Senate Finance Committee have exclusive jurisdiction over changes to the tax laws. Similarly, the House and Senate Appropriations Committees have exclusive jurisdiction over IRS annual appropriations. The Joint Committee does not have legislative jurisdiction, but has significant responsibilities with respect to tax matters and IRS oversight.

Reasons for Change
The Restructuring Commission found that the Congressional committees responsible for IRS oversight "focus on different issues that change from year to year. While these issues are important, there is a lack of coordinated focus on high level and strategic matters. Because the IRS tries to satisfy requests from Congress, this nonintegrated approach to oversight further blurs the ability to set strategic direction and focus on priorities."

The committee believes that Congressional oversight of the IRS should be more coordinated, and should include long-term objectives.

Explanation of Provision
Under the bill, there will be two annual joint hearings of two majority and one minority members of each of the Senate Committees on Finance, Appropriations, and Governmental Affairs and the House Committees on Ways and Means, Ap-

propriations, and Government Reform and Oversight. The first annual hearing is to take place before April 1 of each calendar year and is to review the strategic plans and budget for the IRS (including whether the budget supports IRS objectives). The second annual hearing is to be held after the conclusion of the annual tax filing season, and is to review the progress of the IRS in meeting its objectives under the strategic and business plans, the progress of the IRS in improv-

ing taxpayer service and compliance, progress of the IRS on technology modernization, and the annual filing season. The bill does not modify the existing jurisdiction of the Committees involved in the joint hearings.

* * *

Effective Date

The provision is effective on the date of enactment.

Conference Committee Report (H.R. CONF. REP. NO. 105-599)

Conference Agreement

The conference agreement follows the House bill, with modifications. The conference agreement provides that there will be one annual joint hearing to review: (1) the progress of the IRS in meeting its objectives under the strategic and business plans; (2) the progress of the IRS in improving taxpayer service and compliance; (3) the progress of the IRS on technology modernization; and (4) the annual filing season. The joint review will be held at the call of the Chairman of

the Joint Committee on Taxation, and is to take place before June 1 of each calendar year.

* * *

Effective Date

Same as House bill, except that the requirement for an annual joint review, and report by the Joint Committee on Taxation, shall apply only for calendar years 1999-2003.

[Law at ¶ 6910. CCH Explanation at ¶ 871.]

[¶ 10,750]   Act Sec. 4002.   Joint congressional hearings and coordinated oversight reports (coordinated oversight reports)

House Committee Report (H.R. REP. NO. 105-364, pt. 1)

[Code Sec. 8022]
Present Law

Under the present Congressional committee structure, a number of committees have jurisdiction with respect to IRS oversight. The committees most responsible for IRS oversight are the House Committees on Ways and Means, Appropriations, Government Reform and Oversight, the corresponding Senate Committees on Finance, Appropriations, and Governmental Affairs, and the Joint Committee on Taxation. While these Committees have a shared interest in IRS matters, they typically act independently, and have separate hearings and make separate investigations into IRS matters. Each committee also has jurisdiction over certain issues. For example, the House Ways and Means Committee and the Senate Finance Committee have exclusive jurisdiction over changes to the tax laws. Similarly, the House and Senate Appropriations Committees have exclusive jurisdiction over IRS annual appropriations. The Joint Committee does not have legislative jurisdiction, but has significant responsibilities with respect to tax matters and IRS oversight.

Reasons for Change

The Restructuring Commission found that the Congressional committees responsible for IRS oversight "focus on different issues that change from year to year. While these issues are impor-

tant, there is a lack of coordinated focus on high level and strategic matters. Because the IRS tries to satisfy requests from Congress, this nonintegrated approach to oversight further blurs the ability to set strategic direction and focus on priorities."

The committee believes that Congressional oversight of the IRS should be more coordinated, and should include long-term objectives.

Explanation of Provision
* * *

The bill provides that the Joint Committee is to make annual reports to the Committee on Finance and the Committee on Ways and Means on the overall state of the Federal tax system, together with recommendations with respect to possible simplification proposals and other matters relating to the administration of the Federal tax system as it may deem advisable. The Joint Committee also is to report annually to the Senate Committees on Finance, Appropriations, and Governmental Affairs and the House Committees on Ways and Means, Appropriations, and Government Reform and Oversight with respect to the matters that are the subject of the annual joint hearings of members of such Committees.

Effective Date

The provision is effective on the date of enactment.

Conference Committee Report (H.R. CONF. REP. NO. 105-599)

The conference agreement follows the House bill, with modifications. * * *

In addition, the conference agreement modifies the House bill provision requiring the Joint Committee on Taxation to report on the overall state

of the Federal tax system to provide that such report shall be prepared once in each Congress, but only if amounts necessary to carry out this requirement are specifically appropriated to the Joint Committee on Taxation.

Committee Reports 657

Effective Date
Same as House bill, except that the requirement for an annual joint review, and report by the Joint Committee on Taxation, shall apply only for calendar years 1999-2003.

[Law at ¶ 6920. CCH Explanation at ¶ 873.]

[¶ 10,755]   Act Sec. 4011.   Funding for century date change

House Committee Report (H.R. REP. NO. 105-364, pt. 1)

[Act Sec. 4011]
Present Law
No specific provision.

Reasons for Change
The Committee believes that adequate funding of efforts to resolve this problem is essential.

Explanation of Provision
The bill provides that it is the sense of the Congress that the IRS efforts to resolve the century date change computing problems should be fully funded to provide for certain resolution of such problems.

Effective Date
The provision is effective on the date of enactment.

Conference Committee Report (H.R. CONF. REP. NO. 105-599)

Senate Amendment
The Senate amendment provides that it is the sense of the Congress that the IRS should place resolving the century date change computing problems as a high priority. The Senate amendment also provides that the Commissioner shall expeditiously submit a report to the Congress on the overall impact of the Senate amendment on the ability of the IRS to resolve the century date change computing problems and on the provisions of the Senate amendment that will require significant amounts of computer programming changes prior to December 31, 1999, in order to carry out the provisions.

Effective Date
The Senate amendment provision is effective on the date of enactment.

Conference Agreement
The conference agreement follows the House bill and the Senate amendment with respect to the Sense of the Congress with respect to resolving the century date change conversion problems. The conference agreement does not include the Senate amendment provision requiring the Commissioner to report to the Congress on the impact of the legislation on the ability of the IRS to resolve century date change problems.

Effective Date
Same as the House bill and Senate amendment.

[Law at ¶ 8210. CCH Explanation at ¶ 856.]

[¶ 10,760]   Act Sec. 4021.   Tax law complexity analysis (role of IRS)

House Committee Report (H.R. REP. NO. 105-364, pt. 1)

[Act Sec. 4021]
Present Law
Present law does not require a formal complexity analysis with respect to changes to the tax laws.

Reasons for Change
The Restructuring Commission found a clear connection between the complexity of the Internal Revenue Code and the difficulty of tax law administration and taxpayer frustration. The Committee shares the concern that complexity is a serious problem with the Federal tax system. Complexity and frequent changes in the tax laws create burdens for both the IRS and taxpayers. Failure to address complexity may ultimately reduce voluntary compliance.

The Committee is aware that it may not be possible or desirable to eliminate all complexity in the tax system. There are many objectives of a tax system and particular tax provisions, and simplicity is only one. In some cases other policies, such as fairness, may outweigh concerns about complexity.

Nevertheless, the Committee believes it essential to try to reduce the complexity of the tax system whenever possible. Accordingly, the Committee believes it appropriate to introduce new procedural rules that will help to focus attention on complexity as an issue. Such rules are an important step, but do not take the place of the most effective way to address complexity—that is for the Congress and the Administration to make reducing complexity a priority when drafting tax legislation.

The Committee also believes that encouraging the participation of IRS personnel in drafting legislation will help to highlight administrative and complexity issues while legislation is being developed.

Explanation of Provision
IRS participation in drafting legislation
The bill provides that it is the sense of the Congress that the IRS should provide the Congress with an independent view of tax administration and that the tax-writing committees should hear from front-line technical experts at the IRS during the legislative process with respect to the administrability of pending amendments to the Internal Revenue Code.

* * *

Act Sec. 4021   ¶ 10,760

Effective Date

The requirement for a Tax Complexity Analysis is effective with respect to legislation considered on or after January 1, 1998.

Conference Committee Report (H.R. Conf. Rep. No. 105-599)

Senate Amendment

Role of the IRS

The IRS is to report to the House Ways and Means Committee and the Senate Finance Committee annually regarding sources of complexity in the administration of the Federal tax laws. Factors the IRS may take into account include: (1) frequently asked questions by taxpayers; (2) common errors made by taxpayers in filling out returns; (3) areas of the law that frequently result in disagreements between taxpayers and the IRS; (4) major areas in which there is no or incomplete published guidance or in which the law is uncertain; (5) areas in which revenue agents make frequent errors in interpreting or applying the law; (6) impact of recent legislation on complexity; (7) information regarding forms, including a listing of IRS forms, the time it takes for taxpayers to complete and review forms, the number of taxpayers who use each form, and how the time required changed as a result of recently enacted legislation; and (8) recommendations for reducing

complexity in the administration of the Federal tax system.

* * *

Effective Date

The provision of the Senate amendment requiring the Joint Committee on Taxation to provide a complexity analysis is effective with respect to legislation considered on or after January 1, 1999. The provision requiring the IRS to report on sources of complexity is effective on the date of enactment.

· *Conference Agreement*

Role of the IRS

The conference agreement follows the House bill and the Senate amendment. Under the conference agreement, the Commissioner's report on complexity is to be transmitted to the Congress not later than March 1 of each year.

* * *

Effective Date

The provisions of the conference agreement are effective for calendar years after 1998.

[Law at ¶ 8215. CCH Explanation at ¶ 841.]

[¶ 10,770]   Act Sec. 4022.   Tax law complexity analysis (complexity analysis)

Senate Committee Report (S. Rep. No. 105-174)

[Act Sec. 4022]

Present Law

Present law does not require a formal complexity analysis with respect to changes to the tax laws.

Reasons for Change

The National Commission on Restructuring the IRS found a clear connection between the complexity of the Internal Revenue Code and the difficulty of tax law administration and taxpayer frustration. The Committee shares the concern that complexity is a serious problem with the Federal tax system. Complexity and frequent changes in the tax laws create burdens for both the IRS and taxpayers. Failure to address complexity may ultimately reduce voluntary compliance.

The Committee is aware that it may not be possible or desirable to eliminate all complexity in the tax system. There are many objectives of a tax system and particular tax provisions, and simplicity is only one. In some cases other policies, such as fairness, may outweigh concerns about complexity. Nevertheless, the Committee believes complexity of the tax system should be reduced whenever possible. Accordingly, the Committee believes it appropriate to introduce new procedural rules that will focus attention on complexity. The Committee also believes that the tax-writing committees should receive periodic input from the IRS regarding areas of the law that cause

problems for taxpayers. This input will be valuable in developing future legislation.

Explanation of Provision

* * *

Complexity analysis with respect to current legislation

The bill requires the Joint Committee on Taxation (in consultation with the IRS and Treasury) to provide an analysis of complexity or administrability concerns raised by tax provisions of widespread applicability to individuals or small businesses. The analysis is to be included in any Committee Report of the House Ways and Means Committee or Senate Finance Committee or Conference Report containing tax provisions, or provided to the Members of the relevant Committee or Committees as soon as practicable after the report is filed. The analysis is to include: (1) an estimate of the number and type of taxpayers affected; and (2) if applicable, the income level of affected individual taxpayers. In addition, such analysis should include, if determinable, the following: (1) the extent to which existing tax forms would require revision and whether a new form or forms would be required; (2) whether and to what extent taxpayers would be required to keep additional records; (3) the estimated cost to taxpayers to comply with the provision; (4) the extent to which enactment of the provision would require the IRS to develop or modify regulatory guidance; (5) whether and to what extent the provision can be expected to lead to disputes between taxpayers and the IRS; and (6) how the IRS can be expected to respond to the provision (including the impact on internal training, whether the Internal Revenue Manual would require revision, whether the change would require reprogramming of computers, and the extent to which the IRS would be required to divert or redirect resources in response to the provision).

Conference Committee Report (H.R. CONF. REP. NO. 105-599)

* * *

Complexity analysis

The conference agreement follows the Senate amendment with a modification to provide that a point of order arises in the House of Representatives with respect to the floor consideration of a bill or conference report if the required complexity analysis has not been completed. The point of order may be waived by a majority vote. The point of order is subject to the Constitutional right of each House of the Congress to establish its own rules and procedures; thus, such point of order

Effective Date

The provision requiring the Joint Committee on Taxation to provide a complexity analysis is effective with respect to legislation considered on or after January 1, 1999. The provision requiring IRS to report on sources of complexity is effective on the date of enactment.

may be changed at any time pursuant to the procedures of the House of Representatives.

The conferees intend that the complexity analysis be prepared by the staff of the Joint Committee on Taxation, and that it shall, to the extent feasible, be included in committee or conference committee reports.

Effective Date

The provisions of the conference agreement are effective for calendar years after 1998.

[Law at ¶ 8220. CCH Explanation at ¶ 846.]

[¶ 10,785]   Act Sec. 5001.   Elimination of 18-month holding period for capital gains

Conference Committee Report (H.R. CONF. REP. NO. 105-599)

[Code Sec. 1(h)]

Present Law

The Taxpayer Relief Act of 1997 Act ("the 1997 Act") provided lower capital gains rates for individuals. Generally, the 1997 Act reduced the maximum rate on the adjusted net capital gain of an individual from 28 percent to 20 percent and provided a 10-percent rate for the adjusted net capital gain otherwise taxed at a 15-percent rate. The "adjusted net capital gain" is the net capital gain determined without regard to certain gain for which the 1997 Act provided a higher maximum rate of tax. The 1997 Act retained the prior-law 28-percent maximum rate for net long-term capital gain attributable to the sale or exchange of collectibles, certain small business stock to the extent the gain is included in income, and property held more than one year but not more than 18 months. In addition, the 1997 Act provided a maximum rate of 25 percent for the long-term capital gain attributable to depreciation from real estate held more than 18 months. Beginning in

2001, lower rates of 8 and 18 percent will apply to the gain from certain property held more than five years.

House Bill

No provision.

Senate Amendment

No provision.

Conference Agreement

Under the conference agreement, property held more than one year (rather than more than 18 months) will be eligible for the 10-, 20-, and 25-percent capital gain rates provided by the 1997 Act.

Effective Date

The conference agreement applies to amounts properly taken into account on or after January 1, 1998.

[Law at ¶ 5001, ¶ 5600 and ¶ 5605. CCH Explanation at ¶ 502.]

[¶ 10,790]   Act Sec. 5002.   Deductibility of meals provided for the convenience of the employer

Conference Committee Report (H.R. CONF. REP. NO. 105-599)

[Code Sec. 119(b)]

Present Law

In general, subject to several exceptions, only 50 percent of business meals and entertainment expenses are allowed as a deduction (sec. 274(n)). Under one exception, meals that are excludable from employees' incomes as a de minimis fringe

benefit (sec. 132) are fully deductible by the employer.

In addition, the courts that have considered the issue have held that if substantially all of the meals are provided for the convenience of the employer pursuant to section 119, the cost of such meals is fully deductible because the employer is treated as operating a de minimis eating facility within the meaning of section 132(e)(2) (*Boyd*

Gaming Corp. v. Commissioner[1] and *Gold Coast Hotel & Casino v. I.R.S.*[2]).

House Bill

No provision.

Senate Amendment

No provision.

Conference Agreement

The bill provides that all meals furnished to employees at a place of business for the convenience of the employer are treated as provided for the convenience of the employer under section 119 if more than one-half of employees to whom such meals are furnished on the premises are furnished such meals for the convenience of the employer under section 119. If these conditions are satisfied, the value of all such meals would be excludable from the employee's income and fully deductible to the employer. No inference is intended as to whether such meals are fully deductible under present law.

Effective Date

The provision is effective for taxable years beginning before, on, or after the date of enactment.

[Law at ¶ 5170. CCH Explanation at ¶ 593.]

[¶ 10,795]   Act Sec. 5003.   Normal trade relations

Conference Committee Report (H.R. CONF. REP. NO. 105-599)

[Act Sec. 5003]

Present Law

In the context of U.S. tariff legislation, section 251 of the Trade Expansion Act of 1962 states the principle of "most-favored-nation" (MFN) treatment, requiring tariff treatment to be applied to all countries equally. Specifically, the products of a country given MFN treatment are subject to rates of duty found in column 1 of the Harmonized Tariff Schedule (HTS) of the United States. Products from countries not eligible for MFN treatment under U.S. law are subject to higher rates of duty (found in column 2 of the HTS). Under current U.S. law, only six countries are subject to column 2 treatment: Afghanistan, Cuba, Laos, North Korea, Serbia and Montenegro, and Vietnam. The remaining U.S. trading partners are subject to either conditional or unconditional MFN treatment, or to even more preferential rates than MFN under free trade agreements (Israel, Canada, and Mexico) and under unilateral grants of tariff preference (the Generalized System of Preferences, the Caribbean Basin Initiative, and the Andean Trade Preferences Act).

House Bill

No provision.

Senate Amendment

No provision.

Conference Agreement

The provision would change the terminology used in U.S. trade statutes from "most-favored-nation" (MFN) to "normal trade relations" (NTR) in order to reflect more accurately the nature of the trade relationship in question. The legislation would not change the tariff treatment received by any country.

The Committee has long been concerned that the term "most-favored-nation" is a misnomer and does not accurately reflect the nature of the trading relationship in question. The terminology implies that a country receiving MFN is somehow receiving treatment that is special or better than what a country would normally receive. In reality, however, a country receiving MFN receives nothing more than ordinary or normal treatment. Only six countries receive treatment that is less favorable than this normal treatment. In addition, three countries actually receive tariff treatment that is better than MFN because they participate in a free trade agreement with the United States and numerous others receive treatment more favorable than MFN under unilateral grants of trade preference signifying that the "most" favored terminology is misleading.

The Committee believes that the MFN terminology has led to confusion and a misunderstanding of Congressional and Presidential action concerning the trade statutes. Accordingly, the Subcommittee strongly believes that the terminology should be changed to reflect the true nature of the trading relationship: merely normal relations.

The Committee does not intend that the change in terminology from MFN to NTR have any affect whatsoever on the meaning of any existing U.S. law or practice. It would not change any procedures under existing law for granting or removing MFN status. Rather, the new term is to have the same meaning as MFN as is currently defined in domestic legislation and international agreements and would not change the tariff treatment granted by the United States to any of its trading partners.

[Law at ¶ 8225.]

---

[1] 106 T.C. No. 19 (May 23, 1996).

[2] U.S. D.C. Nev. CV-5-94-1146-HDM(LRL) (September 26, 1996).

[¶ 10,815] Act Sec. 6003(a). Stacking rules for the child credit under the limitations based on tax liability

Senate Committee Report (S. REP. NO. 105-174)

[Code Sec. 24]

Present Law

Present law provides a $500 ($400 for taxable year 1998) tax credit for each qualifying child under the age of 17. A qualifying child is defined as an individual for whom the taxpayer can claim a dependency exemption and who is a son or daughter of the taxpayer (or a descendent of either), a stepson or stepdaughter of the taxpayer or an eligible foster child of the taxpayer. For taxpayers with modified adjusted gross income in excess of certain thresholds, the allowable child credit is phased out. The length of the phase-out range is affected by the number of the taxpayer's qualifying children.

Generally, the maximum amount of a taxpayer's child credit for each taxable year is limited to the excess of the taxpayer's regular tax liability over the taxpayer's tentative minimum tax liability (determined without regard to the alternative minimum foreign tax credit). In the case of a taxpayer with three or more qualifying children, the maximum amount of the taxpayer's child credit for each taxable year is limited to the greater of: (1) the amount computed under the rule described above, or (2) an amount equal to the excess of the sum of the taxpayer's regular income tax liability and the employee share of FICA taxes (and one-half of the taxpayer's SECA tax liability, if applicable) reduced by the earned income credit. In the case of a taxpayer with three or more qualifying children, the excess of the amount allowed in (2) over the amount computed in (1) is a refundable credit.

Nonrefundable credits may not be used to reduce tax liability below a taxpayer's tentative minimum tax. Certain credits not used as result of this rule may be carried over to other taxable years, while others may not. Special stacking rules apply in determining which nonrefundable credits are used in the current year. Generally, the stacking rules require that nonrefundable personal credits be considered first[55] , followed by other credits, business credits, and the investment tax credit. Refundable credits, which are not limited by the minimum tax, are not stacked until after the nonrefundable credits.

Explanation of Provision

The bill clarifies the application of the income tax liability limitation to the refundable portion of the child credit by treating the refundable portion of the child credit in the same way as the other refundable credits. Specifically, after all the other credits are applied according to the stacking rules of the income tax limitation then the refundable credits are applied first to reduce the taxpayer's tax liability for the year and then to provide a credit in excess of income tax liability for the year.

Effective Date

The provision is effective for taxable years beginning after December 31, [1997].

Conference Committee Report (H.R. CONF. REP. NO. 105-599)

The conference agreement follows the Senate amendment * * *

[Law at ¶ 5020. CCH Explanation at ¶ 201.]

[¶ 10,820] Act Sec. 6003(b). Treatment of a portion of the child credit as a supplemental child credit

Senate Committee Report (S. REP. NO. 105-174)

[Code Sec. 32(n)]

Present Law

A portion of the child credit may be treated as a supplemental child credit. The supplemental child credit is treated as provided under the earned income credit and the child credit amount is reduced by the amount of the supplemental child credit.

Explanation of Provision

The bill clarifies that the treatment of a portion of the child credit as a supplemental child credit under the earned income credit (sec. 32) and the offsetting reduction of the child credit (sec. 24) does not affect the total tax credits allowed to the taxpayer or any other tax credit available to the taxpayer. Rather, it simply reduces the otherwise allowable nonrefundable child credit dollar-for-dollar by the amount treated as a supplemental child credit. The bill also clarifies that the amount

---

[55] It is understood that there is also a stacking rule under which the income tax liability limitation applies between the nonrefundable personal credits, including the nonrefundable portion of the child credit. Generally, the nonrefundable portion of the child credit and the other nonrefundable personal credits which do not provide a carryforward are grouped together and stacked first followed by the nonrefundable personal credits which provide a carryforward for purposes of applying the income tax liability limitation. Therefore, if the sum of the taxpayer's nonrefundable credits exceeds the difference between the taxpayer's regular income tax liability and the taxpayer's tentative minimum tax (determined without regard to the alternative minimum foreign tax credit) then the nonrefundable personal credits which do not provide a carryforward would be applied to reduce the income tax liability for that year first and any excess credits which allow a carryforward would be available to reduce the taxpayer's income tax liability in future years.

of the supplemental child credit under section 32(n) is the lesser of (1) the amount by which the taxpayer's total nonrefundable personal credits (as limited by the tax liability limitation of section 26(a)) are increased by reason of the child credit, or (2) the "negative" tax liability of the taxpayer, defined as the excess of taxpayer's total tax credits, including the earned income credit over the sum of the taxpayer's regular income taxes and social security taxes. For purposes of this calculation, subsection 32(n) is not taken into account. The bill also clarifies that the earned income credit rules (e.g., the phaseout of the earned income credit) generally do not apply to the supplemental child credit.

Effective Date

The provision is effective for taxable years beginning after December 31, 1997.

Conference Committee Report (H.R. CONF. REP. NO. 105-599)

The conference agreement follows the Senate amendment * * *

[Law at ¶ 5040. CCH Explanation at ¶ 206.]

[¶ 10,835]   Act Sec. 6004(a)   Clarifications to HOPE and Lifetime Learning tax credits

Senate Committee Report (S. REP. NO. 105-174)

[Code Sec. 25A, Code Sec. 6050S and Act Sec. 6004(a)(3)]

Present Law

Individual taxpayers are allowed to claim a nonrefundable HOPE credit against Federal income taxes up to $1,500 per student for qualified tuition and fees paid during the year on behalf of a student (i.e., the taxpayer, the taxpayer's spouse, or a dependent of the taxpayer) who is enrolled in a post-secondary degree or certificate program at an eligible post-secondary institution on at least a half-time basis. The HOPE credit is available only for the first two years of a student's post-secondary education. The credit rate is 100 percent of the first $1,000 of qualified tuition and fees and 50 percent on the next $1,000 of qualified tuition and fees. The HOPE credit amount that a taxpayer may otherwise claim is phased out for taxpayers with modified adjusted gross income (AGI) between $40,000 and $50,000 ($80,000 and $100,000 for joint returns). For taxable years beginning after 2001, the $1,500 maximum HOPE credit amount and the AGI phaseout range will be indexed for inflation. The HOPE credit is available for expenses paid after December 31, 1997, for education furnished in academic periods beginning after such date.

If a student is not eligible for the HOPE credit (or in lieu of claiming a HOPE credit with respect to a student), individual taxpayers are allowed to claim a nonrefundable Lifetime Learning credit against Federal income taxes equal to 20 percent of qualified tuition and fees paid during the taxable year on behalf of the taxpayer, the taxpayer's spouse, or a dependent. In contrast to the HOPE credit, the student need not be enrolled on at least a half-time basis in order to be eligible for the Lifetime Learning credit, which is available for an unlimited number of years of post-secondary training. For expenses paid before January 1, 2003, up to $5,000 of qualified tuition and fees per taxpayer return will be eligible for the Lifetime Learning credit (i.e., the maximum credit per taxpayer return will be $1,000). For expenses paid after December 31, 2002, up to $10,000 of qualified tuition and fees per taxpayer return will be eligible for the Lifetime Learning credit (i.e., the maximum credit per taxpayer return will be $2,000). The Lifetime Learning credit amount that a taxpayer may otherwise claim is phased out over the same modified AGI phase-out range as applies for purposes of the HOPE credit. The Lifetime Learning credit is available for expenses paid after June 30, 1998, for education furnished in academic periods beginning after such date.

Section 6050S provides that certain educational institutions and other taxpayers engaged in a trade or business must file information returns with the IRS and certain individual taxpayers, as required by regulations prescribed by the Secretary of the Treasury, containing information on individuals who made payments for qualified tuition and related expenses or to whom reimbursements or refunds were made of such expenses.

Explanation of Provision

The bill clarifies that, under section 6050S, information returns containing information with respect to qualified tuition and fees must be filed by a person that is not an eligible educational institution only if such person is engaged in a trade or business of making payments to any individual under an insurance arrangement as reimbursements or refunds (or similar payments) of qualified tuition and related expenses. As under present law, section 6050S will continue to require the filing of information returns by persons engaged in a trade or business if, in the course of such trade or business, the person receives from any individual interest aggregating $600 or more for any calendar year on one or more qualified education loans.

Effective Date

The provision is effective as if included in the 1997 Act—i.e., for expenses paid after December 31, 1997, for education furnished in academic periods beginning after such date.

Conference Committee Report (H.R. CONF. REP. NO. 105-599)

The conference agreement follows the Senate amendment * * *

[Law at ¶ 6080 and ¶ 8239. CCH Explanation at ¶ 226.]

[¶ 10,840] Act Sec. 6004(b). Deduction for student loan interest

Senate Committee Report (S. REP. NO. 105-174)

[Code Sec. 221]
Present Law

Certain individuals who have paid interest on qualified education loans may claim an above-the-line deduction for such interest expenses, up to a maximum deduction of $2,500 per year. The deduction is allowed only with respect to interest paid on a qualified education loan during the first 60 months in which interest payments are required. In this regard, required payments of interest do not include nonmandatory payments, such as interest payments made during a period of loan forbearance. Months during which the qualified education loan is in deferral or forbearance do not count against the 60-month period. No deduction is allowed to an individual if that individual is claimed as a dependent on another taxpayer's return for the taxable year.

A qualified education loan generally is defined as any indebtedness incurred to pay for the qualified higher education expenses of the taxpayer, the taxpayer's spouse, or any dependent of the taxpayer as of the time the indebtedness was incurred in attending (1) post-secondary educational institutions and certain vocational schools defined by reference to section 481 of the Higher Education Act of 1965, or (2) institutions conducting internship or residency programs leading to a degree or certificate from an institution of higher education, a hospital, or a health care facility conducting postgraduate training.

Explanation of Provision

The bill clarifies that the student loan interest deduction may be claimed only by a taxpayer who is legally obligated to make the interest payments pursuant to the terms of the loan.

Effective Date

The provision is effective for interest payments due and paid after December 31, 1997, on any qualified education loan.

Conference Committee Report (H.R. CONF. REP. NO. 105-599)

The conference agreement follows the Senate amendment, with the following modifications, additions, and deletions.
* * *
1. Education Incentives of the 1997 Act
* * *

Deduction for student loan interest

The conference agreement clarifies that a "qualified education loan" means any indebtedness incurred solely to pay qualified higher education expenses. Thus, revolving lines of credit generally would not constitute qualified education loans unless the borrower agreed to use the line of credit to pay only qualifying education expenses. The conference agreement further provides Treasury with authority to issue regulations regarding the calculation of the 60-month period in the case of consolidated loans, collapsed loans, and loans made before the date of enactment of the Taxpayer Relief Act of 1997 (August 5, 1997) for purposes of determining the deductibility of interest paid on such loans. In this regard, the conferees expect that such regulations would mirror the guidance contained in Notice 98-7 issued regarding the establishment of the 60-month period with respect to such loans for reporting purposes. The provision is effective for interest payments due and paid after December 31, 1997, on any qualified education loan.
* * *

[Law at ¶ 5250. CCH Explanation at ¶ 242.]

[¶ 10,845] Act Sec. 6004(c)(1) and 6004(d). Education IRAs

Senate Committee Report (S. REP. NO. 105-174)

[Code Sec. 530]
Present Law

Section 530 provides that taxpayers may establish "education IRAs," meaning certain trusts or custodial accounts created exclusively for the purpose of paying qualified higher education expenses of a named beneficiary. Annual contributions to education IRAs may not exceed $500 per designated beneficiary, and may not be made after the designated beneficiary reaches age 18. Contributions to an education IRA may not be made by certain high-income taxpayers—i.e., the contribution limit is phased out for taxpayers with modified adjusted gross income between $95,000 and $110,000 ($150,000 and $160,000 for taxpayers filing joint returns). No contribution may be made to an education IRA during any year in which any contributions are made by anyone to a qualified State tuition program on behalf of the same beneficiary.

Until a distribution is made from an education IRA, earnings on contributions to the account generally are not subject to tax.[56] In addition, distributions from an education IRA are excludable from gross income to the extent that the distribution does not exceed qualified higher education expenses incurred by the beneficiary during the year the distribution is made (provided that a HOPE credit or Lifetime Learning credit is not claimed with respect to the beneficiary for the same taxable year). The earnings portion of an education IRA distribution not used to pay qualified higher education expenses is includible in the gross income of the distributee and generally is subject to an additional 10-percent tax.[57] However, the additional 10-percent tax does not apply if a distribution is made of excess contributions above the $500 limit (and any earnings attributable to such excess contributions) if the distribution is made on or before the date that a return is required to be filed (including extensions of time) by the contributor for the year in which the excess contribution was made. In addition, section 530 allows tax-free rollovers of account balances from an education IRA benefiting one family member to an education IRA benefiting another family member. Section 530 is effective for taxable years beginning after December 31, 1997.

Explanation of Provision

Consistent with the legislative history to the 1997 Act, the bill provides that any balance remaining in an education IRA will be deemed to be distributed within 30 days after the date that the designated beneficiary reaches age 30 (or, if earlier, within 30 days of the date that the beneficiary dies). The bill further clarifies that, in the event of the death of the designated beneficiary, the balance remaining in an education IRA may be distributed (without imposition of the additional 10-percent tax) to any other (i.e., contingent) beneficiary or to the estate of the deceased designated beneficiary. If any member of the family of the deceased beneficiary becomes the new designated beneficiary of an education IRA, then no tax will be imposed on such redesignation and the account will continue to be treated as an education IRA.

Under the bill, the additional 10-percent tax provided for by section 530(d)(4) will not apply to a distribution from an education IRA, which (although used to pay for qualified higher education expenses) is includible in the beneficiary's gross income solely because the taxpayer elects to claim a HOPE or Lifetime Learning credit with respect to the beneficiary. The bill further provides that

the additional 10-percent tax will not apply to the distribution of any contribution to an education IRA made during a taxable year if such distribution is made on or before the date that a return is required to be filed (including extensions of time) by the *beneficiary* for the taxable year during which the contribution was made (or, if the beneficiary is not required to file such a return, April 15th of the year following the taxable year during which the contribution was made). In addition, the bill amends section 4973(e) to provide that the excise tax penalty applies under that section for each year that an excess contribution remains in an education IRA (and not merely the year that the excess contribution is made).

The bill clarifies that, in order for taxpayers to establish an education IRA, the designated beneficiary must be a life-in-being. The bill also clarifies that, under rules contained in present-law section 72, distributions from education IRAs are treated as representing a pro-rata share of the principal (i.e., contributions) and accumulated earnings in the account.[58]

The bill also provides that, if any qualified higher education expenses are taken into account in determining the amount of the exclusion under section 530 for a distribution from an education IRA, then no deduction (under section 162 or any other section), or exclusion (under section 135) or credit will be allowed under the Internal Revenue Code with respect to such qualified higher education expenses.

In addition, because the 1997 Act allows taxpayers to redeem U.S. Savings Bonds and be eligible for the exclusion under present-law section 135 (as if the proceeds were used to pay qualified higher education expenses) provided the proceeds from the redemption are contributed to an education IRA (or to a qualified State tuition program defined under section 529) on behalf of the taxpayer, the taxpayer's spouse, or a dependent, the bill conforms the definition of "eligible educational institution" under section 135 to the broader definition of that term under present-law section 530 (and section 529). Thus, for purposes of section 135, as under present-law sections 529 and 530, the term "eligible educational institution" is defined as an institution which (1) is described in section 481 of the Higher Education Act of 1965 (20 U.S.C. 1088) and (2) is eligible to participate in Department of Education student aid programs.

---

[56] However, education IRAs are subject to the unrelated business income tax ("UBIT") imposed by section 511.

[57] This 10-percent additional tax does not apply if a distribution from an education IRA is made on account of the death, disability, or scholarship received by the designated beneficiary.

[58] For example, if an education IRA has a total balance of $10,000, of which $4,000 represents principal (i.e., contributions) and $6,000 represents earnings, and if a distribution of $2,000 is made from such an account, then $800 of that distribution will be treated as a return of principal (which under no event is includible in the gross income of the distributee) and $1,200 of the distribution will be treated as accumulated earnings. In such a case, if qualified higher education expenses of the beneficiary during the year of the distribution are at least equal to the $2,000 total amount of the distribution (i.e., principal plus earnings), then the entire earnings portion of the distribution will be excludable

under section 530, provided that a Hope credit or Lifetime Learning credit is not claimed for that same taxable year on behalf of the beneficiary. If, however, the qualified higher education expenses of the beneficiary for the taxable year are less than the total amount of the distribution, then only a portion of the earnings will be excludable from gross income under section 530. Thus, in the example discussed above, if the beneficiary incurs only $1,500 of qualified higher education expenses in the year that a $2,000 distribution is made, then only $900 of the earnings will be excludable from gross income under section 530 (i.e., an exclusion will be provided for the pro-rata portion of the earnings, based on the ratio that the $1,500 of qualified higher education expenses bears to the $2,000 distribution) and the remaining $300 of the earnings portion of the distribution will be includible in the distributee's gross income.

Effective Date

The provisions are effective as if included in the 1997 Act—i.e., for taxable years beginning after December 31, 1997.

Conference Committee Report (H.R. CONF. REP. NO. 105-599)

The conference agreement follows the Senate amendment, with the following modifications, additions, and deletions.

1. Education Incentives of the 1997 Act

Education IRAs

The conference agreement clarifies that for purposes of the special rules regarding tax-free rollovers and changes of designated beneficiaries, the new beneficiary must be under the age of 30.

* * *

[Law at ¶ 5150, ¶ 5190, ¶ 5420 and ¶ 5940. CCH Explanation at ¶ 231 and ¶ 236.]

[¶ 10,850] Act Sec. 6004(c)(2) and 6004(c)(3). Qualified State tuition programs

Senate Committee Report (S. REP. NO. 105-174)

[Code Sec. 529]

Present Law

Section 529 provides tax-exempt status to "qualified State tuition programs," meaning certain programs established and maintained by a State (or agency or instrumentality thereof) under which persons may (1) purchase tuition credits or certificates on behalf of a designated beneficiary that entitle the beneficiary to a waiver or payment of qualified higher education expenses of the beneficiary, or (2) make contributions to an account that is established for the purpose of meeting qualified higher education expenses of the designated beneficiary of the account. The term "qualified higher education expenses" means expenses for tuition, fees, books, supplies, and equipment required for the enrollment or attendance at an eligible post-secondary educational institution, as well as room and board expenses (meaning the minimum room and board allowance applicable to the student as determined by the institution in calculating costs of attendance for Federal financial aid programs under sec. 472 of the Higher Education Act of 1965) for any period during which the student is at least a half-time student.

Section 529 also provides that no amount shall be included in the gross income of a contributor to, or beneficiary of, a qualified State tuition program with respect to any distribution from, or earnings under, such program, except that (1) amounts distributed or educational benefits provided to a beneficiary (e.g., when the beneficiary attends college) will be included in the beneficiary's gross income (unless excludable under another Code section) to the extent such amounts or the value of the educational benefits exceed contributions made on behalf of the beneficiary, and (2) amounts distributed to a contributor or another distributee (e.g., when a parent receives a refund) will be included in the contributor's/distributee's gross income to the extent such amounts exceed contributions made on behalf of the beneficiary. Earnings on an account may be refunded to a contributor or beneficiary, but the State or instrumentality must impose a more than de minimis monetary penalty unless the refund is (1) used for qualified higher education expenses of the beneficiary, (2) made on account of the death or disability of the beneficiary, or (3) made on account of a scholarship received by the designated beneficiary to the extent the amount refunded does not exceed the amount of the scholarship used for higher education expenses.

A transfer of credits (or other amounts) from one account benefiting one designated beneficiary to another account benefiting a different beneficiary will be considered a distribution (as will a change in the designated beneficiary of an interest in a qualified State tuition program), unless the beneficiaries are members of the same family. For this purpose, the term "member of the family" means persons described in paragraphs (1) through (8) of section 152(a)—e.g., sons, daughters, brothers, sisters, nephews and nieces, certain in-laws, etc—and any spouse of such persons.

Explanation of Provision

The bill clarifies that, under rules contained in present-law section 72, distributions from qualified State tuition programs are treated as representing a pro-rata share of the principal (i.e., contributions) and accumulated earnings in the account.

In addition, the bill modifies section 529(e)(2) to clarify that—for purposes of tax-free rollovers and changes of designated beneficiaries—a "member of the family" includes the spouse of the original beneficiary.

Effective Date

The provisions are effective for distributions made after December 31, 1997.

Conference Committee Report (H.R. CONF. REP. NO. 105-599)

The conference agreement follows the Senate amendment * * *

[Law at ¶ 5150 and ¶ 5410. CCH Explanation at ¶ 228.]

[¶ 10,855]   Act Sec. 6004(e)(1).   Enhanced deduction for corporate contributions of computer technology and equipment

Senate Committee Report (S. REP. NO. 105-174)

[Code Sec. 170(e)(6)]

Present Law

In computing taxable income, a taxpayer who itemizes deductions generally is allowed to deduct the fair market value of property contributed to a charitable organization. However, in the case of a charitable contribution of inventory or other ordinary-income property, short-term capital gain property, or certain gifts to private foundations, the amount of the deduction is limited to the taxpayer's basis in the property. In the case of a charitable contribution of tangible personal property, a taxpayer's deduction is limited to the adjusted basis in such property if the use by the recipient charitable organization is unrelated to the organization's tax-exempt purpose.

The Taxpayer Relief Act of 1997 provided that certain contributions of computer and other equipment to eligible donees to be used for the benefit of elementary and secondary school children qualify for an augmented deduction. Under this special rule, the amount of the augmented deduction available to a corporation making a qualified contribution generally is equal to its basis in the donated property plus one-half of the amount of ordinary income that would have been realized if the property had been sold. However, the augmented deduction cannot exceed twice the basis of the donated property. To qualify for the augmented deduction, the contribution must satisfy various requirements.

The legislative history of the provision states that the special tax treatment for contributions of computer and other equipment was to be effective for contributions made during a three-year period in taxable years beginning after December 31, 1997, and before January 1, 2001.[59] However, as a result of a drafting error, the statutory provision does not apply to contributions made during taxable years beginning after December 31, 1999.

Explanation of Provision

The bill corrects the termination date of the provision to provide that the special rule applies to contributions made during taxable years beginning after December 31, 1997, and before December 31, 2000.

In addition, the bill clarifies that the requirements set forth in section 170(e)(6)(B)(ii)-(vii) apply regardless of whether the donee is an educational organization or a tax-exempt charitable entity. Similarly, the rule in section 170(e)(6)(ii)(I) regarding subsequent contributions by private foundations is clarified to permit contributions to either educational organizations or tax-exempt charitable entities described in section 170(e)(6)(B)(i).

Effective Date

The provision is effective as of August 5, 1997, the date of enactment of the 1997 Act.

Conference Committee Report (H.R. CONF. REP. NO. 105-599)

The conference agreement follows the Senate amendment * * *

[Law at ¶ 5220. CCH Explanation at ¶ 696.]

[¶ 10,860]   Act Sec. 6004(f).   Treatment of cancellation of certain student loans

Senate Committee Report (S. REP. NO. 105-174)

[Code Sec. 108(f)]

Present Law

Under present law, an individual's gross income does not include forgiveness of loans made by tax-exempt educational organizations if the proceeds of such loans are used to pay costs of attendance at an educational institution or to refinance outstanding student loans and the student is not employed by the lender organization. The exclusion applies only if the forgiveness is contingent on the student's working for a certain period of time in certain professions for any of a broad class

of employers. In addition, the student's work must fulfill a public service requirement.

Explanation of Provision

The bill clarifies that gross income does not include amounts from the forgiveness of loans made by educational organizations and certain tax-exempt organizations to refinance *any* existing student loan (and not just loans made by educational organizations). In addition, the bill clarifies that refinancing loans made by educational organizations and certain tax-exempt organizations must be made pursuant to a program of the refinancing organization (e.g., school or pri-

---

[59] H. Rept. 105-220, p. 374.

vate foundation) that requires the student to fulfill a public service work requirement.

Effective Date

The provision is effective as of August 5, 1997, the date of enactment of the 1997 Act.

Conference Committee Report (H.R. CONF. REP. NO. 105-599)

The conference agreement follows the Senate amendment * * *

[Law at ¶ 5160. CCH Explanation at ¶ 241.]

[¶ 10,865]   Act Sec. 6004(g).   Qualified zone academy bonds
Senate Committee Report (S. REP. NO. 105-174)

[Code Sec. 1397E and Act. Sec. 6004(g)(1)]

Present Law

Certain financial institutions (i.e., banks, insurance companies, and corporations actively engaged in the business of lending money) that hold "qualified zone academy bonds" are entitled to a nonrefundable tax credit in an amount equal to a credit rate (set monthly by the Treasury Department[60]) multiplied by the face amount of the bond (sec. 1397E). The credit rate applies to all such bonds issued in each month. A taxpayer holding a qualified zone academy bond on the credit allowance date (i.e., each one-year anniversary of the issuance of the bond) is entitled to a credit. The credit is includible in gross income (as if it were an interest payment on the bond), and may be claimed against regular income tax and AMT liability.

"Qualified zone academy bonds" are defined as any bond issued by a State or local government, provided that (1) at least 95 percent of the proceeds are used for the purpose of renovating, providing equipment to, developing course materials for use at, or training teachers and other school personnel in a "qualified zone academy"—meaning certain public schools located in empowerment zones or enterprise communities or with a certain percentage of students from low-income families—and (2) private entities have promised to make contributions to the qualified zone academy with a value equal to at least 10 percent of the bond proceeds.

A total of $400 million of "qualified zone academy bonds" may be issued in each of 1998 and 1999. The $400 million aggregate bond cap will be allocated each year to the States according to their respective populations of individuals below the poverty line.[61] Each State, in turn, will allocate the credit to qualified zone academies within such State. A State may carry over any unused allocation into subsequent years.

Explanation of Provision

The bill clarifies that, for purposes of section 6655(g)(1)(B), the credit for certain holders of qualified zone academy bonds may be claimed for estimated tax purposes. Similarly, the bill clarifies for purposes of section 6401(b)(1) the manner in which the credit is taken into account when determining whether a taxpayer has made an overpayment of tax.

Effective Date

The provisions are effective for obligations issued after December 31, 1997.

Conference Committee Report (H.R. CONF. REP. NO. 105-599)

The conference agreement follows the Senate amendment * * *

[Law at ¶ 5070, ¶ 5090, ¶ 5100, ¶ 5680, ¶ 5690 and ¶ 8239. CCH Explanation at ¶ 244.]

[¶ 10,875]   Act Sec. 6005(a).   Contribution limitations for active participation in an IRA
Senate Committee Report (S. REP. NO. 105-174)

[Code Sec. 219(g)]

Present Law

Under present law, if a married individual (filing a joint return) is an active participant in an employer-sponsored retirement plan, the $2,000 IRA deduction limit is phased out over the following levels of adjusted gross income ("AGI"):

Taxable years beginning in:	Phase-out range
1997	$ 40,000—$50,000
1998	$ 50,000—$60,000
1999	$ 51,000—$61,000
2000	$ 52,000—$62,000
2001	$ 53,000—$63,000
2002	$ 54,000—$64,000
2003	$ 60,000—$70,000
2004	$ 65,000—$75,000
2005	$ 70,000—$80,000
2006	$ 75,000—$85,000
2007	$ 80,000—$100,000

---

[60] The Treasury Department will set the credit rate each month at a rate estimated to allow issuance of qualified zone academy bonds without discount and without interest cost to the issuer.

[61] See Rev. Proc. 98-9, which sets forth the maximum face amount of qualified zone academy bonds that may be issued for each State during 1998; IRS Proposed Rules (REG-119449-97), which provides guidance to holders and issuers of qualified zone academy bonds.

An individual is not considered an active participant in an employer-sponsored retirement plan merely because the individual's spouse is an active participant. The $2,000 maximum deductible IRA contribution for an individual who is not an active participant, but whose spouse is, is phased out for taxpayers with AGI between $150,000 and $160,000.

Explanation of Provision

The bill clarifies the intent of the Act relating to the AGI phase-out ranges for married individuals who are active participants in employer-sponsored plans and the AGI phase-out range for spouses of such active participants as described above.

Effective Date

The provision is effective as if included in the 1997 Act, i.e., for taxable years beginning after December 31, 1997.

Conference Committee Report (H.R. CONF. REP. NO. 105-599)

The conference agreement follows the Senate amendment * * *

[Law at ¶ 5240. CCH Explanation at ¶ 356.]

[¶ 10,880]   Act Sec. 6005(b)(1).   Contribution limit to Roth IRAs

Senate Committee Report (S. REP. NO. 105-174)

[Code Sec. 408A(c)]
Present Law

An individual who is an active participant in an employer-sponsored plan may deduct annual IRA contributions up to the lesser of $2,000 or 100 percent of compensation if the individual's adjusted gross income ("AGI") does not exceed certain limits. For 1998, the limit is phased-out over the following ranges of AGI: $30,000 to $40,000 in the case of a single taxpayer and $50,000 to $60,000 in the case of married taxpayers. An individual who is not an active participant in an employer-sponsored retirement plan (and whose spouse is not an active participant) may deduct IRA contributions up to the limits described above without limitation based on income. An individual who is not an active participant in an employer-sponsored retirement plan (and whose spouse is such an active participant) may deduct IRA contributions up to the limits described above if the AGI of the such individuals filing a joint return does not exceed certain limits. The limit is phased for out for such individuals with AGI between $150,000 and $160,000.

An individual may make nondeductible contributions up to the lesser of $2,000 or 100 percent of compensation to a Roth IRA if the individual's AGI does not exceed certain limits. An individual may make nondeductible contributions to an IRA to the extent the individual does not or cannot make deductible contributions to an IRA or contributions to a Roth IRA. Contributions to all an individual's IRAs for a taxable year may not exceed $2,000.

Explanation of Provision

The bill clarifies the intent of the Act that an individual may contribute up to $2,000 a year to all the individual's IRAs. Thus, for example, suppose an individual is not eligible to make deductible IRA contributions because of the phase-out limits, and is eligible to make a $1,000 Roth IRA contribution. The individual could contribute $1,000 to the Roth IRA and $1,000 to a nondeductible IRA.

Effective Date

The provision is effective as if included in the 1997 Act, i.e., for taxable years beginning after December 31, 1997.

Conference Committee Report (H.R. CONF. REP. NO. 105-599)

The conference agreement follows the Senate amendment * * *

[Law at ¶ 5370. CCH Explanation at ¶ 331.]

[¶ 10,885]   Act Sec. 6005(b)(2)(B) and 6005(b)(2)(C).   Limits based on modified adjusted gross income

Senate Committee Report (S. REP. NO. 105-174)

[Code Sec. 408A(c)(3)]
Present Law

The $2,000 Roth IRA maximum contribution limit is phased out for individual taxpayers with adjusted gross income ("AGI") between $95,000 and $110,000 and for married taxpayers filing a joint return with AGI between $150,000 and $160,000. The maximum deductible IRA contribution is phased out between $0 and $10,000 of AGI in the case of married couples filing a separate return.

Explanation of Provision

The bill clarifies the phase-out range for the Roth IRA maximum contribution limit for a married individual filing a separate return and conforms it to the range for deductible IRA (cont'd) contributions. Under the bill, the phase-out range for married individuals filing a separate return will be $0 to $10,000 of AGI.

Effective Date

The provision is effective as if included in the 1997 Act, i.e., for taxable years beginning after December 31, 1997.

Conference Committee Report (H.R. CONF. REP. NO. 105-599)

The conference agreement follows the Senate amendment * * *

[Law at ¶ 5370. CCH Explanation at ¶ 325.]

[¶ 10,890]   Act Sec. 6005(b)(4)(A) and 6005(b)(4)(B).   Conversions of IRAs into Roth IRAs

Senate Committee Report (S. REP. NO. 105-174)

[Code Sec. 72(t) and Code Sec. 408A]

Present Law

A taxpayer with adjusted gross income of less than $100,000 may convert a present-law deductible or nondeductible IRA into a Roth IRA at any time. The amount converted is includible in income in the year of the conversion, except that if the conversion occurs in 1998, the amount converted is includible in income ratably over the 4-year period beginning with the year in which the conversion occurs.[62] Amounts includible in income as a result of the conversion are not taken into account in determining whether the $100,000 threshold is exceeded. The 10-percent tax on early withdrawals does not apply to conversions of IRAs into Roth IRAs.

In general, distributions of earnings from a Roth IRA are excludable from income if the individual has had a Roth IRA for at least 5 years and certain other requirements are satisfied. The 5-year holding period with respect to conversion Roth IRAs begins from the year of the conversion. (Distributions that are excludable from income are referred to as qualified distributions.)

Present law does not contain a specific rule addressing what happens if an individual dies during the 4-year spread period for 1998 conversions.

Explanation of Provision

Distributions of converted amounts

Distributions before the end of the 4-year spread

The bill modifies the rules relating to conversions of IRAs into Roth IRAs in order to prevent taxpayers from receiving premature distributions from a Roth conversion IRA while retaining the benefits of 4-year income averaging. In the case of conversions to which the 4-year income inclusion rule applies, income inclusion will be accelerated with respect to any amounts withdrawn before the final year of inclusion. Under this rule, a taxpayer that withdraws converted amounts prior to the last year of the 4-year spread will be required to include in income the amount otherwise includible under the 4-year rule, plus the lesser of (1) the taxable amount of the withdrawal, or (2) the remaining taxable amount of the conversion (i.e., the taxable amount of the conversion not

included in income under the 4-year rule in the current or a prior taxable year). In subsequent years (assuming no such further withdrawals), the amount includible in income under the 4-year will be the lesser of (1) the amount otherwise required under the 4-year rule (determined without regard to the withdrawal) or (2) the remaining taxable amount of the conversion.

Under the bill, application of the 4-year spread will be elective. The election will be made in the time and manner prescribed by the Secretary. If no election is made, the 4-year rule will be deemed to be elected. An election, or deemed election, with respect to the 4-year spread cannot be changed after the due date for the return for the first year of the income inclusion (including extensions).

The following example illustrates the application of these rules.

Example: Taxpayer A has a nondeductible IRA with a value of $100 (and no other IRAs). The $100 consists of $75 of contributions and $25 of earnings. A converts the IRA into a Roth IRA in 1998 and elects the 4-year spread. As a result of the conversion, $25 is includible in income ratably over 4 years ($6.25 per year). The 10-percent early withdrawal tax does not apply to the conversion. At the beginning of 1999, the value of the account is $110, and A makes a withdrawal of $10. Under the proposal, the withdrawal would be treated as attributable entirely to amounts that were includible in income due to the conversion. In the year of withdrawal, $16.25 would be includible in income (the $6.25 includible in the year of withdrawal under the 4-year rule, plus $10 ($10 is less than the remaining taxable amount of $12.50 ($25-$12.50)). In the next year, $2.50 would be includible in income under the 4-year rule. No amount would be includible in income in year 4 due to the conversion.

Application of early withdrawal tax to converted amounts

The bill modifies the rules relating to conversions to prevent taxpayers from receiving premature distributions (i.e., within 5 years) while retaining the benefit of the nonpayment of the

---

[62] If the conversion is accomplished by means of a withdrawal and a rollover into a Roth IRA, the 4-year rule applies if the withdrawal is made during 1998 and the rollover occurs within 60 days of the withdrawal. In such a case, the 4-year period begins with the year in which the withdrawal was made. For purposes of this discussion, such conversions are treated as occurring in 1998.

early withdrawal tax. Under the bill, if converted amounts are withdrawn within the 5-year period beginning with the year of the conversion, then, to the extent attributable to amounts that were includible in income due to the conversion, the amount withdrawn will be subject to the 10-percent early withdrawal tax.[63]

Applying this rule to the example above, the $10 withdrawal would be subject to the 10-percent early withdrawal tax (unless as exception applies).

Application of 5-year holding period

The bill will also eliminate the special rule under which a separate 5-year holding period begins for purposes of determining whether a distribution of amounts attributable to a conversion is a qualified distribution; thus, the 5-year holding rule for Roth IRAs will begin with the year for which a contribution is first made to a Roth IRA. A subsequent conversion will not start the running of a new 5-year period.

Ordering rules

Ordering rules will apply to determine what amounts are withdrawn in the event a Roth IRA contains both conversion amounts (possibly from different years) and other contributions. Under these rules, regular Roth IRA contributions will be deemed to be withdrawn first, then converted amounts (starting with the amounts first converted). Withdrawals of converted amounts will be treated as coming first from converted amounts that were includible in income. As under present law, earnings will be treated as withdrawn after contributions. For purposes of these rules, all Roth IRAs, whether or not maintained in separate accounts, will be considered a single Roth IRA.

Corrections

In order to assist individuals who erroneously convert IRAs into Roth IRAs or otherwise wish to change the nature of an IRA contribution, contributions to an IRA (and earnings thereon) may be transferred in a trustee-to-trustee transfer from any IRA to another IRA by the due date for the taxpayer's return for the year of the contribution (including extensions). Any such transferred contributions will be treated as if contributed to the transferee IRA (and not to the transferor IRA). Trustee-to-trustee transfers include transfers between IRA trustees as well as IRA custodians, apply to transfers from and to IRA accounts and annuities, and apply to transfers between IRA accounts and annuities with the same trustee or custodian.

Effect of death on 4-year spread

Under the bill, in general, any amounts remaining to be included in income as a result of a 1998 conversion will be includible in income on the final return of the taxpayer. If the surviving spouse is the sole beneficiary of the Roth IRA, the spouse may continue the deferral by including the remaining amounts in his or her income over the remainder of the 4-year period.

Calculation of AGI limit for conversions

The bill clarifies the determination of AGI for purposes of applying the $100,000 AGI limit on IRA conversions into Roth IRAs. Under the bill, the conversion amount (to the extent otherwise includible in AGI) is subtracted from AGI as determined under the rules relating to IRAs (sec. 219) for the year of distribution. Thus, for example, the AGI-based phase out of the exemption from the disallowance for passive activity losses from rental real estate activities (sec. 469(i)(3)) would be applied taking into account the amount of the conversion that is includible in AGI, and then the amount of the conversion would be subtracted from AGI in determining whether a taxpayer is eligible to convert an IRA into a Roth IRA.

Effective Date

The provision is effective as if included in the 1997 Act, i.e., for taxable years beginning after December 31, 1997.

Conference Committee Report (H.R. CONF. REP. NO. 105-599)

The conference agreement follows the Senate amendment, with the following modifications, additions, and deletions.

* * *

2. Savings and Investment Incentives of the 1997 Act

Conversion of IRAs into Roth IRAs

The conferees wish to clarify that for purposes of determining the $100,000 adjusted gross income ("AGI") limit on IRA conversions to Roth IRAs, the conversion amount is not taken into account. Thus, for this purpose, AGI (and all AGI-based phaseouts) are to be determined without taking into account the conversion amount. For purposes of computing taxable income, the conversion amount (to the extent otherwise includible in AGI) is to be taken into account in computing the AGI-based phaseout amounts. The conferees wish to clarify that the language of the Senate Finance committee report (appearing in connection with section 6005(b) of the Senate amendment) relating to calculation of AGI limit for conversions is superceded.

* * *

[Law at ¶ 5370. CCH Explanation at ¶ 301, 305, 311, 315 and 321.]

---

[63] The otherwise available exceptions to the early withdrawal tax, e.g., for distributions after age 59-1/2, would apply.

[¶ 10,895]   Act Sec. 6005(c).   Penalty-free distributions for education expenses and purchase of first homes

Senate Committee Report (S. REP. NO. 105-174)

[Code Sec. 402]

Present Law

The 10-percent early withdrawal tax does not apply to distributions from an IRA if the distribution is for first-time homebuyer expenses, subject to a $10,000 life-time cap, or for higher education expenses. These exceptions do not apply to distributions from employer-sponsored retirement plans. A distribution from an employer-sponsored retirement plan that is an "eligible rollover distribution" may be rolled over to an IRA. The term "eligible rollover distribution" means any distribution to an employee of all or a portion or the balance to the credit of the employee in a qualified trust, except the term does not include certain periodic distributions, distributions based on life or joint life expectancies and distributions required under the minimum distribution rules. Generally, distributions from cash or deferred arrangements made on account of hardship are eligible rollover distributions. An eligible rollover distribution which is not transferred directly to another retirement plan or an IRA is subject to 20-percent withholding on the distribution.

Explanation of Provision

Under present law, participants in employer sponsored retirement plans can avoid the early withdrawal tax applicable to such plans by rolling over hardship distributions to an IRA and withdrawing the funds from the IRA. The bill modifies the rules relating to the ability to roll over hardship distributions from employer-sponsored retirement plans(including section 403(b) plans) in order to prevent such avoidance of the 10-percent early withdrawal tax. The bill provides that distributions from cash or deferred arrangements and similar arrangements made on account of hardship of the employee are not eligible rollover distributions. Such distributions will not be subject to the 20-percent withholding applicable to eligible rollover distributions.

Effective Date

The provision is effective for distributions after December 31, 1998.

Conference Committee Report (H.R. CONF. REP. NO. 105-599)

The conference agreement follows the Senate amendment * * *

[Law at ¶ 5150, ¶ 5330 and ¶ 5340. CCH Explanation at ¶ 361.]

[¶ 10,915]   Act Sec. 6005(d).   Individual capital gains rate reductions

Senate Committee Report (S. REP. NO. 105-174)

[Code Sec. 1(h)]

Present Law

The 1997 Act provided lower capital gains rates for individuals. Generally, the 1997 Act reduced the maximum rate on the adjusted net capital gain of an individual from 28 percent to 20 percent and provided a 10-percent rate for the adjusted net capital gain otherwise taxed at a 15-percent rate. The "adjusted net capital gain" means the net capital gain determined without regard to certain gain for which the 1997 Act provided a higher maximum rate of tax. The 1997 Act generally retained a 28-percent maximum rate for the long-term capital gain from collectibles, certain long-term capital gain included in income from the sale of small business stock, and the net capital gain determined by including all capital gains and losses properly taken into account after July 28, 1997, from property held more than one year but not more than 18 months and all capital gains and losses properly taken into account for the portion of the taxable year before May 7, 1997. In addition, the 1997 Act provided a maximum rate of 25 percent for the long-term capital gain attributable to real estate depreciation ("unrecaptured section 1250 gain").

Beginning in 2001 and 2006, lower rates of 8 and 18 percent will apply to certain property held more than five years.

The amounts taxed at the 28- and 25- percent rates may not exceed the individual's net capital gain and also are reduced by amounts otherwise taxed at a 15-percent rate.

Under the provisions of the 1997 Act, net short-term capital losses and long-term capital loss carryovers reduce the amount of adjusted net capital gain before reducing amounts taxed at the maximum 25- and 28-percent rates.

The 1997 Act failed to coordinate the new multiple holding periods with certain provisions of the Code.

Explanation of Provision

Under the bill, the "adjusted net capital gain" of an individual is the net capital gain reduced (but not below zero) by the sum of the 28-percent rate gain and the unrecaptured section 1250 gain.

"28-percent rate gain" means the amount of net gain attributable to collectibles gains and losses, an amount of gain equal to the gain excluded from gross income on the sale of certain small business stock under section 1202,[64] long-

---

[64] For example, assume an individual has $300,000 gain from the sale of qualified stock in a small business corporation and assume that section 1202(b) limits the gain that

may be taken into account under section 1202(a) to $240,000. $120,000 of the gain (50 percent of $240,000) is excluded from gross income under section 1202(a). The

term capital gains and losses properly taken into account after July 28, 1997, from property held more than one year but not more than 18 months, the net short-term capital loss for the taxable year and the long-term capital loss carryover to the taxable year. Long-term capital gains and losses properly taken into account before May 7, 1997, also are included in computing 28-percent rate gain.

"Unrecaptured section 1250 gain" means the amount of long-term capital gain (not otherwise treated as ordinary income) which would be treated as ordinary income if section 1250 recapture applied to all depreciation (rather than only to depreciation in excess of straight-line depreciation) from property held more than 18 months (one year for amounts properly taken into account after May 6, 1997, and before July 29, 1997).[65] The unrecaptured section 1250 depreciation is reduced (but not below zero) by the excess (if any) of amount of losses taken into account in computing 28-percent gain over the amount of gains taken into account in computing 28-percent rate gain.

The bill contains several conforming amendments to coordinate the multiple holding periods with other provisions of the Code. Inherited property (sec. 1223 (11) and (12)) and certain patents (sec. 1235) are deemed to have a holding period of more than 18 months, allowing the 10- and 20-percent rates to apply. Amounts treated as ordinary income by reason of section 1231(c) will be allocated among categories of net section 1231 gain in accordance with IRS forms or regulations. The bill clarifies that the amount treated as long-term capital gain or loss on a section 1256 con-tract is treated as attributable to property held for more than 18 months.

Under the bill, in applying section 1233(b) where the substantially identical property has been held more than one year but not more than 18 months, any gain on the closing of the short sale will be considered gain from property held not more than 18 months, and the substantially identical property will have be treated as held for one year on the day before the earlier of the date of the closing of the short sale or the date the property is disposed of. In applying section 1233(d) where, on the date of the short sale, the substantially identical property has been held more than 18 months, any loss on the closing of the short sale will be treated as a loss from the sale or exchange of a capital asset held more than 18 months. Finally, in applying section 1092(f), any loss with respect to the option shall be treated as a loss from the sale or exchange of a capital asset held more than 18 months, if at the time the loss is realized, gain on the sale or exchange of the stock would be treated as gain from the sale or exchange of a capital asset held more than 18 months.[66]

The bill reorders the rate structure under sections 1(h)(1) and 55(b)(3) without any substantive change.

The bill makes minor technical changes, including a provision to reduce the minimum tax preference on certain small business stock to 28 percent, beginning in 2006.[67]

Effective Date

The provision applies to taxable years ending after May 6, 1997.

Conference Committee Report (H.R. CONF. REP. NO. 105-599)

The conference agreement follows the Senate amendment * * *
[Law at ¶ 5001, ¶ 5110, ¶ 5120, ¶ 5600 and ¶ 5605. CCH Explanation at ¶ 501, ¶ 503, ¶ 505, ¶ 506, ¶ 508, ¶ 510, ¶ 512, ¶ 515, ¶ 518, ¶ 521, ¶ 523 and ¶ 524.]

[¶ 10,920] Act Sec. 6005(e)(1). Exclusion of gain on the sale of a principal residence owned and used less than two years (special rules for joint returns)

Senate Committee Report (S. REP. NO. 105-174)

[Code Sec. 121(b)]
Present Law
Under present law, a taxpayer generally is able to exclude up to $250,000 ($500,000 if married filing a joint return) of gain realized on the sale or exchange of a principal residence. To be eligible for the exclusion, the taxpayer must have owned the residence and used it as a principal residence for at least two of the five years prior to the sale or exchange. A taxpayer who fails to meet these requirements by reason of a change of place of employment, health, or unforeseen circumstances is able to exclude a fraction of the taxpayer's

---

(Footnote Continued)

$180,000 of gain that is included in gross income is included in the computation of net capital gain, and $120,000 of that gain is taken into account under section 1(h)(5)(i)(III), as added by the bill, in computing 28-percent rate gain. The maximum effective regular tax rate on the $240,000 of gain to which the 50-percent section 1202 exclusion applies is 14 percent and the maximum rate on the remaining $60,000 of gain is 20 percent.

[65] In the case of a disposition of a partnership interest held more than 18 months, the amount of the individual's long-term capital gain which would be treated as ordinary income under section 751(a) if section 1250 applied to all depreciation, will be taken into account in computing unre-captured section 1250 gain.

[66] Any loss treated as a long-term capital loss by reason of section 1233(d) or 1092(f) will be taken into account in computing 28-percent rate gain where the property causing such loss to be treated as a long-term capital loss was held not more than 18 months on the applicable date.

[67] Thus, the maximum rate under the minimum tax will be 17.92% (.64 times 28%).

realized gain equal to the fraction of the two years that the requirements are met.

Explanation of Provision
* * *

In addition, the bill provides that if a married couple filing a joint return does not qualify for the $500,000 maximum exclusion, the amount of the maximum exclusion that may be claimed by the couple is the sum of each spouse's maximum exclusion determined on a separate basis.

Effective Date

The provision is effective as if included in section 312 of the 1997 Act.

Conference Committee Report (H.R. CONF. REP. NO. 105-599)

The conference agreement follows the Senate amendment * * *

[Law at ¶ 5180. CCH Explanation at ¶ 248.]

[¶ 10,925] Act Sec. 6005(e)(2). Exclusion of gain on the sale of a principal residence owned and used less than two years (exclusion for taxpayers failing to meet certain requirements)

Senate Committee Report (S. REP. NO. 105-174)

[Code Sec. 121(c)(1)]

Present Law
Under present law, a taxpayer generally is able to exclude up to $250,000 ($500,000 if married filing a joint return) of gain realized on the sale or exchange of a principal residence. To be eligible for the exclusion, the taxpayer must have owned the residence and used it as a principal residence for at least two of the five years prior to the sale or exchange. A taxpayer who fails to meet these requirements by reason of a change of place of employment, health, or unforeseen circumstances is able to exclude a fraction of the taxpayer's realized gain equal to the fraction of the two years that the requirements are met.

Explanation of Provision
The bill clarifies that an otherwise qualifying taxpayer who fails to satisfy the two-year ownership and use requirements is able to exclude an amount equal to the fraction of the $250,000 ($500,000 if married filing a joint return), not the fraction of the realized gain which is equal to the fraction of the two years that the ownership and use requirements are met. For example, an unmarried taxpayer who owns and uses a principal residence for one year then sells at realized gain of $500,000 may exclude $125,000 of gain (one-half of $250,000) not $250,000 of gain (one-half of the realized gain). Similarly, an unmarried taxpayer who owns and uses a principal residence for one year then sells at a realized gain of $50,000 may exclude the entire $50,000 of gain since it is less than one half of $250,000. The exclusion is not limited to $25,000 (one-half of the $50,000 realized gain).

* * *

Effective Date
The provision is effective as if included in section 312 of the 1997 Act.

Conference Committee Report (H.R. CONF. REP. NO. 105-599)

The conference agreement follows the Senate amendment * * *

[Law at ¶ 5180. CCH Explanation at ¶ 246.]

[¶ 10,930] Act Sec. 6005(e)(3). Effective date of the exclusion of gain on the sale of a principal residence

Senate Committee Report (S. REP. NO. 105-174)

[Act Sec. 6005(e)(3)]

Present Law
The exclusion for gain on sale of a principal residence under the 1997 Act generally applies to sales or exchanges occurring after May 6, 1997. A taxpayer may elect, however, to apply prior law to a sale or exchange (1) made before the date of enactment of the Act, (2) made after the date of enactment pursuant to a binding contract in effect on such date, or (3) where a replacement residence was acquired on or before the date of enactment (or pursuant to a binding contract in effect on the date of enactment) and the prior-law rollover provision would apply.

Explanation of Provision
The bill clarifies that a taxpayer may elect to apply prior law with respect to a sale or exchange on the date of enactment of section 312 of the 1997 Act.

Effective Date
The provision is effective as if included in section 312 of the 1997 Act.

Act Sec. 6005(e)(3) ¶ 10,930

Conference Committee Report (H.R. CONF. REP. NO. 105-599)

The conference agreement follows the Senate amendment * * *

[Law at ¶ 8240. CCH Explanation at ¶ 251.]

[¶ 10,935] Act Sec. 6005(f). Rollover of gain from sale of qualified stock

Senate Committee Report (S. REP. NO. 105-174)

[Code Sec. 1045]
Present Law

The 1997 Act provided that gain from the sale of qualified small business stock held by an individual for more than six months can be "rolled over" tax-free to other qualified small business stock.

Explanation of Provision

Under the bill, a partnership or an S corporation can roll over gain from qualified small busi-

ness stock held more than six months if (and only if) at all times during the taxable year all the interests in the partnership or S corporation are held by individuals, estates[68], and trusts with no corporate beneficiaries.

Effective Date

The provision applies to sales on or after August 5, 1997, the date of enactment of the 1997 Act.

Conference Committee Report (H.R. CONF. REP. NO. 105-599)

The conference agreement follows the Senate amendment, with the following modifications, additions, and deletions. * * *

2. Savings and Investment Incentives of the 1997 Act
* * *

Small business stock rollover

The conference agreement provides that rules similar to the rules contained in subsections (f) through (k) of section 1202 will apply for purposes of the rollover provision (sec. 1045). Under these rules, for example, the benefit of a tax-free roll-

over with respect to the sale of small business stock by a partnership will flow through to a partner who is not a corporation if the partner held its partnership interest at all times the partnership held the small business stock. A similar rule applies to S corporations. The conference agreement does not contain any provision limiting the types of partners or shareholders that a partnership or S corporation may have in order for the benefits of section 1045 to apply to a noncorporate partner or shareholder.
* * *

[Law at ¶ 5580. CCH Explanation at ¶ 531.]

[¶ 10,945] Act Sec. 6006(a). Clarification of the small business exemption

Senate Committee Report (S. REP. NO. 105-174)

[Code Sec. 55]
Present Law

The corporate alternative minimum tax is repealed for small corporations for taxable years beginning after December 31, 1997. A small corporation is one that had average gross receipts of $5 million or less for a prior three-year period. A corporation that meets the $5 million gross receipts test will continue to be treated as a small corporation exempt from the alternative minimum tax so long as its average gross receipts do not exceed $7.5 million.

Explanation of Provision

The provision clarifies the application of the $5 million and $7.5 million gross receipts tests that a corporation must meet to be a small corporation exempt from the AMT. Under the provision, in order for a corporation to qualify as a small corporation exempt from the AMT for a taxable year, the corporation's average gross receipts for all 3-taxable-year periods beginning after December

31, 1993 and ending before such taxable year must be $7.5 million or less. The $7.5 million amount is reduced to $5 million for the corporation's first 3-taxable-year period (or portion thereof) beginning after December 31, 1993, and ending before the taxable year for which the exemption is claimed.

If a corporation's first taxable year beginning after December 31, 1997 (the first year the exemption is available) is its first taxable year (and the corporation does not lose its status as a small corporation because it is aggregated with one or more corporations under section 448(c)(2) or treated as having a predecessor corporation under section 448(c)(3)(D)), the corporation will be treated as an exempt small corporation for such year regardless of its gross receipts for such year.

The operation of the gross receipts tests for the small corporation AMT exemption is demonstrated by the following examples.

---

[68] The term "estate" is intended to include both the estate of a decedent and the estate of an individual in bankruptcy.

Example 1.—Assume a calendar-year corporation was in existence on January 1, 1994. In order to qualify as a small corporation for 1998 (the first year the exemption is available), (1) the corporation's average gross receipts for the 3-taxable-year period 1994 through 1996 must be $5 million or less and (2) the corporation's average gross receipts for the 1995 through 1997 period must be $7.5 million or less. If the corporation qualifies for 1998, the corporation will qualify for 1999 if its average gross receipts for the 3-taxable-year period 1996 through 1998 also is $7.5 million or less. If the corporation does not qualify for 1998, the corporation cannot qualify for 1999 or any subsequent year.

Example 2.—Assume a calendar-year corporation is first incorporated in 1999 and is neither aggregated with a related, existing corporation under section 448(c)(2) nor treated as having a predecessor corporation under section 448(c)(3)(D). The corporation will qualify as a small corporation for 1999 regardless of its gross receipts for such year. In order to qualify as a small corporation for 2000, the corporation's gross receipts for 1999 must be $5 million or less.[69] If the corporation qualifies for 2000, the corporation also will qualify for 2001 if its average gross receipts for the 2-taxable-year period 1999 through 2000 is $7.5 million or less. If the corporation does not qualify for 2000, the corporation cannot qualify for 2001 or any subsequent year. If the corporation qualifies for 2001, the corporation will qualify for 2002 if its average gross receipts for the 3-taxable-year period 1999 through 2001 is $7.5 million or less.

Effective Date

The provision is effective for taxable years beginning after December 31, 1997.

Conference Committee Report (H.R. CONF. REP. NO. 105-599)

The conference agreement follows the Senate amendment * * *

[Law at ¶ 5110. CCH Explanation at ¶ 566.]

[¶ 10,950]   Act Sec. 6006(b).   Election to use AMT depreciation for regular tax purposes

Senate Committee Report (S. REP. NO. 105-174)

[Code Sec. 168]

Present Law

For regular tax purposes, depreciation deductions for certain shorter-lived tangible property may be determined using the 200-percent declining balance method over 3-, 5-, 7-, or 10-year recovery periods (depending on the type of property). For alternative minimum tax ("AMT") purposes, depreciation on such property placed in service after 1986 and before 1999 is computed by using the 150-percent declining balance method over the longer class lives prescribed by the alternative depreciation system of section 168(g). A taxpayer may elect to use the methods and lives applicable to AMT depreciation for regular tax purposes.

The 1997 Act conformed the recovery periods (but not the methods) used for purposes of the AMT depreciation to the recovery periods used for purposes of the regular tax, for property placed in service after 1998. The 1997 Act did not make a conforming change to the election to use the pre-1998 AMT recovery methods and recovery periods for regular tax purposes.

Explanation of Provision

For property placed in service after 1998, a taxpayer would be allowed to elect, for regular tax purposes, to compute depreciation on tangible personal property otherwise qualified for the 200-percent declining balance method by using the 150-percent declining balance method over the recovery periods applicable to the regular tax (rather than the longer class lives of the alternative depreciation system of sec. 168(g)).

Effective Date

The provision is effective for property placed in service after December 31, 1998.

Conference Committee Report (H.R. CONF. REP. NO. 105-599)

The conference agreement follows the Senate amendment * * *

[Law at ¶ 5210. CCH Explanation at ¶ 571.]

---

[69] The gross receipts for 1999 must be annualized under section 448(c)(3)(B) if the 1999 taxable year is less than 12 months.

[¶ 10,970] Act Sec. 6007(a)(1). Clarification of effective date for indexing of generation-skipping exemption

Senate Committee Report (S. REP. NO. 105-174)

[Code Sec. 2631(c) and Act Sec. 6007(a)(2)]

Present Law

The 1997 Act provided for the indexation of the $1 million exemption from generation-skipping transfers effective for decedents dying after December 31, 1998.

Explanation of Provision

The provision clarifies that the indexing of the exemption from generation-skipping transfers is effective with respect to all generation-skipping transfers (i.e., direct skips, taxable terminations, and taxable distributions) made after 1998.

With respect to existing trusts, transferors are permitted to make a late allocation of any additional GST exemption amount attributable to indexing adjustments in accordance with the present-law rules applicable to late allocations as set forth in sections 2632 and 2642, and the regu-

lations promulgated thereunder. For example, assume an individual transferred $2 million to a trust in 1995, and allocated his entire $1 million GST exemption to the trust at that time (resulting in an inclusion ratio of .50). Assume further that in 2001, the GST exemption has increased to $1,100,000 as the result of indexing, and that the value of the trust assets is now $3 million. If the individual is still alive in 2001, he is permitted to make a late allocation of $100,000 of GST exemption to the trust, resulting in a new inclusion ratio of 1-(($1,500,000+100,000)/$3,000,000), or .467.

Effective Date

The provision is effective for generation-skipping transfers (i.e., direct skips, taxable terminations, and taxable distributions) made after December 31, 1998.

Conference Committee Report (H.R. CONF. REP. NO. 105-599)

The conference agreement follows the Senate amendment * * *

[Law at ¶ 5790. CCH Explanation at ¶ 431.]

[¶ 10,975] Act Sec. 6007(b)(1)(A). Conversion of qualified family-owned business exclusion into a deduction

Senate Committee Report (S. REP. NO. 105-174)

[Code Sec. 2057]

Present Law

The qualified family-owned business provision in the 1997 Act provides an exclusion from estate taxes for certain qualified family-owned business interests. It is unclear whether the provision provides an exclusion of value or an exclusion of property from the estate, and thus it is unclear how the new provision interacts with other provisions in the Internal Revenue Code (e.g., secs. 1014, 2032A, 2056, 2612, and 6166).

Explanation of Provision

The provision converts the qualified family-owned business exclusion into a deduction, and redesignates section 2033A as section 2057. Except as provided below, the requirements of the qualified family-owned business provision otherwise remain unchanged. The qualified family-owned business deduction is not available for generation-skipping transfer tax purposes.

Effective Date

The provision is effective with respect to estates of decedents dying after December 31, 1997.

Conference Committee Report (H.R. CONF. REP. NO. 105-599)

The conference agreement follows the Senate amendment * * *

[Law at ¶ 5760 and ¶ 5770. CCH Explanation at ¶ 401.]

[¶ 10,980] Act Sec. 6007(b)(1)(B). Coordination between unified credit and family-owned business provision

Senate Committee Report (S. REP. NO. 105-174)

[Code Sec. 2057(a)]

Present Law

The 1997 Act effectively increased the amount of lifetime gifts and transfers at death that are exempt from unified estate and gift tax from $600,000 to $1,000,000 over the period 1997 to 2006, through increases in an individual's unified credit. In addition, the 1997 Act provided a limited exclusion for certain family-owned business

interests. The exclusion for family-owned business interests may be taken only to the extent that the exclusion for family-owned business interests, plus the amount effectively exempted by the unified credit, does not exceed $1.3 million. As a result, for years after 1998, the maximum amount of exclusion for family-owned business interests is reduced by increases in the dollar amount of transfers effectively exempted through the unified credit.

Because the structure of the 1997 Act increases the unified credit over time (until 2006) while decreasing over the same period the benefit of the closely-held business exclusion, the estate tax on estates with family-owned businesses increases over time until 2006. This increase in estate tax results from the fact that increases in the unified credit provide a benefit at the decedent's lowest estate tax brackets, while the exclusion for family-owned businesses provides a benefit at the decedent's highest estate tax brackets.

Explanation of Provision

Under the provision, if an executor elects to utilize the qualified family-owned business deduction, the estate tax liability is calculated as if the estate were allowed a maximum qualified family-owned business deduction of $675,000 and an applicable exclusion amount under section 2010 (i.e., the amount exempted by the unified credit) of $625,000, regardless of the year in which the decedent dies. If the estate includes less than $675,000 of qualified family-owned business interests, the applicable exclusion amount is increased on a dollar-for-dollar basis, but only up to the applicable exclusion amount generally available for the year of death.

For example, assume the decedent dies in 2005, when the applicable exclusion amount under section 2010 is $800,000 [950,000.—CCH]. If the estate includes qualified family-owned business interests valued at $675,000 or more, the estate

tax liability is calculated as if the estate were allowed a qualified family-owned business deduction of $675,000, and the applicable exclusion amount under section 2010 is limited to $625,000. If the estate includes qualified family-owned business interests of $500,000 or less, all of the qualified family-owned business interests could be deducted from the estate, and the applicable exclusion amount under section 2010 is $800,000. If the estate includes qualified family-owned business interests valued between $500,000 and $675,000, all of the qualified family-owned business interests could be deducted from the estate, and the applicable exclusion amount under section 2010 is calculated as the excess of $1.3 million over the amount of qualified family-owned business interests. (For example, if the qualified family-owned business interests were valued at $600,000, the applicable exclusion amount under section 2010 is $700,000.)

If a recapture event occurs with respect to any qualified family-owned business interest, the total amount of estate taxes potentially subject to recapture is calculated as the difference between the actual amount of estate tax liability for the estate, and the amount of estate taxes that would have been owed had the qualified family-owned business election not been made.

Effective Date

The provision is effective for decedents dying after December 31, 1997.

Conference Committee Report (H.R. CONF. REP. NO. 105-599)

The conference agreement follows the Senate amendment * * *

[Law at ¶ 5770. CCH Explanation at ¶ 406.]

[¶ 10,985]   Act Sec. 6007(b)(2).   Clarification of businesses eligible for family-owned business provision

Senate Committee Report (S. REP. NO. 105-174)

[Code Sec. 2057(b)(3)]

Present Law

In order to be eligible to exclude from the gross estate a portion of the value of a family-owned business, the sum of (1) the adjusted value of family-owned business interests includible in the decedent's estate, and (2) the amount of gifts of family-owned business interests to family members of the decedent that are not included in the decedent's gross estate, must exceed 50 percent of the decedent's adjusted gross estate.

Explanation of Provision

The provision clarifies the formula for determining the amount of gifts of family-owned business interests made to members of the decedent's family that are not otherwise includible in the decedent's gross estate.

Effective Date

The provision is effective with respect to decedents dying after December 31, 1997.

Conference Committee Report (H.R. CONF. REP. NO. 105-599)

The conference agreement follows the Senate amendment * * *

[Law at ¶ 5770. CCH Explanation at ¶ 411.]

Act Sec. 6007(b)(2)   ¶ 10,985

[¶ 10,990]   Act Sec. 6007(b)(3) 6007(b)(6) and 6007(b)(7).   Other modifications to the qualified family-owned business provision

Senate Committee Report (S. REP. NO. 105-174)

[Code Sec. 2057]

Present Law

The qualified family-owned business provision incorporates by cross-reference several other provisions of the Code, including a number of provisions in section 2032A and the personal holding company rules of section 543(a).

Explanation of Provision

The provision modifies section 2033A(g) (relating to the security requirements for noncitizen qualified heirs) by deleting the cross-reference to section 2033A(i)(3)(M), which does not appear to be appropriate. The provision also makes rules similar to those set forth in section 2032A(h) and (i) (relating to conversions and exchanges of property under sections 1031 and 1033) applicable for purposes of section 2033A. Finally, the provision clarifies that, in identifying assets that produce (or are held for the production of) income of a type described in section 543(a), section 543(a) is applied without regard to section 543(a)(2)(B) (the dividend requirement for corporate entities).

Effective Date

The provision is effective with respect to estates of decedents dying after December 31, 1997.

Conference Committee Report (H.R. CONF. REP. NO. 105-599)

The conference agreement follows the Senate amendment, with the following modifications, additions, and deletions.   * * *

3. Estate and Gift Tax Provisions of the 1997 Act

* * *

Qualification for an estate tax deduction for qualified family-owned business interest in the case of cash leases by decedent to family member

The conference agreement clarifies that an interest in property will not be disqualified, in whole or in part, as an interest in a family-owned business where the decedent leases that interest on a net cash basis to a member of the decedent's family who uses the leased property in an active business. The rental income derived by the decedent from the net cash lease in those circumstances is not treated as personal holding company income for purposes of Code section 2057.

* * *

[Law at ¶ 5770. CCH Explanation at ¶ 426.]

[¶ 10,995]   Act Sec. 6007(b)(5).   Clarification of "trade or business" requirement for family-owned business provision

Senate Committee Report (S. REP. NO. 105-174)

[Code Sec. 2057(e)(1) and Code Sec. 2057(f)]

Present Law

A qualified family-owned business interest is defined as any interest in a trade or business that meets certain requirements—e.g., the decedent and members of his family must own certain percentages of the trade or business, the decedent or members of his family must have materially participated in the trade or business for five of the eight years preceding the decedent's death, and the qualified heir or members of his family must materially participate in the trade or business for at least five years of any eight-year period within 10 years following the decedent's death.

Explanation of Provision

The provision clarifies that an individual's interest in property used in a trade or business may qualify for the qualified family-owned business provision as long as such property is used in a trade or business by the individual or a member of the individual's family. Thus, for example, if a brother and sister inherit farmland upon their father's death, and the sister cash-leases her portion to her brother, who is engaged in the trade or business of farming, the "trade or business" requirement is satisfied with respect to both the brother and the sister. Similarly, if a father cash-leases farmland to his son, and the son materially participates in the trade or business of farming the land for at least five of the eight years preceding his father's death, the pre-death material participation and "trade or business" requirements are satisfied with respect to the father's interest in the farm.

Effective Date

The provision is effective with respect to estates of decedents dying after December 31, 1997.

Conference Committee Report (H.R. CONF. REP. NO. 105-599)

The conference agreement follows the Senate amendment * * *

[Law at ¶ 5770. CCH Explanation at ¶ 421.]

[¶ 11,015] Act Sec. 6007(b)(7). Clarification that interests eligible for family-owned business provision must be passed to a qualified heir

Senate Committee Report (S. REP. NO. 105-174)

[Code Sec. 2057(i)(3)]

Present Law

The 1997 Act provided a new exclusion for qualified family-owned business interests. One of the requirements for the exclusion is that such interests must pass to a "qualified heir," which includes members of the decedent's family and any individual who has been actively employed by the trade or business for at least 10 years prior to the date of the decedent's death.

Explanation of Provision

The provision clarifies that qualified family-owned business interests must pass to a qualified heir in order to qualify for the deduction. For this purpose, if all beneficiaries of a trust are qualified heirs (and in such other circumstances as the Secretary of the Treasury may provide), property passing to the trust may be treated as having passed to a qualified heir.

Effective Date

The provision is effective with respect to estates of decedents dying after December 31, 1997.

Conference Committee Report (H.R. CONF. REP. NO. 105-599)

The conference agreement follows the Senate amendment * * *

[Law at ¶ 5770. CCH Explanation at ¶ 416.]

[¶ 11,020] Act Sec. 6007(c). Clarification of interest on installment payment of estate tax on holding companies

Senate Committee Report (S. REP. NO. 105-174)

[Code Sec. 6166(b)(7)(A) and Code Sec 6166(b)(8)(A)]

Present Law

If certain conditions are met, a decedent's estate may elect to pay the estate tax attributable to certain closely-held businesses over a 14-year period. The 1997 Act provided for a 2-percent interest rate on the estate tax on first $1 million in value of interests in qualified closely-held businesses, and a rate equal to 45 percent of the regular deficiency rate on the amount in excess of the portion eligible for the 2-percent rate, but also provided that none of interest on the deferred payment of estate taxes is deductible for income or estate tax purposes. Interests in holding companies and non-readily-tradeable business interests are not eligible for the 2-percent rate.

Explanation of Provision

The provision clarifies that deferred payments of estate tax on holding companies and non-readily-tradable business interests do not qualify for the 2-percent interest rate, but instead are subject to a rate of 45 percent of the regular deficiency rate. Such interest payments are not deductible for income or estate tax purposes

Effective Date

The provision generally is effective for decedents dying after December 31, 1997.

Conference Committee Report (H.R. CONF. REP. NO. 105-599)

The conference agreement follows the Senate amendment * * *

[Law at ¶ 6160. CCH Explanation at ¶ 436.]

[¶ 11,025] Act Sec. 6007(d). Clarification on declaratory judgment jurisdiction of U.S. Tax Court regarding installment payment of estate tax

Senate Committee Report (S. REP. NO. 105-174)

[Code Sec. 7479(a)]

Present Law

If certain conditions are met, a decedent's estate may elect to pay estate tax attributable to certain closely-held business over a 14-year period. The 1997 Act provided that the U.S. Tax Court would have jurisdiction to determine whether the estate of a decedent qualifies for the 14-year installment payment of estate tax.

Explanation of Provision

The provision clarifies that the jurisdiction of the U.S. Tax Court to determine whether an estate qualifies for installment payment of estate tax on closely-held businesses extends to determining which businesses in an estate are eligible for the deferral.

Effective Date

The provision is effective for decedents dying after the date of enactment of the 1997 Act.

Act Sec. 6007(d)   ¶ 11,025

Conference Committee Report (H.R. CONF. REP. NO. 105-599)

The conference agreement follows the Senate amendment * * *

[Law at ¶ 6710. CCH Explanation at ¶ 441.]

[¶ 11,030]   Act Sec. 6007(e).   Clarification of rules governing revaluation of gifts

Senate Committee Report (S. REP. NO. 105-174)

[Code Sec. 2001, Code Sec. 6501(c) and Act Sec. 6007(e)]

Present Law

The valuation of a gift becomes final for gift tax purposes after the statute of limitations on any gift tax assessed or paid has expired. The 1997 Act extended that rule to apply for estate tax purposes, provided for a lengthened statute of limitations for gift tax purposes if certain information is not disclosed with the gift tax return, and provided jurisdiction to the U.S. Tax Court to determine the value of any gift.

Explanation of Provision

The provision clarifies that in determining the amount of taxable gifts made in preceding calendar periods, the value of prior gifts is the value of such gifts as finally determined, even if no gift tax was assessed or paid on that gift. For this purpose, final determinations include, e.g., the value reported on the gift tax return (if not challenged by the IRS prior to the expiration of the statute of limitations), the value determined by the IRS (if not challenged in court by the taxpayer), the value determined by the courts, or the value agreed to by the IRS and the taxpayer in a settlement agreement.

Effective Date

The provision is effective with respect to gifts made after the date of enactment of the 1997 Act.

Conference Committee Report (H.R. CONF. REP. NO. 105-599)

The conference agreement follows the Senate amendment * * *

[Law at ¶ 5740, ¶ 5780, ¶ 6400 and ¶ 8245. CCH Explanation at ¶ 446.]

[¶ 11,035]   Act Sec. 6007(g).   Clarification with respect to post-mortem conservation easements

Senate Committee Report (S. REP. NO. 105-174)

[Code Sec. 2031(c)]

Present Law

A deduction is allowed for estate tax purposes for a contribution of a qualified real property interest to a charity (or other qualified organization) exclusively for conservation purposes (sec. 2055(f)). The 1997 Act also provided an election to exclude from the taxable estate 40 percent of the value of any land subject to a qualified conservation easement that meets certain requirements. The 1997 Act provided that the executor of the decedent's estate, or the trustee of a trust holding the land, could grant a qualifying easement after the decedent's death, as long as the easement is granted prior to the date of the election (gener-

ally, within nine months after the date of the decedent's death).

Explanation of Provision

The provision clarifies that, in the case of a qualified conservation contribution made after the date of the decedent's death, an estate tax deduction is allowed under section 2055(f). However, no income tax deduction is allowed to the estate or the qualified heirs with respect to such post-mortem conservation easements.

Effective Date

The provision is effective with respect to estates of decedents dying after December 31, 1997.

Conference Committee Report (H.R. CONF. REP. NO. 105-599)

The conference agreement follows the Senate amendment * * *

[Law at ¶ 5750. CCH Explanation at ¶ 451.]

[¶ 11,045]   Act Sec. 6008(a).   Amendments to Title VII of the 1997 Act relating to incentives for the District of Columbia (census tracts)

Senate Committee Report (S. REP. NO. 105-174)

[Code Sec. 1400]
Present Law
Designation of D.C. Enterprise Zone

Certain economically depressed census tracts within the District of Columbia are designated as the "D.C. Enterprise Zone," within which businesses and individual residents are eligible for special tax incentives. The census tracts that compose the D.C. Enterprise Zone for purposes of the wage credit, expensing, and tax-exempt financing incentives include all census tracts that presently are part of the D.C. enterprise community and census tracts within the District of Columbia where the poverty rate is not less than 20 percent. The D.C. Enterprise Zone designation generally will remain in effect for five years for the period from January 1, 1998, through December 31, 2002.

* * *

Explanation of Provisions
Eligible census tracts

The bill clarifies that the determination of whether a census tract in the District of Columbia satisfies the applicable poverty criteria for inclusion in the D.C. Enterprise Zone for purposes of the wage credit, expensing, and special tax-exempt financing incentives (poverty rate of not less than 20 percent) or for purposes of the zero-percent capital gains rate (poverty rate of not less than 10 percent) is based on 1990 decennial census data. Thus, data from the 2000 decennial census would not result in the expansion or other reconfiguration of the D.C. Enterprise Zone.

* * *

Effective Date

The provisions are effective as of August 5, 1997, the date of enactment of the 1997 Act.

Conference Committee Report (H.R. CONF. REP. NO. 105-599)

The conference agreement follows the Senate amendment * * *

[Law at ¶ 5700. CCH Explanation at ¶ 574.]

[¶ 11,050]   Act Sec. 6008(b).   Amendments to Title VII of the 1997 Act relating to incentives for the District of Columbia (qualified D.C. Zone business)

Senate Committee Report (S. REP. NO. 105-174)

[Code Sec. 1400A]
Present Law
* * *
Empowerment zone wage credit, expensing, and tax-exempt financing

The following tax incentives generally are available in the D.C. Enterprise Zone: (1) a 20-percent wage credit for the first $15,000 of wages paid to D.C. residents who work in the D.C. Enterprise Zone; (2) an additional $20,000 of expensing under Code section 179 for qualified zone property placed in service by a "qualified D.C. Zone business"; and (3) special tax-exempt financing for certain zone facilities.

Qualified D.C. Zone business

For purposes of the increased expensing under section 179, as well as for purposes of the zero percent capital gains rate (described below), a corporation or partnership is a qualified D.C. Zone business if: (1) the sole trade or business of the corporation or partnership is the active conduct of a "qualified business" (defined below) within the D.C. Zone; (2) at least 50 percent (80 percent for purposes of the zero percent capital gains rate) of the total gross income of such entity is derived from the active conduct of a qualified business within the D.C. Zone; (3) a substantial portion of the use of the entity's tangible property (whether owned or leased) is within the D.C. Zone; (4) a substantial portion of the entity's intangible property is used in the active conduct

of such business; (5) a substantial portion of the services performed for such entity by its employees are performed within the D.C. Zone; and (6) less than 5 percent of the average of the aggregate unadjusted bases of the property of such entity is attributable to (a) certain financial property, or (b) collectibles not held primarily for sale to customers in the ordinary course of an active trade or business. Similar rules apply to a qualified business carried on by an individual as a proprietorship.

In general, a "qualified business" means any trade or business. However, a "qualified business" does not include any trade or business that consists predominantly of the development or holding of intangibles for sale or license. In addition, a qualified business does not include any private or commercial golf course, country club, massage parlor, hot tub facility, suntan facility, racetrack or other facility used for gambling, liquor store, or certain large farms (so-called "excluded businesses"). The rental of residential real estate is not a qualified business. The rental of commercial real estate is a qualified business only if at least 50 percent of the gross rental income from the real property is from qualified D.C. Zone businesses. The rental of tangible personal property to others also is not a qualified business unless at least 50 percent of the rental of such property is by qualified D.C. Zone businesses or by residents of the D.C. Zone.

Act Sec. 6008(b)   ¶ 11,050

For purposes of the tax-exempt financing provisions, the term "D.C. Zone business" generally is defined as for purposes of the increased expensing under section 179. However, a qualified D.C. Zone business for purposes of the tax-exempt financing provisions includes a business located in the D.C. Zone that would qualify as a D.C. Zone business if it were separately incorporated. In addition, under a special rule applicable only for purposes of the tax-exempt financing rules, a business is not required to satisfy the requirements applicable to a D.C. Zone business until the end of a startup period if, at the beginning of the startup period, there is a reasonable expectation that the business will be a qualified D.C. Zone business at the end of the startup period and the business makes bona fide efforts to be such a business. With respect to each property financed by a bond issue, the startup period ends at the beginning of the first taxable year beginning more than two years after the later of (1) the date of the bond issue financing such property, or (2) the date the property was placed in service (but in no event more than three years after the date of bond issuance). In addition, if a business satisfies certain requirements applicable to a qualified D.C.

Zone business for a three-year testing period following the end of the start-up period and thereafter continues to satisfy certain business requirements, then it will be treated as a qualified D.C. Zone business for all years after the testing period irrespective of whether it satisfies all of the requirements of a qualified D.C. Zone business.

* * *

Explanation of Provisions
* * *

Qualified D.C. Zone business

The bill modifies section 1400B(c) to clarify that a proprietorship can constitute a D.C. Zone business for purposes of the zero-percent capital gains rate.

The bill also clarifies that qualified D.C. Zone businesses that take advantage of the special tax-exempt financing incentives do not become subject to a 35-percent zone resident requirement after the close of the testing period.

* * *

Effective Date

The provisions are effective as of August 5, 1997, the date of enactment of the 1997 Act.

Conference Committee Report (H.R. Conf. Rep. No. 105-599)

The conference agreement follows the Senate amendment * * *

[Law at ¶ 5710. CCH Explanation at ¶ 580.]

[¶ 11,055]   Act Sec. 6008(c).   Amendments to Title VII of the 1997 Act relating to incentives for the District of Columbia (zero-percent capital gains rate)

Senate Committee Report (S. Rep. No. 105-174)

[Code Sec. 1400B]

Present Law
* * *

Zero-percent capital gains rate

A zero-percent capital gains rate applies to capital gains from the sale of certain qualified D.C. Zone assets held for more than five years. For purposes of the zero-percent capital gains rate, the D.C. Enterprise Zone is defined to include all census tracts within the District of Columbia where the poverty rate is not less than 10 percent. Only capital gain that is attributable to the 10-year period beginning January 1, 1998, and ending December 31, 2007, is eligible for the zero-percent rate.

In general, qualified "D.C. Zone assets" mean stock or partnership interests held in, or tangible property held by, a D.C. Zone business. Such assets must generally be acquired after December 31, 1997, and before January 1, 2003. However, under a special rule, qualified D.C. Zone assets include property that was a qualified D.C. Zone asset in the hands of a prior owner, provided that at the time of acquisition, and during substantially all of the subsequent purchaser's holding period, either (1) substantially all of the use of the

property is in a qualified D.C. Zone business, or (2) the property is an ownership interest in a qualified D.C. Zone business.

* * *

Explanation of Provisions
* * *

Zero-percent capital gains rate

The bill clarifies that there is no requirement that D.C. Zone business property be acquired by a subsequent purchaser prior to January 1, 2003, to be eligible for the special rule applicable to subsequent purchasers.

In addition, the bill clarifies that the termination of the D.C. Enterprise Zone designation at the end of 2002 will not, by itself, result in property failing to be treated as a qualified D.C. Zone asset for purposes of the zero-percent capital gains rate, provided that the property otherwise continues to qualify were the D.C. Zone designation in effect.

* * *

Effective Date

The provisions are effective as of August 5, 1997, the date of enactment of the 1997 Act.

Conference Committee Report (H.R. CONF. REP. NO. 105-599)

The conference agreement follows the Senate amendment * * *   [Law at ¶ 5720. CCH Explanation at ¶ 583.]

[¶ 11,060] Act Sec. 6008(d). Amendments to Title VII of the 1997 Act relating to incentives for the District of Columbia (first-time homebuyer credit)

Senate Committee Report (S. REP. NO. 105-174)

[Code Sec. 1400C]

Present Law
* * *

First-time homebuyer tax credit

First-time homebuyers of a principal residence in the District are eligible for a tax credit of up to $5,000 of the amount of the purchase price, except that the credit phases out for individual taxpayers with adjusted gross income ("AGI") between $70,000 and $90,000 ($110,000-$130,000 for joint filers). The credit is available with respect to property purchased after the date of enactment and before January 1, 2001. Any excess credit may be carried forward indefinitely to succeeding taxable years.

Explanation of Provisions
* * *

First-time homebuyer credit

The bill clarifies that, for purposes of the first-time homebuyer credit, a "first-time homebuyer" means any individual if such individual (and, if married, such individual's spouse) did not have a present ownership interest in a principal residence in the District of Columbia during the one-year period ending on the date of the purchase of the principal residence to which the credit applies.

The bill also clarifies that the phaseout of the credit for individual taxpayers with adjusted gross income between $70,000 and $90,000 ($110,000-$130,000 for joint filers) applies only in the year the credit is generated, and does not apply in subsequent years to which the credit may be carried over.

In addition, the bill clarifies that the term "purchase price" means the adjusted basis of the principal residence on the date the residence is purchased. Newly constructed residences are treated as purchased by the taxpayer on the date the taxpayer first occupies such residence.

The bill clarifies that the first-time homebuyer credit is a nonrefundable personal credit and would provide that the first-time homebuyer credit is claimed after the credits described in Code sections 25 (credit for interest on certain home mortgages) and 23 (adoption credit).

Finally, the bill clarifies that the first-time homebuyer credit would be available only for property purchased after August 4, 1997, and before January 1, 2001. Thus, the credit is available to first-time home purchasers who acquire title to a qualifying principal residence on or after August 5, 1997, and on or before December 31, 2000, irrespective of the date the purchase contract was entered into.

Effective Date

The provisions are effective as of August 5, 1997, the date of enactment of the 1997 Act.

Conference Committee Report (H.R. CONF. REP. NO. 105-599)

The conference agreement follows the Senate amendment * * *   [Law at ¶ 5010, ¶ 5030 and ¶ 5730. CCH Explanation at ¶ 577.]

[¶ 11,095] Act Sec. 6009(a). Clarification of qualification for reduced rate of excise tax on certain hard ciders

Senate Committee Report (S. REP. NO. 105-174)

[Code Sec. 5041]

Present Law

Distilled spirits are taxed at a rate of $13.50 per proof gallon; beer is taxed at a rate of $18 per barrel (approximately 58 cents per gallon); and still wines of 14 percent alcohol or less are taxed at a rate of 1.07 per wine gallon. The Code defines still wines as wines containing not more than 0.392 gram of carbon dioxide per hundred milliliters of wine. Higher rates of tax are applied to wines with greater alcohol content, to sparkling wines (e.g., champagne), and to artificially carbonated wines.

Certain small wineries may claim a credit against the excise tax on wine of 90 cents per wine gallon on the first 100,000 gallons of still wine produced annually (i.e., net tax rate of 17 cents per wine gallon on wines with an alcohol content of 14 percent or less). No credit is allowed on sparkling wines. Certain small breweries pay a reduced tax of $7.00 per barrel (approximately 22.6 cents per gallon) on the first 50,000 barrels of beer produced annually.

Hard cider is a wine fermented solely from apples or apple concentrate and water, containing no other fruit product and containing at least one-half of one percent and less than 7 percent alcohol by volume. Once fermented, eligible hard cider may not be altered by the addition of other fruit juices, flavor, or other ingredients that alter the flavor that results from the fermentation process.

Act Sec. 6009(a) ¶ 11,095

The 1997 Act provided a lower excise tax rate of 22.6 cents per gallon on hard cider. Qualifying small producers that produce 250,000 gallons or less of hard cider and other wines in a calendar year may claim a credit of 5.6 cents per wine gallon on the first 100,000 gallons of hard cider produced. This credit produces an effective tax rate of 17 cents per gallon, the same effective rate as that applied to small producers of still wines having an alcohol content of 14 percent or less. This credit is phased out for production in excess of 100,000 gallons but less than 250,000 gallons annually.

Explanation of Provision

The bill clarifies that the 22.6-cents-per-gallon tax rate applies only to apple cider that otherwise would be a still wine subject to a tax rate of $1.07 per wine gallon, i.e., still wines having an alcohol content of 14 percent or less.

Effective Date

The provision is effective as if included in the 1997 Act.

Conference Committee Report (H.R. CONF. REP. NO. 105-599)

The conference agreement follows the Senate amendment * * *

[Law at ¶ 5960. CCH Explanation at ¶ 731.]

[¶ 11,100]   Act Sec. 6009(b).   Election for 1987 partnerships to continue exception from treatment of publicly traded partnerships as corporations

Senate Committee Report (S. REP. NO. 105-174)

[Code Sec. 7704]
Present Law
In general

In the case of an electing 1987 partnership that elects to be subject to a 3.5-percent tax on gross income from the active conduct of a trade or business, the general rule treating a publicly traded partnership as a corporation does not apply. The 3.5-percent tax was intended to approximate the corporate tax the partnership would pay if it were treated as a corporation for Federal tax purposes.

Tax on partnership

The 3.5-percent tax is imposed on the electing 1987 partnership under the provision (sec. 7704(g)(3)). The provision does not specifically make inapplicable, however, the general rule that a partnership as such is not subject to income tax, but rather, the partners are liable for the tax in their separate or individual capacities (sec. 701).

Estimated tax payments

The provision does not specifically make applicable the requirements for payment of estimated tax that apply generally to payments of corporate tax.

Explanation of Provisions
Tax on partnership

The technical correction clarifies that the 3.5-percent tax is paid by the partnership. The general rule of section 701(a) that a partnership as such is not subject to income tax, but rather, the partners are liable for the tax in their separate or individual capacities does not apply to the payment of the 3.5-percent tax by the partnership.

Estimated tax payments

The technical correction provides that the corporate estimated tax payment rules of section 6655 are applied to the 3.5-percent tax payable by an electing 1987 partnership in the same manner as if the partnership were a corporation and the tax were imposed under section 11 (relating to corporate tax rates). References in section 11 to taxable income are to be applied for this purpose as if they were references to gross income of the partnership for the taxable year from the active conduct of trades and businesses by the partnership.

Effective Date
Tax on partnership

The provision is effective as if enacted with the 1997 Act.

Estimated tax payments

The provision is effective for taxable years beginning after the date of enactment.

Conference Committee Report (H.R. CONF. REP. NO. 105-599)

The conference agreement follows the Senate amendment * * *

[Law at ¶ 6840. CCH Explanation at ¶ 676.]

[¶ 11,105]   Act Sec. 6009(c).   Depreciation limitations for electric vehicles

Senate Committee Report (S. REP. NO. 105-174)

[Code Sec. 280F]
Present Law

Annual depreciation deductions with respect to passenger automobiles are limited to specified dollar amounts, indexed for inflation. Any cost not recovered during the 6-year recovery period of such vehicles may be recovered during the years succeeding the recovery period, subject to similar limitations. The recovery-period limitations are trebled for vehicles that are propelled primarily by electricity.

Explanation of Provision

The depreciation limitations applicable to post-recovery periods under section 280F are trebled for vehicles that are propelled primarily by electricity.

Effective Date

The provision is effective for property placed in service after August 5, 1997 and before January 1, 2005.

Conference Committee Report (H.R. CONF. REP. NO. 105-599)

The conference agreement follows the Senate amendment * * *

[Law at ¶ 5270. CCH Explanation at ¶ 592.]

[¶ 11,110]   Act Sec. 6009(d).   Combined employment tax reporting demonstration project

Senate Committee Report (S. REP. NO. 105-174)

[Code Sec. 6103]
Present Law

Traditionally, Federal tax forms are filed with the Federal Government and State tax forms are filed with individual states. This necessitates duplication of items common to both returns. Some States have recently been working with the IRS to implement combined State and Federal reporting of certain types of items on one form as a way of reducing the burdens on taxpayers. The State of Montana and the IRS have cooperatively developed a system to combine State and Federal employment tax reporting on one form. The one form would contain exclusively Federal data, exclusively State data, and information common to both: the taxpayer's name, address, TIN, and signature.

The Internal Revenue Code prohibits disclosure of tax returns and return information, except to the extent specifically authorized by the Internal Revenue Code (sec. 6103). Unauthorized disclosure is a felony punishable by a fine not exceeding $5,000 or imprisonment of not more than five years, or both (sec. 7213). An action for civil damages also may be brought for unauthorized disclosure (sec. 7431). No tax information may be furnished by the Internal Revenue Service ("IRS") to another agency unless the other agency establishes procedures satisfactory to the IRS for safeguarding the tax information it receives (sec. 6103(p)).

Implementation of the combined Montana-Federal employment tax reporting project had been hindered because the IRS interprets section 6103 to apply that provision's restrictions on disclosure to information common to both the State and Federal portions of the combined form, although these restrictions would not apply to the State with respect to the State's use of State-requested information if that information were supplied separately to both the State and the IRS.

The 1997 Act permits implementation of a demonstration project to assess the feasibility and desirability of expanding combined reporting in the future. There are several limitations on the demonstration project. First, it is limited to the State of Montana and the IRS. Second, it is limited to employment tax reporting. Third, it is limited to disclosure of the name, address, TIN, and signature of the taxpayer, which is information common to both the Montana and Federal portions of the combined form. Fourth, it is limited to a period of five years.

Explanation of Provision

The provision permits Montana to use this information as if it had collected it separately by eliminating Federal penalties for disclosure of this information. The provision also corrects a cross-reference to the provision.

Effective Date

The provision is effective as of the date of enactment of the 1997 Act (August 5, 1997), and will expire on the date five years after the date of enactment of the 1997 Act.

Conference Committee Report (H.R. CONF. REP. NO. 105-599)

The conference agreement follows the Senate amendment * * *

[Law at ¶ 6110. CCH Explanation at ¶ 589.]

[¶ 11,115]   Act Sec. 6009(e).   Modification of operation of elective carryback of existing net operating losses of the National Railroad Passenger Corporation ("Amtrak")

Senate Committee Report (S. REP. NO. 105-174)

[Act Sec. 6009(e)]

Present Law

The 1997 Act provides elective procedures that allow Amtrak to consider the tax attributes of its predecessors (i.e., those railroads that were relieved of their responsibility to provide intercity rail passenger service as a result of the Rail Passenger Service Act of 1970) in the use of Amtrak's net operating losses. The benefit allowable under these procedures is limited to the least of: (1) 35 percent of Amtrak's existing qualified carryovers, (2) the net tax liability for the carryback period, or (3) $2,323,000,000. One half of the amount so calculated will be treated as a payment of the tax imposed by chapter 1 of the Internal Revenue Code of 1986 for Amtrak's taxable year ending December 31, 1997, and a similar amount for Amtrak's taxable year ending December 31, 1998.

The availability of the elective procedures is conditioned on Amtrak (1) agreeing to make payments of one percent of the amount it receives to each of the non-Amtrak States to offset certain transportation related expenditures and (2) using the balance for certain qualified expenses. Non-Amtrak States are those States that are not receiving Amtrak service at any time during the period beginning on the date of enactment and ending on the date of payment.

Explanation of Provision

The provision provides that the term "non-Amtrak State" means any State that is not receiving intercity passenger rail service from Amtrak as of the date of enactment of the 1997 Act (August 5, 1997). Thus, a State will not lose its status as a non-Amtrak State with respect to any payment by reason of acquiring Amtrak service with any payment from Amtrak under the 1997 Act provision.

Effective Date

The provision is effective as if included in section 977 of the 1997 Act.

Conference Committee Report (H.R. CONF. REP. NO. 105-599)

The conference agreement follows the Senate amendment * * *

[Law at ¶ 8250. CCH Explanation at ¶ 694.]

[¶ 11,125]   Act Sec. 6010(a)(1).   Exception from constructive sales rules for certain debt positions

Senate Committee Report (S. REP. NO. 105-174)

[Code Sec. 1259(b)(2)]

Present Law

A taxpayer is required to recognize gain (but not loss) upon entering into a constructive sale of an "appreciated financial position," which generally includes an appreciated position with respect to any stock, debt instrument or partnership interest. An exception is provided for positions with respect to debt instruments that have an unconditionally payable principal amount, that are not convertible into the stock of the issuer or a related person, and the interest on which is either fixed, payable at certain variable rates or based on certain interest payments on a pool of mortgages.

Explanation of Provision

The provision clarifies that, to qualify for the exception for positions with respect to debt instruments, the position would either have to meet the requirements as to unconditional principal amount, non-convertibility and interest terms or, alternatively, be a hedge of a position meeting these requirements. A hedge for purposes of the provision includes any position that reduces the taxpayer's risk of interest rate or price changes or currency fluctuations with respect to another position.

Effective Date

The provision is generally effective for constructive sales entered into after June 8, 1997.

Conference Committee Report (H.R. CONF. REP. NO. 105-599)

The conference agreement follows the Senate amendment * * *

[Law at ¶ 5620. CCH Explanation at ¶ 536.]

[¶ 11,130]   Act Sec. 6010(a)(2).   Definition of forward contract under constructive sales rules

Senate Committee Report (S. REP. NO. 105-174)

[Code Sec. 1259(d)(1)]

Present Law

A constructive sale of an appreciated financial position generally results when the taxpayer enters into a forward contact to deliver the same or substantially identical property. A forward contract for this purpose is defined as a contract that provides for delivery of a substantially fixed amount of property at a substantially fixed price.

Explanation of Provision

The provision clarifies that the definition of a forward contract includes a contract that provides for cash settlement with respect to a substantially fixed amount of property at a substantially fixed price.

Effective Date

The provision is generally effective for constructive sales entered into after June 8, 1997.

Conference Committee Report (H.R. CONF. REP. NO. 105-599)

The conference agreement follows the Senate amendment * * *

[Law at ¶ 5620. CCH Explanation at ¶ 541.]

[¶ 11,135]   Act Sec. 6010(a)(3).   Treatment of mark-to-market gains of electing traders

Senate Committee Report (S. REP. NO. 105-174)

[Code Sec. 475(f)(1)(D)]

Present Law

Securities and commodities traders may elect application of the mark-to-market accounting rules. Gain or loss recognized by an electing taxpayer under these rules is treated as ordinary gain or loss.

Under the Self-Employment Contributions Act ("SECA"), a tax is imposed on an individual's net earnings from self-employment ("NESE"). Gain or loss from the sale or exchange of a capital asset is excluded from NESE.

A publicly-traded partnership generally is treated as a corporation for Federal tax purposes. An exception to this rule applies if 90 percent or more of the partnership's gross income consists of passive-type income, which includes gain from the sale or disposition of a capital asset.

Explanation of Provision

The provision clarifies that gain or loss of a securities or commodities trader that is treated as ordinary solely by reason of election of mark-to-market treatment is not treated as other than gain or loss from a capital asset for purposes of determining NESE for SECA tax purposes, determining whether the passive-type income exception to the publicly-traded partnership rules is met or for purposes of any other Code provision specified by the Treasury Department in regulations.

Effective Date

The provision applies to taxable years of electing securities and commodities traders ending after the date of enactment of the 1997 Act.

Conference Committee Report (H.R. CONF. REP. NO. 105-599)

The conference agreement follows the Senate amendment * * *

[Law at ¶ 5380. CCH Explanation at ¶ 551.]

[¶ 11,140]   Act Sec. 6010(a)(4).   Special effective date for constructive sale rules

Senate Committee Report (S. REP. NO. 105-174)

[Act Sec. 6010(a)(4)]

Present Law

The constructive sales rules contain a special effective date provision for decedents dying after June 8, 1997, if (1) a constructive sale of an appreciated financial position occurred before such date, (2) the transaction remains open for not less than two years, (3) the transaction remains open at any time during the three years prior to the decedent's death, and (4) the transaction is not closed within the 30-day period beginning on the date of enactment of the 1997 Act. If the requirements of the special effective date pro-

vision are met, both the appreciated financial position and the transaction resulting in the constructive sale are generally treated as property constituting rights to receive income in respect of a decedent under section 691. However, gain with respect to a position in a constructive sale transaction that accrues after the transaction is closed is not included in income in respect of a decedent.

Explanation of Provision

The provision clarifies the special effective date rule to provide that the rule does not apply if the constructive sale transaction is closed at any time prior to the end of the 30th day after the date of enactment of the 1997 Act.

Effective Date

The provision is effective for decedents dying after June 8, 1997.

Conference Committee Report (H.R. CONF. REP. NO. 105-599)

The conference agreement follows the Senate amendment * * *

[Law at ¶ 8255. CCH Explanation at ¶ 546.]

[¶ 11,145]   Act Sec. 6010(b).   Gain recognition for certain extraordinary dividends

Senate Committee Report (S. REP. NO. 105-174)

[Code Sec. 1059]

Present Law

A corporate shareholder generally can deduct at least 70 percent of a dividend received from another corporation. This dividends received deduction is 80 percent if the corporate shareholder owns at least 20 percent of the distributing corporation and generally 100 percent if the shareholder owns at least 80 percent of the distributing corporation.

Section 1059 of the Code requires a corporate shareholder that receives an "extraordinary dividend" to reduce the basis of the stock with respect to which the dividend was received by the nontaxed portion of the dividend. Whether a dividend is "extraordinary" is determined, among other things, by reference to the size of the dividend in relation to the adjusted basis of the shareholder's stock. In addition, dividends resulting from non pro rata redemptions, partial liquidations, and certain other redemptions are extraordinary dividends. Pursuant to a provision of the 1997 Act, gain is recognized to the extent the reduction in basis of stock exceeds the basis in the stock with respect to which an extraordinary dividend is received. Prior to the 1997 Act, the recognition of such gain generally was deferred until the stock to which the adjustment related was sold or disposed of.

The consolidated return regulations provide basis adjustment rules with respect to dividends paid within a consolidated group of corporations.

These rules provide that a dividend paid from one member of a group to its parent reduces the parent's basis in the stock of the payor and if such reduction exceeds the parent's basis, an "excess loss account" is created or increased. Excess loss accounts generally are not restored to income until the occurrence of certain specified events (e.g., when the corporation to which the excess loss account relates leaves the consolidated group). Legislative history indicates that, except as provided in regulations, the extraordinary dividend provisions do not apply to result in a double reduction in basis in the case of distributions between members of an affiliated group filing consolidated returns or in the double inclusion of earnings and profits.

Explanation of Provision

The provision provides the Treasury Department regulatory authority to coordinate the basis adjustment rules of section 1059 and the consolidated return regulations. It is expected that these rules generally would provide that, except as provided in regulations to be issued,[72] section 1059 will not cause current gain recognition to the extent that the consolidated return regulations require the creation or increase of an excess loss account with respect to a distribution.

Effective Date

The provision generally is effective for distributions after May 3, 1995.

Conference Committee Report (H.R. CONF. REP. NO. 105-599)

The conference agreement follows the Senate amendment, with the following modifications, additions, and deletions. * * *

5. Revenue Increase Provisions of the 1997 Act

   Coordination between basis adjustment rules relating to extraordinary dividends and similar rules applicable to consolidated returns

   With respect to the Senate amendment regarding gain recognition for certain extraordinary dividends, the conference agreement clarifies that

Congress intends that, except as provided in regulations to be issued, section 1059 does not cause current gain recognition to the extent that the consolidated return regulations require the creation or increase of an excess loss account with respect to a distribution. Thus, current Treas. Reg. sec. 1.1059(e)-1(a) does not result in gain recognition with respect to distributions within a consolidated group to the extent such distribution results in the creation or increase of an excess loss account under the consolidated return regulations. * * *

[Law at ¶ 5590. CCH Explanation at ¶ 626.]

---

[72] Thus, current Treas. reg. sec. 1.1059(e)-1(a) will not result in gain recognition with respect to distributions within a consolidated group to the extent such distribution results in the creation or increase of an excess loss account under the consolidated return regulations.

[¶ 11,150] Act Sec. 6010(c).   Treatment of certain corporate distributions

Senate Committee Report (S. REP. No. 105-174)

[Code Sec. 351(c), Code Sec. 355(e)(3)(A), Code Sec. 368(a)(2)(H) and Act Sec. 6010(c)]

Present Law

The 1997 Act (sec. 1012(a)) requires a distributing corporation ("distributing") to recognize corporate level gain on the distribution of stock of a controlled corporation ("controlled") under section 355 of the Code if, pursuant to a plan or series of related transactions, one or more persons acquire a 50-percent or greater interest (defined as 50 percent or more of the voting power or value of the stock) of either the distributing or controlled corporation (Code sec. 355(e)). Certain transactions are excepted from the definition of acquisition for this purpose, including, under section 355(e)(3)(A)(iv), the acquisition by a person of stock in a corporation if shareholders owning directly or indirectly stock possessing more than 50 percent of the voting power and more than 50 percent of the value of the stock in distributing or any controlled corporation before such acquisition own directly or indirectly stock possessing such vote and value in such distributing or controlled corporation after such acquisition.[73]

In the case of a 50-percent or more acquisition of either the distributing corporation or the controlled corporation, the amount of gain recognized is the amount that the distributing corporation would have recognized had the stock of the controlled corporation been sold for fair market value on the date of the distribution. The Conference Report to the 1997 Act states that no adjustment to the basis of the stock or assets of either corporation is allowed by reason of the recognition of the gain.[74]

The 1997 Act (sec. 1012(b)(1)) also provides that, except as provided in regulations, section 355 shall not apply to the distribution of stock from one member of an affiliated group of corporations (as defined in section 1504(a)) to another member of such group (an intragroup spin-off) if such distribution is part of a such a plan or series of related transactions pursuant to which one or more persons acquire stock representing a 50-percent or greater interest in a distributing or controlled corporation, determined after the application of the rules of section 355(e).

In addition, the 1997 Act (sec. 1012(b)(2)) provides that in the case of any distribution of stock of one member of an affiliated group of corporations to another member under section 355, the Treasury Department has regulatory authority under section 358(g) to provide adjustments to the basis of any stock in a corporation which is a member of such group, to reflect appropriately the proper treatment of such distribution.

The 1997 Act (sec. 1012(c)) also modified certain rules for determining control immediately after a distribution in the case of certain divisive transactions in which a controlled corporation is distributed and the transaction meets the requirements of section 355. In such cases, under section 351 and modified section 368(a)(2)(H) with respect to reorganizations under section 368(a)(1)(D), those shareholders receiving stock in the distributed corporation are treated as in control of the distributed corporation immediately after the distribution if they hold stock representing a greater than 50 percent interest in the vote and value of stock of the distributed corporation.

The effective date (Act section 1012(d)(1)) states that the forgoing provisions of the 1997 Act apply to distributions after April 16, 1997, pursuant to a plan (or series of related transactions) which involves an acquisition occurring after such date (unless certain transition provisions apply).

Explanation of Provision

Acquisition of a 50-percent or greater interest

The bill clarifies that the acquisitions described in Code section 355(e)(3)(A) are disregarded in determining whether there has been an acquisition of a 50-percent or greater interest in a corporation. However, other transactions that are part of a plan or series of related transactions could result in an acquisition of a 50-percent or greater interest.

In the case of acquisitions under section 355(e)(3)(A)(iv), the provision clarifies that the acquisition of stock in the distributing corporation or any controlled corporation is disregarded to the extent that the percentage of stock owned directly or indirectly in such corporation by each person owning stock in such corporation immediately before the acquisition does not decrease.

Example: Shareholder A owns 10 percent of the vote and value of the stock of corporation D (which owns all of corporation C). There are nine other equal shareholders of D. A also owns 100 percent of the vote and value of the stock of unrelated corporation P. D distributes C to all the shareholders of D. Thereafter, pursuant to a plan or series of related transactions, D (worth 100x) merges with corporation P (worth 900x). After the merger, each of the former shareholders of corporation D owns stock of the merged entity reflecting the vote and value attributable to that shareholder's respective 10 percent former stock ownership of D. Each of the former shareholders of D owns 1 percent of the stock of the merged corporation, except that shareholder A (who owned 100 percent of corporation P and 10 percent of corporation D before the merger) now owns 91 percent of the stock of the merged corpo-

---

[73] This exception (as certain other exceptions) does not apply if the stock held before the acquisition was acquired pursuant to a plan (or series of related transactions) to acquire a 50-percent or greater interest in the distributing or a controlled corporation.
[74] The 1997 Act does not limit the otherwise applicable Treasury regulatory authority under section 336(e) of the Code. Nor does it limit the otherwise applicable provisions of section 1367 with respect to the effect on shareholder stock basis of gain recognized by an S corporation under this provision.

ration. In determining whether a 50-percent or greater interest in D has been acquired, the interest of each of the continuing shareholders is disregarded only to the extent there has been no decrease in such shareholder's direct or indirect ownership. Thus, the 10 percent interest of A, and the 1 percent interest of each of the nine other former shareholder of D, is not counted. The remaining 81 percent ownership of the merged corporation, representing a decrease of nine percent in the interests of each of the nine former shareholders other than A, is counted in determining the extent of an acquisition. Therefore, a 50-percent or greater interest in D has been acquired.

Treasury regulatory authority

The bill also clarifies that the regulatory authority of the Treasury Department under section 358(c) applies to distributions after April 16, 1997, without regard to whether a distribution involves a plan (or series of related transactions) which involves an acquisition.

As stated in the Conference Report to the 1997 Act, with respect to the Treasury Department regulatory authority under section 358(c) as applied to intragroup spin-off transactions that are not part of a plan or series of related transactions that involve an acquisition of a 50-percent or greater interest under new section 355(f), it is expected that any Treasury regulations will be applied prospectively, except in cases to prevent abuse.

Section 351(c) and section 368(a)(2)(H) "control immediately after" requirement

In general, the 1997 Act modifications to the control immediately after requirement of Section 351(c) and section 368(a)(2)(H) were intended to minimize certain differences in the results of a transaction involving a contribution of assets to controlled corporation prior to a section 355 spin-off that could occur depending on whether the distributing or controlled corporation were acquired subsequent to the spin-off.

The bill clarifies that in the case of certain divisive transactions in which a corporation contributes assets to a controlled corporation and then distributes the stock of the controlled corporation in a transaction that meets the requirements of section 355 (or so much of section 356 as relates to section 355), solely for purposes of determining the tax treatment of the transfers of property to the controlled corporation by the distributing corporation, the fact that the shareholders of the distributing corporation dispose of part or all of the distributed stock shall not be taken into account for purposes of the control immediately after requirement of section 351(a) or 368(a)(1)(D). For purposes of determining the tax treatment of transfers of property to the controlled corporation by parties other than the distributing corporation, the disposition of part or all of the distributed stock continues to be taken into account, as under prior law, in determining whether the control immediately after requirement is satisfied.

Example 1: Distributing corporation D transfers appreciated business X to subsidiary C in exchange for 100 percent of C stock. D distributes its stock of C to D shareholders. As part of a plan or series of related transactions, C merges into unrelated acquiring corporation A, and the C shareholders receive 25 percent of the vote or value of A stock. If the requirements of section 355 are met with respect to the distribution, then the control immediately after requirement will be satisfied solely for purposes of determining the tax treatment of the transfers of property by D to C. Accordingly, the business X assets transferred to C and held by A after the merger will have a carryover basis from D. Section 355(e) will require D to recognize gain as if the C stock had been sold at fair market value.

Example 2: Distributing corporation D transfers appreciated business X to subsidiary C in exchange for 85 percent of C stock. Unrelated persons transfer appreciated assets to C in exchange for the remaining 15 percent of C stock. D distributes all its stock of C to D shareholders. As part of a plan or series of related transactions, C merges into acquiring corporation A; and the interests attributable to the D shareholders' receipt of C stock with respect to their D stock in the distribution represent 25 percent of the vote and value of A stock. If the requirements of section 355 are met with respect to the distribution, then the control immediately after requirement will be satisfied solely for purposes of determining the tax treatment of the transfers of property by D to C. Section 355(e) will require recognition of gain as if the C stock had been sold for fair market value. The business X assets transferred to C and held by A after the merger will have a carryover basis from D. The persons other than D who transferred assets to C for 15 percent of C stock will recognize gain on the appreciation in their assets transferred to C if the control immediately after requirement is not satisfied after taking into account any post-spin-off dispositions that would have been taken into account under prior law.

Example 3: The facts are the same as in example 2, except that the interests attributable to the D shareholders' receipt of C stock with respect to their D stock in the distribution represent 55 percent of the vote and value of A stock in the merger. If the requirements of section 355 are met with respect to the distribution, then the control immediately after requirement will be satisfied solely for purposes of determining the tax treatment of the transfers by D to C. The business X assets in C (and in A after the merger) will therefore have a carryover basis from D. Because the D shareholders retain more than 50 percent of the stock of A, section 355(e) will not apply. The persons other than D who transferred property for the 15 percent of C stock will recognize gain on the appreciation in their assets transferred to C if the control immediately after requirement is not satisfied after taking into account any post-spin-off dispositions that would have been taken into account under prior law.

Effective Date

The provision generally is effective for distributions after April 16, 1997.

Conference Committee Report (H.R. CONF. REP. NO. 105-599)

The conference agreement follows the Senate amendment * * *

[Law at ¶ 5290, 5310, 5320 and 8255. CCH Explanation at ¶ 601.]

[¶ 11,155]   Act Sec. 6010(d).   Application of section 304 to certain international transactions

Senate Committee Report (S. REP. NO. 105-174)

[Code Sec. 304]

Present Law

Under section 304, if one corporation purchases stock of a related corporation, the transaction generally is recharacterized as a redemption. Under section 304(a), as amended by the 1997 Act, to the extent that a section 304 transaction is treated as a distribution under section 301, the transferor and the acquiring corporation are treated as if (1) the transferor had transferred the stock involved in the transaction to the acquiring corporation in exchange for stock of the acquiring corporation in a transaction to which section 351(a) applies, and (2) the acquiring corporation had then redeemed the stock it is treated as having issued. In the case of a section 304 transaction, both the amount which is a dividend and the source of such dividend is determined as if the property were distributed by the acquiring corporation to the extent of its earnings and profits and then by the issuing corporation to the extent of its earnings and profits (sec. 304(b)(2)). Section 304(b)(5), as added by the 1997 Act, provides special rules that apply if the acquiring corporation in a section 304 transaction is a foreign corporation. Under section 304(b)(5), the earnings and profits of the acquiring corporation that are taken into account are limited to the portion of such earnings and profits that (1) is attributable to stock of such acquiring corporation held by a corporation or individual who is the transferor (or a person related thereto) and who is a U.S. shareholder (within the meaning of section 951(b)) of such corporation and (2) was accumulated during periods in which such stock was owned by such person while such acquiring corporation was a controlled foreign corporation. For purposes of this rule, except as otherwise provided by the Secretary of the Treasury, the rules of section 1248(d) (relating to certain exclusions from earnings and profits) apply. The Secretary is to prescribe regulations as appropriate, including regulations determining the earnings and profits that are attributable to particular stock of the acquiring corporation.

For foreign tax credit purposes, under section 902, a U.S. corporation that receives a dividend from a foreign corporation in which it owns at least 10 percent of the voting stock is treated as if it had paid the foreign income taxes paid by the foreign corporation which are attributable to such dividend. The Internal Revenue Service issued rulings providing that a domestic corporation that is a transferor in a section 304 transaction may compute foreign taxes deemed paid under section 902 on the dividends from both a foreign acquiring corporation and a foreign issuing corporation. Rev. Rul. 92-86, 1992-2 C.B. 199; Rev. Rul. 91-5, 1991-1 C.B. 114. Both rulings involve section 304 transactions in which both the domestic transferor and the foreign acquiring corporation are wholly owned by a domestic parent corporation.

Explanation of Provision

Under the provision, in the case of a section 304 transaction in which the acquiring corporation or the issuing corporation is a foreign corporation, the Secretary of the Treasury is to prescribe regulations providing rules to prevent the multiple inclusion of an item of income and to provide appropriate basis adjustments, including rules modifying the application of sections 959 and 961 in the case of a section 304 transaction. It is expected that such regulations will provide for an exclusion from income for distributions from earnings and profits of the acquiring corporation and the issuing corporation that represent previously taxed income under subpart F. It further is expected that such regulations will provide for appropriate adjustments to the basis of stock held by the corporation treated as receiving the distribution or by the corporation that had the prior inclusion with respect to the previously taxed income. No inference is intended regarding the treatment of previously taxed income in a section 304 transaction under present law. The 1997 Act amendments to section 304, including the modifications under this provision, are not intended to change the foreign tax credit results reached in Rev. Rul. 92-86 and 91-5.

The provision also eliminates the cross-reference to the rules of section 1248(d) for purposes of determining the earnings and profits to be taken into account under section 304(b)(5).

Effective Date

The provision generally is effective for distributions or acquisitions after June 8, 1997.

Conference Committee Report (H.R. CONF. REP. NO. 105-599)

The conference agreement follows the Senate amendment * * *

[Law at ¶ 5280. CCH Explanation at ¶ 631.]

[¶ 11,160] Act Sec. 6010(e)(1). Certain preferred stock treated as "boot"—treatment of transferor

Senate Committee Report (S. REP. NO. 105-174)

[Code Sec. 351(g)]

Present Law

The 1997 Act amended section 351 of the Code to provide that in the case of a person who transfers property to a controlled corporation and receives nonqualified preferred stock, section 351(b) will apply to such person. Section 351(b) provides that if section 351(a) of the Code would apply to an exchange but for the fact that there is received, in addition to stock permitted to be received under section 351(a), other property or money, then gain but no loss to such recipient shall be recognized. The Conference Report to the 1997 Act states that if nonqualified preferred stock is received, gain but not loss shall be recognized.

Explanation of Provision

The bill clarifies that section 351(b) applies to a transferor who transfers property in a section 351 exchange and receives nonqualified preferred stock in addition to stock that is not treated as "other property" under that section. Thus, if a transferor received only nonqualified preferred stock but the transaction in the aggregate otherwise qualified as a section 351 exchange, such a transferor would recognize loss and the basis of the nonqualified preferred stock and of the property in the hands of the transferee corporation would reflect the transaction in the same manner as if that particular transferor had received solely "other property" of any other type. As under the 1997 Act, the nonqualified preferred stock continues to be treated as stock received by a transferor for purposes of qualification of a transaction under section 351(a), unless and until regulations may provide otherwise.

Effective Date

The provision applies to transactions after June 8, 1997.

Conference Committee Report (H.R. CONF. REP. NO. 105-599)

The conference agreement follows the Senate amendment * * *

[Law at ¶ 5290. CCH Explanation at ¶ 616.]

[¶ 11,165] Act Sec. 6010(e)(2). Certain preferred stock treated as "boot"—statute of limitations

Senate Committee Report (S. REP. NO. 105-174)

[Code Sec. 354(a)]

Present law

Under the 1997 Act, certain preferred stock received in otherwise tax-free transactions is treated as "other property." Exchanges of stock in certain recapitalizations of family-owned corporations are excepted from this rule. A family-owned corporation is defined as any corporation if at least 50 percent of the total voting power and value of the stock of such corporation is owned by the same family for five years preceding the recapitalization. In addition, a recapitalization does not qualify for the exception if the same family does not own 50 percent of the total voting power and value of the stock throughout the three-year period following the recapitalization.

Explanation of Provision

The bill provides that the statutory period for the assessment of any deficiency attributable to a corporation failing to be a family-owned corporation shall not expire before the expiration of three years after the date the Secretary of the Treasury is notified by the corporation (in such manner as the Secretary may prescribe) of such failure, and such deficiency may be assessed before the expiration of such three-year period notwithstanding the provisions of any other law or rule of law which would otherwise prevent such assessment.

Effective Date

The provision applies to transactions after June 8, 1997.

Conference Committee Report (H.R. CONF. REP. NO. 105-599)

The conference agreement follows the Senate amendment * * *

[Law at ¶ 5300. CCH Explanation at ¶ 621.]

¶ 11,160   Act Sec. 6010(e)(1)

[¶ 11,170]   Act Sec. 6010(f).   Establish IRS continuous levy and improve debt collection

Senate Committee Report (S. REP. NO. 105-174)

[Code Sec. 6331]
Present Law

If any person is liable for any internal revenue tax and does not pay it within 10 days after notice and demand by the IRS, the IRS may then collect the tax by levy upon all property and rights to property belonging to the person, unless there is an explicit statutory restriction on doing so. A levy is the seizure of the person's property or rights to property. A levy on salary and wages is continuous from the date it is first made until the date it is fully paid or becomes unenforceable.

The 1997 Act provides that a continuous levy is also applicable to non-means tested recurring Fed-

eral payments and specified wage replacement payments.

Explanation of Provision

The provision clarifies that the IRS must approve the use of a continuous levy before it may take effect.

Effective Date

The provision is effective for levies issued after the date of enactment of the 1997 Act (August 5, 1997).

Conference Committee Report (H.R. CONF. REP. NO. 105-599)

The conference agreement follows the Senate amendment * * *

[Law at ¶ 6280. CCH Explanation at ¶ 266.]

[¶ 11,175]   Act Sec. 6010(g).   Clarification regarding aviation gasoline excise tax

Senate Committee Report (S. REP. NO. 105-174)

[Code Sec. 4041, Code Sec. 6421 and Code Sec. 9502]
Present Law

Before enactment of the 1997 Act, aviation gasoline was subject to a 19.3-cents-per-gallon tax rate, with 15 cents per gallon being deposited in the Airport and Airway Trust Fund and 4.3 cents per gallon being retained in the General Fund. The 1997 Act extended the 15-cents-per-gallon rate for 10 years, through September 30, 2007, and expanded deposits to the Trust Fund to include revenues from the 4.3-cents-per-gallon rate. The tax does not apply to fuel used in flight

segments outside the United States or to flight segments from the United States to foreign countries.

Explanation of Provision

The bill clarifies the application of the gasoline tax refund provisions to aviation gasoline used in flight segments outside the United States and to flight segments from the United States to foreign countries.

Effective Date

The provision is effective as if included in the 1997 Act.

Conference Committee Report (H.R. CONF. REP. NO. 105-599)

The conference agreement follows the Senate amendment * * *

[Law at ¶ 5840, ¶ 6380 and ¶ 6930. CCH Explanation at ¶ 701.]

[¶ 11,178]   Act Sec. 6010(h)(3) and 6010(h)(4).   Extension of diesel fuel excise taxes to kerosene

Conference Committee Report (H.R. CONF. REP. NO. 105-599)

[Code Sec. 4082(d)(1) and Code Sec. 4082(d)(3)]

The conference agreement follows the Senate amendment, with the following * * * additions * * *.

* * *

5. Revenue Increase Provisions of the 1997 Act
* * *

Extension of diesel fuel excise taxes to kerosene

The conference agreement includes clarifications of the rules under which aviation grade kerosene may be removed for use as aviation fuel without payment of the highway excise taxes.
* * *

[Law at ¶ 5860. CCH Explanation at ¶ 729 and ¶ 730.]

Act Sec. 6010(h)(3)   ¶ 11,178

[¶ 11,180] Act Sec. 6010(h)(5). Clarification of requirement that registered fuel terminals offer dyed fuel[75]

Senate Committee Report (S. REP. NO. 105-174)

[Code Sec. 4101]

Present Law

The 1997 Act provides that fuel terminals are eligible to register to handle non-tax-paid diesel fuel and kerosene only if the terminal operator offers both undyed (taxable) and dyed (nontaxable) fuel.

Explanation of Provision

The bill clarifies that the Code requires terminals eligible to handle non-tax-paid diesel to offer dyed diesel fuel and terminals eligible to handle non-tax-paid kerosene (including diesel fuel #1 and kerosene-type aviation fuel) to offer dyed kerosene. The bill does not require that a terminal offer for sale kerosene as a condition of receiving diesel fuel on a non-tax-paid basis. Similarly, the proposal does not require terminals that sell only kerosene to offer diesel fuel as a condition of receiving non-tax-paid kerosene.

Effective Date

The provision is effective as if included in the 1997 Act.

Conference Committee Report (H.R. CONF. REP. NO. 105-599)

The conference agreement follows the Senate amendment * * *

[Law at ¶ 5890. CCH Explanation at ¶ 726.]

[¶ 11,185] Act Sec. 6010(i). Clarification of treatment of prepaid telephone cards

Senate Committee Report (S. REP. NO. 105-174)

[Code Sec. 4251]

Present Law

A 3-percent excise tax is imposed on amounts paid for local and toll (long-distance) telephone service and teletypewriter exchange service. The tax is collected by the provider of the service from the consumer. In the case of so-called "prepaid telephone cards", the tax is treated as paid when the card is transferred by any telecommunications carrier to any person who is not a telecommunications carrier.

A "prepaid telephone card" is defined as any card or other similar arrangement which permits its holder to obtain communications services and pay for such services in advance.

Explanation of Provision

The bill inserts the word "any" prior to "other similar arrangement" to clarify that payment to a telecommunications carrier from a third party such as a joint venture credit card company is treated as payment made by the holder of the credit card to obtain communication services and the tax is treated as paid in a manner similar to that applied to prepaid telephone cards. The tax applies to payments if the rights to telephone service for which payments are made can be used in whole or in part for telephone service that, if purchased directly, would be subject to the 3-percent excise tax on telephone service. Also, the tax applies without regard to whether telephone service ultimately is provided pursuant to the transferred rights.

Effective Date

The provision is effective as if included in the 1997 Act.

Conference Committee Report (H.R. CONF. REP. NO. 105-599)

The conference agreement follows the Senate amendment * * *

[Law at ¶ 5920. CCH Explanation at ¶ 746.]

[¶ 11,190] Act Sec. 6010(j). Modify UBIT rules applicable to second-tier subsidiaries

Senate Committee Report (S. REP. NO. 105-174)

[Code Sec. 512(b)(13)]

Present Law

In general, interest, rents, royalties and annuities are excluded from the unrelated business income ("UBI") of tax-exempt organizations. However, section 512(b)(13) treats otherwise excluded rent, royalty, annuity, and interest income as UBI if such income is received from a taxable or tax-exempt subsidiary that is controlled by the parent tax-exempt organization.

Under the provision, interest, rent, annuity, or royalty payments made by a controlled entity to a tax-exempt organization are subject to the unre-

---

[75] S. 1173, as passed by the Senate, and H.R. 2400, as passed by the House, would delay the effective date of this requirement for two years, until July 1, 2000.

lated business income tax to the extent the payment reduces the net unrelated income (or increases any net unrelated loss) of the controlled entity. In this regard, section 512(b)(13)(B)(i)(I) cross references a non-existent Code section.

The provision generally applies to taxable years beginning after the date of enactment. However, the provision does not apply to payments made during the first two taxable years beginning on or after the date of enactment if such payments are made pursuant to a binding written contract in effect as of June 8, 1997, and at all times thereafter before such payment.

Explanation of Provision

The bill clarifies that rent, royalty, annuity, and interest income that would otherwise be ex-cluded from UBI is included in UBI under section 512(b)(13) if such income is received or accrued from a taxable or tax-exempt subsidiary that is controlled by the parent tax-exempt organization. The bill further clarifies that the provision does not apply to any payment received or accrued during the first two taxable years beginning on or after the date of enactment if such payment is received or accrued pursuant to a binding written contract in effect on June 8, 1997, and at all times thereafter before such payment (but not pursuant to any contract provision that permits optional accelerated payments).

Effective Date

The provision is effective as of August 5, 1997, the date of enactment of the 1997 Act.

Conference Committee Report (H.R. CONF. REP. NO. 105-599)

The conference agreement follows the Senate amendment * * *

[Law at ¶ 5400 and ¶ 8255. CCH Explanation at ¶ 686.]

[¶ 11,195]   Act Sec. 6010(k).   Application of foreign tax credit holding period rule to RICs

Senate Committee Report (S. REP. NO. 105-174)

[Code Sec. 853 and Code Sec. 901(k)(4)]
Present Law

Section 901(k), as added by the 1997 Act, generally imposes a holding period requirement for claiming foreign tax credits with respect to dividends. Under section 901(k), foreign tax credits with respect to a dividend from a foreign corporation or a regulated investment company (a "RIC") are disallowed if the shareholder has not held the stock for more than 15 days in the case of common stock or more than 45 days in the case of preferred stock. This disallowance applies both to foreign tax credits for foreign withholding taxes that are paid on the dividend where the dividend-paying stock is not held for the required period and to indirect foreign tax credits for taxes paid by a lower-tier foreign corporation or a RIC where any of the stock in the required chain of ownership is not held for the required period. Foreign taxes for which credits are disallowed under section 901(k) may be deducted.

Under section 853, a RIC may elect to flow through to its shareholders the foreign tax credits for foreign taxes paid by the RIC. Under this election, the RIC is not entitled to a deduction or credit for foreign taxes paid; the shareholders of an electing RIC are treated as having paid their proportionate shares of the foreign taxes paid by the RIC. Accordingly, foreign tax credits are claimed at the shareholder level and not at the RIC level.

Explanation of Provision

Under the provision, the flow-through election of section 853 does not apply to any foreign taxes paid by the RIC for which a credit is disallowed under section 901(k) because the RIC did not satisfy the applicable holding period. Accordingly, such taxes are deductible at the RIC level. The election of section 853 applies only to foreign taxes with respect to which the RIC has satisfied any applicable holding period requirement.

Effective Date

The provision is effective for dividends paid or accrued more than 30 days after the date of enactment of the 1997 Act.

Conference Committee Report (H.R. CONF. REP. NO. 105-599)

The conference agreement follows the Senate amendment, with the following modifications, additions, and deletions.

* * *

5. Revenue Increase Provisions of the 1997 Act

* * *

Holding period requirement for claiming foreign tax credits with respect to dividends

The 1997 Act added section 901(k), which denies a shareholder foreign tax credits normally available with respect to a dividend if the shareholder has not held the stock for a minimum period during which it is not protected from risk of loss. Section 901(k)(4), "Exception for certain taxes paid by securities dealers," provides an exception for foreign tax credits with respect to certain dividends received on stock held in the active conduct of a securities business in a foreign country. The Ways and Means and Finance committee reports provide that the exception is available only for dividends received on "stock which the shareholder holds in its capacity as a dealer in securities." H. Rept. 105-148, 105th Cong., 1st Sess. 546 (1997); S. Rept. 105-33, 105th Cong., 1st Sess 176 (1997). The conference agreement clarifies that the exception of section 901(k)(4) is available only for dividends received on stock that the shareholder holds in its capacity as a dealer in securities.

[Law at ¶ 5520 and ¶ 5550. CCH Explanation at ¶ 666.]

* * *

[¶ 11,200]   Act Sec. 6010(m).   Clarification of allocation of basis of properties distributed by a partnership

Senate Committee Report (S. REP. NO. 105-174)

[Code Sec. 751(c)]

Present Law

Present law, as amended by the 1997 Act, provides rules for allocating basis to property in the hands of a partner that receives a distribution from a partnership. Under these rules, basis is first allocated to unrealized receivables and inventory items in an amount equal to the partnership's adjusted basis in each property. If the basis to be allocated is less than the sum of the adjusted bases of the properties in the hands of the partnership, then, to the extent a decrease is required to make the total adjusted bases of the properties equal the basis to be allocated, the decrease is allocated (as described below) for adjustments that are decreases. To the extent of any basis not allocated to inventory and unrealized receivables under the above rules, basis is allocated to other distributed properties, first to the extent of each distributed property's adjusted basis to the partnership. Any remaining basis adjustment, if an increase, is allocated among properties with unrealized appreciation in proportion to their respective amounts of unrealized appreciation (to the extent of each property's appreciation), and then in proportion to their respective fair market values. If the remaining basis adjustment is a decrease, it is allocated among properties with unrealized depreciation in proportion to their respective amounts of unrealized depreciation (to the extent of each property's depreciation), and then in proportion to their respective adjusted bases (taking into account the adjustments already made).

For purposes of these rules, "unrealized receivables" has the meaning set forth in section 751(c) (as provided in sec. 732(c)(1)(A)(i)). Section 751(c) provides that the term "unrealized receivables" includes certain accrued but unreported income. In addition, the last two sentences of section 751(c) provide that for purposes of certain specified partnership provisions (sections 731, 741 and 751), the term "unrealized receivables" includes certain property the sale of which will give rise to ordinary income (for example, depreciation recapture under sections 1245 or 1250), but only to the extent of the amount that would be treated as ordinary income on a sale of that property at fair market value.

Explanation of Provision

The technical correction clarifies that for purposes of the allocation rules of section 732(c), "unrealized receivables" has the meaning in section 751(c) including the last two sentences of section 751(c), relating to items of property that give rise to ordinary income. Thus, in applying the allocation rules of section 732(c) to property listed in the last two sentences of section 751(c), such as property giving rise to potential depreciation recapture, the amount of unrealized appreciation in any such property does not include any amount that would be treated as ordinary income if the property were sold at fair market value, because such amount is treated as a separate asset for purposes of the basis allocation rules.[77]

For example, assume that a partnership has 3 partners, A, C and D. The partnership has 6 assets. Three are capital assets each with adjusted basis equal to fair market value of $20,000. The other three are depreciable equipment each with adjusted basis of $5,000 and fair market value of $30,000. Each of the pieces of equipment would have $25,000 of depreciation recapture if sold by the partnership for its $30,000 value. A has a basis in its partnership interest of $60,000. Assume that one of the capital assets and one of the pieces of equipment is distributed to A in liquidation of its interest. A is treated as receiving three assets: (1) depreciation recapture (an unrealized receivable) with a basis to the partnership of zero and a value of $25,000; (2) a piece of equipment with a basis to the partnership of $5,000 and a value of $5,000 (its $30,000 value reduced by the $25,000 of depreciation recapture); and (3) a capital asset with a basis to the partnership of $20,000 and a value of $20,000.

Under the provision, as clarified by the technical correction, A's $60,000 basis in its partnership interest is allocated as follows. First, basis is allocated to the depreciation recapture, an unrealized receivable, in an amount equal to the partnership's adjusted basis in it, or zero (sec. 732(c)(1)(A)(i)). Then basis is allocated to the extent of each of the other distributed properties' adjusted basis to the partnership, or $5,000 for the equipment (not including the depreciation recapture), and $20,000 to the capital asset. A's remaining $35,000 of basis is allocated next among properties (other than inventory and unrealized receivables) with unrealized appreciation, in proportion to their respective amounts of unrealized appreciation (to the extent of each property's appreciation), but neither of the distributed properties to which basis may be allocated has unrealized appreciation. Basis is then allocated then in proportion to the properties' respective fair market values ($5,000 for the equipment and $20,000 for the capital asset). Thus, of the remaining $35,000, $7,000 is allocated to the equipment, so that its total basis in the partner's hands is $12,000; and $28,000 is allocated to the capital

---

[77] Treasury regulations under section 751(b) provide for a similar bifurcation of assets among potential ordinary income amounts and other amounts in applying the definition of "unrealized receivables" for purposes of that section. Treas. Reg. 1.751-1(c)(4).

asset, so that its total basis in the partner's hands is $48,000.

Effective Date

The provision is effective as if enacted with the 1997 Act.

Conference Committee Report (H.R. CONF. REP. NO. 105-599)

The conference agreement follows the Senate amendment * * *

[Law at ¶ 5500. CCH Explanation at ¶ 681.]

[¶ 11,205]   Act Sec. 6010(o)(3).   Clarification of provision expanding the limitations on deductibility of premiums and interest with respect to life insurance, endowment and annuity contracts (master contracts and additional covered lives)

Senate Committee Report (S. REP. NO. 105-174)

[Code Sec. 264(f)]
Present Law

Master contracts

The 1997 Act provided limitations on the deductibility of interest and premiums with respect to life insurance, endowment and annuity contracts. Under the pro rata interest disallowance provision added by the Act, an exception is provided for any policy or contract owned by an entity engaged in a trade or business, covering an individual who is an employee, officer or director of the trade or business at the time first covered. The exception applies to any policy or contract owned by an entity engaged in a trade or business, which covers one individual who (at the time first insured under the policy or contract) is (1) a 20-percent owner of the entity, or (2) an individual (who is not a 20-percent owner) who is an officer, director or employee of the trade or business.[76] The provision is silent as to the treatment of coverage of such an individual under a master contract.

* * *

Additional covered lives

The 1997 Act provision limiting the deductibility of certain interest and premiums is effective generally with respect to contracts issued after June 8, 1997. To the extent of additional covered lives under a contract after June 8, 1997, the contract is treated as a new contract.

Explanation of Provision

Master contracts

The technical correction clarifies that if coverage for each insured individual under a master contract is treated as a separate contract for purposes of sections 817(h), 7702, and 7702A of the Code, then coverage for each such insured individual is treated as a separate contract, for purposes of the exception to the pro rata interest disallowance rule for a policy or contract covering an individual who is a 20-percent owner, employee, officer or director of the trade or business at the time first covered. A master contract does not include any contract if the contract (or any insurance coverage provided under the contract) is a group life insurance contract within the meaning of Code section 848(e)(2). No inference is intended that coverage provided under a master contract, for each such insured individual, is not treated as a separate contract for each such individual for other purposes under present law.

* * *

Additional covered lives

The technical correction clarifies that the treatment of additional covered lives under the effective date of the 1997 Act provision applies only with respect to coverage provided under a master contract, provided that coverage for each insured individual is treated as a separate contract for purposes of Code sections 817(h), 7702 and 7702A, and the master contract or any coverage provided thereunder is not a group life insurance contract within the meaning of Code section 848(e)(2).

Effective Date

The provisions are effective as if included in the 1997 Act.

Conference Committee Report (H.R. CONF. REP. NO. 105-599)

The conference agreement follows the Senate amendment * * *

[Law at ¶ 5260. CCH Explanation at ¶ 556.]

---

[76] The exception also applies in the case of a joint-life policy or contract under which the sole insureds are a 20-percent owner and the spouse of the 20-percent owner. A joint-life contract under which the sole insureds are a 20-percent owner and his or her spouse is the only type of policy or contract with more than one insured that comes within the exception.

[¶ 11,210]   Act Sec. 6010(o)(4).   Clarification of provision expanding the limitations on deductibility of premiums and interest with respect to life insurance, endowment and annuity contracts (reporting)

Senate Committee Report (S. REP. NO. 105-174)

[Code Sec. 264(f)(5)(A), Code Sec. 6724(d)(1) and Code Sec. 6724(d)(2)]

Present Law
* * *

Reporting

The provision does not apply to any policy or contract held by a natural person; however, if a trade or business is directly or indirectly the beneficiary under any policy or contract, the policy or contract is treated as held by the trade or business and not by a natural person. In addition, the provision includes a reporting requirement. Specifically, the provision provides that the Treasury Secretary shall require such reporting from policyholders and issuers as is necessary to carry out the rule applicable when the trade or business is directly or indirectly the beneficiary under any policy or contract held by a natural person. Any report required under this reporting requirement is treated as a statement referred to in Code section 6724(d)(1) (relating to information returns). The provision does not specifically refer to Code section 6724(d)(2) (relating to payee statements).
* * *

Explanation of Provision
* * *

Reporting

The technical correction clarifies that the required reporting to the Treasury Secretary is an information return (within meaning of sec. 6724(d)(1)), and any reporting required to be made to any other person is a payee statement (within the meaning of sec. 6724(d)(2)). Thus, the $50-per-report penalty imposed under sections 6722 and 6723 of the Code for failure to file or provide such an information return or payee statement apply. It is clarified that the Treasury Secretary may require reporting by the issuer or policyholder of any relevant information either by regulations or by any other appropriate guidance (including but not limited to publication of a form).

* * *

Effective Date

The provisions are effective as if included in the 1997 Act.

Conference Committee Report (H.R. CONF. REP. NO. 105-599)

The conference agreement follows the Senate amendment * * *

[Law at ¶ 5260 and ¶ 6520. CCH Explanation at ¶ 561.]

[¶ 11,215]   Act Sec. 6010(p).   Clarification to the definition of modified adjusted gross income for purposes of the earned income credit phaseout

Senate Committee Report (S. REP. NO. 105-174)

[Code Sec. 32(c) and Act Sec. 6010(p)]

Present Law

The earned income credit ("EIC") is phased out above certain income levels. For individuals with earned income (or modified adjusted gross income ("modified AGI"), if greater) in excess of the beginning of the phaseout range, the maximum credit amount is reduced by the phaseout rate multiplied by the amount of earned income (or modified AGI, if greater) in excess of the beginning of the phaseout range. For individuals with earned income (or modified AGI, if greater) in excess of the end of the phaseout range, no credit is allowed. The definition of modified AGI used for the phase out of the earned income credit is the sum of: (1) AGI with certain losses disregarded, and (2) certain nontaxable amounts not generally included in AGI. The losses disregarded are: (1) net capital losses (if greater than zero);

(2) net losses from trusts and estates; (3) net losses from nonbusiness rents and royalties; (4) 75 percent of the net losses from business, computed separately with respect to sole proprietorships (other than in farming), sole proprietorships in farming, and other businesses.[78] The nontaxable amounts included in modified AGI which are generally not included in AGI are: (1) tax-exempt interest; and (2) nontaxable distributions from pensions, annuities, and individual retirement arrangements (but only if not rolled over into similar vehicles during the applicable rollover period).

Explanation of Provision

The bill clarifies that the two nontaxable amounts that are added to adjusted gross income to compute modified AGI for purposes of the EIC phaseout are additions to adjusted gross income and not disregarded losses.

---

[78] The 1997 Act increased the amount of net losses from businesses, computed separately with respect to sole proprietorships (other than farming), sole proprietorships in farm-ing, and other businesses disregarded from 50 percent to 75 percent.

Effective Date

The provision is effective for taxable years beginning after December 31, 1997.

Conference Committee Report (H.R. CONF. REP. NO. 105-599)

The conference agreement follows the Senate amendment * * *

[Law at ¶ 5040 and ¶ 8255. CCH Explanation at ¶ 211.]

[¶ 11,225]   Act Sec. 6011(b)(1).   Treatment of PFIC option holders

Senate Committee Report (S. REP. NO. 105-174)

[Code Sec. 1297 and Code Sec. 1298]

Present Law

Under the provisions of subpart F, a controlled foreign corporation (a "CFC") is defined generally as any foreign corporation if U.S. persons own more than 50 percent of the corporation's stock (measured by vote or value), taking into account only those U.S. persons that own at least 10 percent of the stock (measured by vote only) (sec. 957). Stock ownership includes not only stock owned directly, but also stock owned indirectly through a foreign entity or constructively (sec. 958). Pursuant to the constructive ownership rules, a person that has an option to acquire stock generally is treated as owning such stock (secs. 958(b) and 318(a)(4)).

The U.S. 10-percent shareholders of a CFC are subject to current U.S. tax on their pro rata shares of certain income of the CFC and their pro rata shares of the CFC's earnings invested in certain U.S. property (sec. 951). For purposes of determining the U.S. shareholder's includible pro rata share of the CFC's income and earnings, only stock held directly or indirectly through a foreign entity (and not stock held constructively) is taken into account (secs. 951(b) and 958(a)).

A foreign corporation is a passive foreign investment company (a "PFIC") if it satisfies a passive income test or a passive assets test for the taxable year (sec. 1297). A U.S. shareholder of a PFIC generally is subject to U.S. tax, plus an interest charge, on distributions from a PFIC and gain realized upon a disposition of PFIC stock (sec. 1291). Alternatively, the U.S. shareholder may elect either to be subject to current U.S. tax on the shareholder's share of the PFIC's earnings or, in the case of PFIC stock that is marketable, to mark to market the PFIC stock (secs. 1293 and 1296). For purposes of the PFIC provisions, constructive ownership rules apply (sec. 1298(a)). Under these rules, an option to acquire stock is treated as stock for purposes of applying the interest charge regime to a disposition of such option, and the holding period for stock acquired pursuant to the exercise of an option includes the holding period for such option (sec. 1298(a)(4) and prop. Treas. reg. secs. 1.1291-1(d) and (h)(3)).

A corporation that is a CFC is also a PFIC if it meets the passive income test or the passive assets test. Under section 1297(e), as added by the 1997 Act, a corporation is not treated as a PFIC with respect to a shareholder during the period after December 31, 1997 in which the corporation is a CFC and the shareholder is a U.S. shareholder (within the meaning of section 951(b)) thereof. Under this rule eliminating the overlap between the PFIC and CFC provisions, a shareholder that is subject to the subpart F rules with respect to a corporation is not also subject to the PFIC rules with respect to such corporation.

Explanation of Provision

Under the provision, the elimination of the overlap between the PFIC and the CFC provisions generally does not apply to a U.S. person with respect to PFIC stock that such person is treated as owning by reason of an option to acquire such stock. Accordingly, for example, the PFIC rules continue to apply to a U.S. person that holds only an option on stock of a corporation that is a CFC because such person does not own stock of such corporation directly or indirectly through a foreign entity and therefore is not subject to the current inclusion rules of subpart F with respect to such corporation. However, under the provision, the elimination of the overlap will apply to a U.S. person that holds an option on stock if such stock is held by a person that is subject to the current inclusion rules of subpart F with respect to such stock and is not a tax-exempt person. Accordingly, an option holder is not subject to the PFIC rules with respect to an option if the option is on stock that is held by a non-tax-exempt person that is subject to the current inclusion rules of subpart F with respect to such stock.

Effective Date

The provision is effective for taxable years of U.S. persons beginning after December 31, 1997 and taxable years of foreign corporations ending with or within such taxable years of U.S. persons.

Conference Committee Report (H.R. CONF. REP. NO. 105-599)

The conference agreement follows the Senate amendment * * *

[Law at ¶ 5650. CCH Explanation at ¶ 641.]

Act Sec. 6011(b)(1)   ¶ 11,225

[¶ 11,230] Act Sec. 6011(b)(2). Application of attribution rules under PFIC provisions

Senate Committee Report (S. REP. NO. 105-174)

[Code Sec. 1298(a)(2)(B)]
Present Law

Special attribution rules apply to the extent that the effect is to treat stock of a passive foreign investment company ("PFIC") as owned by a U.S. person. In general, if 50 percent or more in value of the stock of a corporation is owned (directly or indirectly) by or for any person, such person is considered as owning a proportionate part of the stock owned directly or indirectly by or for such corporation, determined based on the person's proportionate interest in the value of such corporation's stock. However, this 50-percent limitation does not apply in the case of a corporation that is a PFIC. Accordingly, a person that is a shareholder of a PFIC is considered as owning a proportionate part of the stock owned directly or indirectly by or for such PFIC, without regard to whether such shareholder owns at least 50 percent of the PFIC's stock by value.

A corporation is not treated as a PFIC with respect to a shareholder during the qualified portion of the shareholder's holding period for the stock of such corporation. The qualified portion of the shareholder's holding period generally is the portion of such period which is after the effective date of the 1997 Act and during which the shareholder is a United States shareholder (as defined in sec. 951(b)) and the corporation is a controlled foreign corporation.

If a corporation is not treated as a PFIC with respect to a shareholder for the qualified portion of such shareholder's holding period, it is unclear whether the attribution rules that apply with respect to stock owned by or for such corporation apply without regard to the requirement that the shareholder own 50 percent or more of the corporation's stock.

Explanation of Provision

The provision clarifies that the attribution rules apply without regard to the provision that treats a corporation as a non-PFIC with respect to a shareholder for the qualified portion of the shareholder's holding period. Accordingly, stock owned directly or indirectly by or for a corporation that is not treated as a PFIC for the qualified portion of the shareholder's holding period nevertheless will be attributed to such shareholder, regardless of the shareholder's ownership percentage of such corporation.

Effective Date

The provision is effective for taxable years of U.S. persons beginning after December 31, 1997 and taxable years of foreign corporations ending with or within such taxable years of U.S. persons.

Conference Committee Report (H.R. CONF. REP. NO. 105-599)

The conference agreement follows the Senate amendment * * *

[Law at ¶ 5660. CCH Explanation at ¶ 636.]

[¶ 11,235] Act Sec. 6011(c)(2). Interaction between the PFIC provisions and other mark-to-market rules

Senate Committee Report (S. REP. NO. 105-174)

[Code Sec. 1291(d)]
Present Law

A U.S. shareholder of a passive foreign investment company (a "PFIC") generally is subject to U.S. tax, plus an interest charge, on distributions from a PFIC and gain realized upon a disposition of PFIC stock (sec. 1291). As an alternative to this interest charge regime, the U.S. shareholder may elect to be subject to current U.S. tax on the shareholder's share of the PFIC's earnings (sec. 1293). Section 1296, as added by the 1997 Act, provides another alternative available in the case of a PFIC the stock of which is marketable; under section 1296, a U.S. shareholder of a PFIC may make a mark-to-market election with respect to the stock of the PFIC.

The interest charge regime generally does not apply to distributions from, and dispositions of stock of, a PFIC for which the U.S. shareholder has made either a mark-to-market election under section 1296 or an election to include the PFIC's earnings in income currently (sec. 1291(d)(1)). However, special coordination rules provide for limited application of the interest charge regime in the case of a U.S. shareholder that makes a mark-to-market election under section 1296 later than the beginning of the shareholder's holding period for the PFIC stock (sec. 1296(j)).

Under section 475(a), a dealer in securities is required to mark to market certain securities held by the dealer. Under section 475(f), as added by the 1997 Act, a trader in securities may elect to mark to market securities held in connection with the person's trade or business as a trader in securities. Other provisions similarly allow stock to be marked to market (e.g., sec. 1092(b)(1) and temp. Treas. reg. Sec. 1.1092-4T).

Explanation of Provision

Under the provision, the interest charge regime generally does not apply to distributions from, and dispositions of stock of, a PFIC where the U.S. shareholder has marked to market such stock under section 475 or any other provision (in the same manner that such regime does not apply where the shareholder has marked to market such stock under section 1296). In addition, under the provision, coordination rules like those provided in section 1296(j) apply in the case of a U.S. shareholder that marks to market PFIC stock under section 475 or any other provision later than the beginning of the shareholder's holding period for the PFIC stock.

Effective Date

The provision is effective for taxable years of U.S. persons beginning after December 31, 1997

and taxable years of foreign corporations ending with or within such taxable years of U.S. persons. No inference is intended regarding the treatment of PFIC stock that was marked to market prior to the effective date of the provision.

Conference Committee Report (H.R. CONF. REP. NO. 105-599)

The conference agreement follows the Senate amendment * * *

[Law at ¶ 5630. CCH Explanation at ¶ 651.]

[¶ 11,240]   Act Sec. 6011(c)(3).   Application of PFIC mark-to-market rules to RICs

Senate Committee Report (S. REP. NO. 105-174)

[Code Sec. 1296]
Present Law

Under section 1296, as added by the 1997 Act, a shareholder of a passive foreign investment company (a "PFIC") may make a mark-to-market election with respect to the stock of the PFIC, provided that such stock is marketable. Under this election, the shareholder includes in income each year an amount equal to the excess, if any, of the fair market value of the PFIC stock as of the close of the taxable year over the shareholder's adjusted basis in such stock. The shareholder is allowed a deduction for the excess, if any, of the shareholder's adjusted basis in the PFIC stock over its fair market value as of the close of the taxable year, but only to the extent of any net mark-to-market gains with respect to such stock included by the shareholder under section 1296 for prior years.

The mark-to-market election of section 1296 is effective for taxable years of U.S. persons beginning after December 31, 1997 and taxable years of foreign corporations ending with or within such taxable years of U.S. persons. Prior to the enactment of section 1296, a proposed Treasury regulation provided for a mark-to-market election with respect to PFIC stock held by certain regulated investment companies ("RICs") (prop. Treas. reg.

sec. 1.1291-8). Under this mark-to-market election, gains but not losses were recognized.

Section 1296(j) provides rules applicable in the case of a shareholder that makes a mark-to-market election under section 1296 later than the beginning of the shareholder's holding period for the PFIC stock. Special rules apply in the case of a RIC that makes such a mark-to-market election under section 1296 with respect to PFIC stock that the RIC had previously marked to market under the proposed Treasury regulation.

Explanation of Provision

Under the provision, for purposes of determining allowable deductions for any excess of the shareholder's adjusted basis in PFIC stock over the fair market value of the stock as of the close of the taxable year, deductions are allowed to the extent not only of prior mark-to-market inclusions under section 1296 but also of prior mark-to-market inclusions under the proposed Treasury regulation applicable to a RIC that holds stock in a PFIC.

Effective Date

The provision is effective for taxable years of U.S. persons beginning after December 31, 1997 and taxable years of foreign corporations ending with or within such taxable years of U.S. persons.

Conference Committee Report (H.R. CONF. REP. NO. 105-599)

The conference agreement follows the Senate amendment * * *

[Law at ¶ 5640. CCH Explanation at ¶ 646.]

[¶ 11,245]   Act Sec. 6011(f).   Information reporting with respect to certain foreign corporations and partnerships

Conference Committee Report (H.R. CONF. REP. NO. 105-599)

[Code Sec. 6038(a) and Code Sec. 6038(e)]

The conference agreement follows the Senate amendment, with the following * * * additions * * *.

* * *

7. Foreign Tax Provisions of the 1997 Act
  Information reporting with respect to certain foreign corporations and partnerships
  Present law, as amended by the 1997 Act, provides that reporting rules apply to controlled for-

eign corporations and foreign partnerships (sec. 6038). The conference agreement clarifies that guidance relating to the furnishing of required information is to be provided by the Secretary of the Treasury (not specifically through regulations), and conforms the use of the defined term, foreign business entity.

* * *

[Law at ¶ 6050. CCH Explanation at ¶ 683.]

[¶ 11,255] Act Sec. 6012(a). Travel expenses of Federal employees participating in a Federal criminal investigation

Senate Committee Report (S. REP. NO. 105-174)

[Code Sec. 162(a)]
Present Law

Unreimbursed ordinary and necessary travel expenses paid or incurred by an individual in connection with temporary employment away from home (e.g., transportation costs and the cost of meals and lodging) are generally deductible, subject to the two-percent floor on miscellaneous itemized deductions. Travel expenses paid or incurred in connection with indefinite employment away from home, however, are not deductible. A taxpayer's employment away from home in a single location is indefinite rather than temporary if it lasts for one year or more; thus, no deduction is permitted for travel expenses paid or incurred in connection with such employment (sec. 162(a)). If a taxpayer's employment away from home in a single location lasts for less than one year, whether such employment is temporary or indefinite is determined on the basis of the facts and circumstances.

The 1997 Act provided that the one-year limitation with respect to deductibility of expenses while temporarily away from home does not include any period during which a Federal employee is certified by the Attorney General (or the Attorney General's designee) as traveling on behalf of the Federal Government in a temporary duty status to investigate or provide support services to the investigation of a Federal crime. Thus, expenses for these individuals during these periods are fully deductible, regardless of the length of the period for which certification is given (provided that the other requirements for deductibility are satisfied).

Explanation of Provision

The provision clarifies that prosecuting a Federal crime or providing support services to the prosecution of a Federal crime is considered part of investigating a Federal crime.

Effective Date

The provision is effective for amounts paid or incurred with respect to taxable years ending after the date of enactment of the 1997 Act.

Conference Committee Report (H.R. CONF. REP. NO. 105-599)

The conference agreement follows the Senate amendment * * *

[Law at ¶ 5205. CCH Explanation at ¶ 256.]

[¶ 11,260] Act Sec. 6012(d). Magnetic media returns for partnerships having more than 100 partners

Conference Committee Report (H.R. CONF. REP. NO. 105-599)

[Code Sec. 6724(c)]

The conference agreement follows the Senate amendment, with the following * * * additions * * *.

* * *

6. Individual and Business Simplification Provisions of the 1997 Act

Magnetic media returns for partnerships having more than 100 partners

Present law, as amended by the 1997 Act, provides that the Treasury Secretary is to require partnerships with more than 100 partners to file returns on magnetic media (sec. 6011(e)). Present law also imposes a penalty in the case of failure to meet magnetic media requirements. The conference agreement clarifies that the penalty under section 6724(c) for failure to comply with the requirement of filing returns on magnetic media applies to the extent such a failure occurs with respect to more than 100 information returns, in the case of a partnership with more than 100 partners.

* * *

[Law at ¶ 6520. CCH Explanation at ¶ 682.]

[¶ 11,265] Act Sec. 6012(e). Effective date for provisions relating to electing large partnerships, partnership returns required on magnetic media, and treatment of partnership items of individual retirement arrangements

Senate Committee Report (S. REP. NO. 105-174)

[Act Sec. 6012(e)]
Present Law

Rules for simplified flowthrough and simplified audit procedures for electing large partnerships, as well as a March 15 due date for furnishing information to partners of an electing large partnership, were added to present law by the 1997 Act. The 1997 Act also added a rule providing that partnership returns are required on magnetic media, and modified the treatment of partnership items of individual retirement arrangements. The 1997 Act statement of managers provided that these provisions apply to partnership taxable years beginning after December 31, 1997. The statute provided that the rules for simplified flowthrough for electing large partnerships apply to partnership taxable years beginning after December 31, 1997 (Act sec. 1221(c)), although the statute also provided that all the provisions apply to partnership taxable years ending on or after December 31, 1997 (Act sec. 1226).

Explanation of Provision

The technical correction provides that these provisions apply to partnership taxable years beginning after December 31, 1997.

Effective Date

The provision is effective as if enacted in the 1997 Act.

Conference Committee Report (H.R. CONF. REP. NO. 105-599)

The conference agreement follows the Senate amendment * * *

[Law at ¶ 8265. CCH Explanation at ¶ 671.]

[¶ 11,270]   Act Sec. 6012(g).   Modification of distribution rules for REITs

Senate Committee Report (S. REP. NO. 105-174)

[Code Sec. 857(d)(3)(A)]

Present Law

In general, a real estate investment trust ("REIT") is an entity that receives most of its income from passive real estate investments and meets certain other requirements. A REIT receives conduit treatment (i.e., one level of tax) for income distributed to its shareholders. A REIT generally must distribute 95 percent of its earnings (sec. 857(a)(1)). An entity loses its status as a REIT if it retains non-REIT earnings and profits (sec. 857(a)(2)). A REIT simplification provision in the 1997 Act provides that any distribution from a REIT will be deemed to first come from the earliest earnings and profits of the entity. As a result, in the case of a REIT with accumulated REIT earnings and profits that inherits subsequently earned non-REIT earnings and profits (e.g., by way of merger with a C corporation), that the entity must distribute both the accumulated REIT earnings and profits as well as the inherited non-REIT earnings and profits under the 1997 Act provision in order to retain its REIT status.

Explanation of Provision

The provision amends the simplification provision to provide that any distribution from a REIT will be deemed to first come from earnings and profits that were generated when the entity did not qualify as a REIT. The provision does not change the requirement that a REIT must distribute 95 percent of its REIT earnings, or any other requirement.

Effective Date

The provision is effective for taxable years beginning after August 5, 1997.

Conference Committee Report (H.R. CONF. REP. NO. 105-599)

The conference agreement follows the Senate amendment * * *

[Law at ¶ 5530. CCH Explanation at ¶ 661.]

[¶ 11,275]   Act Sec. 6013(a).   Clarification of treatment of revocable trusts for purposes of the generation-skipping transfer tax

Senate Committee Report (S. REP. NO. 105-174)

[Code Sec. 645, Code Sec. 2652 and Code Sec. 2654]

Present Law

The 1997 Act provided an irrevocable election to treat a qualified revocable trust as part of the decedent's estate for Federal income tax purposes. For this purpose, a qualified revocable trust is any trust (or portion thereof) which was treated as owned by the decedent with respect to whom the election is being made, by reason of a power in the grantor (i.e., trusts that are treated as owned by the decedent solely by reason of a power in a nonadverse party would not qualify). A conforming change was also made to section 2652(b) for generation-skipping transfer tax purposes.

Explanation of Provision

The provision clarifies that the election to treat a qualified revocable trust as part of the decedent's estate would apply for generation-skipping transfer tax purposes only with respect to the application of section 2654(b) (describing when a single trust may be treated as two or more trusts). The election has no other effect for generation-skipping transfer tax purposes.

Effective Date

The provision applies to decedents dying after the date of enactment of the 1997 Act.

Act Sec. 6013(a)   ¶ 11,275

Conference Committee Report (H.R. CONF. REP. NO. 105-599)

The conference agreement follows the Senate amendment * * *

[Law at ¶ 5450, ¶ 5800 and ¶ 5810. CCH Explanation at ¶ 433.]

[¶ 11,280]   Act Sec. 6013(b).   Provision of regulatory authority for simplified reporting of funeral trusts terminated during the taxable year

Senate Committee Report (S. REP. NO. 105-174)

[Code Sec. 685(b) and Code Sec. 685(f)]

Present Law

The 1997 Act provided an election which allows the trustee of a qualified pre-need funeral trust to elect special tax treatment for such a trust, to the extent the trust would otherwise be treated as a grantor trust. As part of this provision, the Secretary of the Treasury was granted regulatory authority to prescribe rules for simplified reporting of all trusts having a single trustee.

Explanation of Provision

The provision clarifies that a pre-need funeral trust may continue to qualify for these special rules for the 60-day period after the decedent's death, even though the trust ceases to be a grantor trust during that time. In addition, the provision extends the Secretary's regulatory authority to include rules providing for the inclusion of trusts terminated during the year (e.g., in the event of the death of the beneficiary) in the simplified reporting.

Effective Date

The provision applies to decedents dying after the date of enactment of the 1997 Act.

Conference Committee Report (H.R. CONF. REP. NO. 105-599)

The conference agreement follows the Senate amendment * * *

[Law at ¶ 5490. CCH Explanation at ¶ 456.]

[¶ 11,285]   Act Sec. 6014(a)(1), 6014(a)(2) and 6014(b)(1).   Transfers of bulk imports of wine to wineries or beer to breweries

Conference Committee Report (H.R. CONF. REP. NO. 105-599)

[Code Sec. 5043(a)(2), Code Sec. 5054(a)(1) and Code Sec. 5054(a)(2)]

The conference agreement follows the Senate amendment, with the following * * * additions * * *.

* * *

8. Excise Tax and Other Simplification Provisions of the 1997 Act

* * *

Transfers of bulk imports of wine to wineries or beer to breweries

Prior to the 1997 Act, imported beer and wine always were taxed upon importation (secs. 5043 and 5054). The 1997 Act added provisions for non-tax-paid transfers of bulk imports to breweries and wineries (secs. 5364 and 5418). The conference agreement conforms the provisions imposing tax in all cases on importation to recognize these allowed transfers. Under the conference agreement, liability for tax payment shifts to the brewery or winery when bulk imports are transferred with payment of tax, just as those parties are liable for payment of tax on domestically produced beer and wine.

* * *

[Law at ¶ 5970, ¶ 5990 and ¶ 6000. CCH Explanation at ¶ 732 and ¶ 743.]

[¶ 11,290]   Act Sec. 6014(a)(3) and 6014(b)(2).   Refunds when wine returned to wineries or beer returned to breweries

Conference Committee Report (H.R. CONF. REP. NO. 105-599)

[Code Sec. 5044(a) and Code Sec. 5056]

The conference agreement follows the Senate amendment, with the following * * * additions * * *.

* * *

8. Excise Tax and Other Simplification Provisions of the 1997 Act

Refunds when wine returned to wineries or beer returned to breweries

The 1997 Act added a provision that tax is refunded when tax-paid wine is returned to a winery or tax-paid beer is returned to a brewery (secs. 5044 and 5056). The Code provisions allowing these refunds speak of beverages produced in the United States. A separate provision of the 1997 Act provided that beer and wine imported "in bulk" would be taxed under the rules for domestically produced beverages. The conference agreement provides that the refund provisions are coordinated with the provision on tax treatment of bulk imports.

* * *

[Law at ¶ 5980 and ¶ 6000. CCH Explanation at ¶ 733 and ¶ 743.]

[¶ 11,295] Act Sec. 6014(b)(3). Clarification of provision allowing wine imported in bulk to be transferred to a U.S. winery without payment of tax

Senate Committee Report (S. REP. NO. 105-174)

[Code Sec. 5364]

Present Law

Wine is subject to an excise tax ranging from $1.07 per gallon to $3.40 per gallon, depending on its alcohol content. Distilled spirits are subject to excise tax at a rate of $13.50 per proof gallon. A tax credit equal to the difference between the distilled spirits tax rate and the wine tax rate is allowed for wine that is blended into distilled spirits products (sec. 5010). The wine excise tax is imposed on removal of the beverage from a winery, or on importation. The 1997 Act included a provision allowing wine to be imported in bulk and transferred to a U.S. winery without payment of tax (generally until the wine is removed from the winery).

U.S. law defines wine generally as alcohol that is derived from fruit or fruit residues ("natural wine"). Natural wine may not be fortified with grain or other non-fruit derived alcohol if produced in the U.S. Certain other countries allow wine that is marketed as a natural wine to be fortified with alcohol from other sources. U.S. law follows the laws of the country of origin in classifying imported wine.

Explanation of Provision

The provision clarifies that the provision of the 1997 Act liberalizing rules for bulk importation of wine applies only to alcohol that would qualify as a natural wine if produced in the United States.

Effective Date

The provision is effective as if included in the 1997 Act.

Conference Committee Report (H.R. CONF. REP. NO. 105-599)

The conference agreement follows the Senate amendment * * *

[Law at ¶ 6010. CCH Explanation at ¶ 741.]

[¶ 11,315] Act Sec. 6015(c). Treatment of certain disability payments to public safety employees

Senate Committee Report (S. REP. NO. 105-174)

[Act Sec. 6015(c)]

Present Law

Under present law, certain payments made on behalf of full-time employees of any police or fire department organized and operated by a State (or any political subdivision, agency, or instrumentality thereof) are excludable from income. This treatment applies to payments made on account of heart disease or hypertension of the employee and that were received in 1989, 1990, or 1991 pursuant to a State law as amended on May 19, 1992, which irrebuttably presumed that heart disease and hypertension are work-related illnesses (but only for employees separating from service before July 1, 1992). Claims for refund or credit for overpayments resulting from the provision may be filed up to 1 year after August 5, 1997, without regard to the otherwise applicable statute of limitations.

Explanation of Provision

In order to address problems taxpayers are encountering with the IRS in seeking refunds under the present-law provision, the bill clarifies the scope of the provision.

The bill provides that payments made on account of heart disease or hypertension of the employee and that were received in 1989, 1990, or 1991 pursuant to a State law as described under present law, or received by an individual referred to in such State law under any other statute, ordinance, labor agreement, or similar provision as a disability pension payment or in the nature of a disability pension payment attributable to employment as a police officer or as a fireman will be excludable from income.

Effective Date

The provision is effective as if included in the Taxpayer Relief Act.

Conference Committee Report (H.R. CONF. REP. NO. 105-599)

The conference agreement follows the Senate amendment * * *

[Law at ¶ 8270. CCH Explanation at ¶ 261.]

[¶ 11,325]   Act Sec. 6016(a)(1).   Application of requirements for SIMPLE IRAs in the case of mergers and acquisitions

Senate Committee Report (S. REP. NO. 105-174)

[Code Sec. 408(p)]

Present Law

If an employer maintains a qualified plan and a SIMPLE IRA in the same year due to an acquisition, disposition or similar transaction the SIMPLE IRA is treated as a qualified salary reduction arrangement for the year of the transaction and the following calendar year provided rules similar to the special coverage rules of section 410(b)(6)(C) apply. There is a similar provision with respect to an employer who, because of an acquisition, disposition or similar transaction, fails to be an eligible employer because such employer employs more than 100 employees. In this situation, the employer is treated as an eligible employer for two years following the transaction provided rules similar to the coverage rules of section 410(b)(6)(C)(i) apply.

Explanation of Provision

The bill conforms the treatment applicable to SIMPLE IRAs upon acquisition, disposition or similar transaction for purposes of (1) the 100 employee limit, (2) the exclusive plan requirement, and (3) the coverage rules for participation. In the event of such a transaction, the employer will be treated as an eligible employer and the arrangement will be treated as a qualified salary reduction arrangement for the year of the transaction and the two following years, provided rules similar to the rules of section 410(b)(6)(C)(i)(II) are satisfied and the arrangement would satisfy the requirements to be a qualified salary reduction arrangement after the transaction if the trade or business that maintained the arrangement prior to the transaction had remained a separate employer.

Effective Date

The provision is effective as if included in the Small Business Job Protection Act of 1996.

Conference Committee Report (H.R. CONF. REP. NO. 105-599)

The conference agreement follows the Senate amendment * * *

[Law at ¶ 5360. CCH Explanation at ¶ 366.]

[¶ 11,330]   Act Sec. 6016(a)(2).   Treatment of Indian tribal governments under section 403(b)

Senate Committee Report (S. REP. NO. 105-174)

[Act Sec. 6016(a)(2)]

Present Law

Any 403(b) annuity contract purchased in a plan year beginning before January 1, 1995, by an Indian tribal government is treated as purchased by an entity permitted to maintain a tax-sheltered annuity plan. Such contracts may be rolled over into a section 401(k) plan maintained by the Indian tribal government in accordance with the rollover rules of section 403(b)(8). An employee participating in a 403(b) annuity contract of the Indian tribal government may roll over amounts from such contract to a section 401(k) plan maintained by the Indian tribal government whether or not the annuity contract is terminated.

Explanation of Provision

The bill clarifies that an employee participating in a 403(b)(7) custodial account of the Indian tribal government may roll over amounts from such account to a section 401(k) plan maintained by the Indian tribal government.

Effective Date

The provision is effective as if included in the Small Business Job Protection Act of 1996.

Conference Committee Report (H.R. CONF. REP. NO. 105-599)

The conference agreement follows the Senate amendment * * *

[Law at ¶ 8275. CCH Explanation at ¶ 371.]

[¶ 11,335]   Act Sec. 6017.   Simplified refund provisions for tax on gasoline, diesel fuel and kerosene

Conference Committee Report (H.R. CONF. REP. NO. 105-599)

[Code Sec. 6427(i)(2)]

The conference agreement follows the Senate amendment, with the following * * * additions * * *.

* * *

10. Transportation Equity Act for the 21st Century ("TEA 21") (1998)
Simplified refund provisions for tax on gasoline, diesel fuel and kerosene

TEA 21 included a provision combining the Code refund provisions for gasoline, diesel fuel, and kerosene and reducing the minimum claim amount. Under TEA 21, claims may be filed once a $750 threshold is reached for gasoline, diesel fuel, and kerosene combined, and overpayments attributable to multiple calendar quarters may be aggregated in determining whether this threshold is met (rather than claims being filed only with respect to a single calendar quarter). The confer-ence agreement adds a provision conforming a current Code timing provision to reflect the por-tion of the TEA 21 provision that allows aggrega-tion of multiple calendar quarters into a single refund claim.

[Law at ¶ 6390. CCH Explanation at ¶ 730.]

[¶ 11,345] Act Sec. 6018(f). Treatment of adoption tax credit carryovers

Senate Committee Report (S. REP. NO. 105-174)

[Code Sec. 23(b)(2)(A)]
Present Law

Under present law taxpayers are allowed a maximum nonrefundable credit against income tax liability of $5,000 per child for qualified adop-tion expenses paid or incurred by the taxpayer. In the case of a special needs adoption, the maxi-mum credit amount is $6,000 ($5,000 in the case of a foreign special needs adoption). To the extent the otherwise allowable credit exceeds the tax liability limitation of section 26 (reduced by other personal credits) the excess is carried forward as an adoption credit into the next taxable year, up to a maximum of five taxable years.

The credit is phased out ratably for taxpayers with modified adjusted gross income (AGI) above $75,000, and is fully phased out at $115,000 of modified AGI. For these purposes modified AGI is computed by increasing the taxpayer's AGI by the amount otherwise excluded from gross income under Code sections 911, 931, or 933 (relating to the exclusion of income of U.S. citizens or re-sidents living abroad; residents of Guam, Ameri-can Samoa, and the Northern Mariana Islands, and residents of Puerto Rico, respectively).

Explanation of Provision

The bill clarifies that the AGI phaseout only applies in the year that the credit is generated and is not reapplied to further reduce any car-ryforward amounts.

Effective Date

The provision is effective as if included in the Small Business Job Protection Act of 1996.

Conference Committee Report (H.R. CONF. REP. NO. 105-599)

The conference agreement follows the Senate amendment * * *

[Law at ¶ 5010 and ¶ 8280. CCH Explanation at ¶ 221.]

[¶ 11,355] Act Sec. 6019(a) and 6019(b). Disclosure requirements for apostolic organizations

Senate Committee Report (S. REP. NO. 105-174)

[Code Sec. 6104]
Present Law

Section 501(d) provides tax-exempt status to certain religious or apostolic associations or corpo-rations, if such associations or corporations have a common treasury or community treasury, even if such associations or corporations engage in busi-ness for the common benefit of the members, but only if the members thereof include (at the time of filing their returns) in their gross income their entire pro rata shares, whether distributed or not, of the taxable income of the association or corpo-ration for such year.[79] Any amount so included in the gross income of a member is treated as a dividend received. The effect of section 501(d) is to exempt the religious and apostolic associations or corporations which conduct communal activi-ties (such as farming) from the Federal corporate-level income tax and the undistributed-profits tax, provided that members claim their shares of the corporation's income on their own individual returns.

Section 6033 generally requires tax-exempt or-ganizations to file annual information returns, and such information returns are available for public inspection under sections 6104(b) and 6104(e), except that public disclosure is not re-quired of the identity of contributors to an organi-zation. Section 501(d) entities must include with their annual information return (Form 1065) a Schedule K-1 that identifies the members of the association or corporation and their ratable por-tions of net income and expenses.

Explanation of Provision

The provision amends sections 6104(b) and 6104(e) to provide that public disclosure is not required of a Schedule K-1 filed by a religious or apostolic organization described in section 501(d).

---

[79] Under section 501(d), the requirement of a "common treasury" or "community treasury" is satisfied when all of the income generated from property owned by the organiza-tion is placed into a common fund that is maintained by such organization and is used for the maintenance and support of its members, with all members having equal, undivided interests in this common fund, but no right to claim title to any part thereof. See *Twin Oaks Community, Inc. v. Commissioner*, 87 T.C. 1233, at 1254 (1986). See also Rev. Rul. 78-100, 1978-1 C.B. 162 (sec. 501(d) entity must be supported by internally operated business activities rather than merely being supported by wages of members who are engaged in outside employment).

Act Sec. 6019(a) ¶ 11,355

Effective Date

The provision is effective on the date of enactment.

Conference Committee Report (H.R. CONF. REP. NO. 105-599)

The conference agreement follows the Senate amendment * * *

[Law at ¶ 6120. CCH Explanation at ¶ 691.]

[¶ 11,360]   Act Sec. 6019(c).   Disclosure of returns and return information

Conference Committee Report (H.R. CONF. REP. NO. 105-599)

[Code Sec. 6103(e)(6)]

The conference agreement follows the Senate amendment, with the following * * * additions * * *

* * *

9. **Taxpayer Bill of Rights 2 (1996)**

Disclosure of returns and return information

The rules regarding disclosure of returns and return information were amended in 1996 to permit certain disclosures in two additional circumstances. Present law provides that, in the case of a deficiency with respect to a joint return of individuals who are no longer married or no longer residing in the same household, the Treasury Secretary is permitted to disclose to one such individual whether there has been an attempt to collect the deficiency from the other individual, the general nature of such collection activities, and the amount collected (sec. 6103(e)(8)). Present law also provides that if the Treasury Secretary determines that a person is liable for a penalty for failure to collect and pay over tax, the Secretary is permitted to disclose to that person the name of any other person liable for that penalty, and whether there has been an attempt to collect the deficiency from the other individual, the general nature of such collection activities, and the amount collected (sec. 6103(e)(9)). The conference agreement clarifies that these disclosures, like certain other disclosures permitted under present law, may be made under section 6103(e)(6) to the duly authorized attorney in fact of the person making the disclosure request. The provision takes effect on date of enactment.

* * *

[Law at ¶ 6110. CCH Explanation at ¶ 1295 and ¶ 1432.]

[¶ 11,365]   Act Sec. 6020.   Allow deduction for unused employer social security credit

Senate Committee Report (S. REP. NO. 105-174)

[Code Sec. 196(c)]

Present Law

The general business credit ("GBC") consists of various individual tax credits (including the employer social security credit of Code section 45B) allowed with respect to certain qualified expenditures and activities. In general, the various individual tax credits contain provisions that prohibit "double benefits," either by denying deductions in the case of expenditure-related credits or by requiring income inclusions in the case of activity-related credits. Unused credits may be carried back one year and carried forward 20 years. Section 196 allows a deduction to the extent that certain portions of the GBC expire unused after the end of the carry forward period. Section 196 does not allow a deduction to the extent that the portion of the GBC that expires unused after the end of the carry forward period relates to the employer social security credit.

Explanation of Provision

The provision allows a deduction to the extent that the portion of the GBC relating to the employer social security credit expires unused after the end of the carry forward period.

Effective Date

The provision is effective as if included in the Omnibus Budget Reconciliation Act of 1993.

Conference Committee Report (H.R. CONF. REP. NO. 105-599)

The conference agreement follows the Senate amendment * * *

[Law at ¶ 5230. CCH Explanation at ¶ 586.]

[¶ 11,375]   Act Sec. 6021.   Earned income credit qualification rules

Senate Committee Report (S. REP. NO. 105-174)

[Code Sec. 32(c)]
Present Law

In general

In order to claim the earned income credit ("EIC"), an individual must be an eligible individual. To be an eligible individual, an individual must include a taxpayer identification number ("TIN") for the taxpayer and the taxpayer's spouse and must either have a qualifying child or meet other requirements. In order to claim the EIC without a qualifying child, an individual must not be a dependent and must be over age 24 and under age 65.

Qualifying child

A qualifying child must meet a relationship test, an age test, an identification test, and a residence test. Under the relationship and age tests, an individual is eligible for the EIC with respect to another person only if that other person: (1) is a son, daughter, or adopted child (or a descendent of a son, daughter, or adopted child); a stepson or stepdaughter; or a foster child of the taxpayer (a foster child is defined as a person whom the individual cares for as the individual's child; it is not necessary to have a placement through a foster care agency); and (2) is under the age of 19 at the close of the taxable year (or is under the age of 24 at the end of the taxable year and was a full-time student during the taxable year), or is permanently and totally disabled.

Also, if the qualifying child is married at the close of the year, the individual may claim the EIC for that child only if the individual may also claim that child as a dependent.

To satisfy the identification test, an individual must include on their tax return the name, age, and "TIN" of each qualifying child.

The residence test requires that a qualifying child must have the same principal place of abode as the taxpayer for more than one-half of the taxable year (for the entire taxable year in the case of a foster child), and that this principal place of abode must be located in the United States. For purposes of determining whether a qualifying child meets the residence test, the principal place of abode shall be treated as in the United States for any period during which a member of the Armed Forces is stationed outside the United States while serving on extended active duty.

Explanation of Provision

The bill clarifies that the identification requirement is a requirement for claiming the EIC, rather than an element of the definitions of "eligible individual" and "qualifying child."

Effective Date

The provision is effective as if included in the originally enacted related legislation.

Conference Committee Report (H.R. CONF. REP. NO. 105-599)

The conference agreement follows the Senate amendment * * *

[Law at ¶ 5040. CCH Explanation at ¶ 216.]

[¶ 11,515]   Act Sec. 7001.   Employer deductions for vacation and severance pay

Senate Committee Report (S. REP. NO. 105-174)

[Code Sec. 404(a)]
Present Law

For deduction purposes, any method or arrangement that has the effect of a plan deferring the receipt of compensation or other benefits for employees is treated as a deferred compensation plan (sec. 404(b)). In general, contributions under a deferred compensation plan (other than certain pension, profit-sharing and similar plans) are deductible in the taxable year in which an amount attributable to the contribution is includible in income of the employee. However, vacation pay which is treated as deferred compensation is deductible for the taxable year of the employer in which the vacation pay is paid to the employee (sec. 404(a)(5)).

Temporary Treasury regulations provide that a plan, method, or arrangement defers the receipt of compensation or benefits to the extent it is one under which an employee receives compensation or benefits more than a brief period of time after the end of the employer's taxable year in which the services creating the right to such compensa-

tion or benefits are performed. A plan, method or arrangement is presumed to defer the receipt of compensation for more than a brief period of time after the end of an employer's taxable year to the extent that compensation is received after the 15th day of the 3rd calendar month after the end of the employer's taxable year in which the related services are rendered (the "2-1/2 month" period). A plan, method or arrangement is not considered to defer the receipt of compensation or benefits for more than a brief period of time after the end of the employer's taxable year to the extent that compensation or benefits are received by the employee on or before the end of the applicable 2-1/2 month period. (Temp. Treas. Reg. sec. 1.404(b)-1T A-2).

The Tax Court recently addressed the issue of when vacation pay and severance pay are considered deferred compensation in *Schmidt Baking Co., Inc.*, 107 T.C. 271 (1996). In *Schmidt Baking*, the taxpayer was an accrual basis taxpayer with a fiscal year that ended December 28, 1991. The taxpayer funded its accrued vacation and severance pay liabilities for 1991 by purchasing an irrevocable letter of credit on March 13, 1992. The parties stipulated that the letter of credit represented a transfer of substantially vested interest in property to employees for purposes of section 83, and that the fair market value of such interest was includible in the employees' gross incomes for 1992 as a result of the transfer.[50] The Tax Court held that the purchase of the letter of credit, and the resulting income inclusion, constituted payment of the vacation and severance pay within the 2-1/2 month period. Thus, the vacation and severance pay were treated as received by the employees within the 2-1/2 month period and were not treated as deferred compensation. The vacation pay and severance pay were deductible by the taxpayer for its 1991 fiscal year pursuant to its normal accrual method of accounting.

Reasons for Change

The Committee believes that the decision in *Schmidt Baking* reaches an inappropriate and unintended result. To permit methods such as that used in *Schmidt Baking* to be considered payment or receipt would allow taxpayers to avoid the 2-1/2 month rule and inappropriately accelerate deductions. The Committee believes that the intent of the 2-1/2 rule was clearly to provide that a deduction for deferred compensation is not available for the current taxable year unless the compensation is actually paid to employees within 2-1/2 months after the end of the year. Moreover, previous legislative histories reflect Congressional intent and understanding that compensation actually paid beyond the 2-1/2 month period is deferred compensation.[51]

Further, the Committee is concerned that taxpayers may inappropriately extend the rationale of *Schmidt Baking* to other situations in which a deduction or other tax consequences are contingent upon an item being paid. The Committee does not believe that, as a general rule, letters of credit and similar mechanisms should be considered payment for any purposes of the Code.

Explanation of Provision

Under the bill, for purposes of determining whether an item of compensation is deferred compensation (under Code sec. 404), the compensation is not considered to be paid or received until actually received by the employee. In addition, an item of deferred compensation is not considered paid to an employee until actually received by the employee. The provision is intended to overrule the result in *Schmidt Baking*. For example, with respect to the determination of whether vacation pay is deferred compensation, the fact that the value of the vacation pay is includible in the income of employees within the applicable 2-1/2 month period would not be relevant. Rather, the

vacation pay must have been actually received by employees within the 2-1/2 month period in order for the compensation not to be treated as deferred compensation.

It is intended that similar arrangements, in addition to the letter of credit approach used in *Schmidt Baking*, do not constitute actual receipt by the employee, even if there is an income inclusion. Thus, for example, actual receipt does not include the furnishing of a note or letter or other evidence of indebtedness of the taxpayer, whether or not the evidence is guaranteed by any other instrument or by any third party. As a further example, actual receipt does not include a promise of the taxpayer to provide service or property in the future (whether or not the promise is evidenced by a contract or other written agreement). In addition, actual receipt does not include an amount transferred as a loan, refundable deposit, or contingent payment. Amounts set aside in a trust for employees are not considered to be actually received by the employee.

The provision does not change the rule under which deferred compensation (other than vacation pay and deferred compensation under qualified plans) is deductible in the year includible in the gross income of employees participating in the plan if separate accounts are maintained for each employee.

While *Schmidt Baking* involved only vacation pay and severance pay, there is concern that this type of arrangement may be tried to circumvent other provisions of the Code where payment is required in order for a deduction to occur. Thus, it is intended that the Secretary will prevent the use of similar arrangements. No inference is intended that the result in *Schmidt Baking* is present law beyond its immediate facts or that the use of similar arrangements is permitted under present law.

The provision does not affect the determination of whether an item is includible in income. Thus, for example, using the mechanism in *Schmidt Baking* for vacation pay could still result in income inclusion to the employees, but the employer would not be entitled to a deduction for the vacation pay until actually paid to and received by the employees.

Effective Date

The provision is effective for taxable years ending after the date of enactment. Any change in method of accounting required by the bill is treated as initiated by the taxpayer with the consent of the Secretary of the Treasury. Any adjustment required by section 481 as a result of the change will be taken into account in the year of the change.

---

[50] While the rules of section 83 may govern the income inclusion, section 404 governs the deduction if the amount involved is deferred compensation.

[51] See, e.g., the legislative history to the Omnibus Budget Reconciliation Act of 1987.

Conference Committee Report (H.R. CONF. REP. NO. 105-599)

The conference agreement follows the Senate amendment. As under the Senate amendment, the fact that an item of compensation is includible in employees' incomes or wages within the applicable 2 1/2 month period is not relevant to determining whether an item of compensation is deferred compensation.

As under the Senate amendment, many arrangements in addition to the letter of credit approach used in *Schmidt Baking* do not constitute actual receipt by employees. For example, actual receipt does not include the furnishing of a note or letter or other evidence of indebtedness of the taxpayer, whether or not the evidence is guaranteed by any other instrument or by any third party. As a further example, actual receipt does not include a promise of the taxpayer to provide service or property in the future (whether or not the promise is evidenced by a contract or other written agreement). In addition, actual receipt does not include an amount transferred as a loan, refundable deposit, or contingent payment. Further, amounts set aside in a trust for employees are not considered to be actually received by the employee.

In light of the change being made and its effect on all cases involving this issue, the conferees ask the Secretary to consider whether, on a case-by-case basis, continued challenge of these arrangements for prior years represents the best use of litigation resources.

Effective Date

The provision is effective for taxable years ending after the date of enactment. Any change in method of accounting required by the provision will be treated as initiated by the taxpayer with the consent of the Secretary of the Treasury. Any adjustment required by section 481 as a result of the change will be taken into account over a three-year period beginning with the first year for which the provision is effective.

[Law at ¶ 5350. CCH Explanation at ¶ 591.]

[¶ 11,525]   Act Sec. 7002.   Freeze grandfather status of stapled REITs

Senate Committee Report (S. REP. NO. 105-174)

[Act Sec. 7002]

Present Law

In general

A real estate investment trust ("REIT") is an entity that receives most of its income from passive real estate related investments and that essentially receives pass-through treatment for income that is distributed to shareholders. If an electing entity meets the qualifications for REIT status, the portion of the income that is distributed to the investors each year generally is taxed to the investors without being subjected to a tax at the REIT level. In general, a REIT must derive its income from passive sources and not engage in any active trade or business.

Requirements for REIT status

A REIT must satisfy a number of tests on a year-by-year basis that relate to the entity's (1) organizational structure, (2) source of income, (3) nature of assets, and (4) distribution of income. These tests are intended to allow pass-through treatment only if there is a pooling of investment arrangement, if the entity's investments are basically in real estate assets, and its income is passive income from real estate investment, as contrasted with income from the operation of a business involving real estate. In addition, substantially all of the entity's income must be passed through to its shareholders on a current basis.

Under the organizational structure tests, except for the first taxable year for which an entity elects to be a REIT, the beneficial ownership of the entity must be held by 100 or more persons. Generally, no more than 50 percent of the value of the REIT's stock can be owned by five or fewer individuals during the last half of the taxable year.

Under the source-of-income tests, at least 95 percent of its gross income generally must be derived from rents, dividends, interest and certain other passive sources (the "95-percent test"). In addition, at least 75 percent of its income generally must be from real estate sources, including rents from real property and interest on mortgages secured by real property (the "75-percent test").

For purposes of these tests, rents from real property generally include charges for services customarily rendered in connection with the rental of real property, whether or not such charges are separately stated. Where a REIT furnishes non-customary services to tenants, amounts received generally are not treated as qualifying rents unless the services are furnished through an independent contractor from whom the REIT does not derive any income. In general, an independent contractor is a person who does not own more than a 35-percent interest in the REIT, and in which no more than a 35-percent interest is held by persons with a 35-percent or greater interest in the REIT.

To satisfy the REIT asset requirements, at the close of each quarter of its taxable year, an entity must have at least 75 percent of the value of its assets invested in real estate assets, cash and cash items, and government securities. Not more than 25 percent of the value of the REIT's assets can be invested in securities (other than government securities and other securities described in the preceding sentence). The securities of any one issuer may not comprise more than five percent of the value of a REIT's assets. Moreover, the REIT may not own more than 10 percent of the outstanding securities of any one issuer, determined by voting power.

A REIT is permitted to have a wholly-owned subsidiary subject to certain restrictions. A

REIT's subsidiary is treated as one with the REIT.

The income distribution requirement provides generally that at least 95 percent of a REIT's income (with certain minor exceptions) must be distributed to shareholders as dividends.

Stapled REITs

In a stapled REIT structure, both the shares of a REIT and a C corporation may be traded, but are subject to a provision that they may not be sold separately. Thus, the REIT and the C corporation have identical ownership at all times.

In the Deficit Reduction Act of 1984 (the "1984 Act"), Congress required that, in applying the tests for REIT status, all stapled entities are treated as one entity (sec. 269B(a)(3)). The 1984 Act included grandfather rules, one of which provided that certain then-existing stapled REITs were not subject to the new provision (sec. 136(c)(3) of the 1984 Act). That grandfather rule provided that the new provision did not apply to a REIT that was a part of a group of stapled entities if the group of entities was stapled on June 30, 1983, and included a REIT on that date.

Reasons for Change

In the 1984 Act, Congress eliminated the tax benefits of the stapled REIT structure, out of concern that it could effectively result in one level of tax on active corporate business income that would otherwise be subject to two levels of tax. Congress also believed that allowing a corporate business to be stapled to a REIT was inconsistent with the policy that led Congress to create REITs.

As part of the 1984 Act provision, Congress provided grandfather relief to the small number of stapled REITs that were already in existence. Since 1984, however, many of the grandfathered stapled REITs have been acquired by new owners. Some have entered into new lines of businesses, and most of the grandfathered REITs have used the stapled structure to engage in large-scale acquisitions of assets. The Committee believes that such unlimited relief from a general tax provision by a handful of taxpayers raises new questions not only of fairness, but of unfair competition, because the stapled REITs are in direct competition with other companies that cannot use the benefits of the stapled structure.

The Committee believes that it would be unfair to remove the benefit of the stapled REIT structure with respect to real estate interests that have already been acquired. On the other hand, the Committee believes that future acquisitions of interests in real property by these grandfathered entities, or improvements of property that are tantamount to new acquisitions, should not be accorded the benefits of the stapled REIT structure. Accordingly, the rules of the Committee bill generally apply with respect to real property interests acquired by the REIT or a stapled entity after March 26, 1998, pursuant to transactions not in progress on that date. Further, the Committee is concerned that the some of the benefit of the stapled REIT structure can be derived through mortgages and interests in subsidiaries and partnerships. Accordingly, the Committee bill provides rules for mortgages acquired after March 26, 1998, and indirect acquisitions of real property interests through entities after such date (with transition relief similar to that for direct acquisitions).

Explanation of Provision

Overview

Under the provision, rules similar to the rules of present law treating a REIT and all stapled entities as a single entity for purposes of determining REIT status (sec. 269B) apply to real property interests acquired after March 26, 1998, by an existing stapled REIT, a stapled entity, or a subsidiary or partnership in which a 10-percent or greater interest is owned by an existing stapled REIT or stapled entity (together referred to as the "stapled REIT group"), unless the real property interest is grandfathered as described below. Special rules apply to certain mortgages acquired by the stapled REIT group after March 26, 1998, where a member of the stapled REIT group performs services with respect to the property secured by the mortgage.

Rules for real property interests

In general

The provision generally applies to real property interests acquired by a member of the stapled REIT group after March 26, 1998. Real property interests that are acquired by a member of the REIT group after such date, and which are not grandfathered under the rules described below, are referred to as "nonqualified real property interests".

The provision treats activities and gross income of a stapled REIT group with respect to nonqualified real property interests held by any member of the stapled REIT group as activities and income of the REIT for certain purposes in the same manner as if the stapled REIT group were a single entity. This treatment applies for purposes of the following provisions that depend on a REIT's gross income: (1) the 95-percent test (sec. 856(c)(2)); (2) the 75-percent test (sec. 856(c)(3)); (3) the "reasonable cause" exception for failure to meet either test (sec. 856(c)(6)); and (4) the special tax on excess gross income for REITs with net income from prohibited transactions (sec. 857(b)(5)).

Thus, for example, where a stapled entity leases nonqualified real property from the REIT and earns gross income from operating the property, such gross income will be subject to the provision. The REIT and the stapled entity will be treated as a single entity, with the result that the lease payments from the stapled entity to the REIT would be ignored. The gross income earned by the stapled entity from operating the property will be treated as gross income of the REIT, with the result that either the 75-percent or 95-percent test might not be met and REIT status might be lost. Similarly, where a stapled entity leases property from a third party after March 26, 1998, and uses that property in a business, the gross income it derives will be treated as income of the REIT because the lease would be a nonqualified real property interest.

Grandfathered real property interests

Under the provision, all real property interests acquired by a member of the stapled REIT group after March 26, 1998, are treated as nonqualified real property interests subject to the general rules described above, unless they qualify under one of the grandfather rules. An option to acquire real property is generally treated as a real property interest for purposes of the provision. However, a real property interest acquired by exercise of an option after March 26, 1998, is treated as a nonqualified real property interest, even though the option was acquired before such date.

Under the provision, grandfathered real property interests include properties acquired by a member of the stapled REIT group after March 26, 1998, pursuant to a written agreement which was binding on March 26, 1998, and all times thereafter. Grandfathered properties also include certain properties, the acquisition of which were described in a public announcement or in a filing with the Securities and Exchange Commission on or before March 26, 1998.

A real property interest does not generally lose its status as a grandfathered interest by reason of a repair to, an improvement of, or a lease of, the real property. Thus, if a REIT leases a grandfathered real property to a stapled entity, a renewal of the lease does not cause the property to lose its grandfathered status, whether the renewal is pursuant to the terms of the lease or otherwise. Similarly, if a REIT owns a grandfathered real property interest that is leased to a third party and, at the expiration of that lease, the REIT leases the property to a stapled entity, the interest would remain a grandfathered interest. Finally, if a stapled entity leases a grandfathered property interest from a third party and the property is repaired or improved, the interest would remain a grandfathered interest except as described below.

An improvement of a grandfathered real property interest will cause loss of grandfathered status and become a nonqualified real property interest in certain circumstances. Any expansion beyond the boundaries of the land of the otherwise grandfathered interest occurring after March 26, 1998, will be treated as a non-qualified real property interest to the extent of such expansion. Moreover, any improvement of an otherwise grandfathered real property interest (within its land boundaries) that is placed in service after December 31, 1999, is treated as a separate nonqualified real property interest in certain circumstances. Such treatment applies where (1) the improvement changes the use of the property and (2) its cost is greater than (a) 200 percent of the undepreciated cost of the property (prior to the improvement) or (b) in the case of property acquired where there is a substituted basis, the fair market value of the property on the date that the property was acquired by the stapled entity or the REIT. There is an exception for improvements placed in service before January 1, 2004, pursuant to a binding contract in effect on December 31, 1999, and at all times thereafter. The rule treating improvements as nonqualified real property interests could apply, for example, if a member of the stapled REIT group constructs a building

after December 31, 1999, on previously undeveloped raw land that had been acquired on or before March 26, 1998.

Ownership through entities

If a REIT or stapled entity owns, directly or indirectly, a 10-percent-or-greater interest in a corporate subsidiary or partnership (or other entity described below) that owns a real property interest, the above rules apply with respect to a proportionate part of the entity's real property interest, activities and gross income. Thus, any real property interest acquired by such a subsidiary or partnership that is not grandfathered under the rules described above is treated as a nonqualified real property interest held by the REIT or stapled entity in the same proportion as its ownership interest in the entity. The same proportion of the subsidiary's or partnership's gross income from any nonqualified real property interest owned by it or another member of the stapled REIT group will be treated as income of the REIT under the rules described above. However, an interest in real property acquired by a grandfathered 10-percent-or-greater partnership or subsidiary is treated as grandfathered if such interest would be a grandfathered interest if held directly by the REIT or stapled entity. Thus, for example, if a REIT contributes a grandfathered real property interest to a partnership 10 percent or more of which is owned on March 26, 1998, the interest will not cease to be a grandfathered interest.[52]

Similar rules attributing the proportionate part of the subsidiary's or partnership's real property interests and gross income will apply when a REIT or stapled entity acquires a 10-percent-or-greater interest (or in the case of a previously-owned entity, acquires an additional interest) after March 26, 1998, with exceptions for interests acquired pursuant to binding written agreements or public announcements described above. Transition relief can apply to both an entity's assets and the interest in the entity under the above rules. Thus, if on March 26, 1998, and at all times thereafter, a stapled entity has a binding written contract to buy 10-percent or more of the stock of a corporation and the corporation also has a binding written contract to buy real property, no portion of the property will be treated as a nonqualified real property interest as a result of the transaction.

Under the above rules, gross income of a REIT or stapled entity with respect to a nonqualified real property interest held by a 10-percent-or-greater partnership or subsidiary is subject to the rules for nonqualified real property interests only in proportion to the interest held in the partnership or subsidiary. For example, assume that a stapled entity has a contract to manage a nonqualified real property interest held by a partnership in which the stapled entity owns an 85-percent interest. Under the above rules, for purposes of applying the gross income tests, 85 percent of the partnership's activities and gross income from the property are attributed to the

---

[52] Nevertheless, under the rules below, if the REITs partnership interest increases as a result of the contribution, a portion of each of the partnership's real estate interests,

reflecting the proportionate increase in the partnership interest, will be treated as a nonqualified real property interest.

REIT. As a result, 85 percent of the stapled entity's income from the management contract is ignored under the single-entity analysis described above. The remaining 15 percent of the management fee is not treated as gross income of the REIT because it is not income from a nonqualified real property interest held or deemed held by the REIT or a stapled entity.

Grandfathered real property interests that are deemed owned by a REIT or a stapled entity under the rules for 10-percent-or-greater interests will not be treated as acquired after March 26, 1998, if the REIT or a stapled entity subsequently becomes the actual owner. For example, assume a REIT has a 50-percent interest in a partnership that distributes a grandfathered real property interest to the REIT in complete liquidation of its interest. The 50-percent interest that was previously deemed owned by the REIT will continue to be grandfathered; the remaining 50-percent interest will be a nonqualified real property interest because it was acquired by the REIT after March 26, 1998.

Mortgage rules

Under the provision, special rules apply where a member of the stapled REIT group holds a mortgage (that is not an existing obligation under the rules described below) that is secured by an interest in real property, and a member of the stapled REIT group engages in certain activities with respect to that property. The activities that have this effect under the provision are activities that would result in impermissible tenant service income (as defined in sec.856(d)(7)) if performed by the REIT with respect to property it held. In such a case, all interest on the mortgage that is allocable to that property and all gross income received by a member of the stapled REIT group from the activity will be treated as impermissible tenant service income of the REIT, which is not qualifying income under either the 75-percent or 95-percent tests. For example, assume that the REIT makes a mortgage loan on a hotel owned by a third party which is operated by a stapled entity under a management contract. Unless an exception applies, both the management fees earned by the stapled entity and the interest earned by the REIT will be treated as impermissible tenant services income of the REIT.

An exception to the above rules is provided for mortgages the interest on which does not exceed an arm's-length rate and which would be treated as interest for purposes of the REIT rules. An exception also is available for mortgages that are held by a member of the stapled REIT group on March 26, 1998, and at all times thereafter, and which are secured by an interest in real property on that date, and at all times thereafter (the "existing mortgage exception"). The existing mortgage exception ceases to apply if the mortgage is refinanced and the principal amount is increased in such refinancing.

In the case of a partnership or subsidiary in which the REIT or a stapled entity owns a 10-percent-or-greater interest, a proportionate part of the entity's mortgages, interest and gross income

from activities would be attributed to the REIT or the stapled entity, subject to rules similar to those for nonqualified real property interests. Thus, if a REIT or a stapled entity acquires a 10-percent-or-greater interest in a partnership or corporation after March 26, 1998, no mortgage held by the partnership or subsidiary at such time would qualify for the existing mortgage exception. Similarly, if a REIT or stapled entity owns a 10-percent-or-greater interest in a partnership or subsidiary on March 26, 1998, and the REIT or the stapled entity subsequently acquires a greater interest, a portion of each of the partnership's or subsidiary's mortgages that is the same as the proportionate increase in the ownership interest would fail to qualify for the existing mortgage exception.

Under the provision's priority rules, the mortgage rules do not apply to any part of a real property interest that is owned or deemed owned by the REIT or a stapled entity under the rules for real property interests described above. Thus, for example, if the REIT makes a mortgage loan on real property owned by a stapled entity, the mortgage rules would not apply. If the property is a nonqualified real property interest, the interest on the mortgage would be ignored under the single-entity analysis described above, and the gross income of the stapled entity from the property would be treated as income of the REIT. Similarly, assume that a stapled entity owns 75 percent of the stock of a subsidiary and has a management contract to operate a hotel owned by the subsidiary. Assume also that the REIT makes a mortgage loan for the hotel. Under the real property interest rules, 75 percent of the hotel is treated as owned by the stapled entity. Thus, if the hotel is a nonqualified real property interest, 75 percent of the subsidiary's gross income from the hotel is treated as income of the REIT and 75 percent of the income on the management contract is ignored under the single-entity analysis. With respect to the remaining 25-percent interest in the subsidiary, the real property interest rules do not apply, but the mortgage rules would treat 25 percent of the mortgage interest and 25 percent of management contract income as impermissible tenant services income of the REIT.

Other rules

For purposes of both the real property interest and mortgage rules, if a stapled REIT is not stapled as of March 26, 1998, and at all times thereafter, or if it fails to qualify as a REIT as of such date or any time thereafter, no assets of any member of the stapled REIT group would qualify under the grandfather rules. Thus, all of the real property interests held by the group would be nonqualified real property interests and none of the mortgages held by the group would qualify for the existing mortgage exception.

For a corporate subsidiary owned by a stapled entity, the 10-percent ownership test would be met if a stapled entity owns, directly or indirectly, 10 percent or more of the corporation's stock, by either vote or value.[53] For this purpose, any change in proportionate ownership that is

---

[53] The provision does not apply to a stapled REIT's ownership of a corporate subsidiary, although the REIT would be subject to the normal restrictions on a REIT's ownership of stock in a corporation.

attributable solely to fluctuations in the relative fair market values of different classes of stock is not taken into account. For interests in partnerships, the ownership test would be met if either the REIT or a stapled entity owns, directly or indirectly, a 10-percent or greater interest in the partnership's assets or net profits. Interests in other entities, such as trusts, are treated in the same manner as 10-percent-or-greater interests in partnerships or corporations if the REIT or a stapled entity owns, directly or indirectly, 10 percent or more of the beneficial interests in the entity.

Under the provision, terms used that are also used in the stapled stock rules (sec. 269B) or the REIT rules (sec. 856) have the same meanings as under those rules.

The Secretary of the Treasury is given authority to prescribe such guidance as may be necessary or appropriate to carry out the purposes of the provision, including guidance to prevent the double counting of income and to prevent transactions that would avoid the purposes of the provision.

Effective Date

The provision is effective for taxable years ending after March 26, 1998.

Conference Committee Report (H.R. CONF. REP. NO. 105-599)

The conference agreement generally follows the Senate amendment with the following technical modifications. The conference agreement clarifies that a real property interest acquired pursuant to the exercise of a put option, buy-sell agreement or an agreement relating to a third party default that was binding on March 26, 1998, and at all times thereafter, is generally treated as a grandfathered real property interest. It is the intention of the conferees that this rule apply only to substantive economic arrangements that are outside of the control of the stapled REIT group. The conference agreement clarifies that a renewal of a lease of property from a third party to a member of the stapled REIT group, like a lease or renewal between group members, does not generally terminate grandfather status, whether the renewal is pursuant to the terms of the lease or otherwise.[2] However, renewal of a lease can cause loss of grandfather status if the property is improved to the extent that grandfather status would be lost under the improvement rules described above. Moreover, the conference agreement provides that, for leases and renewals entered into after March 26, 1998 (whether from members of the stapled REIT group or third parties), grandfather status is lost if the rent on the lease or renewal exceeds an arm's length rate.

The conference agreement makes certain changes to the rule attributing ownership of real property interests, mortgages and other items from a partnership or subsidiary in which the REIT or a stapled entity owns a 10-percent-or-greater interest, directly or indirectly. Under the conference agreement, the percentage ownership interest in a partnership is to be determined by the owner's share of capital or profits, whichever is larger. The conference agreement clarifies that an interest in real property acquired by a 10-percent-or-greater partnership or subsidiary pursuant to a binding written agreement, public announcement, SEC filing, put option, buy-sell agreement or agreement relating to a third-party default (a "qualified transaction") is treated as grandfathered if such interest would be a grandfathered interest if acquired directly by the REIT or stapled entity. The conference agree-

ment also provides that the exception for 10-percent-or- greater interests in partnerships or subsidiaries acquired pursuant to a qualified transaction applies to interests acquired by any member of the stapled REIT group. The conferees also wish to clarify that all real property interests, mortgages, activities and gross income of a qualified REIT subsidiary are treated as attributes of the REIT for purposes of the provision.

The conference agreement adds a rule that provides that a transfer, direct or indirect, of a grandfathered real property interest between members of a stapled REIT group does not result in a loss of grandfather status if the total direct and indirect interests of both the exempt REIT and stapled entity in the real property interest does not increase as a result of the transfer. If the total direct and indirect interest of the exempt REIT and stapled entity increases, the transferred real property interest will be deemed to lose grandfather status only to the extent of such increase. The provision applies to all types of transfers of real property interests among group members, such as sales, contributions and distributions, whether taxable or tax-free. Moreover, the provision applies both to direct transfers of real property interests and transfers of such interests indirectly through transfer of interests in 10-percent-or-greater owned partnerships and subsidiaries. The application of the new provision is illustrated by the following examples. First, assume that an exempt REIT sells a portion of a grandfathered real property interest to a stapled entity. The real property interest remains grandfathered because there is no increase in the total interests of the REIT and the stapled entity (100 percent both before and after the transfer). Second, assume that a grandfathered real property interest is contributed by a stapled entity to a partnership or subsidiary in which the stapled entity owns a 10-percent-or-greater interest (either prior to, or as a result of, the contribution). The real property interest remains grandfathered because the previous total interests of the exempt REIT and stapled entity (the stapled entity's 100-percent interest) are not increased by the transfer.[3] Third, assume a REIT owns a 50-per-

---

[2] In the case of a lease from a third party, a renewal will not qualify if there is a significant time period between the two tenancies.

[3] Nevertheless, if the REIT's interest in the partnership or subsidiary increases as a result of the contribution, a

cent interest in a partnership that distributes a grandfathered real property interest to the REIT in complete liquidation of its interest. The 50-percent interest that was previously deemed owned by the REIT will continue to be grandfathered; the remaining 50-percent interest will become a non-grandfathered interest because it represents an increase in the total direct and indirect interests of the REIT and stapled entity in the real property interest. Fourth, assume that a partnership in which an exempt REIT or stapled entity owns a 10-percent or greater interest terminates as a result of a sale of 50 percent or more of the total partnership interests during a 12-month period that does not involve the REIT or a stapled entity (sec. 708(b)(1)(B)). Grandfather status of real property interests owned by the partnership is not lost in the transfer because, as a result of the termination, the partnership's assets are deemed contributed to a new partnership and interests in that partnership are deemed distributed to the purchasing and other partners in proportion to their interests (Treas. reg. sec. 1.708-1(b)(1)(iv)). Thus, there is no change in the total interest of the REIT and stapled entity in the partnership's assets.

The conference agreement adds a provision intended to deal with the special situation of so-called "UPREIT" partnerships (see Treas. reg. 1.701-2(d)(example 4)), which generally treats 100 percent of the real property interests, mortgages, activities and gross income of such partnerships as interests, activities and gross income of the REIT or stapled entity that owns a partnership interest. The provision applies where (i) an exempt REIT or stapled entity owned directly or indirectly) at least a 60-percent interest in a partnership as of March 26, 1998, (ii) 90 percent or more of the interests in the partnership (other than those held by the exempt REIT or stapled entity) are or will be redeemable or exchangeable

for consideration with a value determined with reference to the stock of the REIT or stapled entity or both. The provision also applies to an interest in a partnership formed after March 26, 1998, which meets the provision's other requirements, where the partnership was formed to mirror the stapling of an exempt REIT and a stapled entity in connection with an acquisition agreed to or announced on or before March 26, 1998. If, as of January 1, 1999, more than one partnership owned (directly or indirectly) by either an exempt REIT or stapled entity meets the requirements of the provision, only the largest such partnership (determined by aggregate asset bases) is treated as meeting such requirements.

The conference agreement provides that, for purposes of the exception to the mortgage rules for mortgages held on March 26, 1998, an increase in interest payable on a mortgage (except pursuant to an interest arrangement, such as variable interest, under the mortgage's terms as of March 26, 1998), or an increase in interest payable as a result of a refinancing, causes the mortgage to cease to qualify for the exception unless the new interest rate meets an arm's-length standard.

The conferees also wish to clarify that in the event that a stapled REIT group ceases to be stapled, the rules treating assets, activities and gross income of members or the stapled REIT group as attributes of the REIT apply only to the portion of the year in which the group was a stapled REIT group. Similarly, where a REIT's or stapled entity's interest in a partnership or subsidiary changes during the year, the rules treating a proportionate part of the assets, activities and gross income of the partnership or subsidiary as attributes of the REIT or stapled entity also apply on a partial-year basis.

[Law at ¶ 8285. CCH Explanation at ¶ 655.]

[¶ 11,535]   Act Sec. 7003.   Make certain trade receivables ineligible for mark-to-market treatment

Senate Committee Report (S. REP. NO. 105-174)

[Code Sec. 475]
Present Law

In general, dealers in securities are required to use a mark-to-market method of accounting for securities (sec. 475). Exceptions to the mark-to-market rule are provided for securities held for investment, certain debt instruments and obligations to acquire debt instruments and certain securities that hedge securities. A dealer in securities is a taxpayer who regularly purchases securities from or sells securities to customers in the ordinary course of a trade or business, or who regularly offers to enter into, assume, offset, assign, or otherwise terminate positions in certain types of securities with customers in the ordinary course of a trade or business. A security includes (1) a share of stock, (2) an interest in a widely held or publicly traded partnership or trust, (3)

an evidence of indebtedness, (4) an interest rate, currency, or equity notional principal contract, (5) an evidence of an interest in, or derivative financial instrument in, any of the foregoing securities, or any currency, including any option, forward contract, short position, or similar financial instrument in such a security or currency, or (6) a position that is an identified hedge with respect to any of the foregoing securities.

Treasury regulations provide that if a taxpayer would be a dealer in securities only because of its purchases and sales of debt instruments that, at the time of purchase or sale, are customer paper with respect to either the taxpayer or a corporation that is a member of the same consolidated group, the taxpayer will not normally be treated as a dealer in securities. However, the regulations allow such a taxpayer to elect out of this excep-

(Footnote Continued)

portion of each of the entity's real property interests other than the interest contributed, reflecting the proportionate

tion to dealer status.[54] For this purpose, a debt instrument is customer paper with respect to a person if: (1) the person's principal activity is selling nonfinancial goods or providing nonfinancial services; (2) the debt instrument was issued by the purchaser of the goods or services at the time of the purchase of those goods and services in order to finance the purchase; and (3) at all times since the debt instrument was issued, it has been held either by the person selling those goods or services or by a corporation that is a member of the same consolidated group as that person.

Reasons for Change

Congress enacted the mark-to-market rules of section 475 to provide a more accurate reflection of the income of securities dealers. The Committee does not believe that these provisions were intended to be used by taxpayers whose principal activity is selling goods and services to obtain a deduction for loss in value of their receivables at a time earlier than otherwise would be permitted.

Explanation of Provision

The provision provides that certain trade receivables are not eligible for mark-to-market treatment. A trade receivable is covered by the provision if it is a note, bond or debenture arising out of the sale of goods by a person the principal activity of which is selling or providing non-financial goods and services and it is held by such person or a related person at all times since it was issued.

Under the provision, a receivable meeting the above definition is not treated as a security for purposes of the mark-to-market rules (sec. 475). Thus, such receivables are not marked-to-market, even if the taxpayer qualifies as a dealer in other securities. Because trade receivables cease to meet the above definition when they are disposed of (other than to a related person), a taxpayer who regularly sells trade receivables is treated as a dealer in securities as under present law, with the result that the taxpayer's other securities would be subject to mark-to-market treatment unless an exception to section 475 applies (such as that for securities identified as held for investment).

Effective Date

The provision generally is effective for taxable years ending after the date of enactment. Adjustments required under section 481 as a result of the change in method of accounting generally are required to be taken into account ratably over the four-year period beginning in the first taxable year for which the provision is in effect. However, where the taxpayer terminates its existence or ceases to engage in the trade or business that generated the receivables (except as a result of a tax-free transfer), any remaining balance of the section 481 adjustment is taken into account entirely in the year of such cessation or termination (see sec. 5.04(c) of Rev. Proc. 97-37, 1997-33 I.R.B. 18).

Conference Committee Report (H.R. CONF. REP. NO. 105-599)

The conference agreement follows the Senate amendment with modifications. The conferees wish to clarify that the new provision applies to trade receivables arising from services performed by independent contractors, as well as employees. Thus, for example, if a taxpayer's principal activity is selling non-financial services and some or all of such services are performed by independent contractors, no receivables that the taxpayer accepts for services can be marked-to-market under the new provision. The conferees intend that, pursuant to the authority granted by section 475(g)(1), the Secretary of the Treasury is authorized to issue regulations to prevent abuse of the new exception, including through independent contractor arrangements.

The conference agreement provides that, to the extent provided in Treasury regulations, trade receivables that are held for sale to customers by the taxpayer or a related person may be treated

as "securities" for purposes of the mark-to-market rules, and transactions in such receivables could result in a taxpayer being treated as a dealer in securities (sec. 475(c)(1)). It is the intention of the conferees that, unlike the Senate amendment, a taxpayer will not be treated as a dealer in securities based on sales to unrelated persons of receivables subject to the new provision unless the regulatory exception for receivables held for sale to customers applies.

It is the intention of the conferees that, for trade receivables that are excepted from the statutory mark-to-market rules (sec. 475) under the new provision, mark-to-market or lower-of-cost-or-market will not be treated as methods of accounting that clearly reflect income under general tax principles (see sec. 446(b)).

[Law at ¶ 5380. CCH Explanation at ¶ 554.]

---

[54] Treas. reg. sec. 1.475(c)-1(b), issued December 23, 1996; the "customer paper election."

[¶ 11,545]   Act Sec. 7004.   Exclusion of minimum required distributions from AGI for Roth IRA conversions

JCT Description of Roth Financing Amendment No. 2339 (JCX-31-98)

[Code Sec. 408A(c)(3)(C)(i)]

Present Law

Under present law, uniform minimum distribution rules generally apply to all types of tax-favored retirement vehicles, including qualified retirement plans and annuities, individual retirement arrangements ("IRAs") other than Roth IRAs, and tax-sheltered annuities (sec 403(b)).

Under present law, distributions are required to begin no later than the participant's required beginning date (sec. 401(a)(9)). The required beginning date means the April 1 of the calendar year following the later of.(1) the calendar year in which the employee attains age 70-1/2, or (2) the calendar year in which the employee retires. In the case of an employee who is a 5-percent owner (as defined in section 416), the required beginning date is April 1 of the calendar year following the calendar year in which the employee attains age 70-1/2. The Internal Revenue Service has issued extensive Regulations for purposes of calculating minimum distributions. In general, minimum distributions are includible in gross income in the year of distribution. An excise tax equal to 50 percent of the required distribution applies to the extent a required distribution is not made.

Under present law, all or any part of amounts held in a deductible or nondeductible IRA may be converted into a Roth IRA. Only taxpayers with adjusted gross income ("AUI") of $100,000 or less are eligible to convert an IRA into a Roth IRA. In the case of a married taxpayer, AGI is the combined AGI of the couple. Married taxpayers filing a separate return are not eligible to make a conversion.

Description of Proposal

The proposal would modify the definition of AGI to exclude required minimum distributions from the taxpayer's AGI solely for purposes of determining eligibility to convert from an IRA to a Roth IRA. As under present law, the required minimum distribution would not be eligible for conversion and would be includible in gross income.

Effective Date

The proposal would be effective for taxable years beginning after December 31, 2004.

Conference Committee Report (H.R. CONF. REP. NO. 105-599)

The conference agreement follows the Senate amendment.

Effective Date

Same as Senate amendment.

[Law at ¶ 5370. CCH Explanation at ¶ 323.]

[¶ 11,555]   Act Sec. 8001.   Limited tax benefits under the Line Item Veto Act

Conference Committee Report (H.R. CONF. REP. NO. 105-599)

[Act Sec. 8001]

Present Law

The Line Item Veto Act amended the Congressional Budget and Impoundment Act of 1974 to grant the President the limited authority to cancel specific dollar amounts of discretionary budget authority, certain new direct spending, and limited tax benefits. The Line Item Veto Act provides that the Joint Committee on Taxation is required to examine any revenue or reconciliation bill or joint resolution that amends the Internal Revenue Code of 1986 prior to its filing by a conference committee in order to determine whether or not the bill or joint resolution contains any "limited tax benefits," and to provide a statement to the conference committee that either (1) identifies each limited tax benefit contained in the bill or resolution, or (2) states that the bill or resolution contains no limited tax benefits. The conferees determine whether or not to include the Joint Committee on Taxation statement in the conference report. If the conference report includes the information from the Joint Committee on Taxation identifying provisions that are limited tax benefits, then the President may cancel one or more of those, but only those, provisions that have been identified. If such a conference report contains a statement from the Joint Committee on Taxation that none of the provisions in the conference report are limited tax benefits, then the President has no authority to cancel any of the specific tax provisions, because there are no tax provisions that are eligible for cancellation under the Line Item Veto Act. If the conference report contains no statement with respect to limited tax benefits, then the President may cancel any revenue provision in the conference report that he determines to be a limited tax benefit.

Conference Statement

The Joint Committee on Taxation has determined that H.R. 2676 contains the following provisions that constitute limited tax benefits within the meaning of the Line Item Veto Act:

Section 3105 (relating to administrative appeal of adverse IRS determination of tax-exempt status of bond issue)

Section 3445(c) (relating to State fish and wildlife permits)

[Law at ¶ 8290. CCH Explanation at ¶ 1137, ¶ 1234 and ¶ 30,025.]

[¶ 11,575]   Review of Milwaukee and Waukesha IRS Offices

Conference Committee Report (H.R. CONF. REP. NO. 105-599)

Present Law

A task force was initiated in January, 1998, to conduct an investigation of the equal employment opportunity process in the IRS' Milwaukee and Waukesha, Wisconsin offices.

House Bill

No provision.

Senate Amendment

The Senate amendment directs the IRS Commissioner to appoint an independent expert in employment and personnel matters to review the investigation conducted by the task force and report to Congress with recommendations for action not later than July 1, 1999. The review should include a determination of the accuracy and validity of such investigation; and if determined necessary by the expert, a further investi-

gation of such offices relating to: (1) the equal employment opportunity process; and (2) any alleged discriminatory employment-related actions, including any alleged violation of Federal law.

Effective Date

The Senate amendment provisions is effective on date of enactment.

Conference Agreement

The conference agreement follows the House bill. However, the conferees intend that the task force continue to its conclusion. The conferees intend that the General Accounting Office review the report of the task force and report to the House Committee on Ways and Means and the Senate Committee on Finance.

[CCH Explanation at ¶ 879.]

[¶ 11,580]   Moratorium regarding regulations under Notice 98-11

Conference Committee Report (H.R. CONF. REP. NO. 105-599)

Present Law

Overview

U.S. citizens and residents and U.S. corporations are taxed currently by the United States on their worldwide income, subject to a credit against U.S. tax on foreign-source income for foreign income taxes paid with respect to such income. A foreign corporation generally is not subject to U.S. tax on its income from operations outside the United States.

Income of a foreign corporation generally is taxed by the United States when it is repatriated to the United States through payment to the corporation's U.S. shareholders, subject to a foreign tax credit. However, various regimes imposing current U.S. tax on income earned through a foreign corporation are reflected in the Code. One anti-deferral regime set forth in the Code is the controlled foreign corporation rules of subpart F (secs. 951-964).

A controlled foreign corporation ("CFC") is defined generally as any foreign corporation if U.S. persons own more than 50 percent of the corporation's stock (measured by vote or value), taking into account only those U.S. persons that own at least 10 percent of the stock (measured by vote only) (sec. 957). Stock ownership includes not only stock owned directly, but also stock owned indirectly or constructively (sec. 958).

The United States generally taxes the U.S. 10-percent shareholders of a CFC currently on their pro rata shares of certain income of the CFC (so-called "subpart F income") (sec. 951). In effect, the Code treats those shareholders as having received a current distribution out of the CFC's subpart F income. Such shareholders also are subject to current U.S. tax on their pro rata shares of the CFC's earnings invested in U.S. property (sec. 951). The foreign tax credit may reduce the U.S. tax on these amounts.

Subpart F income includes, among other items, foreign base company income (sec. 952). Foreign

base company income, in turn, includes foreign personal holding company income, foreign base company sales income, foreign base company services income, foreign base company shipping income and foreign base company oil related income (sec. 954). Foreign personal holding company income includes, among other items, dividends, interest, rents, and royalties. An exception from foreign personal holding company income applies to certain dividends and interest received from a related person which is created or organized in the same country as the CFC and which has a substantial part of its assets in that country, and to certain rents and royalties received from a related person for the use of property in the same country in which the CFC was created or organized (the so-called "same-country exception").

Foreign base company sales income includes income derived by a CFC from certain related-party transactions, including the purchase of personal property from a related person and its sale to any person, the purchase of personal property from any person and its sale to a related person, and the purchase or sale of personal property on behalf of a related person, where the property which is purchased or sold is manufactured outside the country in which the CFC was created or organized and the property is purchased or sold for use or consumption outside such foreign country. A special branch rule applies for purposes of determining a CFC's foreign base company sales income. Under this rule, a branch of a CFC is treated as a separate corporation (only for purposes of determining the CFC's foreign base company sales income) where the activities of the CFC through the branch outside the CFC's country of incorporation have substantially the same effect as if such branch were a subsidiary.

Because of differences in U.S. and foreign laws, it is possible for a taxpayer to enter into transactions that are treated in one manner for U.S. tax purposes and in another manner for foreign tax purposes. These transactions are referred to as

Act Sec. 8001   ¶ 11,580

hybrid transactions. For example, a hybrid transaction may involve the use of an entity that is treated as a corporation for purposes of the tax law of one jurisdiction but is treated as a branch or partnership for purposes of the tax law of another jurisdiction.

Notice 98-11 and the regulations issued thereunder

Notice 98-11, issued on January 16, 1998, addressed the treatment of hybrid branches under the subpart F provisions of the Code. The Notice stated that the Treasury Department and the Internal Revenue Service have concluded that the use of certain arrangements involving hybrid branches is contrary to the policy and rules of subpart F. The hybrid branch arrangements identified in Notice 98-11 involve structures that are characterized for U.S. tax purposes as part of a CFC but are characterized for purposes of the tax law of the country in which the CFC is incorporated as a separate entity. The Notice stated that regulations will be issued to prevent the use of hybrid branch arrangements to reduce foreign tax while avoiding the corresponding creation of subpart F income. The Notice stated that such regulations will provide that the branch and the CFC will be treated as separate corporations for purposes of subpart F. The Notice also stated that similar issues raised under subpart F by certain partnership or trust arrangements will be addressed in separate regulation projects.

On March 23, 1998, temporary and proposed regulations were issued to address the issues raised in Notice 98-11 and to address certain partnership and other issues raised under subpart F. Under the regulations, certain payments between a CFC and its hybrid branch or between hybrid branches of the CFC (so-called "hybrid branch payments") are treated as giving rise to subpart F income. The regulations generally provide that non-subpart F income of the CFC, in the amount of the hybrid branch payment, is recharacterized as subpart F income of the CFC if: (1) the hybrid branch payment reduces the foreign tax of the payor, (2) the hybrid branch payment would have been foreign personal holding company income if made between separate CFCs, and (3) there is a disparity between the effective tax rate on the payment in the hands of the payee and the effective tax rate that would have applied if the income had been taxed in the hands of the payor. The regulations also apply to other hybrid branch arrangements involving a partnership, including a CFC's proportionate share of any hybrid branch payment made between a partnership in which the CFC is a partner and a hybrid branch of the partnership or between hybrid branches of such a partnership. Under the regulations, if a partnership is treated as fiscally transparent by the CFC's taxing jurisdiction, the recharacterization rules are applied by treating the hybrid branch payment as if it had been made directly between the CFC and the hybrid branch, or as if the hybrid branches of the partnership were hybrid branches of the CFC, as applicable. If the partnership is treated as a separate entity by the CFC's taxing jurisdiction, the recharacterization rules are applied to treat the partnership as if it were a CFC.

The regulations also address the application of the same-country exception to the foreign personal holding company income rules under subpart F in the case of certain hybrid branch arrangements. Under the regulations, the same-country exception applies to payments by a CFC to a hybrid branch of a related CFC only if the payment would have qualified for the exception if the hybrid branch had been a separate CFC incorporated in the jurisdiction in which the payment is subject to tax (other than a withholding tax). The regulations provide additional rules regarding the application of the same-country exception in the case of certain hybrid arrangements involving a partnership.

The regulations generally apply to amounts paid or accrued pursuant to hybrid branch arrangements entered into or substantially modified on or after January 16, 1998. As a result, the regulations generally do not apply to amounts paid or accrued pursuant to hybrid branch arrangements entered into before January 16, 1998 and not substantially modified on or after that date.

In the case of certain hybrid arrangements involving partnerships, the regulations generally apply to amounts paid or accrued pursuant to such arrangements entered into or substantially modified on or after March 23, 1998. As a result, the regulations generally do not apply to amounts paid or accrued pursuant to such arrangements entered into before March 23, 1998 and not substantially modified on or after that date.

House Bill

No provision.

Senate Amendment

The Senate amendment provides that no temporary or final regulations with respect to Notice 98-11 may be implemented prior to six months after the date of enactment of this provision. This moratorium applies to the regulations with respect to hybrid branches and to the regulations with respect to hybrid arrangements involving partnerships. It is intended that the moratorium delaying implementation of the regulations would not require a modification to the effective dates of the regulations. No inference is intended regarding the authority of the Department of the Treasury or the Internal Revenue Service to issue the Notice or the regulations.

Effective Date

Date of enactment.

Conference Agreement

The conference agreement does not include the Senate amendment. The conferees have agreed not to include the Senate amendment because the Department of the Treasury has withdrawn Notice 98-11 and has announced its intention to withdraw the temporary and proposed regulations issued under Notice 98-11, and to reissue regulations in proposed form to be finalized no earlier than January 1, 2000. See Notice 98-35, 1998-26 I.R.B. 1. The conferees expect that the Congress will consider the international tax policy issues relating to the treatment of hybrid transactions under the subpart F provisions of the Code, and will consider taking legislative action as deemed appropriate. In this regard, the conferees expect that the Congress will consider the impact of any legislation or administrative guidance in this area on affected taxpayers and industries. The conferees strongly recommend that the Department of the Treasury also take into account the impact of any administrative guidance in this area on affected taxpayers and industries. No inference is intended regarding the authority of the Department of the Treasury or the Internal Revenue Service to issue the Notice or the regulations, or to issue any other notice or regulation which reaches the same or similar results with respect to the treatment of hybrid transactions under subpart F.

[CCH Explanation at ¶ 633.]

[¶ 11,585] Sense of the Senate regarding Notices 98-5 and 98-11

Conference Committee Report (H.R. CONF. REP. NO. 105-599)

Present Law

Overview

U.S. citizens and residents and U.S. corporations are taxed currently by the United States on their worldwide income. U.S. persons may credit foreign taxes against U.S. tax on foreign-source income. The amount of foreign tax credits that can be claimed in a year is subject to a limitation that prevents taxpayers from using foreign tax credits to offset U.S. tax on U.S.-source income. Separate limitations are applied to specific categories of income.

A foreign corporation generally is not subject to U.S. tax on its income from operations outside the United States. Income of a foreign corporation generally is taxed by the United States when it is repatriated to the United States through payment to the corporation's U.S. shareholders, subject to a foreign tax credit. However, various regimes imposing current U.S. tax on income earned through a foreign corporation are reflected in the Code. One anti-deferral regime set forth in the Code is the controlled foreign corporation rules of subpart F (secs. 951-964).

A controlled foreign corporation ("CFC") is defined generally as any foreign corporation if U.S. persons own more than 50 percent of the corporation's stock (measured by vote or value), taking into account only those U.S. persons that own at least 10 percent of the stock (measured by vote only) (sec. 957). Stock ownership includes not only stock owned directly, but also stock owned indirectly or constructively (sec. 958).

The United States generally taxes the U.S. 10-percent shareholders of a CFC currently on their pro rata shares of certain income of the CFC (so-called "subpart F income") (sec. 951). In effect, the Code treats those shareholders as having received a current distribution out of the CFC's subpart F income. Such shareholders also are subject to current U.S. tax on their pro rata shares of the CFC's earnings invested in U.S. property (sec. 951). The foreign tax credit may reduce the U.S. tax on these amounts.

Subpart F income includes, among other items, foreign base company income (sec. 952). Foreign base company income, in turn, includes foreign personal holding company income, foreign base company sales income, foreign base company services income, foreign base company shipping income and foreign base company oil related income (sec. 954). Foreign personal holding company income includes, among other items, dividends, interest, rents, and royalties. An exception from foreign personal holding company income applies to certain dividends and interest received from a related person which is created or organized in the same country as the CFC and which has a substantial part of its assets in that country, and to certain rents and royalties received from a related person for the use of property in the same country in which the CFC was created or organized (the so-called "same-country exception").

Foreign base company sales income includes income derived by a CFC from certain related-party transactions, including the purchase of personal property from a related person and its sale to any person, the purchase of personal property from any person and its sale to a related person, and the purchase or sale of personal property on behalf of a related person, where the property which is purchased or sold is manufactured outside the country in which the CFC was created or organized and the property is purchased or sold for use or consumption outside such foreign country. A special branch rule applies for purposes of determining a CFC's foreign base company sales income. Under this rule, a branch of a CFC is treated as a separate corporation (only for purposes of determining the CFC's foreign base company sales income) where the activities of the CFC through the branch outside the CFC's country of incorporation have substantially the same effect as if such branch were a subsidiary.

Because of differences in U.S. and foreign laws, it is possible for a taxpayer to enter into transactions that are treated in one manner for U.S. tax purposes and in another manner for foreign tax purposes. These transactions are referred to as hybrid transactions. For example, a hybrid transaction may involve the use of an entity that is treated as a corporation for purposes of the tax law of one jurisdiction but is treated as a branch or partnership for purposes of the tax law of another jurisdiction.

Notices 98-5 and 98-11

Notice 98-5, issued on December 23, 1997, addresses the treatment of certain types of transactions under the foreign tax credit provisions of the Code. The Notice states that the Treasury Department and the Internal Revenue Service have concluded that the use of certain transactions creates the potential for foreign tax credit abuse. The Notice states that such transactions typically involve either: (1) the acquisition of an asset that generates an income stream (e.g., royalties or interest) subject to a foreign withholding tax, or (2) the effective duplication of tax benefits through the use of certain structures designed to exploit inconsistencies between U.S. and foreign tax laws. The Notice includes five specific transactions as illustrations of arrangements creating the poten-

Act Sec. 8001 ¶ 11,585

tial for foreign tax credit abuse. The Notice states that it is intended that regulations will be issued to disallow foreign tax credits for abusive transactions in cases where the reasonably expected economic profit from the transaction is insubstantial compared to the value of the foreign tax credits expected to be obtained as a result of the arrangement. The Notice further states that it is intended that regulations generally will apply with respect to such transactions for taxes paid or accrued on or after December 23, 1997. Regulations have not yet been issued under Notice 98-5.

Notice 98-11, issued on January 16, 1998, addressed the treatment of hybrid branches under the subpart F provisions of the Code. The Notice stated that the Treasury Department and the Internal Revenue Service have concluded that the use of certain arrangements involving hybrid branches is contrary to the policy and rules of subpart F. The hybrid branch arrangements identified in Notice 98-11 involve structures that are characterized for U.S. tax purposes as part of a CFC but are characterized for purposes of the tax law of the country in which the CFC is incorporated as a separate entity. The Notice stated that regulations will be issued to prevent the use of hybrid branch arrangements to reduce foreign tax while avoiding the corresponding creation of subpart F income. The Notice stated that such regulations will provide that the branch and the CFC will be treated as separate corporations for purposes of subpart F. The Notice also stated that similar issues raised under subpart F by certain partnership or trust arrangements will be addressed in separate regulation projects.

On March 23, 1998, temporary and proposed regulations were issued to address the issues raised in Notice 98-11 and to address certain partnership and other issues raised under subpart F. Under the regulations, certain payments between a CFC and its hybrid branch or between hybrid branches of the CFC (so-called "hybrid branch payments") are treated as giving rise to subpart F income. The regulations generally provide that non-subpart F income of the CFC, in the amount of the hybrid branch payment, is recharacterized as subpart F income of the CFC if: (1) the hybrid branch payment reduces the foreign tax of the payor, (2) the hybrid branch payment would have been foreign personal holding company income if made between separate CFCs, and (3) there is a disparity between the effective tax rate on the payment in the hands of the payee and the effective tax rate that would have applied if the income had been taxed in the hands of the payor. The regulations also apply to other hybrid branch arrangements involving a partnership, including a CFC's proportionate share of any hybrid branch payment made between a partnership in which the CFC is a partner and a hybrid branch of the partnership or between hybrid branches of such a partnership. Under the regulations, if a partnership is treated as fiscally transparent by the CFC's taxing jurisdiction, the recharacterization rules are applied by treating the hybrid branch payment as if it had been made directly between the CFC and the hybrid branch, or as if the hybrid branches of the partnership were hybrid branches of the CFC, as

applicable. If the partnership is treated as a separate entity by the CFC's taxing jurisdiction, the recharacterization rules are applied to treat the partnership as if it were a CFC.

The regulations also address the application of the same-country exception to the foreign personal holding company income rules under subpart F in the case of certain hybrid branch arrangements. Under the regulations, the same-country exception applies to payments by a CFC to a hybrid branch of a related CFC only if the payment would have qualified for the exception if the hybrid branch had been a separate CFC incorporated in the jurisdiction in which the payment is subject to tax (other than a withholding tax). The regulations provide additional rules regarding the application of the same-country exception in the case of certain hybrid arrangements involving a partnership.

The regulations generally apply to amounts paid or accrued pursuant to hybrid branch arrangements entered into or substantially modified on or after January 16, 1998. As a result, the regulations generally do not apply to amounts paid or accrued pursuant to hybrid branch arrangements entered into before January 16, 1998 and not substantially modified on or after that date.

In the case of certain hybrid arrangements involving partnerships, the regulations generally apply to amounts paid or accrued pursuant to such arrangements entered into or substantially modified on or after March 23, 1998. As a result, the regulations generally do not apply to amounts paid or accrued pursuant to such arrangements entered into before March 23, 1998 and not substantially modified on or after that date.

House Bill

No provision.

Senate Amendment

The Senate amendment provides that it is the sense of the Senate that the Department of the Treasury and the Internal Revenue Service should withdraw Notice 98-11 and the regulations issued thereunder, and that the Congress, and not the Department of the Treasury or the Internal Revenue Service, should determine the international tax policy issues relating to the treatment of hybrid transactions under the subpart F provisions of the Code.

The Senate amendment further provides that it is the sense of the Senate that the Department of the Treasury and the Internal Revenue Service should limit any regulations issued under Notice 98-5 to the specific transactions described therein. In addition, such regulations should: (a) not affect transactions undertaken in the ordinary course of business, (b) not have an effective date any earlier than the date of issuance of proposed regulations, and (c) be issued in accordance with normal regulatory procedures which include an opportunity for comment. Nothing in this sense of the Senate should be construed to limit the ability of the Department of the Treasury or the Internal Revenue Service to address abusive transactions.

Effective Date

Date of enactment.

Conference Agreement

Notices 98-5 and 98-11

The conference agreement does not include the Senate amendment. The conferees are aware that the Department of the Treasury has withdrawn Notice 98-11 and has announced its intention to withdraw the temporary and proposed regulations issued under Notice 98-11, and to reissue regulations in proposed form to be finalized no earlier than January 1, 2000. See Notice 98-35, 1998-26 I.R.B. 1. The conferees expect that the Congress will consider the international tax policy issues relating to the treatment of hybrid transactions under the subpart F provisions of the Code, and will consider taking legislative action as deemed appropriate. In this regard, the conferees expect that the Congress will consider the impact of any legislation or administrative guidance in this area on affected taxpayers and industries. The conferees strongly recommend that the Department of the Treasury also take into account the impact of any administrative guidance in this area on affected taxpayers and industries. No inference is intended regarding the authority of the Department of the Treasury or the Internal Revenue Service to issue the Notice or the regulations, or to issue any other notice or regulation which reaches the same or similar results with respect to the treatment of hybrid transactions under subpart F.

The conferees believe that regulations under Notice 98-5 should be issued in accordance with normal regulatory procedures which include an opportunity for public comment. The conferees acknowledge recent actions by the Department of the Treasury to address legitimate taxpayer concerns regarding Notice 98-5 without compromising the ability of the Department of the Treasury or the Internal Revenue Service to address abusive transactions.

The conferees are concerned about the potential disruptive effect of the issuance of an administrative notice that describes general principles to be reflected in regulations that will be issued in the future, but provides that such future regulations will be effective as of the date of issuance of the notice. The conferees strongly encourage the Department of the Treasury and the Internal Revenue Service to limit similar types of action in the future.

Other matters

The conferees are aware of the Department of the Treasury's commitment to withdraw temporary and proposed regulations issued on March 2, 1998, with respect to a special sourcing rule under the foreign sales corporation provisions, and to reinstate the rule contained in the prior temporary regulations. See Temp. Treas. Reg. sec. 1.927(e)-1T, T.D. 8764 (March 2, 1998). In good faith reliance on this commitment, the conferees are deferring action on this issue at this time.

[CCH Explanation at ¶ 633.]

[¶ 11,590]   Financial management advisory group

Conference Committee Report (H.R. CONF. REP. NO. 105-599)

Present Law

No provision.

House Bill

The House bill directs the Commissioner to convene a financial management advisory group consisting of individuals with expertise in governmental accounting and auditing from both the private sector and the Government to advise the Commissioner on financial management issues.

Effective Date

The House bill provision is effective on the date of enactment.

Senate Amendment

No provision.

Conference Agreement

The conference agreement does not include the House bill provision. However, the conferees expect that the Chairman of the Oversight Board will consider establishing a financial management subcommittee to advise the Commissioner on financial management issues.

[CCH Explanation at ¶ 861.]

Committee Reports
Surface Transporation Revenue Act of 1998
Introduction
[¶ 15,001]

The Intermodal Surface Transportation and Efficiency Bill (ISTEA) was introduced in the House on September 4, 1997, as H.R. 2400. H.R. 2400 was reported by the House Ways and Means Committee on March 27, 1998 (H.R. REP. NO. 105-467, pt. 3) and passed by the House on April 1, 1998. On April 2, 1998, the Senate substituted its version of the ISTEA legislation (S. 1173) in lieu of the version passed by the House (H.R. 2400) and approved it by a voice vote. A conference report for H.R. 2400 was filed and agreed to by both the House and Senate on May 22, 1998. President Clinton signed the Transportation Equity Act for the 21st Century (P.L. 105-178) on June 9, 1998. Title IX of P.L. 105-178 is the Surface Transportation Revenue Act of 1998.

This section includes the pertinent texts of the controlling committee reports that explain the changes enacted in P.L. 105-178. The following material is the official wording of the relevant House and Conference Committee Reports in Act Section order. The Technical Explanation of the "Intermodal Surface Transportation Revenue Act of 1997" Relating to the Extension of Highway Trust Fund Excise Taxes and Highway Trust Fund Provisions published in the Congressional Record on October 8, 1998 has been included as background for the Senate Finance Committee Amendment. Headings have been added for convenience in locating the committee reports. Any omission of text is indicated by asterisks (* * *). References are following to the official reports:

● House Ways and Means Committee Report (H.R. 2400), dated March 27, 1998, and published in the FEDERAL EXCISE TAX REPORTER at ¶ 65,101, is referred to as House Committee Report (H.R. REP. NO. 105-467, pt. 3).

● The Technical Explanation of the "Intermodal Surface Transportation Revenue Act of 1997" Relating to the Extension of Highway Trust Fund Excise Taxes and Highway Trust Fund Provisions, published in the Congressional Record on October 8, 1998, is referred to as Senate Explanation of Committee Amendment (143 CONG. REC. 139, S10707—S10709). For additional discussion of the Senate Explanation of Committee Amendment, see 143 CONG. REC. 139, S10522-10622.

● Intermodal Surface Transportation Efficiency Act (ISTEA) Conference Report, filed May 22, 1998, is referred to as Conference Committee Report (H.R. CONF. REP. NO. 105-550).

[¶ 15,015] Act Sec. 9002(a) and 9002(b). Highway-related taxes and exemptions (tax rates)

Senate Explanation of Committee Amendment
(143 CONG. REC. 139, S10707—S10709)

[Code Sec. 4041(a)(1)(C)(iii)(I), Code Sec. 4041(a)(2)(B), Code Sec. 4041(m)(1)(A), Code Sec. 4051(c), Code Sec. 4071(d), Code Sec. 4081(d)(1), Code Sec. 4221(a), Code Sec. 4481(e), Code Sec. 4482(c)(4), Code Sec. 4482(d) and Code Sec. 4483(g)]

Present Law
1. Highway Trust Fund Excise Taxes and Other Related Tax Provisions
   Highway transportation excise taxes

The current highway transportation excise taxes consist of:

(1) taxes on gasoline, diesel fuel, kerosene, and special motor fuels;

(2) a retail sales tax imposed on trucks and trailers having gross vehicle weights in excess of prescribed thresholds;

(3) a tax on manufacturers of tires designed for use on heavy highway vehicles; and

Act Sec. 9002(a) ¶ 15,015

(4) an annual use tax imposed on trucks and tractors having taxable gross weights in excess of prescribed thresholds.

Special motor fuels include liquefied natural gas ("LNG"), benzol, naphtha, liquefied petroleum gas (e.g., propane), natural gasoline, and any other liquid (e.g., ethanol and methanol) other than gasoline or diesel fuel. Compressed natural gas ("CNG") also is subject to tax as a special motor fuel, but at a lower rate than other special motor fuels.

With the exception of 4.3 cents per gallon of the motor fuels excise tax rates, these taxes are scheduled to expire after September 30, 1999.

Highway motor fuels taxes

The current highway motor fuels excise tax rates are shown in Table 1.

TABLE 1.—FEDERAL HIGHWAY TRUST FUND MOTOR FUELS EXCISE TAX RATES, AS OF OCTOBER 1, 1997

[Rates shown in cents per gallon]

Highway Fuel	Tax Rate[2]
Gasoline[3]	18.3
Diesel fuel[4]	24.3
Special motor fuels generally	18.3[5]
CNG	4.3[6]

[1] The rates shown include the 4.3-cents-per-gallon tax rate which is transferred to the Highway Fund beginning on October 1, 1997, pursuant to the Taxpayer Relief Act of 1997.

[2] Effective on October 1, 1997, an additional 0.1-cent-per-gallon rate is imposed on these motor fuels to finance the Leaking Underground Storage Tank Trust Fund.

[3] Gasoline used in motorboats and in certain off-highway recreational vehicles and small engines is subject to tax in the same manner and at the same rates as gasoline used in highway vehicles. 6.8 cents per gallon of the revenues from the tax on gasoline used in these uses is retained in the General Fund; the remaining 11.5 cents per gallon is deposited in the Aquatic Resources Trust Fund (motorboat and small engine gasoline), the Land and Water Conservation Fund ($1 million of motorboat gasoline tax revenues), and the National Recreational Trails Trust Fund (the "Trails Trust Fund") (off-highway recreational vehicles).

[4] Kerosene is taxed at the same rate as diesel fuel.

[5] The rate is 13.6 cents per gallon for propane, 11.9 cents per gallon for liquefied natural gas, and 11.3 cents per gallon for methanol fuel from natural gas, in each case based on the relative energy equivalence of the fuel to gasoline.

[6] The statutory rate is 48.54 cents per thousand cubic feet ("MCF").

Present law includes numerous exemptions (including partial exemptions for specified uses of taxable fuels or for specified fuels) typically for governments or for uses not involving use of (and thereby change to) the highway system. Because the gasoline and diesel fuel taxes generally are imposed before the end use of the fuel is known, many of these exemptions are realized through refunds to end users of tax paid by a party that processed the fuel earlier in the distribution chain. These exempt uses and fuels include:

(1) use in State and local government and nonprofit educational organization vehicles;

(2) use in buses engaged in transporting students and employees of schools;

(3) use in private local mass transit buses having a seating capacity of at least 20 adults (not including the driver) when the buses operate under contract with (or are subsidized by) a State or local governmental unit;

(4) use in private intercity buses serving the general public along scheduled routes (totally exempt from the gasoline tax and exempt from 17 cents per gallon of the diesel tax); and

(5) use in off-highway uses such as farming.

LNG, propane, CNG, and methanol derived from natural gas are subject to reduced tax rates based on the energy equivalence of these fuels to gasoline.

* * *

Non-fuel Highway Fund excise taxes

In addition to the highway motor fuels excise tax revenues, the Highway Fund receives revenues produced by three excise taxes imposed exclusively on heavy highway vehicles or tires. These taxes are:

(1) A 12-percent excise tax imposed on the first retail sale of highway vehicles, tractors, and trailers (generally, trucks having a gross vehicle weight in excess of 33,000 pounds and trailers having such a weight in excess of 26,000 pounds);

(2) An excise tax imposed at graduated rates on highway tires weighing more than 40 pounds; and

(3) An annual use tax imposed on highway vehicles having a taxable gross weight of 55,000 pounds or more. (The maximum rate for this tax is $550 per year, imposed on vehicles having a taxable gross weight over 75,000 pounds.)

* * *

Explanation of Provisions

1. Highway Fund provisions

  a. Extension of existing Highway Fund excise taxes

Under the Committee amendment, the scheduled expiration date of the current Highway Fund excise taxes on motor fuels and heavy highway vehicles and tires is extended for six years, from September 30, 1999 through September 30, 2005.

* * *

Conference Committee Report (H.R. Conf. Rep. No. 105-550)

Tax rates

The conference agreement follows the Senate amendment.

* * *

Effective Date

Date of enactment.

¶ 15,015 Act Sec. 9002(a)

[Law at ¶ 5845, ¶ 5853, ¶ 5857, ¶ 5923, ¶ 5925,
¶ 5927, ¶ 6145 and ¶ 6365. CCH Explanation at
¶ 750.]

[¶ 15,025]   Act Sec. 9002(c) and 9002(d).   Transfers of revenues to Highway Trust Fund

Senate Explanation of Committee Amendment
(143 CONG. REC. 139, S10707—S10709)

[Code Sec. 9503(b), Code Sec. 9503(c)(1), Code
Sec. 9503(c)(2), Code Sec. 9503(c)(3), Code Sec.
9503(c)(4)(A)(i), Code Sec. 9503(c)(5)(A) and
Code Sec. 9503(e)(3)]

Present Law
* * *

2. Highway Trust Fund Expenditure Provisions

In general

Dedication of excise tax revenues to the Highway Fund and expenditures from the Highway Fund are governed by provisions of the Code (sec. 9503).[4] Under present law, revenues from the highway excise taxes, as imposed through September 30, 1999, are dedicated to the Highway Fund. Also, the Highway Fund earns interest on its cash balances each year from investments in Treasury securities. Further, the Code authorizes expenditures (subject to appropriations) from the Fund through September 30, 1997, for the purposes provided in authorizing legislation, as in effect on the date of enactment of the Intermodal Surface Transportation Efficiency Act of 1991.

Highway Fund provisions also govern transfer of 11.5 cents per gallon of the revenues from the tax imposed on gasoline used in motorboats, small engines, and off-highway recreational vehicles. Those revenues are transferred from the Highway Fund (after being received from the General Fund) to the Aquatic Resources Trust Fund, the Land and Water Conservation Fund, and the National Recreational Trails Trust Fund, respectively, through September 30, 1997.

Present-law Highway Fund expenditure purposes

Overview

The Highway Fund is divided into two accounts, a Highway Account and a Mass Transit Account, each of which is the funding source for specific programs.

Highway and Mass Transit Account expenditure purposes have been revised with passage of each authorization Act enacted since establishment of the Highway Trust Fund in 1956. In general, expenditures authorized under those Acts (as the Acts were in effect on the date of enactment of the most recent such authorizing Act) are approved Highway Fund expenditure purposes.[5] Authority to make expenditures from the Highway Fund expired after September 30, 1997. Thus, no Highway Fund monies may be spent for a purpose not approved by the tax-writing committees of Congress. Further, no Highway Fund

expenditures may occur after September 30, 1997, without such approval. Highway Fund spending further is limited by two, internal to the Highway Fund, anti-deficit provisions. The first of these provisions limits the unfunded Highway Account authorizations at the end of any fiscal year to amounts not exceeding revenues projected to be collected for that Account by the dedicated excise taxes during the two following fiscal years. The second anti-deficit provision similarly limits unfunded Mass Transit Account authorizations to the dedicated excise taxes expected to be collected during the next fiscal year. Because of these two provisions, the highway transportation excise taxes typically are scheduled to expire at least two years after current authorizing Acts. If either of these provisions is violated, spending for specified programs funded by the relevant Trust Fund Account is to be reduced proportionally, in much the same manner as would occur under a general Budget Act sequester.

Highway Account

The Highway Fund's Highway Account receives revenues from all non-fuel highway transportation excise taxes and revenues from all but 2.85 cents per gallon (2.0 cents prior to October 1, 1997) of the highway motor fuels excise taxes. Programs financed from the Highway Account include expenditures for the following general purposes:

(1) Federal-aid highways, including the Interstate System, National Highway System, parkways and park roads, forest and public lands highways, Indian reservation roads, scenic highways, and certain overseas highways (includes construction and planning);

(2) Highway resurfacing and repair;

(3) Bridge replacement and repair;

(4) Surface transportation programs;

(5) Congestion mitigation and air quality improvement;

(6) Highway safety programs and research and development, including a share of the cost of National Highway Traffic Safety Administration ("NHTSA") programs and university research centers;

(7) Transportation research, technology, and training;

(8) Traffic control grants and traffic control signal projects;

(9) Intermodal urban projects and mass transit (including carpool and vanpool) grants;

---

[4] The Highway Trust Fund statutory provisions were placed in the Internal Revenue Code in 1982.
[5] The authorizing Acts which currently are referenced in the Highway Trust Fund are the Highway Revenue Act of

1956, Titles I and II of the Surface Transportation Assistance Act of 1982, the Surface Transportation and Uniform Relocation Act of 1987, and the Intermodal Surface Transportation Efficiency Act of 1991.

(10) Magnetic levitation technology deployment;

(11) Intelligent transportation systems;

(12) Certain administrative costs of the Federal Highway Administration and NHTSA;

(13) Grants to the Internal Revenue Service for motor fuels tax and highway use tax enforcement activities;

(14) Wetlands and other habitat mitigation; and

(15) Certain other highway and transit-related programs (including bicycle pathways and pedestrian walkways and fringe and corridor parking facilities).

Mass Transit Account

The Highway Fund's Mass Transit Account receives revenues equivalent to 2.85 cents per gallon (2.0 cents prior to October 1, 1997) of the highway motor fuels excise taxes. Mass Transit Account monies are available through September 30, 1997, for capital and capital-related expenditures under sections 5338(a)(1) and (b)(1) of Title 49, United States Code, or the Intermodal Surface Transportation Efficiency Act of 1991.

The capital and capital-related mass transit programs include new rail or busway facilities, rail rolling stock, buses, improvement and maintenance of existing rail and other fixed guideway systems, and upgrading of bus systems.

* * *

Explanation of Provisions
* * *

c. Extension and modification of Highway Fund provisions[8]

The current September 30, 1997 expiration date of authority to spend monies from the Highway Fund is extended for six years, from October 1, 1997 through September 30, 2003.

The Code provisions governing purposes for which monies in the Highway Fund may be spent is updated to include the purposes provided in S. 1173, as enacted.

* * *

Conference Committee Report (H.R. CONF. REP. NO. 105-550)

Transfers of revenues to Highway Trust Fund

The conference agreement follows the Senate amendment.

* * *

[Law at ¶ 6940. CCH Explanation at ¶ 750.]

[¶ 15,035]   Act Sec. 9003.   Highway-related taxes and exemptions (motor fuel exemptions and alcohol fuels credits)

Senate Explanation of Committee Amendment
(143 CONG. REC. 139, S10707—S10709)

[Code Sec. 40(e)(1), Code Sec. 40(h), Code Sec. 4041(b)(2), Code Sec. 4041(k)(3), Code Sec. 4081(c)(4)(A), Code Sec. 4081(c)(5), Code Sec. 4081(c)(8), Code Sec. 4091(c)(1), Code Sec. 4091(c)(5), Code Sec. 4483(g) and Code Sec. 6427(f)(4)]

Present Law
* * *

Ethanol and methanol derived from renewable sources (e.g., biomass) are eligible for income tax benefits (the "alcohol fuels credit") equal to 54 cents per gallon (ethanol) and 60 cents per gallon (methanol).[1] In addition, small ethanol producers are eligible for a separate 10-cents-per-gallon credit.[2] The 54-cents-per-gallon ethanol and 60-cents-per-gallon renewable source methanol tax credits may be claimed through reduced excise taxes paid on gasoline and special motor fuels as well as through credits against income tax.[3]

* * *

Explanation of Provisions
* * *

b. Extension and modification of ethanol tax provisions

The current tax benefits for ethanol and renewable source methanol are extended for seven years from their currently scheduled expiration dates; the ethanol benefits are modified to reduce the benefit levels during the extension period. The modified ethanol benefit levels are as follows: 2001 and 2002—53 cents per gallon; 2003 and 2004—52 cents per gallon; and, 2005 through 2007—51 cents per gallon. The extension and the

---

[8] S. 1173 would authorize expenditures for a Congestion Mitigation and Air Quality Program ("CMAQ") pursuant to which State transportation departments (or other project sponsors) would be permitted to enter into agreements with public and private entities to implement certain environmental projects, including programs to promote the use of alternative fuels by privately owned vehicles by underwriting the costs of converting vehicles to alternative fuels.

The Committee amendment provides that to the extent that payments received under the program are not taxable under present law when received, no credit or other deduction is allowed, and a reduction in basis may be required, with respect to property (or other expenditures) financed directly or indirectly with the CMAQ monies. No inference

is intended from this provision as to the treatment of amounts received under other Federal grant programs.

[1] The alcohol fuels credit is scheduled to expire after December 31, 2000, or earlier, if the Highway Fund excise taxes actually expire before that date.

[2] The small ethanol producer credit is available on up to 15 million gallons of ethanol produced by persons whose annual production capacity does not exceed 30 million gallons.

[3] Authority to claim the ethanol and renewable source methanol tax benefits through excise tax reductions is scheduled to expire after September 30, 2000 (or earlier, if the underlying excise taxes actually expire before September 30, 2000).

¶ 15,035   Act Sec. 9003

modifications apply to both the alcohol fuels credit and the associated excise tax provisions.
* * *

Conference Committee Report (H.R. CONF. REP. NO. 105-550)

* * *

Motor fuel exemptions and alcohol fuels credits	*Effective Date*
	Date of enactment.

The conference agreement follows the Senate amendment.

Effective Date

Date of enactment.

[Law at ¶ 5065 and ¶ 5857. CCH Explanation at ¶ 760.]

[¶ 15,055]   Act Sec. 9004.   Highway Trust Fund provisions (interest on balances, expenditure authority, anti-deficit provisions and technical corrections)

House Committee Report (H.R. REP. NO. 105-467, pt. 3)

[Code Sec. 9503(b)(6), Code Sec. 9503(c)(7), Code Sec. 9503(e)(4) and Code Sec. 9503(f)]

[*Present Law*]
* * *

B. Highway Trust Fund, Aquatic Trust Resources Fund, and National Recreational Trails Trust Fund expenditure provisions

1. Present-law provisions

In general

Dedication of excise tax revenues to the Highway Fund and expenditures from the Highway Fund are governed by provisions of the Code (sec. 9503).[6] Under present law, revenues from the highway excise taxes, as imposed through September 30, 1999, are dedicated to the Highway Fund. Also, the Highway Fund earns interest on its cash balances each year from investments in Treasury securities (sec. 9602). Further, the Code authorizes expenditures (subject to appropriations) from the Highway Fund through September 30, 1998, for the purposes provided in authorizing legislation, as in effect on the date of enactment of Public Law 105-130.

Highway Fund provisions also govern transfer of 11.5 cents per gallon of the revenues from the tax imposed on gasoline used in motorboats, small engines, and off-highway recreational vehicles. Those revenues are transferred from the Highway Fund (after being received from the General Fund) to the Aquatic Fund, the Land and Water Fund, and the Trails Fund, respectively, through September 30, 1998.

Present-law Highway Fund expenditure purposes

Overview

The Highway Fund is divided into two accounts: a Highway Account and a Mass Transit Account, each of which is the funding source for specific programs.

Highway and Mass Transit Account expenditure purposes have been revised with passage of each authorization Act enacted since establishment of the Highway Fund in 1956. In general, expenditures authorized under those Acts (as the Acts were in effect on the date of enactment of the most recent such authorizing Act) are approved Highway Fund expenditure purposes.[7] Authority to make expenditures from the Highway Fund is currently scheduled to expire after September 30, 1998. Thus, no Highway Fund monies may be spent for a purpose not approved by the tax-writing committees of Congress. Further, no Highway Fund expenditures may occur after September 30, 1998, without such approval.

Highway Fund spending further is limited by two anti-deficit provisions, which are internal to the Highway Fund. The first of these provisions limits the unfunded Highway Account authorizations at the end of any fiscal year to amounts not exceeding the unobligated balance plus revenues projected to be collected for that Account by the dedicated excise taxes during the two following fiscal years. The second anti-deficit provision similarly limits unfunded Mass Transit Account authorizations to the dedicated excise taxes expected to be collected during the next fiscal year. Because of these two provisions, the highway transportation excise taxes typically are scheduled to expire at least two years after current authorizing Acts. If either of these provisions is violated, spending for specified programs funded by the relevant Trust Fund Account is reduced proportionately, in much the same manner as would occur under a general Budget Act sequester.

Highway Account

The Highway Fund's Highway Account receives revenues from all non-fuel highway transportation excise taxes and revenues from all but 2.85 cents per gallon [8] (2.0 cents prior to October 1, 1997) of the highway motor fuels excise taxes. Programs financed from the Highway Account include expenditures for the following general purposes:

(1) Federal-aid highways, including the Interstate System, National Highway System, forest

---

[6] The Highway Fund statutory provisions were placed in the Internal Revenue Code in 1982.

[7] The authorizing Acts which currently are referenced in the Highway Fund (for the Highway Account) are the Highway Revenue Act of 1956, Titles I and II of the Surface Transportation Assistance Act of 1982, the Surface Transportation and Uniform Relocation Act of 1987, the Intermodal Surface Transportation Efficiency Act of 1991, and Public Law 105-130.

[8] A technical correction (to 2.86 cents per gallon) is included in Title VI ("Tax Technical Corrections Act of 1997") of H.R. 2676 as passed by the House on November 5, 1997.

and public lands highways, scenic highways, and certain overseas highways (includes construction and planning and traffic control projects);

(2) Interstate highway resurfacing and repair;

(3) Bridge replacement and repair;

(4) Surface transportation programs;

(5) Congestion mitigation and air quality improvement;

(6) Highway safety programs and research and development, including a share of the cost of National Highway Traffic Safety Administration ("NHTSA") programs and university research centers;

(7) Transportation research, technology, and training;

(8) Intermodal urban projects and mass transit (including carpool and vanpool) grants;

(9) Intelligent transportation systems;

(10) Transportation enhancements (including transportation-related historic restoration, scenic beautification, removal of billboards);

(11) Construction of ferry boats and ferry terminal facilities;

(12) Certain administrative costs of the Federal Highway Administration and NHTSA;

(13) Grants to the Internal Revenue Service for motor fuels tax and highway use tax enforcement activities; and

(14) Certain other highway and transit-related programs (including bicycle pathways and pedestrian walkways).

Mass transit account

The Highway Fund's Mass Transit Account receives revenues equivalent to 2.85 cents per gallon [9] (2.0 cents prior to October 1, 1997) of the highway motor fuels excise taxes. Mass Transit Account monies are available through September 30, 1998, for capital and capital-related expenditures under sections 5338(a)(1) and (b)(1) of Title 49, United States Code, or the Intermodal Surface Transportation Efficiency Act of 1991.

The capital and capital-related mass transit programs include new rail or busway facilities, rail rolling stock, buses, improvement and maintenance of existing rail and other fixed guideway systems, and upgrading of bus systems.

* * *

Reasons for Change

H.R. 2400, as reported by Transportation and Infrastructure, authorizes expenditures (through contract authority and discretionary spending subject to appropriations) for Highway Fund and Aquatic Fund programs during fiscal years 1998 through 2003. H.R. 2400 further provides that Highway Fund spending and revenues are not considered for certain budget calculations. The excise taxes which constitute a dedicated revenue source for these programs currently are scheduled to expire after September 30, 1999. Thus, absent an extension of these taxes, contemplated highway, mass transit, and boat safety programs will not be funded. The Committee revenue title does not extend the present-law scheduled expiration date of the tax subsidies for ethanol and renewa-

ble-source methanol (i.e., present law is retained without change).

Because excise taxes dedicated to trust funds (and exemptions therefrom) are assumed to be permanent under Congressional budget scorekeeping rules, the extension of the highway excise taxes without affirmative extension of the alcohol fuels tax subsidies results in increased revenues relative to the budget baseline.

* * *

Explanation of Provisions

* * *

2. Extension and modification of Highway Fund expenditure authority

The current September 30, 1998, expiration date of authority to spend monies from the Highway Fund is extended through September 30, 2003, and the Code provisions governing purposes for which monies in the Highway Fund may be spent are updated to include the purposes provided in H.R. 2400, as enacted.

Provisions are incorporated into the Highway Fund clarifying that expenditures from the Highway Fund may occur only as provided in the Code. Clarification further is provided that the expiration date for expenditures allowed from the Highway Fund does not preclude disbursements to liquidate contracts which are validly entered into before that date. Expenditures for contracts entered into or for amounts otherwise obligated after that date (or for other non-contract authority purposes permitted by non-Code provisions) are not permitted, notwithstanding the provisions of any subsequently enacted authorization or appropriations legislation. If any such subsequent non-tax legislation provides for expenditures not provided for in the Code, or if any executive agency autchorizes such expenditures in contravention of the Code restrictions, excise tax revenues otherwise to be deposited in the Highway Fund will be retained in the General Fund beginning on the date of enactment of such legislation or the date of such executive agency action.

The Committee is aware that one of the Highway Fund expenditure purposes which it approves in the bill is a provision of contract authority for monies to be transferred to the Internal Revenue Service (the "IRS") for acquisition and operation of a computerized motor fuels tracking system. This system (commonly referred to as the Excise Fuel Information Reporting System, or "Ex-FIRS") would track all deliveries of motor fuel into, and all removals of such fuel from, every registered fuels terminal facility in the United States using information reported electronically by the terminals. The Senate highway bill provides for similar expenditures, except the funds would not be provided pursuant to contract authority. The Highway Fund has authorized tax compliance expenditures for several years; however, those authorizations also were not contract authority. As a result of overall discretionary spending limits, the Department of Transportation ("DOT") either has not requested appropriations of revenues that would go the IRS or has sought to impose restrictions on the transfer that in substance would give DOT control over the

---

[9] See footnote 8, supra.

¶ 15,055   Act Sec. 9004

excise tax collection system. The Transportation and Infrastructure provisions of H.R. 2400 provide for transfer of these monies without DOT restrictions on IRS tax compliance efforts. The Committee expresses its strong intent that the conference agreement on H.R. 2400 include contract authority for the financing of the ExFIRS system without DOT restrictions on IRS compliance efforts.

The Federal highway motor fuels excise tax system has been plagued by evasion throughout the past decade. The Committee has approved provisions restructuring the motor fuels taxes on numerous occasions to limit evasion opportunities. These efforts have been successful as evidenced by the approximately $1 billion in increased diesel fuel tax revenues from improved compliance in the first year after changes made in 1993. The computerized tracking system provided for under the Transportation and Infrastructure provisions of H.R. 2400 provides needed funds to expand efforts to eliminate motor fuels tax evasion. These efforts are supported both by taxpayers and tax collectors. The Committee believes that a system supported by all parties which will increase tax collections through improved compliance should be funded in the bill.

Provisions governing administration of the Highway Fund

The Code rules providing for investment of Highway Fund balances in interest-bearing Treasury securities are modified to provide that no interest will be credited to the Highway Fund after September 30, 1998. Further, on October 1, 1998, the cash balance of the Highway Account in excess of $8 billion and the cash balance of the Mass Transit Account in excess of $5.5 billion will be transferred from the Highway Fund to the General Fund.

The anti-deficit provisions of the Mass Transit Account are conformed to those of the Highway Account so that permitted obligations will be determined by reference to two years of projected revenues.

Highway Fund technical corrections and "deadwood" repeal

Two technical corrections to the Taxpayer Relief Act of 1997 (the "1997 Act") are included:

(1) Clarification is provided that excise tax revenues attributable to LNG, CNG, propane, and methanol from natural gas (all of which are subject to reduced energy equivalent rates, as indicated in Table 1 are divided between the Highway and Mass Transit Accounts of the Highway Fund in the same proportions as gasoline tax revenues are divided between those two accounts.

(2) Clarification is provided that the amount of gasoline and diesel fuel tax revenues deposited into the Mass Transit Account is 2.86 cents per gallon (rather than 2.85 cents per gallon as erroneously provided in the 1997 Act).

A provision of the 1997 Act providing that (1) the transfer of additional motor fuels tax revenues to the Highway Fund and (2) a one-time adjustment to fuels tax deposit requirements do not affect the operation of certain provisions of the 1991 highway legislation is repealed as deadwood.

* * *

Conference Committee Report (H.R. CONF. REP. NO. 105-550)

Senate Amendment
* * *

Highway Trust Fund expenditure authority

The Senate amendment is the same as the House bill with respect to extending the Highway Trust fund expenditure authority through September 30, 2003. The Senate amendment updates the expenditure purposes for the Highway and Mass Transit Accounts to the purposes as included in the current Senate authorizing legislation (H.R. 2400 as amended by the Senate).

The Senate amendment also is the same as the House bill with respect to specifying that expenditures from the Highway Trust Fund may occur only as provided in the Internal Revenue Code, and the clarification relating to liquidations of contract authority.

Highway Trust Fund anti-deficit provisions

The Senate amendment is the same as the House bill.

Highway Trust Fund technical corrections

The Senate amendment is the same as the House bill.

1997 transfer of 4.3 cents-per-gallon tax revenues

The Senate amendment is the same as the House bill.

Effective Date

Date of enactment.

Conference Agreement
* * *

Interest on Highway Trust Fund balances; unspent balances

The conference agreement follows the House bill, with a modification deleting the cancellation of a portion of the Mass Transit Account balance.

Highway Trust Fund expenditure authority

The conference agreement follows the House bill and the Senate amendment by updating the Highway Trust Fund expenditure purposes to include the purposes in the current authorizing legislation (H.R. 2400) as enacted and as in effect on the date of enactment.

Highway Trust Fund anti-deficit provisions

The conference agreement follows the House bill and the Senate amendment.

Highway Trust Fund technical corrections

The conference agreement follows the House bill and the Senate amendment. 1997 transfer of 4.3-cents-per-gallon tax revenues

The conference agreement follows the House bill and the Senate amendment.

Effective Date

Date of enactment.

[Law at ¶ 6940. CCH Explanation at ¶ 751.]

Act Sec. 9004   ¶ 15,055

[¶ 15,075]   Act Sec. 9005.   Aquatic Resources Trust Fund

House Committee Report (H.R. REP. NO. 105-467, pt. 3)

[Code Sec. 9503(b)(4)(D), Code Sec. 9503(c)(4)(A)(ii), Code Sec. 9504(b)(2), Code Sec. 9504(c), Code Sec. 9504(d) and Code Sec. 9504(e)]

[Present Law]

A. Present-Law Highway Trust Fund, Aquatic Resources Trust Fund, and National Recreational Trails Trust Fund Excise Taxes
* * *

Aquatic Resources Trust Fund and National Recreational Trails Trust Fund taxes

Gasoline and special motor fuels used in motorboats and in certain off-highway recreational vehicles and in small engines are subject to tax in the same manner and at the same rates as gasoline and special motor fuels used in highway vehicles. Of the tax revenues from these uses, 6.8 cents per gallon is retained in the General Fund; the remaining 11.5 cents per gallon is deposited in the Aquatic Resources Trust Fund ("Aquatic Fund") (motorboat gasoline and special motor fuels and small-engine gasoline), the Land and Water Conservation Fund ("Land and Water Fund") ($1 million of motorboat fuels tax revenues), and the National Recreational Trails Trust Fund (the "Trails Fund") (fuels used in off-highway recreational vehicles).[5] Transfers to these Funds are scheduled to terminate after September 30, 1998. Transfers to the Trails Fund are contingent on appropriations occurring from that Trust Fund; to date, no appropriations have been enacted.

B. Highway Trust Fund, Aquatic Resources Trust Fund, and National Recreational Trails Trust Fund Expenditure Provisions

1. Present-law provisions

In general

Dedication of excise tax revenues to the Highway Fund and expenditures from the Highway Fund are governed by provisions of the Code (sec. 9503).[6] Under present law, revenues from the highway excise taxes, as imposed through September 30, 1999, are dedicated to the Highway Fund. Also, the Highway Fund earns interest on its cash balances each year from investments in Treasury securities (sec. 9602). Further, the Code authorizes expenditures (subject to appropriations) from the Highway Fund through September 30, 1998, for the purposes provided in authorizing legislation, as in effect on the date of enactment of Public Law 105-130.

Highway Fund provisions also govern transfer of 11.5 cents per gallon of the revenues from the tax imposed on gasoline used in motorboats, small engines, and off-highway recreational vehicles. Those revenues are transferred from the Highway Fund (after being received from the General Fund) to the Aquatic Fund, the Land and Water

Fund, and the Trails Fund, respectively, through September 30, 1998.
* * *

Transfers from Highway Fund to Aquatic Fund and to Land and Water Fund

Transfers of recreational motorboat gasoline and special fuels tax revenues from the Highway Fund to the Boat Safety Account of the Aquatic Fund currently are limited to a maximum of $70 million per fiscal year. Any excess motorboat fuels tax revenues are transferred to the Land and Water Fund ($1 million per year) and to the Sport Fish Restoration Account of the Aquatic Fund.[10] The authority to transfer revenues to the Aquatic Fund is scheduled to expire after September 30, 1998.

Expenditures from the Boat Safety Account and Land and Water Fund are subject to appropriation Acts. The Sport Fish Restoration Account has a permanent appropriation, and all moneys transferred to that Account are automatically appropriated in the fiscal year following the fiscal year of receipt.

Expenditures are authorized from the Boat Safety Account, as follows:

(1) One-half of the amount allocated to the Account are for State boating safety programs; and

(2) One-half of the amount allocated to the Account are for operating expenses of the Coast Guard to defray the cost of services provided for recreational boating safety.
* * *

Reasons for Change

H.R. 2400, as reported by Transportation and Infrastructure, authorizes expenditures (through contract authority and discretionary spending subject to appropriations) for Highway Fund and Aquatic Fund programs during fiscal years 1998 through 2003. H.R. 2400 further provides that Highway Fund spending and revenues are not considered for certain budget calculations. The excise taxes which constitute a dedicated revenue source for these programs currently are scheduled to expire after September 30, 1999. Thus, absent an extension of these taxes, contemplated highway, mass transit, and boat safety programs will not be funded. The Committee revenue title does not extend the present-law scheduled expiration date of the tax subsidies for ethanol and renewable-source methanol (i.e., present law is retained without change).
* * *

* * * Further, the Committee believes that it is appropriate to transfer the full amount of fuels taxes imposed on motorboats and small engines to the relevant Trust Fund accounts; therefore, the

---

[5] Nonhighway recreational fuels taxes are the taxes imposed on (1) fuel used in vehicles and equipment on recreational trails or back country terrain or (2) fuel used in camp stores and other outdoor recreational equipment. Such revenues do not include small-engine gasoline tax revenues, which are transferred to the Aquatic Fund. "Small-engine" fuel means gasoline used as a fuel in the nonbusiness use of

small-engine outdoor power equipment (to the extent of the Highway Fund tax rate).

[6] The Highway Fund statutory provisions were placed in the Internal Revenue Code in 1982.

[10] The maximum balance that may accumulate in the Boat Safety Account is $70 million.

Committee determined that the 6.8-cents-per-gallon general fund portion of fuels taxes imposed on motorboats and small engines should be deposited in the Aquatic Fund for boating safety and environmental programs. * * *

Explanation of Provisions

* * *

3. Provisions affecting the Aquatic Fund

Extension of revenue transfers; increase in tax rate transferred

Transfer of motorboat gasoline and special motor fuels taxes to the Boat Safety Account of the Aquatic Fund and of small-engine gasoline taxes to the Wetlands sub-account of the Aquatic Fund is extended through September 30, 2003. In addition, the 6.8-cents-per-gallon portion of the tax on gasoline and special motor fuels used in motorboats and on small-engine gasoline that currently is retained in the General Fund is transferred to the Aquatic Fund, effective generally for revenues from taxes imposed after September 30, 2000. This provision is phased-in, with the transfer to the Aquatic Fund of 3.4 cents per gallon of the revenues from taxes imposed during the period October 1, 1999 through September 30, 2000.

Extension and modification of expenditure authority.

Expenditure authority for the Boat Safety Account of the Aquatic Fund is extended through September 30, 2003. The expenditure purposes of the Aquatic Fund are conformed to those in effect as of the date of enactment of H.R. 2400. Also, the provisions governing amounts transferred to the Boat Safety Account are modified to conform to expenditure levels anticipated in H.R. 2400. Transfers of motorboat fuels tax revenues to the Boat Safety Account are changed to equal one-half of such revenues each fiscal year, with a limit on the balance in that Account equal to no more than one-half of the prior fiscal year's motorboat fuels tax revenues.

Provisions identical to those described above for the Highway Fund are incorporated into the Aquatic Fund clarifying that expenditures from the Aquatic Fund may occur only as provided in the Code.

* * *

Conference Committee Report (H.R. Conf. Rep. No. 105-550)

Senate Amendment

Revenue transfers

The Senate amendment extends the transfers of 11.5 cents per gallon of motorboat fuels tax revenues to the Boat Safety Account of the Aquatic Fund and of smallengine gasoline tax revenues to the Wetlands sub-account of the Aquatic Fund through September 30, 2003.

Effective Date

October 1, 1998.

Expenditure authority

The Senate amendment is the same as the House bill with respect to the extension of the expenditure authority for the Boat Safety Account through September 30, 2003. The expenditure purposes of the Aquatic Fund are conformed to those in effect in the Senate amendment as of the date of enactment.

The Senate amendment clarifying that expenditures from the Aquatic Fund may occur only as provided in the Code is the same as the House bill provision.

Effective Date

October 1, 1998.

Conference Agreement

Revenue transfers

The conference agreement follows the House bill and the Senate amendment with respect to extension of transfers of 11.5 cents per gallon of motorboat fuels tax revenues to the Boat Safety Account and Wetlands sub-Account of the Aquatic Fund through September 30, 2003. The conference agreement follows the House bill in transferring additional motorboat fuels tax and small-engine gasoline revenues to the Aquatic Fund. The conference agreement provides that an additional 1.5 cents per gallon of taxes imposed during fiscal years 2002 and 2003, and an additional 2 cents per gallon thereafter, will be transferred to the Aquatic Fund.

Effective Date

October 1, 1998.

Expenditure authority

The conference agreement follows the House bill and the Senate amendment with respect to the extension of the expenditure authority for the Boat Safety Account through September 30, 2003. The expenditure purposes of the Aquatic Fund (including those of the Sport Fish Restoration Account) are conformed to those purposes in effect in the authorizing provisions of the bill as of the date of enactment.

The conference agreement follows the House bill and the Senate amendment with respect to the clarification that expenditures from the Aquatic Fund may occur only as provided in the Code.

Effective Date

October 1, 1998.

[Law at ¶ 6940 and ¶ 6950. CCH Explanation at ¶ 752.]

[¶ 15,095]   Act Sec. 9006.   Rail fuels excise tax

Senate Explanation of Committee Amendment
(143 CONG. REC. 139, S10707—S10709)

[Code Sec. 4041(a)(1)(C)(ii), Code Sec. 6421(f)(3)(B)(ii)-(iii) and Code Sec. 6427(l)(3)(B)(ii)-(iii)]

Present Law
* * *

Excise tax on diesel fuel used in rail transportation

Diesel fuel used in trains is subject to a 5.65-cents-per-gallon excise tax. Of this amount, 0.1 cent per gallon is dedicated to the Leaking Underground Storage Tank Trust Fund; this rate is scheduled to expire after March 31, 2005. The remaining 5.55 cents per gallon is a General Fund tax, with 4.3 cents per gallon being permanently imposed and 1.25 cents per gallon being imposed through September 30, 1999.

* * *

Explanation of Provisions
* * *

2. Repeal 1.25 cents per gallon of tax rate on rail diesel fuel

The Committee amendment repeals the 1.25-cents-per-gallon rate on rail diesel fuel that is scheduled to expire after September 30, 1999. The repeal is effective on May 16, 1999.

* * *

Conference Committee Report (H.R. CONF. REP. NO. 105-550)

The conference agreement follows the Senate amendment, except for the effective date.

Effective Date

November 1, 1998.

[Law at ¶ 5840, ¶ 6380 and ¶ 6390. CCH Explanation at ¶ 727.]

[¶ 15,105]   Act Sec. 9007.   Purposes for which Amtrak NOL monies may be used in non-Amtrak states

Conference Committee Report (H.R. CONF. REP. NO. 105-550)

[Act Sec. 9007]

Present Law

The 1997 Act provides elective procedures that allow Amtrak to consider the tax attributes of its predecessors in the use of its net operating losses. The election is conditioned on Amtrak agreeing to make payments equal to one percent of the amount it receives as a result of the election to each of the non Amtrak States. The non-Amtrak states are required to spend these monies to finance qualified expenses. Qualified expenses include the capital costs connected with the provision of intercity passenger rail and bus service, the purchase of intercity rail service from Amtrak, and the payment of interest and principle on obligations incurred for a qualified purpose. Any amounts not spent for qualified purposes by 2010 must be returned to the Treasury.

House Bill

No provision.

Senate Amendment

The Senate amendment expands the list of qualified expenses to include: (1) capital expenditures related to State-owned rail operations in the State; (2) projects eligible to receive funding under section 5309, 5310, or 5311 of Title 49; (3) projects that are eligible to receive funding under section 130 or 152 of Title 23; (4) upgrading and maintenance of intercity primary and rural air service facilities, including the purchase of air service between primary and rural airports and regional hubs; and (5) the provision of passenger ferryboat service within the State.

Effective Date

The provision is effective as if included in the Taxpayer Relief Act of 1997 (effective on August 5, 1997).

Conference Agreement

The conference agreement follows the Senate amendment with further additions to the list of qualified expenses. Additional qualified purposes added by the conference agreement include harbor improvements and certain highway improvements that are eligible to receive funding under section 103, 133, 144, and 149 of Title 23.

Effective Date

The conference agreement follows the Senate amendment.

[Law at ¶ 8392 and CCH Explanation at ¶ 694.]

[¶ 15,115]   Act Sec. 9008.   Requirement that motor fuels terminals offer dyed fuel

House Committee Report (H.R. REP. NO. 105-467, pt. 3)

[Act Sec. 9008]
[*Present Law*]

A. Present-law Highway Trust Fund, Aquatic Resources Trust Fund, and National Recreational Trails Trust Fund Excise Taxes
* * *

Administration of highway motor fuels excise taxes

The gasoline, diesel fuel, and kerosene excise taxes are imposed on removal of the fuel from a refinery or on importation, unless the fuel is transferred by pipeline or barge to a registered terminal facility. In such a case, tax is imposed on removal of the fuel from the terminal facility (i.e., at the "terminal rack").[1] A large majority of these taxes are imposed at the terminal rack. The special motor fuels tax, which accounts for a relatively small portion of motor fuels tax revenues, is imposed at the retail level. Present law imposes tax on all gasoline, diesel fuel, and kerosene that is removed from a terminal facility, except diesel fuel that is destined for nontaxable use (including a partially taxable use in an intercity bus or a train) and that is indelibly dyed in accordance with Treasury Department regulations. Effective July 1, 1998, as a condition of holding untaxed fuel, terminals that sell diesel fuels must offer both dyed and undyed fuel to their customers and terminals that sell kerosene must offer both dyed and undyed kerosene. The person holding an inventory position in the terminal at the time the fuel is removed from that facility (the "position holder") is liable for payment of the tax.
* * *

Explanation of Provisions
* * *

6. Delay in effective date of new requirement for approved diesel fuel or kerosene terminals

A present-law provision requiring motor fuels terminal facilities, as a condition of storing non-tax-paid fuel, to offer to their customers both undyed and dyed fuel if they distribute diesel fuel or kerosene is delayed for two years, to July 1, 2000. This provision does not affect the general rules relating to imposition of tax on diesel fuel and kerosene.

The Committee continues to support the diesel fuel and kerosene tax compliance provisions, as enacted in 1993 and 1997 respectively. Notwithstanding this general support, the Committee believes that the delay in the terminal registration requirement described above is appropriate to allow it to evaluate market responses to these tax compliance measures. Industry representatives have assured the Committee that, where demand for untaxed, dyed diesel fuel or kerosene exists, fuel will be made available without a Federal requirement. The Committee intends to monitor market responses in this area to ensure that untaxed, dyed fuel is made available (either by manual dyeing or through computerized dye injection processes) where consumers require the fuel.

* * *

Conference Committee Report (H.R. CONF. REP. NO. 105-550)

Senate Amendment

The Senate amendment is the same as in the House bill.

Conference Agreement

The conference agreement follows the House bill and the Senate amendment.

[Law at ¶ 8395. CCH Explanation at ¶ 723.]

[¶ 15,125]   Act Sec. 9009.   Motor fuels tax refund procedure

House Committee Report (H.R. REP. NO. 105-467, pt. 3)

[Code Sec. 6421(d)(2), Code Sec. 6427(i)(2)(A), Code Sec. 6427(i)(4)-(5) and Code Sec. 6427(k)(2)]

[*Present Law*]

A. Present-Law Highway Trust Fund, Aquatic Resources Trust Fund, and National Recreational Trails Trust Fund Excise Taxes
* * *

Highway fuels tax exemptions

Present law includes numerous exemptions (including partial exemptions for specified uses of

taxable fuels or for specified fuels) typically for governments or for uses not involving use of the highway system. Because the gasoline and diesel fuel taxes generally are imposed before the end use of the fuel is known, many of these exemptions are realized through refunds to end users of tax paid by a party that processed the fuel earlier in the distribution chain. These exempt uses and fuels include:

(1) use in State and local government and non-profit educational organization vehicles;

---

[1] Gasoline and diesel motor fuel may be removed from a refinery without payment of tax only if the party removing the fuel and all subsequent parties before its removal from a terminal facility are registered with the Internal Revenue Service. If fuel is sold to an unregistered party before leaving the terminal facility, tax immediately is imposed.

This tax does not preclude imposition of a second tax at the terminal rack; however, the second tax may be refunded upon request. This dual tax regime was enacted in 1990 in response to reports that fuel was being removed tax-free from terminals upon a claim that tax had already been paid, when in fact it had not been paid.

(2) use in buses engaged in transporting students and employees of schools;

(3) use in private local mass transit buses having a seating capacity of at least 20 adults (not including the driver) when the buses operate under contract with (or are subsidized by) a State or local governmental unit;

(4) use in private intercity buses serving the general public along scheduled routes (totally exempt from the gasoline tax and exempt from 17 cents per gallon of the diesel tax); and

(5) use in off-highway uses such as farming.
* * *

Explanation of Provisions
* * *

7. Simplify fuels tax refund procedures

Consumers that use previously taxed highway motor fuels in a nontaxable use may file claims for refunds with the Internal Revenue Service. In general, claims for the first three calendar quarters may be filed quarterly if the tax to be refunded exceeds prescribed thresholds.[16] Consumers not satisfying the prescribed dollar thresholds, and all fourth quarter refunds, are claimed through income tax credits.

The amendment consolidates the fuels tax refund thresholds to allow quarterly claims to be filed once an aggregate year-to-date refund of $750 or more for all motor fuels is due. Additionally, fourth quarter refund claims are allowed under the same rules as those applicable to the first three calendar quarters. The provision is effective for claims filed after September 30, 1998.

* * *

Conference Committee Report (H.R. CONF. REP. NO. 105-550)

The conference agreement follows the House bill.

[Law at ¶ 6380 and ¶ 6390. CCH Explanation at ¶ 729.]

[¶ 15,135]   Act Sec. 9010.   Tax treatment of parking and transit benefits

Senate Explanation of Committee Amendment
(143 CONG. REC. 139, S10707—S10709)

[Code Sec. 132(f)(2)(A)-(B), Code Sec. 132(f)(4) and Code Sec. 132(f)(6)]

Present Law
* * *

Exclusion from income for employer-provided transportation benefits

Under present law, up to $170 per month of employer-provided parking is excludable from gross income and wages for employment tax purposes. Effective with respect to taxable years beginning after December 31, 1997, no amount is includible in income or wages merely because an employer offers an employee a choice between cash and employer-provided parking. The amount of cash offered is includible in income only if the employee chooses the cash instead of parking. If an employee chooses parking, the value of the parking is excludable from income as under present law. Employees may exclude a maximum of $65 per month from gross income for the value of employer-provided transit passes or vanpooling in an employer-provided vehicle. In order for the exclusion to apply, the employer-provided transit passes and vanpooling must be provided in addition to and not in lieu of any compensation that is otherwise payable to the employee.
* * *

Explanation of Provisions
* * *

4. Exclusion from income for employer-provided transportation benefits

The Committee amendment permits employers to offer employees the option of electing cash compensation in lieu of any qualified transportation benefit, or a combination of any of these benefits. Qualified transportation benefits include employer-provided transit passes, parking and vanpooling. Thus, no amount is includible in gross income or wages merely because the employee is offered the choice of cash or such benefits. The amount of cash offered is includible in income and wages only to the extent the employee elects cash. In addition, the Committee amendment increases the exclusion for transit passes and vanpooling to $100 per month for taxable years beginning after December 31, 2002. The $100 amount is indexed as under present law.

Conference Committee Report (H.R. CONF. REP. NO. 105-550)

The conference agreement follows the Senate amendment. Thus, as under the Senate amendment, no amount is includible in gross income or wages merely because the employee is offered the choice of cash in lieu of one or more qualified transportation benefits, or a combination of such benefits. In addition, no amount is includible in income or wages merely because the employee is offered a choice among qualified transportation benefits.

---

[16] Under present law, gasoline tax refund claims may be filed quarterly for any of the first three calendar quarters if the quarterly refund claim equals or exceeds $1,000. Diesel fuel tax refund claims for the first three calendar quarters may be filed in any quarter in which the aggregate diesel fuel tax refund for the year equals $750 or more.

Effective Date	[**Law at ¶ 5185. CCH Explanation at ¶ 253.**]

The conference agreement follows the Senate amendment.

[¶ 15,145]   Act Sec. 9011   National Recreational Trails Trust Fund

House Committee Report (H.R. REP. NO. 105-467, pt. 3)

[Code Sec. 9503(b)(4)(D), Code Sec. 9503(c)(6) and Code Sec. 9511]

[Present Law]

A. Present-Law Highway Trust Fund, Aquatic Resources Trust Fund, and National Recreational Trails Trust Fund Excise Taxes
* * *

Aquatic Resources Trust Fund and National Recreational Trails Trust Fund taxes

Gasoline and special motor fuels used in motorboats and in certain off-highway recreational vehicles and in small engines are subject to tax in the same manner and at the same rates as gasoline and special motor fuels used in highway vehicles. Of the tax revenues from these uses, 6.8 cents per gallon is retained in the General Fund; the remaining 11.5 cents per gallon is deposited in the Aquatic Resources Trust Fund ("Aquatic Fund") (motorboat gasoline and special motor fuels and small-engine gasoline), the Land and Water Conservation Fund ("Land and Water Fund") ($1 million of motorboat fuels tax revenues), and the National Recreational Trails Trust Fund (the "Trails Fund") (fuels used in off-highway recreational vehicles).[5] Transfers to these Funds are scheduled to terminate after September 30, 1998. Transfers to the Trails Fund are contingent on appropriations occurring from that Trust Fund; to date, no appropriations have been enacted.

B. Highway Trust Fund, Aquatic Resources Trust Fund, and National Recreational Trails Trust Fund Expenditure Provisions

1. Present-law provisions

In general

Dedication of excise tax revenues to the Highway Fund and expenditures from the Highway Fund are governed by provisions of the Code (sec. 9503).[6] Under present law, revenues from the highway excise taxes, as imposed through September 30, 1999, are dedicated to the Highway Fund. Also, the Highway Fund earns interest on its cash balances each year from investments in Treasury securities (sec. 9602). Further, the Code authorizes expenditures (subject to appropriations) from the Highway Fund through September 30, 1998, for the purposes provided in authorizing legislation, as in effect on the date of enactment of Public Law 105-130.

Highway Fund provisions also govern transfer of 11.5 cents per gallon of the revenues from the tax imposed on gasoline used in motorboats, small engines, and off-highway recreational vehicles. Those revenues are transferred from the Highway

Fund (after being received from the General Fund) to the Aquatic Fund, the Land and Water Fund, and the Trails Fund, respectively, through September 30, 1998.
* * *

Transfers from Highway Fund to the Trails Fund

The Trails Fund was established in the Intermodal Surface Transportation Act of 1991 ("1991 Act"). Amounts are authorized to be transferred from the Highway Fund into the Trails Fund equivalent to revenues received from "nonhighway recreational fuel taxes" (not to exceed $30 million per year under an obligational ceiling set in the 1991 Act), subject to amounts actually being appropriated to the Trails Fund. No monies have been transferred to date, since no amounts have been appropriated to the Trails Fund. The authority to transfer revenues to the Trails Fund is scheduled to expire after September 30, 1998.

Nonhighway recreational fuels taxes are the taxes imposed (to the extent attributable to the 11.5 cents per gallon rate) on (1) fuel used in vehicles and equipment on recreational trails or back country terrain, or (2) fuel used in camp stoves and other outdoor recreational equipment. Such revenues do not include small-engine gasoline tax revenues which are transferred to the Aquatic Fund.

Expenditures are authorized from the Trails Fund, subject to appropriations, for allocations to States for use on trails and trail-related projects as set forth in the 1991 Act. Authorized uses include (1) acquisition of new trails and access areas, (2) maintenance and restoration of existing trails, (3) State environmental protection education programs, and (4) program administrative costs.
* * *

Reasons for Change
* * *

Finally, the Committee concluded that a separate Trails Fund is not necessary, because no revenues have been deposited in the present Trust Fund since its inception and because similar expenditure programs are financed from the Highway Fund under the bill.

Explanation of Provisions
* * *

8. Repeal of Trails Fund

The Code provisions establishing the National Recreational Trails Trust Fund (the "Trails Fund") and providing for transfer of revenues to the Trails Fund is repealed, effective on the date of the bill's enactment. (As described above, no

---

[5] Nonhighway recreational fuels taxes are the taxes imposed on (1) fuel used in vehicles and equipment on recreational trails or back country terrain or (2) fuel used in camp stoves and other outdoor recreational equipment. Such revenues do not include small-engine gasoline tax revenues, which are transferred to the Aquatic Fund. "Small-engine"

fuel means gasoline used as a fuel in the nonbusiness use of small-engine outdoor power equipment (to the extent of the Highway Fund tax rate).

[6] The Highway Fund statutory provisions were placed in the Internal Revenue Code in 1982.

transfers have occurred to date because transfers are contingent on appropriations being enacted, and no funds have been appropriated from the Trails Fund.) Under H.R. 2400, Highway Fund expenditures are authorized for similar purposes to those of the Trails Fund.

Conference Committee Report (H.R. CONF. REP. NO. 105-550)

Senate Amendment

The Senate amendment is the same as the House bill.

Conference Agreement

The conference agreement follows the House bill and the Senate amendment. (Under authoriz-ing provisions of the bill, Highway Trust Fund expenditures are authorized for similar purposes to those of the Trails Fund.)

[Law at ¶ 6940 and ¶ 6955. CCH Explanation at ¶ 753.]

[¶ 15,155]   Act Sec. 9012.   Limited tax benefits in the revenue title subject to the Line Item Veto Act

Conference Committee Report (H.R. CONF. REP. NO. 105-550)

[Act Sec. 9012]

Present Law

The Line Item Veto Act amended the Congressional Budget and Impoundment Act of 1974 to grant the President the limited authority to cancel specific dollar amounts of discretionary budget authority, certain new direct spending, and limited tax benefits. The Line Item Veto Act provides that the Joint Committee on Taxation is required to examine any revenue or reconciliation bill or joint resolution that amends the Internal Revenue Code of 1986 prior to its filing by a conference committee in order to determine whether or not the bill or joint resolution contains any "limited tax benefits," and to provide a statement to the conference committee that either (1) identifies each limited tax benefit contained in the bill or resolution, or (2) states that the bill or resolution contains no limited tax benefits. The conferees determine whether or not to include the Joint Committee on Taxation statement in the conference report. If the conference report includes the information from the Joint Committee on Taxation identifying provisions that are limited tax benefits, then the President may cancel one or more of those, but only those, provisions that have been identified. If such a conference report contains a statement from the Joint Committee on Taxation that none of the provisions in the conference report are limited tax benefits, then the President has no authority to cancel any of the specific tax provisions, because there are no tax provisions that are eligible for cancellation under the Line Item Veto Act.

Conference Statement

The Joint Committee on Taxation has determined that the revenue title to H.R. 2400 contains no provision involving limited tax benefits within the meaning of the Line Item Veto Act.

[Law at ¶ 8400. CCH Explanation at ¶ 30,025.]

Effective Dates
IRS Restructuring and Reform Act of 1998
¶ 20,001

This CCH-prepared table presents the general effective dates for major law provisions added, amended or repealed by the IRS Restructuring and Reform Act of 1998. Entries are listed in Code Section order.

Code Sec.	Act Sec.	Act Provision Subject	Effective Date
	1001(a)	Reorganization of the Internal Revenue Service—in general	Date of enactment
	1001(b)	Reorganization of the Internal Revenue Service—savings provisions	Date of enactment
	1002	IRS mission to focus on taxpayers' needs	Date of enactment
	1103(a)-(e)(3)	Treasury Inspector General for tax administration	Date of enactment
	1201	Improvements in personnel flexibilities	Date of enactment
	1202	Voluntary separation incentive payments	Date of enactment
	1203	Termination of employment for misconduct	Date of enactment
	1204	Basis for evaluation of Internal Revenue Service employees	Evaluations conducted on or after date of enactment
	1205	Employee training program	Date of enactment
	2001(a)-(b)	Electronic filing of tax and information returns	Date of enactment
	2001(d)	Electronic filing of tax and information returns—annual reports	Date of enactment
	2002(b)	Due date for certain information returns—study relating to time for providing notice to recipients	Date of enactment
	2003(c)	Paperless electronic filing—establishment of procedures for other information	Date of enactment
	2003(d)	Paperless electronic filing—internet availability	Date of enactment
	2003(e)	Paperless electronic filing—procedures for authorizing disclosure electronically	Date of enactment
	2004	Return-free tax system	Date of enactment
	2005	Access to account information	Date of enactment
	3000	Short title	Date of enactment

Code Sec.	Act Sec.	Act Provision Subject	Effective Date
	3105	Administrative appeal of adverse IRS determination of tax-exempt status of bond issue	Date of enactment
	3201(c)	Relief from joint and several liability arising on a joint return—separate form for applying for spousal relief	Any tax liability arising after date of enactment and any tax liability arising on or before date of enactment but remaining unpaid as of such date, generally
	3201(d)	Relief from joint and several liability arising on a joint return—separate notice to each filer	Any tax liability arising after date of enactment and any tax liability arising on or before date of enactment but remaining unpaid as of such date, generally
	3414	Threat of audit prohibited to coerce tip reporting alternative commitment agreements	Date of enactment
	3421(a)	Approval process for liens, levies, and seizures	Date of enactment, generally
	3421(b)	Approval process for liens, levies, and seizures—review process	Date of enactment, generally
	3443	Uniform asset disposal mechanism	Date of enactment
	3445(c)	Procedures for seizure of residences and businesses—state fish and wildlife permits	Date of enactment
	3462(d)	Preparation of statement relating to offers-in-compromise	Proposed offers-in-compromise and installment agreements submitted after date of enactment
	3463(a)	Notice of deficiency to specify deadlines for filing Tax Court petition	Notices mailed after December 31, 1998
	3465(b)	Procedures relating to appeals of examinations and collections—appeals officer in each state	Date of enactment
	3465(c)	Procedures relating to appeals of examinations and collections—appeals videoconferencing alternative for rural areas	Date of enactment
	3468(b)	Prohibition on requests to taxpayers to give up rights to bring actions	Date of enactment
	3501(a)	Explanation of joint and several liability	Date of enactment

Code Sec.	Act Sec.	Act Provision Subject	Effective Date
	3501(b)	Explanation of joint and several liability—right to limit liability	Date of enactment
	3502	Explanation of taxpayers' rights in interviews with IRS	Date of enactment
	3503(a)	Disclosure of criteria for examination selection	Date of enactment
	3503(b)	Disclosure of criteria for examination selection—transmission to committees of Congress	Date of enactment
	3504	Explanation of appeals and collection process	Date of enactment
	3506	Statements regarding installment agreements	Date of enactment
	3508	Disclosure to taxpayers—conditions under which return information may be disclosed to parties outside IRS	Date of enactment
	3701	Cataloging complaints	Date of enactment
	3703	Payment of taxes	Date of enactment
	3705(a)	IRS employee contacts—notice	60 days after date of enactment, generally
	3705(b)	IRS employee contacts—single contact	60 days after date of enactment
	3705(c), (d)	IRS employee contacts—telephone helpline in Spanish, other telephone hotline options	January 1, 2000
	3706	Use of pseudonyms by IRS employees	Requests made after date of enactment
	3707(a)(1), (a)(2)(B)	Illegal tax protester designation—prohibition	Date of enactment
	3707(a)(2)(A)	Illegal tax protester designation—prohibition	January 1, 1999
	3707(b)	Illegal tax protester designation—designation of nonfilers allowed	Date of enactment
	3709	Listing of local IRS telephone numbers and addresses	Date of enactment
	3801	Administration of penalties and interest	Date of enactment
	3802	Confidentiality of tax return information	Date of enactment
	3803	Study of noncompliance with internal revenue laws by taxpayers	Date of enactment
	3804	Study of payments made for detection of underpayments and fraud	Date of enactment

Code Sec.	Act Sec.	Act Provision Subject	Effective Date
	4011	Century date change	Date of enactment
	4021	Role of the IRS	Date of enactment
	4022(a)	Tax law complexity analysis—Commissioner study	Date of enactment
	4022(b)	Tax law complexity analysis—analysis to accompany certain legislation	Legislation considered on and after January 1, 1999
	5003	Clarification of designation of normal trade relations	Date of enactment
	6001	Technical corrections—short title	Date of enactment
	6002	Technical corrections—definitions	Date of enactment
	6004(a)(3)	Hope and lifetime learning credits	Expenses paid after December 31, 1997 (in tax years ending after such date), for education furnished in academic periods beginning after such date
	6004(g)(1)	Incentives for education zones	Obligations issued after December 31, 1997
	6005(a)(2)	Restoration of IRA deduction for certain taxpayers	Tax years beginning after December 31, 1997
	6005(b)(8)(C)	Excess contributions to Roth IRAs	Tax years beginning after December 31, 1997
	6005(e)(3)	Exclusion of gain from sale of principal residence—election with respect to sales on or before August 5, 1997	Effective as if originally included in Act. Sec. 312 of the Taxpayer Relief Act of 1997
	6007(a)(2)	Cost-of-living adjustments relating to estate and gift tax provisions—exemption from generation-skipping tax	Estates of decedents dying, and gifts made, after December 31, 1997
	6007(e)(1)	Gifts may not be revalued for estate tax purposes after expiration of statute of limitations	Gifts made after August 5, 1997
	6009(e)	Elective carryback of existing carryovers of National Railroad Passenger Corporation	August 5, 1997
	6010(a)(4)	Constructive sales treatment for appreciated financial positions—special rule applicable to certain decedents	Decedents dying after June 8, 1997, generally

Code Sec.	Act Sec.	Act Provision Subject	Effective Date
	6010(c)(1)	Application of Code Sec. 355 to distributions in connection with acquisitions and to intragroup transactions—effective date	Distributions after April 16, 1997, generally
	6010(h)(1)	Kerosene taxed as diesel fuel—conforming amendment	July 1, 1998
	6010(h)(2)	Kerosene taxed as diesel fuel	July 1, 1998
	6010(j)(3)	Expansion of look-through rule for interest, annuities, royalties and rents derived by subsidiaries of tax-exempt organizations—conforming amendment for binding contracts	Tax years beginning after August 5, 1997
	6010(n)	Modifications to tax years to which unused credits may be carried	Credits arising in tax years beginning after December 31, 1997
	6010(o)(3)(B)	Expansion of denial of deduction for certain amounts paid in connection with insurance—conforming amendment for master contracts	Contracts issued after June 8, 1997, in tax years ending after such date
	6010(p)(3)	Improved enforcement of the application of the earned income credit—extension procedures applicable to mathematical or clerical errors	Tax years beginning after December 31, 1997
	6010(q)	Treatment of exception from installment sales rules for sales of property by manufacturer to dealer—coordination with Code Sec. 481	Tax years beginning after August 5, 1998
	6011(g)	Transfers of property to foreign partnerships subject to information reporting comparable to information reporting for such transfers to foreign corporations	Transfers made after August 5, 1997, generally
	6012(b)(4)	Payment of tax by commercially acceptable means	May 5, 1998
	6012(b)(5)	Payment of tax by commercially acceptable means	May 5, 1998
	6012(e)	Effective date for simplification relating to electing large partnerships	Partnership tax years beginning after December 31, 1997
	6015(b)	Extension of moratorium on application of certain nondiscrimination rules to state and local governments	Tax years beginning on or after August 5, 1997, generally
	6015(c)(1)-(2)	Treatment of certain disability benefits received by former police officers or firefighters	August 5, 1997

Code Sec.	Act Sec.	Act Provision Subject	Effective Date
	6016(a)(2)(A)-(B)	Modifications of section 403(b)	August 20, 1996
	6018(a)	Clarification of employment tax status of certain fishermen	Payments made after December 31, 1997
	6018(c)	Definition of highly compensated employees; repeal of family aggregation	Years beginning after December 31, 1996, generally
	6018(d)(1)-(2)	Depreciation under income forecast method	Property placed in service after September 13, 1995, generally
	6018(e)	Extension of airport and airway trust fund excise taxes	August 27, 1996, generally
	6018(f)(2)	Adoption assistance	Tax years beginning after December 31, 1996
	6018(g)	Modifications of rules relating to foreign trusts having one or more U.S. beneficiaries	Transfers of property after February 6, 1995
	7002	Termination of exception for certain real estate investment trusts from the treatment of stapled entities	Tax years ending after March 26, 1998
1(g)(3)(C),(D)	6007(f)(1)	Repeal of tax on transfers to trusts at less than fair market value—conforming amendment	Sales or exchanges after August 5, 1997
1(h)(5)	5001(a)(1)	Lower capital gains rates to apply to property held more than 1 year	Tax years ending after December 31, 1997
1(h)(6)(A)	5001(a)(2)	Lower capital gains rates to apply to property held more than 1 year	Tax years ending after December 31, 1997
1(h)(7)(A)	5001(a)(3)	Lower capital gains rates to apply to property held more than 1 year	Tax years ending after December 31, 1997
1(h)(13)	5001(a)(4)	Lower capital gains rates to apply to property held more than 1 year	Tax years ending after December 31, 1997
1(h)	6005(d)(1)	Maximum capital gains rates for individuals	Tax years ending after May 6, 1997
23(b)(2)(A)	6018(f)(1)	Adoption assistance	Tax years beginning after December 31, 1996
23(c)	6008(d)(6)	Tax incentives for revitalization of the District of Columbia—conforming amendment	August 5, 1997
24(d)	6003(a)	Child tax credit	Tax years beginning after December 31, 1997
25(e)(1)(C)	6008(d)(7)	Tax incentives for revitalization of the District of Columbia—conforming amendment	August 5, 1997

¶ 20,001

Code Sec.	Act Sec.	Act Provision Subject	Effective Date
32(c)(1)(F)	6021(a)	Identification requirement for individuals eligible for earned income credit	Returns due after September 21, 1996, generally
32(c)(1)(G)	6021(b)(2)	Identification requirement for qualifying children under earned income credit—individuals who do not include TIN, etc., of any qualifying child	Tax years beginning after December 31, 1990
32(c)(2)(B)	6010(p)(2)	Improved enforcement of the application of the earned income credit—workfare payments not included in earned income	Tax years beginning after December 31, 1997
32(c)(3)(A)	6021(b)(3)	Identification requirement for qualifying children under earned income credit—conforming amendment	Tax years beginning after December 31, 1990
32(c)(3)(D)	6021(b)(1)	Identification requirement for qualifying children under earned income credit	Tax years beginning after December 31, 1990
32(c)(5)	6010(p)(1)	Improved enforcement of the application of the earned income credit	Tax years beginning after December 31, 1997
32(m)-(n)	6003(b)	Supplemental child credit	Tax years beginning after December 31, 1997
34(b)	6023(24)(B)	Miscellaneous clerical and deadwood changes	Date of enactment
42(j)(4)(D)	6004(g)(5)	Incentives for education zones	Obligations issued after December 31, 1997
45A(b)(1)(B)	6023(1)	Miscellaneous clerical and deadwood changes	Date of enactment
49(b)(4)	6004(g)(6)	Incentives for education zones	Obligations issued after December 31, 1997
50(a)(5)(C)	6004(g)(7)	Incentives for education zones	Obligations issued after December 31, 1997
55(b)(3)	6005(d)(2)	Maximum rate of tax on net capital gain of noncorporate taxpayers	Tax years ending after May 6, 1997
55(e)(1)	6006(a)	Exemption from alternative minimum tax for small corporations	Tax years beginning after December 31, 1997
57(a)(7)	6005(d)(3)	Maximum capital gains rate for individual—minimum tax	Tax years ending after May 6, 1997
59(a)(3)-(4)	6011(a)	Election to use simplified section 904 limitation for alternative minimum tax	Tax years beginning after December 31, 1997
59(b)	6023(2)	Miscellaneous clerical and deadwood changes	Date of enactment
66(c)	3201(b)	Relief from joint and several liability arising on a joint return—equita-	Any tax liability arising after date of en-

¶ 20,001

Code Sec.	Act Sec.	Act Provision Subject	Effective Date
		ble relief for individuals not filing joint return	actment and any tax liability arising on or before date of enactment but remaining unpaid as of such date, generally
72(e)(9)	6004(d)(3)(B)	Education individual retirement accounts	Tax years beginning after December 31, 1997
72(n)	6023(3)	Miscellaneous clerical and deadwood changes	Date of enactment
72(t)(2)(A)	3436(a)	Waiver of early withdrawal tax for IRS levies on employer-sponsored retirement plans or IRAs	Distributions made after December 31, 1999
72(t)(3)(A)	6023(4)	Miscellaneous clerical and deadwood changes	Date of enactment
72(t)(8)(E)	6005(c)(1)	Distributions from certain plans may be used without penalty to purchase first homes	Distributions in tax years beginning after December 31, 1997
108(f)(2)	6004(f)(1)	Treatment of cancellation of certain student loans	Discharges of indebtedness after August 5, 1997
108(f)(3)	6004(f)(2)	Treatment of cancellation of certain student loans	Discharges of indebtedness after August 5, 1997
119(b)	5002	Clarification of exclusion of meals for certain employees	Tax years beginning before, on, or after date of enactment
121(b)(2)	6005(e)(1)	Exclusion of gain from sale of principal residence	Sales and exchanges after May 6, 1997, generally
121(c)(1)	6005(e)(2)	Exclusion of gain from sale of principal residence	Sales and exchanges after May 6, 1997, generally
135(c)(2)(C)	6004(d)(9)	Education individual retirement accounts	Tax years beginning after December 31, 1997
135(c)(3)	6004(c)(1)	Modifications of qualified state tuition programs	Tax years beginning after December 31, 1997, generally
135(d)(2)	6004(d)(4)	Education individual retirement accounts	Tax years beginning after December 31, 1997
142(f)(3)(A)	6023(5)	Miscellaneous clerical and deadwood changes	Date of enactment
162(a)	6012(a)	Treatment of traveling expenses of certain federal employees engaged in criminal investigations	Amounts paid or incurred with respect to tax years ending after August 5, 1997

¶ 20,001

Code Sec.	Act Sec.	Act Provision Subject	Effective Date
168(c)	6006(b)	Repeal of separate depreciation lives for minimum tax purposes	August 5, 1997
170(e)(6)(B)	6004(e)(1)-(2)	Contributions of computer technology and equipment for elementary or secondary school purposes	Tax years beginning after December 31, 1997
170(e)(6)(C)	6004(e)(3)	Contributions of computer technology and equipment for elementary or secondary school purposes	Tax years beginning after December 31, 1997
170(e)(6)(F)	6004(e)(4)	Contributions of computer technology and equipment for elementary or secondary school purposes	Tax years beginning after December 31, 1997
196(c)(6)-(8)	6020	Credit for portion of employer social security taxes paid with respect to employee cash tips	Taxes paid after December 31, 1993
219(g)(1),(7)	6005(a)(1)	Restoration of IRA deduction for certain taxpayers—special rule for spouses who are not active participants	Tax years beginning after December 31, 1997
221(d)	6004(b)(2)	Deduction for interest on education loans	Interest payments due and paid after December 31, 1997, and the portion of the 60-month period referred to in Code Sec. 221(d) after December 31, 1997
221(e)(1)	6004(b)(1)	Deduction for interest on education loans	Interest payments due and paid after December 31, 1997, and the portion of the 60-month period referred to in Code Sec. 221(d) after December 31, 1997
264(a)(3)	6010(o)(1)	Expansion of denial of deduction for certain amounts paid in connection with insurance—plan of systematic borrowing of increases in cash value	Contracts issued after June 8, 1997, in tax years ending after such date
264(a)(4)	6010(o)(2)	Expansion of denial of deduction for certain amounts paid in connection with insurance—interest on policy loans	Contracts issued after June 8, 1997, in tax years ending after such date
264(f)(4)(E)	6010(o)(3)(A)	Expansion of denial of deduction for certain amounts paid in connection with insurance—pro rata allocation of interest expense to policy cash values	Contracts issued after June 8, 1997, in tax years ending after such date
264(f)(5)(A)	6010(o)(4)(A)	Expansion of denial of deduction for certain amounts paid in connec-	Contracts issued after June 8, 1997, in tax

Code Sec.	Act Sec.	Act Provision Subject	Effective Date
		tion with insurance—pro rata allocation of interest expense to policy cash values	years ending after such date
264(f)(8)(A)	6010(o)(5)	Expansion of denial of deduction for certain amounts paid in connection with insurance—aggregation rules	Contracts issued after June 8, 1997, in tax years ending after such date
280F(a)(1)(C)	6009(c)	Exemption of incremental cost of clean fuel vehicle from limits on depreciation for vehicles	Property placed in service after August 5, 1997 and before January 1, 2005
304(b)(5)(B)-(C)	6010(d)(1)	Tax treatment of redemptions involving related corporations—special rule for acquisitions by foreign corporations	Distributions and acquisitions after June 8, 1997, generally
304(b)(6)	6010(d)(2)	Tax treatment of redemptions involving related corporations—avoidance of multiple inclusions	Distributions and acquisitions after June 8, 1997, generally
351(c)	6010(c)(3)(A)	Application of Code Sec. 355 to distributions in connection with acquisitions and to intragroup transactions—determination of control in certain divisive transactions	Transfers after August 5, 1997, generally
351(g)(1)(B)-(C)	6010(e)(1)	Certain preferred stock treated as boot	Transactions after June 8, 1997, generally
354(a)(2)(C)	6010(e)(2)	Certain preferred stock treated as boot	Transactions after June 8, 1997, generally
355(e)(3)(A)	6010(c)(2)	Application of Code Sec. 355 to distributions in connection with acquisitions and to intragroup transactions	Distributions after April 16, 1997, generally
368(a)(2)(H)	6010(c)(3)(B)	Application of Code Sec. 355 to distributions in connection with acquisitions and to intragroup transactions—determination of control in certain divisive transactions	Transfers after August 5, 1997, generally
402(c)(4)(C)	6005(c)(2)(A)	Denial of rollover treatment for transfers of hardship distributions to individual retirement plans	Distributions made after December 31, 1998
403(b)(8)(B)	6005(c)(2)(B)	Denial of rollover treatment for transfers of hardship distributions to individual retirement plans	Distributions made after December 31, 1998
404(a)(9)(C)-(D)	6015(d)	Gratuitous transfers for the benefit of employees	Transfers made by trusts to, or for the use of, an employee stock ownership plan after August 5, 1997

Code Sec.	Act Sec.	Act Provision Subject	Effective Date
404(a)	7001	Clarification of deduction for deferred compensation	Tax years ending after date of enactment
408(d)(7)	6018(b)(1)-(2)	Establishment of savings incentive match plans for employees of small employers	Tax years beginning after December 31, 1996
408(p)(2)(D)	6016(a)(1)(A)	Establishment of savings incentive match plans for employees of small employers	Tax years beginning after December 31, 1996
408(p)(2)	6016(a)(1)(C)	Establishment of savings incentive match plans for employees of small employers	Tax years beginning after December 31, 1996
408(p)(8)-(9)	6015(a)	Matching contributions of self-employed individuals not treated as elective employer contributions	Years beginning after December 31, 1996
408(p)(10)	6016(a)(1)(B)	Establishment of savings incentive match plans for employees of small employers	Tax years beginning after December 31, 1996
408A(c)(3)(A)-(C)	6005(b)(2)	Establishment of nondeductible tax-free individual retirement accounts—contribution limits based on modified adjusted gross income	Tax years beginning after December 31, 1997
408A(c)(3)(A)	6005(b)(1)	Establishment of nondeductible tax-free individual retirement accounts—contribution limits based on modified adjusted gross income	Tax years beginning after December 31, 1997
408A(c)(3)(C)	7004(a)	Modification of AGI limit for conversions to Roth IRAs	Tax years beginning after December 31, 2004
408A(d)(1)	6005(b)(5)(B)	Establishment of nondeductible tax-free individual retirement accounts—exclusion of qualified distributions	Tax years beginning after December 31, 1997
408A(d)(2)(B)	6005(b)(3)(A)	Establishment of nondeductible tax-free individual retirement accounts—distributions within nonexclusion period	Tax years beginning after December 31, 1997
408A(d)(2)(C)	6005(b)(3)(B)	Establishment of nondeductible tax-free individual retirement accounts—distributions of excess contributions and earnings	Tax years beginning after December 31, 1997
408A(d)(3)(A)	6005(b)(4)(A)	Establishment of nondeductible tax-free individual retirement accounts—rollovers from IRAs other than Roth IRA	Tax years beginning after December 31, 1997
408A(d)(3)(D)-(G)	6005(b)(6)(B)	Establishment of nondeductible tax-free individual retirement accounts—conversion of excess contributions	Tax years beginning after December 31, 1997

Code Sec.	Act Sec.	Act Provision Subject	Effective Date
408A(d)(3)(F),(G)	6005(b)(4)(B)	Establishment of nondeductible tax-free individual retirement accounts—rollovers from IRAs other than Roth IRA	Tax years beginning after December 31, 1997
408A(d)(4)	6005(b)(5)(A)	Establishment of nondeductible tax-free individual retirement accounts—aggregation and ordering rules	Tax years beginning after December 31, 1997
408A(d)(6)	6005(b)(6)(A)	Establishment of nondeductible tax-free individual retirement accounts—adjustments before due date for trustee-to-trustee transfers	Tax years beginning after December 31, 1997
408A(d)(7)	6005(b)(7)	Establishment of nondeductible tax-free individual retirement accounts—adjustments before due date for trustee-to-trustee transfers	Tax years beginning after December 31, 1997
408A(f)	6005(b)(9)	Establishment of nondeductible tax-free individual retirement accounts—individual retirement plan defined	Tax years beginning after December 31, 1997
475(c)	7003(a)	Certain customer receivables ineligible for mark-to-market treatment	Tax years ending after date of enactment, generally
475(f)(1)(D)	6010(a)(3)	Constructive sales treatment for appreciated financial positions—election of mark to market for dealers in commodities and for traders in securities or commodities	Tax years ending after August 5, 1997, generally
475(g)	7003(b)	Certain customer receivable ineligible for mark-to-market treatment—regulations	Tax years ending after date of enactment, generally
501(n)(3)	6023(6)	Miscellaneous clerical and deadwood changes	Date of enactment
501(o)	6023(7)	Miscellaneous clerical and deadwood changes	Date of enactment
512(b)(13)(A)	6010(j)(1)	Expansion of look-through rule for interest, annuities, royalties and rents derived by subsidiaries of tax-exempt organizations	Tax years beginning after August 5, 1997, generally
512(b)(13)(B)	6010(j)(2)	Expansion of look-through rule for interest, annuities, royalties and rents derived by subsidiaries of tax-exempt organizations	Tax years beginning after August 5, 1997, generally
512(b)(17)(B)	6023(8)	Miscellaneous clerical and deadwood changes	Date of enactment
529(c)(3)(A)	6004(c)(2)	Modifications of qualified state tuition programs	January 1, 1998, generally

¶ 20,001

Code Sec.	Act Sec.	Act Provision Subject	Effective Date
529(e)(2)	6004(c)(3)	Modifications of qualified state tuition programs	January 1, 1998, generally
530(b)(1)(E)	6004(d)(2)(A)	Education individual retirement accounts	Tax years beginning after December 31, 1997
530(b)(1)	6004(d)(1)	Education individual retirement accounts	Tax years beginning after December 31, 1997
530(d)(1)	6004(d)(3)(A)	Education individual retirement accounts	Tax years beginning after December 31, 1997
530(d)(2)(D)	6004(d)(5)	Education individual retirement accounts	Tax years beginning after December 31, 1997
530(d)(4)(B)	6004(d)(6)	Education individual retirement accounts	Tax years beginning after December 31, 1997
530(d)(4)(C)	6004(d)(7)	Education individual retirement accounts	Tax years beginning after December 31, 1997
530(d)(5)	6004(d)(8)(A)	Education individual retirement accounts	Tax years beginning after December 31, 1997
530(d)(6)	6004(d)(8)(B)	Education individual retirement accounts	Tax years beginning after December 31, 1997
530(d)(7)	6004(d)(2)(B)	Education individual retirement accounts	Tax years beginning after December 31, 1997
530(d)(8)	6004(d)(2)(C)	Education individual retirement accounts	Tax years beginning after December 31, 1997
543(d)(5)(A)	6023(9)	Miscellaneous clerical and deadwood changes	Date of enactment
641(c),(d)	6007(f)(2)	Repeal of tax on transfers to trusts at less than fair market value—conforming amendment	Sales or exchanges after August 5, 1997
645	6013(a)(1)	Certain revocable trusts treated as part of estate	Estates of decedents dying after August 5, 1997
646	6013(a)(1)	Certain revocable trusts treated as part of estate	Estates of decedents dying after August 5, 1997
664(d)(1)(C),(2)(C)	6010(r)	Limitations on charitable remainder trust eligibility for certain trusts	Transfers in trust after July 28, 1997, generally
672(f)(3)(B)	6011(c)(1)	Election of mark to market for marketable stock in passive foreign investment company	Tax years of U.S. persons beginning after December 31, 1997 and tax years of for-

Code Sec.	Act Sec.	Act Provision Subject	Effective Date
			eign corporations ending with or within such tax years of U.S. persons
685(b)	6013(b)(1)	Treatment of funeral trusts	Tax years ending after August 5, 1997
685(f)	6013(b)(2)	Treatment of funeral trusts	Tax years ending after August 5, 1997
751(c)	6010(m)	Allocation of basis among properties distributed by partnership	Distributions after August 5, 1997
774(d)(2)	6012(c)	Simplified flow-through for electing large partnerships	Partnership tax years beginning after December 31, 1997
853(c)	6010(k)(2)	Holding period requirement for certain foreign taxes—notice of withholding taxes paid by regulated investment company	Dividends paid or accrued after September 4, 1997
853(e),(f)	6010(k)(1)	Holding period requirement for certain foreign taxes paid by regulated investment company—treatment of taxes not allowed as credit under Code Sec. 901(k)	Dividends paid or accrued after September 4, 1997
857(d)(3)(A)	6012(g)	Modification of earnings and profits rules for determining whether REIT has earnings and profits from non-REIT year	Tax years beginning after August 5, 1997
871(f)(2)(B)	6023(10)	Miscellaneous clerical and deadwood changes	Date of enactment
901(k)(4)(A)	6010(k)(3)	Holding period requirement for certain foreign taxes paid by regulated investment company—exception for certain taxes paid by securities dealers	Dividends paid or accrued after September 4, 1997
991	6011(e)(1)	Repeal of excise tax on transfers to foreign entities; recognition of gain on certain transfers to foreign trusts and estates	August 5, 1997
1017(a)(2)	6023(11)	Miscellaneous clerical and deadwood changes	Date of enactment
1045(a)	6005(f)(1)	Rollover of gain from qualified small business stock to other qualified small business stock	Sales after August 5, 1997
1045(b)(5)	6005(f)(2)	Rollover of gain from qualified small business stock to other qualified small business stock	Sales after August 5, 1997
1059(g)(1)	6010(b)	Tax treatment of certain extraordinary dividends received by corporate shareholders—authority to issue regulations	Distributions after May 3, 1995, generally

¶ 20,001

Code Sec.	Act Sec.	Act Provision Subject	Effective Date
1223(11), (12)	5001(a)(5)	Lower capital gains rates to apply to property held more than 1 year	January 1, 1998
1223(11),(12)	6005(d)(4)	Holding period for property acquired from decedent or certain qualified real property transferred to qualified heir	Tax years ending after May 6, 1997
1235(a)	5001(a)(5)	Lower capital gains rates to apply to property held more than 1 year	January 1, 1998
1235(a)	6005(d)(4)	Holding period for sales or exchanges of patents	Tax years ending after May 6, 1997
1250(d)(4)(D)	6023(12)	Miscellaneous clerical and deadwood changes	Date of enactment
1259(b)(2)	6010(a)(1)	Constructive sales treatment for appreciated financial positions	Constructive sales after June 8, 1997, generally
1259(d)(1)	6010(a)(2)	Constructive sales treatment for appreciated financial positions	Constructive sales after June 8, 1997, generally
1291(d)(1)	6011(c)(2)	Election of mark to market for marketable stock in passive foreign investment company	Tax years of U.S. persons beginning after December 31, 1997 and tax years of foreign corporations ending with or within such tax years of U.S. persons
1296(d)	6011(c)(3)	Election of mark to market for marketable stock in passive foreign investment company	Tax years of U.S. persons beginning after December 31, 1997 and tax years of foreign corporations ending with or within such tax years of U.S. persons
1297(e)(4)	6011(b)(1)	U.S. shareholders of controlled foreign corporations not subject to PFIC inclusion	Tax years of U.S. persons beginning after December 31, 1997 and tax years of foreign corporations ending with or within such tax years of U.S. persons
1297(e)	6011(d)	Valuation of assets for passive foreign investment company determination	Tax years of U.S. persons beginning after December 31, 1997 and tax years of foreign corporations ending with or within such tax years of U.S. persons

¶ 20,001

Code Sec.	Act Sec.	Act Provision Subject	Effective Date
1298(a)(2)(B)	6011(b)(2)	U.S. shareholders of controlled foreign corporations not subject to PFIC inclusion	Tax years of U.S. persons beginning after December 31, 1997 and tax years of foreign corporations ending with or within such tax years of U.S. persons
1361(e)(4)	6007(f)(3)	Repeal of tax on transfers to trusts at less than fair market value— conforming amendment	Sales or exchanges after August 5, 1997
1397E(d)(4)(B)	6004(g)(2)	Incentives for education zones	Obligations issued after December 31, 1997
1397E(g)	6004(g)(4)	Incentives for education zones	Obligations issued after December 31, 1997
1397E(h)	6004(g)(3)	Incentives for education zones	Obligations issued after December 31, 1997
1400(b)(2)(B)	6008(a)	Tax incentives for revitalization of the District of Columbia	August 5, 1997
1400A(a)	6008(b)	Tax incentives for revitalization of the District of Columbia	August 5, 1997
1400B(b)(5)	6008(c)(1)	Tax incentives for revitalization of the District of Columbia	August 5, 1997
1400B(b)(6)	6008(c)(2)	Tax incentives for revitalization of the District of Columbia	August 5, 1997
1400B(c)	6008(c)(3)	Tax incentives for revitalization of the District of Columbia	August 5, 1997
1400B(d)(2)	6008(c)(4)	Tax incentives for revitalization of the District of Columbia	August 5, 1997
1400C(b)(1)	6008(d)(1)	Tax incentives for revitalization of the District of Columbia	August 5, 1997
1400C(c)(1)	6008(d)(2)	Tax incentives for revitalization of the District of Columbia	August 5, 1997
1400C(e)(2)(B)	6008(d)(3)	Tax incentives for revitalization of the District of Columbia	August 5, 1997
1400C(e)(3)	6008(d)(4)	Tax incentives for revitalization of the District of Columbia	August 5, 1997
1400C(i)	6008(d)(5)	Tax incentives for revitalization of the District of Columbia	August 5, 1997
2001(f)	6007(e)(2)(B)	Gifts may not be revalued for estate tax purposes after expiration of statute of limitations	Gifts made after August 5, 1997
2031(c)(6)	6007(g)(2)	Estate tax with respect to land subject to qualified conservation easement	Estates of decedents dying after December 31, 1997
2031(c)(9),(10)	6007(g)(1)	Estate tax with respect to land subject to qualified conservation easement	Estates of decedents dying after December 31, 1997

¶ 20,001

Code Sec.	Act Sec.	Act Provision Subject	Effective Date
2033A, 2057	6007(b)(1)(A)	Family-owned business interests—redesignation as Code Sec. 2057	Estates of decedents dying after December 31, 1997
2057(a)	6007(b)(1)(B)	Family-owned business interests—allowance of deduction	Estates of decedents dying after December 31, 1997
2057(b)(2)(A)	6007(b)(1)(C)	Family-owned business interests—includible family-owned business interests	Estates of decedents dying after December 31, 1997
2057(b)(3)	6007(b)(2)	Family-owned business interests—includible gifts of interests	Estates of decedents dying after December 31, 1997
2057(c)	6007(b)(1)(D)	Family-owned business interests—adjusted gross estate	Estates of decedents dying after December 31, 1997
2057(e)(1)	6007(b)(5)(A)	Qualified family-owned business interests	Estates of decedents dying after December 31, 1997
2057(e)(2)(C)	6007(b)(3)(A)	Qualified family-owned business interest	Estates of decedents dying after December 31, 1997
2057(e)(2)(D)	6007(b)(3)(B)	Qualified family-owned business interest	Estates of decedents dying after December 31, 1997
2057(e)(2)	6007(b)(3)(C)	Qualified family-owned business interest	Estates of decedents dying after December 31, 1997
2057(f)(2)(C)	6007(b)(4)(B)	Family-owned business interests—adjusted tax difference	Estates of decedents dying after December 31, 1997
2057(f)(2)	6007(b)(4)(A)	Family-owned business interests—additional estate tax	Estates of decedents dying after December 31, 1997
2057(f)(3)	6007(b)(5)(B)	Family-owned business interests—failure to materially participate in business or dispositions of interests	Estates of decedents dying after December 31, 1997
2057(g)(1)	6007(b)(6)	Family-owned business interests—security requirements for noncitizen qualified heirs	Estates of decedents dying after December 31, 1997
2057(i)(3)(L)-(P)	6007(b)(7)	Family-owned business interests—other definitions and applicable rules	Estates of decedents dying after December 31, 1997
2504(c)	6007(e)(2)(B)[G]	ifts may not be revalued for estate tax purposes after expiration of statute of limitations—conforming amendment	Gifts made after August 5, 1997

¶ 20,001

Code Sec.	Act Sec.	Act Provision Subject	Effective Date
2631(c)	6007(a)(1)	Cost-of-living adjustments relating to estate and gift tax provisions—exemption from generation-skipping tax	Generation-skipping transfers made after December 31, 1998
2652(b)(1)	6013(a)(3)	Certain revocable trusts treated as part of estate	Estates of decedents dying after August 5, 1997
2652(b)(1)	6013(a)(4)(A)	Certain revocable trusts treated as part of estate	Estates of decedents dying after August 5, 1997
2654(b)	6013(a)(4)(B)	Certain revocable trusts treated as part of estate	Estates of decedents dying after August 5, 1997
3121(a)(5)	6023(13)	Miscellaneous clerical and deadwood changes	Date of enactment
3401(a)(19)	6023(14)	Miscellaneous clerical and deadwood changes	Date of enactment
3401(a)(21)	6023(15)	Miscellaneous clerical and deadwood changes	Date of enactment
4041(l)	6010(g)(1)	Airport and airway trust fund excise taxes—fuel taxes	October 1, 1997
4052(f)(2)	6014(c)	Modifications to retail tax on heavy trucks	January 1, 1998
4082(d)(1)	6010(h)(3)	Kerosene taxed as diesel fuel—certain kerosene exempt from dying requirement	July 1, 1998
4082(d)(3)	6010(h)(4)	Kerosene taxed as diesel fuel—certain kerosene exempt from dying requirement	July 1, 1998
4091(a)(2)	6014(d)	Allowance or credit of refund for tax-paid aviation fuel purchased by registered producer of aviation fuel	Fuel acquired by the producer after September 30, 1997
4092(b)	6023(16)	Miscellaneous clerical and deadwood changes	Date of enactment
4101(e)(1)	6010(h)(5)	Kerosene taxed as diesel fuel—certain approved terminals of registered persons required to offer dyed diesel fuel and kerosene for nontaxable purposes	July 1, 2000
4221(c)	6023(17)	Miscellaneous clerical and deadwood changes	Date of enactment
4222(d)	6023(17)	Miscellaneous clerical and deadwood changes	Date of enactment
4251(d)(3)	6010(i)	Application of communications tax to prepaid telephone cards	Amounts paid in calendar months beginning after October 4, 1997

Code Sec.	Act Sec.	Act Provision Subject	Effective Date
4946(c)(5)-(7)	1101(c)(1)	Internal Revenue Service Oversight Board—conforming amendments	Date of enactment, generally
4973(b)	6005(b)(8)(B)	Excess contributions to Roth IRAs	Tax years beginning after December 31, 1997
4973(e)(1)	6004(d)(10)(A)	Education individual retirement accounts	Tax years beginning after December 31, 1997
4973(e)(2)(B)-(C)	6004(d)(10)(B)	Education individual retirement accounts	Tax years beginning after December 31, 1997
4973(f)	6005(b)(8)(A)	Excess contributions to Roth IRAs	Tax years beginning after December 31, 1997
4973	6023(18)(A)	Miscellaneous clerical and deadwood changes	Date of enactment
4975(c)(3)	6023(19)(A)	Miscellaneous clerical and deadwood changes	Date of enactment
4975(i)	6023(19)(B)	Miscellaneous clerical and deadwood changes	Date of enactment
5041(b)(6)	6009(a)	Modification of tax treatment of hard cider—hard cider containing less than 7 percent alcohol treated as wine	October 1, 1997
5043(a)(2)	6014(b)(1)	Transfer to bonded wine cellars of wine imported in bulk without payment of tax	April 1, 1998
5044(a)	6014(b)(2)	Transfer to bonded wine cellars of wine imported in bulk without payment of tax	April 1, 1998
5054(a)(1)	6014(a)(1)	Transfer to brewery of beer imported in bulk without payment of tax	April 1, 1998
5054(a)(2)	6014(a)(2)	Transfer to brewery of beer imported in bulk without payment of tax	April 1, 1998
5056	6014(a)(3)	Transfer to brewery of beer imported in bulk without payment of tax	April 1, 1998
5364	6014(b)(3)	Transfer to bonded wine cellars of wine imported in bulk without payment of tax	April 1, 1998
6011(f)-(g)	2001(c)	Electronic filing of tax and information returns—promotion of electronic filing and incentives	Date of enactment
6013(e)	3201(e)(1)	Relief from joint and several liability on joint return—conforming amendments	Any tax liability arising after date of enactment and any tax liability arising on or before date of enactment but remaining unpaid as of such date, generally

Code Sec.	Act Sec.	Act Provision Subject	Effective Date
6013	6011(e)(2)	Repeal of excise tax on transfers to foreign entities; recognition of gain on certain transfers to foreign trusts and estates	August 5, 1997
6015	3201(a)	Relief from joint and several liability on joint return	Any tax liability arising after date of enactment and any tax liability arising on or before date of enactment but remaining unpaid as of such date, generally
6038(a)(2)	6011(f)(1)	Controlled foreign partnerships subject to information reporting comparable to information reporting for controlled foreign corporations	Annual accounting periods beginning after August 5, 1997
6038(a)(3)	6011(f)(2)	Controlled foreign partnerships subject to information reporting comparable to information reporting for controlled foreign corporations	Annual accounting periods beginning after August 5, 1997
6038(e)(4)	6011(f)(3)	Controlled foreign partnerships subject to information reporting comparable to information reporting for controlled foreign corporations	Annual accounting periods beginning after August 5, 1997
6039(a)(1)	6023(20)	Miscellaneous clerical and deadwood changes	Date of enactment
6050R(b)(2)(A)	6023(21)	Miscellaneous clerical and deadwood changes	Date of enactment
6050S(a)	6004(a)(2)	Hope and lifetime learning credits	Expenses paid after December 31, 1997 (in tax years ending after such date), for education furnished in academic periods beginning after such date
6050S(b)(2)(C)	3712(a)	Reporting requirements in connection with education tax credit	Returns required to be filed with respect to tax years beginning after December 31, 1998
6050S(d)(2)	3712(b)(1)	Reporting requirements in connection with education tax credit—conforming amendment	Returns required to be filed with respect to tax years beginning after December 31, 1998
6050S(e)	3712(b)(2)	Reporting requirements in connection with education tax credit—conforming amendment	Returns required to be filed with respect to tax years beginning after December 31, 1998

Code Sec.	Act Sec.	Act Provision Subject	Effective Date
6061	2003(a)	Paperless electronic filing—in general	Date of enactment
6071(b)-(c)	2002(a)	Due date for certain information returns—information returns filed electronically	Returns required to be filed after December 31, 1999
6103(d)(5)	6009(d)	Combined employment tax reporting demonstration project	August 5, 1997
6103(e)(1)(A)	6007(f)(4)	Repeal of tax on transfers to trusts at less than fair market value—conforming amendment	Sales or exchanges af ter August 5, 1997
6103(e)(6)	6019(c)	Exempt organizations required to provide copy of return	Date of enactment
6103(f)(5)	3708	Provision of confidential information to Congress by whistleblowers	Date of enactment
6103(h)(4)(A)	6023(22)	Miscellaneous clerical and deadwood changes	Date of enactment
6103(h)(5)	1101(b)	Internal Revenue Service Oversight Board—restriction on disclosure of return information to Oversight Board members	Date of enactment, generally
6103(k)(8)-(9)	6012(b)(2)	Payment of tax by commercially acceptable means	May 5, 1998
6103(l)(10)	3711(b)(1)-(2)	Offset of past-due, legally enforceable state income tax obligations against overpayments—disclosure of certain information to states requesting refund offsets for past-due, legally enforceable state income tax obligations	Refunds payable under section 6402 of the Internal Revenue Code of 1986 after December 31, 1999
6103(l)(17)	3702(a)	Archive of records of IRS	Requests made by the Archivist of the U.S. after date of enactment
6103(p)(3)(A)	3702(b)(1)	Archive of records of IRS—conforming amendment	Requests made by the Archivist of the U.S. after date of enactment
6103(p)(4)(F)	3702(b)(3)	Archive of records of IRS—conforming amendment	Requests made by the Archivist of the U.S. after date of enactment
6103(p)(4)	3702(b)(2)	Archive of records of IRS—conforming amendment	Requests made by the Archivist of the U.S. after date of enactment
6104(b)	6019(a)	Exempt organizations required to provide copy of return	Date of enactment
6104(e)(1)(C)	6019(b)	Exempt organizations required to provide copy of return	Date of enactment
6109(a)	3710	Identification of return preparers	Date of enactment

Code Sec.	Act Sec.	Act Provision Subject	Effective Date
6110(b)(1)	3509(a)	Disclosure of Chief Counsel advice	Any Chief Counsel advice issued more than 90 days after date of enactment, generally
6110(f)(1)	3509(c)(1)	Disclosure of Chief Counsel advice—conforming amendment	Any Chief Counsel advice issued more than 90 days after date of enactment, generally
6110(i)-(m)	3509(b)	Special rules for disclosure of Chief Counsel advice	Any Chief Counsel advice issued more than 90 days after date of enactment, generally
6110(j)	3509(c)(2)	Disclosure of Chief Counsel advice—conforming amendment	Any Chief Counsel advice issued more than 90 days after date of enactment, generally
6110(k)(1)(B)	3509(c)(3)	Disclosure of Chief Counsel advice—conforming amendment	Any Chief Counsel advice issued more than 90 days after date of enactment, generally
6159(c)-(d)	3467(a)	Guaranteed availability of installment agreements	Date of enactment
6159(d)	3462(c)(2)	Offers-in-compromise—conforming amendment	Proposed offers-in-compromise and installment agreements submitted after date of enactment
6166(b)(7)(A)	6007(c)(1)	Modifications to rate of interest on portion of estate tax deferred under Code Sec. 6166	Estates of decedents dying after December 31, 1997
6166(b)(8)(A)	6007(c)(2)	Modifications to rate of interest on portion of estate tax extended under Code Sec. 6166	Estates of decedents dying after December 31, 1997
6211(c)	6012(f)	Treatment of partnership items in deficiency proceedings	Partnership tax years ending after August 5, 1997
6212(a)	1102(b)	Commissioner of Internal Revenue; other officials—notice of right to contact office included in notice of deficiency	Date of enactment
6213(a)	3463(b)	Notice of deficiency to specify deadlines for filing Tax Court petition—later filing deadlines specified on notice of deficiency to be binding	Notices mailed after December 31, 1998

Code Sec.	Act Sec.	Act Provision Subject	Effective Date
6213(a)	3464(a)	Refund or credit of overpayments before final determination—Tax Court proceedings	Date of enactment
6230(c)(5)(A)	3201(e)(2)	Relief from joint and several liability on joint return—conforming amendments	Any tax liability arising after date of enactment and any tax liability arising on or before date of enactment but remaining unpaid as of such date, generally
6231(a)(7)	3507(a)	Notification of change in tax matters partner	Selections of tax matters partners made by the IRS after date of enactment
6304	3466(a)	Application of certain fair debt collection procedures	Date of enactment
6311(e)(1)	6012(b)(1)	Payment of tax by commercially acceptable means	May 5, 1998
6320	3401(a)	Due process in IRS collection actions—notice and opportunity for hearing upon filing of notice of lien	Collection actions initiated after 180 days after date of enactment
6323(b)(10)	3435(b)	Increase in amount of certain property on which lien not valid—expansion of treatment of passbook loans	Date of enactment
6323(b)	3435(a)(1)	Increase in amount of certain property on which lien not valid	Date of enactment
6323(i)	3435(a)(2)	Increase in amount of certain property on which lien not valid—inflation adjustment	Date of enactment
6323(j)(1)(D)	1102(d)(1)(A)	Commissioner of Internal Revenue; other officials—conforming amendments relating to National Taxpayer Advocate	Date of enactment
6325(b)(4)	3106(a)	Civil action for release of erroneous lien	Date of enactment
6330	3401(b)	Due process in IRS collection actions—notice and opportunity for hearing before levy	Collection actions initiated after 180 days after date of enactment
6331(h)(1)	6010(f)	Continuous levy on certain payments	Levies issued after August 5, 1997
6331(i)-(j)	3433(a)	Levy prohibited during pendency of refund proceedings	Unpaid tax attributable to tax years beginning after December 31, 1998
6331(j)-(k)	3444(a)	Codification of IRS administrative procedures for seizure of tax-	Date of enactment

Code Sec.	Act Sec.	Act Provision Subject	Effective Date
		payer's property—no levy before investigation of status of property	
6331(k)-(l)	3462(b)	Offers-in-compromise—levy prohibited while offer-in-compromise pending or installment agreement pending or in effect	Offers-in-compromise pending on or made after December 31, 1999
6334(a)(2)	3431(a)	Modifications to certain levy exemption amounts—fuel, etc.	Levies issued after date of enactment
6334(a)(3)	3431(b)	Modifications to certain levy exemption amounts—books, etc.	Levies issued after date of enactment
6334(a)(13)	3445(a)	Procedures for seizure of residences and businesses	Date of enactment
6334(e)	3445(b)	Procedures for seizure of residences and businesses—levy allowed in certain circumstances	Date of enactment
6334(g)(1)	3431(c)	Modifications to certain levy exemption amounts—conforming amendment	Levies issued after date of enactment
6335(e)(1)(A)	3441(a)	Prohibition on sales of seized property at less than minimum bid	Sales made after date of enactment
6335(e)(4)	3441(b)	Cross reference to penalty for violation	Sales made after date of enactment
6340(a)	3442(a)(1)	Accounting of sales of seized property	Seizures occurring after date of enactment
6340(c)	3442(a)(2)	Accounting of sales of seized property—accounting to taxpayer	Seizures occurring after date of enactment
6343(d)(2)(D)	1102(d)(1)(B)	Commissioner of Internal Revenue; other officials—conforming amendments relating to National Taxpayer Advocate	Date of enactment
6343(e)	3432(a)	Release of levy upon agreement that amount is uncollectible	Levies imposed after December 31, 1999
6344(b)	1104(b)(1)	Other personnel—conforming amendments	Date of enactment
6401(b)(1)	6022	Alternative minimum tax for individuals and corporations	Tax years beginning after December 31, 1986, generally
6402(a)	3711(c)(1)	Offset of past-due, legally enforceable state income tax obligations against overpayments—conforming amendment	Refunds payable under section 6402 of the Internal Revenue Code of 1986 after December 31, 1999
6402(d)(2)	3711(c)(2)	Offset of past-due, legally enforceable state income tax obligations against overpayments—conforming amendment	Refunds payable under section 6402 of the Internal Revenue Code of 1986 after December 31, 1999

¶ 20,001

Code Sec.	Act Sec.	Act Provision Subject	Effective Date
6402(e)-(k)	3711(a)	Offset of past-due, legally enforceable state income tax obligations against overpayments	Refunds payable under section 6402 of the Internal Revenue Code of 1986 after December 31, 1999
6402(f)	3711(c)(3)	Offset of past-due, legally enforceable state income tax obligations against overpayments—conforming amendment	Refunds payable under section 6402 of the Internal Revenue Code of 1986 after December 31, 1999
6402(h)	3711(c)(4)	Offset of past-due, legally enforceable state income tax obligations against overpayments—conforming amendment	Refunds payable under section 6402 of the Internal Revenue Code of 1986 after December 31, 1999
6402(j)	3505(a)	Explanation of reason for refund disallowance	Disallowances after 180 days after date of enactment
6404(g)-(h)	3305	Suspension of interest and certain penalties where Secretary fails to contact individual taxpayer	Tax years ending after date of enactment
6404(h)-(i)	3309	Abatement of interest on underpayments by taxpayers in Presidentially declared disaster areas	Disasters declared after December 31, 1997, with respect to tax years beginning after December 31, 1997, generally
6416(b)(5)	6023(23)	Miscellaneous clerical and deadwood changes	Date of enactment
6421(a)-(b)	6023(24)(C)	Miscellaneous clerical and deadwood changes	Date of enactment
6421(c)	6010(g)(3)	Gasoline sold for certain exempt purposes	October 1, 1997
6421(i)-(k)	6023(24)(A)	Miscellaneous clerical and deadwood changes	Date of enactment
6427(d)	6016(b)(1)-(2)	Extension of airport and airway trust fund excise taxes	August 27, 1996, generally
6427(f)(3)	6023(25)	Miscellaneous clerical and deadwood changes	Date of enactment
6427(i)(1)-(2)(A)	6023(26)(B)	Miscellaneous clerical and deadwood changes	Date of enactment
6427(i)(2)(B)	6017	Simplified fuel tax refund procedures	October 1, 1998
6427(m)-(r)	6023(26)(A)	Miscellaneous clerical and deadwood changes	Date of enactment
6427(q)(2)	6023(16)	Miscellaneous clerical and deadwood changes	Date of enactment
6501(c)(4)	3461(b)	Procedures relating to extensions of statute of limitations by agree-	Requests to extend period of limitations

Code Sec.	Act Sec.	Act Provision Subject	Effective Date
		ment—notice to taxpayer of right to refuse or limit extension	made after December 31, 1999, generally
6501(c)(9)	6007(e)(2)(A)	Gifts may not be revalued for estate tax purposes after expiration of statute of limitations—modification of application of statute of limitations	Gifts made in calendar years ending after August 5, 1997
6501(m)	6023(27)	Miscellaneous clerical and deadwood changes	Date of enactment
6502(a)	3461(a)	Procedures relating to extensions of statute of limitations by agreement—authority to extend 10-year collection period after assessment	Requests to extend the period of limitations made after December 31, 1999, generally
6503(f)	3106(b)(3)	Civil action for release of erroneous lien	Date of enactment
6511(h)-(i)	3202	Suspension of statute of limitations on filing refund claims during periods of disability	Periods of disability before, on, or after date of enactment, unless barred by any law or rule of law as of date of enactment
6512(a)(5)-(6)	3464(b)	Refund or credit of overpayments before final determination—other proceedings	Date of enactment
6512(b)(1)	3464(c)	Refund or credit of overpayments pending appeal	Date of enactment
6601(f)	3301(b)	Elimination of interest rate differential on overlapping periods of interest on tax overpayments and underpayments—conforming amendment	Interest for periods beginning after date of enactment, generally
6611(g)(1)	6010(l)	Interest on underpayments not reduced by foreign tax credit carrybacks—conforming amendment	Foreign tax credit carrybacks arising in tax years beginning after August 5, 1997
6621(a)(1)(B)	3302	Increase in overpayment rate payable to taxpayers other than corporations	Interest for the second and succeeding calendar quarters beginning after date of enactment
6621(d)	3301(a)	Elimination of interest rate differential on overlapping periods of interest on tax overpayments and underpayments	Interest for periods beginning after date of enactment, generally
6631	3308	Notice of interest charges	Notices issued after December 31, 2000

Code Sec.	Act Sec.	Act Provision Subject	Effective Date
6651(h)	3303	Mitigation of penalty on individual's failure to pay for months during period of installment agreement	Determining additions to tax for months beginning after December 31, 1999
6656(c)(2)	3304(b)	Mitigation of failure to deposit penalty—expansion of exemption for first-time deposits	Deposits required to be made after the 180th day after date of enactment
6656(e)(1)	3304(c)	Mitigation of failure to deposit penalty—periods apply to current liabilities unless designated otherwise	Deposits required to be made after December 31, 2001
6656(e)	3304(a)	Mitigation of failure to deposit penalty	Deposits required to be made after the 180th day after date of enactment, generally
6672(b)	3307	Personal delivery of notice of penalty under section 6672	Date of enactment
6724(c)	6012(d)	Due date for furnishing information to partners of electing large partnerships	Partnership tax years beginning after December 31, 1997
6724(d)(1)(B)	6010(o)(4)(B)	Expansion of denial of deduction for certain amounts paid in connection with insurance—returns relating to reporting with respect to certain life insurance and annuity contracts	Contracts issued after June 8, 1997, in tax years ending after such date
6724(d)(2)	6010(o)(4)(C)	Expansion of denial of deduction for certain amounts paid in connection with insurance—returns relating to reporting with respect to certain life insurance and annuity contracts	Contracts issued after June 8, 1997, in tax years ending after such date
6751	3306	Procedural requirements for imposition of penalties and additions to tax	Notices issued and penalties assessed after December 31, 2000
7122(c)	3462(a)	Offers-in-compromise—standards for evaluation of offers-in-compromise	Proposed offers-in-compromise and installment agreements submitted after date of enactment
7122(d)	3462(c)(1)	Offers-in-compromise—review of rejections of offers-in-compromise and installment agreements	Proposed offers-in-compromise and installment agreements submitted after date of enactment
7123-7124	3465(a)	Procedures relating to appeals of examinations and collections—dispute resolution procedures	Date of enactment

¶ 20,001

Code Sec.	Act Sec.	Act Provision Subject	Effective Date
7213(d)-(e)	3413(b)	Software trade secrets protection—unauthorized disclosure of software	Summonses issued and software acquired after date of enactment, generally
7217	1105	Prohibition on executive branch influence over taxpayer audits and other investigations	Requests made after date of enactment
7421(a)	3201(e)(3)	Relief from joint and several liability on joint return—conforming amendments	Any tax liability arising after date of enactment and any tax liability arising on or before date of enactment but remaining unpaid as of such date, generally
7422(j)-(k)	3104(a)	Refund actions by estates which have elected the installment payment method	Any claim for refund filed after date of enactment
7426(a)(4)	3106(b)(1)	Civil action for release of erroneous lien	Date of enactment
7426(b)(5)	3106(b)(2)(A)	Civil action for release of erroneous lien	Date of enactment
7426(g)	3106(b)(2)(B)	Civil action for release of erroneous lien	Date of enactment
7426(h)-(i)	3102(b)	Civil damages for collection actions—damages allowed in civil actions by persons other than taxpayers	Actions of IRS officers or employees after date of enactment
7429(a)(1)	3434(a)	Approval required for jeopardy and termination assessments and jeopardy levies	Taxes assessed and levies made after date of enactment
7430(b)(4)-(5)	6012(h)	Awarding of administrative costs	Civil actions or proceedings commenced after August 5, 1997
7430(c)(1)(B)	3101(a)	Expansion of authority to award costs and certain fees—increase in attorney's fees	Costs incurred more than 180 days after date of enactment
7430(c)(2)	3101(b)	Expansion of authority to award costs and certain fees—award of administrative costs incurred after 30-day letter	Costs incurred more than 180 days after date of enactment
7430(c)(3)	3101(c)	Expansion of authority to award costs and certain fees—award of fees for certain additional services	Costs incurred and services performed more than 180 days after date of enactment
7430(c)(4)(B)	3101(d)	Expansion of authority to award costs and certain fees—determination of whether position of United States is substantially justified	Costs incurred more than 180 days after date of enactment

¶ 20,001

Code Sec.	Act Sec.	Act Provision Subject	Effective Date
7430(c)(4)(D)	6014(e)	Application of net worth requirement for awards of litigation costs	Proceedings commenced after August 5, 1997
7430(c)(4)(E)	3101(e)(1)	Expansion of authority to award costs and certain fees—taxpayer treated as prevailing if judgement is less than taxpayer's offer	Costs incurred more than 180 days after date of enactment
7430(g)	3101(e)(2)	Expansion of authority to award costs and certain fees—taxpayer treated as prevailing if judgement is less than taxpayer's offer	Costs incurred more than 180 days after date of enactment
7431(c)(2)-(3)	3101(f)	Expansion of authority to award costs and certain fees—award of attorneys fees in unauthorized inspection and disclosure cases	Costs incurred more than 180 days after date of enactment
7431(g)-(h)	6012(b)(3)	Payment of tax by commercially acceptable means	May 5, 1998
7433(a)-(b),(d)	3102(a)(1)-(2)	Civil damages for collection actions—extension to negligence actions	Actions of IRS officers or employees after date of enactment
7433(b)	3102(c)(2)	Civil damages for collection actions—conforming amendment	Actions of IRS officers or employees after date of enactment
7433(e)	3102(c)(1)	Civil damages for collection ac tions—civil damages for IRS violations of bankruptcy procedures	Actions of IRS officers or employees after date of enactment
7434(b)(3)	6023(29)	Miscellaneous clerical and deadwood changes	Date of enactment
7436(c)(1)	3103(b)(1)	Increase in size of cases permitted on small case calendar—conforming amendments	Proceedings com menced after date of enactment
7443(b)(4)-(5)	3401(c)(1)	Due process in IRS collection actions—review by special trial judges allowed	Collection actions initiated after 180 days after date of enactment
7443(c)	3401(c)(2)	Due process in IRS collection actions—review by special trial judges allowed	Collection actions initiated after 180 days after date of enactment
7443A(b)(3)	3103(b)(1)	Increase in size of cases permitted on small case calendar—conforming amendments	Proceedings commenced after the date of enactment
7463	3103(a)	Increase in size of cases permitted on small case calendar	Proceedings commenced after date of enactment
7479(a)(1),(2)	6007(d)	Clarification of judicial review of eligibility for extension of time for payment of estate tax	Estates of decedents dying after August 5, 1997

¶ 20,001

Code Sec.	Act Sec.	Act Provision Subject	Effective Date
7479(c)	3104(b)	Refund actions by estates which have elected the installment payment method—extension of time to file refund suit	Any claim for refund filed after date of enactment
7491	3001	Burden of proof	Court proceedings arising in connection with examinations commencing after date of enactment, generally
7502(c)	2003(b)	Paperless electronic filing—acknowledgment of electronic filing	Date of enactment
7525	3411(a)	Confidentiality privileges relating to taxpayer communications	Communications made on or after date of enactment
7526	3601(a)	Low income taxpayer clinics	Date of enactment
7602(c)-(e)	3417(a)	Notice of IRS contact of third parties	Contacts made after 180 days after date of enactment
7602(d)	3412	Limitation on financial status audit techniques	Date of enactment
7603(b)(2)(J)	3413(c)	Software trade secrets protection—application of special procedures for third-party summonses	Summonses issued and software acquired after date of enactment, generally
7603(b)	3416(a)	Service of summonses to third-party recordkeepers permitted by mail	Summonses served after date of enactment
7608(b)(1)	1103(e)(4)	Treasury Inspector General for tax administration	Date of enactment
7609(a)(1)	3415(a)	Taxpayers allowed motion to quash all third-party summonses	Summonses served after date of enactment
7609(a)(3)-(5)	3415(c)(1)	Taxpayers allowed motion to quash all third-party summonses—conforming amendments	Summonses served after date of enactment
7609(c)	3415(c)(2)	Taxpayers allowed motion to quash all third-party summonses—con. forming amendment	Summonses served after date of enactment
7609(e)(2)	3415(c)(3)	Taxpayers allowed motion to quash all third-party summonses—conforming amendment	Summonses served after date of enactment
7609(f)	3415(c)(4)	Taxpayers allowed motion to quash all third-party summonses—conforming amendment	Summonses served after date of enactment
7609(g)	3415(c)(5)	Taxpayers allowed motion to quash all third-party summonses—conforming amendment	Summonses served after date of enactment

¶ 20,001

Code Sec.	Act Sec.	Act Provision Subject	Effective Date
7609(i)(1)-(3)	3415(c)(6)	Taxpayers allowed motion to quash all third-party summonses—conforming amendments	Summonses served after date of enactment
7609(j)	3415(b)	Taxpayers allowed motion to quash all third-party summonses—coordination with other authority	Summonses served after date of enactment
7611(f)(1)	1102(e)(3)	Commissioner of Internal Revenue; other officials—additional conforming amendments	Date of enactment
7612	3413(a)	Software trade secrets protection—special procedures for summonses for computer software	Summonses issued and software acquired after date of enactment, generally
7702B(e)(2)	6023(28)	Miscellaneous clerical and deadwood changes	Date of enactment
7704(g)(3)(C)	6009(b)	Election for 1987 partnerships to continue exception from treatment of publicly traded partnerships as corporations—payment of estimated taxes	Tax years beginning after date of enactment
7802	1101(a)	Internal Revenue Service Oversight Board	Date of enactment, generally
7803	1102(a)	Commissioner of Internal Revenue; other officials	Date of enactment, generally
7804	1104(a)	Other personnel	Date of enactment
7805(d)	3704	Clarification of authority of secretary relating to the making of elections	Date of enactment
7811(a)	1102(c)	Commissioner of Internal Revenue; other officials—expansion of authority to issue taxpayer assistance orders	Date of enactment
7811(b)(2)(D)	1102(d)(1)(C)	Commissioner of Internal Revenue; other officials—conforming amendments relating to National Taxpayer Advocate	Date of enactment
7811(c)	1102(d)(1)(D)	Commissioner of Internal Revenue; other officials—conforming amendments relating to National Taxpayer Advocate	Date of enactment
7811(d)(1)	1102(d)(2)	Commissioner of Internal Revenue; other officials—conforming amendments relating to National Taxpayer Advocate	Date of enactment
7811(d)(2)	1102(d)(1)(E)	Commissioner of Internal Revenue; other officials—conforming amendments relating to National Taxpayer Advocate	Date of enactment
7811(e)-(f)	1102(d)(3)	Commissioner of Internal Revenue; other officials—conforming	Date of enactment

Code Sec.	Act Sec.	Act Provision Subject	Effective Date
		amendments relating to National Taxpayer Advocate	
7811(e)	1102(d)(1)(F)	Commissioner of Internal Revenue; other officials—conforming amendments relating to National Taxpayer Advocate	Date of enactment
7811(f)	1102(d)(1)(G)	Commissioner of Internal Revenue; other officials—conforming amendments relating to National Taxpayer Advocate	Date of enactment
7872(f)(2)(B)	6023(30)	Miscellaneous clerical and deadwood changes	Date of enactment
8021(e)	4001	Expansion of duties of the Joint Committee on Taxation	Requests made after date of enactment
8021(f)	4001	Expansion of duties of the Joint Committee on Taxation	Date of enactment
8022(3)	4002	Coordinated oversight reports	Date of enactment
9502(b)	6010(g)(2)	Airport and airway trust fund excise taxes—increased trust fund deposits	Taxes received in the Treasury on and after October 1, 1997
9502(e)	6023(31)	Miscellaneous clerical and deadwood changes	Date of enactment
9503(c)(1)	9015(a)	Highway trust fund	Date of enactment
9503(e)(3)	9015(a)	Highway trust fund	Date of enactment
9504(b)(2)(A), (B), (C)	9015(b)	Boat safety account and sport fish restoration account	Date of enactment
9504(c)	9015(c)	Boat safety account and sport fish restoration account	Date of enactment
9811(e)-(f)	6015(e)	Amendments to the Internal Revenue Code of 1986 to implement the Newborns' and Mothers' Health Protection Act of 1996 and the Mental Health Parity Act of 1996	Group health plans for plan years beginning on or after January 1, 1998

Effective Dates

Surface Transportation Revenue Act of 1998

¶ 20,005

This CCH-prepared table presents the general effective dates for major law provisions added, amended or repealed by the Surface Transportation Revenue Act of 1998 (P.L. 105-178), enacted June 9, 1998. Entries are listed in Code Section order.

Code Sec.	Act Sec.	Act Provision Subject	Effective Date
	9007	Additional qualified expenses available to nonAmtrak states—amendments to section 977(e)(1)(B) of the Taxpayer Relief Act of 1997	August 5, 1997
	9008	Delay in effective date of new requirement for approved diesel or kerosene terminals—amendment to section 1032(f) of the Taxpayer Relief Act of 1997	June 9, 1998
40(e)(1)	9003(a)(3)	Extension of tax benefits for alcohol fuels—credit for alcohol used as fuel	June 9, 1998
40(h)	9003(b)(1)	Modification of tax benefits for alcohol fuels	January 1, 2001
132(f)(2)(A), (B)	9010(b)(2)	Election to receive taxable cash compensation in lieu of nontaxable qualified transportation fringe benefits—inflation adjustment only after 1999	Tax years beginning after December 31, 1998
132(f)(2)(A)	9010(c)(1)	Election to receive taxable cash compensation in lieu of nontaxable qualified transportation fringe benefits—increase in maximum exclusion for employer-provided transit passes	Tax years beginning after December 31, 2001
132(f)(4)	9010(a)	Election to receive taxable cash compensation in lieu of nontaxable qualified transportation fringe benefits—no constructive receipt	Tax years beginning after December 31, 1997
132(f)(6)(A)	9010(c)(2)	Election to receive taxable cash compensation in lieu of nontaxable qualified transportation fringe benefits—increase in maximum exclusion for employer-provided transit passes	Tax years beginning after December 31, 2001
132(f)(6)	9010(b)(1)	Election to receive taxable cash compensation in lieu of nontaxable qualified transportation fringe benefits—inflation adjustment only after 1999	Tax years beginning after December 31, 1998

Code Sec.	Act Sec.	Act Provision Subject	Effective Date
4041(a)(1)(C)	9002(a)(1)(A)	Extension of highway-related taxes	June 9, 1998
4041(a)(1)(C)	9006(a)	Repeal of 1.25 cent tax rate on rail diesel fuel	June 9, 1998
4041(a)(2)(B)	9002(a)(1)(B)	Extension of highway-related taxes	June 9, 1998
4041(b)(2)(A)-(D)	9003(b)(2)(A)	Modification of tax benefits for alcohol fuels	January 1, 2001
4041(b)(2)(C)	9003(a)(1)(A)	Extension of tax benefits for alcohol fuels	June 9, 1998
4041(k)(3)	9003(a)(1)(B)	Extension of tax benefits for alcohol fuels	June 9, 1998
4041(m)(1)(A)	9002(a)(1)(C)	Extension of highway-related taxes	June 9, 1998
4051(c)	9002(a)(1)(D)	Extension of highway-related taxes	June 9, 1998
4071(d)	9002(a)(1)(E)	Extension of highway-related taxes	June 9, 1998
4081(c)(4)(A)	9003(b)(2)(B)	Modification of tax benefits for alcohol fuels	January 1, 2001
4081(c)(5)	9003(b)(2)(C)	Modification of tax benefits for alcohol fuels	January 1, 2001
4081(c)(8)	9003(a)(1)(C)	Extension of tax benefits for alcohol fuels	June 9, 1998
4081(d)(1)	9002(a)(1)(F)	Extension of highway-related taxes	June 9, 1998
4091(c)(1)	9003(b)(2)(D)	Modification of tax benefits for alcohol fuels	January 1, 2001
4091(c)(5)	9003(a)(1)(D)	Extension of tax benefits for alcohol fuels	June 9, 1998
4221(a)	9002(b)(1)	Extension of certain exemptions	June 9, 1998
4481(e)	9002(a)(1)(G)	Extension of highway-related taxes	June 9, 1998
4482(c)(4)	9002(a)(1)(H)	Extension of highway-related taxes	June 9, 1998
4483(g)	9002(b)(2)	Extension of certain exemptions	June 9, 1998
6156(e)(2)	9002(a)(2)(B)	Extension of highway-related taxes	June 9, 1998
6412(a)(1)	9002(a)(2)(A)	Extension of highway-related taxes	June 9, 1998
6421(d)(2)	9009(b)(3)	Simplified fuel tax refund procedures—conforming amendment	October 1, 1998
6421(f)(3)(B)	9006(b)(1)	Repeal of 1.25 cent tax rate on rail diesel fuel—conforming amendment	June 9, 1998
6427(f)(4)	9003(a)(2)	Extension of tax benefits for alcohol fuels—extension of refund authority	June 9, 1998
6427(i)(2)(A)	9009(a)	Simplified fuel tax refund procedures	October 1, 1998
6427(i)(4)-(5)	9009(b)(1)	Simplified fuel tax refund procedures—conforming amendment	October 1, 1998
6427(k)(2)	9009(b)(2)	Simplified fuel tax refund procedures—conforming amendment	October 1, 1998
6427(l)(3)(B)	9006(b)(2)	Repeal of 1.25 cent tax rate on rail diesel fuel—conforming amendment	June 9, 1998

Code Sec.	Act Sec.	Act Provision Subject	Effective Date
9503(b)(1)(C)-(F)	9002(f)(1)	Extension of highway-related taxes and trust fund—clerical amendment	June 9, 1998
9503(b)(4)(D)	9005(a)(1)	Aquatic resources trust fund—increased transfers	June 9, 1998
9503(b)(4)(D)	9011(b)(2)	Repeal of National Recreational Trails Trust Fund—conforming amendment	June 9, 1998
9503(b)(6)	9004(c)	Limitation on expenditure authority	June 9, 1998
9503(b)	9002(c)(1)	Extension of deposits into, and certain transfers from, trust fund	June 9, 1998
9503(c)(1)(C), (D)	9002(d)(1)(B)	Extension and expansion of expenditures from trust fund—highway account	June 9, 1998
9503(c)(1)	9002(d)(1)(A)	Extension and expansion of expenditures from trust fund—expansion of purposes	June 9, 1998
9503(c)(1)	9002(f)(4)	Extension of highway-related taxes and trust fund—clerical amendment	June 9, 1998
9503(c)(2)(A)	9002(f)(2), (3)	Extension of highway-related taxes and trust fund—clerical amendment	June 9, 1998
9503(c)(2), (3)	9002(c)(1)	Extension of deposits into, and certain transfers from, trust fund	June 9, 1998
9503(c)(3)	9002(c)(3)	Extension of deposits into, and certain transfers from, trust fund—conforming amendment	June 9, 1998
9503(c)(4)(A), (5)(A)	9002(c)(2)(A)	Extension of deposits into, and certain transfers from, trust fund—motorboat and small-engine fuel tax transfers	June 9, 1998
9503(c)(4)(A)	9005(a)(2)	Aquatic resources trust fund—increased transfers	June 9, 1998
9503(c)(6)	9011(b)(1)	Repeal of National Recreational Trails Trust Fund—conforming amendment	June 9, 1998
9503(c)(7)	9004(b)	Repeal of limitation on expenditures added by Taxpayer Relief Act of 1997	Taxes received in the Treasury after September 30, 1997
9503(e)(2)	9002(e)(1)	Technical correction relating to transfers to mass transit account	Taxes received in the Treasury after September 30, 1997
9503(e)(3)(A)-(C)	9002(d)(2)(B)	Extension and expansion of expenditures from trust fund—mass transit account	June 9, 1998
9503(e)(3)	9002(d)(2)(A)	Extension and expansion of expenditures from trust fund—mass transit account	June 9, 1998

¶ 20,005

Code Sec.	Act Sec.	Act Provision Subject	Effective Date
9503(e)(3)	9002(f)(5)	Extension of highway-related taxes and trust fund—clerical amendment	June 9, 1998
9503(e)(4)	9004(d)	Modification of mass transit account rules on adjustments of apportionments	June 9, 1998
9503(f)	9004(a)	Determination of trust fund balances after September 30, 1998	October 1, 1998
9504(b)(2)(A)	9005(b)(1)	Aquatic resources trust fund—expansion of expenditure authority from boat safety account	June 9, 1998
9504(b)(2)(A)	9005(f)(1)	Aquatic resources trust fund—clerical amendment	June 9, 1998
9504(b)(2)(B)	9005(b)(2)	Aquatic resources trust fund—expansion of expenditure authority from boat safety account	June 9, 1998
9504(b)(2)(B)	9005(f)(2)	Aquatic resources trust fund—clerical amendment	June 9, 1998
9504(b)(2)(B)-(C)	9005(b)(3)	Aquatic resources trust fund—expansion of expenditure authority from boat safety account	June 9, 1998
9504(b)(2)(C)	9005(f)(3)	Aquatic resources trust fund—clerical amendment	June 9, 1998
9504(c)	9005(c)	Aquatic resources trust fund—extension and expansion of expenditure authority from boat safety account	June 9, 1998
9504(c)	9005(f)(4)	Aquatic resources trust fund—clerical amendment	June 9, 1998
9504(d)-(e)	9005(d)	Aquatic resources trust fund—limitation on expenditure authority	June 9, 1998
9511	9011(a)	Repeal of National Recreational Trails Trust Fund	June 9, 1998

Code Section to Explanation Table
¶ 25,001

¶ 25,001

¶ **25,001**

Code Sections Added, Amended or Repealed

The list below notes all the Code Sections or subsections of the Internal Revenue Code that were added, amended or repealed by the IRS Restructuring and Reform Act of 1998 and the Surface Transportation Revenue Act of 1998 (P.L. 105-178). The first column indicates the Code Section added, amended or repealed and the second column indicates the Act Section. The Code Sections are listed under the pertinent Acts.

¶ 25,005

IRS Restructuring and Reform Act of 1998

Code Sec.	Act Sec.	Code Sec.	Act Sec.
1(g)(3)(C)-(D)	6007(f)(1)	162(a)	6012(a)
1(h)	6005(d)(1)	168(c)	6006(b)(2)
1(h)(5)	5001(a)(1)	168(c)(2)	6006(b)(1)
1(h)(6)(A)	5001(a)(2)	170(e)(6)(B)(iv)	6004(e)(2)
1(h)(7)(A)(i)-(ii)	5001(a)(3)	170(e)(6)(B)(vi)-(vii)	6004(e)(1)
1(h)(13)	5001(a)(4)	170(e)(6)(C)(ii)(I)	6004(e)(3)
23(b)(2)(A)	6018(f)(1)	170(e)(6)(F)	6004(e)(4)
23(c)	6008(d)(6)	196(c)(6)-(8)	6020(a)
24(d)(1)-(5)	6003(a)(1)(A)-(C)	219(g)(1)	6005(a)(1)(A)
24(d)(3)	6003(a)(2)	219(g)(7)	6005(a)(1)(B)
25(e)(1)(C)	6008(d)(7)	221(d)	6004(b)(2)
32(c)(1)(F)	6021(a)	221(e)(1)	6004(b)(1)
32(c)(1)(G)	6021(b)(2)	264(a)(3)	6010(o)(1)
32(c)(2)(B)(v)	6010(p)(2)	264(a)(4)	6010(o)(2)
32(c)(3)(A)(ii)-(iv)	6021(b)(3)	264(f)(4)(E)	6010(o)(3)(A)
32(c)(3)(D)(i)	6021(b)(1)	264(f)(5)(A)(iv)	6010(o)(4)(A)
32(c)(5)(A)	6010(p)(1)(A)	264(f)(8)(A)	6010(o)(5)
32(c)(5)(B)(iii)	6010(p)(1)(B)	280F(a)(1)(C)(ii)	6009(c)
32(c)(5)(B)(iv)(III)	6010(p)(1)(C)	304(b)(5)(B)-(C)	6010(d)(1)
32(c)(5)(C)	6010(p)(1)(C)	304(b)(6)	6010(d)(2)
32(m)-(n)	6003(b)(1)	351(c)	6010(c)(3)(A)
34(b)	6023(24)(B)	351(g)(1)(A)-(C)	6010(e)(1)
39(a)(2)	6010(n)(1)-(2)	354(a)(2)(C)(ii)(III)	6010(e)(2)
42(j)(4)(D)	6004(g)(5)	355(e)(3)(A)	6010(c)(2)(A)
45A(b)(1)(B)	6023(1)	355(e)(3)(A)(iv)	6010(c)(2)(B)
49(b)(4)	6004(g)(6)	368(a)(2)(H)(ii)	6010(c)(3)(B)
50(a)(5)(C)	6004(g)(7)	402(c)(4)(A)-(C)	6005(c)(2)(A)
55(b)(3)	6005(d)(2)	403(b)(8)(B)	6005(c)(2)(B)
55(e)(1)	6006(a)	404(a)(9)(C)-(D)	6015(d)
57(a)(7)	6005(d)(3)	404(a)(11)	7001(a)
59(a)(3)-(4)	6011(a)	408(d)(7)	6018(b)(2)
59(b)	6023(2)	408(d)(7)(B)	6018(b)(1)
66(c)	3201(b)	408(p)(2)(C)(i)(II)	6016(a)(1)(C)(i)
72(e)(9)	6004(d)(3)(B)	408(p)(2)(D)(i)	6016(a)(1)(A)
72(n)	6023(3)	408(p)(2)(D)(iii)	6016(a)(1)(C)(ii)
72(t)(2)(A)(iv)-(vii)	3436(a)	408(p)(8)-(9)	6015(a)
72(t)(3)(A)	6023(4)	408(p)(10)	6016(a)(1)(B)
72(t)(8)(E)	6005(c)(1)(A)-(B)	408A(c)(3)(A)	6005(b)(1)
108(f)(2)	6004(f)(1)	408A(c)(3)(A)(ii)	6005(b)(2)(A)
108(f)(3)	6004(f)(2)	408A(c)(3)(B)	6005(b)(2)(B)(i)-(ii)
119(b)(4)	5002(a)	408A(c)(3)(C)(i)	6005(b)(2)(C)
121(b)(2)	6005(e)(1)	408A(c)(3)(C)(i)	7004(a)
121(c)(1)	6005(e)(2)	408A(d)(1)	6005(b)(5)(B)
135(c)(2)(C)	6004(d)(9)(A)-(B)	408A(d)(2)(B)	6005(b)(3)(A)
135(c)(3)	6004(c)(1)	408A(d)(2)(C)	6005(b)(3)(B)
135(d)(2)	6004(d)(4)	408A(d)(3)(A)(iii)	6005(b)(4)(A)
142(f)(3)(A)(ii)	6023(5)	408A(d)(3)(D)-(G)	6005(b)(6)(B)

Code Sec.	Act Sec.	Code Sec.	Act Sec.
408A(d)(3)(F)-(G)	6005(b)(4)(B)	1397E(h)	6004(g)(3)
408A(d)(4)	6005(b)(5)(A)	1400(b)(2)(B)	6008(a)
408A(d)(6)	6005(b)(6)(A)	1400A(a)	6008(b)
408A(d)(7)	6005(b)(7)	1400B(b)(5)	6008(c)(1)
408A(f)	6005(b)(9)	1400B(b)(6)	6008(c)(2)
475(c)(4)	7003(a)	1400B(c)	6008(c)(3)
475(f)(1)(D)	6010(a)(3)	1400B(d)(2)	6008(c)(4)
475(g)(1)-(3)	7003(b)	1400C(b)(1)	6008(d)(1)
501(n)(3)	6023(6)	1400C(c)(1)	6008(d)(2)
501(o)	6023(7)	1400C(e)(2)(B)	6008(d)(3)
512(b)(13)(A)	6010(j)(1)	1400C(e)(3)	6008(d)(4)
512(b)(13)(B)(i)(I)	6010(j)(2)	1400C(i)	6008(d)(5)
512(b)(17)(B)(ii)(II)	6023(8)	2001(f)	6007(e)(2)(B)
529(c)(3)(A)	6004(c)(2)	2031(c)(6)	6007(g)(2)
529(e)(2)	6004(c)(3)	2031(c)(9)-(10)	6007(g)(1)
530(b)(1)	6004(d)(1)	2033A	6007(b)(1)(A)
530(b)(1)(E)	6004(d)(2)(A)	2057	6007(b)(1)(A)-(B)
530(d)(1)	6004(d)(3)(A)	2057(b)(2)(A)	6007(b)(1)(C)
530(d)(2)(D)	6004(d)(5)	2057(b)(3)	6007(b)(2)
530(d)(4)(B)(ii)-(iv)	6004(d)(6)	2057(c)	6007(b)(1)(D)
530(d)(4)(C)	6004(d)(7)	2057(e)(1)	6007(b)(5)(A)
530(d)(5)	6004(d)(8)(A)	2057(e)(2)	6007(b)(3)(C)
530(d)(6)	6004(d)(8)(B)	2057(e)(2)(C)	6007(b)(3)(A)
530(d)(7)	6004(d)(2)(B)	2057(e)(2)(D)(ii)	6007(b)(3)(B)
530(d)(8)	6004(d)(2)(C)	2057(f)(2)	6007(b)(4)(A)
543(d)(5)(A)(ii)	6023(9)	2057(f)(2)(C)	6007(b)(4)(B)
641(c)-(d)	6007(f)(2)	2057(f)(3)	6007(b)(5)(A)
645	6013(a)(1)	2057(g)(1)	6007(b)(6)
646	6013(a)(1)	2057(i)(3)(L)-(P)	6007(b)(7)
664(d)(1)(C)	6010(r)	2504(c)	6007(e)(2)(B)[(C)]
664(d)(2)(C)	6010(r)	2631(c)	6007(a)(1)
672(f)(3)(B)	6011(c)(1)	2652(b)(1)	6013(a)(3)
685(b)	6013(b)(1)	2652(b)(1)	6013(a)(4)(A)
685(f)	6013(b)(2)	2654(b)	6013(a)(4)(B)
751(c)	6010(m)	3121(a)(5)(F)	6023(13)(A)
774(d)(2)	6012(c)	3121(a)(5)(G)	6023(13)(B)
853(c)	6010(k)(2)	3121(a)(5)(I)	6023(13)(C)
853(e)-(f)	6010(k)(1)	3401(a)(19)	6023(14)
857(d)(3)(A)	6012(g)	3401(a)(21)	6023(15)
871(f)(2)(B)	6023(10)	4041(l)	6010(g)(1)
901(k)(4)(A)	6010(k)(3)	4052(f)(2)	6014(c)
991	6011(e)(1)	4082(d)(1)	6010(h)(3)
1017(a)(2)	6023(11)	4082(d)(3)	6010(h)(4)
1045(a)	6005(f)(1)(A)-(B)	4091(a)(2)	6014(d)
1045(b)(5)	6005(f)(2)	4092(b)	6023(16)
1059(g)(1)	6010(b)	4101(e)(1)	6010(h)(5)
1223(11)-(12)	5001(a)(5)	4221(c)	6023(17)
1223(11)-(12)	6005(d)(4)	4222(d)	6023(17)
1235(a)	5001(a)(5)	4251(d)(3)	6010(i)
1235(a)	6005(d)(4)	4946(c)(5)-(7)	1101(c)(1)
1250(d)(4)(D)	6023(12)	4973	6023(18)(A)
1259(b)(2)(A)-(C)	6010(a)(1)(A)-(C)	4973(b)(1)(A)	6005(b)(8)(B)(i)
1259(d)(1)	6010(a)(2)	4973(b)(2)(C)	6005(b)(8)(B)(ii)
1291(d)(1)	6011(c)(2)	4973(e)(1)	6004(d)(10)(A)
1296(d)	6011(c)(3)	4973(e)(2)(B)-(C)	6004(d)(10)(B)
1297(e)(4)	6011(b)(1)	4973(f)(1)(A)	6005(b)(8)(A)(i)
1297(e)-(f)	6011(d)	4973(f)(2)(B)	6005(b)(8)(A)(ii)
1298(a)(2)(B)	6011(b)(2)	4975(c)(3)	6023(19)(A)
1361(e)(4)	6007(f)(3)	4975(i)	6023(19)(B)
1397E(d)(4)(B)	6004(g)(2)	5041(b)(6)	6009(a)
1397E(g)	6004(g)(4)	5043(a)(2)	6014(b)(1)

Code Sec.	Act Sec.	Code Sec.	Act Sec.
5044(a)	6014(b)(2)	6320	3401(a)
5054(a)(1)	6014(a)(1)(A)-(B)	6323(b)(4)	3435(a)(1)(A)
5054(a)(2)	6014(a)(2)	6323(b)(7)	3435(a)(1)(B)
5056	6014(a)(3)	6323(b)(10)	3435(b)(1)-(3)
5364	6014(b)(3)	6323(i)(4)	3435(a)(2)
6011(f)-(g)	2001(c)	6323(j)(1)(D)	1102(d)(1)(A)
6013(e)	3201(e)(1)	6325(b)(4)	3106(a)
6013(g)(1)(A)	6011(e)(2)	6330	3401(b)
6013(g)(5)	6011(e)(2)	6331(h)(1)	6010(f)
6013(h)(1)	6011(e)(2)	6331(i)-(j)	3433(a)
6015	3201(a)	6331(j)-(k)	3444(a)
6038(a)(2)	6011(f)(1)	6331(k)-(l)	3462(b)
6038(a)(3)	6011(f)(2)	6334(a)(2)	3431(a)
6038(e)(4)	6011(f)(3)	6334(a)(3)	3431(b)
6039(a)(1)	6023(20)	6334(a)(13)	3445(a)
6050R(b)(2)(A)	6023(21)	6334(e)	3445(b)
6050S(a)	6004(a)(2)	6334(g)(1)	3431(c)(1)-(2)
6050S(b)(2)(C)(ii)-		6335(e)(1)(A)(i)	3441(a)
(iv)	3712(a)(1)	6335(e)(4)	3441(b)
6050S(b)(2)(C)(iii)	3712(a)(2)	6340(a)	3442(a)(1)(A)-(B)
6050S(b)(2)(C)(iv)	3712(a)(3)	6340(c)	3442(a)(2)
6050S(d)(2)	3712(b)(1)	6343(d)(2)(D)	1102(d)(1)(B)
6050S(e)	3712(b)(2)	6343(e)	3432(a)
6061	2003(a)(1)	6344(b)	1104(b)(1)
6061(b)	2003(a)(2)	6401(b)(1)	6022(a)
6071(b)-(c)	2002(a)	6402(a)	3711(c)(1)
6103(d)(5)	6009(d)	6402(d)(2)	3711(c)(2)
6103(e)(1)(A)(ii)-(iv)	6007(f)(4)	6402(e)-(k)	3711(a)
6103(e)(6)	6019(c)	6402(f)	3711(c)(3)(A)-(B)
6103(f)(5)	3708(a)	6402(h)	3711(c)(4)
6103(h)(4)(A)	6023(22)	6402(j)	3505(a)
6103(h)(5)	1101(b)	6404(g)-(h)	3305(a)
6103(k)(8)-(9)	6012(b)(2)	6404(h)-(i)	3309(a)
6103(l)(10)	3711(b)(1)	6416(b)(5)	6023(23)
6103(l)(10)	3711(b)(2)	6421(a)	6023(24)(C)
6103(l)(17)	3702(a)	6421(b)	6023(24)(C)
6103(p)(3)(A)	3702(b)(1)	6421(c)	6010(g)(3)(A)-(B)
6103(p)(3)(A)	6012(b)(4)	6421(i)-(k)	6023(24)(A)
6103(p)(4)	3702(b)(2)	6427(d)	6016(b)(1)-(2)
6103(p)(4)(F)(ii)	3702(b)(3)	6427(f)(3)	6023(25)
6104(b)	6019(a)	6427(i)(1)	6023(26)(B)
6104(e)(1)(C)	6019(b)	6427(i)(2)(A)	6023(26)(B)
6109(a)	3710(a)	6427(i)(2)(B)	6017(a)
6110(b)(1)	3509(a)	6427(m)-(r)	6023(26)(A)
6110(f)(1)	3509(c)(1)	6427(q)(2)	6023(16)
6110(i)-(m)	3509(b)	6501(c)(4)(A)-(B)	3461(b)(1)-(2)
6110(j)(1)(B)	3509(c)(2)	6501(c)(9)	6007(e)(2)(A)
6110(j)(2)	3509(c)(2)	6501(m)	6023(27)
6110(k)(1)(B)	3509(c)(3)	6502(a)	3461(a)(1)-(2)
6159(c)-(d)	3467(a)	6503(f)	3106(b)(3)
6159(d)[(e)]	3462(c)(2)	6511(h)-(i)	3202(a)
6166(b)(7)(A)(iii)	6007(c)(1)	6512(a)(4)-(6)	3464(b)
6166(b)(8)(A)(iii)	6007(c)(2)	6512(b)(1)	3464(c)
6211(c)	6012(f)(1)-(2)	6601(f)	3301(b)
6212(a)	1102(b)	6611(g)(1)	6010(l)
6213(a)	3463(b)	6621(a)(1)(B)	3302(a)
6213(a)	3464(a)(1)-(2)	6621(d)	3301(a)
6230(c)(5)(A)	3201(e)(2)	6631	3308(a)
6231(a)(7)	3507(a)	6651(h)	3303(a)
6304	3466(a)	6656(c)(2)	3304(b)(1)
6311(e)(1)	6012(b)(1)	6656(e)	3304(a)

Code Sec.	Act Sec.	Code Sec.	Act Sec.
6656(e)(1)	3304(c)	7525	3411(a)
6672(b)(1)	3307(a)	7526	3601(a)
6672(b)(2)	3307(b)(1)	7602(c)-(e)	3417(a)
6672(b)(3)	3307(b)(2)	7602(d)	3412
6724(c)	6012(d)	7603(a)-(b)	3416(a)
6724(d)(1)(B)(xv)-(xvii)	6010(o)(4)(B)	7603(b)(2)(H)-(J)	3413(c)
6724(d)(2)(Y)-(AA)	6010(o)(4)(C)	7608(b)(1)	1103(e)(4)
6751	3306(a)	7609(a)(1)	3415(a)
7122(c)	3462(a)	7609(a)(3)-(5)	3415(c)(1)
7122(d)	3462(c)(1)	7609(c)	3415(c)(2)
7123	3465(a)(1)	7609(e)(2)	3415(c)(3)
7124	3465(a)(1)	7609(f)	3415(c)(4)(A)
7213(d)-(e)	3413(b)	7609(f)(3)	3415(c)(4)(B)
7217	1105(a)	7609(g)	3415(c)(5)
7421(a)	3201(e)(3)	7609(i)	3415(c)(6)(A)
7422(j)-(k)	3104(a)	7609(i)(1)	3415(c)(6)(B)
7426(a)(4)	3106(b)(1)	7609(i)(2)	3415(c)(6)(C)(i)-(ii)
7426(b)(5)	3106(b)(2)(A)	7609(i)(3)	3415(c)(6)(D)
7426(g)(1)-(3)	3106(b)(2)(B)	7609(j)	3415(b)
7426(h)-(i)	3102(b)	7611(f)(1)	1102(e)(3)
7429(a)(1)	3434(a)	7612	3413(a)
7430(b)(4)-(5)	6012(h)	7613	3413(a)
7430(c)(1)(B)(iii)	3101(a)(1)	7702B(e)(2)	6023(28)
7430(c)(1)(B)(iii)	3101(a)(2)	7704(g)(3)(C)	6009(b)(1)
7430(c)(2)	3101(b)	7802	1101(a)
7430(c)(3)	3101(c)	7803	1102(a)
7430(c)(4)(B)(iii)-(iv)	3101(d)	7804	1104(a)
7430(c)(4)(D)	6014(e)	7805(d)	3704
7430(c)(4)(E)	3101(e)(1)	7811(a)	1102(c)
7430(g)	3101(e)(2)	7811(b)(2)(D)	1102(d)(1)(C)
7431(c)(2)-(3)	3101(f)	7811(c)	1102(d)(1)(D)
7431(g)-(h)	6012(b)(3)	7811(d)(1)	1102(d)(2)
7433(a)	3102(a)(1)(A)	7811(d)(2)	1102(d)(1)(E)
7433(b)	3102(a)(1)(B)(i)-(ii)	7811(e)	1102(d)(1)(F)
7433(b)	3102(c)(2)	7811(e)-(f)	1102(d)(3)
7433(d)(1)	3102(a)(2)	7811(f)	1102(d)(1)(G)
7433(e)	3102(c)(1)	7872(f)(2)(B)	6023(30)
7434(b)(3)	6023(29)	8021(e)-(f)	4001(a)
7436(c)(1)	3103(b)(1)	8022(3)	4002(a)
7443[A](b)(3)-(5)	3401(c)(1)	9502(b)	6010(g)(2)
7443[A](c)	3401(c)(2)	9502(e)	6023(31)
7443A(b)(3)	3103(b)(1)	9503(c)(1)	9015(a)
7463	3103(a)	9503(e)(3)	9015(a)
7479(a)(1)-(2)	6007(d)	9504(b)(2)(A)	9015(b)
7479(c)	3104(b)	9504(b)(2)(B)	9015(b)
7491	3001(a)	9504(b)(2)(C)	9015(b)
7502(c)	2003(b)	9504(c)	9015(b)
		9811(e)-(f)	6015(e)

¶ **25,005**

Surface Transportation Revenue Act of 1998

Code Sec.	Act Sec.	Code Sec.	Act Sec.
40(e)(1)	903(a)(3)(A)-(B)	6427(f)(4)	903(a)(2)
40(h)	903(b)(1)	6427(i)(2)(A)	909(a)
132(f)(2)(A)	910(c)(1)	6427(i)(4)-(5)	909(b)(1)
132(f)(2)(A)-(B)	910(b)(2)(A)-(B)	6427(k)(2)	909(b)(2)
132(f)(4)	910(a)(1)	6427(l)(3)(B)(ii)-(iii)	906(b)(2)(A)-(B)
132(f)(6)	910(b)(1)	9503(b)	902(c)(1)(A)-(B)
132(f)(6)(A)	910(c)(2)	9503(b)(1)(C)-(F)	902(f)(1)
4041(a)(1)(C)(ii)(II)-		9503(b)(4)(D)	905(a)(1)
(III)	906(a)(1)-(2)	9503(b)(4)(D)	911(b)(2)
4041(a)(1)(C)(iii)(I)	902(a)(1)(A)	9503(b)(6)	904(c)
4041(a)(2)(B)	902(a)(1)(B)	9503(c)(1)	902(d)(1)(A)
4041(b)(2)	903(b)(2)(A)i)-(ii)	9503(c)(1)	902(d)(1)(B)(i)-(ii)
4041(b)(2)(C)	903(a)(1)(A)	9503(c)(2)(A)(i)(II)-	
4041(k)(3)	903(a)(1)(B)	(IV)	902(f)(2)
4041(m)(1)(A)	902(a)(1)(C)	9503(c)(2)(A)(ii)	902(f)(3)
4051(c)	902(a)(1)(D)	9503(c)(2)-(3)	902(c)(1)(A)-(B)
4071(d)	902(a)(1)(E)	9503(c)(3)	902(c)(3)
4081(c)(4)(A)	903(b)(2)(B)	9503(c)(4)(A)(i) and	
4081(c)(5)	903(b)(2)(C)	(5)(A)	902(c)(2)(A)
4081(c)(8)	903(a)(1)(C)	9503(c)(4)(A)(ii)	905(a)(2)
4081(d)(1)	902(a)(1)(F)	9503(c)(6)	911(b)(1)
4091(c)(1)	903(b)(2)(D)	9503(c)(7)	904(b)(1)
4091(c)(5)	903(a)(1)(D)	9503(e)(2)	902(e)(1)
4221(a)	902(b)(1)	9503(e)(3)	902(d)(2)(A)
4481(e)	902(a)(1)(G)	9503(e)(3)	902(d)(2)(B)(i)-(iii)
4482(c)(4)	902(a)(1)(H)	9503(e)(4)	904(d)
4482(d)	902(a)(1)(I)	9503(f)	904(a)(1)
4483(g)	902(b)(2)	9504(b)(2)	905(b)(1)-(3)
6156(e)(2)	902(a)(2)(B)	9504(c)	905(c)(1)-(2)
6412(a)(1)	902(a)(2)(A)(i)-(ii)	9504(d)-(e)	905(d)
6421(d)(2)	909(b)(3)	9511	911(a)
6421(f)(3)(B)(ii)-(iii)	906(b)(1)(A)-(B)		

Table of Amendments to Other Acts

¶ 25,010

IRS Restructuring and Reform Act of 1998

Amended Act Sec.	H.R. 2676 Act Sec.	Par. (¶)	Amended Act Sec.	H.R. 2676 Act Sec.	Par. (¶)
TITLE 5 U.S.C.			**TAXPAYER RELIEF ACT OF 1997—**	continued	
5109(b)-(c)	1102(e)(2)	8015	1032(a)	6010(h)(1)	8255
9501	1201(a)	8025	1032(e)(12)(A)	6010(h)(2)	8255
9502	1201(a)	8025	1041(b)(2)	6010(j)(3)	8255
9503	1201(a)	8025	1084(d)	6010(o)(3)(B)	8255
9504	1201(a)	8025	1085(a)(3)	6010(p)(3)	8255
9505	1201(a)	8025	1088(b)(2)(C)	6010(q)	8255
9506	1201(a)	8025	1144(c)(1)-(2)	6011(g)	8260
9507	1201(a)	8025	1213(b)	6012(b)(5)	8265
9508	1201(a)	8025	1226	6012(e)	8265
9509	1201(a)	8025	1505(d)(2)	6015(b)	8270
9510	1201(a)	8025	1529(a)	6015(c)(1)	8270
INSPECTOR GENERAL ACT OF 1978			1529(b)(1)(B)	6015(c)(2)	8270
2(3)(A)-(B)	1103(a)	8020	1601(d)(4)(A)	6016(a)(2)(A)	8275
8D(a)(1)-(3)	1103(e)(2)(A)	8020	1601(d)(4)(A)(ii)	6016(a)(2)(B)	8275
8D(a)(4)	1103(b)(1)	8020	**SMALL BUSINESS JOB PROTECTION ACT OF 1996**		
8D(b)	1103(e)(1)	8020	1116(b)(2)(C)	6018(a)	8280
8D(b)	1103(e)(2)(B)	8020	1431(c)(1)(E)	6018(c)	8280
8D(b)(1)-(3)	1103(b)(2)(A)-(B)	8020	1604(b)(3)	6018(d)(1)-(2)	8280
8D(c)-(d)	1103(e)(2)(C)	8020	1609(h)(1)	6018(e)	8280
8D(e)(1)-(3)	1103(b)(3)(A)-(D)	8020	1807(c)(3)	6018(f)(2)	8280
8D(f)	1103(b)(4)	8020	1903(b)	6018(g)	8280
8D(g)	1103(b)(5)	8020	**TRADE EXPANSION ACT OF 1962**		
8D(g)-(h)	1103(b)(6)(A)-(C)	8020	251	5003(b)(1)	8225
8D(h)-(l)	1103(b)(7)	8020	**TRADE ACT OF 1974**		
8G	1103(e)(3)(A)-(C)	8020	402	5003(b)(2)(A)	8225
9(a)(1)(L)(i)-(ii)	1103(c)(1)(A)-(C)	8020	601(9)	5003(b)(2)(B)	8225
TECHNICAL AND MISCELLANEOUS REVENUE ACT OF 1988			**UNITED STATES CANADA FREE-TRADE AGREEMENT IMPLEMENTATION ACT OF 1988**		
6231	1204(d)	8040	302(a)(3)(C)	5003(b)(3)	8225
TAXPAYER RELIEF ACT OF 1997			**NORTH AMERICAN FREE TRADE AGREEMENT IMPLEMENTATION ACT**		
201(c)(2)(A)	6004(a)(3)	8239	202(n)	5003(b)(4)	8225
226(a)	6004(g)(1)	8239	**URUGUAY ROUND AGREEMENTS ACT**		
301(a)(2)	6005(a)(2)	8240	135(a)(2)	5003(b)(5)	8225
302(b)	6005(b)(8)(C)	8240			
312(d)[e](2)	6005(e)(3)	8240			
501(f)	6007(a)(2)	8240			
506(e)(1)	6007(e)(1)	8245			
977(e)(2)	6009(e)	8250			
1001(d)(3)(C)	6010(a)(4)	8255			
1012(d)(1)	6010(c)(1)	8255			

¶ 25,010

Surface Transportation Revenue Act of 1998

Table of Act Sections Not Amending Internal Revenue Code Sections

¶ 25,015

IRS Restructuring and Reform Act of 1998

Act Sections Amending Code Sections
¶ 25,020

IRS Restructuring and Reform Act of 1998

Act Sec.	Code Sec.	Act Sec.	Code Sec.
1101(a)	7802	3201(e)(3)	7421(a)
1101(b)	6103(h)(5)	3202(a)	6511(h)-(i)
1101(c)(1)	4946(c)(5)-(7)	3301(a)	6621(d)
1102(a)	7803	3301(b)	6601(f)
1102(b)	6212(a)	3302(a)	6621(a)(1)(B)
1102(c)	7811(a)	3303(a)	6651(h)
1102(d)(1)(A)	6323(j)(1)(D)	3304(a)	6656(e)
1102(d)(1)(B)	6343(d)(2)(D)	3304(b)(1)	6656(c)(2)
1102(d)(1)(C)	7811(b)(2)(D)	3304(c)	6656(e)(1)
1102(d)(1)(D)	7811(c)	3305(a)	6404(g)-(h)
1102(d)(1)(E)	7811(d)(2)	3306(a)	6751
1102(d)(1)(F)	7811(e)	3307(a)	6672(b)(1)
1102(d)(1)(G)	7811(f)	3307(b)(1)	6672(b)(2)
1102(d)(2)	7811(d)(1)	3307(b)(2)	6672(b)(3)
1102(d)(3)	7811(e)-(f)	3308(a)	6631
1102(e)(3)	7611(f)(1)	3309(a)	6404(h)-(i)
1103(e)(4)	7608(b)(1)	3401(a)	6320
1104(a)	7804	3401(b)	6330
1104(b)(1)	6344(b)	3401(c)(1)	7443[A](b)(3)-(5)
1105(a)	7217	3401(c)(2)	7443[A](c)
2001(c)	6011(f)-(g)	3411(a)	7525
2002(a)	6071(b)-(c)	3412	7602(d)
2003(a)(1)	6061	3413(a)	7612
2003(a)(2)	6061(b)	3413(a)	7613
2003(b)	7502(c)	3413(b)	7213(d)-(e)
3001(a)	7491	3413(c)	7603(b)(2)(H)-(J)
3101(a)(1)	7430(c)(1)(B)(iii)	3415(a)	7609(a)(1)
3101(a)(2)	7430(c)(1)(B)(iii)	3415(b)	7609(j)
3101(b)	7430(c)(2)	3415(c)(1)	7609(a)(3)-(5)
3101(c)	7430(c)(3)	3415(c)(2)	7609(c)
3101(d)	7430(c)(4)(B)(iii)-(iv)	3415(c)(3)	7609(e)(2)
3101(e)(1)	7430(c)(4)(E)	3415(c)(4)(A)	7609(f)
3101(e)(2)	7430(g)	3415(c)(4)(B)	7609(f)(3)
3101(f)	7431(c)(2)-(3)	3415(c)(5)	7609(g)
3102(a)(1)(A)	7433(a)	3415(c)(6)(A)	7609(i)
3102(a)(1)(B)(i)-(ii)	7433(b)	3415(c)(6)(B)	7609(i)(1)
3102(a)(2)	7433(d)(1)	3415(c)(6)(C)(i)-(ii)	7609(i)(2)
3102(b)	7426(h)-(i)	3415(c)(6)(D)	7609(i)(3)
3102(c)(1)	7433(e)	3416(a)	7603(a)-(b)
3102(c)(2)	7433(b)	3417(a)	7602(c)-(e)
3103(a)	7463	3431(a)	6334(a)(2)
3103(b)(1)	7436(c)(1)	3431(b)	6334(a)(3)
3103(b)(1)	7443A(b)(3)	3431(c)(1)-(2)	6334(g)(1)
3104(a)	7422(j)-(k)	3432(a)	6343(e)
3104(b)	7479(c)	3433(a)	6331(i)-(j)
3106(a)	6325(b)(4)	3434(a)	7429(a)(1)
3106(b)(1)	7426(a)(4)	3435(a)(1)(A)	6323(b)(4)
3106(b)(2)(A)	7426(b)(5)	3435(a)(1)(B)	6323(b)(7)
3106(b)(2)(B)	7426(g)(1)-(3)	3435(a)(2)	6323(i)(4)
3106(b)(3)	6503(f)	3435(b)(1)-(3)	6323(b)(10)
3201(a)	6015	3436(a)	72(t)(2)(A)(iv)-(vii)
3201(b)	66(c)	3441(a)	6335(e)(1)(A)(i)
3201(e)(1)	6013(e)	3441(b)	6335(e)(4)
3201(e)(2)	6230(c)(5)(A)	3442(a)(1)(A)-(B)	6340(a)

Act Sec.	Code Sec.	Act Sec.	Code Sec.
3442(a)(2)	6340(c)	6004(c)(1)	135(c)(3)
3444(a)	6331(j)-(k)	6004(c)(2)	529(c)(3)(A)
3445(a)	6334(a)(13)	6004(c)(3)	529(e)(2)
3445(b)	6334(e)	6004(d)(1)	530(b)(1)
3461(a)(1)-(2)	6502(a)	6004(d)(2)(A)	530(b)(1)(E)
3461(b)(1)-(2)	6501(c)(4)(A)-(B)	6004(d)(2)(B)	530(d)(7)
3462(a)	7122(c)	6004(d)(2)(C)	530(d)(8)
3462(b)	6331(k)-(l)	6004(d)(3)(A)	530(d)(1)
3462(c)(1)	7122(d)	6004(d)(3)(B)	72(e)(9)
3462(c)(2)	6159(d)[(e)]	6004(d)(4)	135(d)(2)
3463(b)	6213(a)	6004(d)(5)	530(d)(2)(D)
3464(a)(1)-(2)	6213(a)	6004(d)(6)	530(d)(4)(B)(ii)-(iv)
3464(b)	6512(a)(4)-(6)	6004(d)(7)	530(d)(4)(C)
3464(c)	6512(b)(1)	6004(d)(8)(A)	530(d)(5)
3465(a)(1)	7123	6004(d)(8)(B)	530(d)(6)
3465(a)(1)	7124	6004(d)(9)(A)-(B)	135(c)(2)(C)
3466(a)	6304	6004(d)(10)(A)	4973(e)(1)
3467(a)	6159(c)-(d)	6004(d)(10)(B)	4973(e)(2)(B)-(C)
3505(a)	6402(j)	6004(e)(1)	170(e)(6)(B)(vi)-(vii)
3507(a)	6231(a)(7)	6004(e)(2)	170(e)(6)(B)(iv)
3509(a)	6110(b)(1)	6004(e)(3)	170(e)(6)(C)(ii)(I)
3509(b)	6110(i)-(m)	6004(e)(4)	170(e)(6)(F)
3509(c)(1)	6110(f)(1)	6004(f)(1)	108(f)(2)
3509(c)(2)	6110(j)(1)(B)	6004(f)(2)	108(f)(3)
3509(c)(2)	6110(j)(2)	6004(g)(2)	1397E(d)(4)(B)
3509(c)(3)	6110(k)(1)(B)	6004(g)(3)	1397E(h)
3601(a)	7526	6004(g)(4)	1397E(g)
3702(a)	6103(l)(17)	6004(g)(5)	42(j)(4)(D)
3702(b)(1)	6103(p)(3)(A)	6004(g)(6)	49(b)(4)
3702(b)(2)	6103(p)(4)	6004(g)(7)	50(a)(5)(C)
3702(b)(3)	6103(p)(4)(F)(ii)	6005(a)(1)(A)	219(g)(1)
3704	7805(d)	6005(a)(1)(B)	219(g)(7)
3708(a)	6103(f)(5)	6005(b)(1)	408A(c)(3)(A)
3710(a)	6109(a)	6005(b)(2)(A)	408A(c)(3)(A)(ii)
3711(a)	6402(e)-(k)	6005(b)(2)(B)(i)-(ii)	408A(c)(3)(B)
3711(b)(1)	6103(l)(10)	6005(b)(2)(C)	408A(c)(3)(C)(i)
3711(b)(2)	6103(l)(10)	6005(b)(3)(A)	408A(d)(2)(B)
3711(c)(1)	6402(a)	6005(b)(3)(B)	408A(d)(2)(C)
3711(c)(2)	6402(d)(2)	6005(b)(4)(A)	408A(d)(3)(A)(iii)
3711(c)(3)(A)-(B)	6402(f)	6005(b)(4)(B)	408A(d)(3)(F)-(G)
3711(c)(4)	6402(h)	6005(b)(5)(A)	408A(d)(4)
3712(a)(1)	6050S(b)(2)(C)(ii)-(iv)	6005(b)(5)(B)	408A(d)(1)
3712(a)(2)	6050S(b)(2)(C)(iii)	6005(b)(6)(A)	408A(d)(6)
3712(a)(3)	6050S(b)(2)(C)(iv)	6005(b)(6)(B)	408A(d)(3)(D)-(G)
3712(b)(1)	6050S(d)(2)	6005(b)(7)	408A(d)(7)
3712(b)(2)	6050S(e)	6005(b)(8)(A)(i)	4973(f)(1)(A)
4001(a)	8021(e)-(f)	6005(b)(8)(A)(ii)	4973(f)(2)(B)
4002(a)	8022(3)	6005(b)(8)(B)(i)	4973(b)(1)(A)
5001(a)(1)	1(h)(5)	6005(b)(8)(B)(ii)	4973(b)(2)(C)
5001(a)(2)	1(h)(6)(A)	6005(b)(9)	408A(f)
5001(a)(3)	1(h)(7)(A)(i)-(ii)	6005(c)(1)(A)-(B)	72(t)(8)(E)
5001(a)(4)	1(h)(13)	6005(c)(2)(A)	402(c)(4)(A)-(C)
5001(a)(5)	1223(11)-(12)	6005(c)(2)(B)	403(b)(8)(B)
5001(a)(5)	1235(a)	6005(d)(1)	1(h)
5002(a)	119(b)(4)	6005(d)(2)	55(b)(3)
6003(a)(1)(A)-(C)	24(d)(1)-(5)	6005(d)(3)	57(a)(7)
6003(a)(2)	24(d)(3)	6005(d)(4)	1223(11)-(12)
6003(b)(1)	32(m)-(n)	6005(d)(4)	1235(a)
6004(a)(2)	6050S(a)	6005(e)(1)	121(b)(2)
6004(b)(1)	221(e)(1)	6005(e)(2)	121(c)(1)
6004(b)(2)	221(d)	6005(f)(1)(A)-(B)	1045(a)

¶ **25,020**

Act Sec.	Code Sec.	Act Sec.	Code Sec.
6005(f)(2)	1045(b)(5)	6010(g)(1)	4041(l)
6006(a)	55(e)(1)	6010(g)(2)	9502(b)
6006(b)(1)	168(c)(2)	6010(g)(3)(A)-(B)	6421(c)
6006(b)(2)	168(c)	6010(h)(3)	4082(d)(1)
6007(a)(1)	2631(c)	6010(h)(4)	4082(d)(3)
6007(b)(1)(A)	2033A	6010(h)(5)	4101(e)(1)
6007(b)(1)(A)-(B)	2057	6010(i)	4251(d)(3)
6007(b)(1)(C)	2057(b)(2)(A)	6010(j)(1)	512(b)(13)(A)
6007(b)(1)(D)	2057(c)	6010(j)(2)	512(b)(13)(B)(i)(I)
6007(b)(2)	2057(b)(3)	6010(k)(1)	853(e)-(f)
6007(b)(3)(A)	2057(e)(2)(C)	6010(k)(2)	853(c)
6007(b)(3)(B)	2057(e)(2)(D)(ii)	6010(k)(3)	901(k)(4)(A)
6007(b)(3)(C)	2057(e)(2)	6010(l)	6611(g)(1)
6007(b)(4)(A)	2057(f)(2)	6010(m)	751(c)
6007(b)(4)(B)	2057(f)(2)(C)	6010(n)(1)-(2)	39(a)(2)
6007(b)(5)(A)	2057(e)(1)	6010(o)(1)	264(a)(3)
6007(b)(5)(B)	2057(f)(3)	6010(o)(2)	264(a)(4)
6007(b)(6)	2057(g)(1)	6010(o)(3)(A)	264(f)(4)(E)
6007(b)(7)	2057(i)(3)(L)-(P)	6010(o)(4)(A)	264(f)(5)(A)(iv)
6007(c)(1)	6166(b)(7)(A)(iii)	6010(o)(4)(B)	6724(d)(1)(B)(xv)-(xvii)
6007(c)(2)	6166(b)(8)(A)(iii)		
6007(d)	7479(a)(1)-(2)	6010(o)(4)(C)	6724(d)(2)(Y)-(AA)
6007(e)(2)(A)	6501(c)(9)	6010(o)(5)	264(f)(8)(A)
6007(e)(2)(B)	2001(f)	6010(p)(1)(A)	32(c)(5)(A)
6007(e)(2)(B)[(C)]	2504(c)	6010(p)(1)(B)	32(c)(5)(B)(iii)
6007(f)(1)	1(g)(3)(C)-(D)	6010(p)(1)(C)	32(c)(5)(B)(iv)(III)
6007(f)(2)	641(c)-(d)	6010(p)(1)(C)	32(c)(5)(C)
6007(f)(3)	1361(e)(4)	6010(p)(2)	32(c)(2)(B)(v)
6007(f)(4)	6103(e)(1)(A)(ii)-(iv)	6010(r)	664(d)(1)(C)
6007(g)(1)	2031(c)(9)-(10)	6010(r)	664(d)(2)(C)
6007(g)(2)	2031(c)(6)	6011(a)	59(a)(3)-(4)
6008(a)	1400(b)(2)(B)	6011(b)(1)	1297(e)(4)
6008(b)	1400A(a)	6011(b)(2)	1298(a)(2)(B)
6008(c)(1)	1400B(b)(5)	6011(c)(1)	672(f)(3)(B)
6008(c)(2)	1400B(b)(6)	6011(c)(2)	1291(d)(1)
6008(c)(3)	1400B(c)	6011(c)(3)	1296(d)
6008(c)(4)	1400B(d)(2)	6011(d)	1297(e)-(f)
6008(d)(1)	1400C(b)(1)	6011(e)(1)	991
6008(d)(2)	1400C(c)(1)	6011(e)(2)	6013(g)(1)(A)
6008(d)(3)	1400C(e)(2)(B)	6011(e)(2)	6013(g)(5)
6008(d)(4)	1400C(e)(3)	6011(e)(2)	6013(h)(1)
6008(d)(5)	1400C(i)	6011(f)(1)	6038(a)(2)
6008(d)(6)	23(c)	6011(f)(2)	6038(a)(3)
6008(d)(7)	25(e)(1)(C)	6011(f)(3)	6038(e)(4)
6009(a)	5041(b)(6)	6012(a)	162(a)
6009(b)(1)	7704(g)(3)(C)	6012(b)(1)	6311(e)(1)
6009(c)	280F(a)(1)(C)(ii)	6012(b)(2)	6103(k)(8)-(9)
6009(d)	6103(d)(5)	6012(b)(3)	7431(g)-(h)
6010(a)(1)(A)-(C)	1259(b)(2)(A)-(C)	6012(b)(4)	6103(p)(3)(A)
6010(a)(2)	1259(d)(1)	6012(c)	774(d)(2)
6010(a)(3)	475(f)(1)(D)	6012(d)	6724(c)
6010(b)	1059(g)(1)	6012(f)(1)-(2)	6211(c)
6010(c)(2)(A)	355(e)(3)(A)	6012(g)	857(d)(3)(A)
6010(c)(2)(B)	355(e)(3)(A)(iv)	6012(h)	7430(b)(4)-(5)
6010(c)(3)(A)	351(c)	6013(a)(1)	646
6010(c)(3)(B)	368(a)(2)(H)(ii)	6013(a)(1)	645
6010(d)(1)	304(b)(5)(B)-(C)	6013(a)(3)	2652(b)(1)
6010(d)(2)	304(b)(6)	6013(a)(4)(A)	2652(b)(1)
6010(e)(1)	351(g)(1)(A)-(C)	6013(a)(4)(B)	2654(b)
6010(e)(2)	354(a)(2)(C)(ii)(III)	6013(b)(1)	685(b)
6010(f)	6331(h)(1)	6013(b)(2)	685(f)

Act Sec.	Code Sec.	Act Sec.	Code Sec.
6014(a)(1)(A)-(B)	5054(a)(1)	6023(12)	1250(d)(4)(D)
6014(a)(2)	5054(a)(2)	6023(13)(A)	3121(a)(5)(F)
6014(a)(3)	5056	6023(13)(B)	3121(a)(5)(G)
6014(b)(1)	5043(a)(2)	6023(13)(C)	3121(a)(5)(I)
6014(b)(2)	5044(a)	6023(14)	3401(a)(19)
6014(b)(3)	5364	6023(15)	3401(a)(21)
6014(c)	4052(f)(2)	6023(16)	4092(b)
6014(d)	4091(a)(2)	6023(16)	6427(q)(2)
6014(e)	7430(c)(4)(D)	6023(17)	4221(c)
6015(a)	408(p)(8)-(9)	6023(17)	4222(d)
6015(d)	404(a)(9)(C)-(D)	6023(18)(A)	4973
6015(e)	9811(e)-(f)	6023(19)(A)	4975(c)(3)
6016(a)(1)(A)	408(p)(2)(D)(i)	6023(19)(B)	4975(i)
6016(a)(1)(B)	408(p)(10)	6023(20)	6039(a)(1)
6016(a)(1)(C)(i)	408(p)(2)(C)(i)(II)	6023(21)	6050R(b)(2)(A)
6016(a)(1)(C)(ii)	408(p)(2)(D)(iii)	6023(22)	6103(h)(4)(A)
6016(b)(1)-(2)	6427(d)	6023(23)	6416(b)(5)
6017(a)	6427(i)(2)(B)	6023(24)(A)	6421(i)-(k)
6018(b)(1)	408(d)(7)(B)	6023(24)(B)	34(b)
6018(b)(2)	408(d)(7)	6023(24)(C)	6421(a)
6018(f)(1)	23(b)(2)(A)	6023(24)(C)	6421(b)
6019(a)	6104(b)	6023(25)	6427(f)(3)
6019(b)	6104(e)(1)(C)	6023(26)(A)	6427(m)-(r)
6019(c)	6103(e)(6)	6023(26)(B)	6427(i)(1)
6020(a)	196(c)(6)-(8)	6023(26)(B)	6427(i)(2)(A)
6021(a)	32(c)(1)(F)	6023(27)	6501(m)
6021(b)(1)	32(c)(3)(D)(i)	6023(28)	7702B(e)(2)
6021(b)(2)	32(c)(1)(G)	6023(29)	7434(b)(3)
6021(b)(3)	32(c)(3)(A)(ii)-(iv)	6023(30)	7872(f)(2)(B)
6022(a)	6401(b)(1)	6023(31)	9502(e)
6023(1)	45A(b)(1)(B)	7001(a)	404(a)(11)
6023(2)	59(b)	7003(a)	475(c)(4)
6023(3)	72(n)	7003(b)	475(g)(1)-(3)
6023(4)	72(t)(3)(A)	7004(a)	408A(c)(3)(C)(i)
6023(5)	142(f)(3)(A)(ii)	9015(a)	9503(c)(1)
6023(6)	501(n)(3)	9015(a)	9503(e)(3)
6023(7)	501(o)	9015(b)	9504(b)(2)(A)
6023(8)	512(b)(17)(B)(ii)(II)	9015(b)	9504(b)(2)(B)
6023(9)	543(d)(5)(A)(ii)	9015(b)	9504(b)(2)(C)
6023(10)	871(f)(2)(B)	9015(b)	9504(c)
6023(11)	1017(a)(2)		

¶ 25,020

Surface Tranportation Revenue Act of 1998

Act Sec.	Code Sec.	Act Sec.	Code Sec.
902(a)(1)(A)	4041(a)(1)(C)(iii)(I)	903(a)(3)(A)-(B)	40(e)(1)
902(a)(1)(B)	4041(a)(2)(B)	903(b)(1)	40(h)
902(a)(1)(C)	4041(m)(1)(A)	903(b)(2)(A)i)-(ii)	4041(b)(2)
902(a)(1)(D)	4051(c)	903(b)(2)(B)	4081(c)(4)(A)
902(a)(1)(E)	4071(d)	903(b)(2)(C)	4081(c)(5)
902(a)(1)(F)	4081(d)(1)	903(b)(2)(D)	4091(c)(1)
902(a)(1)(G)	4481(e)	904(a)(1)	9503(f)
902(a)(1)(H)	4482(c)(4)	904(b)(1)	9503(c)(7)
902(a)(1)(I)	4482(d)	904(c)	9503(b)(6)
902(a)(2)(A)(i)-(ii)	6412(a)(1)	904(d)	9503(e)(4)
902(a)(2)(B)	6156(e)(2)	905(a)(1)	9503(b)(4)(D)
902(b)(1)	4221(a)	905(a)(2)	9503(c)(4)(A)(ii)
902(b)(2)	4483(g)	905(b)(1)-(3)	9504(b)(2)
902(c)(1)(A)-(B)	9503(b)	905(c)(1)-(2)	9504(c)
902(c)(1)(A)-(B)	9503(c)(2)-(3)	905(d)	9504(d)-(e)
902(c)(2)(A)	9503(c)(4)(A)(i) and (5)(A)	906(a)(1)-(2)	4041(a)(1)(C)(ii)(II)-(III)
902(c)(3)	9503(c)(3)	906(b)(1)(A)-(B)	6421(f)(3)(B)(ii)-(iii)
902(d)(1)(A)	9503(c)(1)	906(b)(2)(A)-(B)	6427(l)(3)(B)(ii)-(iii)
902(d)(1)(B)(i)-(ii)	9503(c)(1)	909(a)	6427(i)(2)(A)
902(d)(2)(A)	9503(e)(3)	909(b)(1)	6427(i)(4)-(5)
902(d)(2)(B)(i)-(iii)	9503(e)(3)	909(b)(2)	6427(k)(2)
902(e)(1)	9503(e)(2)	909(b)(3)	6421(d)(2)
902(f)(1)	9503(b)(1)(C)-(F)	910(a)(1)	132(f)(4)
902(f)(2)	9503(c)(2)(A)(i)(II)-(IV)	910(b)(1)	132(f)(6)
902(f)(3)	9503(c)(2)(A)(ii)	910(b)(2)(A)-(B)	132(f)(2)(A)-(B)
903(a)(1)(A)	4041(b)(2)(C)	910(c)(1)	132(f)(2)(A)
903(a)(1)(B)	4041(k)(3)	910(c)(2)	132(f)(6)(A)
903(a)(1)(C)	4081(c)(8)	911(a)	9511
903(a)(1)(D)	4091(c)(5)	911(b)(1)	9503(c)(6)
903(a)(2)	6427(f)(4)	911(b)(2)	9503(b)(4)(D)

Provisions Dropped in Conference

¶ 30,001

The following proposed law changes originally included in the House or Senate versions of the IRS Restructuring and Reform Act of 1998, were dropped by the conferees. References to the Senate bill are to the IRS Restructuring and Reform Bill of 1998 (H.R. 2676), as passed by the Senate on May 7, 1998. References to the House bill are to the IRS Restructuring and Reform Bill of 1997 (H.R. 2676), as passed by the House on November 5, 1997.

Revenue Raisers

Clarification of the phaseout range for the 5-percent estate and gift surtax to phase out the benefits of the unified credit and graduated rates (Senate Sec. 6007(a)(1)).

Reduction of the carryback period for excess foreign tax credits from two years to one year and extension of the carryforward period from five years to seven years (Senate Sec. 5002).

Use of the mathematical and clerical error procedures to deny the dependent care tax credit, child tax credit, and earned income credit if statutory age restrictions are not satisfied (Senate Sec. 5003).

Addition of any vaccine against rotavirus gastroenteritis to the list of taxable vaccines (Senate Sec. 5006).

Restriction of special net operating loss carryback rules for specified liability losses (Senate Sec. 5007).

Extension of the IRS user fee program for letter rulings (Senate Sec. 5009).

Elimination of the distinction between the assumption of a liability and the acquisition of an asset subject to a liability under Code Sec. 357 (Senate Sec. 3301A)

International Transactions

A moratorium on temporary and final regulations with respect to Notice 98-11, relating to the treatment of hybrid branches under subpart F (Code Secs. 951-964) (Senate Sec. 3713(a)(1)).

A sense of the Senate provision that the IRS should withdraw Notice 98-11 and limit regulations issued under Notice 98-5, relating to the foreign tax credit, to the specific transactions described therein (Senate Sec. 3713(a)(2) and (b)).

These provisions were dropped in light of the IRS's recent withdrawal of Notice 98-11. See ¶ 633 for additional details.

Excise taxes

Clarifications regarding the effect of certain transfers to the Highway Trust Fund and the Mass Transit Account portions of highway motor fuels taxes (Senate Sec. 6009(a) and (b); House Sec. 608(a) and (b)).

Taxpayer Rights

Tax Court jurisdiction over the responsible person penalty (Senate Sec. 3104).

Limiting IRS participation in a "conference of right" to IRS national office personnel (Senate Sec. 3707).

IRS Restructuring

Requiring the IRS Oversight Board to issue a study on whether the IRS has the necessary resources to prevent tax avoidance attributable to unlawful transfer pricing methods (Senate Sec. 3803).

Requiring the IRS to convene a financial management advisory group to advise the Commissioner on financial management issues (House Sec. 412). The conference committee report, however, indicates that it expects the Chairman of the Oversight Board to consider establishing such a committee. See ¶ 861.

Iowa Demonstration Project

The creation an employment tax demonstration project in Iowa (Senate Sec. 3715).

Recent Tax Legislation and the Line Item Veto Act

¶ 30,025

Though none of the revenue provisions in the Surface Transportation Revenue Act of 1998 (P.L. 105-178) were subject to the Line Item Veto, the IRS Restructuring and Reform Act of 1998 identifies two provisions as limited tax benefits which would have been vulnerable to cancellation under the Line Item Veto Act (P.L. 104-130) (Act Sec. 8001 of the IRS Restructuring and Reform Act of 1998). On June 25, 1998, the U.S. Supreme Court struck down the Line Item Veto Act as unconstitutional under the Presentment Clause (*Clinton v. City of New York,* SCt, 98-2 USTC ¶ 50,504). Thus, the two provisions identified under Act Sec. 8001 will in no event be selectively vetoed. The identified provisions were:

(1) section 3105 (relating to administrative appeal of an adverse IRS determination of tax-exempt status of a bond issue); and

(2) section 3445(c) (relating to levy exemptions in cases involving State fish and wildlife permits).

Prior to the Supreme Court's decision in *Clinton v. City of New York,* the President was given the authority under the Line Item Veto Act to "cancel" limited tax benefits (provisions benefiting 100 or fewer taxpayers) contained in a revenue or reconciliation bill or joint resolution. A canceled provision would then be "without legal force or effect." For practical purposes, exercise of a line item veto would repeal a portion of the Act.

Procedurally, the Joint Committee on Taxation was required by the Line Item Veto Act to prepare a statement identifying each limited tax benefit contained in a bill or resolution. Conferees then determined whether to include the statement in the conference report. The President had five days after enactment of a law to cancel one or more of the identified provisions.

If the conference report did not identify provisions subject to cancellation, the President could determine on his own which provisions were subject to cancellation. A "special message" to Congress from the President would provide notification of the cancellations. In response, the House and Senate could enact a "disapproval bill" rendering the identified cancellations as "null and void."

Justice Stevens delivered the 6-3 decision in *Clinton* rendering the selective cancellation rules void. The Court's opinion leaves no room for procedures which would allow the President to amend or repeal selective portions of a bill. The only Presidential veto procedure allowable under Article I, §7 of the U.S. Constitution is for the President to return the *entire* bill, *before* it becomes law. There is no constitutional authority for any post-enactment amendment or repeal by the President.

The Court rejected government arguments that President's past utilizations of line item veto power were merely exercises of discretionary authority allowed under the Balanced Budget Act and the Taxpayer Relief Act (in which provisions were canceled). By giving the President unilateral power to change the text of enacted statutes, the Line Item Veto Act clearly violated Constitutional procedures for creating a law. The text created by the President under his authority to cancel certain provisions would not have been voted on by either House or presented to the President for signature, as required under Article I. It would thus not be able to "become a law" pursuant to Article I, §7, according to the Supreme Court.

As a result of the Supreme Court's decision in *Clinton v. City of New York,* the two provisions in the Taxpayer Relief Act of 1997 (P.L. 105-34) that were canceled must be considered reinstated. Act Sec. 968 of the Taxpayer Relief Act of 1997 would make the sale of stock of a qualified refiner or processor to a farmer's cooperative eligible for gain deferral under Code Sec. 1042. This provision was discussed at ¶ 369 of CCH's *1997 Tax Law Legislation: Law, Explanation and Analysis.* Act Sec. 1175 of the Taxpayer Relief Act of 1997 would amend Code Sec. 954 to temporarily exclude certain overseas income derived in the active conduct of a banking, financing, or similar business from the definition of personal holding company income. This provision was discussed at ¶ 942 of CCH's *1997 Tax Law Legislation: Law, Explanation and Analysis.*

Committee Report at ¶ 11,555.

Miscellaneous Clerical and Deadwood Changes

¶ 30,050

The IRS Restructuring and Reform Act of 1998 makes numerous changes to the Internal Revenue Code necessitated by the repeal or lapse of law (deadwood) as well as numerous clerical amendments stemming from prior legislation (Act Sec. 6023 of the 1998 Act). There is no committee report for these provisions.

The following Code Sections are amended to reflect these changes:

(1) Code Sec. 34(b) relating to credits for certain uses of gasoline and special fuels;

(2) Code Sec. 45A(b)(1)(B) relating to the work opportunity credit;

(3) Code Sec. 59(b) relating to exemption from alternative minimum tax for income eligible for the Puerto Rico Economic Activity credit;

(4) Code Sec. 72(n) relating to annuities under retired serviceman's family protection plan or survivor benefit plan;

(5) Code Sec. 72(t)(3) relating to the 10-percent additional tax on early distributions from qualified retirement plans;

(6) Code Sec. 142(f)(3)(A), relating to exempt facility bonds;

(7) Code Sec. 501(n)(3) relating to the organizational requirements of charitable risk pools;

(8) Code Sec. 501(o) relating to the treatment of hospitals participating in provider-sponsored organizations;

(9) Code Sec. 512(b)(17)(B)(ii) relating to unrelated business taxable income;

(10) Code Sec. 543(d)(5)(A) relating to personal holding companies and business computer software royalties;

(11) Code Sec. 871(f)(2) relating to exclusion for annuities received under qualified plan by nonresident aliens;

(12) Code Sec. 1017(a) relating to discharge of indebtedness,

(13) Code Sec. 1250(d)(4)(D) relating to basis of property acquired in an involuntary conversion;

(14) Code Sec. 3121(a)(5) relating to the definition of FICA wages;

Code Secs. 3401(a)(19) and (21) relating to definition of wages for income tax withholding purposes;

(15) Code Sec. 4092(b) relating to exemption from excise tax for fuel used in commercial aviation;

(16) Code Sec. 4221(c) and Code Sec. 4222(d) relating to exemption from manufacturers excise tax;

(17) Code Sec. 4973 relating to tax on excess contributions to tax-exempt plans;

(18) Code Sec. 4975(c)(3) and (i) relating to tax on prohibited transactions;

(19) Code Sec. 6039(a) relating to information returns required in connection with the exercise of an incentive stock option;

(20) Code Sec. 6050R(b)(2) relating to information reporting for certain purchases of fish;

(21) Code Sec. 6103(h)(4) relating to disclosure of return information in judicial and administrative tax proceedings;

(22) Code Sec. 6416(b)(5) relating to return of excise tax paid with respect to installment accounts;

(23) Code Secs. 6421(a), (b), (j) and (k) relating to credits or refunds of gasoline tax;

(24) Code Sec. 6427(f)(3), (i) (n), (p), (q), and (r) relating to fuels not used for a taxable purpose;

(25) Code Sec. 6501(m) to clarify that the period for assessing a deficiency attributable to an election (or revocation) to claim the orphan drug credit (Code Sec. 45C(d)(4)) may not expire before the date 1 year after the date on which the IRS is notified of the election (or revocation);

(26) Code Sec. 7434(b)(3) relating to civil damages for fraudulent filing of information returns;

(27) Code Sec. 7702(B)(e)(2) relating to treatment of qualified long-term care health insurance;

(28) Code Sec. 7872(f)(2) relating to below market interest rate loans; and

(29) Code Sec. 9502(e) relating to airport and airway trust fund transfers.

★ *Effective date.* Theses provisions are all effective on the date of enactment (Act Sec. 6023(32) of the IRS Restructuring and Reform Act of 1998).

Sample Client Letter: Financial and Retirement Planning

¶ 50,001

Dear Client:

The complex federal tax legislation that Congress just passed—the IRS Restructuring and Reform Act of 1998—creates significant financial and retirement planning opportunities, while also creating some tax traps for the unwary. Despite its name, the new law isn't just about a new organization chart for the IRS. The provisions curbing IRS abuses and giving taxpayers valuable rights if audited have received much publicity. In addition, however, this law also takes up where the Taxpayer Relief Act of 1997 (TRA'97) left off, fine-tuning and adding new provisions to the tax rules on capital gains and losses, IRAs and Roth IRA conversions, sales of a principal residence, education tax incentives, and exceptions to the estate and gift tax. As a result, every taxpayer needs to review whether his or her financial and retirement plans should be revised to maximize tax benefits.

The IRS Restructuring and Reform Act introduces additional rules for computing capital gains and losses. Although the IRS had anticipated many of these changes in its tax forms last year, the new law not only makes this treatment official, but also confirms the burden it puts on investors to carefully keep track of capital gains and losses. In an important change to the rules imposed by TRA '97, the new law eliminates the 18-month holding period that was required to obtain the lowest applicable capital gains rate. Now, an asset need only be held "more than 12 months." This change is retroactive to January 1, 1998.

The new law also coordinates the lower capital gain rates with other tax rules, such as those for inherited property or short-sale and covered-call option holding periods. Furthermore, under the new law, those who can take advantage of the tax-free rollover treatment for capital gains on small business stock now have the flexibility of using S corporations and partnerships to do so.

One of the more significant tax breaks for homeowners in a long time—the $500,000/$250,000 exclusion of gain on the sale of a principal residence—has just gotten easier to qualify for in certain situations. In particular, those taxpayers on the move who fail to satisfy the full two-year ownership and use requirement may now be entitled to a portion of the tax benefits. These homeowners can now exclude an amount equal to the fraction of the exclusion proportional to their use of the house as a principal residence over the two-year term.

Roth IRAs, which should be considered by virtually every taxpayer, are the recipients of more good news than bad under the new law. The good news is that, starting in the tax year 2005 in determining whether a taxpayer can meet the $100,000 adjusted gross income (AGI) limit for eligibility to convert regular IRAs into Roth Conversion IRAs, individuals over age 70½ may exclude from their AGI computation any required distributions from retirement plans. This provides an important break not only for some current retirees, but also for those planning how to maximize tax benefits when they retire in the future. However, a loophole that unexpectedly allowed immediate, penalty-free withdrawals for Roth Conversion IRAs has been plugged.

The new education tax breaks have also been the focus of some loophole closing. Education IRAs are now generally subject to a penalty tax if they are not used up before the beneficiary reaches age 30, and only taxpayers who are directly obligated on a student loan are allowed to deduct the interest under the new rules.

Those who own small businesses need to reevaluate their financial and estate plans because of changes to the estate tax made by the 1998 Act. The TRA '97 exclusion for family owned businesses has been changed to a *deduction* from a person's estate and is now coordinated with the gradual increase in the estate tax unified credit scheduled through 2006. The new law also clarifies the rules governing how a business qualifies for family-owned business treatment. Generation-skipping trusts and conservation contributions also may require review as the result of the 1998 Act.

Finally, one word of warning about the new taxpayer rights provision that has been getting much press—the switching of the burden of proof from the taxpayer to the IRS. This rule applies only to certain civil court cases and, more importantly, does not mean that taxpayers should no longer keep meticulous records of their financial transactions.

We would be pleased to assist you in separating the opportunities from the pitfalls in planning your financial and retirement strategies in light of Congress's latest changes to the tax law.

Sincerely yours,

Sample Client Letter: Tax Planning for Individuals

¶ 50,002

Dear Client:

The IRS Restructuring and Reform Act of 1998, a complex tax law just passed by Congress, directly affects individual taxpayers in a variety of important ways. But the most important part of the new law from an immediate tax planning perspective has nothing to do with IRS reform. The new law clarifies and expands many of the important tax breaks initiated in last year's historic tax-cut legislation, including capital gain tax rate reductions, Roth IRAs, and a myriad of other provisions. The new law also provides a long list of new taxpayer rights, intended not only to help those already caught in the IRS audit and collections process, but also to help taxpayers avoid IRS problems in the first place. Finally, the new law also reorganizes the IRS under a new structure that is intended to discourage abusive tactics by its agents.

Changes to TRA '97: Technical corrections to the Taxpayer Relief Act of 1997 (TRA'97) were enacted as part of the IRS Restructuring and Reform Bill because Congress did not want to wait to develop a separate law to get these important provisions passed. Among the 40-plus changes to TRA'97 made by the 1998 tax law that will affect individuals, these rank high in importance:

★ The 18-month holding period that was required in order to obtain the lowest applicable capital gains rate has been eliminated. Now, an asset need only be held "more than 12 months." This change is retroactive to January 1, 1998.

★ Capital gains and losses are subject to a complicated netting process, which can result in an increase or decrease in up to 8% in tax liability depending upon how a taxpayer times the recognition of gains and losses. Investors who take the time to do some careful tax planning in this area can be amply rewarded.

★ The lower 20 percent maximum capital gains rate has been coordinated with other provisions in the tax code, such as holding periods for gains relating to inherited property, patents, short sales and covered-call options.

★ Homeowners who move before they have owned and used the house as their principal residence for two years now get a bigger piece of the $500,000/$250,000 capital gain exclusion under the new law when they sell.

★ Roth Conversion IRAs (Roth IRAs set up with funds from regular IRAs) will be available to more people who retire and receive distributions from existing retirement plans. Under the new rules, starting in the 2005 tax year, individuals over age 70½ can exclude minimum required distributions from the amount of income used to determine whether a taxpayer meets the $100,000 adjusted gross income eligibility limit for Roth Conversion IRAs.

★ Education tax breaks, new for 1998, have been limited in two ways: Education IRA funds are made subject to a penalty if not distributed before a beneficiary reaches age 30; and student loan interest can only be deducted by the person primarily liable on the loan.

★ Family-held businesses now need to coordinate estate plans to fit within the correction in the new law that pairs more precisely the family-owned business deduction with the gradual rise in the unified gift and estate tax credit.

New taxpayer rights: Taxpayer rights have been greatly expanded by the new law. The new taxpayer rights provisions combine to form powerful protections against the unfairness not only of IRS actions but also of certain sections of the tax code itself. The most important taxpayer rights provisions, some of which lend themselves to protective tax planning as well as audit and collection safeguards, include:

★ Shifting the burden of proof in some situations from the taxpayer to the IRS.

★ Creating a confidentiality privilege for certain nonattorneys.

★ Making innocent spouse relief easier to achieve.

★ Inaugurating a broader offers-in-compromise program.

★ Suspending some interest and penalties for adjustments made by the IRS more than 18 months after filing a timely return.

★ Creating a new National Taxpayer Advocate Office within the IRS.

★ Imposing new lien, levy and collection safeguards including a 30-day hearing period and higher exemptions.

★ Allowing some medical impairments to excuse late filed refund claims.

★ Restricting the IRS from using lifestyle audits as an examination technique.

This latest tax law to come out of Congress covers considerable ground and probably affects you in at least several ways. If you have any questions about the new law, or if you would like to schedule an appointment to discuss your particular tax situation in depth, please do not hesitate to call.

Sincerely yours,

Sample Client Letter: Small Business Tax Breaks

¶ 50,003

Dear Client:

With the recent passage of the sizable IRS Restructuring and Reform Act of 1998, small businesses have good cause to celebrate. Many new taxpayer rights provisions now allow businesses to function more smoothly despite IRS audit or collection efforts. But perhaps more importantly, the new law also expands, clarifies, and fine-tunes many of the most significant small-business oriented provisions in the Taxpayer Relief Act of 1997. Some of these provisions can just be pulled off the shelf and implemented when the need arises, while others require careful planning in order to fully realize certain tax benefits.

Taxpayer rights. Much of the testimony before the Senate in hearings this past May and last September involved horror stories of small businesses dealing with IRS agents' abusive tactics. The new law attempts to level the playing field for a small business when dealing with the IRS in certain key areas. Some of the more important new provisions include:

★ Improving the offers-in-compromise procedure in which businesses and other taxpayers can work out a negotiated settlement of an outstanding tax liability. These improvement not only include more liberal acceptance criteria but also a requirement that the IRS suspend collection activities during the compromise process or while the taxpayer appeals.

★ Imposing procedural safeguards upon the IRS while an issue is in the collections process. When a business is contesting a tax liability, it may find itself caught by a rapidly-advancing IRS collection machine in which the IRS may seize assets vital to the business. The new law requires the IRS to give 30 days notice before any levy or seizure. During this period the taxpayer can request a hearing by IRS Appeals and immediately halt the collection process.

★ Shifting the burden of proof to the IRS in a tax case in which the taxpayer introduces credible evidence relevant to a disputed issue.

★ Extending the confidentiality privilege in administrative proceedings and certain civil tax cases to tax advisors authorized to practice before the IRS.

Small business provisions. The 1998 Reform Act makes "technical corrections" to the Taxpayer Relief Act of 1997 that are favorable for small businesses. Many of these "corrections" have important substantive significance.

★ Partnerships and S corporations can roll over gain on qualified small business stock, provided all interests in the partnership or S corporation are held by individuals, estates, or certain trusts.

★ Employers that maintain both a defined benefit plan and a SIMPLE IRA plan in the same tax year because of a merger, acquisition, disposition or similar transaction are eligible to treat the SIMPLE plan as a salary reduction plan from the date of the transaction through the following two tax years.

★ For purposes of the small business exemption from the corporate minimum tax, if a corporation's first tax year after December 31, 1997 (the first year the exemption is available) is its first tax year and the corporation is not treated as having a predecessor, the corporation will be treated as an exempt small business

¶ 50,003

regardless of its receipts for the year. It will, therefore, not be subject to the $5 million and $7.5 million gross receipts test until the following tax year.

Family-owned businesses and the estate tax. The Act also changes the TRA '97 exclusion for family-owned businesses to a deduction and coordinates the family-owned business provision with the phased-in increase in the unified credit. Although the Act clarifies the trade or business requirement and expands the definition of a qualified heir, careful planning is still required to ensure that the business meets the complex eligibility requirements.

This wide-ranging legislation most probably affects you, your business and your estate planning in several ways. If you have any questions concerning the new tax or you would like to schedule an appointment to discuss in depth its impact on you and your business, please do not hesitate to call.

Sincerely yours,

Sample Client Letter: Taxpayer Relief Act Follow-Up

¶ 50,004

Dear Client:

Flush with a federal budget surplus, Congress is entering into a new era of pro-taxpayer legislation. Last year, it enacted the historic Taxpayer Relief Act of 1997 (TRA'97), the largest tax-cut legislation in 16 years. This year—even before turning to the annual budget—Congress has already passed the extensive IRS Restructuring and Reform Act of 1998. This Act not only reorganizes the IRS and arms taxpayers with valuable rights to assert against IRS audits and collections, but, equally as important, it improves and fine-tunes capital gains relief, Roth IRAs, child credits, education tax incentives, estate tax reductions and dozens of other provisions originally enacted in TRA'97.

This letter is intended to alert you to the changes made to the more important TRA'97 provisions. Due to the significant nature of these changes, we are recommending that all our clients reexamine tax strategies initiated after TRA'97 in order to continue to maximize tax benefits under the new Act.

Congress has changed the rules in over 40 of the original provisions in the Taxpayer Relief Act of 1997. Some are technical corrections that affect a small number of taxpayers. Others are more sweeping, affecting virtually all taxpayers in some way. Here is our "top 10" list of changes:

★ The 18-month holding period for long-term capital assets eligible for the lower capital gain rates set by TRA'97 has been eliminated. Instead, property held for more than one year will qualify for the favorable rates, effective for tax years ending after 1997.

★ Congress has now made it clear that the complicated netting process for capital gains and losses can result in an increase or decrease of up to 8% in tax liability depending upon how a taxpayer times the recognition of gains and losses. Investors who take the time to do some careful tax planning in this area can be amply rewarded.

★ Roth Conversion IRAs (Roth IRAs set up with funds from regular IRAs) will be available to more people who retire and receive distributions from existing retirement plans. Under the new rules, starting in the 2005 tax year, an individual over age 70½ can exclude minimum required distributions from the amount of income used to determine whether a taxpayer meets the $100,000 adjusted gross income eligibility limit for Roth Conversion IRAs. This provision affects individuals planning for their future retirement as well as those who are presently retired.

★ Roth Conversion IRA owners also need to watch more carefully how they withdraw money from their Roth IRAs for emergencies and other needs. The new law imposes penalties on some, but not all, early withdrawals. Planning can help preserve an extra degree of the flexibility for the Roth IRA owner.

★ Homeowners who move because of a change in employment, health or unforseen circumstances before they have owned and used the house as their principal residence for the required two years now get a potentially bigger piece of the $500,000/$250,000 capital gain exclusion under the new law. When they sell, they may exclude a fraction of the exclusion amount based on the fraction of the two years that the ownership and use requirement is satisfied. Advance planning in anticipation of a possible move can help increase this exclusion.

★ Education tax breaks, new for 1998, have been circumscribed in two ways. Funds in an education IRA, a new IRA that offers tax-free earnings for higher education, must be used by the time the beneficiary turns age 30. The new law has closed a potential loophole by imposing a penalty on funds still on hand. By planning to shift benefits to other family members who are under age 30, however, taxpayers can still avoid the penalty.

★ Student loan interest can be deducted for the first time beginning in 1998. Knowing how to take out a student loan and who should take out that loan has taken a new planning twist as the 1998 Act makes it clear that student loan interest can only be deducted by the person primarily liable on the loan.

★ The TRA'97 exclusion for family owned businesses has been converted into a *deduction* from the estate and is now coordinated with the unified credit. Other changes clarify qualification for the deduction and may open up new estate planning opportunities. As a result of these and other changes in the transfer tax laws, including indexing of the $1 million GST (generation-skipping transfer tax) exemption, all estate plans should be reviewed.

★ For certain families, clarification of the "stacking" rules for computing the new child credit will increase the refundable portion of the credit beginning in 1998.

★ Individuals will have an easier time obtaining innocent spouse relief which is now available with respect to *all* tax understatements attributable to erroneous, rather than grossly erroneous, items of the other spouse. Also, divorced and legally separated couples can elect separate tax liability even if they filed jointly.

In addition to those tax law revisions highlighted above, there are many other changes made by the new 1998 tax law which may affect your personal situation. If you have any questions or wish to make an appointment to discuss your situation in depth, please do not hesitate to call.

Sincerely yours,

INDEX

References are to explanation paragraph (¶) numbers.

FAM